More praise for *The Complete Works of Isaac Babel*

"Babel's . . . tropes, in Peter Constantine's hardworking translation, explode off the page. . . . [He provides] unblinking witness and electric, heroically wrought prose."　　　—John Updike, *The New Yorker*

"Babel is altogether the artist, drawing the reader completely into a new view of the world."　　　—Alfred Kazin, *New York Review of Books*

"A talent of great energy and boldness."　　　—Lionel Trilling

"*The Complete Works of Isaac Babel* is the most comprehensive edition of his writings in any language and the one that does the most justice to his genius."　　　—Gregory Freidin, chairman, Department of Slavic Languages and Literature, Stanford University

"The best Russia has to offer."
　　　—Maxim Gorky, about Isaac Babel, to Andre Malraux, 1926

"The publication of this book, containing the totality of Babel's surviving work, is a literary event and cause for celebration. . . . It's impossible not to recommend this volume."
　　　—Erik Tarlhoff, *San Francisco Chronicle*

"[I]t's impossible to say enough about the monumental *Complete Works of Isaac Babel*, which . . . brings us face-to-face with the stark beauty and even starker terror of the human soul."
　　　—David L. Ulin, *Los Angeles Times*

"[An] overdue tribute to an artist whose irrepressible personality, and refusal to leave Russia, sealed his fate."　　　—*Philadelphia Inquirer*

"When the planes hit the Twin Towers, I was just a couple hundred pages into the collection, watching the great Jewish Russian-language writer find his voice at the beginning of the 20th century. His sardonic, anguished stories of brutality—whether committed by idealistic revolutionaries, Jewish gangsters or Cossacks out to rob and kill a few Jews for kicks—suddenly seemed painfully relevant, almost too much so to read."　　　—Polly Shulman, *Newsday*

The
COMPLETE
WORKS

of

Isaac Babel

EDITED BY NATHALIE BABEL

TRANSLATED WITH NOTES BY
PETER CONSTANTINE

INTRODUCTION BY CYNTHIA OZICK

W. W. NORTON & COMPANY
NEW YORK LONDON

All photographs courtesy of Nathalie Babel
Frontispiece photograph: Isaac Babel, circa 1931, Molodenovo
Afterword photograph: Isaac Babel with daughter, Nathalie, 1935, Paris
Chronology photograph: Isaac Babel, July 1930, previously unpublished in book form,
sent by Isaac Babel to his sister in Brussels with the handwritten inscription,
"My life is spent fighting this man."

The stories "Elya Isaakovich and Margarita Prokofievna" and Mama, Rimma, and Alla"
appeared in earlier translation in *The Lonely Years* by Isaac Babel, originally
published by Farrar, Straus & Company in 1964. Copyright © 1964, renewed 1992 by
Farrar, Straus and Giroux, LLC.

For information about permission to reproduce selections from this book, write to
Permissions, W. W. Norton & Company, Inc., 500 Fifth Avenue, New York, NY 10110

Manufacturing by The Haddon Craftsmen, Inc.
Book design by Mary Wirth
Cartography by Jacques Chazaud
Production manager: Julia Druskin

Library of Congress Cataloging-in-Publication Data

Babel', I. (Isaak), 1894–1941.
[Works. English. 2001]
The complete works of Isaac Babel / edited by Nathalie Babel ; translated by Peter
Constantine ; introduction by Cynthia Ozick.
p.   cm.
Includes bibliographical references.
ISBN 0-393-04846-2
1. Babel' I. (Isaak), 1894–1941—Translations into English. I. Babel, Nathalie.
II. Constantine, Peter, 1963– III. Ozick, Cynthia. IV. Title.
PG3476.B2 A23 2001
891.73'42—dc21   2001044036
ISBN 0-393-32824-4 pbk.

W. W. Norton & Company, Inc., 500 Fifth Avenue, New York, N.Y. 10110
www.wwnorton.com

W. W. Norton & Company Ltd., Castle House, 75/76 Wells Street, London W1T 3QT

1 2 3 4 5 6 7 8 9 0

To the memory of my father,
Isaac Emmanuelovich Babel,
and of my mother,
Evgenia Borisovna Babel.

CONTENTS

Contents

II. The Odessa Stories

III. The Red Cavalry Stories

IV. The Red Cavalry Cycle: Additional Stories   335

V. The Red Cavalryman: Articles   363

XIII. Plays

XIV. Screenplays

INTRODUCTION
by Cynthia Ozick

On May 15, 1939, Isaac Babel, a writer whose distinction had earned him the Soviet privilege of a dacha in the country, was arrested at Peredelkino and taken to Moscow's Lubyanka prison, headquarters of the secret police. His papers were confiscated and destroyed—among them half-completed stories, plays, film scripts, translations. Six months later, after three days and nights of hellish interrogation, he confessed to a false charge of espionage. The following year, a clandestine trial was briefly held in the dying hours of January 26; Babel recanted his confession, appealed to his innocence, and at 1:40 the next morning was summarily shot by a firing squad. He was forty-five. His final plea was not for himself, but for the power and truth of literature: "Let me finish my work."

What Kafka's art hallucinates—trial without cause, an inescapable predicament directed by an irrational force, a malignant social order—Babel is at last condemned to endure in the living flesh. Kafka and Babel can be said to be the twentieth century's European coordinates: they are separated by language, style, and temperament; but where their fevers intersect lies the point of infection. Each was an acutely conscious Jew. Each witnessed a pogrom while still very young, Kafka in enlightened Prague, Babel under a Czarist regime that promoted harsh legal disabilities for Jews. Each invented a type of literary modernism, becoming a movement in himself, indelible, with no possibility of successors. To be influenced by Kafka is to end in parody; and because the wilderness of an astoundingly variegated experience is incised, unduplicatably, in the sinews of Babel's prose, no writer can effectively claim to be his disciple.

But of course they are opposites: Kafka ingrown, self-dissatisfied, indifferent to politics; hardly daring, despite genius, to feel entitlement to his own language; endlessly agonizing over a broken engagement; rarely leaving home. And here is Babel, insouciant, reckless, a womanizer, half a vagabond, a horseman, a propagandist, the father of three by three different women, only one of them legally his wife. Then why bring up Kafka when speaking of Babel? Kafka at least died in his bed. Babel was murdered by the criminal agency of a cynically criminal government. Kafka requested that his writing be destroyed, and was not obeyed. Babel's name and work were erased—as if he had never written at all—until 1954, when, during a "thaw," he was, in Soviet terminology, rehabilitated.

Yet taken together, they tell us what we in our time are obliged to know about the brutal tracings of force and deception, including self-deception. Kafka alone is not enough; his interiors are too circumscribed. Babel alone is not enough; his landscapes are too diffuse. Kafka supplies the grandly exegetical metaphor: the man who thinks but barely lives, the metaphysician who is ultimately consumed by a conflagration of lies. Babel, by contrast, lives, lives, lives! He lives robustly, inquisitively, hungrily; his appetite for unpredictable human impulse is gargantuan, inclusive, eccentric. He is trickster, rapscallion, ironist, wayward lover, imprudent impostor—and out of these hundred fiery selves insidious truths creep out, one by one, in a face, in the color of the sky, in a patch of mud, in a word. Violence, pity, comedy, illumination. It is as if he is an irritable membrane, subject to every creaturely vibration.

Babel was born in Odessa, a cosmopolitan and polyglot city that looked to the sea and beyond. It was, he wrote,

> the most charming city of the Russian Empire. If you think about it, it is a town in which you can live free and easy. Half the population is made up of Jews, and Jews are a people who have learned a few simple truths along the way. Jews get married so as not to be alone, love so as to live through the centuries, save money so they can buy houses and give their wives astrakhan jackets, love children because,

let's face it, it is good and important to love one's children. The poor Odessa Jews get very confused when it comes to officials and regulations, but it isn't all that easy to get them to budge in their opinions, their very antiquated opinions. You might not be able to budge these Jews, but there's a whole lot you can learn from them. To a large extent it is because of them that Odessa has this light and easy atmosphere.

There is much of the affectionate and mirthful Babel in this paragraph: the honest yet ironic delight in people exactly as they are, the teasing sense of laughing entitlement ("so as to live through the centuries"), prosperity and poverty rubbing elbows, ordinary folk harried by officialdom, confusion and stubbornness, love and loneliness. As for poor Jews, Babel began as one of these, starting life in the Moldavanka, a mixed neighborhood with a sprinkling of mobsters. What he witnessed there, with a bright boy's perceptiveness, catapulted him early on into the capacious worldliness that burst out (he was twenty-nine) in the exuberant tales of Benya Krik and his gang—tough but honorable criminals with a Damon Runyonesque strain.

Lionel Trilling, among the first to write seriously about Babel in English, mistook him for "a Jew of the ghetto." If "ghetto" implies a narrow and inbred psyche, then Babel stands for the reverse. Though he was at home in Yiddish and Hebrew, and was familiar with the traditional texts and their demanding commentaries, he added to these a lifelong infatuation with Maupassant and Flaubert. His first stories were composed in fluent literary French. The breadth and scope of his social compass enabled him to see through the eyes of peasants, soldiers, priests, rabbis, children, artists, actors, women of all classes. He befriended whores, cabdrivers, jockeys; he knew what it was to be penniless, to live on the edge and off the beaten track. He was at once a poet of the city ("the glass sun of Petersburg") and a lyricist of the countryside ("the walls of sunset collapsing into the sky"). He was drawn to spaciousness and elasticity, optimism and opportunity, and it was through these visionary seductions of societal freedom, expressed politically, that he welcomed the Revolution.

He not only welcomed it; he joined it. In order to be near Maxim Gorky, his literary hero, Babel had been living illegally in St.

Petersburg, one of the cities prohibited to Jews under the hobbling restrictions of the Czarist Pale of Settlement. With the advent of the Revolution the Pale dissolved, discriminatory quotas ceased, censorship vanished, promises multiplied, and Babel zealously attached himself to the Bolshevik cause. In 1920, as a war correspondent riding with the Red Calvary to deliver Communist salvation to the reluctant Polish villages across the border, he fell into disenchantment. "They all say they're fighting for justice and they all loot," he wrote in his diary. "Murderers, it's unbearable, baseness and crime. . . . Carnage. The military commander and I ride along the tracks, begging the men not to butcher the prisoners." Six years later, Babel published his penetratingly authoritative *Red Cavalry* stories, coolly steeped in pity and blood, and found instant fame.

With Stalin's ascension in 1924, new tyrannies began to mimic the old. Postrevolutionary literary and artistic ferment, much of it experimental, ebbed or was suppressed. Censorship returned, sniffing after the subversive, favoring the coarse flatness of Socialist Realism. Babel's wife, Evgenia, whom he had married in 1919, emigrated to Paris, where his daughter Nathalie was born in 1929. His mother and sister, also disaffected, left for Brussels. Babel clung to Moscow, hotly wed to his truest bride, the Russian tongue, continuing his work on a cycle of childhood stories and venturing into writing for theater and film. The film scripts, some designed for silent movies, turned out to be remarkable: they took on, under the irresistible magnetism of the witnessing camera and the innovation of the present tense, all the surreal splendor of Babel's most plumaged prose. Several were produced and proved to be popular, but eventually they failed to meet Party guidelines, and the director of one of them, an adaptation of Turgenev, was compelled to apologize publicly.

Unable to conform to official prescriptiveness, Babel's publications grew fewer and fewer. He was charged with "silence"—the sin of Soviet unproductivity—and was denied the privilege of traveling abroad. His last journey to Paris occurred in 1935, when André Malraux intervened with the Soviet authorities to urge Babel's attendance at a Communist-sponsored International Congress of Writers for the Defense of Culture and Peace—after which Babel never again met with his wife and daughter. Later that year, back in Moscow, he set up a second household with Antonina Pirozhkova, with whom he fathered a second daughter; through an earlier liaison, he was already the father of a son. But if Babel's personal life was unpredictable, disorganized, and rash, his art was otherwise. He wrested his sentences out of a purifying immediacy. Like Pushkin, he said, he was in pursuit of "precision and brevity." His most pointed comment on literary style appears in "Guy de Maupassant," a cunning seriocomic sexual fable fixed on the weight and trajectory of language itself. The success of a phrase, the young narrator instructs, "rests in a crux that is barely discernible. One's fingertips must grasp the key, gently warming it. And then the key must be turned once, not twice." But even this is not the crux. The crux (Babel's severest literary dictum) is here: "No iron spike can pierce a human heart as icily as a period in the right place."

A writer's credo, and Babel's most intimate confession. Stand in awe of it, yes—but remember also that this same master of the white bone of truth, this artist of the delicately turned key, was once a shameless propagandist for the Revolution, capable of rabid exhortations: "Beat them, Red Fighters, clobber them to death, if it is the last thing you do! Right away! This minute! Now!" "Slaughter them, Red Army fighters! Stamp harder on the rising lids of their rancid coffins!" While it is a truism that every utopia contains the seeds of dystopia, Babel, after all, was granted skepticism almost from the start. Out of skepticism came disillusionment; out of disillusionment, revulsion. And in the end, as the tragic trope has it, the Revolution devoured its child.

Babel's art served as a way station to the devouring. He was devoured because he would not, could not, accommodate to falsehood; because he saw and he saw, with an eye as merciless as a klieg light; and because, like Kafka, he surrendered his stories to voices and passions tremulous with the unforeseen. If we wish to complete, and transmit, the literary configuration of the twentieth century—the image that will enduringly stain history's retina—now is the time (it is past time) to set Babel beside Kafka. Between them, they leave no nerve unshaken.

CYNTHIA OZICK

PREFACE

by Nathalie Babel

*I*n most countries, there is extraordinary significance attached to the publication of the complete works of famous writers. It is the crowning of a career, often posthumous. In the case of Isaac Babel, such efforts have been defeated until now. There have been competing publishers, different countries, and numerous translators, translating the same materials, sometimes ineptly, sometimes excellently. Large sections appeared in magazines and literary journals between publications in Russia and in other countries. The first postwar volume of Babel's stories in the Soviet Union, albeit censured, was published in Moscow in 1957 and, since then, many compilations have appeared in a variety of languages in Russia, Western Europe, and the United States. An extensive two-volume collection* was published in Moscow in 1990–1991, although it still contains omissions from the 1957 version.

This unfortunate situation was due, of course, to Babel's having been a Soviet citizen, living in the Soviet Union. It is attributable also to his mysterious disappearance in 1939, exacerbated by the fact that his name was not officially heard again until 1954. Since we have now learned what actually happened to him, and since great efforts and scholarly endeavors have been made to gather his writings, it has finally become possible to prepare, with some considered confidence, the complete works of Isaac Babel.

---

* Isaak Babel: Sochineniia, Moscow, Khudozhestvennaya Literatura, 1990–1991.

Among Babel's little-known works are his screenplays, some of which were written in collaboration with Sergei Eisenstein. In 1998, Peter Constantine approached me with the idea of translating these screenplays. His suggestion about the screenplays fell on fertile soil, for I saw in it the possibility of realizing a dream I had long nourished to have a reliable and complete edition of my father's work. Peter's initial idea therefore grew into a much larger endeavor, which has resulted in the present book. In this W. W. Norton edition, all of Babel's known writings, uncensored and/or forgotten, have been assembled for the first time in any language.

As these works illustrate, and as anyone can surmise who has ever read anything about him, he was an enigma. Although his complete literary works are now in print with this long-awaited edition, a comprehensive biography about him has yet to be written. A number of people, including scholars, graduate students, and journalists, are attempting this difficult task. In addition, documentary films about his life have been made in the Netherlands and Germany, both using historical footage of Russia during the Revolution to illustrate the confusion of the times. They show huge rebelling crowds, and scenes with Cossacks, Russian workers, Poles, and Jews. It seems easier to show this period of history in film than to draw a written portrait of my father, a man so elusive and contradictory.

So, who was Isaac Emmanuelovich Babel?

Was he a Soviet writer, a Russian writer, or a Jewish writer?

As a Soviet writer, he shows and experiences a profound dichotomy between acceptance of the ideals of the Revolution and repulsion for its methods. As a Russian writer, he expresses both nostalgia for the old world and desire for the new. As a Jewish writer, he was well versed in Hebrew and the Talmud. Yet he wrote in Russian. His work reveals what many have called a "Jewish sensibility." However, when he used the typical Jewish themes found in Yiddish literature, they were always interwoven with Russian cultural archetypes.

Babel's work defies categorization. Simply put, in my personal view, the juxtaposition of compatibles and incompatibles keeps Babel's prose in a state of constant tension and gives it its unique character. Approaching Babel with expectations based on traditional Russian literature might lead either to disappointment or to a feeling of discovery. His prose does not merely draw on past themes and forms, but is the forging of a new manner of writing, which reflected new times. Babel's readers are not only students of Russian literature and history or of the Russian Revolution. They belong to different cultures, different religions, and different social classes. They have no single national tradition.

Critics have taken various positions and a great deal of research and passion has been invested in solving questions of Babel's personal convictions and literary style. Actually, the critical literature on Babel's works fills bookcases, compared to the mere half shelf of his own writings. Babel started writing as an adolescent, but he himself considered that his career as a man of letters, writing "clearly and concisely," began only in 1924. It was then that his stories, which were to become the volumes entitled *Red Cavalry* and *The Odessa Stories* started to appear. The young writer burst upon the literary scene and instantly became the rage in Moscow. The tradition in Russia being to worship poets and writers, Babel soon became one of the happy few, a group that included Soviet writers, who enjoyed exceptional status and privileges in an otherwise impoverished and despotic country. He was allowed to travel abroad and to stay in Western Europe for relatively long periods of time. In the late 1930s, he was given a villa in the writers' colony of Peredelkino, outside Moscow. No secret was ever made of his having a wife and daughter in Paris. At the same time, hardly anyone outside of Moscow knew of two other children he had fathered. As a matter of fact, Babel had many secrets, lived with many ambiguities and contradictions, and left many unanswered questions behind him.

During his lifetime, Babel was loved, admired, and respected as a writer. The following entry from the first volume of the second edition of the *Small Soviet Encyclopedia* of March 1937 provides an insightful description of the man and the writer. I will quote from this article, since I find it well documented, critically sound, and psychologically perceptive. It shows what Babel was striving for and what he in fact achieved. Moreover, it is astonishing to note the date of publication, the year 1937, when the ground was very shaky for Jews and intellectuals. It seems that when the books were already printed in March 1937, the publishers did not have time to revise the contents of the encyclopedia according to the Party's latest interpretations of Soviet history. They did, however, manage to glue by hand an addendum of "corrections" into each of the sixty-one thousand copies of the first volume before they were distributed, explaining the need for the revision of several of the articles. Fortunately for us, the entry on Babel was neither "corrected" nor removed.

Babel, Isaac Emmanuelovich (born 1894)—Soviet writer; son of an Odessa merchant. His first stories appeared in 1916, although the height of his literary activity occurred during the years 1923–1924. Babel's literary output is small in volume. His basic genre was the "novella" or short story, most of which can be grouped into three thematic cycles: "Odessa Stories," mainly about the exploits of the gangsters of Odessa (the film scenario of "Benya Krik" and the play "Sunset" also fall under this theme); the collection of stories "Red Cavalry"—impressions of the 1920 campaign of the army of Budyonny, in which Babel took part; and autobiographical stories ("The Story of My Dovecote," etc.). . . .

An aesthete with a heightened interest in all the colorful revelations of the human character, inclined towards the abstract intellectual humanism and to romanticism, expressing through his whole life and work the agonizing sensation of his own dilettante weaknesses, Babel admired the heroic spirit of the Revolutionary and saw the Revolution as essentially elemental, accepting it without fear.

In his portrayal of Red Cavalry soldiers, as with the gangsters of Odessa, Babel expresses both admiration and horror of their strength and natural daring, through his own intellectual's skeptical irony. This creates an original combination of heroics and humor. Characteristically, in his book "Red Cavalry," Babel focuses his attention less on the colorful episodes of military life, and more on the wild escapades of the partisans.

Typical for Babel is his primordial florid imagery, his original synthesis of romanticism and sharp naturalism, of the physiological and the erotic, which at times becomes pathological. His great mastery is in his concise picturesque story telling, his bright and witty communication of local color and life (for example—the subtly humorous depiction of Jewish life in "Odessa Stories").

The stories which he published after his long silence in 1931–1932, including the fragment "Gapa Guzhva"—which touches

separately on the theme of collectivization, are similar in nature to his
earlier literary work.

L. KAGAN

Indeed, the author of this "politically incorrect" article was on dangerous ground. One wonders whatever happened to Mr. Kagan.

By this time, the Great Purges were in full swing. Stalin held the
country in his fist. His Revolutionary comrades, his generals, writers,
anarchists, so-called Trotskyites, and their associates were arrested, tortured, and shot. The political terror penetrated all spheres of life,
including literary and cultural circles. It was only a matter of time
before my father's turn would come. He surely must have known that
he himself had been under the vigilant surveillance of the secret police
for some years.

On May 15, 1939, Babel was arrested. He disappeared. Not a
trace, not a word. He vanished. His lodgings were searched and every
scrap of paper was confiscated—correspondence, drafts, manuscripts,
everything. None of it has ever resurfaced. His name, his works, were
officially erased as though he had never existed. There was only
silence. How could a man so friendly, so socially astute, so famous, not
be able to pass a word to the outside? And so the guessing began, and
slowly, a sort of myth emerged. He never existed, but by his nonexistence, he became famous. I have been asked many times in my life,
"Do you know how he died? Do you know where? Do you know why?"
There is another question also often asked. "Why did he go back to
the Soviet Union? The times were already bad. Didn't he know it?
Why didn't he stay in Paris with his family?" Babel came to Paris in
the summer of 1935, as part the delegation of Soviet writers to the
International Congress of Writers for the Defense of Culture and
Peace. He probably knew this would have been his last chance to
remain in Europe. As he had done numerous times for some ten years,
he asked my mother to return with him to Moscow. Although he knew
the general situation was bad, he nevertheless described to her the
comfortable life that the family could have there together. It was the
last opportunity my mother had to give a negative answer, and she
never forgot it. Perhaps it helped her later on to be proven completely
right in her fears and her total lack of confidence in the Soviet Union.

My mother described to me these last conversations with my father many times.

So, why did he go back to Moscow in 1935? For many years, Babel had battled with the dilemma of his life situation. During his lengthy visits to Paris dating from 1926, he could express his thoughts without fear of possible betrayal. According to his close friend Boris Souvarine,* for example, Babel had a great knowledge of high political spheres in the Soviet Union, of its plots, manipulations and daily practices. He knew very well the nature of Stalin's character and private life, and had no illusions about Stalin's monstrous intentions and crimes.

Another person with intimate knowledge of Babel's political views at the time was Yuri Annenkov.† In his memoirs, Annenkov wrote of his many encounters with Babel in Paris and of the letters he received from him through the early 1930s. In 1932, Babel returned to Paris to visit his family, after an absence of three years. Annenkov wrote, "Babel's moods had changed significantly in the past months. It's true, he was still a big joker, but his topics of conversation were different. The last stay in the Soviet Union and the growing repression of creative art through the demands and instructions of the State had completely disillusioned him. To write within the framework of 'the barrack mentality of Soviet ideology' was intolerable for him, yet he didn't know how he could manage to live otherwise."**

Annenkov described another visit with Babel in 1932, noting that the conversation had just one subject: how to manage to live further.

---

*Boris Souvarine (1895–1984), historian and writer of Russian origin, who settled in Paris. On Lenin's personal recommendation, he became a member of the Committee for the Third International (1919), later a member of the Executive Committee of the Komintern (1921-1924), and a member of the French Communist Party, which he helped to create and from which he was expelled in 1924. Author of *Staline: Aperçu historique du Bolchevisme* (1935), the first biography and historical study of Joseph Stalin, and *Dernières conversations avec Babel*, Ed. Counterpoint, 1979, later a chapter in his book *Souvenirs sur Panait Istrati, Isaac Babel, et Pierre Pascal*, Ed. Gérard Lebovici, Paris, 1985. Souvarine was considered the foremost French specialist on Kremlin politics. The first monograph on his life and work, *Boris Souvarine: le premier désenchanté du communisme*, by Jean Louis Panné, was published in Paris in 1993 by Robert Laffont. The title speaks for itself.

†Yuri Pavlovich Annenkov (1889–1974), famous Russian portraitist, painter, printmaker, scientific draftsman, theater designer, cartoonist, writer, critic, stage manager. Left the USSR in 1924 and settled in Paris. His memoirs of his meetings with well-known artists, writers, and political figures were published in 1996 (*People and Portraits: A Tragic Cycle*, Vols. 1–2, published by the Inter-Language Literary Associates, New York, 1996).

**Annenkov, pp. 305–306.

"I have a family: a wife and daughter," said Babel, "I love them and have to provide for them. Under no circumstances do I want them to return to Sovietland. They must remain here in freedom. But what about myself? Should I stay here and become taxi driver, like the heroic Gaito Gazdanov? But you see, he has no children! Should I return to our proletarian revolution? Revolution indeed! It's disappeared! The proletariat? It flew off, like an old buggy with a leaky roof, that's lost its wheels. And it stayed wheelless. Now, dear brother, it's the Central Committees that are pushing forward—they'll be more effective. They don't need wheels—they have machine guns instead. All the rest is clear and needs no further commentary, as they say in polite society. . . . Maybe I won't become a taxi driver after all, although, as you know, I passed the driving test long ago. Here a taxi driver has more freedom than the rector of a Soviet university. . . . Driver or no driver, I'm going to become a free man.[*]

On July 27, 1933, Babel wrote to Annenkov that he had received a strange summons from Moscow and was departing immediately, "in the most dramatic conditions and no money and a lot of debts everywhere. . . . Live well without me. Don't forget Evgenia Borisovna[†] while I'm gone. . . . I kiss you. I'm glad that I'm going to Moscow. All the rest is bitter and uncertain."[**]

This turned out to be the last letter Yuri Annenkov ever received from my father. In their correspondence, Babel sounds to me like a man divided in his heart, a man pulled with equal force in two different directions.

In 1933, Babel still had a powerful political protector, his beloved mentor Alexei Maximovich Gorky. Gorky had played a critical and irreplaceable role in Babel's life. Babel wrote in 1924, "At the end of 1916, I happened to meet Gorky. I owe everything to this meeting and to this day speak the name of Alexei Maximovich with love and reverence. He published my first stories in the November 1916 issue of *Letopis*. Alexei Maximovich taught me extremely important things and sent me into the world, at a time when it was clear that my two or three

---

[*] As above.
[†] Evgenia Borisovna Babel, born Gronfein. My parents were married on August 9, 1919, in Odessa.
[**] Annenkov, p. 307.

tolerable attempts as a young man were at best successful by accident, that I would not get anywhere with literature, and that I wrote amazingly badly."*

During a trip to Italy in the spring of 1933, shortly before returning to the Soviet Union, my father visited Gorky in Sorrento. His death in 1936 was a great personal loss for Babel and signaled the inevitable coming tragedy.

One of Babel's main preoccupations was money. All his adult life, Babel had money problems and worried about them. Not that he did not make money. On the contrary, he made a lot of money. In the 1920s, his stories were published and republished in book form. In one year (1924–1925), four collections of stories and two screenplays were published. He also received payment for foreign editions. In the 1930s, he worked for film studios in Moscow, Kiev, and Leningrad and was extremely well paid for his efforts. He not only wrote original scripts, but also revised the screenplays of others, without attribution to himself. Apparently, he was the main author of *The Gorky Trilogy*, which appeared only after his arrest and without his name in the film credits.

Babel's problem was not the absence of money, but his inability to manage it. Above all, he felt the obligation to take care of his relatives abroad. His sister Meri Emmanuelovna Chapochnikoff had left in 1924 to join her fiancé, who was studying medicine in Belgium; my mother Evgenia Borisovna had left in 1925, taking with her a lifelong hatred of the Bolsheviks; and his mother, the last one to leave, joined her daughter in Brussels in 1926.

As I noted in my introduction to *The Lonely Years*, "Money matters tormented him. To make more money, he had to work under increasingly difficult conditions. Moreover, the impractical Babel would let his generosity run away with him. Whether he was in Moscow or in Paris, distant relatives, friends and friends of friends were continually imploring him for financial assistance. A few weeks after his return to the Soviet Union from a trip abroad, he would find himself totally impoverished, his Soviet friends having finished the job that had begun in

---

*Excerpt from an autobiographical sketch by Babel that appeared in Lidin, Vladimir (ed.), *"Pisateli: avtobiografii i portrety sovremennykh russkikh prozaikov"* ("Authors: Autobiographies and Portraits of Contemporary Russian Writers") Sovremennyie Problemi (Contemporary Problems), Moscow, 1926, pp. 27–29.

Paris. Above all, Babel feared that his economic position would affect his work. His life centered on writing."[*]

His inability to imagine himself as anything but a writer played a critical role in his refusal to leave the USSR. His stays abroad made him understand that he could not make a comfortable living as an émigré writer.

As Cynthia Ozick observed in a review of Babel's *1920 Diary*, "By remaining in the Soviet Union and refusing finally to bend his art to Soviet directives, Babel sacrificed his life to his language."[†]

Souvarine remembers what he called Babel's leitmotiv, "I am a Russian writer. If I did not live with the Russian people, I would cease being a writer. I would be like a fish out of water."[**] Actually, my mother would use these words almost verbatim to explain my father's absence and why I had no brothers and sisters, whom I had always wanted. This romantic ideal of the writer, which was only part of the story, stayed with me for a very long part of my life. It took many years to let it go.

For Babel, it is clear that there was no one ideal solution. In the end, a man's destiny is his own.

In 1954, after many years of official silence, Babel's name was heard again. A typed half sheet of ordinary paper, accepted as an official document, declared, "The sentence of the Military College dated 26 January 1940 concerning Babel I. E. is revoked on the basis of newly discovered circumstances and the case against him is terminated in the absence of elements of a crime." The news took a couple of years to leak out of Moscow to the rest of Europe. Several decades later in the early 1990s, following the breakup of the Soviet Union, some brave souls were able to get access to the KGB's archives on Babel. Minute records had been kept about the arrest and interrogations of the accused.

As we now know, his trial took place on January 26, 1940, in one of Lavrenti Beria's private chambers. It lasted about twenty minutes. The sentence had been prepared in advance and without ambiguity:

---

[*] *Isaac Babel: The Lonely Years 1925–1939. Unpublished Stories and Private Correspondence.* Edited with an Intoduction by Nathalie Babel, published by Farrar, Straus and Co., 1964.

[†] Cynthia Ozick, "The Year of Writing Dangerously," *The New Republic*, May 8, 1995.

[**] Boris Souvarine, *Souvenirs sur Panait Istrati, Isaac Babel, et Pierre Pascal,* Ed. Gérard Lebovici, Paris 1985, p. 34.

death by firing squad, to be carried out immediately. Babel had been accused and convicted of "active participation in an anti-Soviet Trotskyite organization" and of "being a member of a terrorist conspiracy, as well as spying for the French and Austrian governments."

Babel's last recorded words in the proceedings were, "I am innocent. I have never been a spy. I never allowed any action against the Soviet Union. I accused myself falsely. I was forced to make false accusations against myself and others. . . . I am asking for only one thing— let me finish my work." He was shot the next day and his body was thrown into a communal grave. All of this horrific information was revealed in the early 1990s, a relatively short time ago.

Considering that revelations about my father have been coming to light for almost fifty years, a large portion of my life, I understand why it has never been possible to put an end to grieving. In this edition, I have also included in the afterword a few of my own memoirs, which illustrate how his absence affected me personally. For many years now, I have been involved with attempting to bring together and to light what is recognized as the body of Babel's work. I hope the present ambitious project will provide further insights into his personality, as well as a greater knowledge and appreciation of his literary legacy.

NATHALIE BABEL
Washington, D.C.
March 2001

FOREWORD

by Peter Constantine

*O*ne of the great tragedies of twentieth century literature took place in the early morning hours of May 15, 1939, when a cadre of agents from the Soviet secret police burst into the house of Isaac Babel in Peredelkino, arrested him, and gathered up the many stacks of unpublished manuscripts in his office. From that day on, Babel, one of the foremost writers of his time, became a nonperson in the Soviet Union. His name was blotted out, removed from literary dictionaries and encyclopedias, and taken off school and university syllabi. He became unmentionable in any public venue. When the film director Mark Donskoi's famous Gorky trilogy premiered the following year, Babel, who had worked on the screenplay, had been removed from the credits.

Babel was executed in 1940. It was only in 1954, fourteen years later, that he was officially exonerated, but his books were only warily republished in the Soviet Union, and in censored form. And yet today, sixty-two years after his arrest and the subsequent silence surrounding his name, Babel is considered, both inside and outside Russia, to be among the most exciting—and at times unsettling—writers of the twentieth century.

Babel is one of the great masters of the short story, and for the translator a great and challenging master of style. It has been fascinating to see his style change from work to work. We are familiar with terms such as Proustian, Chekhovian, and Nabokovian, but, as I soon realized, the term "Babelian" is harder to define.

Babel burst onto the literary scene after the Bolshevik Revolution of 1917, becoming within a few years one of Russia's most original and highly regarded authors—"the best Russia has to offer," as Maxim Gorky wrote to André Malraux in 1926. Babel began his career during a time when Russian culture, society, and language were in total upheaval. World War I, the February and October Revolutions of 1917, and the Civil War left in their wake poverty, hunger, and social instability. At the same time, the promise of limitless change was in the air. The people of Russia felt that they were being given the opportunity to participate in an exhilarating and unprecedented social experiment which, if World Communism was to have its way, would be a global one.

The abrupt social changes on all levels, the abolition of imperial censorship, and the new feeling of liberty drove writers of Babel's generation—Mayakovsky, Pasternak, Zamyatin, Bulgakov—to write in new ways about new topics with an unprecedented vigor. Babel did this with a vengeance. His themes were steeped in the brutal realism of the times: In the arctic night of Petersburg a Chinese man, seeing a desperate prostitute, holds up a loaf of bread—"With his blue fingernail he draws a line across the crust. One pound. Glafira [the prostitute] raises two fingers. Two pounds." A teenage girl tries to help her younger sister abort her baby with a clothes hanger—their mother walks in on them just in time. The morgues of Petersburg are filled with corpses—the narrator gazes at a dead aristocratic couple and, looking at the noblewoman, thinks, "In death she keeps a stamp of beauty and impudence. She sobs and laughs disdainfully at her murderers." Starving wet nurses feeding undersized infants in state-run maternity wards beg the narrator for a crust of bread.

These were contemporary topics that before Babel nobody had dared touch. When the valiant Red Cavalry rode into Poland, in what was intended to be the first step that would carry the glories of Communism to Europe and the world, Babel rode along. He brought back with him a series of stories that presented a literary portrait of war that has awed and haunted readers for almost eighty years.

One apt definition of "Babelian" might be: a trenchant and unrelenting literary re-creation of a world in war and turmoil. And yet this is a limited definition, for it leaves out Babel's irrepressible sense of

humor in his stories, plays, and screenplays. In the screenplay *Roaming Stars*, Babel describes a production of *King Lear* in the hinterlands of Volhynia, where Lear's daughters appear onstage as "[two] stout, middle-aged Jewish women, the third is a girl of about six . . . the actresses are also wearing lacquered officer's boots with spurs." In the play *Sunset*, Babel portrays a synagogue scene that the Moscow Arts Theater cut out of its 1928 production of the play because the scene was deemed too irreverent toward Judaism. As the carters chant and pray, Arye-Leib, the synagogue *shamas*, discusses market prices with them:

ARYE-LEIB (serenely): *Lifnei adonai ki vo, ki vo* . . . *Oy*, I am standing, *oy*, I am standing before God . . . where do oats stand?
SECOND JEW (without interrupting his prayer): A ruble and four, a ruble and four!
ARYE-LEIB: I'm going crazy!

In translating *The Complete Works of Isaac Babel*, I was constantly struck by the different registers of Babel's voice in different stories. The minute I thought I had pinned down Babel's style, it transformed itself into something very different in the next story. Babel's first published piece, "Old Shloyme," which opens this volume, has absolutely nothing in common with the style, content, language, or rhythm of the second story, "At Grandmother's," or with the story after that, or with any of the other stories. The Odessa stories, traditionally thought of as a stylistic unit threaded through with feisty Babelian color, are, on closer scrutiny, just as disparate. In the first Odessa story, "The King," the author-narrator draws us into the wild gangster world of Odessa with his elegant and surprising prose: "The tables, draped in velvet, coiled through the yard like a snake on whose belly patches of every color had been daubed, and these orange and red velvet patches sang in deep voices." The second Odessa story, "Justice in Parentheses," begins on a very different note: "My first run-in was with Benya Krik, my second with Lyubka Shneiweis. Do you understand the meaning of these words? Can you drink in their full essence?" Here the narrator Zudechkis, a small-time wheeler-dealer who operates on the fringes of Odessa's Jewish underworld, suddenly steps into the foreground. The story is told from his perspective and in his subtly Yiddling words, "At five o'clock in the morning—or no, it must have been four, and then again, maybe it wasn't even four yet—the King entered my bedroom, grabbed me, if you will pardon the expression, by my back, dragged me out of bed. . . ." In the next story, "How Things Were Done in Odessa," the primary narrator is an unworldly Jew, described as having glasses on his nose and autumn in his heart.

The Red Cavalry stories are, stylistically speaking, just as varied. There is the "I" of Isaac Babel and the "I" of Kiril Lyutov, the very Russian war correspondent (who might go as far as admitting that his mother is Jewish). "Lyutov" was also the identity that Babel assumed in real life as a way of surviving among the fiercely anti-Semitic Cossacks of the Red Cavalry. There are also other narrators, such as the murderous Cossack Balmashov. When these characters are the narrators, the tone, style, and grammar in the stories begin to go awry. Babel is a master at re-creating the Cossacks' wild, ungrammatical speech filled with skewed and half-understood Communist doctrine. In "Salt," for instance, the entire story is narrated in the voice of a Cossack whose ranting jumble ranges from Communist jargon to folk verse:

> I want to tell you of some ignorant women who are harmful to us. I set my hopes on you, that you who travel around our nation's fronts have not overlooked the far-flung station of Fastov, lying afar beyond the mountains grand, in a distant province of a distant land, where many a jug of home-brewed beer we drank with merriment and cheer.

Babel is one of the few writers who goes out of his way never to repeat himself. Each of his many reports from Petersburg, Georgia, or France is original, almost as if more than one reporter were at work. The two plays sound and feel completely different from each other, and the screenplays are so different from one another in style and presentation—that it is hard to believe (even for the translator who has pored over every word and comma) that they were written by the same writer.

I have found in translating other authors, such as Anton Chekhov and Thomas Mann, that after a few stories I was steering toward a

Chekhovian or Mannian style I felt worked in English. Not so with Babel. Each of the 147 texts in this volume, from the shortest story to the longest play, had to be treated on its own terms. Babel is not only one of the greatest storytellers of European literature, but also one of its greatest stylists.

PETER CONSTANTINE
New York
March 2001

ACKNOWLEDGMENTS

*T*he purpose of this volume is to present in one edition everything known to have been written by Isaac Babel. In this light, we call the volume *Complete Works,* even though this term may not include all of Babel's literary heritage, since his files of manuscripts were seized by the police upon his arrest. But as there is little hope that any of that material survives or can be recovered, we use the word "complete."

The realization of this volume has been a long-term dream and struggle. The struggle has been made easier by my good fortune in working with Peter Constantine, who took it upon himself to translate anew all available original manuscripts and the first publications in Russian—a long and arduous task. As this is the first time that a single person has translated all of Babel's work into English, this volume has a unique coherence and consistency that I believe is true to Babel's voice in Russian. Peter was not only meticulous in his choice of words and phrasing, but also in his research in order to clarify the text and provide notes where necessary. He also was of great help to me in organizing and editing this large and unwieldy collection of materials, and in supporting me with frequent practical advice and unflagging enthusiasm.

I approached Gregory Freidin without warning to request that he prepare a biographical and literary chronology of Babel's life and works. Gregory's exceptional knowledge allowed us to sort out many conflicting or incomplete items of information. I thank him for his graciousness in completing this task.

Special thanks are also due to Robert Weil, my editor at W. W.

Norton, who embraced the challenge of giving new life to Babel's work through what he knew would be a difficult project. His editorial advice and his steadfast guidance have earned my heartfelt gratitude. Without the professional perseverance and affectionate encouragement of my friend and literary agent, Jennifer Lyons, this work would not have been completed. I thank her warmly.

When it came to my own contribution, I chose to forego writing a traditional introduction in favor of speaking of the connections between Babel and myself, connections that have not been obvious despite his being my father. No research or scholar could help me there. I had only myself, the blank page, and the past. Enter my friend Christine Galitzine. I cannot hope to acquit my debt merely with thanks, or even the feelings of profound gratitude and affection that I feel for her. As she became more and more interested in this project, she also became more indispensable to my being able to advance it. Through her knowledge of English, French, and Russian, as well as her own literary and administrative gifts, she was able to understand my thoughts and sentiments deeply and to help me render them onto the printed page. Indeed, her involvement in this work led her to make a detour while traveling in France, to visit the town of Niort, which occupies a large place in my life and my recollections. Upon arrival there, she went immediately to the information office to ask whether the old jail still existed. Unfazed, the French lady in charge told her that the jail remained in the same location that it had been for the last three hundred years. Christine came back with photos, brochures, maps, and historic and geographic information—an act which moved me deeply and helped me to confront more peacefully these difficult episodes of my life.

This publication is also the realization of a dream of my husband, Richard Harvey Brown, who for over thirty years has hoped that I would be able to master my memories sufficiently to bring this volume to print. His benevolence and loving support throughout these struggles also should be publicly acknowledged.

NATHALIE BABEL BROWN

*I*would like to thank Nathalie Babel for offering me this project, and for her constant support and encouragement. I owe particular thanks to my Russian editor, Anneta Greenlee, for her tireless checking of my translation against the Russian original for stylistic nuance. My translation owes much to her specialized knowledge of early-twentieth-century Russian language and literature. I am also grateful to Katya Ilina for her help in editing Isaac Babel's *1920 Diary*, and for the weeks she spent studying the many editions of Babel works, checking for editorial variations and instances of Soviet censorship.

I am also indebted to my editor at Norton, Robert Weil, for his insightful and knowledgeable editing and particularly for his expertise in American and European Jewish literature. I am also grateful to Jason Baskin and Nomi Victor, editors at Norton, and to David Cole for copyediting the manuscript.

I am indebted to Professor Gregory Freidin for his help and advice, and for his specialized knowledge of Isaac Babel's life and works, and to Christine Galitzine for her knowledge of pre-Revolutionary Russia.

I am thankful to Peter Glassgold for his initial suggestion that I translate Isaac Babel, and for his helpful editorial advice. I am thankful also to my agent, Jessica Wainwright, for her encouragement and constant support as I worked on the translation. I also wish to thank Jennifer Lyons, the agent of the Babel estate, for her help and input.

I am deeply indebted to the resources of the New York Public Library, where I did all my research and annotation. I owe special gratitude to Edward Kasinec, curator of the Slavic and Baltic Division, for his erudite advice and for the many times he personally located materials for me that were hidden in obscure Soviet publications of the 1920s and 1930s. I am also grateful to Tanya Gizdavcic, librarian of the Slavic and Baltic Division, for her help in locating material, and to Serge Gleboff, Robert Davis, Lev Chaban, and Hee-Gwone Yoo for their help and advice.

I would like to thank Paul Glasser at YIVO for his helpful explanations of Yiddish expressions. I would also like to express my appreciation to Karina Vamling from the Linguistics Department of the University of Lund, Sweden, for her explanations of Georgian expressions in Isaac Babel's texts and the information she provided on aspects of Georgian and Caucasian politics that Babel referred to, and to Peter Gasiorowski of the University of Poznan, Poland, for his linguistic advice on expressions used in the *1920 Diary*. I am also grateful to Thomas Fiddick for his help—I benefited greatly from his books and articles on the Russian-Polish war of 1920. I am thankful as well to Patricia Herlihy for her encouragement: I found her book *Odessa: A History, 1794–1914* a great help in putting early-twentieth-century Odessa—the Odessa of Babel's early years—into perspective. I found the extensive annotations in the German translation of the *1920 Diary* by Peter Urban very helpful, as I did the scholarly and bibliographical work on Babel by Efraim Sicher. I am also grateful for Professor Sicher's valuable corrections and suggestions for the footnotes of this edition.

My very special thanks to Burton Pike, who inspired, helped, and advised me throughout the project.

PETER CONSTANTINE

THE
COMPLETE
WORKS
OF
ISAAC BABEL

I

❖

Early Stories

W hen the twenty-one-year-old Isaac Babel arrived in St. Petersburg in 1916, he found the city in wild but stimulating upheaval. It was still the capital of Russia and the center of Russian literature and art, where the foremost writers of the day lived and published. But the city was shaken by World War I. The Imperial government was losing control, and calls for change, which were to lead to the Revolution and Civil War, were in the air. Perhaps most important for a young writer was that the Czarist censorship was crumbling, which meant that daring new subjects could be treated in new ways, a characteristic that was to stay with Babel throughout his writing career. His first published story, "Old Shloyme" (1913), dealt with the subversive subject of Jews forced by officially sanctioned anti-Semitism to renounce their religion. In the story, a young Jew gives in to the pressure to Russianize himself, "to leave his people for a new God," while the old Jew, though never interested in religion or tradition, cannot bring himself to give them up. In the subsequent stories, Babel touches on other taboo subjects: Jewish men mixing with Christian women, prostitution, teenage pregnancy, and abortion.

These early stories also reveal Babel's growing interest in using language in new and unusual ways. He has a young woman offer herself to her lover, "and the lanky fellow wallowed in businesslike bliss." Odessa matrons, "plump with idleness and naively corseted are passionately squeezed behind bushes by fervent students of medicine or law." Babel describes the Czarina as "a small woman with a tightly powdered face, a consummate schemer with an indefatigable passion for power." In a forest scene, "green leaves bent toward one another, caressed each other with their flat hands." We also see the recurring motifs of sun and sunset, which are to play an important role in Babel's later writing.

Babel's piquant brand of realism soon caught the eye of Maxim Gorky, who was to be the single most influential literary figure in the Soviet Union during the 1920s and 1930s, and who was particularly instrumental in helping young Soviet writers. Gorky published Babel's stories "Elya Isaakovich and Margarita Prokofievna," and "Mama, Rimma, and Alla" in 1916 in his literary magazine LETOPIS, which marked the beginning of Gorky's mentoring of Babel's career. This mentoring was to last until Gorky's death exactly twenty years later.

OLD SHLOYME

*A*lthough our town is small, its inhabitants few in number, and although Shloyme had not left this town once in sixty years, you'd be hard-pressed to find a single person who was able to tell you exactly who Shloyme was or what he was all about. The reason for this, plain and simple, is that he was forgotten, the way you forget an unnecessary thing that doesn't jump out and grab you. Old Shloyme was precisely that kind of thing. He was eighty-six years old. His eyes were watery. His face—his small, dirty, wrinkled face—was overgrown with a yellowish beard that had never been combed, and his head was covered with a thick, tangled mane. Shloyme almost never washed, seldom changed his clothes, and gave off a foul stench. His son and daughter-in-law, with whom he lived, had stopped bothering about him—they kept him in a warm corner and forgot about him. His warm corner and his food were all that Shloyme had left, and it seemed that this was all he needed. For him, warming his old broken bones and eating a nice, fat, juicy piece of meat were the purest bliss. He was the first to come to the table, and greedily watched every bite with unflinching eyes, convulsively cramming food into his mouth with his long bony fingers, and he ate, ate, ate till they refused to give him any more, even a tiny little piece. Watching Shloyme eat was disgusting: his whole puny body quivered, his fingers covered with grease, his face so pitiful, filled with the dread that someone might harm him, that he might be forgotten. Sometimes his daughter-in-law would play a little trick on Shloyme. She would serve the food, and then act as if she had overlooked him.

The old man would begin to get agitated, look around helplessly, and try to smile with his twisted, toothless mouth. He wanted to show that food was not important to him, that he could perfectly well make do without it, but there was so much pleading in the depths of his eyes, in the crease of his mouth, in his outstretched, imploring arms, and his smile, wrenched with such difficulty, was so pitiful, that all jokes were dropped, and Shloyme received his portion.

And thus he lived in his corner—he ate and slept, and in the summer he also lay baking in the sun. It seemed that he had long ago lost all ability to comprehend anything. Neither his son's business nor household matters interested him. He looked blankly at everything that took place around him, and the only fear that would flutter up in him was that his grandson might catch on that he had hidden a dried-up piece of honey cake under his pillow. Nobody ever spoke to Shloyme, asked his advice about anything, or asked him for help. And Shloyme was quite happy, until one day his son came over to him after dinner and shouted loudly into his ear, "Papa, they're going to evict us from here! Are you listening? Evict us, kick us out!" His son's voice was shaking, his face twisted as if he were in pain. Shloyme slowly raised his faded eyes, looked around, vaguely comprehending something, wrapped himself tighter in his greasy frock coat, didn't say a word, and shuffled off to sleep.

From that day on Shloyme began noticing that something strange was going on in the house. His son was crestfallen, wasn't taking care of his business, and at times would burst into tears and look furtively at his chewing father. His grandson stopped going to high school. His daughter-in-law yelled shrilly, wrung her hands, pressed her son close to her, and cried bitterly and profusely.

Shloyme now had an occupation, he watched and tried to comprehend. Muffled thoughts stirred in his long-torpid brain. "They're being kicked out of here!" Shloyme knew why they were being kicked out. "But Shloyme can't leave! He's eighty-six years old! He wants to stay warm! It's cold outside, damp. . . . No! Shloyme isn't going anywhere! He has nowhere to go, nowhere!" Shloyme hid in his corner and wanted to clasp the rickety wooden bed in his arms, caress the stove, the sweet, warm stove that was as old as he was. "He grew up here, spent his poor, bleak life here, and wants his old bones to be buried in the small local cemetery!" At moments when such thoughts came to him, Shloyme became unnaturally animated, walked up to his son, wanted to talk to him with passion and at great length, to give him advice on a couple of things, but . . . it had been such a long time since he had spoken to anyone, or given anyone advice. And the words froze in his toothless mouth, his raised arm dropped weakly. Shloyme, all huddled up as if ashamed at his outburst, sullenly went back to his corner and listened to what his son was saying to his daughter-in-law. His hearing was bad, but with fear and dread he sensed something terrifying. At such moments his son felt the heavy crazed look of the old man, who was being driven insane, focused on him. The old man's two small eyes with their accursed probing, seemed incessantly to sense something, to question something. On one occasion words were said too loudly—it had slipped the daughter-in-law's mind that Shloyme was still alive. And right after her words were spoken, there was a quiet, almost smothered wail. It was old Shloyme. With tottering steps, dirty and disheveled, he slowly hobbled over to his son, grabbed his hands, caressed them, kissed them, and, not taking his inflamed eyes off his son, shook his head several times, and for the first time in many, many years, tears flowed from his eyes. He didn't say anything. With difficulty he got up from his knees, his bony hand wiping away the tears; for some reason he shook the dust off his frock coat and shuffled back to his corner, to where the warm stove stood. Shloyme wanted to warm himself. He felt cold.

From that time on, Shloyme thought of nothing else. He knew one thing for certain: his son wanted to leave his people for a new God. The old, forgotten faith was kindled within him. Shloyme had never been religious, had rarely ever prayed, and in his younger days had even had the reputation of being godless. But to leave, to leave one's God completely and forever, the God of an oppressed and suffering people—that he could not understand. Thoughts rolled heavily inside his head, he comprehended things with difficulty, but these words remained unchanged, hard, and terrible before him: "This mustn't happen, it mustn't!" And when Shloyme realized that disaster was inevitable, that his son couldn't hold out, he said to himself, "Shloyme, old Shloyme! What are you going to do now?" The old man looked around helplessly, mournfully puckered his lips like a child, and wanted to burst into the bitter tears of an old man. But there were no relieving tears. And then, at the moment his heart began aching, when his mind grasped the boundlessness of the disaster, it was then that Shloyme looked at his warm corner one last time and decided that no one was going to kick him out of here, they would never kick him out. "They will not let old Shloyme eat the dried-up piece of honey cake lying under his pillow! So what! Shloyme will tell God how he was wronged! After all, there is a God, God will take him in!" Shloyme was sure of this.

In the middle of the night, trembling with cold, he got up from his bed. Quietly, so as not to wake anyone, he lit a small kerosene lamp. Slowly, with an old man's groaning and shivering, he started pulling on his dirty clothes. Then he took the stool and the rope he had prepared the night before, and, tottering with weakness, steadying himself on the walls, went out into the street. Suddenly it was so cold. His whole body shivered. Shloyme quickly fastened the rope onto a hook, stood up next to the door, put the stool in place, clambered up onto it, wound the rope around his thin, quivering neck, kicked away the stool with his last strength, managing with his dimming eyes to glance at the town he had not left once in sixty years, and hung.

There was a strong wind, and soon old Shloyme's frail body began swaying before the door of his house in which he had left his warm stove and the greasy Torah of his forefathers.

AT GRANDMOTHER'S

*O*n Sabbaths after six classes I came home late. Walking through the streets didn't seem to me pointless. I could daydream remarkably well as I walked, and I felt that everything, everything around me was part of my being. I knew the signs, the stones of the houses, the windows of the stores. I knew them in a very special way, a very personal way, and I was firmly convinced that I saw the fundamental secret within them—what we grown-ups call the "essence" of things. Everything about them was deeply imprinted on my soul. When grown-ups mentioned a store in my presence, I envisioned its sign, the worn, golden letters, the little scratch in the left corner, the young lady with the tall coiffure at the cash register, and I remembered the air around this store that was not around any other. I pieced together from these stores, from the people, the air, the theater posters, my own hometown. To this day I remember, feel, and love this town—feel it, as one feels one's mother's scent, the scent of her caresses, words, and smiles, and I love this town because I grew up in it, was happy, melancholy, and dreamy in it. Passionately and singularly dreamy.

I always walked down the main street—that is where most of the people were.

The Sabbath I want to tell you about was a Sabbath in early spring. At that time of year, our air does not have the quiet tenderness, so sweet in central Russia, resting upon its peaceful streams and modest valleys. Our air has a sparkling, light coolness that blows with a shallow, chilly passion. I was no more than a young boy then and didn't understand a thing, but I felt the spring, and I blossomed and reddened in the chill.

The walk lasted a long time. I stared at the diamonds in the jeweler's window, read the theater posters from A to Z, and once I even studied the pale pink corsets with their long, wavy suspenders in Madam Rosalie's store. As I was about to walk on, I collided with a tall student who had a big black mustache. He smiled at me and asked, "So you're examining these closely, are you?" I was mortified. Then he patronizingly patted me on the back and said in a superior tone, "Keep up the good work, dear colleague! My compliments! All the best!" He roared with laughter, turned, and walked away. I felt very flustered, avoided looking at Madam Rosalie's display window, and quickly headed for home.

I was supposed to spend the Sabbath at my grandmother's. She had her own room at the very end of the apartment, behind the kitchen. A stove stood in the corner of this room, Grandmother always felt cold. The room was hot and stuffy, which made me feel melancholy and want to escape, to get out into the open.

I dragged my belongings over to Grandmother's, my books, my music stand, and my violin. The table had already been set for me. Grandmother sat in the corner. I ate. We didn't say a word. The door was locked. We were alone. There was cold gefilte fish for dinner with horseradish (a dish worth embracing Judaism for), a rich and delicious soup, roasted meat with onions, salad, compote, coffee, pie, and apples. I ate everything. I was a dreamer, it is true, but a dreamer with a hearty appetite. Grandmother cleared away the dishes. The room became tidy. There were wilting flowers on the windowsill. What grandmother loved best among all living things were her son, her grandson, Mimi her dog, and flowers. Mimi came over, rolled herself up on the sofa, and immediately fell asleep. She was kind of a lazy pooch, but a splendid dog, good, clever, small, and pretty. Mimi was a pug dog. Her coat was light-colored. Even in old age she didn't get flabby or heavy, but managed to remain svelte and slim. She lived with us for a long time, from birth to death, the whole fifteen years of her dog life, and, needless to say, she loved us, and most of all our severe and unbending grandmother. I shall tell about what tight-mouthed, secretive friends they were another time. It is a very interesting and tender story.

So there we were, the three of us—Grandmother, Mimi, and me. Mimi slept. Grandmother, kind, wearing her holiday silk dress, sat in the corner, and I was supposed to study. That day was difficult for me. There were six classes in the high school, and Mr. Sorokin, the music teacher, was supposed to come, and Mr. L., the Hebrew teacher, to make up the lesson I had missed, and then maybe Peysson, my French teacher. I had to prepare for all these lessons. I could deal with L. easily enough, we were old friends, but the music and the scales—what anguish! First of all, I started on my homework. I spread out my notebooks and painstakingly began to do my mathematics problems. Grandmother didn't interrupt me, God forbid. The tension inside her, and her reverence for my work, gave her face a dazed look. Her eyes, round, yellow, transparent, never left me. I would turn a page—and her eyes would slowly follow my hand. Another person might have suffered greatly under her persistent, watchful, unwavering stare, but I was used to it.

Then Grandmother listened to me recite my lessons. It has to be said that her Russian was bad—she had her own peculiar way of mangling words, mixing Russian with Polish and Hebrew. Needless to say, she couldn't read or write Russian, and would hold books upside down. But that didn't deter me from reciting my lesson from beginning to end. Grandmother listened without understanding a word, but to her the music of the words was sweet, she bowed before science, believed me, believed in me, and wanted me to become a "bogatir"*—that is what she called a rich man. I finished my lessons and began reading a book. At the time, I was reading "First Love" by Turgenev. I liked everything in it, the clear words, the descriptions, the conversations, but the scene that made me shiver all over was the one in which Vladimir's father strikes Zinaida's cheek with a whip. I could hear the whip's whistling sound—its lithe leather body sharply, painfully, instantly biting into me. I was seized by an indescribable emotion. At that point in the book I had to stop reading, and pace up and down the room. And Grandmother sat there stock-still, and even the hot, stupefying air did not stir, as if it sensed I was studying and shouldn't be disturbed. The heat in the room kept rising. Mimi began snoring. Until then there had

*The grandmother is mixing up *Bogatir,* a Herculean hero in Russian folklore, with *bogaty,* "rich man."

been silence, a ghostly silence, not a sound. Everything seemed uncanny at that moment and I wanted to run away from it all, and yet I wanted to stay there forever. The darkening room, Grandmother's yellow eyes, her tiny body wrapped in a shawl silent and hunched over in the corner, the hot air, the closed door, and the clout of the whip, and that piercing whistle—only now do I realize how strange it all was, how much it meant to me. I was snatched out of this troubled state by the doorbell. Sorokin had come. I hated him at that moment, I hated the scales, the incomprehensible, pointless, shrill music. I must admit that Sorokin was quite a nice fellow. He wore his black hair cropped very short, had large red hands, and beautiful thick lips. On that day, under Grandmother's watchful stare, he had to work for a whole hour, even longer, he had to push himself to the limit. For all of this he got absolutely no recognition. The old woman's eyes coldly and persistently followed his every move, remaining distant and indifferent. Grandmother had no interest in outside people. She demanded that they fulfill their obligations to us, and nothing more. We began our lesson. I wasn't frightened of Grandmother, but for a full hour I had to brave poor Sorokin's boundless zeal. He felt extremely ill-at-ease in this remote room, in the presence of a dog peacefully asleep and a coldly watchful, hostile old woman. Finally he took his leave. Grandmother gave him her hard, wrinkled, large hand with indifference, without shaking it. On his way out, he stumbled into a chair.

I also survived the following hour, Mr. L.'s lesson, longing for the moment that the door would close behind him too.

Evening came. Faraway golden dots ignited in the sky. Our courtyard, a deep cage, was dazzled by the moon. A woman's voice next door sang the ballad "Why I Am Madly in Love." My parents went to the theater. I became melancholy. I was tired. I had read so much, studied so much, seen so much. Grandmother lit a lamp. Her room immediately became quiet. The dark, heavy furniture was softly illuminated. Mimi woke up, walked through the room, came back to us again, and waited for her supper. The maid brought in the samovar. Grandmother was a tea lover. She had saved a slice of honey cake for me. We drank large quantities. Sweat sparkled in Grandmother's deep, sharp wrinkles. "Are you sleepy?" she asked. "No," I said. We began to talk. And once more I heard Grandmother's stories. Long ago, many, many years ago, there was a Jew who ran a tavern. He was poor, married, burdened with children, and traded in bootleg vodka. The commissar came and tormented him. Life became difficult. He went to the *tsaddik* and said, "Rabbi! The commissar is vexing me to death! Speak to God on my behalf!" "Go in peace," the *tsaddik* said to him. "The commissar will calm down." The Jew left. At the threshold of his tavern he found the commissar. He was lying there dead, with a purple, swollen face.

Grandmother fell silent. The samovar hummed. The woman next door was still singing. The moon still dazzled. Mimi wagged her tail. She was hungry.

"In olden times, people had beliefs!" Grandmother said. "Life on earth was simpler. When I was a girl, the Poles rebelled. Near where we lived was a count's estate. Even the Czar came to visit the count. Seven days and seven nights they made merry. At night I ran over to the count's castle and looked through the bright windows. The count had a daughter and the finest pearls in the world. Then came the uprising. Soldiers dragged him out onto the square. We all stood there crying. The soldiers dug a pit. They wanted to blindfold the old man. He said, "That will not be necessary!" The count stood before the soldiers and ordered, "Fire!" He was a tall, gray-haired man. The muzhiks loved him. Just as they began burying him, a messenger came galloping up. He brought a pardon from the Czar.

The samovar had gone out. Grandmother drank her last, cold glass of tea, and sucked on a piece of sugar with her toothless mouth.

"Your grandfather," she began, "knew many stories, but he had no beliefs whatsoever, he only believed in people. He gave away all his money to his friends, and when his turn came to ask them for something they kicked him down the stairs, and he lost his mind."

And then Grandmother told me about my grandfather, a tall, haughty, passionate, and despotic man. He played the violin, wrote literary works at night, and knew all the languages. He was governed by an unquenchable thirst for knowledge and life. A general's daughter fell in love with their eldest son, who traveled a lot, played cards, and died in Canada at the age of thirty-seven. All Grandmother had left was one son and me. It was all over. Day slips into evening, and death slowly approaches. Grandmother falls silent, lowers her head, and begins crying.

"Study!" she suddenly said forcefully. "Study and you can have everything—wealth and glory. You must know everything. Everyone will fall on their knees before you and bow to you. Let them envy you. Don't believe in people. Don't have friends. Don't give them your money. Don't give them your heart!"

Grandmother stops talking. Silence. Grandmother is thinking of bygone years and sorrows, is thinking about my fate, and her severe testament rests heavily, eternally, on my weak, young shoulders. In the dark corner, the incandescent cast-iron stove is blazing intensely. I'm suffocating, I can't breathe, I want to run out into the air, into the open, but I don't have the strength to lift my drooping head.

Dishes clatter in the kitchen. Grandmother goes there. We're going to have supper. I hear her angry, metallic voice. She is shouting at the maid. I feel strange and troubled. Just a short while ago she had been breathing peace and sorrow. The maid snaps back at her. Grandmother's unbearably shrill voice rings out in an uncontrollable rage, "Get out of here, you dreck! I'm the mistress here. You are destroying my property. Get out of here!" I cannot bear her deafening voice of steel. I can see Grandmother through the half-open door. Her face is distorted, her lips are trembling thinly and relentlessly, her throat has thickened, as if it were bulging out. The maid answers back. "Get out of here," Grandmother says. Then there is silence. The maid bows, and quietly, as if she were afraid of offending the silence, slips out of the room.

We eat our dinner without talking. We eat our fill, abundantly and long. Grandmother's transparent eyes are staring immovably—what they are staring at, I do not know. After supper, she [. . .]*

• • •

More than that I do not see because I fall into a deep sleep, a child's sleep behind seven locks in Grandmother's hot room.

*Gap in manuscript.

ELYA ISAAKOVICH

AND

MARGARITA PROKOFIEVNA

*G*ershkovich came out of the police chief's office with a heavy heart. He had been informed that if he didn't leave Oryol on the first train, he would have to leave town in a chain gang. And leaving meant he would lose business.

With briefcase in hand, gaunt, unhurried, he walked down the dark street. At the corner, a tall female figure called out to him, "Will you come with me, sweetie?"

Gershkovich raised his head, looked at her through his shimmering spectacles, thought it over, and guardedly said, "I'll come."

The woman took him by the arm. They walked around the corner.

"So where will we go? To a hotel?"

"I want something for the whole night," Gershkovich answered. "How about your place?"

"That'll cost you three rubles, Papa."

"Two," Gershkovich said.

"Not worth my while, Papa!"

• • •

He managed to haggle her down to two-and-a-half rubles. They began walking.

The prostitute's room was small, nice, and clean, with frayed curtains and a pink lamp.

When they entered, the woman took off her coat, unbuttoned her blouse, and winked at him.

"Hey!" Gershkovich said, knitting his brow. "Stop messing around!"

"You're in a bad mood, Papa."

She came over and sat on his knee.

"Well, I'll be damned!" Gershkovich said. "You must weigh at least five *pood*!"

"Four-point-three *pood*!"

She gave him a long kiss on his graying cheek.

• • •

"Hey!" Gershkovich said, knitting his brow again. "I'm tired, I want to go to sleep."

The prostitute stood up. Her face had become hard.

"You a Jew?"

He looked at her through his spectacles and answered, "No."

"Papa," the prostitute said slowly, "that'll be ten rubles."

He got up and walked to the door.

"Five," the woman said.

Gershkovich came back.

"Make up the bed for me," the Jew said wearily, then took off his jacket and looked for a place to hang it. "What's your name?"

"Margarita."

"Change the sheets, Margarita."

The bed was wide and covered with a soft eiderdown.

Gershkovich slowly started undressing. He took off his white socks, stretched his sweaty toes, locked the door with the key, put the key under his pillow, and lay down. Margarita yawned, and slowly took off her dress, squinted, squeezed out a pimple on her shoulder, and began plaiting a thin braid for the night.

"Papa, what's your name?"

"Eli. Elya Isaakovich."

"A tradesman?"

"Well, if you want to call it a trade . . ." Gershkovich answered vaguely.

Margarita blew out the night-light and lay down. . . .

• • •

"Well, I'll be damned!" Gershkovich said. "That's a whole lot of woman here."

Soon they were asleep.

• • •

Next morning the sun's bright light filled the room. Gershkovich woke up, dressed, and walked to the window.

"We have sea, and you have fields," he said. "Great."

"Where you from?" Margarita asked.

"Odessa," Gershkovich answered. "The number-one town, a good town." And he smiled slyly.

"It looks like you pretty much feel nice and fine everywhere," Margarita said.

"You can say that again," Gershkovich said. "Wherever there's people it's nice and fine."

"You're such a fool!" Margarita said, propping herself up on the bed. "People are evil."

"No," Gershkovich said. "People are good. They've been taught to think that they're evil, and they ended up believing it."

Margarita thought for a while, and then smiled.

"You're funny," she said slowly, and she ran her eyes carefully over him.

"Turn around, I'm going to get dressed."

Then they ate breakfast, drank tea with hard rolls. Gershkovich taught Margarita how to spread butter on a roll in a special way and to put the sausage on top.

"Try it! Though I have to be on my way now.

"Here are three rubles for you, Margarita," he said on his way out. "Believe me, rubles don't come easy nowadays."

Margarita smiled.

"You skinflint, you! So give me three. You coming back this evening?"

"Yes, I am."

That evening Gershkovich brought dinner with him—a herring, a bottle of beer, sausages, apples. Margarita was wearing a dark, high-buttoned dress. They talked as they ate.

"Nowadays you can't get by on fifty rubles a month," Margarita said. "And what with this job, if you don't dress up, you don't get no cabbage soup. You have to take into account that I have to pay fifteen for this room."

"Back in Odessa," Gershkovich said pensively, straining to cut the herring into equal parts, "for ten rubles you can get a room in the Moldavanka fit for a Czar."

"You have to take into account that people tumble all over the place in my room, what with the drunks and everything."

"Every man must bear his burden," Gershkovich said, and started talking about his family, his faltering business dealings, his son who had been called up by the army.

Margarita listened, resting her head on the table, and her face was attentive, quiet, and thoughtful.

After supper, he took off his jacket, painstakingly wiped his spectacles with a piece of cloth, and sat down at the table to write some business letters. Margarita washed her hair.

Gershkovich wrote unhurriedly, carefully, raising his eyebrows, stopping to think, and when he dipped his pen into the inkwell, he never once forgot to shake off the extra ink.

After he finishing writing he had Margarita sit down on his notebook.

"Well, I'll be damned, but you sure are a lady with bulk! Do me a favor and keep sitting there, Margarita Prokofievna."

Gershkovich smiled, his spectacles shimmered, and his eyes became small, more sparkling, full of laughter.

The next day he left town. As he paced up and down the platform, a few minutes before the train was to leave, Gershkovich noticed Margarita walking quickly toward him with a small parcel in her hands. There were pies in the parcel, and oily blotches had seeped through the paper.

Margarita's face was red, pitiful, her chest agitated from walking so quickly.

"Greetings to Odessa!" she said. "Greetings. . . ."

"Thank you," Gershkovich answered. He took the pies, raised his eyebrows, thought about something for a moment, and bent forward.

The third bell rang. They stretched their hands out to each other.

"Good-bye, Margarita Prokofievna."

"Good-bye, Elya Isaakovich."

Gershkovich went inside the railway car. The train began moving.

MAMA, RIMMA,
AND ALLA

*F*rom early in the morning the day had been going badly.

The day before, the maid had begun putting on airs and walked out. Barbara Stepanovna ended up having to do everything herself. Then the electric bill came first thing in the morning. And then the student boarders, the Rastokhin brothers, came up with a completely unexpected demand. They had allegedly received a telegram from Kaluga in the middle of the night informing them that their father had been taken ill, and that they had to come to him at all costs. They were therefore vacating the room, and could they have the sixty rubles back that they had given Barbara Stepanovna "on loan."

To this Barbara Stepanovna answered that it was quite irregular to vacate a room in April, when there is no one to rent it to, and that it was difficult for her to return the money, as it was given to her not on loan but as a payment for the room, regardless of the fact that the payment had been made in advance.

The Rastokhin brothers disagreed with Barbara Stepanovna. The discussion became drawn-out and unfriendly. The students were stubborn, infuriating louts in long, clean frock coats. When they realized that getting their money back was a lost cause, the older brother suggested that Barbara Stepanovna give them her sideboard and pier glass as collateral.

Barbara Stepanovna turned purple, and retorted that she would not tolerate being spoken to in such a tone, that the Rastokhins' suggestion was utter rubbish, that she knew the law, her husband being a member of the district court in Kamchatka, and so on. The younger Rastokhin flared up and told her that he didn't give a hoot that her husband was a member of the district court in Kamchatka, that it was quite obvious that once she got her hands on a kopeck there was no prying it loose, that they would remember their stay at Barbara Stepanovna's—with all that clutter, dirt, and mess—to their dying day, and that although the district court in Kamchatka was quite far away, the Moscow Justice of the Peace was just around the corner.

And that was how the discussion ended. The Rastokhins marched out haughtily and in silent fury, and Barbara Stepanovna went to the kitchen to make some coffee for her other boarder, a student by the name of Stanislaw Marchotski. There had been loud and insistent ringing from his room for quite a few minutes.

Barbara Stepanovna stood in front of the spirit stove in the kitchen. A nickel pince-nez, rickety with age, sat on her fat nose; her graying hair was disheveled, her pink morning coat full of stains. She made the coffee, and thought how these louts would never have spoken to her in such a tone if there hadn't been that eternal shortage of money, that unfortunate need to constantly snatch, hide, cheat.

When Marchotski's coffee and fried eggs were ready, she brought his breakfast to his room.

Marchotski was a Pole—tall, bony, light blond, with long legs and well-groomed fingernails. That morning he was wearing a foppish gray dressing gown with ornamental military clasps.

He faced Barbara Stepanovna with resentment.

"I've had enough of there never being a maid around!" he said. "I have to ring for a whole hour, and then I'm late for my classes."

It was true that all too often the maid wasn't there, and that Marchotski had to ring and ring, but this time he had a different reason for his resentment.

The evening before, he had been sitting on the living room sofa with Rimma, Barbara Stepanovna's oldest daughter. Barbara Stepanovna had seen them kissing two or three times and hugging in the darkness. They sat there till eleven, then till midnight, then Stanislaw laid his head on Rimma's breast and fell asleep. After all, who in his youth has not dozed off on the edge of a sofa with his head propped on the breast of a high school girl, met by chance on life's winding path? It is not necessarily such a bad thing, and more often than not there are no consequences, but one does have to show a little consideration for others, not to mention that the girl might well have to go to school the next day.

It wasn't until one-thirty in the morning that Barbara Stepanovna declared quite sourly that it was time to show some consideration. Marchotski, brimming with Polish pride, pursed his lips and took umbrage. Rimma cast an indignant look at her mother.

The matter had ended there. But the following morning it was quite clear that Stanislaw hadn't forgotten the incident. Barbara Stepanovna gave him his breakfast, salted the fried eggs, and left.

It was eleven in the morning. Barbara Stepanovna opened the drapes in her daughters' room. The gentle rays of the weak sun gleamed on the dirty floor, on the clothes scattered throughout the room, on the dusty bookshelf.

The girls were already awake. The eldest, Rimma, was thin, small, quick-eyed, black-haired. Alla was a year younger—she was seventeen—larger than her sister, pale, sluggish in her movements, with delicate, pudgy skin, and a sweetly pensive expression in her blue eyes.

When her mother left the room, she started speaking. Her heavy bare arm lay on the blanket, her little white fingers hardly moving.

"I had a dream, Rimma," she said. "Imagine—a strange little town, small, Russian, mysterious. . . .The light gray sky is hanging very low, and the horizon is very close. The dust in the streets is also gray, smooth, calm. Everything is dead. Not a single sound can be heard, not a single person can be seen. And suddenly I feel like I'm walking down some side streets I don't know, past quiet little wooden houses. I wander into blind alleys, then I find my way out into the streets again, but I can only see ten paces ahead, and I keep walking on and on. Somewhere in front of me is a light cloud of whirling dust. I approach it and see wedding carriages. Mikhail and his bride are in one of them. His bride is wearing a veil, and her face is happy. I walk up to the carriages, I seem to be taller than everyone else, and my heart aches a little. Then they all notice me. The carriages stop. Mikhail comes up to me, takes me by the arm, and slowly leads me into a side street. 'Alla, my friend,' he says in a flat voice, 'all this is very sad, I know. But there's nothing I can do, because I don't love you.' I walk next to him, my heart shudders, and more gray streets keep opening up before us."

Alla fell silent.

"A bad dream," she added. "But, who knows? Maybe because it's bad, everything will turn out well and he'll send me a letter."

"Like hell he will!" Rimma answered. "You should have been a little more clever and not run off to see him. By the way, I intend to have a word or two with Mama today!" she said suddenly.

Rimma got up, dressed, and went over to the window.

Spring lay over Moscow. The long somber fence outside their window, which stretched almost the whole length of the side street, glistened with warm dampness.

Outside the church, in its front yard, the grass was damp, green. The sun softly gilded the lackluster chasubles, and twinkled over the dark face of the icon standing on the slanting column by the entrance to the churchyard.

The girls went into the dining room. Barbara Stepanovna was sitting there, carefully eating large portions of food, intently studying the rolls, the coffee, the ham, through her spectacles. She drank the coffee with loud short gulps, and ate the rolls quickly, greedily, almost furtively.

"Mama!" Rimma said to her severely, proudly raising her pretty little face. "I'd like to have a little chat with you. You needn't blow up. We can settle this quietly, once and for all. I can no longer live with you. Set me free."

"Fine," Barbara Stepanovna answered calmly, raising her colorless eyes to look at Rimma. "Is this because of yesterday?"

"Not because of yesterday, but it has to do with yesterday. I'm suffocating here."

"And what do you intend to do?"

"I'll take some classes, learn stenography, right now the demand—"

"Right now stenographers are crawling out of the woodwork! You think the jobs will come running—"

"I won't come to you for help, Mama!" Rimma said shrilly. "I won't come to you for help. Set me free!"

"Fine," Barbara Stepanovna said again. "I'm not holding you back."

"I want you to give me my passport."

"I'm not giving you your passport."

The conversation had been unexpectedly restrained. Now Rimma felt that the passport matter gave her a reason to start yelling.

"Well, that's marvelous!" she shouted, with a sarcastic laugh. "I can't go anywhere without my passport!"

"I'm not giving you your passport!"

"I'll go turn myself into a kept woman!" Rimma yelled hysterically. "I shall give myself to a policeman!"

"Who do you think will want you?" Barbara Stepanovna answered, critically eyeing her daughter's shivering little body and flushed face. "You think a policeman can't find a better—"

"I'll go to Tverskaya Street!" Rimma shouted. "I'll find myself some old man—I don't want to live with her, with this stupid, stupid, stupid—"

"Ah, so this is how you speak to your mother," Barbara Stepanovna said, standing up with dignity. "We can't make ends meet, everything is falling apart around us, we're short of everything, all I ask is for a few minutes of peace and quiet, but you . . . Wait till your father hears about this!"

"I'm going to write him myself, to Kamchatka!" Rimma shouted in a frenzy. "I'll get my passport from him!"

Barbara Stepanovna walked out of the room. Rimma, small and disheveled, paced excitedly up and down the room. Angry, isolated phrases from her future letter to her father tore through her brain.

"Dear Papa!" she would write. "You are busy, I know, but I have to tell you everything. May the allegation that Stanny dozed on my breast lie heavy on Mama's conscience! It was an embroidered cushion that he was dozing on, but the center of gravity lies elsewhere. As Mama is your wife, you will doubtless side with her, but I can't stay here any longer, she is a difficult person! If you want, Papa, I can come to you in Kamchatka, but I will need my passport!"

Rimma paced up and down, while Alla sat on the sofa and watched her. Quiet and mournful thoughts lay heavily on her soul.

"Rimma is fussing about," she thought, "while I am completely desolate! Everything is painful, nothing makes sense!"

She went to her room and lay down. Barbara Stepanovna came in wearing a corset. She was thickly and naively powdered, flushed, perplexed, and pitiful.

"I just remembered that the Rastokhins are leaving today. I have to give them back their sixty rubles. They threatened to take me to court. There are some eggs in the cupboard. Make some for yourself—I'm going down to the pawnbroker.

•   •   •

When Marchotski came home from his classes at around six in the evening, he found the entrance hall filled with packed suitcases. There was noise coming from the Rastokhins' rooms—they were obviously arguing. Right there in the entrance hall Barbara Stepanovna, some-how, with lightning speed and desperate resolution, managed to borrow ten rubles from Marchotski. It was only when he got back to his room that he realized how stupid he had been.

His room was different from all the other rooms in Barbara Stepanovna's apartment. It was neat, filled with bibelots, and covered with carpets. Drawing utensils, foppish pipes, English tobacco, ivory paper knives were carefully laid out on the tables.

Before Stanislaw even managed to change into his dressing gown, Rimma quietly slipped into his room. He gave her a chilly reception.

"Are you angry, Stanny?" the girl asked.

"I am not angry," the Pole answered. "It is just that in the future I would prefer not to be encumbered with having to bear witness to your mother's excesses."

"It'll all be over very soon," Rimma said. "Stanny, I'm going to be free!"

She sat down next to him on the sofa and embraced him.

"I am a man," Stanny began. "This platonic business is not for me, I have a career before me."

He gruffly told her the things that men more or less say to certain women when they've had enough. There's nothing to talk to them about, and flirting with them is pointless, as it is quite obvious they are not prepared to get down to business.

Stanny said that he was consumed by desire; it was hampering his work, making him nervous. The matter had to be settled one way or the other—he didn't care in the least which, as long as it was settled.

"Why are you saying such things to me?" Rimma asked him pen-sively. "What is all this 'I am a man' about, and what do you mean by

'the matter has to be settled'? Why is your face so cold and nasty? And why can we talk about nothing else but that one thing? This is so sad, Stanny! Spring is in the streets, it's so beautiful, and we are in such an ugly mood."

Stanny didn't answer. They both remained silent.

A fiery sunset was sinking over the horizon, flooding the distant sky with a scarlet glow. On the opposite horizon a volatile, slowly thickening darkness was descending. The room was illuminated by the last glowing light. On the sofa, Rimma leaned more and more tenderly toward the student. They were doing what they always did at this exquisite hour of the day.

Stanislaw kissed the girl. She rested her head on the pillow and closed her eyes. They both burst into flame. Within a few minutes, Stanislaw was kissing her incessantly, and in a fit of malicious, unquenchable passion began shoving her thin, burning body about the room. He tore her blouse and her bodice. Rimma, with parched mouth and rings under her eyes, offered her lips to be kissed, while with a distorted, mournful grin she defended her virginity. Suddenly there was a knock at the door. Rimma began rushing about the room, clutching the hanging strips of her torn blouse to her breast.

They eventually opened the door. It turned out to be a friend of Stanislaw's. He eyed Rimma with ill-concealed derision as she rushed past him. She slipped into her room furtively, changed into another blouse, and went to stand by the chilly windowpane to cool down.

·　·　·

The pawnbroker only gave Barbara Stepanovna forty rubles for the family silver. Ten rubles she had borrowed from Marchotski, and the rest of the money she got from the Tikhonovs, walking all the way from Strastny Boulevard to Pokrovka. In her dismay, she forgot that she could have taken a tram.

At home, besides the raging Rastokhins, she found Mirlits, a barrister's assistant, waiting for her. He was a tall young man with decaying stumps for teeth, and foolish, moist gray eyes.

Not too long ago, the shortage of money had driven Barbara Stepanovna to consider mortgaging a cottage her husband owned in Kolomna. Mirlits had brought over a draft of the mortgage. Barbara

Stepanovna felt that something was wrong with the draft, and that she ought to get some more advice before signing. But she told herself that she was being beset by altogether too many problems of every kind. To hell with everything—boarders, daughters, rudeness.

After the business discussion, Mirlits uncorked a bottle of Crimean Muscat-Lunelle that he had brought with him—he knew Barbara Stepanovna's weakness. They drank a glass each and right away had another. Their voices rang louder, Barbara Stepanovna's fleshy nose grew red, and the stays of her corset expanded and bulged out. Mirlits was telling a jovial story and burst out laughing. Rimma sat silently in the corner, wearing the blouse into which she had changed.

After Barbara Stepanovna and Mirlits finished the Muscat-Lunelle, they went for a walk. Barbara Stepanovna felt that she was just a tiny bit tipsy. She was a little ashamed about this, but at the same time couldn't care less because there was simply too much hardship in life, so everything could go to hell.

Barbara Stepanovna came back earlier than she had anticipated, because the Boikos, whom she had intended to visit, had not been home. She was taken aback by the silence that lay over the apartment. Usually at this time of the day the girls were always fooling around with the students, giggling, running about. The only noise came from the bathroom. Barbara Stepanovna went to the kitchen. There was a little window there from which one could see what was going on in the bathroom.

She went to the little window and saw a strange and most unusual scene.

The stove for boiling the bathwater was red-hot. The bath was filled with steaming water. Rimma was kneeling next to the stove. In her hands she held a pair of curling irons. She was heating them over the fire. Alla was standing naked next to the bath. Her long braids were undone. Tears were rolling down her cheeks.

"Come here," Alla told Rimma. "Listen, can you maybe hear its heart beating?"

Rimma laid her head on Alla's soft, slightly swollen belly.

"It's not beating," she answered. "Anyway there's no doubt about it."

"I'm going to die," Alla whispered. "I'm going to get scalded by the water! I won't be able to bear it! Not the curling irons! You don't know how to do it!"

"Everyone does it this way," Rimma told her. "Stop whimpering, Alla. You can't have that baby."

Alla was about to climb into the tub, but she didn't manage to, because at that very moment she heard the unforgettable, quiet, wheezing voice of her mother call out. "What are you doing in there, girls?"

Two or three hours later, Alla was lying on Barbara Stepanovna's wide bed, tucked in, caressed, and wept over. She had told her mother everything. She felt relieved. She felt like a little girl who had overcome a silly childish fear.

Rimma moved about the bedroom carefully and silently, tidying up, making tea for her mother, forcing her to eat something, seeing to it that the room would be clean. Then she lit the icon lamp in which the oil had not been refilled for at least two weeks, undressed, trying hard not to make any noise, and lay down next to her sister.

Barbara Stepanovna sat at the table. She could see the icon lamp, its even, darkish red flame dimly illuminating the Virgin Mary. Her tipsiness, somehow strange and light, still bubbled in her head. The girls quickly fell asleep. Alla's face was broad, white, and peaceful. Rimma nestled up against her, sighed in her sleep, and shuddered.

Around one in the morning, Barbara Stepanovna lit a candle, placed a sheet of paper in front of her, and wrote a letter to her husband:

Dear Nikolai,

Mirlits came by today, a very decent Jew, and tomorrow I'm expecting a gentleman who will give me money for the house. I think I'm doing things right, but I'm getting more and more worried, because I lack confidence.

I know you have your own troubles, your work, and I shouldn't be bothering you with this, but things at home, Nikolai, are somehow not going all too well. The children are growing up, life nowadays is more demanding—courses, stenography—girls want more freedom. They need their father, they need someone to maybe yell at them, but I simply don't seem to be able to. I can't help thinking that your leaving for Kamchatka was a mistake. If you were here, we would have moved to Starokolenny Street, where there is a very bright little apartment available.

Rimma has lost weight and looks rather bad. For a whole month we were ordering cream from the dairy across the street, and the girls started looking much better, but now we have stopped ordering it. At times my liver acts up a little, and at times it doesn't. Write me more often. After your letters I am a bit more careful, I don't eat herring and my liver doesn't bother me. Come and see us, Kolya, we could all unwind. The children send you their greetings. With loving kisses,

Your Barbara.

THE PUBLIC LIBRARY

*O*ne feels right away that this is the kingdom of books. People working at the library commune with books, with the life reflected in them, and so become almost reflections of real-life human beings.

Even the cloakroom attendants—not brown-haired, not blond, but something in between—are mysteriously quiet, filled with contemplative composure.

At home on Saturday evenings they might well drink methylated spirits and give their wives long, drawn-out beatings, but at the library their comportment is staid, circumspect, and hazily somber.

And then there is the cloakroom attendant who draws. In his eyes there is a gentle melancholy. Once every two weeks, as he helps a fat man in a black vest out of his coat, he mumbles, "Nikolai Sergeyevich approves of my drawings, and Konstantin Vasilevich also approves of them. . . . In the first thing I was originating . . . but I have no idea, no idea where to go!"

The fat man listens. He is a reporter, a married man, gluttonous and overworked. Once every two weeks he goes to the library to rest. He reads about court cases, painstakingly copies out onto a piece of paper the plan of the house where the murder took place, is very pleased, and forgets that he is married and overworked.

The reporter listens to the attendant with fearful bewilderment, and wonders how to handle such a man. Do you give him a ten-kopeck coin on your way out? He might be offended—he's an artist. Then again, if you don't he might also be offended—after all, he's a cloak-room attendant.

In the reading room are the more elevated staff members, the librarians. Some, the "conspicuous ones," possess some starkly pronounced physical defect. One has twisted fingers, another has a head that lolled to the side and stayed there. They are badly dressed, and emaciated in the extreme. They look as if they are fanatically possessed by an idea unknown to the world.

Gogol would have described them well!

The "inconspicuous" librarians show the beginnings of bald patches, wear clean gray suits, have a certain candor in their eyes, and a painful slowness in their movements. They are forever chewing something, moving their jaws, even though they have nothing in their mouths. They talk in a practiced whisper. In short, they have been ruined by books, by being forbidden from enjoying a throaty yawn.

Now that our country is at war, the public has changed. There are fewer students. There are very few students. Once in a blue moon you might see a student painlessly perishing in a corner. He's a "white-ticketer," exempt from service. He wears a pince-nez and has a delicate limp. But then there is also the student on state scholarship. This student is pudgy, with a drooping mustache, tired of life, a man prone to contemplation: he reads a bit, thinks about something a bit, studies the patterns on the lampshades, and nods off over a book. He has to finish his studies, join the army, but—why hurry? Everything in good time.

A former student returns to the library in the figure of a wounded officer with a black sling. His wound is healing. He is young and rosy. He has dined and taken a walk along the Nevsky Prospekt. The Nevsky Prospekt is already lit. The late edition of the *Stock Exchange News* has already set off on its triumphal march around town. Grapes lying on millet are displayed in the store window at Eliseyev's. It is still too early to make the social rounds. The officer goes to the public library for old times' sake, stretches out his long legs beneath the table where he is sitting, and reads *Apollon*. It's somewhat boring. A female student is sitting opposite him. She is studying anatomy, and is copying a picture of a stomach into her notebook. It looks like she might be of Kalugan origin—large-faced, large-boned, rosy, dedicated, and robust. If she has a lover, that would be perfect—she's good material for love.

Beside her is a picturesque tableau, an immutable feature of every public library in the Russian Empire: a sleeping Jew. He is worn out. His hair is a fiery black. His cheeks are sunken. There are bumps on his forehead. His mouth is half open. He is wheezing. Where he is from, nobody knows. Whether he has a residence permit or not, nobody knows. He reads every day. He also sleeps every day. There is a terrible, ineradicable weariness in his face, almost madness. A martyr to books—a distinct, indomitable Jewish martyr.

Near the librarians' desk sits a large, broad-chested woman in a gray blouse reading with rapturous interest. She is one of those people who suddenly speaks with unexpected loudness in the library, candidly and ecstatically overwhelmed by a passage in the book, and who, filled with delight, begins discussing it with her neighbors. She is reading because she is trying to find out how to make soap at home. She is about forty-five years old. Is she sane? Quite a few people have asked themselves that.

There is one more typical library habitué: the thin little colonel in a loose jacket, wide pants, and extremely well-polished boots. He has tiny feet. His whiskers are the color of cigar ash. He smears them with a wax that gives them a whole spectrum of dark gray shades. In his day he was so devoid of talent that he didn't manage to work his way up to the rank of colonel so that he could retire a major general. Since his retirement he ceaselessly pesters the gardener, the maid, and his grandson. At the age of seventy-three he has taken it into his head to write a history of his regiment.

He writes. He is surrounded by piles of books. He is the librarians' favorite. He greets them with exquisite civility. He no longer gets on his family's nerves. The maid gladly polishes his boots to a maximal shine.

Many more people of every kind come to the public library. More than one could describe. There is also the tattered reader who does nothing but write a luxuriant monograph on ballet. His face: a tragic edition of Hauptmann's. His body: insignificant.

There are, of course, also bureaucrats riffling through piles of *The Russian Invalid* and the *Government Herald*. There are the young provincials, ablaze as they read.

It is evening. The reading room grows dark. The immobile figures sitting at the tables are a mix of fatigue, thirst for knowledge, ambition.

Outside the wide windows soft snow is drifting. Nearby, on the Nevsky Prospekt, life is blossoming. Far away, in the Carpathian Mountains, blood is flowing.

C'est la vie.

NINE

*T*here are nine people. All waiting to see the editor. The first to enter the editor's office is a broad-shouldered young man with a loud voice and a bright tie. He introduces himself. His name: Sardarov. His occupation: rhymester. His request: to have his rhymes published. He has a preface written by a well-known poet. And if need be, an epilogue, too.

The editor listens. He is an unruffled, pensive man, who has seen a thing or two. He is in no rush. The upcoming issue has gone to press. He reads through the rhymes:

> *O, dolefully the Austrian Kaiser groans,*
> *And I too emit impatient moans.*

The editor says that, unfortunately, for this reason and that, and so on. The magazine is currently looking for articles on cooperatives or foreign affairs.

Sardarov juts out his chest, excuses himself with exquisite politeness bordering on the caustic, and noisily marches out.

The second person to enter the editor's office is a young lady—slim, shy, very beautiful. She is there for the third time. Her poems are not intended for publication. All she wants to know, and absolutely nothing more, is if there's any point in her continuing to write. The editor is extremely pleasant to her. He sometimes sees her walking along the Nevsky Prospekt with a tall gentleman who, from time to time, gravely buys her half a dozen apples. His gravity is ominous. Her poems testify to this. They are a guileless chronicle of her life.

"You want my body," the girl writes. "So take it, my enemy, my friend! But where will my soul find its dream?"

"He'll be getting his hands on your body any day now, that's pretty clear!" the editor thinks. "Your eyes look so lost, weak, and beautiful. I doubt your soul will be finding its dream anytime soon, but you'll definitely make quite a spicy woman!"

In her poems the girl describes life as "madly frightening" or "madly marvelous," in all its little aggravations: "Those sounds, sounds, sounds that me enfold, those sounds eternal, so drunken and so bold."

One thing is certain: once the grave gentleman's enterprise comes to fruition, the girl will stop writing poetry and start visiting midwives.

After the girl, Lunev, a small and nervous man of letters, enters the editor's office. Here things get complicated. On a former occasion Lunev had blown up at the editor. He is a talented, perplexed, hapless family man. In his fluster and scramble for rubles he is unable to discriminate who he can afford to shout at and who not. First he blew up at the editor, and then, to his own and the editor's amazement, handed over the manuscript, suddenly realizing how foolish all this was, how hard life was, and how unlucky he was, oh, how very unlucky! He had already begun having palpitations in the waiting room, and now the editor informed him that his "little daubs" weren't all that bad, but, *au fond*, you couldn't really classify them as literature, they were, well . . . Lunev feverishly agreed, unexpectedly muttering, "Oh, Alexander Stepanovich! You are such a good man! And all the while I was so horrible to you! But it can all be seen from another perspective! Absolutely! That is all I want to elucidate, there is more to it than meets the eye, I give you my word of honor!" Lunev turns a deep crimson, scrapes together the pages of his manuscript with quaking fingers, endeavoring to be debonair, ironic, and God knows what else.

After Lunev, two stock figures found in every editorial office come in. The first is a lively, rosy, fair-haired lady. She emits a warm wave of perfume. Her eyes are naive and bright. She has a nine-year-old son, and this son of hers, "you wouldn't believe it, but he simply writes and writes, day and night, at first we didn't pay any attention, but then all our friends and acquaintances were so impressed, and my husband, you know, he works in the Department of Agricultural Betterment, a very practical man, you know, he will have nothing to do with modern literature, not Andreyev, not Nagrodskaya, but even he couldn't stop laughing—I have brought along three notebooks. . . ."

The second stock figure is Bykhovsky. He is from Simferopol. He is a very nice, lively man. He has nothing to do with literature, he doesn't really have any business with the editor, he doesn't really have anything to say to him, but he is a subscriber, and has dropped by for a little chat and to exchange ideas, to immerse himself in the hurly-burly of Petrograd life. And he *is* immersing himself. The editor mumbles something about politics and cadets, and Bykhovsky blossoms, convinced that he is taking an active part in the nation's public life.

The most doleful of the visitors is Korb. He is a Jew, a true Ahasuerus. He was born in Lithuania, and had been wounded in a pogrom in one of the southern towns. From that day on his head has been hurting very badly. He went to America. During the War he somehow turned up in Antwerp and, at the age of forty-four, joined the French Foreign Legion. He was hit on the head in Maubeuge. Now it won't stop shaking. Korb was somehow evacuated to Russia, to Petrograd. He gets a pension from somewhere, rents a ramshackle little place in a stinking basement in Peski, and is writing a play called *The Czar of Israel*. Korb has terrible headaches, he cannot sleep at night, and paces up and down in his basement, deep in thought. His landlord, a plump, condescending man who smokes black four-kopeck cigars, was angry at first, but then was won over by Korb's gentleness and his diligence at writing hundreds of pages, and finally came to like him. Korb wears an old, faded Antwerp frock coat. He doesn't shave his chin, and there is a tiredness and fanatical determination in his eyes. Korb has headaches, but he keeps on writing his play, and the play's opening line is: "Ring the bells, for Judah hath perished!"

After Korb, three remain. One is a young man from the provinces. He is unhurried, lost in thought, takes a long time to settle into a chair, and stays settled there for a long time. His sluggish attention comes to rest on the pictures on the wall, the newspaper clippings on the table, the portraits of the staff. What is it exactly that he wants?—It is not that he really wants anything . . . He worked for a newspaper—What newspaper?—A newspaper in the provinces . . . Well, all he really wants to know is what the circulation of this magazine is and how much it pays. The young man is told that such information is not handed out to just anybody. If he were a writer, that would be another matter, if not, well then . . . The young man says that he isn't really a writer or anything, and that he hasn't really done this kind of work before, but he could take to, well, working as an editor, for instance.

The young "editor" exits, and Smursky enters. He too is a man with a background. He worked as an agriculturist in the district of Kashin in the province of Tver. A tranquil district, a wonderful province! But Smursky was drawn to Petrograd. He applied for a position as an agriculturist, and also submitted twenty manuscripts to an editor. Two had been accepted, and Smursky had come to the conclusion that his future lay in literature. Now he is no longer applying for a position as an agriculturist. He walks about town in a morning coat with his briefcase in hand. He writes a lot, and every day, but little is ever published.

The ninth visitor is none other than Stepan Drako, "the man who walked around the world on foot, bon vivant extraordinare, and public speaker."

ODESSA

*O*dessa is a horrible town. It's common knowledge. Instead of say-ing "a great difference," people there say "two great differences," and *"tuda i syuda,"** they pronounce *"tudoyu i syudoyu"*! And yet I feel that there are quite a few good things one can say about this important town, the most charming city of the Russian Empire. If you think about it, it is a town in which you can live free and easy. Half the pop-ulation is made up of Jews, and Jews are a people who have learned a few simple truths along the way. Jews get married so as not to be alone, love so as to live through the centuries, hoard money so they can buy houses and give their wives astrakhan jackets, love children because, let's face it, it is good and important to love one's children. The poor Odessa Jews get very confused when it comes to officials and regula-tions, but it isn't all that easy to get them to budge in their opinions, their very antiquated opinions. You might not be able to budge these Jews, but there's a whole lot you can learn from them. To a large extent it is because of them that Odessa has this light and easy atmosphere.

The typical Odessan is the exact opposite of the typical Petrogradian. Nowadays it is a cliché how well Odessans do for themselves in Petrograd. They make money. Because they are dark-haired, limpid blondes fall in love with them. And then, Odessans have a tendency to settle on the Kamenno-Ostrovsky Prospect. People will claim that what I am saying smacks of tall tales. Well, I assure you that these are not tall

*"Here and there."

tales! There is much more to this than meets the eye. Dark-haired Odessans simply bring with them a little lightness and sunshine.

But I have a strong hunch that Odessa is about to provide us with much more than gentlemen who bring with them a little sunshine and a lot of sardines packed in their original cans. Any day now, we will fully experience the fecund, revivifying influence of the Russian south, Russian Odessa—perhaps, *qui sait*, the only Russian town where there is a good chance that our very own, sorely needed, homegrown Maupassant might be born. I can even see a small, a very small sign, heralding Odessa's great future: Odessa's chanteuses (I am referring to Izya Kremer*). These chanteuses might not have much in the way of a voice, but they have a joy, an expressive joy, mixed with passion, lightness, and a touching, charming, sad feeling for life. A life that is good, terrible, and, *quand même et malgré tout*, exceedingly interesting.

I saw Utochkin,[†] a *pur sang* Odessan, lighthearted and profound, reckless and thoughtful, elegant and gangly, brilliant and stuttering. He has been ruined by cocaine or morphine—ruined, word has it, since the day he fell out of an airplane somewhere in the marshes of Novgorod. Poor Utochkin, he has lost his mind. But of one thing I am certain: any day now the province of Novgorod will come crawling down to Odessa.

The bottom line is: this town has the material conditions needed to nurture, say, a Maupassantesque talent. In the summer, the bronze, muscular bodies of youths who play sports glisten on beaches, as do the powerful bodies of fishermen who do not play sports, the fat, potbellied, good-natured bodies of the "businessmen," and the skinny, pimply dreamers, inventors, and brokers. And a little distance from the sea, smoke billows from the factories, and Karl Marx plies his familiar trade.

In Odessa there is an impoverished, overcrowded, suffering Jewish ghetto, an extremely self-satisfied bourgeoisie, and a very Black Hundred** city council.

In Odessa there are sweet and oppressive spring evenings, the spicy aroma of acacias, and a moon filled with an unwavering, irresistible light shining over a dark sea.

---

*Izya Kremer, 1885–1956, Odessan Jewish folksinger.

[†] Sergei Isayevich Utochkin, 1874–1916, aviation pioneer, was the first to fly from Moscow to St. Petersburg, in 1911.

**Chernosotentsy (Black Hundred), a right-wing, anti-Semitic group responsible for

In Odessa the fat and funny bourgeois lie in the evenings in their white socks on couches in front of their funny, philistine dachas, digesting their meals beneath a dark and velvety sky, while their powdered wives, plump with idleness and naively corseted, are passionately squeezed behind bushes by fervent students of medicine or law.

In Odessa the destitute "*luftmenshen*" roam through coffeehouses trying to make a ruble or two to feed their families, but there is no money to be made, and why should anyone give work to a useless person—a "*luftmensh*"?

In Odessa there is a port, and in the port there are ships that have come from Newcastle, Cardiff, Marseilles, and Port Said; Negroes, Englishmen, Frenchmen, and Americans. Odessa had its moment in the sun, but now it is fading—a poetic, slow, lighthearted, helpless fading.

"But Odessa is just a town like any other," the reader will argue. "The problem is that you are extremely biased, that's all."

Well, fine. So I am biased, I admit it. Maybe I'm even extremely biased, but *parole d'honneur*, there *is* something to this place! And this something can be sensed by a person with mettle who agrees that life is sad, monotonous—this is all very true—but still, *quand même et malgré tout*, it is exceedingly, exceedingly interesting.

And now my thoughts move on from my Odessan discourse to higher matters. If you think about it, doesn't it strike you that in Russian literature there haven't been so far any real, clear, cheerful descriptions of the sun?

Turgenev poeticized the dewy morning, the calm night. With Dostoyevsky you feel the uneven, gray road along which Karamazov walks to the tavern, the mysterious and heavy fog of Petersburg. The gray roads and the shrouds of fog that stifle people and, stifling them, distorts them in the most amusing and terrible way, giving birth to the fumes and stench of passions, making people rush around frenetically in the hectic humdrum pace. Do you remember the life-giving, bright sun in Gogol, a man who, by the way, was from the Ukraine? But such descriptions are few and far between. What you always get is "The Nose," "The Overcoat," "The Portrait," and "Notes of a Madman." Petersburg defeated Poltava. Akaki Akakiyevich, modestly enough but with terrible competence, finished off Gritsko, and Father Matvei finished off what Taras began.* The first person to talk about the sun in a Russian book, to talk about it with excitement and passion, was Gorky. But precisely because he talks about it with excitement and passion, it still isn't quite the real thing.

Gorky is a forerunner, and the most powerful forerunner of our times. Yet he is not a minstrel of the sun, but a herald of the truth. If anything is worth singing the praises of, then you know what it is: the sun! There is something cerebral in Gorky's love for the sun. It is only by way of his enormous talent that he manages to overcome this obstacle.

He loves the sun because Russia is rotten and twisted, because in Nizhny, Pskov, and Kazan, the people are pudgy, heavy, at times incomprehensible, at times touching, at times excessive, and at times boring to the point of distraction. Gorky knows why he loves the sun, why the sun must be loved. It is this very awareness that hides the reason why Gorky is a forerunner, often magnificent and powerful, but still a forerunner.

And on this point Maupassant is perhaps off the mark, or right on the mark. A stagecoach rumbles along a road scorched by the heat, and in it, in this stagecoach, sits a fat, crafty young man by the name of Polyte, and a coarse, healthy peasant girl. What they are doing there and why, is their business. The sky is hot, the earth is hot. Polyte and the girl are dripping with sweat, and the stagecoach rumbles along the road scorched by the bright heat. And that's all there is to it.

In recent times there has been a growing trend of writing about how people live, love, kill, and how representatives are elected in the provinces of Olonetsk, or Vologda, not to mention Arkhangelsk. All this is written with total authenticity, verbatim, the way people speak in Olonetsk and Vologda. Life there, as it turns out, is cold, extremely wild. It is an old story. And the time is approaching where we will have had more than enough of this old story. In fact, we have already had enough. And I think to myself: the Russians will finally be drawn to the

---

*Babel is implying that a cold, northern Petersburg frame of mind overpowered Gogol's earlier brighter southern "Poltavan" style, and that the somber and tragic Akaki Akakiyevich, the protagonist of "The Overcoat," superseded Gritsko, the lively and witty protagonist of "Evenings on a farm near Dikanka." Father Matvei Konstantinovsky was a fanatical ascetic priest who influenced Gogol's later writing. Taras is the protagonist of Gogol's story "Taras Bulba."

south, to the sea, to the sun! "Will be drawn," by the way, is wrong. They already *have* been drawn, for many centuries. Russia's most important path has been her inexhaustible striving toward the southern steppes, perhaps even her striving for "the Cross of Hagia Sophia."*

It is high time for new blood. We are being stifled. Literature's Messiah, so long awaited, will issue from there—from the sun-drenched steppes washed by the sea.

* Constantinople's Cathedral of Hagia Sophia, the seat of Russian and Greek Orthodox Christianity.

THE AROMA OF
ODESSA

I am wandering between tables, making my way through the crowd, catching snippets of conversation. S., a female impersonator, walks past me. In his pale youthful face, in his tousled soft yellow hair, in his distant, shameless, weak-spirited smile is the stamp of his peculiar trade, the trade of being a woman. He has an ingratiating, leisurely, sinuous way of walking. His hips sway, but barely. Women, real women, love him. He sits silently among them, his face that of a pale youth and his hair soft and yellow. He smiles faintly at something, and the women smile faintly and secretively back—what they are smiling at only S. and the women know.

On the other side of the café a man in a blue caftan and a peasant shirt tied with a strap hurries past in patent-leather boots. They call him the "Bard of Russian Song." On the bard's nose is a pince-nez, and in his soul the petty anxiety of a petty man. The bard's face is that of a worldly pharmacist. Why even mention his name.

I make my way between tables where retired colonels with brilliantined mustaches have found a haven for their shamed Czarist uniforms and play lotto with Jewish boys. Fat, serene wives of movie-theater owners, thin cash-register girls ("true union members"), and fleshy, flabby, sagacious café-chantant agents, currently unemployed, also sit with the colonels.

Our times have knocked these people off their feet, misfortune has driven them to the Palais Royal, and to Paraskeva and other Greek cafés to make a quick ruble trading in turquoise rings. At the club you can learn a lot about their desires and ideals, and who their idols are. Go to the reading room, where portraits of Gorky, Vinaver, and Linovsky* hang on the walls. On the table you will find an old issue of *Divertissement*. Take it from me, a very interesting magazine! A life filled with mirth, wine, love, and death will open out before you. You can read about the clever and beautiful Jenny Molten, who came to Russia in the bloom of her youth. You can read about her successes and her admirers, of the papa's boys who love her body, and the little men, downtrodden by life, who love her soul. You can read of her nomadic life, of the barrels of wine she has drunk, the crates of oranges she has eaten, of her husband, the husband of a café-chantant diva, and of her death. About the death of Jenny Molten you will read at the end. Someone else besides Jenny Molten who has died is Naumenko or Karasulenko, our passionate, trusting, drunk, kindhearted, hysterical Russian chanteuse. She died on a bed strewn with flowers and doused in perfume. Telegrams were found in her room from officials, warrant officers, and second lieutenants. According to these telegrams the second lieutenants were about to rush to her side, to kiss her. They were indignant about something, even threatening.

But in *Divertissement* you will also find serious articles with advice on professional matters and portraits of the editor, a handsome man with a black mustache and languid eyes. His mustache, his eyes, his noble demeanor point unmistakably to one thing: the editor was loved, and never squandered his money on little chanteuses. There are also stories in *Divertissement* about wrestling champions, of their first victories, the arenas bathed in light, the Parisian crowds, the Parisian women applauding ecstatically, the crowd carrying the smooth, powerful body of the wrestler on its shoulders. In every issue of *Divertissement* there are also jokes about Odessa Jews, about Café Fankoni,[†] about brokers taking dance classes and Jewesses riding trams.

Divertissement smells of Odessa and Odessa's hot, homegrown lingo. The whole club on Preobrazhenskaya Street smells of Odessa, and that might well be the only reason I began talking about it. These

---

* Maxim Moseyevich Vinaver, 1863–1923, Jewish politician, activist, and writer who emigrated to Paris, where he became the editor of the Russian-French Jewish journal *Evreiskaya Tribuna*. Nikolai Osipovich Linovsky, a Jewish writer who wrote under the pseudonym Pruzhansky.

† An elegant and expensive Odessan café that attracted a wealthy international clientele.

days the aroma of one's native town is very important. This is the fourth year that warriors from afar have flooded it without respite. The horns of large ocean liners no longer roar, fine coal dust no longer wafts over the harbor. The brilliant sun lights the quiet, untroubled waters. There is no *Bavaria* pulling into port, there are no money changers, no tall, strong German and American sailors roaming through the town in packs, there are no taverns in the port where through waves of tobacco smoke one can see the drunk drooping heads of Englishmen, while a gramophone, rasping and proud, plays "Rule Britannia." During the war, ruined people have flocked to our town, strange Jews who are foreign to us—refugees from Latvia and Poland. Serbs and Rumanians have come. But nobody who loves Odessa can say a word against these Rumanians. They have brought life back to Odessa. They remind us of the days when the streets were full of trade, when we had Greeks trading in coffee and spices, German sausage makers, French book peddlers, and Englishmen in steamship offices. The Rumanians have opened restaurants, play music with cymbals, fill taverns with their fast, foreign speech. They have sent us handsome officers with yellow boots and tall, elegant women with red lips. These people fit the style of our town.

Not that it is a problem if the other newcomers do not fit Odessa's style. Odessa stands strong, she hasn't lost her astonishing knack for assimilating people. A proud, cunning Polish Jew comes to Odessa, and before long we've turned him into a loud, gesticulating fellow who is as quick to flare up or calm down as the best of us. We're still busy grinding them down. Soon the time will come when all the ex-Czarist officers who are used to life in the capital and their regiments in Mezhibozh will leave, and then all the red-bearded Jews, who walk dully down our streets, littering them dully with sunflower-seed shells, will go back to their gray Kozlovs and Tulas. The horns of ocean liners will once more blare in our harbor, and in our taverns old gramophones will once more croak words about Britannia ruling the waves. Our storehouses will be filled with oranges, coconuts, pepper, and Málaga wine, and in our granaries the greenish dust of pouring grain will rise.

INSPIRATION

I felt sleepy and was in a bad mood. Just then Mishka dropped in to read me the novella he had written. "Lock the door," he said, and pulled a bottle of wine out of his coat pocket. "This is an evening to celebrate! I have finished my novella! I think this is the real thing. Let's drink to it!"

Mishka's face was pale and clammy.

"Only fools will say that there's no such thing as happiness on earth," he said. "Happiness is inspiration! Yesterday I wrote the whole night through and didn't even notice the sun rising. Then I walked through town. Early in the morning it's striking: dew, silence, and almost nobody out and about. Everything is limpid, and the day begins bluish cold, spectral, and gentle. Let's drink to it! There's no mistake, this novella is definitely a turning point in my life."

Mishka poured himself some wine and drank. His fingers trembled. He had remarkably beautiful hands—slim, white, and smooth, with fingers delicately pointed at the tip.

"You know, I have to place this novella," he continued. "They'll all want it. They print such rubbish nowadays. Connections are the most important thing. I've already put out feelers. Sukhotin will take care of everything."

"Mishka," I said to him. "You need to go through your novella again; I don't see a single correction."

"Nonsense! There'll be time enough for that! Back home, everyone's making fun of me. *Rira bien, qui rira le dernier.* I'm not going to say anything. Just wait a year, then they'll all come running!"

The bottle was almost empty.

"You've already had enough to drink, Mishka!"

"I need to get myself on a roll," he answered. "Last night I smoked forty cigarettes."

He took out his notebook. It was very thick, very thick indeed. I thought of asking him to leave it with me. But then I saw his pale forehead, with a swollen vein protruding, and his dangling tie, crooked and pitiful.

"Well, Mr. Tolstoy," I said to him. "When you write your memoirs, don't forget to include me."

Mishka smiled.

"You bastard!" he said. "You don't value our friendship at all!"

I made myself comfortable. Mishka leaned over his notebook. The room was quiet and the lights were dim.

"My aim in this novella," Mishka said, "has been to come up with a new way of writing that is filled with cloudy dreams, subtle shadows and allusions. . . . How I loathe, loathe life's folly!"

"Enough preamble, start reading!" I said to him.

He began. I listened carefully. It wasn't easy. The story was clumsy and boring. A clerk had fallen in love with a ballerina and kept lounging around under her window. She left town. The clerk fell ill because his dreams of love had come to nothing.

It wasn't long before I stopped listening. The words were trite and boring, slippery as polished wood. Nothing was clear—not what the clerk was like, not what she was like.

I looked at Mishka. His eyes were sparkling. He was grinding his dead cigarette butts between his fingers. His dull, gaunt face, horribly distorted with sterile creative ardor, his yellow, fat, protruding nose, and puffy, pale-pink lips, all gradually brightened as he was gripped by the burgeoning power of his creative rapture.

He read with agonizing slowness, and when he finished, he awkwardly put his notebook away and looked at me.

"Well, Mishka," I said to him slowly. "You see, you need to think it through a little . . . The idea is quite original, it is very tender and everything, but, you see, it does need a little work . . . you see, it sort of needs to be edited down a little."

"I've been working on it for three years!" Mishka said. "Of course there are still a few rough edges, but as a whole it's fine, isn't it?"

Mishka had sensed something. His lips trembled. He hunched forward and took a terribly long time to light a cigarette.

"Mishka," I said to him. "What you've written is marvelous. Your technique isn't quite there yet, but *ça viendra*. Damn it, there's so much in that head of yours!"

Mishka turned around, looked at me, and his eyes were like those of a child—tender, radiant, and happy.

"Let's go out into the street," he said. "Let's go out, I can't breathe." The streets were dark and quiet.

Mishka squeezed my hand hard and said, "The one thing that I feel with utter conviction is that I have talent! My father wants me to look for a position somewhere. But I won't! In autumn I'm off to Petrograd. Sukhotin will take care of everything." He fell silent, lit another cigarette with the one he was just finishing, and spoke more quietly. "At times my inspiration is so strong that I'm in agony! At such times I know that what I am doing I am doing right! I sleep badly, always nightmares and anguish. I toss and turn for hours before I fall asleep. In the morning my head feels heavy, painful, terrible. I can only write at night, when I am alone, when there is silence, when my soul is burning. Dostoyevsky always wrote at night, drinking a whole samovar of tea—me, I have my cigarettes . . . you know, there's a blanket of smoke beneath my ceiling."

We reached Mishka's house. His face was lit by a street lamp. A fierce, thin, yellow, happy face.

"We'll get there, damn it!" he said, and squeezed my hand tighter. "Everyone makes it big in Petrograd!"

"Anyway, Mishka," I said, "you've got to keep working."

"Sashka, my friend!" he replied, grinning at me broadly and patronizingly. "I'm no fool, I know what I know. Don't worry, I'm not about to start resting on my laurels. Come by tomorrow. We'll go through it again."

"Very well," I said. "I'll come by."

We parted. I went home. I felt very depressed.

DOUDOU

*B*ack in those days I was a medical orderly in the hospital in the town of N. One morning General S., the hospital administrator, brought in a young girl and suggested she be taken on as a nurse. Needless to say, she was hired.

The new nurse was called *la petite Doudou*. She was kept by the general, and in the evenings danced at the café chantant.

She had a lithe, springy gait, the exquisite, almost angular gait of a dancer. In order to see her, I went to the café chantant. She danced an amazing *tango acrobatique,* with what I'd call chastity mixed with a vague, tender passion.

At the hospital she worshiped all the soldiers, and looked after them like a servant. Once, when the chief surgeon was walking through the halls, he saw Doudou on her knees trying to button up the underpants of a pockmarked, apathetic little man called Dyba.

"Dyba! Aren't you ashamed of yourself?" the surgeon called out. "You should have gotten one of the men to do that!"

Doudou raised her calm, tender face and said: "*Oh, mon docteur,* do you think I have never seen a man in his underpants before?"

I remember on the third day of Passover they brought us a badly injured French airman, a Monsieur Drouot. Both his legs had been smashed to bits. He was a Breton—strong, dark, and taciturn. His hard cheeks had a slight bluish tint. It was so strange to see his powerful torso, his strong, chiseled neck, and his broken, helpless legs.

They put him in a small, private room. Doudou would sit with him for hours. They spoke warmly and quietly. Drouot talked about his flights and how he was all alone, none of his family was here, and how sad it all was. He fell in love with her (it was clear to all), and looked at her as was to be expected: tenderly, passionately, pensively. And Doudou, pressing her hands to her breast, told Sister Kirdetsova in the corridor with quiet amazement: "*Il m'aime, ma soeur, il m'aime.*"*

That Saturday night she was on duty and was sitting with Drouot. I was in a neighboring room and saw them. When Doudou arrived, he said: "*Doudou, ma bien aimée!*" He rested his head on her breast and slowly started kissing her dark blue silk blouse. Doudou stood there without moving. Her fingers quivered and picked at the buttons of her blouse.

"What is it you want?" Doudou asked him.

He answered something.

Doudou looked at him carefully and pensively, and slowly undid her lace collar. Her soft, white breast appeared. Drouot sighed, winced, and clung to her. Doudou closed her eyes in pain. But still, she noticed that he was uncomfortable, and so she unhooked her bodice. He clasped Doudou close, but moved sharply and moaned.

"You're in pain!" Doudou said. "You must stop. You mustn't—"

"Doudou!" he said. "I'll die if you leave!"

I left the window. But I still saw Doudou's pale, pitiful face. I saw her try desperately not to hurt him, I heard the moan of passion and pain.

The story got out. Doudou was dismissed—in short, she was fired. The last I saw of her she was standing in the hall, bidding me farewell. Heavy, bright tears fell from her eyes, but she was smiling so as not to upset me.

"Good-bye!" Doudou said, stretching out her slim, white-gloved hand to me. "*Adieu, mon ami!*" She fell silent and then added, looking me straight in the eye: "*Il géle, il meurt, il est seul, il me prie, dirai-je non?*"†

At that moment, Dyba, filthy and small, hobbled in at the end of the hall. "I swear to you," Doudou said to me in a soft, shaking voice. "I swear to you, if Dyba had asked me to, I would have done the same for him."

*"He loves me, Sister, he loves me."
†"He is cold, he is dying, he is alone, he begs me to, would I say no?"

SHABOS-NAKHAMU

*M*orning came, evening came—it was the fifth day. Morning came, evening came—the sixth day. On the sixth day, on Friday evening, one prays. Having prayed, one puts one's best hat on and goes for a stroll through the shtetl and then hurries home for dinner. At home a Jew will empty a glass of vodka—and neither God nor the Talmud forbid him to empty two—he will eat gefilte fish and raisin cake. After dinner he feels quite jovial. He talks to his wife and then dozes off, one eye shut, his mouth hanging open. He dozes, but in the kitchen Gapka, his wife, hears music—as if a blind fiddler had come from the shtetl and was playing beneath the window.

This is how things go with your average Jew. But Hershele is not your average Jew. It wasn't by chance that he was famous in all of Ostropol, in all of Berdichev, and in all of Vilyuisk.

Hershele celebrated only one Friday evening in six. On other Fridays he sat in the cold darkness with his family. His children cried. His wife hurled reproaches at him, each as heavy as a cobblestone. Hershele answered her with poetry.

Once, word has it, Hershele decided to act with foresight. He set off on a Wednesday to go to a fair to make some money by Friday. Where there's a fair there's a goyish gentleman, where there's a goyish gentleman there are sure to be ten Jews hovering about. But you'll be lucky to squeeze three *groschen* out of ten Jews. They all listened to Hershele's routine, but quickly disappeared into thin air when the time came to pay up.

His stomach empty as a wind instrument, Hershele shuffled back home.

"What did you earn?" his wife asked him.

"Everlasting life," he answered. "Both the rich and the poor promised it to me."

Hershele's wife had only ten fingers, but she had many more curses. Her voice boomed like mountain thunder.

"Other women have husbands who are like husbands! All my husband knows how to do is feed his wife jokes! Come New Year, may God rip out his tongue, his arms, and his legs!"

"Amen!" Hershele said.

"Candles burn in every window as if people were burning oak trees in their houses. My candles are thin as matchsticks, and they give off so much smoke that it rises all the way to heaven! Everyone has made their white bread already, but my husband brings me firewood as wet as newly washed hair!"

Hershele did not say a word. First, why throw kindling on a fire when it is blazing brightly? Second, what can one say to a ranting wife when she is absolutely right?

The time came when his wife got tired of shouting. Hershele went to lie down on his bed and think.

"Why don't I go see Rabbi Boruchl?" he thought.

(As is common knowledge, Rabbi Boruchl had a tendency to fall into a black melancholia, and there was no better cure for him than Hershele's jokes.)

"Why don't I go see Rabbi Boruchl? It's true that the *tsaddik*'s helpers keep the meat and only give me bones. Meat is better than bones, but bones are better than air. Let's go to Rabbi Boruchl!"

Hershele got up and went to harness his mare. She looked at him severely and morosely.

"This is great, Hershele!" her eyes said. "Yesterday you didn't give me any oats, the day before yesterday you didn't give me any oats, and I didn't get anything today either. If I don't get any oats by tomorrow, I'm going to have to give my life some serious thought."

Hershele could not bear her penetrating stare. He lowered his eyes and patted her soft lips. Then he sighed so loudly that the horse understood. Hershele decided to go to Rabbi Boruchl on foot.

When Hershele set out, the sun stood high in the sky. The hot road ran on ahead. White oxen slowly pulled carts piled high with fragrant hay. Muzhiks sat on these piles, their legs dangling, and waved their long whips. The sky was blue and the whips were black.

About five versts down the road, Hershele came to a forest. The sun was beginning to set. Soft fires raged in the sky. Barefoot girls chased cows from the pastures. The cows' pink udders swung heavily with milk.

In the forest, Hershele was met by a cool, quiet twilight. Green leaves bent toward one another, caressed each other with their flat hands, and, softly whispering high in the trees, returned to their places, rustling and quivering.

Hershele did not notice their whispering. An orchestra as large as the ones at Count Potocki's feasts was playing in his belly. The road before him was long. An airy darkness drifted from the edges of the earth, closed over Hershele's head, and scattered over the world. Unmoving lamps lit up in the sky. The world fell silent.

It was night when Hershele came to the inn. A light flickered through the small window by which Zelda the landlady was sitting, sewing swaddling clothes in the warm room. Her belly was so large it looked as if she were about to give birth to triplets. Hershele looked at her small red face and blue eyes and greeted her.

"May I rest here awhile, mistress?"

"You may."

Hershele sat down. His nostrils flared like a blacksmith's bellows. Hot flames were burning in the stove. In a large cauldron water was boiling, pouring steam over the waiting, snow-white dumplings. A plump chicken was bobbing up and down in a golden soup. The aroma of raisin pie wafted from the oven.

Hershele sat on the bench writhing like a woman in labor. His mind was hatching more plots in a minute than King Solomon had wives.

It was quiet in the room; the water was boiling, and the chicken bobbing in the golden soup.

"Where is your husband?"

"My husband went to the goyish gentleman to pay the money for the rent." The landlady fell silent. Her childish eyes widened. Suddenly she said, "I am sitting here at the window, thinking. And I would like to ask you a question, Mr. Jew. I am sure you wander about the world quite a bit, and that you've studied with a rabbi and know about our Jewish ways. Me, I never studied with anyone. Tell me, Mr. Jew, will Shabos-Nakhamu come to us soon?"

"Aha!" Hershele thought. "Not a bad little question! In God's garden all kinds of potatoes grow!"

"I am asking this because my husband promised that when Shabos-Nakhamu comes to us, we will go visit my mother, and he said I'll buy you a new dress, and a new wig, and we'll go to Rabbi Motalemi to ask that a son be born to us, and not a daughter, all of this when Shabos-Nakhamu comes. I think he's someone from the other world."

"You are not mistaken!" Hershele answered. "God placed these words in your mouth. You will have a son and a daughter. I am Shabos-Nakhamu, mistress!"

The swaddling clothes slipped from Zelda's knees. She rose and banged her small head against a beam, for Zelda was tall and plump, flushed and young. Her breasts jutted up like two taut sacks filled with seed. Her blue eyes opened wide, like those of a child.

"I am Shabos-Nakhamu, mistress!" Hershele said again. "This is the second month that I am walking the earth helping people. It is a long path from heaven down to earth. My shoes are falling apart. I have brought you greetings from all your loved ones."

"From Auntie Pesya?" the woman shouted. "And from Papa, and Auntie Golda? You know them?"

"Who doesn't?" Hershele answered. "I was speaking to them just the way I'm speaking to you now!"

"How are they doing up there?" the woman asked, clutching her belly with trembling fingers.

"They are doing badly," Hershele said dolefully. "How should a dead person be doing? There are no feasts up there!"

The woman's eyes filled with tears.

"It is cold up there," Hershele continued. "They are cold and hungry. They eat just what angels eat, nobody in that world is allowed to eat more than angels. And what do angels need? All they need is a swig of water—up there, you won't see a glass of vodka in a hundred years!"

"Poor Papa!" the devastated woman whispered.

"At Passover he gets one *latke*. And a blin has to last him a day and a night!"

"Poor Auntie Pesya!" the woman stammered.

"I myself have to go hungry!" Hershele said, turning his head away as a tear rolled down his nose and fell into his beard. "And I'm not allowed to complain, as they think of me as one of them."

Hershele didn't get any further.

With fat feet slapping over the floor, the woman ran to get plates, bowls, glasses, and bottles. When Hershele started eating, the woman was completely convinced that he was a man from the other world.

To start with, Hershele ate chopped liver with finely diced onions doused in fat. Then he had a glass of the best vodka (orange peels floated in it). Then he had fish, mashing soft potatoes into the aromatic broth, and he poured on the side of his plate half a jar of red horseradish—a horseradish that would have driven five fully decked-out counts to tears of envy.

After the fish, Hershele busied himself with the chicken, and spooned down the soup in which droplets of fat swam. The dumplings, dipped in melted butter, fled into Hershele's mouth like hares fleeing a hunter. I need not dwell on what happened to the pies—what else could have happened to them if one takes into account that at times a whole year would pass without Hershele ever seeing a pie?

After the meal, the woman collected all the things she wanted to send with Hershele to the other world for Papa, Auntie Golda, and Auntie Pesya. For her father she packed a new prayer shawl, a bottle of cherry liqueur, a jar of raspberry jam, and a pouch of tobacco. For Auntie Pesya she brought out some warm gray stockings. For Auntie Golda she packed an old wig, a large comb, and a prayerbook. She also gave Hershele some shoes for himself, a loaf of bread, fat cracklings, and a silver coin.

"Greet everyone from me, Mr. Shabos-Nakhamu! Greet everyone from me!" she called after Hershele as he left, carrying the heavy bundle. "Or why don't you stay a little longer, until my husband comes back?"

"No," Hershele said. "I must hurry! Do you think you are the only one I have to see?"

In the dark forest the trees were sleeping, the birds were sleeping, the green leaves were sleeping. The stars that stand watch over us had gone pale and began flickering.

After about a verst, Hershele stopped to catch his breath, heaved the bundle off his shoulder, sat on it, and thought things through.

"One thing I must tell you, Hershele!" he said to himself. "There's no lack of fools in this world! The mistress of the inn is a fool, but her husband might well be a clever man with big fists and fat cheeks—and a long whip! What if he comes home and then hunts you down in the forest?"

Hershele did not waste time weighing the odds. He immediately buried his bundle and marked the place so that he could find it again.

Then he ran off toward the opposite side of the forest, took off all his clothes, threw his arms around the trunk of a tree, and waited. He did not have to wait long. As dawn approached he heard the lashes of a whip, the smacking lips of a horse, and the clattering of hooves. It was the innkeeper in full pursuit of Mr. Shabos-Nakhamu.

The innkeeper pulled his cart up to Hershele, who stood naked, hugging the tree. He reined in his horse and looked at Hershele with an expression as foolish as that of a monk coming face-to-face with the devil.

"What are you doing?" the innkeeper asked him in a cracked voice.

"I am a man from the other world," Hershele told him dolefully. "I was robbed—they took some important papers which I was taking to Rabbi Boruchl."

"I know who robbed you!" the innkeeper shouted. "I myself have some accounts to settle with him! Which way did he go?"

"I cannot tell you which way he went!" Hershele whispered bitterly. "But give me your horse, and I shall catch him in an instant! Just wait for me here. Undress, stand by the tree, hug it, and don't move an inch until I return! This tree is a holy tree! Many things in our world depend on it!"

Hershele had been quick to size this man up. One glance had been enough to tell him that husband and wife were not all that far apart. And, sure enough, the innkeeper took off his clothes, went over to the tree, and stood by it. Hershele jumped into the cart and rode off. He dug up his things, put them in the cart, and rode to the edge of the forest.

Hershele left the horse, slung the bundle over his shoulder, and continued along the road that led to Rabbi Boruchl's house.

The sun had already risen. The birds sang, closing their eyes. The innkeeper's mare, her head hanging low, pulled the empty cart back to where she had left her master.

The innkeeper, naked beneath the rays of the rising sun, stood waiting for her huddled against the tree. He felt cold. He was shifting from one foot to the other.

ON THE FIELD
OF HONOR

*T*he following stories are the beginning of my notes on the War.
Their plots were taken from books written by French soldiers
and officers who took part in the battles. In some passages I have
altered the plot and the narrative form, in others I tried to stay as close
as possible to the original.

On the Field of Honor

The German batteries were shelling the villages with heavy artillery.
The peasants were running for Paris. They dragged with them cripples,
freaks, women in labor, dogs, sheep, goods and chattels. The sky,
sparkling with heat and azure, slowly turned crimson, heavy, and clouded with smoke.

The sector near N was occupied by the Thirty-seventh Infantry
Regiment. Losses were great. The regiment was preparing to counterattack. Captain Ratin was making his rounds of the trenches. The sun
was at its zenith. The neighboring sector sent word that all the officers
of the Fourth Company had fallen. The Fourth Company was continuing its resistance.

Ratin saw the shape of a man about three hundred meters from the
trenches. It was private Bidou, Simpleton Bidou. He was cowering in a
wet pit, which had been made by an exploding shell. The soldier was
doing what obscene old men in villages and depraved boys in public
lavatories do. I don't think I need say more.

"Bidou! Button yourself up!" the captain yelled in disgust. "Why are you here?"

"I . . . I can't tell you . . . I'm frightened, Captain!"

"You've found yourself a wife here, you swine! You have the gall to tell me to my face that you're a coward? You have abandoned your comrades just when the regiment is about to attack? *Bien, mon cochon!*"

"I swear to you, Captain, I've tried everything! 'Bidou!' I said to myself. 'Be reasonable!' I drank a whole bottle of pure spirits for courage! *Je ne peux pas, capitaine.* I'm frightened, Captain!"

The simpleton lay his head on his knees, clutched it with both hands, and began to cry. Then he looked up at the captain, and through the slits of his porcine eyes flickered timid, tender hope.

Ratin was a quick-tempered man. He had lost two brothers in the war and had a wound in his neck that hadn't healed. A wave of blasphemous abuse poured over the soldier, a dry hot torrent of the repulsive, frenzied, and nonsensical words that send blood pounding to the temples, and drive one man to kill another.

Instead of answering, Bidou quietly shook his round, red-haired, tousled head, the heavy head of the village idiot.

No power on earth could have made him stand up. The captain came right to the edge of the pit and whispered very quietly.

"Get up, Bidou, or I will piss on you from head to toe."

He did as he said. Captain Ratin was not a man to joke with. A reeking stream splashed forcefully over the soldier's face. Bidou was an idiot, a village idiot, but he could not bear this insult. He gave a long, inhuman howl. The miserable, solitary, forlorn howl spread over the harrowed fields. He jumped up, wrung his hands, and bolted over the field toward the German trenches. An enemy bullet struck him in the chest. Ratin finished him off with two shots from his revolver. The soldier's body didn't even twitch. It was left lying in no-man's-land, between enemy lines.

Thus died Celestin Bidou, a Norman peasant from Ori, twenty-one years of age, on the bloodstained fields of France.

The story I have told here is true. Captain Gaston Vidal wrote of it in his book *Figures et anecdotes de la Grand Guerre.* He had witnessed the event. He also fought for France, Captain Vidal did.

The Deserter

Captain Gémier was an outstanding man, and a philosopher too. On the battlefield he never hesitated, in private life he was capable of overlooking minor offenses. It is no small thing for a man to be able to overlook minor offenses. He loved France with a soul-devouring fervor, and his hatred for the barbarians who were defiling her ancient soil was relentless, unquenchable, and lifelong.

What more can one say about Gémier? He loved his wife, brought up his children to be good citizens, was a Frenchman, a patriot, a Parisian, and a lover of books and beautiful things.

Then one fine rosy spring morning, Captain Gémier was informed that an unarmed soldier had been found between French and enemy lines. The soldier's intention to defect was obvious, his guilt clear, and he was brought back under guard.

"Is that you, Beaugé?"

"Yes, Captain!" the soldier replied, saluting.

"I see you took advantage of the dawn to catch a breath of fresh air!" Silence.

"*C'est bien!* You may leave the two of us alone!"

The other soldiers left. Gémier locked the door. The soldier was twenty years old.

"You know what awaits you! *Voyons,* explain yourself!"

Beaugé told him everything. He said that he was sick of war.

"I'm sick of war, *mon capitaine.* No sleep for six nights because of the shelling!"

He had a horror of war. He had not wanted to go to the other side as a traitor, but to give himself up.

In a word, our little Beaugé was unexpectedly eloquent. He told the captain that he was only twenty—*mon dieu, c'est naturel,* one makes mistakes at twenty. He had a mother, a fiancée, *des bons amis.* His whole life lay before him, before twenty-year-old Beaugé, and he would have ample time to make up for his transgression against France.

"Captain, what would my mother say if she found out that I was shot like a wretched criminal?"

The soldier fell to his knees.

"Don't try that with me, Beaugé!" the captain told him. "The other soldiers saw you. We get five soldiers like you, and the whole company is poisoned. *C'est la défaite. Cela jamais.** You are going to die, Beaugé, but I shall save your honor. The local authorities will not be informed of your disgrace. Your mother will be told that you fell on the field of honor. Let's go!"

The soldier followed his superior officer. When they got to the forest, the captain stopped, took out his revolver, and held it out to Beaugé.

"This is how you can avoid a court-martial. You will shoot yourself! I will come back in five minutes. By then everything must be over!"

Gémier walked away. Not a sound interrupted the silence of the forest. The captain returned. Beaugé was waiting for him, hunched over.

"I can't, Captain!" he whispered. "I don't have the strength."

And he recommenced the same long story—his mother, his fiancée, his friends, the life that lay before him.

"I am giving you another five minutes, Beaugé! Don't waste my time!"

When the captain returned, he found the soldier lying on the ground, sobbing, his fingers twitching weakly on the revolver.

Gémier helped the soldier to his feet and, looking him in the eye, said in a quiet, friendly voice, "Beaugé, my friend. Could it be that you don't know how to do it?"

He slowly took the revolver from the young boy's wet hands, walked away three paces, and shot him in the head.

• • •

This incident is also described in Gaston Vidal's book. And the soldier was in actual fact called Beaugé. I am not fully sure if this captain's name really was Gémier. Vidal's story is dedicated "with deep reverence" to a certain Firmin Gémier—and I believe this dedication might well indicate that the captain's name was indeed Gémier. Furthermore, Vidal maintains that the captain was "a patriot, a soldier, a good father and a man who was capable of overlooking minor offences." And that is quite a commendable trait in a man—being able to overlook minor offenses.

*"That would mean defeat. Never."

Papa Marescot's Family

We occupy a village that we have taken from the enemy. It is a tiny Picardy village, lovely and modest. Our company has been bivouacked in the cemetery. Surrounding us are smashed crucifixes and fragments of statues and tombstones wrecked by the sledgehammer of an unknown defiler. Rotting corpses have spilled out of coffins shattered by shells. A picture worthy of you, Michelangelo!

A soldier has no time for mysticism. A field of skulls has been dug up into trenches. War is war. We're still alive. If it is our lot to increase the population of this chilly little hole, we should at least make these decaying corpses dance a jig to the tune of our machine guns.

A shell had blown off the cover of one of the vaults. This so I could have a shelter, no doubt about it. I made myself comfortable in that hole, *que voulez vous, on loge ou on peut.**

So—it's a wonderful, bright spring morning. I am lying on corpses, looking at the fresh grass, thinking of Hamlet. He wasn't that bad a philosopher, the poor prince. Skulls spoke to him in human words. Nowadays, that kind of skill would really come in handy for a lieutenant of the French army.

"Lieutenant, there's some civilian here who wants to see you!" a corporal calls out to me.

What the hell does a civilian want in these nether regions?

A character enters. A shabby, shriveled little old man. He is wearing his Sunday best. His frock coat is bespattered with mud. A half-empty sack dangles from his cowering shoulders. There must be a frozen potato in it—every time he moves, something rattles in the sack.

"*Eh bien,* what do you want?"

"My name, you see, is Monsieur Marescot," the civilian whispers, and bows. "That is why I've come . . ."

"So?"

"I would like to bury Madame Marescot and the rest of my family, Monsieur Lieutenant."

"What?"

"My name, you see, is Papa Marescot." The old man lifts his hat

* "What do you expect, one holes up where one can."

from his gray forehead. "Perhaps you have heard of me, Monsieur Lieutenant!"

Papa Marescot? I have heard this name before. Of course I have heard it. This is the story: Three days ago, at the beginning of our occupation, all nonenemy civilians had been issued the order to evacuate. Some left, others stayed. Those who stayed hid in cellars. But their courage was no match for the bombardment—the stone defense proved hopeless. Many were killed. A whole family had been crushed beneath the debris of a cellar. It was the Marescot family. Their name had stuck in my mind, a true French name. They had been a family of four, the father, mother, and two daughters. Only the father survived.

"You poor man! So you are Marescot? This is so sad. Why did you have to go into that damned cellar, why?"

The corporal interrupted me.

"It looks like they're starting up again, Lieutenant!"

That was to be expected. The Germans had noticed the movement in our trenches. The volley came from the right flank, then it moved farther left. I grabbed Papa Marescot by the collar and pulled him down. My boys ducked their heads and sat quietly under cover, no one as much as sticking his nose out.

Papa Marescot sat pale and shivering in his Sunday best. A five-inch kitten was meowing nearby.

"What can I do for you, Papa? This is no time to beat about the bush! As you can see, we're at each other's throats here!"

"*Mon lieutenant,* I've told you everything. I would like to bury my family."

"Fine, I'll send the men to collect the bodies."

"I have the bodies with me, Monsieur Lieutenant!"

"What?"

He pointed to the sack. In it were the meager remains of Papa Marescot's family.

I shuddered with horror.

"Very well, Papa, I will have my men bury them."

He looked at me as if I had just uttered the greatest idiocy.

"When this hellish din has died down," I continued, "we shall dig an excellent grave for them. Rest assured, *père Marescot,* we will take care of everything."

"But I have a family vault."

"Splendid, where is it?"

"But . . . but . . ."

" 'But what?

"But we're sitting in it as we speak, *mon lieutenant.*"

The Quaker

"Thou shalt not kill" one of the Commandments dictates. This is why Stone, a Quaker, enlisted in the Drivers Corps. He could serve his country without committing the mortal sin of murder. His wealth and education could have secured him a higher post, but, a slave to his conscience, he humbly accepted an insignificant position and the company of people he found coarse.

Who was Stone? He was a bald dome on top of a long stick. The Lord had given him this body with only one objective: to raise Stone's thoughts above the sorrows and cares of this world. His every move was nothing more than a victory of spirit over matter. Regardless of how bad things were, when he was sitting at the wheel of his car he bore himself with the wooden firmness of a preacher in his pulpit. No one ever saw him laugh.

One morning Stone was off duty and decided to go for a walk to pay homage to the Lord in the midst of His creation. An enormous Bible under his arm, Stone strode with his long legs over meadows revived by spring. The blue sky, the twittering of the sparrows in the grass, filled him with joy.

Stone sat down, opened his Bible—but at that very moment he saw an untethered horse, its scrawny ribs jutting out, appear by the bend in the path. Stone immediately heard the powerful voice of duty calling him from within. Back home, he was a member of the Society for the Protection of Animals. He went up to the beast, patted its soft lips, and, forgetting his walk, set off for the stables, clutching his Bible. On the way, he stopped to let the horse drink at a well.

The stableboy was a young man named Bekker. His ways had always triggered righteous indignation in Stone: at every posting, Bekker left inconsolable fiancées.

"I could report you to the major!" the Quaker told him. "But I hope that this time a simple warning will be enough! You are going to look after this poor sick horse, which deserves a much better fate than you do!"

And he marched off with a measured, solemn gait, ignoring the guffaws behind him. The young man's square, protruding chin convincingly testified of his invincible stubbornness.

A few days passed. The horse was still wandering about neglected. This time, Stone told Bekker severely, "Son of Satan!" this is more or less how he started his speech. "The Lord Almighty may well allow you to destroy your soul, but your grievous sins should not be allowed to fall upon an innocent mare! Look at her, you wretch! She is stomping about, greatly unsettled. I am certain you are treating her roughly, as is to be expected from a criminal like you! I shall say this one last time, you Devil's progeny: head to your own damnation as fast as you see fit, but look after this horse, or you will have me to answer to!"

From that day on, Stone felt that Providence had invested him with a special mission: to care for the fate of the abused quadruped. He felt that people, sinful as they were, were unworthy of respect. But for animals he felt an indescribable compassion. His exhausting duties did not hinder him from keeping his inviolable promise to God.

At night the Quaker would often get out of his car (he slept in it, huddled on the seats) in order to make sure that the horse was at a suitable distance from Bekker's nail-studded boot. In good weather, Stone would even mount the beloved animal. The poor nag, trotting along with an air of importance, would carry Stone's long, scrawny body over the green fields, while Stone, his face yellowish and sallow and his lips pressed tight, would picture the immortal, toy-soldierlike figure of the Knight of the Mournful Countenance trotting on his mare Rosinante, over flowers and pastures green.

Stone's zeal bore fruit. The stableboy felt Stone's relentless eyes upon him, and used every trick in the book not to be caught in the act, but when he was alone with the mare, he vented on her all the fury of his base soul. He felt an inexplicable dread of the taciturn Quaker, and he hated him because of this, and despised himself. The only way he could raise himself in his own esteem was to taunt the horse which the Quaker had taken under his wing. Such is the despicable pride of man. Locking himself in the stables with the horse, the stableboy pricked her hairy, sagging lips with red-hot needles, lashed her across the spine with a wire whip, and threw salt in her eyes. When he finally let the tortured animal totter fearfully to its stall, blinded by stinging salt and swaying like a drunkard, the stableboy threw himself in the hay and laughed his heart out, enjoying his revenge to the fullest.

There was a change at the front. Stone's division was relocated to a more dangerous position. His religious beliefs did not permit him to kill, but they did permit him to be killed. The Germans were advancing on the Isère. Stone was transporting the injured. All around him, men of various nationalities were dying at an incredible rate. Old generals, spotlessly clean, their faces swollen, stood on hilltops and monitored the area with field glasses. There was a ceaseless barrage of cannon fire. A stench rose from the earth, the sun rummaged through the mangled corpses.

Stone forgot his horse. But within a week his conscience began gnawing at him, and he found an opportunity to return to the area where he had been stationed before. He found the horse in a dark shed made of a few rickety planks. The mare was so weak she could barely stand. Her eyes were covered with a grimy film. She neighed weakly when she saw her true friend, and lay her faltering muzzle on his hand.

"It isn't my fault," the stableboy told Stone cheekily. "We're not being given any oats."

"Fine," Stone said. "I'll go get some oats."

He looked up at the sky that shone through a hole in the roof, and went outside.

I came across him a few hours later and asked him whether the road he was driving down wasn't too dangerous. He seemed more intense than usual. The last few blood-drenched days had left a deep mark on him, it was as if he were in mourning for himself.

"I haven't run into any trouble this far," he mumbled. "But things might well end up badly." And suddenly he added, "I'm heading for the forage stores. I need some oats."

The following morning a search party of soldiers that was sent out to look for him found him dead at the wheel of his car. A bullet had penetrated his forehead. The car had crashed into a ditch.

Thus died Stone, the Quaker, on account of his love for a horse.

THE SIN OF JESUS

*A*rina had a little room by the grand stairway near the guest rooms, and Sergei, the janitor's assistant, had a room near the service entrance. They had done a shameful deed together. Arina bore Sergei twins on Easter Sunday. Water flows, stars shine, muzhiks feel lust, and Arina again found herself in a delicate condition. She is in her sixth month, the months just roll by when a woman is pregnant, and Sergei ends up being drafted into the army—a fine mess! So Arina goes to him and says, "Listen, Sergunya, there's no point in me sitting around waiting for you. We won't see each other for four years, and I wouldn't be surprised if I had another brood of three or four by the time you come back. Working in a hotel, your skirt is hitched up more often than not. Whoever takes a room here gets to be your lord and master, Jews or whatever. When you come back from the army my womb will be worn out, I'll be washed up as a woman, I don't think I'll be of any use to you."

"True enough," Sergei said, nodding his head.

"The men who want to marry me right now are Trofimich the contractor, he's a rude roughneck, Isai Abramich, a little old man, and then there's the warden of Nilolo-Svyatskoi Church, he's very feeble, but your vigor has rattled my soul to pieces! As the Lord is my witness, I'm all chewed up! In three months I'll be rid of my burden, I'll leave the baby at the orphanage, and I'll go marry them."

When Sergei heard this he took off his belt and gave Arina a heroic beating, aiming for her belly.

"Hey!" the woman says to him. "Don't beat me on the gut, remember it's your stuffing in there, not no one else's!"

She received many savage wallops, he shed many a bitter tear, the woman's blood flowed, but that's neither here nor there. The woman went to Jesus Christ and said:

"This and that, Lord Jesus. Me, I'm Arina, the maid from the Hotel Madrid & Louvre on Tverskaya Street. Working in a hotel, your skirt is hitched up more often than not. Whoever takes a room there gets to be your lord and master, Jews or whatever. Here on earth walks a humble servant of Yours, Sergei the janitor's assistant. I bore him twins last year on Easter Sunday."

And she told him everything.

"And what if Sergei didn't go to the army?" the Savior pondered.

"The constable would drag him off."

"Ah, the constable," the Savior said, his head drooping. "I'd forgotten all about him. Ah!—and how about if you led a pure life?"

"For four years!" the woman gasped. "Do you mean to say that everyone should stop living a life? You're still singing the same old tune! How are we supposed to go forth and multiply? Do me a favor and spare me such advice!"

Here the Savior's cheeks flushed crimson. The woman had stung him to the quick, but he said nothing. You cannot kiss your own ear, even the Savior knew that.

"This is what you need to do, humble servant of the Lord, glorious maidenly sinner Arina!" the Savior proclaimed in all his glory. "I have a little angel prancing about up in heaven, his name is Alfred, and he's gotten completely out of hand. He keeps moaning, 'Why, O Lord, did you make me an angel at twenty, a fresh lad like me?' I'll give you, Arina, servant of God, Alfred the angel as a husband for four years. He'll be your prayer, your salvation, and your pretty-boy, too. And there's no way you'll get a child from him, not even a duckling, because there's a lot of fun in him, but no substance."

"That's just what I need!" maid Arina cried. "It's their substance that has driven me to the brink of the grave three times in two years!"

"This will be a sweet respite for you, child of God, a light prayer, like a song. Amen."

And thus it was decided. Alfred, a frail, tender youth, was sent down, and fluttering on his pale blue shoulders were two wings, rippling in a rosy glow like doves frolicking in the heavens. Arina hugged him, sobbing with emotion and female tenderness.

"My little Alfredushka, my comfort and joy, my one-and-only!"

The Savior gave her instructions that, before going to bed, she had to take off the angel's wings, which were mounted on hinges, just like door hinges, and she had to take them off and wrap them in a clean sheet for the night, because at the slightest frolic the wings could break, as they were made of infants' sighs and nothing more.

The Savior blessed the union one last time, and called over a choir of abbots for the occasion, their voices thundering in song. There was nothing to eat, not even a hint of food—that wouldn't have been proper—and Arina and Alfred, embracing, descended to earth on a silken rope ladder. They went to Petrovka, that's were the woman dragged him to, she bought him lacquered shoes, checkered tricot trousers (by the way, not only was he not wearing pants, he was completely in the altogether), a hunting frock, and a vest of electric-blue velvet.

"As for the rest, sweetie," she said, "we'll find that at home."

That day Arina did not work in the hotel, she took the day off. Sergei came and made a big to-do outside her room, but she wouldn't open, and called out from behind her door, "Sergei Nifantich, I'm busy washing my feet right now and would be obliged if you would distance yourself without all that to-do!"

He left without saying a word. The angelic power was already taking effect.

Arina cooked a meal fit for a merchant—ha, she was devilishly proud, she was! A quart of vodka, and even some wine, Danube herring with potatoes, a samovar filled with tea. No sooner had Alfred eaten this earthly abundance than he keeled over into a deep sleep. Arina managed to snatch his wings off their hinges just in time. She wrapped them up, and then carried Alfred to her bed.

Lying on her fluffy eiderdown, on her frayed, sin-ridden bed, is a snow-white wonder, an otherworldly brilliance radiating from him. Shafts of moonlight mix with red rays and dart about the room, trippling over their feet. And Arina weeps, rejoices, sings, and prays. The unheard of, O Arina, has befallen you in this shattered world, blessed art thou among women!

They had drunk down the whole quart of vodka. And it was pretty obvious, too. As they fell asleep, Arina rolled over onto Alfred with the hot, six-month gut that Sergei had saddled her with. You can imagine the weight! It wasn't enough that she was sleeping next to an angel, it wasn't enough that the man next to her wasn't spitting on the wall, or snoring, or snorting—no it wasn't enough for this lusty, crazed wench! She had to warm her bloated, combustible belly even more. And so she crushed the Lord's angel, crushed him in her drunken bliss, crushed him in her rapture like a week-old infant, mangled him beneath her, and he came to a fatal end, and from his wings, wrapped in the sheet, pale tears flowed.

Dawn came, the trees bowed down low. In the distant northern woods, every fir tree turned into a priest, every fir tree genuflected.

The woman comes again before the throne of the Savior. She is strong, her shoulders wide, her red hands carrying the young corpse.

"Behold, Lord!"

This was too much for Jesus' gentle soul, and he cursed the woman from the bottom of his heart.

"As it is in the world, Arina, so it shall be with you!"

"But Lord!" the woman said to him in a low voice. "Was it I who made my body heavy, who brewed the vodka, who made a woman's soul lonely and stupid?"

"I do not wish to have anything further to do with you," Lord Jesus exclaimed. "You have crushed my angel, you trollop, you!" And Arina was hurled back down to earth on a purulent wind, to Tverskaya Street, to her sentence at the Madrid & Louvre. There all caution had been thrown to the winds. Sergei was carousing away the last few days before he had to report as a recruit. Trofimich, the contractor, who had just come back from Kolomna, saw how healthy and red-cheeked she was.

"Ooh what a nice little gut!" he said, among other things.

Isai Abramich, the little old man, came wheezing over when he heard about the little gut.

"After all that has happened," he said, "I cannot settle down with you lawfully, but I can definitely still lie with you."

Six feet under, that's where he should be lying, and not spitting into her soul like everyone else! It was as if they had all broken loose from their chains—dishwashers, peddlers, foreigners. A tradesman likes to have some fun.

And here ends my tale.

Before she gave birth—the remaining three months flew by quickly—Arina went out into the backyard behind the janitor's room, raised her horribly large belly to the silken skies, and idiotically uttered, "Here you are, Lord, here is my gut! They bang on it as if it were a drum. Why, I don't know! And then, Lord, I end up like this again! I've had enough!"

Jesus drenched Arina with his tears. The Savior fell to his knees.

"Forgive me, my Arinushka, sinful God that I am, that I have done this to you!"

"I will not forgive you, Jesus Christ!" Arina replied. "I will not!"

AN EVENING WITH
THE EMPRESS

*S*iberian salmon caviar and a pound of bread in my pocket. Nowhere to go. I am standing on Anichkov Bridge, huddling against Klodt's horses. A heavy evening is descending from Morskaya. Orange lights wrapped in gauze roam along the Nevsky Prospekt. I need shelter. Hunger is plucking at me the way a clumsy brat plucks at the strings of a violin. My mind skims over all the apartments abandoned by the bourgeoisie. The Anichkov Palace shimmers into view in all its squat splendor. There's my shelter!

It isn't hard to slip into the entrance hall unnoticed. The palace is empty. An unhurried mouse is scratching away in one of the chambers. I am in the library of the Dowager Empress Maria Fyodorovna.* An old German is standing in the middle of the room, stuffing cotton wool in his ears. He is about to leave. Luck kisses me on the lips! I know this German! I once typed a report for him, free of charge, about the loss of his passport. This German belongs to me, from his puffy head to his good-natured toes. We decide that I have an appointment with Lunacharsky† in the library, and that I am waiting for him.

The melodic ticking of the clock erases the German from the room. I am alone. Balls of crystal blaze above me in the silky yellow

---

* Empress Maria Fyodorovna (Princess Dagmar of Denmark), 1847–1928, wife of Czar Alexander III.
† Anatoly Lunacharsky, 1875–1933, Marxist critic and playwright, was the USSR's first Commissar of Education.

---

light. A warmth beyond description rises from the steam pipes of the central heating. The deep divans wrap my frozen body in calm.

A quick inspection yields results. I discover a potato pie in the fireplace, a saucepan, a pinch of tea and sugar. And behold! The spirit stove just stuck its bluish little tongue out.

That evening I ate like a human being. I spread the most delicate of napkins on an ornate little Chinese table glittering with ancient lacquer. I washed down each piece of my brown ration bread with a sip of sweet, steaming tea, its coral stars dancing on the faceted sides of the glass. The bulging velvet palms of the cushion beneath me caressed my bony hips. Outside the windows, fluffy snow crystals fell on the Petersburg granite deadened by the hard frost.

Light streamed down the warm walls in glittering lemon torrents, touching book spines that responded with a bluish gold twinkle.

The books, their pages molding and fragrant, carried me to faraway Denmark. Over half a century ago they had been given to the young princess as she left her small, chaste country for savage Russia. On the austere title pages, the ladies of the court who had raised her bade her farewell in three slanting lines, in fading ink, as did her friends from Copenhagen, the daughters of state councilors, her tutors, parchment professors from the Lycée, and her father, the King, and her mother, the Queen, her weeping mother. Long shelves of small plump books with blackened gilt edges, children's Bibles speckled with timid ink splotches, clumsy little prayers written to Lord Jesus, morocco-leather volumes of Lamartine and Chénier containing dried flowers crumbling to dust. I leaf through the gossamer pages that have survived oblivion, and the image of a mysterious country, a thread of exotic days, unfurls before me: low walls encircling the royal gardens, dew on the trimmed lawns, the drowsy emerald canals, the tall King with chocolate sideburns, the calm ringing of the bell above the palace cathedral and, maybe, love—a young girl's love, a fleeting whisper in the heavy halls. Empress Maria Fyodorovna, a small woman with a tightly powdered face, a consummate schemer with an indefatigable passion for power, a fierce female among the Preobrazhensky Grenadiers, a ruthless but attentive mother, crushed by the German woman,* unfurls the scroll of her long, somber life before me.

* Empress Maria Fyodorovna's daughter-in-law, Empress Alexandra, 1872–1918, wife of Czar Nicholas II.

It was very late that night when I tore myself from this sorrowful and touching chronicle, from the specters with their blood-drenched skulls. The balls of crystal covered in swirls of dust were still blazing peacefully above me on the ornate brown ceiling. Next to my tattered shoes, leaden rivulets had crystallized on the blue carpet. Exhausted by my thoughts and the silent heat, I fell asleep.

In the depths of the night I made my way toward the exit over the dully glinting parquet of the corridors. Alexander III's study was a high-ceilinged box with boarded-up windows facing the Nevsky Prospekt. Mikhail Alexandrovich's* rooms were the lively apartment of a cultivated officer who likes his exercise. The walls were decorated with bright, pink-patterned wallpaper. Little porcelain bibelots, of the naive and redundantly fleshy genre of the seventeenth century, lined the low mantelpieces.

Pressed against a column, I waited for a long time for the last court lackey to fall asleep. He dropped his wrinkled jowls, clean-shaven out of age-old habit, the lantern weakly gilding his high, lolling forehead.

At one in the morning I was out in the street. The Nevsky Prospekt welcomed me into its sleepless womb. I went to the Nikolayevsky Station to sleep. Let those who have fled this city know that there is still a place in Petersburg where a homeless poet can spend the night.

* Grand Duke Mikhail Alexandrovich, 1878–1918, brother of Czar Nicholas II.

CHINK

A vicious night. Slashing wind. A dead man's fingers pluck at the frozen entrails of Petersburg. The crimson pharmacies on street corners freeze over. A pharmacist's prim head lolls to the side. The frost grips the pharmacy by its purple heart. And the pharmacy's heart dies.

The Nevsky Prospekt is empty. Ink vials shatter in the sky. It is two in the morning. The end. A vicious night.

A young girl and a gentleman are sitting by the railing of the Café Bristol. Two whimpering backs. Two freezing ravens by a leafless bush.

"If, with the help of Satan, you manage to succeed the deceased Czar, then see if the masses will follow you, you mother-killers! Just you try! The Latvians will back them, and those Latvians are Mongols, Glafira!"

The man's jowls hang on both sides of his face like a rag peddler's sacks. In the man's reddish brown pupils wounded cats prowl.

"I beg you, for the love of Christ, Aristarkh Terentich! Please go to Nadezhinskaya Street! Who will walk up to me if I'm sitting with a man?"

A Chinese in a leather jacket walks past. He lifts a loaf of bread above his head. With his blue fingernail he draws a line across the crust. One pound. Glafira raises two fingers. Two pounds.

A thousand saws moan in the ossified snow of the side streets. A star twinkles in the hard, inky firmament.

The Chinese man stops and mumbles to her through clenched teeth, "You a dirty one? Huh?"

"I'm a nice clean girl, comrade!"

"Pound."

On Nadezhinskaya Street, Aristarkh looks back with sparks in his eyes.

"Darling," the girl says to the Chinese man in a hoarse voice, "I've got my godfather with me. Will you let him sleep in a corner?"

The Chinese man slowly nods his head. O great wisdom of the East!

"Aristarkh Terentich," the girl yells casually, leaning against the smooth leather shoulder. "My acquaintance is inviting you to join us for company!"

Aristarkh Terentich immediately livens up.

"For reasons beyond the control of management, he is currently not employed," she whispers, wriggling her shoulders. "But he had a past with meat and potatoes in it!"

"Definitely. I am pleased to make your acquaintance. Aristarkh Terentich Sheremetsev."

At the hotel they were served Chinese liquor and weren't even asked to pay.

Late at night, the Chinese man slipped out of bed into the darkness of the room.

"Where are you going?" Glafira asked gruffly, twisting her legs.

There was a large sweat stain under her back.

The Chinese man went over to Aristarkh, who was sleeping on the floor by the washstand. He shook the old man's shoulders and pointed to Glafira.

"Oh, yes, yes, pal!" Aristarkh prattled from the floor, "A definite yes!" And with quick little steps he hobbled over to the bed.

"Get away from me, you dog!" Glafira shouted. "Your Chinaman's finished me off already!"

"She won't do it, pal!" Aristarkh hissed quickly. "You ordered her to, but she isn't obeying!"

"He friend!" the Chinese man said. "He do! Big harlot!"

"You are an elderly gentleman, Aristarkh Terentich," the girl whispered, letting the old man climb into bed with her. "What's got into your head?"

Period.

A TALE ABOUT
A WOMAN

*O*nce upon a time there was a woman, her name was Xenia. Large bosom, round shoulders, blue eyes. That was the kind of woman she was. If only you and I had such a woman!

Her husband was killed on the battlefield. Three years she lived without a husband, working in the house of a rich family. The rich family wanted a hot meal three times a day. Wood they never burned, nothing but coal. The heat from the coals was unbearable—in coals fiery roses glow.

For three years the woman cooked for the rich family, and she was virtuous with the menfolk. But where do you hide a gigantic bosom like that? Can you tell me?

The fourth year she goes to the doctor. "My head feels all heavy," she says to him. "One minute I'm ablaze with fire, the next I'm all weak."

And this, believe it or not, is what the doctor tells her: "Is there no menfolk running around in your courtyard? *Oy,* woman!"

"I wouldn't dare," Xenia said, bursting into tears. "I'm a delicate girl!"

And indeed she was a delicate girl. Xenia's bitter tears made her eyes bluer.

Old mother Morozikha took matters in hand.

Old mother Morozikha was the midwife and potion-maker for the whole street. The likes of her are ruthless with a woman's insides. Give her half a chance to steam them out, and you'll be lucky if even a blade of grass will ever grow there again.

"Xenia," she says, "I'll fix things for you! A dryness has cracked the soil. All it needs is some God-sent rain. A mushroom needs to sprout up in a woman, all soggy and rank."

And she brought him. Valentin Ivanovich was his name. Not much to look at, but quite a joker, and he could make up nice ditties. He didn't have a body worth mentioning, his hair was long, and he was covered with a rainbow scattering of pimples. But did Xenia need a bull? He was a man, and could make up nice ditties. Could you find anything better in the world? Xenia cooked a hundred blini and raisin pies. Three eiderdowns were laid on her bed, and six pillows, all nice and fluffy— all for you to roll around in, Valentin!

Evening came, the guests squeezed into the tiny room behind the kitchen, everyone downed a glass of vodka. Old mother Morozikha had put on a silk kerchief, you wouldn't believe how respectable she looked. And Valentin spoke wonderful words to Xenia: "Ah, Xenia, my sweet one! I am a neglected man in this world, a dog-tired youth! Do not think of me lackadaisically! Night will descend with stars and black fans—O can a man express his soul in a poem? O, timid man that I am!"

Word upon word. Needless to say, they emptied two whole bottles of vodka and three of wine. Not to mention five rubles' worth of food— no joke!

Our Valentin's face flushed to a dark maroon, and he began hollering poetry.

Old mother Morozikha got up from the table.

"Well, I'll be off, may the Lord be with me!" she said. "There'll be love between the two of you, so when you lie down together on the stove bench, pull off his boots. With men, you can wash sheets till you're blue in the face."

But the liquor was beginning to kick in. Valentin grabbed his hair and started tearing at it. "I," he shouts, "am having visions. The moment I have a few drinks, I start having visions. Xenia, I can see you lying dead, your face looks sickening. And I am the priest, I am walking behind your coffin, swinging the censer!"

At this point, needless to say, he raised his voice.

Well, Xenia was only human. She too had loosened her blouse, unfastening a button or two.

"Don't shout, Valentin Ivanovich," she whispered. "Don't shout, the master and mistress will hear."

But tell me, can you hold a man back once he is seized by melancholia?

"You have offended me most deeply!" Valentin wept convulsively. "Oh, what snakes people are! What did they want? They wanted to buy my soul! I," he went on, "was born out of wedlock, but I am still a nobleman's son! Are you listening to me, you scullery maid, you?"

"I will be sweet to you, Valentin Ivanovich."

"Leave me be!"

He rose and flung open the door.

"Leave me be! I am going out into the world!"

But how was he to go out into the world, poor soul, soused out of his mind as he was? He collapsed onto the bed, puked on the, if you will pardon the expression, sheets, and fell asleep, the humble servant of God.

Old mother Morozikha was already rolling up her sleeves.

"Well, that's the end of that," she said. "We'd better carry him outside."

The women carried Valentin out into the street and laid him down outside the gate. They went back in, and there stood the mistress, in a nightcap and the most elegant pantaloons.

"You entertain men here at night and act most scandalously!" she scolded her cook. "I want you to pack your bags and leave my God-fearing household by tomorrow morning! I have my unmarried daughter to think of!"

Xenia sat in the hall, weeping till dawn.

"Grandma Morozikha, ah, Grandma Morozikha," she whimpered, "what have you done to me, poor young woman that I am! I'm ashamed of myself, how can I even dare look at God's world, and what can I expect to see in God's world now?"

Xenia cried and carried on, surrounded by raisin pies, snowy featherbeds, holy icon lamps, and wine. And her warm shoulders shook.

"It was a blunder," old mother Morozikha said to her. "We should have gone for a simpler fellow, we should have gone for Mitya."

And morning set up shop once more. The girls carrying milk went from house to house. It was a blue and frosty morning.

THE BATHROOM WINDOW

I have an acquaintance, a Madam Kebchik. In her day, Madam Kebchik assures me, "nothing in the world" would have induced her to take less than five rubles.

Now she has a nice, respectable apartment, and in this apartment she has two girls, Marusya and Tamara. There are more requests for Marusya than for Tamara. One of the windows of the girls' room has a view of the street, the other window, just an air vent near the ceiling, has a view of the bathroom. When I realized this, I said to Fanya Osipovna Kebchik, "How about putting a ladder by the little window in the bathroom in the evenings, so I can climb up and peek into Marusya's room? I'll give you five rubles."

"You rogue, you!" Fanya Osipovna said, and agreed.

She got her five rubles quite often. I made use of the little window when Marusya had clients.

Everything went without a hitch, but one time an extremely foolish thing happened. I was standing on the ladder. Luckily, Marusya hadn't turned off the light. Her guest was a pleasant, unassuming fellow with one of those large, harmless mustaches. He undressed in a prim and proper fashion: he took off his collar, looked in the mirror, noticed a pimple under his mustache, studied it, and pressed it out with a handkerchief. He took off a boot and examined it too—was there a scratch on the sole?

They kissed, undressed, and smoked a cigarette. I got ready to climb down. At that moment I felt the ladder sliding away under me. I tried to grab hold of the window, but it gave way. The ladder fell with a crash and there I was, dangling in the air.

Suddenly the whole apartment exploded with alarm. Everyone came running, Fanya Osipovna, Tamara, and an official I didn't know in a Ministry of Finance uniform. They helped me down. My situation was pitiful. Marusya and her lanky client came into the bathroom.

The girl looked at me, froze, and said quietly, "What a bastard, oh, what a bastard!"

She fell silent, stared at us foolishly, went over to the lanky man, and for some reason kissed his hand and started crying.

"My dear, O God, my dear!" she said, between kisses and sobs.

The lanky man stood there like a total idiot. My heart was pounding wildly. I dug my nails into my palms and went over to Madam Kebchik.

Within a few minutes, Marusya knew everything. All was forgiven and forgotten. But I was still wondering why she had kissed the lanky fellow.

"Madam Kebchik," I said. "Put up the ladder one last time, and you can have ten rubles."

"Your mind's even more unsteady than that ladder of yours!" the landlady answered, and agreed.

So there I was again, standing by the little window. I looked through it and saw Marusya, her thin arms wrapped around her client, kissing him with slow kisses, tears flowing from her eyes.

"My darling!" she whispered. "O God, my sweet darling!" And she gave herself to him with all the passion of a woman in love. She looked at him as if he, this lanky fellow, were the only man in the world.

And the lanky fellow wallowed in businesslike bliss.

BAGRAT-OGLY AND
THE EYES OF HIS BULL

I saw a bull of unparalleled beauty lying by the side of the road.
A boy was bending over it, crying.

"This boy is Bagrat-Ogly," said a snake charmer who was eating his
scanty meal nearby. "Bagrat-Ogly, son of Kazim."

"He is as exquisite as twelve moons," I said.

"The green cloak of the Prophet will never cover the rebellious
whiskers of Kazim," the snake charmer said. "He was a quarrelsome
man, and left his son nothing but a pauper's hut, his plump wives, and
a bull that was unrivaled. But Allah is great!"

"*Allah il'Allah!*" I said.

"Allah is great," he repeated, pushing away his basket of snakes.
"The bull grew up to become the mightiest bull in Anatolia. Memed-
khan, a neighbor, sick with envy, castrated it last night. Now no one
will bring their cows to Bagrat-Ogly in the hope of conception. Now
no one will pay Bagrat-Ogly a hundred piasters for the love of his
bull. He is a pauper, Bagrat-Ogly. He weeps by the side of the road.

The silence of the mountains unfurled its violet banners above us.
The snows glittered on the peaks. Blood trickled down the legs of the
mutilated bull and bubbled onto the grass. And, hearing the bull moan,
I looked into its eyes and saw the bull's death and my own death, and I
fell to the ground in measureless torment.

"Traveler!" the boy then called, his face as rosy as the dawn. "You
writhe, and foam bubbles from the corners of your lips. A black illness
is fettering you with the ropes of its convulsions."

"Bagrat-Ogly!" I answered, sunk in exhaustion. "In the eyes of your bull I saw the reflection of the ever-watchful malice of our neighbors, the Memed-khans of this world. In the moist depths of its eyes I saw mirrors in which rage the green fires of the treachery of our neighbors, the Memed-khans of this world. In the eyes of the mutilated bull I saw my youth, barren and cut down, the prime of my life thrashing its way through the thorny undergrowth of indifference. The deserts of Syria, Arabia, and Kurdistan, which I have fathomed thrice, I saw within the eyes of your bull, O Bagrat-Ogly, and their flat sands leave me no hope. The hatred of the whole world has penetrated the eye sockets of your bull. Flee from the malice of our Memed-khan neighbors, O Bagrat-Ogly, and may the old snake charmer hoist his basket of pythons onto his back and flee at your side!"

And filling the ravines with my moans, I rose to my feet. I drank in the fragrance of the eucalyptus and walked away. A many-headed dawn soared above the mountains like a thousand swans. The steel waters of the Bay of Trebizond sparkled in the distance, and I saw the sea and the yellow decks of the feluccas. The freshness of the grass poured over the ruins of a Byzantine wall. The bazaars of Trebizond and the carpets of Trebizond rose before me. I came across a young highlander at a fork in the road outside the city. On his outstretched hand sat a pigeon hawk chained by its talon. The highlander walked with a light gait. The sun surfaced above our heads. And a sudden calm descended on my wanderer's soul.

LINE AND COLOR

I first met Alexander Fyodorovich Kerensky* on December 20, 1916, in the dining room of the Ollila Spa. We were introduced by Zatsareni, a barrister from Turkestan. I had heard that Zatsareni had had himself circumcised at the age of forty. That disgraced imbecile Grand Duke Peter Nikolayevich, who was banished to Tashkent, prized Zatsareni's friendship very highly. The Grand Duke used to walk about Tashkent stark naked, married a Cossack woman, lit candles before a portrait of Voltaire as if it were an icon of Jesus Christ, and had the boundless flatlands of Amu-Dari drained. Zatsareni was a good friend to him.

So, there we were at the Ollila Spa. Ten kilometers away shimmered the blue granite walls of Helsingfors.† O Helsingfors, love of my heart! O sky, pouring down onto the esplanades and soaring high like a bird!

So, there we were at the Ollila Spa. Northern flowers were withering in vases. Antlers spread across the murky ceilings. The air of the dining room was filled with the fragrance of pine trees, the cool breasts of Countess Tyszkiewicz, and the British officers' silk underwear.

At the table, a courteous converted Jew from the police department was sitting next to Kerensky. To his right, a Norwegian by the name of

---

* Alexander Fyodorovich Kerensky, 1881–1970, served as Minister of Justice, Minister of War, and provisional Prime Minister of Russia after the 1917 Russian Revolution.

† A former name (Swedish) for Helsinki, which until Finland's declaration of independence in 1917 was Russian.

Nickelsen, the owner of a whaling vessel. To his left, Countess Tyszkiewicz, as beautiful as Marie Antoinette.

Kerensky ate three pieces of cake and went with me for a walk in the forest. Fröken Kristi hurried past us on skis.

"Who was that?" Kerensky asked me.

"That was Nickelsen's daughter, Fröken Kristi," I said. "She's beautiful, isn't she?"

Then we saw old Johannes's sledge.

"Who was that?" Kerensky asked.

"That was old Johannes," I said. "He brings cognac and fruit from Helsingfors. Can it be that you don't know old Johannes the coachman?"

"I know everyone here," Kerensky replied, "but I can't see anyone."

"Are you nearsighted, Alexander Fyodorovich?"

"Yes, I'm nearsighted."

"You need glasses, Alexander Fyodorovich."

"Never!"

"If you think about it," I said to him with the brashness of youth, "you are not merely blind, you are as good as dead. The line—that divine trait, that queen of the world—has escaped you forever. You and I are walking through this enchanted garden, this marvelous Finnish forest. To our dying day we will not encounter anything better, and you, you cannot even see the rosy, ice-crusted edges of the waterfall, over there, on the river. The weeping willow, leaning over the waterfall—you cannot see its Japanese delicacy. The red trunks of the pine trees heaped with snow! The granular sparkle that scintillates over the snows! It begins as a frozen line above the tree's wavy surface, like Leonardo's line, crowned by the reflection of the blazing clouds. And what about Fröken Kristi's silk stockings, and the line of her maturing legs? I beg of you, Alexander Fyodorovich, buy some spectacles!"

"My dear boy," he answered, "don't waste your gunpowder! That half-ruble coin you want me to squander on a pair of spectacles is the one coin that will never leave my pocket! You can keep that line of yours with its repulsive reality. You are living the sordid life of a trigonometry teacher, while I am enveloped by wonders, even in a hole like Klyazma! Why do I need the freckles on Fröken Kristi's face when I, who can barely make her out, can imagine everything I want to imagine about her? Why do I need these clouds in the Finnish sky, when I can see a dreamy ocean above my head? Why do I need lines when I have colors? For me the whole world is a gigantic theater in which I am the only spectator without opera glasses. The orchestra plays the prelude to the third act, the stage is far away as in a dream, my heart swells with delight, I see Juliet's crimson velvet, Romeo's violet silk, and not a single false beard—and you want to blind me with a pair of half-ruble spectacles?"

That evening I left for town. O Helsingfors, refuge of my dreams!

I saw Alexander Fyodorovich again half a year later, in June of 1917, after he had become Supreme Commander of the Russian army and master of our fate.

That day the Troitsky drawbridge had been lifted. The Putilov workers were heading for the arsenal. Burning tramcars lay in the streets like dead horses.

The mass rally had gathered at the House of the People. Alexander Fyodorovich gave a speech on Russia, our mother and our wife. The crowd smothered him with its sheepskin-coat passion. Could he, the only spectator without opera glasses, even see the bristling passion of the sheepskin coats? I have no idea. But after him, Trotsky came to the podium, twisted his lips, and, in a voice that chased away one's last hopes, said:

"My Comrades and Brothers!"

YOU MISSED THE BOAT,
CAPTAIN!

*T*he *Halifax* pulled into Odessa's port. It had come from
London for a cargo of Russian wheat.

On the twentieth-seventh of January, the day of Lenin's funeral,
the ship's colored crew—three Chinese, two Negroes, and a Malay—
called the captain to the deck. In town orchestras were thundering and
a blizzard howled.

"Captain O'Nearn!" the Negroes said. "As there's no loading to do
today, can we go ashore this evening?"

"You will stay where you are!" O'Nearn told them. "A wind-force-
nine gale is blowing right now, and it's getting stronger. The
Beaconsfield has gotten stuck in the ice at Sanzheyka, and the barome-
ter is pointing to where I wish it weren't! In weather like this, the crew
has to stay with the vessel. Stay where you are!"

And Captain O'Nearn went off to see the first mate. The two had
a good laugh, lit cigars, and pointed at the city, where the blizzard and
the orchestras writhed and howled in abject grief.

The two Negroes and the three Chinese loitered about the deck.
They blew on their frozen palms, stamped their rubber boots, and
peered into the captain's cabin, the door of which stood ajar. The velvet
of the sofas, the heated cognac, and the soft tobacco fumes came wafting out into the wind-force-nine gale.

"Boatswain!" O'Nearn yelled, seeing the sailors. "Our deck is not a
boulevard! Throw them in the hold!"

"Yes, sir!" shouted the boatswain, a pillar of red meat covered with red hair. "Yes, sir!" And he grabbed the Malay by the scruff of his neck. He dragged him to the side of the deck facing the open sea, and shoved him onto a rope ladder. The Malay jumped down and went scampering over the ice. The three Chinese and the two Negroes followed close at his heels.

"Did you throw them in the hold?" the captain yelled from his cabin, which was warmed by cognac and delicate smoke.

"I threw them, sir!" shouted the boatswain, a pillar of red meat, standing in the storm by the gangway like a sentinel.

The wind blew in from the sea at force nine, like nine rounds of fire discharged by the frozen batteries of the sea. White snow raged above the mounds of ice. And over the hardened waves five contorted commas with singed faces and flapping jackets frantically scampered toward the shore, toward the piers. They clambered onto the icy embankments with scraping hands, and ran through the port and into the town, which was quaking in the wind.

A detachment of stevedores with black flags was marching over the square to the pedestal where Lenin's monument was to be raised. The two Negroes and the Chinese marched beside the stevedores, panting, shaking hands with people, overcome with the joy of escaped convicts.

That very minute in Moscow, on Red Square, Lenin's body was being lowered into his tomb. Back in Odessa, sirens wailed, the blizzard howled, and the crowds marched in columns. And on board the *Halifax* the impermeable boatswain was standing alone in the storm by the gangway like a sentinel. Under his equivocal guard, Captain O'Nearn drank cognac in his smoky cabin.

He had relied on his boatswain, Captain O'Nearn had, and so the captain had missed the boat.

THE END OF
ST. HYPATIUS

*Y*esterday I was at the St. Hypatius Monastery, and Father Hillarion, the last of the resident monks, showed me the abode of the Romanov boyars.

The Muscovites had come here in 1613 to ask Mikhail Fyodorovich* to ascend the throne.

I saw the worn corner where Sister Martha, the Czar's mother, used to pray, her gloomy bedchamber, and the turret from which she watched the wolf hunts in the Kostroma forests.

Father Hillarion and I crossed the ancient little bridges on which the snow was piled high, and startled the ravens that had nested in the boyars' tower. We went up to the church, which was indescribably beautiful.

The church, painted carmine and azure, encircled by a wreath of snows, stood out against the smoke-blackened northern sky like a peasant woman's motley kerchief with its design of Russian flowers.

The lines of the modest cupolas were chaste, the blue side buildings potbellied, and the patterned transom of the windows sparkled in the sun with a needless brilliance.

In this deserted church I found the iron gates that had been a gift of Ivan the Terrible, and looked at the ancient icons, the dank decay of ruthless holiness.

The saints—possessed, naked muzhiks with withered thighs—

---

* Mikhail Fyodorovich Romanov, 1596–1645, was the first Czar of the Romanov dynasty.

writhed on the flaking walls, and next to them the Russian Holy Virgin was portrayed, a thin peasant woman with parted knees and sagging breasts that looked like two extra green arms.

The ancient icons wrapped my cheerful heart in the chill of their deathly passions, and I barely managed to escape them and their sepulchral saints.

Their God lay in the church, cleansed and ossified, like a cadaver that has been washed on its deathbed but left unburied.

Father Hillarion wandered alone among his corpses. His left foot had a limp; he tended to doze off, kept scratching his dirty beard, and soon began to bore me.

I threw open Ivan the Terrible's gates and ran under the black arches out onto the square, where the Volga, shackled in ice, twinkled at me.

Kostroma's smoke rose high, cutting through the snow. Muzhiks clothed in a yellow halo of frost were dragging flour on sledges, and their dray-horses slammed their iron hooves into the ice.

On the river the chestnut dray-horses, covered with hoarfrost and steam, breathed noisily, the rosy lightning flashes of the north darted into the pines, and the crowds, the faceless crowds, crawled over the frozen slopes.

A fiery wind blew on them from the Volga. Many of the women tumbled into the snowdrifts, but they kept climbing higher, heading for the monastery like invading columns.

Women's laughter thundered over the mountain, samovar pots and tubs traveled up the slope, impish sleighs groaned as they veered.

Ancient crones were hauling great loads up the high mountain, the mountain of St. Hypatius, and dragged goats on leashes and infants sleeping in little sledges.

"Damn you all!" I shouted when I saw them, and stepped back from the outrageous invasion. "You're all going to Sister Martha to ask her son, Mikhail Romanov, to ascend the throne!"

"Get out of our way!" one of the women yelled, stepping forward. "Stop wasting our time! We're not here to have babies with you!" And, harnessing herself again to her sleigh, she hauled it into the courtyard of the monastery, practically knocking the confused monk off his feet. She dragged her washtubs, her geese, and her hornless gramophone into the cradle of the Muscovite Czars, declaring that her name was

Savicheva, and demanding that she be allotted apartment number nineteen in the archbishop's chambers.

To my amazement, Savicheva *was* allotted an apartment, as were all the others behind her. I was told that the Union of Textile Workers had constructed forty apartments in the burned-out building for the workers of the Kostroma United Flax Mills, and that today was the day they were moving into the monastery.

Father Hillarion stood at the gates counting goats and women. Then he invited me in to drink tea, and silently laid out the table with cups he had stolen in the courtyard when the treasures of the Romanov boyars were being packed off to the museum.

We drank tea from these cups till sweat dripped from our faces, while the women's bare feet trampled on windowsills in front of us: the women were washing the windows of their new apartments.

Then, as if by prearrangement, smoke billowed from all the chimneys, and a cock scampered onto the tomb of Abbot Sioni and began squawking. The accordion of one of the women, having labored its way through a prelude, sang a tender song, and some little old woman in a homespun overcoat poked her head into Father Hillarion's cell and asked him to lend her a pinch of salt for her cabbage soup.

Evening had already fallen when the little old woman appeared. Purple clouds surged above the Volga, the thermometer on the outside wall registered forty degrees below zero, gigantic fires died out, flashing over the river. A determined young man obstinately climbed a frozen ladder to the iron bar above the gates in order to hang up a flimsy lamp and a sign with a legion of letters on it, "USSR—RSFSR," along with the emblem of the Textile Union, the hammer and sickle, and the figure of a woman standing at a loom from which rays surged in all directions.

II

❧

The Odessa Stories

I n 1921, Isaac Babel's first two Odessa stories, "The King" and "Justice in Parenthesis," were published in the Odessa magazines Moryak and Na Pomoshch, beginning a series of stories that was to continue into the 1930s about the city and its strange and colorful Jewish gangster class that were to become some of Babel's most acclaimed stories. This section contains all these stories.

Babel was particularly fascinated by the new Jewish classes emerging from the social upheavals of the early twentieth century. The RED CAVALRY stories, published during the same period as the Odessa stories, reveal Babel's fascination with the new Jewish fighters who have managed to break out of the strictures of the Jewish shtetl culture and transform themselves into wild, fast-riding cavalrymen. The Jewish characters of the Odessa stories are just as unconventional and surprising. The carters, peddlers, cantors, and not-so-pious synagogue SHAMASES who "jumped onto the tables and sang out above the din of the seething flourishes" at a gangster wedding, are not the conventional Jewish figures one might expect to find in even the wildest of Jewish shtetls. There is Benya the King with his "refined gangster

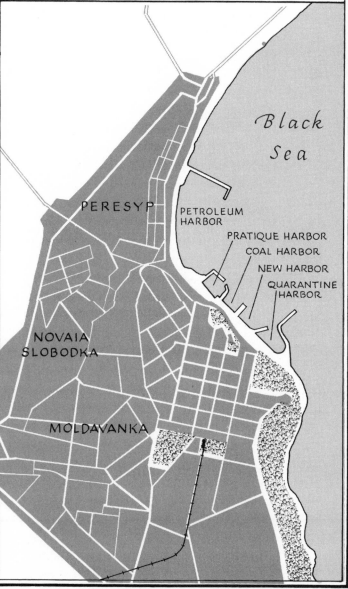

Babel's Odessa

NEW ARBOR

Platon Mole

QUARANTINE HARBOR

St.

ALEXANDROVSKY PARK

Staro Porto-Franskaya St.

500 yds

500 m

Black Sea

PERESYP

PETROLEUM HARBOR

PRATIQUE HARBOR

COAL HARBOR

NEW HARBOR

QUARANTINE HARBOR

NOVAIA SLOBODKA

MOLDAVANKA

chic"; his father, Mendel, a carter "known as a ruffian even in carting cir-cles"; the murderous Madam Shneiweis (Snow-white in Yiddish), who is known as Lyubka the Cossack; Yid-and-a-Half, the millionaire; little old Pesya-Mindl, cook and procuress; and Manka, the aged matriarch of the Jewish bandits from the shantytowns beyond the factory districts.

The stories are set in the Moldavanka, a real Odessa neighborhood "crowded with suckling babies, drying rags, and conjugal nights filled with big-city chic and soldierly tirelessness."

THE KING

The wedding ceremony ended, the rabbi sank into a chair, then he left the room and saw tables lined up the whole length of the courtyard. There were so many of them that the end stuck out of the gates onto Gospitalnaya Street. The tables, draped in velvet, coiled through the yard like a snake on whose belly patches of every color had been daubed, and these orange and red velvet patches sang in deep voices.

The rooms had been turned into kitchens. A rich flame, a drunk, plump flame, forced its way through the smoke-blackened doors. Little old women's faces, wobbly women's chins, beslobbered breasts, baked in the flame's smoky rays. Sweat, red as blood, pink as the foam of a rabid dog, dripped from these blobs of rampant, sweet-odored human flesh. Three cooks, not counting the scullery maids, prepared the wedding feast, and over them eighty-year-old Reizl reigned, traditional as a Torah scroll, tiny and hunchbacked.

Before the feast began, a young man unknown to the guests wormed his way into the courtyard. He asked for Benya Krik. He took Benya Krik aside.

"Listen, King!" the young man said. "I have a couple of words I need to tell you. Aunt Hannah from Kostetskaya Street, she sent me."

"So?" Benya Krik, nicknamed "the King," answered. "So what's these couple of words?"

"Aunt Hannah, she sent me to tell you that a new chief of police took over at the police station yesterday."

"I've known that since the day before yesterday," Benya Krik answered. "Well?"

"The chief of police called the whole station together and gave a speech . . ."

"A new broom is always eager to sweep," Benya Krik answered. "He wants a raid. So?"

"But when does he want to raid, King, do you know that?"

"Tomorrow."

"King, it's going to be today!"

"Who told you that, boy?"

"Aunt Hannah, she said so. You know Aunt Hannah?"

"I know Aunt Hannah. So?"

"The chief called the whole station together and gave them a speech: 'We must finish off Benya Krik,' he said, 'because when you have His Majesty the Czar, you can't have a King too. Today, when Krik gives away his sister in marriage, and they will all be there, is when we raid!' "

"So?"

"Then the cops began to get worried. They said, 'If we raid them today, during his feast, Benya will get angry and a lot of blood will flow.' But the chief said, 'Our self-respect is more important to me!' "

"Good, you can go," the King said.

"So what do I tell Aunt Hannah about the raid?"

"Tell her Benya he knows from the raid."

And the young man left. Three or four of Benya's friends followed him. They said they would be back in about half an hour. And they were back in half an hour. That was that.

At the table, the guests did not sit in order of seniority. Foolish old age is just as pitiful as cowardly youth. Nor in order of wealth. The lining of a heavy money bag is sewn with tears.

The bride and groom sat at the table's place of honor. It was their day. Beside them sat Sender Eichbaum, the King's father-in-law. That was his due. You should know the story of Sender Eichbaum, because it's a story definitely worth knowing.

How did Benya Krik, gangster and King of gangsters, make himself Eichbaum's son-in-law? How did he make himself the son-in-law of a man who owned one milch cow short of sixty? It all had to do with a robbery. A year or so earlier Benya had written a letter to Eichbaum.

"Monsieur Eichbaum," he wrote. "I would be grateful if you could place twenty thousand rubles by the gate of number 17, Sofiyefskaya Street, tomorrow morning. If you do not, then something awaits you, the like of which has never before been heard, and you will be the talk of all Odessa. Sincerely yours, Benya the King."

Three letters, each clearer than the one before, remained unanswered. Then Benya took action. They came by night, nine men carrying long sticks. The sticks were wound with tarred oakum. Nine burning stars flared up in Eichbaum's cattle yard. Benya smashed the barn's locks and started leading the cows out, one by one. They were met by a man with a knife. He felled the cows with one slash and plunged his knife into their hearts. On the ground drenched with blood the torches blossomed like fiery roses, and shots rang out. The dairy maids came running to the cowshed, and Benya chased them away with shots. And right after him other gangsters began shooting into the air because if you don't shoot into the air you might kill someone. And then, as the sixth cow fell with a death bellow at the King's feet, it was then that Eichbaum came running out into the courtyard in his long johns.

"Benya! Where will this end?" he cried.

"If I don't have the money, you don't have the cows, Monsieur Eichbaum. Two and two make four."

"Benya, come into my house!"

And inside the house they came to an agreement. They divided the slaughtered cows between them, Eichbaum was promised immunity and given a certificate with a stamp to that effect. But the miracle came later.

At the time of the attack, that terrible night when the slashed cows bellowed and calves skidded in their mothers' blood, when torches danced like black maidens, and the milkmaids scattered and screeched before the barrels of the amicable Brownings—that terrible night, old Eichbaum's daughter, Zilya, had run out into the yard, in a low-cut chemise. And the King's victory turned into his downfall.

Two days later, without warning, Benya gave back all the money he had taken from Eichbaum, and then came in the evening on a social call. He wore an orange suit, and underneath his cuff a diamond bracelet sparkled. He entered the room, greeted Eichbaum, and asked him for the hand of his daughter, Zilya. The old man had a small stroke, but recovered—there were at least another twenty years of life in him.

"Listen, Eichbaum," the King told him. "When you die, I'll have you buried in the First Jewish Cemetery, right by the gates. And, Eichbaum, I will have a monument of pink marble put up for you. I will make you the Elder of the Brodsky Synagogue. I will give up my career, Eichbaum, and I will go into business with you as a partner. We will have two hundred cows, Eichbaum. I will kill all the dairymen except you. No thief shall walk the street you live in. I shall build you a dacha at the Sixteenth Stop* . . . and don't forget, Eichbaum, you yourself were no rabbi in your youth. Who was it who forged that will? I think I'd better lower my voice, don't you? And your son-in-law will be the King, not some snotface! The King, Eichbaum!"

And he got his way, that Benya Krik, because he was passionate, and passion holds sway over the universe. The newlyweds stayed for three months in fertile Bessarabia, among grapes, abundant food, and the sweat of love. Then Benya returned to Odessa to marry off Dvoira, his forty-year-old sister, who was suffering from goiter. And now, having told the story of Sender Eichbaum, we can return to the marriage of Dvoira Krik, the King's sister.

For the dinner at this wedding, they served turkeys, roasted chicken, geese, gefilte fish, and fish soup in which lakes of lemon shimmered like mother-of-pearl. Above the dead goose heads, flowers swayed like luxuriant plumes. But do the foamy waves of the Odessan Sea throw roasted chickens onto the shore?

On this blue night, this starry night, the best of our contraband, everything for which our region is celebrated far and wide, plied its seductive, destructive craft. Wine from afar heated stomachs, sweetly numbed legs, dulled brains, and summoned belches as resonant as the call of battle horns. The black cook from the *Plutarch*, which had pulled in three days before from Port Said, had smuggled in big-bellied bottles of Jamaican rum, oily Madeira, cigars from the plantations of Pierpont Morgan, and oranges from the groves of Jerusalem. This is

* Bolshoi Fontan, an elegant resort spa outside Odessa.

what the foamy waves of the Odessan Sea throw onto the shore, and this is what Odessan beggars sometimes get at Jewish weddings. They got Jamaican rum at Dvoira Krik's wedding, and that's why the Jewish beggars got as drunk as unkosher pigs and began loudly banging their crutches. Eichbaum unbuttoned his vest, mustered the raging crowd with a squinting eye, and hiccuped affectionately. The orchestra played a flourish. It was like a regimental parade. A flourish, nothing more than a flourish. The gangsters, sitting in closed ranks, were at first uneasy in the presence of outsiders, but soon they let themselves go. Lyova Katsap smashed a bottle of vodka over his sweetheart's head, Monya Artillerist fired shots into the air. But the peak of their ecstasy came when, in accordance with ancient custom, the guests began bestowing gifts on the newlyweds. The synagogue *shamases* jumped onto the tables and sang out, above the din of the seething flourishes, the quantity of rubles and silver spoons that were being presented. And here the friends of the King proved what blue blood was worth, and that Moldavanka chivalry was still in full bloom. With casual flicks of the hand they threw gold coins, rings, and coral necklaces onto the golden trays.

The Moldavanka aristocrats were jammed into crimson vests, their shoulders encased in chestnut-colored jackets, and their fleshy legs bulged in sky-blue leather boots. Drawing themselves up to their full height and sticking out their bellies, the bandits clapped to the rhythm of the music and, shouting "Oy, a sweet kiss for the bride!," threw flowers at her, and she, forty-year-old Dvoira, Benya Krik's sister, the sister of the King, deformed by illness, with her swollen goiter and eyes bulging out of their sockets, sat on a mountain of pillows next to a frail young man who was mute with melancholy who had been bought with Eichbaum's money.

The gift-giving ceremony was coming to an end, the *shamases* were growing hoarse, and the bass fiddle was clashing with the violin. A sudden faint odor of burning spread over the courtyard.

"Benya," Papa Krik, the old carter, known as a ruffian even in carting circles, shouted. "Benya! You know what? I think the embers have blazed up again!"

"Papa!" the King said to his drunken father. "Please eat and drink and don't let these foolish things be worrying you!"

And Papa Krik followed his son's advice. He ate and drank. But the cloud of smoke became ever more poisonous. Here and there patches of sky were turning pink, and suddenly a tongue of fire, narrow as a sword, shot high into the air. The guests got up and started sniffing, and their women yelped. The gangsters looked at one another. And only Benya, who seemed not to notice anything, was inconsolable.

"My feast! They're ruining it!" he shouted in despair. "My friends, please, eat, drink!"

But at that moment the same young man who had come at the beginning of the feast appeared again in the courtyard.

"King!" he said. "I have a couple of words I need to tell you!"

"Well, speak!" the King answered. "You always got a couple words up your sleeve!"

"King!" the young man said with a snigger. "It's so funny—the police station's burning like a candle!"

The storekeepers were struck dumb. The gangsters grinned. Sixty-year-old Manka, matriarch of the Slobodka* bandits, put two fingers in her mouth and whistled so shrilly that those sitting next to her jumped up.

"Manka! You're not at work now!" Benya told her. "Cool down!"

The young man who had brought this startling news was still shaking with laughter.

"About forty of them left the station to go on the raid," he said, his jaws quivering. "They hadn't gone fifteen yards when everything went up in flames! Run and see for yourselves!"

But Benya forbade his guests to go look at the fire. He himself went with two friends. The police station was in flames. With their wobbling backsides, the policemen were running up and down the smoke-filled staircases, throwing boxes out of the windows. The prisoners made a run for it. The firemen were bristling with zeal, but it turned out that there wasn't any water in the nearby hydrant. The chief of police, the new broom so eager to sweep, stood on the opposite sidewalk, chewing on his mustache which hung into his mouth. The new broom stood completely still. Benya walked past and gave him a military salute.

---

* Slobodka was a rough shantytown neighborhood on the outskirts of Odessa.

"A very good day to you, Your Excellency!" he said sympathetically. "What bad luck! A nightmare!" He stared at the burning building, shook his head, and smacked his lips: "Ai-ai-ai!"

·   ·   ·

When Benya came back home, the lantern lights in the courtyard were already going out and dawn was breaking across the sky. The guests had dispersed, and the musicians were asleep, their heads leaning against the necks of their bass fiddles. Only Dvoira hadn't gone to sleep yet. With both hands she was edging her timid husband toward the door of their nuptial chamber, looking at him lustfully like a cat which, holding a mouse in its jaws, gently probes it with its teeth.

JUSTICE IN
PARENTHESES

*M*y first run-in was with Benya Krik, my second with Lyubka Shneiweis. Do you understand the meaning of these words? Can you drink in their full essence? On this road to hell, Seryozhka Utochkin* was missing. I did not run into him this time around, which is why I am still here to tell the tale. Like a bronze colossus, he will tower above the town—red-haired, gray-eyed Utochkin. Everyone will have to scamper through his bronze legs.

But I must not send my tale down side streets, even if on these side streets chestnuts are ripening and acacias are in bloom. I'll start with Benya, and then go on to Lyubka Shneiweis. And that will be that. Then I can say I put the period where it belongs.

I became a broker. Becoming an Odessan broker, I sprouted leaves and shoots. Weighed down with leaves and shoots, I felt unhappy. What was the reason? The reason was competition. Otherwise I would not have even wiped my nose on Justice. I never learned a trade. All there is in front of me is air, glittering like the sea beneath the sun, beautiful, empty air. The shoots need to be fed. I have seven of them, and my wife is the eighth shoot. I did not wipe my nose on Justice. No, Justice wiped its nose on me. What was the reason? The reason was competition.

The cooperative store had been given the name "Justice." Nothing

* Sergei Isayevich Utochkin, 1874–1916, aviation pioneer, was the first man in Odessa to own a car and had a reputation for devil-may-care driving.

bad can be said about that store. Sinful is he who speaks ill of it. It was run by six partners, "*primo di primo*," specialists, if anything, in their line. Their store was full of merchandise, and the policeman they had standing outside was Motya from Golovkovskaya. What more do you want? Can you want more? This deal was suggested to me by the Justice bookkeeper. I give you my word of honor, it was a proper deal, an honest deal! With a clothes brush I brushed my body and sent it over to Benya. The King acted as if he did not notice my body. So I cleared my throat and said: "Ready when you are, Benya."

The King was having light refreshments. A carafe of vodka, a fat cigar, a big-bellied wife in her seventh or eighth month, I wouldn't want to lie to you. The terrace was surrounded by nature and wild vines.

"Ready when you are, Benya," I said.

"When?" he asked me.

"Well, now that you ask me," I said to the King, "I have to tell you my opinion. If you ask *me*, the best time of all would be Sabbath night going on Sunday. By the way, none other than Motya from Golovkovskaya will be on guard. We *could* do this on a weekday, but why turn a nice and easy job into a job that isn't nice and easy?"

That was my opinion. And the King's wife also agreed.

"Baby," Benya said to her. "I want you to go take a rest on the sofa now."

Then with slow fingers he tore the gold band off his cigar and turned to Froim Stern.

"Tell me, Grach, are we busy on the Sabbath, or are we not busy on the Sabbath?"

But Froim Stern is quick-witted. He is a red-haired man with only one eye in his head. Froim cannot afford to give an open answer.

"On the Sabbath," he said, "you were thinking of dropping by the Mutual Credit Society."

Grach acted as if he had nothing more to say, and calmly turned his one eye to the farthest corner of the terrace.

"Excellent," Benya Krik said to him. "Remind me about Zudechkis on the Sabbath, make yourself a note, Grach!" Then the King turned to me: "Go back to your family, Zudechkis. Sabbath evening, I might very well be dropping in at the Justice. Take my words with you, Zudechkis, and get going."

The King speaks little and speaks politely. This frightens people so much that they never question him. I left his courtyard and set off down Gospitalnaya Street, turned on Stepovaya, and then stopped to ponder Benya's words. I probed them by touch and by weight, bit down on them with my front teeth, and realized that they had not been the words that I needed.

"I might very well," the King had said, pulling the gold band off his cigar with slow fingers. The King speaks little and speaks politely. Who can fathom the meaning of the King's few words? I might very well be dropping by, or I might very well not be dropping by? Between yes and no, a five-thousand-ruble commission hangs in the air. Not to mention the two cows that I keep for my needs—I have nine mouths at home snatching for food! Who gave me the right to run risks? After the Justice bookkeeper came to see me, didn't he drop by at Bunzelmann's? And then didn't Bunzelmann run straight to Kolya Shtift? And Kolya is a fellow who is hotheaded beyond belief. The words of the King lay like a stone block across the road where hunger roamed, multiplied by nine. To make a long story short, I whispered a little warning in Bunzelmann's ear. He was going in to see Kolya just as I was coming out from seeing Kolya. It was hot, and he was sweating. "Relax, Bunzelmann," I said to him. "You're rushing for nothing, and you're sweating for nothing! This is my deal, *und damit Punktum*, like the Germans say!"

And then the fifth day came. And then the sixth day came. The Sabbath came strolling through the streets of the Moldavanka. Motya was already standing guard, and I was already asleep in my bed, and Kolya was busy working at the Justice. He had loaded half a cart, and was aiming to load another half. Suddenly there was a rumpus in the alley, the clattering of iron-reinforced wheels, and Motya from Golovkovskaya grabbed hold of the telegraph pole and yelled, "Shall I push it over?"

"Not yet!" Kolya yelled back. (The thing is, the telegraph pole could be toppled when push came to shove.)

A cart rolled slowly into the alley and pulled up in front of the store. Kolya thought the police were on their way, and his heart tore itself to shreds, because he really hated the idea of the deal going sour.

"Motya!" he yelled. "When I fire my gun, the pole topples!"

"Understood!"

Kolya Shtift went back into the store, and all his helpers followed him. They lined up against the wall and drew their revolvers. Ten eyes and five revolvers were trained on the door, and outside there was the booby-trapped telegraph pole. The youths were bristling with impatience.

"Scram, you cops, you!" one of the eager youths hissed. "Scram or we'll finish you off!"

"Shut up!" Benya Krik growled, jumping down from the loft. "Where d'you see cops, you lunkhead? It's me, the King!"

A bit more and there would have been trouble. Benya knocked Shtift down and snatched the revolver from his hands. Men started descending from the loft like rain. You couldn't tell who was who in the darkness.

"Ha! Interesting!" Kolya shouted. "So now Benya is out to kill me!"

It was the first time in his life that the King had been mistaken for a policeman. This was worth a good laugh. The gangsters laughed out loud. They turned on their flashlights, splitting their sides with laughter, rolling on the floor, gasping for air.

Only the King did not laugh.

"They will be saying in Odessa," he began in a serious tone, "in Odessa they will be saying the King was tempted by his friend's earnings."

"They will say it only once," Shtift said. "No one will dare say it twice."

"Kolya," the King continued in a solemn, quiet voice. "Do you believe me, Kolya?"

And here the gangsters stopped laughing. Each of them was holding a burning lantern, but laughter wormed its way out of the Justice store.

"What do you want me to believe you about, King?"

"Do you believe me, Kolya, that I had nothing to do with all of this?"

And the King sat down sadly on a chair, covered his eyes with a dusty sleeve, and began to cry. This was how proud this man was, he should burn in hell! And all the gangsters, each and every one of them, saw their King crying because his pride was hurt.

Then the two men stood opposite each other. Benya stood, and Shtift stood. They apologized to each other, they kissed each other on the lips, and they shook hands with such force that it looked as if they were trying to tear each other's arms off. Dawn was already beginning to blink its bleary eye, Motya had already left for the police station to sign out, two full carts had hauled off what had once been known as the Justice Cooperative Store, while the King and Kolya were still distraught, still bowing to each other, still throwing their arms around each other's necks, kissing each other tenderly like drunks.

Who was Fate hunting down that morning? Fate was hunting down me, Zudechkis, and Fate cornered me.

"Kolya!" the King finally said. "Who arranged for you to come here to the Justice?"

"Zudechkis. What about you, Benya? Who had you come here?"

"Zudechkis!"

"Benya!" Kolya exclaimed. "Is he to be left alive?"

"Most definitely not," Benya said, and he turned to one-eyed Stern, who was chuckling in a corner because the two of us don't see eye to eye. "Froim! You go order a brocaded coffin, and I'll go over to Zudechkis. And you, Kolya, once you've started something you have to finish it, which is why my wife and I would like to cordially invite you to visit us in our home in the morning, to partake of breakfast with us and our family."

At five o'clock in the morning—or no, it must have been four, and then again, maybe it wasn't even four yet—the King entered my bedroom, grabbed me, if you will pardon the expression, by my back, dragged me out of bed, laid me down on the floor, and placed his foot on my nose. Hearing various sounds and so on, my wife jumped out of bed and asked Benya, "Monsieur Krik, why have you taken umbrage at my Zudechkis?"

"What do you mean, 'why'?" Benya said, without removing his foot from the bridge of my nose, and tears began to trickle from his eyes. "He has cast a shadow on my name, he has disgraced me before my companions, you can bid him farewell, Madam Zudechkis, because my honor is more important to me than my happiness, which is why he cannot live!"

Continuing to cry, he began stomping on me. My wife, seeing that

I was quite distressed, started yelling. This occurred at four-thirty, but she didn't finish with Benya until around eight. She let him have it—*oy!*—how she let him have it! It was a joy to behold!

"Why are you angry at my Zudechkis?" she shouted, standing on the bed, while I, writhing on the floor, looked up at her with admiration. "Why beat up my Zudechkis? Why? Because he wanted to feed nine little hungry fledglings? You—ha!—you're so very grand! The King! The son-in-law of a rich man, rich yourself, and your father rich too! You are a man with the world at your feet! What is one bungled deal for Benchik, when next week will bring seven successful ones? How dare you beat my Zudechkis! How dare you!"

She saved my life.

The children woke up and began yelling in unison with my wife. Benya still ruined as much of my health as he knew he needed to ruin. He left two hundred rubles for my doctor's bill, and walked out. I was taken to the Jewish hospital. On Sunday I was dying, on Monday I felt better, on Tuesday I took a turn for the worse.

This is my first story. Who was to blame, and what was the reason? Was Benya really to blame? Let us not try to pull the wool over each other's eyes. There is no other like Benya the King! He stamps out lies in his quest for justice—justice in parentheses as well as justice without parentheses. But what are you to do when everyone else is as unruffled as a pickled fish? The others don't care for justice, and don't look for it, which is even worse!

I recovered—escaping from Benya's hands only to fall into Lyubka's! I have told you about Benya, and I will tell you about Lyubka Shneiweis. But let us stop here. Then I can say I put the period where it belongs.

HOW THINGS WERE
DONE IN ODESSA

I was the one who began.

"Reb Arye-Leib," I said to the old man. "Let's talk about Benya Krik. Let's talk about his lightning-quick beginning and his terrible end. Three shadows block the path of my thoughts. There is Froim Grach. The steel of his actions—doesn't it bear comparison to the power of the King? There is Kolka Pakovsky. The rage of that man had everything it takes to rule. And could not Chaim Drong tell when a star was on the rise? So why was Benya Krik the only one to climb to the top of the ladder while everyone else was clinging to the shaky rungs below?"

Reb Arye-Leib remained silent as he sat on the cemetery wall. Before us stretched the green calm of the graves. A man thirsting for an answer must stock up with patience. A man in possession of facts can afford to carry himself with aplomb. That is why Arye-Leib remained silent as he sat on the cemetery wall. Finally he began his tale:

"Why him? Why not the others, you want to know? Well then, forget for a while that you have glasses on your nose and autumn in your heart. Forget that you pick fights from behind your desk and stutter when you are out in the world! Imagine for a moment that you pick fights in town squares and stutter only on paper. You are a tiger, you are a lion, you are a cat. You can spend the night with a Russian woman, and the Russian woman will be satisfied by you. You are twenty-five years old. If the sky and the earth had rings attached to them, you would grab these rings and pull the sky down to the earth. And your papa is the carter Mendel Krik. What does a papa like him think about? All he thinks about is downing a nice shot of vodka, slugging someone in their ugly mug, and about his horses—nothing else. You want to live, but he makes you die twenty times a day. What would you have done if you were in Benya Krik's shoes? You wouldn't have done a thing! But he did. Because he is the King, while you only thumb your nose at people when their back is turned!

"He, Benchik, went to Froim Grach, who even back then peered at the world with only one eye and was just what he is now. And Benya told Froim, 'Take me on. I want to come on board your ship. The ship I end up on will do well by me.'

"Grach asked him, 'Who're you, where d'you come from, what's your bread and butter?'

"'Try me, Froim,' Benya answered, 'and let's stop wasting time spreading kasha on the table.'

"'Fine, we won't waste time spreading kasha on the table,' Grach said. 'I'll try you.'

"And the gangsters called a council together to decide about Benya Krik. I wasn't at that council, but word has it that they did call together a council. The elder back then was the late Lyovka Bik.

"'Anyone know what's going on under Benchik's hat?' the late Bik asked.

"And one-eyed Grach gave his opinion.

"'Benya talks little, but he talks with zest. He talks little, but you want that he'll say more.'

"'If that's so, we'll try him out on Tartakovsky,' the late Bik pronounced.

"'We'll try him out on Tartakovsky,' the council decided, and those who still housed a trace of conscience turned red when they heard this decision. Why did they turn red? If you listen, you'll find out.

"Tartakovsky was known as 'Yid-and-a-Half' or 'Nine-Raids.' They called him 'Yid-and-a-Half' because there wasn't a single Jew who had as much chutzpah or money as Tartakovsky had. He was taller than the tallest Odessa policeman, and heavier than the fattest Jewess. And they called Tartakovsky 'Nine-Raids' because the firm of Lyovka Bik and Company had launched not eight raids and not ten, but exactly nine raids against his business. To Benya, who was not yet King, fell the honor of carrying out the tenth raid on Yid-and-a-Half. When Froim informed Benya of this, Benya said yes, and left, slamming the door behind him. Why did he slam the door? If you listen, you'll find out.

"Tartakovsky has the soul of a murderer, but he's one of us. He sprang forth from us. He is our blood. He is our flesh, as if one mama had given birth to us. Half of Odessa works in his stores. Not to mention, his own Moldavankans have given him quite a bit of grief. They abducted him twice and held him for ransom, and once, during a pogrom, they buried him with chanters. The Slobodka* thugs were beating up Jews on Bolshaya Arnautskaya. Tartakovsky ran away from them and came across the funeral march with chanters on Sofiyskaya Street.

"'Who are they burying with chanters?' he asked.

"The passersby told him that Tartakovsky was being buried. The procession marched to the Slobodka Cemetery. Then our boys yanked a machine gun out of the coffin and started shooting at the Slobodka thugs. But Yid-and-a-Half had not foreseen this. Yid-and-a-Half got the fright of his life. What boss in his place would not have been frightened?

"A tenth raid on a man who had already been buried once was a crass deed. Benya, who back then wasn't yet the King, knew this better than anyone else. But he said yes to Grach and on that very same day wrote Tartakovsky a letter, typical of those letters:

> Most esteemed Rubin Osipovich,
>
> I would be grateful if by the Sabbath you could place by the rain-water barrel a . . . , and so on. Should you choose to refuse, which you have opted to do lately, a great disappointment in your family life awaits you.
>
> Respectfully yours,
> Ben Zion Krik

"Tartakovsky, not one to dither, was quick to answer:

---

* A poor neighborhood on the outskirts of Odessa.

Benya,

If you were an idiot, I would write you as to an idiot. But from what I know of you, you aren't one, and may the Lord prevent me from changing my mind. You, as is plain to see, are acting like a boy. Is it possible that you are not aware that this year the crop in Argentina has been so good that we can stand on our heads but we still can't unload our wheat? And I swear to you on a stack of Bibles that I'm sick and tired of having to eat such a bitter crust of bread and witness such trouble after having worked all my life like the lowliest carter. And what do I have to show for my life sentence of hard labor? Ulcers, sores, worries, and no sleep! Drop your foolish thoughts, Benya.

> Your friend, a far better one than you realize,
> Rubin Tartakovsky

"Yid-and-a-Half had done his part. He had written a letter. But the mail didn't deliver it to the right address. Getting no answer, Benya became angry. The following day he turned up at Tartakovsky's office with four friends. Four masked youths with revolvers burst into the room.

"'Hands up!' they shouted, waving their pistols.

"'Not so loud, Solomon!' Benya told one of the youths, who was yelling louder than the rest. 'Don't get so jumpy on the job!' and he turned to the shop assistant, who was white as death and yellow as clay, and asked him:

"'Is Yid-and-a-Half here?'

"'He's not here,' said the shop assistant, whose family name was Muginshtein, his first name Josif, and who was the unmarried son of Aunt Pesya, the chicken seller on Seredinskaya Square.

"'So who's in charge when the boss is out?' they asked poor Muginshtein.

"'I'm in charge when the boss is out,' the shop assistant said, green as green grass.

"'In that case, with God's help, please open the safe!' Benya ordered, and a three-act opera began.

"Nervous Solomon stuffed money, papers, watches, and jewelry into a suitcase—the late Josif Muginshtein stood in front of him with his hands in the air, while Benya told stories from the life of the Jewish people.

"'Well, ha! If he likes playing Rothschild,' Benya said about Tartakovsky, 'then let him roast in hell! I ask you, Muginshtein, as one asks a friend: he gets my business letter—so how come he can't take a five-kopeck tram to come visit me at home, drink a shot of vodka with my family, and eat what God has seen fit to send us? What stopped him from baring his soul to me? Couldn't he have said—Benya, you know, such and such, but here's my balance sheet, just give me a couple of days to catch my breath, to get things rolling—don't you think I'd have understood? Pigs at a trough might not see eye to eye, but there is no reason why two grown men can't! Do you see what I'm saying, Muginshtein?'

"'I see what you're saying,' Muginshtein answered, lying, because he was at a loss as to why Yid-and-a-Half, a respected, wealthy man, one of the foremost men in town, should want to take a tram so he could have a bite to eat with the family of Mendel Krik, a carter.

"But all the time misfortune was loitering beneath the windows, like a beggar at dawn. Misfortune burst loudly into the office. And though this time it came in the guise of the Jew Savka Butsis, it was as drunk as a water carrier.

"'Ooh, ooh, ah!' Savka the Jew shouted. 'I'm sorry I'm so late, Benchik!' And he stamped his feet and waved his hands. Then he fired, and the bullet hit Muginshtein in the stomach.

"Are words necessary here? There was a man, and now there's none. An innocent bachelor, living his life like a little bird on a branch, and now he's dead from sheer idiocy. In comes a Jew looking like a sailor and doesn't shoot at a bottle in a fairground booth to win a prize—he shoots at a living man! Are words necessary here?

"'Everyone out!' Benya shouted, and as he ran out last, managed to tell Butsis, 'On my mother's grave, Savka, you'll be lying next to him!'

"So tell me, a young gentleman like you who cuts coupons on other people's bonds, how would you have acted in Benya Krik's position? You wouldn't know what to do? Well, he did! That's why he was King, while you and I are sitting here on the wall of the Second Jewish Cemetery, holding up our hands to keep the sun out of our eyes.

"Aunt Pesya's unfortunate son didn't die right away. An hour after they got him to the hospital, Benya turned up. He had the senior doctor called in and the nurse, and, without taking his hands out of the pockets of his cream-colored pants, told them, 'I have a whole lot of interest that your patient, Josif Muginshtein, recovers. Just in case, let me introduce myself—Ben Zion Krik. Give him camphor, oxygen, a private room, from the depths of your heart! If you don't, then every doctor here, even if they're doctors of philosophy, will be doled out six feet of earth!'

"And yet, Muginshtein died that same night. It was only then that Yid-and-a-Half raised hell in all Odessa. 'Where do the police begin and Benya end?' he wailed.

"'The police end where Benya begins,' levelheaded people answered, but Tartakovsky wouldn't calm down, and to his amazement saw a red automobile with a music box for a horn playing the first march from the opera *I Pagliacci* on Seredinskaya Square. In broad daylight the car raced over to the little house in which Aunt Pesya lived. Its wheels thundered, it spat smoke, gleamed brassily, reeked of gasoline, and honked arias on its horn. A man jumped out of the automobile and went into the kitchen where little Aunt Pesya was writhing on the earthen floor. Yid-and-a-Half was sitting on a chair waving his arms. 'You ugly hooligan!' he shouted, when he saw the man. 'You damn bandit, may the earth spit you out! A nice style you've picked for yourself, going around murdering live people!'

"'Monsieur Tartakovsky,' Benya Krik said to him quietly. 'For two days and nights I have been crying for the dear deceased as if he were my own brother. I know that you spit on my young tears. Shame on you, Monsieur Tartakovsky! What fireproof safe have you hidden your shame in? You had the heart to send a paltry hundred rubles to the mother of our dear deceased Josif. My hair, not to mention my brain, stood on end when I got word of this!'

"Here Benya paused. He was wearing a chocolate jacket, cream pants, and raspberry-red half boots.

"'Ten thousand down!' he bellowed. 'Ten thousand down, and a pension till she dies—may she live to be a hundred and twenty! If it's 'no,' then we leave this house together, Monsieur Tartakovsky, and go straight to my car!'

"Then they started arguing. Yid-and-a-Half swore at Benya. Not that I was present at this quarrel, but those who were, remember it well. They finally agreed on five thousand cash in hand, and fifty rubles a month.

"'Aunt Pesya!' Benya then said to the disheveled old woman rolling on the floor. 'If you want my life, you can have it, but everyone makes mistakes, even God! This was a giant mistake, Aunt Pesya! But didn't God Himself make a mistake when he settled the Jews in Russia so they could be tormented as if they were in hell? Wouldn't it have been better to have the Jews living in Switzerland, where they would've been surrounded by first-class lakes, mountain air, and Frenchmen galore? Everyone makes mistakes, even God. Listen to me with your ears, Aunt Pesya! You're getting five thousand in hand and fifty rubles a month till you die—may you live to be a hundred and twenty! Josif's funeral will be first-class. Six horses like lions, two hearses with garlands, chanters from the Brodsky Synagogue, and Minkovsky himself will come to chant the burial service for your departed son!'

"And the funeral took place the next morning. Ask the cemetery beggars about this funeral! Ask the synagogue *shamases,* the kosher poultry sellers, or the old women from the Second Poorhouse! Such a funeral Odessa had never seen, nor will the world ever see the like of it. On that day the policemen wore cotton gloves. In the synagogues, draped with greenery, their doors wide open, the electricity was on. Black plumes swayed on the white horses pulling the hearse. Sixty chanters walked in front of the procession. The chanters were boys, but they sang with women's voices. The elders of the Kosher Poultry Sellers Synagogue led Aunt Pesya by the hand. Behind the elders marched the members of the Society of Jewish Shop Assistants, and behind the Jewish shop assistants marched the barristers, the doctors, and the certified midwives. On one side of Aunt Pesya were the chicken sellers from the Stary Bazaar, and on the other the esteemed dairymaids from the Bugayevka, wrapped in orange shawls. They stamped their feet like gendarmes on parade. From their broad hips came the scent of sea and milk. And behind them plodded Rubin Tartakovsky's workers. There were a hundred of them, or two hundred, or two thousand. They wore black frock coats with silk lapels, and new boots that squeaked like piglets in a sack.

"And now I will speak as God spoke on Mount Sinai from the burning bush! Take my words into your ears. Everything I saw, I saw with my own eyes, sitting right here on the wall of the Second Cemetery, next to lisping Moiseika and Shimshon from the funeral home. I, Arye-Leib, a proud Jew living among the dead, saw it with my own eyes.

"The hearse rolled up to the synagogue in the cemetery. The coffin was placed on the steps. Aunt Pesya was shaking like a little bird. The cantor climbed out of the carriage and began the funeral service. Sixty chanters supported him. And at that very moment the red automobile came flying around the corner. It was honking *I Pagliacci* and came to a stop. The people stood, silent as corpses. The trees, the chanters, the beggars stood silent. Four men got out from under the red roof, and with quiet steps carried to the hearse a wreath of roses of a beauty never before seen. And when the funeral ended, the four men lifted the coffin onto their steel shoulders, and with burning eyes and protruding chests, marched with the members of the Society of Jewish Shop Assistants.

"In front walked Benya Krik, who back then nobody was yet calling the King. He was the first to approach the grave. He climbed onto the mound, and stretched out his arm.

"'What are you doing, young man?' Kofman from the Burial Brotherhood shouted, running up to him.

"'I want to give a speech,' Benya Krik answered.

"And he gave a speech. All who wanted to hear it heard it. I, Arye-Leib, heard it, as did lisping Moiseika, who was sitting next to me on the wall.

"'Ladies and gentlemen,' Benya Krik said. 'Ladies and gentlemen,' he said, and the sun stood above his head, like a guard with a rifle. 'You have come to pay your last respects to an honest toiler, who died for a copper half-kopeck. In my own name, and in the name of all those who are not present, I thank you. Ladies and gentlemen! What did our dear Josif see in his life? One big nothing! What did he do for a living? He counted someone else's money. What did he die for? He died for the whole working class. There are men who are already doomed to die, and there are men who still have not begun to live. And suddenly a bullet, flying toward the doomed heart, tears into Josif, when all he has seen of life is one big nothing. There are men who can drink vodka, and there are men who can't drink vodka but still drink it. The former get pleasure from the agony and joy, and the latter suffer for all those who drink vodka without being able to drink it. Therefore, ladies and gentlemen, after we have prayed for our poor Josif, I ask you to accompany Saveli Butsis, a man unknown to you but already deceased, to *his* grave.'

"Having finished his speech, Benya Krik came down from the mound. The people, the trees, and the cemetery beggars stood silent. Two gravediggers carried an unpainted coffin to an adjacent grave. The cantor, stuttering, ended the prayer. Benya threw the first spadeful of earth and walked over to Savka. All the barristers and ladies with brooches followed him like sheep. He had the cantor chant the full funeral rites for Savka, and sixty chanters sang with him. Savka had never dreamt of such a funeral—you can trust the word of Arye-Leib, an aged old man.

"Word has it that it was on that day that Yid-and-a-Half decided to close shop. Not that I myself was there. But I saw with my own eyes, the eyes of Arye-Leib—which is my name—that neither the cantor, nor the choir, nor the Burial Brotherhood asked to get paid for the funeral. More I couldn't see, because the people quietly slipped away from Savka's grave and started running, as if from a fire. They flew off in carriages, in carts, and on foot. And the four men who had arrived in the red automobile left in it. The musical horn played its march, the car lurched and hurtled off.

"'The King!' lisping Moiseika, who always grabs the best seat on the wall, said, following the car with his eyes.

"Now you know everything. You know who was the first to pronounce the word 'King.' It was Moiseika. Now you know why he didn't call one-eyed Grach that, nor raging Kolka. You know everything. But what use is it if you still have glasses on your nose and autumn in your heart? . . ."

LYUBKA THE COSSACK

*I*n the Moldavanka, on the corner of Dalnitskaya and Balkovskaya
Streets, stands Lyubka Shneiweis's house. In this house there is a
wine cellar, an inn, an oat store, and a dovecote for a hundred Kryukov
and Nikolayev doves. All these as well as lot number forty-six in the
Odessa quarry belong to Lyubka Shneiweis, nicknamed Lyubka the
Cossack—only the dovecote is the property of Yevzel, a retired soldier
with a medal. On Sundays, Yevzel goes to Okhotnitskaya Square and
sells doves to officials from town and to the boys of the neighborhood.
Also living in Lyubka's courtyard, besides the watchman, are Pesya-
Mindl, cook and procuress, and Zudechkis, the manager, a small Jew
with a build and beard like those of our Moldavanka Rabbi, Ben
Zkharia. There are many stories I can tell about Zudechkis. The first is
the story of how Zudechkis became the manager of the inn that
belonged to Lyubka, nicknamed the Cossack.

About ten years ago Zudechkis was the middleman in the sale of a
horse-drawn threshing machine to a landowner, and in the evening he
brought the landowner over to Lyubka's to celebrate the sale. This
landowner had not only a mustache, but also a goatee, and wore lacquered shoes. Pesya-Mindl served him gefilte fish, followed by a very
nice young lady by the name of Nastya. The landowner stayed the
night, and in the morning Yevzel woke Zudechkis, who was lying
curled up by Lyubka's door.

"Well!" Yevzel said to him. "Last night you were boasting about
how the landowner bought a threshing machine through you! Well, let

me inform you that he stayed the night and then at dawn, like the lowest of the low, made a run for it. That'll be two rubles for the food and four rubles for the young lady. I can see you're a slippery old con!"

But Zudechkis wouldn't pay. So Yevzel shoved him into Lyubka's room and locked the door.

"Well!" the watchman said. "You're going to stay right here till Lyubka gets back from the quarry, and with the help of God she will beat the soul out of you! Amen!"

"Jailbird!" Zudechkis shouted after the soldier, and looked around the room. "All you know about is your doves, you jailbird! But I still have some faith in God who will lead me out of here, the way He led all the Jews first out of Egypt and then out of the desert!"

There was much more that the little middleman wanted to tell Yevzel, but the soldier had taken the key and left, his shoes thumping. Then Zudechkis turned around and saw the procuress, Pesya-Mindl, sitting by the window reading *The Miracles and Heart of the Baal-Shem*. She was reading the Hasidic book with gilt edges, and rocking an oak cradle with her foot. In the cradle lay Lyubka's son, Davidka, crying.

"I see you have a nice setup here in this Sakhalin prison camp!" Zudechkis said to Pesya-Mindl. "The child lies there, bawling its lungs out so that a man feels pity at the sight of it, while you, you fat woman, sit here like a stone in the woods and don't even give him a bottle."

"*You* give him a bottle!" Pesya-Mindl answered, without looking up from her book. "That's if he'll take a bottle from you, you old crook! He's as big as a pork butcher, and all he wants is his mama's milk, while his mama gallops around her quarries, drinks tea with Jews in the Medved Tavern, buys contraband down by the harbor, and thinks of her son as she might think of last year's snow!"

"*Oy*, poor Zudechkis!" the small middleman then said to himself. "You have fallen into the hands of the Pharaoh himself!" And he went over to the eastern wall of the room, muttered the whole Morning Prayer with addenda, and then took the crying infant in his arms. Davidka looked at him in bewilderment and waved his little crimson legs covered in infant's sweat, and the old man started walking up and down the room and, rocking like a *tsaddik* in prayer, began singing an endless song.

"Ah-ah-ah," he began singing. "Now all the children will get nothing-and-a-half, but our little Davidka will get some buns, so he will sleep both night and day . . . ah-ah-ah, now all the children will get a good punch in the . . ."

Zudechkis showed Lyubka's son his fist with its gray hairs, and repeated the song about getting nothing-and-a-half and buns until the boy fell asleep and the sun had reached the middle of the shining sky. It reached the middle and began quivering like a fly weakened by the heat. Wild muzhiks from Nerubaiska and Tatarka who were staying at Lyubka's inn crawled under their carts and fell into a wild and sonorous sleep; a drunken workman went out to the gates and, dropping his plane and his saw, collapsed on the ground and began snoring then and there, surrounded by the golden flies and the blue lightning of July. Wrinkled German settlers who had brought Lyubka wine from the borders of Bessarabia sat nearby in the shade. They lit their pipes, and the smoke from their curved chibouks blended with the silver stubble of their old, unshaven cheeks. The sun hung from the sky like the pink tongue of a thirsty dog, the immense sea rolled far away to Peresip, and the masts of distant ships swayed on the emerald water of Odessa Bay. The day sat in an ornate boat, the day sailed toward evening, and halfway toward evening, at five o'clock, Lyubka came back from town. She rode in on a little roan horse with a large belly and an overgrown mane. A fat-legged young man in a calico shirt opened the gate for her, Yevzel grabbed hold of the bridle of her horse, at which point Zudechkis called down to Lyubka from his prison cell, "My respects, Madam Shneiweis, and good day to you! You simply go off on a three-year trip, and throw your hungry child at me!"

"Shut your ugly trap!" Lyubka shouted back at the old man, and jumped off the horse. "Who's that yelling out my window?"

"It's Zudechkis, a slippery old con," the soldier with the medal explained to his mistress, and began telling her the whole story about the landowner, but didn't get to the end because Zudechkis interrupted him, yelling with all his might.

"This is an outrage!" he yelled, hurling down his skullcap. "This is an outrage to throw a child at a stranger and simply go off on a three-year trip! Come here this instant and give him your breast!"

"You wait till I come up there, you crook!" Lyubka muttered, and ran to the stairs. She came into the room and pulled her breast out of her dusty blouse.

The child stretched toward her and gnawed at her monstrous nipple, but didn't strike milk. A vein protruded on the mother's brow, and, shaking his skullcap, Zudechkis said to her, "You're such a greedy woman, Lyubka! You want everything for yourself! You snatch at the whole world, the way a child snatches at a tablecloth to get at breadcrumbs! You always have to have the best wheat and the best grapes! You want to bake white bread in the blaze of the sun, while your little baby, your sweet little pumpkin, is drying up without milk!"

"How am I supposed to have milk!" the woman yelled, kneading her breast. "The *Plutarch* pulled into port today and I had to cover fifteen versts in the heat! But don't think you can hoodwink me with your stories, you old Jew! Give me my six rubles!"

But again Zudechkis wouldn't pay. He rolled up his sleeve, and jabbed his thin, dirty elbow into Lyubka's mouth.

"Choke, you jailbird!" he shouted, and spat into the corner.

Lyubka stood there for a while with the foreign elbow in her mouth, then took it out, locked the door, and went out into the courtyard. Waiting for her there was Mr. Trottyburn, who resembled a pillar of red meat. Mr. Trottyburn was the chief engineer on the *Plutarch*. He had brought Lyubka two sailors. One of the sailors was an Englishman, the other a Malay. The three of them were lugging into the courtyard contraband they had brought from Port Said. The box was heavy. They dropped it on the ground, and out of the box tumbled cigars tangled with Japanese silk. A horde of women came running to the box, and two wandering gypsy women came slyly edging nearer.

"Get out of here! Scum!" Lyubka yelled at them, and led the sailors to the shade of an acacia tree.

They sat down at a table. Yevzel brought them wine, and Mr. Trottyburn began unwrapping his merchandise. Out of his bale he took cigars and delicate silks, cocaine and metal jiggers, uncut tobacco from the state of Virginia, and black wine bought on the Island of Chios. Each item had a special price, and each figure was washed down with Bessarabian wine with its bouquet of sunshine and bedbugs. Twilight was already flooding the courtyard, twilight was flooding in like an evening wave over a wide river, and the drunken Malay, completely taken aback, poked Lyubka's breast with his finger. He poked it with one finger, then with each of his fingers, one after the other.

His yellow and tender eyes hung above the table like paper lanterns on a Chinese street. He started singing, barely audibly, and toppled onto the ground as Lyubka punched him with her fist.

"A nice literate fellow, that one!" Lyubka said to Mr. Trottyburn. "That Malaysian's making me lose my last drop of milk, while that Jew up there won't stop badgering me for it!"

And she pointed at Zudechkis, who was standing by the window, washing his socks. A small lamp was smoking in Zudechkis's room, his tub frothed and hissed, he leaned out the window sensing that they were talking about him, and in despair started yelling down to them.

"Save me, you people!" he yelled, waving his hands.

"Shut your ugly trap!" Lyubka yelled back, and burst out laughing. "Shut up!"

She threw a stone at the old man, but didn't manage to hit him. She then grabbed an empty wine bottle. But Mr. Trottyburn, the chief engineer, took the bottle away from her, aimed, and flung it through the open window.

"Miss Lyubka," the chief engineer said, rising, pulling his drunken legs toward himself. "Many worthy individuals have come to me, Miss Lyubka, to trade, but I trade with no one, not with Mr. Kuninson nor with Mr. Bats, nor with Mr. Kupchik, no one but you, because I find your conversation so agreeable, Miss Lyubka."

And, gaining a foothold on his wobbly legs, he grabbed his sailors by their shoulders—the one an Englishman, the other a Malay—and began dancing with them through the cooling courtyard. The men from the *Plutarch* danced in deeply pensive silence. An orange star had slid right down to the edge of the horizon and was staring them in the face. Then they took their money, grabbed each other by the hand, and went out into the street, swaying the way hanging lamps sway on a ship. From the street they could see the sea, the black waters of Odessa Bay, little toy flags on sunken masts, and piercing lights that had ignited in the spacious depths. Lyubka walked her dancing guests to the intersection. She stayed back alone in the empty street, laughed to herself, and went home. The sleepy young man in the calico shirt locked the gates behind her, Yevzel brought his mistress the proceeds of the day, and she went upstairs to sleep. There Pesya-Mindl, the procuress, was already slumbering, and Zudechkis was rocking the oak cradle with his bare feet.

"How you've tortured us, you shameless woman!" he said, and took the child out of the cradle. "But here, watch me and you might learn a thing or two, you foul mother, you!"

He laid a thin comb on Lyubka's breast and put her son into her bed. The child stretched toward his mother, pricked himself on the comb, and started to cry. Then the old man pushed the bottle toward him, but Davidka turned away from the bottle.

"Is this some spell you're putting on me, you old swindler?" Lyubka muttered, dozing off.

"Shut up, you foul mother, you!" Zudechkis said to her. "Shut up and learn, may the devil take you!"

The baby pricked himself on the comb again, hesitantly took the bottle, and began sucking.

"There!" Zudechkis said, and burst out laughing. "I have weaned your child! I can teach you a thing or two, may the devil take you!"

Davidka lay in his cradle, sucking on his bottle and dribbling blissfully. Lyubka woke up, opened her eyes, and closed them again. She saw her son, and the moon forcing its way through her window. The moon jumping into black clouds, like a straying calf.

"Well, fair enough," Lyubka said. "Unlock the door for Zudechkis, Pesya-Mindl, and let him come tomorrow for a pound of American tobacco."

And the following day Zudechkis came for a pound of uncut tobacco from the state of Virginia. He was given it, and a quarter pound of tea was thrown in. And within a week, when I came to buy a dove from Yevzel, I ran into the new manager of Lyubka's courtyard. He was tiny, like our Rabbi Ben Zkharia. Zudechkis was the new manager. He stayed at his post for fifteen years, and during that period I heard a great number of stories about him. And if I can manage, I will tell them one after another, because they are very interesting stories.

THE FATHER

*F*roim Grach had once been married. That was long ago—twenty years have passed since then. His wife had borne him a daughter and had died in childbirth. The girl was named Basya. Her grandmother on her mother's side lived in Tulchin. The old woman did not like her son-in-law. She said about him, "Froim is a carter by profession, he has black horses, but his soul is blacker than his horses' coats."

The old woman did not like her son-in-law and took away the newborn girl. She lived twenty years with the girl and then died. Then Basya came back to her father. That's how it happened.

On Wednesday, the fifth, Froim Grach was carting wheat from the Dreyfus Company warehouses down to the port to load on the *Caledonia*. As evening fell, he finished working and went home. At the corner of Prokhorovskaya Street he came across Ivan Pyatirubel, the blacksmith.

"My respects, Grach!" Ivan Pyatirubel said. "There's some woman banging on your door."

Grach drove on and saw a gigantic woman standing in his courtyard. Her hips were enormous, and her cheeks brick red.

"Papa!" the woman shouted in a deafening bass voice. "The devil is snatching at me already, I'm so bored! I've been waiting for you all day. . . . You know, Grandma died in Tulchin."

Grach stood in his cart staring at his daughter.

"Don't prance about in front of the horses!" he shouted in despair. "Grab the bridle there! You trying to finish off my horses?"

Grach stood on the cart waving his whip. Basya grabbed the shaft horse's bridle and led the horses to the stable. She unharnessed them and went to busy herself in the kitchen. She hung her father's foot bindings on a line, scrubbed the sooty teapot with sand, and warmed up a large meatball in the cast-iron pot.

"What unbearable dirt, Papa!" she said, grabbed the rancid sheepskins from the floor and threw them out the window. "But I'll get rid of this dirt!" she shouted, and gave her father his food.

The old man drank vodka out of an enameled teapot and ate his meatball, which smelled of happy childhood. Then he picked up his whip and walked out the gates. Basya came out after him. She had put on a pair of men's boots, an orange dress, and a hat covered with birds, and sat down next to him on the bench. The evening slouched past the bench; the shining eye of the sunset fell into the sea beyond Peresip, and the sky was red, like a red-letter day on a calendar. All trading had ended on Dalnitskaya Street, and the gangsters drove by on the shadowy street to Ioska Samuelson's brothel. They rode in lacquered carriages and were dressed up in colorful jackets, like hummingbirds. They were goggle-eyed, one leg resting on the running board, their steel hands holding bouquets of flowers wrapped in cigarette paper. The lacquered cabs moved at a walking pace, and in each carriage sat one man with a bouquet; the drivers, sticking out on their high seats, were covered in bows like best men at weddings. Old Jewish women in bonnets lazily watched the flow of this everyday procession—they were indifferent to everything, these old Jewish women, it was only the sons of shopkeepers and dockworkers who envied the kings of the Moldavanka.

Solomonchik Kaplun, the grocer's son, and Monya Artillerist, the smuggler's son, were among those who tried to turn their eyes away from the splendor of other men's success. Both of them walked past Basya swaying like girls who have just discovered love. They whispered to each other and mimicked with their arms how they would embrace her, if she wanted them to. And Basya immediately wanted them to, because she was a simple girl from Tulchin, that self-seeking, nearsighted little town. She weighed a good five *pood* and a few pounds over, had lived all her life among the viperous offspring of Podolian brokers, itinerant booksellers, and lumber dealers, and she had never before seen anyone like Solomonchik Kaplun. This is why when she saw him she started shuffling her fat feet, which had been squeezed into men's boots, and said to her father, "Papa!" she said in a thundering voice. "Look at that sweetie of a gentleman! Look at his little dolly feet! I could eat them up!"

"Aha, Mr. Grach," whispered an old Jew named Golubchik sitting next to them. "I see your child wants to roam in the pasture."

"That's all I need!" Froim told Golubchik, twirling his whip a little, and then went home to sleep, and slept soundly because he didn't believe the old man. He didn't believe the old man, but he turned out to be entirely wrong. Golubchik was the one who was right. Golubchik was the matchmaker on our street, at night he read prayers for the well-to-do who had passed away, and he knew all there was to know about life. Froim Grach was wrong. Golubchik was the one who was right.

And, truth to tell, from that day on Basya spent all her evenings outside the gates. She sat on the bench, sewing herself a trousseau. Pregnant women sat next to her. Heaps of sackcloth unfurled over her powerful, bandy knees. The pregnant women were filled with all kinds of things, the way a cow's udder in a pasture fills with the rosy milk of spring, and then their husbands, one by one, came from work. The quarrelsome women's husbands wrung out their tousled beards beneath the water fountain, and then made way for the hunchbacked old women. The old women washed fat babies in troughs, they slapped their grandsons' shiny bottoms, and bundled them up in their frayed skirts. And so Basya from Tulchin saw life in the Moldavanka, our generous mother, a life crowded with suckling babies, drying rags, and conjugal nights filled with big-city chic and soldierly tirelessness. The girl wanted such a life for herself too, but she was quick to realize that the daughter of one-eyed Grach could not count on a suitable match. That was when she stopped calling her father "Father."

"You redheaded thief!" she yelled at him in the evenings. "You redheaded thief! Come get your grub!"

And this went on until Basya had sewed herself six nightgowns and six pairs of bloomers with lace frills. Having finished sewing the hem of the lace, she began crying in a faint little voice not at all like her usual voice, and through her tears said to the unshakeable Grach: "Every girl has her interests in life!" she told him. "I'm the only one who has to live like a night watchman in someone else's warehouse. Either do something with me, Papa, or I shall kill myself off!"

Grach heard his daughter out, and on the following day put on a sailcloth cloak and went to visit Kaplun the grocer on Privoznaya Square.

A golden sign sparkled above Kaplun's store. It was the best store on Privoznaya Square. Inside was the aroma of many seas and wonderful lives unknown to us. A boy was sprinkling the cool depths of the store with a watering can, singing a song suitable only for adults to sing. Solomonchik, the owner's son, stood behind the counter. On the counter were olives that had come from Greece, Marseilles butter, coffee beans, Lisbon Malaga, sardines from the firm of "Philippe and Canot," and cayenne pepper. Kaplun himself was sitting in his vest in the sun on a glassed-in porch eating a watermelon, a red watermelon with black seeds, slanting seeds like the eyes of sly Chinese girls. Kaplun's stomach lay on the table in the sun, and there was nothing the sun could do with him. But then the grocer saw Grach in his sailcloth cloak and turned pale.

"Good day to you, Monsieur Grach," he said, and moved to the side. "Golubchik informed me that you'd be dropping by, and I have prepared a pound of tea for you, an absolute rarity!"

And he began talking about a new variety of tea that had been brought to Odessa on Dutch ships. Grach listened to him patiently, but then interrupted him, because he was a simple man with no tricks up his sleeve.

"I'm a simple man with no tricks up my sleeve," Froim said. "I stay with my horses and I work hard at my work. I'm ready to throw in some new linen and a few coins for Basya, and I needn't tell you that I myself stand behind her—and whoever thinks that's not enough can burn in hell!"

"Why should we burn?" Kaplun answered in a quick jabber, caressing the carter's arm. "No need for such words, Monsieur Grach. We know you well as a man who can lend another a helping hand, not to mention that your talk might offend a man—you're no Cracow rabbi, you know, and though I myself didn't stand beneath wedding wreaths with no niece of Moses Montefiore, we must consider . . . we must consider Madame Kaplun, a grand lady—God himself has no idea what that woman wants—"

"Me, I know, I know that Solomonchik wants my Basya," Grach interrupted the grocer. "But Madame Kaplun doesn't want me."

"That's right! I don't want you!" shouted Madame Kaplun, who had been listening by the door, and she came into the glass veranda, hot all over, her chest fluttering. "I don't want you, Grach, as man doesn't want death! I don't want you, as a bride doesn't want her face to be covered with pimples! Don't forget that our dear late granddaddy was a grocer, and we must keep up *la branche*."

"You can keep your *la branche*!" Grach told the heated Madame Kaplun, and went home.

Basya was waiting for him there in her orange dress. But without even glancing at her, the old man spread out a sheepskin coat under the cart and went to sleep, and he slept until Basya's powerful arm dragged him out from under the cart.

"You redheaded thief!" the girl said in a whisper, not at all like her usual whisper. "Why do I have to put up with your carter's ways, and why are you as mute as a log, you redheaded thief!"

"Basya!" Grach said to her. "Solomonchik wants you, but Madame Kaplun doesn't want me. She wants a grocer's girl."

The old man adjusted his sheepskin coat and crawled back under the cart, and Basya went running out of the courtyard.

All of this happened on a Sabbath, a day of rest. The purple eye of the sunset, rummaging over the earth, stumbled upon Grach in the evening, snoring under his cart. An impulsive ray bumped into the sleeping man, and with its blazing reproach led him to Dalnitskaya Street, which lay dusty and shimmering like green rye in the wind. Tatars were walking up Dalnitskaya Street, Tatars and Turks with their mullahs. They were returning from a pilgrimage to Mecca and going back to their homes on the Orenburg Steppes and in Transcaucasia. A steamship had brought them to Odessa, and they were going from the harbor to the inn of Lyubka Shneiweis, nicknamed Lyubka the Cossack. The Tatars wore striped, rigid robes, and they covered the streets with the bronze sweat of the deserts. White towels were wound around their fezzes, indicating they had worshiped at the shrine of the Prophet. The pilgrims walked to the corner of the street and headed for Lyubka's courtyard, but they couldn't get in because a big crowd of people had gathered by the gates. Lyubka Shneiweis, her bag by her side, was beating a drunken muzhik, pushing him out into the street. She was punching him in the face, her fist clenched like a tambourine, while with her other hand she was holding him up so he wouldn't collapse. Streams of blood were trickling between the muzhik's teeth and down past his ears. He was lost in thought, looking at Lyubka as if she were a complete stranger. Then he collapsed onto the stones and fell asleep. Lyubka gave him a kick and went back inside her store. Yevzel, her watchman, closed the gates behind her, and waved at Froim Grach, who was walking by.

"My respects, Grach!" he shouted. "If you want to see a real slice of life, come into our courtyard—you'll have a good laugh!"

And the watchman took Grach to a wall where the pilgrims who had arrived the night before had settled down. An old Turk in a green turban, an old Turk as green and light as a leaf, was lying on the grass. He was covered in pearly sweat, breathing with difficulty, and his eyes were rolling.

"There!" Yevzel said, adjusting the medal on his shabby jacket. "There you have a scene from the real-life opera 'Turkish Sickness.' He's dying, this old man is, but no one must call a doctor, because they think that whoever dies on the road back from the Muhammadan God is a fortunate and wealthy man. . . . Halvah!" Yevzel shouted at the dying man, and burst out laughing. "The doctor has come to cure you!"

The Turk looked up at the watchman with childish terror and hatred, and turned away. Yevzel, pleased with himself, took Grach to the wine cellar on the other side of the courtyard. In the cellar, lamps were already burning, and music was playing. Old Jews with massive beards were playing Rumanian and Jewish songs. Mendel Krik was at a table drinking wine from a green glass, describing how his own sons—Benya, the older one, and Lyovka, the younger—had maimed him. He yelled out his story in a hoarse and terrifying voice, showed his smashed teeth, and let those around him poke the wounds on his belly. The Volhynian *tsaddiks*, with their porcelain faces, stood behind his chair and listened to Mendel Krik's bragging with numb bewilderment. They were astonished at everything they heard, and Grach despised them for it.

"Old braggart!" he mumbled, and ordered wine.

Then Froim called over the owner, Lyubka the Cossack. She was standing by the door spouting curses and downing shots of vodka.

"What!" she shouted at Froim, squinting at him in fury.

"Madam Lyubka," Froim said, beckoning her to sit next to him. "You are a clever woman, and I have come to you as I would to my very own mama. I have faith in you, Madam Lyubka—first and foremost in God, then in you."

"What!" Lyubka yelled, and quickly marched around the cellar before coming to sit next to him.

And Grach said, "In the settlements," he said, "the Germans are having a rich wheat harvest, but in Constantinople groceries go for a song. In Constantinople you can buy a *pood* of olives for three rubles, and then sell them here for thirty kopecks a pound! The grocers are really doing well now, Madam Lyubka, they've grown big and fat, and if one approaches them with a delicate touch, one could come away quite happy. But I'm all alone now on the job, the late Lyovka Bik has died, and I have no one left to turn to, and I'm all alone, as God is alone in heaven.

"Benya Krik!" Lyubka said to him. "You tried Benya out on Tartakovsky, so why not Benya?"

"Benya Krik?" Grach repeated, full of amazement. "He's a bachelor too, now that I think of it!"

"He's a bachelor," Lyubka said. "Hook him up with Basya, give him money, make the rounds with him."

"Benya Krik," the old man repeated, like an echo, a distant echo. "I hadn't thought of him."

Froim Grach got up, muttering and stuttering, Lyubka marched off, and he tagged along behind her. They crossed the courtyard and went up to the second floor. There on the second floor lived the women that Lyubka kept for her guests.

"Our bridegroom is with Katyusha," Lyubka said to Grach. "Wait for me in the hall!" And she went to the room at the other end, where Benya was in bed with a woman named Katyusha.

"Enough slobbering!" Lyubka told the young man. "You have to set yourself up first, Benchik, and then you can slobber away. Froim Grach is looking for you. He needs a man for a job but can't find one."

Then she told him everything she knew about Basya and about Grach's business.

"I'll think it over," Benya told her, covering Katyusha's bare legs with the sheet. I'll think it over. Let the old man wait a bit."

"Wait a bit," Lyubka told Grach, who was still standing in the hall. "Wait a bit, he's thinking it over."

Lyubka brought him a chair, and he sank into boundless waiting. He waited patiently, like a muzhik in a government office. Behind the wall, Katyusha moaned and burst out laughing. The old man dozed off for two hours, maybe more. Evening had long turned into night, the sky had turned black, and its Milky Ways had filled with gold, brilliance, and coolness. Lyubka's cellar was locked up already, the drunks lay like broken furniture in the courtyard, and the old mullah with the green turban had died around midnight. Then music came over the sea—hunting horns and trumpets from the English ships—the music came over the sea and faded away, but Katyusha, unfailing Katyusha, was still incandescing her rosy-painted Russian paradise for Benya Krik. She moaned behind the wall and burst out laughing. Old Froim sat motionless in front of her door. He waited till one in the morning, and then he knocked.

"Hey!" he called. "Are you making fun of me?"

Benya finally opened the door.

"Monsieur Grach!" he said, flustered, smiling, and covering himself with a sheet. "When we're young, we see girls like them's merchandise, but they're just straw that catches fire by itself."

He got dressed, made Katyusha's bed, shook out her pillow, and went out into the street with the old man. They walked until they came to the Russian cemetery, and there at the cemetery the interests of Benya Krik and gnarled old Grach the gangster intersected. Their interests intersected because Basya would bring her future husband three thousand rubles as a dowry, two thoroughbred horses, and a pearl necklace. They also intersected because Kaplun would have to pay two thousand rubles to Benya, Basya's bridegroom. Kaplun of Privoznaya Square was guilty of family pride. He had grown rich on Constantinople olives, he showed no mercy for Basya's first love, and that was why Benya decided to take on the task of relieving Kaplun of two thousand rubles.

"I'll take on this task, Papa!" he said to his future father-in-law. "With the help of God we shall punish all grocers!"

These words were uttered at dawn, after night had already past. And here now a new story begins, the story of the fall of the house of Kaplun, the tale of its slow ruin, of arson and gunshots in the night. And all this—the fate of arrogant Kaplun and the fate of Basya—was decided that night when Basya's father and her sudden fiancé sauntered past the Russian cemetery. Young men were pulling girls behind the fences, and kisses echoed on the gravestones.

FROIM GRACH

*I*n 1919, Benya Krik's men ambushed the rear guard of the Volunteer Army,[*] slit all the officers' throats, and captured part of their supply unit. As a reward, they demanded that the Odessa soviet allow them three days of "peaceful insurrection," but as they were not given permission, they looted all the stores lining the Alexandrovsky Boulevard. Then they set their sights on the Mutual Credit Society. They let all the customers enter first, and then requested that the porters carry all the bags of money and valuables outside to a car parked nearby. Within a month Benya Krik's men were being lined up and shot. There were people who said that Aron Peskin, a workshop owner, had had a hand in their capture and arrest. What kind of workshop it was, nobody knew. There was a machine in it—a long device with a warped lead roller—and on the floor, surrounded by sawdust, lay pasteboards for binding books.

One spring morning Misha Yablochko, one of Peskin's friends, knocked on the door of his workshop.

"The weather's great outside," Misha said to him. "You see before you a man who is about to grab a bottle of vodka along with some food and go for a ride to Arkadia.[†] Don't laugh—sometimes I love to just walk away from it all!"

Peskin put on his jacket and set out with Misha Yablochko in his

---

[*] The counterrevolutionary army (the Whites) fighting the Bolshevik forces in southern Russia and Ukraine from 1918–1920 under generals Kornilov, Denikin, and Wrangel.

[†] A resort area outside Odessa by the sea.

buggy to Arkadia. They rode about until evening. At dusk, Misha Yablochko entered the room in which Madame Peskin was bathing her fourteen-year-old daughter in a tub.

"Greetings," Misha said, lifting his hat. "We had such a nice time. The air there—simply out of this world! Though talking to your husband is like pulling teeth. What a tiresome man he is!"

"You can say that again!" Madame Peskin said, grabbing her daughter by the hair and yanking her head every which way. "Where is he, that vagabond?"

"He's unwinding outside in the garden."

Misha lifted his hat again, excused himself, and left in his buggy. Madame Peskin went straight outside. Her husband was sitting there in a Panama hat, leaning against the garden table with a grin on his face.

"You vagabond!" Madame Peskin said to him. "How dare you just sit there laughing, while that daughter of yours is driving me to an early grave! She won't wash her hair! I want you to go inside right now and have a word with her!"

Peskin sat there silently, still grinning.

"You fool!" Madame Peskin said. She peered under her husband's Panama hat and started screaming.

The neighbors came running.

"He's not alive," she told them. "He's dead!"

That wasn't true. Peskin had been shot twice in the chest and his skull was broken, but he was still alive. They took him to the Jewish hospital. Doctor Silberberg in person operated on the wounded man, but Peskin was out of luck. He died under the knife. That same night the Cheka* arrested a man nicknamed The Georgian, and his friend Kolya Lapidus. One of them was Misha Yablochko's coachman, the other had lain in wait for the buggy in Arkadia by the bend in the road that leads from the seashore out into the steppes. The two arrested men were shot after a brief interrogation. But Misha Yablochko managed to slip the net. He disappeared from sight, and a few days later an old woman selling sunflower seeds came hobbling into Froim Grach's yard.

---

* The Odessa branch of the "Extraordinary Commission" set up in 1917 to investigate counterrevolutionary activities. The Cheka later became the KGB.

She was carrying a basket of seeds on her arm. One of her eyebrows was arched in a furry, coal-black line above her eye, the other, barely visible, lay sagging on her eyelid. Froim Grach was sitting near the stable with his legs apart, playing with Arkadi, his grandson. The boy had come tumbling out of his daughter Basya's powerful womb three years ago. Froim held out his finger to Arkadi, who grabbed it and began to swing from it as if it were a crossbeam.

"You little scoundrel, you!" Froim said to his grandson, peering at him with his single eye.

The old woman came up to him with her furry eyebrow and her men's boots tied with string.

"Froim," she said. "I tell you these people have not a drop of soul in them. They don't say a word, they just kill us in their cellars like dogs. And they don't give us a chance to open our mouths before we die. We should tear these men to pieces with our teeth, and rip out their hearts! Why are you silent?" the old woman—Misha Yablochko—asked Froim. "Our men are waiting for you to break your silence!"

Misha got up, moved the basket to his other arm, and left, lifting his black eyebrow. He ran into three girls with braided hair walking with their arms around each other's waists outside the church on Alekseyevskaya Square.

"Hello girls," Misha Yablochko said to them. "Sorry I can't invite you for tea and cake."

He scooped up some sunflower seeds with a little glass mug, poured them into the pockets of their dresses, and walked off, disappearing around the church.

Froim Grach remained alone in his yard. He sat motionless, his single eye staring into the distance. Mules captured from imperialist troops were munching hay in the stables, and fattened mares were grazing with their foals on the meadow. Carters were playing cards in the shade of the chestnut trees and drinking wine from broken cups. Hot gusts of air swept over the whitewashed walls, and the sun in its blue rigidity poured over the yard. Froim got up and went out into the street. He crossed Prokhorovskaya Street, which was blackening the sky with the destitute, melting smoke of its kitchens, and Tolkuchy market, where people laden with curtains and drapes were trying to sell them to each other. He walked up Ekaterininskaya Street, made a turn by the statue of the Empress, and went inside the building of the Cheka.

"I am Froim," he told the commandant. "I want to see the boss."

The chairman of the Cheka back then was Vladislav Simen, who had come from Moscow. When he heard that Froim was there to see him, he called in Borovoi, one of his investigators, and asked for information on him.

"A first-rate fellow!" Borovoi told him. "Odessa begins and ends with him!"

And old Froim, in his canvas overalls, red-haired and big as a house, a patch over one eye and his cheek disfigured, was led into the office by the commandant.

"You know who you're killing off, boss?" he said as he walked into the room. "You're killing off all the lions! And you know what you'll be left with if you keep it up? You'll be left with shit!"

Simen leaned forward and opened his desk drawer.

"Don't worry, I'm clean," Froim told him. "Nothing in my hands, nothing in my boots—and I didn't leave nobody waiting outside neither. Let my boys go, boss! Just name your price!"

Simen had the old man sit down in an armchair, and offered him some cognac. Borovoi left the room and called together all the investigators who had come from Moscow.

Borovoi told them how it was one-eyed Froim and not Benya Krik who was the real boss of the forty thousand Odessa thugs. Froim might never show his hand, but he was the brains behind everything—the looting of the factories and the Odessa Treasury, and the ambushing of both the anti-Bolshevik army and its allies. Borovoi waited for Froim to come out of Simen's office so he could have a word with him. But Froim did not appear. Tired of waiting, Borovoi went to look for him. He searched through the whole building until he finally looked out into the backyard. Froim Grach was lying there stretched out under a tarpaulin by a wall covered in ivy. Two Red Army men stood by his body, smoking.

"Strong as an ox," the older of the two said when he saw Borovoi. "Strength like you wouldn't believe! If you don't butcher an old man like that, he'll live forever. He had ten bullets in him and he was still going strong!"

The Red Army man's face reddened, his eyes sparkled, and his cap slipped to the side.

"You're shooting your mouth off!" the second soldier cut in. "He died just like they all do!"

"No, not like they all do!" the older soldier shouted. "Some holler and beg, some don't say a word! So what do you mean, 'like they all do'?"

"To me they're all the same," the younger Red Army man repeated obstinately. "They all look the same, I can't even tell them apart!"

Borovoi bent down and pulled back the tarpaulin. The old man's face was frozen in a grimace.

Borovoi went back to his office. It was a round chamber with walls covered in satin. A meeting was under way about new rules for prosecuting cases. Simen was reprimanding the staff on the irregularities he had come upon, about the haphazard way verdicts were written up, and the absurd method with which protocols of the investigations were drawn up. The investigators were to split into groups and work with legal experts, so that from now on matters would be conducted according to the codes and statutes instituted by the Cheka headquarters in Moscow.

Borovoi sat in his corner, listening. He sat alone, far away from the rest. Simen came up to him after the meeting and took him by the hand.

"I know you're angry at me, Sasha," Simen said to him, "but you mustn't forget that now we are the power, the state power! You must remember that!"

"I'm not angry at you," Borovoi said, turning away. "It's just that you're not an Odessan, you can't understand what the old man represented."

They sat side by side, the chairman of the Cheka, who had just turned twenty-three, and his subordinate. Simen was holding Borovoi's hand in his and pressing it.

"Tell me one thing as a Chekist, as a revolutionary," Simen said to him after a moment of silence. "What use would that man have been to the society we are building?"

"I don't know," Borovoi said, staring motionlessly in front of him. "I suppose no use at all."

He pulled himself together and chased away his memories. Then, livening up, he continued telling the Chekists who had come from Moscow about the life of Froim Grach, about his ingenuity, his elusiveness, his contempt for his fellow men, all the amazing tales that were now a thing of the past.

THE END OF
THE ALMSHOUSE

*I*n the days of the famine, no one lived better in all Odessa than the almsfolk of the Second Jewish Cemetery. Kofman, the cloth merchant, had built an almshouse for old people by the wall of the cemetery in memory of his wife Isabella, a fact that became the butt of many a joke at Café Fankoni.* But Kofman turned out to be right in the end. After the Revolution, the old men and women who found refuge by the cemetery immediately grabbed positions as gravediggers, cantors, and body washers. They got their hands on an oak coffin with a silver-tasseled pall, and rented it out to the poor.

There were no planks to be found anywhere in Odessa in those days. The rental coffin did not stand idle. The dead would lie in the oak coffin at home and at the funeral service—but then they were pitched into their graves wrapped in a shroud. This was a forgotten Jewish custom.

Wise men had taught that one is not to hinder the union of worm and carrion—carrion is unclean. "For dust thou art and unto dust shalt thou return."

Because of the revival of the forgotten custom, the rations of the old folk grew in ways which in those days no one could even dream of. In the evenings they got drunk in Zalman Krivoruchka's cellar, and threw their leftover scraps to poorer companions.

Their prosperity remained undisturbed until the rebellion in the

---

* An elegant and expensive café that attracted a wealthy international clientele.

German settlements. The Germans killed Garrison Commander Gersh Lugovoy.

He was buried with honors. The troops marched to the cemetery with bands, field kitchens, and machine guns on *tachankas*. Speeches were given and vows made over his open grave.

"Comrade Gersh joined the Revolutionary Social Democratic Workers Party of the Bolsheviks in 1911, where he held the position of propagandist and liaison agent!" Lenka Broytman, the division commander, yelled at the top of his lungs. "Comrade Gersh was arrested along with Sonya Yanovskaya, Ivan Sokolov, and Monozon in the town of Nikolayev in 1913. . . ."

Arye-Leib, the elder of the almshouse, lay in waiting with his comrades. Lenka hadn't yet finished his farewell speech over the grave when the old men heaved up the coffin in order to tip it onto its side so that the deceased, covered with a flag, would come tumbling out. Lenka discreetly jabbed Arye-Leib with his boot spur.

"Beat it!" he hissed. "Go on, beat it! . . . Gersh served the Republic . . ."

Before the eyes of the horrified old folk, Lugovoy was buried along with the oak coffin, the tassels, and the black pall onto which the Star of David and verses from an ancient Hebrew prayer for the dead had been woven in silver.

"We've all just attended our own funeral!" Arye-Leib told his comrades after the burial. "We have fallen into Pharaoh's hands!" And he rushed off to see Broydin, the overseer of the cemetery, with a request that planks for a new coffin and cloth for a pall be issued immediately. Broydin made promises, but did nothing. His plans did not include the enrichment of the old folk.

"My heart aches more for the unemployed municipal employees than for these entrepreneurs," he told the others at the office.

Broydin made promises, but did nothing. In Zalman Krivoruchka's wine cellar, Talmudic curses rained down on his head and the heads of the Union of Municipal Workers. The old folk cursed Broydin's bone marrow and that of the members of the union, along with the fresh seed in the wombs of their wives. They called down every kind of paralysis and boil upon each and every one of them.

The old folk's income shrank. Their rations now consisted of bluish soup with boiled fish bones, with a second course of barley kasha without a single dab of butter in it.

An aged Odessan is ready enough to eat any kind of soup, regardless what it's made of, as long as there's garlic, pepper, and a bay leaf in it. There were none of these in the old folk's soup.

The Isabella Kofman Almshouse shared in the common lot. The rage of its famished inmates grew. Their rage rained down upon the head of the person who least expected it. This person was Dr. Judith Shmayser, who had come to the almshouse to administer smallpox vaccinations.

The Provincial Executive Committee had issued an order for mandatory vaccination. Judith Shmayser laid out her instruments on the table and lit a little alcohol burner. Outside the windows stood the emerald walls of the cemetery hedges. The blue tongue of the flame mingled with the June lightning.

Meyer Beskonechny, a haggard old man, stood closest to Judith. He watched her preparations sullenly.

"I'll give you a jab now," Judith said to him, beckoning him over with her tweezers. She pulled his thin, bluish strap of an arm out of his rags.

"There's nowhere for you to jab me," the old man said, jerking back his arm.

"It's not going to hurt," Judith exclaimed. "It doesn't hurt when you're given a jab in the flesh."

"I don't have no flesh!" Meyer Beskonechny said. "There's nowhere for you to jab."

Muffled sobs came from one of the corners. Doba-Leya, a former cook at circumcision feasts, was sobbing. Meyer twisted his decayed cheeks.

"Life is shit," he muttered. "The world's a brothel, everyone's a swindler!"

The pince-nez on Judith's nose bounced, her breasts swelled out of her starched coat. She opened her mouth to explain the benefits of vaccination, but Arye-Leib, the elder of the almshouse, stopped her.

"Young lady," he said. "Our mamas gave birth to us just like your mama gave birth to you! And this woman, our mama, gave birth to us so we would live, not so we would suffer! She wanted for us to live well, and she was as right as a mother can be. A person who is pleased with what Broydin provides him, that person is not worth the material that went into him. Your aim, young lady, is to inoculate smallpox, and with God's help, you are inoculating it. Our aim is to live out our life, not torture it! But we are not achieving our aim!"

Doba-Leya, a whiskered old woman with a leonine face, started sobbing even louder on hearing these words. She sobbed in a deep bass.

"Life is shit," Meyer Beskonechny repeated. "Everyone's a swindler!"

Paralyzed Simon-Volf, screeching and twisting his hands, clutched at the steering wheel of his invalid cart and went rolling toward the door. His yarmulke slid over his swollen, crimson head. Thirty growling and grimacing old men and women tumbled out onto the cemetery walk behind Simon-Volf. They shook their crutches and brayed like starving donkeys.

When he saw them, the watchman slammed the cemetery gates shut. The amazed gravediggers stopped digging and raised their shovels, clumps of earth and grass roots still clinging to them.

The noise brought out bearded Broydin in his tight little jacket, leggings, and cycling cap.

"You swindler!" Simon-Volf shouted. "There's nowhere for us to be jabbed! We've got no meat on our arms!"

Doba-Leya began snarling and growling. She grabbed Simon-Volf's invalid cart and tried to ram Broydin with it. Arye-Leib, as always, began spouting allegories and parables that crept up on byways toward an end that was not always clearly apparent.

He began with the parable about Rabbi Osiya, who had given his property to his children, his heart to his wife, his fear to God, and his levy to Caesar, keeping for himself only a place beneath an olive tree where the setting sun shone the longest. From Rabbi Osiya, Arye-Leib moved on to planks for a new coffin, and to rations.

Broydin spread his long-legginged legs, and listened without raising his eyes. The brown fringe of his beard lay motionless on his new jacket. He seemed immersed in sad, tranquil thought.

"Forgive me, Arye-Leib," Broydin sighed, turning to the cemetery sage. "Forgive me, but I must say that I cannot but see ulterior motives and political goals here. Standing behind you, I cannot but see people who know exactly what they are doing, just as you know exactly what you are doing."

Broydin raised his eyes. In a flash they filled with the white water of fury. He trained the trembling hills of his pupils on the old folk.

"Arye-Leib!" Broydin said in his powerful voice. "I want you to read this telegram from the Tatar Republic, where an immense number of Tatars are starving like madmen! Read the petition of the Petersburg proletariat who are working and waiting, hungering by their benches!"

"I don't have time to wait!" Arye-Leib interrupted Broydin. "I have no time!"

"There are people," Broydin continued without listening, "who have it worse than you do, and there are thousands of people who have it worse than the people who have it worse than you do! You are sowing trouble, Arye-Leib, and a whirlwind is what you shall reap. You are as good as dead if I turn my back on you. You will die if I go my way and you go yours. You will die, Arye-Leib. You will die, Simon-Volf. You will die, Meyer Beskonechny. But tell me one thing, just one thing, before you die—do we have a Soviet government, or could it be that we do not? If we do not have a Soviet government, if it's all in my imagination, then I would be grateful if you would be so kind as to take me back to Mr. Berzon's on the corner of Deribasovskaya and Ekaterininskaya Streets, where I worked as a tailor sewing vests all my life! Tell me, Arye-Leib, is the Soviet government all in my imagination?"

And Broydin came right up to the old cripples. His quivering pupils broke loose and went hurtling over the groaning, petrified herd like searchlights, like tongues of flame. Broydin's leggings crackled, and sweat stewed on his furrowed face. He came closer and closer to Arye-Leib, demanding an answer to whether it was all in his imagination that the Soviet government was now in power.

Arye-Leib remained silent. This silence might have been the end of him, had not Fedka Stepun appeared at the end of the walk, barefoot and in a sailor's shirt.

Fedka had been shell-shocked near Rostov and lived in a hut next to the cemetery, recovering. He wore a whistle on an orange police cord and carried a revolver without a holster.

Fedka was drunk. The locks of his rock-hard curls rested on his forehead. Beneath his locks his face, with its high cheekbones, was twisted by convulsions. He walked up to Lugovoy's grave, which was surrounded by wilted wreaths.

"Where were you, Lugovoy, when I took Rostov?" Fedka asked the dead man.

Fedka gnashed his teeth, blew his police whistle, and pulled the revolver from his belt. The revolver's burnished muzzle glittered.

"They've trampled on the czars," Fedka shouted. "There are no czars! Let them all lie without coffins!"

Fedka was clutching his revolver. His chest was bare. On it were tattooed the name "Riva" and a dragon, its head inclined toward a nipple.

The gravediggers crowded around Fedka with their raised shovels. The women who were washing corpses came out of their sheds ready to join Doba-Leya in her howling. Roaring waves beat against the locked cemetery gates.

People with dead relatives on wheelbarrows demanded to be let in. Beggars banged their crutches against the fence.

"They've trampled on the czars!" Fedka shouted, firing into the sky.

The people came hopping and jumping up the cemetery walk. Broydin's face slowly turned white. He raised his hand, agreed to all the demands of the almsfolk, and, with a soldierly about-turn, went back to his office. At that very instant the gates burst open. Pushing their wheelbarrows in front of them, the relatives of the dead briskly hurried down the paths. Self-proclaimed cantors sang *"El moley rakhim"** in piercing falsettos over open graves. In the evening the old folk celebrated their victory at Krivoruchka's. They gave Fedka three quarts of Bessarabian wine.

"Hevel havolim," Arye-Leib said, clinking glasses with Fedka. "You're one of us, one of us! *Kuloy hevel."*[†]

The mistress of the wine cellar, Krivoruchka's wife, was washing glasses behind the partition.

"When a Russian man is blessed with a good character," Madame Krivoruchka commented, "it's a rare luxury!"

---

*Hebrew: *El maley rakhamim,* "God is filled with mercy." A prayer traditionally chanted at burials.

[†]Hebrew quotations from the Bible (Ecclesiastes 12:8), *Hevel havolim,* "vanity of vanities," and *Kuloy hevel,* "All is vanity."

Fedka was led out of the wine cellar after one in the morning.

"*Hevel havolim.*" He muttered the dire, incomprehensible words as he tottered along Stepovaya Street. "*Kuloy hevel.*"

On the following day the old folk of the almshouse were each given four sugar cubes, and there was meat in their borscht. In the evening they were taken to the Odessa City Theater to a performance organized by the Department of Social Assistance. A performance of *Carmen*. It was the first time in their lives that these invalids and cripples saw an Odessa theater's gilt tiers, the velvet of its loges, and the oily sparkle of its chandeliers. During intermission they were given liver-sausage sandwiches.

An army truck took them back to the cemetery. It rolled through the deserted streets, banging and sputtering. The old folk slept with full stomachs. They belched in their sleep and shuddered with satiation, like dogs who have run so much they can run no more.

The next morning, Arye-Leib got up earlier than the rest. He faced east to say his prayers and saw a notice pinned to the door, in which Broydin announced that the almshouse was going to be closed for renovations and that all its wards were to report immediately to the local Department of Social Assistance for their employability to be reassessed.

The sun emerged over the green treetops of the cemetery grove. Arye-Leib raised his hand to his eyes. A tear dropped from the spent hollows.

The shining chestnut walk stretched toward the mortuary. The chestnuts were in bloom, the trees bore tall white blossoms on their spreading boughs. An unknown woman with a shawl tied tautly under her breasts was working in the mortuary. Everything had been redone—the walls decorated with fir branches, the tables scraped clean. The woman was washing an infant. She nimbly turned it from side to side, the water pouring in a diamond stream over its crushed, blotchy little back.

Broydin was sitting on the mortuary steps in his leggings. He sat there like a man of leisure. He took off his cap and wiped his forehead with a yellow handkerchief.

"That's exactly what I said to Comrade Andreychik at the union," said the melodious voice of the unknown woman. "We're not afraid of work! Let them go ask about us in Ekaterinoslav—Ekaterinoslav knows how we work.*

"Make yourself at home, Comrade Blyuma, make yourself at home," Broydin said placidly, sticking his yellow handkerchief into his pocket. "I'm easy enough to get along with, yes, I'm easy enough to get along with!" he repeated, and turned his sparkling eyes to Arye-Leib, who had dragged himself all the way up to the stoop. "As long as you don't spit in my kasha."

Broydin did not finish what he was saying. A buggy harnessed to a large black horse pulled up at the gate. Out of the buggy stepped the director of the Communal Economics Department, wearing a fine shirt. Broydin rushed over to help him out of the buggy and, bowing and scraping, took him to the cemetery.

The former tailor's apprentice showed his director a century of Odessan history resting beneath the granite tombstones. He showed him the vaults and memorials of the wheat exporters, shipping brokers, and merchants who had built Russia's Marseille on the site of Khadzhibei.† They all lay here, their faces toward the gate, the Ashkenazis, Gessens, and Efrussis—the lustrous misers and philosophical bon vivants, the creators of wealth and Odessa anecdotes. They lay beneath their labradorite and rose-marble memorials, shielded by chains of acacias and chestnut trees from the plebes clumped against the wall.

"They wouldn't let us live while they were alive," Broydin said, kicking a memorial with his boot. "And after their death they wouldn't let us die."

Inspired, he told the director of the Communal Economics Department about his reorganization program for the cemetery and his campaign plan against the Jewish Burial Brotherhood.

"And get rid of them over there too," the director said, pointing to the beggars who had gathered by the gate.

"I am already seeing to that," Broydin answered. "Step by step, everything's being taken care of."

---

* Broydin has hired cemetery workers from outside Odessa to take over the funerary duties of the old folk from the almshouse. Ekaterinoslav in Eastern Ukraine has been renamed Dnipropetrovsk.
†Khadzhibei was the small settlement where in 1794 Czarina Catherine II decided to build a powerful Black Sea harbor, which she then renamed Odessa.

"Well, keep up the good work," Mayorov,* the director, said. "I see you have things under control here. Keep up the good work!"

He placed his boot on the buggy's footboard, but suddenly remembered Fedka.

"By the way, who was that clown back there?"

"Just some shell-shocked fellow," Broydin said, lowering his eyes. "There are times when he loses control of himself—but he's been straightened out, and he apologizes."

"That Broydin knows his onions," Mayorov told his companion, as they drove off. "He's handling things well."

The large horse took Mayorov and the director of the Department of Public Services into town. On the way, they passed the old men and women who had been thrown out of the almshouse. They were hobbling along the road in silence, bent under their bundles. Spirited Red Army fighters were herding them into lines. The invalid carts of the paralyzed were screeching. Asthmatic whistling and humble wheezing tore from the chests of the retired cantors, wedding jesters, circumcision-feast cooks, and washed-up sales clerks.

The sun stood high in the sky. The heat tore into the hearts of the heaps of rags dragging themselves along the earth. Their journey lay along a joyless, scorched, stony high road, past shacks of straw and clay, fields smothered by rocks, gutted houses mangled by shells, and past the plague mound.† This inexpressibly sad Odessan high road led from the town to the cemetery.

---

*Mikhail Moisevich Mayorov (born Meyer Biberman), 1890–1938, like Broydin also originally a tailor by profession, became the director of the Communal Economics Department in July 1920.

†A huge sepulchral mound in which victims of the 1812 plague were buried.

SUNSET

One day Lyovka, the youngest of the Kriks, saw Lyubka's daughter Tabl. "Tabl" in Yiddish means dove. He saw her and left home for three days and nights. The dust of other streets and the geraniums in other people's windows were a comfort to him. After three days and nights, Lyovka came back home and found his father in the front garden. His father was eating supper. Madame Gorobchik was sitting next to her husband with murder in her eyes.

"Get out of here, you lout!" Papa Krik said to Lyovka when he saw him.

"Papa, pick up your tuning fork and tune your ears," Lyovka said to him.

"What might be the issue?"

"There is this girl," Lyovka said. "She's got blond hair on her head. Her name is Tabl. 'Tabl' in Yiddish means dove. I've clapped my eyes on that girl!"

"You've clapped your eyes on a slop bucket!" Papa Krik said. "And her mother is a gangster!"

On hearing these paternal words, Lyovka rolled up his sleeves and raised a sacrilegious hand to his father. But Madame Gorobchik jumped up from her chair and threw herself between them.

"Mendel!" she screeched. "Bash in Lyovka's ugly kisser! Lyovka, he ate eleven from my meatballs!"

"What? You ate eleven meatballs from your mother?" Mendel shouted, lunging at his son. But Lyovka dodged his blow and ran out of the yard, and Benchik, his older brother, ran with him. They roamed the streets until nightfall, seething like yeast in which vengeance is brewing, and finally Lyovka turned to his brother Benya, who within a few months was destined to become Benya the King: "Benchik," he said, "let's act now, and people will be lining up to kiss our feet. Let's kill Papa. The Moldavanka no longer calls him Mendel Krik. The Moldavanka is calling him Mendel the Pogrom. Let's kill Papa—can we wait any longer?"

"No, the time hasn't come yet," Benya answered. "But the time is coming. Listen to its footsteps and make way for it. You must step aside, Lyovka."

And Lyovka stepped aside to make way for time. Time, that ancient bookkeeper, set out, and along the way met Dvoira, the King's sister, Manasseh, the carter, and a Russian girl called Marusya Yevtushenko.

Ten years ago I still knew men who might have wanted Dvoira, the daughter of Mendel the Pogrom, but now goiter is dangling beneath her chin and her eyes are bulging from their sockets. Nobody wants Dvoira. And yet only recently an elderly widower with grown daughters appeared. He wanted a cart and two horses. When Dvoira heard the news, she rushed off to wash her green dress and hung it in the yard to dry. She wanted to call at the widower's to find out how old he was, what kind of horses he wanted, and whether she could get him. But Papa Krik didn't like widowers. He took the green dress, hid it in his cart, and left for work. Dvoira heated up the flatiron so she could press her dress, but the dress was nowhere to be found, and Dvoira threw herself on the ground and had a fit. Her brothers dragged her to the water pipe and poured water over her. So, my friends, can you see the workings of their father's, Mendel the Pogrom's, hand?

And now to Manasseh, the old carter, who harnessed Maid of Honor and Solomon the Wise. To his misfortune, he heard that old Butsis, Froim Grach, and Chaim Drong had their horses shod with rubber. Following their example, Manasseh went over to Pyatirubel and had Solomon the Wise shod with rubber. Manasseh loved Solomon the Wise, but Papa Krik told him, "I'm not Chaim Drong and I'm not Czar Nicholas II, that my horses should go to work in rubber soles!" And he grabbed Manasseh by the collar, lifted him up into his cart, and went riding out of the courtyard with him. Manasseh was dangling from Papa Krik's outstretched arm as from a gallows. The sunset was boiling in the skies, a sunset thick as jam, the bells of Alekseyevsky Church moaned, and the sun was sinking behind Blizhniye Melnitsy,* and Lyovka, the younger son of the house, ran after the cart like a dog running after its master.

An immense crowd followed the Kriks as if they were an ambulance cart, Manasseh still hanging from Papa Krik's iron grip.

"Papa, you are crushing my heart with your outstretched hand!" Lyovka shouted over to his father. "Drop my heart, let it roll in the dust!"

But Mendel didn't even turn around. The horses galloped, the wheels thundered, and the people enjoyed the circus. The cart veered into Dalnitskaya Street, to Ivan Pyatirubel the blacksmith. Mendel threw Manasseh against the wall of the smithy and then hurled him onto a heap of scrap iron. Lyovka ran off to get a bucket of water, and threw it over the old carter Manasseh. So, my friends, can you see the workings of Papa Krik's, Mendel the Pogrom's, hand?

"Time is coming," Benchik had said, and his brother had stepped aside to make way for time. And so Lyovka stood to the side until Marusya Yevtushenko got knocked up.

"Marusya's got knocked up," people whispered, and Papa Krik laughed when he heard them.

"Marusya's got knocked up," he said, laughing like a boy. "Woe unto Israel! And who is this Marusya?"

Benya was just coming out of the stables and laid his hand on his father's shoulder.

"I am a fan of women's!" Benchik said sternly to his papa, and gave him twenty-five rubles, because he wanted the cleanup to be done by a doctor in a hospital, and not at Marusya's house.

"I'll give her the money," his papa said, "and she can do a cleanup, or I won't live to see a happy day."

And the following morning, at the usual time, he harnessed Baby Burglar and Loving Wife, and drove off. But around lunchtime, Marusya Yevtushenko came to the Kriks' courtyard.

---

*"Near Mills," a poor factory and shantytown suburb.

"Benchik," she said, "I loved you, you bastard!"

And she hurled ten rubles in his face. Put two fivers together and they never come to more than a tenner.

"We're going to kill Papa," Benchik said to Lyovka, and they sat down on a bench by the gates, and next to them sat Semyon, Anisim the janitor's son, who was seven years old. And who would have thought that a little seven-year-old ragamuffin already has love in his heart as well as hatred? Who would think that he loved Mendel the Pogrom? But love him he did.

The brothers sat on the bench trying to figure out how old their papa was, and how long the hidden tail of years behind his admitted sixty might be, and Semyon, the janitor's son, was sitting next to them.

At that hour the sun had not yet reached Blizhniye Melnitsy. It poured into the clouds like the blood of a gouged boar, and the carts of old Butsis went rumbling through the streets, returning from work. The milkmaids were already milking the cows for the third time, and Madame Parabellum's women were dragging the pails of evening milk up onto her stoop. Madame Parabellum stood on the stoop and clapped her hands.

"Women! My own women, and the rest too!" she shouted. "Berta Ivanovna, ice-cream makers, and kefir makers! Come get your evening milk!"

Berta Ivanovna, a German language teacher who received two quarts of milk per lesson, was the first to be poured her portion. Right after her came Dvoira Krik, with an eye out to check how much water Madame Parabellum might have added to her milk and how much baking soda.

But Benya pulled his sister aside.

"This evening, if you see the old man has killed us, then go right up to him and smash his head in with your iron colander. And may that be the end of the firm of Mendel Krik and Sons!"

"Amen! And joyful the day will be!" Dvoira answered, and went outside the gates. And she saw that Semyon, Anisim's son, was no longer in the courtyard and that the whole of the Moldavanka was coming over to the Kriks'.

The Moldavanka was arriving in droves, as if a wake were being held in the Kriks' yard. The people came running as they come running to a country fair on the second day of Passover. Ivan Pyatirubel the blacksmith came with his pregnant daughter-in-law and his grandchildren. Old Butsis brought along his niece, who had just come on a boat from Kamenets-Podolsk. Tabl came with a Russian man. She was leaning on his arm and twirling the ribbon of her braid. Last of all came Lyubka, galloping in on her roan stallion. And only Froim Grach came all alone, redheaded as rust, one-eyed, and in a sailcloth cloak.

The people sat down in the front garden and unpacked the food they had brought with them. Workers took off their shoes, sent their children to get beer, and rested their heads on their wives' stomachs. And Lyovka said to Benchik, his brother, "Mendel the Pogrom is our father," he said, "Madame Gorobchik is our mother, and these people here are dogs! We are working for dogs!"

"We must think things through," Benya answered, but no sooner had he uttered these words than there was a roll of thunder on Golovkovskaya Street. The sun soared up into the sky and spun like a red bowl on the tip of a spear. Old Krik's cart came flying toward the gates. Darling Wife was covered in lather, and Baby Burglar was straining in his harness. The old man raised his whip over the crazed horses. His powerful legs were firmly planted on the cart, crimson sweat was seething on his face, and he was singing a song in a drunken voice. And suddenly Semyon, Anisim's son, slithered through somebody's legs like a snake and went scuttling out onto the street, shouting at the top of his voice, "Turn back the cart, Uncle Krik! Your sons want to give you a beating!"

But it was too late. Papa Krik flew into the courtyard with his foaming horses. He lifted his whip, opened his mouth, and—was struck dumb. The people sitting in his front garden were staring at him. Benya was standing on the left side of the yard by the dovecote. Lyovka was standing on the right side of the yard by the janitor's hut.

"People, neighbors!" Mendel Krik said barely audibly, lowering his whip. "Take a look at my own flesh and blood lifting a hand to strike me!"

And the old man jumped off the cart and hurled himself at Benya and smashed his nose with his fist. Lyovka came running, and did all he could do. He shuffled his father's face like a fresh deck of cards. But the old man was sewn of the devil's hide, and the stitches of this hide were reinforced with cast iron. The old man wrenched Lyovka's arms back and threw him on the ground next to his brother. He sat on Lyovka's chest, and the women closed their eyes so as not to see the old man's broken teeth and his face covered with blood. And at that moment the people of the indescribable Moldavanka heard Dvoira's voice and fast steps.

"This is for Lyovka," she said, "and for Benchik, and for me, Dvoira, and for all the others!" And she smashed her father's head with the heavy iron colander. The people jumped up and came running toward them, waving their arms. They dragged the old man to the water pipe as Dvoira had once been dragged, and turned on the faucet. Blood flowed like water into the gutter, and the water flowed like blood. Madame Gorobchik elbowed her way through the crowd, hopping up to them like a sparrow.

"Don't be silent, Mendel," she said in a whisper. "Yell something, Mendel.

But she heard the silence in the courtyard, and saw that the old man had just come from work, that the horses had not been unharnessed, and that nobody had poured water on the heated wheels, and so she went scuttling through the courtyard like a three-legged dog. And the honorable citizens drew closer. Papa Krik lay with his beard pointing upward.

"He's done for!" Froim Grach said, and turned away.

"Cashed in his rubles!" Chaim Drong said, but Ivan Pyatirubel the blacksmith waved his finger right in front of Chaim's nose.

"Three against one," Pyatirubel said. "A disgrace for all Moldavanka, but it's not night yet. I have yet to meet a fellow who could finish off old Krik!"

"It *is* night!" Arye-Leib cut in, suddenly appearing out of nowhere. "It *is* night, Ivan Pyatirubel. *Oy,* Russian man, do not say it isn't, when everything around you yells that it is!"

And Arye-Leib squatted down next to Papa Krik and wiped his mouth with a handkerchief, kissed his forehead, and told him about King David, the King of all the Jews, who had many wives, much land and treasure, and who could always weep when the time was right.

"Stop whining, Arye-Leib!" Chaim Drong shouted, thumping him on the back. "Don't read us a funeral service, you're not in your cemetery now!" He turned to Papa Krik and said, "Get up, you old drayman! Wet your whistle, say something foul like you always do, you old rough-neck, and get a couple of carts ready for the morning—I have some trash I want carted off!"

And all the people waited to see what Mendel would say about the carts. But for a long time he said nothing. Then he opened his eyes and his mouth, caked with dirt and hair, blood seeping from his lips.

"I don't have no carts," Papa Krik said. "My sons have killed me. Let them take over."

And yet they who were to take over Mendel Krik's bitter inheritance were not to be envied. They were not to be envied because all the hay troughs in the stable had long been rotting away, and half the wheels needed to be refitted. The sign above the gates had fallen apart, you couldn't read a single word, and none of the carters had even a single pair of underpants left. Half the town owed money to Mendel Krik, but his horses licked the numbers written in chalk on the walls as they browsed for oats in their feeding troughs. All day long muzhiks came to the dumbfounded heirs demanding money for chaff and barley. All day long women came to get their golden rings and nickel-plated samovars out of pawn. Peace left the house of the Kriks, but Benya, who within a few months was destined to become Benya the King, did not give up, and ordered a new sign: "Horse-Carting Establishment Mendel Krik & Sons." He wanted this to be written in gold letters on a sky-blue background with garlands of horseshoes painted bronze surrounding them. He also bought a bale of sailcloth ticking so that underwear for his carters could be made, and an unheard-of amount of timber to repair the carts. He hired Pyatirubel for a whole week and wrote out receipts for each customer. And—you can believe what I am telling you—by the evening of the following day he was more worn out than if he had made fifteen trips from the Watermelon Docks to the Odessa Tovarnaya Railroad Depot. And in the evening—you can believe what I am telling you—he didn't find so much as a crumb of bread or a single washed plate. Try fathoming the passionate barbarism of Madame Gorobchik! The dirt lay unswept in the rooms, an unprecedented pot of jellied veal was thrown to the dogs. And Madame Gorobchik stood by her husband's bed like a mud-drenched crow on an autumn branch.

"Keep an eye on them," Benchik told his younger brother, "keep our two newlyweds under a microscope, because I tell you Lyovka, it looks to me like they're cooking something up."

That is what Lyovka was told by his brother Benchik, who could see through everything with the eyes of Benya the King, but Lyovka, the second fiddle, didn't believe him and went to sleep. His papa was already snoring on the boards, while Madame Gorobchik was tossing and turning. She kept spitting onto the wall and the floor. Her malicious character kept her from sleeping. But in the end she too fell asleep. The stars scattered in front of the window like urinating soldiers, green stars on a blue field. A gramophone at Petka Ovsyanitsy's house across the street played Jewish songs. Then the gramophone fell silent. The night went about its business, and the air, the rich air, poured through the window to Lyovka, the youngest of the Kriks. He loved the air, Lyovka did. He lay there, breathing, dozing, frolicking with the air. He savored this richness until he heard rustling and creaking from his father's bed. Lyovka closed his eyes and made his ears stand to attention. Papa Krik raised his head like a mouse sniffing the air, and got out of bed. The old man pulled a bag of money out from under his pillow and swung his boots over his shoulder. Lyovka let him go—for where could he get to, the old dog? So Lyovka crept after his father, and also saw Benchik come creeping along the wall on the other side of the courtyard. The old man stole quietly to the carts and stuck his head in the stable. He whistled to the horses, and the horses came running to rub their muzzles on Mendel's head. Night was in the courtyard, night filled with stars, blue air, and silence.

"Sh!" Lyovka said, laying his finger on his lips, and Benchik, who came creeping from the other side of the yard, also laid his finger on his lips. Papa whistled to the horses as if they were little children, and then went running between the carts and up to the gate.

"Anisim," he said in a soft voice, tapping against the window of the janitor's shed. "Anisim, dear friend, unlock the gates for me."

Anisim, rumpled as hay, came crawling out of the janitor's shed.

"I beg you, master," he said. "Don't grovel before me, a simple man. Go back to your bed, master."

"You will open the gates for me," Papa whispered even more softly. "I know you will, my friend."

"Go back inside, Anisim," Benchik said, coming over to the janitor's shed and laying his hand on his papa's shoulder. And right before his eyes Anisim saw Mendel the Pogrom's face, white as paper, and he turned away so that he would not see his master with such a face.

"Don't hit me, Benchik," old Krik said, stepping back. "When will your father's torture end?"

"Oh, low-down father!" Benchik said. "How could you say what you just said?"

"I could!" Mendel shouted, and banged his fist against his head. "I could, Benchik!" he yelled with all his might, staggering like an epileptic. "This courtyard around me, in which I have served a sentence for half my life. This courtyard has seen me be the father of my children, the husband of my wife, the master of my horses. It has seen my glory, and that of my twenty stallions and my twelve iron-reinforced carts. It has seen my legs, unshakable as pillars, and my arms, my evil arms. But now unlock the gates for me, my dear sons, today let me for once do as I wish! Let me leave this courtyard that has seen too much!"

"Papa," Benya said to him without raising his eyes. "Go back inside to your wife."

But there was no point in going back inside to Madame Gorobchik. She herself came rushing out and threw herself on the ground, kicking the air with her old yellow legs.

"Oy!" she shouted, rolling on the ground. "Mendel the Pogrom and bastard sons! What have you done to me, you bastards? What have you done to my hair, my body, where are my teeth, where is my youth?"

The old woman shrieked, tore her blouse from her shoulders, and, getting to her feet, went running in circles like a dog trying to bite its tail. She scratched her sons' faces, she kissed her sons' faces, and ripped at their cheeks.

"You old thief!" Madame Gorobchik yelled, hobbling around her husband, twisting his mustache and tugging at it. "You're an old thief, my darling Mendel!"

All the neighbors were awakened by her yelling. Everyone came running to the gate, and bare-bellied children began tooting on their whistles. All Moldavanka came running, eager for scandal. And Benya

Krik, gray with shame in front of everyone, barely managed to jostle his "newlyweds" back into the house. He chased the people away with a stick, herding them toward the gates, but Lyovka, his younger brother, grabbed him by the collar and shook him like a pear tree.

"Benchik," he said, "we are torturing the old man! Tears are gnawing at me, Benchik!"

"Tears are gnawing at you, are they?" Benchik said to Lyovka, and sucking the spit together in his mouth, spat in Lyovka's face. "You are the lowest of the low," he whispered. "You disgust me! Don't tie my hands, and don't get tangled between my feet!"

And Lyovka didn't tie his hands. He slept in the stables until dawn and then disappeared from the house. The dust of other streets and the geraniums in other people's windows were a comfort to him. The young man walked the roads of sorrow, disappeared for two days and nights, came back on the third day, and saw the blue sign floating above the Kriks' house. The blue sign struck him to the heart, and the velvet tablecloths knocked his eyes right off their feet. The velvet tablecloths were spread over tables, and a large crowd of guests was laughing in the front garden. Dvoira was walking among the guests in a white headdress, starched women glittered in the grass like enameled teapots, and staggering workmen, who had already thrown off their jackets, grabbed Lyovka and pushed him into the house. Mendel Krik, the eldest of the Kriks, was sitting there, his face bruised. Usher Boyarsky, the owner of the firm Chef d'oeuvre, his hunchbacked cutter Efim, and Benya Krik, were all circling around the disfigured father.

"Efim," Usher Boyarsky said to his cutter, "be so kind as to come a little closer and measure Monsieur Krik for one of our *prima* striped suits, like he's family, and make so bold as to inquire what material the gentleman would prefer—English naval double-breasted, English civilian single-breasted, Lodz *demi-saison*, or thick Moscow cloth?"

"What kind of suit would you prefer?" Benchik asked Papa Krik. "Confess to Monsieur Boyarsky."

"What you feel in your heart is good enough for your father," Papa Krik said, wiping away a tear, "that's the kind of suit you'll have him make."

"Well, since Papa isn't a navy man," Benya interrupted his father, "a civilian would suit him better. First of all choose a suit for him for everyday use."

Monsieur Boyarsky bent forward and cupped his ear.

"What, pray, might you have in mind?"

"This is what I have in mind. . . ."

III

❧

The Red Cavalry Stories

In late May 1920, the First Cavalry of the Soviet Red Army, under the command of General Budyonny, rode into Volhynia, today the border region of western Ukraine and eastern Poland. The Russian-Polish campaign was under way, the new Soviet government's first foreign offensive, which was viewed back in Moscow as the first step toward spreading the doctrines of World Revolution to Poland, then to Europe, then to the world.

Babel chronicled this campaign in his RED CAVALRY stories, later to become the most well-known and enduring of his literary legacy. These loosely linked stories take the reader from the initial triumphant assault against the "Polish masters" to the campaigns of the summer of 1920, and the increasingly bitter defeats that led to the wild retreat of the cavalry in the autumn. Babel blends fiction and fact, creating a powerful effect that is particularly poignant in his rendering of the atrocities of war. The stories were published in magazines and newspapers between 1923 and 1926; the reading public was torn between delight at Babel's potent new literary voice and horror at the brutality portrayed in the stories. In 1926, thirty-four of the stories were included in the book KONARMIA (translated into English as

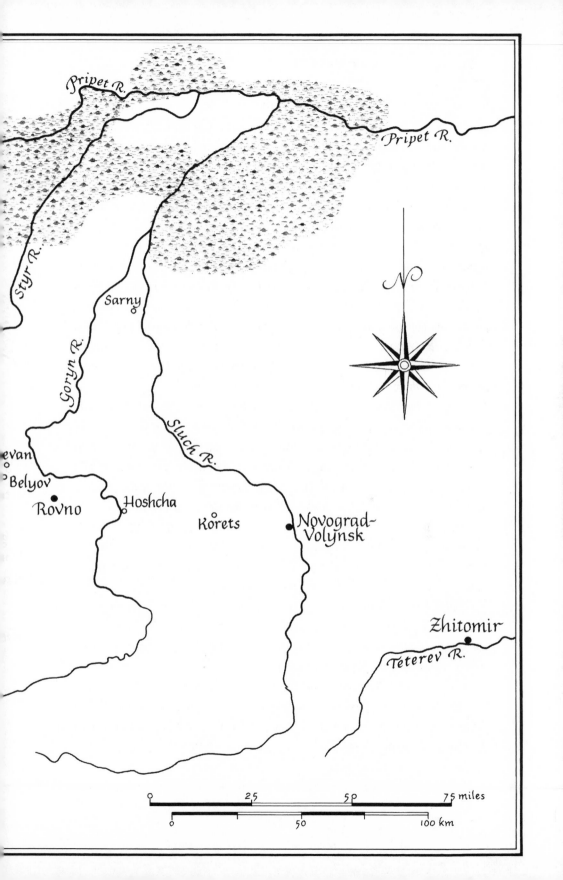

Pripet R.

Pripet R.

Styr R.

Sarny

Goryn R.

Sluch R.

evan

Belyov

Rovno

Hoshcha

Korets

Novograd-
Volynsk

Zhitomir

Teterev R.

N

0   25   50   75 miles

0   50   100 km

RED CAVALRY), *which quickly went into eight editions and was translated into English, French, Italian, Spanish, and German. It immediately turned Babel into an international literary figure and made him into one of the Soviet Union's foremost writers.*

The stories, as Babel himself repeatedly stressed, were fiction set against a real backdrop. Literary effect was more important to Babel than historical fact. Babel might also have felt more comfortable reconfiguring military strategy that might still have been classified when the stories began appearing in newspapers and magazines in the first years after the war. Novograd-Volynsk, for instance, the town in the first story, lies on the river Slucz, not on the Zbrucz as the story indicates. (The Zbrucz runs along the western frontier of Volhynia, along the former border between the kingdom of Poland and Russia.) Also, Novograd-Volynsk was not occupied by the Red Cavalry, but by the Soviet 14th Army. As the historian Norman Davies has pointed out, a high road from Warsaw to Brest had been built by serfs under Nicholas I, but it lay two hundred miles beyond the front at Novograd-Volynsk, and so could not have been cluttered by the rear guard.

One of Babel's strategies for creating a sharper feeling of reality in his stories was to mix real people with fictional characters. This was to have serious repercussions. General Budyonny, for instance, the real-life commander of the cavalry, often comes across in the stories as brutal, awkward, and irresolute. Babel makes fun of his oafish and uneducated Cossack speech. In the story "Czesniki," Budyonny is asked to give his men a speech before battle: "Budyonny shuddered, and said in a quiet voice, 'Men! Our situations . . . well, it's . . . bad. A bit more liveliness, men!'"

Babel had, of course, no way of knowing that General Budyonny was to become a Marshal of the Soviet Union, First Deputy Commissar for Defense, and later "Hero of the Soviet Union." Another real character in the stories, Voroshilov, the military commissar, also does not always come across particularly well. The implication in "Czesniki" is that Voroshilov overrode the other commanders' orders, resulting in an overhasty attack that led to defeat. Voroshilov happened to be a personal friend of Stalin; he had become the People's Commissar of Defense by the time the RED CAVALRY *collec-*

tion was in print, and was destined to become Head of State. These were dangerous men to cross.

In these stories Babel uses different narrators, such as Lyutov, the young intellectual journalist, hiding his Jewishness and struggling to fit in with the Cossacks, and Balmashov, the murderous, bloodthirsty Cossack.

The Soviet Union wanted to forget this disastrous campaign, its first venture at bringing Communism to the world. Babel's Red Cavalry stories, however, kept the fiasco in the public eye, both in the Soviet Union and abroad, throughout the 1920s and 1930s, and ever since.

CROSSING THE
RIVER ZBRUCZ

*T*he commander of the Sixth Division reported that Novograd-Volynsk was taken at dawn today. The staff is now withdrawing from Krapivno, and our cavalry transport stretches in a noisy rear guard along the high road that goes from Brest to Warsaw, a high road built on the bones of muzhiks by Czar Nicholas I.

Fields of purple poppies are blossoming around us, a noon breeze is frolicking in the yellowing rye, virginal buckwheat is standing on the horizon like the wall of a faraway monastery. Silent Volhynia is turning away, Volhynia is leaving, heading into the pearly white fog of the birch groves, creeping through the flowery hillocks, and with weakened arms entangling itself in the underbrush of hops. The orange sun is rolling across the sky like a severed head, gentle light glimmers in the ravines among the clouds, the banners of the sunset are fluttering above our heads. The stench of yesterday's blood and slaughtered horses drips into the evening chill. The blackened Zbrucz roars and twists the foaming knots of its rapids. The bridges are destroyed, and we wade across the river. The majestic moon lies on the waves. The water comes up to the horses' backs, purling streams trickle between hundreds of horses' legs. Someone sinks, and loudly curses the Mother of God. The river is littered with the black squares of the carts and filled with humming, whistling, and singing that thunders above the glistening hollows and the snaking moon.

Late at night we arrive in Novograd. In the quarters to which I am assigned I find a pregnant woman and two red-haired Jews with thin necks, and a third Jew who is sleeping with his face to the wall and a blanket pulled over his head. In my room I find ransacked closets, torn pieces of women's fur coats on the floor, human excrement, and fragments of the holy Seder plate that the Jews use once a year for Passover.

"Clean up this mess!" I tell the woman. "How can you live like this?"

The two Jews get up from their chairs. They hop around on their felt soles and pick up the broken pieces of porcelain from the floor. They hop around in silence, like monkeys, like Japanese acrobats in a circus, their necks swelling and twisting. They spread a ripped eiderdown on the floor for me, and I lie down by the wall, next to the third, sleeping Jew. Timorous poverty descends over my bed.

Everything has been killed by the silence, and only the moon, clasping its round, shining, carefree head in its blue hands, loiters beneath my window.

I rub my numb feet, lie back on the ripped eiderdown, and fall asleep. I dream about the commander of the Sixth Division. He is chasing the brigade commander on his heavy stallion, and shoots two bullets into his eyes. The bullets pierce the brigade commander's head, and his eyes fall to the ground. "Why did you turn back the brigade?" Savitsky, the commander of the Sixth Division, shouts at the wounded man, and I wake up because the pregnant woman is tapping me on the face.

"*Pan*,"* she says to me, "you are shouting in your sleep, and tossing and turning. I'll put your bed in another corner, because you are kicking my papa."

She raises her thin legs and round belly from the floor and pulls the blanket off the sleeping man. An old man is lying there on his back, dead. His gullet has been ripped out, his face hacked in two, and dark blood is clinging to his beard like a clump of lead.

"*Pan*," the Jewess says, shaking out the eiderdown, "the Poles were hacking him to death and he kept begging them, 'Kill me in the back-yard so my daughter won't see me die!' But they wouldn't inconvenience themselves. He died in this room, thinking of me. . . . And now I want you to tell me," the woman suddenly said with terrible force, "I want you to tell me where one could find another father like my father in all the world!"

* Polish for "Sir" or "Mr."

THE CHURCH IN NOVOGRAD

*Y*esterday I took a report over to the military commissar who had been billeted to the house of a Catholic priest who had fled. In the kitchen I was met by *Pani** Eliza, the Jesuit's housekeeper. She gave me a cup of amber tea and some sponge cake. Her sponge cakes had the aroma of crucifixion. Within them was the sap of slyness and the fragrant frenzy of the Vatican.

In the church next to the house the bells were howling, tolled by the crazed bell ringer. It was an evening filled with the stars of July. *Pani* Eliza, shaking her attentive gray hair, kept on heaping cookies on my plate, and I delighted in the Jesuitical fare.

The old Polish woman addressed me as "*Pan*," gray old men with ossified ears stood to attention near the door, and somewhere in the serpentine darkness slithered a monk's soutane. The *Pater* had fled, but he had left behind his curate, *Pan* Romuald.

Romuald was a eunuch with a nasal voice and the body of a giant, who addressed us as "Comrade." He ran his yellow finger along the map, circling the areas where the Poles had been defeated. He counted the wounds of his fatherland with rasping ecstasy. May gentle oblivion engulf the memory of Romuald, who betrayed us without pity and was then shot without so much as a second thought. But that evening his tight soutane rustled at all the portieres and swept through all the corridors in a frenzy, as he smiled at everyone who wanted a drink of vodka. That evening the monk's shadow crept behind me

*"Mrs." in Polish.

---

wherever I went. *Pan* Romuald could have become a bishop if he had not been a spy.

I drank rum with him. The breath of an alien way of life flickered beneath the ruins of the priest's house, and *Pan* Romuald's ingratiating seduction debilitated me. O crucifixes, tiny as the talismans of a courtesan! O parchment of the Papal Bull and satin of women's love letters moldering in blue silken waistcoats!

I can see you now, you deceptive monk with your purple habit, your puffy, swollen hands, and your soul, tender and merciless like a cat's! I can see the wounds of your God, oozing with the seed, the fragrant poison that intoxicates young maidens.

We drank rum, waiting for the military commissar, but he still hadn't come back from headquarters. Romuald had collapsed in a corner and fallen asleep. He slept and quivered, while beyond the window an alley seeped into the garden beneath the black passion of the sky. Thirsting roses swayed in the darkness. Green lightning bolts blazed over the cupolas. A naked corpse lay on the embankment. And the rays of the moon streamed through the dead legs that are pointing upward.

So this is Poland, this is the arrogant grief of the Rzeczpospolita Polska!* A violent intruder, I unroll a louse-ridden straw mattress in this church abandoned by its clergymen, lay under my head a folio in which a Hosanna has been printed for Jozef Pilsudski,† the illustrious leader of the Polish nobility.

Hordes of beggars are converging on your ancient towns, O Poland! The song of all the enslaved is thundering above them, and woe unto you, Rzeczpospolita Polska, and woe unto you, Prince Radziwill, and you Prince Sapieha,** who have risen for an hour.

My military commissar has still not returned. I go look for him at the headquarters, the garden, the church. The doors of the church are wide open, I enter, and suddenly come face-to-face with two silver skulls flashing up from the lid of a shattered coffin. Aghast, I stumble

---

* Poland's official name after 1918.

† Jozef Klemens Pilsudski, 1867–1935, the first Chief of State of Poland after its independence from Russia in 1918, and commander-in-chief of the Polish army.

** Janusz Radziwill, 1880–1967, politician belonging to an important Polish-Lithuanian princely family; Eustachy Sapieha, 1881–1963, was Polish envoy to London in 1919–20 and Polish Foreign Minister in 1920–21. Later he was a leader of the monarchist movement.

back and fall down into the cellar. The oak staircase leads up to the altar from here, and I see a large number of lights flitting high up, right under the cupola. I see the military commissar, the commander of the special unit, and Cossacks carrying candles. They hear my weak cry and come down to haul me out from the basement.

The skulls turn out to have been carved into the church catafalque and no longer frighten me. I join the others on their search of the premises, because it turned out that *that* was what they were doing in the church, conducting a search, as a large pile of military uniforms had been found in the priest's apartment.*

With wax dripping from our hands, the embroidered gold horse heads on our cuffs glittering, we whisper to one another as we circle with clinking spurs through the echoing building. Virgin Marys, covered with precious stones, watch us with their rosy, mouselike eyes, the flames flicker in our fingers, and rectangular shadows twist over the statues of Saint Peter, Saint Francis, Saint Vincent, and over their crimson cheeks and curly, carmine-painted beards.

We continue circling and searching. We run our fingers over ivory buttons and suddenly icons split open, revealing vaults and caverns blossoming with mold. This church is ancient and filled with secrets. Its lustrous walls hide clandestine passages, niches, and noiseless trapdoors.

You foolish priest, hanging the brassieres of your female parishioners on the nails of the Savior's cross! Behind the holy gates we found a suitcase of gold coins, a morocco-leather sackful of banknotes, and Parisian jewelers' cases filled with emerald rings.

We went and counted the money in the military commissar's room. Columns of gold, carpets of paper money, wind gusts blowing on our candle flames, the raven madness in the eyes of *Pani* Eliza, the thundering laughter of Romuald, and the endless roar of the bells tolled by *Pan* Robacki, the crazed bell ringer.

"I have to get away from here," I said to myself, "away from these winking Madonnas conned by soldiers."

---

* The humorous implication here is that when the narrator first saw the Cossack commanders carrying candles, he had assumed that these hard-line Communist fighters had come to the church to pray.

A LETTER

*H*ere is a letter home dictated to me by Kurdyukov, a boy in our regiment. This letter deserves to be remembered. I wrote it down without embellishing it, and am recording it here word for word as he said it.

Dearest Mama, Evdokiya Fyodorovna,

I hasten in these first lines of my letter to set your mind at rest and to inform you that by the grace of the Lord I am alive and well, and that I hope to hear the same from you. I bow most deepest before you, touching the moist earth with my white forehead. (There follows a list of relatives, godfathers, and godmothers. I am omitting this. Let us proceed to the second paragraph.)

Dearest Mama, Evdokiya Fyodorovna Kurdyukova, I hasten to inform you that I am in Comrade Budyonny's Red Cavalry Regiment, and that my godfather Nikon Vasilich is also here and is at the present time a Red Hero. He took me and put me in his special detachment of the Polit-otdel* in which we hand out books and newspapers to the various positions: the Moscow ZIK *Izvestia*,† the Moscow *Pravda,* and our own merciless newspaper the *Krasny Kavalerist,*** which every fighter on the front wants to read and then

---

* A political organ of the new Soviet government charged with the ideological education of the military during the Russian Civil War and the Russo-Polish War of 1920.

† The newspaper published by the Central Executive Committee, which was the executive branch of the new Bolshevik government.

** *The Red Cavalryman.*

go and heroically hack the damn Poles to pieces, and I am living real marvelous at Nikon Vasilich's.

Dearest Mama, Evdokiya Fyodorovna, send me anything that you possibly in any way can. I beg you to butcher our speckled pig and make a food packet for me, to be sent to Comrade Budyonny's Polit-otdel unit, addressed to Vasily Kurdyukov. All evenings I go to sleep hungry and bitterly cold without any clothes at all. Write to me a letter about my Stepan—is he alive or not, I beg you to look after him and to write to me about him, is he still scratching himself or has he stopped, but also about the scabs on his forelegs, have you had him shod, or not? I beg you dearest Mama, Evdokiya Fyodorovna, to wash without fail his forelegs with the soap I hid behind the icons, and if Papa has swiped it all then buy some in Krasnodar, and the Lord will smile upon you. I must also describe that the country here is very poor, the muzhiks with their horses hide in the woods from our Red eagles, there's hardly no wheat to be seen, it's all scrawny and we laugh and laugh at it. The people sow rye and they sow oats too. Hops grow on sticks here so they come out very well. They brew home brew with them.

In these second lines of this letter I hasten to write you about Papa, that he hacked my brother Fyodor Timofeyich Kurdyukov to pieces a year ago now. Our Comrade Pavlichenko's Red Brigade attacked the town of Rostov, when there was a betrayal in our ranks. And Papa was with the Whites back then as commander of one of Denikin's companies. All the folks that saw Papa says he was covered in medals like with the old regime. And as we were betrayed, the Whites captured us and threw us all in irons, and Papa caught sight of my brother Fyodor Timofeyich. And Papa began hacking away at Fyodor, saying: you filth you, red dog, son of a bitch, and other things, and hacked away at him until sundown until my brother Fyodor Timofeyich died. I had started writing you a letter then, about how your Fyodor is lying buried without a cross, but Papa caught me and said: you are your mother's bastards, the roots of that whore, I've plowed your mother and I'll keep on plowing her my whole damn life till I don't have a drop of juice left in me, and other things. I had to bear suffering like our Savior Jesus Christ. I managed to run away from Papa in the nick of time and join up with the Reds again, Comrade Pavlichenko's company. And our brigade got the order to go to the town of Voronezh to get more men, and we got more men and horses too, bags, revolvers, and everything we needed.

About Voronezh, beloved Mama Evdokiya Fyodorovna, I can describe that it is indeed a marvelous town, a bit larger I think than Krasnodar, the people in it are very beautiful, the river is brilliant to the point of being able to swim. We were given two pounds of bread a day each, half a pound of meat, and sugar enough so that when you got up you drank sweet tea, and the same in the evenings, forgetting hunger, and for dinner I went to my brother Semyon Timofeyich for blini or goose meat and then lay down to rest. At the time, the whole regiment wanted to have Semyon Timofeyich for a commander because he is a wild one, and that order came from Comrade Budyonny, and Semyon Timofeyich was given two horses, good clothes, a cart specially for rags he's looted, and a Red Flag Medal, and they really looked up to me as I am his brother. Now when some neighbor offends you, then Semyon Timofeyich can completely slash him to pieces. Then we started chasing General Denikin, slashed them down by the thousand and chased them to the Black Sea, but Papa was nowhere to be seen, and Semyon Timofeyich looked for him in all the positions, because he mourned for our brother Fyodor. But only, dearest Mama, since you know Papa and his stubborn character, do you know what he did? He impudently painted his red beard black and was in the town of Maykop in civilian clothes, so that nobody there knew that he is he himself, that very same police constable in the old regime. But truth will always show its head—my godfather Nikon Vasilich saw him by chance in the hut of a townsman, and wrote my brother Semyon Timofeyich a letter. We got on horses and galloped two hundred versts—me, my brother Semyon, and boys which wants to come along from our village.

And what is it we saw in the town of Maykop? We saw that people away from the front, they don't give a damn about the front, and it's all full of betrayal and Yids like in the old regime. And my brother Semyon Timofeyich in the town of Maykop had a good row with the Yids who would not give Papa up and had thrown him in jail under lock and key, saying that a decree had come not to hack to pieces prisoners, we'll try him ourselves, don't be angry, he'll get what he deserves. But then Semyon Timofeyich spoke and proved that he was the commander of a regiment, and had been given all the medals of the Red Flag by Comrade Budyonny, and threatened to hack to pieces everyone who argued over Papa's person without handing him over, and the boys from the Cossack villages threatened them too. But then, the moment Semyon got hold of Papa, Semyon began whipping him, and lined up all the fighters in the yard as befits military order. And then Semyon splashed water all over Papa's beard and the color flowed from the beard. And Semyon asked our Papa, Timofey Rodyonich, "So, Papa, are you feeling good now that you're in my hands?"

"No," Papa said, "I'm feeling bad."

Then Semyon asked him, "And my brother Fyodor, when you were hacking him to pieces, did he feel good in your hands?"

"No," Papa said, "Fyodor was feeling bad."

Then Semyon asked him, "And did you think, Papa, that someday you might be feeling bad?"

"No," Papa said, "I didn't think that I might be feeling bad."

Then Semyon turned to the people and said, "And I believe, Papa, that if I fell into your hands, I would find no mercy. So now, Papa, we will finish you off!"

Timofey Rodyonich began impudently cursing Semyon, by Mama and the Mother of God, and slapping Semyon in the face, and Semyon sent me out of the yard, so that I cannot, dearest Mama, Evdokiya Fyodorovna, describe to you how they finished off Papa, because I had been sent out of the yard.

After that we stopped at the town of Novorossisk. About that town one can say that there isn't a single bit dry anywhere anymore, just water, the Black Sea, and we stayed there right until May, and then we set off for the Polish Front where we are slapping the Polish masters about in full swing.

I remain your loving son, Vasily Timofeyich Kurdyukov. Mama, look in on Stepan, and the Lord will smile upon you.

This is Kurdyukov's letter, without a single word changed. When I had finished, he took the letter and hid it against the naked flesh of his chest.

"Kurdyukov," I asked the boy, "was your father a bad man?"

"My father was a vicious dog," he answered sullenly.

"And your mother?"

"My mother's good enough. Here's my family, if you want to take a look."

He held out a tattered photograph. In it was Timofey Kurdyukov, a wide-shouldered police constable in a policeman's cap, his beard neatly combed. He was stiff, with wide cheekbones and sparkling, colorless, vacant eyes. Next to him, in a bamboo chair, sat a tiny peasant woman in a loose blouse, with small, bright, timid features. And against this provincial photographer's pitiful backdrop, with its flowers and doves, towered two boys, monstrously big, dull-witted, broad-faced, goggle-eyed, and frozen as if standing at attention: the Kurdyukov brothers, Fyodor and Semyon.

THE RESERVE CAVALRY
COMMANDER

A wail spreads over the village. The cavalry is trampling the grain and trading in horses. The cavalrymen are exchanging their worn-out nags for the peasants' workhorses. One can't argue with what the cavalrymen are doing—without horses there can be no army.

But this isn't much of a comfort to the peasants. They are stubbornly gathering outside the headquarters, dragging behind them struggling old nags tottering with weakness. The muzhiks' breadwinners have been taken away from them, and with a surge of bitter valor, aware that this valor will not last long, they hurry to rant despairingly at the authorities, at God, and at their bitter lot.

Chief of Staff Z.* is standing on the front porch in full uniform. His inflamed eyelids half closed, he listens to the muzhiks' complaints with evident attention. But his attention is only a ploy. Like all disciplined and weary bureaucrats, he has a knack for shutting down all cerebral activity during empty moments of existence. During these moments of blissful empty-headedness our chief of staff recharges his worn-out instrument.

And this is what he is doing this time too, with the muzhiks.

To the soothing accompaniment of their desperate and disjointed clamor, Chief of Staff Z. cautiously follows his brain's soft wisps, those precursors of clear and energetic thought. He waits for the necessary pause, grasps the final muzhik sob, yells in a commanderial fashion, and returns to his office to work.

* Konstantin Karlovich Zholnarkevich, the staff commander in the *1920 Diary*.

But on this particular occasion even yelling would not have been necessary. Galloping up to the porch on an Anglo-Arabian steed came Dyakov,* a former circus rider and now commander of the Reserve Cavalry—red-faced with a gray mustache, a black cape, and wide red Tatar trousers with silver stripes.

"The Father Superior's blessing on all the honest filth of the earth!" he shouted, reining in his horse in front of the porch, and at that very instant a shabby little horse that had been given in exchange by the Cossacks collapsed in front of him.

"There, you see, Comrade Commander!" a muzhik shouted, slapping his thighs in despair. "There you have what your people are giving our people! Did you see what they've given us? And we're supposed to farm with that?"

"For this horse," Dyakov proclaimed distinctly and momentously, "for this horse, my highly esteemed friend, you have every right to request fifteen thousand rubles from the Reserve Cavalry, and if this horse were a trifle livelier, you, my dearest of friends, would be entitled to twenty thousand rubles. Just because a horse falls does not mean it's *factual*! If a horse falls but then gets up—that is a horse. If, to invert what I am saying, the horse does not get up—then that is not a horse. But I do believe I can make this lively little mare spring to her feet again!"

"Lord in Heaven and Mother of God!" the muzhik cried, throwing his hands up in the air. "How is this poor thing supposed to get up? It's on its last legs!"

"You are insulting this horse, my dear fellow!" Dyakov answered with fierce conviction. "Pure blasphemy, my dear fellow!" And he deftly swung his athlete's body out of his saddle. Splendid and deft as if in the circus ring, he stretched his magnificent legs, his trousers girded by cords around the knees, and walked up to the dying animal. She peered at him dolefully with a severe, penetrating eye, licked some invisible command from his crimson palm, and immediately the feeble mare felt bracing power flow from this sprightly, gray, blossoming Romeo. Her muzzle lolling, her legs skidding under her, feeling the whip tickling her stomach with imperious impatience, the mare slowly and deliber-

---

* For Dyakov, see *1920 Diary*, entries 7/13/20, and 7/16/20.

ately rose onto her legs. And then we all saw Dyakov's slender hand with its fluttering sleeve run through her dirty mane, and his whining whip swatting her bleeding flanks. Her whole body shivering, the mare stood on all four legs without moving her timid, doglike, lovestruck eyes from Dyakov.

"So you see—this is a horse," Dyakov said to the muzhik, and added softly, "and you were complaining, my dearest of friends!"

Throwing his reins to his orderly, the commander of the Reserve Cavalry jumped the four stairs in a single leap and, swirling off his operatic cloak, disappeared into the headquarters.

PAN APOLEK

*T*he wise and wonderful life of *Pan* Apolek went straight to my head, like an old wine. Among the huddling ruins of Novograd-Volynsk, a town crushed in haste, fate threw at my feet a gospel that had remained hidden from the world. There, surrounded by the guileless shine of halos, I took a solemn oath to follow the example of *Pan* Apolek. The sweetness of dreamy malice, the bitter contempt for the swine and dogs among men, the flame of silent and intoxicating revenge—I sacrificed them all to this oath.

• • •

An icon was hanging high on the wall in the home of the Novograd priest, who had fled. It bore the inscription: "The Death of John the Baptist." There was no doubt about it: in the portrayal of John I saw a man I had seen somewhere before.

I remember the gossamer stillness of a summer morning hung on the bright, straight walls. The sun had cast a ray straight on the foot of the icon. Sparkling dust swarmed in it. The tall figure of John came straight at me from the blue depths of the niche. A black cape hung triumphantly on that inexorable, repulsively thin body. Droplets of blood shone in the cape's round buckles. His head had been hacked diagonally off the flayed neck. It lay on an earthen platter that was held by the large yellow fingers of a warrior. The face of the dead man seemed familiar. I was touched by a mysterious premonition. The hacked-off head on the earthen platter was modeled after *Pan* Romuald, the curate of the priest who had fled. Out of his snarling mouth curled the tiny body of a snake, its scales shining brightly. Its head, a tender pink, was bristling with life, and stood out powerfully against the deep background of the cape.

I was amazed at the painter's artistry, his dark inventiveness. I was even more amazed the following day when I saw the red-cheeked Virgin Mary hanging above the matrimonial bed of *Pani* Eliza, the old priest's housekeeper. Both paintings bore the marks of the same brush. The meaty face of the Virgin Mary was a portrait of *Pani* Eliza. And this is where I found the key to the mystery of the Novograd icons. And the key led me to *Pani* Eliza's kitchen, where on fragrant evenings the shadows of old servile Poland gather, with the holy fool of a painter at their center. But was *Pan* Apolek a holy fool, peopling the local villages with angels, and elevating lame Janek, the Jewish convert, to sainthood?

Pan Apolek had come here thirty years ago on a summer day like any other with blind Gottfried. The two friends, Apolek and Gottfried, had gone to Shmerel's tavern on the Rovno high road, two versts from the edge of the town. In his right hand Apolek was holding a box of paints, and with his left hand leading the blind concertina player. The melodious tread of their reinforced German boots echoed with calmness and hope. A canary-yellow scarf hung from Apolek's thin neck, and three chocolate-brown feathers swung on the blind man's Tyrolean hat.

The newcomers had placed the paints and the concertina on a windowsill in the tavern. The artist unwound his scarf, which was neverending, like a fairground magician's ribbon. Then he went out into the yard, took off all his clothes, and poured freezing water over his thin, feeble, pink body. Shmerel's wife brought them raisin vodka and a bowl of meat cutlets stuffed with rice. Gottfried ate his fill, and then placed his concertina on his bony knees. He sighed, threw his head back, and flexed his thin fingers. The chords of the Heidelberg songs echoed against the walls of the Jewish tavern. With his scratchy voice Apolek accompanied the blind man. It was as if the organ had been brought from the Church of Saint Indegilda to Shmerel's tavern and the muses, with their quilted scarves and reinforced German boots, had seated themselves in a row upon this organ.

The two men sang till sunset, then they put the concertina and the paints into canvas sacks. *Pan* Apolek bowed deeply and gave Brayna, the taverner's wife, a sheet of paper.

"My dear *Pani* Brayna," he said. "Please accept from the hands of a wandering artist, upon whom the Christian name of Apollinarius has been bestowed, this portrait as a sign of our most humble gratitude for your sumptuous hospitality. If the Lord Jesus Christ sees fit to lengthen my days and give strength to my art, I will come back and add color to this portrait. There shall be pearls in your hair and a necklace of emeralds upon your breast."

Drawn on a small sheet of paper with a red pencil, a pencil red and soft like clay, was *Pani* Brayna's laughing face, surrounded by a mass of copper curls.

"My money!" Shmerel shouted when he saw his wife's portrait. He grabbed a stick and started running after the two men. But as he ran, Shmerel remembered Apolek's pink body with water splashing all over it, the sun in his little courtyard, and the soft sound of the concertina. The taverner's soul drooped, and, putting the stick down, he went back home.

The following morning, Apolek showed the priest of Novograd his diploma from the Munich Academy, and laid out before him twelve paintings with biblical motifs. They had been painted with oil on boards of thin cypress wood. On his table the *Pater* saw the burning purple of cloaks, the emerald sparkle of fields, and blossoming blankets of flowers flung over the plains of Palestine.

Pan Apolek's saints, a multitude of simple, jubilating elders with gray beards and red faces, were encircled by streams of silk and potent evening skies.

That same day, *Pan* Apolek was commissioned to do paintings for the new church. And over Benedictine wine, the *Pater* said to the artist: "Sancta Maria! My dear *Pan* Apollinarius, from what wondrous realms has your joyous grace descended upon us?"

Apolek worked with great zeal, and within a month the new church was filled with the bleating of herds, the dusty gold of setting suns, and straw-colored cow udders. Buffaloes with worn hides struggled under their yokes, dogs with pink muzzles trotted in front of the large flocks of sheep, and plump infants rocked in cradles that hung from the trunks of tall palm trees. The tattered brown habits of

Franciscan monks crowded around a cradle. The group of wise men stood out with their shining bald heads and their wrinkles red like wounds. The small, wrinkled old face of Pope Leo XIII twinkled with its fox-like smile from the group of wise men, and even the priest of Novograd was there, running the fingers of one hand through the carved beads of a Chinese rosary while with his other, free hand, he blessed the infant Jesus.

For five months Apolek inched along the walls, the cupola, and the choir stalls, fastened to the wooden scaffolding.

"You have a predilection for familiar faces, my dear *Pan* Apolek," the priest once said, recognizing himself among the wise men and *Pan* Romuald in the severed head of John the Baptist. The old *Pater* smiled, and sent a tumbler of cognac up to the artist working beneath the cupola.

Apolek finished the Last Supper and the Stoning of Mary Magdalene. Then one Sunday he unveiled the walls. The distinguished citizens the priest had invited recognized Janek the lame convert in the Apostle Paul, and in Mary Magdalene Elka, a Jewish girl of unknown parentage and mother of many of the urchins roaming the streets. The distinguished citizens demanded that the blasphemous images be painted over. The priest showered threats over the blasphemer, but Apolek refused to paint over the walls.

And so an unprecedented war broke out, with the powerful body of the Catholic Church on one side, and the unconcerned icon painter on the other. The war lasted for three decades. The situation almost turned the gentle idler into the founder of a new heresy; in which case he would have been the most whimsical and ludicrous fighter among the many in the slippery and stormy history of the Church of Rome, a fighter roaming the earth in blessed tipsiness with two white mice under his shirt and with a collection of the finest little brushes in his pocket.

"Fifteen zloty for the Virgin Mary, twenty-five zloty for the Holy Family, and fifty zloty for the Last Supper portraying all the client's family. The client's enemy can be portrayed as Judas Iscariot, for which an extra ten zloty will be added to the bill," *Pan* Apolek informed the peasants after he had been thrown out of the Novograd church.

There was no shortage of commissions. And when a year later the archbishop of Zhitomir sent a delegation in response to the frenzied epistles of the Novograd priest, they found the monstrous family portraits, sacrilegious, naive, and flamboyant, in the most impoverished, foul-smelling hovels. Josephs with gray hair neatly parted in the middle, pomaded Jesuses, many-childed village Marys with parted knees. The pictures hung in the icon corners, wreathed with garlands of paper flowers.

"He has bestowed sainthood upon you people during your lifetime!" the bishop of Dubno and Novokonstantinov shouted at the crowd that had come to defend Apolek. "He has endowed you with the ineffable attributes of the saints, you, thrice fallen into the sin of disobedience, furtive moonshiners, ruthless moneylenders, makers of counterfeit weights, and sellers of your daughters' innocence!"

"Your holiness!" lame-footed Witold, the town's cemetery watchman and procurer of stolen goods, then said to the bishop. "Where does our all-forgiving Lord God see truth, and who will explain it to these ignorant villagers? Is there not more truth in the paintings of *Pan* Apolek, who raises our pride, than in your words that are filled with abuse and tyrannical anger?"

The shouts of the crowd sent the bishop running. The agitation in the villages threatened the safety of the clerics. The painter who had taken Apolek's place could not work up the courage to paint over Elka and lame Janek. They can still be seen today above a side altar of the Novograd church: Janek, as Saint Paul, a timorous cripple with the shaggy black beard of a village apostate, and Elka as the whore from Magdala, decrepit and crazed, with dancing body and fallen cheeks.

The battle with the priest lasted three decades. Then the Cossack flood chased the old monk out of his aromatic stone nest, and Apolek— O fickle fortune!—settled into *Pani* Eliza's kitchen. And here I am, a passing guest, imbibing the wine of his conversation in the evenings.

What do we converse about? About the romantic days of the Polish nobility, the fanatical frenzy of women, the art of Luca della Robbia,* and the family of the Bethlehem carpenter.

"There is something I have to tell you, Mr. Clerk," Apolek tells me secretively before supper.

---

* Luca della Robbia, 1399–1482, Florentine sculptor.

"Yes," I answer. "Go ahead, Apolek, I'm listening."

But *Pan* Robacki, the lay brother of the church—stern, gray, bony, and with large ears—is sitting too close. He unfolds a faded screen of silence and animosity before us.

"I have to tell you, *Pan*," Apolek whispers, taking me aside, "that Jesus Christ, the son of Mary, was married to Deborah, a Jerusalem girl of low birth—"

"*O, ten czlowiek!*"* *Pan* Robacki shouts in despair. "This man not dies in his bed! This man the peoples will be killing!"

"After supper," Apolek murmurs in a gloomy voice. "After supper, if that will suit you, Mr. Clerk."

It suits me. Inflamed by the beginning of Apolek's story, I pace up and down the kitchen waiting for the appointed time. And outside the window night stands like a black column. Outside the window the bristling, dark garden has fallen still. The road to the church flows beneath the moon in a sparkling, milky stream. The earth is covered with a dismal sheen, a necklace of shining berries is draped over the bushes. The aroma of lilacs is clean and strong as alcohol. The seething oily breath of the stove drinks in this fresh poison, killing the stuffy resinous heat of the spruce wood lying about the kitchen floor.

Apolek is wearing a pink bow tie and threadbare pink trousers, and is puttering about in his corner like a friendly graceful animal. His table is smeared with glue and paint. He is working in quick small movements. A hushed, melodic drumming comes drifting from his corner: it is old Gottfried tapping with his trembling fingers. The blind man is sitting rigidly in the greasy yellow lamplight. His bald head is drooping as he listens to the incessant music of his blindness and the muttering of Apolek, his eternal friend.

"... And what the priests and the Evangelist Mark and the Evangelist Matthew are telling you, *Pan* Clerk, is not truth. But truth can be revealed to you, *Pan*, for I am prepared for fifty marks to paint your portrait in the form of Saint Francis on a background of green and sky. He was a very simple saint, *Pan* Francis was. And if you have a bride in Russia, *Pan* Clerk, women love Saint Francis, although not all women, *Pan*."

And from his spruce-wood-scented corner he began telling me the

---

* Polish: "Oh, this man!"

tale of the marriage of Jesus to Deborah. According to Apolek, Deborah already had a bridegroom, a young Israelite who traded in ivory. But Deborah's wedding night ended in bewilderment and tears. The woman was gripped by fear when she saw her husband approach her bed. Hiccups bulged in her throat and she vomited all the food she had eaten at the wedding table. Shame fell upon Deborah, on her father, her mother, and on all her kin. The bridegroom abandoned her with words of ridicule, and called all the guests together. And Jesus, filled with pity at seeing the anguish of the woman who was thirsting for her husband but also fearing him, donned the robes of the newlywed man and united himself with Deborah as she lay in her vomit. Afterward she went out to the wedding guests, loudly exulting like a woman proud of her fall. And only Jesus stood to the side. His body was drenched with mortal sweat, for the bee of sorrow had stung his heart. He left the banquet hall unnoticed, and went into the desert east of Judea, where John the Baptist awaited him. And Deborah gave birth to her first son. . . ."

"So where is that son?" I yelled.

"The priests have hidden him," Apolek said with gravity, raising his thin, cold finger to his drunkard's nose.

"*Pan* Artist!" Robacki suddenly shouted, stepping out of the shadows, his gray ears quaking. "What you saying? But this is outrage!"

"*Tak, tak,*" Apolek said, cringing and grabbing hold of Gottfried. "*Tak, tak, panie.*"*

Apolek pulled the blind man toward the door, but stopped by the doorpost and beckoned me with his finger.

"Saint Francis with a bird on your sleeve," he whispered, winking at me. "A dove or a goldfinch, you can choose, *Pan* Clerk!"

And he disappeared with his blind eternal friend.

"Oh, what foolishness!" Robacki, the church lay brother, said. "This man not dies in his bed!"

Pan Robacki opened his mouth wide and yawned like a cat. I wished him a good night, and went home, to my plundered Jews, to sleep.

The vagrant moon trailed through the town and I tagged along, nurturing within me unfulfillable dreams and dissonant songs.

---

* Polish: "Yes, yes, gentlemen."

ITALIAN SUN

*Y*esterday I was sitting once more under a heated garland of green spruce twigs in *Pani* Eliza's servants' quarters. I sat by the warm, lively, crackling stove, and then returned to my lodgings late at night. Below, in the ravine, the silent Zbrucz rolled its glassy, dark waves.

The burned-out town—broken columns and the hooks of evil old women's fingers dug into the earth—seemed to me raised into the air, comfortable and unreal like a dream. The naked shine of the moon poured over the town with unquenchable strength. The damp mold of the ruins blossomed like a marble bench on the opera stage. And I waited with anxious soul for Romeo to descend from the clouds, a satin Romeo singing of love, while backstage a dejected electrician waits with his finger on the button to turn off the moon.

Blue roads flowed past me like rivulets of milk trickling from many breasts. On my way back, I had been dreading running into Sidorov, with whom I shared my room, and who at night brought his hairy paw of dejection down upon me. That night, luckily, harrowed by the milk of the moon, Sidorov did not say a single word to me. I found him writing, surrounded by books. On the table a hunchbacked candle was smoking—the sinister bonfire of dreamers. I sat to the side, dozed, dreams pouncing around me like kittens. And it wasn't until late that night that I was awakened by an orderly who had come to take Sidorov to headquarters. They left together. I immediately hurried over to the table where Sidorov had been writing, and leafed through his books.

There was an Italian primer, a print of the Roman Forum, and a street map of Rome. The map was completely marked up with crosses. I leaned over the sheet of paper covered with writing and, with clenched fingers and an expiring heart, read another man's letter. Sidorov, the dejected murderer, tore the pink cotton wool of my imagination to shreds and dragged me into the halls of his judicious insanity. I began reading on the second page, as I did not dare look for the first one:

•   •   •

. . . shot through the lungs, and am a little off my head, or, as Sergey always says, flying mad. Well, when you go mad, idiotically mad, you don't go, you fly. Anyway, let's put the horsetail to one side and the jokes to the other. Back to the events of the day, Victoria, my dear friend.

I took part in a three-month Makhno campaign*—the whole thing a grueling swindle, nothing more! Only Volin is still there. Volin is wearing apostolic raiment and clamoring to be the Lenin of anarchism. Terrible. And Makhno listens to him, runs his fingers through his dusty wire curls, and lets the snake of his peasant grin slither across his rotten teeth. And I'm not all that sure anymore if there isn't a seed of anarchy in all this, and if we won't wipe your prosperous noses for you, you self-proclaimed Tsekists from your self-proclaimed Tsekhs,† "made in Kharkov," your self-proclaimed capi-tal.** Your strapping heroes prefer not to remember the sins of their anarchist youth, and now laugh at them from the heights of their governmental wisdom! To hell with them!

Then I ended up in Moscow. How did I end up in Moscow? The boys had treated someone unjustly, something to do with requisitions or something. Well, fool that I am, I defended him. So they let me have it, and rightly so. My wound was not even worth mentioning, but in Moscow, O Victoria, in Moscow I was struck dumb by the misery all around. Every day the hospital nurses would bring me a nibble of kasha. Bridled with reverence, they brought it in on a large tray, and I despised this shock-brigade kasha, this unregimented

---

* Nestor Ivanovich Makhno, 1889–1934, the Ukrainian anarchist leader.

† A pun: the Tsekists are members of the Tseka, the Central Committee of the Bolshevik Party. A "tsekh," however, is a simple guild.

** Today, Kharkiv, a city in northeastern Ukraine. The "self-proclaimed" capital in the sense that Kharkiv replaced Kiev as the capital of the Ukrainian S.S.R from 1917 until 1934.

treatment in regimented Moscow. Then, in the Soviet Council, I ran into a handful of anarchists. All fops and dithering old men! I managed to get all the way to the Kremlin with my plan for some real work. But they patted me on the back and promised to give me a nice deputy position if I changed my ways. I did not change my ways. And what came next? Next came the front, the Red Cavalry, and the damn soldiers stinking of blood and corpses.

Save me, Victoria! Governmental wisdom is driving me insane, boredom is inebriating me. If you won't help me I will die like a dog without a five-year plan! And who wants a worker to die unplanned? Surely not you, Victoria, my bride who will never be my wife. See, I'm becoming maudlin again, damn it to hell!

But let's get to the point now. The army bores me. I cannot ride because of my wound, which means I cannot fight. Use your connections, Victoria, have them send me to Italy! I am studying the language, and I'll be speaking it within two months. The land down there is smoldering, things there are almost ready. All they need is a few shots. One of these shots I shall fire. It is high time that their King be sent to join his ancestors. That is very important. He is a nice old fellow who plays for popularity and has himself photographed with the tamer socialists for family magazines.

But don't say anything about shots or kings at the Tseka or the People's Commissariat for Foreign Affairs. They will pat you on the head and coo: "What a romantic he is!" Just tell them plain and simple: "He's sick, he's angry, he's drunk with depression, he wants some Italian sun and he wants some bananas! Does he deserve it, or doesn't he? He'll recuperate, and *basta*! And if not, then send him to the Odessa Cheka.* They're very sensible there!"

The things I am writing you are so foolish, so unfairly foolish, Victoria, my dear friend.

Italy has seeped into my heart like an obsession. Thinking about that country that I have never seen is as sweet to me as a woman's name, as your name, Victoria. . . .

I read the letter through and then went to lie down on my dirty, crumpled bed, but sleep would not come. On the other side of the wall the pregnant Jewess was crying heartfelt tears, her lanky husband

---

* The Odessa branch of the "Extraordinary Commission" set up in 1917 to investigate counterrevolutionary activities. The Cheka later became the KGB.

answering with mumbling groans. They were lamenting the things that had been stolen, and blaming each other for their bad luck. Then, before daybreak, Sidorov came back. The dwindling candle was expiring on the table. He pulled another candle end out of his boot and pressed it with unusual pensiveness onto the drowned wick. Our room was dark, gloomy, everything in it breathed a damp, nocturnal stench, and only the window, lit up by the fire of the moon, shone like salvation.

He came over, my agonizing neighbor, and hid the letter. Bending forward, he sat down at the table and opened the picture album of Rome. The magnificent book with its gilt-edged pages stood opposite his expressionless, olive-green face. The jagged ruins of the Capitol and the Coliseum, lit by the setting sun, glittered over his hunched back. The photograph of the royal family was also there. He had inserted it between the large, glossy pages. On a piece of paper torn from a calendar was the picture of the pleasant, frail King Victor Emmanuel with his black-haired wife, Crown Prince Umberto, and a whole brood of princesses.

It is night, a night full of distant and painful sounds, with a square of light in the damp darkness, and in this square is Sidorov's deathly face, a lifeless mask hovering over the yellow flame of the candle.

GEDALI

*O*n the eve of the Sabbath I am always tormented by the dense sorrow of memory. In the past on these evenings, my grandfather's yellow beard caressed the volumes of Ibn Ezra. My old grandmother, in her lace bonnet, waved spells over the Sabbath candle with her gnarled fingers, and sobbed sweetly. On those evenings my child's heart was gently rocked, like a little boat on enchanted waves.

I wander through Zhitomir looking for the timid star.* Beside the ancient synagogue, beside its indifferent yellow walls, old Jews, Jews with the beards of prophets, passionate rags hanging from their sunken chests, are selling chalk, bluing, and candle wicks.

Here before me lies the bazaar, and the death of the bazaar. Slaughtered is the fat soul of abundance. Mute padlocks hang on the stores, and the granite of the streets is as clean as a corpse's bald head. The timid star blinks and expires.

Success came to me later, I found the star just before the setting of the sun. Gedali's store lay hidden among the tightly shut market stalls. Dickens, where was your shadow that evening?† In this old junk store you would have found gilded slippers and ship's ropes, an antique compass and a stuffed eagle, a Winchester hunting rifle with the date "1810" engraved on it, and a broken stewpot.

Old Gedali is circling around his treasures in the rosy emptiness of

---

* The star that signals nightfall and the beginning of evening prayers for the Sabbath.
† A reference to Charles Dickens's novel *The Old Curiosity Shop*.

the evening, a small shopkeeper with smoky spectacles and a green coat that reaches all the way to the ground. He rubs his small white hands, tugs at his gray beard, lowers his head, and listens to invisible voices that come wafting to him.

This store is like the box of an intent and inquisitive little boy who will one day become a professor of botany. This store has everything from buttons to dead butterflies, and its little owner is called Gedali. Everyone has left the bazaar, but Gedali has remained. He roams through his labyrinth of globes, skulls, and dead flowers, waving his cockerel-feather duster, swishing away the dust from the dead flowers.

We sit down on some empty beer barrels. Gedali winds and unwinds his narrow beard. His top hat rocks above us like a little black tower. Warm air flows past us. The sky changes color—tender blood pouring from an overturned bottle—and a gentle aroma of decay envelops me.

"So let's say we say 'yes' to the Revolution. But does that mean that we're supposed to say 'no' to the Sabbath?" Gedali begins, enmeshing me in the silken cords of his smoky eyes. "Yes to the Revolution! Yes! But the Revolution keeps hiding from Gedali and sending gunfire ahead of itself."

"The sun cannot enter eyes that are squeezed shut," I say to the old man, "but we shall rip open those closed eyes!"

"The Pole has closed my eyes," the old man whispers almost inaudibly. "The Pole, that evil dog! He grabs the Jew and rips out his beard, *oy*, the cur! But now they are beating him, the evil dog! This is marvelous, this is the Revolution! But then the same man who beat the Pole says to me, 'Gedali, we are requisitioning your gramophone!' 'But gentlemen,' I tell the Revolution, 'I love music!' And what does the Revolution answer me? 'You don't know what you love, Gedali! I am going to shoot you, and then you'll know, and I cannot *not* shoot, because I am the Revolution!'"

"The Revolution cannot *not* shoot, Gedali," I tell the old man, "because it is the Revolution."

"But my dear *Pan*! The Pole did shoot, because he is the counter-revolution. And you shoot because you are the Revolution. But Revolution is happiness. And happiness does not like orphans in its house. A good man does good deeds. The Revolution is the good deed done by good men. But good men do not kill. Hence the Revolution is done by bad men. But the Poles are also bad men. Who is going to tell Gedali which is the Revolution and which the counterrevolution? I have studied the Talmud. I love the commentaries of Rashi and the books of Maimonides. And there are also other people in Zhitomir who understand. And so all of us learned men fall to the floor and shout with a single voice, 'Woe unto us, where is the sweet Revolution?' "

The old man fell silent. And we saw the first star breaking through and meandering along the Milky Way.

"The Sabbath is beginning," Gedali pronounced solemnly. "Jews must go to the synagogue."

"*Pan* Comrade," he said, getting up, his top hat swaying on his head like a little black tower. "Bring a few good men to Zhitomir. *Oy,* they are lacking in our town, *oy,* how they are lacking! Bring good men and we shall give them all our gramophones. We are not simpletons. The International,* we know what the International is. And I want the International of good people, I want every soul to be accounted for and given first-class rations. Here, soul, eat, go ahead, go and find happiness in your life. The International, *Pan* Comrade, you have no idea how to swallow it!"

"With gunpowder," I tell the old man, "and seasoned with the best blood."

And then from the blue darkness young Sabbath climbed onto her throne.

"Gedali," I say to him, "today is Friday, and night has already fallen. Where can I find some Jewish biscuits, a Jewish glass of tea, and a piece of that retired God in the glass of tea?"

"You can't," Gedali answers, hanging a lock on his box, "you can't find any. There's a tavern next door, and good people used to run it, but people don't eat there anymore, they weep."

He fastened the three bone buttons of his green coat. He dusted himself with the cockerel feathers, sprinkled a little water on the soft palms of his hands, and walked off, tiny, lonely, dreamy, with his black top hat, and a large prayer book under his arm.

The Sabbath begins. Gedali, the founder of an unattainable International, went to the synagogue to pray.

---

* The Third Communist International, 1919–1943, an organization founded in Moscow by the delegates of twelve countries to promote Communism worldwide.

MY FIRST GOOSE

*S*avitsky, the commander of the Sixth Division, rose when he saw me, and I was taken aback by the beauty of his gigantic body. He rose—his breeches purple, his crimson cap cocked to the side, his medals pinned to his chest—splitting the hut in two like a banner splitting the sky. He smelled of perfume and the nauseating coolness of soap. His long legs looked like two girls wedged to their shoulders in shiny riding boots.

He smiled at me, smacked the table with his whip, and picked up the order which the chief of staff had just dictated. It was an order for Ivan Chesnokov to advance to Chugunov-Dobryvodka with the regiment he had been entrusted with, and, on encountering the enemy, to proceed immediately with its destruction.

". . . the destruction of which," Savitsky began writing, filling the whole sheet with his scrawl, "I hold the selfsame Chesnokov completely responsible for. Noncompliance will incur the severest punitive measures, in other words I will gun him down on the spot, a fact that I am sure that you, Comrade Chesnokov, will not doubt, as it's been quite a while now that you have worked with me on the front. . . ."

The commander of the Sixth Division signed the order with a flourish, threw it at the orderlies, and turned his gray eyes, dancing with merriment, toward me.

I handed him the document concerning my assignment to the divisional staff.

"See to the paperwork!" the division commander said. "See to the paperwork, and have this man sign up for all the amusements except for those of the frontal kind.* Can you read and write?"

"Yes, I can," I answered, bristling with envy at the steel and bloom of his youth. "I graduated in law from the University of Petersburg."

"So you're one of those little powder puffs!" he yelled, laughing. "With spectacles on your nose! Ha, you lousy little fellow, you! They send you to us, no one even asks us if we want you here! Here you get hacked to pieces just for wearing glasses! So, you think you can live with us, huh?"

"Yes, I do," I answered, and went to the village with the quartermaster to look for a place to stay.

The quartermaster carried my little traveling trunk on his shoulder. The village street lay before us, and the dying sun in the sky, round and yellow as a pumpkin, breathed its last rosy breath.

We came to a hut with garlands painted on it. The quartermaster stopped, and suddenly, smiling guiltily, said, "You see we have a thing about spectacles here, there ain't nothing you can do! A man of high distinguishings they'll chew up and spit out—but ruin a lady, yes, the most cleanest lady, and you're the darling of the fighters!"

He hesitated for a moment, my trunk still on his shoulder, came up very close to me, but suddenly lunged away in despair, rushing into the nearest courtyard. Cossacks were sitting there on bundles of hay, shaving each other.

"Fighters!" the quartermaster began, putting my trunk on the ground. "According to an order issued by Comrade Savitsky, you are required to accept this man to lodge among you. And no funny business, please, because this man has suffered on the fields of learning!"

The quartermaster flushed and marched off without looking back. I lifted my hand to my cap and saluted the Cossacks. A young fellow with long, flaxen hair and a wonderful Ryazan face walked up to my trunk and threw it out into the street. Then he turned his backside toward me, and with uncommon dexterity began emitting shameless sounds.

"That was a zero-zero caliber!" an older Cossack yelled, laughing out loud. "Rapid-fire!"

---

* The division commander is punning, substituting the word *udovolstvie,* "amusements," for *prodovolstvie,* "provisions."

The young man walked off, having exhausted the limited resources of his artistry. I went down on my hands and knees and gathered up the manuscripts and the old, tattered clothes that had fallen out of my trunk. I took them and carried them to the other end of the yard. A large pot of boiling pork stood on some bricks in front of the hut. Smoke rose from it as distant smoke rises from the village hut of one's childhood, mixing hunger with intense loneliness inside me. I covered my broken little trunk with hay, turning it into a pillow, and lay down on the ground to read Lenin's speech at the Second Congress of the Comintern,* which *Pravda* had printed. The sun fell on me through the jagged hills, the Cossacks kept stepping over my legs, the young fellow incessantly made fun of me, the beloved sentences struggled toward me over thorny paths, but could not reach me. I put away the newspaper and went to the mistress of the house, who was spinning yarn on the porch.

"Mistress," I said, "I need some grub!"

The old woman raised the dripping whites of her half-blind eyes to me and lowered them again.

"Comrade," she said, after a short silence. "All of this makes me want to hang myself!"

"Goddammit!" I muttered in frustration, shoving her back with my hand. "I'm in no mood to start debating with you!"

And, turning around, I saw someone's saber lying nearby. A haughty goose was waddling through the yard, placidly grooming its feathers. I caught the goose and forced it to the ground, its head cracking beneath my boot, cracking and bleeding. Its white neck lay stretched out in the dung, and the wings folded down over the slaughtered bird.

"Goddammit!" I said, poking at the goose with the saber. "Roast it for me, mistress!"

The old woman, her blindness and her spectacles flashing, picked up the bird, wrapped it in her apron, and hauled it to the kitchen.

"Comrade," she said after a short silence. "This makes me want to hang myself." And she pulled the door shut behind her.

---

* The Third Communist International, 1919–1943, an organization founded in Moscow by the delegates of twelve countries to promote Communism worldwide.

In the yard the Cossacks were already sitting around their pot. They sat motionless, straight-backed like heathen priests, not once having looked at the goose.

"This fellow'll fit in here well enough," one of them said, winked, and scooped up some cabbage soup with his spoon.

The Cossacks began eating with the restrained grace of muzhiks who respect one another. I cleaned the saber with sand, went out of the courtyard, and came back again, feeling anguished. The moon hung over the yard like a cheap earring.

"Hey, brother!" Surovkov, the oldest of the Cossacks, suddenly said to me. "Sit with us and have some of this till your goose is ready!"

He fished an extra spoon out of his boot and handed it to me. We slurped the cabbage soup and ate the pork.

"So, what are they writing in the newspaper?" the young fellow with the flaxen hair asked me, and moved aside to make room for me.

"In the newspaper, Lenin writes," I said, picking up my *Pravda*, "Lenin writes that right now there is a shortage of everything."

And in a loud voice, like a triumphant deaf man, I read Lenin's speech to the Cossacks.

The evening wrapped me in the soothing dampness of her twilight sheets, the evening placed her motherly palms on my burning brow.

I read, and rejoiced, waiting for the effect, rejoicing in the mysterious curve of Lenin's straight line.

"Truth tickles all and sundry in the nose,"* Surovkov said when I had finished. "It isn't all that easy to wheedle it out of the pile of rubbish, but Lenin picks it up right away, like a hen pecks up a grain of corn."

That is what Surovkov, the squadron commander, said about Lenin, and then we went to sleep in the hayloft. Six of us slept there warming each other, our legs tangled, under the holes in the roof which let in the stars.

I dreamed and saw women in my dreams, and only my heart, crimson with murder, screeched and bled.

---

* A pun on "truth," *Pravda*, which is also the name of the Russian daily that the narrator is reading to the Cossacks.

THE RABBI

"All things are mortal. Only a mother is accorded eternal life. And when a mother is not among the living, she leaves behind a memory that no one has yet dared to defile. The memory of a mother nourishes compassion within us, just as the ocean, the boundless ocean, nourishes the rivers that cut through the universe."

These were Gedali's words. He uttered them gravely. The dying evening wrapped him in the rosy haze of its sadness.

"In the ardent house of Hasidism," the old man said, "the windows and doors have been torn out, but it is as immortal as a mother's soul. Even with blinded eyes, Hasidism still stands at the crossroads of the winds of history."

That is what Gedali said, and, after having prayed in the synagogue, he took me to Rabbi Motale, the last rabbi of the Chernobyl dynasty.

Gedali and I walked up the main street. White churches glittered in the distance like fields of buckwheat. A gun cart moaned around the corner. Two pregnant Ukrainian women came out through the gates of a house, their coin necklaces jingling, and sat down on a bench. A timid star flashed in the orange battles of the sunset, and peace, a Sabbath peace, descended on the slanted roofs of the Zhitomir ghetto.

"Here," Gedali whispered, pointing at a long house with a shattered facade.

We went into a room, a stone room, empty as a morgue. Rabbi Motale sat at a table surrounded by liars and men possessed. He was wearing a sable hat and a white robe, with a rope for a belt. The rabbi was sitting, his eyes closed, his thin fingers digging through the yellow fluff of his beard.

"Where have you come from, Jew?" he asked me, lifting his eyelids.

"From Odessa," I answered.

"A devout town," the rabbi said. "The star of our exile, the reluctant well of our afflictions! What is the Jew's trade?"

"I am putting the adventures of Hershele of Ostropol* into verse."

"A great task," the rabbi whispered, and closed his eyelids. "The jackal moans when it is hungry, every fool has foolishness enough for despondency, and only the sage shreds the veil of existence with laughter . . . What did the Jew study?"

"The Bible."

"What is the Jew looking for?"

"Merriment."

"Reb Mordkhe," the rabbi said, and shook his beard. "Let the young man seat himself at the table, let him eat on the Sabbath evening with other Jews, let him rejoice that he is alive and not dead, let him clap his hands as his neighbors dance, let him drink wine if he is given wine!"

And Reb Mordkhe came bouncing toward me, an ancient fool with inflamed eyelids, a hunchbacked little old man, no bigger than a ten-year-old boy.

"*Oy*, my dear and so very young man!" ragged Reb Mordkhe said, winking at me. "*Oy*, how many rich fools have I known in Odessa, how many wise paupers have I known in Odessa! Sit down at the table, young man, and drink the wine that you will not be given!"

We all sat down, one next to the other—the possessed, the liars, the unhinged. In the corner, broad-shouldered Jews who looked like fishermen and apostles were moaning over prayer books. Gedali in his green coat dozed by the wall like a bright bird. And suddenly I saw a youth behind Gedali, a youth with the face of Spinoza, with the powerful forehead of Spinoza, with the sickly face of a nun. He was smoking and twitching like an escaped convict who has been tracked down and brought back to his jail. Ragged Reb Mordkhe sneaked up on him

* In Yiddish folklore, a trickster. See Babel's story "Shabos-Nakhamu."

from behind, snatched the cigarette from his mouth, and came running over to me.

"That is Ilya, the rabbi's son," Mordkhe wheezed, turning the bloody flesh of his inflamed eyelids to me, "the damned son, the worst son, the disobedient son!"

And Mordkhe threatened the youth with his little fist and spat in his face.

"Blessed is the Lord," the voice of Rabbi Motale Bratslavsky rang out, and he broke the bread with his monastic fingers. "Blessed is the God of Israel, who has chosen us among all the peoples of the world."

The rabbi blessed the food, and we sat down at the table. Outside the window horses neighed and Cossacks shouted. The wasteland of war yawned outside. The rabbi's son smoked one cigarette after another during the silence and the prayers. When the dinner was over, I was the first to rise.

"My dear and so very young man," Mordkhe muttered behind me, tugging at my belt. "If there was no one in the world except for evil rich men and destitute tramps, how would holy men live?"

I gave the old man some money and went out into the street. Gedali and I parted, and I went back to the railroad station. There at the station, on the propaganda train of the First Cavalry, I was greeted by the sparkle of hundreds of lights, the enchanted glitter of the radio transmitter, the stubborn rolling of the printing presses, and my unfinished article for the *Krasny Kavalerist*.*

---

* The newspaper *The Red Cavalryman*.

THE ROAD TO BRODY

I mourn for the bees. They have been destroyed by warring armies. There are no longer any bees in Volhynia.

We desecrated the hives. We fumigated them with sulfur and detonated them with gunpowder. Smoldering rags have spread a foul stench over the holy republics of the bees. Dying, they flew slowly, their buzzing barely audible. Deprived of bread, we procured honey with our sabers. There are no longer any bees in Volhynia.

The chronicle of our everyday crimes oppresses me as relentlessly as a bad heart. Yesterday was the first day of the battle for Brody. Lost on the blue earth, we suspected nothing—neither I, nor my friend Afonka Bida. The horses had been fed grain in the morning. The rye stood tall, the sun was beautiful, and our souls, which did not deserve these shining, soaring skies, thirsted for lingering pain.

"In our Cossack villages the womenfolk tell tales of the bee and its kind nature," my friend began. "The womenfolk tell all sorts of things. If men wronged Christ, or if no wrong was done, other people will have to figure out for themselves. But if you listen to what the womenfolk of the Cossack villages tell, Christ is hanging tormented on the cross, when suddenly all kinds of gnats come flying over to plague him! And he takes a good look at the gnats and his spirits fall. But the thousands of little gnats can't see his eyes. At that moment a bee flies around Christ. 'Sting him!' a gnat yells at the bee. 'Sting him for us!'—'That I cannot do,' the bee says, covering Christ with her wings. 'That I cannot do, he belongs to the carpenter class.' One has to understand the bees," Afonka, my platoon commander, concluded. "I hope the bees hold out. We're fighting for them too!"

Afonka waved dismissively and started to sing. It was a song about a light bay stallion. Eight Cossacks in Afonka's platoon joined in the song.

The light bay stallion, Dzhigit was his name, belonged to a junior Cossack captain who got drunk on vodka the memorial day of the Beheading of Saint John, sang Afonka sleepily, his voice taut like a string. Dzhigit had been a loyal horse, but on feast days the Cossack's carousing knew no bounds. He had five jugs of vodka on the memorial day of the Beheading of Saint John. After the fourth jug, the junior Cossack captain mounted his steed and rode up to heaven. The climb was long, but Dzhigit was a true horse. They rode into heaven, and the Cossack reached for his fifth jug. But the last jug had been left back on earth. He broke down and wept, for all his efforts had been in vain. He wept, and Dzhigit pointed his ears, and turned to look at his master. Afonka sang, clinking and dozing.

The song drifted like smoke. We rode toward the sunset, its boiling rivers pouring over the embroidered napkins of the peasants' fields. The silence turned rosy. The earth lay like a cat's back, covered with a thick, gleaming coat of grain. The mud hamlet of Klekotov crouched on a little hill. Beyond the pass, the vision of deadly, craggy Brody awaited us. But in Klekotov a loud shot exploded in our faces. Two Polish soldiers peered out from behind a hut. Their horses were tied to a post. A light enemy battery came riding up the hill. Bullets unfurled like string along the road.

"Run for it!" Afonka yelled.

And we fled.

Brody! The mummies of your trampled passions have breathed their irresistible poison upon me. I had felt the fatal chill of your eye sockets filled with frozen tears. And now, in a tumbling gallop, I am being carried away from the smashed stones of your synagogues. . . .

THE *TACHANKA** THEORY

*H*eadquarters sent me a coachman, or, as we generally say here, a vehicular driver. His name is Grishchuk. He is thirty-nine years old.

He had spent five years in a German prison camp, escaped a few months ago, walked across Lithuania and northwest Russia, reached Volhynia, only, in Byelov, to fall into the hands of what must be the world's most brainless draft commission, which reconscripted him into active service. He had been a mere fifty versts from his home in the Kremenec District. He has a wife and children in the Kremenec District. He hasn't been home for five years and two months. The Draft Commission made him my vehicular driver, and now I am no longer a pariah among the Cossacks.

I have a *tachanka* and a driver for it. *Tachanka!* That word has become the base of the triangle on which our way of fighting rests: hack to pieces—*tachanka*—blood.

The simplest little open carriage, the *britzka,* the kind you would see some cleric or petty official riding in, has, through a whim of all the civil strife, become a terrible and fast-moving war machine, creating new strategies and tactics, twisting the traditional face of war, spawning *tachanka* heroes and geniuses. Such was Makhno,[†] who had made the *tachanka* the crux of his secretive and cunning strategy, abolishing infantry, artillery, even cavalry, and replaced that clumsy hodgepodge by

---

* An open carriage or buggy with a machine gun mounted on the back.
† The Ukrainian anarchist leader.

mounting three hundred machine guns onto *britzkas*. Such was Makhno, as innovative as nature: hay carts lined up in military formation to conquer towns. A wedding procession rolls up to the headquarters of a provincial executive committee, opens fire, and a frail little cleric, waving the black flag of anarchy, demands that the authorities immediately hand over the bourgeois, hand over the proletariat, hand over music and wine.

An army of *tachankas* is capable of unprecedented mobility.

Budyonny was just as adept at demonstrating this as Makhno was. To hack away at such an army is difficult, to corner it impossible. A machine gun buried under a stack of hay, a *tachanka* hidden in a peasant's shed, cease to be military targets. These hidden specks—the hypothetically existing but imperceptible components of a whole—when added up result in the new essence of the Ukrainian village: savage, rebellious, and self-seeking. Makhno can bring an army like this, its ammunition concealed in all its nooks and crannies, into military readiness within an hour, and can demobilize it even faster.

Here, in Budyonny's Red Cavalry, the *tachanka* does not rule so exclusively. But all our machine gun detachments travel only in *britzkas*. Cossack fantasy distinguishes two kinds of *tachanka*, "German settler" and "petty official," which is not fantasy but a real distinction.

The petty official *britzkas*, those rickety little carts built without love or imagination, had rattled through the wheat steppes of Kuban carrying the wretched, red-nosed civil servants, a sleep-starved herd of men hurrying to autopsies and inquests, while the settler *tachankas* came to us from the fat German settlements of the Volga regions of Samara and the Urals. The broad oaken seat backs of the settler *tachankas* are covered with simple paintings, plump garlands of rosy German flowers. The sturdy cart decks are reinforced with steel. The frame rests on soft, unforgettable springs. I can feel the ardor of many generations in these springs, now bouncing over the torn-up high roads of Volhynia.

I am experiencing the delight of first possession. Every day after we eat, we put on the harnesses. Grishchuk leads the horses out of the stable. They are becoming stronger with every passing day. With proud joy I notice a dull sheen on their groomed flanks. We rub the horses' swollen legs, trim their manes, throw Cossack harnesses—a tangled, withered mesh of thin straps—over their backs, and drive out of the yard at a fast trot. Grishchuk is sitting sideways on the box. My seat is covered with a bright sackcloth and hay smelling of perfume and tranquillity. The high wheels creak in the white, granular sand. Patches of blooming poppies color the earth, ruined churches glow on the hills. High above the road, in a niche wrecked by shells, stands the brown statue of Saint Ursula with bare round arms. And narrow, ancient letters form an uneven chain on the blackened gold of her pediment: "Glory Be to Jesus and the Mother of God."

Lifeless Jewish shtetls cluster around the foot of the Polish nobles' estates. The prophetic peacock, a passionless apparition in the blue vastness, glitters on brick walls. The synagogue, enmeshed in a tangle of huts, crouches eyeless and battered, round as a Hasidic hat, on the barren earth. Narrow-shouldered Jews hover sadly at crossroads. And the image of southern Jews flares up in my memory—jovial, potbellied, sparkling like cheap wine. There is no comparison between them and the bitter aloofness of these long bony backs, these tragic yellow beards. In their fervent features, carved by torture, there is no fat or warm pulse of blood. The movements of the Galician and the Volhynian Jew are abrupt, brusque, and offensive to good taste, but the power of their grief is filled with dark grandeur, and their secret contempt for the Polish masters is boundless. Looking at them, I understood the fiery history of these faraway hinterlands, the stories of Talmudists who leased out taverns, of rabbis who dabbled in moneylending, of girls who were raped by Polish mercenaries and over whom Polish magnates dueled.

DOLGUSHOV'S DEATH

*T*he veils of battle swept toward the town. At midday, Korotchaev, the disgraced commander of the Fourth Division, who fought alone and rode out seeking death, flew past us in his black Caucasian cloak. As he came galloping by, he shouted over to me, "Our communications have been cut, Radzivillov and Brody are in flames!"

And off he charged—fluttering, black, with eyes of coal.

On the plain, flat as a board, the brigades were regrouping. The sun rolled through the crimson dust. Wounded men sat in ditches, eating. Nurses lay on the grass and sang in hushed voices. Afonka's scouts roamed over the field, looking for dead soldiers and ammunition. Afonka rode by two paces from me and, without turning his head, said, "We got a real kick in the teeth! Big time! They're saying things about our division commander—it looks like he's out. Our fighters don't know what's what!"

The Poles had advanced to the forest about three versts away from us, and set up their machine guns somewhere nearby. Flying bullets whimper and yelp; their lament has reached an unbearable pitch. The bullets plunge into the earth and writhe, quaking with impatience. Vytyagaichenko, the commander of the regiment, snoring in the hot sun, cried out in his sleep and woke up. He mounted his horse and rode over to the lead squadron. His face was creased with red stripes from his uncomfortable sleep, and his pockets were filled with plums.

"Son of a bitch!" he said angrily, spitting out a plum stone. "A damn waste of time! Timoshka, hoist the flag!"

"Oh, so we're going for it?" Timoshka asked, pulling the flagpole out of the stirrup, and unrolling the flag on which a star had been painted, along with something about the Third International.*

"We'll see what happens," Vytyagaichenko said, and suddenly shouted wildly, "Come on, girls, onto your horses! Gather your men, squadron leaders!"

The buglers sounded the alarm. The squadrons lined up in a column. A wounded man crawled out of a ditch and, shading his eyes with his hand, said to Vytyagaichenko, "Taras Grigorevich, I represent the others here. It looks like you're leaving us behind."

"Don't worry, you'll manage to fight them off," Vytyagaichenko muttered, and reared his horse.

"We sort of think we won't be able to fight them off, Taras Grigorevich," the wounded man called after Vytyagaichenko as he rode off.

Vytyagaichenko turned back his horse. "Stop whimpering! Of course I won't leave you!" And he ordered the carts to be harnessed.

At that very moment the whining, high-pitched voice of my friend Afonka Bida burst out, "Let's not set off at full trot, Taras Grigorevich! It's five versts. How are we supposed to hack them down if our horses are worn out? Why the rush? You'll be there in time for the pear pruning on St. Mary's Day!"

"Slow trot!" Vytyagaichenko ordered, without raising his eyes.

The regiment rode off.

"If what they're saying about the division commander is true," Afonka whispered, reining in his horse, "and they're getting rid of him, well then thank you very much—we might as well kill off the cattle and burn down the barn!"

Tears flowed from his eyes. I looked at him in amazement. He spun like a top, held his cap down, wheezed, and then charged off with a loud whoop.

Grishchuk, with his ridiculous *tachanka*,† and I stayed behind, rushing back and forth among walls of fire until the evening. Our divisional staff had disappeared. Other units wouldn't take us in. The reg-

---

* The Third Communist International, 1919–1943, an organization founded in Moscow by the delegates of twelve countries to promote Communism worldwide.
† An open carriage or buggy with a machine gun mounted on the back.

iments pushed forward into Brody but were repelled. We rode to the town cemetery. A Polish patrol jumped up from behind the graves, put their rifles to their shoulders, and started firing at us. Grishchuk spun his *tachanka* around. It shrieked with all its four wheels.

"Grishchuk!" I yelled through the whistling and the wind.

"What damn stupidity!" he shouted back morosely.

"We're done for!" I hollered, seized by the exhilaration of disaster. "We're finished!"

"All the trouble our womenfolk go to!" he said even more morosely. "What's the point of all the matchmaking, marrying, and in-laws dancing at weddings?"

A rosy tail lit up in the sky and expired. The Milky Way surfaced from under the stars.

"It makes me want to laugh!" Grishchuk said sadly, and pointed his whip at a man sitting at the side of the road. "It makes me want to laugh that women go to such trouble!"

The man sitting by the roadside was Dolgushov, one of the telephonists. He stared at us, his legs stretched out in front of him.

"Here, look," Dolgushov said, as we pulled up to him. "I'm finished . . . know what I mean?"

"I know," Grishchuk answered, reining in the horses.

"You'll have to waste a bullet on me," Dolgushov said.

He was sitting propped up against a tree. He lay with his legs splayed far apart, his boots pointing in opposite directions. Without lowering his eyes from me, he carefully lifted his shirt. His stomach was torn open, his intestines spilling to his knees, and we could see his heart beating.

"When the Poles turn up, they'll have fun kicking me around. Here's my papers. Write my mother where, what, why."

"No," I replied, and spurred my horse.

Dolgushov placed his blue palms on the ground and looked at his hands in disbelief.

"Running away?" he muttered, slumping down. "Then run, you bastard!"

Sweat slithered over my body. The machine guns hammered faster and faster with hysterical tenacity. Afonka Bida came galloping toward us, encircled by the halo of the sunset.

"We're kicking their asses!" he shouted merrily. "What're you up to here, fun and games?"

I pointed at Dolgushov and moved my horse to the side.

They spoke a few words, I couldn't hear what they said. Dolgushov held out his papers. Afonka slipped them into his boot and shot Dolgushov in the mouth.

"Afonka," I said, riding up to him with a pitiful smile. "*I* couldn't have done that."

"Get lost, or I'll shoot you!" he said to me, his face turning white. "You spectacled idiots have as much pity for us as a cat has for a mouse!"

And he cocked his trigger.

I rode off slowly, without looking back, a feeling of cold and death in my spine.

"Hey! Hey!" Grishchuk shouted behind me, and grabbed Afonka's hand. "Cut the crap!"

"You damn lackey bastard!" Afonka yelled at Grishchuk. "Wait till I get my hands on him!"

Grishchuk caught up with me at the bend in the road. Afonka was not with him. He had ridden off in the opposite direction.

"Well, there you have it, Grishchuk," I said to him. "Today I lost Afonka, my first real friend."

Grishchuk took out a wrinkled apple from under the cart seat.

"Eat it," he told me, "please, eat it."

THE COMMANDER OF
THE SECOND BRIGADE

General Budyonny, in his red trousers with the silver stripes, stood by a tree. The commander of the Second Brigade had just been killed. The general had appointed Kolesnikov to replace him.

Only an hour ago, Kolesnikov had been a regimental captain. A week ago Kolesnikov had been a squadron leader.

The new brigade commander was summoned to General Budyonny. The general waited for him, standing by the tree. Kolesnikov came with Almazov, his commissar.

"The bastards are closing in on us," the general said with his dazzling grin. "We win, or we die like dogs. No other options. Understood?"

"Understood," Kolesnikov answered, his eyes bulging from their sockets.

"You run for it, I'll have you shot," the general said with a smile, and he turned and looked at the commander of the special unit.

"Yes, General!" the commander of the special unit said.

"So start rolling, Koleso!"* one of the Cossacks standing nearby shouted cheerfully.

Budyonny swiftly turned on his heel and saluted his new brigade commander. The latter lifted five young red fingers to his cap, broke into a sweat, and walked along the plowed field. The horses were waiting for him fifty yards away. He hung his head, placing one long and

*A pun: Koleso, short for Kolesnikov, means "wheel."

crooked leg in front of the other with agonizing slowness. The fire of the sunset swept over him, as crimson and implausible as impending doom.

And suddenly, on the outstretched earth, on the yellow, harrowed nakedness of the fields, we saw nothing but Kolesnikov's narrow back, his dangling arms, and his hanging head with its gray cap.

His orderly brought him his horse.

He jumped into the saddle and galloped to his brigade without looking back. The squadrons were waiting for him on the main road, the high road to Brody.

A moaning hurrah, shredded by the wind, drifted over to us.

Aiming my binoculars, I saw the brigade commander on his horse circling through columns of thick dust.

"Kolesnikov has taken over the brigade," said our lookout, who was sitting in a tree above our heads.

"So he has," Budyonny answered, lighting a cigarette and closing his eyes.

The hurrahs faded. The cannonade died down. Pointless shrapnel burst above the forest. And we heard the great, silent carnage.

"He's a good boy," Budyonny said, getting up. "Wants honors. Looks like he'll make it." And Budyonny had the horses brought over, and rode off to the battlefield. His Staff followed him.

As it happened, I was to see Kolesnikov again that very night, about an hour after the Poles had been finished off. He was riding in front of his brigade, alone, on a brown stallion, dozing. His right arm was hanging in a sling. A cavalry Cossack was carrying the unfurled flag about ten paces behind him. The men at the head of the squadron lazily sang bawdy ditties. The brigade stretched dusty and endless, like peasant carts heading to a market fair. At the rear, tired bands were gasping.

That evening, as Kolesnikov rode, I saw in his bearing the despotic indifference of a Tatar khan and saw in him a devotee of the glorified Kniga, the willful Pavlichenko, and the captivating Savitsky.

SASHKA CHRIST

Sashka, that was his real name, and Christ is what we called him because he was so gentle. He had been one of the shepherds of his Cossack village and had not done any heavy work since he was fourteen, when he had caught the evil disease.

This is what had happened. Tarakanich, Sashka's stepfather, had gone to the town of Grozny for the winter, and had joined a guild there. The guild was working well—it was made up of Ryazan muzhiks. Tarakanich did carpentry for them, and his income increased. When he realized that he could not manage the work alone anymore, he sent home for the boy to come and be his assistant—the village could survive the winter well enough without him. Sashka worked with his stepfather for a week. Then Saturday came, and they put their tools away and sat down to drink some tea. Outside it was October, but the air was mild. They opened the window, and put on a second samovar. A beggar woman was loitering near the windows. She knocked on the frame and said, "A good day to you! I see you're not from these parts. You can see what state I'm in, no?"

"What is it about your state?" Tarakanich said. "Come in, you old cripple!"

The beggar woman scrambled up and clambered into the room. She came over to the table and bowed deeply. Tarakanich grabbed her by her kerchief, pulled it off, and ruffled her hair. The beggar woman's hair was gray, ashy, and hanging in dusty tatters.

"Ooh, will you stop that, you naughty handsome man you!" she said. "You're a joke a minute, you are! But please, don't be disgusted by me just because I'm a little old woman," she quickly whispered, scampering onto the bench.

Tarakanich lay with her. The beggar woman turned her head to the side and laughed.

"Ooh, luck is raining on this little old woman's field!" she laughed. "I'll be harvesting two hundred *pood* of grain an acre!"

And she suddenly noticed Sashka, who was drinking his tea at the table, not looking up as if his life depended on it.

"Your boy?" she asked Tarakanich.

"More or less mine," Tarakanich answered. "My wife's."

"Ooh, look at him staring at us," the old woman said. "Hey, come over here!"

Sashka went over to her—and he caught the evil disease. But the evil disease had been the last thing on their minds. Tarakanich gave the beggar woman some leftover bones and a silver fiver, a very shiny one.

"Polish the fiver nicely with sand, holy sister," Tarakanich said to her, "and it'll look even better. If you lend it to the Almighty on a dark night, it will shine instead of the moon."

The old cripple tied her kerchief, took the bones, and left. And within two weeks the muzhiks realized what had happened. The evil disease made them suffer. They tried to cure themselves all winter long, dousing themselves with herbs. And in spring they returned to the Cossack village and their peasant work.

The village was about nine versts from the railroad. Tarakanich and Sashka crossed the fields. The earth lay in its April wetness. Emeralds glittered in the black ditches. Green shoots hemmed the soil with cunning stitches. A sour odor rose from the ground, as from a soldier's wife at dawn. The first herds trickled down from the hills, the foals played in the blue expanse of the horizon.

Tarakanich and Sashka walked along barely visible paths.

"Let me be one of the shepherds, Tarakanich," Sashka said.

"What for?"

"I can't bear that the shepherds have such a wonderful life."

"I won't allow it."

"Let me be one, Tarakanich, for the love of God!" Sashka repeated. "All the saints came from shepherds."

"Sashka the Saint!" the stepfather laughed. "He caught syphilis from the Mother of God!"

They passed the bend in the road by Red Bridge, then the grove and the pasture, and saw the cross on the village church.

The women were still puttering around in their vegetable gardens, and Cossacks were sitting among the lilacs, drinking vodka and singing. It was another half verst to Tarakanich's hut.

"Let us pray that everything is fine," Tarakanich said, crossing himself.

They walked over to the hut and peeked in the little window. Nobody was there. Sashka's mother was in the shed milking the cow. They crept over to her silently. Tarakanich came up behind her and laughed out loud.

"Motya, Your Excellency," he shouted, "how about some food for your guests!"

The woman turned around, began to shake, and rushed out of the shed and ran circling around the yard. Then she came back into the shed and, trembling, pressed her head on Tarakanich's chest.

"How silly and ugly you look," Tarakanich said, gently pushing her away. "Where are the children?"

"The children have left the yard," the woman said, her face ashen, and ran out again, throwing herself onto the ground.

"Oh, Aleshonka!" she shrieked wildly. "Our babies have gone, feet first!"

Tarakanich waved at her dismissively and went over to the neighbors. The neighbors told him that a week ago the Lord had taken the boy and the girl with typhus. Motya had written him a letter, but he probably hadn't gotten it. Tarakanich went back to the hut. The woman was stoking the oven.

"You got rid of them quite nicely, Motya," Tarakanich said. "Rip you to pieces, that's what I should do!"

He sat down at the table and fell into deep grief—and grieved till he fell asleep. He ate meat and drank vodka, and did not see to his work around the farm. He snored at the table, woke up, and snored again. Motya prepared a bed for herself and her husband, and another for Sashka to the side. She blew out the light, and lay down next to her husband. Sashka tossed and turned on the hay in his corner. His eyes were open, he did not sleep, but saw, as if in a dream, the hut, a star shining through the window, the edge of the table, and the horse collars under his mother's bed. A violent vision took hold of him; he surrendered to it and rejoiced in his waking dream. It was as if two silver strings hung from the sky, entwined into a thick rope to which a cradle was fastened, a rosewood cradle with carvings. It swung high above the earth but far from the sky, and the silver rope swayed and glittered. Sashka was lying in this cradle, fanned by the air. The air, loud as music, rose from the fields, and the rainbow blossomed above the unripe wheat.

Sashka rejoiced in his waking sleep, and closed his eyes so as not to see the horse collars under his mother's bed. Then he heard panting from the bed, and thought that Tarakanich must be pawing his mother.

"Tarakanich," he said loudly. "There's something I need to talk to you about."

"In the middle of the night?" Tarakanich yelled angrily. "Sleep, you fleabag!"

"I swear by the Holy Cross that there's something I need to talk to you about," Sashka said. "Come out into the yard!"

And in the yard, beneath the unfading stars, Sashka said to his stepfather, "Don't wrong my mother, Tarakanich, you're tainted."

"You should know better than to cross me, boy!" Tarakanich said.

"I know, but have you seen my mother's body? She has legs that are clean, and a breast that is clean. Don't wrong her, Tarakanich. We're tainted."

"Boy!" his stepfather said. "Avoid my blood and my wrath! Here are twenty kopeks, go to sleep and your head will be clearer in the morning."

"I don't need the twenty kopeks," Sashka muttered. "Let me go join the shepherds."

"I won't allow that," Tarakanich said.

"Let me join the shepherds," Sashka muttered, "or I'll tell Mother what we are. Why should she suffer with such a body?"

Tarakanich turned around and went into the shed to get an axe.

"Saint Sashka," he said in a whisper, "you wait and see, I'll hack you to pieces!"

"You'd hack me to pieces on account of a woman?" the boy said, barely audibly, and leaned closer to his stepfather. "Take pity on me and let me join the shepherds."

"Damn you!" Tarakanich said, and threw away the axe. "So go join the shepherds!"

And Tarakanich went back into the hut and slept with his wife.

That same morning Sashka went to the Cossacks to be hired, and from that day on he lived as a village shepherd. He became known throughout the whole area for his simple heart, and the people of the village gave him the nickname Sashka Christ, and he lived as a shepherd until he was drafted. The old men, who had nothing better to do, came out to the pasture to chat with him, and the women came running to Sashka for respite from their husbands' rough ways, and were not put off by Sashka's love for them or by his illness. Sashka's draft call came in the first year of the war. He fought for four years, and then returned to the village, where the Whites were running the show. Sashka was urged to go to the village of Platovskaya, where a detachment was being formed to fight the Whites. A former cavalry sergeant-major—Semyon Mikhailovich Budyonny—was running things in that detachment, and he had his three brothers with him: Emelian, Lukian, and Denis. Sashka went to Platovskaya, and there his fate was sealed. He joined Budyonny's regiment, his brigade, his division, and finally his First Cavalry Army. He rode to the aid of heroic Tsaritsyn,[*] joined with Voroshilov's Tenth Army, and fought at Voronezh, Kastornaya, and at the Generalsky Bridge on the Donets. In the Polish Campaign, Sashka was transferred to the cavalry transport unit, because he had been wounded and was considered an invalid.

So that's how everything had come about. I had recently met Sashka Christ, and took my little suitcase and moved over to his cart. Many times we watched the sunrise and rode into the sunset. And whenever the obdurate will of war brought us together, we sat in the evenings on a sparkling earth mound,[†] or boiled tea in our sooty kettle in the woods, or slept next to each other on harvested fields, our hungry horses tied to our legs.

---

[*] Renamed Stalingrad in 1925 in honor of Joseph Stalin, who had played a major role in the defense of the city against General Denikin's White Russian Army. Today Volgograd.

[†] *Zavalinka:* a mound of earth around a Russian peasant hut that protects it from the weather and is often used for sitting outside.

THE LIFE OF MATVEY
RODIONOVICH PAVLICHENKO

*D*ear comrades, brothers, fellow countrymen! Hear in the name of mankind the life story of Red General Matvey Pavlichenko. This general had been a mere swineherd, a swineherd on the estate of Lidino of which Nikitinsky was master, and, until life gave him battle stripes, this swineherd tended his master's pigs, and then with those battle stripes our little Matvey was given cattle to herd. Who knows— had he been born in Australia, my friends, our Matvey, son of Rodion, might well have worked his way up to elephants, yes, our Matyushka would have herded elephants, but unfortunately there are no elephants to be found in our district of Stavropol. To be perfectly honest, there is no animal larger than a buffalo in all the lands of Stavropol. And the poor fellow would not have had any fun with buffaloes—Russians don't enjoy taunting buffaloes. Give us poor orphans a mare on Judgment Day, and I guarantee you we will know how to taunt her till her soul goes tearing out of her sides.

So here I am, herding my cattle, cows crowding me from all sides, I'm doused in milk, I stink like a slit udder, all around me calves and mouse-gray bullocks roam. Freedom lies all around me in the fields, the grass of all the world rustles, the skies above me open up like a many-buttoned concertina, and the skies, my brothers, the skies we have in the district of Stavropol, can be very blue. So there I am, herding the beasts and playing my flute to the winds with nothing better to do, when an old man comes up to me and tells me, "Go, Matvey," he says to me, "go to Nastya."

"What for?" I ask him. "Or are you maybe pulling my leg, old man?"

"Go to her," he says. "She wants you."

So I go to her.

"Nastya!" I say to her, and all my blood runs dark. "Nastya," I say to her, "or are you making fun of me?"

But she does not speak a word, runs straight past me, running as fast as her legs can carry her, and she and I run together until we're out on the meadow, dead tired, flushed, and out of breath.

"Matvey," Nastya says to me at this point. "On the third Sunday before this one, when the spring fishing season began and the fishermen came back to shore, you were walking with them, and you let your head hang. Why did you let your head hang, or is it that a thought is squeezing down on your heart? Answer me!"

And I answer her.

"Nastya," I say to her. "I have nothing to tell you, my head is not a gun, it has neither a fore-sight nor back-sight, and you know my heart full well, Nastya, it is empty, completely empty, except perhaps for being doused in milk—it's a terrible thing how I stink of milk!"

And I can see that Nastya is about to burst into laughter at my words.

"I swear by the Holy Cross," she says, bursting into laughter, laughing loudly, laughing with all her might, her laughter booming across the steppes as if she were pounding a drum, "I swear by the Holy Cross, you sure know how to sweet-talk a girl!"

So we exchange a few foolish words, and soon enough we're married. Nastya and me began living together as best we could, and we did our best. We felt hot all night, we felt hot all winter, all night we went naked and tore the hide off each other. We lived it up like devils, until the day the old man came to me again.

"Matvey," he says. "The other day the master touched your wife in all those places, and the master is going to have her."

And I say to him, "No," I say to him, "it cannot be, and please excuse me, old man, or I shall kill you right here and now."

The old man rushed off without another word, and I must have marched a good twenty versts over land that day, yes, that day a good chunk of earth passed beneath my feet, and by evening I sprouted up in the estate of Lidino, in the house of my merry master Nikitinsky. The old man was sitting in his drawing room busy taking apart three saddles, an English, a dragoon, and a Cossack saddle, and I stood rooted by his door like a burdock, I stood rooted there for a good hour. Then he finally clapped eyes on me.

"What do you want?"

"I want to quit."

"You have a grudge against me?"

"I don't have a grudge, but I want to quit."

At this point he turned his eyes away, leaving the high road for the field path, put the red saddlecloths on the floor—they were redder than the Czar's banners, his saddlecloths were—and old Nikitinsky stepped on them, puffing himself up.

"Freedom to the free," he tells me, all puffed up. "Your mothers, all Orthodox Christian women, I gave the lot of them a good plowing! You can quit, my dear little Matvey, but isn't there one tiny little thing you owe me first?"

"Ho, ho!" I answer. "What a joker! May the Lord strike me dead if you're not a joker! It is *you* who still owes *me* my wage!"

"Your wage!" my master thunders, shoving me down onto my knees, kicking me and yelling in my ear, cursing the Father, the Son, and the Holy Ghost. "You want your wage, but the bull's yoke you ruined seems to have slipped your mind! Where is my bull's yoke? Give me back my bull's yoke!"

"I will give you back your bull's yoke," I tell my master, raising my foolish eyes up at him as I kneel there, lower than the lowest of living creatures. "I'll give you back your bull's yoke, but don't strangle me with debts, master, just wait awhile!"

So, my dear friends, my Stavropol compatriots, fellow countrymen, my comrades, my very own brothers: for five years the master waited with my debts, five years I lost, until, lost soul that I was, finally the year '18 came!* It rode in on merry stallions, on Kabardinian steeds! It brought big armies with it and many songs. O, my sweet year '18! O, for us to dance in each other's arms just one more time, my sweet darling year '18! We sang your songs, drank your wine, proclaimed your

*1918, the year following the Bolshevik Revolution.

truth, but all that's left of you now is a few scribblers! Yet, ah, my love, it was not the scribblers back then who came flying through Kuban, shooting the souls of generals to Kingdom Come! No! It was me, Matvey Rodionovich, who lay outside Prikumsk in a pool of my own blood, and from where I, Matvey Rodionovich, lay to the estate of Lidino was a mere five versts. And I rode to Lidino alone, without my regiment, and as I entered the drawing room, I entered peacefully. People from the local authorities were sitting there in the drawing room, Nikitinsky was serving them tea, groveling all over them. When he saw me his face tumbled to pieces, but I lifted my fur hat to him.

"Greetings," I said to the people there. "Greetings. May I come in, your lordship, or how shall we handle this?"

"Let's handle this nicely, correctly," one of the men says, who, judging by the way he speaks, must be a land surveyor. "Let us handle things nicely, correctly, but from what I see, Comrade Pavlichenko, it seems you have ridden quite a distance, and dirt has crossed your face from side to side. We, the local authorities, are frightened of such faces. Why is your face like that?"

"Because you are the local cold-blooded authorities," I answer. "Because in my face one cheek has been burning for five years now, burning when I'm in a trench, burning when I'm with a woman, and it will be burning at my final judgment! At my final judgment!" I tell him, and look at Nikitinsky with fake cheerfulness. But he no longer has any eyes—there are now two cannonballs in the middle of his face, ready and in position under his forehead, and with these crystal balls he winks at me, also with fake cheerfulness, but so abominably.

"My dear Matyusha," he says to me, "we've known each other so long now, and my wife Nadyezhda Vasilevna, whose mind has come unhinged on account of the times we're living in, she was always kind to you, Nadyezhda Vasilevna was, and you, my dear Matyusha, always looked up to her above all others! Wouldn't you like to at least see her, even though her mind has come unhinged?"

"Fine," I tell him, and follow him into another room, and there he started clasping my hands, the right one, then the left.

"Matyusha!" he says. "Are you my fate or are you not?"

"No," I tell him. "And stop using such words! God has dropped us lackeys and run. Our fate is a chicken with its head cut off, our life is not worth a kopeck! Stop using such words and let me read you Lenin's letter!"

"Lenin wrote me, Nikitinsky, a letter?"

"Yes, he wrote you a letter," I tell him, and take out the order book, open it to an empty page, and read—though I'm illiterate to the bottom of my soul. "In the name of the people," I read, "for the establishment of a future radiant life, I order Pavlichenko—Matvey Rodionovich—to deprive, at his discretion, various persons of their lives."

"There we are," I tell him. "That is Lenin's letter to you!"

And he says to me, "No!"

"No," he says, "my dear Matyusha, even if life has gone tumbling to the devil, and blood has become cheap in Holy Mother Russia! But regardless of how much blood you want, you'll get it anyway, and you'll even forget my last dying look, so wouldn't it be better if I just show you my secret hideaway?"

"Show me," I tell him. "Maybe it'll be for the better."

And again we went through the rooms, climbed down into the wine cellar, where he pulled out a brick, and behind this brick lay a little case. In it, in this case, were rings, necklaces, medals, and a pearl-studded icon. He threw the case over to me and stood there rigidly.

"Take it!" he says. "Take what is most holy to the Nikitinskys, and go off to your den in Prikumsk!"

And here I grabbed him by the neck, by the hair.

"And what about my cheek?" I tell Nikitinsky. "How am I supposed to live with my cheek this way?"

And he burst out laughing for all he was worth, and stopped struggling to get away.

"A jackal's conscience," he says, and does not struggle. "I speak to you as to an officer of the Russian Empire, and you, you scum, were suckled by a she-wolf. Shoot me, you son of a bitch!"

But shoot him I did not—I did not owe him a shot. I just dragged him up to the sitting room. There in the sitting room Nadyezhda Vasilevna was wandering about completely mad, with a drawn saber in her hand, looking at herself in the mirror. And when I dragged Nikitinsky into the sitting room, Nadyezhda Vasilevna runs to sit in the chair, and she is wearing a velvet crown and feathers on her head. She sat in the chair and saluted me with the saber. Then I started kicking Nikitinsky, my master, I kicked him for an hour, maybe even more than an hour, and I really understood what life actually is. With one shot, let me tell you, you can only get rid of a person. A shot would have been a pardon for him and too horribly easy for me, with a shot you cannot get to a man's soul, to where the soul hides and what it looks like. But there are times when I don't spare myself and spend a good hour, maybe even more than an hour, kicking the enemy. I want to understand life, to see what it actually is.

THE CEMETERY IN
KOZIN

*T*he cemetery in a shtetl. Assyria and the mysterious decay of the East on the overgrown, weed-covered fields of Volhynia.

Gray, abraded stones with letters three hundred years old. The rough contours of the reliefs cut into the granite. The image of a fish and a sheep above a dead man's head. Images of rabbis wearing fur hats. Rabbis, their narrow hips girded with belts. Beneath their eyeless faces the wavy stone ripple of curly beards. To one side, below an oak tree cleft in two by lightning, stands the vault of Rabbi Azriil, slaughtered by Bogdan Khmelnitsky's Cossacks. Four generations lie in this sepulcher, as poor as the hovel of a water carrier, and tablets, moss-green tablets, sing of them in Bedouin prayer:

> *"Azriil, son of Anania, mouth of Jehovah.*
> *Elijah, son of Azriil, mind that has wrestled with oblivion.*
> *Wolf, son of Elijah, prince taken from his Torah in his nineteenth spring.*
> *Judah, son of Wolf, Rabbi of Krakow and Prague.*
> *O death, O mercenary, O covetous thief, why did you not, albeit one single time, have mercy upon us?"*

PRISHCHEPA

I'm making my way to Leshniov, where the divisional staff has set up quarters. My traveling companion, as usual, is Prishchepa, a young Cossack from Kuban, a tireless roughneck, a Communist whom the party kicked out, a future rag looter, a devil-may-care syphilitic, an unflappable liar. He wears a crimson Circassian jacket made of fine cloth, with a ruffled hood trailing down his back. As we rode, he told me about himself.

A year ago Prishchepa had run away from the Whites. As a reprisal, they took his parents hostage and killed them at the interrogation. The neighbors ransacked everything they had. When the Whites were driven out of Kuban, Prishchepa returned to his Cossack village.

It was morning, daybreak, peasant sleep sighed in the rancid stuffiness. Prishchepa hired a communal cart and went through the village picking up his gramophone, kvas jugs, and the napkins that his mother had embroidered. He went down the street in his black cloak, his curved dagger in his belt. The cart rattled behind him. Prishchepa went from one neighbor's house to the next, the bloody prints of his boots trailing behind him. In huts where he found his mother's things or his father's pipe, he left hacked-up old women, dogs hung over wells, icons soiled with dung. The people of the village smoked their pipes and followed him sullenly with their eyes. Young Cossacks had gathered on the steppes outside the village and were keeping count. The count rose and the village fell silent. When he had finished, Prishchepa returned to his ransacked home. He arranged his reclaimed furniture the way he remembered it from his childhood, and ordered vodka to be brought to him. He locked himself in the hut and for two days drank, sang, cried, and hacked tables to pieces with his saber.

On the third night, the village saw smoke rising above Prishchepa's hut. Seared and gashed, he came staggering out of the shed pulling the cow behind him, stuck his revolver in her mouth, and shot her. The earth smoked beneath his feet, a blue ring of flame flew out of the chimney and melted away, the abandoned calf began wailing. The fire was as bright as a holy day. Prishchepa untied his horse, jumped into the saddle, threw a lock of his hair into the flames, and vanished.

THE STORY OF
A HORSE

One day Savitsky, our division commander, took for himself a
white stallion belonging to Khlebnikov, the commander of the
First Squadron. It was a horse of imposing stature, but with a somewhat raw build, which always seemed a little heavy to me. Khlebnikov
was given a black mare of pretty good stock and good trot. But he mis-
treated the mare, hankered for revenge, waited for an opportunity, and
when it came, pounced on it.

After the unsuccessful battles of July, when Savitsky was dismissed
from his duties and sent to the command personnel reserves,
Khlebnikov wrote to army headquarters requesting that his horse be
returned to him. On the letter, the chief of staff penned the decision:
"Aforementioned stallion is to be returned to primordial owner." And
Khlebnikov, rejoicing, rode a hundred versts to find Savitsky, who was
living at the time in Radzivillov, a mangled little town that looked like
a tattered old whore. The dismissed division commander was living
alone, the fawning lackeys at headquarters no longer knew him. The
fawning lackeys at headquarters were busy angling for roasted chickens
in the army commander's smiles, and, vying to outgrovel each other,
had turned their backs on the glorious division commander.

Drenched in perfume, looking like Peter the Great, he had fallen
out of favor. He lived with a Cossack woman by the name of Pavla,
whom he had snatched away from a Jewish quartermaster, and twenty
thoroughbreds which, word had it, were his own. In his yard, the sun
was tense and tortured with the blindness of its rays. The foals were

wildly suckling on their mothers, and stableboys with drenched backs were sifting oats on faded winnowing floors. Khlebnikov, wounded by the injustice and fired by revenge, marched straight over to the barricaded yard.

"Are you familiar with my person?" he asked Savitsky, who was lying on some hay.

"Something tells me I've seen you somewhere before," Savitsky said to him with a yawn.

"In that case, here is the chief of staff's decision," Khlebnikov said gruffly. "And I would be obliged, Comrade of the reserve, if you would look at me with an official eye!"

"Why not?" Savitsky mumbled appeasingly. He took the document and began reading it for an unusually long time. He suddenly called over the Cossack woman, who was combing her hair in the coolness under the awning.

"Pavla!" he yelled. "As the Lord's my witness, you've been combing your hair since this morning! How about heating a samovar for us!"

The Cossack woman put down her comb, took her hair in both hands, and flung it behind her back.

"You've done nothing but bicker all day, Konstantin Vasilevich," she said with a lazy, condescending smile. "First you want this, then you want that!"

And she came over to Savitsky; her breasts, bobbing on her high heels, squirmed like an animal in a sack.

"You've done nothing but bicker all day," the woman repeated, beaming, and she buttoned up the division commander's shirt.

"First I want this, then I want that," the division commander said, laughing, and he got up, clasped Pavla's acquiescing shoulders, and suddenly turned his face, deathly white, to Khlebnikov.

"I am still alive, Khlebnikov," he said, embracing the Cossack woman tighter. "My legs can still walk, my horses can still gallop, my hands can still get hold of you, and my gun is warming next to my skin."

He drew his revolver, which had lain against his bare stomach, and stepped closer to the commander of the First Squadron.

The commander turned on his heels, his spurs yelped, he left the yard like an orderly who has received an urgent dispatch, and once again rode a hundred versts to find the chief of staff—but the chief of staff sent him packing.

"I have already dealt with your matter, Commander!" the chief of staff said. "I ordered that your stallion be returned to you, and I have quite a few other things to deal with!"

The chief of staff refused to listen, and finally ordered the errant commander back to his squadron. Khlebnikov had been away a whole week. During that time we had been transferred to the Dubno forest to set up camp. We had pitched our tents and were living it up. Khlebnikov, from what I remember, returned on the twelfth, a Sunday morning. He asked me for some paper, a good thirty sheets, and for some ink. The Cossacks planed a tree stump smooth for him, he placed his revolver and the paper on it, and wrote till sundown, filling many sheets with his smudgy scrawl.

"You're a real Karl Marx, you are!" the squadron's military commissar said to him in the evening. "What the hell are you writing there?"

"I am describing various thoughts in accordance with the oath I have taken," Khlebnikov answered, and handed the military commissar his petition to withdraw from the Communist Party of the Bolsheviks.

• • •

"The Communist Party," his petition went, "was, it is my belief, founded for the promotioning of happiness and true justice with no restrictings, and thus must also keep an eye out for the rights of the little man. Here I would like to touch on the matter of the white stallion who I seized from some indescribably counterrevolutionary peasants, and who was in a horrifying condition, and many comrades laughed brazenly at that condition, but I was strong enough to withstand that laughing of theirs, and gritting my teeth for the Common Cause, I nursed the stallion back to the desired shape, because, let it be said, Comrades, I am a white-stallion enthusiast and have dedicated to white stallions the little energy that the Imperial War and the Civil War have left me with, and all these stallions respond to my touch as I respond to his silent wants and needs! But that unjust black mare I can neither respond to, nor do I need her, nor can I stand her, and, as all my comrades will testify, there's bound to be trouble! And yet the Party is unable to return to me, according to the chief of staff's decision, that which is my very own, handing me no option but to write this here petition with tears that do not befit a fighter, but which flow endlessly, ripping my blood-drenched heart to pieces!"

. . .

This and much more was written in Khlebnikov's petition. He spent the whole day writing it, and it was very long. It took me and the military commissar more than an hour to struggle through it.

"What a fool you are!" the military commissar said to him, and tore it up. "Come back after dinner and you and I will have a little talk."

"I don't need your little talk!" Khlebnikov answered, trembling. "You and I are finished!"

He stood at attention, shivering, not moving, his eyes darting from one side to the other as if he were desperately trying to decide which way to run. The military commissar came up to him but couldn't grab hold of him in time. Khlebnikov lunged forward and ran with all his might.

"We're finished!" he yelled wildly, jumped onto the tree stump, and began ripping his jacket and tearing at his chest.

"Go on, Savitsky!" he shouted, throwing himself onto the ground. "Kill me!"

We dragged him to a tent, the Cossacks helped us. We boiled some tea for him, and rolled him some cigarettes. He smoked, his whole body shivering. And it was only late in the evening that our commander calmed down. He no longer spoke about his deranged petition, but within a week he went to Rovno, presented himself for an examination by the Medical Commission, and was discharged from the army as an invalid on account of having six wounds.

That's how we lost Khlebnikov. I was very upset about this because Khlebnikov had been a quiet man, very similar to me in character. He was the only one in the squadron who owned a samovar. On days when there was a break in the fighting, the two of us drank hot tea. We were rattled by the same passions. Both of us looked upon the world as a meadow in May over which women and horses wander.

KONKIN

*S*o there we were making mincemeat of the Poles at Belaya Tserkov. So much so that the trees were rattling. I'd been hit in the morning, but managed to keep on buzzing, more or less. The day, from what I remember, was toppling toward evening. I got cut off from the brigade commander, and was left with only a bunch of five proletarian Cossacks tagging along after me. All around me everyone's hugging each other with hatchets, like priests from two villages, the sap's slowly trickling out of me, my horse is cut up and bleeding. Need I say more?

Me and Spirka Zabuty ended up riding off a ways from the forest. We look—and yes, two and two does make four!—no less than a hundred and fifty paces away, we see a dust cloud which is either the staff or the cavalry transport. If it's the staff—that's great, if it's the cavalry transport—that's even better! The boys' tattered clothes hung in rags, their shirts barely covering their manhood.

"Zabuty!" I yell over to Spirka, telling him he's a son of a whore, that his mother is a you-know-what, or whatever (I leave this part up to you, as you're the official orator here). "Isn't that *their* staff that's riding off there?"

"You can bet your life it's their staff!" Spirka yells back. "The only thing is, we're two and they're eight!"

"Let's go for it, Spirka!" I shout. "Either way, I'm going to hurl some mud at their chasubles! Let's go die for a pickle and World Revolution!"

And off we rode. They were eight sabers. Two of them we felled with our rifles. I spot Spirka dragging a third to Dukhonin's head-quarters to get his papers checked. And me, I take aim at the big King of Aces. Yes, brothers, a big, red-faced King of Aces, with a chain and a gold pocket watch. I squeezed him back toward a farm. The farm was full of apple and cherry trees. The horse that the Big Ace was rid-ing was nice and plump like a merchant's daughter, but it was tired. So the general drops his reins, aims his Mauser at me, and puts a hole in my leg.

"Ha, fine, sweetheart!" I think to myself. "I'll have you on your back with your legs spread wide in no time!"

I got my wheels rolling and put two bullets in his horse. I felt bad about the horse. What a Bolshevik of a stallion, a true Bolshevik! Copper-brown like a coin, tail like a bullet, leg like a bowstring. I want-ed to present him alive to Lenin, but nothing came of it. I liquidated that sweet little horse. It tumbled like a bride, and my King of Aces fell out of his saddle. He dashed to one side, then turned back again and put another little loophole in my body. So, in other words, I had already gotten myself three decorations for fighting the enemy.

"Jesus!" I think to myself. "Just watch him finish me off by mis-take!"

I went galloping toward him, he'd already pulled his saber, and tears are running down his cheeks, white tears, the milk of man.

"You'll get me a Red Flag Medal!" I yell. "Give yourself up while I'm still alive, Your Excellency!"

"I can't do that, *Pan!*" the old man answers. "Kill me!"

And suddenly Spirka is standing before me like a leaf before a blade of grass.* His face all lathered up with sweat, his eyes as if they're dan-gling on strings from his ugly mug.

"Konkin!" he yells at me. "God knows how many I've finished off! But you have a general here, he's got embroidery on him, I'd like to fin-ish him off myself!"

"Go to the Turk!" I tell Zabuty, and get furious. "It's my blood that's on his embroidery!"

---

* From the Russian folktale *The Little Humpbacked Horse,* in which the hero summons his magic horse with, "Appear before me like a leaf before a blade of grass!"

And with my mare I edge the general into the barn, where there was hay or something. It was silent in there, dark, cool.

"*Pan,* think of your old age!" I tell him. "Give yourself up to me, for God's sake, and we can both have a rest."

And he's against the wall, panting with his whole chest, rubbing his forehead with a red finger.

"I can't," he says. "If I do, you'll kill me. I will only give my saber to Budyonny!"

He wants me to bring him Budyonny! O, Lord in Heaven! And I can tell the old man's on his last legs.

"*Pan!*" I shout at him, sobbing and gnashing my teeth. "On my proletarian honor, I myself am the commander-in-chief. Don't go looking for embroidery on me, but the title's mine. You want my title? I am the musical eccentric and salon ventriloquist of Nizhny . . . Nizhny, a town on the Volga!"

Then the devil got into me. The general's eyes were blinking like lanterns in front of me. The Red Sea parted before me. His snub enters my wound like salt, because I see that the old man doesn't believe me. So, my friends, what I did is, I closed my mouth, pulled in my stomach, took a deep breath, and demonstrated, in the proper way, our way, the fighter's way, the Nizhny way—demonstrated to this Polish nobleman my ventriloquy.

The old man went white in the face, clutched his heart, and sat on the ground.

"Do you now believe Konkin the Eccentric, commissar of the Third Invincible Cavalry Brigade?"

"A commissar?" he shouts.

"A commissar," I tell him.

"A Communist?" he shouts.

"A Communist," I tell him.

"At my hour of death," he shouts, "at my last breath, tell me, my dear Cossack friend, are you a Communist, or are you lying to me?"

"I am a Communist," I tell him.

So there's grandpa, sitting on the ground, kissing some kind of amulet or something, breaks his saber in half, and in his eyes two sparks flare up, two lanterns above the dark steppes.

"Forgive me," he says, "but I cannot give myself up to a Communist."

And he shakes my hand. "Forgive me," he says, "and finish me off like a soldier."

Konkin, the political commissar of the N. Cavalry Brigade and three-time Knight of the Order of the Red Flag, told us this story with his typical antics during a rest stop one day.

"So, Konkin, did you and the *Pan* come to some sort of an agreement in the end?"

"Can you come to an agreement with someone like that? He was too proud. I begged him again, but he wouldn't give in. So we took his papers, those he had with him, we took his Mauser, and the old fool's saddle, the one I'm sitting on right now. Then I see all my life flowing out of me in drops, a terrible tiredness grabs hold of me, my boots are full of blood, I lost interest in him."

"So you put the old man out of his misery?"

"Well, I guess I did."

BERESTECHKO

We were advancing from Khotin to Berestechko. Our fighters were dozing in their saddles. A song rustled like a stream running dry. Horrifying corpses lay on thousand-year-old burial mounds. Muzhiks in white shirts raised their caps and bowed as we passed. The cloak of Division Commander Pavlichenko was fluttering ahead of the staff officers like a gloomy banner. His ruffled hood hung over his cloak, his curved saber at his side.

We rode past the Cossack burial mounds and the tomb of Bogdan Khmelnitsky. An old man with a mandolin came creeping out from behind a gravestone and with a child's voice sang of past Cossack glory. We listened to the song in silence, then unfurled the standards, and burst into Berestechko to the beat of a thundering march. The inhabitants had put iron bars over their shutters, and silence, a despotic silence, had ascended to the shtetl throne.

I happened to be billeted in the house of a redheaded widow, who was doused with the scent of widow's grief. I washed off the dirt of the road and went out into the street. An announcement was already nailed up on telegraph poles that Divisional Military Commissar Vinogradov would be giving a speech on the Second Congress of the Comintern.* Right outside the house a couple of Cossacks were getting ready to shoot an old silver-bearded Jew for espionage. The old man was screeching, and tried to break free. Kudrya from the machine gun

* The Third Communist International, 1919–1943, an organization founded in Moscow by the delegates of twelve countries to promote Communism worldwide.

detachment grabbed his head and held it wedged under his arm. The Jew fell silent and spread his legs. Kudrya pulled out his dagger with his right hand and carefully slit the old man's throat without spattering himself. Then he knocked on one of the closed windows.

"If anyone's interested," he said, "they can come get him. It's no problem."

And the Cossacks disappeared around the corner. I followed them, and then wandered through Berestechko. Most of the people here are Jewish, and only on the outskirts have a few Russian townspeople, mainly tanners, settled. The Russians live cleanly, in little white houses behind green shutters. Instead of vodka, they drink beer or mead, and in their front gardens grow tobacco which, like Galician peasants, they smoke in long curved pipes. That they are three diligent and entrepreneurial races living next to each other awakened in all of them an obstinate industriousness that is sometimes inherent in a Russian man, if he hasn't become louse-ridden, desperate, and besotted with drink.

Everyday life, which once flourished, has blown away. Little sprouts that had survived for three centuries still managed to blossom in Volhynia's sultry hotbed of ancient times. Here, with the ropes of profit, the Jews had bound the Russian muzhiks to the Polish *Pans* and the Czech settlers to the factory in Lodz. These were smugglers, the best on the frontier, and almost always warriors of the faith. Hasidism kept this lively population of taverners, peddlers, and brokers in a stifling grip. Boys in long coats still trod the ancient path to the Hasidic cheder, and old women still brought daughters-in-law to the *tsaddik* with impassioned prayers for fertility.

The Jews live here in large houses painted white or a watery blue. The traditional austerity of this architecture goes back centuries. Behind the houses are sheds that are two, sometimes three stories high. The sun never enters these sheds. They are indescribably gloomy and replace our yards. Secret passages lead to cellars and stables. In times of war, people hide in these catacombs from bullets and plunder. Over many days, human refuse and animal dung pile up. Despair and dismay fill the catacombs with an acrid stench and the rotting sourness of excrement.

Berestechko stinks inviolably to this day. The smell of rotten herring emanates from everyone. The shtetl reeks in expectation of a new era, and, instead of people, fading reflections of frontier misfortune wander through it. I had had enough of them by the end of the day, went beyond the edge of the town, climbed the mountain, and reached the abandoned castle of the Counts Raciborski, the recent owners of Berestechko.

The silence of the sunset turned the grass around the castle blue. The moon rose green as a lizard above the pond. Looking out the window, I could see the estate of the Raciborskis—meadows and fields of hops hidden beneath the crepe ribbons of dusk.

A ninety-year-old countess and her son had lived in the castle. She had tormented him for not having given the dying clan any heirs, and—the muzhiks told me this—she used to beat him with the coachman's whip.

A rally was gathering on the square below. Peasants, Jews, and tanners from the outlying areas had come together. Above them flared Vinogradov's ecstatic voice and the clanking of his spurs. He gave a speech about the Second Congress of the Comintern, and I roamed along the walls where nymphs with gouged eyes danced their ancient round dance. Then on the trampled floor, in a corner, I found the torn fragment of a yellowed letter. On it was written in faded ink:

> *Berestechko, 1820, Paul, mon bien aimé, on dit que l'empereur Napoléon est mort, est-ce vrai? Moi, je me sens bien, les couches ont été faciles, notre petit héros achéve sept semaines. . . .**

Below me, the voice of the divisional military commissar is droning on. He is passionately haranguing the bewildered townspeople and the plundered Jews: "You are the power. Everything here belongs to you. There are no masters. I shall now conduct an election for the Revolutionary Committee."

---

* Berestechko, 1820, my beloved Paul, I hear that Emperor Napoleon is dead. Is it true? I feel well; it was an easy birth, our little hero is already seven weeks old.

SALT

*D*ear Comrade Editor,
   I want to tell you of some ignorant women who are harmful to us. I set my hopes on you, that you who travel around our nation's fronts, have not overlooked the far-flung station of Fastov, lying afar beyond the mountains grand, in a distant province of a distant land, where many a jug of home-brewed beer we drank with merriment and cheer. About this aforementioned station, there is much you can write about, but as we say back home: you can shovel till the cows come home, but the master's dung heap never gets no smaller. So I will only describe what my eyes have seen in person.

   It was a quiet, glorious night seven days ago when our well-deserved Red Cavalry transport train, loaded with fighters, stopped at that station. We were all burning to promote the Common Cause and were heading to Berdichev. Only, we notice that our train isn't moving in any way at all, our Gavrilka is not beginning to roll, and the fighters begin mistrusting and asking each other: "Why are we stopping here?" And truly, the stop turned out to be mighty for the Common Cause, because the peddlers, those evil fiends among whom there was a count-less force of the female species, were all behaving very impertinently with the railroad authorities. Recklessly they grabbed the handrails, those evil fiends, they scampered over the steel roofs, frolicked, made trouble, clutching in each hand sacks of contraband salt, up to five *pood* in a sack. But the triumph of the capitalist peddlers did not last long. The initiative showed by the fighters who jumped out of the train made it possible for the struggling railroad authorities to emit sighs from their breasts. Only the female species with their bags of salt stayed around. Taking pity, the soldiers let some of the women come into the railroad cars, but others they didn't. In our own railroad car of the Second Platoon two girls popped up, and after the first bell there comes an imposing woman with a baby in her arms: "Let me in, my dear Cossacks," she says. "I have been suffering through the whole war at train stations with a suckling baby in my arms, and now I want to meet my husband, but the way the railroad is, it is impossible to get through! Don't I deserve some help from you Cossacks?"

"By the way, woman," I tell her, "whichever way the platoon decides will be your fate." And, turning to the platoon, I tell them that here we have a woman who is requesting to travel to her husband at an appointed place and that she does, in fact, have a child with her, so what will your decision be? Let her in or not?

"Let her in," the boys yell. "Once we're done with her, she won't be wanting that husband of hers no more!"

"No," I tell the boys quite politely, "I bow to your words, platoon, but I am astonished to hear such horse talk. Recall, platoon, your lives and how you yourselves were children with your mothers, and therefore, as a result, you should not talk that way!"

And the Cossacks said, "How persuasive he is, this Balmashov!" And they let the woman into the railroad car, and she climbs aboard thankfully. And each of the fighters, saying how right I am, tumble all over each other telling her, "Sit down, woman, there in the corner, rock your child the way mothers do, no one will touch you in the corner, so you can travel untouched to your husband, as you want, and we depend upon your conscience to raise a new change of guard for us, because what is old grows older, and when you need youth, it's never around! We saw our share of sorrow, woman, both when we were drafted and then later in the extra service, we were crushed by hunger, burned by cold. So just sit here, woman, and don't be frightened!"

The third bell rang and the train pulled out of the station. The glorious night pitched its tent. And in that tent hung star lanterns. And the fighters remembered the nights of Kuban and the green star of Kuban. And thoughts flew like birds. And the wheels clattered and clattered.

With the passing of time, when night was relieved of its watch and the red drummers drummed in the dawn on their red drums, then the Cossacks came to me, seeing that I am sitting sleepless and am unhappy to the fullest.

"Balmashov," the Cossacks say to me, "why are you so horribly unhappy and sitting sleepless?"

"I bow to you deeply, O fighters, and would like to ask you the small favor of letting me speak a few words with this citizen."

And trembling from head to toe, I rise from my bunk from which sleep had run like a wolf from a pack of depraved dogs, and walk up to her, take the baby from her arms, rip off the rags it's swaddled in and its diaper, and out from the diaper comes a nice fat forty-pound sack of salt.

"What an interesting little baby, Comrades! It does not ask Mommy for titty, doesn't peepee on mommy's skirty, and doesn't wake people from their sleep!"

"Forgive me, my dear Cossacks," the woman cut into our conversation very coolly, "it wasn't me who tricked you, it was my hard life."

"I, Balmashov, forgive your hard life," I tell the woman. "It doesn't cost Balmashov much. What Balmashov pays for something, that is the price he sells it for! But address yourself to the Cossacks, woman, who elevated you as a toiling mother of the republic. Address yourself to these two girls, who are now crying for having suffered under us last night. Address yourself to our women on the wheat fields of Kuban, who are wearing out their womanly strength without husbands, and to their husbands, who are lonely too, and so are forced against their will to rape girls who cross their paths! And you they didn't touch, you improper woman, although you should have been the first to be touched! Address yourself to Russia, crushed by pain!"

And she says to me, "As it is I've lost my salt, so I'm not afraid of calling things by their real name! Don't give me that about saving Russia—all you care about is saving those Yids, Lenin and Trotsky!"

"Right now our topic of conversation is not the Yids, you evil citizen! And by the way, about Lenin I don't really know, but Trotsky is the dashing son of the Governor of Tambov who, turning his back on his high social rank, joined the working classes. Like prisoners sentenced to hard labor, Lenin and Trotsky are dragging us to life's road of freedom, while you, foul citizen, are a worse counterrevolutionary than that

White general waving his sharp saber at us from his thousand-ruble horse. You can see him, that general, from every road, and the worker has only one dream—to kill him! While you, you dishonest citizen, with your bogus children who don't ask for bread and don't pee in their pants, you one doesn't see. You're just like a flea, you bite and bite and bite!"

And I truthfully admit that I threw that citizen off the moving train and onto the embankment, but she, being brawny as she was, sat up, shook out her skirts, and went on her deceitful way. Seeing this uninjured woman and Russia all around her, the peasant fields without an ear of corn, the raped girls, and the comrades, many of whom were heading for the front but few of whom would ever return, I wanted to jump from the train and either kill myself or kill her. But the Cossacks took pity on me and said, "Just shoot her with that rifle."

And I took the loyal rifle from the wall and wiped that blot off the face of the working land and the republic.

And we, the fighters of the Second Platoon, swear before you, dear Comrade Editor, and before you, dear Comrades of the editorial office, that we will deal relentlessly with all the traitors who pull us into the pit and want to turn back the stream and cover Russia with corpses and dead grass.

In the name of all the fighters of the Second Platoon,

Nikita Balmashov, Fighter of the Revolution.

EVENING

O statutes of the RCP!* You have laid impetuous rails across the rancid dough of Russian prose. You have transformed three bachelors, their hearts filled with the passion of Ryazan Jesuses, into editors of the *Krasny Kavalerist*.† You have transformed them so that day after day they can churn out a rambunctious newspaper filled with courage and rough-and-ready mirth.

Galin with his cataract, consumptive Slinkin, and Sychev with his withered intestines shuffle through the barren soil of the rear lines, spreading the revolt and fire of their news sheet through the ranks of dashing, pensioned-off Cossacks, reserve cheats who have registered as Polish translators, and girls sent out to our Polit-otdel train** from Moscow for recuperation.

By evening the newspaper is ready—a dynamite fuse placed under the cavalry. The cross-eyed lantern of the provincial sun expires in the sky, the lights of the printing press scatter in all directions and burn uncontrollably like the passion of a machine. And then, toward midnight, Galin comes out of the railroad car shuddering from the bite of his unrequited love for Irina, our train's washerwoman.

"Last time," Galin says, pale and blind, his shoulders narrow, "last

* The Russian Communist Party

† *The Red Cavalryman,* the newspaper distributed to the Red Cavalry forces and for which Babel also wrote pieces. See *The Red Cavalryman:* Articles, Part V in this book.

** The train belonging to the Polit-otdel, the political organ of the new Soviet government charged with the ideological education of the military.

time, Irina, we discussed the shooting of Nicholas the Bloody, executed by the proletariat of Ekaterinburg. Now we will proceed to the other
tyrants who died like dogs. Peter III was strangled by Orlov, his wife's
lover. Paul was torn to pieces by his courtiers and his own son. Nikolai
Palkin poisoned himself, his son perished March first, his grandson
drank himself to death. It is important for you to know all this, Irina!"

And raising his blank eye, filled with adoration, to the washerwoman, Galin rummages relentlessly through the crypts of murdered
emperors. He is standing stoop-shouldered, bathed in the rays of the
moon hovering high above like a nagging splinter, the printing presses
are hammering somewhere nearby, and the radio station is shining with
clear light. Irina nestles against the shoulder of Vasily the cook as she
stands listening to Galin's dull and nonsensical mutterings of love.
Above her, the stars are dragging themselves through the black seaweed
of the sky. The washerwoman yawns, makes the sign of the cross over
her puffy lips, and stares wide-eyed at Galin.

Next to Irina, rough-faced Vasily yawns. Like all cooks he scorns
mankind. Cooks: they constantly have to handle the meat of dead animals and the greed of the living, which is why, when it comes to politics, a cook always seeks things that have nothing to do with him. This
goes for Vasily too. Hiking his pants up to his nipples, he asks Galin
about the civil lists of various kings, the dowries of Czars' daughters.
Then he yawns and says, "It's night, Irina, another day will be rolling in
tomorrow. Let's go crush some fleas."

They closed the kitchen door, leaving Galin alone, with the moon
hovering high above like a nagging splinter. I sat opposite the moon on
the embankment by the sleeping pond, wearing my spectacles, with
boils on my neck, my feet bandaged. My confused poetic brain was
digesting the class struggle when Galin came up to me with his twinkling cataracts.

"Galin," I said, overcome with self-pity and loneliness, "I am sick,
my end is near, I am tired of life in the Red Cavalry!"

"You're a wimp!" Galin said, and the watch on his bony wrist
showed one in the morning. "You're a wimp, and we end up having to
put up with wimps like you! We're cracking the nut for you, and soon
enough you will be able to see the meat inside, at which point you'll
take your thumb out of your mouth and sing the glories of the new life

in striking prose—but for the time being, just sit where you are, nice and quiet, you wimp, and stop getting in the way with all your whimpering!"

He came closer to me, fixed the bandages which had slipped off my itching sores, and let his head loll onto his pigeon breast. The night comforted us in our anguish; a light breeze rustled over us like a mother's skirt, and the weeds below us glittered with freshness and moisture.

The roaring machines of the train's printing press screeched and fell silent. Dawn drew a line across the edge of the earth, the kitchen door creaked and opened a crack. Four feet with fat heels came thrusting out into the coolness, and we saw Irina's loving calves and Vasily's big toe with its crooked black nail.

"Vasilyok," the woman whispered in a throaty, expiring voice. "Get out of my bed, you troublemaker!"

But Vasily only jerked his heel and moved closer to her.

"The Red Cavalry," Galin said to me, "the Red Cavalry is a public conjuring trick pulled off by our Party's Central Committee. The curve of the Revolution has thrown the Cossack marauders, saddled with all kinds of prejudices, into the forefront, but the Central Committee is going to weed them out with its iron rake."

Then Galin began talking about the political education of the First Cavalry. He spoke long, in a dull voice, with complete clarity. His eyelid fluttered over his cataract.

AFONKA BIDA

$\mathcal{W}$e were fighting by Leshniov. A wall of enemy cavalry rose all around us. The new Polish strategy was uncoiling like a spring, with an ominous whistle. We were being pushed back. It was the first time in our campaign that we felt on our own backs the devilish sharpness of flank attacks and breaches in the rear lines—slashes from the very weapons that had served us so well.

The front at Leshniov was being held by the infantry. Blond and barefoot, Volhynian muzhiks shuffled along crooked trenches. This infantry had been plucked from behind its plows the day before to form the Red Cavalry's infantry reserve. The peasants had come along eagerly. They fought with the greatest zeal. Their hoarse peasant ferocity amazed even the Budyonny fighters. Their hatred for the Polish landowners was built of invisible but sturdy material.

In the second phase of the war, when our whooping had lost its effect on the enemy's imagination, and cavalry attacks on our opponents, burrowed in their trenches, had become impossible, this ragtag infantry could have proved extremely useful to the Red Cavalry. But our poverty got the upper hand: there were three muzhiks to every rifle, and the cartridges that were issued didn't fit. The venture had to be dropped, and this true peasant home guard was sent back to its villages.

But back to the fighting at Leshniov. Our foot soldiers had dug themselves in three versts from the shtetl. A hunched youth with spectacles was walking up and down in front of them, a saber dangling at his side. He moved along in little hops, with a piqued look on his face, as if his boots were pinching him. This peasant *ataman*,* chosen and cherished by the muzhiks, was a Jew, a half-blind Jewish youth, with the sickly, intent face of a Talmudist. In battle, he showed circumspect and coolheaded courage that reflected the absentmindedness of a dreamer.

It was after two o'clock on a crystalline July day. A gossamer rainbow of heat glittered in the air. A festive stripe of uniforms and horse manes braided with ribbons came sparkling from behind the hills. The youth gave the signal for the men to take their positions. The muzhiks, shuffling in their bast sandals, ran to their posts and took aim. But it turned out to be a false alarm. It was Maslak's[†] colorful squadrons that came riding up the Leshniov high road, their emaciated but spirited horses trotting at a steady pace. In fiery pillars of dust, magnificent banners were fluttering on gilded poles weighed down by velvet tassels. The horsemen rode with majestic and insolent haughtiness. The tattered foot soldiers came crawling out of their trenches and, their mouths hanging open, watched the light-footed elegance of the unruffled stream.

In front of the regiment, riding a bowlegged steppe horse, was Brigade Commander Maslak, filled with drunken blood and the putridness of his fatty juices. His stomach lay like a big cat on the silver-studded pommel of his saddle. When Maslak saw the muzhik foot soldiers, his face turned a merry purple, and he beckoned Platoon Commander Afonka Bida to come over. We had given the platoon commander the nickname "Makhno"** because he looked so much like him. Maslak and Bida whispered for about a minute. Then Bida turned toward the First Squadron, leaned forward, and in a low voice ordered, "Charge!" The Cossacks, one platoon after another, broke into a trot. They spurred their horses and went galloping toward the trenches from which the muzhik foot soldiers were peering, dazzled by the sight.

"Prepare to engage!" sang Afonka's voice, dismal and as if he were calling from far away.

Maslak, wheezing and coughing, relishing the spectacle, rode off to

---

* Term for Cossack leader.

[†] Maslakov, commander of the First Brigade of the Fourth Division, a relentless partisan who was soon to betray the Soviet regime. [Footnote by Isaac Babel.]

** The Ukrainian anarchist leader.

the side, and the Cossacks charged. The poor muzhik foot soldiers ran, but it was too late. The Cossack lashes were already cutting across their tattered jackets as the horsemen circled the field, twirling their whips with exquisite artistry.

"What's all this nonsense about?" I shouted over to Afonka.

"Just a bit of fun," he shouted back, fidgeting in his saddle, and he dragged a young man out of the bushes in which he was hiding.

"Just a bit of fun!" he yelled, clobbering away at the terrified young man.

The fun ended when Maslak, tired and majestic, waved his plump hand.

"Foot soldiers! Stop gawking!" Afonka yelled, haughtily straightening his frail body. "Go catch some fleas!"

The Cossacks grinned at each other and gathered into formation. The foot soldiers vanished without a trace. The trenches were empty. And only the hunched Jewish youth stood in the same spot as before, eyeing the Cossacks haughtily through his spectacles.

The gunfire from the direction of Leshniov did not let up. The Poles were encircling us. We could see the single figures of their mounted scouts through our binoculars. They came galloping from the shtetl and disappeared again like jack-in-the-boxes. Maslak gathered together a squadron and divided it on either side of the high road. A sparkling sky hung above Leshniov, indescribably void as always in hours of danger. The Jew threw his head back and blew mournfully and loud on his metallic pipe. And the foot soldiers, the battered foot soldiers, returned to their positions.

Bullets flew thickly in our direction. Our brigade staff came under machine gun fire. We rushed into the forest and fought our way through the bushes on the right side of the high road. Branches, hit, cracked heavily above us. By the time we had managed to cut our way through the bushes, the Cossacks were no longer positioned where they had been. The division commander had ordered them to retreat toward Brody. Only the muzhiks sent a few snarling shots out of their trenches, and Afonka, trailing behind, went chasing after his platoon.

He was riding on the outermost edge of the road, looking around him and sniffing at the air. The shooting died down for a few moments. Afonka decided to take advantage of the lapse and began galloping at full speed. At that moment a bullet plunged into his horse's neck. Afonka galloped on another hundred paces or so, and then, right in front of our line, his horse abruptly bent its forelegs and sank to the ground.

Afonka casually pulled his wedged foot out of the stirrup. He sat on his haunches and poked about in the wound with his copper-brown finger. Then he stood up again and ran his agonized eyes over the glittering horizon.

"Farewell, Stepan," he said in a wooden voice, and, taking a step away from the dying horse, bowed deeply to it. "How will I return to my quiet village without you? Who am I to throw your embroidered saddle on? Farewell, Stepan!" he repeated more loudly, then choked, squeaked like a mouse in a trap, and began wailing. His gurgling howls reached our ears, and we saw Afonka frantically bowing like a possessed woman in a church. "But you'll see! I won't give in to goddamn fate!" he yelled, lifting his hands from his ashen face. "You'll see! From now on I'm going to hack those cursed Poles to pieces with no mercy at all! Right down to their gasping hearts, right down to their very last gasp, and the Mother of God's blood! I swear this to you, Stepan, before my dear brothers back home!"

Afonka lay down with his face on the horse's wound and fell silent. The horse turned its deep, sparkling, violet eye to its master, and listened to his convulsive wheezing. In tender oblivion it dragged its fallen muzzle over the ground, and streams of blood, like two ruby-red harness straps, trickled over its chest covered in white muscles.

Afonka lay there without moving. Maslak walked over to the horse, treading daintily on his fat legs, slid his revolver into its ear, and fired. Afonka jumped up and swung his pockmarked face to Maslak.

"Take the harness off, Afanasi, and go back to your unit," Maslak said to him gently.

And from our slope we saw Afonka, bent under the weight of the saddle, his face raw and red like sliced meat, tottering toward his squadron, boundlessly alone in the dusty, blazing desert of the fields.

Late that evening I saw him at the cavalry transport. He was sleeping on a cart which held all his "possessions"—sabers, uniform jackets, and pierced gold coins. His blood-caked head with its wrenched, dead mouth, lay as if crucified on the saddle's bow. Next to him lay the harness of the dead horse, the inventive and whimsical raiment of a Cossack racer: breastplates with black tassels, pliant tail cruppers studded with colored stones, and the bridle embossed with silver.

Darkness thickened around us. The cavalry transport crawled heavily along the Brody high road. Simple stars rolled through Milky Ways in the sky, and distant villages burned in the cool depths of the night. Orlov, the squadron subcommander, and big-mustached Bitsenko were sitting right there on Afonka's cart discussing his grief.

"He brought the horse all the way from home," long-mustached Bitsenko said. "Where's one to find another horse like that?"

"A horse—that's a friend," Orlov answered.

"A horse—that's a father," Bitsenko sighed. "The horse saves your life more times than you can count. Bida is finished without his horse."

In the morning Afonka was gone. The skirmishes near Brody began and ended. Defeat was replaced by fleeting victory, we had a change of division commander, but Afonka was still nowhere to be seen. And only a terrible rumbling from the villages, the evil and rapacious trail of Afonka's marauding, showed us his difficult path.

"He's off somewhere getting a horse," the men of the squadron said about him, and on the endless evenings of our wanderings I heard quite a few tales of this grim, savage pillaging.

Fighters from other units ran into Afonka about ten versts from our position. He lay in wait for Polish cavalrymen who had fallen behind, or scoured the forests looking for herds hidden by the peasants. He set villages on fire and shot Polish elders for hiding horses. Echoes of the frenzied one-man battle, the furtive ransacking robbery of a lone wolf attacking a herd, reached our ears.

Another week passed. The bitter events of the day crowded out the tales of Afonka's sinister bravado, and we began to forget our "Makhno." Then the rumor went round that Galician peasants had slaughtered him somewhere in the woods. And on the day we entered Berestechko, Yemelyan Budyak from the First Squadron went to the division commander to ask if he could have Afonka's saddle and the yellow saddlecloths. Yemelyan wanted to ride in the parade on a new saddle, but it was not to be.

We entered Berestechko on August 6. Fluttering in front of our division was our new division commander's Asiatic quilted jacket and his red Cossack coat. Lyovka, the division commander's brutal lackey, walked behind him leading his stud mare. A military march filled with protracted menace resounded through the pretentious, destitute streets. The town was a colorful forest of dead-end alleys and decrepit and convulsive planks and boards. The shtetl's heart, corroded by time, breathed its despondent decay upon us. Smugglers and philistines hid in their large, shadowy huts. Only *Pan* Ludomirski, a bell ringer in a green frock coat, met us at the church.

We crossed the river and entered deeper into the petit-bourgeois settlement. We were nearing the priest's house when Afonka suddenly came riding around the corner on a large stallion.

"Greetings," he called out in a barking voice, and, pushing the fighters apart, took his old position in the ranks.

Maslak stared into the colorless distance.

"Where did you get that horse?" he wheezed, without turning around.

"It's my own," Afonka answered, and rolled himself a cigarette, wetting the paper with a quick dart of his tongue.

One after the other, the Cossacks rode up to greet him. A monstrous pink pustule shone repugnantly in his charred face where his left eye had been.

The following morning Bida went carousing. He smashed Saint Valentine's shrine in the church and tried to play the organ. He was wearing a jacket that had been cut from a blue carpet and had an embroidered lily on its back, and he had combed his sweat-drenched forelock* over his gouged-out eye.

After lunch he saddled his horse and fired his rifle at the knocked-out windows of the castle of the Count Raciborski. Cossacks stood around him in a semicircle. They tugged at the stallion's tail, prodded its legs, and counted its teeth.

"A fine figure of a horse!" Orlov, the squadron subcommander, said.

"An exemplary horse," big-mustached Bitsenko confirmed.

---

* Ukrainian Cossacks shaved their heads, leaving only a forelock, known as a *chub*.

AT SAINT VALENTINE'S

*O*ur division occupied Berestechko yesterday evening. The headquarters have been set up in the house of Father Tuzynkiewicz.
Dressed as a woman, Tuzynkiewicz had fled Berestechko before our
troops entered the town. All I know about him is that he had dealt with
God in Berestechko for forty-five years, and that he had been a good
priest. The townspeople make a point of this, telling us he was even
loved by the Jews. Under Tuzynkiewicz, the old church had been ren-
ovated. The renovations had been completed on the day of the church's
three-hundredth anniversary, and the bishop had come from Zhitomir.
Prelates in silk cassocks had held a service in front of the church.
Potbellied and beatific, they stood like bells on the dewy grass. Faithful
streams flowed in from the surrounding villages. The muzhiks bent
their knees, kissed priestly hands, and on that day clouds never before
seen flamed in the sky. Heavenly banners fluttered in honor of the
church. The bishop himself kissed Tuzynkiewicz on the forehead and
called him the Father of Berestechko, *Pater Berestechkae.*

I heard this tale in the morning at the headquarters, where I was
checking over the report of our scout column that was on a reconnaissance
mission near Lvov in the district of Radziekhov. I read the documents.
The snoring of the orderlies behind me bespoke our never-ending homelessness. The clerks, sodden with sleeplessness, wrote orders to the
division, ate pickles, and sneezed. It wasn't until midday that I got away,
went to the window, and saw the church of Berestechko, powerful and
white. It shone in the mild sun like a porcelain tower. Flashes of mid-

day lightning sparkled on its shining flanks. The lightning's arcs began at the ancient green cupolas and ran lightly downward. Pink veins glimmered in the white stone of the portal, and above it were columns as thin as candles.

Then organ music came pouring into my ears, and that instant an old woman with disheveled yellow hair appeared outside the doors of the headquarters. She moved like a dog with a broken paw, hobbling in circles, her legs tottering. The pupils of her eyes, filled with the white liquid of blindness, oozed tears. The sounds of the organ, now drawn-out, now rapid, came fluttering over to us. Their flight was difficult, their wake reverberated plaintive and long. The old woman wiped her eyes with her yellow hair, sat on the floor, and began kissing the tops of my boots. The organ fell silent and then burst into a laughter of bass notes. I took the old woman by the arm and looked around. The clerks were pounding their typewriters and the orderlies snored ever louder, the spurs on their boots ripping the felt under the velvet upholstery of the sofas. The old woman kissed my boots tenderly, hugging them as she would an infant. I led her to the door and locked it behind me. The church towered strikingly before us, like a stage set. Its side doors were open, and on the graves of Polish officers lay horses' skulls.

We hurried into the churchyard, went through a dark corridor, and arrived in a square-shaped room, which had been built as an extension to the chancel. Sashka, the nurse of the Thirty-first Regiment, was puttering about in there, rummaging through a pile of silk that somebody had thrown on the floor. The cadaverous aroma of brocade, scattered flowers, and fragrant decay seeped into her nostrils, tickling and poisonous. Then Cossacks entered the room. They burst into guffaws, grabbed Sashka by the arms, and flung her with gusto onto a pile of cloth and books. Sashka's body, blossoming and reeking like the meat of a freshly slaughtered cow, was laid bare, her raised skirts revealing the legs of a squadron woman, slim, cast-iron legs, and dim-witted Kurdyukov, the silly fool, sat on top of Sashka, bouncing as if he were in a saddle, pretending to be in the grip of passion. She pushed him off and rushed out the door. We passed the altar, and only then did we enter the nave of the church.

The church was filled with light, filled with dancing rays, columns of air, and an almost cool exultation. How can I ever forget Apolek's painting, hanging over the right side-altar? In this painting twelve rosy *Paters* are rocking a cradle girdled with ribbons, with a plump infant Jesus in it. His toes are stretched out, his body lacquered with hot morning sweat. The child is writhing on his fat, wrinkly back, and twelve apostles in cardinals' miters are bending over the cradle. Their faces are meticulously shaven, flaming cloaks are billowing over their bellies. The eyes of the Apostles sparkle with wisdom, resolution, and cheer. Faint grins flit over the corners of their mouths, and fiery warts have been planted on their double chins—crimson warts, like radishes in May.

This church of Berestechko had its private and beguiling approach to the death agonies of the sons of man. In this church the saints marched to their deaths with the flair of Italian opera singers, and the black hair of the executioners shone like the beard of Holofernes. Here, above the altar, I saw the sacrilegious painting of John the Baptist, which had also sprung from Apolek's heretical, intoxicating brush. In this painting the Baptist was beautiful in the ambiguous and reticent way that drives the concubines of kings to shed their half-lost honor and their blossoming lives.

At first I did not notice the signs of destruction in the church, or didn't think they looked too bad. Only the shrine of Saint Valentine had been smashed. Lying around it were shreds of decayed wadding and the saint's ridiculous bones, which, if they resembled anything, looked like chicken bones. And Afonka Bida was still playing the organ. Afonka was drunk, wild, his body was lacerated. He had come back to us only yesterday with the horse he had seized from local farmers. Afonka was obstinately trying to play a march, and someone was badgering him in a sleepy voice, "Enough, Afonka, enough, let's go eat!" But Afonka wouldn't give up. Many more of Afonka's songs followed. Each sound was a song, and one sound was torn from the other. The song's dense tune lasted for a moment and then crossed over into another. I listened, looked around—the signs of destruction didn't look too bad. But *Pan* Ludomirski, the bell ringer of the Church of Saint Valentine and husband of the old blind woman, thought otherwise.

Ludomirsky had suddenly appeared out of nowhere. He walked through the church with measured steps, his head lowered. The old man could not bring himself to cover the scattered relics because a simple man, a lay person, may not touch what is holy. The bell ringer threw himself on the blue slabs of the floor, lifted his head, his blue nose jutting up above him like a flag above a corpse. His blue nose quivered above him and at that moment a velvet curtain by the altar swayed, rustled, and fell open. In the depths of the niche, against the backdrop of a sky furrowed with clouds, ran a bearded little figure wearing an orange Polish caftan—barefoot, his mouth lacerated and bleeding. A hoarse wail assailed our ears. The man in the orange caftan was being pursued by hatred, and his pursuer had caught up with him. The man lifted his arm to ward off the blow, and blood poured from it in a purple stream. The young Cossack standing next to me yelled out and, ducking, started to run, even though there was nothing to run from, because the figure in the niche was only Jesus Christ—the most unusual portrayal of the Son of God I have ever seen in my life.

Pan Ludomirski's Savior was a curly-headed Jew with a scraggly little beard and a low, wrinkled forehead. His sunken cheeks were tinted with carmine, and thin, red-brown eyebrows curved over eyes that were closed in pain.

His mouth was wrenched open, like a horse's mouth, his Polish caftan fastened with a precious girdle, and from under the caftan jutted crooked little porcelain feet, painted, bare, pierced by silver nails.

Pan Ludomirski stood under the statue in his green frock coat. He stretched his withered arm toward us and cursed us. The Cossacks stared at him with wide eyes and let their straw-colored forelocks hang. In a thundering voice, the bell ringer of the Church of Saint Valentine cursed us in the purest Latin. Then he turned away, fell to his knees, and clasped the feet of the Savior.

Back at the headquarters, I wrote a report to the division commander about the insult to the religious feelings of the local population. A decree was issued that the church be closed, and the guilty parties were charged with a breach of discipline and sent before the military tribunal.

SQUADRON COMMANDER
TRUNOV

*A*t noon we brought the bullet-ridden body of Trunov, our squadron commander, back to Sokal. He had been killed that morning in a battle with enemy airplanes. All the hits had caught Trunov in the face; his cheeks were riddled with wounds, his tongue torn out. We washed the dead man's face as best we could so that he would look less horrifying, placed his Caucasian saddle at the head of his coffin, and dug him a grave in a stately spot—in the public park in the middle of the town, right by the fence. Our squadron rode there on horseback. The regimental staff and the divisional military commissar were also present. And at two in the afternoon, by the cathedral clock, our rickety little cannon fired the first shot. The cannon saluted Squadron Commander Trunov with its timeworn three-inch bore, did a full salute, and we carried the coffin to the open pit. The coffin was open, the clean midday sun lit the lanky corpse, lit his mouth filled with smashed teeth and his carefully polished boots, their heels placed together as at a drill.

"Fighters!" Regimental Captain Pugachov said, as he eyed the dead man and walked up to the edge of the pit. "Fighters!" he said, standing at attention, shaking with emotion. "We are burying Pashka Trunov, an international hero! We are according Pashka the final honor!"

Pugachov raised his eyes, burning with sleeplessness, to the sky and shouted out his speech about the dead fighters of the First Cavalry, that proud phalanx which pounds the anvil of future centuries with the hammer of history. Pugachov shouted out his speech loudly, clenched the hilt of his curved Chechen saber, and scuffed the earth with his tat-tered boots and their silver spurs. After his speech the orchestra played the "Internationale," and the Cossacks took leave of Pashka Trunov. The whole squadron leaped onto their horses and fired a volley into the air, our three-inch cannon hissed toothlessly a second time, and we sent three Cossacks to find a wreath. They whirled off at full gallop, firing as they rode and plunging from their saddles in a display of acrobatics, and brought back armfuls of red flowers. Pugachov scattered the flow-ers around the grave, and we stepped up to Trunov for the last kiss. I touched my lips on an unblemished patch of forehead crowned by his saddle, and then left to go for a walk through the town, through goth-ic Sokal, which lay in its blue dust and in Galicia's dejection.

A large square stretched to the left of the park, a square surround-ed by ancient synagogues. Jews in long, torn coats were cursing and shoving each other on this square. Some of them, the Orthodox, were extolling the teachings of Adassia, the Rabbi of Belz, which led the Hasidim of the moderate school, students of Rabbi Iuda of Husyatyn, to attack them. The Jews were arguing about the Kabbala, and in their quarrel shouted the name of Elijah, Gaon of Vilna, the persecutor of the Hasidim.

Ignoring war and gunfire, the Hasidim were cursing the name of Elijah, the Grand Rabbi of Vilna, and I, immersed in my sorrow over Trunov, joined in the jostling and yelled along with them to ease my pain, until I suddenly saw a Galician before me, sepulchral and gaunt as Don Quixote.

This Galician was wearing a white linen garment that reached down to his ankles. He was dressed as for burial or as for the Eucharist, and led a bedraggled little cow tied to a rope. Over its wide back darted the tiny wriggling head of a snake. On the snake's head was a teetering wide-brimmed hat made of village straw. The pitiful little cow tagged along behind the Galician. He led her with impor-tance, and his lanky body cut into the hot brilliance of the sky like a gallows.

He crossed the square with a stately stride and went into a crooked little alley seasoned with sickeningly thick smoke. In the charred little hovels, in beggarly kitchens, were Jewesses who looked like old Negro women, Jewesses with boundless breasts. The Galician walked past them and stopped at the end of the alley before the pediment of a shattered building.

There by the pediment, near a crooked white column, sat a gypsy blacksmith shoeing horses. The gypsy was pounding the horses' hooves with a hammer, shaking his greasy hair, whistling, and smiling. A few Cossacks with horses were standing around him. My Galician walked up to the blacksmith, gave him a dozen or so baked potatoes without a word, and turned and walked off, not looking up at anyone. I was about to follow him, but one of the Cossacks, waiting for his horse to be shod, stopped me. This Cossack's name was Seliverstov. He had left Makhno* some time ago and was serving in the Thirty-third Cavalry Regiment.

"Lyutov," he said, shaking my hand, "you can't keep from picking quarrels with everyone! You've got the devil in you! Why did you finish off Trunov this morning?"

And from the scraps of gossip he had heard, Seliverstov yelled foolish gibberish at me, about how that very morning I had given Trunov, my squadron commander, a good beating. Seliverstov hurled all kinds of reproaches at me, reproached me in front of all the Cossacks, but there wasn't a grain of truth in what he said. It was true that Trunov and I had argued that morning, because Trunov wasted so much time dawdling with the prisoners. He and I had argued, but Pashka Trunov is dead, he will no longer be judged in this world, and I would be the last to do so. I will tell you why we quarreled.

We had taken some men prisoner at dawn today near the train station. There were ten of them. They were in their underwear when we took them. A pile of clothes lay next to the Poles—it was a trick, so that we couldn't tell the officers from the regular men by their uniforms. They had taken off their clothes themselves, but this time Trunov decided to find out the truth.

"All officers, step forward!" he commanded, walking up to the prisoners and pulling out his revolver.

Trunov had already been wounded in the head that morning. His head was bandaged with a rag, and blood trickled from it like rain from a haystack.

* The Ukrainian anarchist leader.

"Officers! Own up!" he repeated, and began prodding the Poles with the butt of his revolver.

Suddenly a thin old man with yellow cheekbones, a drooping mustache, and a large, bare bony back, came forward.

"End of this war!" the old man said with incomprehensible delight. "All officers run away, end of this war!"

And the Pole held out his blue hands to Trunov.

"Five fingers," he said, sobbing, twisting his large, wilted hands from side to side. "I raising with these five fingers my family!"

The old man gasped, swayed, and broke into tears of delight. He fell on his knees before Trunov, but Trunov pushed him back with his saber.

"Your officers are dogs!" Trunov said. "Your officers threw their uniforms here, but I'm going to finish off whoever they fit! We're going to have a little fitting!"

And Trunov picked out an officer's cap from the pile of rags and put it on the old man's head.

"It fits," Trunov murmured, stepping up closer to him, "it fits." And he plunged his saber into the prisoner's gullet.

The old man fell, his legs twitching, and a foamy, coral-red stream poured from his neck. Then Andryushka Vosmiletov, with his sparkling earring and his round villager's neck, sidled up to the dying man. Andryushka unbuttoned the dying Pole's trousers, shook him lightly, and pulled the trousers off. He flung them onto his saddle, grabbed another two uniforms from the pile, and then trotted off, brandishing his whip. At that moment the sun came out from behind the clouds. It nimbly enveloped Andryushka's horse, its cheerful trot, the carefree swish of its docked tail. Andryushka rode along the path to the forest—our cavalry transport was in the forest, the carters of the transport yelling and whistling, and making signs to Vosmiletov like to a deaf man.

The Cossack was already halfway there when Trunov, suddenly falling to his knees, hoarsely yelled after him.

"Andrei!" he shouted, lowering his eyes to the ground. "Andrei!" he repeated without looking up. "Our Soviet Republic is still alive, it's too early to be divvying up her property! Bring back those rags, Andrei!"

But Vosmiletov didn't even turn around. He rode at his amazing Cossack trot, his horse pertly swatting its tail, as if to shoo us away.

"Treason!" Trunov mumbled in disbelief. "Treason!" he said, quickly shouldering his gun and shooting, missing in his haste. This time Andrei stopped. He turned his horse toward us, bouncing on his saddle like a woman, his face red and angry, his legs jerking.

"Listen, countryman!" he yelled, riding closer, and immediately calming down at the sound of his own deep and powerful voice. "I should knock you to Kingdom Come to where your you-know-what mother is! Here you've caught a dozen Poles, and make a big song-and-dance of it! We've taken hundreds and didn't come running to you for help! If you're a worker, then do your job!"

Andryushka threw the trousers and the two uniforms off his saddle, snorted, turned away from the squadron commander, and came over to help me draw up a list of the remaining prisoners. He loafed about and snorted unusually loudly. The prisoners howled and ran away from him. He ran after them and gathered them under his arms, the way a hunter grips an armful of reeds and pushes them back to see a flock of birds flying to the river at dawn.

Dealing with the prisoners, I exhausted my repertoire of curses, and somehow managed to write up eight of the men, the numbers of their units, the type of gun they carried, and moved on to the ninth prisoner. The ninth was a young man who looked like a German acrobat from a good circus, a young man with a white, German chest, sideburns, a tricot undershirt, and a pair of long woolen drawers. He turned the nipples on his high chest toward me, threw back his sweaty blond hair, and told me the number of his unit. Andryushka grabbed him by his drawers and sternly asked him, "Where did you get those?"

"My mama knitted them," the prisoner answered, suddenly tottering.

"She's a great knitter, that mama of yours—looks factory-made," Andryushka said, looking more closely at the drawers, and ran his fingertips over the Pole's neat nails. "Yes, a great knitter—us, we never got to wear nothing like that."

He felt the woolen drawers again and took the ninth man by the hand in order to take him over to the other prisoners who were already on my list. But at that moment I saw Trunov creeping out from behind a mound. Blood was trickling from his head like rain from a haystack and the dirty rag had come undone and was hanging down. He crawled on his stomach holding his carbine in his hands. It was a Japanese carbine, lacquered and with a powerful shot. From a distance of twenty paces, Pashka shot the young Pole's skull to pieces and his brains spattered onto my hands. Trunov ejected the empty cartridges from his carbine and came over to me.

"Cross that one off," he said, pointing at my list.

"I'm not crossing him off," I answered, quaking. "From what I see, Trotsky's orders don't apply to you!"

"Cross that one off the list!" Trunov repeated, pressing his black finger down onto the paper.

"I'm not crossing him off!" I yelled with all my might. "There were ten of them, now there are eight—back at headquarters, Trunov, they're not going to let you get away with this!"

"At headquarters they'll chalk it up to the rotten life we live," Trunov said, coming up to me, all tattered, hoarse, and covered in soot. But then he stopped, raised his blood-drenched face to the sky, and said with bitter reproach, "Buzz, buzz! And there comes another one buzzing!"

And Trunov pointed to four dots in the sky, four bombers that came floating out from behind the shining, swanlike clouds. These were machines from the air squadron of Major Fauntleroy, large, armored machines.

"To horse!" the platoon commanders yelled when they saw the airplanes, and took the squadron at a fast trot into the woods. But Trunov did not ride with his squadron. He stayed back at the station building, huddled silently against the wall. Andryushka Vosmiletov and two machine-gunners, two barefoot fellows in crimson breeches, stood next to him, increasingly anxious.

"Run for it, boys!" Trunov said to them, and the blood began to drain from his face. "Here's a message to Pugachov from me."

And Trunov scrawled gigantic peasant letters on a crookedly torn piece of paper.

"As I have to perish today," he wrote, "I see it my duty to add two dead toward my possible shooting down of the enemy, and at the same time I am handing over my command to Platoon Commander Semyon Golov."

He sealed the letter, sat down on the ground, and took off his boots with great difficulty.

"For you," he said, handing the machine-gunners the message and his boots. "These boots are new."

"Good luck to you, Commander," the machine-gunners muttered back to him, shifting from one foot to the other, hesitating to leave.

"And good luck to you too," Trunov said, "whatever happens." And he went over to the machine guns that stood on a mound by the station hut. Andryushka Vosmiletov, the rag looter, was waiting for him there.

"Yes, whatever happens," Trunov said to him, and aimed his machine gun. "So you're staying with me, Andryushka?"

"Jesus Christ!" Andryushka answered, terrified, started sobbing, went white, and burst out laughing. "Damned Mother of Lord Jesus Christ!"

And he aimed the second machine gun at the airplanes.

The airplanes came flying over the station in tighter circles, rattled fussily high in the air, plunged, drew arcs, and the sun rested its pink rays on the sparkle of their wings.

In the meantime we, the Fourth Squadron, sat in the forest. There, in the forest, we awaited the outcome of the unequal battle between Pashka Trunov and Major Reginald Fauntleroy of the American forces. The major and three of his bombers proved their ability in this battle. They descended to three hundred meters, and first shot Andryushka and then Trunov. None of the rounds our men fired did the Americans any harm. The airplanes turned and flew away without even noticing our squadron hidden in the forest. And that was why, after waiting for half an hour, we were able to go pick up the bodies. Andryushka Vosmiletov's body was taken by two of his kinsmen who were serving in our squadron, and we took Trunov, our deceased squadron commander, to the gothic town of Sokal and buried him there in a stately spot—in a flower bed, in the public park in the middle of the town.

IVAN AND IVAN

*D*eacon Aggeyev had deserted from the front twice. For this he had been sent to Moscow's "regiment of the branded." Sergei Sergeyevich Kamenev,[*] the commander in chief, had inspected this regiment at Mozhaysk before it was to be sent to the front.

"I have no use for them," the commander in chief had said. "Send them back to Moscow to clean latrines."

In Moscow the branded regiment was somehow absorbed into an infantry company. The deacon also ended up in it. He arrived at the Polish front, where he claimed to be deaf. Barsutsky, the medical assistant from the first-aid detachment, after going back and forth with him for a week, was amazed at the deacon's obstinacy.

"To hell with that deaf man!" Barsutsky said to Soychenko, the medical orderly. "Go see if you can get a cart from the cavalry transport, we'll send the deacon to Rovno for a checkup."

Soychenko went to the transport and got three carts. Akinfiev was the driver of the first cart.

"Ivan," Soychenko said to him, "you're going to take the deaf man to Rovno."

"Take him I can," Akinfiev answered.

"Be sure to get me a receipt."

"Will do," Akinfiev said. "And what was it that caused it, this deafness of his?"

---

[*] Sergei Sergeyevich Kamenev, 1881–1963, was the commander in chief of the Eastern Front.

"To save his own goods and chattels a man will gladly set fire to another man's hide," Soychenko, the medical orderly, said. "That's what caused it. He's a damn four-flusher, that's what he is, not deaf!"

"Take him I can," Akinfiev repeated, and drove off after the other carts.

Three carts pulled up in front of the first-aid station. In the first cart sat a nurse who was being transferred to the rear lines, the second cart had been brought for a Cossack with an inflamed kidney, and in the third cart sat Ivan Aggeyev, the deacon.

Having arranged everything, Soychenko called the medical assistant.

"There goes that damn four-flusher," he said. "I'm putting him on the Revolutionary Tribunal cart* against receipt. They'll be off any minute now."

Barsutsky looked out the window, saw the carts, and went running out of the house, red-faced and hatless.

"Hey, I know you're going to cut his throat!" he yelled to Ivan Akinfiev. "I want the deacon in another cart!"

"Wherever you put him," the Cossacks standing nearby said, laughing, "our Ivan's going to get him."

Ivan Akinfiev, whip in hand, was also standing there next to his horses.

"Greetings, Comrade Medical Assistant," he said politely, taking off his cap.

"Greetings, my friend," Barsutsky answered. "You're going to have to put the deacon in another cart, you wild beast!"

"It would interest me to know," Akinfiev began in a whiny voice, and his upper lip shivered, slid up, and began quivering over his dazzling teeth, "it would interest me to know, if this is right behavior or behavior that is not right, that when the enemy is tormenting us unbelievably, when the enemy is pounding our last breath out of us, when the enemy is clinging to our legs like a lead weight and tying our hands with snakes, is it correct behavior for us to clog our ears at such a deadly hour?"

* The Revolutionary Tribunals were set up by the Bolsheviks after the October Revolution in 1918 to combat counterrevolutionary elements, abuse of power, speculation, and desertion from the Soviet army. The Revolutionary Tribunal carts were used to transport any personnel, prisoners, and supplies that connected with the tribunals' military work.

"Our Ivan thinks like a commissar!" Korotkov, the driver of the first cart, shouted.

"So what if he thinks like a commissar!" Barsutsky muttered, and turned away. "We all do. But we have to stick to the rules."

"But our deaf friend, he can hear perfectly well!" Akinfiev suddenly interrupted. He twirled his whip with his fat fingers, laughed, and winked at the deacon. The deacon sat on the cart, his large shoulders drooping, his head trembling.

"Well then, go with God!" the medical assistant yelled in desperation. "I hold you responsible, Ivan!"

"I'll gladly be held responsible," Ivan Akinfiev said slowly, and lowered his head. "Make yourself comfortable," he said to the deacon, without looking back at him. "Make yourself even more comfortable," he repeated, and took the reins in his hands.

The carts formed a line and hurried off one after the other along the high road. Korotkov drove in front and Akinfiev at the back, whistling a tune and waving the reins. They rode this way some fifteen versts, but as evening fell they came up against a sudden enemy attack.

On that day, July 22, the Poles in a swift maneuver had mangled the rear lines of our army, stormed the shtetl of Kozin, and had taken prisoner many of our fighters of the Eleventh Division. The squadrons of the Sixth Division rushed off to Kozin to counterattack the enemy. The lightning maneuvers of the units threw the cavalry transport into turmoil, and the Revolutionary Tribunal carts rolled through the raging throes of battle for two days and nights, and it was only on the third night that they came out onto the road along which the rearguard staff was retreating. It was on this road at midnight where I ran into the three carts.

Numb with despair, I ran into them after the battle at Khotin. In the battle at Khotin my horse had been killed. After I lost him, I climbed onto an ambulance cart, and gathered up wounded men until evening. Then all the able-bodied men were kicked off the ambulance cart, and I was left behind near a destroyed hut. Night came galloping toward me on swift steeds. The wailing of the transport carts deafened the universe; on the earth enveloped by screams the roads faded away. Stars slithered out of the cool gut of the sky, and on the horizon abandoned villages flared up. With my saddle on my shoulders I walked along a torn-up field path, stopping by a bend to answer the call of nature. Relieved, I buttoned myself up, but suddenly felt droplets falling on my hand. I switched on my flashlight, turned around, and saw lying on the ground the body of a Pole, drenched in my urine. A notebook and scraps of Pilsudski's proclamation* lay next to the corpse. The Pole's notebook had a list of his expenses, a schedule of performances at the Krakow Dramatic Theater, and an entry indicating the birthday of a woman by the name of Marie-Louisa. I picked up Pilsudski's proclamation, wiped the stinking liquid from my unknown brother's skull, and walked on, bent under the weight of my saddle.

At that moment, there was a groaning of wheels close by.

"Halt!" I yelled. "Who goes there?"

Night came galloping toward me on swift steeds, flames danced on the horizon.

"We're from the Revolutionary Tribunal," a voice smothered by darkness called back.

I rushed forward and ran right into the cart.

"They killed my horse!" I said loudly. "His name was Lavrik."

No one answered. I climbed onto the cart, put the saddle under my head, fell asleep, and slept till dawn, warmed by the rotting hay and the body of Ivan Akinfiev, my chance neighbor. In the morning, the Cossack woke up later than I did.

"Thank God it's light enough to see again," he said, took his revolver out from under his little trunk, and fired a shot next to the deacon's ear. The deacon was sitting right in front of us, driving the horses. Airy gray hair fluttered over his large, balding skull. Akinfiev fired another shot next to the deacon's other ear, and slipped the revolver back into its holster.

"Good day to you, Ivan!" he said to the deacon, grunting as he pulled on his boots. "So we'll grab a bite, huh?"

"Hey!" I yelled. "What the hell d'you think you're doing?"

"Not enough, that's what I'm doing!" Akinfiev answered, unpacking the food. "It's the third day now he's been pretending."

Then Korotkov, who I knew from the Thirty-first Regiment, yelled back from the first cart, telling me the whole story of the deacon from

---

* Jozef Klemens Pilsudski, 1867–1935, the first Chief of State of Poland after its independence from Russia in 1918, and commander in chief of the Polish army.

the beginning. Akinfiev listened carefully, cupping his ear, and then from under his saddle pulled out a roasted leg of ox. It was wrapped in a sackcloth and had straw all over it.

The deacon climbed over to us from the box, carved off a slice of green meat with his knife, and gave everyone a piece. After breakfast, Akinfiev wrapped the leg of ox in the sackcloth and slid it into the hay.

"Ivan," he said to Deacon Aggeyev, "let's drive out the devil. We have to stop anyway, since the horses need water."

He took a medicine bottle out of his pocket and a Tarnovsky syringe,* and gave them to the deacon. They climbed off the cart and walked about twenty paces into the field.

"Nurse!" Korotkov yelled from the first cart. "Adjust your eyes for distance, and you'll be dazzled by Akinfiev's endowment!"

"I you-know-what you and your endowments," the woman muttered, and turned away.

Akinfiev pulled up his shirt. The deacon knelt in front of him and gave him his injection. Then he wiped the syringe with a rag and held it up to the light. Akinfiev pulled his trousers up. He waited a moment, went behind the deacon, and fired another shot right next to his ear.

"My humblest thanks, Ivan," he said, buttoning up his trousers.

The deacon laid the medicine bottle on the grass and got up from his knees. His airy hair flew up.

"I will answer to a higher judge," he said dully. "You are not above me, Ivan."

"Nowadays everyone judges everyone else," the driver of the second cart, who looked like a boisterous little hunchback, interrupted. "They even sentence you to death, just like that!"

"Or even better," Deacon Aggeyev said, straightening up, "kill me, Ivan."

"Don't talk nonsense, Deacon!" Korotkov, whom I knew from before, said, coming up to him. "You should realize what kind of man you're riding with here. A lesser man would have shot you down like a duck, you wouldn't have had time to quack, yet he's trying to fish the truth out of you, and teach you a thing or two, you defrocked cleric!"

---

* A device for treating syphilis.

"Or even better," the deacon repeated obstinately, stepping forward, "kill me, Ivan."

"As it is, you'll kill yourself, you bastard," Akinfiev answered, going white and breaking into a lisp. "You're digging your own pit and burying yourself in it!"

Akinfiev waved his arms, tore his collar open, and fell down on the ground in a fit.

"O my dear little sweetheart!" he yelled wildly, and threw sand into his face. "O my bittersweet darling, my sweet darling Soviet power!"

"Ivan," Korotkov said, coming up to him, tenderly laying his hand on his shoulder. "Don't thrash about, my dear friend, don't be sad. Come, we have to go now."

Korotkov filled his mouth with water and spat it into Akinfiev's face, and then carried him over to the cart. The deacon sat on the box again, and we drove off.

There were no more than two versts left to the shtetl of Verba. Countless transport carts had crowded into the town that morning. They were from the Eleventh, the Fourteenth, and the Fourth Divisions. Jews in waistcoats, with raised shoulders, stood in their doorways like bedraggled birds. Cossacks went from yard to yard collecting rags and eating unripe plums. The moment we arrived, Akinfiev curled up on the hay and fell asleep, and I took a blanket from his cart and went to look for some shade to lie down in. But the fields on both sides of the road were covered with excrement. A bearded muzhik in copper-rimmed spectacles and a Tyrolean hat was sitting by the wayside reading a newspaper. He waved to me and said, "We call ourselves human, but we make more filth than the jackals! One is ashamed to face the earth!"

And he turned away and went back to reading his newspaper through his large spectacles.

I headed for the forest to the left, and saw the deacon approaching me.

"Where are you off to, countryman?" Korotkov yelled to him from the first cart.

"To relieve myself," the deacon mumbled. He grabbed my hand, and kissed it. "You are a fine gentleman," he whispered with a grimace, shuddering and gasping for air. "I beg you, whenever you have a free moment, to write a letter to the town of Kasimov, so my wife can mourn for me."

"Are you deaf, Father Deacon, or not?" I shouted into his face.

"Excuse me?" he said. "Excuse me?" And he cupped his ear.

"Are you deaf, Aggeyev, or not?"

"That's exactly it, deaf!" he quickly said. "Three days ago I could hear perfectly well, but Comrade Akinfiev crippled my hearing with a shot. He was supposed to deliver me to Rovno, Comrade Akinfiev was, but I really doubt he'll deliver me there."

And the deacon fell to his knees and crawled headfirst between the carts, completely entangled in his disheveled, priestly hair. Then he got up from his knees, pulled himself free from in between the carts, and went over to Korotkov, who gave him some tobacco. They rolled cigarettes and lit them for each other.

"That's better," Korotkov said, and made some space next to him.

The deacon sat down, and both were silent.

Then Akinfiev woke up. He rolled the leg of ox out of the sackcloth, carved off a slice of green meat with his knife, and gave everyone a piece. At the sight of the festering meat I felt overcome by weakness and desperation, and gave my piece back.

"Farewell, boys!" I said. "Good luck to you all!"

"Farewell," Korotkov said.

I took my saddle from the cart and left. As I walked off, I heard the endless muttering of Akinfiev.

"Ivan, you made a big mistake, my friend," he was saying to the deacon. "You should have trembled at my name, but you just got into my cart without a second thought. You could still have escaped before you ran into me, but now I'm going to hurt you, Ivan, you can bet on it, I'm really going to hurt you!"

THE CONTINUATION
OF THE STORY OF
A HORSE

*F*our months ago, Savitsky, our former division commander, took away the white stallion belonging to Khlebnikov, commander of the First Squadron. Khlebnikov had left the army shortly after, and today Savitsky received a letter from him.

Khlebnikov to Savitsky

And no anger upon the Budyonny army can I have longer, my sufferings in that army I understand and keep within my heart purer than anything holy. But to you, Comrade Savitsky, as an international hero, the working masses of Vitebsk, where I am the chairman of the District Revolutionary Committee, send the proletarian cry: "Give us World Revolution!" And we hope that that white stallion will trot beneath you on soft paths for many a year to come in aid of Freedom so beloved by all, and the Brother Republics in which we must keep a sharp eye out for the provincial authorities and the district units in an administrative respect. . . .

Savitsky to Khlebnikov

My true and dear Comrade Khlebnikov,

Which letter you wrote me is very commendable for the Common Cause, all the more after your foolishness when the good of your own hide made your eyes blind and you de-joined our Communist Party of the Bolsheviks. Our Communist Party, Comrade Khlebnikov, is an iron column of fighters sacrificing their blood in the front lines, and when blood flows from iron, then it is no joke, Comrade, but victory or death. The same goes for the Common Cause, the dawn of which I do not expect to see because the fighting is heavy and I have to change commanding officers every two weeks. Thirty days I have been fighting in the rear guard, covering the retreat of the invincible First Red Cavalry, and finding myself facing powerful gunfire from airplanes and artillery. Tardy was killed, Likhmanikov was killed, Gulevoy was killed, Trunov was killed, and the white stallion is no longer under me, so with the change in our fortunes of war, Comrade Khlebnikov, do not expect to see your beloved Division Commander Savitsky ever again. To tell you the truth, we shall meet again in the Kingdom of Heaven, although, from what people say, the old man up there in heaven isn't running a kingdom, but an all-out whorehouse, and as it is we have enough clap down here on earth—so, who knows, we might not get to see each other after all. Farewell, Comrade Khlebnikov.

THE WIDOW

*S*hevelyov, the regimental captain, is dying in an ambulance cart. A woman is sitting at his feet. Night, pierced by the flashes of the cannonade, is stooping over the dying man. Lyovka, the division commander's driver, is warming up food in a pot. Lyovka's forelock is hanging over the fire, the hobbled horses are crackling in the bushes. Lyovka is stirring the pot with a twig and talking to Shevelyov, who is stretched out in the ambulance cart.

"I worked in the town of Temryuk, Comrade, as a circus rider and also as a lightweight wrestler. The women in a small town like that get very bored, so when the little ladies saw me, all the walls came tumbling down. 'Lev Gavrilich,' they'd say to me, 'surely you won't turn down a little à la carte appetizer—you won't find it a waste of your time.' So I went with one of them to a tavern. We order two portions of veal, we order a jug of vodka, we sit there nice and quiet, we drink, I look, and what do I see? Some sort of gentleman bustling over toward me, nicely dressed, clean, but I notice that he is full of himself, not to mention that he was two sheets to the wind.

" 'If you will pardon me,' he says to me, 'what, if I may ask, is your nationality?'

" 'For what reason are you touching me about my nationality when I am in the company of a lady?' I ask him.

"And he: 'You? You are an athlete?' he says. 'In French wrestling they'd finish you off in the twinkle of an eye. Show me your nationali—' Yet I, believe it or not, still don't catch what's going on.

"So I ask him, 'Why do you—I don't even know your name—why do you try to provoke the kind of misunderstanding where one man or the other will have to lose his life, in other words, lie flat on his back awaiting his last breath?'"

"Lie flat on his back awaiting his last breath!" Lyovka repeats enthusiastically, stretching his arms up to the sky, letting the night envelop him like an aura. The tireless wind, the clean wind of the night, sings, fills itself with sound, and gently rocks the soul. The stars, blazing in the darkness like wedding rings, fall on Lyovka, become entangled in his hair, and expire on his tousled head.

"Lyovka, come here," Shevelyov suddenly whispers to him with blue lips. "The gold I have is for Sashka," the wounded man whispers. "The rings, the harness—everything's hers. We did our best to get by, I want to reward her. My clothes, my underwear, my medal for selfless heroism, are for my mother on the Terek. Send them to her with a letter and write in the letter: The regimental captain sends his regards, and don't cry. The house is yours, old woman, enjoy it. If anyone lays a finger on you, go straight to Budyonny and tell him, 'I'm Shevelyov's mama!' My horse, Abramka, I offer to the regiment, I am offering the horse in memory of my soul."

"Don't worry, I'll see to the horse," Lyovka mumbles. "Sashka!" he yells to the woman, waving to her. "You heard what he said? Swear before him—will you be sure to give the old woman what's hers or won't you?"

"I you-know-what the old woman!" Sashka says, and walks off into the bushes, holding her head high like a blind woman.

"Will you give her her miserable share?" Lyovka asks, catching up with her and grabbing her by the throat. "Say it here in front of him!"

"I'll give it to her, let me go!"

And then, having forced the declaration out of her, Lyovka grabbed the pot from the fire and began pouring soup into the dying man's rigid mouth. Cabbage soup trickled down Shevelyov's face, the spoon clanked against his sparkling, dead teeth, and bullets sang with growing mournfulness and force through the dense expanses of the night.

"They're shooting with rifles, the bastards," Lyovka said.

"The damn lackeys!" Shevelyov answered. "They're ripping open our right flank with their machine guns."

And Shevelyov, closing his eyes, stately as a corpse on a slab, listened to the battle with his large, waxen ears. Next to him, Lyovka was chewing meat, crunching and panting. When he had finished, Lyovka licked his lips and pulled Sashka into a ditch.

"Sash," he said, trembling, burping, his hands fidgeting. "Sash, as the Lord is my witness, we're covered in vice like yard dogs with lice. You only live once and then you die! Let me have you, Sash—I'll serve you, even if it's with my blood! His time's up, Sash, but the Lord has plenty more days in store for us!"

They sat down in the tall grass. The wavering moon crept from behind the clouds and stopped over Sashka's bare knee.

"You're warming each other," Shevelyov mumbled, "but it looks like the Fourteenth Division has been routed."

Lyovka crunched and panted in the bushes. The misty moon loitered in the sky like a beggar woman. Distant gunfire floated in the air. Feather grass rustled on the troubled earth onto which August stars fell.

Then Sashka returned to her previous place. She changed the wounded man's bandages and raised the flashlight over the festering wound.

"By tomorrow you'll be gone," Sashka said, wiping the cold sweat off Shevelyov. "By tomorrow you'll be gone. Death's already in your guts."

At that moment a heavy, many-voiced blast hit the earth. Four fresh enemy brigades, sent into battle under a unified command, had fired their first shell at Busk, lighting up the Bug watershed and severing our communications. Obedient blazes rose on the horizon, and heavy birds of cannon fire soared up from the flames. Busk was burning and Lyovka sped through the forest with the rattling cart of the commander of Division Six. He gripped the red reins tightly; the lacquered wheels banged against tree stumps. Shevelyov's ambulance cart came flying behind, Sashka checking the horses, which were straining at their harnesses.

They came to a clearing in the forest where there was a first-aid station. Lyovka unharnessed the horses and set out for the medical officer to ask for a horse blanket. He walked through the forest, which was filled with carts. Nurses' bodies jutted out from under their carts, timid dawn trudged over the soldiers' sheepskins. The sleeping men's boots lolled in a jumble, their pupils pointed to the sky, the black pits of their mouths askew.

The medical officer did have a horse blanket. Lyovka returned to Shevelyov, kissed his forehead, and pulled the blanket over his head. Then Sashka came up to the cart. She had knotted her kerchief under her chin and shaken the straw out of her dress.

"Pavlik," she said. "Jesus Christ in Heaven." And she lay herself against the dead man, covering him with her massive body.

"Her grief's killing her," Lyovka said. "Say what you want, she had it good with him. Now she'll have to take on the whole squadron again. It's tough."

And he drove off to Busk, where the headquarters of the Sixth Cavalry Division had been set up.

There, about ten versts from town, the battle against the Savinkov Cossacks was raging. The traitors were fighting us under the command of Cossack Captain Yakovlev, who had gone over to the Poles. They fought with courage. It was the second day our division commander was out with the troops, and as Lyovka did not find him at the headquarters, he went back to his hut, cleaned his horses, poured water over the wheels of his cart, and lay down to sleep on the threshing floor in the shed. The shed was filled with fresh hay, as arousing as perfume. Lyovka slept himself out, and then sat down to eat. His landlady boiled him some potatoes, which she doused in buttermilk. Lyovka was still sitting at the table when the funereal wail of trumpets and the clatter of many hooves resounded in the street. A squadron with bugles and banners rode along the winding Galician street. Shevelyov's body, covered with flags, was lying on a gun carriage. Sashka was riding behind the coffin on Shevelyov's stallion. A Cossack song came drifting from the back rows.

The squadron marched along the main street and turned toward the river. Lyovka, barefoot and without a cap, ran after the marching detachment and grabbed the reins of the squadron commander's horse.

Neither the division commander, who had stopped by the crossroads to salute the dead commander, nor his staff could hear what Lyovka was saying to the squadron commander.

"Drawers . . . mother on the Terek . . ." came wafting over to us in fragments on the breeze. Lyovka was shouting incoherently.

The squadron commander, without listening any further, freed his reins and pointed at Sashka. The woman shook her head and rode on. Lyovka jumped onto her horse behind her, grabbed her by the hair, pulled her head back, and slammed his fist into her face. Sashka wiped the blood away with the hem of her skirt and rode on. Lyovka slipped off her saddle, shook his forelock out of his face, and tied his red scarf around his hips. And the howling bugles led the squadron to the sparkling shore of the River Bug.

Lyovka came back to us later that day, his eyes glittering, and shouted, "I gave it to her! 'When the time comes,' she says, 'I'll send it to his mother. I won't forget him,' she says, 'I'll remember him.' 'You'd better remember him, you evil snake! If you forget, we'll come around and remind you! And if you forget a second time, we'll come around and remind you a second time!'"

ZAMOSC

The division commander and his staff were lying on a harvested field about three versts from Zamosc. The troops were going to attack the town that evening. Our orders were that we were to spend the night in Zamosc, and the division commander was waiting for a report of victory.

It was raining. Wind and darkness blew over the sodden earth. Stars were extinguished in the swelling ink of the clouds. Exhausted horses sighed and stamped their hooves in the darkness. We had nothing to give them to eat. I tied my horse's reins to my foot, wrapped myself in my cloak, and lay down in a waterlogged pit. The wet earth wrapped me in its comforting sepulchral embrace. The mare tugged at her reins, pulling at my leg. She found a tuft of grass and began nibbling at it. I fell asleep and dreamed of a threshing floor covered with hay. The dusty gold of threshed corn droned over it. Sheaves of wheat flew into the sky, the July day turned into evening, and the thickets of the sunset arched back over the village.

I lay stretched out on my silent bed of hay, and the hay caressing the nape of my neck drove me out of my mind. Then the barn doors opened with a whistle. A woman in a ball gown came up to me. She released one of her breasts from the black lace of her bodice and carefully offered it to me, like a wet nurse about to suckle an infant. She laid her breast on mine. An agonizing warmth shook the foundations of my soul, and drops of sweat—living, flowing sweat—seethed between our nipples.

"Margot!" I wanted to shout. "The earth is dragging me away with the rope of its wretchedness like a stubborn dog, and yet I have managed to see you again!"

I wanted to shout these words, but my jaws, clamped shut by a sudden frost, would not unclench.

Then the woman moved away from me and fell to her knees.

"Lord Jesus," she said, "take unto Thee the soul of Thy departed slave!"

She pressed two worn five-kopeck coins onto my lids and stuffed fragrant hay into the opening of my mouth. A moan tried in vain to flutter through my clenched jaws; my expiring pupils slowly rolled beneath the copper coins; I could not unclasp my hands, and . . . I awoke.

A muzhik with a tangled beard was lying in front of me. He held a rifle in his hands. My horse's back cut the sky like a black crossbeam. The reins gripped my foot in a tight noose, pulling it upward.

"You fell asleep, countryman," the muzhik said, and smiled with nocturnal, sleepless eyes. "That horse has dragged you a good half verst!"

I untied the reins and got up. Blood was trickling down my face, slashed by thistles.

Right there, not two paces away from me, lay the front line. I could see the chimneys of Zamosc, the thievish lights in the ravines of its ghetto, and the watchtower with its shattered lantern. The damp sunrise poured down on us like waves of chloroform. Green rockets soared over the Polish camp. They flashed in the air, came showering down like roses beneath the moon, and expired.

And in the silence I heard the distant breath of a moan. The smoke of a furtive murder encircled us.

"They're killing someone," I said. "Who is it they're killing?"

"The Pole's on a rampage," the muzhik told me. "The Pole is slashing the Yids' throats."

The muzhik moved the rifle from his right hand to his left. His beard had slid completely to one side. He looked at me fondly. "These nights on the front line are long," he said. "There's no end to these nights. One itches all over to talk to someone, but where d'you find this someone?"

The muzhik passed me his cigarette for me to light mine.

"It's all the fault of those Yids," he said. "That's how we see it, and that's how the Poles see it. After the war there'll be hardly any of them left. How many Yids you reckon there's in the world?"

"Around ten million," I answered, and began to bridle my horse.

"There'll be two hundred thousand of them left!" the muzhik yelled, grabbing me by the arm, afraid that I was about to leave. But I climbed onto my saddle and galloped off in the direction of our headquarters.

The division commander was preparing to ride off. The orderlies were standing at attention before him, dozing on their feet. Squadrons of dismounted horsemen crept over wet hillocks.

"They've turned the screws on us," the division commander whispered, and rode off.

We followed him along the road to Sitaniec.

It began raining again. Dead mice floated down the roads. Autumn surrounded our hearts with traps. Trees, upright naked corpses, stood swaying at crossroads.

We arrived in Sitaniec in the morning. I was with Volkov, the staff quartermaster. He found us a hut at the edge of the village.

"Wine," I told the mistress of the house. "Wine, meat, and bread!"

The old woman sat down on the floor and fed the calf she had hidden under her bed.

"*Nic niema*,"* she answered indifferently, "and I don't remember a time when there ever was anything."

I sat at the table, took off my revolver, and fell asleep. A quarter of an hour later I opened my eyes and saw Volkov hunched over the windowsill. He was writing a letter to his bride.

"Highly esteemed Valya," he wrote. "Do you remember me?"

I read the first line, and then took some matches out of my pocket and lit a pile of straw lying on the floor. Unfettered flames flashed up and came moving toward me. The old woman hurled herself chest-first onto the fire and extinguished it.

"What you doing, *Pan*?" the old woman gasped, staggering back in horror.

* Polish: "There's nothing."

Volkov turned around and stared at her with his empty eyes, and went back to writing his letter.

"I'm going to burn you, old woman," I muttered, drowsily. "I'm going to burn you and that stolen calf of yours."

"*Czekaj!*"* she shouted in a high-pitched voice. She ran out into the hall and came back with a jug of milk and some bread.

We had barely eaten half the bread when we heard shots rattling outside in the yard. There were many shots. They went on rattling and got on our nerves. We finished the milk, and Volkov went out into the yard to see what was going on.

"I've saddled your horse," he called through the window. "They've shot mine full of holes. The Poles have set up their machine guns less than a hundred paces from here!"

So the two of us ended up with one horse. She barely managed to take us out of Sitaniec. I sat in the saddle, and Volkov climbed on behind.

Transport carts rolled, roared, and sank in the mud. The morning seeped out of us like chloroform seeping over a hospital table.

"You married, Lyutov?" Volkov suddenly said, sitting behind me.

"My wife left me," I answered, dozing off for a few seconds, and I dreamed that I was sleeping in a bed.

Silence.

Our horse totters.

"Two more versts and this mare will be finished," Volkov says, sitting behind me.

Silence.

"We've lost the campaign," Volkov mutters, and begins to snore.

"Yes," I say.

* Polish: "Wait."

TREASON

Comrade Investigator Burdenko. Answering your question, my Party Membership Number is twenty-four zero-zero, issued to Nikita Balmashov by the Krasnodar Party Committee. My life history I would describe as domestic until 1914, as I worked on my father's fields, and I went from the fields into the ranks of the imperialists to defend Citizen Poincaré and the butchers of the German Revolution Ebert-Noske,* who, it looks like, were fast asleep one day and in their dreams saw how they could help St. Ivan, my Cossack village in the District of Kuban. And so the string kept unraveling all the way until Comrade Lenin, together with Comrade Trotsky, turned my beast of a bayonet to point it at new and better guts and paunches. From that time on I've been carrying number twenty-four zero-zero on the watchful tip of my bayonet, and I find it shameful and laughable to hear your words, Comrade Investigator Burdenko, this impossible sham about some unknown hospital in N. I neither fired at this hospital nor attacked it—I couldn't have. We were wounded, the three of us, in other words, Fighter Golovitsyn, Fighter Kustov, and me, not to mention that we had a fever in our bones and so didn't attack, but were crying, standing there in our hospital shirts out on the square among the free people of Jewish nationality! And as for the destruction of the three windowpanes, which we destroyed with an officer's revolver, I declare

---

*Raymond Poincaré, 1860–1932, president of France, supported the Imperialist Russian forces against the Bolsheviks in the Russian Civil War. Ebert and Noske were held responsible for the suppression of the Spartacus Rebellion in Germany.

from the bottom of my heart that these windowpanes did not corre-
spond to their purpose, as they were in the storeroom, which did not
need them. And Dr. Yaveyn, seeing our bitter gunshot, only laughed
with lots of chuckles, standing by the window of his hospital, and this
too can be corroborated by the aforementioned free Jews of the shtetl
of Kozin. As to Dr. Yaveyn, I also submit the following material,
Comrade Investigator, that he laughed when we, the three wounded
men, in other words Fighter Golovitsyn, Fighter Kustov, and me, initially presented ourselves for cure, and from his very first words, he
informed us far too roughly, 'You, fighters, will each take a bath in the
tub, and this very instant remove your weapons and clothes, as I'm worried they might be infectious—I want them out of here and dropped off
at the storeroom!' And as Fighter Kustov saw a beast before him and
not a man, he stepped forward with his broken leg and expressed himself, that the only people who need fear an infection from his sharp
Kuban saber are the enemies of our Revolution, and Fighter Kustov
also expressed an interest in knowing if at the storeroom one would find
among the things there a Party Fighter or, on the contrary, someone
from the partyless masses. And here Dr. Yaveyn obviously saw that we
were well able to recognize treason. He turned his back and without
another word and—again with lots of chuckles—sent us to the ward
where we also went, limping with broken legs, waving our crippled
arms, holding each other up, as the three of us are from the same
Cossack village of St. Ivan, in other words Fighter Golovitsyn, Fighter
Kustov, and me, we have the selfsame fate, and he who has a ripped-off
leg, he holds on to his comrade's arm, and he who is missing an arm,
he leans on his comrade's shoulder! Following the order issued, we went
to the ward where we expected to encounter Cultural and Educational
Work and devotion to the Cause, but what did we see in the ward? We
saw Red Army soldiers, only infantrymen, sitting on neat beds, playing
checkers, and with them nurses of tall build, smooth, standing by the
windows, fluttering their eyelashes. When we saw this, we stood there
as if lightning had struck us.

"You're done with fighting, boys?" I shout to the wounded.

"We're done with fighting," the wounded answer, and they move
their checkers made of bread pellets.

"Too soon," I tell the wounded, "too soon have you finished fighting, infantry, when the enemy walks on soft paws not fifteen versts from this town, and when you can read of our international situation in the *Krasny Kavalerist* newspaper, that it's one big disaster and that the horizon is full of black clouds!" But my words bounced off the heroic infantry like sheep dung from a regimental drum, and instead of a discussion the sisters of mercy led us off to some bunks and started all that drivel again about how we should hand in our weapons as if we had already been defeated! They agitated Kustov beyond words, and he began tearing at the wound on his left shoulder above his bleeding heart of a fighter and proletarian. Seeing his struggle, the nurses were quiet, but they only were quiet for the shortest time, and then again the partyless masses began making fun, and in the night the nurses sent volunteers ready to rip our clothes off us as we slept, or force us for Cultural and Educational Work to play theater roles in women's clothes, which is unseemly.

Unmerciful sisters! They tried more than once to trick us out of our clothes with sleeping powders, so that we started sleeping in shifts with one eye open, and we even went to the latrine in full uniform and with our revolvers. And suffering like this for a week and a day, so that we were already ranting and seeing visions, finally, waking on the accused morning of August 4, we noted on ourselves the following change: that we are lying there in shirts with numbers on them, like prisoners, without weapons and without the clothes sewn by our mothers, poor doddering old women from Kuban. And the sun, we see, is shining nice and bright, but the trench infantry, among who we three Red Cavalrymen are suffering, is hooliganizing us! And along with them the unmerciful sisters, who the night before gave us sleeping powders and now are wiggling their fresh breasts, bringing us trays with cococoa to drink, and milk enough in this cococoa to drown in! This whole frolicking merry-go-round makes the infantry bang their crutches on the ground so loud it's dreadful, and they pinch our bottoms like we're buyable females, yelling that Budyonny's First Cavalry has also finished fighting. But no, my curly-headed Comrades, you who have stuffed yourselves with such splendid paunches that rattle like machine guns in the night! Budyonny's First Cavalry has not yet finished fighting! So what we did was we excused ourselves as if we had to go answer a call of nature. Then the three of us went down into the courtyard and from the courtyard we went with our fevers and blue boils to Citizen Boyderman, the chairman of the Revolutionary Committee, without whom, Comrade Investigator Burdenko, it would never have come to this misunderstanding with the shooting—in other words, if it hadn't been for him, I mean if it hadn't been for the chairman of the Revolutionary Committee, who made us lose our senses completely. And even though we cannot present hard evidence about Citizen Boyderman, when we came in to the office of the chairman of the Revolutionary Committee, we noticed that he was a citizen of advanced years in a sheepskin coat, of Jewish nationality, sitting at the table, and the table is so full of papers that it is a terrible sight to see. And Citizen Boyderman's eyes dart first to one side, then to the other, and it is clear he has no idea what these papers are. These papers are a misery to him, even more so when unknown but deserving fighters come threatening, demanding rations, while one after the other local workers interrupt, informing him of the counterrevolution in the surrounding villages. And also regular workers suddenly appear who wish to get married at the Revolutionary Committee as soon as possible and without red tape. And we too announced with loud voices the incidents of treason at the hospital, but Citizen Boyderman only stared at us and his eyes darted again first to one side and then to the other, and he patted us on the shoulder, which already is not an Authority, and unworthy of an Authority! He didn't issue any resolution at all, and only announced, "Comrade Fighters, if you have compassion for the Soviet State, then leave these premises!" But we would not agree to do this, in other words, leave the premises, but demanded a full verification of his person, which, when he would not do that, we lost consciousness. And having lost consciousness, we went out onto the square in front of the hospital, where we disarmed the militia which was made up of one cavalry individual, and with tears in our eyes destroyed the three poor-quality windowpanes in the aforementioned storeroom. Dr. Yaveyn, during this unallowable action, made faces and chuckled, and all that at the very moment when four days later Comrade Kustov was to die of his illness!

In his short Red life, Comrade Kustov was endlessly distressed about treason, which one moment is winking at us from the window, the next is making fun of the coarse proletariat. But the proletariat,

Comrades, knows full well how coarse treason is, and we are pained by that, our soul is burning, and its fire rips apart the prison of our bodies.

Treason, I tell you, Comrade Investigator Burdenko, grins at us from the window, treason creeps in its socks through our house, treason has flung its boots over its shoulders, so that the floorboards of the house it is about to ransack will not creak.

CZESNIKI

*T*he Sixth Division had gathered in the forest near the village of Czesniki and waited for the signal to attack. But Pavlichenko, commander of the Sixth Division, was waiting for the Second Brigade, and would not give the signal. So Voroshilov* rode up to the division commander and prodded his chest with the muzzle of his horse.

"We're dawdling, Division Commander," he said, "we're dawdling!"

"The Second Brigade is proceeding as you ordered at full trot to the place of engagement," Pavlichenko answered in a hollow voice.

"We're dawdling, Division Commander, we're dawdling!" Voroshilov repeated, tugging at his reins.

Pavlichenko took a step back.

"In the name of conscience," he shouted, wringing his clammy fingers, "in the name of conscience, do not rush me, Comrade Voroshilov."

"Do not rush me?" hissed Klim Voroshilov, the political representative of the Revolutionary War Council, closing his eyes. He sat on his horse, silent, his eyes closed, his lips moving. A Cossack wearing bast sandals and a bowler hat stared at him in amazement. The galloping squadrons went crashing through branches, roaring through the forest like the wind. Voroshilov combed his horse's mane with his Mauser.

"Army Commander!" he yelled, turning to Budyonny. "Say a few words to your troops before we ride! There he is, the Pole, standing on top of the hill like a pretty picture, laughing at you!"

* Kliment Yefremovich Voroshilov, 1881–1969, was a close friend and colleague of Stalin's, and cofounder with Budyonny of the Red Cavalry.

As a matter of fact, we could see the Poles through our binoculars. The army staff jumped onto their horses and the Cossacks streamed toward Budyonny from all sides.

Ivan Akinfiev, the former vehicular driver of the Revolutionary Tribunal, rode past sitting sidesaddle, and prodded me with his stirrup.

"What? You're with the troops now, Ivan?" I called out to him. "You've got no ribs left!"

"I you-know-what these ribs," Akinfiev called back. "Let's hear what the man has to say!"

He rode on and pushed his way through right up to Budyonny.

Budyonny shuddered, and said in a quiet voice: "Men! Our situations . . . well, it's . . . bad. A bit more liveliness, men!"

"To Warsaw!" the Cossack in the bast sandals and the bowler hat yelled, his eyes wild, and he slashed the air with his saber.

"To Warsaw!" Voroshilov shouted, rearing his horse and vaulting into the center of the squadrons.

"Fighters and Commanders!" he shouted passionately. "In Moscow, our ancient capital, there rages a power never before seen! A government of workers and peasants, the first in the world, orders you, fighters and commanders, to attack the enemy and bring back victory!"

"Draw your sabers!" Pavlichenko sang out from far behind the army commander, and his fat crimson lips glistened foam-speckled through the ranks. Pavlichenko's red Cossack coat hung in tatters, his repulsive, meaty face was twisted. He saluted Voroshilov with the blade of his precious saber.

"In accordance with my duty to the revolutionary pledge," said the commander of Division Six, wheezing, his eyes darting around, "I hereby report to the Revolutionary War Council that the Second Invincible Cavalry Brigade is at the present time moving at a fast trot to the place of engagement!"

"Well, get on with it," Voroshilov answered, waving him away. He tugged at his reins and rode off, with Budyonny at his side. On their long-limbed chestnut mares they rode next to each other in identical military jackets and glittering silver-embroidered trousers. The fighters, whooping, flocked after them, and pale steel gleamed in the purulence of the autumn sun. But I did not hear solidarity in the howls of the Cossacks, and, waiting for the attack, I went into the forest, into its heart, to our provision station.

A wounded Red Army soldier lay there in a delirium, and Styopka Duplishchev, a young, dim-witted Cossack, was rubbing down Hurricane, the division commander's thoroughbred stallion, which was descended from Lyulyusha, the Rostov record holder. The wounded man was rambling, reminiscing about Shuya, about a heifer and some sort of flax strands. Duplishchev, to drown out the pitiful muttering, was singing a song about an orderly and a fat general's wife. He sang louder and louder, waving his currycomb and patting the horse. But he was interrupted by Sashka, puffy Sashka, the lady of all the squadrons. She rode up to Duplishchev and jumped off her horse.

"So we'll do it, or what?" Sashka said to him.

"Get out of here," the young Cossack answered, turning his back to her, and began plaiting ribbons into Hurricane's mane.

"You stick to your word, Styopka!" Sashka told him. "Or are you just a lump of boot wax?"

"Get out of here!" Styopka answered. "I stick to my word."

He plaited all the ribbons into the horse's mane, and suddenly turned to me in despair. "Just look at that! See how she tortures me, Kiril Vasilich? For a whole month already you wouldn't believe what I've had to put up with! Wherever I turn to, she's there, wherever I run to, she blocks my path, always wanting me to let the stallion have a go. But the division commander tells me every day, 'Styopka,' he tells me, 'with a stallion like this one, many will be coming to ask you to let the stallion have a go, but don't let him, not before he's four!'"

"I bet you you won't be letting anyone before he's fifteen," Sashka muttered, and turned away. "And when he's fifteen, you'll be drooling bubbles, for all I know!"

She went over to her mare, tightened the saddle strap, and was about to ride off.

The spurs on her boots clattered, her lace stockings were full of straw and spattered with dirt, her monstrous breasts went swinging toward her back.

"And to think I brought a ruble with me," Sashka said to herself, shoving her spurred boot into the stirrup. "I brought it with me but now I'll have to take it away again."

She took out two fifty-kopeck coins, jingled them in her palm, and hid them again in her cleavage.

"So we'll do it, or what?" Duplishchev said, his eyes fixed on the silver, and he brought over the stallion.

Sashka went to a sloping place in the clearing and had her mare stand there.

"You'd be amazed, but you're the only one in these mudfields who's got a stallion," she said to Styopka, pushing Hurricane into position. "My mare's a frontline war horse, two years now she hasn't been humped, so I says to myself—why not get her some good blood?"

Sashka finished with the stallion, and then led her horse to the side.

"So, sweetie, we got our stuffing now," she whispered, kissing her mare's wet, skewbald lips from which slobbering strands of spittle hung. She rubbed her cheek against the mare's muzzle, and suddenly noticed the noise thudding through the forest.

"The Second Brigade's coming back," Sashka said sternly, turning to me. "We must go, Lyutov!"

"Coming back, not coming back, I don't give a damn!" Duplishchev shouted, the words getting stuck in his throat. "You've had your feast, now pay the priest!"

"My money's nice and fine where it is!" Sashka muttered, and leaped onto her mare.

I dashed after her, and we rode off in full gallop. Duplishchev's howl and the light thud of a gunshot rang out behind us.

"Just look at that!" the Cossack boy yelled as loudly as he could, running through the forest.

The wind hopped through the branches like a crazed rabbit, the Second Brigade went flying through the Galician oak trees, the placid dust of the cannonade rose above the earth as above a peaceful hut. And at a sign from the division commander, we launched our attack, the unforgettable attack on Czesniki.

AFTER THE BATTLE

*T*he story of my fight with Akinfiev is as follows:

On the thirty-first came the attack on Czesniki. The squadrons had gathered in the forest next to the village, and hurled themselves at the enemy at six in the evening. The enemy was waiting for us on a hill three versts away. We galloped the three versts on our totally exhausted horses, and when we got to the hill we saw a deadly wall of black uniforms and pale faces. They were Cossacks who had betrayed us at the beginning of the Polish Campaign and had been rounded up into a brigade by Cossack Captain Yakovlev. The Cossack captain formed his horsemen into a square formation, and waited with his saber unsheathed. A gold tooth flashed in his mouth and his black beard lay on his chest like an icon on the chest of a corpse. The enemy's machine guns fired at twenty paces; wounded men fell in our lines. We went trampling over them and hurled ourselves at the enemy, but his square formation did not waver, and we turned and ran.

So the Savinkov Cossacks gained a short-lived victory over the Sixth Division. They gained the victory because they did not turn their faces from the lava flow of our oncoming squadrons. The Cossack captain stood firm that time, and we ran without reddening our sabers with the traitors' contemptible blood.

Five thousand men, our whole division, poured down the slope with no one in pursuit. The enemy stayed on the hill, unable to believe their illogical victory and muster their wits to set out in pursuit after us. That is why we survived and went bounding into the valley unharmed, where we were met by Vinogradov, our military commissar. Vinogradov was dashing about on his crazed horse trying to send the fleeing Cossacks back into battle.

"Lyutov!" he yelled when he saw me. "Get those fighters to turn around or I'll rip your soul out!"

Vinogradov pounded his tottering stallion with the butt of his Mauser, howled, and tried rounding up the men. I got away from him and rode up to Gulimov, a Kirghiz, who was galloping past.

"Gulimov! Get back up there!" I yelled to him. "Turn back your horse!"

"Turn back your own damn horse!" Gulimov yelled back. His eyes darted about thievishly and he fired a shot, singeing the hair above my ear.

"Turn your own horse back," Gulimov hissed, grabbed my shoulder with one hand, and tried unsheathing his saber with the other. The saber was jammed in its sheath, the Kirghiz shuddered and looked around. He held my shoulder tightly and brought his head closer and closer.

"Yours first," he whispered almost inaudibly, "and mine will follow." And he tapped me lightly on the chest with the blade of his saber, which he had managed to unsheathe.

I felt a wave of nausea from death's closeness and its tight grip. With the palm of my hand I pushed away the Kirghiz's face, hot as a stone in the sun, and scratched it with all my might. Warm blood rippled under my nails, tickling them. I rode away from Gulimov, out of breath as after a long journey. My horse, my tormented friend, trotted slowly. I rode without looking where I was going, I rode without turning around, until I came across Vorobyov, the commander of the First Squadron. Vorobyov was looking for his quartermasters and couldn't find them. He and I made our way to Czesniki and sat down on a bench along with Akinfiev, the former vehicular driver of the Revolutionary Tribunal. Sashka, the nurse of the Thirty-first Cavalry Regiment, came by, and two commanders sat down on the bench with us. The commanders sat there in silence, dozing. One of them was shell-shocked, shaking his head uncontrollably and winking with one bloated eye. Sashka went to tell the people at the field hospital about him, and then came back to us, dragging her horse behind her by the reins. Her mare resisted, her hooves skidding in the wet mud.

"So where are you sailing off to?" Vorobyov asked the nurse. "Sit down here with us, Sash!"

"I'm not sitting with you!" Sashka answered, and slapped her mare on the belly. "No way!"

"What d'you mean?" Vorobyov shouted, laughing. "Or have you had second thoughts about drinking tea with men?"

"It's you that I've had second thoughts about!" she told the commander, hurling away the reins. "Yes, I've had second thoughts about drinking tea with you, after I saw you all today and saw what heroes you all are, and how disgusting you are, Commander!"

"So when you saw it," Vorobyov muttered, "how come you didn't join in the shooting?"

"Join in the shooting?" Sashka shouted in desperation, tearing off her nurse's band. "What am I supposed to shoot with? This?"

Here Akinfiev, the former vehicular driver of the Revolutionary Tribunal, with whom I still had some unfinished business to settle, came up to us.

"You've got nothing to shoot with, Sash," he said soothingly. "No one's blaming you for that! I blame those who get all mixed up in battle and forget to load cartridges in their revolvers!" A spasm suddenly shot over his face. "You rode in the attack!" he shouted at me. "You rode but didn't put any cartridges in! Why?"

"Back off, Ivan," I said to Akinfiev. But he wouldn't back off, and kept coming closer to me, an epileptic with a twisted spine and no ribs.

"The Pole shot at you, yes, but you didn't shoot at him!" he muttered, twisting and turning with his shattered hip. "Why?"

"The Pole did shoot at me," I told him brusquely, "but I didn't shoot at the Pole!"

"So you're a Molokan,* right?" Akinfiev whispered, stepping back.

"So I'm a Molokan!" I said, louder than before. "What do you want?"

"What I want is for you to be aware," Akinfiev yelled in wild triumph, "aware that you're a Molokan, because in my books all Molokans should be shot dead, they believe in God!"

---

* Members of a Bible-centered religious movement among the Russian peasantry that broke away from the Russian Orthodox Church in the sixteenth century.

A crowd gathered, and Akinfiev yelled on about wimps without stopping. I wanted to walk away, but he ran after me, and caught up with me, and punched me in the back with his fist.

"You didn't put any cartridges in!" Akinfiev whispered in a breathless voice right next to my ear, and with his large thumbs began trying to wrench my mouth open. "You believe in God, you traitor!"

He tugged and tore at my mouth. I pushed the epileptic back and hit him in the face. He keeled over onto his side, hit the ground, and began to bleed.

Sashka went over to him with her dangling breasts. She poured water over him, and pulled out of his mouth a long tooth which was swaying in the blackness like a birch tree on a bare country road.

"These bantams know just one thing," Sashka said, "and that's how to belt each other in the mouth. With a day like this and everything, I just want to shut my eyes!"

There was anguish in her voice, and she took wounded Akinfiev with her, while I staggered off into the village of Czesniki, which was sliding around in the relentless Galician rain.

The village floated and bulged, crimson clay oozing from its gloomy wounds. The first star flashed above me and tumbled into the clouds. The rain whipped the willow trees and dwindled. The evening soared into the sky like a flock of birds and darkness laid its wet garland upon me. I was exhausted, and, crouching beneath the crown of death, walked on, begging fate for the simplest ability—the ability to kill a man.

THE SONG

When we were quartered in the village of Budziatycze, it was my lot to end up with an evil landlady. She was a widow, she was poor. I broke many locks on her storerooms, but found no provisions.

All I could do was to try and outsmart her, and one fine day, coming home early before dusk, I caught her closing the door of the stove, which was still warm. The hut smelled of cabbage soup, and there might well have been some meat in that soup. I did smell meat in her soup and laid my revolver on the table, but the old woman denied everything. Her face and black fingers were gripped by spasms, she glowered at me with fear and extraordinary hatred. Nothing would have saved her—I would have made her own up with my revolver if Sashka Konyayev, in other words Sashka Christ, hadn't suddenly turned up.

He came into the hut with his concertina under his arm, his exquisite legs shuffling in battered boots.

"How about a song?" Sashka said, looking at me, his eyes filled with blue and dreamy ice crystals. "How about a song?" he said, and sat down on the bench and played a prelude.

The pensive prelude came as if from far away. He stopped, and his blue eyes filled with longing. He turned away, and, knowing what I liked, started off on a song from Kuban.

"Star of the fields," he sang, "star of the fields over my native hut, and my mother's hand, so sorrowful. . . ."

I loved that song. Sashka knew this, because both of us, both he and I, had first heard this song back in '19 in the shallows of the Don in the Cossack village of Kagalnitskaya.

A hunter who poached in the protected waters there had taught it to us. There, in the protected waters, fish spawn and countless flocks of birds nest. The fish multiply in the shallows in incredible numbers, you can scoop them up with a ladle or even with your bare hands, and if you dip your oar in the water, it just stands there upright—a fish will have grabbed it and will carry it away. We saw this with our own eyes, we will never forget the protected waters of Kagalnitskaya. Every government has banned hunting there—a good ban—but back in '19 a war was raging in the shallows, and Yakov the hunter, who plied his forbidden trade right before our eyes, gave Sashka Christ, our squadron singer, a concertina as a present so that we would look the other way. He taught Sashka his songs. Many of them were soulful, old songs. So we forgave the roguish hunter, for we needed his songs: back then, no one could see the war ever ending, and Sashka covered our arduous paths with melody and tears. A bloody trail followed our paths. The songs soared over this trail. That is how it was in Kuban and on our campaigns against the Greens,* and that is how it was in the Urals and in the Caucasian foothills, and that is how it is to this very day. We need these songs, no one can see this war ever ending, and Sashka Christ, our squadron singer, is too young to die.

And this evening too, cheated of my landlady's cabbage soup, Sashka calmed me with his soft, wavering voice.

"Star of the fields," he sang, "star of the fields over my native hut, and my mother's hand, so sorrowful. . . ."

And I listened, stretched out in a corner on my rotting bedding. A dream was wracking my bones, the dream shook the putrid hay beneath me, and through the dream's burning torrent I could barely make out the old woman, who was standing by the wall, her withered cheek propped on her hand. She hung her ravaged head and stood fixed by the wall, not moving even after Sashka had finished playing. Sashka finished and put down his concertina, yawned, and burst out laughing

---

* Defectors from the Imperial army and later also from the new Soviet army, who banded together in guerrilla groups. They were called "Greens" because they hid in forests. Both the Whites and the Reds tried to organize them under their influence, creating bands of Red Greens and White Greens.

sleep, and then, noticing the chaos in the widow's hut, he wiped the debris from the bench and brought in a bucket of water.

"You see, deary, what your boss is up to?" the landlady said to him, pointing at me and rubbing her back against the door. "Your boss came in here, yelled at me, stamped his foot, broke all the locks in my house, and shoved his gun at me. It is a sin before the Lord to shove a gun at me—I'm a woman, after all!"

She rubbed her back against the door again and threw a sheepskin coat over her son. Her son lay snoring beneath an icon on a large bed covered with rags. He was a deaf-mute boy with a white, water-swollen head and gigantic feet, like those of a grown muzhik. His mother wiped the snot from his nose and came back to the table.

"Mistress," Sashka said to her, caressing her shoulder, "if you wish, I could be really nice to you."

But it was as if the woman hadn't heard what he had said.

"I didn't see no cabbage soup at all," she said, her cheek propped on her hand. "It ran away, my cabbage soup, and people shove their guns at me, so that even when a nice man comes along and I get a chance to tumble a little, I've ended up feeling so drab, I can't even enjoy sinning!"

She dragged out her mournful lament and, mumbling, rolled her deaf-mute son to the wall. Sashka lay with her on the rag-covered bed while I tried to sleep, conjuring up dreams so that I would doze off with pleasant thoughts.

THE RABBI'S SON

*D*o you remember Zhitomir, Vasily? Do you remember the River Teterev, Vasily, and that night in which the Sabbath, the young Sabbath, crept along the sunset crushing the stars with the heel of her red slipper?

The thin horn of the moon dipped its arrows in the black waters of the Teterev. Little, funny Gedali, the founder of the Fourth International,* who took us to Rabbi Motale Bratslavsky for evening prayer. Little, funny Gedali, shaking the cockerel feathers of his top hat in the red smoke of the evening. The candles' predatory pupils twinkled in the rabbi's room. Broad-shouldered Jews crouched moaning over prayer books, and the old jester of the Chernobyl line of *tsaddiks* jingled copper coins in his frayed pocket.

You remember that night, Vasily? Outside the window horses neighed and Cossacks shouted. The wasteland of war yawned outside and Rabbi Motale Bratslavsky, clutching his tallith with his withered fingers, prayed at the eastern wall. Then the curtains of the cabinet fell open, and in the funerary shine of the candles we saw the Torah scrolls wrapped in coverings of purple velvet and blue silk, and above the Torah scrolls hovered the humble, beautiful, lifeless face of Ilya, the rabbi's son, the last prince of the dynasty.

And then, Vasily, two days ago the regiments of the Twelfth Army

---

* See the story "Gedali," in which Gedali envisions an ideal International that would supplant the Third Communist International founded in Moscow in 1919 to promote Communism worldwide.

opened the front at Kovel. The victors' haughty cannonade thundered through the town. Our troops were shaken and thrown into disarray. The Polit-otdel train* crept along the dead spine of the fields. The typhoid-ridden muzhik horde rolled the gigantic ball of rampant soldier death before it. The horde scampered onto the steps of our train and fell off again, beaten back by rifle butts. It panted, scrambled, ran, was silent. And after twelve versts, when I no longer had any potatoes to throw to them, I threw a bundle of Trotsky leaflets at them. But only one of them stretched out a dirty, dead hand to grab a leaflet. And I recognized Ilya, the son of the Zhitomir rabbi. I recognized him straightaway, Vasily! It was so painful to see the prince, who had lost his trousers, his back snapped in two by the weight of his soldier's rucksack, that we broke the rules and dragged him up into the railroad car. His naked knees, clumsy like the knees of an old woman, knocked against the rusty iron of the steps. Two fat-breasted typists in sailor blouses dragged the dying man's timid, lanky body along the floor. We laid him out in the corner of the train's editorial compartment. Cossacks in red Tatar trousers fixed his slipped clothing. The girls, their bandy bovine legs firmly planted on the floor, stared coolly at his sexual organs, the withered, curly manhood of the emaciated Semite. And I, who had met him during one of my nights of wandering, packed the scattered belongings of Red Army soldier Ilya Bratslavsky into my suitcase.

I threw everything together in a jumble, the mandates of the political agitator and the mementos of a Jewish poet. Portraits of Lenin and Maimonides lay side by side—the gnarled steel of Lenin's skull and the listless silk of the Maimonides portrait. A lock of woman's hair lay in a book of the resolutions of the Sixth Party Congress, and crooked lines of Ancient Hebrew verse huddled in the margins of Communist pamphlets. Pages of *The Song of Songs* and revolver cartridges drizzled on me in a sad, sparse rain. The sad rain of the sunset washed the dust from my hair, and I said to the young man, who was dying on a ripped mattress in the corner, "Four months ago, on a Friday evening, Gedali the junk dealer took me to your father, Rabbi Motale, but back then, Bratslavsky, you were not in the Party."

* The train sent out by the Polit-otdel, the political organ of the new Soviet government charged with the ideological education of the military.

"I was in the Party back then," the young man answered, scratching his chest and twisting in his fever. "But I couldn't leave my mother behind."

"What about now, Ilya?"

"My mother is just an episode of the Revolution," he whispered, his voice becoming fainter. "Then my letter came up, the letter 'B,' and the organization sent me off to the front. . . ."

"So you ended up in Kovel?"

"I ended up in Kovel!" he shouted in despair. "The damn kulaks opened the front. I took over a mixed regiment, but it was too late. I didn't have enough artillery."

He died before we reached Rovno. He died, the last prince, amid poems, phylacteries, and foot bindings. We buried him at a desolate train station. And I, who can barely harness the storms of fantasy raging through my ancient body, I received my brother's last breath.

IV
❧

The Red Cavalry Cycle:
Additional Stories

The seven additional RED CAVALRY stories in this section were not included in Babel's book KONARMIA (RED CAVALRY), published in 1926. Most of them appeared in magazines in the late 1920s and 1930s after the book had come out, while "And Then There Were Nine" and the fragment "And Then There Were Ten" were not published during Babel's lifetime. The last piece, "A Letter to the Editor," appeared in the magazine OKTYABR in October 1924. It was a response to General Budyonny's vitriolic article with the punning title "Babism Bablya" ("Babel's woman-ishness"), in which he condemned Babel's RED CAVALRY stories and their portrayal of himself and other real commanders.

MAKHNO'S BOYS

$\mathcal{T}$he previous night, six Makhno* fighters raped a maid. When I heard this the following morning, I decided to find out what a woman looks like after being raped six times. I found her in the kitchen. She stood bent over a tub, washing clothes. She was a fat girl with blooming cheeks. Only a tranquil life on fertile Ukrainian soil can douse a Jewish girl in such bovine juices, lend her face such a lusty gloss. The girl's legs, fat, brick-red, bulging like globes, gave off the luscious stench of freshly carved meat, and it seemed to me that all that remained of yesterday's virginity were her cheeks, more flushed than usual, and her lowered eyes.

Young Kikin, the errand boy at Makhno's headquarters, was also in the kitchen. He was known at the headquarters as something of a simpleton—he had a tendency to walk about on his hands at the most unsuitable moments. More than once I found him in front of the mirror, stretching out his leg in his tattered trousers. He would wink at himself, slap himself on his bare, boyish stomach, sing marching tunes, and make triumphant grimaces which made even him guffaw. This boy's imagination worked with incredible vigor. Today I again found him busy on one of his special projects—he was sticking strips of gold paper on a German helmet.

"How many of them did you accommodate yesterday, Ruhlya?" he asked the girl, narrowing his eyes as he eyed the decorated helmet.

She remained silent.

* Nestor Ivanovich Makhno, 1889–1934, the Ukrainian anarchist leader.

"You accommodated six of them," he continued, "but there are girls who can accommodate up to twenty. Our boys did a Krapivno house-wife and they kept pounding and pounding away at her till they ran out of steam. But she was a good deal fatter than you are."

"Go get me some water," the girl said.

Kikin brought a bucket of water from the yard. He shuffled over to the mirror in his bare feet, put the helmet with the gold ribbons on his head, and carefully peered at his reflection. His image in the mirror fascinated him. He stuck his fingers in his nose and avidly watched it change shape under the pressure from within.

"I'll be going out on a mission," he said to the Jewess. "Don't you say a word to no one! Stetsenko's taking me into his squadron. At least they give you a real uniform, people respect you, and I'll have some real fighter pals, not like here, where we're just some dinky little flea-ridden outfit. Yesterday, when they grabbed you and I was holding you down by the head, I said to Matvey Vasilich, Hey, Matvey Vasilich, I said to him, four have already had a go, and I still get to keep holding and holding her down! You've already had her twice, Matvey Vasilich, and just because I'm underage and not in your gang, everyone can just push me around! And you yourself, Ruhlya, must have heard what he said to me—We, he said to me, don't push you around, Kikin! Once all my orderlies have had a go, it'll be your turn. He did say I could, and then, when they were already dragging you out into the woods, Matvey Vasilich tells me, You can do her now, Kikin, if you wish!—No way do I wish, Matvey Vasilich! I tell him, not after Vaska has had her, I'd never get over it till I die!"

Kikin grunted and fell silent. Barefoot, lanky, sad, his stomach bare, the glittering helmet on his straw-colored head, he lay down on the floor and stared into the distance.

"The whole world reckons the Makhno gang is all heroic and everything!" he said morosely. "But when you start hanging out with them, you soon see that they all harbor some grudge or other!"

The Jewess lifted her flushed face from the tub, glanced over at the boy, and left the kitchen with the heavy gait of a cavalryman whose numb legs have just touched the ground after a very long ride. Left alone, the boy looked dully around the kitchen, sighed, rested his palms on the floor, swung his legs in the air, and, with his heels together, quickly walked around on his hands.

A HARDWORKING
WOMAN

Three Makhno fighters—Gniloshkurov and two others—had come to an agreement with a woman about her love services. For two pounds of sugar, she agreed to take on the three of them, but when the third one's turn came, she couldn't hold out and went reeling around the room. The woman scrambled out into the yard, where she ran straight into Makhno.* He lashed her with his whip, tearing her upper lip, and Gniloshkurov got it too.

This happened in the morning, at nine o'clock. After that the day went by with much activity, and now it's night, the rain is drizzling, whispering and unyielding. It is rustling beyond the wall. In front of me, outside the window, hangs a single star. The town of Kamenka has drowned in the haze—the teeming ghetto is filled with teeming darkness and the inexorable bustling of the Makhno fighters. Someone's horse neighs softly like a pining woman; beyond the edge of the shtetl sleepless *tachankas*† creak, and the cannonade, falling silent, lies down to sleep on the black, wet earth.

Only Makhno's window is ablaze in a faraway street. It cuts through the gloom of the autumn night like an exhilarated searchlight, flashing, drenched with rain. There, in Makhno's headquarters, a brass band is playing in honor of Antonina Vasilevna, a nurse who was spending her first night with Makhno. The thick, melancholy trumpets blow louder and louder, and the partisans, huddled together beneath

* The anarchist leader.
† An open carriage or buggy with a machine gun mounted on the back.

my window, listen to the thundering of old marches. Three partisans are sitting beneath my window—Gniloshkurov and his comrades—and then Kikin, a crazed Cossack, comes rushing over to join them. He kicks his legs up in the air, does a handstand, chirps and sings, and has difficulty calming down, like an epileptic after a fit.

"Oat-head!" Gniloshkurov suddenly whispers to Kikin. "Oat-head," he repeats morosely. "How can it be that she let two more have a go after me without so much as batting an eyelash? There I was, putting my belt back on, and she looks at me and says to me, '*Merci* for spending some time with me, Papa, you are so charming! My name is Anelya—that's what I'm called, Anelya.' So you see, Oat-head, I think to myself she must have been chewing some bitter herbs since the morning, and then Petka wanted to have a go at her too!"

"Then Petka wanted to have a go at her too," fifteen-year-old Kikin chimes in, sitting down and lighting a cigarette. " 'Young man,' she tells Petka, 'would you please be kind enough, I'm at the end of my rope!' And she jumps up and starts spinning like a top, and the boys spread their arms and won't let her out the door, and she keeps begging and begging." Kikin stands up, his eyes flash, and he begins to laugh. "She escapes," Kikin continues, "and then right there at the door, who does she run into? Makhno himself. 'Halt!' he yells. 'I bet you have the clap! I'm going to hack you up here and now!' And he starts lashing her, and she—she still wants to give him some lip!"

"It must also be said," Petka Orlov's pensive and tender voice interrupts Kikin, "it must also be said, that there is greed among people, ruthless greed! I told her—'There's three of us, Anelya! Bring a girl-friend along, share the sugar with her, she'll help you!' 'No,' she says, 'I can cope well enough, I have three children to feed, it's not like I'm a virgin or something.' "

"A hardworking woman!" Gniloshkurov, still sitting beneath my window, assures Petka. "Hardworking to the last!"

And he falls silent. I can still hear the sound of water. The rain is continuing to stutter, bubble, and moan on the roofs. The wind grabs the rain and shoves it to the side. The triumphant blowing of the trumpets falls silent in Makhno's courtyard. The light in his room has dimmed by half. Gniloshkurov rises from the bench, splicing the dim glimmer of the moon. He yawns, tugs his shirt up, and scratches his remarkably white stomach, and then goes over to the shed to sleep. Petka Orlov's tender voice floats after him.

"In Gulya-Polye there was this out-of-town muzhik called Ivan Golub," Petka says. "He was a quiet muzhik—no drinking, he was cheerful when he worked, lifted too much of a load, got himself a rupture, and died. The people of Gulya-Polye mourned him and the whole village walked behind his coffin. They walked, even though he was a stranger."

And at the door of the shed, Petka begins muttering the story of the late Ivan, muttering more and more softly and tenderly.

"There is ruthlessness among people," Gniloshkurov says to him, yawning, "there really is, I tell you."

Gniloshkurov falls asleep, and the two others with him, and I remain alone by the window. My eyes explore the soundless dark, the beast of memory tears at me, and sleep will not come.

. . . She had sat in the main street selling berries since the morning. The Makhno fighters had paid her in abolished banknotes. She had the plump, airy body of a blonde. Gniloshkurov, his stomach jutting out, was sunning himself on a bench. He dozed, waited, and the woman, anxious to sell off her wares, gazed at him with her blue eyes, and blushed slowly and tenderly.

"Anelya," I whisper her name. "Anelya."

GRISHCHUK

Our second trip to the shtetl ended badly. We had set out in the cart to find some fodder, and were heading back around midday. Grishchuk's back was bobbing gently up and down before my eyes. Right outside the village, he laid his reins carefully together, sighed, and slipped down from the box, crawled over my knees, and sprawled out across the cart. His cooling head rocked gently, the horses trotted on slowly, and a yellowing fabric of peace settled on his face like a shroud.

"Didn't eat nothing," he politely answered my cry of alarm, and wearily closed his eyelids.

That was how we rolled into the village—the coachman sprawled out across the cart.

At our lodgings I gave him some bread and a potato to eat. He ate sluggishly, dozing and shaking himself awake. Then he went out into the middle of the yard and lay down on his back, his arms spread wide.

"If you never tell me anything, Grishchuk," I said to him in exasperation, "how am I supposed to understand your pain?"

He said nothing and turned away. It was only that night, as we lay warming each other in the hay, that he shared with me a chapter from his mute novel.

Russian prisoners of war had worked building German fortifications along the North Sea coast. During the harvest season they were herded together and sent into the heart of Germany. A lone, crazed farmer took on Grishchuk. His madness consisted in his never speaking. He beat and starved Grishchuk until Grishchuk learned to communicate with him by hand signals. They lived together peacefully and in silence for four years. Grishchuk didn't learn the language because he never heard it spoken. After the German Revolution* he returned to Russia. His master had walked him to the edge of the village. They stopped at the side of the high road. The German pointed at the church, at his heart, at the boundless and empty blue of the horizon. He laid his gray, tousled head on Grishchuk's shoulder. They stood in a silent embrace. And then the German, throwing up his arms, ran back to his house with quick, faltering, stumbling steps.

* The abortive German November Revolution of 1918.

ARGAMAK

I decided to join the ranks at the front. The division commander grimaced when he heard this.

"Why the hell d'you want to go there? If you let your mouth hang open for a second, they shoot you point-blank!"

I held my ground. And that wasn't all. My choice fell on the most active division, the Sixth. I was assigned to the Fourth Squadron of the Twenty-third Cavalry Regiment. The squadron was commanded by Baulin, a Bryansk factory metalworker, who was a mere boy. He had grown a beard to inspire respect. Ash-blond tufts covered his chin. In his twenty-two years, Baulin had let nothing ruffle him. This quality, found in thousands of Baulins, proved an important element in the victory of the Revolution. Baulin was hard, taciturn, and headstrong. The path of his life had been decided. He had no doubts about the rightness of this path. Deprivation came easy to him. He could sleep sitting up. He slept pressing one arm against the other, and when he woke, his path from oblivion to full alertness was seamless.

One could expect no mercy under Baulin's command. My service started with an unusual omen of success—I was given a horse. There weren't any horses in the reserve stables or with the peasants. Chance helped. The Cossack Tikhomolov had killed two captured officers without authorization. He had been instructed to take them to the brigade headquarters, as enemy officers could give important information. Tikhomolov did not take them there. It was decided that he would be tried before the Revolutionary Tribunal,* but then they changed their minds. Squadron Commander Baulin came up with a punishment much harsher than anything the tribunal could have inflicted—he took Tikhomolov's stallion Argamak away from him, and sent Tikhomolov off to the transport carts.

The agony I had to suffer with Argamak was beyond what a man can endure. Tikhomolov had brought his horse from the Terek, where he was from. The stallion had been trained in the Cossack trot, that specific Cossack hard trot—dry, violent, sudden. Argamak's stride was long, extended, obstinate. With this devilish stride he carried me off, out of the lines, separating me from the squadron. I lost my sense of direction, roamed for days on end looking for my unit, ended up in enemy territory, slept in ravines, tried to tag along with other regiments but was chased away by them. My horsemanship was limited to the fact that in the Great War I had served with an artillery unit in the Fifteenth Infantry Division. Most of the time we had spent sitting on ammunition carts; we rarely rode out on raids. I didn't have an opportunity to get used to Argamak's cruel, bounding trot. Tikhomolov had bestowed on his horse all the devils of his downfall. I shook like a sack on the stallion's long, dry spine. I rode his back to pieces. Sores appeared on it. Metallic flies preyed upon these sores. Hoops of baked black blood girded the horse's flanks. Bad shoeing made Argamak trip, his hind legs became swollen at the breeching strap and turned elephantine. Argamak grew thin. His eyes filled with the fire one sees in tortured horses, the fire of hysteria and obstinacy. He no longer let me saddle him.

"You've liquidated that horse, four-eyes!" my platoon commander said.

The Cossacks said nothing in my presence, but behind my back plotted like plunderers in drowsy treachery. They didn't even ask me to write letters for them anymore.

The cavalry took Novograd-Volynsk. In a single day we had to cover seventy, eighty versts. We were getting close to Rovno. Rest days

---

* The Revolutionary Tribunals were the organs of military justice representing the Revolutionary Military Council. They investigated crimes committed by military personnel and dealt with prisoners of war. Revolutionary Tribunal detachments were present in each army division and brigade.

were annulled. Night after night I had the same dream: I am riding Argamak at full trot. Campfires are burning by the roadside. The Cossacks are cooking food. I ride past them, they don't even look up. A few call out a greeting, others don't even turn around, they're not interested in me. What does this mean? Their indifference indicates that there is nothing unusual in my horsemanship, I ride like everyone else, there's no reason for them to look at me. I gallop off and am happy. My thirst for peace and happiness was never quenched in my waking hours, which is why I dreamed these dreams.

There was no sign of Pashka Tikhomolov. He was watching me from somewhere on the fringes of the march, in the bumbling tail of carts crammed full with looted rags.

"Pashka keeps asking what's with you," my platoon commander said to me one day.

"Why, he has a problem with me?"

"It looks like he does."

"I reckon he feels I've done him wrong."

"Why, you reckon you didn't do him wrong?"

Pashka's hatred followed me through forests and over rivers. I felt it on my hide and shuddered. He nailed his bloodshot eyes on my path.

"Why did you saddle me with an enemy?" I asked Baulin.

Baulin rode past, yawning.

"Not my problem," he answered without looking back. "It's your problem."

Argamak's back healed a little, then his wounds opened up again. I put three saddlecloths under his saddle, but I could not really ride him, the wounds weren't healing. The knowledge that I was sitting on an open wound made me cringe.

A Cossack from our platoon, his name was Bizyukov, was Tikhomolov's countryman from the Terek, and he knew Pashka's father.

"His father, Pashka's father, he breeds horses for fun," Bizyukov told me one day. "A rough rider, sturdy. He comes to a herd, he picks out a horse on the spot, and they bring it to him. He stands face-to-face with the horse, his legs planted firm, glares at it. What does he want? This is what he wants: he waves his fist and punches the horse right between the eyes—the horse is dead. 'Why did you finish off the horse, Kalistrat?'—'I had a terrible desire for this horse, but I wasn't fated to ride it. The horse didn't take to me, but my desire for this horse was deadly!' He's a rough rider, let me tell you!"

And then Argamak, who had survived Pashka's father, who had been chosen by him, fell into my hands. How was this to end? I weighed many plans in my mind. The war had released me from other worries. The cavalry attacked Rovno. The town was taken. We stayed there for two days. The following night the Poles pushed us out. They engaged us in a skirmish to get their retreating units through. Their maneuver worked. The Poles were covered by a storm, lashing rain, a violent summer storm that tumbled onto the world in floods of black water. We cleared out of Rovno for a day. During the nocturnal battle we lost Dundic, the Serb, one of our bravest men. Pashka Tikhomolov also fought in this battle. The Poles attacked his transport carts. The area there was flat, without any cover. Pashka lined up his carts in a battle formation known only to him. It was, doubtless, how the Romans lined up their chariots. Pashka had a machine gun. He had probably stolen it and hidden it, for an emergency. With this machine gun he repelled the attack, saved his possessions, and led the whole transport to safety, except for two carts whose horses had been shot.

"What do you intend to do with your best fighters, marinate them?" they asked Baulin at headquarters a few days after the battle.

"If I'm letting them marinate, there must be a reason, right?"

"Careful, you'll run into trouble."

No amnesty was proclaimed for Pashka, but we knew that he was coming back. He came wearing galoshes on his bare feet. His toes had been hacked off, ribbons of black gauze hung from them. The ribbons dragged behind him like a train. In the village of Budziatycze, Pashka appeared at the square in front of the church where our horses stood tied to the hitching post. Squadron Commander Baulin was sitting on the church, steps, his feet soaking in a steaming bucket. His toes were rotting. They were pink, the way steel is pink before it is forged. Tufts of young straw-blond hair tumbled over Baulin's forehead. The sun burned on the bricks and tiles of the church. Bizyukov, standing next to Baulin, popped a cigarette into Baulin's mouth and lit it. Tikhomolov, dragging his tattered train behind him, went up to the hitching post. His galoshes shuffled. Argamak stretched his long neck and neighed to his master in greeting, a quiet, rasping neigh, like that of a horse in a desert. Pus coiled like lace between the strips of torn flesh on the horse's back. Pashka stood next to the horse. The dirty ribbons lay still on the ground.

"So that's how things stand," the Cossack said, barely audibly.

I stepped forward.

"Let's make peace, Pashka. I'm glad the horse is going back to you. I can't handle him. Let's make peace?"

"It's not Easter yet, for people to make peace," the platoon commander said from behind me, rolling a cigarette. His Tatar trousers loose, his shirt open over his copper chest, he was resting on the church steps.

"Kiss him three times, Pashka,"* mumbled Bizyukov, Tikhomolov's countryman, who knew Kalistrat, Pashka's father. "He wants to kiss three times."

I was alone among these men whose friendship I had not managed to win.

Pashka stood in front of the horse as if rooted there. Argamak, breathing strong and free, stretched his muzzle to him.

"So that's how things stand," the Cossack repeated. He turned to me sharply, and said emphatically, "I will not make peace with you."

He walked away, dragging his galoshes down the chalk-white, heat-baked street, his bandages sweeping the dust of the village square. Argamak walked behind him like a dog. The reins swung beneath his muzzle, his long neck hung low. Baulin continued soaking the reddish steel of his feet's rotting flesh in the tub.

"Why did you saddle me with an enemy?" I said to him. "None of this is my fault."

The squadron commander raised his head.

"I can see right through you!" he said. "Right through you! What you want is to live without enemies, you'll do anything not to have enemies."

"Kiss him three times," Bizyukov muttered, turning away.

A fiery spot burned on Baulin's forehead. His cheek twitched.

"You know what you end up with like that?" he said in a gasping voice. "You end up being bored! To goddamn hell with you!"

* A manifestation of friendship symbolizing the Holy Trinity.

It was obvious I had to leave. I got myself transferred to the Sixth Squadron. Things went better there. The long and the short of it was that Argamak had taught me some of Tikhomolov's horsemanship. Months passed. My dream had become a reality. The Cossacks' eyes stopped following me and my horse.

THE KISS

At the beginning of August, headquarters sent us to Budziatycze to regroup. The Poles had occupied it at the beginning of the war, but we had been quick to win it back. Our brigade entered the shtetl at dawn. I arrived later in the day. The best billets had already been taken, and I ended up at the schoolmaster's house. He was a paralyzed old man sitting in an armchair in a low-ceilinged room, among buckets with fruit-bearing lemon trees. On his head was a Tyrolean hat with a feather. His gray beard lay on his chest, which was covered with cigarette ash. Babbling, his eyes fluttering, he seemed to be asking me for something. I washed, went to the headquarters, and didn't come back until night. My orderly, Mishka Surovtsev, a cunning Cossack from Orenburg, gave me a full report: besides the paralyzed old man, there was also a daughter present, Elizaveta Alekseyevna Tomilina, and her five-year-old son who was also called Mishka, like Surovtsev. The daughter, the widow of an officer who had fallen in the Great War, was a respectable woman but, according to Surovtsev's information, would be willing to make herself available to a proper gentleman.

"I can arrange things," he told me, and went off to the kitchen, where he began clattering about with plates. The schoolmaster's daughter helped him. As they cooked, Surovtsev told her of my brave feats, how I had knocked two Polish officers out of their saddles in a battle, and how much the Soviet authorities respected me. He was answered by the restrained, soft voice of Tomilina.

"Where d'you sleep?" Surovtsev asked her as he left the kitchen. "You should come sleep closer to us, we're living, breathing people."

He brought me some fried eggs in a gigantic frying pan, and put it on the table.

"She's up for it," he said, sitting down. "She just hasn't come out and said it yet."

At that very instant we heard whispering, rattling, and heavy, careful steps. We didn't have time to finish eating our war meal, when some old men on crutches and old women with kerchiefs on their heads came hobbling through the house. They dragged little Mishka's bed into the dining room, into the lemon-tree forest, next to his grandfather's armchair. The feeble guests, readying themselves to defend Elizaveta Alekseyevna's honor, huddled together in a flock, like sheep in a storm, and, barricading the door, spent the whole night silently playing cards, whispering, "My trick," and falling silent at every sound. I was so mortified, so embarrassed, that I simply could not fall asleep behind that door, and could barely wait for the sun to rise.

"For your information," I told Tomilina when I ran into her in the hall, "for your information, I have a law degree and am a member of the so-called intelligentsia!"

Rigid, her arms dangling, she stood there in her old-fashioned housedress, which clung tightly to her slim body. Without blinking, she looked straight at me with widening blue eyes sparkling with tears.

Within two days we were friends. The schoolmaster's family, a family of kind, weak people, lived in boundless fear and uncertainty. Polish officials had convinced them that Russia had fallen in fire and barbarity, like Rome. They were overcome with a childlike, fearful joy when I told them of Lenin, the Moscow Arts Theater, of a Moscow in which the future was raging. In the evenings, twenty-two-year-old Bolshevik generals with scraggly red beards came to visit us. We smoked Moscow cigarettes, we ate meals that Elizaveta Alekseyevna prepared with army provisions, and sang student songs. Leaning forward in his armchair, the paralyzed old man listened avidly, his Tyrolean hat bobbing to the rhythm of our songs. Through all these days the old man was in the clutches of a sudden, stormy, vague hope, and, in order not to let anything darken his happiness, he did his best to overlook the foppish bloodthirstiness and loudmouthed simplicity with which in those days we solved all the problems of the world.

After our victory over the Poles—the family counsel decided—the Tomilins would move to Moscow. We would have a celebrated professor cure the old man, Elizaveta Alekseyevna would take classes, and we would put Mishka in the selfsame school that his mother had once gone to at Patriarkhy Prudy. The future seemed incontestably ours, and war was merely a stormy prelude to happiness, happiness, the core of our being. The only things that remained unresolved were the specific details, and nights passed in discussing these details, mighty nights, in which the candle end was mirrored in the dull bottle of our home-brewed vodka. Elizaveta Alekseyevna, blossoming, was our silent listener. I have never met a more impulsive, free, or timorous being. In the evenings, cunning Surovtsev, in the wicker cart he had requisitioned back in Kuban, drove us up the hill to where the abandoned house of the Counts Gasiorowski shone in the flames of the sunset. The horses, thin but long-bodied and thoroughbred, were running in step in their red reins. A carefree earring swayed on Surovtsev's ear. Round towers rose up from a pit that was overgrown with a yellow tablecloth of flowers. The ruined walls drew a crooked line flooded with ruby-red blood across the sky. A dog-rose bush hid its berries, and blue steps, the remains of the flight of stairs that Polish kings had once mounted, shone in the thickets. Once, as I sat there, I pulled Elizaveta Alekseyevna's head toward me and kissed her. She slowly pulled away, got up, and leaned against the wall, holding on to it with both hands. She stood there motionless, and around her, around her dazzled head, swirled a fiery dusty ray. Shuddering, as if she had just heard something, Tomilina raised her head and let go of the wall. She ran down the hill, her uncertain steps becoming faster. I called out to her, she didn't answer. Below, red-cheeked Surovtsev lay sprawled out in his wicker cart.

At night, when everyone was asleep, I crept to Elizaveta Alekseyevna's room. She sat reading, holding her book at arm's length. Her hand, lying on the table, seemed lifeless. She turned when I knocked, and rose.

"No," she said, looking me in the eyes, "please, dearest, no." And, embracing my head with her long, bare arms, she gave me an increasingly violent, never-ending, silent kiss.

"Where d'you sleep?" Surovtsev asked her as he left the kitchen. "You should come sleep closer to us, we're living, breathing people."

He brought me some fried eggs in a gigantic frying pan, and put it on the table.

"She's up for it," he said, sitting down. "She just hasn't come out and said it yet."

At that very instant we heard whispering, rattling, and heavy, careful steps. We didn't have time to finish eating our war meal, when some old men on crutches and old women with kerchiefs on their heads came hobbling through the house. They dragged little Mishka's bed into the dining room, into the lemon-tree forest, next to his grandfather's armchair. The feeble guests, readying themselves to defend Elizaveta Alekseyevna's honor, huddled together in a flock, like sheep in a storm, and, barricading the door, spent the whole night silently playing cards, whispering, "My trick," and falling silent at every sound. I was so mortified, so embarrassed, that I simply could not fall asleep behind that door, and could barely wait for the sun to rise.

"For your information," I told Tomilina when I ran into her in the hall, "for your information, I have a law degree and am a member of the so-called intelligentsia!"

Rigid, her arms dangling, she stood there in her old-fashioned housedress, which clung tightly to her slim body. Without blinking, she looked straight at me with widening blue eyes sparkling with tears.

Within two days we were friends. The schoolmaster's family, a family of kind, weak people, lived in boundless fear and uncertainty. Polish officials had convinced them that Russia had fallen in fire and barbarity, like Rome. They were overcome with a childlike, fearful joy when I told them of Lenin, the Moscow Arts Theater, of a Moscow in which the future was raging. In the evenings, twenty-two-year-old Bolshevik generals with scraggly red beards came to visit us. We smoked Moscow cigarettes, we ate meals that Elizaveta Alekseyevna prepared with army provisions, and sang student songs. Leaning forward in his armchair, the paralyzed old man listened avidly, his Tyrolean hat bobbing to the rhythm of our songs. Through all these days the old man was in the clutches of a sudden, stormy, vague hope, and, in order not to let anything darken his happiness, he did his best to overlook the foppish bloodthirstiness and loudmouthed simplicity with which in those days we solved all the problems of the world.

After our victory over the Poles—the family counsel decided—the Tomilins would move to Moscow. We would have a celebrated professor cure the old man, Elizaveta Alekseyevna would take classes, and we would put Mishka in the selfsame school that his mother had once gone to at Patriarkhy Prudy. The future seemed incontestably ours, and war was merely a stormy prelude to happiness, happiness, the core of our being. The only things that remained unresolved were the specific details, and nights passed in discussing these details, mighty nights, in which the candle end was mirrored in the dull bottle of our home-brewed vodka. Elizaveta Alekseyevna, blossoming, was our silent listener. I have never met a more impulsive, free, or timorous being. In the evenings, cunning Surovtsev, in the wicker cart he had requisitioned back in Kuban, drove us up the hill to where the abandoned house of the Counts Gasiorowski shone in the flames of the sunset. The horses, thin but long-bodied and thoroughbred, were running in step in their red reins. A carefree earring swayed on Surovtsev's ear. Round towers rose up from a pit that was overgrown with a yellow tablecloth of flowers. The ruined walls drew a crooked line flooded with ruby-red blood across the sky. A dog-rose bush hid its berries, and blue steps, the remains of the flight of stairs that Polish kings had once mounted, shone in the thickets. Once, as I sat there, I pulled Elizaveta Alekseyevna's head toward me and kissed her. She slowly pulled away, got up, and leaned against the wall, holding on to it with both hands. She stood there motionless, and around her, around her dazzled head, swirled a fiery dusty ray. Shuddering, as if she had just heard something, Tomilina raised her head and let go of the wall. She ran down the hill, her uncertain steps becoming faster. I called out to her, she didn't answer. Below, red-cheeked Surovtsev lay sprawled out in his wicker cart.

At night, when everyone was asleep, I crept to Elizaveta Alekseyevna's room. She sat reading, holding her book at arm's length. Her hand, lying on the table, seemed lifeless. She turned when I knocked, and rose.

"No," she said, looking me in the eyes, "please, dearest, no." And, embracing my head with her long, bare arms, she gave me an increasingly violent, never-ending, silent kiss.

The shrill ring of the telephone in the next room pushed us apart. An orderly was calling from headquarters.

"We're pulling out!" he said over the phone. "You are to report to the brigade commander now!"

I rushed out of the house without even putting on my hat, stuffing my papers into my bag as I ran. Horses were being brought out of yards, horsemen galloped yelling through the darkness. The brigade commander, tying his cloak, told us that the Poles had broken through our lines near Lublin, and that we had been ordered to execute a bypass maneuver. Both regiments pulled out an hour later. The old man, awoken from his sleep, anxiously followed me with his eyes through the leaves of a lemon tree.

"Promise me you will return," he kept saying, his head wagging.

Elizaveta Alekseyevna, a fur jacket over her batiste nightdress, accompanied us out onto the street. An invisible squadron raced past violently. At the curve in the road by the field I turned to look back—Elizaveta Alekseyevna was bending down to fix the jacket of little Mishka, who was standing in front of her, and the erratic light of the lamp burning on the windowsill streamed over the tender bones of her nape.

After riding a hundred kilometers without rest, we joined forces with the Fourteenth Cavalry Division and, fighting, we began our retreat. We slept in our saddles. At rest stops, we fell to the ground overwhelmed with exhaustion, and our horses, pulling at their reins, dragged us fast asleep through the harvested fields. It was the beginning of autumn and the soundless, drizzling Galician rain. Huddled together in a bristling silent herd, we dodged and circled, fell into the Poles' waiting net, but managed to slip out again just before they could close it. We lost all sense of time. When we were quartered in the church in Toscza, it did not even occur to me that we were only nine versts from Budziatycze. Surovtsev reminded me, we exchanged glances.

"The problem is that the horses are exhausted," he said cheerfully. "Otherwise we could go."

"We couldn't anyway," I replied. "They'd notice if we left in the middle of the night."

And we went. We tied gifts to our saddles—a clump of sugar, a fox-fur wrap, and a live, two-week-old goat kid. The road went through a swaying wet forest, a metallic star strayed through the crowns of the oaks. In less than an hour we arrived at the shtetl, its burned-out center filled with trucks, pale with flour dust, and with machine-gun-cart harnesses and broken shafts. Without dismounting, I knocked on the familiar window. A white cloud flitted through the room. Wearing the same batiste nightdress with its hanging lace, Tomilina came rushing out onto the porch. She took my hand in her hot hand and led me into the house. Men's underclothes were hanging out to dry on the broken branches of the lemon trees, and unknown men were sleeping in camp beds lined up in tight rows like in a field hospital. With crooked, hardened mouths they yelled out hoarsely in their sleep, breathing greedily and loud, their dirty feet jutting out. The house was occupied by our War Spoils Commission, and the Tomilins had been bundled off into a single room.

"When will you take us away from here?" Elizaveta Alekseyevna asked, clasping my hand.

The old man woke, his head wagging. Little Mishka cuddled the goat kid, and brimmed over with happy, soundless laughter. Above him stood Surovtsev, puffing himself up. Out of the pockets of his Cossack trousers he shook spurs, shot-through coins, and a whistle hanging on a yellow string. In this house occupied by the War Spoils Commission there was nowhere to hide, and Tomilina and I went to the wooden shed where the potatoes and beehive frames were kept in winter. There, in the shed, I saw what an inevitably pernicious path that kiss had been, the path that had begun by the castle of the Counts Gasiorowski.

Surovtsev came knocking shortly before dawn.

"When will you take us from here?" Elizaveta Alekseyevna asked, turning her head away.

I stood there silently, and then walked over to the house to say good-bye to the old man.

"The problem is we're running out of time," Surovtsev said, blocking my way. "Get on your horse, we've got to go!"

He jostled me out onto the street and brought me my horse. Elizaveta Alekseyevna gave me her chilled hand. As always, she held her head high. The horses, well rested overnight, carried us off at a brisk trot. The flaming sun rose through the black tangle of the oak trees. The rejoicing morning filled my whole being.

A glade in the forest opened up before us. I directed my horse toward it, and, turning back to Surovtsev, called out to him, "We could have stayed a bit longer. You came for me too early!"

"Too early?" he said, riding up closer to me, pushing away the wet branches that dropped their sparkling raindrops. "If it wasn't for the old man, I'd have come for you even earlier. He was trying to tell me something and suddenly was all nerves, started squawking, and keeled over. I rush to him, I look, he's dead, dead as a doornail!"

The forest came to an end. We rode over a plowed field without paths. Standing up in his stirrups, looking all around, whistling, Surovtsev sniffed out the right direction and, breathing it in with the air, hunched forward and went galloping toward it.

We arrived in time. The men of the squadron were just being awakened. The sun shone warmly, promising a hot day. That morning our brigade crossed the former border of the Kingdom of Poland.

AND THEN
THERE WERE NINE

*This story is an earlier variation of
"Squadron Commander Trunov."*

Nine prisoners of war are no longer alive. I know that in my heart. When Golov, a platoon commander from the Sormov workers,* killed the gangly Pole, I said to the chief of staff, "The example the platoon commander is setting is demoralizing our fighters. We must draw up a list of prisoners and then send them to headquarters for interrogation."

The chief of staff agreed. I took pencil and paper out of my bag and called Golov over.

"You look at the world through your spectacles," he told me, looking at me with hatred.

"Yes, through my spectacles," I said to him. "And what about you, Golov? How do you look at the world?"

"I look at it through the miserable life of a worker," he said, and went over to the prisoner who was holding a Polish uniform with dangling sleeves. The uniform had been too small for him. The sleeves had barely reached his elbows. Golov examined the prisoner's woolen drawers.

"You an officer?" Golov asked him, shielding his eyes from the sun.

"No," the Pole answered firmly.

"We never got to wear nothing like that!" Golov muttered, and fell silent. He stood there without saying a word, shuddered, looked at the prisoner, and his eyes paled and widened.

* The Sormov Steelworks (19,839 workers in 1917) played a key role in the Revolution and the Civil War.

"My mama knitted them," the prisoner said firmly. I turned around and looked at him. He was a slender young man. Long sideburns curled over his yellowish cheeks.

"My mama knitted them," he repeated, and lowered his eyes.

"She's a great knitter, that mama of yours," Andryushka Burak cut in. He was a young red-cheeked Cossack with silky hair, who earlier had dragged the trousers off a dying Pole. The trousers now lay thrown over his saddle. Laughing, Andryushka rode over to Golov, carefully scooped the uniform out of his hands, threw it over the trousers on his saddle, and, tapping his horse lightly with his whip, rode off.

At that moment the sun came pouring out from behind a cloud, enveloping with dazzling light Andryushka's horse, its lively trot, the carefree swish of its docked tail. In a daze, Golov watched the Cossack ride off. He turned and saw me drawing up the list of prisoners. He saw the young Pole with the curly sideburns. The Pole raised calm eyes filled with youthful arrogance and smiled at Golov's dismay. Golov cupped his hands to his mouth and yelled, "Our Republic is still alive, Andrei! It's too early to be dealing out her property! Bring back those rags!"

Andrei turned a deaf ear. He rode on at a trot, his horse pertly swatting its tail, as if it were shooing us away.

"Treason!" Golov mumbled, morose and rigid, pronouncing the word syllable by syllable. He kneeled, took aim, and fired, but missed. Andrei swerved his horse around and came galloping back toward Golov. His red-cheeked, blossoming face was filled with anger.

"Listen, countryman!" he yelled loudly, suddenly rejoicing in the sound of his powerful voice. "I should knock you to Kingdom Come, Platoon Commander! I should knock you to where your you-know-what mother is! You've got a dozen Poles on your hands, and you're making a big fuss! We've taken hundreds, and didn't come running for your help! If you're a worker, then do your job!"

And, glancing at us triumphantly, Andryushka rode off at a gallop. Platoon Commander Golov did not look up at him. He clutched his forehead. Blood was trickling from his head like rain from a haystack. He lay down on his stomach, crawled toward the stream, and for a long time held his smashed, blood-drenched head in the shallow water.

Nine prisoners of war are no longer alive. I know that in my heart.

Sitting on my horse, I made a list of them arranged in neat columns. In the first column I entered a row of numbers, in the second their names and surnames, and in the third column the units to which they had belonged. All in all there were nine names. The fourth name was Adolf Shulmeister, a clerk from Lodz, a Jew. He kept snuggling up to my horse and caressing my boots with tender, trembling fingers. His leg had been shattered by a rifle butt, and he left behind him a thin track, like a lame, wounded dog. The sun boiled the sparkling sweat on his orange, pockmarked, bald pate.

"You *Jude, Pane*,"* he whispered, frantically caressing my stirrup. "You Jude!" he whimpered, dribbling spittle, writhing with joy.

"Get back in line, Shulmeister," I yelled at the Jew, and suddenly, seized by deathly numbness, slipped off my saddle.

"How come you know?" I asked him breathlessly.

"Your eyes, their sweet Jewish look," he yelped, hopping on one leg, leaving his thin dog's track behind him. "Your sweet Jewish look, *Pane!*"

I barely managed to extricate myself from his condemned man's frenzy. I came back to my senses slowly, as after a concussion.

The chief of staff ordered me to take care of the details and rode off to the units.

The machine guns were dragged up onto the hill like calves on halters. They moved up side by side, like a well-ordered herd, clanking reassuringly. The sun played on their dusty muzzles. And I saw a rainbow on their steel. The Polish youth with the curly sideburns stared at them with village curiosity. He leaned his whole body forward, revealing a view of Golov, who was crawling out of a ditch pale and intent, his smashed head and his rifle raised. I stretched my hands out to Golov and yelled, but the sound choked and bulged in my throat. Golov quickly shot the prisoner in the back of the neck and jumped up to his feet. The surprised Pole turned to him, executing a half spin on his heel, as in a military exercise. With the slow movements of a woman giving herself to a man, he lifted both hands to his nape, slumped to the ground, and died instantly.

A smile of peace and relief flitted over Golov's face. A light flush returned to his cheeks.

---

*"You are a Jew, sir"—Shulmeister uses *vy*, the Russian polite form for "you," *Jude*, the German word for "Jew," and *Pane*, the Polish word for "sir."

"Our mothers don't knit drawers like that for us," he told me slyly. "Cross that one off, and give me a list for eight."

I gave him the list.

"You'll answer for that, Golov!" I said in desperation.

"I will answer for that!" he yelled in unbridled triumph. "But not to you, four-eyes, I'll answer to my own people from the Sormov factory. They know what's what!"

Nine prisoners of war are no longer alive. I know that in my heart. This morning I decided to hold a memorial service for the murdered men. In the Red Cavalry there is no one but me who can do it. Our unit stopped to rest on a ravaged Polish estate. I took out my diary and went into the flower garden, which had remained untouched. Hyacinths and blue roses were growing there.

I began writing about the platoon commander and the nine dead men, but a noise, a familiar noise, interrupted me. Cherkashin, the headquarters lackey, had launched a raid against the beehives. Mitya, a red-cheeked youth from Oryol, was following him, holding a smoking torch in his hand. Their heads were wrapped in their army coats. The slits of their eyes glowed. Swarms of bees charged their conquerors and died by their hives. And I put down my pen. I was horrified at the great number of memorial services awaiting me.

AND THEN
THERE WERE TEN

The following story fragment is an earlier variation of the two stories "Squadron Commander Trunov" and "And Then There Were Nine."

Zavadi Station. This happened yesterday. About thirty Poles were sitting tight in the stone building by the junction of the railroad tracks. The chief of staff himself got involved in this serious business. He strutted in front of our line of men with a revolver in his hand.

"How pointless it is to die at Zavady Station," I thought, and went over to the chief of staff.

The Poles ran [and broke through] our line of men. We brought back ten of them alive. We took them to the field. They looked like a striped blanket laid out on the ground. In front of them, Platoon Commander Golov, mounted, was standing in his stirrups.

"Officers! Own up!" he said, shaking his reins. Blood trickled from his head like rain from a haystack. He had been wounded on the forehead.

"All officers, step forward!" he repeated in a thicker voice, getting off his horse.

Suddenly a lanky man with a drooping little mustache stepped forward from the group.

"End of this war!" the man said with delight, and began crying. "All officers run away, end of this war!"

And the lanky man held out his blue hand to the squadron commander. On his face was an incomprehensible bliss.

"Five fingers," he muttered, sobbing, "I raising with these five fingers my family!"

And, with burning eyes, he slowly waved his large, wilted hand. Golov pushed it back with his saber.

"Your officers threw their uniforms here!" he yelled. "But we're going to have a little fitting now, and whoever the uniforms fit, I'm going to finish off!"

He picked out a cap without a brim from the pile of rags and put it on the lanky man's head.

"It fits," Golov whispered. He stepped up closer to the prisoner, looked him in the eyes, and plunged his saber into his gullet. The lanky man fell, shivered, his legs twitching in a frenzy. A foamy, coral-red stream poured from his neck. A young red-cheeked Cossack with silky hair knelt before the dying man. He unbuttoned the man's [trousers].

A LETTER TO THE EDITOR

This letter from Babel was published in 1924 in the literary magazine Oktyabr, *issue no. 4, in answer to an article by General Budyonny, in which Budyonny attacked Babel for his portrayal of the Red Cavalry and its fighters in his stories, accusing Babel, among other things, of character assassination and "counterrevolutionary lies."*

*I*n 1920, I served in the First Cavalry's Sixth Division, of which Comrade Timoshenko was commander at the time. I witnessed his heroic, military, and revolutionary work with much admiration. This wonderful and pristine image of my beloved division commander long ruled my imagination, and when I set about to write my memoirs of the Polish Campaign, my thoughts often returned to him. But in the process of writing, my aim of keeping within the parameters of historical truth began to shift, and I decided instead to express my thoughts in a literary form. All that remained from my initial outline were a few authentic surnames. Through an unforgivable oversight, however, I did not undertake to remove these surnames, and, to my great consternation, these names have now appeared by mistake in print, as for instance in the piece "Timoshenko and Melnikov,"* published in the third volume of *Krasnaya Nov,* 1924. This oversight came about because I was late handing in the materials for that volume, and the editorial office, not to mention the typesetting department, had put me under extreme pressure, and in this last-minute rush, I overlooked the vital task of changing the original surnames in the final proofs. I need not stress that Comrade Timoshenko has nothing whatsoever in common with the character in that piece, a fact clear to anyone who has ever crossed paths with the former commander of Division Six, one of the most courageous and selfless of our Red Commanders.

I. Babel

* In later editions of *Red Cavalry,* this piece was renamed "The Story of a Horse."

V

The Red Cavalryman: Articles

B abel wrote the following pieces under the non-Jewish nom-de-plume Kiril V. Lyutov, for KRASNY KAVALERIST, THE RED CAVALRYMAN— the newspaper distributed to the fighters of the Cavalry during the Russian-Polish Campaign. In Babel's story "The Letter," a young Cossack had described KRASNY KAVALERIST as "our own merciless newspaper [. . .] which every fighter on the front wants to read and then go and heroically hack the damn Poles to pieces."

The pseudonymous Lyutov is also one of the narrators in the RED CAVALRY stories. Lyutov is very Russian (as opposed to Jewish), one of the young intellectuals of the new Soviet Union, a journalist sent to cover the fighting on the front. He is furthermore the persona whom Babel adopted in his daily life during the Russian-Polish Campaign as a way of deflecting the ruthless anti-Semitism of his Cossack colleagues. Lyutov's role in the KRASNY KAVALERIST pieces is to incite his fellow fighters to action with propaganda and Bolshevik slogans.

conditions he triumphed over the enemy through his exceptional, self-less courage, his unbending persistence, and his immutable self-possession, and through his great influence over the men of the Red Army that was so close to him. If there were more Trunovs among us, the masters of this world would be finished.

WHAT WE NEED
IS MORE MEN LIKE
TRUNOV!

*W*e must add one more name now to our heroic, bloody, and sorrowful list, a name that will never be forgotten by the Sixth Division: the name of Konstantin Trunov, commander of the Thirty-fourth Cavalry Regiment, who died in the line of duty on August 3, near K. Another grave is now hidden by the shadows of the dense forests of Volhynia, another distinguished life marked by self-sacrifice and devotion to duty has been relinquished to the cause of the oppressed, another proletarian heart has been crushed so that its fiery blood will tint the red flags of Revolution. The story of Comr. Trunov's final years of life is inextricably linked with the titanic battle of the Red Army. He emptied his cup to the last drop, participating in every campaign from Tsaritsyn to Voronezh, and from Voronezh to the shores of the Black Sea. In the past he suffered hunger, deprivation, wounds, overwhelming battles fought alongside the best men in the front lines, and finally the bullet of the Polish nobleman which cut down the Stavropol peasant from the faraway steppes who was bringing the word of freedom to people who were strangers to him.

From the first days of the Revolution, Comrade Trunov took his true position without a moment's hesitation. We found him among the organizers of the first detachments of the Stavropol troops. In the Red Army, he subsequently took over the command of the Fourth Stavropol Regiment, the First Brigade of the Thirty-second Division, and the Thirty-fourth Cavalry Regiment of the Sixth Division.

In our military ranks his memory will not pale. Under the harshest

THE KNIGHTS OF
CIVILIZATION

*T*he Polish army has gone berserk. The Polish *Pans,* fatally bitten, expiring like dogs, are writhing in mortal agony, piling up
crimes in stupidity, dying and going to their graves in shame, cursed by
their own people and by others. With the same feeling as before, they
forge ahead not thinking of the future, forgetting that, according to
their European governesses, they are the knights of European civilization, and therefore must act as the guardians of "law and order," a barrier against Bolshevik barbarity.

This is how this Polish barrier protects civilization:

Once upon a time there lived a modest, hardworking pharmacist in
Berestechko, who always did his best. He worked without respite, taking care of his patients, his test tubes, and his prescriptions. He had no
connection to politics at all, and quite possibly thought that Bolsheviks
were monsters with ears above their eyes.

This pharmacist was a Jew. For the Poles that was enough: he was
nothing but a cowering animal! Why even waste a bullet? Beat him, cut
him down, torture him! They were quick to set him up. The peaceful
pharmacist, who had happily saddled himself with hemorrhoids working with his little bottles, was accused of having somewhere, at some
time, for some reason, killed a Polish officer, and was therefore an
accomplice of the Bolsheviks.

What followed takes us back to the most oppressive years of the
Spanish Inquisition. If I had not seen that lacerated face and that shattered body with my own eyes, I would never have believed that such

shocking evil could exist in our era, cruel and bloody though it is. The pharmacist's body had been scorched with white-hot iron pokers, stripes like those on an officer's uniform had been burned into his legs ("We see you're in cahoots with those Cossack-Bolsheviks!"), burning needles had been driven under his nails, a Red Army star had been cut into his chest, his hair had been torn out, one hair at a time.

All this had been done at a leisurely pace, accompanied by little jibes at Communism and Jewish commissars.

But this wasn't all! The animalized Polish *Pans* razed the pharmacy to the ground and trampled on all the medicines. Not a single bottle was left untouched. Now the little town will doubtless perish without medical help. You will not find any powder against toothache in Berestechko. The population of twenty thousand has been left defenseless in the face of epidemics and disease.

And so now the Polish masters are perishing. Thus the evil, rabid dogs expire. Beat them, Red Fighters, clobber them to death, if it is the last thing you do! Right away! This minute! Now!

DISPATCH OFFICE,
SHAPE UP!

*D*ear Comrade Zdanevich,

The ceaseless battles of this past month have thrown us completely off track. We are living under trying circumstances: endless advances, marches, and retreats. We are entirely cut off from what is generally called "cultured" life. We haven't seen a single newspaper in the past month, and we have absolutely no idea what is going on in the world at large. It is as if we were living in a forest. As a matter of fact, that is exactly what we are doing—we are trudging through forests.

I don't even know if my reports are getting through to you. When things end up this way, one feels like throwing in the towel. The most absurd rumors have begun circulating among our fighters, who are living in complete ignorance of what is happening. The harm this does is inestimable. It is vital that immediate measures be taken to supply the Sixth Division, our largest division, with our *Krasny Kavalerist* and other regional newspapers.

As a personal favor, I beg you to issue an order to the dispatch office, that it (1) send me at least a three-week run of our paper, and enclose any other regional papers it might have; (2) send me at least five copies of our paper on a daily basis at the following address: Sixth Division Headquarters, War Correspondent K. Lyutov. Please be sure they do this, so I can at least somehow get my bearings.

How are things at the editorial office? My work has not been moving ahead the way it ought to. We are completely exhausted. For a whole week now I haven't been able to sit down for half an hour to dash off a few words.

I hope things will now shape up a little.

Please write me your intentions, plans, and requirements—this will serve as a link for me to the outside world.

With Comradely Greetings,
K. Lyutov

MURDERERS WHO
HAVE YET TO BE CLUBBED
TO DEATH

*T*hey wrought revenge on the workers in 1905. They set off on punitive expeditions in order to shoot and smother our dark slave-villages through which a fleeting breeze of freedom had blown.

In October 1917, they threw off their masks and went after the Russian proletariat with fire and sword. For almost three years they hacked at the land that had already been hacked to pieces. It looked like they were on their last legs. We left them to die a natural death, but they would not die.

Now we are paying for our mistake. His Excellency Duke Wrangel* is strutting about the Crimea, while the pitiful remnants of the Black Hundred† of the Russian Denikin** gangs are turning up in the ranks of the highly refined and most noble of Polish warriors. The ragtag and bobtail of Russia hurried to the aide of Counts Potocki and Taraszczynski to save culture and law from the Barbarians.

This is how culture was saved in the town of Komarov, occupied on August 28, by the Sixth Cavalry Division.

The valiant boys of Cossack Captain Yakovlev‡ had spent the night

---

* Baron Pyotr Nikolayevich Wrangel, 1827–1928, was the commander of the anti-Bolshevik armies in southern Russia. He managed to hold the Crimea until 1920, after which the Communists forced him to evacuate his troops to Constantinople. This ended the civil war in Russia.

† Chernosotentsy (Black Hundred), a right-wing, anti-Semitic group responsible for pogroms.

** Anton Ivanovich Denikin, 1872–1947, the son of a serf, rose in the ranks of the Russian army. After the Revolution, he became the commander of the anti-Bolshevik forces in southern Russia. In 1920 he resigned his command to General Pyotr Nikolayevich Wrangel.

‡ A Russian Cossack, fought on the side of the Poles, and appears in Babel's diary (8/28/1929, 8/31/1920), and also in the *Red Cavalry* stories "Czesniki" and "After the Battle."

---

in the little town—the same Captain Yakovlev who kept trying to talk us into returning to the sweet and peaceful life of our villages, which have been littered with the bodies of commissars, Yids, and Red Army soldiers.

As our squadrons approached, these knights disappeared into thin air. But before they did, they managed to ply their trade.

We found the town's Jewish population robbed of everything it had, wounded and hacked to pieces. Our soldiers, who have seen a thing or two in their time and have been known to chop off quite a few heads, staggered in horror at what they saw. In the pitiful huts that had been razed to the ground, seventy-year-old men with crushed skulls lay naked in pools of blood, infants, often still alive, with fingers hacked off, and old women, raped, their stomachs slashed open, crouched in corners, with faces on which wild, unbearable desperation had congealed. The living were crawling among the dead, bumping into mangled corpses, their hands and faces covered with sticky, foul-smelling blood, terrified of leaving their houses, fearing that all was not yet over.

Hunched, frightened shadows roamed the streets of the dead town, cowering away from human voices, wailing for mercy at every sound. We came across houses over which a terrible silence hung—a whole family was lying next to an aged grandfather. Father, grandchildren—everyone in twisted, inhuman positions.

All in all, over thirty were killed and about sixty wounded. Two hundred women were raped, many of them tortured to death. To escape the rapists, women had jumped from second- and third-floor windows, breaking limbs and necks. Our medical officers worked all day without respite, and still could not meet the demands for help. The horror of the Middle Ages pales in comparison to the bestiality of the Yakovlev bandits.

The pogrom, needless to say, was carried out according to the rules. First, the officers demanded fifty thousand rubles in protection money from the Jewish population. Money and vodka were immediately brought, but still the officers marched in the front lines of the pogromists and searched the cowering Jewish elders at gunpoint for bombs and machine guns.

Our answer to the Polish Red Cross's laments concerning Russian bestiality is: the event I have just described is only one among a thousand far worse.

The dogs that haven't yet been completely slashed to pieces have begun howling hoarsely. The murderers who haven't yet been completely clubbed to death are crawling out of their graves.

Slaughter them, Red Army fighters! Stamp harder on the rising lids of their rancid coffins!

HER DAY

I had a sore throat. I went to see the nurse of the First Squadron headquarters of the N. Division. A smoky hut, filled with fumes and rankness. The soldiers are lying on benches, smoking, scratching themselves, and using foul language. The nurse has set up shop in a corner. She bandages the wounded, one after the other, without much fuss or unnecessary ado. Some troublemakers hamper her work any way they can, each trying to outdo the other with the most blasphemous, unnatural curses. Suddenly—the alarm is sounded. The order to mount the horses. The squadron forms. We set off.

The nurse has harnessed her horse, tied a sack with oats to its muzzle, packed her bag, and ridden off. Her pitiful, thin dress flutters in the wind, and her frozen red toes show through the holes of her tattered shoes. It is raining. The exhausted horses can barely lift their hooves from the terrible, sucking, viscous Volhynian mud. The damp penetrates to the bone. The nurse has neither cloak nor coat. The men are singing a bawdy song. The nurse quietly hums her own song—about dying for the Revolution, about better days to come. A few men begin singing along with her, and our song, our unceasing call to freedom, spills out into the rainy autumnal dusk.

In the evening—the attack. Shells burst with soft, sinister booms, machine guns rattle faster and faster with feverish dread.

Beneath the most horrifying crossfire, the nurse bandages the wounded with disdainful calm, dragging them away from the battle on her shoulders.

The attack ends. The agonizing advance continues. Night, rain. The soldiers are darkly silent, only the heated whisper of the nurse, comforting the wounded, can be heard. An hour later, the same picture as before—a dark, dirty hut in which the platoon has settled down, and in the corner, by the light of a pitiable dwindling candle, the nurse keeps bandaging, bandaging, bandaging. . . .

Foul curses hang heavily in the air. The nurse, at times unable to restrain herself, snaps back, and the men laugh at her. Nobody helps her, nobody puts straw down for her to sleep on, nobody fluffs up her pillow.

These are our heroic nurses! Lift your hats and bow to them! Soldiers and commanders, honor your nurses! It is high time we distinguished between the camp girls who shame our army and the martyred nurses who ennoble it.

VI

1920 Diary

On June 3, 1920, the day on which the first entry of the 1920 DIARY occurs (the first fifty-four pages of the diary are missing and believed lost), Isaac Babel was twenty-five years old, soon to be twenty-six. He had already made a name for himself as a promising writer and journalist and had, as a war correspondent, joined the Sixth Cavalry Division, commanded by the charismatic Timoshenko (Pavlichenko, in the RED CAVALRY stories), who was later to become a Marshal of the Soviet Union and Commissar of Defense.

The diary that Babel kept during his months with the Red Cavalry was a writer's diary. Babel noted quick impressions that he intended subsequently to develop as motifs and plot lines for the RED CAVALRY stories: "Describe the soldiers and women, fat, fed, sleepy"; "Describe the bazaar, the baskets of cherries"; "Describe what a horseman feels: exhaustion, the horse won't go on, the ride is long, no strength, the burned steppe, loneliness, no one there to help you, endless versts." At times the impressions appear in strings of telegraphic clauses that served Babel as a form of private shorthand, but when Babel is particularly taken by a scene or *situation, he slips into the rich and controlled style that would mark the* RED CAVALRY *stories.*

The RED CAVALRY *stories that grew out of this diary shocked the world with their unforgiving depictions of the desperation and atrocities of the cavalrymen. Particularly daring was the way in which Babel depicted real people, their ranks and names unchanged, in realistic, savage, unflattering circumstances. In this diary, which was not intended for publication, Babel could afford even greater candor. The* RED CAVALRY *stories reveal that the heroic cavalry was made up of wild and ruthless Cossacks who had a skewed notion of Communist doctrine. They were clearly not the glorious harbingers of World Revolution that Soviet propaganda would have liked them to be. This contradiction might be suggested by the stories, but the* 1920 DIARY *states it in the clearest of terms. Babel asks, "What kind of men are our Cossacks? Many-layered: rag-looting, bravado, professionalism, revolutionary ideals, savage cruelty. We are the vanguard, but of what?"*

The 1920 DIARY, *by virtue of its privacy, is Babel's most sincere personal written testimony. His persona, so elusive in his fictional prose, is very clear in this private writing. We see his firm Socialist convictions, his sensitivity, his horror of the marauding ways of his Cossack companions, his ambiguous fascination with "the West and chivalrous Poland," his equivocal stance toward Judaism, with feelings that fluctuate between distaste and tenderness toward the Volhynian Jews, "the former (Ukrainian) Yids."*

It is relatively late in the diary that Babel's optimism about the Soviet Union's chances of winning this war begins to fade. In the final entries, as Babel and his colleagues return to Russia on the fleeing propaganda train in mid-September of 1920, the war has been lost, the Soviet Union defeated.

Within days, the Red Cavalry was to go into reserve. Babel had chronicled its last great campaign.

JUNE 3, 1920. ZHITOMIR

Morning in the train,* came here to get my tunic and boots. I sleep

---

* The Polit-otdel train, equipped with a printing press and radio station, sent to the front for the ideological education of the troops.

with Zhukov, Topolnik,* it's dirty, in the morning the sun shines in my eyes, railroad car dirt. Lanky Zhukov, voracious Topolnik, the whole editorial crew unbelievably dirty people.

Bad tea in borrowed mess tins. Letters home, packages off to Yugrosta,† interview with Pollak, operation to seize Novograd, discipline is weakening in the Polish army, Polish White Guard literature, packets of cigarette paper, matches, former (Ukrainian) Yids, commissars—the whole thing stupid, malicious, feeble, talentless, and surprisingly unconvincing. Mikhailov copying out Polish articles word for word.

The train's kitchen, fat soldiers with flushed faces, gray souls, stifling heat in the kitchen, kasha, noon, sweat, fat-legged washerwomen, apathetic women—printing presses—describe the soldiers and women, fat, fed, sleepy.

Love in the kitchen.

Off to Zhitomir after lunch. A town that is white, not sleepy, yet battered and silent. I look for traces of Polish culture. Women well dressed, white stockings. The Catholic Church.

Bathe at Nuski in the Teterev, a horrible little river, old Jews in the bathing boxes with long, emaciated legs covered with gray hairs. Young Jews. Women are washing clothes in the Teterev. A family, beautiful woman, husband holds the child.

The bazaar in Zhitomir, old cobbler, bluing, chalk, laces.

The synagogue buildings, old architecture—how all this touches my soul.

Watch crystal, 1,200 rubles. Market. A small Jewish philosopher. An indescribable store: Dickens, brooms, and golden slippers. His philosophy: they all say they're fighting for truth yet they all plunder. If only one government at least were good! Wonderful words, his scant beard, we talk, tea and three apple turnovers—750 rubles. An interesting old woman, malicious, practical, unhurried. How greedy for money they all are. Describe the bazaar, the baskets of cherries, the inside of a tavern. A conversation with a Russian woman who came over to borrow a tub. Sweat, watery tea, I'm sinking my teeth into life again, farewell to you, dead men.

---

* Babel's colleagues, reporters for the *Krasny Kavalerist* (*The Red Cavalryman*).

† The Ukrainian division of ROSTA, the Soviet news service agency from 1918 to 1935.

Podolsky, the son-in-law, a half-starved intellectual, something about trade unions and service with Budyonny,* I, needless to say, am Russian, my mother a Jewess, what for?

The Zhitomir pogrom carried out by the Poles, and then, of course, by the Cossacks.

After our vanguard units appeared, the Poles entered the town for three days, Jewish pogrom, cut off beards, they always do, rounded up forty-five Jews in the market, took them to the slaughterhouses, torture, they cut out tongues, wailing over the whole town square. They torched six houses, the Konyukhovsky house, I went to take a look, those who tried to save them were machine-gunned down, they butchered the janitor into whose arms a mother had thrown an infant out of a burning window, the priest put a ladder against the back wall, and so they managed to escape.

The Sabbath is drawing to a close, we leave the father-in-law and go to the *tsaddik*. Didn't get his name. A stunning picture for me, though the decline and decadence are plain to see. Even the *tsaddik*—his broad-shouldered, gaunt body. His son, a refined boy in a long overcoat, I can see petit bourgeois but spacious rooms. Everything nice and proper, his wife a typical Jewess, one could even call her of the modern type.

The faces of the old Jews.

Conversations in the corner about rising prices.

I can't find the right page in the prayer book. Podolsky shows me.

Instead of candles—an oil lamp.

I am happy, large faces, hooked noses, black, gray-streaked beards, I have many thoughts, farewell to you, dead men. The face of the *tsaddik*, a nickel-rimmed pince-nez.

"Where are you from, young man?"

"From Odessa."

"How is life there?"

"People are alive."

"Here it's terrible."

A short conversation.

I leave shattered.

---

* Semyon Mikhailovich Budyonny, the commander of the First Cavalry.

Podolsky, pale and sad, gives me his address, a marvelous evening. I walk, think about everything, quiet, strange streets. Kondratyev with a dark-haired Jewess, the poor commandant with his tall sheepskin hat, he doesn't succeed.

And then nightfall, the train, painted Communist slogans (the contrast with what I saw at the old Jews').

The hammering of the presses, our own electrical generator, our own newspapers, a movie is being shown, the train flashes, rumbles, fat-faced soldiers stand in line for the washerwomen (for two days).

JUNE 4, 1920. ZHITOMIR

Morning—packages off to Yugrosta, report on the Zhitomir pogrom, home, to Oreshnikov, to Narbut.

I'm reading Hamsun.* Sobelman tells me his novel's plot.

A new story of Job, an old man who has lived centuries, his students carried him off to feign a resurrection, a glutted foreigner, the Russian Revolution.

Schulz, what's most important, voluptuousness, Communism, how we are filching apples from the masters, Schulz is chatting away, his bald patch, apples hidden under his shirt, Communism, a Dostoyevskyan figure, there is something interesting there, must give it some thought, that inexhaustible overindulgence of his, Schulz in the streets of Berdichev.

Khelemskaya, she's had pleurisy, diarrhea, has turned yellow, dirty overcoat, applesauce. What're you doing here, Khelemskaya? You've got to get married, a husband, an engineer in a technical office, abortion or first child, that was what your life has been about, your mother, you took a bath once a week, your romance, Khelemskaya, that's how you should live, and you'll adapt to the Revolution.

The opening of a Communist club in the editorial office. That's the proletariat for you: incredibly feeble Jews and Jewesses from the underground. March forward, you pitiful, terrible tribe! Then describe the concert, women singing Ukrainian songs.

Bathing in the Teterev. Kiperman, and how we search for food.

---

* Knut Hamsun, the Norwegian novelist.

What kind of man is Kiperman? What a fool I am, he never paid me back. He sways like a reed, he has a large nose, and he is nervous, possibly insane, yet he managed to trick me, the way he puts off repaying me, runs the club. Describe his trousers, nose, and unruffled speech, torture in prison, Kiperman is a terrible person.

Night on the boulevard. The hunt for women. Four streets, four stages: acquaintance, conversation, awakening of desire, gratification of desire. The Teterev below, an old medical orderly who says that the commissars have everything, wine too, but he is nice about it.

Me and the Ukrainian editors.

Guzhin, whom Khelemskaya complained about today, they're looking for something better. I'm tired. And suddenly loneliness, life flows before me, but what is its significance?

JUNE 5, 1920. ZHITOMIR

Received boots, tunic on the train. Going to Novograd at sunrise. The automobile is a Thornicroft. Everything seized from Denikin. Sunrise in the monastery yard or the schoolyard. Slept in the automobile. Arrived in Novograd at 11. Travel farther in another Thornicroft. Detour bridge. The town is livelier, the ruins appear normal. I take my suitcase. The staff left for Korets. One of the Jewesses gave birth, in a hospital, of course. A gangly hook-nosed man asks me for a job, runs behind me with my suitcase. He promised to come again tomorrow. Novograd is Zvyagel.

A man from the supplies division in a white sheepskin hat, a Jew, and stoop-shouldered Morgan are on the truck. We wait for Morgan, he's at the pharmacy, our little friend has the clap. The automobile has come from Fastov. Two fat drivers. We're flying, a true Russian driver, all our insides thoroughly shook up. The rye is ripening, orderlies gallop by, miserable, enormous, dusty trucks, half-naked, plump, light-blond Polish boys, prisoners, Polish noses.

Korets: describe, the Jews outside the large house, a *yeshiva bokher**
in spectacles, what are they talking about, these old men with their yellow beards, stoop-shouldered merchants, feeble, lonely. I want to stay,

---

* Talmud student.

but the telephone operators roll up the wires. Of course the staff has left. We pick apples and cherries. Moved on at a wild pace. Then the driver, red sash, eats bread with his motor-oil-stained fingers. Six versts short of our goal the magneto floods with oil. Repairs beneath the scorching sun, sweat and drivers. I get there on a hay cart (I forgot: Artillery Inspector Timoshenko (?) [*sic*] is inspecting the cannons in Korets. Our generals.) Evening. Night. The park in Hoshcha. Zotov* and the staff rush on, transport carts go galloping by, the staff left for Rovno, damn it, what bad luck. The Jews, I decide to stay at Duvid Uchenik's, the soldiers try to talk me out of it, the Jews beg me to stay. I wash myself, bliss, many Jews. Are Uchenik's brothers twins? The wounded want to meet me. Healthy bastards, just flesh wounds on their legs, they get about on their own. Real tea, I eat supper. Uchenik's children, a small but shrewd girl with squinting eyes, a shivering six-year-old girl, a fat wife with gold teeth. They sit around me, there's anxiety in the air. Uchenik tells me the Poles were out plundering, then others raided, whooping and hollering, they carried off everything, his wife's things.

The girl: Aren't you a Jew? Uchenik sits watching me eat, the girl sits shivering on his lap. "She is frightened, the cellar and the shooting and your people." I tell them everything will be fine, what the Revolution means, I talk profusely. "Things are bad, we're going to be plundered, don't go to bed."

Night, a lantern in front of the window, a Hebrew grammar, my soul aches, my hair is clean, clean is my sorrow. Sweating from the tea. As backup: Tsukerman with a rifle. A radio-telegrapher. Soldiers in the yard, they chase everyone off to sleep, they chuckle. I eavesdrop on them, they hear something: Halt, who goes there? We'll mow you down!

The hunt for the woman prisoner. Stars, night over the shtetl. A tall Cossack with an earring and a cap with a white top. They had arrested mad Stasova, a mattress, she beckoned with her finger: Let's go, I'll let you have some, I can keep it working all night writhing, hopping, not running away! The soldiers chase everyone off to sleep. They eat supper—fried eggs, tea, stew—indescribable coarseness, sprawled

* Commander of the Cavalry Field Headquarters.

all over the table, Mistress, more! Uchenik in front of his house, he's on sentry duty, what a laugh, "Go off to sleep!" "I'm guarding my house!" A terrible situation with the fugitive madwoman. If they catch her, they'll kill her.

I can't sleep. I meddled, now they say everything's lost.

A difficult night, an idiot with a piglet's body—the radio-telegrapher. Dirty nails and refined manners. Discussion about the Jewish question. A wounded man in a black shirt, a milksop and lout, the old Jews are running, the women have been sent off. Nobody is asleep. Some girls or other on the porch, some soldier asleep on the sofa.

I write in my diary. There is a lamp. The park in front of the window, transport carts roll by. No one's going off to sleep. An automobile has arrived. Morgan is looking for a priest, I take him to the Jews.

Goryn, Jews and old women on the porches. Hoshcha has been ransacked, Hoshcha is clean, Hoshcha is silent. A clean job. In a whisper: Everything's been taken and they don't even weep, they're experts. The Horyn, a network of lakes and tributaries, evening light, here the battle for Rovno took place. Discussions with Jews, my people, they think I'm Russian, and my soul opens up to them. We sit on the high embankment. Peace and soft sighs behind me. I leave to defend Uchenik. I told them my mother is a Jewess, the story, Belaya Tserkov, the rabbi.

June 6, 1920. Rovno

Slept anxiously, just a few hours. I wake up, sun, flies, a good bed, pink Jewish pillows, feathers. The soldiers are banging their crutches. Again: Mistress, we want more! Roasted meat, sugar from a cut-glass chalice, they sit sprawled out, their forelocks* hanging down, dressed in riding gear, red trousers, sheepskin hats, leg stumps swinging boisterously. The women have brick-red faces, they run around, none of them slept. Duvid Uchenik is pale, in a vest. He tells me, Don't leave as long as they're still here. A cart comes by to pick them up. Sun, the cart is waiting across from the park, they're gone. Salvation.

The automobile arrived yesterday evening. At 1 P.M. we leave

---

* Ukrainian Cossacks shaved their heads, leaving only a forelock, known as a *chub.*

Hoshcha for Rovno. The River Horyn is sparkling in the sun. I go for a morning walk. It turns out the mistress of the house hadn't spent the night at home. The maid and her friends were sitting with the soldiers who wanted to rape her, all night till dawn the maid kept feeding them apples, quiet conversations: We've had enough of war, want to get married, go to sleep. The cross-eyed girl became talkative, Duvid puts on his vest, his *tallith*, prays solemnly, offers thanks, flour in the kitchen, dough is being kneaded, they're getting things under way, the maid is a fat, barefoot, thick-legged Jewess with soft breasts, tidying up, talking endlessly. The landlady's speech—what she wants is for everything to end well. The house comes to life.

I travel to Rovno in the Thornicroft. Two fallen horses. Smashed bridges, the automobile on wooden planks, everything creaks, endless line of transport carts, traffic jam, cursing, describe the transport carts in front of the broken bridge at noon, horsemen, trucks, two-wheelers with ammunition. Our truck drives with crazed speed, even though it is completely falling to pieces, dust.

Eight versts short of our goal, it breaks down. Cherries, I sleep, sweat in the sun. Kuzitsky, an amusing fellow, can immediately tell you your future, lays out cards, a medical assistant from Borodyanitsy, in exchange for treatment women offered him their services, roasted chicken, and themselves, he is constantly worried that the chief of the medical division won't let him go, shows me his genuine wounds, when he walks he limps, left a girl on the road forty versts from Zhitomir, go, she told him, because the divisional chief of staff was courting her. Loses his whip, sits half naked, babbles, lies without restraint, photograph of his brother, a former staff cavalry captain, now a division commander married to a Polish countess, Denikin's men shot him.

I'm a medical man.

Dust in Rovno, dusty molten gold flows over the dreary little houses.

The brigade rides past, Zotov at the window, the people of Rovno, the Cossacks' appearance, a remarkably peaceful, self-confident army. Jewish youths and maidens watch them with admiration, the old Jews look on indifferently. Describe the air in Rovno, something agitated and unstable about it, and there are Polish store signs and life.

Describe the evening.

The Khast family. A sly, black-haired girl from Warsaw takes us there. The medical orderly, malicious verbal stench, coquetry, You'll eat with us! I wash up in the hallway, everything is uncomfortable, bliss, I'm dirty and sweat-drenched, then hot tea with my sugar.

Describe this Khast, a complex fury of a man, unbearable voice, they think I don't understand Yiddish, they argue incessantly, animal fear, the father quite inscrutable, a smiling medical orderly, treats the clap (?) [*sic*], smiles, lies low, but seems hotheaded, the mother: We're intellectuals, we own nothing, he's a medical orderly, a worker, we don't mind having them here as long as they're quiet, we're exhausted! A stunning apparition: their rotund son with his cunning and idiotic smile behind the glass of his round spectacles, the fawning conversation, they scrape and bow to me, a gaggle of sisters, all vixens (?) [*sic*]. The dentist, some sort of grandson to whom they all talk with the same whining hysteria as to the old folk, young Jews come over, people from Rovno with faces that are flat and yellow with fear and fish eyes, they talk of Polish taunts, show their passports, there was a solemn decree of Poland annexing Volhynia as well, I recall Polish culture, Sienkiewicz, the women, the empire, they were born too late, now there is class consciousness.

I give my clothes to be laundered. I drink tea incessantly and sweat like a beast and watch the Khasts carefully, intently. Night on the sofa. Undressed for the first time since the day I set out. All the shutters are closed, the electric light burns, the stuffiness is unbearable, many people sleep there, stories of pillaging by Budyonny's men, shivering and terror, horses snort outside the window, transport carts roll down Shkolnaya Street, night. [The following twenty-one pages of the diary are missing.]

July 11, 1920. Belyov

Spent the night with the soldiers of the staff squadron, in the hay. Slept badly, thinking about the manuscripts. Dejection, loss of energy, I know I'll get over it, but when will that be? I think of the Khasts, those worms, I remember everything, those reeking souls, and the cow eyes, and the sudden, high, screeching voices, and the smiling father. The main thing: his smile and he is hotheaded, and many secrets, reeking memories of scandals. The mother, a gigantic figure—she is malicious, cowardly, gluttonous, repugnant, her fixed, expectant stare. The daughter's repulsive and detailed lies, the son's eyes laughing behind his spectacles.

I roam about the village. I ride to Klevan, the shtetl was taken yesterday by the Third Cavalry Brigade of the Sixth Division. Our mounted patrols appeared on the Rovno-Lutsk high road, Lutsk is being evacuated.

8th–12th heavy fighting, Dundic killed, Shadilov, commander of the Thirty-sixth Regiment, killed, many horses fell, tomorrow we'll have the details.

Budyonny's orders concerning our loss of Rovno, the unbelievable exhaustion of the units, the frenzied attacks of our brigades which don't have the same results as before, incessant battles since May 27, if the army isn't given a breather, it will become unfit for battle.

Isn't it premature to issue such orders? No, they make sense: their objective is to rouse the rear lines—Klevan. Burial of six or seven Red Army fighters. I rode behind a *tachanka*. The funeral march, on the way back from the cemetery, a bravura infantry march, no sign of the funeral procession. A carpenter—a bearded Jew—is rushing around the shtetl, he's banging some coffins together. The main street is also Shossova.

My first requisition is a notebook. Menashe, the synagogue *shamas,* goes with me. I have lunch at Mudrik's, the same old story, the Jews have been plundered, their perplexity, they looked to the Soviet regime as saviors, then suddenly yells, whips, Yids. I am surrounded by a whole circle, I tell them about Wilson's note, about the armies of labor, the Jews listen, sly and commiserating smiles, a Jew in white trousers had come to the pine forests to recuperate, wants to go home. The Jews sit on earth mounds,* girls and old men, stillness, stifling, dusty, a peasant (Parfenty Melnik, the one who did his military service at Elizavetopol) complains that his horse has swollen up with milk, they took her foal away, sadness, the manuscripts, the manuscripts—that's what is clouding my soul.

Colonel Gorov, elected by the people, village headman—sixty years old—a pre-reform rat of a nobleman. We talk about the army, about Brusilov, if Brusilov set off, why shouldn't we? Gray whiskers, sputters,

---

* *Zavalinka:* a mound of earth around a hut that protects it from the weather and is often used for sitting on outside.

---

a man of the past, smokes homegrown tobacco, lives in the government building, I feel sorry for the old man.

The clerk of the district government, a handsome Ukrainian. Flawless order. Has relearned everything in Polish, shows me the books, the district statistics: 18,600 people, 800 of whom are Poles, wanted to be united with Poland, a solemn petition of unification with the Polish state.

The clerk is also a pre-reform figure in velvet trousers, with Ukrainian speech, touched by the new times, a little mustache.

Klevan, its roads, streets, peasants, and Communism are far from one another.

Hops-growing, many nurseries, rectangular green walls, sophisticated cultivation.

The colonel has blue eyes, the clerk a silken mustache.

Night, headquarters work at Belyov. What kind of man is Zholnarkevich? A Pole? His feelings? The touching friendship of two brothers.* Konstantin and Mikhail. Zholnarkevich is an old hand, exact, hardworking without overexerting himself, energetic without kicking up a fuss, Polish mustache, slim Polish legs. The headquarters staff is made up of Zholnarkevich and three other clerks toiling away till nightfall.

A colossal job, the positioning of the brigades, no provisions, the main thing: the operational itineraries are handled unobtrusively. The orderlies at the headquarters sleep on the ground. Thin candles burn, the divisional chief of staff in his hat wipes his forehead and dictates, ceaselessly dictates operational reports, orders to the artillery division, we are continuing our advance on Lutsk.

Night, I sleep on the hay next to Lepin,† a Latvian, horses that have broken from their tethers roam about, snatch away the hay from under my head.

July 12, 1920. Belyov

This morning I began my journal of military operations, analyzing the operational reports. The journal is going to be an interesting piece of work.

---

* Konstantin Karlovich Zholnarkevich was the divisional chief of staff, and his brother, Mikhail, was a staff officer.
† A staff officer in the Sixth Cavalry Division.

After lunch I go riding on the horse of Sokolov, the orderly. (He is ill with a relapse of typhus, he lies next to me on the ground in a leather jacket, thin, a man of breeding, a whip in his emaciated hand, he left the hospital, they didn't feed him, and he was bored, he lay there sick on that terrible night of our retreat from Rovno, he had been totally soaked in water, lanky, totters, talks to the people of the house with curiosity but also imperiously, as if all muzhiks were his enemy). Shpakovo, a Czech settlement. A rich region, lots of oats and wheat, I ride through the villages: Peresopnitsa, Milostovo, Ploski, Shpakovo. There is flax, they make sunflower oil out of it, and a lot of buckwheat.

Rich villages, hot noon, dusty roads, transparent sky without clouds, my horse lazy, when I whip it it moves. My first mounted ride. In Milostovo—I take a cart from Shpakovo—I'm going to get a *tachanka* and horses with an order from divisional headquarters.

I'm too softhearted. I look admiringly at the clean, hearty, un-Russian life of the Czechs. A good village elder, horsemen galloping in all directions, constantly new demands, forty cartloads of hay, ten pigs, the agents of the Requisitions Committee—grain, the elder is given a receipt—oats have been received, thank you. Reconnaissance commander of the Thirty-fourth Regiment.

The sturdy huts glitter in the sun, roof tiles, iron, stone, apples, the stone schoolhouse, a demi-urban type of woman, bright aprons. We go to Yuripov, the miller, the richest and best-educated man around here, a typical tall, handsome Czech with a Western European mustache. A wonderful courtyard, a dovecote—I'm touched by that—new mill machinery, former affluence, white walls, an extensive farm, a bright, spacious, single-story house and a nice room, and this Czech most probably has a good family, his father—a poor sinewy old man—all of them good people, a robust son with gold teeth, trim and broad-shouldered. A good wife, probably young, and his children.

The mill has, of course, been modernized.

The Czech has been stuffed full of receipts. They took four of his horses and gave him a note for the Rovno District Commissariat, they took a phaeton and gave him a broken *tachanka* in exchange, and three receipts for flour and oats.

The brigade arrives, red flags, a powerful, unified body, self-assured commanders, experienced, calm eyes of the forelocked Cossacks, dust, silence, order, marching band, they are swallowed into their billets, the brigade commander shouts over to me: We mustn't take anything from here, this is our territory. With worried eyes the Czech watches the dashing young brigade commander bustling about in the distance, chats politely with me, returns the broken *tachanka,* but it falls apart. I don't waste any energy. We go to a second, a third house. The village elder lets us know where there are things to be had. An old man actually does have a phaeton, his son keeps jabbering that it is broken, the front part is damaged—you have a bride, I think to myself, or you ride in it to church on Sundays—it's hot, I feel lazy and sorry for them, the horsemen scavenging through everything, this is what freedom initially looks like. I didn't take anything, even though I could have, I'll never be a true Budyonny fighter.

I'm back, it's evening, a Pole was caught in the rye, they hunted him down like an animal, wide fields, scarlet sun, golden fog, swaying grain, in the village they're driving cattle home, rosy, dusty streets, surprisingly tender forms, flaming tongues, orange flames shoot from the borders of the pearly clouds, the carts raise dust.

I work at the headquarters (my horse galloped nicely), I sleep next to Lepin. He is Latvian, his snout blunt, piglety, spectacles, he seems kind. A general staff man.

Cracks sudden, dull jokes. Hey, woman, when're you going to drop dead? And he grabs hold of her.

There's no kerosene at the headquarters. He says: We're striving toward enlightenment, but we have no light, I'm going to play with the village girls. Stretched out his arm, won't let go, his snout strained, his piggy lips quiver, his glasses shake.

JULY 13, 1920. BELYOV

My birthday. Twenty-six years old. I think of home, of my work, my life is flying past. No manuscripts. Dull misery, I will surmount it. I'm keeping my diary, it will be an interesting piece of work.

The clerks are handsome young men, the young Russians from headquarters sing arias from operettas, they are a little corrupted by the work there. Describe the orderlies, the divisional chief of staff and the others—Cherkashin, Tarasov—rag-looters, lickspittles, fawners, gluttons, loafers, products of the past, they know who their master is.

The work at the headquarters in Belyov. A well-oiled machine, a brilliant chief of staff, routine work, a lively man. They discovered that he is a Pole, relieved him of his duties, and then reinstated him on the order of the division commander. He is loved by all, gets on well with the division commander, what does he feel? He's not a Communist, he's a Pole, yet he is as loyal as a guard dog—try figuring that out!

About our operations.

The position of our units.

Our march on Lutsk.

The makeup of the division, the brigade commanders.

The work flow at headquarters: the directive, then the order, then the operational report, then the intelligence report, we drag the Polit-otdel along, the Revolutionary Tribunal,* the reserve horses.

I ride over to Yasinevichi to exchange my carriage for a *tachanka* and horses. Unbelievable dust, heat. We ride through Peresopnitsa, delight in the fields, my twenty-seventh year, I think the rye and barley are ripe, here and there the oats look very good, the poppies are past their bloom, there are no cherries, the apples aren't ripe, a lot of flax, buckwheat, many trampled fields, hops.

A rich land, but within bounds.

Dyakov, commander of the Reserve Cavalry: a fantastical apparition, red trousers with silver stripes, an embossed belt, a Stavropol Cossack, the body of an Apollo, a cropped gray mustache, forty-five years old, has a son and a nephew, outlandish cursing, things were sent over to him from the Supply Department, he had smashed a table to pieces there, but finally got what he wanted. Dyakov, his men love him: our commander is a hero. He was an athlete, can barely read and write, he says: I'm a cavalry inspector now, a general. Dyakov is a Communist, a daring old Budyonny fighter. He met a millionaire with a lady on his

---

* The polit-otdel was a political organ of the new Soviet government charged with the ideological education of the military during the Russian Civil War and the Russian-Polish War of 1920. The Revolutionary Tribunals, *Revtribunaly*, were the organs of military justice representing the Revolutionary Military Council. They investigated crimes committed by military personnel and dealt with prisoners of war. Detachments of the Revolutionary Tribunal were present in each army division and brigade.

arm: "I say, Mr. Dyakov, did we not meet at my club?"—"I have been in eight countries, when I come out on stage, I need only wink."

Dancer, concertina player, trickster, liar, a most picturesque figure. Has a hard time reading documents, he keeps losing them—all this paperwork, he says, has finished me off, if I walk out, what will they do without me?—cursing, chats with the muzhiks, their mouths hang open.

The *tachanka* and two emaciated horses, describe the horses.

People go to Dyakov with requests, phew, I'm being worn down to the bone, distribute underwear, one thing after the other, fatherly relationship, you (to one of the patients) will end up being the head cattle driver here. I go home. Night. Headquarters work.

We have been billeted in the house of the village elder's mother. The merry mistress of the house keeps up an endless babble, hitches up her skirts and works like a bee for her family and then seven people on top of that.

Cherkashin (Lepin's orderly) is rude and tiresome, won't leave her in peace, we're always asking for something or other, children are loafing about the house, we requisition hay, the hut is full of flies, some children, old people, a bride, soldiers jostle and holler. The old woman is sick. The old people drop by to visit her and are mournfully silent, the lamp.

Night, headquarters, the pompous telephone operator, K. Karlovich writes reports, orderlies, the clerks on duty are sleeping, the village pitch-black, a sleepy clerk is typing an order, K. Karlovich is precise as clockwork, the orderlies arrive silently.

The march on Lutsk. The Second Brigade is leading it, they still haven't managed to take it. Where are our advance units?

JULY 14, 1920. BELYOV

Sokolov has been billeted with us. He is lying on the hay, lanky, Russian, in leather boots. Misha is a nice, red-cheeked fellow from Oryol. Lepin* plays with the maid when no one is watching, he has a blunt, tense face, our landlady keeps up an endless babble, tells tales,

* A staff officer in the Sixth Cavalry Division.

works tirelessly, her old mother-in-law—a shriveled-up little old woman—loves her, Cherkashin, Lepin's orderly, eggs her on, she prattles on without stopping to catch her breath.

Lepin fell asleep at the headquarters, a completely idiotic face, he simply can't wake up. A wail over the village, the cavalrymen are trading in their horses, giving the villagers their worn-out nags, trampling the grain, taking their cattle, complaints to the chief of staff, Cherkashin is arrested for whipping a muzhik. Lepin spends three hours writing a letter to the tribunal, Cherkashin, he writes, had been influenced by the scandalously provocative behavior of the Red Officer Sokolov. My advice: don't put seven men in one hut.

Gaunt, angry Sokolov tells me: We're destroying everything, I hate the war.

Why are they all here in this war—Zholnarkevich, Sokolov? All this is subconscious, inert, unthinking. A nice system.

Frank Mosher.* A shot-down American pilot, barefoot but elegant, neck like a column, dazzlingly white teeth, his uniform covered with oil and dirt. He asks me worriedly: Did I maybe commit a crime by fighting against Soviet Russia? Our position is strong. O the scent of Europe, coffee, civilization, strength, ancient culture, many thoughts, I watch him, can't let him go. A letter from Major Fountleroy: things in Poland are bad, there's no constitution, the Bolsheviks are strong, the socialists the center of attention but not in power. One has to learn the new methods of warfare. What are they telling Western European soldiers? Russian imperialism is out to destroy the nationalities, customs, that's the main thing, to take over all the Slavic lands, what old and tired words these are! An endless conversation with Mosher, I sink into the past, they'll shake you up, Mosher, ha, Mr. Conan Doyle, letters to New York. Is Mosher being sly or not—he keeps asking frantically what Bolshevism is. A sad, heart-warming impression.

I'm getting used to the headquarters, I have what they call a vehicular driver, thirty-nine-year-old Grishchuk, a prisoner in Germany for six years, fifty versts from his home (he is from the Kremenets district), the army won't let him go, he says nothing.

---

* Frank Mosher, the assumed name of Captain Merian Caldwell Cooper, the shot-down American pilot whom Babel interrogated in Belyov. He later achieved fame as the creator and producer of the motion picture *King Kong*.

Division Commander Timoshenko is at headquarters. A colorful figure. A colossus, red half-leather trousers, a red cap, slender, a former platoon commander, a machine-gunner, an artillery warrant officer in the past. Legendary tales. The commissar of the First Brigade had been frightened by the fire—Boys, on your horses!—and Timoshenko had begun lashing at all his commanders with his whip: Kniga,* the regimental commanders, he shoots the commissar—On your horses, you sons of bitches!—goes charging after them, five shots—Comrades, help!—I'll show you!—Help!—a shot through the hand, in the eye, the revolver misfires, and I bawl out the commissar. He fires up the Cossacks, a Budyonny man, when you ride with him into battle, if the Poles don't kill you, he'll kill you.

The Second Brigade attacks Lutsk and withdraws toward evening, the enemy counterattacks, heavy forces, wants to break through to Dubno. We occupy Dubno.

Report: Minsk, Bobruisk, Molodechno, Proskurov, Sventsyany, Sarny, Staro-Konstantinov have been taken, they are entering Galicia where there will be a cav. maneuver—by the River Styr or the Bug. Kovel is being evacuated, heavy forces at Lvov, Mosher's deposition. There will be an assault.

The division commander's gratitude for the battle at Rovno. Issue a statement.

The village silent, a light at the headquarters, arrested Jews. The Budyonny fighters bring Communism, a little old woman weeps. Ha, what a gloomy life these Russians lead! Where is that Ukrainian mirth? The harvest is beginning. The poppies are ripening, I wonder where I can get some grain for the horses and cherry dumplings.

Which divisions are to our left?

Mosher barefoot, noon, dull Lepin.

July 15, 1920. Belyov

Interrogation of defectors. They show us our leaflets. Their power is great, the leaflets help the Cossacks.

---

* Vasily Ivanovich Kniga was the commander of the First Brigade of the Sixth Cavalry Division.

We have an interesting military commissar: Bakhturov,* a fighter, fat, foul-mouthed, always in the front lines.

Describe the job of a war correspondent, what exactly is a war correspondent?

I have to get the operational reports from Lepin, it's torture. The headquarters have been set up in the house of a converted Jew.

At night the orderlies stand in front of the headquarters building.

The harvest has begun. I am learning to tell the plants apart. Tomorrow is my sister's birthday.

A description of Volhynia. The muzhiks live revoltingly, dirty, we eat, poetic Matyash, a womanizer, even when he's talking to an old woman he is still mellifluous.

Lepin is courting the maid.

Our units are one-and-a-half versts from Lutsk. The army is preparing a cavalry attack, is concentrating its forces in Lvov, moving them up to Lutsk.

We've found a Pilsudski† proclamation: Warriors of the Rzecz Pospolita. A touching proclamation. Our graves are white with the bones of five generations of fighters, our ideals, our Poland, our happy home, your Motherland is relying on you, our young freedom is shuddering, one last stand, we will remember you, everything will be for you, Soldiers of the Rzecz Pospolita!

Touching, sad, without the steel of Bolshevik slogans, no promises and words like *order, ideals,* and *living in freedom.*

Victory will be ours!

July 16, 1920. Novoselki

Received an army order: seize the crossings over the River Styr in the Rozhishche-Yalovichi sector.

The headquarters move to Novoselki, twenty-five versts. I ride with the division commander, the staff squadron, the horses gallop, forests, oak trees, forest paths, the division commander's red cap, his

---

* Pavel Vasilevich Bakhturov, the military commissar of the Sixth Cavalry Division from February to August 1920. He had just been decorated with a Red Flag Medal.

† Josef Pilsudski, the commander in chief of the Polish forces.

powerful frame, buglers, beauty, the new army, the division commander and the squadron—one body.

Our billet, our landlord and his wife, young and quite wealthy, they have pigs, a cow, all they ever say: *nemae.**

Zholnarkevich's tale of the sly medical orderly. Two women, he had to deal with them. He gave one of them castor oil—when it got to her, he dashed off to the other one.

A terrible incident, soldiers' love, two sturdy Cossacks came to an agreement with a woman—Can you hold out with two of us?—Yes, I can. One of them did it three times, the other one climbed onto her, she went running around the room dirtying the whole floor, they threw her out, didn't give her any money, she had been too hard-working.

About the Budyonny commanders: are they soldiers of fortune or future usurpers? They are of Cossack background, that's the main thing, describe the provenance of these detachments, all these Timoshenkos and Budyonnys had set up these detachments them-selves, mainly with neighbors from their Cossack villages, now the detachments have been organized by the Soviet government.

The division is carrying out the order it was given, a powerful col-umn is moving from Lutsk to Dubno, the evacuation of Lutsk has obviously been called off, troops and equipment are arriving there.

Our young landlord and his wife: she is tall with traces of village beauty, bustling about among her five children, who are rolling about on the bench. Interesting—each child looks after the next, Mama, give him titty. The mother, well built and flushed, lies sternly among her swarming brood of children. The husband is a good man. Sokolov: These pups should be shot, why keep breeding? The husband: Out of little ones big ones grow.

Describe our soldiers: Cherkashin (today he came back from the tribunal a little browbeaten), insolent, lanky, depraved, what an inhab-itant of Communist Russia, Matyash, a Ukrainian, boundlessly lazy, keen on women, always torpid, his boots unlaced, lazy movements, Misha, Sokolov's orderly, has been to Italy, handsome, messy.

Describe: the ride with the division commander, a small squadron,

* Ukrainian: "there isn't any."

the division commander's retinue, Bakhturov, old Budyonny fighters, a march plays as we set off.

The divisional chief of staff is sitting on a bench, a peasant is choking with fury, points at a mare on her last legs that he has been given in exchange for a good horse. Dyakov comes riding in, the conversation is short, for a horse like this you can get fifteen thousand, for a horse like this, even twenty thousand. If it gets up, then it's a horse.

They are taking away the pigs, chickens, the village wails. Describe our provisions. I sleep in the hut. The horror of their lives. Flies. Research on flies, myriads of them. Five hollering, unhappy little children.

They hide provisions from us.

JULY 17, 1920. NOVOSELKI

I am beginning my war journal from 7/16. I go to Pozha [Pelcha]. The Polit-otdel,* they eat cucumbers there, sun, they sleep barefoot behind the haystacks. Yakovlev[†] promises to help. The day passes with work. Lepin's lip is swollen. He has round shoulders. He's tough to get along with. A new page: I am studying the science of military operations.

Next to one of the huts lies a slaughtered cow that has only recently calved. Her bluish teats lying on the ground, just skin. An indescribable pity! A murdered young mother.

JULY 18, 1920. NOVOSELKI—MALI DOROGOSTAI

The Polish army is gathering in the region of Dubno-Kremenets for a decisive attack. We are paralyzing their maneuver, we are a step ahead of them. The army launches an attack on the southern sector, our division is being held in reserve. Our task: to seize the crossings over the River Styr around Lutsk.

In the morning we arrive in Mali Dorogostai (north of Mlynov), we leave the transport carts behind, also the sick and the administrative staff, it is obvious that an operation is ahead.

* Charged with the ideological education of the military.
† The political commissar of the Sixth Cavalry Division.

We receive an order from the Southwestern Front,* when we cross into Galicia—it will be the first time that Soviet troops will cross the border—we are to treat the population well. We are not entering a conquered nation, the nation belongs to the workers and peasants of Galicia, and to them alone, we are only there to help them set up a Soviet power. The order is important and sensible—will the rag-looters stick to it? No.

We set out. Buglers. The division commander's cap glitters. A discussion with the division commander about the fact that I need a horse. We ride, forests, the fields are being harvested, but the harvest is poor, scanty, here and there two women and two old men. The centuries-old Volhynian forests, majestic green oaks and hornbeams, it is clear why the oak is king.

We ride along forest paths with two staff squadrons, they are always with the division commander, they are handpicked. Describe their horses' garb, sabers in red velvet, curved sabers, vests, carpets over their saddles. Dressed poorly, though each of them has ten service jackets—it's doubtless a matter of chic.

Fields, roads, sun, the wheat is ripening, we are trampling the fields, the harvest is weak, the grain stunted, there are many Czech, German, and Polish settlements. Different people, prosperity, cleanliness, marvelous gardens, we eat unripe apples and pears, everyone wants to be quartered with the foreigners, I also catch myself wishing for that, the foreigners are frightened.

The Jewish cemetery outside Malin, centuries old, the stones have toppled, almost all the same shape, oval at the top, the cemetery is overgrown with weeds, it saw Khmelnitsky,[†] now Budyonny, the unfortunate Jewish population, everything repeats itself, once again the same story of Poles, Cossacks, Jews is repeating itself with striking exactness, what is new is Communism.

More and more often we come across trenches from the last war, barbed wire everywhere, enough for fences for the next ten years,

---

*The Southwestern Front was formed on January 10, 1920, to fight the anti-Bolshevik White Polish Army in the Russian-Polish Campaign and the Imperialist forces of Generals Denikin and Wrangel.

[†] Bogdan Khmelnitsky, the legendary seventeenth-century Cossack leader whose brutal raids in the region were still remembered.

destroyed villages, they are being rebuilt again everywhere, but slowly, there's nothing, no materials of any kind, no cement.

With the Cossacks at the rest stops, hay for the horses, they all have long stories to tell: Denikin, their farms, their leaders, Budyonnys and Knigas, campaigns with two hundred men, plundering raids, the rich, free life of a Cossack, how many officers' heads they have chopped off. They read the newspaper, but the names just don't sink in, how easily they twist everything.

Wonderful camaraderie, unity, love of horses, a horse takes up a quarter of a day, incessant bartering and chatting. A horse's role and life.

Completely wayward attitude toward the leaders—they address them with the familiar "you."

M[ali] Dorogostai was completely destroyed, is being rebuilt.

We ride into the priest's garden. We take hay, eat fruit. A shady, sunny, wonderful garden, a little white church, there had been cows, horses, a priest with a little braid is wandering around in a daze collecting receipts. Bakhturov* is lying on his stomach eating yogurt with cherries, I'll give you a receipt, really, I will!

We've eaten enough of the priest's food to last us a whole year. Word has it he's ruined, is trying to get a position, do you have any openings for a regimental clergyman?

Evening at my quarters. Again *nemae*†—they're all lying, I write in my journal, they give us potatoes with butter. Night in the village, an enormous, crimson fiery circle before my eyes, yellow fields flee from the ravaged village. Night. Lights at the headquarters. There are always lights at headquarters, Karl Karlovich** dictates an order from memory, he never forgets anything, the telephone operators sit with hanging heads. Karl Karlovich served in Warsaw.

JULY 19, 1920. M[ALI] DOROGOSTAI—
SMORDVA—BEREZHTSY

Slept badly last night. Cramps in my stomach. We ate green pears yesterday. I feel dreadful. We're setting off at dawn.

---

* The military commissar of the Sixth Cavalry Division.
† Ukrainian: "there isn't any."
** Konstantin Karlovich Zholnarkevich, the chief of staff of the Sixth Cavalry Division.

The enemy is attacking us in the sector of Mlynov-Dubno. We pushed forward all the way to Radzivillov.

Today at dawn, the decisive attack by all the divisions—from Lutsk to Kremenets. The Fifth, the Sixth Division are concentrated in Smordva, we have reached Kozino.

In other words, we're heading south.

We're pulling out of M. Dorogostai. The division commander is greeting the squadrons, his horse is trembling. Music. We are stretched out along the road. The road is unbearable. We are going via Mlynov to Berezhtsy. A pity we can't enter Mlynov, it's a Jewish shtetl. We get to Berezhtsy, cannonade, the staff heads back, there's a smell of fuel oil, cavalry units are crawling over the slopes. Smordva, the priest's house, young provincial ladies in white stockings, their eyes red from weeping, it has been a long time since I have seen anything like it, the priest's wounded wife, limping, the sinewy cleric, a solid house, the divisional staff and the commander of Division Fourteen, we are waiting for the arrival of the brigades, our staff is on a hill, a truly Bolshevik staff: the division commander, Bakhturov, the military commissars. We're under gunfire, the division commander knows his stuff: he's clever, a go-getter, somewhat of a dandy, self-assured, the bypass movement toward Bokunin was his idea, the attack is held up, orders issued to the brigades. Kolesov and Kniga* came galloping over (the famous Kniga, why is he famous?). Kolesov's superb horse, Kniga has the face of a bakery sales clerk, a diligent Ukrainian. Swift orders, everyone confers, the gunfire gets stronger, shells are falling a hundred paces from us.

The commander of Division Fourteen is of a weaker mettle, a fool, talkative, an intellectual, wants to pass for a Budyonny fighter, curses incessantly—I've been fighting all night—likes to brag a bit. The brigades are winding in long ribbons along the opposite bank, the transport carts are under fire, columns of dust. Budyonny's regiments with their transport carts, carpets across their saddles.

I feel worse and worse. I have a temperature of 39.8. Budyonny and Voroshilov[†] arrive.

---

* Nikolai Petrovich Kolesov was commander of the Third Brigade, and Vasily Ivanovich Kniga was commander of the First Brigade of the Sixth Cavalry Division.

[†] The two founding members of the First Cavalry Army, Semyon Mikhailovich Budyonny, its commander, and Kliment Efremovich Voroshilov, its commissar.

There's a conference. The division commander goes flying past. The battle begins. I'm lying in the priest's garden. Grishchuk is completely impassive. What kind of a man is Grishchuk? Submissiveness, endless silence, boundless indolence. Fifty versts from home, hasn't been home in six years, doesn't run away.

He knows the meaning of authority, the Germans taught him that.

Wounded men start coming in, bandages, bare stomachs, forbearing, unbearable heat, incessant gunfire from both sides, can't doze off. Budyonny and Voroshilov on the porch. A picture of the battle, the cavalrymen return covered with dust, sweating, red, no traces of excitement, they've been slashing, they're professionals, everything done with the utmost calm, that's what sets them apart, self-assuredness, hard work, nurses go flying by on horses, a Zhguchy armored car. In front of us is Count Ledochowski's* mansion, a white building above the lake, not tall, not flamboyant, very noble, memories of my childhood, novels—many more memories. At the medical assistants': a pitiful, handsome young Jew, he might well have been on the count's payroll, gray with worry. If I may ask, what is the situation at the front? The Poles mocked and tormented, he thinks life is about to begin, but the Cossacks don't always behave well.

Echoes of battle—galloping horsemen, reports, the wounded, the dead.

I sleep in the churchyard. Some brigade commander or other is sleeping with his head resting on some young lady's stomach.

I have been sweating, I feel better. I ride to Berezhtsy, the headquarters office is there, a destroyed house, I drink cherry tea, lie down in the landlady's bed, sweat, aspirin powder. It would do me good to sleep a little. I remember—I have a fever, heat, some soldiers in the churchyard kicking up a fuss, others cool, they are coupling their stallions with mares.

Berezhtsy, Sienkiewicz, I drink cherry tea, I'm lying on a spring mattress, next to me lies a child gasping for breath. I dozed off for about two hours. They wake me. I'm drenched in sweat. At night we return to Smordva, from there we continue, a clearing in the forest. Night journey, moon, somewhere in front of us, the squadron.

---

* Ignacy Ledochowski, commander of the Polish Fourteenth Artillery Brigade.

A hut in the forest. The muzhiks and their womenfolk sleep along the walls. Konstantin Karlovich* is dictating. A rare picture: the squadron is sleeping all around, everything is steeped in darkness, nothing can be seen, a chill flows in from the forest, I bump into the horses, at the headquarters everyone's eating, I feel sick and lie down on the ground next to a *tachanka*, I sleep for three hours covered with Barsukov's shawl and coat, it feels good.

JULY 20, 1920. THE HEIGHTS NEAR SMORDVA. PELCHA.

We set out at five in the morning. Rain, damp, we stick to the forests. The operation is going very well, our division commander chose the right bypass maneuver, we're continuing to detour. We're soaked, forest paths. The bypass is taking us through Bokuika to Pelcha. Information: at 10 o'clock Dobryvodka was taken, at twelve o'clock, after negligible resistance, Kozin. We're pursuing the enemy, we go to Pelcha. Forests, forest paths, the squadrons are winding on ahead.

My health is better, for inexplicable reasons.

I am studying the flora of the province of Volhynia, there has been much logging, the clearing in the forest with felled trees, remains of the war, barbed wire, white trenches. Majestic green oaks, hornbeams, many pines, the willow is a majestic and gentle tree, rain in the forest, washed-out roads in the forest, ash trees.

To Pelcha along forest paths. We arrive around ten o'clock. Another village, lanky landlady, boring—*nemae*, very clean, son had been a soldier, gives us eggs, there's no milk, in the hut it's unbearably stuffy, it's raining, washes out all the roads, black squelching mud, it's impossible to get to the headquarters. Sitting all day in the hut, it's warm, there, outside the window, the rain. How boring and banal this kind of life is for me—chicks, a hidden cow, dirt, idiocy. An indescribable sadness lies over the earth, everything is wet, black, autumn, whereas back in Odessa . . .

In Pelcha we captured the transport carts of the Forty-ninth Polish Infantry Regiment. The spoils are being divided outside my window,

---

* Zholnarkevich, the chief of staff of the Sixth Cavalry Division.

completely idiotic cursing, nonstop, other words are boring, they avoid them, as for the cursing: the Mother of Christ, the Goddamn Mother, the peasant women cringe, the Mother of God, the children ask questions—the soldiers curse. Mother of God. I'll shoot you, damn it! I get a document bag and a saddlebag. Describe this dull life. The peasant doesn't go to work on the field. I sleep in the landlady's bed. We heard that England proposed that Sov. Russia and Poland make peace—is it possible this will end soon?

JULY 21, 1920. PELCHA—BORATIN

We have taken Dubno. The resistance, regardless of what we say, has been insignificant. What is going on? The prisoners talk, and it is clear that it is the revolution of the little people. Much can be said about that, the beauty of the Polish pediments, there is something touching about it, Milady. Fate, slighted honor, Jews, Count Ledochowski. Proletarian Revolution. How I drink in the aroma of Europe that flows from over there.

We set out for Boratin by way of Dobryvodka, forests, fields, soft outlines, oak trees, again music and the division commander, and, near-by, the war. A rest stop in Zhabokriki, I eat white bread. Grishchuk sometimes seems dreadful to me—downtrodden. The Germans: that grinding jaw.

Describe Grishchuk.

In Boratin, a hardy, sunny village. Khmil, smiling at his daughter, he is a closemouthed but wealthy peasant, eggs fried in butter, milk, white bread, gluttony, sun, cleanliness, I am recuperating from my illness, to me all these peasants look alike, a young mother. Grishchuk is beaming, they gave him fried eggs with bacon, a wonderful, shadowy threshing shed, clover. Why doesn't Grishchuk run away?

A wonderful day. My interview with Konstantin Karlovich [Zholnarkevich]. What kind of men are our Cossacks? Many-layered: rag-looting, bravado, professionalism, revolutionary ideals, savage cruelty. We are the vanguard, but of what? The population is waiting for liberators, the Jews for freedom—but who arrives? The Kuban Cossacks. . . .

The army commander summons the division commander for a

meeting in Kozin. Seven versts. I ride. Sand. Every house remains in my heart. Clusters of Jews. Faces, ghetto, and we, an ancient people, tormented, we still have strength, a store, I drink excellent coffee, I pour balm on the storekeeper's soul as he listens to the rumpus in his store. The Cossacks are yelling, cursing, climbing up to the shelves, the poor store, the sweaty, red-bearded Jew. . . . I wander endlessly, I cannot tear myself away, the shtetl was destroyed, is being rebuilt, has existed for four hundred years, the ruins of a synagogue, a marvelous destroyed old temple, a former Catholic church, now Russian Orthodox, enchanting whiteness, three wings, visible from afar, now Russian Orthodox. An old Jew—I love talking with our people—they understand me. A cemetery, the destroyed house of Rabbi Azrail, three generations, the tombstone beneath the tree that has grown over it, these old stones, all of the same shape, the same contents, this exhausted Jew, my guide, some family of dim-witted, fat-legged Jews living in a wooden shed by the cemetery, the coffins of three Jewish soldiers killed in the Russian-German war.* The Abramoviches of Odessa, the mother had come to bury him, and I see this Jewess, who is burying her son who perished for a cause that to her is repulsive, incomprehensible, and criminal.

The old and the new cemetery, the shtetl is four hundred years old.

Evening, I walk among the buildings, Jews and Jewesses are reading the posters and proclamations: Poland is the dog of the bourgeoisie, and so on. Insects bring death, and don't remove heaters from the railroad cars.

These Jews are like paintings: lanky, silent, long-bearded, not like ours, fat and jovial. Tall old men hanging around with nothing to do. Most important: the store and the cemetery.

Seven versts back to Boratin, a marvelous evening, my soul is full, our landlord rich, sly girls, fried eggs, lard, our men are catching flies, the Russo-Ukrainian soul. All in all, uninteresting.

JULY 22, 1920. BORATIN

Before lunch, a report to army field headquarters. Nice, sunny weather, rich, solid village, I go to the mill, describe what a water mill

---

* The First World War.

is like, Jewish workman, then I bathe in the cold, shallow stream beneath the weak sun of Volhynia. Two girls are playing in the water, a strange, almost irrepressible urge to talk dirty, rough slippery words.

Sokolov is doing badly. I give him horses to get him to the hospital. The staff leaves for Leshniov (Galicia, we cross the border for the first time). I wait for the horses. It is nice here in the village, bright, stomach full.

Two hours later I leave for Khotin. The road goes through the forest, anxiety. Grishchuk is dull-witted, frightening. I am on Sokolov's heavy horse. I am alone on the road. Bright, clear, not hot, a light warmth. A cart up ahead, five men who look like Poles. A game: we ride, we stop, where are you from? Mutual fear and anxiety. By Khotin we can see our troops, we ride off, gunfire. A wild gallop back, I yank the horse's reins. Bullets buzz, howl. Artillery fire. At times Grishchuk gallops with dark and taciturn energy, and then at dangerous moments he is unfathomable, limp, black, a heavy growth of beard on his jaw. There's no longer anyone in Boratin. Our transport carts have passed beyond it, a mess begins. The transport-cart saga, aversion and vileness. Gusev is in charge. We wait outside Kozin half the night, gunfire. We send out a scout, nobody knows anything, horsemen ride about the place with an intent air, tall German fellow from the district commander's, night, want to sleep, the feeling of helplessness—you don't know where they're taking you, I think it's the twenty or thirty men we chased into the woods, an assault. But where did they get the artillery from? I sleep for half an hour, they say there was an exchange of fire, a line of our men advanced. We move farther. The horses are exhausted, a terrible night, we move in a colossal train of transport carts through the impenetrable darkness, we don't know which villages we're passing through, there's a great blaze to one side, other trains of transport carts cross our path. Has the front collapsed or is this just a transport-cart panic?

Night drags on endlessly, we fall into a ditch. Grishchuk drives strangely, we're rammed from behind by a shaft, there are yells from somewhere far away, we stop every half verst and stand around futilely and for an agonizingly long time.

A rein tears, our *tachanka* no longer responds, we drive off into a field, night, Grishchuk has an attack of savage, blunt, hopeless despair that infuriates me: O may these reins burn in hell, burn, burn! Grishchuk is blind, he admits it, at night he can't see a thing. The train of transport carts leaves us behind, the roads are harsh, black mud, Grishchuk, clutching the remnants of the reins, with his surprising jangling tenor: We're done for, the Poles are going to catch up with us, they're shelling us from all around, our cavalry transport is surrounded. We drive off at random with torn reins. Our *tachanka* screeches, in the distance a heavy gloomy dawn, wet fields. Violet streaks in the sky with black voids. At dawn the shtetl of Verba. Railroad tracks—dead, frail— the smell of Galicia. 4 o'clock in the morning.

July 23, 1920. In Verba

Jews, who have been up all night, stand pitiful, like birds, blue, disheveled, in vests and without socks. A wet and desolate dawn, all of Verba crammed with transport carts, thousands of them, all the drivers look alike, first-aid units, the staff of the Forty-fifth Division, depressing rumors and doubtless absurd, and these rumors are circulating despite our chain of victories. . . . Two brigades of the Eleventh Division have been taken prisoner, the Poles have captured Kozin, poor Kozin, I wonder what will happen there? The strategic position is interesting, the Sixth Division is at Leshniov, the Poles are at Kozin, at Boratin, at our rear lines, we are like squashed pies. We are waiting on the road from Verba. We stand there for two hours, Misha in a tall white cap with a red ribbon gallops over the field. Everyone eats bread with straw, green apples, with dirty fingers and reeking mouths. Dirty, disgusting food. We drive on. Amazing, we come to a standstill every five steps, an endless line of provision carts of the Forty-fifth and the Eleventh Divisions, at times we lose our transport unit, then we find it again. The fields, the trampled rye, villages stripped of food and others not yet completely stripped of food, a hilly region, where are we going? The road to Dubno. Forests, wonderful, ancient, shadowy forests. Heat, shade in the forest. Many trees have been felled for military purposes, a curse upon them, the bare forest clearings with their protruding stumps. The ancient Volhynian forests of Dubno—must find out where they get that fragrant black honey.

Describe the forests.

Krivikha: ruined Czechs, a tasty-looking woman. The horror that follows, she cooks for a hundred men, flies, the commissar's moist and rattled woman, Shurka, wild game with potatoes, they take all the hay, reap the oats, potatoes by the ton, the girl at the end of her tether, the vestiges of a prosperous farm. The pitiful, lanky, smiling Czech, the nice, fleshy foreign woman, his wife.

A bacchanalia. Gusev's tasty-looking Shurka with her retinue, the Red Army scum, cart drivers, everyone tramping about in the kitchen, grabbing potatoes, ham, pies are being baked for them. The heat is unbearable, you can't breathe, clouds of flies. The tortured Czechs. Shouting, coarseness, greed. And yet my meal is marvelous: roast pork with potatoes and marvelous coffee. After the meal I sleep under the trees—a quiet, shady slope, swings are swaying before my eyes. Before my eyes lie quiet green and yellow hills drenched in sunlight, and forests. The forests of Dubno. I sleep for about three hours. Then we're off to Dubno. I ride with Prishchepa, a new acquaintance, caftan, white hood, illiterate Communist, he takes me to see Zhenya. Her husband—*a grober mensh**—rides on his little horse from village to village buying up produce from the peasants. The wife a tasty-looking, languorous, sly, sensual young Jewess, married five months, doesn't love her husband, and, by the way, she's flirting with Prishchepa. I'm the center of attention—*er ist ein* [illegible]†—she keeps staring at me, asks me my surname, doesn't take her eyes off me, we drink tea, I'm in an idiotic bind, I am quiet, slack, polite, and thank her for every gesture. Before my eyes: the life of a Jewish family, the mother comes by, some young ladies or other, Prishchepa is quite the ladies' man. Dubno has changed hands quite a few times. Our side, it seems, didn't plunder it. So once again they are all shivering, once again degradation without end and hatred toward the Poles who tear out their beards. The husband: Will there be freedom to trade, to buy a few things and then sell them right away, no speculating? I tell him yes, there will, everything will be for the better— my usual system—in Russia wondrous things are happening: express trains, free food for children, theaters, the International.** They listen

---

* Yiddish: "an uncouth individual."

† German: "he is a . . ."

** The Third Communist International, 1919–1943, an organization founded in Moscow by the delegates of twelve countries to promote Communism worldwide.

with delight and mistrust. I think to myself: a sky full of diamonds will be yours, everything will be turned upside down, everyone will be uprooted yet again, I feel sorry for them.

The Dubno synagogues. Everything destroyed. Two small ante-rooms remain, centuries, two minute little rooms, everything filled with memories, four synagogues in a row, and then the pasture, the fields, and the setting sun. The synagogues are pitiful, squat, ancient, green and blue little buildings, the Hasidic one, inside, no architecture whatsoever. I go into the Hasidic synagogue. It's Friday. What stunted little figures, what emaciated faces, for me everything that existed for the past 300 years has come alive, the old men bustle about the synagogue, there is no wailing, for some reason they all run back and forth, the praying is extremely informal. It seems that Dubno's most repulsive-looking Jews have gathered. I pray, rather, I almost pray, and think about Hershele,* this is how I should describe him. A quiet evening in the synagogue, this always has an irresistible effect on me, four synagogues in a row. Religion? No decoration at all in the building, everything is white and plain to the point of asceticism, everything is incorporeal and bloodless to a monstrous degree, to grasp it fully you have to have the soul of a Jew. But what does this soul consist of? Is it not bound to be our century in which they will perish?

A little nook in Dubno, four synagogues, Friday evening, Jews and Jewesses by the ruined stones—all etched in my memory. Then evening, herring, I am sad because there's no one to copulate with. Prishchepa and the teasing and exasperating Zhenya, her sparkling Jewish eyes, fat legs, and soft breasts. Prishchepa, his hands slip deeper, and her unyielding gaze, while her fool of a husband is out in the tiny shed feeding his commandeered horse.

We stay the night with other Jews, Prishchepa asks them to play some music, a fat boy with a hard, idiotic face, gasping with terror, says that he is not in the mood. The horse is nearby in the yard. Grishchuk is only fifty versts from home. He does not run away.

The Poles attack in the area of Kozin-Boratin, they are at our rear lines, the Sixth Division is in Leshniov, Galicia. We're marching to

---

* In Yiddish folklore, a trickster. See Babel's story "Shabos-Nakhamu."

Brody, Radzivillov is in front and one brigade is in the rear. The Sixth Division is in hard fighting.

JULY 24, 1920

Morning at army headquarters. The Sixth Division is annihilating the enemy assaulting us in Khotin, the area of battle is Khotin-Kozin, and I think to myself, poor Kozin.

The cemetery, round stones.

Prishchepa and I ride from Krivikha to Leshniov by way of Demidovka. Prishchepa's soul—an illiterate fellow, a Communist, the Kadety* killed his parents, he tells me how he went about his Cossack village collecting his belongings. Colorful, wearing a hood, as simple as grass, will turn into a rag-looter, despises Grishchuk because he doesn't love or understand horses. We ride through Khorupan, Smordva, and Demidovka. Remember the picture: transport carts, horsemen, half-wrecked villages, fields and forests, oak trees, now and then wounded men and my *tachanka*.

We arrive in Demidovka toward evening. A Jewish shtetl, I am on guard. Jews in the steppes, everything is destroyed. We are in a house with a horde of women. The Lyachetskys and the Shvevels,† no, this isn't Odessa. Dora Aronovna, a dentist, is reading Artsybashev,** a Cossack rabble loitering about. She is proud, angry, says that the Poles destroyed all sense of self-respect, despises the Communists for their plebianism, a horde of daughters in white stockings, devout father and mother. Each daughter distinctly individual: one is pitiful, black-haired, bowlegged, the other fleshy, a third housewifely, and all, doubtless, old maids.

The main friction: today is the Sabbath. Prishchepa wants them to roast potatoes, but tomorrow is a day of fasting, *Tishah b'Ab*,‡ and I

---

* Members of the Constitutional Democratic Party, liberal monarchists who were in favor of a more moderate bourgeois revolution as opposed to a proletarian revolution. After the October Revolution, the Kadety actively fought the Bolsheviks.

† Shevel was Babel's mother's maiden name. His aunt, Katya Aronovna, had married into the Lyakhetsky family.

** The author Mikhail Petrovich Artsybashev, 1878–1927.

‡ The ninth day of the month Ab, a Jewish day of mourning commemorating the destruction of the First and Second Temples in Jerusalem.

say nothing because I am Russian. The dentist, pale with pride and self-respect, announces that nobody will dig up potatoes because it is a holy day.

I manage to restrain Prishchepa for quite a while, but then he explodes: Yids, sons-of-bitches, a whole arsenal of curses, all of them hate us and me, dig up potatoes, frightened in the garden that isn't theirs, they blame the Christians, Prishchepa is outraged. How painful it all is—Artsybashev, the orphaned schoolgirl from Rovno, Prishchepa in his hood. The mother wrings her hands: the stove has been lit on the Sabbath, curses fly. Budyonny was here and left again. An argument between a Jewish youth and Prishchepa. A youth with spectacles, black-haired, highly strung, scarlet, inflamed eyelids, inaccurate Russian speech. He believes in God, God is the ideal we carry in our souls, every person has their own God in their soul, if you act badly, God grieves, this nonsense is proclaimed with rapture and pain. Prishchepa is offensively idiotic, he talks of religion in ancient times, mixes Christianity and Paganism, his main point, in ancient times there was the commune, needless to say nothing but rubbish—you have no education whatsoever—and the Jew with his six years of Rovno high-school education quotes Platonov—touching and comical—the clans, the elders, Perun, paganism.

We eat like oxen, fried potatoes, and five glasses of coffee each. We sweat, they serve us everything, it's all terrible, I tell fairy tales about Bolshevism, its blossoming, the express trains, the Moscow textile mills, the universities, the free food, the Revel Delegation, and, to crown it all, my tale about the Chinese, and I enthrall all these poor tortured people. *Tishah b'Ab.* The old woman sobs sitting on the floor, her son, who worships her, says that he believes in God to make her happy, he sings in a pleasant tenor and tells the story of the destruction of the Temple. The terrible words of the prophets: they will eat dung, the maidens will be defiled, the menfolk slaughtered, Israel crushed, angry and dejected words. The lamp smokes, the old woman wails, the youth sings melodiously, the girls in their white stockings, outside the window Demidovka, night, Cossacks, everything just as it had been in the days when the Temple was destroyed. I go to sleep in the wet, reeking yard.

It's a disaster with Grishchuk, he is in a daze, hovering around like a sleepwalker, he is feeding the horses badly, informs me about problems *post factum*, favors the muzhiks and their children.

Machine-gunners have come in from the front lines, they come over to our yard, it is night, they are wrapped in their cloaks. Prishchepa is courting a Jewess from Kremenets, pretty, fleshy, in a smooth dress. She blushes tenderly, her one-eyed father-in-law is sitting nearby, she blossoms, it's nice talking with Prishchepa, she blossoms and acts coquettish—what are they talking about?—then, he wants to go to bed, spend some time with her, she is tormented, who understands her soul better than I? He: We will write to each other. I wonder with a heavy heart: surely she won't give in. Prishchepa tells me she agrees (with him they all agree). I suddenly remember that he seemed to have had syphilis, I wonder: was he fully cured?

The girl later on: I will scream. Describe their initial pussyfooting conversation—how dare you—she is an educated person, she served on the Revolutionary Committee.*

God almighty, I think, the women are hearing all these curses now, they live like soldiers, what happened to their tenderness?

At night rain and storm, we run over to the stable, dirty, dark, damp, cold, the machine-gunners will be sent back to the front lines at dawn, they assemble in the pouring rain, cloaks and freezing horses. Miserable Demidovka.

July 25, 1920

We pull out of Demidovka in the morning. A tortured two hours, they woke the Jewesses at four o'clock in the morning and had them boil Russian meat,† and that on *Tishah b'Ab*. Half-naked and disheveled girls run through wet gardens, Prishchepa is in the grip of lust, he throws himself on the bride of the one-eyed man's son while their cart is being requisitioned, an incredible bout of cursing, the soldiers are eating meat out of the pots, she, I will scream, her face, he pushes her against the wall, a shameless spectacle. Under no circumstances does she want to hand over the cart, they had hidden it in the

---

* Local organs of the Soviet government.
† Nonkosher.

loft, she will make a good Jewess. She wrangles with the commissar, who says that the Jews do not want to help the Red Army.

I lost my briefcase and then found it at the headquarters of the Fourteenth Division in Lishnya.

We head for Ostrov—fifteen versts, there is a road from there to Leshniov, it's dangerous there, Polish patrols. The priest, his daughter looks like Plevitskaya* or a merry skeleton. She is a Kiev student, everyone yearns for civility, I tell my fairy tales, she cannot tear herself away. Fifteen dangerous versts, sentries gallop past, we cross the border, wooden planks. Trenches everywhere.

We arrive at the headquarters. Leshniov. The little town half destroyed. The Russians have fouled up the place pretty badly. A Catholic church, a Uniate church, a synagogue, beautiful buildings, miserable life, a few spectral Jews, a revolting landlady, a Galician woman, flies and dirt, a lanky, shy blockhead, second-grade Slavs. Convey the spirit of destroyed Leshniov, its enfeeblement and its depressing, semi-foreign dirt.

I sleep in the threshing shed. A battle is raging at Brody and at the Tsurovitse crossing. Leaflets about Soviet Galicia. Pastors. Night in Leshniov. How unimaginably sad this all is, and these pitiful Galicians gone wild, and the destroyed synagogues, and trickles of life against a backdrop of horrifying events, of which only reflections come through to us.

JULY 26, 1920. LESHNIOV

The Ukraine in flames. Wrangel[†] has not been annihilated. Makhno[**] is launching raids in the districts of Ekaterinoslav and Poltava. New gangs have appeared, a rebellion near Kherson. Why are they rebelling? Is the Communist jacket too short for them?

What's going on in Odessa? Longing.

Much work, I'm remembering the past. This morning Brody was taken, again the surrounded enemy managed to get out, a sharp order

---

* Nadyezhda Plevitskaya, a celebrated Russian singer and actress.
† Baron Pyotr Nikolaevich Wrangel was the commander of the anti-Bolshevik armies in southern Russia.
** The Ukrainian anarchist leader.

from Budyonny, we've let them get away four times now, we are able to shake them loose but we don't have the strength to hold them.

A meeting in Kozin, Budyonny's speech: We've stopped all maneuvering, from now on frontal attacks, we are losing contact with the enemy, no reconnaissance, no defense, the division commanders show no initiative, lifeless operations.

I talk with Jews, for the first time uninteresting Jews. Nearby, the destroyed synagogue, a red-haired man from Brody, some countrymen of mine from Odessa.

I move in with a legless Jew, affluence, cleanliness, quiet, marvelous coffee, clean children, the father lost both legs on the Italian Front, new house, they're still building, the wife has an eye for profit but is decent, polite, a small shady room, I recover from the Galicians.

I am distressed, I must think things through: Galicia, the World War, and my own fate.

Life in our division. About Bakhturov,* about our division commander, the Cossacks, the marauding, the vanguard's vanguard. I don't belong.

In the evening panic: the enemy pushed us back out of Churovitse, they were a verst and a half away from Leshniov. The division commander went galloping off and came galloping back. And our wanderings begin again, another night without sleep, transport carts, enigmatic Grishchuk, the horses walk quietly; cursing, forests, stars, we stop somewhere. Brody at dawn, all this is horrifying: barbed wire everywhere, burned-out chimneys, a bloodless city, drab houses, word has it there are goods to be had, our men won't hold back, there were factories here, a Russian military cemetery, and, judging by the nameless lonely crosses on the graves, these were Russian soldiers.

The road is completely white, cut-down forests, everything disfigured, Galicians on the road, Austrian uniforms, barefoot with pipes in their mouths, what is in their faces, what mystery of insignificance, commonplaceness, submissiveness.

Radzivillov is worse than Brody, barbed wire on poles, pretty buildings, dawn, pitiful figures, fruit trees plucked bare, bedraggled, yawning Jews, destroyed roads, defiled crucifixes, sterile earth, shattered

---

* The military commissar of the Sixth Cavalry Division.

Catholic churches, where are their priests, smugglers used to be here, and I can see how life used to be.

KHOTIN. JULY 27, 1920

After Radzivillov—endless villages, horsemen charging on, difficult after a sleepless night.

Khotin is the same village where we had been under fire. My quarters are horrifying: abject poverty, bathhouse, flies, an unruffled, gentle, well-built muzhik, a crafty woman, she won't give a thing, I get some lard, potatoes. They live absurdly, wild, the dingy room and the myriad flies, the terrible food, and they don't strive for anything better—and the greed, and the repulsive, immutable way their dwelling is set up, and the hides reeking in the sun, the limitless dirt, exasperate me.

There was a landowner here—Sveshnikov—the factory is destroyed, his manor is destroyed, the majestic skeleton of the factory, a red brick-building, cobbled paths, now no trace of them, the muzhiks indifferent.

Artillery supplies are lagging, I'm immersing myself in headquarters work: the vile work of murder. What is to Communism's credit: at least it doesn't advocate animosity toward the enemy, only toward Polish soldiers.

Prisoners were brought in, a Red Army fighter wounded a perfectly healthy man with two gunshots for no reason whatsoever. The Pole doubles over, moans, they put a pillow under his head.

Zinoviev was killed, a young Communist in red trousers, a rattle in his throat and blue eyelids.

Astonishing rumors are going around—on the 30th, discussions for an armistice will begin.

Night in a reeking hole they call a yard. I can't sleep, it's late, I go over to the headquarters, the situation with the crossings is not all that good.

Late night, red flag, silence, Red Army fighters thirsting for women.

JULY 28, 1920. KHOTIN

The skirmish for the crossing at Churovitse. The Second Brigade is bleeding to death in Budyonny's presence. The whole infantry battalion is wounded, almost completely destroyed. The Poles are in old reinforced trenches. Our men weren't successful. Is the Poles' resistance growing stronger?

There is no sign of slackening due to the prospect of peace.

I'm staying in a poor hut where a son with a big head plays the violin. I terrorize the mistress of the house, she won't give me anything. Grishchuk, sullen as a stone, does not take good care of the horses, it turns out he was schooled by hunger.

A ruined estate, Sveshnikov the landowner, the majestic, destroyed distillery (the symbol of the Russian landed gentry?), when the alcohol was handed out all the fighters drank themselves into a stupor.

I am exasperated, I can't contain my indignation: the dirt, the apathy, the hopelessness of Russian life are unbearable, the Revolution will do some good work here.

The mistress of the house hides the pigs and the cow, talks fast, sugary, and with impotent hatred, is lazy, and I have the impression she is running their household into the ground, her husband believes in a strong government, is charming, gentle, passive, resembles Stroyev.

The village is boring, living here is dreadful. I'm immersing myself in headquarters work. Describe the day, the reverberations of the battle raging only a few versts away from us, the orderlies, Lepin's* hand is swollen.

The Red Army fighters sleep with the women.

A story: How a Polish regiment had laid down its weapons four times, but then each time began defending itself again as we hacked them down.

Evening, quiet, a discussion with Matyazh, he is boundlessly lazy, indolent, snot-nosed, and somehow pleasantly, affectionately lustful. The terrible truth is that all the soldiers have syphilis. Matyazh is almost cured (with practically no treatment). He had syphilis, got treatment for two weeks, he and a fellow countryman were to pay ten silver kopecks in Stavropol, his fellow countryman died, Misha had it many times, Senechka and Gerasya have syphilis, and they all go with women, and back home they have brides. The soldier's curse. Russia's curse—it's horrifying. They swallow ground crystal, at times they drink

---

* A staff officer in the Sixth Cavalry Division.

either carbolic acid or crushed glass. All our fighters: velvet caps, rapes, Cossack forelocks, battle, Revolution, and syphilis. The whole of Galicia is infected.

A letter to Zhenya,* I long for her and home.

Must keep an eye on the Osobotdel† and the Revolutionary Tribunal.**

Will there really be peace talks on the 30th?

An order from Budyonny. We've let the enemy escape a fourth time, we had completely surrounded them at Brody.

Describe Matyazh, Misha. The muzhiks, I want to fathom them. We have the power to maneuver, to surround the Poles, but, when it comes down to it, our grip is weak, they can break free, Budyonny is furious, reprimands the division commander. Write the biographies of the division commander, the military commissar, Kniga,‡ and so on.

JULY 29, 1920. LESHNIOV

In the morning we set out for Leshniov. Again the same landlord as before, black-bearded, legless Froim. During my absence he was robbed of four thousand guldens, they took his boots. His wife, a smooth-tongued bitch, is colder to me, now that she has realized she can't make any money off me, how greedy they are. I talk with her in German. Bad weather begins.

Froim has lame children, there are many of them, I can't tell them apart, he has hidden his cow and his horse.

Galicia is unbearably gloomy, destroyed churches and crucifixes, overcast low-hanging sky, the battered, worthless, insignificant population. Pitiful, inured to the slaughter and the soldiers and the disarray, matronly Russian women in tears, the torn-up roads, stunted crops, no sun, Catholic priests with wide-brimmed hats, without churches. An oppressive anguish emanates from all who are struggling to survive.

---

* Evgenia Borisovna Babel, née Gronfein, Babel's wife.

† Osobii Otdel ("Special Section") was formed in December 1918 to identify and eradicate counterrevolutionary elements in the Red Army.

** The Revolutionary Tribunals were the organs of military justice representing the Revolutionary Military Council.

‡ The commander of the First Brigade of the Sixth Cavalry Division, who had been decorated with a Red Flag Medal.

Are the Slavs the manure of history?

The day passes full of anxiety. The Poles broke through the Fourteenth Division's position to the right of where we are, they've again occupied Berestechko. No information whatsoever, quite a quadrille, they are moving behind our rear lines.

The mood at headquarters. Konstantin Karlovich* is silent. The clerks, that band of gorged, impudent, venereal ruffians, are worried. After a hard, monotonous day, a rainy night, mud—I'm wearing low shoes. And now a really powerful rain is setting in, the real victor.

We trudge through the mud, a fine, penetrating rain.

Cannon and machine gun fire closer and closer. I have an unbearable urge to sleep. There's nothing to feed the horses with. I have a new coachman: a Pole, Gowinski, tall, adept, talkative, bustling, and, needless to say, impudent.

Grishchuk is going home, at times he explodes—"I'm worn out"— he did not manage to learn German because his master had been a severe man, all they did was quarrel, but they never talked.

It also turns out he had starved for seven months, and I didn't give him enough food.

The Pole: completely barefoot, with haggard lips, blue eyes. Talkative and happy-go-lucky, a defector, he disgusts me.

An insurmountable urge to sleep. It's dangerous to sleep. I lie there fully clothed. Froim's two legs are standing on a chair next to me. A little lamp is shining, his black beard, the children are lying on the floor.

I get up ten times—Gowinski and Grishchuk are asleep—anger. I fall asleep around four o'clock, a knock at the door: we must go. Panic, the enemy is right outside the shtetl, machine gun fire, the Poles are getting nearer. Pandemonium. They can't bring the horses out, they break down the gates, Grishchuk with his repulsive despair, there's four of us, the horses haven't been fed, we have to go get the nurse, Grishchuk and Gowinski want to leave her behind, I yell in a voice not my own—the nurse? I'm furious, the nurse is foolish, pretty. We fly up the high road to Brody, I rock and sleep. It's cold, penetrating wind and rain. We have to keep an eye on the horses, the harness is unreliable, the Pole is singing, I'm shivering with cold, the nurse is chattering away

---

* Zholnarkevich, the chief of staff of the Sixth Cavalry Division.

foolishly. I rock and sleep. A new sensation: I can't keep my eyelids open. Describe the inexpressible urge to sleep.

Again we are fleeing from the Pole. There you have it: the cavalry war. I wake up, we have stopped in front of some white buildings. A village? No, Brody.

JULY 30, 1920. BRODY

A gloomy dawn. I've had enough of that nurse. We dropped Grishchuk off somewhere. I wish him good luck.

Where do we go from here? Tiredness is stifling me. It's six o'clock in the morning. We end up with some Galician. The wife is lying on the floor with a newborn baby. He is a quiet little old man, children are lying with his naked wife, there are three or four of them.

There's some other woman there too. Dust soaked down with rain. The cellar. A crucifix. A painting of the Holy Virgin. The Uniates are really neither one thing nor the other. A strong Catholic influence. Bliss—it is warm, some kind of hot stench from the children, from the women. Silence and dejection. The nurse is sleeping, but I can't, bedbugs. There is no hay, I yell at Gowinski. The landlord doesn't have any bread, milk.

The town is destroyed, looted. A town of great interest. Polish culture. An old, rich, distinctive, Jewish population. The terrible bazaars, the dwarves in long coats, long coats and *peyes,* ancient old men. Shkolnaya Street, nine synagogues, everything half destroyed, I take a look at the new synagogue, the architecture [one word illegible, the kondesh/kodesh], the *shamas,* a bearded, talkative Jew: If only there were peace, then we'd have trade. He talks about the Cossacks' looting of the town, of the humiliations inflicted by the Poles. A wonderful synagogue, how lucky we are that we at least have some old stones. This is a Jewish town, this is Galicia, describe. Trenches, destroyed factories, the Bristol, waitresses, "Western European" culture, and how greedily we hurl ourselves onto it. Pitiful mirrors, pale Austrian Jews—the owners. And the stories: there had been American dollars here, oranges, cloth.

The high road, barbed wire, cut-down forests, and dejection, boundless dejection. There's nothing to eat, there's nothing to hope for, war, everyone's as bad as the next, as strange as the next, hostile, wild, life had been quiet and, most important, full of tradition.

Budyonny fighters in the streets. In the shops nothing but lemon fizz, and also the barbershops have opened. At the bazaar the shrews are only selling carrots, constant rain, ceaseless, penetrating, smothering. Unbearable sorrow, the people and their souls have been killed.

At the headquarters: red trousers, self-assuredness, little souls puffing themselves up, a horde of young people, Jews also among them, they are at the personal disposal of the army commander and are in charge of food.

Mustn't forget Brody and the pitiful figures, and the barbershop, and the Jews from the world beyond, and the Cossacks in the streets.

It's a disaster with Gowinski, there's absolutely no fodder for the horses. The Odessan hotel Galpernia, there is hunger in town, nothing to eat, good tea in the evening, I comfort my landlord, pale and panicky as a mouse. Gowinski found some Poles, he took their army caps, someone helped Gowinski. He is unbearable, doesn't feed the horses, is wandering about somewhere, is constantly jabbering away, can't get his hands on anything, is frightened they might arrest him, and they've already tried to arrest him, they came to me.

Night in the hotel, next door a married couple and their conversation, and words and [blacked out] coming from the woman's lips. Oh, you Russians, how disgustingly you spend your nights, and what voices your women have now! I listen with bated breath and feel despondent.

A terrible night in tortured Brody. Must be on the alert. I haul hay for the horses at night. At the headquarters. I can sleep, the enemy is advancing. I went back to my billet, slept deeply with a deadened heart, Gowinski wakes me.

July 31, 1920. Brody, Leshniov

In the morning before we leave, my *tachanka* is waiting on Zolotaya Street, an hour in a bookstore, a German store. All marvelous uncut books, albums, the West, here it is, the West and chivalrous Poland, a chrestomathy, a history of all the Boleslaws,* and for some reason this

---

* A dynasty of medieval Polish kings.

seems to me so beautiful: Poland, glittering garments draped over a decrepit body. I rummage like a madman, leaf through books, it is dark, then a horde pours in and rampant pillaging of office supplies begins, repulsive young men from the War Spoils Commission with a super-military air. I tear myself away from the bookstore in despair.

Chrestomathies, Tetmajer,* new translations, a heap of new Polish national literature, textbooks.

The headquarters are in Stanislavchik or Koziuzkov. The nurse served with the Cheka, very Russian, tender and shattered beauty. She lived with all the commissars, that's my impression, and suddenly: her album from the Kostroma Gymnasium, the schoolmistresses, idealistic hearts, the Romanoff boarding school, Aunt Manya, skating.

Again Leshniov and my old landlord, terrible dirt, the thin veneer of hospitality and respect for the Russians. Despite my kindness there is an air of unfriendliness emanating from these ruined people.

The horses, there's nothing to feed them with, they are growing thin, the *tachanka* is falling apart because of stupid little things, I hate Gowinski, he is such a happy-go-lucky, gluttonous walking disaster. They're no longer giving me any coffee.

The enemy has circumvented us, pushed us back from the river crossings, ominous rumors about a breach of the Fourteenth Division's lines, orderlies gallop off. Toward evening—Grzhimalovka (north of Churovitse). A destroyed village, we got oats, ceaseless rain, my shoes can't make the shortcut to headquarters, a torturing journey, the front line is moving closer to us, I drank some marvelous tea, boiling hot, at first the mistress of the house pretended to be ill, the village has continually been within the range of the battles to secure the crossing. Darkness, anxiety, the Pole is stirring.

Toward evening the division commander came, a marvelous figure of a man, gloves, always out in the front lines, night at the headquarters, Konstantin Karlovich's work.

AUGUST 1, 1920. GRZHIMALOVKA, LESHNIOV

God, it's August, soon we shall die, man's brutality is indestructible. The situation is getting worse at the front. Gunfire right outside the

---

* Kazimierz Przerwa Tetmajer, 1865–1940, Polish poet and writer.

village. They are forcing us back from the crossing. Everyone's left, a few staff people have remained, my *tachanka* is standing by the headquarters, I am listening to the sounds of battle, for some reason I feel good, there are only a few of us, no transport carts, no administrative staff, it's peaceful, simple, Timoshenko's* tremendous sangfroid. Kniga is impassive, Timoshenko—if he doesn't kick them out I'll shoot him, tell him that from me!—and yet he smiles. In front of us the road bloated by rain, machine guns flare up here and there, the invisible presence of the enemy in this gray and airy sky. The enemy has advanced all the way to the village. We are losing the crossing over the Styr. How many times have we headed back to ill-fated Leshniov?

The division commander is off to the First Brigade. It is terrible in Leshniov, we are stopping for two hours, the administrative staff is fleeing, the enemy wall is rising all around.

The battle near Leshniov. Our infantry is in the trenches, this is amazing: barefoot, semi-idiotic Volhynian fellows—the Russian village, and they are actually fighting the Poles, the *Pans*† who oppressed them. Not enough weapons, the cartridges don't fit, the boys are moping about in the stifling hot trenches, they are moved from one clearing to another. A hut by the clearing, an obliging Galician makes some tea for me, the horses are standing in a little hollow.

I went over to a battery, precise, unhurried, technical work.

Under machine gun fire, bullets shriek, a dreadful sensation, we creep along through the trenches, some Red Army fighter is panicking, and, of course, we are surrounded. Gowinski had gone to the road, wanted to dump the horses, then drove off, I found him at the clearing, my *tachanka* destroyed, peripeteia, I look for somewhere to sit, the machine-gunners push me away, they are bandaging a wounded young man, his leg is up in the air, he is howling, a friend whose horse was killed is with him, we strap the *tachanka* together, we drive off, the *tachanka* is screeching, won't turn. I have the feeling that Gowinski will be the death of me, that's fate, his bare stomach, the holes in his shoes, his Jewish nose, and the endless excuses. I move to Mikhail Karlovich's** cart, what a relief,

---

* Commander of the Sixth Cavalry Division.
† Polish: "Lords."
** Mikhail Karlovich Zholnarkevich, staff officer, and brother of Konstantin Karlovich, the divisional chief of staff.

I doze, it's evening, my soul is shaken, transport carts, we come to a halt on the road to Bielavtsy, then go along a road bordered by the forest, evening, cool, high road, sunset, we are rolling toward the front lines, we bring Konstantin Karlovich [Zholnarkevich] some meat.

I am greedy and pitiful. The units in the forest have left, typical picture, the squadron, Bakhturov* is reading a report on the Third International, about how people from all over the world came together, a nurse's white kerchief is flashing through the trees, what is she doing here? We drive back, what kind of man is Mikhail Karlovich? Gowinski's run off, no horses. Night, I sleep in the cart next to Mikhail Karlovich. We're outside Bielavtsy.

Describe the people, the air.

The day has passed, I saw death, white roads, horses between trees, sunrise and sunset. The main thing: Budyonny fighters, horses, troop movements, and war, through the wheat fields walk solemn, barefoot, spectral Galicians.

Night in the wagon.

I chatted with some clerks by their *tachanka* on the edge of the forest.

AUGUST 2, 1920. BIELAVTSY

The problem with my *tachanka*. Gowinski drives toward the shtetl, needless to say he hasn't found a blacksmith. My shouting match with the blacksmith, he jostled a woman, shrieks and tears. The Galicians don't want to fix the *tachanka*. A whole arsenal of devices, persuasion, threats, begging, what proved most effective was the promise of sugar. A long story, one smith is ill, I drag him over to another one, tears, they drag him home. They don't want to wash my clothes, nothing will induce them to.

Finally they fix the *tachanka*.

I am tired. Alarm at the headquarters. We leave. The enemy is closing in, I run to warn Gowinski, heat, I'm afraid of being late, I run through sand, manage to warn him, catch up again with the headquarters staff outside the village, no one will take me, they leave, dejection, I ride for a while with Barsukov, we are rolling toward Brody.

---

* The military commissar of the Sixth Cavalry Division.

I am given an ambulance *tachanka* from the Second Squadron, we drive to the forest, my driver Ivan and I wait there. Budyonny arrives, Voroshilov, it is going to be a decisive battle, no more retreating, all three brigades turn around, I speak with the staff commandant. The atmosphere at the start of a battle, a large field, airplanes, cavalry maneuvers on the field, our cavalry, explosions in the distance, the battle has begun, machine guns, the sun, somewhere the two armies clash, muffled shouts of "Hurrah!" Ivan and I move back, deadly danger, I do not feel fear, but passivity, he seems to be frightened, which way should we drive, Korotchayev's* group turns to the right, we, for some reason, go left, the battle is raging, wounded men on horses catch up with us, one of them, deathly pale—"Brother, take me with you!"—his trousers soaked with blood, he threatens to shoot us if we don't take him, we rein in our horses, he is in a terrible state, Ivan's jacket becomes soaked with blood, a Cossack, we stop, I will bandage him, his wound is light, in the stomach, a rib has been hit, we take another one whose horse has been killed. Describe the wounded man. For a long time we go roving through the fields under fire, we can't see a thing, these indifferent roads, the weeds, we send out horsemen, we come to a high road—which way should we go, Radzivillov or Brody?

The administrative staff is supposed to be at Radzivillov along with all the transport carts, but in my opinion, Brody would be more interesting, the battle is being fought for Brody. Ivan's opinion prevails, some of the cart drivers are saying the Poles are in Brody, the transport carts are fleeing, the army staff has left, we drive to Radzivillov. We arrive in the night. All this time we've been eating carrots and peas, penetrating hunger, we're covered in dirt, haven't slept. I took a hut on the outskirts of Radzivillov. Good choice, my knack for this sort of thing is getting better. An old man, a girl. The buttermilk is marvelous, we had all of it, they're making tea with milk, Ivan is going to get some sugar, machine gun fire, the thunder of carts, we run out of the house, the horse is suddenly limping, that's how things are sometimes, we are running in panic, we're being shot at, we have no idea what's going on, they'll catch us any moment now, we make a dash for the bridge, pandemonium, we fall into the marshes, wild panic, a dead man lying

---

* A brigade commander of the Sixth Cavalry Division.

there, abandoned carts, shells, *tachankas*. Traffic jam, night, terror, carts standing in an endless line, we are moving, a field, we stop, we sleep, stars. What upsets me most in all of this is the lost tea, I'm so upset, it's peculiar. I think about it all night and hate the war.

What a crazy life.

AUGUST 3, 1920

Night in the field, we are rolling toward Brody in a buggy. The town keeps changing hands. The same horrifying picture, the town, half destroyed, is waiting once more. The provision station, I run into Barsukov at the edge of town. I drive over to the headquarters. Deserted, dead, dismal. Zotov[*] is sleeping stretched out on some chairs, like a corpse. Borodulin and Pollak are also asleep. The building of the Bank of Prague, ransacked and gutted, water closets, those bank cashier windows, mirror glass.

Word has it that the division commander is in Klyokotovo, we spent about two hours in devastated Brody with its ominous air, tea in a barbershop. Ivan is standing outside the headquarters. Should we leave, shouldn't we leave. We leave for Klyokotovo, we turn off the Leshniov high road, we don't know—is it ours or Polish, we drive on feeling our way, the horses are exhausted, one of them is limping harder, we eat potatoes in the village, brigades show up, indescribable beauty, a frightful force is moving, endless lines, a big farm, everything in ruins, a thresher, a Clenton locomobile, a tractor, the locomobile is still working, it's a hot day.

The battlefield, I meet the division commander, where is the staff, we've lost Zholnarkevich. The battle begins, artillery cover, explosions nearby, a grim moment, the decisive battle over whether we will stem the Polish offensive or not, Budyonny to Kolesnikov[†] and Grishin: "I'll shoot you!" They leave on foot, pale.

Before that, the terrible field sown with hacked-up men, an inhuman cruelty, inconceivable wounds, crushed skulls, young, white, naked bodies are gleaming in the sun, notebooks lying around, single pages, military booklets, Bibles, bodies in the rye.

[*] Commander of the Cavalry Field Headquarters.
[†] Actually Nikolai Petrovich Kolesov, commander of the Third Brigade.

I absorb these impressions mainly with my mind. The battle begins, I'm given a horse. I see columns forming, chains, they attack, I feel sorry for these poor men—they are not men, they are columns—the gunfire reaches maximum intensity, the carnage is carried out in silence. I ride on, rumors that the division commander is being recalled?

The beginning of my adventures, I ride with the transport carts toward the high road, the battle is growing fiercer, I find the provision station, we're being fired at on the high road, the whistling of shells, explosions a mere twenty paces away, the feeling of hopelessness, the transport carts are flying at full gallop, tag along with the Twentieth Regiment of the Fourth Division, wounded men, the querulous commander: No, he says, not wounded, just a little bang on the head. They're professionals. And everywhere fields, sun, bodies, I sit by the field kitchen, hunger, peas, nothing to feed my horse with.

Field kitchen, talking, we sit on the grass, the regiment suddenly pulls out, I have to go to Radzivillov, the regiment heads for Leshniov and I feel helpless, I am afraid of getting cut off from them. An endless journey, dusty roads, I move to a cart, a Quasimodo, two donkeys, a grim spectacle: the hunchbacked driver, silent, his face dark like the forests of Murom.

We drive, I have a terrible feeling—I am getting farther and farther from the division. Hope flutters up—then suddenly the opportunity to take a wounded man to Radzivillov, the wounded man has a pale, Jewish face.

We ride into the forest, we're fired at, shells a hundred paces away, endless rushing back and forth along the forest edge.

Thick sand, impassable. The ballad of the tortured horses.

An apiary, we search the hives, four huts in the forest—nothing there, everything ransacked, I ask a Red Army fighter for bread, he answers me, "I don't want anything to do with Jews." I'm an outsider, in long trousers, not one of them, I am lonely, we ride on, I am so tired I can barely stay on my mare, I have to look after her myself, we arrive at Konyushkovo, we steal some barley, they tell me: Go take whatever you want, take everything. I go through the village looking for a nurse, the womenfolk are hysterical, within five minutes of our arrival the looting begins, some women are beating their breasts, lamenting, sobbing unbearably, these never-ending horrors are hard to bear, I look for a nurse, insuperable sorrow, I swipe a jug of milk from the regimental commander, snatch a dough-bun out of the hands of a peasant woman's son.

Ten minutes later, we're off. Who'd have thought it! The Poles are somewhere nearby. Back we go again, I don't think I can bear this for much longer, and at a fast trot at that, at first I ride with the commander, then I tag along with the transport carts, I want to move over onto a cart, they all give me the same answer: The horses are tired. You want me to get off so you can sit here, huh? Well, so get yourself up here, just mind the corpses! I look at the sackcloth, corpses are lying under it.

We come to a field, there are many transport carts from the Fourth Division, a battery, again a field kitchen, I look for some nurses, a difficult night, I want to sleep, I have to feed my horse, I lie down, the horses are eating the excellent wheat, Red Army fighters in the wheat, ashen, at the end of their tether. My mare is tormenting me, I run after her, I join a nurse, we sleep on a *tachanka*, the nurse is old, bald, most probably a Jewess, a martyr, unbearable cursing, the vehicular driver keeps trying to push her off, the horses roam about, the vehicular driver won't wake up, he is rough and foulmouthed, she says: Our heroes are terrible people. She covers him, they sleep in each other's arms, the poor old nurse, that driver should be shot, the foul language, the cursing, this is not the nurse's world—we fall asleep. I wake up two hours later—our bridle has been stolen. Despair. Dawn. We are seven versts away from Radzivillov. I ride off willy-nilly. The poor horse, all of us are poor, the regiment moves on. I get going.

For this day, the main thing is to describe the Red Army fighters and the air.

August 4, 1920

I am heading alone to Radzivillov. A difficult road, nobody on it, the horse is tired, with every step I'm afraid of running into Poles. Things turned out well, in the area around Radzivillov there are no units, in the shtetl uneasiness, they send me to the station, the townspeople devastated and completely used to change. Sheko* in the auto-

* Yakov Vasilevich Sheko, the new chief of staff of the Sixth Cavalry Division, who replaced Konstantin Karlovich Zholnarkevich.

mobile. I'm in Budyonny's billet. A Jewish family, young ladies, a group from the Bukhteyev Gymnasium, Odessa, my heart skips a beat.

O joy, they give me cocoa and bread. The news: we have a new division commander, Apanasenko, and a new divisional chief of staff, Sheko. Wonder of wonders.

Zholnarkevich arrives with his squadron, he is pitiable, Zotov informs him he has been replaced: I'll go sell buns on Sukharevka! Of course you're of the new school, he says, you know how to set up units, in the old days I could do that too, but now, without any reserves, I can't.

He has a high fever, he says things that would be better left unsaid, a shouting match with Sheko, he immediately raises his voice: "The general chief of staff ordered you to report to headquarters!"— "I don't have to pass any tests, I'm not some little boy who hangs out at headquarters!" He leaves the squadron and goes off. The old guard is leaving, everything is falling apart, now Konstantin Karlovich [Zholnarkevich] is gone too.

Another impression, both harsh and unforgettable, is the arrival of the division commander on his white horse, along with his orderlies. The whole ragtag from the headquarters comes running with chickens for the army commander, they are patronizing, loutish, Sheko, haughty, asks about the operations, the division commander tells him, smiles, a marvelous, statuesque figure of a man, and despair. Yesterday's battle— the Sixth Division's brilliant success—1,000 horses, three regiments chased back into the trenches, the enemy routed, pushed back, the division headquarters are in Khotin. Whose success is this, Timoshenko's or Apanasenko's?[*] Comrade Khmelnitsky: a Jew,[†] a guzzler, a coward, insolent, but for the army commander a chicken, a piglet, corn on the cob. The orderlies detest him, the insolent orderlies, their only interest: chickens, lard, they eat like pigs, they're fat, the chauffeurs stuff themselves with lard, all this on the porch in front of the house. My horse has nothing to eat.

The mood has changed completely, the Poles are retreating, even

[*] Timoshenko had been the commander of the Sixth Cavalry Division from November 1919 to August 1920, and Apanasenko from August to October 1920.

[†] R. P. Khmelnitsky, Voroshilov's aide-de-camp, was a Jew, who happened to have the same name as Bogdan Khmelnitsky, the legendary seventeenth-century Cossack leader.

though they are still occupying Brody, we're beating them again, Budyonny's pulled us through.

I want to sleep, I can't. The changes in the life of the division will have a significant effect. Sheko in a cart. Me with the squadron. We are riding to Khotin, again at a trot, we've put fifteen versts behind us. I'm billeted with Bakhturov. He is devastated, the division commander is out and he feels he will be next.* The division is shaken, the fighters walk around in silence, what will come next? Finally I have had some supper: meat, honey. Describe Bakhturov, Ivan Ivanovich, and Petro. I sleep in the threshing shed, finally some peace.

AUGUST 5, 1920. KHOTIN

A day of rest. We eat, I wander through the sun-drenched village, we rest, I had some lunch, supper—there is honey, milk.

The main thing: internal changes, everything is topsy-turvy.

I feel so sorry for our division commander it hurts, the Cossacks are worried, a lot of hushed talk, an interesting sight, they gather in groups, whisper to one another, Bakhturov is crestfallen, our division commander was a hero, the new commander won't let him into the room, from 600–6,000, a harsh humiliation, they hurled it in his face, "You are a traitor!" Timoshenko laughed.† Apanasenko is a new and colorful figure of a man, ugly, pockmarked, passionate, haughty, ambitious, he sent an appeal to headquarters at Stavropol and the Don about the disorder in the rear lines, in order to let them know back home that he was a division commander. Timoshenko was more pleasant, cheerful, broadminded, and, perhaps, worse. The two men—I suppose they didn't like each other. Sheko is showing his true colors, unbelievably heavy-handed orders, haughtiness. Work at headquarters now completely changed. There is no transport or administrative staff. Lepin is raising his head—he is hostile, idiotic, answers back to Sheko.**

In the evening music, and dance—Apanasenko trying to be popu-

---

* Bakhturov, the military commissar of the Sixth Cavalry Division, was to be relieved of his duties the following day.

† Timoshenko's tenure as commander of the Sixth Cavalry Division ended with the battle near Brody. He was held responsible for the battle's failure.

** Lepin, as a staff officer, now had to report to Sheko, the new chief of staff.

lar—the circle widens, he chooses a horse for Bakhturov from the Polish ones, now everyone is riding Polish horses, they are marvelous, narrow-chested, tall, English, chestnut horses—I mustn't forget this. Apanasenko has the horses paraded.

All day long, talk of intrigues. A letter to the rear lines.

Longing for Odessa.

Remember the figure, face, cheerfulness of Apanasenko, his love of horses, chooses one for Bakhturov.

About the orderlies who throw their lot in with the "masters." What will Mikheyev, lame Sukhorukov, all the Grebushkos, Tarasovs, and Ivan Ivanoviches do with Bakhturov?* They all follow blindly.

About the Polish horses, about the squadrons galloping through the dust on the tall, golden, narrow-chested, Polish horses. Forelocks, chains, suits tailored out of carpets.

Six hundred horses got stuck in the marshes, unlucky Poles.

AUGUST 6, 1920. KHOTIN

The exact same place. We get ourselves in order, shoe the horses, eat, there is a break in operations.

My landlady is a small, timorous, fragile woman with tortured, meek eyes. Lord, how the soldiers torment her, the endless cooking, we steal honey. Her husband came home, bombs from an airplane chased his horses away. The old man hasn't eaten for five days, now he is going off into the wide world to look for his horses, a saga. An ancient old man.

A sultry day, thick, white silence, my soul rejoices, the horses are standing, oats are being threshed for them, the Cossacks sleep next to them all day long, the horses are resting, that's our top priority.

From time to time Apanasenko flits by, unlike the reserved Timoshenko he is one of us, he is our fatherly commander.

In the morning Bakhturov leaves, his retinue follows, I watch the new military commissar's work, a dull but polished Moscow worker, this is where his strength lies: humdrum but grand visions, three military commissars, absolutely must describe limping Gubanov, the

---

* Now that Bakhturov, their former "master," has lost his tenure.

scourge of the regiment, a desperate fighter, a young, twenty-three-year-old youth, modest Shiryayev, cunning Grishin. They are sitting in the garden, the military commissar is asking them questions, they gossip, talk pompously about World Revolution, the mistress of the house is shaking apples from the trees because all her apples have been eaten, the military commissar's secretary, lanky, with a ringing voice, goes looking for food.

New trends at the headquarters: Sheko* is issuing special orders, bombastic and highfalutin, but short and energetic, he gives the Revolutionary Council his opinion, he acts on his own initiative.

Everyone is pining for Timoshenko,[†] there won't be a mutiny.

Why am I gripped by a longing that will not pass? Because I am far from home, because we are destroying, moving forward like a whirlwind, like lava, hated by all, life is being shattered to pieces, I am at a huge, never-ending service for the dead.

Ivan Ivanovich is sitting on a bench, talking of the days when he spent twenty thousand, thirty thousand. Everyone has gold, everyone ransacked Rostov, threw sacks of money over their saddles and rode off. Ivan Ivanovich dressed and kept women. Night, threshing shed, fragrant hay, but the air is heavy, I am smothered by something, by the sad senselessness of my life.

AUGUST 7, 1920. BERESTECHKO

It is evening now, 8. The lamps in the shtetl have just been lit. There is a funeral service in the room next door. Many Jews, the doleful chants of home, they rock, sit on benches, two candles, the eternal light on the windowsill. The funeral service is for the landlady's granddaughter, who died of fright after their house was looted. The mother is crying, tells me the story as she prays, we stand at the table, I have been pounded by sorrow for two months now. The mother shows me a photograph tattered by teardrops, and they all say what an uncommon beauty she was, some commander ran amok, banging on the door in the night, they dragged them out of bed, the Poles ransacked the house,

---

* The new chief of staff of the Sixth Cavalry Division.
† The former commander of the Sixth Cavalry Division.

then the Cossacks, ceaseless vomiting, she wasted away. The main thing for the Jews—she was a beauty, no other like her in all the shtetl.

A memorable day. In the morning we went from Khotin to Berestechko. I ride with Ivanov, the military commissar's secretary, a lanky, voracious, spineless fellow, a lout—and, believe it or not, he is the husband of Komarova, the singer, "We used to do concerts, I'll write to her to come." A Russian maenad.

The corpse of a slaughtered Pole, a terrible corpse, naked and bloated, monstrous.

Berestechko has changed hands quite a few times. There are historic sites outside Berestechko, Cossack graves. And this is the main thing, everything is repeating itself: Cossack against Pole, or rather serf against *Pan*.

I won't forget this shtetl, covered courtyards, long, narrow, stinking, everything 100–200 years old, the townsfolk more robust than in other places, the main thing is the architecture, the white and watery blue little houses, the little backstreets, the synagogues, the peasant women. Life is almost back on track again. People had led a good life here— respected Jewry, rich Ukrainians, market fairs on Sundays, a specialized class of Russian artisans: tanners trading with Austria, contraband.

The Jews here are less fanatical, better dressed, heartier, they even seem more cheerful, the very old men in long coats, the old women, everything exudes the old days, tradition, the shtetl is saturated in the bloody history of the Polish Jewish ghetto. Hatred for the Poles is unanimous. They looted, tortured, scorched the pharmacist's body with white-hot iron pokers, needles under his nails, tore out his hair, all because a Polish officer had been shot at—sheer idiocy! The Poles have gone out of their minds, they are destroying themselves.

An ancient church, the graves of Polish officers in the churchyard, fresh burial mounds, ten days old, white birch crosses, all this is terrible, the house of the Catholic priest has been destroyed, I find ancient books, precious Latin manuscripts. The priest, Tuzynkiewicz, I find a photograph of him, he is short and fat, he worked here for forty-five years, he lived in one place, a scholar, the assortment of books, many of them in Latin, editions of 1860, that was when Tuzynkiewicz lived. His living quarters are old-fashioned, enormous, dark paintings, photographs of the prelate conventions at Zhitomir, portraits of Pope Pius

X, a nice face, an exquisite portrait of Sienkiewicz*—here he is the essence of the nation. Blanketing all this is the stench of Sukhin's pitiful little soul. How new all this is for me, the books, the soul of the Catholic *Pater,* a Jesuit, I want to fathom the heart and soul of Tuzynkiewicz, and I have. Lepin suddenly plays the piano, touchingly. He sometimes sings in Latvian. Remember: his little bare feet, so droll you could die. What a funny creature.

A terrible incident: the looting of the church, they've ripped down the chasubles, the precious, glittering material is torn and lying on the floor, a sister of mercy dragged off three bundles, they are tearing the linings, the candles have been taken, the receptacles smashed open, the papal bulls thrown out, the money taken—this magnificent church, what its eyes have seen these past 200 years (Tuzynkiewicz's manuscripts), how many counts and serfs, magnificent Italian art, rosy *Paters* rocking the infant Jesus, the magnificent dark Jesus, Rembrandt, a Madonna like that of Murillo, maybe even by Murillo, and the main thing: the pious, well-fed Jesuits, the eerie Chinese figurine behind a veil, Jesus, a little bearded Jew in crimson Polish raiment, a bench, the shattered shrine, the figure of St. Valentine. The beadle, shivering like a bird, squirms, speaks in a jumble of Russian and Polish, I mustn't touch these things, he sobs. These animals are only here to plunder. It's very clear, the old gods are being destroyed.

An evening in the town. The church has been closed. In the late afternoon I go to the castle of Count Raciborski. A seventy-year-old man, his mother ninety. It was just the two of them, they were mad, people say. Describe the two of them. An old, aristocratic Polish house, most probably over a hundred years old, antlers, old bright paintings on the ceilings, remains of antlers, small rooms for the servants upstairs, flagstones, corridors, excrement on the floors, little Jewish boys, a Steinway piano, sofas slashed down to the springs, remember the white, delicate oak doors, French letters dated 1820, *notre petit héros achève 7 semaines.*† My God, who wrote that, when, the letters have been trampled on, I took some relics, a century, the mother is a countess, Steinway piano, park, pond.

---

* Henryk Sienkiewicz, 1846–1916, Polish novelist, author of *Quo Vadis?*.
† French: "our little hero is already seven weeks old."

I cannot tear myself away—I think of Hauptmann, *Elga.*[*]

A rally in the castle park, the Jews of Berestechko, dull Vinokurov,[†] children running around, a Revolutionary Committee is being elected, the Jews twirl their beards, the Jewesses listen to words about the Russian paradise, the international situation, about the uprising in India.

A night filled with anxiety, someone said we should be on the alert, all alone with feeble *mishures,*[**] unexpected eloquence, what did he talk about?

AUGUST 8, 1920. BERESTECHKO

I am settling down in the shtetl. There were fairs here. The peasants sell pears. They are paid with long-abolished banknotes. This place had been bubbling over with life, Jews had exported grain to Austria, human and commodity contraband, the closeness of the border.

Unusual barns, cellars.

I've been billeted with the proprietress of a coach inn, a gaunt, red-headed bitch. Ilchenko bought some cucumbers, reads the *Zhurnal dlya Vsekh,*[‡] and is pontificating about economic policy, the Jews are to blame for everything, a blunt, Slavic creature who filled his pockets during the plundering of Rostov. Some adopted children, the mother recently died. The tale of the pharmacist under whose nails the Poles stuck needles, people gone berserk.

A hot day, the townsfolk are roaming about, they are coming alive again, there will be trade.

Synagogue, Torahs, built thirty-six years ago by an artisan from Kremenets, they paid him fifty rubles a month, gold peacocks, crossed arms, ancient Torahs, the *shamases* show no enthusiasm whatever, wizened old men, the bridges of Berestechko, how they shook, the Poles gave all this a long-faded tint. The little old man at whose house

---

[*] Gerhart Hauptmann, 1862–1946, German dramatist. His play Elga was first performed in 1905.

[†] Aleksander Nikolayevich Vinokurov was the military commissar of the Sixth Cavalry Division. He replaced Bakhturov.

[**] Yiddish: "servant."

[‡] *Magazine for All,* a popular monthly magazine.

Korotchayev, the demoted division commander,* and his Jewish subaltern, are billeted. Korotchayev was chairman of the Cheka somewhere in Astrakhan, rotten to the core. Friendship with the Jew. We drink tea at the old man's. Silence, placidity. I roam about the shtetl, there is pitiful, powerful, undying life inside the Jewish hovels, young ladies in white stockings, long coats, so few fat people.

We are sending out scouts to Lvov. Apanasenko† sends dispatches to the Stavropol Executive Committee, heads will roll on the home front, he is delighted. The battle outside Radzivillov, Apanasenko acts heroically—instantaneous disposition of the troops, he almost opened fire on the retreating Fourteenth Division. We're nearing Radzikhov. Moscow newspapers of July 29. The commencement of the Second Congress of the Third International, finally the unification of all peoples has been realized, everything is clear: two worlds, and a declaration of war. We will be fighting endlessly. Russia has thrown down a challenge. We will march to Europe to subjugate the world. The Red Army has become an international factor.

I have to take a closer look at Apanasenko. *Ataman.***

The quiet old man's funeral service for his granddaughter.

Evening, performance in the count's garden, the theatergoers of Berestechko, an idiot of an orderly, the young ladies of Berestechko, silence descends, I would like to stay here awhile and get to know it.

AUGUST 9, 1920. LASHKOV

The move from Berestechko to Lashkov. Galicia. The division commander's carriage, the division commander's orderly is Lyovka—the one who chases horses like a gypsy. The tale of how he whipped his neighbor Stepan, a former constable under Denikin who had harassed the people, when Stepan came back to the village. They wouldn't just "butcher" him, they beat him in prison, slashed his back, jumped up and down on him, danced, an epic exchange: "Are you feeling good, Stepan?" "I'm feeling bad." "And the people you harassed, did they feel

---

* D. D. Korotchayev had been the provisional commander of the Fourth Cavalry Division from May 1 to June 20, 1920.

† The new commander of the Sixth Cavalry Division.

** Also *hetman,* a Cossack leader.

good?" "No, they felt bad." "And did you think that someday you might be feeling bad?" "No, I didn't." "You should have thought about that, Stepan, because what we think is that if we'd fallen into your hands, you'd have butchered us, so f— it, now, Stepan, we will kill you." When they finally left him he was already getting cold. Another tale about Shurka the nurse. Night, battle, regiments form, Lyovka in the phaeton, Shurka's lover is heavily wounded, gives Lyovka his horse, they take away the wounded man and return to the battle. "Shurka, we only live once, and then we die!" "Well, okay, then." She went to a boarding school in Rostov, gallops with the regiment, she can do fifteen. "But now, Shurka, let's go, we're retreating." The horses got caught up in the barbed wire, he galloped four versts, a village, he sits down, cuts through the barbed wire, the regiment rides through, Shurka leaves the formation. Lyovka prepares supper, they want food, they ate, chatted, go on, Shurka, one more time. Well, okay. But where?

She went galloping after the regiment, he went to sleep. If your wife comes, I'll kill her.

Lashkov is a green, sunny, quiet, rich Galician village. I've been billeted at the deacon's house. His wife has just given birth. Downtrodden people. A clean, new hut, but there's nothing in the hut. Next door typical Galician Jews. They think—he must be Jewish, no? The story: they came plundering, one of them chopped off the heads of two chickens, found the things in the threshing shed, dug up things from the earth, herded everyone together in the hut, the usual story, remember the young man with sideburns. They tell me that the head rabbi lives in Belz, they finished off the rabbis.

We rest, the First Squadron is in my front garden. Night, a lamp is standing on my table, the horses snort quietly, everyone here is a Kuban Cossack, they eat, sleep, cook together, marvelous, silent camaraderie. They're all peasants, in the evenings they sing with rich voices songs that sound like hymns, devotion to horses, small bundles, saddle, bridle, ornate sabers, greatcoat, I sleep surrounded by them.

I sleep in the field during the day. No operations, rest—what a marvelous and necessary thing it is. The cavalry, the horses are recuperating after this inhuman work, people are recuperating from all the cruelty, living together, singing songs with quiet voices, they are telling each other things.

The headquarters are in the school. The division commander at the priest's.

AUGUST 10, 1920. LASHKOV

Our rest continues. Scouts to Radzikhov, Sokolovka, Stoyanov, all in the direction of Lvov. News has come that Aleksandrovsk was taken, gigantic complications in the international situation, will we have to go to war against the whole world?

A fire in the village. The priest's threshing shed is burning. Two horses, thrashing around with all their might, burned. You can't lead a horse out of a fire. Two cows broke out, the hide of one of them split, blood is coming out of the crack, touching and pitiful.

The smoke envelops the entire village, bright flames, plump black billows of smoke, a mass of wood, hot in the face, everything carried out of the priest's house and the church, thrown into the front garden. Apanasenko in a red Cossack jacket, a black coat, clean-shaven face, a terrifying apparition, an ataman.

Our Cossacks, a sad sight, dragging loot out over the back porch, their eyes burning, all of them looking uneasy, ashamed, this so-called habit of theirs is ineradicable. All the church banners, ancient saints' books,* icons are being carried out, strange figures painted whitish pink, whitish blue, monstrous, flat-faced, Chinese or Buddhist, heaps of paper flowers, will the church catch fire, peasant women are wringing their hands in silence, the townspeople, frightened and silent, are running barefoot, everyone sits in front of their hut with a bucket. They are apathetic, cowed, remarkably numb, but they'd drop everything to put out their own fires. They've come to terms with the plundering—the soldiers are circling around the priest's trunks like rapacious, overwrought beasts, they say there's gold in there, one can take it away from a priest, a portrait of Count Andrzej Szceptycki, the Metropolitan of Galicia. A manly magnate with a black ring on his large, aristocratic hand. The lower lip of the old priest, who has served in Lashkov for thirty-five years, is constantly trembling. He tells me about Szceptycki, that he is not "educated" in the Polish spirit, comes from Ruthenian

---

* *Chet'i Menie,* anthologies of Old Church Slavonic writings about the lives of saints, organized by month and date.

grandees, "The Counts of Szceptycki," then they went over to the Poles, his brother is commander in chief of the Polish forces, Andrzej returned to the Ruthenians. His ancient culture, quiet and solid. A good, educated priest who has laid in a supply of flour, chickens, wants to talk about the universities, Ruthenians, the poor man, Apanasenko with his red Cossack jacket is staying with him.

Night—an unusual sight, the high road is brilliantly lit, my room is bright, I'm working, the lamp is burning, calm, the Kuban Cossacks are singing with feeling, their thin figures by the campfires, the songs are totally Ukrainian, the horses lie down to sleep. I go to the division commander. Vinokurov tells me about him—a partisan, an ataman, a rebel, Cossack freedom, wild uprising, his ideal is Dumenko,* an open wound, one has to submit oneself to the organization, a deadly hatred for the aristocracy, clerics, and, most of all, for the intelligentsia, which he cannot stomach in the army. Apanasenko will graduate from a school—how is it different from the times of Bogdan Khmelnitsky?

Late at night. Four o'clock.

August 11, 1920. Lashkov

A day of work, sitting at the headquarters, I write to the point of exhaustion, a day of rest. Toward evening, rain. Kuban Cossacks are staying the night in my room, strange: peaceful and warlike, domestic, and peasants of obvious Ukrainian origin, not all that young.

About the Kuban Cossacks. Camaraderie, they always stick together, horses snort beneath the windows night and day, the marvelous smell of horse manure, of sun, of sleeping Cossacks, twice a day they boil large pails of soup and meat. At night Kuban Cossacks come to visit. Ceaseless rain, they dry themselves and eat their supper in my room. A religious Kuban Cossack in a soft hat, pale face, blond mustache. They are decent, friendly, wild, but somehow more sympathetic, domestic, less foulmouthed, more calm than the Cossacks from Stavropol and the Don.

The nurse came, how clear it all is, must describe that, she is worn

---

* Boris Mokeyevich Dumenko had been the legendary commander of the Fourth Cavalry Divison in 1918, and fought with Stalin, Budyonny, and Voroshilov at the Battle of Tsaritsyn.

out, wants to leave, everyone has had her—the commandant, at least that's what they say, Yakovlev,* and, O horror, Gusev. She's pitiful, wants to leave, sad, talks gibberish, wants to talk to me about something and looks at me with trusting eyes, she says I am her friend, the others, the others are scum. How quickly they have managed to destroy a person, debase her, make her ugly. She is naive, foolish, receptive even to revolutionary phrases, and the silly fool talks a lot about the Revolution, she worked in the Cheka's Culture and Education Division, how many male influences.

Interview with Apanasenko. This is very interesting. Must remember this. His blunt, terrible face, his hard body, like Utochkin's.†

His orderlies (Lyovka), magnificent golden horses, his hangers-on, carriages, Volodya, his adopted son—a small Cossack with an old man's face, curses like a grown man.

Apanasenko, hungry for fame, here we have it: a new class of man. Whatever the operational situation might be, he will always go off and come back again, an organizer of units, totally hostile to officers, four George Crosses, a career soldier, a noncommissioned officer, an ensign under Kerensky, chairman of the Regimental Committee, stripped officers of their stripes, long months on the Astrakhan steppes, indisputable authority, a professional soldier.

About the atamans, there had been many there, they got themselves machine guns, fought against Shkuro and Mamontov,** merged into the Red Army, a heroic epic. This is not a Marxist Revolution, it is a Cossack uprising that wants to win all and lose nothing. Apanasenko's hatred for the rich, an unquenchable hatred of the intelligentsia.

Night with the Kuban Cossacks, rain, it's stuffy, I have some sort of strange itch.

August 12, 1920. Lashkov

The fourth day in Lashkov. A completely downtrodden Galician village. They used to live better than the Russians, good houses, strong

---

* The political commissar of the Sixth Cavalry Division.

† Sergey Utochkin, a celebrated Russian aviation pioneer from Odessa.

** Andrei Grigorevich Shkuro and Konstantin Konstantinovich Mamontov were counterrevolutionary Cossack generals.

sense of decency, respect for priests, the people honest but blood-drained, my landlord's deformed child, how and why was he born, not a drop of blood left in the mother, they are continually hiding something somewhere, pigs are grunting somewhere, they have probably hidden cloth somewhere.

A day off, a good thing—my correspondence, mustn't neglect that.

Must write for the newspaper, and the life story of Apanasenko.

The division is resting, a kind of stillness in one's heart, and people are better, songs, campfires, fire in the night, jokes, happy, apathetic horses, someone reads the newspaper, they stroll around, shoe their horses. What all this looks like, Sokolov is going on leave, I give him a letter home.

I keep writing about pipes, about long-forgotten things, so much for the Revolution, that's what I should be concentrating on.

Don't forget the priest in Lashkov, badly shaven, kind, educated, possibly mercenary: a chicken, a duck, his house, lived well, droll etchings.

Friction between the military commissar and the division commander. He got up and left with Kniga* while Yakovlev, the divisional political commissar, was giving a report, Apanasenko went to the military commissar.

Vinokurov: a typical military commissar, always wants things done his way, wants to put the Sixth Division on track, struggle with the partisan attitude, dull-witted, bores me to death with his speeches, at times he's rude, uses the informal "you" with everyone.

AUGUST 13, 1920. NIVITSA

At night the order comes: head for Busk, thirty-five versts east of Lvov.

We set out in the morning. All three brigades are concentrated in one place. I'm on Misha's horse, it was taught to run and won't go at a walking pace, it goes at a trot. The whole day on horseback with the division commander. The farm at Porady. In the forest, four enemy airplanes, a volley of fire. Three brigade commanders: Kolesnikov,

---

* Vasily Ivanovich Kniga, commander of the First Brigade of the Sixth Cavalry Division.

Korotchayev, Kniga. Vasily Ivanovich [Kniga]'s sly move, headed for Toporov (Chanyz) in a bypass maneuver, didn't run into the enemy anywhere. We are at the Porady farm, destroyed huts, I pull an old woman out of a hatch door, dovecotes. Together with the lookout on the battery. Our attack by the woods.

A disaster—swamps, canals, the cavalry can't be deployed anywhere, attacks in infantry formation, inertia, is our morale flagging? Persistent and yet light fighting near Toporov (in comparison to the Imperialist carnage), they're attacking on three sides, cannot overpower us, a hurricane of fire from our artillery, from two batteries.

Night. All the attacks failed. Overnight the headquarters move to Nivitsa. Thick fog, penetrating cold, horse, roads through forests, campfires and candles, nurses on *tachankas*, a harsh journey after a day of anxiety and ultimate failure.

All day long through fields and forests. Most interesting of all: the division commander, his grin, foul language, curt exclamations, snorting, shrugs his shoulders, is agitated, responsibility for everything, passion—if only he had been there everything would have been fine.

What can I remember? The night ride, the screams of the women in Porady when we began (I broke off writing here, two bombs thrown from an airplane exploded a hundred paces from us, we're at a clearing in the forest west of St[ary] Maidan) taking away their linen, our attack, something we can't quite make out, not frightening at a distance, some lines of men, horsemen riding over a meadow, at a distance this all looks like it is done haphazardly, it does not seem in the least bit frightening.

When we advanced close to the little town, things began to heat up, the moment of the attack, the moment when a town is taken, the feverish, frightening, mounting rattle of the machine guns driving one to hopelessness and despair, the ceaseless explosions and, high up over all of this, silence, and nothing can be seen.

The work of Apanasenko's headquarters, every hour there are reports to the army commander, he is trying to ingratiate himself.

We arrive frozen through, tired, at Nivitsa. A warm kitchen. A school.

The captivating wife of the schoolmaster, she's a nationalist, a sort of inner cheerfulness about her, asks all kinds of questions, makes us tea, defends her *mowa*,* your *mowa* is good and so is my *mowa*, and always laughter in her eyes. And this in Galicia, this is nice, it's been ages since I've heard anything like this. I sleep in the classroom, in the straw next to Vinokurov.†

I've got a cold.

AUGUST 14, 1920

The center of operations—the taking of Busk and the crossing of the Bug. All day long attacking Toporov, no, we've stopped. Another indecisive day. The forest clearing by St[ary] Maidan. The enemy has taken Lopatin.

Toward evening we throw them out. Once again Nivitsa. Spend the night at the house of an old woman, in the yard together with the staff.

AUGUST 15, 1920

Morning in Toporov. Fighting near Busk. Headquarters are in Busk. Force our way over the Bug. A blaze on the other side. Budyonny's in Busk.

Spend the night in Yablonovka with Vinokurov.

AUGUST 16, 1920

To Rakobuty, a brigade made it across.

I'm off to interrogate the prisoners.

Once again in Yablonovka. We're moving on to N[ovy] Milatin, St[ary] Milatin, panic, spend the night in an almshouse.

AUGUST 17, 1920

Fighting near the railroad tracks near Liski. The butchering of prisoners.

Spend the night in Zadvurdze.

---

* Ukrainian: "language."
† The military commissar of the Sixth Cavalry Division.

AUGUST 18, 1920

Haven't had time to write. We're moving on. We set out on August 13. From that time on we've been on the move, endless roads, squadron banners, Apanasenko's horses, skirmishes, farms, corpses. Frontal attack on Toporov, Kolesnikov* in the attack, swamps, I am at an observation point, toward evening a hurricane of fire from two batteries. The Polish infantry is waiting in the trenches, our fighters go, return, horse-holders are leading the wounded, Cossacks don't like frontal attacks, the cursed trenches cloud with smoke. That was the 13th. On the 14th, the division moves to Busk, it has to get there at all cost, by evening we had advanced ten versts. That's where the main operation has to take place: the crossing of the Bug. At the same time they're searching for a ford.

A Czech farm at Adamy, breakfast in the farmhouse, potatoes with milk, Sukhorukov thrives under every regime, an ass-kisser, Suslov dances to his tune, as do all the Lyovkas. The main thing: dark forests, transport carts in the forests, candles above the nurses, rumbling, the tempos of troop movement. We're at a clearing in the forest, the horses are grazing, the airplanes are the heroes of the day, air operations are on the increase, airplane attacks, five-six planes circle endlessly, bombs at a hundred paces, I have an ash-gray gelding, a repulsive horse. In the forest. An intrigue with the nurse: Apanasenko made her a revolting proposition then and there, they say she spent the night with him, now she speaks of him with loathing. She likes Sheko,[†] but the divisional military commissar likes her, cloaking his interest in her with the pretext that she is, as he says, without protection, has no means of transport, no protector. She talks of how Konstantin Karlovich** courted her, fed her, forbade others to write her letters, but everyone kept on writing to her. She found Yakovlev[‡] extremely attractive, and the head of the Registration Department, a blond-haired boy in a red hood asked for her hand and her heart, sobbing like a child. There was also some other story but I couldn't find out anything about it. The saga of the nurse, and the main thing: they talk a lot about her and everyone

---

* Kolesov, commander of the Third Brigade.
[†] The chief of staff of the Sixth Cavalry Division.
** Zholnarkevich, the former chief of staff of the Sixth Cavalry Division.
[‡] The political commissar of the Sixth Cavalry Division.

looks down on her, her own coachman doesn't talk to her, her little boots, aprons, she does favors, Bebel brochures.

*Woman and Socialism.**

One can write volumes about the women in the Red Army. The squadrons set off into battle—dust, rumbling, the baring of sabers, savage cursing—they gallop ahead with hitched-up skirts, dust-covered, fat-breasted, all of them whores, but comrades too, and whores because they are comrades, that's the most important thing, they serve in every way they can, these heroines, and then they're looked down upon, they give water to the horses, haul hay, mend harnesses, steal things from churches and from the townsfolk.

Apanasenko's agitation, his foul language, is it willpower?

Night again in Nivitsa, I sleep somewhere in the straw, because I can't remember anything, everything in me is lacerated, my body aches, a HUNDRED versts by horse.

I spend the night with Vinokurov. His attitude toward Ivanov.[†] What kind of man is this gluttonous, pitiful, tall youth with a soft voice, wilted soul, and sharp mind? The military commissar is unbearably rough with him, swears at him ceaselessly, finds fault with everything: What's up with you—curses fly—You didn't do it? Go pack your things, I'm kicking you out!

I have to fathom the soul of the fighter, I am managing, this is all terrible, they're animals with principles.

Overnight the Second Brigade took Toropov in a nocturnal attack. An unforgettable morning. We move at a fast trot. A terrible, uncanny shtetl, Jews stand at their doors like corpses, I wonder about them: what more are you going to have to go through? Black beards, bent backs, destroyed houses, here there's [illegible], remnants of German efficiency and comfort, some sort of inexpressible, commonplace, and burning Jewish sadness. There's a monastery here. Apanasenko is radiant. The Second Brigade rides past. Forelocks, jackets made out of carpets, red tobacco pouches, short carbines, commanders on majestic horses, a Budyonny brigade. Parade, marching bands, we greet you, Sons of the Revolution. Apanasenko is radiant.

We move on from Toporov—forests, roads, the staff on the road,

* *Die Frau und der Sozialismus* (*Woman and Socialism*) by August Bebel.
† Vinokurov's secretary.

orderlies, brigade commanders, we fly on to Busk at a fast trot, to its eastern part. What an enchanting place (on the 18th an airplane is flying, it will now drop bombs), clean Jewesses, gardens full of pears and plums, radiant noon, curtains, in the houses the remnants of the petite bourgeoisie, a clean and possibly honest simplicity, mirrors, we have been billeted at the house of a fat Galician woman, the widow of a schoolmaster, wide sofas, many plums, unbearable exhaustion from overstrained nerves (a shell came flying, didn't explode), couldn't fall asleep, lay by the wall next to the horses remembering the dust and the horrible jostle in the transport cart, dust—the majestic phenomenon of our war.

Fighting in Busk. It's on the other side of the bridge. Our wounded. Beauty—over there the shtetl is burning. I ride to the crossing, the sharp experience of battle, have to run part of the way because it's under fire, night, the blaze is shining, the horses stand by the huts, a meeting with Budyonny is under way, the members of the Revolutionary War Council* come out, a feeling of danger in the air, we didn't take Busk with our frontal attack, we say good-bye to the fat Galician woman and drive to Yablonovka deep in the night, the horses are barely moving ahead, we spend the night in a pit, on straw, the division commander has left, the military commissar and I have no strength left.

The First Brigade found a ford and crossed the Bug by Poborzhany. In the morning with Vinokurov at the crossing. So here is the Bug, a shallow little river, the staff is on a hill, the journey has worn me out, I'm sent back to Yablonovka to interrogate prisoners. Disaster. Describe what a horseman feels: exhaustion, the horse won't go on, the ride is long, no strength, the burned steppe, loneliness, no one there to help you, endless versts.

Interrogation of prisoners in Yablonovka. Men in their underwear, exhausted, there are Jews, light-blond Poles, an educated young fellow, blunt hatred toward them, the blood-drenched underwear of a wounded man, he's not given any water, a fat-faced fellow pushes his papers at me. You lucky fellows—I think—how did you get away. They crowd around me, they are happy at the sound of my benevolent voice, miser-

---

* *Revvoensoviet,* founded in 1918, were councils in which military commanders and political representatives of the Bolshevik government conferred on military tactics.

able dust, what a difference between the Cossacks and them, they're spineless.

From Yablonovka I return by *tachanka* to the headquarters. Again the crossing, endless lines of transport carts crossing over (they don't wait even a minute, they are right on the heels of the advancing units), they sink in the river, trace-straps tear, the dust is suffocating, Galician villages, I'm given milk, lunch in a village, the Poles have just pulled out of here, everything is calm, the village dead, stifling heat, midday silence, there's no one in the village, it is astounding that there is such light, such absolute and unruffled silence, peace, as if the front were well over a hundred versts away. The churches in the villages.

Farther along the road is the enemy. Two naked, butchered Poles with small, slashed faces are glittering through the rye in the sun.

We return to Yablonovka, tea at Lepin's, dirt, Cherkashin* denigrates him and wants to get rid of him. If you look closely, Cherkashin's face is dreadful. In his body, tall as a stick, you can see the muzhik—he is a drunkard, a thief, and a cunning bastard.

Lepin is dirty, dim-witted, touchy, incomprehensible.

Handsome Bazkunov's long, endless tale, a father, Nizhny-Novgorod, head of a chemistry department, Red Army, prisoner under Denikin, the biography of a Russian youth, his father a merchant, an inventor, dealt with Moscow restaurants. Chatted with him during the whole trip. We are heading for Milatin, plums along the road. In St[ary] Milatin there is a church, the priest's house, the priest lives in a luxurious house, unforgettable, he keeps squeezing my hand, sets off to bury a dead Pole, sits down with us, asks whether our commander is a good man, a typical Jesuitical face, shaven, gray eyes dart around—a pleasure to behold—a crying Polish woman, his niece, begging that her heifer be returned to her, tears and a coquettish smile, all very Polish. Mustn't forget the house, knickknacks, pleasant darkness, Jesuitical, Catholic culture, clean women, and the most aromatic and agitated *Pater*, opposite him a monastery. I want to stay here. We wait for the order for where we are to stay—in Stary Milatin or in Novy Milatin. Night. Panic. Some transport carts, the Poles have broken through somewhere, pandemonium on the road, three rows of transport carts,

* Lepin's orderly.

I'm in the Milatin schoolhouse, two beautiful old maids, it's frightening how much they remind me of the Shapiro sisters from Nikolayev, two quiet, educated Galician women, patriots, their own culture, bedroom, possibly curlers, in thundering, war-torn Milatin, outside these walls transport carts, cannons, fatherly commanders telling tales of their heroic feats, clouds of orange dust, the monastery is enveloped by them. The sisters offer me cigarettes, they breathe in my words of how everything will be marvelous—it's like balm, they have blossomed out, and we speak elegantly about culture.

A knock at the door. The commandant wants me. A fright. We ride over to Novy Milatin. *N. Milatin.* With the military commissar in the almshouse, some sort of town house, sheds, night, vaults, the priest's maid, dark, dirty, myriads of flies, tiredness beyond compare, the tiredness of the front.

Daybreak, we depart, the railroad has to be breached (this all takes place on August 17), the Brody-Lvov railroad.

My first battle, I saw the attack, they gather in the bushes, the brigade commanders ride up to Apanasenko—careful Kniga,* all slyness, rides up, talks up a storm, they point to the hills, there beneath the forest, there over the hollow, they've spotted the enemy, the regiments ride to attack, sabers in the sun, pale commanders, Apanasenko's hard legs, hurrah.

What happened? A field, dust, the staff in the plains, Apanasenko curses in a frenzy, brigade commander—destroy those bastards, f—ing bandits.

The mood before the battle, hunger, heat, they gallop in attack, nurses.

A thunder of hurrahs, the Poles are crushed, we ride out onto the battlefield, a little Pole with polished nails is rubbing his pink, sparsely haired head, answers evasively, prevaricating, hemming and hawing, well, yes, Sheko,† roused and pale, answer, who are you—I'm, he ducks the question, a sort of ensign, we ride off, they take him, a good-looking fellow behind him loads his gun, I shout—"Yakov Vasilevich [Sheko]!" He acts like he didn't hear, rides on, a shot, the little Pole in

---

* Vasily Ivanovich Kniga, commander of the First Brigade of the Sixth Cavalry Division.
† The chief of staff of the Sixth Cavalry Division.

his underwear falls on his face and twitches. Life is disgusting, murderers, it's unbearable, baseness and crime.

They are rounding up the prisoners, undressing them, a strange picture—they undress incredibly fast, shake their heads, all this in the sun, mild embarrassment, all the command personnel is there, embarrassment, but who cares, so cover your eyes. I will never forget that "sort of" ensign who was treacherously murdered.

Ahead—terrible things. We crossed the railroad tracks by Zadvurdze. The Poles are fighting their way along the railroad tracks to Lvov. An attack in the evening at the farm. Carnage. The military commissar and I ride along the tracks, begging the men not to butcher the prisoners, Apanasenko* washes his hands of it. Sheko's tongue ran away with him: "Butcher them all!" It played a horrifying role. I didn't look into their faces, they impaled them, shot them, corpses covered with bodies, one they undress, another they shoot, moans, yells, wheezing, our squadron led the attack, Apanasenko stands to the side, the squadron has dressed up, Matusevich's horse was killed, his face frightening, dirty, he is running, looking for a horse. This is hell. How we bring freedom—terrible. They search a farm, men are dragged out, Apanasenko: Don't waste bullets, butcher them. Apanasenko always says—butcher the nurse, butcher the Poles.

We spend the night in Zadvurdze, bad quarters, I'm with Sheko, good food, ceaseless skirmishes, I'm living a soldier's life, completely worn out, we are waiting in the forest, nothing to eat all day, Sheko's carriage arrives, brings something, I'm often at the observation point, the work of the batteries, the clearings, hollows, the machine guns are mowing, the Poles are mainly defending themselves with airplanes, they are becoming a menace, describe the air attacks, the faraway and seemingly slow hammering of the machine guns, panic in the transport carts, it's harrowing, they are incessantly gliding over us, we hide from them. A new use of aviation, I think of Mosher, Captain Fauntleroy in Lvov, our wanderings from one brigade to the next, Kniga only likes bypass maneuvers, Kolesnikov† frontal attacks, I ride with Sheko on reconnaissance, endless forests, deadly danger, on the hills, bullets are buzzing all around before the attack, the pitiful face of Sukhorukov

---

*The commander of the Sixth Cavalry Division.

† Actually Nikolai Petrovich Kolesov, commander of the Third Brigade.

with his saber, I tag along behind the staff, we await reports, but they advancing, doing bypass maneuvers.

The battle for Barshchovitse. After a day of fluctuations, Polish columns manage in the evening to break through to Lvov. When Apanasenko saw this, he went mad, he is shaking, the brigades are going full force even though they are dealing with a retreating enemy, and the brigades stretch out in endless ribbons, three cavalry brigades are hurled into the attack, Apanasenko is triumphant, snorts, sends out Litovchenko as the new commander of the Third Brigade to replace Kolesnikov, who's been wounded, you see them, there they are, go finish them off, they're running. He meddles in the artillery action, interferes with the orders of the battery commanders, feverish, they were hoping to repeat what had happened at Zadvurdze, but it wasn't to be. Swamps on one side, ruinous fire on the other. March to Ostrov, the Sixth Cavalry Division is supposed to take Lvov from the southeast.

Gigantic losses among the command personnel: Korotchayev, heavily wounded, his adjutant, a Jew, was killed, the commander of the Thirty-fourth Regiment wounded, all the commissars of the Thirty-first Regiment out of action, all the chiefs of staff wounded, above all Budyonny's commanders.

The wounded crawl onto *tachankas*. This is how we're going to take Lvov, the reports to the army commander are written in the grass, brigades gallop, orders in the night, again forests, bullets buzz, artillery fire chases us from one place to another, miserable fear of airplanes, get down off your horse, a bomb's about to explode, there's a revolting sensation in your mouth. Nothing to feed the horses with.

I see now what a horse means to a Cossack and a cavalryman.

Unhorsed cavalrymen on the hot dusty roads, their saddles in their arms, they sleep like corpses on other men's carts, horses are rotting all around, all that's talked about is horses, the customs of barter, the excitement, horses are martyrs, horses are sufferers—their saga, I myself have been gripped by this feeling, every march is an agony for the horse.

Apanasenko's visits to Budyonny with his retinue. Budyonny and Voroshilov at a farm, they sit at a table. Apanasenko's report, standing at attention. The failure of the special regiment: they had planned an attack on Lvov, set out, the special regiment's sentry post was, as always, asleep, it was taken down, the Poles rolled their machine guns within a hundred paces, rounded up the horses, wounded half the regiment.

The Day of the Transfiguration of Our Savior Jesus Christ—19 August—in Barshchovitse, a butchered, but still breathing, village, peace, a meadow, a flock of geese (we dealt with them later—Sidorenko or Yegor chopped up the geese on a block with their sabers), we eat boiled goose. That day, white as they were, they beautified the village, on the green meadows the villagers, festive but feeble, spectral, barely able to crawl out of their hovels, silent, strange, dazed, and completely cowed.

There is something quiet and oppressive about this holiday.

The Uniate priest in Barshchovitse. A ruined, defiled garden, Budyonny's headquarters had been here, and smashed, smoked-out beehives, this is a terrible, barbaric custom—I remember the broken frames, thousands of bees buzzing and fighting by the destroyed hives, their panicking swarms.

The priest explains to me the difference between the Uniate and the Russian Orthodox faith. Sheptitsky is a tall man, he wears a canvas cassock. A plump man, a dark, chubby face, shaved cheeks, sparkling little eyes with a sty.

The advance on Lvov. The batteries are drawing nearer and nearer. A rather unsuccessful skirmish by Ostrov, but still the Poles withdraw. Information on Lvov's defenses—schoolmasters, women, adolescents. Apanasenko will butcher them—he hates the intelligentsia, with him it's deep-rooted, he wants an aristocracy on his own terms, a muzhik and Cossack state.

August 21, a week of battle has passed, our units are four versts outside Lvov.

An order: the whole Red Cavalry is being put under the command of the Western Front.* They are moving us north to Lublin. There will be an attack there. They are withdrawing the army, now four versts from the town, even though it took so much time for them to get there. The Fourteenth Army will replace us. What is this? Madness, or the impossibility of a town being taken by the cavalry? I will remember the forty-five-verst ride from Barshchovitse to Adamy for the rest of my life. I on my little piebald horse, Sheko[†] in his carriage, heat and dust,

---

* *Zapfront* (Zapadnii Front), February 1919 to January 1921, was the central Red Army command of western and northwestern strategic points in Soviet Russia.

[†] The chief of staff of the Sixth Cavalry Division.

the dust of the Apocalypse, stifling clouds, endless lines of transport carts, all the brigades are on the move, clouds of dust from which there is no escape, one is afraid of suffocating, shouting all around, movement, I ride with a squadron over fields, we lose Sheko, the most horrendous part of it begins, the ride on my little horse which can't keep up, we ride endlessly and always at a trot, I am completely exhausted, the squadron wants to overtake the transport carts, we overtake them, I am afraid of being left behind, my horse is drifting along like a bit of fluff, to the point of inertia, all the brigades are on the move, all the artillery, they've each left one regiment behind as a covering force, and these regiments are to reunite with the division at the onset of darkness. In the night we ride through silent, dead Busk. What is special about Galician towns? The mixture of the dirty, ponderous East (Byzantium and the Jews) with the beer-drinking German West. Fifteen km. from Busk. I can't hold out anymore. I change my horse. It turns out that there is no covering on the saddle. Riding is torture. I keep constantly changing position. A rest stop in Kozlov. A dark hut, bread with milk. A peasant, a warm and pleasant person, was a prisoner of war in Odessa, I lie on the bench, mustn't fall asleep, I'm wearing another man's service jacket, the horses in the dark, it's stuffy in the hut, children on the floor. We arrived in Adamy at four in the morning. Sheko is asleep. I leave my horse somewhere, there is hay, and I lie down to sleep.

AUGUST 21, 1920. ADAMY

Frightened Ruthenians. Sun. Nice. I'm ill. Rest. The whole day in the threshing shed. I sleep, feel better toward evening, my head pounds, aches. I'm billeted with Sheko. Yegor, the chief of staff's lackey. We eat well. How we get our food. Vorobyov took over the Second Squadron. The soldiers are pleased. In Poland, where we are heading, there's no need to hold back—with the Galicians, who are completely innocent, we had to be more careful. I'm resting, I'm not in the saddle.

Conversation with Artillery Division Commander Maksimov, our army is out to make some money, what we have is not revolution but an uprising of renegade Cossacks.

They are simply an instrument the party is not above using.

Two Odessans, Manuilov and Boguslavsky,* operational air force military commissar, Paris, London, a handsome Jew, a big talker, articles in a European magazine, the divisional chief of staff's adjutant, Jews in the Red Cavalry, I tell them what's what. Wearing a service jacket, the excesses of the Odessan bourgeoisie, painful news from Odessa. They're being smothered there. What about my father? Have they really taken everything away from him? I have to give some thought to the situation back home.

I'm turning into a sponger.

Apanasenko has written a letter to the officers of the Polish army: You bandits, stop fighting, surrender, you *Pans,* or we will butcher you all!

Apanasenko's letter to the Don headquarters, to Stavropol, there they are making things difficult for our fighters, for the Sons of the Revolution, we are heroes, we have no fear, we will march ahead.

A description of the squadron's rest, they steal hens, the squealing of pigs, agents, musical flourishes on the town square. They wash clothes, thresh oats, come galloping with sheaves. The horses, wiggling their ears, eat oats. The horse is everything. Horse names: Stepan, Misha, Little Brother, Old Girl. Your horse is your savior, you are aware of it every moment, even if you might beat it inhumanly. No one takes care of my horse. They barely take care of it.

AUGUST 22, 1920. ADAMY

Manuilov, the divisional chief of staff's adjutant, has a stomachache. I'm not surprised. Served with Muravyov,† in the Cheka, something to do with military investigation, a bourgeois, women, Paris, air force, something to do with his reputation, and he's a Communist. Boguslavsky, the secretary, frightened, sits silently and eats.

A peaceful day. We march on northward.

I'm billeted with Sheko. I can't do anything. I'm tired, battered. I

---

* Manuilov was the adjutant to Sheko, the divisional chief of staff, and Boguslavsky was staff secretary.

† Mikhail Artemevich Muravyov, a legendary figure who in 1918, during his tenure as commander of the Western Front, instigated the counterrevolutionary Muravyov Revolt for which he was executed.

sleep and eat. How we eat. The system. The provisions depot men and the foragers won't give us anything. The arrival of the Red Army fighters in the village, they search through everything, cook, all night the stoves sputter, the household daughters suffer, the squealing of pigs, they come to the military commissar with receipts. The pitiful Galicians.

The saga of how we eat. We eat well: pigs, hens, geese.

Those who don't take part are "rag-looters" and "wimp."

August 23/24, 1920. Viktov

Ride on to Vitkov in a cart. System of using civilian carts, poor civilians, they are harassed for two, three weeks, are let go, given a pass, are snatched up by other soldiers, are harassed again. An episode: where we are billeted a boy comes back from the transport carts. Night. His mother's joy.

We march into the Krasnostav-Lublin district. We've overtaken the army, which is four versts from Lvov. The cavalry did not manage to take it.

The road to Vitkov. Sun. Galician roads, endless transport carts, factory horses, ravaged Galicia, Jews in shtetls, somewhere an unscathed farm, Czech we imagine, we attack the unripe apples, the beehives.

More details about the beehives another time.

On the road, in the cart, I think, I mourn the fate of the Revolution.

The shtetl is unusual, rebuilt on a single plan after its destruction, little white houses, tall wooden roofs, sadness.

We are billeted with the divisional chief of staff's aides, Manuilov knows nothing about staff work, the hassles of trying to get horses, no one will give us any, we ride on the civilians' carts, Boguslavsky wears lilac-colored drawers, a great success with the girls in Odessa.

The soldiers ask for a theatrical show. They're fed *His Orderly Let Him Down*.

The divisional chief of staff's night: where's the Thirty-third Regiment, where did the Second Brigade go, telephone, orders from army headquarters to the brigade commander, 1, 2, 3!

The orderlies on duty. The setup of the squadrons—Matusevich and Vorobyov,* a former commandant, an unalterably cheerful and, from what I can see, a foolish man.

The divisional chief of staff's night: the division commander wants to see you.

August 25, 1920. Sokal

Finally, a town. We ride through the shtetl of Tartakuv, Jews, ruins, cleanliness of a Jewish kind, the Jewish race, little stores.

I am still ill, I've still not gotten back on my feet after the battles outside Lvov. What stuffy air these shtetls have. The infantry had been in Sokal, the town is untouched, the divisional chief of staff is billeted with some Jews. Books, I saw books. I'm billeted with a Galician woman, a rich one at that, we eat well, chicken in sour cream.

I ride on my horse to the center of town, it's clean, pretty buildings, everything soiled by war, remnants of cleanliness and originality.

The Revolutionary Committee. Requisitions and confiscation. Interesting: they don't touch the peasantry, all the land has been left at its disposal. The peasantry is left alone.

The declarations of the Revolutionary Committee.

My landlord's son—a Zionist and *ein ausgesprochener Nationalist.*† Normal Jewish life, they look to Vienna, to Berlin, the nephew, a young man, is studying philosophy, wants to go to the university. We eat butter and chocolate. Sweets.

Friction between Manuilov and the divisional chief of staff.** Sheko tells him to go to—

"I have my pride," they won't give him a billet, no horse, there's the cavalry for you, this isn't a holiday resort. Books—*polnische, Juden.*‡

In the evening, the division commander in his new jacket, well fed, wearing his multicolored trousers, red-faced and dim-witted, out to have some fun, music at night, the rain disperses us. It is rain-

---

* Now demoted to the rank of squadron commander.
† German: "a vehement nationalist."
** Manuilov was the divisional chief of staff's adjutant, and Sheko, his boss, was the divisional chief of staff.
‡ German: "Polish ones, Jews."

ing, the tormenting Galician rain, it pours and pours, endlessly, hopelessly.

What are our soldiers up to in this town? Dark rumors.

Boguslavsky has betrayed Manuilov. Boguslavsky is a slave.

AUGUST 26, 1920. SOKAL

A look around town with the young Zionist. The synagogues: the Hasidic one is a staggering sight, it recalls three hundred years ago, pale, handsome boys with *peyes,* the synagogue as it was two hundred years ago, the selfsame figures in long coats, rocking, waving their hands, howling. This is the Orthodox party, they support the Rabbi of Belz, the famous Rabbi of Belz, who's made off to Vienna. The moderates support the Rabbi of Husyatin. Their synagogue. The beauty of the altar made by some artisan, the magnificence of the greenish chandeliers, the worm-eaten little tables, the Belz synagogue—a vision of ancient times. The Jews ask me to use my influence so they won't be ruined, they're being robbed of food and goods.

The Yids hide everything. The cobbler, the Sokal cobbler, is a proletarian. His apprentice's appearance, a red-haired Hasid—a cobbler.

The cobbler has been waiting for Soviet rule—now he sees the Yid-killers and the looters, and that there'll be no earnings, he is shaken, and looks at us with distrust. A hullabaloo over money. In essence, we're not paying anything, 15–20 rubles. The Jewish quarter. Indescribable poverty, dirt, the boxed-in quality of the ghetto.

The little stores, all of them open, whiting and resin, soldiers ransacking, swearing at the Yids, drifting around aimlessly, entering homes, crawling under counters, greedy eyes, trembling hands, a strange army indeed.

The organized looting of the stationery store, the owner in tears, they tear up everything, they come up with all kinds of demands, the daughter with Western European self-possession, but pitiful and red-faced, hands things over, is given some money or other, and with her storekeeper's politeness tries to act as if everything were as it should be, except that there are too many customers. The owner's wife is so full of despair that she cannot make head or tail of anything.

At night the town will be looted—everyone knows that.

Music in the evening—the division commander is out to have some fun. In the morning he wrote some letters to Stavropol and the Don. The front will not tolerate the disgraceful goings-on in the rear lines. The same old story.

The division commander's lackeys lead his magnificent horses with their breastplates and cruppers back and forth.

The military commissar and the nurse. A Russian man—a sly muzhik—coarse and sometimes insolent and confused. Has a high opinion of the nurse, sounds me out, asks me all kinds of questions, he is in love.

The nurse goes to say good-bye to the division commander, and this after everything that's happened. Everyone's slept with her. That boor Suslov is in the adjoining room—the division commander is busy, he's cleaning his revolver.

I'm given boots and underwear. Sukhorukov received them and dealt them out himself, he's a super-lackey, describe him.

A chat with the nephew who wants to go to university.

Sokal: brokers and artisans—Communism, they tell me, isn't likely to strike root here.

What battered, tormented people these are.

Poor Galicia, poor Jews.

My landlord has eight doves.

Manuilov has a sharp confrontation with Sheko, he has many sins in his past. A Kiev adventurer. He came to us demoted from having been chief of staff of the Third Brigade.

Lepin. A dark, terrifying soul.

The nurse—twenty-six men and one woman.*

AUGUST 27, 1920

Skirmishes near Znyatin, Dluzhnov. We ride northwest. Half the day with the transport carts. Heading to Laszczow, Komarow. In the morning we set off from Sokal. A regular day with the squadrons: we wander through forests and glades with the division commander, the brigade commanders come, sun, for five hours I haven't gotten off my

* A reference to Maxim Gorky's story, "Twenty-six Men and One Woman."

horse, brigades ride past. Transport cart panic. I left the carts at a clearing in the forest, rode over to the division commander. The squadrons on a hill. Reports to the army commander, a cannonade, there are no airplanes, we ride from one place to another, a regular day. Heavy exhaustion toward evening, we spend the night in Wasylow. We didn't reach Laszczow, our target destination.

The Eleventh Division is in Wasylow or somewhere near there, pandemonium, Bakhturov*—a tiny division, he has lost some of his sparkle. The Fourth Division is mounting successful battles.

AUGUST 28, 1920. KOMAROW

I rode off from Wasylow ten minutes after the squadrons. I am riding with three horsemen. Earth mounds, glades, destroyed farms, somewhere in the greenery are the Red Columns, plums. Gunfire, we don't know where the enemy is, we can't see anybody, machine guns are hammering quite near and from different directions, my heart tenses, and so every day single horsemen are out looking for their field headquarters, they are carrying reports. Toward noon I found my squadron in a ravaged village with all the villagers hiding in their cellars, under trees covered in plums. I ride with the squadrons. I ride into Komarow with the division commander, red hood. A magnificent, unfinished, red church. Before we entered Komarow, after the gunfire (I was riding alone), silence, warm, a bright day, a somewhat strange and translucent calm, my soul ached, all alone, nobody getting on my nerves, fields, forests, undulating valleys, shady roads.

We stop opposite the church.

The arrival of Voroshilov and Budyonny. Voroshilov blows up in front of everyone: "Lack of energy!" He gets heated, a heated individual, the whole army restless, he rides and yells, Budyonny is silent, smiles, white teeth. Apanasenko defends himself: "Let's go inside"— "Why do we keep letting the enemy get away?" Voroshilov shouts. "Without contact you can't strike."

Is Apanasenko worthless?

---

* Pavel Vasilevich Bakhturov, the former military commissar of the Sixth Cavalry Division, had become the military commissar of the Eleventh Division on August 8.

The pharmacist who offers me a room. Rumors of atrocities. I go into the shtetl. Indescribable fear and desperation.

They tell me what happened. Hiding in a hut, they are frightened that the Poles will return. Last night Captain Yakovlev's* Cossacks were here. A pogrom. The family of David Zis, in their home, the old prophet, naked and barely breathing, the butchered old woman, a child with chopped-off fingers. Many of these people are still breathing, the stench of blood, everything turned topsy-turvy, chaos, a mother over her butchered son, an old woman curled up, four people in one hut, dirt, blood under a black beard, they're just lying there in their blood. Jews in the town square, the tormented Jew who shows me everything, a tall Jew takes his place. The rabbi has gone into hiding, everything has been smashed to pieces in his house, he doesn't leave his burrow until evening. Fifteen people have been killed: Hasid Itska Galer, 70 years old, David Zis, synagogue *shamas*, 45 years old, his wife and his daughter, 15 years old, David Trost, his wife, the butcher.

At the house of a raped woman.

Evening—at my landlord's, a conventional home, Sabbath evening, they didn't want to cook until the Sabbath was over.

I look for the nurses, Suslov laughs. A Jewish woman doctor.

We are in a strange, old-fashioned house, they used to have everything here—butter, milk.

At night, a walk through the shtetl.

The moon, their lives at night behind closed doors. Wailing inside. They will clean everything up. The fear and horror of the townsfolk. The main thing: our men are going around indifferently, looting where they can, ripping the clothes off the butchered people.

The hatred for them is the same, they too are Cossacks, they too are savage, it's pure nonsense that our army is any different. The life of the shtetls. There is no escape. Everyone is out to destroy them, the Poles did not give them refuge. All the women and girls can scarcely walk. In the evening a talkative Jew with a little beard, he had a store, his daughter threw herself out of a second-floor window, she broke both arms, there are many like that.

What a powerful and magnificent life of a nation existed here. The

---

* A Cossack captain fighting on the Polish side.

fate of the Jewry. At our place in the evening, supper, tea, I sit drinking in the words of the Jew with the little beard who asks me plaintively if it will be possible to trade again.

An oppressive, restless night.

AUGUST 29, 1920. KOMAROW, LABUNYE, PNEVSK

We pull out of Komarow. During the night our men looted, in the synagogue they threw away the Torah scrolls and took the velvet coverings for their saddles. The military commissar's orderly eyes the phylacteries, wants to take the straps. The Jews smile obsequiously. That is religion.

Everyone is greedily looking at what hasn't yet been taken. They rummage through bones and ruins. They've come here to make some money.

My horse is limping, I take the divisional chief of staff's horse, want to trade, I am too soft, a talk with the village elder, nothing comes of it.

Labunye. A vodka distillery. A hundred thousand liters of spirits. Under guard. Rain, penetrating and incessant. Autumn, everything points to autumn. The Polish family of the bailiff. The horses under a canopy, the Red Army fighters drinking in spite of the prohibition. Labunye is a threatening peril for the army.

Everything is secretive and simple. The people are silent, as if nothing out of the ordinary were going on. Oh, you Russians! Everything breathes secrecy and menace. Sidorenko has calmed down.

The operation to take Zamosc. We are ten versts from Zamosc. There I will ask about R.Y.

The operation, as always, is uncomplicated. Bypass via the west and the north, and then take the town. Alarming news from the Western Front.* The Poles have taken Bialystok.

We ride on. The looted estates of Kulaczkowski near Labunki. White columns. An enchanting, even if manorial, setup. The destruction is beyond belief. The real Poland: bailiffs, old women, white-blond children, rich, semi-European villages with elders, local headmen, all

* The central Red Army command of western and northwestern strategic points in Soviet Russia.

Catholic, beautiful women. Our men are dragging away oats on the estate. The horses stand in the drawing room, black horses. Well—after all, we do have to keep them out of the rain. Extremely precious books in a chest, they didn't have time to take them along: the constitution approved by the Sejm* at the beginning of the eighteenth century, old folios from the times of Nicholas I, the Polish code of laws, precious bindings, Polish manuscripts of the sixteenth century, the writings of monks, old French novels.

There is no destruction upstairs, it was merely searched, all the chairs, walls, sofas have been slashed open, the floors ripped up—not destroyed, just searched. Delicate crystal, the bedroom, the oak beds, powder case, French novels on the tables, many French and Polish books about child care, smashed intimate feminine toiletries, remnants of butter in a butter dish, newlyweds?

A settled way of life, gymnastic equipment, good books, tables, bottles of medicine—everything sacrilegiously besmirched. An unbearable feeling of wanting to run away from the vandals, but they walk about, search, describe how they walk, their faces, hats, their cursing: Goddamn, f—ing Mother of God, the Holy Virgin. They drag sheaves of oats through the impassable mud.

We near Zamosc. A terrible day. The rain is the victor, not letting up even for a minute. The horses can barely pull the carts. Describe this unendurable rain. We wander deep into the night. We are soaked to the bone, tired, Apanasenko's red hood. We bypass Zamosc, the units are three to four versts away from it. The armored trains won't let us pass, they shower us with artillery fire. We stay in the fields, wait for reports, dull rivulets flow. Brigade Commander Kniga in a hut, a report. Our fatherly commander. We cannot do a thing against the armored train. It turns out we didn't know that there was a railroad here, it's not marked on the map, a mix-up, so much for our reconnaissance.

We roam around and keep waiting for them to take Zamosc. Damn it to hell. The Poles keep fighting better and better. Horses and men are shivering. We spend the night in Pnevsk. A fine Polish peasant family. The difference between Poles and Russians is striking. The Poles live more cleanly, cheerfully, play with their children, beautiful icons, beautiful women.

---

* The Polish Parliament.

AUGUST 30, 1920

In the morning we leave Pnevsk. The operation to take Zamosc continues. The weather is as bad as before, rain, slush, impassible roads, we barely slept: on the floor, in the straw, wearing our boots—on constant alert.

Again roaming around. We go with Sheko to the Third Brigade. He goes with his revolver drawn to attack the Zavadi Train Station. Lepin and I stay in the forest. Lepin is squirming. The skirmish at the station. Sheko has a doomed look on his face. Describe the "rapid fire." The station has been taken. We ride along the railroad tracks. Ten prisoners, one of them we arrive too late to save.* A revolver wound? An officer. Blood is flowing out of his mouth. Thick, red, clotting blood is drenching his whole face, it looks terrible, red, covered in his thick blood. The prisoners are all undressed. Trousers have been slung over the squadron leader's saddle. Sheko makes him give them back. They try to make the prisoners put on their clothes, but they won't put anything on. An officer's cap. "And then there were nine." Foul words all around. They want to kill the prisoners. A bald, lame Jew in his drawers who can't keep up with the horse, a terrible face, an officer no doubt, gets on everyone's nerves, he can't walk, they are all in the grip of animal fear, pitiful, unfortunate people, Polish proletarians, one of the Poles is stately, calm, with sideburns, wearing a knitted jersey, he comports himself with dignity, everyone keeps asking if he's an officer. They want to butcher them. A dark cloud gathers over the Jew. A frenzied Putilov worker—They should all be butchered, the scum—the Jew is hopping after us, we always drag prisoners along, and then hand them over to the authorities of the military escort. What happens to them. The rage of the Putilov worker, foaming at the mouth, his saber: I will butcher the scum and won't have to answer for it.

We ride over to the division commander, he is with the First and Second Brigades. We are always within sight of Zamosc, we can see its chimneys, houses, we are trying to take it from all sides. A night attack

---

* See the stories "And Then There Were Nine" and "And Then There Were Ten," in which the Cossacks capture Polish prisoners at the Zavadi Station. Babel and Lepin arrive too late to stop the Cossacks from murdering one of the prisoners.

is in preparation. We are three versts from Zamosc, are waiting for the town to be seized, will spend the night there. Field, night, rain, penetrating cold, we are lying on the wet earth, there's nothing to feed the horses with, it's dark, men ride with messages. The First and the Third Brigades will lead the attack. Kniga and Levda*—a semiliterate Ukrainian who is commander of the Third Brigade—arrive the way they always do. Tiredness, apathy, the unquenchable thirst for sleep, almost desperation. A line advances briskly in the dark, a whole brigade on foot. Next to us a cannon. An hour later the infantry advances. Our cannon is firing continuously, a soft, cracking sound, flames in the night, the Poles are firing rockets, crazed shooting from rifles and machine guns, this is hell, we wait, it's three in the morning. The battle ebbs. Nothing came of it. For us more and more often now things come to nothing. What does this mean? Is the army giving up?

We ride ten versts to Sitaniec to lodge for the night. The rain is getting stronger. An indescribable fatigue. My one and only dream—a billet. My dream becomes a reality. A dismayed old Pole with his wife. The soldiers, needless to say, clean him out. Extreme fear, they've all been hiding in cellars. Heaps of noodles, butter, milk, bliss. I keep unearthing more and more food. A tortured, nice old woman. Delightful melted butter. Suddenly gunfire, bullets whistling about the stables, about the horses' legs. We up and run. Despair. We ride to the other end of the village. Three hours of sleep interrupted by reports, debriefings, anxiety.

AUGUST 31, 1920. CZESNIKI

A meeting with the brigade commanders. A farm. A shady glade. The destruction total. Not even any clothes left. We clean out the last of the oats. An orchard, an apiary, the destruction of the hives, terrible, the bees buzz around in desperation, the hives are detonated with gunpowder, the men wrap themselves in their greatcoats and launch an attack on the hives, a bacchanalia, they drag out the frames with their sabers, the honey streams onto the ground, the bees sting, they are

---

* Kniga was the commander of the First Brigade of the Sixth Cavalry Division, and Levda was commander of the Third Brigade of the Fourteenth Cavalry Division.

smoked out with tarred rags, burning rags. Cherkashin.* In the apiary there is chaos and complete destruction, smoke rises from the ruins.

I am writing in the garden, a glade, flowers, I feel sorrow for all this.

The military order to leave Zamosc, to go to the rescue of the Fourteenth Division, which is being forced back from Komarow. The shtetl has again been taken by the Poles. Poor Komarow. We ride along the flanks and the brigades. Before us, the enemy cavalry—nothing to hold us back, whom should we butcher if not the Cossacks of Captain Yakovlev.† An attack is imminent. The brigades are gathering in the forest—two versts from Czesniki.

Voroshilov and Budyonny are with us all the time. Voroshilov, short, graying, in red trousers with silver stripes, always goading, getting on everyone's nerves, keeps hounding Apanasenko about why the Second Brigade hasn't arrived. We are waiting for the arrival of the Second Brigade. Time is dragging with torturing slowness. Do not rush me, Comrade Voroshilov. Voroshilov: Everything is ruined, f— it to hell.

Budyonny is silent, at times he smiles, showing his dazzling white teeth. We must send the brigade first, and then the regiment. Voroshilov's patience snaps, he sends everyone he has into the attack. The regiment marches past Voroshilov and Budyonny. Voroshilov pulls out his enormous revolver, show the Polish *Pans* no mercy, his cry is met with joy. The regiment flies off helter-skelter, hurrah, go for it, some gallop off, others hold back, others again move in a trot, the horses balk, bowler hats and carpets.** Our squadron launches an attack. We gallop about four versts. They are waiting for us in columns on the hill. Amazing: none of them so much as move. Sangfroid, discipline. An officer with a black beard. I'm being shot at. My sensations. Flight. The military commissars turn. Nothing helps. Luckily, the enemy doesn't pursue us, otherwise we would have had a catastrophe on our hands. We try to gather a brigade together for a second attack, nothing comes of it. Manuilov is threatened with revolvers. The nurses are the heroines.

---

* An orderly at the Sixth Cavalry Division headquarters.
† The Cossack captain fighting on the Polish side.
** Babel is referring to the colorful attire of the Cossacks, some of whom are wearing bowler hats and clothes cut out of carpets, and have draped carpets looted from houses over their saddles.

We ride back. Sheko's* horse is wounded, Sheko has a concussion, his terrible, rigid face. He doesn't understand what is happening, he is crying, we lead his mare. She is bleeding.

The nurse's story: there are nurses who are only out for sympathy, we help the fighters, go through thick and thin with them, I would shoot, but what can I shoot with, a f—ing dick, I don't even have that.

The command staff is crushed, menacing signs of our army's disintegration. Cheerful, foolish Vorobyov† recounts his heroic feats, he went galloping up, four shots point-blank. Apanasenko suddenly turns around: You ruined the attack, you bastard.

Apanasenko in a black mood, Sheko pitiful.

There is talk about how the army isn't in the shape it used to be, it's high time for a rest. What next? We spend the night in Czesniki, we are frozen through, tired, silent—impassable, all-engulfing mud, autumn, destroyed roads, dejection. Before us somber prospects.

SEPTEMBER 1, 1920. TEREBIN

We set out from Czesniki in the night. We stopped there for two hours. Night, cold, on our horses. We are shivering. The military order to retreat, we are surrounded, we have lost contact with the Twelfth Army,** we don't have contact with anybody. Sheko is crying, his head shaking, his face that of a hurt child, he is pitiful, crushed. What bastards people are. Vinokurov‡ wouldn't give him the military order to read—he is not on active duty. Apanasenko gives him his carriage, but I'm not their driver.

Endless conversations about yesterday's attack, lies, sincere regrets, the fighters are silent. That idiot Vorobyov keeps shooting his mouth off. The division commander cuts him off.

The beginning of the end of the First Cavalry Army. Rumors of retreat.

Sheko is a man deep in misfortune.

---

* The chief of staff of the Sixth Cavalry Division.
† Commander of the Second Squadron of the Sixth Cavalry Division.
** The infantry, the main force in the Russian-Polish campaign.
‡ The military commissar of the Sixth Cavalry Division.

Manuilov has a temperature of 40°C, fever, everyone hates him, Sheko harasses him, why? He doesn't know how to comport himself. Borisov, the orderly, cunning, ingratiating, secretive, no one has any pity for him, that's what's dreadful. A Jew?

The Fourth Division saves the army. And that with Timoshenko— the traitor.*

We arrive in Terebin, a half-destroyed village, cold. It's autumn, during the day I sleep in the threshing shed, at night together with Sheko.

My talk with Arzam Slyagit. Riding next to me. We spoke about Tiflis, fruit, sun. I think about Odessa, my soul is torn.

We are dragging Sheko's bleeding horse behind us.

SEPTEMBER 2, 1920. TEREBIN—METELIN

Pitiful villages. Unfinished huts. Half-naked villagers. We ruin them once and for all. The division commander is with the troops. The military order: delay the enemy's advance on the Bug, attack in the area of Wakijow-Hostyne. We fight but without success. Rumors about the weakening of the army's fighting efficiency are becoming more persistent. Desertion. Masses of reports of men going on leave, illness.

The main illness of the division is the absence of command staff, all the commanders are from the ranks, Apanasenko hates the democrats,[†] they don't understand a thing, there's no one who can lead a regiment into an attack.

Squadron commanders are leading regiments.

Days of apathy, Sheko is recovering, he is depressed. Life is tough in the atmosphere of an army whose side has split open.

SEPTEMBER 3, 4, 5, 1920. MALICE

We have moved on to Malice.

Orlov is the new chief of staff's adjutant. A figure from Gogol. A

---

* An ironic comment. After Timoshenko had been relieved of his command of the Sixth Cavalry Division on August 5, 1920, he became the division commander (August 25) of the Fourth Cavalry Division. He was awarded his second Red Flag Medal for his leadership in the Battle for Zamosc.

† Russian Social Democratic Workers Party, of which there was a Leninist and a non-Leninist wing.

pathological liar, his tongue always wagging, a Jewish face, the main thing: the terrifying ease, when you think about it, with which he talks, chatters, lies, he's in pain (he limps), a partisan, a Makhno* fighter, he went to high school, commanded a regiment. His ease frightens me, what is behind it.

Finally Manuilov has fled, and not without scandal—he was threatened with arrest, how addle-brained Sheko is, they had sent him to the First Brigade, sheer idiocy, Army headquarters sent him to the air force. Amen.

I'm billeted with Sheko. Dull, amiable if you know how to stay on his good side, inept, does not have a strong will. I grovel—and so I get to eat. Boguslavsky, languid, half Odessan, dreams of "Odessan girls," from time to time will ride out at night to collect an army order.

The First Platoon of the First Squadron. Kuban Cossacks. They sing songs. Staid. They smile. They're not rowdy.

Levda† reported sick. A cunning Ukrainian. "I have rheumatism. I am too weak to work." Three report sick from the brigades, they're in cahoots. If we're not given any leave, the division will go under, there's no ardor, the horses won't go on, the men are impassive, the Third Brigade, two days in the field, cold, rain.

A sad country, impassable mud, no muzhiks to be seen anywhere, they hide their horses in the forests, women sobbing quietly.

A report from Kniga: Unable to execute my duties without a command staff.

All the horses are in the forests, the Red Army fighters exchange them, a science, a sport.

Barsukov is falling apart. He wants to go to school.

There are skirmishes. Our side is trying to advance on Wakijow-Honiatycki. Nothing comes of it. A strange weakness.

The Pole is slowly but surely pushing us back. The division commander is useless, he has neither the initiative nor the necessary tenacity. His purulent ambition, philandering, gluttony, and probably feverish activity should it be needed.

Our way of life.

---

* The Ukrainian anarchist leader.
† Commander of the Third Brigade of the Fourteenth Cavalry Division.

Kniga writes: The previous ardor no longer exists, the fighters are dragging their feet.

Dispiriting weather all the time, destroyed roads, terrible Russian village mud in which your boots get stuck, there is no sun, it is raining, gloomy, what a cursed land.

I am ill, angina, fever, I can barely move, terrible nights in stifling, smoke-filled huts in the straw, my whole body torn to pieces, flea-bitten, itching, bleeding, there's nothing I can do.

Our operations continue sluggishly, a period of equilibrium in which, however, the ascendancy is beginning to shift to the Poles.

The command staff is passive, doesn't even exist anymore.

I rush over to the nurse to pick up bandages, I have to go through kitchen gardens, impassable mud. The nurse is staying with a platoon. A heroine, even though she copulates with many. A hut, everyone smoking, cursing, changing foot wrappings, a soldier's life, and another person, the nurse. Anyone too squeamish to drink from the same mug as the rest gets thrown out.

The enemy advances. We took Lot, have to give it up again, the enemy pushes us back, not a single attack of ours has brought results, we send off the transport carts, I ride to Terebin on Barsukov's cart, from there on rain, slush, misery, we cross the Bug, Budyatichi. So—it has been decided to relinquish the Bug line.

SEPTEMBER 6, 1920. BUDYATICHI

Budyatichi is occupied by the Forty-fourth Division. Clashes. They are startled by our division pouring in like a wild horde. Orlov:* Hand this place over to us and get out!

The nurse—a proud woman, pretty and somewhat dim-witted—is in tears, the doctor is outraged at the shouts of "Down with the Yids, save Russia!" They are stunned, the quartermaster was thrashed with a whip, the field hospital demolished, pigs are requisitioned and dragged off without receipts or anything, and before everything had been well ordered, all sorts of representatives go to see Sheko to complain. There you have the Budyonny fighters.

---

* The adjutant of the chief of staff of the Sixth Cavalry Division.

The proud nurse, a kind we've never seen before, in white shoes and stockings, a full, shapely leg, they have things nicely organized, respect for human dignity, quick, thorough work.

We are billeted with Jews.

My thoughts of home are becoming increasingly persistent. I see no way out.

SEPTEMBER 7, 1920. BUDYATICHI

We are occupying two rooms. The kitchen is full of Jews. There are refugees from Krylow, a pitiful little bunch of people with the faces of prophets. They sleep side by side. All day long they are boiling and baking, the Jewess works like a slave, sewing, laundering. They pray there too. Children, young girls. The damn bastards, the lackeys, they are continually stuffing themselves, drinking vodka, guffawing, growing fat, hiccuping with lust for women.

We eat every two hours.

A unit is placed on the opposite shore of the Bug, a new phase in the operation.

It's been two weeks now that everyone's been saying more and more doggedly that the army has to be pulled out for a rest. A rest!— our new battle cry.

A delegation turns up, the division commander entertains them, they're constantly eating, his stories about Stavropol, Suslov is growing fatter, the bastard has gotten himself a good deal.

Terrible tactlessness: Sheko, Suslov, Sukhorukov have been put up for a Red Flag Medal.

The enemy is trying to cross over to our side of the Bug, the Fourteenth Division acted quickly and pushed them back.

I am issuing certificates.

I've gone deaf in one ear. The result of my cold? My body is all scratched up, cuts everywhere, I don't feel well. Autumn, rain, everything is depressing, deep mud.

SEPTEMBER 8, 1920. VLADIMIR-VOLYNSK

In the morning I head to the administrative headquarters on a civilian cart. I have to testify, some song and dance about money. Some demi-rearguard sordidness: Gusev, Nalyotov, money at the Revolutionary Tribunal. Lunch with Gorbunov.

Off to Vladimir with the same nags. An arduous ride, insurmountable mud, the roads impassable. We arrive at night. A squabble about the billet, a cold room in a widow's house. Jews—storekeepers. Mama and Papa are old.

Poor Grandma. The gentle, black-bearded husband. The redheaded, pregnant Jewess is washing her feet. The girl has diarrhea. It is cramped, but there is electricity, it's warm.

For supper there are dumplings with sunflower oil—pure bliss. There you have it: Jewish abundance. They think I don't understand Yiddish, they are as cunning as flies. The town is destitute.

Borodin* and I sleep on a featherbed.

SEPTEMBER 9, 1920. VLADIMIR-VOLYNSK

The town is destitute, dirty, hungry, you can't buy anything with money, sweets cost twenty rubles and cigarettes. Dejection. Army headquarters. Gloomy. A council of trade unions, young Jews. I go to the economic councils and the trade unions, dejection, the military members make demands, act like louts. Sickly young Jews.

Magnificent meal—meat, kasha. Our only pleasure is food.

The new military commissar at headquarters—a monkey's face.

My landlord wants to barter for my shawl. I'm not going to let him hoodwink me.

My driver, barefoot with bleary eyes. *Oy* Russia!†

A synagogue. I pray, bare walls, some soldier or other is swiping the electric light bulbs.

The bathhouse. A curse on soldiering, war, the cramming together of young, tormented, still-healthy people gone crazy.

The home life of my landlord and his wife, they are taking care of a few things, tomorrow is Friday, they are already preparing themselves, the old woman is good, the old man a little underhanded, they are only pretending to be poor. They say: Better to starve under the Bolsheviks than to eat fancy bread under the Poles.

---

* An orderly at the headquarters of the Sixth Cavalry Division.
† Babel uses "Rasseya," an archaic folksy name for Russia.

SEPTEMBER 10, 1920. KOVEL

Half the day in the shattered, doleful, terrible train station in Vladimir-Volynsk. Dejection. The black-bearded Jew is working. We arrive in Kovel at night. Unexpected joy: The Polit-otdel train.* Supper with Zdanevich,† butter. I spend the night in the radio station. Blinding light. A miracle. Khelemskaya is having an affair. Lymph glands. Volodya. She took off all her clothes. My prophecy came true.

SEPTEMBER 11, 1920. KOVEL

The town has kept traces of European-Jewish culture. They won't accept Soviet money, a glass of coffee without sugar: fifty rubles. A disgusting meal at the train station: 600 rubles.

Sun, I go from doctor to doctor, have my ear treated, itching.

I visit Yakovlev,** quiet little houses, meadows, Jewish alleys, a quiet hearty life, Jewish girls, youths, old men at the synagogues, perhaps wigs. Soviet power does not seem to have ruffled the surface, these quarters are across the bridge.

Dirt and hunger in the train. Everyone's emaciated, louse-ridden, with sallow faces, they all hate one another, sit locked up in their cubicles, even the cook is emaciated. A striking change. They are living in a cage. Khelemskaya, dirty, puttering about in the kitchen, her connection to the kitchen, she feeds Volodya, a Jewish wife "from a good home."

All day I look for food.

The district in which the Twelfth Army is located. Luxurious establishments: clubs, gramophones, conscientious Red Army fighters, cheerful, life is bubbling up, the newspapers of the Twelfth Army, Central Military News Service, Army Commander Kuzmin‡ who writes articles. As far as work goes, the Polit-otdel seems to be doing well.

---

* A train for the ideological education of the troops, equipped with a printing press and radio station.

† V. Zdanevich, the editor-in-chief of the Red Cavalry newspaper *Krasny Kavalerist*, for which Babel wrote articles. See "Dispatch Office, Shape Up!"

** The political commissar of the Sixth Cavalry Division.

‡ Nikolai Nikolayevich Kuzmin was the provisional commander of the Twelfth Army from August to November 1920.

The life of the Jews, crowds in the streets, the main street is Lutskaya Street, I walk around on my shattered feet, I drink an incredible amount of tea and coffee. Ice cream: 500 rubles. They have no shame. Sabbath, all the stores are closed. Medicine: five rubles.

I spend the night at the radio station. Blinding light, sassy radio-telegraphers, one of them is struggling to play a mandolin. Both read avidly.

SEPTEMBER 12, 1920. KIVERTSY

In the morning, panic at the train station. Artillery fire. The Poles are in town. Unimaginably pitiful flight, carts in five rows, the pitiful, dirty, gasping infantry, cavemen, they run over meadows, throw away their rifles, Borodin the orderly already sees the butchering Poles. The train moves out quickly, soldiers and carts come dashing, the wounded, their faces contorted, jump up into our train cars, a gasping political worker, his pants have fallen down, a Jew with a thin, translucent face, possibly a cunning Jew, deserters with broken arms jump on, sick men from the field hospital.

The institution that calls itself the Twelfth Army. For every fighter there are four rear-line men, two ladies, two trunks filled with things—and even the actual fighter doesn't fight. The Twelfth Army is ruining the front and the Red Cavalry, it exposes our flanks and then sends us to stop up those holes with ourselves. One of their units, the Urals Regiment or the Bashkir Brigade, surrendered, leaving the front open. Disgraceful panic, the army is unfit for combat. The soldier types: The Russian Red Army infantryman is barefoot, not only not modernized, but the embodiment of "wretched Russia," hungry and squat muzhiks, tramps, bloated, louse-ridden.

At Goloby all the sick, the wounded, and the deserters are thrown off the train. Rumors, and then facts: the Provision Unit of the First Cavalry sent into the cul-de-sac of Vladimir-Volynsk has been captured by the enemy, our headquarters has moved to Lutsk, a mass of fighters and equipment of the Twelfth Army has been captured, the army is fleeing.

In the evening we arrive in Kivertsy.

Life in the railway car is hard. The radio-telegraphers keep plotting to get rid of me, one of them still has an upset stomach, he plays the mandolin, the other keeps taunting him because he is an idiot.

Life in the railway car, dirty, malicious, hungry, animosity toward one another, unhealthy. Moscow women smoking, eating like pigs, faceless, many pitiful people, coughing Muscovites, everyone wants to eat, everyone is angry, everyone has an upset stomach.

SEPTEMBER 13, 1920. KIVERTSY

A bright morning, the forest. The Jewish New Year. Hungry. I go into the shtetl. Boys wearing white collars. Ishas Khakl offers me bread and butter. She earns her money "herself," a hardy woman, a silk dress, she has tidied up the house. I am moved to tears, here the only thing that helped was talking things through, we spoke for a long time, her husband is in America, a shrewd, unhurried Jewess.

A long stop at the station. Dejection, like before. We get books from the club, we read avidly.

SEPTEMBER 14, 1920. KLEVAN

We stop in Klevan for a day and a night, the whole time at the station. Hunger, dejection. The town of Rovno won't allow us passage. A railroad worker. We bake shortbread and potatoes at his place. A railroad watchman. They eat, say kind things, don't give us anything. I am with Borodin, his light gait. All day long we look for food, from one watchman to the next. I spend the night in the radio station in the blinding light.

SEPTEMBER 15, 1920. KLEVAN

The third day of our agonizing stop in Klevan begins, the same hunt for food, in the morning we had a lot of tea with shortbread. In the evening I rode to Rovno on a cart of the First Cavalry's Air Force Department. A conversation about our air force, it doesn't exist, all the machines are broken, the pilots don't know how to fly, the planes are old, patched up, completely worthless. The Red Army fighter with a swollen throat—quite a type. He can barely speak, his throat must be completely blocked, inflamed, sticks in his fingers to scrape away the film in his gullet, they told him salt might help, he pours salt down his throat, he hasn't eaten for four days, he drinks cold water because nobody will give him hot. His talk is garbled, about the attack, about the commander, about the fact that they were barefoot, some advanced, others didn't, he beckons with his finger.

Supper at Gasnikova's.

VII

❖

Sketches for the Red Cavalry Stories

The notebooks that Isaac Babel kept while he worked as a war correspondent in the Russian-Polish Campaign of 1920 are the most significant documentation of his writing process. They are terse, quick jottings
of incidents and impressions that he wished to use and develop, first in his
diary and later in the RED CAVALRY stories. Like his diary, his drafts and
sketches are reminders of how he wished to present incidents: "Very simple, A
FACTUAL ACCOUNT, no superfluous descriptions. . . . Pay no attention to
continuity in the story." Babel was very interested in keeping an accurate
account of specific details, such as an individual's military rank or the dates
and tactical implications of incidents—so much so, that he made the dangerous choice of threading real figures and incidents into his stories, not
always showing them in a favorable light. Commander Budyonny was to
become Marshal of the Soviet Union, Voroshilov was Stalin's right-hand
man, and Timoshenko became a Marshal of the Soviet Union and
Commissar of Defense.

As becomes clear from these jottings, Babel's ultimate aim in the stories
he intended to write about the Polish Campaign was literary effect. As he

experienced these events, he was already arranging them as they were to appear, first in his diary, and later in finished prose: "THE SEQUENCE: *Jews. Airplane. Grave. Timoshenko. The letter. Trunov's burial, the salute.*"

The battle near Br[ody]

Pil[sudski's] pro[clamations] 2.

Killed, butchered men, sun, wheat, military booklets, Bible pages. Pilsudski's proclamation?

The battle near Br[ody]

No discussions.—Painstaking choice of words.—Konkin— proverbs: If the Lord does not decree, the bladder will not burst.—His beard is that of Abraham, his deeds are those of an evil man—we're covered in vice like yard dogs with lice.—Gnats will chew at you till their dying breath.—To save his own goods and chattels a man will gladly set fire to another man's hide.

The battle near Br[ody]

1. Decamp from Bielavtsy. The battle by Brody.—I bandage men.— Description of the battle.—Korotchayev.* The death of a wounded man in my arms. Radzivillov. Ivan shoots a horse, the horseman runs away.—On the bridge.—It's a pity about the buttermilk.
2. Departure from Brody. An untouched steam contraption. Farm. I go to answer the call of nature . . . A corpse. A sparkling day. The place is littered with corpses, completely unnoticeable in the rye. Pilsudski's proclamations. Battle, butchery in silence.—The division comman- der.—I move away. Why? I don't have the strength to bear this.
3. Going around in circles. First I went to . . . [written over: Konkin]. Konyushkovo.—The nurse.
4. Radzivillov.

The battle near Br[ody]

1. On the Radzivillov high road. Battle. In Radzivillov. Night. The movement of the horses is the main thing.

---

* A brigade commander of the Sixth Cavalry Division who had been demoted after his provi- sionary tenure as commander of the Fourth Cavalry Division.

2. Night in Brody. The synagogue is next door.
3. (Briefly). Departure from Brody. A corpse. A field littered with corpses. Pilsudski's proclamations. Battle. Kolesnikov and Grishin. I go away.—The wounded platoon commander. A special insert.
4. Konkin. We're going around in circles.—Anti-Semites.
5. The nurse. Night. Desperation. Dawn.
   The length of the episodes—half a page each.
   Battle.
1. Wounded men in the *tachanka*. The heroism of the Cossack. I will shoot him. The death of the wounded man.
2. Night, horses are moving.
3. Brody. Next door.
4. Departure from Brody. Corpses. Pilsudski's proclamations. The battle begins. Kolesnikov and Grishin. The beginning of wandering in circles.
5. Lyovka.
6. Konkin.
7. The nurse.

The battle near Brody II

On Ivan's *tachanka*. Wounded men. Lyovka? Brody or Radzivillov. Buttermilk manqué.

The battle by Klyokotovo. Budyonny with his staff. Got cut off from my unit. Roaming about with the Fourth Division.—The nurse.

The end of the battle. A new division commander* with his retinue. K.K.† in Radzivillov.

Lyovka.

Short chapters?
1. On Ivan's *tachanka*. Death.—Describe the wounded.—Budyonny. Kolesnikov. Grishin.—Roaming about in circles. [. . .]

---

* Iosif Rodionovich Apanasenko took over as commander of the Sixth Cavalry Division on August 5, 1920, from Semyon Konstantinovich Timoshenko.
† Konstantin Karlovich Zholnarkevich was the chief of staff of the Sixth Cavalry Division until August 5, 1920, during the period when Timoshenko was the division commander.

Immediately a description of the battle—dust, sun, details, a picture of a Budyonny battle.—Specifics—the killing of the officer, and so on.—After that we are on our *tachanka,* dead men.—Brody or Radzivillov.

II. The field. Waiting to move to our night camp. The nurse.—The horses are pulling the men.

1. Decamp from Belavtsy. The battle near Brody. On Ivan's *tachanka.*
2. Radzivillov.
3. Entry into Brody. The field by Klyokotovo. A farm. A field sown with corpses. Pilsudski's declarations.—A meeting with the division commander.
4. The battle by Klyokotovo.—Konkin.—The death of the Polish general.
5. Roaming around in circles with the Fourth Division. Night in the field.—The Jewish nurse.
6. In Radzivillov. K.K. [Zholnarkevich]. Sheko.

August 3. The battle near B[rody]. The battle near Brody. My roaming around.

1. The Jewish nurse. What does this mean? I sleep in the field tying the stirrup to my foot. I want to kill my vehicular driver!—The main thing: about the nurse.
2. In Radzivillov.—The visit of K.K. and Timoshenko,* The battle ended with a change in the command staff.
3. Rest. New men. Night in the field. The horses, I tie myself to the stirrup.—Night, corn on the cob, nurse. Dawn. Without a plot.

Dialogues. The battle near Brody

Rest stops. Hay. Threshing sheds. Horses.
Topics?
The cunning orderly.—Arrival at the night camp. Feeding the horses. We drag away the peasants' hay.

Night.—We rested for two hours. On our horses. *The battle near Brody.*—Our bridle has been stolen.

---

*Timoshenko, the commander of the Sixth Division, and his chief of staff, K. K. Zholnarkevich.

Chapter about Brody—in separate fragments—I've been cut off from my division, what that means.

Vasili Rybochkin.

Style: "In Belyov."—Short chapters saturated with content.

Konkin. I find the brigade waiting in suspense. Introduction at the priest's place. What do you want, Moseika? News of heroic Vasili Rybochkin. The army commander's order. The other Rybochkin.—Plays the Cossack.—Then, returning from battle: a gold watch, trunks, a horse.—When I get to Nizhny, ha, will I show them . . . The sister of mercy on the horse. A bitch. The commissar has made a nice profit.—His picture as a clown.—Greetings from Nizhny.—The internationally renowned miracle clown and overseas circus rider.—The procession moves off.

The battle near Lvov

Day by day. Briefly. Dramatic.—Include: the Polish air force. Zadvurdze.

The Polish air force. The battle near Lvov.

The Red Cavalry is retreating. What from? From twenty airplanes.

The secret is out in the open, the cure has been found. Mosher[*] was right. The airplanes are having a strong demoralizing effect. The wounding of Korotchayev.[†]—Major Fauntleroy's letter to his headquarters in New York.—First encounter with Wes[tern] European technology.—The planes take off in the mornings.

The battle near Lvov.—Describe the battle with the airplanes.—Then development.—The battle.—The air squadron sends us packing, follows us, we squirm, relocate from one place to another. The battle near Lvov.—Describe the day.—Development after the story.—The two phases of war.—Our victories, the fruitlessness of our efforts, but the failure is not obvious.

Brody

I have never seen a sadder town.—The origins of Jewry, an impres-

---

[*] Frank Mosher, the assumed name of Captain Merian Caldwell Cooper, the shot-down American pilot that Babel interrogated in Belyov.

[†] A brigade commander of the Sixth Cavalry Division.

sion that will last my whole life. The Brodsky synagogue in Odessa, aristocracy.—Friday evening. The town—a quick walk around the center, it is destroyed. The outskirts, a Jewish town.—A description of the synagogues: the main thing.

1. At the Galician's. Polite death. 2. Synagogues. 3. Night, in the room next door. Talmudists.—Hasidism with blind eye sockets. A vision of ancient times: for the Rabbi of Belz and for the Rabbi of Husyatin. Chandeliers, old men, children. Talmudists.—I have lived through many nights shivering in corridors, but never have I lived through such a damp, boring, dirty night.—She is a nurse, he is from the quartermaster's office.—Through the crack. The woman's foul language.—The history of the synagogue.—Find out about the history of Brody.—They are hiding a shriveled-up little old man—The Rabbi of Belz. [. . .]. Without comparison or historical counterpart.—Simply a story.

Sokal 1.

In the square in front of the synagogue. The quarreling of the Jews. The Cossacks digging a grave. Trunov's body. Timoshenko. An airplane?—An airplane chased the Jews away, then I went up to Tim[oshenko]. A phrase from Melnikov's* letter—and I understand the suffering felt within this army.

The sequence: Jews. Airplane. Grave. Timoshenko. The letter. Trunov's burial, the salute.

The Orthodox Jews, the Rabbi of Belz. I've lost you, Sasha.— Religious carnage, you'd think you were in the eighteenth century, Ilya-Gaon, Baal Shem, if the Cossacks didn't dig the grave (description). The Uniate cleric, his leg like an arc.—The Uniate cleric, what ruin, what ruin, say I there are more important things to think about, an airplane is coming, a spot in the distance, the Cossacks, and you won't even have to go out. Do you all remember Melnikov, his white stallion? His petition to the army. He sends you his greetings and his love.

---

* Parfenti Melnikov, commander of the First Squadron of the Sixth Cavalry Division, who appears as Khlebnikov in "The Story of a Horse" and "The Continuation of the Story of a Horse."

Tim[oshenko] rests his military notebook on the coffin cover to write in it.

Sokal 2.

Go to hell with your "what ruin," we have more important things to deal with here.—Trunov's body with his neatly placed legs and his carefully polished boots.—His head on the saddle, the stirrups around his chest.

—I have lost you, Pava—

Very simple, *a factual account,* no superfluous descriptions.—Stand to attention. We are burying Pavel Trunov. Military commissar, give your speech. And the military commissar gave a speech about Soviet power, about the constitution of the Union of Soviet Republics, and about the blockade.

The past.

I remember, said Tim[oshenko], right now is when we could use him.—We are burying Pavel Trunov, the international hero.—The military commissar, honor the memory of this hero in the presence of the fighters.

Trunov's death

I too would believe in the resurrection of Elijah if it weren't for that airplane that came floating toward us, etc. It dropped bombs with soft thuds. Art[illery] harnesses.

The airplane, the Cossack from inside the grave: I inform you, Comr. Division Commander, that it is highly possible that we will all end up here.—Right you are.—and he went to get the dead man ready. His saddle, stirrups, the band and the delegations from the regiments. We are burying Trunov, the international hero, the military commissar gives a speech that expresses this.

Com[rades], the Communist Party is an iron column, pouring out its blood in the front line. And when blood flows from iron, that is no laughing matter, Comrades, but victory or death. A subject: the military commissar's speech.

Gowinski

A Polish deserter. Where in the world is there an army like ours?

They took him in and sent him right over to me as my coachman. He is shaken, then suddenly whips the horses and sings at the top of his voice.

Rev. chapter.—Af[onka] Bida. They caught him, wanted to kill him—the main thing: why didn't they kill him?—Then they forgot about him, then they put him on the rations list. A subject: how Gowinski was placed on the rations list.

The fire in Lashkov

Galician culture.—The cler[gyman] Szeptycki, description of the icons, chasubles, the womenfolk, how they bury, the church.—Apanasenko at the fire, he looks like Utochkin.*—The Cossacks are ransacking.—All night long my room is brightly lit.—My landlord in Lashkov.—Kuban Cossacks beneath my window.—Also there—the band—the nurse. A proposal? The Galicians are putting out the fire with detestable slackness, they cannot.— Burned horses, singed cows.—The Galicians' apathy.—Apanasenko.

Briefly.—Immediately the fire, Ap[anasenko], the Galicians, the Cossacks.—The pile outside the church, the conversation with the clergyman, Count Szeptycki.—The Metropolitan of Galicia.

Page 1. A miniature.

The books.

Style, scope.—The cemetery in Kozin . . .

The estate of Kulaczkowski, horses in the drawing room—a listing of the books.

A poem in prose.

Books—I grabbed as many as I could, they keep calling me—I cannot tear myself away.—We gallop off—I keep throwing books away—a piece of my soul—I've thrown them all away.—The core—a listing of the books.—Books and battle—Heloise and Abelard. Napoleon.—Anatole France.

LESHNIOV. JULY 29, 1920

The vicissitudes of a cavalry campaign.—Rain is the victor, a

---

* Sergei Utochkin, a celebrated Russian aviation pioneer from Odessa.

Gal[ician] shtetl through a sheet of rain.—Night at Froim's.—A night of anxiety.—Gowinski and Grishchuk.—The highroad to Brody.

Describe the night simply. Beginning: the night will be one of anxiety. The condition of waiting and fatigue.

Milatin

Right away a description of the monastery.—The Catholic priest. Burials. The Polish woman.—Korotchayev. Remembering the days of marching. The horses chomping, the sky shimmers through, we are lying in the hay.—Then at the Jew's. Korotchayev acts like a country squire. The Jew has no revolutionary tendencies.—The demoted division commander.—Then, Korotchayev's star—the Jewish adjutant of the squadron commander.—Kniga.—A tall, immovable man, bulky, like the inspector in Korolenko,* he sits on the sofa, is silent, vodka—a mute scene—a figure behind the enclosure, a Basilian monastery, the monk in a gray cassock, tall, broad-shouldered, fingers his rosary—I stand there—bewitched—then noise, the thunder of transport carts.—A Pole lying in a coffin.—Two orderlies—one of them, Borisov, tiptoes through the yard, his head down, the other—a Kirghiz . . . the body is slashed—uncovered—covered again.—I feel sorry for the Polish woman—I want to be graceful, gallant.—They return from battle—a special calm, their usual way of riding, professionalism! Separate: Milatin, Korotchayev. [. . .]

Milatin 2.

The maid—a tiny, brown, ugly Polish woman—a cow with teats, a young mother. The cool luxury of the room.—The empty, shriveled teats.

The sequence: A sultry, dusty, golden evening.—Transport carts.—Right away a description of the monastery. The *Pater* and his niece, the roads to the monastery.—He conducts burials in secret . . . I make my way to the monastery. The masterful voice of the Catholic priest. (Pay no attention to continuity in the story.) The funeral rites.—A new military order, the arrival of the Cossacks, I leave.—The Cossacks return from battle in businesslike fashion.

* A figure in Vladimir Korolenko's autobiographical novel *The History of My Contemporary*.

Second chapter about Korotchayev.
The maid by the gate—the main figure of trust.

Belyov—Boratin.

A four-day march. Diary. A simple, lengthy narration.—Begin—a marvelous march?—I saw, I remembered—marching in the forests with the division commander, rest stop with Germans, then with the cleric. The regimental clergyman. K[onstantin] K[arlovich Zholnarkevich]. Nighttime at headquarters . . . Headquarters, symbol . . . A battle by Smordva.—My illness. Night in Smordva. A rest stop in Zhabokriki.—Grishchuk.—A meeting in Kozin.

Apanasenko's life story.

Noncommissioned officer. Four St. George Crosses. Son of a swineherd.—Got the village together. He stuck out his neck.—He joined forces with Budyonny.—The Astrakhan campaign.

His epistle to the Poles, which starts out like this: You damn bastards. Compose his epistle.

Lepin

His soul rebels. Wanted to go to the Latvians.* His petition.

Demidovka

Briefly.—Naked Prishchepa.—The blood-drenched pig.—Barsukov.—The synagogue.—The kitchen.

I ride with Prishchepa, Prishchepa's tale, a Jewish shtetl, I prick up my ears (my father is in the Brodsky Synagogue, surrounded by merchants in the choir. Women weep). The father deaf.—A stately old man. The anxious stateliness of the deaf.

Prishchepa, argument with the high school student or with Ida Aronovna.

Chapters: Prishchepa.—The old woman, prayer, the pig.—Ida Aronovna. The rape.—The synagogue.

The form?

* Lepin, one of the staff officers, was Latvian.

Demidovka

The beginning: a description of the family, an analysis of their feelings and beliefs.—How do I come to find out all this? A universal phenomenon. (Their) political Weltanschauung. They have orphans in their house.

2. Our arrival. Potatoes, coffee. Prishchepa's argument with the youth. My tale about Soviet power.—Evening. The shtetl beyond the windows. *Tishah b'Ab.*—The destruction of Jerusalem. A description of the girl from Kremenets. In the house of her *future* father-in-law. In the morning she is in complete disarray, ashen, she defends the cart, a conversation with the commissar. Prishchepa walks around her, presses against her, our girls cook pork, the Kremenets girl is sewing.—Demidovka medical externs.— A dentist—the pride of the family. A description of the family—the father is of the old school, a venerable Jew, new shoots, [. . .], listens to modern ideas, does not interfere, the mother a go-between, the children disperse, life filled with tradition, there's a hunchbacked one, a proud one (the dentist), there's a plump one (married), one has dedicated herself to her family and the household, another is a midwife helping the womenfolk, she will grow old in Demidovka.—Describe each sister separately. (Chekhov's *Three Sisters?*).—A lyrical prelude.—Into this family, which still hasn't broken up, Prishchepa and I have intruded.—The hunchbacked one serves us, then toward morning Dora Aronovna softens up too, how painful it is to see this broken feminine pride. A pretty girl, the only beautiful one, which is why it is so hard for her to get married—she is a blend of shtetl health, very black, moist eyes, Polish slyness, and Warsaw slippers, her ever-anxious parents conceived her in a simple moment of joy, the rest are complex, proud—the only son, sixteen years old, in other words six years of war, is nervous, a dreamer, his mother's favorite.—The wailing of Jeremiah.—The son is reading, the daughters lie on their beds in white stockings.—They bring us everything.—About *Tishah b'Ab*— build on the correspondence of the prayers with what is going on outside the walls.—Shots—the lock, machine-gunners returning from their positions, the Cossacks are out and about.—Dora Aronovna—for us this is a holiday—she is pale with pride.—Prishchepa—we will spill blood.—I capture their attention with a tale—the longest to resist is Dora Aronovna.

1. Description of the family. 2. Potatoes, scandal, we eat,

Prishchepa with eyes clouded with caresses. They are pitiful. We speak about the Poles. Dora Aronovna dreams of W[estern] Eu[rope], in Kiev she had been part of various circles, I tell fairytales,—Prishchepa and the high-school boy.—Evening. The weather is a little gloomy. The shtetl is inexpressibly sad, the bent father-in-law, machine-gunners come, Prishchepa courts the girl, the high-school boy goes to the synagogue.—3. *Tishah b'Ab.*—The wailing of Jeremiah. Night in the yard. Morning. The machine-gunners leave, carts, the girl from Kremenets. Ida Aronovna's pride is crushed.—What is read on *Tishah b'Ab?*

Simple. Briefly. A description of the damp evening.—A description of the shtetl.—Fright in the synagogue.—Prishchepa's courting.

About the bees. A story? The figure of the old Czech. He died—stung all over.

The division commander's day: A conference day. Narrative.
1. The Frenchman. 2. The dispatch bag from the Economic Council. 3. The division commander's morning. At the headquarters. The division commander's lackeys.

Budyatichi. The meeting with the Forty-fourth Div[ision]. The doctor, the nurse [. . .] A proud nurse, good organization of medical setup, the brigade is well organized. Orlov. Get out of here . . . At that moment, elegant Sheko. A scandal with Orlov. The nurse, like a greeting from Russia, things have changed there if such women are coming to the army. A new army, a real one.—A characterization of Orlov. He throws things away.—They pack their things—culture—thermos, blanket, fold-up cots.

VIII

❧

Reports from Petersburg
1918

I saac Babel's reports from Petersburg—stark belletristic articles and short
stories—were published in 1918, the first year of Soviet rule. Russia
had been devastated, not only by World War I, but also by the February and
October Revolutions of 1917, and the Civil War (1918–22) against the
White pro-Monarchist forces. The Bolsheviks had come to power with the
October Revolution, just five months before Babel's first "Report from
Petersburg" appeared in Maxim Gorky's new magazine NOVAYA ZHIZN
(NEW LIFE). Years later, Babel remembered Gorky saying to him, an
unknown twenty-one-year-old writer, the harsh words that were to have
such a formative effect on him: "It is very clear that you don't really know
anything, but that you are good at guessing quite a lot. What you must now
do is go out into the world."

Babel took Gorky's words to heart. He set out in these Petersburg reports
to record with candor and specificity the overwhelming problems faced by different sectors of Russian society as the country endeavored to rebuild itself
along Soviet lines. Imperialist censorship was suddenly gone, and Babel was
among the first writers to address previously unmentionable subjects: the piles

of the murdered overwhelming the morgues, the panicking blind and disabled war veterans, the high incidence of infant mortality, the starvation of animals at the Petersburg Zoo. "My journalistic work gave me a lot, especially in the sense of material," Babel said in an interview fourteen years later in LITERATURNAYA GAZETA. "I managed to amass an incredible number of facts, which proved to be an invaluable creative tool. I struck up friendships with morgue attendants, criminal investigators, and government clerks. Later, when I began writing fiction, I found myself always returning to these 'subjects,' which were so close to me, in order to put character types, situations, and everyday life into perspective. Journalistic work is full of adventure."

We do not think of Babel as a journalist, but in writing these probing reports, he was among the pioneers of investigative journalism—"writing pieces on a range of subjects," as he himself put it, "that was to set a precedent for later journalism."

Babel did not hesitate to criticize the weaknesses of the new Soviet government, but he maintained that it was not the socialist ideal that was at fault, but the incompetent people whom "the curve of the Revolution has thrown . . . into the forefront." As always, Babel calls things here as he sees them. He is particularly unforgiving of the "people of the past, who have jumped onto the bandwagon of the 'people's cause.'"

The first seventeen pieces in this section were published in Gorky's newspaper Novaya Zhizn, until the Bolshevik censor's office closed it down in July 1918, an action that suggested that the newly gained freedom of the press would prove ephemeral.

The reports from Petersburg present one of the most striking pictures of life in the Soviet Union in the days following the Revolution.

FIRST AID

*E*very day people stab each other, throw each other off bridges into the black Neva, hemorrhage from hapless or wretched child-birth. That's how things are, that's how they've always been.

In order to save the little man in the street, who pounds the side-walks of big cities, first-aid centers have been set up.

That is what they call it, "first" or "quick" aid. If you want to know what help you can expect in Petrograd, and how quickly you can expect it, then I can tell you.

A heavy silence hangs over the office of the "first" aid center. There are large rooms, gleaming typewriters, piles of papers, clean-swept floors. There is also a startled young lady who, about three years ago, frantically began writing pamphlets and magazine articles, and who can't be stopped, by fair means or foul. And it might well be bet-ter if she did manage to stop, because for quite a while now people have had absolutely no need for pamphlets or magazines. There is no one else in the office besides the young lady. The young lady is the staff. One could even say she is both the regular and part-time staff in one. As there are no horses, no gasoline, no work, no doctors, no care-takers, and no one to be taken care of, one asks oneself why one would need a staff.

There is really nothing available. There used to be three ambu-lances, "lie-downers" or "non-lie-downers," as the crew calls them. The ambulances are still here, but they are not sent out on calls because there's no gasoline. There hasn't been any gasoline for ages. Recently, one of the people here finally had had enough of this dead-end situation, stuck a badge on his jacket, and marched over to the authorities at Smolny.*

The authorities responded, "The maximum quantity of gasoline dispensed to urban depots is two and a half *poods*."† It is possible that the authorities were mistaken. But what is the point of objecting?

There are also six carts at the fire station that could be used. But at the present time they are not in use. The fire department refuses to provide horses—"We don't even have enough for ourselves!"

So all they have is a single cart. To pull it, they hire two horses from a carter at a cost of a thousand rubles a month.

Of the countless emergency calls that come in, only two or three a day are dealt with. That is all that can be handled. The distances are great and the horses gaunt. To get to an accident—in Vasilevsky, for instance—takes two to three hours. The person has already died, or simply isn't there anymore, having vanished into thin air. If the victim does happen to still be around, he is carted over to the hospital at a leisurely pace, and the cart, after a little rest, sets out again to an accident that was called in five or six hours ago. There is a special book in which all of the center's activities are recorded—the rejection book. When a call cannot be answered, it is entered in this book. It is a thick book, a hefty book, the only book. Other books are not necessary.

The only working cart is manned by a crew of twenty-two—eleven are medical attendants, and eight are medical assistants. It is quite likely that all of them receive wages based on complex pay scales, with increases reflecting the rising cost of living.

The center has no institutions connected with its functions, no exhibits, no hospitals. In many Western European cities, such exhibits hold particular interest as a doleful chronicle of city life. They display instruments of murder and suicide and letters left by suicide victims, silent and eloquent testimonies to human hardship, to the disastrous influence of city and stone.

We don't have that. We have nothing—neither quickness nor aid.

---

* The Petrograd Council, the seat of Lenin's government, situated in the former Smolny Institute for Girls of the Nobility.

† Approximately forty kilograms.

All we have is an undernourished city of three million, rocking wildly on the foundations of its existence. Much blood is shed on its streets and in its houses.

The center, formerly run by the Red Cross, has now been taken over by the city. It is clear that the city will have to do something.

HORSES

What used to be called the Petrograd Slaughterhouses no longer exist. Not a single bull, not a single calf is sent to the cattle yard. The only bulls there now are those outside the entrance of the magnificent, architecturally grand and resplendent main wing—the bronze bulls, symbols of power, abundance, and wealth. These symbols are now orphaned and live their own separate existence. I wander through the cattle yard. It is bizarrely, lethally empty. The white snow shines beneath the bright cold sun of Petropol.* Faintly trodden paths lead in various directions. Powerful, squat buildings, silent and swept clean. Not a single person is around, not a single voice, not a single blade of grass on the ground. Only ravens hover above the places where blood once steamed and freshly expired entrails quivered.

I look for the place where horses are slaughtered, but for a whole quarter of an hour I cannot find a single person in the vast yards who can tell me where it is. Finally I find it. Here the picture is very different. This place is not deserted. Quite the opposite. Dozens of horses—hundreds—stand crestfallen in stalls. They are somnolent with exhaustion, and chew at their own dung and the wooden posts of the fence. The fence is now protected by iron rails. This was done to keep the posts that have already been half eaten by the horses from total destruction.

* The Greek name for St. Petersburg/Petrograd, often used in Russian literature to give the city a classical air.

Wood, half chewed to pieces by starving animals. A nice modern symbol compared to the symbol of bygone days: bronze bulls filled with hearty red meat.

Dozens of Tatars are busy slaughtering the horses. It has become a typical Tatar occupation. Our soldiers, sitting around unemployed, cannot bring themselves to do this kind of work. They cannot, their soul rebels.

This causes damage. The Tatars are completely untrained in their trade. No less than a quarter of all the hides go to waste. The Tatars don't know how to skin horses. There aren't enough old slaughterers left. You'll immediately see why.

A doctor walks with me past the building where the horses are being slaughtered. Butchers carry steaming carcasses, horses fall onto the stone floor and die without a sound. The doctor feeds me boring platitudes about how there is chaos everywhere right now, and chaos in the slaughterhouses too. This and that needs to be done, all kinds of measures are in the offing.

I am aware of the terrible statistics. In the past, thirty to forty horses a day were slaughtered—now the slaughterhouse accommodates five hundred to six hundred horses daily. In January a thousand horses were slaughtered, for March we anticipate ten thousand. The reason: no fodder. The Tatars will pay a thousand, fifteen hundred, two thousand rubles for an emaciated horse. The quality of the slaughtered horses has risen dramatically. In the past, only old and dying horses came to the slaughterhouse. Now you see magnificent working steeds, three- and four-year-olds, being brought in for slaughter. Everyone is selling off their horses: cabbies, carters, private horse owners, local peasants. The "dehorsification" process is advancing with incredible speed, and this before spring, before the work season has begun. We have been losing our steam-power capacity at a catastrophic rate, and animal power, so vital to us, is going the same way. Will anything be left?

Figures show that since October (the month in which the great increase of slaughtering was first registered), enough horses were killed to keep slaughterers busy under normal circumstances for a period of twelve to fifteen years.

I leave the horses' place of rest and head over to the Khutorok Tavern, which is across from the slaughterhouses. It is lunchtime. The tavern is full of Tatars—slaughterers and merchants. The scent of blood, strength, and contentment emanates from them. The sun shines outside the window, thawing the dirty snow and dancing on the dull panes. The sun pours its rays over the scraggly Petrograd market, over the small frozen fish, over the frozen cabbages, over the Yu-Yu cigarettes and the Oriental *guzinaki*.* In the tavern, strapping Tatars chatter in their own language and order two rubles' worth of preserves with their tea. A little muzhik squeezes in next to me. He winks at me, and says that nowadays a Tatar earns himself around five thousand rubles a month, even ten. "They've bought up every single horse, down to the last one!"

Later, I find out that the Russians too are beginning to wise up. They are also joining in. "What d'you expect? In the old days it was the Tatars who ate horses, now the whole country is eating horses, even the masters!"

The sun is shining. A strange thought enters my head: Everyone's doing badly, we're all at the end of our tether. Only the Tatars are doing fine—the merry gravediggers of prosperity! But then the thought vanishes. These Tatars? They're nothing but gravediggers.

* A Georgian sweet made of walnuts or almonds and honey.

PREMATURE BABIES

*H*eated white walls shine with an even light.

The Fontanka River, meager pools seeping over its marshy bed, cannot be seen. The heavy brocade of the embankment, swamped with swollen heaps of pulpy, loose, black, snowy filth, cannot be seen.

Women in gray or black dresses are shuffling about noiselessly in the warm, high-ceilinged rooms. Along the walls, in small metal tubs, lie silent little monsters with wide, serious eyes, the dwarfed fruit of corroded, soulless, stunted women, women from the wood-and-plank outskirts immersed in fog.

When they are brought in, the premature babies weigh a pound, a pound and a half. A chart hangs on each tub—the infant's life curve. These days it isn't really a curve. The lines are leveled out. Life in the one-pound bodies flickers spectrally and despondently.

Another imperceptible facet of our decline: the women who breast-feed the children keep giving them less and less milk.

There aren't many wet nurses. Five for thirty infants. Each wet nurse feeds her own infant and four others. There is even a saying in the wards: "Four others to one of your own."

They have to be breast-fed every three hours. There are no holi-days. You can sleep two hours in a row, not more.

The women, whose breasts are sucked seven times every twenty-four hours by five thin blue mouths, are given three-eighths of a loaf of bread every day.

They are standing around me, five of them, in their monastic attire, big-breasted but thin, telling me: "The doctor says we're not giving the children enough milk, that they're not growing!"—"We'd gladly give them more, but they're sucking our blood dry!"—"If only we were granted the same rations as carters!"—"The authorities told us we're not laborers!"—"Two of us went down to the store, we set off, our knees kept giving way, we stopped, we looked at each other, we just wanted to collapse, we could hardly walk!"

They beg me for ration cards, extra food; they implore, stand along the walls, their faces redden and become strained and pitiful, like petitioners at a government office.

I leave. The supervisor comes running after me. "They're just a little overwrought," she whispers. "Open your mouth and they start crying! What we do is look the other way, cover things up. There's a soldier who comes to see one of them—we turn a blind eye!"

She tells me the story of the woman who is visited by the soldier. She came to the ward a year ago—a tiny, efficient woman. The only large things about her were her heavy, milk-filled breasts. She had more milk than any of the other wet nurses in the ward. A year went by, a year of ration cards, salty smelts, and more and more crooked little bodies expelled one after the other by the faceless, soulless women of Petrograd. Now the tiny, efficient woman has no more milk. They taunt her and she cries, venomously squeezing her empty breast and turning her head away when she breast-feeds.

If only the tiny woman were to be given another three-eighths of a loaf, if only she were granted the same rations as a carter, if only something were done. One really has to give this some thought, it's a pity about these children. If they don't die they will become young men and women. They have to build up a life for themselves—what if they only build up three-eighths of one? That would be a stunted life. And we have seen enough stunted life.

THE DEAD

A week ago I spent a whole morning walking through Petrograd, through the town of poverty and death. The fog, thin but all-powerful, swirled above the murk of the stone streets. Dirty snow turned into dim, glowing black puddles.

The markets were bare. The women crowded around peddlers who were selling things that nobody needed. The peddlers still had taut pink cheeks puffed up with chilled fat. Their eyes, selfish and blue, skimmed over the helpless crowd of women, soldiers in civilian trousers, and old men wearing leather galoshes.

Carts rolled past the market. The carters' faces, absurd and gray, their curses heated and stale from habit. Their horses were gigantic, their loads consisting of broken plush sofas and black barrels. The horses had heavy, shaggy hooves and thick, long manes. But their scrawny ribs stuck out, their legs sliding with feebleness, their tense muzzles hanging low.

I walked on and read about the executions, about how this city of ours spent yet another of its nights. I went to the place where the dead are counted every morning.

In the chapel next to the mortuary a service was being held.

The service is for a soldier.

Three relatives are standing around him. Two workmen and a woman. Thin faces.

The priest prays badly, without grandeur or sorrow. The relatives sense this. They glare at the priest with dull, staring eyes.

I start talking to the watchman.

"At least they're burying this one," he tells me. "We've got a good thirty of them lying in there. They've lain there for three weeks, and every day more come piling in."

Every day the bodies of the executed and the murdered are brought to the mortuary. They bring them on wooden sledges, dump them by the gates, and then leave.

In the past, questions were asked: who was killed, when, by whom. Now they don't bother. "Unidentified male" is written on a slip of paper, and the body is taken to the morgue.

The bodies are brought in by Red Army soldiers, policemen, and all kinds of other people. These deliveries, every morning and night, have been going on for a whole year without a breather, without a break. Recently, the quality of the corpses has risen dramatically. When, out of sheer boredom, someone asks the policemen questions, they simply answer, "Killed in a robbery."

I go into the mortuary accompanied by the watchman. He lifts the sheets and shows me the faces, covered in black blood, of the people killed three weeks ago. They are all young and have sturdy bodies. Their feet are bare and waxen, or stick out in boots or foot wrappings. Yellowish bellies are visible, hair caked with blood. A note is lying on one of the bodies:

"Prince Constantine Eboli de Tricoli."

The watchman pulls back the sheet. I see a lean, well-proportioned body, and a small, grinning, impudent, terrible face. The prince is wearing an English suit and lacquered shoes with black suede tops. He is the only nobleman within these silent walls.

On another table I find his aristocratic friend, Francisca Britti. She survived for two hours in the hospital after she was shot. Her well-proportioned, purple body is bandaged. She is also thin and tall, like the prince. Her mouth is open. Her head is raised in quick, frenzied yearning. Her long white teeth sparkle voraciously. In death she keeps a stamp of beauty and impudence. She sobs and laughs disdainfully at her murderers.

I find out the most important thing: the bodies are not being buried because there is no money to bury them. The hospital does not want to waste money on burials. There are no relatives. The

Commissariat does not pay any attention to the petitions, and replies with pretexts and formalities. The administration will turn to Smolny.*

Of course.

We'll all end up there.

"For now, all this is no problem!" the watchman says. "Let them lie where they are! But when the heat kicks in you'll have to run as far away from that hospital as you can!"

The unclaimed corpses are a burning issue at the hospital. Who will deal with them? It's a matter of principle.

"They killed them—let them come take them away!" the medical assistant says bitterly. "They're clever enough, though, to come and dump them here! We get dozens a day, some executed, some killed in robberies. You wouldn't believe the petitions we've already sent!"

I leave the place where the dead are counted.

It is depressing.

---

* The Petrograd Council, the seat of Lenin's government.

THE PALACE OF
MOTHERHOOD

*L*egend has it that it was built by Rastrelli.

A dark red facade, enlivened by slim columns—those true, silent, and refined monuments to Imperial Petropol*—less solemn in its delicate and simple structure than the magnificent palaces of the Yusupovs and the Stroganovs.

The palace belonged to Razumovsky.[†] Later, girls of noble birth were educated there, orphan girls. These noble orphans had a headmistress. The headmistress lived in twenty-two high-ceilinged, light-blue rooms.

Now there is no Razumovsky, no headmistress. Eight women in bedroom slippers shuffle with the heavy tread of the pregnant through the Rastrellian halls, their large bellies sticking out.

There are only eight. But the palace belongs to them. And this is why it is called the Palace of Motherhood.

Eight women of Petrograd with gray faces and legs swollen from too much walking. Their past: months of standing in lines outside provision stores, factory whistles calling their husbands to the defense of the Revolution, the hard anxiety of war and the upheaval of the Revolution scattering people all over the place.

The recklessness of our destruction is already dispassionately hand-

---

*The Greek name for St. Petersburg/Petrograd often used in Russian literature to give the city a classical air.

[†] Field Marshall Alexei Razumovsky, 1709–1771, was a favorite of Catherine the Great.

ing us its invoice of unemployment and hunger. There are no jobs for the men returning from the front, their wives have no money to give birth, factories raise their frozen chimneys to the skies. A paper fog— paper money and paper of every other kind—flashes eerily past our stunned eyes and vanishes. And the earth keeps turning. People die, people are born.

I enjoy talking about the flickering flame of creation kindled in our empty little rooms. It is good that the buildings of the institute have not been snatched up by requisition and confiscation committees. It is good that oily cabbage soup is not poured from these white tables, and that no discussions of arrests, so common now, are to be heard.

This building will be called the Building of Motherhood. The decree says: "It will assist women in their great and strenuous duty."

This palace breaks with the old jaillike traditions of the Foundling Home, where children died or, at best, were sent on to "foster parents." Children must live. They must be born for "the building of a better life."

That is the idea. But it has to be carried through to the end. We have to make a revolution at some point.

It could be argued that shouldering rifles and firing at each other might occasionally have its good points. But that is hardly a complete revolution. Who knows, it might not even be a revolution at all.

It is important to bear children well. And this, I am fully convinced, is the true revolution.

The Palace of Motherhood opened three days ago. The regional councils sent their first patients. The first step has been taken. Now we must forge ahead.

A school for motherhood is also in the offing. Anyone who wants to attend will be able to. They will teach hygiene, and how to safeguard the lives of infants and mothers. This has to be taught. At the beginning of our century the death rate in our maternity wards reached forty percent. This figure has never dropped below fifteen to twenty percent. Now, due to malnutrition and anemia, the number of deaths is on the rise again.

Women will enter the palace in the eighth month of their pregnancy. They will spend the month and a half before they give birth under peaceful conditions, with enough to eat and reasonable amounts of work. It is free of charge. The bearing of children is a tribute to the state. The state will pay for it.

After giving birth, the mothers stay in the palace for ten, twenty, forty-two days, until they have recovered completely. In the past, they used to leave the wards after three days: "No one to take care of the household, the children have to be fed."

There are also plans to build a school for substitute housewives. The substitutes will look after the homes of the women who are in the palace.

A special museum/exhibition center is also being considered. There, a mother can view a nice simple bed, linen, diagrams of appropriate nutrition, she can view models of syphilitic and variolar sores, read through statistical charts showing the all-too-familiar, and yet the first actual numbers of infant mortality. At the exhibition, a mother will be able to buy linen, swaddling clothes, and medicine at low prices.

This is the embryo of the idea, the revolutionary idea of the "socialization of women."

The first eight wives of workers and sailors have come to these spacious halls. The halls belong to them. The halls must be maintained and expanded.

EVACUEES

There once was a factory, and in this factory untruth reigned. And yet, despite the reign of untruth, smoke rose from the chimneys, the flywheels rolled noiselessly, steel sparkled, the factory's whole body was shaken by the buzzing drone of work.

Then came truth. But truth was badly organized. Steel production died. People were being laid off. Cars dragged them in apathetic bewilderment to the railway station.

According to some immutable law, working people are drifting without purpose, like dust, over the face of the earth.

A few days ago they "evacuated" a Baltic factory. Four working families were dumped in a railroad car. The railroad car was put on a ferry and left there. I don't know if the car was fastened properly or poorly to the ferry. They say it was hardly fastened at all.

Yesterday I saw those four "evacuated" families. They are lying, one next to the other, in the morgue. Twenty-five corpses. Fifteen of them children. Their surnames befit such a mundane catastrophe: Kuzmin, Kulikov, Ivanov. None was over forty-five.

All day in the morgue, women from Vasilevsky and Viborgskaya crowd around the white coffins. Their faces are like those of the drowned—gray.

They weep frugally. Whoever goes to cemeteries knows that we no longer weep at funerals. People are in a hurry, confused. Petty, sharp thoughts incessantly drill into their brains.

The women grieve most for the children, and put ten-kopeck bills in their little crossed hands. The breasts of one of the drowned women, who is clutching a suffocated five-month-old infant, are completely covered with money.

I left. By the wicket gate, in a blind alley, two bent little old women were sitting on a rotting bench. With teary, colorless eyes they watched a burly janitor melting the spongy black snow. Dark streams trickled over the sticky ground.

The old women whispered their everyday gossip: The cabinetmaker's son joined the Red Army and got himself killed. There aren't any potatoes at the market, nor are there likely to be. A Georgian has settled in the courtyard, trades in candy, led the general's daughter—a student—astray, drinks vodka with the militia, gets money from all sides.*

Then one of the old women explained in dark, old-woman's words why twenty-five people fell into the Neva.

"All the engineers have run off from those factories. The German says the land is his. The people said this, said that, then they dumped their apartments and set off for home. So the Kulikovs set off for Kaluga. They started building a raft. Three days they banged away. One drank too much, the other goes bitter and sits down, thinks. And there's no engineers, just dim-witted peasants! They banged the raft together, set sail, all shouting farewells. The river rose, folk and children, women, everyone fell in. But they fixed up everything very nice, they gave eight thousand for the burial, they're doing a funeral service, the coffins are all brocaded, they're really showing their respect for the working people!"

* See "The Georgian, the Kerensky Rubles, and the General's Daughter (A Modern Tale)."

MOSAIC

On Sunday, a day of springtime celebration, Comrade Shpitsberg gives a speech in the grand hall of the Winter Palace.

The title of his speech is "The All-forgiving Persona of Christ and the Vomiting Up of the Anathema of Christianity."

Comrade Shpitsberg calls God "Mr. God," the priests "clerics," "damn clericalists," and, more often than not, "paunchists" (a term he has coined from the word "paunch").

He defines all religions as the "market stalls of charlatans and quacks," denounces the Pope, bishops, archbishops, Jewish rabbis, and even the Tibetan Dalai Lama, "whose excrement the foolish Tibetan democracy considers a medicinal balm."

An attendant is sitting in a niche away from the hall. He is quiet, thin, and clean-shaven. He is surrounded by a horde of people: women, contented workers, unemployed soldiers. The attendant is telling them about Kerensky,* bombs exploding beneath the floors, ministers thrown against the smooth walls of dark, echoing corridors, of the feathers bursting from the pillows of Czar Alexander and Czarina Maria Fyodorovna.

A little old woman interrupts his tale. "Where are they giving the lecture, dearie?" she asked him.

"The Antichrist is in the Nikolayevsky Hall," the attendant answers indifferently.

---

* Alexander Fyodorovich Kerensky, 1881–1970, served as Minister of Justice, Minister of War, and provisional Prime Minister of Russia after the February 1917 Revolution.

A soldier standing nearby laughs. "The Antichrist is in the hall, and you're chattering away here?"

"I'm not frightened," the attendant says with the same indifference as before. "I live with him day and night."

"So you're living it up, ha—"

"No," the attendant says, fixing the soldier with his colorless eyes. "I'm not living it up. Life with him is boring."

And the old man despondently tells the smiling crowd that his devil is short and bashful, walks about in galoshes, and ruins schoolgirls when no one is looking.

The old man doesn't get to finish his tale. Two of his colleagues come and lead him away, saying that since October* he has "lost a few of his marbles."

I walk off deep in thought. This old man had seen the Czar, the Revolt, blood, death, the feathers of the Imperial pillows. And the Antichrist had come to him—the Devil had nothing better to do on earth than to dream of schoolgirls and dodge the guards of the Admiralty Subdistrict.†

Our devils are a humdrum bunch.

•   •   •

Shpitsberg's sermon on the killing off of Mr. God does not seem to be going all that well. The crowd listens sluggishly, applauds feebly. Things were very different a week before at a similar discussion, which contained "a few short words, but anti-religious ones." Four people were noteworthy: a church warden, a frail psalm reader, a retired colonel in a fez, and a stout storekeeper from the Gostiny Dvor Market. They marched up to the platform. Before them stood a crowd of women and taciturn, menacing shopkeepers.

The psalm reader began in an oily voice: "My friends, let us pray." And ended in a little whisper: "Not everyone is asleep, my friends. Some of us have taken a solemn oath at the tomb of Father Ioann.** Set up your parishes once more, my friends!"

---

* The Bolshevik October Revolution in 1917.
† The area surrounding the Winter Palace.
** Father Ioann of Kronstadt, 1829–1908, was the confessor of Czar Alexander III, and was considered capable of performing miracles.

The psalm reader left the platform and, squinting with rage, his scrawny body quaking, added: "The whole thing stinks of rotten fish, my friends. The rabbis—they've come out of this scot-free!"

Then the voice of the church warden thundered: "They slaughtered the spirit of the Russian army!" The colonel with the fez shouted: "We will not let them!" And the storekeeper gave a blunt and deafening roar: "Swindlers!"

Bareheaded women thronged around the meekly smiling priests and chased the speaker off the podium, jamming two workers, Red Guardsmen who had been wounded at Pskov, against the wall. One of them started yelling, shaking his fist: "We know your little tricks! In Kolpino* they hold evening masses till two in the morning now! They've come up with a new service—a rally in a church! We'll make those cupolas shake!"

"You won't shake nothing, you cursed wretch," a woman said in a muffled voice, turning away from him and crossing herself.

At Easter, the crowds stand with burning candles in the Cathedral of our Lady of Kazan. The people's breath makes the small yellow flames flutter. The immense cathedral is packed from wall to wall. The service is unusually long. Priests in sparkling miters proceed though the halls. There is an artful arrangement of electric lights behind the crucifix. It is as if Christ were stretched out across the starry dark blue sky.

In his sermon the priest speaks of the Holy Countenance that is once more averted in unbearable pain. He speaks of everything holy being spat upon, slapped, and of sacrileges committed by ignorant men "who know not what they do." The words of the sermon are mournful, vague, and portentous. "Flock to the church, our last stronghold! The church will not betray you!"

A little old woman is praying by the portal of the cathedral. "How nicely the chorus is chanting," she says to me tenderly. "What nice services these are! Last week the Metropolitan himself conducted the service—never before has there been such holy goodness! The workers from our factory, they too come to the services. The people are tired, they're all crumpled up with worry, and in the church there's quiet and there's singing, you can get away from everything."

* A small town outside St. Petersburg.

QUITE AN
INSTITUTION!

*N*o one was filled with more admirable intentions than the Welfare Commissariat in the days of the "Social Revolution." It started out on quite a grandiose note. It was assigned the most important of tasks: "The instantaneous uplifting of the soul, the decreeing of the realm of love, and the preparation of citizens for a lofty existence and a free commune." The Commissariat headed straight for its goal without once straying from its path.

In the Welfare Commissariat there is a department that goes by the clumsy name of Refuges for Minors Accused of Socially Dangerous Deeds. These refuges were supposed to be established according to new guidelines based on the latest psychological and pedagogical data. And that was exactly how the Commissariat's measures were implemented—according to the newest of guidelines.

One of the directors appointed was an unknown doctor from Murmansk. Another director was a minor railroad functionary—also from Murmansk. This latter social reformer is currently being tried for cohabiting with female wards and for freely spending the funds of the free commune. He writes semiliterate petitions (this director of a refuge for minors), full of backbiting insinuations, smacking of prison-guard penmanship. He writes that he has "dedicated body and soul to the Holy Cause of the people," and that he was betrayed by "counterrevolutionaries."

This man entered the service of the Welfare Commissariat describing himself politically as "a worker of the Party, a true Bolshevik."

It seems that these were the only qualifications necessary to become an educator of juvenile delinquents.

The other educators:

A Latvian woman who knows very little Russian. She seems to have had four years of schooling of some kind.

An ex-dancer who was schooled by life and danced in the ballet for thirty years.

A former Red Army soldier who, prior to being a soldier, had been a sales clerk in a tea store.

A barely literate shop boy from Murmansk.

A shop girl from Murmansk.

There are also five "uncles" (what a knack these people have for Communist terminology!) appointed to look after the boys in the institution.

Their official job description reads: "On duty for a day, sleep for a day, take a day off, do whatever you think needs doing, have whoever shows up mop the floors."

I must also add that in one of the refuges there are twenty-three attendants for forty children.

An audit revealed that the records kept by these attendants, many of whom have already been indicted, were found to be in the following state:

Most of the bills have not been signed, one cannot ascertain from these bills what the moneys were spent on, there are no receivers' signatures. The receipts do not indicate the number of hours for which workers are being paid—a junior employee's traveling expenses for this January alone amounted to 455 rubles!

If you visit the refuge, you will find that there is no schooling or instruction of any kind. Sixty percent of the children are barely literate. No work of any kind is being done. The children's diet consists of root-vegetable soup and herring. A powerful stench has saturated the building, as the sewer pipes are broken. No disinfecting measures have been taken, even though there have already been ten cases of typhoid among the children. There is much illness. In one case, a boy with frostbite on his foot was brought in at eleven o'clock at night, and left to lie in the corridor until morning without receiving treatment of any kind. Escapes are frequent. At night they make the children go to the cold, wet bathrooms naked. They hide the children's clothes out of fear they might escape.

Conclusion:

The Commissariat's Welfare Institution Refuges are nothing more than stinking holes that bear an uncanny resemblance to prereform police lockups. The administrators and educators are people of the past, who have jumped on the bandwagon of the "people's cause" without having the slightest specialization in welfare, the majority of them having had no training whatever in this field. It is unclear what the basis was for them to be hired by the government of the workers and peasants of our nation.

I saw all this with my own eyes—the morose, barefoot children, the pimply, swollen faces of their doleful warders, and the cracked sewer pipes. Our poverty and wretchedness are truly beyond compare.

THE GEORGIAN,
THE KERENSKY RUBLES, AND
THE GENERAL'S DAUGHTER
(A MODERN TALE)

*T*wo sad Georgians are sitting in the Palmyra Restaurant. One of them is old, the other young. The young one is named Ovanes.

•   •   •

Things aren't going well for them. The tea they are served is watery. The young one is eyeing the Russian women. He is an aficionado. The old one is eyeing the gramophone. The old man feels morose, but warm.

•   •   •

The young man is sniffing out the situation.

•   •   •

He has sniffed it out. The young man dons the national costume, a curved saber and soft Caucasian boots.

•   •   •

The horizons are clearing. The Palmyra Restaurant offers to sell the young man almonds and raisins. Ovanes buys them. A woman he knows from the State Inspection Agency will cook *guzinaki* * for them at her house.

•   •   •

* A Georgian sweet made of walnuts or almonds and honey.

The merchandise brings in a profit.

. . .

Days and weeks go by. Ovanes owns a store on Mokhovaya Street selling Oriental sweets.

. . .

Now Ovanes has a store on the Nevsky Prospekt. Petka, his assistant, struts around in shiny new galoshes. Ovanes does not bow to the servant girls he knows, but salutes them. His doorman gets a whole chocolate cake on his name day. Everyone respects Ovanes.

. . .

Meanwhile, General Orlov is living on Kirochnaya Street. His neighbor is Burishkin, a retired medical assistant.

. . .

When General Orlov's daughter, Galichka, graduated from the third class to the second at the institute, the Empress kissed her on the cheek. Friends and relatives were certain that Galichka would marry a communications engineer. Galichka has a slim, shapely foot in a delicate suede shoe.

. . .

The medical assistant Burishkin has served every regime. Burishkin is a sharp man. He has cotton wool in his ears, but at the same time his boots are well polished. You can't find fault with him.

. . .

They found fault with him. Burishkin was fired. He has a lot of free time. He notices it was spring. He writes a petition. His handwriting is beautiful.

. . .

Lightning strikes from a clear blue sky: Galichka moves in with Ovanes.

. . .

The general is so distraught that he starts a friendship with Burishkin. There is a lack of supplies. The government distributes Siberian salmon. The general doesn't see his daughter.

• • •

One morning the general woke up and thought, "They're all a bunch of dunderheads! The Bolsheviks are the real people!" Then he went back to sleep, happy with his thought.

• • •

Galichka sits at the cash register in Ovanes's store. Her friends from the institute work as salesgirls at the store. They have fun. The customers come in droves. The store is just like Abrikosov's. The customers are treated with disdain. Galichka's friends are called Lida and Shurik. Shurik is very lively, she is cuckolding a second lieutenant. Galichka has set up daily hot breakfasts. At the Ministry of Food Provisions, where she worked before, the workers always set up hot breakfasts along Cooperative guidelines.

• • •

The general mulls things over some more.

• • •

The general and his daughter are reconciled. The general eats chocolates every day. Galichka is unusually pretty and tender. Ovanes has acquired a Nikolayevsky greatcoat.* The general is surprised that he has never taken an interest in Georgians. The general studies the history of Georgia and the Caucasian campaigns. Burishkin is forgotten.

The city government distributes Siberian salmon. Pensions are paid out in Kerensky rubles.†

• • •

It is spring. Galichka and her father ride along the Nevsky Prospekt in

---

* A military coat of the former Imperial Army.

† Rubles printed during Kerensky's provisional government, which was in power between February and October 1917.

a carriage. Burishkin's thoughts are rambling—if only he could find some food. There is no bread. The old man is desolate.

• • •

Burishkin decides to buy some *guzinaki* to quell his appetite.

• • •

Ovanes's store is filled with customers. Burishkin stands in line. Lida and Shurik look at him disdainfully. The general is telling Ovanes a joke, and laughing. The Georgian smiles condescendingly. Burishkin is crushed.

• • •

Ovanes does not want to give Burishkin change for his Kerensky rubles. Even though Ovanes has change.

"Have you read the decree about change for Kerensky rubles?" Burishkin asks Ovanes.

"I spit on those decrees!" the Georgian answers.

"It's the only money I have," Burishkin whispers.

"Then give me back the *guzinaki*."

"And what if I bring in the Red Army?"

"I spit on the Red Army!"

"I see!"

• • •

Burishkin is down at the Red Army headquarters. Burishkin tells his story. The commissar dispatches fifty men.

• • •

The squad is at the store. Shurik has fainted. The general, deathly pale and with trembling hands, adjusts his pince-nez with dignity.

• • •

Ovanes's store is searched. They find: flour, oatmeal, sugar, gold bars, Swedish crowns, "Eggo" egg-powder, shoe-sole leather, rice starch, ancient coins, decks of cards, and bottles of "Modern" perfume. It's all over.

• • •

Ovanes is in jail. At night he dreams that nothing happened, that he is in the Palmyra Restaurant looking at women.

• • •

Burishkin is bristling with energy. He is a witness.

• • •

Galichka's abortion went well. She is weak and tender. Shurik's husband became an instructor in the Red Army, participated in a number of battles on the home front, receives a pound of bread a day, is very cheerful, has come back with a regrettable illness. Shurik is being treated by an expensive doctor, and is full of whims and fancies. Her husband says that everyone is sick nowadays.

• • •

The general is cultivating a friendship with Leibzon the chemist. The general has become weak, emaciated. He is beginning to admire Jewish enterprise.

• • •

Lida visits Galichka, who has not yet managed to get over her illness. Her looks have faded, she is working as a secretary in the Smolny,* and spring is having a bad effect on her. She says that it's hard for a woman to get by nowadays. The railroads aren't working, so you can't go on trips to the countryside.

* The Petrograd Council.

THE BLIND

The sign said: "Refuge for Blind Soldiers." I rang the bell by the tall oak doors. Nobody answered. It turned out that the door was open. I went inside, and this is what I saw.

A tall, dark-haired man wearing sunglasses comes down the broad staircase. He taps in front of himself with a reed cane. The blind man has negotiated the staircase, but now many paths lie before him: dark back streets, blind alleys, stairs, side rooms. His cane softly taps the smooth, dimly shimmering walls. The blind man's head points upwards unmoving. He walks slowly, probes for the step with his foot, stumbles, and falls. A rivulet of blood cuts across his protruding white forehead, flows around his temples, and disappears under his sunglasses. The dark-haired man gets up, dips his fingers in his blood, and quietly calls out, "Kablukov!" The door to the adjoining room opens noiselessly. Reed canes shimmer before my eyes. The blind are coming to the aid of their fallen comrade. Some cannot find him, and huddle against the walls, looking upward with their unseeing eyes; others grab him by the arms and help him up from the floor and, hanging their heads, wait for the nurse or the orderly.

The nurse comes. She leads the soldiers to their rooms, and then explains things to me. "This sort of thing happens every day. This building is completely wrong for us, completely wrong! What we need is a level, one-story building with long corridors. Our ward is a death trap, full of stairs and more stairs! Every day they fall!"

• • •

Our government, as everyone knows, wallows in administrative bliss in only two cases: when we need to run for our lives or when we need to be mourned. During periods of evacuation and ruinous mass resettlement, the government's activity takes on a vigor, a creative verve, an ingenious voluptuousness.

I was told how the blind were evacuated from the refuge. The initiative for the move had come from the patients themselves. With the approach of the Germans, the fear of occupation had unleashed extreme agitation in the blind men. The reasons for this agitation are many. The main reason is that all worry is sweet for the blind. Excitement grabs them quickly and unyieldingly, and restless aspiration toward an imaginary goal triumphs over the gloom of their darkness.

The second reason for the evacuation is their peculiar fear of the Germans.

Most of the blind men have come from prisoner-of-war camps. They firmly believe that when the Germans come they will be made to slave and starve again.

"You are blind," the nurses have told them. "You're no use to anyone! They won't do anything to you!"

But the blind men answered, "The German doesn't let anyone slip through his fingers! The German makes everyone work—we've lived with Germans, sister!"

Their fear is touching, and typical of returned prisoners of war.

The blind men asked to be taken to the depths of Russia. Since it looked as if an evacuation was in the works, the authorization was quick to come. And this is where it all started.

With decisiveness stamped on their haggard faces, the blind men, wrapped in their coats, hobbled over to the train station. Their guides later told us what they had to go through. It was raining that day. All night the drenched men huddled together in the rain waiting to board the train. Then, in the cold and dark boxcars, they rattled over the face of their destitute fatherland, went to government offices, waited in dirty reception halls to be handed rations, and, dismayed and silent, followed their tired, angry guides. Some of the blind headed for villages. But the villages wanted nothing to do with them. Nobody wanted to have anything to do with them. These worthless dregs of humanity, of no use to anyone, roamed about the railroad stations like packs of blind dogs looking for shelter. But there was no shelter. They all returned to Petrograd. Petrograd was silent, absolutely silent.

· · ·

There is a single-story house huddling at the side of the main building. In it live peculiar people from a peculiar time, blind men with their families.

I talked with one of the wives, a pudgy young woman in a house-coat and Caucasian slippers. Her husband, sitting right next to her, was an old, bony Pole with an orange-colored face eaten away by poi-son gas.

I asked a few questions, and was quick to get the picture. The sloth-ful little woman was a typical Russian woman of our times, who had been hurled about by the whirlwind of war, shock, and migration. When the war began she had enlisted as a nurse, "out of patriotism." She had gone through a lot: maimed "boys," German air raids, dances at the officers' club, officers in "riding britches," a woman's ailment, love for some delegate or other, then the Revolution, the Campaign, anoth-er love, evacuation, and then the subcommittees.

Somewhere, at some point, she had had parents in Simbirsk, as well as a sister, Varya, and a cousin who was a railway man. But she hadn't had a letter from her parents in a year and a half, and as her sister, Varya, was far away, the warm family aroma had dissipated.

What she now has instead is exhaustion, a body that is coming apart at the seams, a seat by the window, a penchant for idleness, lack-luster eyes that slither gently from one object to another, and her hus-band—a blind Pole with an orange face.

There are quite a few such women in the refuge. They don't leave because there's nowhere to go and no point in going.

"I can't understand what kind of a place we're running here," the head nurse often says to them. "We all live here bunched together, but you people have no right to be here! I don't even know what to call this refuge. By law we're supposed to be a public establishment, but with all of you here, I'm not so sure!"

· · ·

In a dark, low-ceilinged room, two pale, bearded muzhiks sit facing each other on narrow beds. Their glass eyes are fixed. With soft voices they talk about land, wheat, the current price of suckling pigs.

In another room a rickety, apathetic little old man is giving a tall, strong soldier violin lessons. Weak, yelping sounds flow from under the bow in a singing, trembling stream.

I walk on.

In one of the rooms a woman is moaning. I look in and see a girl of about seventeen with a thin crimson face, writhing in pain on a wide bed. Her dark husband sits on a low stool in a corner, weaving a basket with broad hand movements, listening carefully and coldly to her moans.

The girl married him six months ago.

Any minute now a child will be born in this peculiar building filled with peculiar people.

This child will be a true child of our times.

THE EVENING

I'm not about to draw any conclusions. I'm not in the mood.
My story will be simple.

I was walking along Ofitserskaya Street. It was May 14, ten o'clock
at night. I heard a shout coming from inside one of the courtyard gates.
All kinds of people went to peek through this gate: a passing storekeeper, a sharp-eyed shop assistant, a young lady carrying a musical
score, a fat-cheeked maid flushed with spring.

In the depths of the courtyard, by the shed, stood a man in a black
jacket. Calling him a "man," however, might be going somewhat too far.
He was a thin, narrow-chested little fellow of about seventeen. A group of
brawny men howling drawn-out curses was circling around him in new,
squeaking boots. One of the men ran up to him with a bewildered look
and punched him in the face. The little fellow lowered his head silently.

A hand holding a revolver jutted out of a window on the second
floor, and a rapid, wheezing voice yelled, "One thing's for certain—you
won't live! Comrades, I will tear him to pieces! You will not live!"

Hanging his head, the little fellow stood below the window and,
with attentive sadness, peered up at the yelling man. The yelling man
had widened the narrow slits of his lackluster blue eyes to their utmost,
and the rage of his passionate, ridiculous shouting was making him
increasingly incensed. The little fellow stood motionless. A candle was
flickering in the window. The sound of a gunshot resonated like a powerful, velvety note delivered by a baritone.

The little fellow tottered and ducked to the side.

"What are you doing, Comrades?" he whispered. "My God. . . ."

Then I saw the men beating him on the stairs. I was told that they were policemen, and that this building was their regional headquarters. The fellow was a prisoner who had tried to escape.

The fat-cheeked maid and the eager storekeeper were still standing by the gate. The beaten, gray-faced prisoner ran toward them. Seeing him, the storekeeper slammed the gate shut with sudden gusto and leaned against it with his shoulder, his eyes bulging. The prisoner threw himself against the gate, and one of the policemen hit him over the head with the butt of his gun. There was a dull, muffled gasp: "Murder."

I walked down the street, my heart aching, despair seizing hold of me.

The men beating the little fellow were all workers. None of them was over thirty. They dragged him over to the police station. I slipped in behind them. Broad-shouldered men with crimson faces crept along the corridors. The prisoner sat on a wooden bench, surrounded by guards. His insignificant face was covered with blood and filled with doom. The policemen became businesslike, tense, and unhurried. One of them came up to me and, staring me in the eye, said, "What're you doing here? Get out!"

All the doors slammed shut. The police station screened itself off from the outside world. Silence descended. From behind the door came the sound of distant, muffled bustling. A gray-haired guard came over to me.

"Go away, Comrade, you're looking for trouble. They're going to finish him off. See? They've locked the door." Then the guard added, "Killing that dog is too good for him! I'd like to see him try to escape again!"

A few streets away from the police station I saw a café with a lit-up row of windows. Sweet music came drifting out. I was sad. I went inside. The look of the room startled me. It was flooded with the strange light of powerful electric lamps—a hot, white, blinding light. The brilliance made my eyes blur. The blue, red, and white uniforms painted a bright and joyful picture. Young blond heads and the gold of epaulettes, buttons, and cockades glittered beneath the shining lamps, and the black glow of the hard-polished boots shone with precision and exactness. All the tables were occupied by German soldiers. They were smoking long, black cigars, gazing pensively at the blue rings of smoke, and drinking large amounts of coffee with milk. A plump, maudlin old German was serving. He kept telling the band to play Strauss waltzes and Mendelssohn's "Songs Without Words." The soldiers' powerful shoulders moved to the beat of the music, their bright eyes shone with sly confidence. They swaggered before one another and kept looking in the mirror. The cigars and the gold-embroidered uniforms had just been sent to them from Germany. The coffee-gulping Germans included all types: reticent and talkative, handsome and gnarled, laughing and silent. But the stamp of youth lay on all of them. Their thoughts and smiles were calm and confident.

Our hushed Rome of the north was grand and melancholy that night. For the first time this year the streetlights were not lit. The white nights were beginning.

The granite streets lay empty in the milky fog of the spectral night. Women's dark shadows stood out dimly against the wide intersections. The mighty St. Isaac's Cathedral loomed like a single, airy, everlasting stone thought. One could see in the blue, dusky radiance how clean was the delicate granite design of the carriageways. The Neva, imprisoned within its unyielding shores, coldly caressed the gleam of the lights in its dark, smooth waters.

Everything lay silent: the bridges and palaces, and the monuments that were waiting to be torn down, entangled in red bands and ulcerated by scaffolding. No one was out in the streets anymore. All noise had died away. The impetuous light of an automobile dipped out of the thinning darkness and disappeared without a trace.

The bodiless shroud of the night coiled itself around the golden steeples. The silent emptiness hid the most airy and cruel of thoughts.

I WAS STANDING
AT THE BACK

*W*e are like flies in September. We are sitting limply, as if we are about to expire. We have come together for a meeting of the unemployed of the district of Petrogradskaya Storona.

We have been allotted a spacious hall for this meeting. The advancing rays of the sun—wide, hot, white—lie on the walls.

The talk is being given by the chairman of the Committee of the Unemployed.

He is saying, "There are one hundred thousand unemployed. The factories that have come to a standstill cannot be brought back into action. There is no fuel. The Labor Exchange is inefficient. Even though workers are running it, they happen to be workers who are not very clever, not very literate. The Food Distribution Department is not answerable in its operations to anyone. Those distributing bread among the population have the right to declare it unfit for distribution. No good comes of this. No one is being held accountable for anything."

The audience listens passively to the report. It is waiting for the conclusions. The conclusions follow.

"It is essential that these government institutions not employ families as a whole—husband, wife, and children.

"It is essential that the unemployed control the Labor Exchange.

"It is essential that spacious premises be allotted to the Committee of the Unemployed"—and so on and so forth.

Boots gleam with a black sparkle under the chairs. It is common knowledge that an unemployed worker, with a lot of free time and a little money left over from his severance pay, will spit assiduously on his boots every morning to give himself the illusion of activity.

The speaker has stopped. Awkward, subdued men in stunted coats come up to the podium. The unemployed of Petrograd give speeches about their great neediness, the five-ruble assistance, and the supplementary ration cards.

"Our people have gotten so quiet," an aged toothless voice whispers timidly behind me. "Our people have gotten so meek. Look how quiet the people's expressions are."

"One quiets down," another voice answers in a rich and rumbling bass. "Without food, your head doesn't work the way it should. On the one hand it's hot, on the other there's no food. The people, I tell you, have fallen into silence."

"That is true, they have fallen," the old man corroborates.

The orators changed. All were applauded. The intelligentsia took the rostrum. A shy man with a little beard, distracted, coughing, covering his eyes with the palm of his hand, informed the audience that Marx has been misunderstood, that capital should be put to work.

The orators finished speaking, and the public began to disperse. Only the sullen-faced workers stayed behind, waiting for something.

A worker of about forty, with a kind, round face, red with emotion, comes up to the platform. The speech he gives is incoherent.

"Comrades, the chairman has just spoken here, others too. . . . I think that's fine, I don't know how to express my thoughts. At the factory they ask me, 'Who are you with?' I tell them, 'I don't belong to no one, I'm illiterate, give me some work, I'll feed you, I'll feed everyone. The men came to the factory with newspapers, they all yelled their throats out. I was standing at the back, Comrades, I didn't belong to no one, give me some work.' . . . One of them made a great speech—and what do we see? He turns out to be a commissar yelling orders—March around the Labor Exchange!—so what are we supposed to do? March around the Labor Exchange, and then around Petrogradskaya Storona, and then around the whole of Russia? . . . What's the point of all that, Comrade?"

The worker is interrupted. A roar shakes the hall. The applause is deafening.

The orator is bewildered, elated, he waves his arms and kneads his cap.

"Comrades, I don't know how to express my thoughts, but they fired me, and what is there left for me to do now? We all learned about justice. If there is justice, if we are the people, then that means the Treasury is ours, the forests are ours, the estates are ours, all the land and water are ours. Push us forward! We stood at the back, we are completely blameless, we've ended up hanging around jobless on street corners. A man cannot keep on living with such worry. . . . Everyone's our enemy, the Germans and others too, and I wore myself out knocking them down . . . about justice I wanted to say . . . if we could find a little work this summer, and all . . ."

This last orator was successful, the most successful, the only one who was successful. When he came down from the podium, the workers lifted him in the air, clustered around him, and everyone applauded.

He smiled happily.

"It's never been my thing to talk," he said, looking around him. "But from now on, Comrades, I will go to all the meetings, I have to say what's what about work!"

He will go to all the meetings. He will speak. And I am afraid that he will be successful, this last orator of ours.

A BEAST
CAN'T TALK

*T*he woman's face is smiling, gentle, a radiant white. An old monkey stares at her from its cage with cold scrutiny.

The parrots, seized by tedious malaise, begin screeching with unbearable shrillness. They rub the wires with their silvery tongues, their curled talons grab the bar, they open and close their gray, tin-flute beaks like birds dying of thirst. The white and pink bodies of the parrots rhythmically rock on the wires of the cage.

An Egyptian dove looks at the woman with its red sparkling eye.

Guinea pigs, heaped into a quivering pile, squeak and poke their white hairy snouts out of their cage.

The woman does not give the hungry animals any food. She cannot afford nuts or fruit drops.

A monkey, dying of old age and lack of food, raises itself with great effort and clambers onto the pole, dragging its swollen, gray, hairy rear behind it.

Hanging its dispassionate snout, coolly opening its legs, the monkey turns its dull, vacant eyes to the woman and begins performing the kind of foul act with which dim-witted old men in villages and boys behind backyard rubbish heaps entertain themselves.

A blush floods the woman's pale cheeks, her eyelashes flutter and close over her blue eyes. She moves her neck with charming, sly embarrassment.

Soldiers and adolescent boys standing around the woman guffaw. She goes on a quick round of the zoo and comes back to the monkey's cage.

"You old dog, you," she whispers reproachfully. "You have gone completely out of your mind, you shameless wretch!"

The woman takes a piece of bread out of her pocket and holds it out to the monkey.

Getting up with difficulty, the animal approaches her without moving its eyes from the moldy piece of bread.

"People are sitting around starving," a soldier nearby mutters.

"What can a beast do? A beast can't talk!"

The monkey carefully eats the piece of bread, moving its jaws cautiously. The sun's rays touch the woman's squinting eyes. Her eyes sparkle, and she throws a sidelong glance at the hunched, furry little figure.

"Silly boy," she whispers with a smile. Her chintz skirt billows, and brushes against the soldier's glossy boots, and with slowly swaying hips she walks toward the exit, where the swollen sun is drilling the gray street.

The woman leaves—the soldier follows her.

The boys and I stay behind, watching the chewing monkey. An old Polish woman who works in the building is standing next to me, muttering briskly that people have turned their backs on God, that all the animals are going to starve to death, and that people have now started the religious processions again—they have remembered God, but it is too late!

Thin tears stream from the old woman's eyes, and she wipes them out of her wrinkles with gaunt, nimble fingers. Her bent body shudders, and she continues muttering about people, about God, and about the monkey.

• • •

A few days ago, three gray-bearded elders came to the zoo. They were the members of the commission that had been charged with evaluating which animals appeared the least valuable. Such animals would be shot, as there was a shortage of food.

The elders walked along the deserted, clean-swept alleys. A zookeeper was explaining things. A visiting group of Tatar animal trainers, with meek Tatar maids in tow, walked behind the old men of the commission.

The elders stopped by the cages. A group of two-humped camels rose onto their long legs in greeting and licked the elders' hands, expressing the resigned bewilderment of souls confused by hunger. Bucks butted their soft, stunted horns against the iron bars.

An elephant walked endlessly up and down the embankment, rolling and unrolling its trunk. But no one gave him anything.

The commissioners deliberated, and the zookeeper continued desolately reporting the facts.

Over the winter, eight lions and tigers had died in the zoo. They had been fed bad horse meat. The beasts had been poisoned.

Out of thirty-six monkeys, only two had survived. Thirty-four had died of consumption and malnutrition. A monkey does not stay alive for more than a year in Petrograd.

One of the two elephants fell—the better one. Hunger had made him fall. The zoo sprang into action and gave him a *pood* of bread and a *pood* of hay. That didn't help.

The zoo no longer has any snakes. Their cages stand empty. All the boa constrictors, those illustrious specimens of the breed, have died.

The elders walked the deserted little paths. The silent crowd of Tatar animal trainers and their meek Tatar maids followed them.

The sun is over their heads. The motionless rays have turned the earth white. The beasts slumber behind the fences on the smooth sand.

There are no visitors. Three yellow-haired Finnish girls with braids quietly sneak by. They are refugees from Vilnius. This is a special treat for them.

The foliage, which has just turned green, is covered with a hot film of dust. The lonely blue sun shines high in the sky.

FINNS

*In July 1917, Finland declared its independence from Russia. In this
story, the Finns who are on Soviet territory are not sure where there
allegiance should lie, and matters are further confused by a series of contradictory military orders sent to the Soviet troops stationed at the new
Soviet-Finnish border. "Tatar" and "Turkic" in this story refer to the
Finns.*

The Reds have been forced to the border. Helsingfors, Abo, and
Vyborg* have fallen. It became apparent that things were going
badly for the Reds. Then headquarters sent to the far north for help.

A month ago, at a deserted Finnish station where the sky is translucent and tall pine trees stand motionless, I saw the men that had been
gathered together for the final battle.

They had come from Kom and Murmansk, from the frozen lands
on the edge of the tundra.

They gathered in a low wooden shed filled with damp gloom.

Black bodies, side by side, lay motionless on the ground. A hazy
light strayed over hairless Tatar faces. The men wore elk-skin boots,
and black furs covered their shoulders.

A curved dagger hung from each man's waistband. Taut fingers
rested on the tarnished barrels of archaic weapons.

Turkic elders were lying in front of me—round-headed, dispassionate, silent.

A Finnish officer was giving a speech.

"Tomorrow's battle will be at Belo-Ostrova by the last bridge!" he
said. "There we shall find out who will be master in our land!"

The officer was not very convincing. He was thinking aloud, slowly grinding out his words with painful thoroughness.

*Helsingfors was the former name for Helsinki. Turku is a city to the northwest of Helsinki,
and Vyborg, a city in northwestern Russia on the gulf of Finland, seventy miles northwest of St.
Petersburg.

He fell silent, stepped back, and, lowering his head, listened to the others.

A discussion began, a peculiar discussion. I had never heard anything like it in Russia.

Silence reigned in the wooden shed filled with damp gloom. Beneath black fur hats, hard faces, spectrally distorted in the haze, were gazing down, vacantly silent.

Slowly and arduously, soft voices began permeating the morose silence. A fifteen-year-old boy spoke with the cold gravity of an old man, and the old men resembled the youth in every way.

"Let's go help them," some of the Finns said.

They left the shed and, their weapons rattling, gathered into formation by the forest.

The others stayed put where they were. A pale boy of about sixteen held out to the officer a newspaper in which Russia's order for all Reds crossing the border to disarm was printed.

The boy handed him the newspaper and quietly muttered a few words.

"What did he just say?" I asked the Finnish interpreter.

The Finn turned to me, fixed me with his cold eyes, and said point-blank, "I won't tell you! I'm not telling you anything anymore!"

The Finns who had stayed back with the boy got up.

In place of an answer they shook their shaven heads, went outside, and, crestfallen, huddled together in a silent group by the low wall.

The officer, his face ashen, crept out after them, fumbling for his revolver with trembling hands. He pointed it at the lifeless, yellow, high-cheeked face of the youth standing in front of the group. The youth peered at him through his narrow eyes, turned away, and crouched down.

The officer walked away, slumped down onto a tree stump, threw away his revolver, and covered his eyes with his hands.

Evening descended on the earth. A red flush lit up the edges of the sky. The silence of spring and night enveloped the forest. The discarded revolver lay on the ground. The officer stood at the edge of the forest, handing out cartridges to whomever passed by.

I saw a little muzhik in a heavy cloth coat not far from the detachment that was preparing for battle. He was sitting on a thick tree stump. In front of him stood a bowl of kasha, a mess tin full of borscht, and a loaf of bread.

The muzhik was eating, choking with greed. He moaned, leaned back, wheezed, and dug his black fingers into the gnarled lumps of hardened kasha. There was enough food for three.

Realizing that I was Russian, the muzhik lifted his dull blue eyes up to me. His eyes squinted, slithered over the loaf of bread, and winked at me.

"They gave me kasha and some dry tea. They want to sweet-talk me into taking them to the position, as I'm from Petrozavodsk.* But what for? These Finns know what's what, and they know what they're doing. They won't come out of this alive. The Reds brought in all those damn roughnecks who can't wait to arrest everyone—Why else did you bring us here? they ask. Those Finns, they know what's what. I'm sure the Germans[†] will kill everyone.

I saw all of this at a deserted Finnish railroad station a month ago.

---

* Petrozavodsk, the capital of Karelia in northwestern Russia, near the Finnish border.
[†] General Graf Rüdiger von der Goltz was leading a force of twelve thousand German soldiers to uphold the nationalist forces of the Finnish general Carl Gustaf Mannerheim against the Red Guards, who were challenging Finland's newly established independence from Russia.

A NEW LIFE

*W*e are in a damp, dark barn. Kosarenko is slicing potatoes with a small knife. A fat-legged, barefoot girl raises her moist, freckled face, heaves a sack filled with seedlings onto her back, and leaves. We follow her.

Midday, blindingly blue, resounds with the silence of the intense heat. The circling flight of swallows is lightly silhouetted against the shining puffs of white cloud. Flower beds and little paths, eagerly engulfed by the whispering grass, are outlined with austere sharpness.

The girl presses the potatoes with a nimble hand into the furrowed earth. Kosarenko turns his head to the side, and his thin lips curl into a smile. Soft shadows flit over his dry skin and cover his yellowish face with a faint ripple of wrinkles. His bright eyes narrow pensively as they skim blankly over flowers, grass, a log lying to the side.

"The Czar's own regiment wasn't too far away from where we were," Kosarenko whispers in my direction. "More princes than you could shake a stick at! Sukhikh was the colonel of the guard, he went to school with the Czar himself! He was given our regiment and the title of aide-de-camp—now he could pay off one or two of his debts, as he wasn't really one of the rich ones!"

Kosarenko had already told me all about the great princes, about Skoropadsky,* the general he had served under, about the

---

* Pavel Petrovich Skoropadsky, a Czarist general. On April 29, 1918, he launched a German-supported coup in the Ukraine, assumed the traditional hereditary title of Ataman, and established a conservative regime. He was forced to resign on December 14, 1918.

battles in which the Russian guard had perished.

We are sitting on a bench adorned with a smiling, potbellied little Cupid. A gilt inscription shines on the facade of the airy building in front of us: "Officers' Club of the Finland Life-Guard Regiment." A stained-glass mosaic has been nailed over with planks. A bright hall glimmers through a crack. Its walls are covered with paintings, and white, carved furniture has been stacked in a corner.

"Comrade," the fat-legged girl says to Kosarenko. "The delegate said I was to plant the garden beds. I planted the garden beds."

The girl leaves. Her blouse stretches tightly over her fleshy back, her powerful nipples bounce energetically beneath the calico, protruding like quivering hillocks. The empty sack in the girl's hands shows the sun its black holes.

· · ·

The camp of the Finland Regiment had been turned into a wasteland. Now the land belongs to the Red Army. It decided to turn this wasteland into a vegetable garden, and has sent ten Red Army fighters to do it. This is what I was told about these men: "They are lazy, finicky, insolent, and loud. They don't know how to work, they don't want to work, and they will not work. So we sent them back and hired some civilians instead."

There were a thousand healthy young men in the regiment without anything better to do than eat and talk all day. The garden that belongs to these thousand men is being tended by two underfed Finns, as impassive as death, and by a few girls from the Petersburg outskirts.

They are being paid eleven rubles a day, and they also get a pound of bread. They are supervised by an agronomist. The agronomist keeps looking people in the eye and saying, "We destroyed everything, but now we've begun to rebuild, even though everything isn't perfect, we are rebuilding. Next week we'll buy forty cows!"

Having mentioned the cows, the agronomist will quickly flit away, but then slowly come sidling back and, suddenly, with a malevolent wheezing whisper, mumble into one's ear, "It's tragic. There are no workers. It's tragic."

· · ·

I'm in the field. The heat has cracked the earth. The sun is above me. Next to me are cows—real ones, not Red Army ones. I am happy. I roam about just like a spy, stamping my boots into the crumbling earth.

The Finns bounce behind the plow.

Of the ten Red Army fighters, only one has remained. He is harrowing the soil. The harrow is being wielded by clumsy, perplexed hands, the horses are trotting, the barbs are merely skimming over the surface of the soil.

The Red Army fighter is a muzhik with quite a few tricks up his sleeve. They wanted to restation him in town along with the others. He resisted—here the mutton soup wasn't bad, and life was free and easy.

Now he is running after the galloping horses and the somersaulting harrow. Sweating but pompous, his eyes bulging, he yells at me hotly, "Out of the way!"

And the girls: they're watering the beds, working unhurriedly, taking breaks, clasping their hands around their knees, and with sly, singsong whispers bandying shameless urban ditties among themselves.

"I've put on ten pounds," one of the girls said, her eyes darting about. She was a little hunchback with a thin, grayish face. "It's not worth running away to work at some factory on Grebetskaya Street. If state work was always available in the country, then maybe I'd have had some milk for my baby."

• • •

Lunch break. The sun is high. The walls are white. The flies are buzzing lazily. Kosarenko and I are lying on the trampled grass.

The girls heave the spades onto their shoulders and slowly leave the garden. A Finn, puffing at his pipe, his watery blue eyes darting about, unharnesses one of the horses. The Red Army fighter is sleeping in the sun, his leg with its bast shoe lolling to the side, his twisted black mouth hanging open.

Silence. Kosarenko stares at the ground deep in thought, and slowly whispers, "I've been a sergeant major for twenty-two years, and I can safely say that nothing surprises me no more. But I will tell you that I myself wasn't sure if I was dreaming or if what my eyes were seeing was really true. I was in the barracks with them—nothing to do, everyone sleeping, the floor covered with herring, trash, spilled cabbage soup! How long can we go on like this?"

He stares at me with unblinking eyes.

"I don't know, Kosarenko, I guess for as long as we can."

"There's no one to work with, look!"

I look. The Finn has unharnessed the horses and is sitting on a tree stump, vacantly arranging his foot wrappings, the Red Army fighter is sleeping, the deserted yard is bathed in white sultriness, the long line of stables boarded up.

At a distance from us, on the facade of the airy building, the gilt letters shine: "Officers' Club . . ." Next to me Kosarenko is snoring. He has already forgotten what he was talking about. The sun has overpowered him.

AN INCIDENT ON THE
NEVSKY PROSPEKT

I turn from the Liteiny Prospekt onto the Nevsky Prospekt. In front of me walks a young, one-armed man, swaying. He is in uniform. His empty sleeve is pinned to the black cloth of his jacket.

The young man sways. He looks cheerful to me. It is three in the afternoon. Soldiers are selling lilies of the valley, and generals are selling chocolate. It is spring, warm, bright.

I had been mistaken, the one-armed man is not cheerful. He walks up to the wooden fence, which is brightly decorated with posters, and sits down on the hot asphalt of the sidewalk. His body slides down, saliva dribbles out of his distorted mouth, his head, narrow and yellow, lolls to the side.

Slowly people start gathering. They have gathered. We stand there sluggish, whispering, eyeing each other with dull, dumbfounded eyes.

A golden-haired lady is quicker than the rest. She is wearing a wig, has light-blue eyes, bluish cheeks, a powdered nose, and bouncing false teeth. She has fully grasped the situation: the poor invalid has fainted from hunger after returning from a German prison camp.

Her blue cheeks bob up and down. "Ladies and gentlemen!" she says. "The Germans are filling the streets of our capital with their cigar smoke while our poor martyrs . . ."

We all gather around the outstretched body in an unhurried but attentive herd. We are all touched by the lady's words.

Prostitutes drop little sugar cubes into the soldier's cap with anxious haste, a Jew buys potato pancakes from a stand, a foreigner throws a bright stream of new ten-kopeck coins, a young lady from one of the stores brings out a cup of coffee.

The invalid writhes on the asphalt, drinks the coffee from the Chinese cup, and chews sweet pies.

"Like a beggar on a church porch!" he mutters, hiccuping, his cheeks flooding with bright tears. "Just like a beggar, just like they've all come to a circus, my God!"

The lady asks us to go on our way. She asks us to show some tact. The invalid rolls onto his side. His stretched-out leg pops up into the air like the leg of a toy clown.

At that moment a carriage pulls up at the curb. A sailor climbs out, followed by a blue-eyed girl with white stockings and suede shoes. She is pressing an armful of flowers to her breast.

The sailor stands in front of the wooden fence, his legs apart. The invalid raises his limp neck and peers timidly at the sailor's bare neck, his carefully curled hair, and his drunk and joyful face covered with specks of powder.

The sailor slowly takes out his wallet and throws a forty-ruble note into the hat. The young man scrapes it up with his rigid, black fingers and raises his watery, canine eyes to the sailor.

The sailor sways on his long legs, takes a step backward, and winks slyly and tenderly at the soldier on the ground.

Stripes of flame light up the sky. An idiot's smile stretches the soldier's lips, we hear a wheezing, yowling laugh, and a stifling stench of alcohol pours from his mouth.

"Lie where you are, Comrade," the sailor tells him, "lie where you are!"

It is spring on the Nevsky Prospekt, warm, bright. The sailor's wide back slowly recedes. The blue-eyed girl, leaning against his round shoulder, smiles quietly. The cripple, wriggling on the asphalt, is overcome by an abrupt, joyous, and nonsensical fit of laughter.

THE MOST HOLY
PATRIARCH

*T*wo weeks ago Tikhon,* the Patriarch of Moscow, received a group of delegations from the parochial councils, the ecclesiastical academy, and religious-educational societies.

Representatives of the delegations—monks, clergymen, and laymen—made speeches. I recorded the speeches and am reporting them here.

"Socialism is the religion of swine groveling in the mud!"

"Ignorant men are marauding through towns and villages, pyres are smoking, the blood of those slaughtered for their faith is flowing! They tell us, 'This is socialism!' Our response is, 'This is robbery, the destruction of the Russian land, the challenging of the Holy Eternal Church!' "

"Ignorant men are proclaiming brotherhood and equality. They stole these slogans from Christianity and have heinously distorted them to the utmost, shameful degree."

There is a quick procession of curly-haired priests, black-bearded church wardens, short, breathless generals, and little girls in white dresses.

They prostrate themselves before the Patriarch, striving to kiss the beloved boot hidden beneath the cassock's sweeping purple silk, and grapple for the patriarchal hand, unable to muster the strength to tear themselves from the faltering, bluish fingers.

---

* Tikhon of Moscow became the Patriarch of the Russian Orthodox Church following the Bolshevik Revolution of 1917. He was canonized in 1989.

The Patriarch is sitting in a gilded armchair. He is surrounded by bishops, archbishops, archimandrites, and monks. White flower petals are caught in the silk of his sleeves. The tables and the carpet runners are covered with flowers.

Reams of titles flow with sugary clarity from the lips of the generals—"Your Holiness, Holy Father beloved of God, Czar of Our Church." Following ancient custom, they bow deeply before the Patriarch, awkwardly touching the floor with their hands. The monks watch the procession of reverence with stern discretion, and make way for the delegates with haughty apprehension.

The people crane their trembling necks. They are standing trapped in the vise of steaming bodies, singing hymns and breathing heavily in the stifling heat. The priests flit about in all directions, pressing their flapping cassocks between their boots.

The golden chair is hidden by the round priestly backs. A time-worn lassitude rests on the Patriarch's thin wrinkles, lighting up the yellowness of his quietly shivering cheeks, which are sparsely covered with silver hair.

Strident voices thunder with unrelenting fervor. The mounting ecstasy of the word torrents pours forth unimpeded. The archimandrites rush up to the podium, hastily bowing their wide backs, and a wall of black grows silently and swiftly, coiling around the holy chair. The white miter is hidden from the fervent eyes. A harsh voice pierces the ears of the congregation with impatient words: "The restoration of the Patriarchy to Moscow is the first sign that the state of Russia will once again arise from the ashes. The church believes that her true sons, led in the name of the Lord by Tikhon, Patriarch of Moscow and all Russia, will tear the mask from the blood-drenched face of our motherland!

"As in ancient times of trouble, Russia lifts her tortured eyes with hope to her one true leader, who in these days of anarchy has shouldered the holy burden of unifying the shattered church!"

Strident voices thunder. Upright and frail, his head high, the Patriarch trains his unflinching gaze on the speakers. He listens with the dispassion and alacrity of a condemned man.

•   •   •

Around the corner lies a dead horse, its four legs pointing straight up to the sky.

The evening is flushed.

The street is silent.

Orange streams of heat flow between the smooth houses.

Sleeping cripples lie on the church porch. A wrinkled official is chewing an oat cake. The nasal tones of blind men ring out in the crowd huddling in front of the church. A fat woman is lying flat on the ground before the crimson glimmer of the icons. A one-armed soldier, his immobile eyes staring into space, mutters a prayer to the Virgin Mary. He discreetly brushes his hand over the icons, and with nimble fingers swipes the fifty-ruble notes.

Two old beggar women press their faces against the colorful stone wall of the church.

I overhear their whispering.

"They are waiting for them to come out. This isn't no service. The Patriarch and all his men have gathered in the church. They're having a discussion."

The swollen feet of the beggar women are wound in red rags. White tears dampen their inflamed lids.

I go and stand next to the official. He is chewing without lifting his eyes, spittle bubbling in the corners of his purplish lips.

The bells chime heavily. The people huddle by the wall and are silent.

AT THE STATION:
A SKETCH FROM LIFE

*T*his happened about two years ago at a godforsaken railway station not far from Penza. In the corner of the station a group had gathered. I joined them. It turned out that they were sending a soldier off to war. Someone, drunk, was playing a concertina, raising his face to the sky. A hiccuping youth, a factory hand by the look of him, his thin body quaking, reached out his hand to the man with the concertina and whispered, "Come, make our souls weep, Vanya!"

Then the youth walked away and, turning his back to the crowd, slyly and carefully poured some eau de cologne into a glass of Khanzha liquor.

A bottle of lusterless liquid was passed from hand to hand. Everyone drank from it. The soldier's father was sitting pale and silent on the ground nearby. The soldier's brother was vomiting incessantly. He keeled over, his face lolling into the vomit, and passed out.

The train pulled in. They began saying their good-byes. The soldier's father kept trying to stand up—he couldn't open his eyes, let alone get on his feet.

"Get up, Semyonich," the factory hand said. "Give your son your blessing!"

The old man didn't answer. The others started shaking him. A button on his fur hat hung loose. A constable came up to them.

"How disgusting!" he muttered. "The man is dead and they're shaking him."

It turned out to be true. The old man had passed out and died. The soldier looked around in dismay. His concertina trembled in his hands and emitted some sounds.

"Just look at you!" the soldier said. "Just look at you!"

"The concertina is for Petka," he added, holding out the concertina.

The stationmaster came out onto the platform.

"Damn loafers!" he muttered. "Some place they've picked to gather! Prokhor, you son of a bitch, ring the second bell!"

The constable hit the bell twice with the large iron key to the station toilet. (The bell's tongue had been ripped out long ago.)

"You should be bidding your father farewell," they told the soldier, "and you're just standing around like an idiot!"

The soldier bent down, kissed his father's dead hand, crossed himself, and dully walked over to the railway car. His brother was still lying in his own vomit.

They took the old man away. The crowd began to disperse.

"That's sobriety for you," an old merchant standing next to me said. "They die like flies, those sons of bitches!"

"Well, brother, don't talk to me about sobriety!" a bearded muzhik said roughly. "Our people is a people that drinks. Our eyes need to be all fuzzy."

"What did you say?" the merchant asked him.

"Take a look," the muzhik said, pointing at the field. "It's black and endless."

"So?"

"Well, nothing, really. You see the murk? The people's eyes have to be like that too—murky."

ON PALACE SQUARE

*A*long-armed Italian, old, shabby, shivering with cold, ran across the stage and, placing his finger to his lips, whistled up at the sky. Two airplanes, their engines rattling, twirled above him. The pilots waved scarves at Signor Antonio's little bald patch. The crowd shouted, "Hurrah!" Signor Antonio jumped up and down on the planks covered with a red carpet, waving at the twinkling little stars. And, surrounded by howling boys, he yelped, "You want the Barinka, huh? The Marseillaise, huh?" And, wriggling, he began whistling the Marseillaise.

This took place on Palace Square by the Victory Statue in front of the Winter Palace. Draped in orange, yellow, and crimson sheets, magicians came somersaulting across the stage. Shivering torches thrown by a juggler's practiced hand flashed through the air.

Fireworks soared over the Neva. The black water blazed with purple light, cannon thunder rumbled beside us, howling and frightening like enemy fire.

"Herr Biene," I heard a meticulous German voice behind my back. "Even at the Duke of Baden's birthday celebration in 1912 we didn't see the likes of this, did we?"

"Oh," Herr Biene's raucous and condescending voice came from behind my back. "*Der Grossherzog von Baden ist, mit Respekt zu sprechen, ein Schuft.*"*

---

* German: "The Grand Duke of Baden, with all due respect, is a scoundrel."

By the Victory Statue, lights illuminated the red carpet. I went over to the Neva. At the Nikolayevsky Bridge, on the deck of a minesweeper next to the searchlight, a sailor with a shiny brillianteened head stood silently.

"On me, on me!" the urchins on the riverbank called out.

The sailor turned the searchlight and flooded a red-haired, green-freckled ragamuffin with unbearable light.

"On the fortress!"

"On the sky!"

The ray, swift as a shot, threw a foggy radiant blemish on the sky.

Then a potbellied old man in a chocolate coat and bowler hat came up. A bony old woman and their two flat-chested daughters in starched dresses followed him.

"Comrade!" the old man said. "As we have just come in from Luga, one hopes, as the saying goes, that one will not miss out on anything."

The searchlight of minesweeper number such-and-such of the Baltic fleet left the Peter-and-Paul Fortress and headed for the visitor from Luga. It latched on to his belly covered by the chocolate coat, flooded it with radiance, and cast haloes around the heads of his flat-chested daughters.

THE CONCERT IN
KATERINENSTADT

This piece, a precursor to Babel's later stories that were to mix fiction with actual events and real people, is set in Katerinenstadt (later renamed Marx). This town was one of the many old German settlements in the Volga region that Babel visited in 1918 as a member of the first produce expedition organized by Sergei Malyshev (nicknamed the "Red Merchant"), who was one of the chief trade administrators in the early years of the Soviet Union. "With Lenin's approval, he loaded a series of trains with goods useful to peasants, and sent these trains to the Volga region to exchange the goods for wheat" ("The Ivan and Maria").

*W*indermayer slowly comes up to the platform in the middle of the tavern. He is blind. His drowsy son hands him a concertina with dark bronze casings. We listen to a song he had brought with him from Tyrol.

I am sitting by the window. The day fades over the market square. Pastor Kühlberg comes out of the church, his head bowed deep in thought. The mysterious crowd surges in gentle waves over the trampled ground.

Mad Gottlieb moves around by the counter where the tavern keeper is standing. His Richard Wagner face is framed by a solemn mane of yellowish gray hair. A disdainful and heavy head is perched on the worn-out and insignificant little body of this man, who long ago slipped into insanity.

Windermayer has finished his Tyrolian song. He is holding a Bible for the blind.

"Windermayer! Play the song of the Heidelberg students!"

Two swollen white pupils hover in the gloom. They are like the eyes of a blinded bird.

"The young people are opening a Marx Club today, Diesenhoff is closing his tavern."

"What are you going to do, Windermayer?"

"I haven't been to my fatherland for fifty-two years. I'm going back to Tübingen."

Two weeks ago I came to Katerinenstadt with some unusual people—a group of cripples. We had formed a provision detachment for invalids, and set out for the German settlements on the Volga to acquire some grain.

I can see them now from the window. They are hobbling over the market square with tapping wooden legs. They have kitted themselves out with shining boots, and are wearing their George Crosses. The Council of Workers Deputies of Katerinenstadt is opening its first club today. The council is giving a ball in honor of the destitute and the liberated.

The cripples disperse into different taverns. They order cutlets, each the size of a fist, their teeth tear at white buns with rosy brown crusts, and on the tables bowls of fried potatoes, crumbly, crisp, and hot potatoes, are steaming. Heavy drops of yellow, glowing butter drip from their trembling chins.

The local peasants are summoned to the festivities by pealing bells. The hunched-over lay brothers are barely visible in the thickening darkness and the emerging stars. Drawing their balding heads into their bony shoulders, they hang tightly on to the moving bell-cables. Washed over by the darkness, the lay brothers bang the slow clappers against the sides of the Katerinenstadt bells.

I saw the Bauers and the Müllers who had come from the settlements in the morning to go to church. Now they are sitting on the square again—blue-eyed, silent, wrinkled and bowed by work. A steady weak glow burns in every pipe. Old German women and yellow-haired girls sit rigidly on the benches.

The house in which the club is located is on the other side of the square. Its windows are lit. Cavalrymen on Kirghiz horses ride slowly up to the gates. The horses have been seized from slaughtered officers near Uralsk.* Curved sabers hang at the soldiers' sides, and they are wearing wide-brimmed gray hats with dangling red ribbons.

A group of commissars, German village craftsmen with red scarves

---

* A city in western Kazakstan, now named Oral.

around their necks, come out of the council. They take off their hats, cross the square, and head for the club. Through the lit-up windows we can see portraits of Marx and Lenin framed by garlands. *Genosse** Tietz, chairman and former locksmith, wearing a black frock coat, is walking in front of the commissars.

The sound of the bells ceases abruptly, hearts shudder. Pastor Kühlberg and *Pater* Uhljahm stand by the statue of the Virgin Mary next to the Roman Catholic church. A military band is playing the exquisite rhythms of the "Internationale" loudly and off-key. *Genosse* Tietz walks up to the podium. He's about to give a speech.

The hunched Germans stiffen on the benches. A weak flame smolders in every pipe. The stars shine above our heads. The rays of the moon have reached the Volga.

Windermayer is receiving his last pay tonight. His concertina with the dark bronze casings is lying to the side. Diesenhoff, the tavern keeper, is counting out the money.

The madman with Wagner's face is sleeping at the bar in his tattered frock coat, his high, yellow forehead lolling on the counter. Diesenhoff's customers have fed him for twenty-two years.

The blind man's son counts the money the tavern keeper has given his father.

In the club, the broad wicks of the kerosene lamps burn with increasing brightness, the flames mixing with cigarette smoke.

"So you're closing your tavern, Diesenhoff?" a German coming in from the street says to the old man.

Diesenhoff answers without turning around, mumbling disdainfully in a low voice, "Why keep it open? The storehouses are empty, there's no trade, they've chased away all the good customers. But you won't have to go far, Gustav. There, on the other side of the square—word has it that things are quite jolly over there."

"What about Windermayer?"

"He'll go back to Tübingen to retire."

"*Blödsinn!*† Wait for me here, Windermayer, I'll go talk to Tietz. You can play at the club!"

---

* German: Comrade.
† German: "Nonsense!"

Gustav leaves. We see him descending the stairs, his tall shape dwindling in the hall. He takes Tietz to the side and they stand talking by the wall.

The blind man waits in the empty tavern, his thin fingers resting on the concertina. I'm still sitting by the window. Gottlieb is sleeping at the counter, his proud empty head glowing dimly. One of the commissars is standing on the platform and, waving his arms, gives a speech to the people.

IX

❧

Reports from Georgia

1922–1924

In 1921, Joseph Stalin and Grigory Ordzhonikidze, the Georgian Bolshevik leaders in Moscow, outmaneuvered Lenin and sent the Red Army to occupy Georgia. They quickly established a Soviet regime, brutally crushing the local Communist factions and the Mensheviks, the non-Leninist wing of the Russian Social Democratic Workers Party, which had played a leading role in the administration of the region since the Russian February Revolution of 1917. Early in 1922, Babel traveled through Tiblisi, Sokhumi, and the towns and villages along the Georgian, Abkhazian, and Ajarian seacoasts, to report on the progress of the Sovietification of the region.

In these reports Babel traces much of what is wrong in the Georgia of 1922 back to Czarist Imperial Russia, which had gained control of the region through a series of annexations in the nineteenth century. Babel condemns the Russian nobility, which had set out in the early 1900s to turn Georgia's Black Sea coast into a Russian Riviera that would eclipse France's Côte d'Azur. He is even more unforgiving about the four years of Menshevik influence that followed the Russian Revolution. But, as always, he does not refrain from criticizing the misguided methods of the new Soviet regime.

AT THE WORKERS'
RETREAT

*B*eyond the veranda is the night, full of slow sounds and majestic darkness. An inexhaustible rain patrols the violet clefts of the mountains, and the gray rustling silk of its watery walls hangs over the cool and menacing dusk of the ravines. The blue flame of our candle flickers through the tireless murmur of the drumming water like a distant star, and twinkles on the wrinkled faces carved by the heavy, eloquent chisel of labor.

Three old tailors, gentle as nursemaids, the charming M. who not too long ago lost an eye at his loom, and I who am worn out by the bitter, agonizing dust of our towns, are sitting on the veranda that extends into the night, the boundless, aromatic night. An ineffable calm rubs our sore, exhausted muscles with its maternal palms, and we sip our tea, unhurriedly and dreamily—three gentle tailors, the charming M., and I, a downtrodden but enthusiastic workhorse.

You petite bourgeoisie, as talentless and hopeless as a storekeeper's paunch, who built these "little dachas" for yourselves, if only you could see us rest in them! If only you could see our faces, ravaged by the steel-jawed machines, brighten up!

This silent, masculine kingdom of peace, these vulgar dachas that the miraculous power of events transformed into Workers' Retreats, embody the elusive and noble essence of careful, silent indolence, so revitalizing and peaceful. Oh, the peerless gesture of a worker's resting hands chastely frugal and wisely deliberate! I watch with fixed rapture these unswerving, convulsive black hands, used to the complex and unflagging soul of the machine. It is the machine that has given the exhausted body its resigned, silent, and deliberate immobility. How much I learned of the philosophy of respite and the principles of resuscitating depleted energy on that noisy, clear evening, as the tailors and metal workers drank tea on the terrace in the Workers' Retreat in Mtskhet.*

Tipsy with tea, the boisterous champagne of the poor, we slowly and fervently sweat as we lovingly exchange subdued words and reminisce about how the Workers' Retreats came to be.

A year has passed since their birth. It was only last February that the Georgian Trade Union Commission came to Mtskhet for an initial survey. They found the dachas in a terrible state, uninhabitable, filthy, dilapidated. The Trade Union went to work with unflagging zeal to launch this blessed undertaking, the bourgeoisie pitching in to the extent its modest means allowed. As is well known, the penalties the Trade Union has imposed on storekeepers of every kind for violating labor laws have reached the comforting sum of six hundred million rubles. So a hundred and fifty million of this sum was spent turning the tumbledown dachas into Workers' Retreats—from which it clearly follows that the bourgeoisie's money, for which it had spat blood (emphasis on the blood), is supporting Georgia's first workers' spas, for which we bow our heads in thanks. There is an unshakable confidence in the air that, due to the intrinsic nature of the bourgeoisie, the influx of enforced donations will not flag, and will allow the Trade Union to unfurl a model Workers' Town over the blossoming slopes of Mtskhet in lieu of the present dachas. Unfortunately, the grandiloquent compliments paid the bourgeoisie above are tainted by the memory of the astonishing and heroic battles the owners of the dachas fought in their war against the Trade Union. The owners threatened to go "all the way to the Czar." And they did. Their path was long, and paved with the delicate poison of juridical pettifoggery. But "the Czar" (spelled VZIK† in the new orthography) was prompt and just. The petitioners departed with a speed inversely proportional to the slowness of their arrival. The lesson that the dacha owners learned in their tireless quest for

---

* Mtskhet, the ancient capital of Georgia.
† The Executive Committee of the Soviet Union.

truth was that they had been born a good twenty years too late. An insightful lesson.

The dachas are set up to hold sixty people. The Department of Labor Protection intends to increase their capacity to a thousand, a thousand five hundred people per season, calculating a two-week stay per worker. In certain cases this stay can be extended up to a month. But one does have certain reservations, since in the overwhelming majority of cases a two-weeks' stay is not enough for our workers' worn-out constitutions.

The period of construction and reconstruction of the Mtskhet dachas is still continuing. Thus advice proffered with goodwill and love can be quite beneficial. For instance, the food which is, all told, healthy and abundant, should be increased at breakfast and dinnertime. Not to mention that it would be nice if they could eradicate the god-awful dormitory structure of these Workers' Retreats. We get sick and tired of it, we who have to live in furnished rooms, offices, and barracks. What we need in the blissful two weeks in which we get to stretch our wracked and wheezing chests is a little corner of cleanliness, coziness, and with a modicum of seclusion.

A library is already up and running. That's good. Little evening concerts will begin next week to entertain the resting workers. For the time being, we subsist on *durachok*.* But, by God, with what fire, with what unspent ebullience and passion we play this endless, tender game that warms us like a grandfatherly sheepskin coat. I will never forget these simple, shining faces bent over the tattered cards, and for a long time to come I will carry within me the memory of the happy, restrained laughter ringing beneath the sound of the dying rain and the mountain winds.

* A simple Russian card game.

KAMO AND *SHAUMIAN*

*W*ere my heart not fluttering so wildly with joy, I would perhaps be better able to describe what happened in a clearer and more objective manner.

First and foremost, the sentence of the People's Court of Ajaristan:* Oh, what a sentence filled with dry erudition and fiery pathos, arrayed in the inexorable armor of law and frothing with the bile of indignation! The laws of the emperors now slumbering with their gods, the starched norms of international "courtesy," the ancient dust of Roman Law, the Treaty of Krasin with Lloyd George,† the ambiguous decrees of ambiguous conventions and conferences, and, finally, the Soviet decrees dripping with the red juice of revolt, were all contained within the incontrovertible verdict pronounced by an ordinary and grimy worker from Batum.**

Why was this done? It was done to show the thrice-miraculous passing of the camel of justice through the needle's eye of bourgeois institutions. It was done in order to compel polyglot trickery to serve the cause of truth, and nimbly to push those evasive scoundrels loafing around the shores of Batum against the wall. Messrs. Christi and Papadopoulos—virtuosos of lyrical loquacity and maritime agents with a dexterity worthy of the Knights of Malta—and Messrs. Skrembi, the

---

* Ajaria, in southwestern Georgia on the coast of the Black Sea.
† A trade agreement between the new Soviet Union and Great Britain, signed by Krasin and Lloyd George.
** Batumi, the capital of Ajaria.

shipping magnates, are now writhing in a trap which the blunt hands of a laborer set up by mashing the twigs of our shadowy history with the tempestuous blood of the present (proving that you do not have to be a professor of international law to move mountains).

At the Black Sea Transport docks the *George* and the *Edwig* are flying the red flag. The warehouses of the Knights of Malta have been requisitioned, and even the intervention of the Italian consul, appealing to the highest political echelons, has not managed to incite the clouds to release their salutary rain of transport payment.

The *George* and the *Edwig* (formerly the *Rossiya* and the *Maria*) have been smuggled out of their Russian and Georgian ports in the most underhanded way in order to sail through the Suez Canal and into the Red Sea under a foreign flag. But the world closed in on the Maltese. Three hundred unemployed ships lie moored at the shores of Marseilles, millions of tons are idly rotting on the docks of London, Trieste, and Constantinople. Thousands of sailors are starving. The shipping routes of the world have fallen into disuse, smothered by the catastrophic sport of Parisian diplomacy.* There is no cargo for Haifa, Jaffa, or San Francisco. Europe can only load cargo in Soviet ports. And so Messrs. Skrembi, having plucked up their courage and insured their stolen ships from Bolshevik seizure, set sail for Soviet ports.

Messrs. Skrembi will receive their insurance money. We seized their ships.

The red waterlines of *Kamo* and *Shaumian* blossom on the blue waters like the flames of the setting sun. The exquisite outlines of Turkish feluccas rock around them, green fezzes burn on the barges like boat lanterns, the smoke of the steamships is rising unhurriedly to the blinding skies of Batum.

The mighty hulls of the *Kamo* and the *Shaumian* stand out like giants among the multicolored miniatures surrounding them, their snow-white decks shine and sparkle, and the slant of their masts cuts the horizon with an austere and powerful line.

Were my heart not fluttering so persistently with joy, I would perhaps be better able to describe what happened in a clearer and more objective manner.

---

* The Treaty of Versailles, signed on June 28, 1919.

But today we shall brush all orderliness aside, as we would brush away a midsummer fly.

Groups of old Black Sea sailors are sitting cross-legged on the wooden piers. They sit, mellow and still, like Arabs at leisure, unable to tear their eyes from the black lacquered sides of the ships.

A crowd of us climb on board the dethroned *George*. We are enthralled by its engine, fine-tuned like clockwork and sparkling with the red copper of its pipes and the pearly glaze of its cylinders. We are surrounded by mountains of crystal in the passenger lounge paneled with marble and oak, and by the severe cleanliness of the cabins and the aromatic paint of the walls.

"It was completely remodeled only two months ago," the old boatswain assigned to the *Shaumian* tells me. "It cost them forty thousand pounds sterling. If I die on this boat, more I cannot ask of the Lord! Forty thousand pounds—how much is that in our money, Yakov?"

"Forty thousand pounds," Yakov repeats pensively, swaying on his bare feet. "With our money, you can't even say."

"How right you are!" the boatswain exclaims triumphantly. "And the *Edwig* cost just as much. Try counting that up in our money!"

"In our money," swaying Yakov repeats stubbornly, "there is no way I can count that up."

And Yakov's blissful, crimson face, filled with sly delight and suppressed laughter, droops toward the deck. His fingers snap ecstatically in the air, and his shoulders keep sinking lower.

"Could it be that you are three sheets to the wind today, Yakov?" the new captain of the *Kamo* asks him as he walks past.

"I am not three sheets to the wind, Comrade Captain," Yakov explains. "But in the case of a case such as today's, I am in full steam, as our vessel is preparing to embark for Odessa. Not to mention, I think this whole thing is terribly funny . . . it's as if—for example, Comrade Captain—you were to wickedly snatch away my wife. It isn't that she's glamorous or anything, but, for me, poor man that I am, she'll do. . . . Anyway, so you've taken her away from me, right? Well, a year goes by, and then, after that, another year goes by, and as I'm walking along I suddenly run into my old woman, and what do I see? She's as smooth as a hog, dressed up and wearing shoes, nice and fat, with earrings, money in her pocket, and on her head the differentest hairdos, her face quite beckoning, an indescribable facade, and so impossibly impressive you wouldn't believe it. So, Comrade Captain, in the case of such a case, can't I let off some steam now that the vessel is about to embark?"

"Let off some steam, Yakov!" the captain answers, laughing. "But don't forget to shut the valves."

"Aye-aye, Captain!" Yakov shouts.

We all went back to the engine room, which was fine-tuned like clockwork.

WITHOUT A HOMELAND

During the Russian Civil War, many Russian crews stayed with their ships when the ship owners or captains defected, or when the ships were confiscated by foreign powers. In this piece, Babel describes the absurd situation of former Russian vessels being rerequisitioned by the new Soviet government, and the subsequent expatriation of the Russian crews, who were perceived as traitors to the Soviet cause.

*A*nd so it came to be that we did catch the thief. The thief's pockets turned out to be quite deep. In them we found two freighters. The robbers' arrogant flag descended dolefully, and another flag, stained with the blood of battle and the purple of victory, soared to the top of the mast. Speeches were made and cannons were fired in celebration. Some people did grind their teeth. But let them grind them all they want.

So let us continue. Once upon a time there were three oil tankers in the Black Sea: the *Ray*, the *Light*, and the *Splendor*.* The *Light* died of natural causes, but the *Ray* and the *Splendor* fell into the aforementioned pocket. And so it came to be that three days ago we pulled the *Ray*, now the *Lady Eleonora*, out of that pocket—a solid three-mast vessel carrying a hundred thousand *poods*† of oil, with sparkling crystal in its cabins, a powerful black hull, and the red veins of its oil pipes and polished silver of its cylinders shining. A very useful *Lady*. One assumes she will be able refill the extinct furnaces of the Soviet shores with Soviet oil.

The *Lady* is already waiting at the Black Sea transport dock, the very same spot where the *Shaumian* had been brought.** There are still gentlemen in purple suspenders and lacquered shoes roaming around her flat decks. Their dry, shaven faces are twisted with grimaces of

---

* The Russian names of the ships are *Luch*, *Svyet*, and *Blesk*.
† 13,418 barrels of oil.
** See the previous story, "Kamo and Shaumian."

exhaustion and displeasure. Their toiletry cases and canary cages are being brought up from their cabins. The gentlemen curse each other in wheezing voices, and listen for automobile horns wafting through the rain and fog.

The pale flame of crimson roses—the shapely legs in gray silk stockings—the chatter of faraway tongues—the mackintoshes of portly men and the steel columns of their pressed trousers—the shrill, boisterous scream of automobile engines.

The canaries, the toiletry cases, and the passengers are packed into the automobiles and disappear. All that remains is the rain, the relentless rain of Batum, murmuring from the surface of the dark waters, covering the leaden swelling of the sky, and swarming beneath the pier like millions of angry, stubborn mice. A crowd of people also remains, huddling next to the *Lady Eleonora*'s coal bunkers. A mute and gloomy snowdrift of wilting blue sailors' shirts, extinguished cigarettes, callused fingers, and cheerless silence. These are the people no one cares about.

The Russian consul in Batum told the former crew of the seized ships, "You call yourselves Russians, but I don't know you from Adam! Where were you when Russia was tottering under the unbearable strain of a lopsided battle? You want to keep your old jobs, but weren't you the ones who started the engines, raised the anchor, and swung the signal lights during those dark hours when enemies and mercenaries were stripping our devastated Soviet ports of their last possessions? One has to earn the honor of becoming a citizen of our Workers' State! You have not earned this honor!"

So there they are, huddling by the coal bunkers of the *Lady Eleonora*, locked in a cage of rain and solitude, these people without a homeland.

"This is strange," an old stoker says to me. "Who are we? We're Russians, but we're not citizens. Here they won't allow us in, and there they chase us away. The Russians won't have anything to do with me, and the English never had anything to do with me in the first place. Where should I go, and how can I start over again? Four thousand ships are lying idle in New York, and three hundred in Marseilles. Everyone tells me to go back where I came from. But I came from Ryazan* thirty years ago."

* City in western Russia, about 120 miles southeast of Moscow.

"You shouldn't have made a run for it, you foolish stoker!" I tell him. "Who were you running from?"

"I know, I know," the old man answers. "You're right."

In the evening, like a morose herd, they went with their knapsacks down to the port to board a foreign boat heading for Constantinople. They were pushed and jostled on the gangway by the gray mackintoshes and the trunks of the perfumed ladies. A crimson captain with gold brocade on his cap shouted at them from the bridge, "Get away from there, you dogs! I've had enough of you, you freeloading scum! Out of the way! Let the passengers pass!"

They were standing next to a pile of ropes on the stern. Then the ropes were needed and they were driven to the other end of the ship. They loafed about on deck, stunned, timorous, silent, with their stained sailors' shirts and their little waiflike bundles. When the ship whistled its departure, and the ladies on board started throwing flowers to the people who were seeing them off, the old stoker went to the railing and yelled over to me in despair, "If we were at least subjects of some country or other, that bald-headed dog wouldn't be bullying us like this!"

MUSLIM SEMINARIES AND
SOVIET SCHOOLS

A crucial and imperceptible battle is being waged with hidden and muffled doggedness. It is being waged everywhere, on the bleak slopes of inaccessible mountains and in the humid valleys of Lower Ajaria.* One camp has a mosque and a fanatical *hocha,* a teacher of the Koran, the other an unprepossessing little hut with some of its doors and windows missing, and a red banner with "Workers' School" written in faded lettering. In a few days I will head out into the mountains to take a close look at the tortuous tactics of the battle for cultural predominance. I will set out on the inscrutable zigzagging trek that one has to undertake to reach these muffled and remote villages that are still saturated with the blind and poisonous poetry of feudalism and religious stagnation. In the meantime, I will share with you a few facts that I have collected from my review of the work of the People's Commissariat of Education.

Influencing a person's soul requires vision and circumspection. Under the difficult conditions of the East, these qualities must be multiplied by ten and pushed to the limit. A situation that is crystal clear. But the Menshevik cavalry of enlightenment[†] thought otherwise. They imported the guileless ardor of shortsighted national chauvinism into

---

*Part of Ajaria, an autonomous republic of the USSR from 1922 to 1991, located in southwestern Georgia, adjacent to the Black Sea and the Turkish border.

[†] The non-Leninist wing of the Russian Social Democratic Workers' Party. The Mensheviks played a leading role in the initial postrevolutionary administration in Ajaria. "Cavalry of enlightenment" refers to their educational programs.

the tottering kingdom of the Ajarian Mullah. The results were not surprising. The population ended up ferociously despising anything that came from the government. The state school serving a dozen villages had ten to fifteen students, while the Muslim seminary was bursting at the seams with the sheer abundance of its pupils. The peasants brought the *hochas* money, food, and building supplies for repair work, while the Menshevik school deteriorated and emptied out, which undermined not only the authority of its founders (that would have been only a minor misfortune), but also gnawed away at the basic foundation of the culture that these prereform schools had brought with them.

And so the Mensheviks left a legacy, a cursed legacy. Now we were faced with getting rid of it. Not an easy task. Mistrust had been fanned in the Muslim peasants, and passions burst into flame. The basic battle over alphabets wound its roots around the immense task of political education. The Congress of Ajarian Executive Committee Members was fully aware of this. It prescribed a method of careful gradualism and ideological competition which is now beginning to bear fruit.

The Muslim seminaries were left alone. They coexisted with the Soviet schools. On top of this, the People's Commissariat of Education persistently set about opening schools in those places where religious schools already existed. It was not uncommon for *hochas* to be asked to teach the Turkish language in Soviet schools, and the *hochas* came and brought with them large crowds of children. The decree that Turkish had to be taught, while the official administrative language was to remain Georgian, played a decisive role.

We have now had the experience of a year and a half of work. What are the results? They are highly propitious. The rift has been completed. The scholastic cadaver of the Muslim seminaries has been crushed by the vital workers' system of teaching that is inherent in our schools. The children are literally running from the *hochas'* classes, jumping out of windows, at times breaking down doors to run and hide from their severe tutors. The number of pupils studying in Soviet schools is sharply rising. And this victory was achieved without a single repressive measure, without a shadow of coercion. Unstoppable change and the power of the self-evident have brought this about with unparalleled speed and clarity. Our vital task is clear: we must fortify these bloodless and momentous conquests and expand them, but . . .

there are so many "buts" at this point that I shall have to begin a new paragraph.

The Ajaristan People's Commissariat of Education has no money. It wouldn't even be worth touching on this routine fact had not the Ajaristan People's Commissariat of Education's lack of money reached legendary proportions. Suffice it to say that the teachers' wages for the last seven months—from January through August—were only paid a few days ago, thanks to a four-billion-ruble credit that was finally allotted by the Ajarian Council of People's Commissars after almost a year of reflection. If one considers the unbearable conditions that a cultural worker thrown into the wild gorges of Upper Ajaria has to endure, cut off from the outside world in the winter, trapped with distrustful peasants who are in need of tireless and drawn-out processing—all of this without any form of pay—then it is a true miracle that these cultural workers do not simply run away. The basic preparation of the teaching staff has been taken over by the People's Commissariat of Education. There is now a Teacher's College in Khutsubani, where about two dozen Ajarian youths are studying, and very soon the first staff of Muslim teachers will graduate. These will be teachers equally proficient in Georgian and Turkish, imbued with belief in Soviet power and familiar with the basics of modern pedagogy. A pedagogical institute with the same goals will be opened in Batum in the coming school year. This institute will have to be given particular attention. Crumbs from the Menshevik pedagogical table have proved quite a hindrance to the work at hand, as has the problem of our workers having not yet adapted to the particular characteristics of the population. Everything will change the moment the true flesh-and-blood Ajarians return to their villages as teachers and propagandists. They will be welcomed with honor, trust, and love.

They will return as teachers and propagandists. I use the word "propagandist" deliberately. It is not coincidental that to implement the new school system, our districts have welded together a triad made up of a local director from the People's Education Committee, a representative of the Party Committee, and an instructor from the People's Commissariat of Education. The little hut with its red banner with "Workers' School" written in faded lettering is the core to which we must in the future attach a reading room, a model workshop, and a cultural movie theater. There is no better way of penetrating the half-opened hearts of these mountain people. In a village, a teacher must be, all in one, the People's Commissariat of Education, the Chief Political Educator, and the Agitation and Propaganda Minister of the Party Committee. In the coming year several schools are already beginning small model weaving workshops and courses in silkworm breeding. The success of these enterprises is preordained. Even women, veiled Ajarian women, are eagerly participating in these courses.

But as far as the repairing of school buildings is concerned, things couldn't be worse. Most of the buildings are no more than dilapidated hovels. The local Executive Committees have declared themselves ready to help rebuild the schools in whatever way they can. Compared to last year, when the peasants believed that they were showing immeasurable indulgence toward the government by even sending their children to school, the Executive Committee's current readiness to help shows an important change in attitude. But a village can only offer what it has. The villages have no steel, glass, tiles, and no learning materials. Let us hope that the recently renewed staff of the Ajaristan People's Commissariat of Education will show some persistence in this. Needless to say, there is not much it can do if the central Tbilisi institutions will not help by sending supplies such as textbooks and handicraft manuals.

TOBACCO

A weak-eyed little old woman turns to the People's Commissariat for Social Security for help.

"There is no tobacco," the official at the People's Commissariat for Social Security tells her in consternation. "We've run out of it. You can forget tobacco!"

What role does tobacco play here? Murky waters. But let us continue.

A schoolmistress goes to the People's Commissariat of Education.

"We did have tobacco, but there's none left," the comrade from the People's Commissariat of Education venomously shouts in response to her request. "You can kiss tobacco good-bye! Another month or two and we'll have seen the very last of it!"

And finally, the garbage man roughly demands his due from the Department of Municipal Economy.

"Where are we supposed to find tobacco?" the comrade from the Department of Municipal Economy yells angrily. "Do you think it's sprouting here on my palms, huh? Or are you perhaps suggesting we start a tobacco plantation in the little garden in front of the building?"

Amazing Abkhazia! Little old ladies smoke tobacco with the same fervor garbage men do, and the primmest schoolmistress doesn't lag far behind.

Murky waters. And how sadly these waters shimmer when a decisive complaint is lodged in the Department of Tobacco Cultivation.

In 1914, the tobacco harvest in Abkhazia had risen to a million *poods.* That was a record number, and all the conditions indicated that it would continue to rise steadily. Even before the war, the tobacco from Sukhumi triumphed decisively over the Kuban and Crimean tobaccos. The factories of Petrograd, Rostov-on-Don, and southern Russia worked with the Sukhumi crop. Exports grew with every passing year. The former tobacco monopolists—Macedonia, Turkey, Egypt—had to acknowledge the incomparable quality of their new competitor's crop. The most delicate assortments, issued by the illustrious factories of Cairo, Alexandria, and London, acquired new status from the Abkhazian tobacco blend. Our product was quick to clinch its reputation as one of the best in the world, and foreign capital headed briskly for the Abkhazian coast, building gigantic storehouses and setting up industrialized tobacco plantations.

In the years before the war the price of tobacco fluctuated, depending on its quality, from fourteen to thirty rubles a *pood.* The average yield per hectare was eighty to a hundred *poods.* The most prevalent size of a peasant plantation was three to four hectares. The pioneers of tobacco culture on the shores of Abkhazia were Greeks and Armenians. Then the inhabitants of the region made successful use of the pioneers' experiment and turned the cultivation of tobacco into the area's economic mainstay. The Sukhumi farmers' profits grew, in spite of the thievery of the wholesalers and the Czar's imperial administration. Now it is clear why "tobacco comes in all qualities"—because it is embraced by everyone, from frail little old ladies to diligent schoolmistresses.

After 1914, the war began plying its ruinous trade. Waves of migrants crushed the delicate crop, the first onslaught of the Revolution inevitably deepening the crisis, and then the dire Mensheviks obliterated what was left.

In the fertile and enchanted garden we call Abkhazia, one quickly learns to vehemently detest the Mensheviks, that species of sluggish wood louse that left its tracks in full manifestation of its creative genius. During the two years that they ruled, they managed to wreck all the vital establishments of the city, opened up Abkhazia's wealth of timber to the plunder of foreign sharks, and, with the declaration of a tobacco monopoly, finally dealt a fatal blow to the nerve of the region. The monopoly wasn't half the evil. A government, conducting intelligent economic policies, will resort to measures that are even more drastic, but it will resort to them cleverly. The Menshevik monopoly was calculated to cause the quick demise of the tobacco industry. Parallel to the fact that the low government price did not reflect the manufacturing cost, there was also the problem of prices on the foreign market exceeding the fixed rate by four hundred percent. What recourse did a planter have under such circumstances? None. He gladly extricated himself from this dead-end situation.

Under the aegis of enlightened seafarers, Abkhazia's tobacco industry came to a peaceful end. To put it in starker terms: not even a pound of newly harvested tobacco ended up on the markets between 1918 and 1920. The plantations were given over to maize, a situation accelerated by a suspension of grain imports from Soviet Russia. The gaping wound began oozing and has remained open.

Such was the legacy of the Mensheviks. And here—when one considers how the present Soviet government is going about liquidating this sad legacy—one frankly has to admit that there is neither enough know-how nor a systematic rigor. It is true that the new Soviet government abolished the monopoly—but this only to make room for official mayhem. Petitions lodged by the tobacco industry are looked at every two weeks, at which point the most contradictory responses rain down upon the bewildered heads of the planters. All kinds of institutions have a hand in running the tobacco industry, but none of them are putting much effort into it. There is right now an unsettled dispute between the Committee of Exports and the People's Commissariat of Abkhazia about who will dispose of the rest of the tobacco funds left over after the Menshevik tenure. During the year and a half of Soviet rule, about half a million *poods* of tobacco was disposed of without a plan and at minimal prices, in order to cover ongoing government expenses. As for the future, the yield of 1922 will barely reach ten thousand *poods* of fresh tobacco. The dwindling plantations are not being restored. Vague permissions, vague prohibitions, cumbersome footnotes to bulky paragraphs, have resulted in the complete bewilderment of the planters, who, as it is, have been uncertain of what the future has in store for them. Without that certainty there will be no revival. And therefore the farmer is planting maize on his hectare of land, which can bring him at best a wholesale revenue of ten, fifteen million. Tobacco, an average yield of which can bring him a revenue of seventy-five to a hundred million, is neglected. The material conditions of the Abkhazian peasant have drastically worsened. His clothes are tattered and he lives in a dilapidated house, which he cannot renovate for lack of money.

The eagerness to plant tobacco is universal. The only thing the planter is appealing for is a strict law regulating the tobacco industry. Whether this will be in the form of taxes paid in produce or in the form of trade regulations, the economic institutions must decide what is best for the country and the workers. But clarity is vital. It is high time boundaries were laid on the confusion of understanding and the unbalancing of minds. Otherwise the hands of the tobacco gold mines are threatening to grow rigid for a long time to come. This will not serve the federation well.

GAGRY

*B*y the will of the reigning despot, the city was raised on the cliff. Palaces were built for the chosen few, and huts for those who would serve the chosen few. Lights danced on the remote shore, and bursting moneybags with decaying lungs dragged themselves to the resplendent despot's cliff.*

Life flowed as it was meant to flow. The palaces blossomed, the huts rotted. The decaying lungs of the select few grew strong, the strong lungs of those who served them declined and withered away, but the wayward old prince untiringly chased swans over his ponds, laid out flower beds, and clambered up steep slopes to erect more palaces and huts on inaccessible peaks, nothing but palaces and huts. In St. Petersburg they thought of declaring the prince insane and putting him under guard. Then war broke out. The prince was declared a genius and appointed head of the Medical Department. History reports with amazement how Prince Oldenburg healed five million sick and wounded, but as for Gagry, the brainchild of his stubborn and idle fantasy, who will tell about Gagry?

First came the war, followed immediately by the Revolution. The ebb and flow of red banners. Fashionable sanatoriums lost their patients, nurses lost their bread and butter. The thunder of battle on the high roads, and heavy silence crouching in distant corners. A wild thunderstorm descended upon the whole of Russia, hurling its unneed-

---

* In the early 1900s, Prince Alexander Oldenburg, who was married to a niece of Czar Nicholas II, began to develop the town of Gagry in northwestern Georgia as a resort for the rich.

ed ballast onto its faraway shores, the bodies of rats fleeing from ships. And moribund Gagry, this stately absurdity, fell apart on its devastated hill, forgotten by everyone, not producing anything.

Even now this doleful, wild little town makes a terrible impression. It resembles a beautiful woman bespattered with rain and mud, or a group of Spanish dancers appearing in a starving Volga village. The ponds that were laid out around the palace have turned into swamps, and their poisonous breath saps the last strength from the pitiful, spectral population. Unimaginable people with saffron faces, on crutches and in civil service uniforms, wander among the gloomy fairground booths that huddle by the granite walls of the multistoried giants. Goya's madness and Gogol's hatred could not have invented anything more horrifying. Prereform officialdom—ruined debris, mindless visions of the past, scorched by poverty and malaria and somehow trapped among the living—still roams about here as a desolate symbol of the dead city.

For five years Gagry did nothing, because there was nothing it could do or was able to do. All it knows how to do is to consume—it is a town of nurses, restaurateurs, bellhops, and bathhouse attendants, who learned the science of spa tips and lackey chic from their old master.

And so this year the new owner is reopening the season in Gagry for the first time. The sanatoriums are being cleaned and prepared. They are awaiting sick comrades from Soviet Russia and the Transcaucasia. The sanatoriums are scheduled to accommodate 150 to 200 beds. The possibilities for Gagry are great. Only the question of food, still a big problem, casts a dark shadow on the situation, but the buildings of the resort and the former Oldenburg Palace, though their contents have become markedly depleted,* are still beautiful. The Department of Spas, as is well known, has not been exactly overworking these days, but it has begun to show some signs of life.

There is now a timid smile of anticipation on the town's sagging cheeks. Gagry is hoping for new birds and new songs. These exhausted, ill, but indefatigable birds that have reinvigorated the limitless expanses of our country—may they add a particle of their vital energy in order to bring back to life the healing resort, which until now has been badly run and has gone to seed, but still has the right to exist.

---

* "Depleted" as a result of the October Revolution and the Russian Civil War. The palace that Prince Oldenburg built for himself in 1907 is today the Chaika (Seagull) Hotel.

IN CHAKVA

*T*ea. Picking tea: here, all effort, hope, and attention is aimed at these two words as at a target. The ancient slopes of Chakva* are covered by orderly rows of carefully tended bushes. In their simple greenness you will not see fruits, flowers, or pods. An eye thirsting for the moist fields of Ceylon, expecting the yellow plains of China, will flit indifferently over the green shoots, looking for "tea." And who will recognize tea in the tiny, lilac bud crowning the dwarfish tip of the bush, or in the fresh leaf hiding beneath the bud, looking just like millions upon millions of other ordinary little leaves? They will be recognized, found, and plucked by the inhumanly deft machine lodged in the hands of the local Greeks, and in the small, red, perforated fingers of their ten-year-old daughters.

All these Achillideses, Ambarzakises, and Theotokises have come down to Chakva from their Ajarian ravines covered in the blue clouds of the eternal mists to pick tea. Their untiring cooperative associations, made up of children, crawl slowly over the eroded terraces. Elusive hands fly over the bushes like a swarm of fleeting birds. Their experienced unwavering eyes seek out the two little leaves in the inexhaustible labyrinth of green, and let him who does not believe in the unattainable know that there are girls who, in a single working day, manage to bring in a harvest of a hundred and fifty pounds of these weightless buds and stems.

* A village eleven miles from Batumi, the capital of Ajaria.

Red-bearded horsemen trot on mangy nags along the rosy paths of Chakva. Gentle buffaloes, their yokes creaking, drag bullock carts with freshly plucked leaves into the valley. Olive-skinned Greeks, the elders of the cooperative association, clamber over the hills, flick open their notebooks, unhurriedly shout at the workers, and suddenly break into rollicking song as wild as the tunes of Balaklava fishermen. But the horsemen, the buffaloes, and the olive-skinned Greeks are all drawn toward the valley, to that flat piece of land shackled in cement, where lies the inalienable estate belonging to Zhen Lao—his tea factory.

Zhen Lao is known far and wide as Ivan Ivanovich. Everyone on both sides of the high road going from Chakva to Batum knows him. This unshakable renown is not great in size, but it is inexhaustible in depth. Twenty-seven years ago, a tea enthusiast and tea magnate, Popov, had brought the twenty-year-old Lao from central China, from the sacred thickets of the East where a European's foot had yet to tread. The former slave on the plantation of a Mandarin, the current Ivan Ivanovich was destined to become a pioneer in the tea business in Russia and its incontestable leader. And only on the boundless flat soil of China, where people are as uncountable as the bamboo stems of a tropical forest, only in that mysterious land, fertilized by faceless millions, could the fiery passion, the inexorable activity, the abrupt and deliberate Asiatic temperament of Zhen Lao come into its own.

All threads lead to him. The buffaloes, descending from the hills, see the terraces of the cement rectangles adjoining the factory. An Australian sun shines above the lacy, rubicund landscape of Chakva. Giant rectangles, strewn with an emerald carpet of drying tea, look like freshly laundered white tablecloths shining beneath a crystalline stream of electric light. But tea-drying in the open is a remnant of old primitive ways, and is only perpetuated because there is not enough covered space for the thirty thousand pounds of fresh leaf picked daily on the plantations.

After the leaves have been left to wither for twenty-four hours, they are rolled through the presses. Only then do the leaves begin to turn into the black aromatic strands that we recognize. Next comes the process of fermentation. The leaves, touched by the brown, moist poison of decay, are ready to be dried. In a hermetic oven, which looks like a village hut, an endless iron grill revolves, with tea spread over it in an even layer. In this steam hut, which is as complex as an engine and tightly sealed, the tea is exposed to slow and even heating. The drying process is repeated twice. Once the tea is removed from the oven after the second drying, it is ready. It is now dark and tattered, but lacks aroma. The mechanical sifters provide the finishing touch. These machines are simple, their work easy enough to understand, but it is at this stage of production that the key to success lies. The imperceptible properties of tea here reveal their tyranny, their delicate perfidy inaccessible to the uninitiated.

The mechanical sifter is a mesh drum divided into sectors, each sector having different-sized openings in its mesh netting. The drum rotates quickly, sifts the tea, dropping the smallest and most valuable leaves through the first sectors. The closer we get to the refuse vent, the larger are the openings in the meshes, and the coarser the sifted tea. Beneath each sector is a wooden box into which falls the tea that has been sifted by that part of the drum. This is why each box has its own specific quality of tea. Box number two and three have the best-quality tea because the sorter drops the buds and the upper leaves into them. The other boxes have the lower quality from the sifting of older and coarser leaves.

After the sorting comes the packing. And that's that. This is the system: on the third or fourth day after the green leaves arrive from the plantation, the tea enters the factory's storehouses, where it lies for a few months and acquires its specific aroma.

This is the system, but it is as bare as a human skeleton lacking meat, muscle, and skin. Yet we're not discussing the system here. The hidden life of material, the seemingly simple but actually elusive transformation of the leaf, the tyrannical inconstancy of its basic properties— all this requires indefatigable, ceaseless attention, and experience refined over decades. The end result can be affected by the slightest change in temperature, a half hour too much withering or drying, intangible aspects of the harvest. And it is no secret that hasty planting, neglect of the plantation, and barbarous indiscriminate sorting to meet wartime needs have lowered the quality of Russian Chakva tea, though it could be raised to a level that would even satisfy the intolerant taste of the planter from central China. Come to the tea factory on any beautiful day on which Chakva looks like the chiseled environs of Melbourne, and have Zhen Lao bring you a sample in a white porcelain teacup. In this fragrant, coral liquid, whose density resembles the density and texture of a Spanish wine, you will experience the sweet and mortal infusion of sacred, faraway grasses.

Flooded with the lavish gold of an unforgettable sunset, I walk over to the tangerine groves. The low trees are weighed down by fruit in whose deep emerald tones it is difficult to guess the future fiery red copper of ripeness. Scattered workers spray the trees with lime and dig furrows around them.

We pass by the bamboo thickets, which play quite a large role in the Chakva economy, and arrive at the forbidden and impenetrable boundaries of the forests of the estate. Here are 30,634 acres of completely unexploited land, an inexhaustible wealth that extends to the far reaches of the mountain peaks. And until now our daring axe has not mustered the courage to penetrate these dark, cool depths. Chakva's forestry project, which was initiated a few years ago, came to a halt. Money is needed to continue it, and for the time being there isn't any.

The crimson circle of the setting sun hangs above the sea. Tender blood flows from the tattered rosy clouds. The sun floods the blue squares of the sea with its colorful flames, reaches the bend in the shore, where one can see, inside an arched window, the yellow faces of Zhen Lao and his family—tiny and gentle Chinese women.

The crowns of club palms motionlessly border the toylike roads. The silvery, dusty eucalyptus leaves cut through the flushed plains of the sky—and all this splendor intoxicates the soul with the most subtle lines of Japanese silk.

RENOVATIONS AND
REFURBISHMENT

A little history. This is important, so that one can see how correctly sometimes (unfortunately not always), and with what flair, the NEP* is being implemented in certain towns (unfortunately not all towns).

Last year the economy of the city of Sukhumi† reached a point beyond which catastrophe lies. The Mensheviks ran it completely into the ground. Nor did the first months following Sovietization bring significant improvement. The Department of Municipal Economy was busy with the distribution of furniture and useless knickknacks. The hospital was on its last legs. The water distribution system, primitive and not designed to support the present growth of the city, was suffering prolonged interruptions. The registry of buildings, such as commercial and other profitable enterprises, had not been carried out. The buildings were casually falling to ruin. The electric station, ransacked by the Mensheviks, was on its last legs. And, most of all, it was not understood how vitally important it was to restore our cities, the cradle of our proletariat. The Department of Municipal Economy had neither the authority nor the means—a familiar picture. And when realization of the danger came, the clock of the city's economy was already well past the eleventh hour.

The important thing is not that one of our institutions is doing its

* The "New Economic Policy" of the Soviet government after the Revolution during the transition from capitalism to socialism.
† The capital city of Abkhazia.

job well: the great effort of the Russian Federation, renovating and refurbishing itself, has found here, in this small mirror, its true reflection. What is exhilarating is that this difficult and complex problem, a relatively recent one, has here been dealt with in a corner far removed from the center and nourished by the scant resources provided by an extremely bad provincial communication system.

A worker in a leather cap is sitting at the table. The tumultuous waves of "bourgeois elements" crash against this table: the solicitations of a poorly understood NEP, the dangerous insinuations of the contractors, the suspect calculations of all kinds of merchants, the capricious demands of engineers, the complaints of old women.

One of the generators at the electric station has broken down. The station is overloaded. And so an expedition is preparing to set out for Poti, where a powerful turbo-generator that was taken there by the Mensheviks is lying idle. The projected outcome of the expedition is the complete electrification of Abkhazia: adapting factories to electric power, the effective development of industry, the full provision of energy to the city, and the electrification of the villages. If the generator can be secured, all the work can be completed within a few months.

The water distribution system. The little river that supplies it does not provide it with a sufficient quantity of water. A project for a new water distribution system and sewerage has already been developed, and the preliminary surveys have been initiated. The Department of Municipal Economy is trying to acquire some forest terrain for exploitation, in exchange for which it has pledged to complete all work on the city's water distribution and sewer system by next summer.

Finances. Six months ago, the Department of Municipal Economy had nothing but debts. Now, with its own funds, it supports the schools of the People's Commissariat of Education, the hospital of the People's Commissariat of Health, and the orphanage founded by the Department of Social Assistance. All this has been accomplished with a judicious system of leasing, and a trade policy without the tight yoke of taxation.

"Give us three years," the director of the Department of Municipal Economy says, "and you will not recognize Sukhumi. Things were bad a year ago, now they are getting better, and in three years they will be very good. We are ready for electrification. The water distribution system and the sewerage will be ready in a matter of months. We have started paving the streets. We are initiating the refurbishment of the dacha suburbs. We have improved sanitation, and easily dealt with this year's epidemic. By summer we will have a municipal ice factory functioning. We are racking our brains as to how to set up a repair fund for the wholesale purchase of building materials and setting up loans for homeowners and the community. We will be receiving goods a hundred percent cheaper than on the regular market. We will use these as a solid foundation for the repairs of the city buildings. The electrification will allow us to arrange a proper forestry industry as well as open a carbide factory, for which we have all the arrangements in place. Come visit Sukhumi in three years and you won't recognize the place!"

And I believe him. The three hours I spent in the Sukhumi Department of Municipal Economy—a quite ordinary provincial Department of Municipal Economy—have convinced me of the truth in these proud words.

PARIS AND JULIET

*T*his happened not too long ago. A British flag was hoisted above the *Paris*. The *Paris* was the Russian steamer *Juliet*, abducted by the Whites in 1919.* *Juliet* sailed the Mediterranean and the Sea of Marmara for four years, and then joined the Anatolian Line. Last December, she sailed from Constantinople to Zunguldak for coal. In Zunguldak her first officer went to the maritime agent.

"*Effendi,*"† the first officer said. "Your harbor is cluttered with ships, and my turn for loading coal is going to take a long time, and I'll be late getting to Ergli, *Effendi!*"

"*Yakshi!*"** the Turk said, tapping his hand on his forehead, his heart, and wherever else custom has it.

And by nightfall *Juliet* set out for Ergli. She had sailed about fifteen miles from shore when Gavrilichenko, the first officer, took a revolver in each hand and climbed up to the bridge.

"Comrades!" he said to the crew. "We will not head for Ergli, but home to Odessa. If anyone has any objections, he can come up to the bridge and throw me overboard!"

No one had any objections. Gavrilichenko put away his revolvers. The helmsman turned the steering wheel. *Juliet* headed home to Odessa.

---

* The White pro-monarchist forces in the Black Sea region had commandeered many ships of the Russian navy during the Russian Civil War (1918–1922).
† Turkish: "Sir."
** Turkish: "Fine!"

Juliet sailed with extinguished lights, and fought hard to survive a gale of unprecedented strength. The wind was blowing at force eleven, and in Novorossiysk, the gigantic *Transbalt* had torn loose from its anchor. The *Kapnaro* and the *Admiral De Roiter* had been lost at sea, but *Juliet,* with her extinguished lights and broken propeller, without coal and managing to dodge her hunters, headed home for Odessa.

Juliet's light hull bobbed on the unfathomable waves, her radio and her siren echoed through the black, unfathomable depths, but the vessel with the shattered propeller, dragged in tow by an icebreaker, arrived in Odessa. And today the British flag flying above the *Paris* was lowered. Orchestras, Komsomols, and sailors came down to the port. The British flag fell slowly onto the stern like an injured bird, and our red flag climbed the difficult pole of our six-year ascent.

The English sailors laughed as they left the ship, and the Russian sailors laughed as they boarded it. Then everyone went down to the wardroom, drank wine, and danced on the decks, pounding their heels harder than the God of yore hurled his toothless thunderclaps.

Because all this was extremely funny. The English sailors lost nothing, handing over the goods their masters had stolen, and we won everything, regaining the steamer that had been illegally seized by its former masters.

The proletariat lost nothing on that day, and that was why everyone drank wine and stomped their feet harder than God hurled His thunderclaps.

X

❧

Reports from France

1935

B*abel arrived suddenly and unexpectedly in Paris in 1935. The International Congress of Writers for the Defense of Culture had been called together under the chairmanship of André Malraux and André Gide for the purpose of discussing ways of opposing fascism and war. Over two hundred official delegates from thirty-eight countries participated, speaking before an audience of over two thousand in Paris' Palais de la Mutualité. The world's foremost writers attended, among them E. M. Forster, Aldous Huxley, Bertold Brecht, and Robert Musil.*

When the Soviet delegation arrived in Paris, Malraux and Gide were outraged that Isaac Babel and Boris Pasternak had not been brought to France as part of the Soviet delegation. As Malraux told his biographer Jean Lacouture in a 1972 interview, "Gide and I went to the Soviet embassy to demand, in view of the importance of the Congress, that the French proletariat be given the opportunity of hailing the artists it most admired, namely Pasternak and Babel. . . . The ambassador immediately called Moscow." As a result, Stalin's personal secretary contacted Babel and Pasternak and ordered them to present themselves immediately at an air base from which they were to be flown directly to Paris in a Soviet Air Force plane. Pasternak, bedridden in a clinic where he was convalescing from a "nervous condition," was too ill to fly, and Babel offered to accompany him by train. By the time they arrived, the conference was already in its third day, but both Babel and Pasternak gave impromptu speeches that were received with great acclaim. As Babel wrote on June 27 to his mother and sister, who were living in Brussels, "I'll spend the short time assigned to me in Paris roaming around in search of material like a hungry wolf." Babel did not return to Moscow with the Soviet delegation, but spent a few months with his wife and daughter Nathalie, who were living in Paris.

The following pieces, published two years later in the Soviet Union in PIONER, are the result.

THE CITY OF LIGHT

*S*ince my earliest childhood I have heard people speak of the great city. The French call it "La Ville de Lumière"—the city of light. In the West it is considered the capital of the world.

Our train pulled in at Gare du Nord. We stepped out onto the platform, and experienced something along the lines of disappointment. Dirt, clamor, no discernible order anywhere. Where signs cautioned "Do Not Walk" people were walking. Where it said "No Smoking" everyone smoked. The crowds were singing and laughing. A group of youngsters were kissing loudly in a din of whistle and song.

We left the station. We saw gloomy, smoke-blackened three-story houses, and piles of garbage on the streets. The day of our arrival was stifling. A yellow sun hung heavily above the hot flagstones. In sidewalk cafés, stout men had taken off their jackets and sat at ease in their shirts and vests, talking loudly, reminding me of my fellow townspeople back in Odessa—the same kind of nimble, trivial, self-assured folk.

We did not find what we had expected: there was no solemnity, punctiliousness, or ostentatious splendor, no particular sparkle, no imposing buildings. What we found was an old-fashioned jumble of a town. Next to the wide, glittering boulevards lay narrow back alleys and cul-de-sacs through which crowds thronged in loud disorder.

After we had stayed awhile in Paris, taking in all we encountered (though we didn't always know what things were, or their importance), we gradually began to understand why so many artists from all over the world come to Paris for a week or month but end up staying for the rest of their lives in this city, which itself evolved like a work of art.

The city is a thousand years old. People from every nation, from every walk of life, live here—it is a world in miniature. Its diversity is unmatched. There isn't a tongue you will not hear spoken in Paris, and no human emotion that is not expressed in one of these countless tongues. Every wine can be tasted. A Frenchman I met fervently assured me that the best Ukrainian borscht was not to be found in Poltava but in Paris, in a little side street off the Champs-Élysées. And he was right. Les Champs-Élysées—the Elysian Fields—how strange this name sounds to our ears! The French consider it the most beautiful boulevard in the world. It stretches from the Place de la Concorde to the ancient and eternal Bois de Boulogne, and in its wide, triumphant course it passes crystal fountains and green public gardens, rainwater glittering and gushing over its marble flagstones.

Little by little we cast off our initial impressions to make way for new ones. There were few children on the boulevards, but an abundance of old men and women, reading newspapers, knitting, watching children, talking tirelessly of food, and discussing what the weather was like last Thursday—I must confess that these people managed to cure me of my distaste for what is commonly known as "weather talk." It is the city dweller's attempt, however feeble, to get close to nature.

On the streets the crowds were restless and conceited. When a street musician appears, he is immediately surrounded by people snatching up leaflets on which the words of a song are written, which they all then sing along with him. When a tram conductor speaks sharp words to a passenger, a merry hullabaloo breaks out that lasts a good half hour. One might be misled into thinking that these people lead a superficial existence. At first you think: Is it possible that these flighty, brazen people gave birth to art of such peerless beauty, clarity, and simplicity? Is it possible that these are the people who gave us Balzac and Hugo, Voltaire and Robespierre? One needs time to sense wherein lie the mystery and delight of this city and of its people, and of the magnificent country as a whole, nurtured with love, thoughtfulness, and taste.

There are publishing houses in Paris that are centuries old, and sitting in little bookstores you will more often than not find a great-great-grandson, the direct descendant of the man who founded the store some three hundred years ago, in an era when wolves and bears roamed the outskirts of Moscow. Here the accumulation of wealth, knowledge, and technical expertise began centuries earlier than it did in Russia. The culture of France does not manifest itself with fanfare—vigilance and earnestness are necessary to penetrate its depths.

If there is such a thing as national character, then the French, when seen from a broad perspective, are a philosophical people of clear, exact, elegant thought, with deep meanings often hidden behind jokes. Regardless of their reputation, the French are not an open people— they do not wear their hearts on their sleeves. The problem is that the power of the capitalists and the political system of capitalist government disfigure the wonderful face of this country, shattering its nerve centers.

FRENCH SCHOOLS

*S*een from a Soviet viewpoint, French schools are badly organized. Here France has lagged behind along with the most underdeveloped nations of Europe, with old, scholastic teaching methods, with cramming as the basis of teaching.

Children spend up to ten hours a day in school. They enter school when they are six. There is much homework and the requirements are harsh. Physical education is only now beginning to catch on. The French schoolboy is a puny, tormented creature. Our children differ very favorably from French children in strength and uncomplicated, healthy cheerfulness. The ancient French school buildings resemble bastions and fortresses. They are morose and prisonlike. These buildings, and the routine of school life, serve to smother and cow a child's imagination. Cramming for Latin and Greek begins already after the second school year. When the French have completed their education, they know the ancient languages and the classical authors, but the price is an overwhelming strain on their physical strength. And the French themselves are the first to confess that more than half of what they have studied in school is so inapplicable to life, so false and scholastic, that they regret the time and energy they have wasted all these years.

The teaching is better organized in the schools run by the Jesuit Order, one of the ablest, most persistent, and educated orders of the Catholic Church. The poison of religious education seeps into the children's consciousness with such delicate furtiveness, through methods so wily and exhaustive, that its danger should not be underestimated. The

Jesuits have the best teachers, the best equipment, hot breakfasts, adept after-school programs, and a pleasant, soft countenance. Many working men and women become entangled in this trap and are molded in a spirit advantageous to the Jesuits.

A very different wind blows in schools of higher education. The Sorbonne, a network of Parisian universities, is made up of gigantic, gray, cold buildings, but inside bubbles a cheerful, multilingual, energetic crowd.

Anyone can walk into the Sorbonne, sign up for a course, pay a few dozen francs, and attend. Let us say you have studied archaeology or geography. At the Sorbonne you can walk up to a famous professor and tell him, "I would like you to examine me in the course you are teaching in geography." This professor is then compelled to examine you and issue you a certificate. You needn't even be signed up.

Is this a good system? That I do not know. But at least it is not weighed down by bureaucracy.

TOWN AND COUNTRY

I rode along on the surprising French highways, a map by my side. Considering the number of kilometers I had put behind me, I should have been deep in the countryside by now. But on either side of the road stood dull, eyeless walls without windows or doors. I drove through this morose medley of warehouses or armories, and asked the first man I came across where the countryside might be.

"You've passed it," he told me.

The walls I had taken to be those of armories or depots turned out to shelter living, breathing people, not plows and grain. Wealthy French farmers (kulaks, as good, honest people call them back home), build their houses with windows and doors that face the inner courtyards, raising self-contained fortresses that differ from medieval castles only in their commonplaceness and size. "Dog eat dog"—that is what is written in invisible letters on these walls. Each farmstead is an enemy of the next, each farm pitted against the other.

The soul delights when this somber vista changes into the panorama of a little town. One comes across them quite often, serene, both gothic and romantic, hidden in greenery and enveloped by flowers. Much in France is timeworn, but much has also been newly built. The earth has been worked and adorned by the hands of many generations. This labor was fostered by the blessed climate of the south.

I will never forget the days I spent in Marseilles, on the Mediterranean shore "beneath skies eternally blue," beneath the brilliant, generous sun. The fresh sea breeze sways the branches of palms and of lemon, orange, and olive trees. The cheerful southern streets start by the sea. But Marseilles also has an old quarter where the sun does not seep through. The alleys there are narrow, and the houses medieval and six, seven stories high. The sun does not penetrate the tight shafts between these medieval bastions crowded close together in the damp, winding corridors of the little streets, where two vehicles cannot fit side by side, and the stench of the desolate apartments is stupefying. High up between the houses hangs the washing. Down below in the streets and the passageways, people cook food on little coal stoves, disseminating pungent, spicy odors. Moors, Arabs, and Negroes, the downtrodden workforce of the Port of Marseilles, live here in poverty. Five hundred meters away the emerald sea glitters, the water reflecting the nimble white hulls of the yachts, and above the sea rises the elegant quarter with its villas and palaces, while the powerful, surging bodies of expensive cars rocket through the streets. Comrades, that's capitalism for you!

COURT OF JUSTICE AND PARLIAMENT

*T*he chambers of the criminal court. The judge is presiding, and around him is such a howl and din, such a racket, that it is impossible to figure out who the defendant is, who the counsel for the defense, or which side is which.

The sentence is passed in quite a casual, offhand manner: Two years. Three years. Six months. The defendant may leave!

At first one is amused by all this hullabaloo. But then, when it turns out that these sentences, passed with a casual flick of the wrist in this loud market-square jumble, send people to prison for years of hard labor, one's mood changes. There are a great number of cases, so the hearing moves forward with bulletlike speed, conducted by a presiding judge, to whom a lavish shower of witticisms appear the height of *bon ton*. A typical hearing:

"*Bonjour,* my friend. So we meet at last. I take it you have ended up here by mistake? You are completely innocent, am I right? But as we have all gathered here, would you perhaps be so kind as to give us a detailed account of how you pulled off all those low-down tricks?"

Defense attorneys are second in order of importance in the French judicial system. Regardless of how insignificant a case may be, the defense attorney sees it as his duty to be as verbose as possible, brimming over with pathos and histrionic gestures as he delves into the mists of time. He is followed the way an actor is followed on the stage, and assessed by the audience as an actor might be. And what is more, this performance does not hinder the presiding judge from going on with other things, chatting with his colleagues, doing paperwork. Nor does the performance hinder the presiding judge at the end from leaning toward the other two judges, ancient men reminiscent of Egyptian mummies, one sitting to his right and one to his left, and casually saying, "Three years. You may go, my friend. Gendarmes, take him away."

There is not much more order in the French Parliament. A beautiful, semicircular hall, usually about three-quarters empty: The delegates do not listen to the speaker, but talk loudly among themselves, write letters, and read newspapers. The speaker is not talking to them, but to the stenographer. The parliamentary hall jumps to life when a renowned speaker takes the podium or if some scandal is under way—of which there never seems to be a lack.

THE POPULAR FRONT

*T*he last elections strengthened the role and importance of the Communist faction in the French Parliament. The French Communists have been the architects of the Popular Front against Fascism. The parties of the Communists, Socialists, and Radicals have joined forces to mount a collective action in a united Popular Front.

The current French government is supported by the Popular Front. Socialists and Radicals are now represented in the government, and the Communists support it in the name of the struggle against the terrible menace hanging over the world, the struggle against Fascism. The Communists stand at the head of the people's battle for peace, for a France that is happy and free.

I shall never forget July 14, 1935, Bastille Day, which I spent in Paris. The prison which the rebelling masses had torn down on July 14, 1789, had stood on the Place de la Bastille, an event which began the French Revolution that overthrew the king and toppled the feudal system, launching a new era in the history of man. This day is celebrated. The people of Paris pour into the streets, dance night and day, and rejoice as only children and sages can. On July 14, 1935, the old *Place* that has seen so much saw millions of proletarians pledging an oath of unity and battle.

In the first rows of the march were the leaders of the Popular Front. Sidewalks, windows, and window ledges were filled with hundreds of thousands of people. The French crowd brims over with mirth. It laughs and horses around; firecrackers crackle, joyful tunes roar out of key. After the leaders of the Popular Front came the Central Committees of the three parties, and after them, in a separate group, representatives of the Popular Front: writers, artists, and scientists.

The degree of applause and noise with which the crowd greeted each of the leaders of the three parties made it clear on whose side the people of Paris were. The Parisian workers' most enthusiastic approbation, the most boisterous applause, was accorded to the Central Committee of the Communist Party.

It was a workers' demonstration, a procession of men and women with rough, callused hands and with Phrygian caps on their heads. At the same time a second demonstration, with different people and different ideals, was marching up the Champs-Élysées. My comrades and I took a taxi and rode from the Place de la Bastille to the Champs-Élysées. The area between the two demonstrations seemed dead. There were no children or old men and women on the boulevards, the squares, or the embankments. Only rows of soldiers, their weapons stacked in racks, stood in the public gardens.

On the Champs-Élysées we saw another world, another state of mind. Here too the crowds were French. On the Place de la Bastille the masses were shouting, "Long live Soviet Russia!" while on the Champs-Élysées the frenzied crowd was yelling, "To the gallows with the Soviets!" and "Down with Soviet Russia!"

A cheerful crowd of laborers was marching on the Place de la Bastille, while here, on the Champs-Élysées, Fascists in black shirts and black caps were marching, stamping their boots in military fashion.

THE POWER OF
MONEY

The workers are in support of the current French government because it is fighting for peace, against Fascism, and is in the process of strengthening its ties with the Soviet Union. And yet France is still a bourgeois country, and the main power behind it is the power of money. The government cannot abolish that power, but it has been endeavoring to loosen the grip that the bankers and financial bigwigs have over the country. This endeavor is supported not only by France's workers and farmers, but also by a large section of the intelligentsia and a section of the petite bourgeoisie that is being smothered by bankers and factory magnates.

At the head of the French national bank, the main financial institution of the country, there had been a board of twelve directors. These twelve men had been the cornerstone of France's economy.

The government disbanded the board of twelve, appointed a new director of the bank, and so knocked the single most powerful weapon out of the hands of the bankers and speculators.

We have all heard the surprising reports about the extent to which the press is bribed in bourgeois countries. But on arriving here, we came face-to-face with this daily crime, and the only surprise was how simple the whole process was.

Someone found deposits of lead or zinc somewhere in Morocco or Algeria. They found about a hundred pounds of it—in other words, the deposits could in no way be considered of any industrial significance. The speculators, however, were not about to let such a chance slip through their fingers. This very moment a stock-trading enter-prise is being launched with a capital of about a million francs, with the aim of putting new mines into operation. In order to raise the mil-lion francs, a hundred thousand pieces of paper have been issued—shares which have to be sold. But the whole thing is a sham, there is no zinc worth mentioning, and selling the stocks is difficult. So a phone call is made to a journalist, who is told, "Here's ten thousand francs. How about writing that you were there and saw the zinc pits with your own eyes?"

And within three days the following article appears in a news-paper:

"The richest deposits of lead, zinc, and copper . . . stunning land-scape . . . all those wishing to grow rich should buy these stocks."

One article is published, a second, a third—all by the reporter "on location," and there are lots of pictures. Anyone who buys bonds at a hundred francs will earn two hundred francs within a year. And the public rushes off to invest its last centime.

All this came about as a result of extensive and deceitful publicity. In France there are people known as *rentiers*, "pensioners." More often than not these *rentiers* come in the form of a little old man and a little old woman who, having managed to amass a little capital, sit in the sun twiddling their thumbs without having to work, and spend their time hatching plans for how they can get rich. One newspaper tells them, "Invest all your money in zinc!" Another trumpets, "Invest in copper mines!" After much pondering, they make up their minds. They believe that their ten thousand francs will turn into twenty thousand within a year. But the truth is that they will never see those twenty thousand francs—nor the ten thousand they invested. I mentioned old-age pen-sioners. But needless to say, they are not the only ones affected. There are quite a few people here who believe that living at the expense of others is not only not criminal, but constitutes their most cherished dream.

That's how things stand.

There is falsehood all around—it is both bought and sold. Even in the theater. If I have money, then I can go to Paris, proclaim that I am a renowned singer, and hold a press conference. Fifty articles are writ-ten analyzing my voice, my mode of singing, proclaiming that the crowds carry me on their shoulders through the streets of Moscow, and, needless to say, the public comes in droves. One thing is certain: the worse my voice, the more I have to pay for publicity.

This canker is devouring France, so wonderful in its diversity and wealth, this country of great scientists, poets, and artists.

THE RED BELT

*P*aris is girdled by small towns. They are considered her suburbs, and most of her mills and factories, businesses and establishments are there. The votes of the masses working there belong to the Communist Party, and most of the towns surrounding Paris are Communist municipalities. This belt tied tightly around Paris is a red belt.

One of the places our Soviet delegation visited (we were attending the International Congress of Writers for the Defense of Culture) was Villejuif, one of the Red suburbs of Paris. The mayor of Villejuif, Vaillant-Couturier, is a member of the French Communist Party, a writer and journalist, and the editor in chief of the newspaper *l'Humanité*.* The transition from the capital, with its intricate, contradictory, frightening apparatus of the bourgeois state, to Villejuif, a hotbed of the future, was striking.

There is no noticeable border marking where Paris ends and the small surrounding towns begin. The endless city stretches over dozens of kilometers, the quarters becoming poorer the farther one gets from the center, and one sees more and more factory overalls being worn, which soon enough become the predominant dress.

We arrived in Villejuif and went straight to the town hall. Everyone addresses each other as "Comrade," and in all the offices there is so

---

*Paul Vaillant-Couturier, 1892–1937, renowned Communist politician, author, and journalist, had been editor in chief of *l'Humanité*, France's Communist newspaper, since 1926. He met Babel at the conference in Paris, where both were speakers.

much esprit de corps, simplicity, and sincerity, that we immediately felt as if we were back home. We understood not only with our minds but also with our hearts that the world of Communist ideals is as wide and boundless as the earth.

In the town hall we spent a few hours talking to Vaillant-Couturier. People came to this Communist mayor on the most unusual business—workers, the bourgeoisie, speculators, and military men.

Most of the people who came were out of work. One of them complained to the mayor, "My boss, that damn dog, laid me off, and now he refuses to sign a paper so that I can get my severance pay! Please help me, Vaillant!"

And Vaillant helps him. Then and there he writes a note to the "damn dog":

"Dear Sir, etc., etc., I suggest that you immediately pay in full the money owed to Monsieur so-and-so. Should you refuse to do so, then . . ."

One feels certain that the "damned dog" will not "refuse to do so." The worker takes the note and thanks the mayor.

Within half an hour the boss comes rushing in, disheveled and distraught.

"Monsieur Vaillant, I swear that deep in my soul I too am a Communist, but I swear that I do not owe that man a hundred francs! You are ruining me! You're adding things up all wrong. The workers live better than I do! I'm ruined! I don't even have enough money to pay off the mounting interest."

Vaillant pats him on the shoulder. "Don't worry, my friend! Soon enough all your troubles will be over! When France becomes Communist you will no longer have to pay any interest, and the state will no longer have to pay any unemployment!"

A cold chill runs down the boss's spine, and he leaves deep in thought.

The best school in France has been built in the Communist municipality of Villejuif.* Its architecture is uncommonly attractive and cheerful—it is exquisitely built. There is a large fresco by Lurçat and classrooms full of light and harmony. There are flower beds, halls for

---

* L'École Karl Marx, built by the French architect André Lurçat, 1894–1970, had been inaugurated July 9, 1933, two years before Babel's visit to Villejuif. The school had aroused international attention because of its avant-garde architecture and Marxist curriculum.

physical education, and a movie theater. This school is the eighth wonder of the world for the people of France, who are used to dour, medieval school buildings. Even the official government could not help but be impressed by the brilliance and simplicity of the building and the innovative methods of teaching. The Minister of Education had expressed the wish to participate in the ceremony opening the school. However, he had been given to understand that the prospect of his participation was not viewed with much enthusiasm. He got the message.

A Red belt surrounds Paris, and the hour is approaching when, to the joy of all progressive men and women, the Red suburbs will unite with a Red Paris.

XI

❧

Stories, 1925–1938

B*y 1925, Isaac Babel was beginning to gain fame and notoriety throughout the Soviet Union. In the previous two years, his* Red Cavalry *stories had appeared in quick succession in newspapers and literary magazines, and had been received with great enthusiasm by readers and critics. But they were received with outrage by the powerful commanders who found themselves appearing in the stories in a most unfavorable light. General Budyonny, Division Commander Timoshenko, and Squadron Commander Melnikov (who had been portrayed in the "The Story of a Horse" as having a breakdown that prompted him to leave the cavalry and to resign his membership in the Communist Party), wrote outraged letters and articles that were printed in major newspapers and magazines.* This added greatly to Babel's mystique, and after the* Red Cavalry *stories came out as a book in 1926, it was reprinted eight times over the next few years.*

In the stories in this section, Babel broadened his range of subject matter, dealing more directly than before with autobiographical material and

---

* In reaction to the protests, Babel changed some of the names in later editions of the stories. Timoshenko, for instance, became Savitsky, and Melnikov became Khlebnikov.

---

writing in longer forms. He intended to collect the stories he wrote based on his childhood in a single volume under the title THE STORY OF MY DOVECOTE, and began working on a novel, VELIKAYA KRINITSA, named after a Ukrainian village (Velikaya Staritsa) that he visited in the spring of 1930. The novel was to be about the effects of enforced collectivization on farmers, a dangerous subject for a book during the Stalin era. Two chapters of this novel have survived as separate stories, "Gapa Guzhva," which was to be the first chapter, and "Kolyvushka," which was not published during Babel's lifetime.

Some of Babel's most celebrated stories are from this period. As Maxim Gorky wrote to Romain Rolland in 1928, "Babel is the great hope of Russian literature."

THE STORY OF
MY DOVECOTE

For Maxim Gorky

*A*s a child I wanted a dovecote very badly. In all my life I have never desired anything more intensely. I was nine years old when my father promised to give me the money to buy some planks and three pairs of doves. The year was 1904. I was getting ready for the examinations for the preparatory class of the Nikolayev Lycée. My family lived in Nikolayev, in the province of Kherson. This province no longer exists; our town was absorbed into the district of Odessa.

I was only nine years old, and was frightened of the examinations. In both Russian and mathematics I could not afford to get less than five, the highest grade. The Jewish entry quota for our lycée was harsh, only five percent. Out of forty boys, only two Jews could be admitted into the preparatory class. The teachers would come up with the most cunning questions for these two boys; nobody was given the kind of complicated questions we were. So my father promised to buy me doves on condition that I manage to get two five-pluses. He tormented me more than I can say, I tumbled into a never-ending daydream—the long, desperate dream of a child—and though I went to the examination immersed in that dream, I still fared better than the rest.

I was good at learning. The teachers, though they tried every trick, did not manage to waylay my mind and my sharp memory. I was good at learning, and so got two fives. But then the situation changed. Khariton Efrussi,* the grain merchant who exported wheat to

---

* The Efrussi family was one of the oldest and wealthiest Jewish merchant families in Odessa.

Marseilles, proffered a five-hundred-ruble bribe for his son, I was given a five-minus instead of a five, and the lycée admitted Efrussi Junior in my place. My father was deeply pained by this. From the time I was six, he had taught me all the subjects you could imagine. That minus drove him to desperation. He wanted to beat Efrussi up, or to hire two dock-workers to beat him up, but mother talked him out of it, and I began preparing myself for the examination next year for the following grade. Behind my back, my family talked my tutor into going over the lessons for both the preparatory class and the first class within one year, and, as we were completely desperate, I ended up learning three books by heart. These books were Smirnovsky's grammar, Yevtushevsky's book of mathematical problems, and Putsikovich's introduction to Russian history. Children no longer study these books, but I learned them by heart, line by line, and the following year Karavayev, the schoolmaster, gave me those unattainable five-pluses in my Russian language examination.

Karavayev was a ruddy-faced, indignant man who had been a student in Moscow. He was barely thirty. His manly cheeks blossomed with the flush seen on the cheeks of peasant children. He had a wart on his face from which a tuft of ashen, feline hair sprouted. Also present at the examination besides Karavayev was the deputy warden, who was considered an important figure not only in the lycée but in the whole province. The deputy warden asked me about Peter I, and a blankness came over me, a feeling that the end, the abyss, was near, a dry abyss surrounded by delight and despair.

I knew by heart the passage about Peter the Great in Putsikovich's book and Pushkin's poems. I recited the poems in sobs. Faces swarmed into my eyes, mixing and shuffling deep inside like a fresh deck of cards, while I, shivering, straight-backed, shouted out Pushkin's verses with all my might, as fast as I could. I went on shouting the verses for a long time, nobody interrupting my crazed rambling. Across my crimson blindness, across the freedom that had taken hold of me, I only saw Pyatnitsky's old face leaning forward with its silvery beard. He did not interrupt me, but turned to Karavayev, who was rejoicing in Pushkin and me, and whispered, "What a nation! The devil is in these Yids!"

When I finished he said, "Very good, off you go now, my little friend."

I left the classroom and went out into the corridor, and there, leaning against the unpainted wall, I woke from the convulsions of my dreams. Russian boys were playing all around me, the school bell hung nearby over the official-looking flight of stairs, a watchman was dozing on a broken chair. I gazed at him and began to come back to my senses. Children came creeping toward me from all sides. They wanted to poke me and get me to play with them, but suddenly Pyatnitsky appeared in the corridor. Passing by me, he stopped for an instant, his frock coat undulating in a heavy slow wave over his back. I saw emotion in his large, fleshy, gentlemanly back, and I went up to him.

"Children," he told the schoolboys. "Leave this boy alone!" And he laid his fat, tender hand on my shoulder. "My little friend," Pyatnitsky said, turning to me. "You can go and tell your father that you have been accepted into the first class."

A magnificent star shone on his chest, medals tinkled by his lapel, and hemmed in by the murky walls, moving between them like a barge moves through a deep canal, his large, black, uniformed body marched off on rigid legs and disappeared through the doors of the headmaster's office. A little attendant brought him tea with solemn ceremony, and I ran home to our store.

In our store a muzhik customer sat scratching his head in the grip of indecision. When my father saw me, he abandoned the muzhik and drank in my story without a moment's doubt. He shouted to his sales clerk to close the store, and rushed over to Sobornaya Street to buy me a cap with the school emblem on it. My poor mother barely managed to wrest me away from my delirious father. She stood there, pale, trying to foresee my fate. She kept caressing me and then pushing me away in disgust. She said that a list of all the children admitted into the lycée was always published in the newspapers, and that God would punish us and that people would laugh at us, if we bought a school uniform ahead of time. My mother was pale, she was trying to foresee my fate in my eyes, and looked at me with bitter pity, as if I were a little cripple, for she was the only one who fully realized how luckless our family was.

All the men of our clan had been too trusting of others and too quick to take unconsidered action. We had never had any luck in anything. My grandfather had once been a rabbi in Belaya Tserkov, had been chased out of town for blasphemy, and then lived in scandal and poverty for another forty years, learned foreign languages, and started going insane in his eightieth year. My Uncle Lev, my father's brother, studied at the Yeshiva in Volozhin, evaded conscription in 1892, and abducted the daughter of a quartermaster serving in the Kiev military district. Uncle Lev took this woman to California, to Los Angeles, where he abandoned her, and he died in a madhouse among Negroes and Malays. After his death, the American police sent us his belongings—a large trunk reinforced with brown iron hoops—from Los Angeles. In this trunk were dumbbells, locks of a woman's hair, Uncle's *tallith*, whips with gilded tips, and herbal tea in little boxes trimmed with cheap pearls. The only men left in the family were mad Uncle Simon, who lived in Odessa, my father, and me. But my father was too trusting of others, he offended people with his exhilarating welcome of first love. They did not forgive him for this, and so cheated him. This was why my father believed that his life was governed by a malevolent fate, an inscrutable being that pursued him and that was unlike him in every way. So in our family I was my mother's only hope. Like all Jews, I was short in stature, weak, and plagued by headaches from too much study. My mother could see this clearly. She had never been blinded by her husband's destitute pride and his incomprehensible belief that our family would one day be stronger and richer than other people in this world. She did not foresee any success for us, was frightened of buying a school uniform ahead of time, and only acceded to my having my picture taken by a portrait photographer.

On September 20, 1905, a list of all those who had managed to enter the first class was posted outside the lycée. My name was on that list. My whole family went to look at this piece of paper—even Grandpa Shoyl, my great-uncle, went to the lycée. I loved this braggart of an old man because he sold fish in the market. His fat hands were moist, covered with fish scales, and reeked of wonderful, cold worlds. Shoyl was also different from other people because of his fabricated stories about the Polish uprising of 1861. In the distant past, he had been an innkeeper in Skvira. He had witnessed the soldiers of Nicholas I shoot Count Godlewski and other Polish insurgents. But then again, maybe he hadn't witnessed this. Now I know that Shoyl was no more than an old fool and a naive teller of tall tales, but I have not forgotten those little tales of his, they were good tales. So even foolish Shoyl went over to the lycée to read the list that had my name on it, and in the evening he danced and stamped his feet at our beggarly feast.

My father organized a feast of celebration and invited his comrades—grain merchants, estate brokers, and itinerant salesmen who sold agricultural machines in our region. These itinerant salesmen sold machines to everyone. Both muzhiks and landowners were afraid of them, as they could not get rid of them without buying something. Of all the Jews, the itinerant salesmen are the most worldly and cheerful. At our feast they sang drawn-out Hasidic songs made up of only three words, but with many funny intonations. Only those who have celebrated Passover with the Hasidim, or who have visited their boisterous synagogues in Volhynia, know the charm of these intonations. Old Liberman, who taught me Hebrew and the Torah, also came to our house that evening. My family always addressed him as Monsieur Liberman. He drank more Bessarabian wine than he should have, the traditional silk strings slipped out from under his red vest, and he called out a toast in my honor in Hebrew. In this toast the old man congratulated my parents, and said that by passing this examination I had won a victory over all my foes, I had won a victory over the fat-cheeked Russian boys and the sons of our roughneck rich. Thus in ancient times had David, the King of the Jews, won a victory over Goliath, and just as I had triumphed over Goliath, so too would our people, through its sheer power of mind, triumph over the foes that surround us, eager for our blood. Monsieur Liberman wept, pronounced these words weeping, drank some more wine, and yelled, "*Vivat!*" The dancing guests took him into the circle and danced with him the ancient quadrille, as at a shtetl wedding. Everyone was joyful at our feast, even my mother took a little sip of wine, though she did not like vodka and did not understand how anyone could. Which is why she thought all Russians were mad, and why she could not understand how women could live with Russian husbands.

But our happy days were to begin later. For my mother they began when she started making me sandwiches in the morning before I left for school, when we went from store to store buying festive supplies— a pencil box, a piggybank, a schoolbag, new books with hard covers, and notebooks with glossy covers. No one in the world has a stronger response to new things than children. They shudder at the smell that new things give off, like dogs at the scent of a rabbit, and experience a madness, which later, when one is an adult, is called inspiration. And this clean, childish feeling of ownership of new things infected my mother too. It took us a whole month to get used to the pencil box and the morning twilight, when I would drink tea at the edge of the large, brightly lit table and gather my books into my schoolbag. It took us a whole month to get used to our happy life, and it was only after the first school term that I remembered the doves.

I had gotten everything ready for them—the one and a half rubles and the dovecote made out of a box by Grandpa Shoyl. The dovecote was given a coat of brown paint. It had nests for twelve pairs of doves, a series of little slats on its roof, and special grating I had invented so that it would be easier for other doves to come in too. Everything was ready. On Sunday, October 22, I set off to the wild game market, but I ran into unexpected obstacles along the way.

The story I am relating here, in other words my entry into the first class of the lycée, took place in the autumn of 1905. Czar Nicholas was in the process of giving the Russian people a constitution, and orators in threadbare coats were clambering onto podiums outside the buildings of the town councils and giving speeches to the people. On the streets at night shots were fired, and my mother did not want to let me go to the wild game market. Early in the morning on October 20, the boys from next door were flying a kite right outside the police station, and our water carrier, abandoning all his duties, strolled pomaded and red-faced along the street. Then we saw the sons of Kalistov, the baker, drag a leather vaulting horse out onto the street and start to do their exercises right in the middle of the road. Nobody tried to stop them. Semernikov, the constable, was even egging them on to jump higher. Semernikov was wearing a homemade silk waistband, and his boots that day had been polished to a shine they had never before achieved. An out-of-uniform constable frightened my mother more than anything else, and it was because of him that she would not let me go out. But I crept out onto the street through backyards, and ran all the way to the wild game market, which lay behind the train station.

Ivan Nikodimich, the dove seller, was sitting at his usual place in the market. Besides doves, he was also selling rabbits and a peacock. The peacock, its tail fanned out, sat on a perch, darting its dispassionate head from one side to the other. Its foot was tied with a twisted string, the other end of the string lay wedged under Ivan Nikodimich's wicker chair. The moment I got there, I bought from the old man a pair of cherry-red doves with wonderful ruffled tails, and a pair of crested ones, and hid them in a sack under my shirt. I still had forty kopecks after my purchase, but the old man wouldn't give me a male and female Kryukov dove for that price. What I liked about Kryukov doves was their beaks, which were short, mottled, and amiable. Forty kopecks was the right price for them, but the old man overpriced them and turned away his yellow face, harrowed by the unsociable passions of the bird-catcher. As the market started closing, Ivan Nikodimich called me over, seeing that there weren't going to be any other buyers. Things turned out my way, things turned out badly.

Shortly before noon, or a little after, a man in felt boots walked across the square. He walked lightly on swollen feet, his lively eyes twinkling in his haggard face.

"Ivan Nikodimich," he said, as he walked past the bird-catcher. "Gather up your bits and bobs, in town the nobles of Jerusalem are being given a constitution. On Rybnaya Street they've just served Grandpa Babel a helping of death."

He made his way lightly among the cages, like a barefoot plowman walking along a field path.

"This is wrong!" Ivan Nikodimich muttered after him. "This is wrong!" he shouted more adamantly, gathering up the rabbits and the peacock, and pushing the Kryukov doves into my hands for forty kopecks.

I hid them under my shirt and watched the people run from the market. The peacock on Ivan Nikodimich's shoulder was the last to disappear. It sat like the sun in a damp autumn sky, like July on a rosy riverbank, a scorching July in long cold grass. There was no one left at the market, and shots were thundering not too far away. Then I ran to the train station, cut across the little park, which suddenly seemed to turn upside down, and I dashed into a deserted alley tamped with yellow earth. At the end of the alley sat legless Makarenko in a wheelchair, in which he rode around town selling cigarettes from a tray. The boys from our street bought cigarettes from him, the children liked him, I went running toward him in the alley.

"Makarenko," I said, breathless from running, and patted the legless man on the shoulder. "Have you seen Shoyl?"

The cripple didn't answer, his rough face of red fat and fists and iron was shining translucently. He was fidgeting in his chair, his wife, Katyusha, turning her puffed-up backside toward us, was riffling through things that lay scattered on the ground.

"How many have you counted?" the legless man asked her, pitching away from the woman with his whole body, as if he knew in advance that he wouldn't be able to bear her answer.

"Seven pairs of spats," Katyusha said, without straightening up, "six duvet covers, now I'm counting the bonnets."

"Bonnets!" Makarenko shouted, choked, and made a sound as if he were sobbing. "Obviously, God has chosen me to bear the Cross, Katyusha! People are carting off whole bales of cloth—these people get nice and proper things, and what do we get? Bonnets!"

And sure enough, a woman with a beautiful, fiery face went running down the alley. She was holding a bunch of fezzes in one hand and a bolt of cloth in the other. In a happy, desperate voice she was calling out to her children, who had disappeared. A silk dress and a blue jacket trailed after her scuttling body, and she didn't hear Makarenko, who went rushing after her in his wheelchair. The legless man couldn't catch up with her. His wheels rattled, he moved the levers with all his might.

"Madame!" he yelled deafeningly. "Madamochka! Where did you get the calico?"

But the woman with the scuttling dress was no longer to be seen. A rickety cart came flying around the corner where she had just disappeared. A young peasant was standing upright in the cart.

"Where's everyone run off to?" the young man asked, raising the red reins above his nags, who were straining in their collars.

"Everyone's on Sobornaya Street," Makarenko whined in an imploring voice. "Everyone's there, my dearest, my very dearest friend! Whatever you can grab, bring it here to me—I'll buy everything!"

The young man leaned forward over the front of his cart and whipped his skewbald nags. They bounced in their dirty cruppers like colts and went galloping off. The yellow alley was once again left yellow and empty. The legless man glared at me with his dead eyes.

"Well, am I not the man that God singled out?" he said lifelessly. "Am I not the Son of Man, huh?"

And he stretched out a hand flecked with leprosy.

"What've you got there in that bag?" he said, snatching away the sack that had warmed my heart.

The cripple's fat hand turned the sack upside down and he pulled out a cherry-red dove. The bird lay in his palm, its feet sticking up.

"Doves!" Makarenko said, and rolled up to me with squeaking wheels. "Doves!" he repeated, and slapped me across the face.

He hit me hard with the palm of his hand, crushing the bird. Katyusha's puffed-up backside loomed before my eyes, and I fell down in my new overcoat.

"Their seed has to be stamped out!" Katyusha said, getting up from the bonnets. "I cannot abide their seed and their stinking men!"

She also said other things about our seed, but I no longer heard anything. I lay on the ground, the innards of the crushed bird trickling down the side of my face. They trickled, winding and dribbling, down my cheek, blinding me. The dove's tender entrails slithered over my forehead, and I closed my uncaked eye so that I would not see the world unravel before me. This world was small and ugly. A pebble lay in front of my eyes, a pebble dented like the face of an old woman with a large jaw. A piece of string lay near it and a clump of feathers, still breathing. My world was small and ugly. I closed my eyes so I wouldn't see it, and pressed myself against the earth that lay soothing and mute beneath me. This tamped earth did not resemble anything in our lives. Somewhere far away disaster rode across it on a large horse, but the sound of its hooves grew weaker and vanished, and silence, the bitter silence that can descend on children in times of misfortune, dissolved the boundary between my body and the unmoving earth. The earth smelled of damp depths, of tombs, of flowers. I breathed in its scent and cried without the slightest fear. I walked down a foreign street filled with white boxes, walked in my raiment of blood-drenched feathers, alone on sidewalks swept clean as on a Sunday, and I cried more bitterly, more fully and happily than I would ever cry again. Whitened wires hummed above my head, a little mongrel mutt was running in front of me, in a side street a young muzhik in a vest was smashing a window frame in the house of Khariton Efrussi. He was smashing it with a wooden hammer, his whole body steeped in the movement. He breathed in deeply, smiled in all directions the gentle smile of drunkenness, of sweat and hearty strength. The whole street was filled with the crackling, crashing song of shattering wood. All this muzhik wanted was to flex his back, to sweat, and to yell out bizarre words in an unknown, not Russian language. He shouted them and sang, opening his blue eyes wide, until a religious procession appeared on the street, marching from the town council.

Old men with painted beards were carrying the portrait of a neatly combed Czar, banners with sepulchral saints fluttered above the religious procession, inflamed old women were running in front of it. When the muzhik in the vest saw the procession, he pressed the hammer to his chest and went running after the banners, while I, waiting for the procession to pass, carefully made my way to our house. It was empty. Its white doors stood open, the grass by the dovecote was trampled down. Kuzma, our janitor, was the only one who had not left our courtyard. Kuzma was sitting in the shed, laying out Shoyl's dead body.

"The wind brings you in like a bad splinter," the old man said when he saw me. "You were gone for ages! See how the townsfolk have hacked our Grandpa down?"

Kuzma began sniffling, turned away, and pulled a perch out of the fly of Grandpa's trousers. Two perches had been shoved into Grandpa—one into his fly, the other into his mouth—and although Grandpa was dead, one of the perches was still alive and quivering.

"Just our Grandpa's been hacked down, no one else!" Kuzma said, throwing the perches to the cat. "You should have heard him curse their goddamn mothers up and down! What a sweet man he was. You should lay two fivers on his eyes."

But back then, just ten years old, I had no idea what dead people needed fivers for.

"Kuzma," I whispered, "save us!"

And I went over to the janitor, embraced his old, bent back with its crooked shoulders, and peered at Grandpa Shoyl from behind the janitor's back. Grandpa Shoyl was lying there in the sawdust, his chest crushed, his beard pointing up, rugged shoes on his bare feet. His legs, spread apart, were dirty, purple, dead. Kuzma was bustling around them. He bound Grandpa's jaws, and kept looking to see if there was anything else he had to do for the deceased. He was bustling about as if some new object had just been delivered to his house. He only calmed down after he finished combing the dead man's beard.

"He cursed their goddamn mothers," he said, smiling, and looked at the corpse lovingly. "If they had been Tatars attacking him, he'd have fought them off—but it was Russians who came, women too, damn Russians; those damn Russians think it's an insult to forgive someone, I know those Russians well!"

The janitor poured sawdust under the dead man. He took off his carpenter's apron and grabbed hold of my hand.

"Let's go to your father," he mumbled, squeezing my hand harder and harder. "Your father's been looking for you since this morning, he must be half dead with worry!"

And I went with Kuzma to the house of the tax inspector, where my parents had hidden from the pogrom.

FIRST LOVE

*W*hen I was ten years old I fell in love with a woman by the name of Galina Apollonovna. Her surname was Rubtsov. Her husband, an officer in the army, had gone to the Japanese War and returned in October 1905. He brought many trunks back with him. These trunks were full of Chinese things: folding screens, precious weapons—all in all, thirty *poods*. Kuzma told us that Rubtsov had bought them with money he had made serving in the engineering corps of the Manchurian Army. Others said the same thing. People found it hard to gossip about the Rubtsovs, because the Rubtsovs were happy. Their house lay right next to our property. Their glass veranda cut into a piece of our land, but my father had not quarreled with them about it. Old Rubtsov, the tax inspector, was known in our town as a fair man, he counted Jews among his acquaintances. And when his son, the officer, returned from the Japanese War, we all saw how lovingly and happily he and his wife settled down together. For days on end Galina Apollonovna would hold her husband's hand. She didn't take her eyes off him, as she hadn't seen him for a year and a half. But I was horrified at her gaze, and looked away, shivering. In the two of them I was watching the strange and shameful life of all the people in the world, and I wanted to fall into a magic sleep to forget this life that surpassed all my dreams. Sometimes Galina Apollonovna would walk about her room in red shoes and a Chinese dressing gown, her braid hanging loose. Beneath the lace of her low-cut chemise I could see the deepening onset of her pressed-down breasts, white and swollen, and on her dressing gown dragons, birds, and hollow trees embroidered in silk.

All day she trailed about the house, a vague smile on her wet lips, bumping into the trunks that had not yet been unpacked and the exercise ladders that lay around on the floor. Whenever Galina bruised her leg, she would lift her dressing gown above her knees and croon to her husband, "Kiss my little booboo!"

And the officer, bending his long legs in dragoon's breeches, spurs, and tight kidskin boots, got down on the dirty floor, and, smiling, shuffled crawling on his knees to her and kissed the bruised spot, the spot where her garter had left a puffy crease. I saw those kisses from my window. They caused me great suffering, but it is not worth describing because the love and jealousy of a ten-year-old boy resembles in every way the love and jealousy of a grown man. For two weeks I did not go to my window and avoided Galina, until a coincidence threw us together. The coincidence was the pogrom that broke out in 1905 in Nikolayev and other towns inside the Jewish Pale. A crowd of hired killers ransacked my father's store and killed my Grandpa Shoyl. All this happened without me. That morning I had been out buying doves from Ivan Nikodimich, the hunter. For five of my ten years I had dreamed with all the fervor of my soul about having doves, and then, when I finally managed to buy them, Makarenko the cripple smashed the doves against the side of my face. After that Kuzma had taken me to the Rubtsovs. A cross had been drawn in chalk on the Rubtsovs' gate, no one would harm them, and they had hidden my parents. Kuzma took me to their glass veranda. There, in the green rotunda, sat my mother and Galina.

"We're going to have to wash our face," Galina said to me. "We're going to have to wash it, my little rabbi. Our whole little face is covered in feathers, and the feathers are all bloody."

She hugged me and led me along the corridor with its sharp aroma. My head was leaning against Galina's hip, and her hip moved and breathed. We went into the kitchen, and she put my head under the tap. A goose was frying on the tiled oven, flickering kitchenware hung along the walls, and next to the kitchenware, in the cook's corner, hung Czar Nicholas I, decorated with paper flowers. Galina washed off the remains of the dove that were caking my cheeks.

"As handsome as a bridegroom, my pretty little boy," she said, then kissed me on the lips with her puffy mouth and turned away.

"Your Papa," she suddenly whispered, "your Papa is very troubled right now. All day long he has been wandering aimlessly through the streets. Go to the window and call him!"

Outside the window I saw the empty street with the enormous sky above it, and my red-haired father walking along. He wasn't wearing a hat, and his red hair was tousled and wispy. His paper shirtfront was twisted to the side and fastened haphazardly with a button, but not the right one. Vlasov, a haggard workman in patched-up soldier's rags, was doggedly following my father.

"No, we don't need it!" he was saying in a fervent, wheezing voice, patting my father tenderly with both hands. "We don't need freedom just so the Yids can trade freely! Just give a working man a life of bright . . . brightfulness . . . for all his big horrible toil! Give it to him, my friend! You hear me? Give it to him!"

The workman was patting my father, beseeching him. In his face, flashes of pure drunken inspiration alternated with drowsy despondence.

"Like wimps, that's what our lives should be like," he muttered, swaying on unsteady legs. "Our lives should be just like wimps, only without that God of the Old Betrievers*—it's from Him the Jews make a profit, no one else does!"

And Vlasov began shouting desperately about the God of the "Old Betrievers," who took pity on no one but the Jews. Vlasov howled, stumbled, and tried to catch up with his mysterious God, but at that moment a mounted Cossack patrol blocked his path. An officer in striped trousers, wearing a silver parade belt, was riding at the head of the detachment. A tall peaked cap was perched on his head. The officer rode slowly, without looking left or right. He rode as if he were riding through a ravine where one can only look forward.

"Captain," my father whispered, when the Cossack reached his side. "Captain," my father repeated, falling to his knees in the mud and clasping his head.

---

* Vlasov mispronounces *Staro-Ver* ("Old Believer") as *Stalo-Ver* ("Started-Believing"), and comically identifies the Old Believers with the Jews. The Old Believers were an archconservative Christian sect that had split from the Russian Orthodox Church in the seventeenth century.

"What can I do for you?" the officer answered, still looking forward, lifting his hand in its lemon suede glove to his peaked cap.

Up ahead, at the corner of Rybnaya Street, thugs were smashing our store and throwing out into the street boxes of nails, tools, and also the new portrait photograph of me in my lycée uniform.

"Over there," my father said, without getting up from his knees. "They're smashing everything I've worked for all my life, Captain! Why are they doing this?"

The officer muttered something, tapped his cap with his lemon suede glove, and tugged the reins, but his horse didn't move. My father had crawled on his knees in front of it, brushing against its kindly, short, slightly shaggy legs.

"I will see to it!" the captain said, tugged at the reins, and rode off. The Cossacks followed him.

They sat dispassionately on their high saddles, riding through their imaginary ravine, and disappeared around the corner of Sobornaya Street.

Galina again pushed me toward the window.

"Get your Papa to come home," she said. "He hasn't eaten anything since this morning."

And I leaned out the window.

My father turned around when he heard my voice.

"My darling son," he called out with indescribable tenderness.

He and I went up to the veranda of the Rubtsovs, where mother was lying in the green rotunda. Next to her bed lay dumbbells and an exercise machine.

"Those damn kopecks!" my mother said to us as we came in. "People's lives, and children, and our luckless luck. You gave them everything! Those damn kopecks!" she shouted in a hoarse voice unlike her own. She shuddered convulsively, and lay quiet on the bed.

Then, in the silence, I began to hiccup. I stood by the wall with my cap pulled down and couldn't stop hiccuping.

"Shame on you, my pretty little boy," Galina said, smiling her haughty smile at me, and tapping me with the stiff flap of her dressing gown. She went over to the window in her red shoes and began to hang Chinese curtains on the extraordinary rod. Her bare arms drowned in the silk, the live braid moved over her hip. I looked at her with delight.

Learned boy that I was, I looked at her as at a distant stage lit by many lights. And I imagined I was Miron, the son of the coal merchant who sold coal on our street corner. I imagined myself in the Jewish Self-defense Brigade. I could see myself walking around, just like Miron, in tattered shoes tied together with string. A dingy rifle hangs on a green strap from my shoulder, and I'm kneeling by the old wooden fence, firing shots at the murderers. Beyond the fence lies a vacant lot with heaps of dusty coal. My old rifle shoots badly, the murderers with their beards and white teeth are edging ever closer to me. I feel the proud sensation of impending death, and high, high up, high in the blue heavens, I see Galina. I see an opening cut into the wall of a gigantic fortress built with myriads of bricks. This crimson building looms over the side street with its badly tamped gray earth. On the parapet stands Galina. With her haughty smile she smiles from that inaccessible opening, her husband, the half-dressed officer, standing behind her back, kissing her neck.

In my attempt to stop hiccuping, I imagined all this in order to make my loving her more bitter, hot, and hopeless, and perhaps because so much grief is overwhelming for a ten-year-old boy. These foolish fantasies helped me forget the death of the doves and the death of Shoyl. I would have perhaps forgotten these deaths if Kuzma had not come onto the veranda with that terrible Jew, Aba.

It was twilight when they came. A weak little lamp, hiding in a corner, shone on the veranda—a twinkling lamp, a disciple of misfortune.

"I have prepared Grandfather," Kuzma said as he came in. "Now he's lying nice and pretty—I brought the *shamas* too so he can say some words over the old man."

And Kuzma pointed to *shamas* Aba.

"Let him whine a little," Kuzma said amiably. "Stuff a *shamas'* guts, and the *shamas* will pester God all night."

Kuzma stood on the threshold, his good-natured, broken nose jutting in all directions, and warmly began telling us how he had bound the dead man's jaw. But my father interrupted him.

"I would be thankful, Reb Aba, if you would pray over the deceased, I will pay you," my father said.

"Pay me? But I'm worried you won't pay," Aba answered in a weary voice, laying his squeamish bearded face on the tablecloth. "I am worried that you will take my ruble and run off to Argentina, to Buenos Aires, and open a wholesale business there with that ruble of mine! A wholesale business!" Aba said. He chewed his disdainful lips and picked up the newspaper *Son of the Fatherland*, which was lying on the table. In this newspaper there was an article about the Czar's manifesto of October 17, and about freedom.

"Citizens of free Russia," Aba read haltingly, and chewed his beard, which he had stuffed into his mouth. "Citizens of free Russia, Happy Easter to you all, Christ has risen!" The old *shamas* held the shaking newspaper sideways in front of him. He read it drowsily, in a singsong voice, pronouncing the Russian words he did not know in the strangest way. Aba's pronunciation of these words resembled the muffled babble of a Negro who has just arrived at a Russian port from his native land. It even made my mother laugh.

"I am being sinful," she shouted, leaning out of the rotunda. "You are making me laugh, Aba! You should tell us how you and your family are doing?"

"Ask me about something else," Aba mumbled without releasing his beard from between his teeth, and continued reading the newspaper.

"Ask him something else," my father repeated, walking over to the middle of the room. His eyes, smiling at us through their tears, suddenly began rolling and fixed themselves on a spot invisible to all.

"Oy, Shoyl!" my father uttered in a flat, false, theatrical voice. "*Oy, beloved Shoyl!*"

We saw that he was getting ready to start hollering, and my mother forewarned us.

"Manus!" she shouted, tearing at my father's breast, her hair becoming instantly disheveled. "Look what a state our child is in, can't you hear him hiccuping? Can't you?"

Father fell silent.

"Rakhel," he said timorously, "I cannot tell you how unhappy I am about Shoyl."

Aba went to the kitchen and came back with a glass of water.

"Drink, you little *shlemazl*," he said, coming over to me. "Drink this water, which will help you as much as incense helps a dead man!"

And sure enough, the water did not help me in the least. My hiccups became stronger and stronger. A growl tore out of my chest. A swelling, pleasant to the touch, expanded in my throat. The swelling breathed, widened, covered my gullet, and came bulging out over my collar. Within the swelling gurgled my torn breath. It gurgled like boiling water. By nightfall I was no longer the silly little boy I had been all my life, but had turned into a writhing heap. My mother, now taller and shapelier, wrapped herself in her shawl and went to Galina, who stood watching stiffly.

"My dear Galina," my mother said in a strong, melodious voice. "We are imposing on you and dear Nadyezhda Ivanovna, and all your family so much. My dear Galina, I am so embarrassed!"

With fiery cheeks my mother jostled Galina toward the door, and then came hurrying over to me, stuffing her shawl into my mouth to smother my groans.

"Hold on, my little darling," mother whispered. "Hold on for Mama."

But even if I could have held on, I wouldn't have, because I no longer felt any shame at all.

That was how my illness began. I was ten years old at the time. The following morning I was taken to the doctor. The pogrom continued, but no one touched us. The doctor, a fat man, diagnosed an illness of the nerves.

He told us to go to Odessa as quickly as we could, to the specialists, and to wait there for the warm weather and bathing in the sea.

And that is what we did. A few days later I left for Odessa with my mother to stay with Grandfather Levy-Itskhok and Uncle Simon. We left in the morning on a ship, and by midday the churning waters of the Bug changed to the heavy green waves of the sea. This was the beginning of my life in the house of my crazed Grandfather Levy-Itskhok. And I bade farewell forever to Nikolayev, where I had lived the first ten years of my childhood.

KARL-YANKEL

*I*n the days of my childhood there was a smithy in Peresyp* that belonged to Jonas Brutman. Horse dealers, carters—known as *bindyuzhniks* in Odessa—and butchers from the town slaughterhouses gathered in this smithy. It was on the Balta Road, and it was quite handy as a lookout post for intercepting muzhiks carting oats and Bessarabian wine into town. Jonas was a small, timid man, but he knew his way around wine. In him dwelled the soul of an Odessa Jew.

In my day he had three growing sons. He only came up to their waists. It was on the beach of Peresyp that I first reflected on the power of the forces in nature. The boys, three fattened bulls with crimson shoulders and feet big as shovels, carried shriveled-up little Jonas to the water the way one carries an infant. And yet it had been he, and no one else, who had sired them. There was no doubt about that. The black-smith's wife went to the synagogue twice a week, on Friday evenings and on the morning of the Sabbath. It was a Hasidic synagogue, where on Passover they whirled themselves into an ecstasy like dervishes. Jonas's wife paid tribute to the emissaries sent by the Galician *tsaddiks* to our southern provinces. The blacksmith did not interfere in his wife's relationship with God. After work, he went to a wine shop next to the slaughterhouses, and there, sipping his cheap pink wine, listened meek-ly to what people were talking about—politics and the price of cattle.

His sons resembled their mother in strength and build. As soon as

---

* Odessa's eastern suburb by the harbor.

they came of age, two of the boys went and joined the partisans. The elder was killed at Voznesensk, the other, Semyon, went over to Primakov* and joined a Red Cossack division. He was chosen to be commander of a Cossack regiment. He and a few other shtetl youths were the first in this unexpected breed of Jewish fighters, horsemen, and partisans.

The third son became a blacksmith like his father. He works at the Ghen plow factory.[†] He has not married and has not sired anyone.

The children of Semyon, the Cossack commander, tagged along from place to place with his division. But the old woman needed a grandchild to whom she could tell stories about the Baal-Shem. She was expecting a grandchild from her youngest daughter Paulina. Paulina was the only one in the whole family who resembled little old Jonas. She was timid, nearsighted, and had delicate skin. Many came around asking for her hand in marriage. Paulina chose Ofsey Byelotserkovsky. We could not understand why she chose him. Even more surprising was the news that the young couple was happy. A woman runs her household as she wills, an outsider cannot see pots breaking. But in this case it was Ofsey Byelotserkovsky who was to break the pots. A year into their marriage, he dragged Brana Brutman, his mother-in-law, to court. The old woman had taken advantage of Ofsey's being away on a business trip and Paulina's being in the hospital for a breast inflammation to abduct her newborn grandson and take him to the neighborhood charlatan, Naftula Gerchik. And there, in the presence of ten doddering wrecks—ten ancient and impoverished men, denizens of the Hasidic synagogue—the rites of circumcision were performed.

Ofsey Byelotserkovsky did not find out what had happened until after his return. Ofsey had put himself forward as a candidate to join the Party. He decided to seek the advice of Bychach, the secretary of the local cell of the State Trade Committee.

"You've been morally bespattered!" Bychach told him. "You must pursue this matter further."

---

*Vitaly Markovich Primakov, 1897–1937, a Red Commander who had taken part in the storming of the Winter Palace. In 1918, he had formed the first Red Cossack Regiment, and was later both commander and military commissar of the Eighth Cavalry Division.

[†] One of the largest agricultural machinery factories of the time.

Odessa's public prosecutor's office decided to set up a model public trial at the Petrovsky factory.* Naftula Gerchik, the neighborhood charlatan, and Brana Brutman, sixty-two years of age, found themselves on the defendants' bench.

Naftula was as much an Odessan fixture as the statue of the Duke of Richelieu.† Naftula used to walk past our windows on Dalnitskaya Street carrying his tattered, grease-stained midwife's bag. In that bag he kept his simple instruments. Sometimes he took a little knife out of it, sometimes a bottle of vodka and a piece of honey cake. He'd sniff the honey cake before he drank his vodka, and having drunk it would rattle off some prayers. Naftula was as redheaded as the first redheaded man on earth. When he sliced off what was his due, he did not strain off the blood through a glass funnel, but sucked it with puckered lips. The blood smudged his tousled beard. He appeared tipsy before the guests. His bearlike eyes twinkled cheerfully. Redheaded as the first redheaded man on earth, he whimpered a blessing over the wine. With one hand Naftula pitched his vodka into his mouth's overgrown, crooked, fire-spitting pit, while in the other he held a plate. On this plate lay the little knife, reddened with the infant's blood, and some gauze. As he collected his money, Naftula went from guest to guest with his plate, elbowing his way through the women, falling on them, grabbing their breasts. "Fat mamas!" he howled for the whole street to hear, his little coral eyes glittering. "Go churn out some boys for Naftula, thresh some corn on your bellies! Do your best for Naftula! Go churn out some boys, fat mamas!"

The husbands threw money onto his plate. The women wiped away the blood from his beard. The courtyards of Glukhaya and Gospitalnaya Streets did not lack offspring. They seethed with children, as the mouths of rivers seethe with roe. Naftula went trudging around with his bag, like a tax collector. Orlov, the investigating magistrate, brought Naftula's rounds to an end.

The investigating magistrate thundered from the bench, endeavoring to prove that the neighborhood charlatan was a priest in a cult.

---

* One of the largest steelworks of the time. Its more than eight thousand workers had played a key role in the Revolution. Holding this trial at the Petrovsky factory indicated that the new Soviet government wanted to make a landmark case out of it.

† A French émigré nobleman, governor general of Odessa from 1803–1814, on whom Lord Byron modeled his Don Juan. The famous bronze statue of him was sculpted by Ivan Martos.

"Do you believe in God?" he asked Naftula.

"Let him who won two thousand believe in God," the old man answered.

"Were you not surprised when Comrade Brana Brutman came to you at such a late hour in the rain, carrying a newborn in her hands?"

"I am surprised when a person does something reasonable," Naftula said. "When a person does idiotic things, then I'm not surprised!"

These answers did not satisfy the investigating magistrate. The matter of the glass funnel came next. He charged that by sucking blood with his lips, the defendant was exposing children to the danger of infection. Naftula's head, that shaggy nut of his, hung almost to the ground. He sighed, closed his eyes, and wiped his drooping mouth with his fist.

"What are you muttering about, Comrade Gerchik?" the judge asked him.

Naftula fixed his extinguished eyes on Orlov, the investigating magistrate.

"The late Monsieur Zusman, your late Papa," Naftula said to him with a sigh, "he had a head the likes of which you can't find nowhere in the world. And praised be God, that your papa did not have an apoplectic fit when he had me come over to perform your *bris*. And we can all see plain enough that you grew into a big man in the Soviet government, and that Naftula did not snip off along with that little piece of *shmokhtes* anything you might have needed later on."

He blinked with his bearlike eyes, shook his red-haired nut, and fell silent. There were volleys of laughter, thunderous guffawing salvos. Orlov, né Zusman, waved his arms in the air and shouted out something that could not be heard in the cannonade. He demanded that the record reflect that . . . Sasha Svetlov, one of the satirists of the *Odessa News,* sent him a note from the press box. "You're a nincompoop, Syoma," the note went. "Finish him off with irony, only what is funny will kill! Your Sasha."

The room quieted down when they brought Byelotserkovsky to the witness box.

Byelotserkovsky reiterated what was in his deposition. He was lanky and wore riding breeches and cavalry jackboots. According to Ofsey, the Tiraspol and Balta Party Committees had been fully cooperative in the business of acquiring livestock feed. In the heat of the negotiations he had received a telegram announcing the birth of his son. After discussing the matter with the Balta Party Committee's head of operations, he decided not to interrupt the transaction and to restrict himself to dispatching a congratulatory telegram. He did not return home for another two weeks. Sixty-four thousand *poods* of livestock feed had been gathered throughout the region. No one was at home, except for the witness Kharchenko—a neighbor and laundress by profession—and his infant son. His wife was away at the hospital, and the witness Kharchenko was rocking the cradle and was engaged in the now-obsolete practice of singing a lullaby. Knowing the witness to be an alcoholic, he did not find it necessary to try making out the words of this song, but he was taken aback to hear her call the boy Yankel, when he had expressly given instructions that his son be named Karl, in honor of our esteemed teacher Karl Marx. Unwrapping the child's swaddling clothes, he came face-to-face with his misfortune.

The investigating magistrate asked a few questions, the defense did not. The bailiff led in the witness Paulina Byelotserkovskaya. She staggered toward the bar. The bluish tremor of recent motherhood twisted her face, and there were drops of sweat on her forehead. She looked over to her father, the little blacksmith, dressed to the nines in a bow tie and new boots as if for a feast, and to her mother's coppery, gray-mustached face. The witness Paulina Byelotserkovskaya did not answer the question as to what she knew about the matter at hand. She said that her father was a poor man, who had worked in the smithy on the road to Balta for forty years. Her mother had given birth to six children, of whom three had died. One brother was a Red commander, the other worked in the Ghen factory. "My mother is very devout, everyone knows that, and she always suffered because her children were not religious. She could not bear the idea that her grandchildren would not be Jews. You must take into consideration in what kind of a family my mother was raised. Everyone knows the shtetl of Medzhibozh,* the women there are still wearing wigs."

"Will the witness please tell us," a sharp voice interrupted her. Paulina fell silent, the drops of sweat darkening on her forehead as if

---

* A shtetl in Western Ukraine in the District of Khmelnitsky where the founder of Hasidism, Israel ben Eliezer the "Baal Shem Tov," was from.

blood were seeping through her delicate skin. "Will the witness please tell us," repeated the voice of Samuel Lining, a former barrister. Were the Sanhedrin* to exist nowadays, Lining would have been its head. But the Sanhedrin no longer exists, and Lining, who had learned to read and write Russian at twenty-five, had begun in his fourth decade to write appeals to the government indistinguishable from the treatises of the Talmud. The old man had slept throughout the trial. His jacket was covered in cigarette ash. But he had woken up when Paulina Byelotserkovskaya had appeared. "Will the witness please tell us"—his fishlike rows of bobbing blue teeth were clacking—"if you had been aware of your husband's decision to name his son Karl?"

"Yes."

"What name did your mother give him?"

"Yankel."

"And what about you, Comrade Witness? What do you call your son?"

"I call him 'sweetie.' "

"And why 'sweetie,' of all things?"

"I call all children 'sweetie.' "

"Let us proceed," Lining said. His teeth slipped out, but he caught them with his nether lip and slid them back into his mouth. "Let us proceed. In the evening, when the child was taken over to the defendant Gerchik, you were not at home. You were at the hospital. Is my statement in accordance with the facts?"

"I was at the hospital."

"At what hospital were you being treated?"

"The one in Nezhinskaya Street, at Dr. Drizo's."

"Dr. Drizo was treating you?"

"Yes."

"Are you sure of this?"

"Why wouldn't I be?"

"I would like to introduce this here document into evidence." Lining's lifeless face rose over the table. "From this document the court will ascertain that during the period of time in question, Dr. Drizo was away at a congress of pediatricians in Kharkov."

* The highest court of the ancient Jewish nation.

The investigating magistrate did not object to the introduction of the document.

"Let us proceed," Lining said, his teeth clacking.

The witness leaned her whole body against the bar. Her whisper was barely audible.

"Maybe it wasn't Dr. Drizo," she said, resting her whole weight against the bar. "I can't remember everything. I am exhausted."

Lining raked his pencil through his yellow beard. He rubbed his stooping back against the bench and joggled his false teeth.

Paulina was asked to produce her official medical report, but she told the court she had misplaced it.

"Let us proceed," the old man said.

Paulina ran her palm over her forehead. Her husband sat at the end of the bench, away from the other witnesses. He sat there stiffly, his long legs in their cavalry boots pulled in under him. The rays of the sun fell on his face, packed with a framework of minute, spiteful bones.

"I will find my medical record," Paulina whispered, and her hands slid off the bar.

At that moment a bawling baby was heard. A child was crying and mewling outside the doors.

"You see, Paulina?" the old woman suddenly yelled out in a hoarse voice. "The child hasn't been fed since this morning! He's shriveling up with hollering!" Startled Red Army fighters snatched up their rifles. Paulina began to slide lower and lower, her head falling back to the floor. Her arms flew up, flailed, and then tumbled down.

"The court is adjourned!" the public prosecutor shouted.

An uproar erupted in the room. Byelotserkovsky stalked over to his wife with cranelike steps, a green sheen on his hollow cheeks.

"Feed the child!" people were shouting from the back rows, cupping their hands like megaphones around their mouths.

"They're already feeding him!" a woman's voice shouted back. "You think they were waiting for you?"

"The daughter's tangled up in all of this," said a worker sitting next to me. "The daughter's got her hand in it."

"It's a family thing," the man sitting next to him said. "One of those dark, nighttime jobs. At night they go tangling up things that in daylight you just can't untangle."

The sun cut through the room with its slanting rays. The crowd stirred heavily, breathing fire and sweat. Elbowing my way through, I reached the corridor. The door to the Red Corner* stood ajar. I could hear Karl-Yankel's mewling and slurping inside. Lenin's portrait hung in the Red Corner, the portrait in which he is giving a speech from the armored car on the square in front of the Finland Station. It was surrounded by multicolored production graphs showing the Petrovsky factory's output. The walls were lined with banners and rifles on wooden mounts. A woman worker with a Kirghiz face, her head bent forward, was feeding Karl-Yankel, a plump little fellow about five months old with knitted socks and a white tuft of hair on his head. Fastened to the Kirghiz woman by his mouth, he gurgled, banging her breast with his little clenched fist.

"What are they shouting for?" the Kirghiz woman said. "There's always someone who'll feed a baby."

There was also a girl of about seventeen puttering about the room in a red kerchief, her cheeks puffed out like pine cones. She was wiping dry Karl-Yankel's changing-mat.

"He's going to be a fighter, he is," the girl said. "Look at those punches he's throwing!"

The Kirghiz woman gently pulled her nipple out of Karl-Yankel's mouth. He began growling, and in desperation threw back his head with its white tuft of hair. The woman took out her other breast and gave it to him. He looked at her nipple with dull eyes that suddenly lit up. The Kirghiz woman looked at Karl-Yankel, squinting her black eyes at him.

"Not a fighter, no," she crooned, fixing the boy's cap. "He'll be an aviator. He will fly through the sky, he will."

In the other room the hearing had resumed.

A battle was now raging between the investigating magistrate and the experts who were giving vague and inconclusive testimony. The public prosecutor got up from his seat and began banging the desk with his fist. I could see the public in the first few rows—Galician *tsaddiks*, their beaver hats resting on their knees. They had come to the Petrovsky factory, where, according to the Warsaw papers, the Jewish

* A reading room in public buildings that contained Communist Party literature and the works of Marx and Lenin.

religion was being put on trial. The faces of the rabbis sitting in the first row hovered in the stormy, dusty brightness of the sun.

"Down with them!" shouted a member of the Young Communist League who had managed to fight his way right up to the podium.

The battle raged with growing force.

Karl-Yankel, staring blankly at me, sucked at the Kirghiz woman's breast.

The straight streets that my childhood and youth walked unfurled outside the window—Pushkin Street went to the train station, Malo-Arnautskaya Street jutted out into the park by the sea.

I grew up on these streets. Now it was Karl-Yankel's turn. But nobody had fought over me the way they were fighting over him, nobody had cared much about me.

"I can't believe that you won't be happy, Karl-Yankel," I whispered to myself . "I can't believe you won't be happier than me."

THE AWAKENING

*A*ll the people of our circle—middlemen, storekeepers, clerks in banks and steamship offices—sent their children to music lessons. Our fathers, seeing they had no prospects of their own, set up a lottery for themselves. They built this lottery on the bones of their little children. Odessa was in the grip of this craze more than any other town. And sure enough, over the last few decades our town had sent a number of child prodigies onto the stages of the world. Mischa Elman, Zimbalist, Gawrilowitsch all came from Odessa—Jascha Heifetz started out with us.*

When a boy turned four or five, his mother took the tiny, frail creature to Mr. Zagursky. Zargursky ran a factory that churned out child prodigies, a factory of Jewish dwarfs in lace collars and patent leather shoes. He went hunting for them in the Moldavanka slums and the reeking courtyards of the old bazaar. Zagursky gave them the first push, then the children were sent off to Professor Auer[†] in Petersburg. There was powerful harmony in the souls of these little creatures with their swollen blue heads. They became acclaimed virtuosi. And so—my father decided to keep up with them. I had passed the age of child prodigies—I was almost fourteen—but because of my height and frail-

---

*Mischa Elman, 1891–1967; Efrem Zimbalist, 1890–1985; Ossip Gawrilowitsch, 1878–1936; and Jascha Heifetz, 1901–1987, were among the foremost violinists and conductors of the twentieth century.

[†] Leopold Auer, 1845–1930, world-famous professor of violin at the St. Petersburg Conservatory.

---

ness I could be mistaken for an eight-year-old. Therein lay all our hopes.

I was brought to Zagursky. Out of respect for my grandfather, he agreed to take me at a ruble a lesson—a low fee. My grandfather was the laughingstock of the town, but also its ornament. He walked the streets in a top hat and tattered shoes, and provided answers to the murkiest questions. People asked him what a Gobelin was, why the Jacobins had betrayed Robespierre, how synthetic silk was made, what a cesarean section was. My grandfather knew the answers to all these questions. It was out of respect for his knowledge and madness that Zagursky charged us only a ruble a lesson. And he put a lot of effort into me, fearing Grandfather, though putting any effort into me was pointless. Sounds scraped out of my violin like iron filings. These sounds cut even into my own heart, but my father would not give up. All anyone talked about at home was Mischa Elman; the Czar himself had absolved him from military service. Zimbalist, from what my father had heard, had been presented to the King of England and had played at Buckingham Palace. Gawrilowitsch's parents had bought two houses in Petersburg. The child prodigies brought wealth to their parents. My father was prepared to resign himself to a life of poverty, but he needed fame.

"It's unthinkable," people who went out dining with my father at his expense assured him, "absolutely unthinkable, that the grandson of a grandfather like his wouldn't become . . ."

But I had other things in my head. Whenever I practiced my violin I placed books by Turgenev or Dumas on my music stand, and, as I scraped away, devoured one page after another. During the day I told stories to the neighborhood boys, at night I put them down on paper. Writing was a hereditary occupation in our family. Grandpa Levy-Itskhok, who had gone mad in his old age, had spent his life writing a novel with the title *The Headless Man*. I followed in his footsteps.

Laden with violin case and music scores, I dragged myself over to Zagursky's on Witte Street, formerly Dvoryanskaya Street.* There, along the walls, Jewesses sat, waiting flushed and hysterical for their

---

* The street had been renamed in honor of Sergei Witte, an Odessan who had been Russia's Minister of Finance.

turn. They pressed to their weak knees violins more magnificent than those destined to play at Buckingham Palace.

The door of the inner sanctum opened. Large-headed, freckled children came bustling out of Zagursky's chamber, their necks thin as flower stalks, a convulsive flush on their cheeks. Then the door closed, swallowing up the next dwarf. In the adjacent room Zagursky, with his red curls, bow tie, and thin legs, sang and conducted in ecstasy. The founder of this freakish lottery filled the Moldavanka and the back alleys of the old bazaar with specters of pizzicato and cantilena. This incantation of his was then fine-tuned to a diabolical brilliancy by old Professor Auer.

I had no business being a member of his sect. I too was a dwarf just as they were, but I heard a different calling in the voice of my ancestors.

This was an arduous apprenticeship for me. One day I set out from home, laden with my music, my violin, its case, and the sum of twelve rubles, the fee for a month of lessons. I walked down Nezhinskaya Street, and should have turned into Dvoryanskaya Street to get to Zagursky's place. Yet I walked down Tiraspolskaya and ended up in the port. My allotted three hours flew past in the Prakticheskaya harbor. That was the beginning of my liberation. Zagursky's waiting room was never to see me again. More important things were occupying my mind. My classmate Nemanov and I got in the habit of going on board the *Kensington* to visit an old sailor called Mr. Trottyburn. Nemanov was a year younger than I, but from the time he was eight years old he had engaged in the most complex trading you could imagine. He was a genius at anything having to do with trade, and always delivered what he promised. Now he is a millionaire in New York, the general manager of General Motors, a company as powerful as Ford. Nemanov took me along because I obeyed his every command. He bought smuggled tobacco pipes from Mr. Trottyburn. These pipes had been carved by the old sailor's brother in Lincoln.

"Mark my words, gentlemen," Mr. Trottyburn said to us. "You have to make your children with your own hands. Smoking a factory-made pipe is like sticking an enema tube in your mouth. Do you know who Benvenuto Cellini was? He was a master! My brother in Lincoln could tell you about him. My brother lives and lets live. The one thing he believes in is that you have to make your children with your own hands, you can't leave that sort of thing to others. And he is right, gentlemen!"

Nemanov sold Trottyburn's pipes to bank managers, foreign consuls, and rich Greeks. He made a hundred percent profit.

The pipes of the Lincoln master exuded poetry. Each and every one of them contained a thought, a drop of eternity. A little yellow eye twinkled from their mouthpieces. Their cases were lined with satin. I tried to imagine how Matthew Trottyburn, the last of the pipe-carving masters, lived in an England of old, defying the winds of change.

"He is right, gentlemen, you have to make your children with your own hands!"

The heavy waves by the harbor wall separated me more and more from a home reeking of onions and Jewish fate. From the Prakticheskaya harbor I moved on to the breakwater. There, on a stretch of sandbar, the boys of Primorskaya Street hung out. They went without pants from morning till night, they dove under fishing boats, stole coconuts for food, and waited for the time when carts carrying watermelons rolled in from Kherson and Kamenki, and they could split these watermelons open on the moorings of the dock.

My dream now was to learn how to swim. I was ashamed of admitting to those bronzed boys that I, though born in Odessa, had not even seen the sea until I was ten, and that I still could not swim at fourteen.

How late I learned the essential things in life! In my childhood, nailed to the Gemara,* I led the life of a sage, and it was only later, when I was older, that I began to climb trees.

It turned out that the ability to swim was beyond my reach. The hydrophobia of my ancestors, the Spanish rabbis and Frankfurt money changers, dragged me to the bottom. Water would not carry me. Battered, doused in salt water, I went back to the shore, to my violin and my music scores. I was attached to my instruments of crime, and dragged them along with me. The battle of the rabbis with the sea lasted until the local water god—Efim Nikitich Smolich, a proofreader for the *Odessa News*—took pity on me. In that athletic chest of his there was a warmth for Jewish boys. Nikitich led crowds of frail little crea-

---

* Part of the Talmud, the Gemara is a rabbinical commentary on the Mishna, the first codification of ancient Jewish oral laws.

tures, gathering them up from the bedbug-ridden hovels of the Moldavanka. He took them to the beach, built sand castles with them, exercised and dived with them, taught them songs, and, baking in the hard rays of the sun, told them tales of fishermen and animals. To grown-ups, Nikitich explained that he was simply a devotee of natural philosophy. Nikitich's stories made the Jewish children collapse with laughter. They squealed and frolicked like puppies. The sun spattered them with creeping freckles, freckles the color of lizards.

Nikitich silently watched me combat the waves single-handed. Seeing that there was no hope I would ever learn to swim on my own, he let me join the other little lodgers of his heart. His cheerful heart was completely devoted to us. It was never disdainful, never miserly, and never agitated. He lay among us by the breakwater, the king of these melon and kerosene waters, with his copper shoulders, his head that of an aging gladiator, and his lightly crooked, bronze legs. I loved him as only a boy afflicted with hysteria and headaches can love an athlete. I didn't leave his side, and tried to please him every way I could.

"Calm down," he told me. "Steady your nerves, and swimming will come of its own accord. . . . What do you mean, the water won't hold you up? Why shouldn't it?"

Seeing how I was reaching out to him, Nikitich made an exception for me among all his pupils, and invited me to come up to his place, a clean, spacious garret covered in mats, and showed me his dogs, his hedgehog, his tortoise, and his doves. In gratitude for his generosity I brought him a tragedy I had written the night before.

"I knew you were a scribbler!" Nikitich said. "You have that look in your eyes. You're no longer looking at things."

He read my play, shrugged his shoulders, ran his fingers through his stiff, gray locks, and paced up and down the garret.

"I believe," he said in a slow drawl, pausing between words, "that there is a divine spark in you."

We went out into the street. The old man stopped, banged his stick hard on the sidewalk, and peered at me.

"There's something lacking in your work, but what is it? That you are young is no problem—that will pass in time. What you lack is a feel for nature."

He pointed his stick at a tree with a reddish trunk and a low crown.

"What kind of tree is that?"

I didn't know.

"What's growing on this bush?"

I didn't know that either. We walked through the little park on Aleksandrovsky Boulevard. The old man poked at all the trees with his stick, grabbed my shoulder whenever a bird flew by, and had me listen to their different calls.

"What bird is that singing?"

I couldn't answer. The names of birds and trees, what families they belonged to, where the birds flew, on which side the sun rose, when the dew was at its heaviest—all this was unknown to me.

"And you have the audacity to write? A man who does not exist in nature the way a stone or an animal exists in it will not write a single worthwhile line in all his life. Your landscapes resemble descriptions of stage sets. Goddamn it! What could your parents have been thinking of these past fourteen years?"

What had they been thinking of? Of contested bills and the mansions of Mischa Elman. I didn't tell Nikitich that, I remained silent.

At home, at the dinner table, I didn't touch my food—it wouldn't go down.

"A feel for nature!" I thought. My God, why hadn't this occurred to me? Where could I find someone to tell me what the different birdcalls and the names of trees were? How much did I know about these things? I could perhaps identify lilacs—that is, if they were in bloom. Lilacs and acacias. Deribasovskaya and Grecheskaya Streets were lined with acacias.

At dinner, Father told us a new story about Jascha Heifetz. On his way to Robyn's, father had run into Mendelson, Jascha's uncle. It turned out that the boy was getting eight hundred rubles a performance: "So go ahead and add up how much that comes to at fifteen concerts a month!"

I added it up. The result was twelve thousand a month. As I multiplied the number, carrying the four in my head, I looked out the window. My music teacher, Mr. Zagursky, wearing a lightly billowing cape, red ringlets jutting out from under his soft hat, and propping himself up with his cane, came marching through our cement yard. It cannot be said that he had been quick to notice my absence: more than three months had already passed since the day my violin had sunk to the sandy bottom off the breakwater.

Zagursky came up to our front door. I rushed off to the back door. It had been boarded up the night before to keep out thieves. So I locked myself in the toilet. Within half an hour my whole family had gathered outside the toilet door. The women were crying. Auntie Bobka, quivering with sobs, was grinding her fat shoulder against the door. My father was silent. He began speaking more quietly and distinctly than ever before in his life.

"I am an officer," my father said, "I have an estate. I ride out on hunts. The muzhiks pay me rent. I sent my son to the Cadet Corps. There is no reason for me to lose any sleep over my son."

He fell silent. The women sniffled. Then a terrible blow came crashing against the toilet door. My father began throwing himself on it with his whole body; he took runs and hurled himself against it.

"I am an officer!" he howled. "I ride out on hunts! I will kill him! That's it!"

The hook went hurtling off the door, but the bolt was still there, held by a single nail. The women threw themselves on the floor, grappling for my father's legs. Raving, he tried to tear himself loose. Hearing the rumpus, my old grandmother, my father's mother, came hurrying in.

"My child," she said to him in Yiddish. "Our sorrow is great, it knows no bounds. The last thing we need in our house is blood. I do not want to see blood in our house!"

My father moaned. I heard his footsteps receding. The latch was hanging on its last nail.

I sat in my fortress till nightfall. When everybody had gone to bed, Auntie Bobka took me to my grandmother's. It was a long walk. The moonlight froze on unknown shrubs, on nameless trees. An invisible bird whistled once and then was quiet, perhaps it had fallen asleep. What kind of bird was it? What was it called? Was there dew in the evenings? Where was the constellation of the Great Bear in the sky? On what side did the sun rise?

We walked along Pochtovaya Street. Auntie Bobka held my hand tightly so that I wouldn't run away. She was right. I was thinking of running away.

IN THE BASEMENT

I was a boy who told lies. This came from reading. My imagination was always aroused. I read during class, between classes, on my way home, and under the table at night, hidden by the tablecloth that hung down to the floor. Reading books, I missed out on everything the world around me had to offer: skipping classes to go to the port, the coming of billiards to the coffee shops along Grecheskaya Street, swimming at Langeron.* I had no friends. Who would have wanted to spend time with someone like me?

One day I saw the brightest student in our class, Mark Borgman, with a book about Spinoza. He had just read it and was dying to tell the boys around him about the Spanish Inquisition. What he told them was nothing but scientific prattle. There was no poetry in Borgman's words. I could not stop myself from cutting in. To whoever would listen, I talked about old Amsterdam, about the gloom of the ghetto, about the philosopher diamond cutters. I added quite a lot of spice to what I had read in books. I couldn't resist. My imagination sharpened dramatic scenes, altered endings, steeped the beginnings in more mystery. Spinoza's death, his lonely death in freedom, appeared to me in my imagination as a battle. The Sanhedrin had tried to compel the dying man to repent, but he held fast. It was at this point that I blended in Rubens. I imagined Rubens standing at the head of Spinoza's bed, casting a death mask of the corpse's face.

* A beach in Odessa, named after the French count, Alexander Langeron, who was governor general of Odessa from 1816–1822.

My schoolmates listened to my outlandish tale with open mouths. I told my tale with gusto. When the bell rang we reluctantly dispersed. Borgman came up to me during the following break, took me by the arm, and we went for a walk together. Soon we were seeing eye to eye. Borgman wasn't a bad specimen of top student. To his powerful brain, high school learning was only a scribble in the margin of the book of life. And he sought that book with ardor. Even as foolish little twelve-year-olds, we were all very aware that a wondrous and erudite life lay before him. He didn't even prepare for classes, he just sat there and listened. This reserved, sober boy was drawn to me because of my knack for twisting things, even the simplest things you could imagine.

That year we moved up to the third class. My report card was full of three-minuses.* I was so strange, with all the outlandish gibberish bouncing through my mind, that my teachers, after much deliberation, decided against giving me twos.

At the beginning of summer, Borgman invited me to come to his dacha. His father was the director of the Russian Bank for International Trade. He was one of those men who was turning Odessa into a Marseilles or Naples. The core of the old Odessa merchant was within him. He was one of those pleasant but skeptical bon vivants who avoided speaking Russian, preferring instead the rough, choppy language of the Liverpool ship captains. When an Italian opera came to Odessa in April, Borgman invited the whole cast to dinner. The puffy banker, the last of the Odessa merchants, had a little two-month liaison with the buxom prima donna. She took with her memories that did not burden her conscience along with a necklace chosen with taste but not costing too much.

The old man also held the position of Argentinean consul, and was chairman of the stock exchange committee. And I had been invited to his house. My Auntie Bobka ran out into the courtyard trumpeting the news. She dressed me up as best she could. I took the train to the six-teenth stop at Bolshoy Fontan.† The dacha stood on a low, red cliff right by the shore. A flower garden of fuchsias and clipped thuya shrubs covered the cliff.

---

* The equivalent of a C-minus. Five was the highest grade, one the lowest.
† "Large Fountain" was an elegant beach spa outside Odessa.

I came from a loud, impoverished family. The Borgman dacha filled me with awe. White wicker chairs glittered in walks covered with foliage. The dinner table was filled with flowers, the windows fitted with green casings. A low wooden colonnade opened up before the house.

The bank director came to the dacha in the evenings. After dinner he placed his wicker chair at the very edge of the cliff in front of the shifting plain of the sea, stretched out his legs in his white trousers, lit a cigar, and began to read the *Manchester Guardian*. The guests, Odessa ladies, played poker on the veranda. A narrow samovar with ivory handles was sputtering on the edge of the table.

The women—card-playing gourmands, sluttish coquettes, and furtive debauchees with large hips and perfumed undergarments—fluttered black fans and staked their gold. The sun pierced its way to them through the copse of wild vines. Its fiery globe was immense. Copper sparks weighed down the women's black hair. Flashes of sunset pierced their diamonds—diamonds that hung everywhere: in the deep hollows of breasts pressed apart, from powdered ears, and on plump and bluish female fingers.

Evening fell. A bat rustled by. The sea rolled blacker against the red cliff. My twelve-year-old heart surged with the cheer and ease of others' wealth. My friend and I ambled hand in hand down the long walks. Borgman told me that he would become an aviation engineer. There was a rumor that his father would be appointed the London representative of the Russian Bank for International Trade. Borgman would be educated in England.

At our house, Auntie Bobka's house, no one talked of such things. I had nothing with which I could match this uninterrupted splendor. So I told Borgman that although things back at my place were very different, my grandfather Levy-Itskhok and my uncle had traveled the whole world over and had thousands of adventures under their belts. I described these adventures one after the other. Within seconds, I lost all sense of reality, and took Uncle Volf from the Russian-Turkish War to Alexandria and Egypt.

Night rose in the poplars, stars pressed down on stooping branches. I spoke with wild gesticulations. The fingers of the future aviation engineer trembled in my hand. He emerged with difficulty from the hallucination, and promised to come visit me at my place the following Sunday. Braced by his promise, I took the ferry back home to Auntie Bobka's.

The whole following week I imagined I was a bank director. I brought about millions of transactions with Singapore and Port Said. I acquired a yacht, and sailed it single-handedly. By Sabbath reality struck. Little Borgman was to come visiting the following day. Nothing of what I had told him actually existed. What did exist was far more extraordinary than anything I had invented, but at the age of twelve I had no idea how to grapple with the truth of my world. Grandpa Levy-Itskhok, a rabbi chased out of his shtetl for forging Count Branitsky's signature on promissory notes, was considered a madman by neighbors and street boys alike. Uncle Simon-Volf I could not stand because of his loud eccentricity, full of mad fire, yelling, and harassment. Auntie Bobka was the only one I could count on. She was very proud that the son of a bank director was my friend. She saw this friendship as the beginning of a bright career and baked a fruit strudel and a poppy-seed pie for our guest. Into that pie she put the heart of our tribe, the heart that had withstood so many tribulations. We hid my grandfather, with his tattered top hat and his swollen feet bound in rags, with our neighbors the Apelkhots, and I begged him not to show himself until our guest left. I also dealt with Simon-Volf. He went off with his profiteer pals to drink tea at the Medved Tavern. Tea there was braced with vodka, and it was safe to assume that Simon-Volf would be delayed. It has to be said that my family was not your typical Jewish family. There were drunks in our clan, we had run away with the daughters of generals and then abandoned them before crossing the border, and our grandfather had forged signatures and written blackmailing letters for abandoned wives.

All my efforts went into keeping Simon-Volf away for the whole day. I gave him the three rubles I had managed to save up. Spending three rubles took some doing, Simon-Volf would come back late, and the bank director's son would never know that the tales of my uncle's kindness and strength were all lies. It must, however, be said that were one to appraise things purely with one's heart, then my tale could be seen as true and not a lie at all. But when you first came face-to-face with the loud and dirty Simon-Volf, this intangible truth was not to be discerned.

On Sunday morning, Bobka put on her brown, raw-cloth dress. Her fat, kindly breasts bounced in all directions. She tied on her kerchief with the black floral print, the kind of kerchief worn in the synagogue on Yom Kippur and Rosh Hashanah. Bobka arranged the pies, jam, and pretzels on the table and waited. We lived in the basement. Borgman raised his eyebrows as he walked over the corridor's crooked floor. A barrel of water stood by the entrance. The instant Borgman was inside, I began entertaining him with every conceivable marvel. I showed him the alarm clock which my grandfather had constructed down to the last screw—a lamp was hooked up to the clock, and every time the clock reached a full or half hour, the lamp would light up. I also showed him our little keg of shoe wax. Grandpa Levy-Itskhok had invented that shoe wax recipe, and he would not reveal it to anyone. Then Borgman and I read a few pages from my grandfather's manuscript. He wrote in Yiddish, on square sheets of yellow paper large as maps. The manuscript was called *The Headless Man*. In it was a description of all Levy-Itskhok's neighbors over a period of sixty years—first in Skvira and Belaya Tserkov, then in Odessa. Undertakers, cantors, Jewish drunks, cooks at *bris* feasts, and the charlatans who performed the ritual operation—these were Levy-Itskhok's characters. They were all loud and offensive people, with crude speech and fleshy noses, pimply faces, and twisted backsides.

As we were reading, Bobka appeared in her brown dress. She came floating in, engulfed by her fat, kindly breasts, carrying a tray on which stood a samovar. I introduced them. "Pleased to meet you," Bobka said, reaching out her sweaty, stiff fingers and doing a little scraping bow. I couldn't have wished for things to go better. Our neighbors the Apelkhots wouldn't let Grandfather leave their place. I dragged out all his treasures one by one: grammars of every language you could imagine, and sixty-six volumes of the Talmud. Borgman was dazzled by the keg of shoe wax, the wondrous alarm clock, and the mountain of Talmuds—all things one would never see in any other home.

We each drank two glasses of tea with our strudel. Bobka left, bowing her head and shuffling backward out of the room. I fell into a joyful state of mind, struck a pose, and began declaiming the verses that I loved more than anything in the world. Antony, bending over Caesar's dead body, speaks to the people of Rome.

Friends, Romans, countrymen, lend me your ears;
I come to bury Caesar, not to praise him.

That is how Antony begins his performance. I gasped and pressed my hand to my heart.

He was my friend, faithful and just to me:
But Brutus says he was ambitious;
And Brutus is an honorable man.
He hath brought many captives home to Rome
Whose ransoms did the general coffers fill:
Did this in Caesar seem ambitious?
When that the poor have cried, Caesar hath wept:
Ambition should be made of sterner stuff:
Yet Brutus says he was ambitious;
And Brutus is an honorable man.

Brutus's face hovered before my eyes, in the mists of the universe. His face turned whiter than chalk. The people of Rome began closing in on me menacingly. I raised my arm—Borgman's eyes obediently followed it—my clenched fist was quaking, I raised my arm, and through the window saw Uncle Simon-Volf walk through the yard with Leykakh the junk dealer. They were carrying a rack made of antlers, and a red trunk with handles in the form of lions' jaws. Bobka also saw them from the window. Forgetting my guest, she came running into the room and grabbed hold of me with trembling hands.

"Oy, Bubele! He's been buying furniture again!"

Borgman rose in his school uniform, and bowed to Auntie Bobka in bewilderment. They were pounding on the door. The thud of boots and the clatter of the trunk being dragged across the floor came rumbling from the corridor. The thundering voices of Simon-Volf and red-headed Leykakh were deafening. Both were tipsy.

"Bobka!" Simon-Volf yelled. "Guess how much I paid for these horns!"

He blared like a trumpet, but there was a hint of uncertainty in his voice. Drunk though he was, he knew how much we hated redheaded Leykakh, who spurred him on to keep buying things, flooding our place with useless and ridiculous furniture.

Bobka stood there in silence. Leykakh said something to Simon-Volf in his wheezing voice. To drown out his snakelike hissing and my anxiety, I started shouting Anthony's words.

> *But yesterday the word of Caesar might*
> *Have stood against the world; now lies he there.*
> *And none so poor to do him reverence.*
> *O masters, if I were disposed to stir*
> *Your hearts and minds to mutiny and rage,*
> *I should do Brutus wrong, and Cassius wrong,*
> *Who, you all know, are honorable men . . .*

Suddenly there was a thud. Bobka had fallen down, knocked off her feet by her husband's blow. She must have made a sharp remark about the antlers. The daily ritual began. Simon-Volf's brassy voice thundered to high heaven.

"You are squeezing the last drop out of me!" my uncle roared. "You are squeezing out of me the last drop so you can stuff those damn pig snouts of yours! My soul's been crushed by work, I've nothing left to work with, no hands, no legs, nothing! You've hung a millstone around my neck, a goddamn millstone!"

He heaped Yiddish curses on Bobka and me, he wished that our eyes would fall out, that our children would rot and wither in their mothers' wombs, that we would not live to bury each other, and that we would be dragged by our hair to a pauper's grave.

Little Borgman stood up. He looked around the room, his face pale. He did not understand the ins and outs of Jewish blasphemy, but he was familiar enough with Russian swearing. And Simon-Volf did not refrain from slipping into Russian. The bank director's son stood there kneading his cap. My eyes saw him double as I struggled to shout away all the evil in the world. My mortal agony and Caesar's death became one. I was dead and I was shouting. A wheeze rose from the depths of my being.

> *If you have tears, prepare to shed them now.*
> *You all do know this mantle: I remember*
> *The first time ever Caesar put it on;*

'Twas on a summer's evening, in his tent,
That day he overcame the Nervii:
Look, in this place ran Cassius' dagger through:
See what a rent the envious Casca made:
Through this the well-beloved Brutus stabb'd;
And as he pluck'd his cursed steel away,
Mark how the blood of Caesar follow'd it . . .

No one would have had the power to drown out Simon-Volf. Bobka sat on the floor, sobbing and blowing her nose. Leykakh, unruffled, was dragging the trunk along behind the partition. And it was at this very moment that my crazed grandfather got it into his head to come to my rescue. He tore himself loose from the Apelkhots next door, crawled over to the window, and began sawing away at his violin, most probably so that people wouldn't hear Simon-Volf's cursing. Borgman looked out the window, which was at ground level, and stumbled back in horror. My poor grandfather was twisting his rigid blue mouth into wild grimaces. He had on his crooked top hat and his black quilted cloak with its bone buttons; the remnants of what had been shoes clung to his elephantine feet. His sooty beard hung in tatters and blew into the window. Borgman ran for the door.

"Please don't worry," he muttered, as he ran for freedom. "Please don't worry."

His uniform and his cap with the raised brim flashed through the yard.

With Borgman's departure my agitation began to subside. I waited for evening to come. After Grandfather lay down in his cot and went to sleep, having filled a sheet of paper with Yiddish scribbles (describing the Apelkhots, at whose house, through my ministrations, he had spent the whole day), I went out into the corridor. It had a dirt floor. I moved through the darkness, barefoot, in my long, patched-up nightshirt. The cobblestones shimmered like blades of light through the cracks in the boards. The barrel of water stood as always in the corner. I lowered myself into it. The water cut me in two. I plunged my head under, choked, and came up for air. Our cat gazed at me sleepily from high up on a shelf. The second time I held out longer. The water swished around me, swallowing my moan. I opened my eyes and saw

my billowing shirt and my legs pressed against each other. Again I did-
n't have enough strength. I came up. My grandfather was standing next
to the barrel in his nightshirt. His single tooth jiggled in his mouth.

"My grandson." He spoke these words distinctly and with contempt. "I shall go and drink some castor oil so that I will have something to dump on your grave."

I started shouting and thrashing, plunging into the water with all
my might. I was pulled up by my grandfather's weak hand. I cried for
the first time that day, and the world of tears was so immense and beautiful that everything except my tears disappeared from before my eyes.

When I regained consciousness, I was lying wrapped in blankets in
my bed. Grandfather was pacing up and down the room, whistling. Fat
Bobka was warming my hands on her breasts.

"Oy, how he is shivering, our silly little boy!" Bobka said. "And how
does he have the strength to shiver like that?"

Grandfather tugged at his beard, whistled, and began walking up
and down the room again. In the next room Simon-Volf was snoring
with tormented breath. He always yelled himself out during the day,
and so never woke in the night.

GAPA GUZHVA

Gapa Guzhva is the first chapter of the novel Velikaya Krinitsa *that Babel worked on in the early 1930s. Although friends of Babel's reported that they knew of subsequent chapters that he had completed, only two chapters, this and "Kolyvushka," have survived. Both this story and "Kolyvushka" (which was unpublished during Babel's lifetime) dealt with the devastating effects of Stalin's enforced collectivization—a dangerous subject matter for a novel at the time.*

Six weddings were held in Velikaya Krinitsa on Shrovetide in 1930. They were celebrated with a wild abandon, the likes of which had not been seen for a long time. Old customs were reborn. The father of one of the bridegrooms got drunk and demanded that he be allowed to try out the bride, a custom that had been discontinued some twenty years back. The father-in-law had already taken off his sash and thrown it to the ground. The bride, shaking with laughter, was tugging at the old man's beard. He puffed out his chest closer and closer to her, guffawed, and stamped his boots. And yet there was not much for the old man to be worried about. Of the six sheets that were hung up over the huts after the wedding night, only two were stained with virginal blood. As for the other brides, they had gone on late-night walks and come back soiled. One of the sheets was grabbed by a Red Army soldier who was home on leave, and Gapa Guzhva climbed up for the other one. She jumped onto the roof, kicking away the men behind her, and clambered up the pole, which bent and swayed under her weight. She tore down the reddened rag and came sliding down the pole. A table and a stool stood on the gable of the roof, and on the table was a half liter bottle of vodka and slices of cold meat. Gapa tipped the bottle into her mouth, and with her free hand waved the sheet. The crowd down below roared and danced. The stool slid out from under her, shook, and fell apart. Berezan herdsmen, driving their oxen to Kiev, stared at the woman drinking vodka on the roof under the sky.

"She's no woman, that one!" the villagers told them. "Our widow's the devil, she is!"

Gapa threw bread, twigs, and plates from the roof. She finished the vodka and smashed the bottle against the chimney ledge. The muzhiks who had gathered below roared. The widow jumped off the roof, untied her shaggy-bellied mare who stood dozing by the wooden fence, and rode off to get some wine. She came back weighed down with flasks, as a Circassian tribesman is weighed down with ammunition. Her horse was panting heavily and tossing its muzzle. Its belly, heavy with foal, surged and bulged, and equine madness quivered in its eyes.

At the weddings, the villagers danced holding handkerchiefs, with lowered eyes, their boots shuffling in one spot. Only Gapa whirled around, as they do in the towns. She danced with Grishka Savchenko, her lover. They held each other as if they were wrestling. They tugged at each other's shoulders with headstrong anger. They drummed the ground with their boots, and tumbled down as if they had been knocked off their feet.

The third day of the wedding feasts began. The couples' best men wore their sheepskin coats inside out and ran smeared with soot through the village, banging on oven doors. Bonfires were lit in the streets. People jumped through them, horns painted on their foreheads. Horses were harnessed to troughs that were dragged hurtling through the flames over clods of grass. Men fell to the ground, overpowered by sleep. Housewives threw broken pots and pans into their yards. The newlyweds washed their feet and climbed into tall beds, and only Gapa was still dancing alone in an empty shed. She whirled in circles, holding a tarred boat pole in her hand, her hair untied. She pounded the pole against the walls, leaving sticky black wounds, the thuds jolting the shed.

"We bring fire and death," Gapa whispered, waving the pole over her head.

Planks and straw rained down on her as the walls caved in.

She danced with loose hair among the ruins, in the din and dust of the crumbling wattle and the flying splinters of the breaking planks. Her delicate red-rimmed boots whirled through the rubble, drumming the ground.

Night fell. The bonfires were dying out in the thawing snow pits.

The shed lay in a tangled heap on the hill. A light began to flicker in the village council hut across the street. Gapa threw away her pole and ran over to the hut.

"Ivashko!" she yelled, as she rushed into the room. "Come have some fun with us, let's drink our life away!"

Ivashko was the representative of the Regional Commission for Collectivization. For two months now he had been trying to talk the villagers into collectivizing. He was sitting in front of a pile of crumpled, tattered papers, his hands resting on the table. The skin on either side of his forehead was wrinkled, and in his eyes hung the pupils of an ailing cat. Above them bulged the arches of his bare pink eye sockets.

"Are you sneering at our peasants?" Gapa yelled, stamping her foot.

"I'm not sneering," Ivashko said gloomily. "But it would be inappropriate for me to join you all."

Gapa danced past him, tapping her feet and waving her arms.

"Come break bread with us," she said to him. "And then tomorrow we'll do exactly as you say, Comrade Representist! We will tomorrow, not today!"

Ivashko shook his head.

"It would be inappropriate for me to break bread with you," he said. "You people aren't human—you bark like dogs! I've lost fifteen pounds since I came here!"

He chewed his lip and closed his eyes. He stretched out his hand, groped for his canvas bag, got up, staggered forward, and made his way toward the door with dragging feet, as if he were walking in his sleep.

"Comrade Ivashko is pure gold," Kharchenko, the council secretary, said after he had left. "He's a kind fellow, but our village has been too rough on him."

An ash-blond forelock* hung over Kharchenko's button nose and pimples. He was reading a newspaper, his feet resting on the bench.

"Just wait till the judge from Voronkov† comes over," Kharchenko said, turning a page of his newspaper. "Then you'll all sit up straight."

Gapa slipped a bag of sunflower seeds out of her cleavage.

"How come all you think about's your duties, Comrade Secretary?"

---

* It was a custom among Ukrainian villagers to shave their heads except for a forelock.
† A town southeast of Kiev.

she asked. "Why are you afraid of death? Who ever heard of a muzhik turning away from death?"

Outside, a swollen black sky was seething around the village belfry, and wet huts crouched and slithered away. The stars struggled to ignite above them, and the wind crept along the ground.

Gapa heard the dull murmur of an unfamiliar, husky voice in the front room of her hut. A woman pilgrim had come to spend the night and was sitting on the bench above the stove with her legs pulled in under her. The icon lamp's crimson threads of flame threw a net on the wall. A stillness hung over the clean hut. An odor of apple liquor seeped from the walls and partitions. Gapa's fat-lipped daughters, craning their necks, were staring at the beggar woman. Short horsy hair covered their heads, and their lips were large and puffed out. A dead, greasy sheen lay on their narrow foreheads.

"Keep up your lies, Grandma Rakhivna," Gapa said, leaning against the wall. "I love it when you tell your lies."

Rakhivna sat on the bench above the stove with her head against the low ceiling, plaiting her hair into braids, which she then coiled in rows over her little head. Her washed, misshapen feet rested on the edge of the stove.

"There's three patriarchs in this world," the old woman said, lowering her wrinkled face. "Our government has imprisoned the Patriarch of Moscow, the Jerusalem Patriarch is living among Turks. It is the Antioch Patriarch who now rules all of Christianity. He sent forty Greek priests onto Ukrainian soil to curse the churches from which our government took down the bells. The Greek priests passed Kholodny Yar, they've already been seen at Ostrogradsk, and come next Sunday they'll be here in Velikaya Krinitsa!"

Rakhivna closed her eyes and fell silent. The light of the icon lamps flickered over the hollows of her feet.

"The judge from Voronkov," the old woman suddenly said. "He collectivized the whole of Voronkov in a single day! He stuck nine squires in a cold cell, and on the following day they were to march in the chain gangs to Sakhalin. I tell you, daughter, there's people everywhere, Christ is gloried everywhere! The squires were kept in a cold cell all night—then in come the guards to take them, the guards open the dungeon door, and what do their eyes behold in the full light of the morning? Nine squires dangling from the rafters on their belts!"

Before she lay down, Rakhivna fussed about for a long time, sorting through her rags, whispering to her God as she would have whispered to her old man lying next to her. Then her breathing suddenly became light. Grishka Savchenko, the husband of one of the village women, was lying on a bench by the wall. He lay curled up, right on the edge as if he had been crushed, his back twisted, his vest bunched up over it, and his head sunk in pillows.

"A man's love," Gapa said, prodding and shaking him. "I know all there is to know about a man's love. They turn their snouts away from their wives and shuffle off, like this one here! *He* didn't go home to his wife Odarka, no, he didn't!"

Half the night they rolled on the bench in the darkness, their lips tightly clenched, their arms stretching out in the darkness. Gapa's braid went flying over the pillow. At dawn Grishka started up, moaned, and fell asleep with a snarl on his lips. Gapa gazed at her daughters' brown shoulders, low foreheads, thick lips, and dark breasts.

"What camels!" she said to herself. "How could they have come from me?"

Darkness receded from the oak-framed window. Dawn opened a violet streak in the clouds. Gapa went out into the yard. The wind enveloped her like cold river water. She harnessed her sledge and loaded it with sacks of wheat—during the wedding celebrations everyone had run out of flour. The road slithered through the fog and mist of dawn.

It snowed all day. At the mill they couldn't start grinding till the following evening. At the edge of the village, short-legged Yushko Trofim, wearing a soaked cap, came out from inside a sheet of snow to meet Gapa. His shoulders, covered in a sea of flakes, were surging and falling.

"Well, they finally got up," he muttered. He came up to her sledge and raised his bony black face up to her.

"What's that supposed to mean?" Gapa asked him. She pulled at her reins.

"All the big men came to our village last night," Trofim said. "They've already dragged off that old biddy staying with you and arrested her. The head of the Collectivization Commission and the secretary of the District Party Committee. They've nabbed Ivashko and now the Voronkov judge is stepping in."

Trofim walked off, his walrus whiskers bobbing, snowflakes slithering down them. Gapa shook the reins but then tugged at them again.

"Trofim! What did they drag the old biddy off for?"

Trofim stopped and yelled back from far away through the whirling, flying snow.

"They said it was because of her propaganda campaign about the world coming to an end!"

He walked on, limping on one foot, and in an instant his wide back was swallowed up by the sky that melted into the earth.

Gapa rode up to her hut and tapped on the window with her whip. Her daughters were lounging around the table dressed in shawls and shoes as if they were at a feast.

"Mama," the oldest said. "Odarka came over while you were out and took her husband back home."

The daughters set the table and lit the samovar. Gapa ate, and then went to the village council, where she found the elders of Velikaya Krinitsa sitting in silence along the walls. The window, smashed some time back during a debate, was boarded up, the glass of the lamps had worn thin, and a sign saying "No Smoking" had been nailed to the pockmarked walls. The judge from Voronkov, his shoulders hunched, sat at the table reading. He was reading through the record ledger of the village council of Velikaya Krinitsa. He had raised the collar of his shabby little coat. Kharchenko, the council secretary, was sitting next to him, drawing up a formal charge against his own village. On columned sheets of paper he was entering all the crimes, arrears, and fines—all the wounds, visible and invisible. When Judge Osmolovsky from Voronkov had arrived in the village, he had refused to call a general meeting of the citizens, as the representatives before him had done. He did not give speeches, but simply asked for a list of quota dodgers and former merchants, an inventory of their property, crops, and farmsteads.

The elders of Velikaya Krinitsa sat quietly on the benches, while Kharchenko's bustling, whistling pen crackled through the silence. There was a flurry of movement when Gapa came into the room. Evdokim Nazarenko's face lit up when he saw her.

"Here's our number one activist, Comrade Judge!" Evdokim said, guffawing and rubbing his palms together. "Our widow here has been actively ruining all our village youths."

Gapa stopped by the door and narrowed her eyes. A sneer flitted over Judge Osmolovsky's lips, and he crinkled his thin nose.

"Good morning," he said, nodding to her.

"She was the first one to sign up for the collective farm," Evdokim said, trying to chase away the brewing storm with a gush of words. "But then the good people of the village had a chat with her, and she designed up."

Gapa didn't move. Her face flushed brick red.

"The good people of the village say that in the collective farm everyone is to sleep under the same blanket!" she said in her sonorous voice.

Her eyes twinkled in her fixed face.

"Well, I for one am against sleeping wholesale! *We* like sleeping in twos, and we like our home-brewed vodka, goddamn it!"

The muzhiks burst out laughing, but immediately fell silent. Gapa peered at the judge. He raised his inflamed eyes and nodded to her. Then he slumped even lower, took his head in his thin, red-haired hands, and once again immersed himself in the record ledger of Velikaya Krinitsa. Gapa turned around, and her stately back flashed out of the room.

In the yard, Grandpa Abram, overgrown with raw flesh, was sitting on some wet planks with his knees pulled up. A yellow mane of hair hung to his shoulders.

"What's wrong?" Gapa asked him.

"I'm sad," the old man said.

Back at home, her daughters were already in bed. Late at night, a little slanting flame, its mercurial tongue flickering, hovered across the road in the hut of Nestor Tyagay, a member of the Young Communist League. Judge Osmolovsky was lodging there. A sheepskin coat had been laid out on a bench, and his supper was waiting for him. A bowl of yogurt, an onion, and a thick slice of bread. The judge took off his spectacles and covered his aching eyes with his palms. He was known throughout the district as Comrade Two-Hundred-and-Sixteen-Percent—that had been the percentage of grain which he had managed to exact from the renegade town of Voronkov. Osmolovsky's percentage had given rise to tales, songs, and folk legends.

He chewed the bread and the onion, and spread out in front of him

Pravda, the instructions of the District Committee, and the collectivization reports of the People's Commissariat for Agriculture. It was late, after one in the morning, when the door opened and Gapa, her shawl tied across her chest, came in.

"Judge," she said to him, "what's going to happen to the whores?"

Osmolovsky raised his eyes, his face covered in rippled light.

"They will no longer exist."

"Won't the whores be allowed to earn their living?"

"They will," the judge said. "But in a different, better way."

Gapa stared into a corner of the room with unseeing eyes. She fingered the necklace that hung across her chest.

"I'm glad to hear that!"

Her necklace clinked. Gapa left, closing the door behind her.

The piercing, frenzied night hurled itself down on her with thickets of low-hanging clouds—twisted ice floes lit up by black sparks. Silence spread over Velikaya Krinitsa, over the flat, sepulchral, frozen desert of the village night.

KOLYVUSHKA

*F*our men entered Ivan Kolyvushka's courtyard: Ivashko, the representative of the Regional Commission for Collectivization, Evdokim Nazarenko, the head of the village council, Zhitnyak, the chairman of the newly formed kolkhoz,* and Adrian Morinets. Adrian walked like a tower that had uprooted itself and was on the march. Ivashko had hurried past the barns, pressing his canvas briefcase to his side, and came bursting into Kolyvushka's house. Kolyvushka's wife and two daughters were sitting by the window spinning yarn on blackened spindles. They looked like nuns, with their kerchiefs, their long bodices, and their small, clean, bare feet. Photographs of Czarist ensigns, schoolmistresses, and townsfolk at their dachas hung on the walls between embroidered towels and cheap mirrors. Ivan Kolyvushka came into the house after his guests, and took off his hat.

"How much tax does Kolyvushka pay?" Ivashko asked, turning to face the others.

Evdokim, the village council head, watched the whirling wheels of the spindles with his hands in his pockets.

Ivashko snorted when he was told that Kolyvushka paid two hundred and sixteen rubles.

"Surely he can swing more than that!"

"It looks like he can't."

Zhitnyak stretched his dry lips in a thin line. Evdokim continued

---

* Collective farm.

watching the spindles. Ivan Kolyvushka stood in the doorway and winked at his wife, who went and pulled a receipt out from behind an icon and handed it to Ivashko, the representative of the Collectivization Commission.

"And what about the seed fund?" Ivashko asked abruptly, impatiently digging his foot into the floorboards.

Evdokim raised his eyes and looked around the room.

"This household has already been cleaned out, Comrade Representative," Evdokim said. "This isn't the kind of household that doesn't pay its share."

The whitewashed walls curved up into a low, warm cupola over the guests' heads. The flowers in glass jars, the plain cupboards, the polished benches, all sparkled with an oppressive cleanliness. Ivashko jumped up and hurried out the door, his briefcase swinging.

"Comrade Representative!" Kolyvushka called out, hurrying after him. "So will instructions be sent to me, or what?"

"You'll be notified!" Ivashko shouted, his arms dangling, and rushed off.

Adrian Morinets, inhumanly large, rushed after him. Timish, the cheerful bailiff, bobbed past the gate close at Ivashko's heel, wading with his long legs through the mud of the village street.

"What's this all about?" Kolyvushka called out, waving him over and grabbing him by the sleeve. The bailiff, a long cheerful stick, bent forward and opened his mouth, which was packed with a purple tongue and set with rows of pearls.

"They are about to confiscate your house."

"What about me?"

"You'll be sent off for resettlement."

And Timish rushed after Ivashko and the others with cranelike steps.

A horse harnessed to a sledge was standing in Kolyvushka's courtyard, and the red reins had been thrown over some sacks of wheat piled up in the sledge. There was a tree stump with an axe stuck in it in the middle of the yard by a stooping lime tree. Kolyvushka ran his fingers over his hat, pushed it back, and sat down. The mare came over to him, dragging the sledge behind her. She hung out her tongue and then curled it up. She was with foal, and her belly was heavily swollen. She playfully nudged and nuzzled her master's shoulder. Kolyvushka looked down at his feet. The trampled snow lay in ripples around the tree stump. Hunching over, Kolyvushka grabbed the axe, held it up high in the air for an instant, and brought it down on the horse's forehead. One of her ears lunged back, the other fluttered and then slumped down. She moaned and bolted to the side, the sledge toppling over, the wheat flying in curved ribbons over the snow. She reared her forelegs into the air, tossing back her muzzle, and got caught in the spikes of a harrow by the shed. Her eyes peered out from under a streaming curtain of blood. She sang out in lament. The foal turned within her. A vein puffed up on her belly.

"Forgive me!" Ivan said, stretching out his hand to her. "Forgive me, my one and only!"

He held out his palm to her. The mare's ear hung limply, her eyes rolled, rings of blood sparked around them, her muzzle lay in a straight line with her neck. She curled back her upper lip in despair. She stretched out her neck and scuttled forward, pulling the jumping harrow behind her. Ivan raised the axe over his head. The blow hit her between the eyes, her foal again turned inside her tumbling belly. Ivan walked across the yard to the shed and dragged out the winnowing fan. He swung the axe down with wide, slow blows, smashing the machine, dragging the axe into the drum and the delicate grid of the wheels. His wife came out onto the stoop in her long bodice.

"Mother!" Kolyvushka heard her faraway voice. "Mother! He's smashing everything up!"

The door opened. Out of the house came an old woman in canvas trousers, steadying herself on a stick. Yellow hair hung over the hollows of her cheeks, and her shirt clung to her thin body like a shroud. The old woman stepped into the snow with her shaggy stockings.

"Murderer!" she said to her son, grabbing the axe out of his hand. "Do you remember your father? Do you remember your brothers in the labor camps?"

The neighbors began to gather in the yard. The muzhiks stood in a semicircle and looked away. A woman lunged forward and began to shriek.

"Shut up, you foolish cow!" her husband told her.

Kolyvushka stood leaning against the wall. His rasping breath echoed through the courtyard. It was as if he were working strenuously, panting heavily.

Kolyvushka's Uncle Terenti was shuffling about the gate, trying to lock it.

"I am a man!" Kolyvushka suddenly said to the people around him. "I am a man, a villager like you! Have you never seen a man before?"

Terenti hustled the villagers out of the yard. The gates creaked and fell shut. They swung open again in the evening, and a sledge piled high with possessions came sweeping out of the yard, the women perched on bales like frozen birds. A cow, tethered by her horn, came trotting behind. The sledge passed the outskirts of the village and disappeared into the flat, snowy desert. The wind spiraled in this desert, pummeling and moaning, scattering its blue waves behind which stretched the metallic sky, through which a mesh of diamonds wound sparkling.

Kolyvushka walked down the street to the village council, his eyes fixed straight ahead. A meeting of the new kolkhoz named "Renaissance" was under way. Hunchbacked Zhitnyak sat slouching behind the desk.

"The great change in our lives—what's this great change all about?" he said.

The hunchback's hands pressed against his torso, and then went flying up.

"Fellow villagers! We are redirecting ourselves into dairy production and market gardening! This is of momentous importance! Our fathers and grandfathers trudged over great treasures with their boots, and the time has now come for us to dig these treasures up! Is it not a disgrace, is it not an outrage that though we are only some sixty versts from our regional capital, we haven't developed our farming according to scientific methods? Our eyes were closed, my fellow villagers, we've been running away from ourselves! What does sixty versts mean? Does anyone here know? In our country that is equal to an hour—but even that one hour belongs to us! It is worth its weight in gold!"

The door of the village council opened. Kolyvushka came in and walked over to the wall in his voluminous fur jacket and tall sheepskin hat. Ivashko's fingers jumped and went scuttling into the pile of papers in front of him.

"I must ask all individuals without a voting right to immediately leave this meeting," he said, looking down at the papers.

Outside the window, beyond the dirty glass, the sunset was spilling out in green emerald streams. In the twilight of the village hut, sparks glittered faintly in the raw clouds of rough tobacco. Ivan Kolyvushka took off his hat, and his mop of black hair came pouring forth.

He walked up to the table around which the committee was sitting: Ivga Movchan, a woman who worked as a farmhand, Evdokim, the head of the village council, and silent Adrian Morinets.

"My people!" Ivan Kolyvushka said, stretching out his hand and laying a bunch of keys on the table. "My people, I am cutting all ties with you!"

The iron keys clanked and lay on the blackened boards. Adrian's haggard face appeared from within the darkness.

"Where will you go, Ivan?"

"My people won't have me, maybe the earth will!"

Kolyvushka walked out quietly, his head lowered.

"It's a trick!" Ivashko yelled the moment the door fell shut. "It's a provocation! He's gone to get his rifle, that's what! He's gone to get his rifle!"

Ivashko banged his fist on the table. Words about panic and the need to keep calm tried to struggle through his lips.

Adrian's face again retreated into its dark corner. "No, Comrade Chairman," he said from within the darkness. "I don't think he went to get his rifle."

"I have a proposal to make!" Ivashko shouted.

The proposal was that a guard be set up outside Kolyvushka's place. Timish the bailiff was voted to be the guard. Grimacing, he took a bentwood chair out onto the stoop, slumped down on it, and laid his shotgun and his truncheon by his feet. From the heights of the stoop, from the heights of his village throne, Timish bantered with the girls, whistled, shouted, and thumped his shotgun on the ground. The night was lilac and heavy, like a bright mountain crystal. Veins of frozen rivulets lay across it. A star sank into a well of black clouds.

The following morning Timish reported that there had been no incidents. Kolyvushka had spent the night at Grandpa Abram's, an old man overgrown with raw flesh.

In the evening Abram had hobbled off to the well.

"Why go there, Grandpa Abram?" Kolyvushka asked.

"I'm going to put on a samovar," Grandpa said.

They slept late. Smoke rose above the hut. Their door remained shut.

"He's run for it!" Ivashko said at the kolkhoz meeting. "Are we going to cry tears over him? What d'you think, villagers?"

Zhitnyak sat at the table, his sharp, quivering elbows spread wide, entering the particulars of the confiscated horses. The hump on his back cast a moving shadow.

"How much more are we going to stuff down our throats?" Zhitnyak pronounced philosophically as he wrote. "Now we suddenly need everything in the world! We need crop sprinklers, we need plows, tractors, pumps! Gluttony, that's what this is! Our whole country has been seized by gluttony!"

The horses that Zhitnyak entered in the book were all bay or skewbald, with names like "Boy" and "Little Miss." Zhitnyak had the owners sign against their surnames.

He was interrupted by a noise, a faraway, muffled clatter of hooves. A tidal wave was rolling toward Velikaya Staritsa* and came crashing over it. A crowd poured over the ravished street, legless cripples hobbling in front. An invisible banner was fluttering above their heads. They slowed as they arrived at the village council and drew into formation. A circle opened in their midst, a circle of ruffled-up snow, a gap as for a priest during a church procession. Kolyvushka was standing in the circle, his shirt hanging loose beneath his vest, his head completely white. The night had silvered his gypsy locks, not a black hair was left. Flakes of snow, weak birds carried by the wind, drifted across the warming sky. An old man with broken legs jostled his way forward and peered avidly at Kolyvushka's white hair.

"Tell us, Ivan," the old man said, raising his arms. "Tell us what is in your soul!"

"Where will you chase me to, my fellow villagers?" Kolyvushka whispered, looking around. "Where shall I go? I was born here among you."

---

* The actual village that Babel visited in the spring of 1930 and decided to base his novel on. In the novel's first chapter, "Gapa Guzhva," the same village appears as Velikaya Krinitsa. Babel had decided to change the name of the village so as not offend the inhabitants.

The crowd began to rumble. Morinets elbowed his way to the front.

"Let him be," he said in a low, trembling voice, the cry trapped in his powerful chest. "Let him be! Whose share will he grab?"

"Mine!" Zhitnyak said, and burst out laughing. He walked up to Kolyvushka, shuffling his feet, and winked at him.

"I slept with a woman last night!" the hunchback said. "When we got up she made pancakes, and me and her, we gobbled them down like we was hogs—ha, we blew more farts than you could shake a stick at—"

The hunchback stopped in midsentence, his guffaws broke off, and the blood drained from his face.

"So you've come to line us up against the wall?" he asked in a lower voice. "You've come to bully us with that white head of yours, to turn the thumbscrews on us? But we won't let you, the time for thumbscrews has passed!"

The hunchback came nearer on his thin, bowed legs. Something whistled inside him like a bird.

"You should be killed," he whispered, an idea flitting through his mind. "I'll go get my gun and finish you off."

His face brightened. He gave Kolyvushka's hand a spirited tap and hurried off into the house to get Timish's gun. Kolyvushka wavered for a moment, and then walked off. His silver head disappeared in the tangled mesh of houses. He stumbled as he walked, but then his strides grew firmer. He took the road to Ksenevka.

No one ever saw him again in Velikaya Staritsa.

THE ROAD

I left the crumbling front in November 1917. At home my mother packed underwear and dried bread for me. I arrived in Kiev the day before Muravyov began shelling the city.* I was trying to get to Petersburg. For twelve days and nights I hid with Chaim Tsiryulnik in the basement of his Hotel Bessarabka. The commander of Soviet Kiev issued me a pass to leave the city.

In all the world there is no more cheerless sight than the Kiev train station. For many years makeshift wooden barracks have defaced the town outskirts. Lice crackled on wet planks. Deserters, smugglers, and gypsies were all crowded together in the station. Old Galician women urinated standing on the platform. The low sky was furrowed with clouds full of rain and gloom.

Three days went by before the first train left. At first it stopped every verst; then it gathered speed, its wheels rattling faster, singing a powerful song. This filled everyone in our transport car with joy. Fast travel filled people with joy in 1918. At night, the train gave a jolt and stopped. The door of our car opened, and we saw the green glimmer of snow before us. A station telegrapher in soft Caucasian boots and a fur coat tied with a strap climbed aboard. The telegrapher stretched out his hand and tapped his finger on his open palm. "Put all travel permits here!"

Right by the door an old woman lay quietly curled up on some

---

* Mikhail Artemevich Muravyov, 1880–1918, was the commander in chief of the Southern Revolutionary Front. He was shelling Kiev in order to occupy it for the Bolsheviks.

bundles. She was heading for Lyuban to her son, who was a railroad worker. Dozing next to me was a schoolmaster, Yehuda Veynberg, and his wife. The schoolmaster had married a few days earlier, and was taking his young wife to Petersburg. They had been whispering throughout the journey about new structured methods in teaching, and then dozed off. Their hands were clasped even in sleep.

The telegrapher read their permit signed by Lunacharsky,* pulled a Mauser with a thin, dirty muzzle from under his coat, and shot the schoolmaster in the face.

A big, hunchbacked muzhik in a fur cap with dangling earflaps was standing behind the telegrapher. The telegrapher winked at him, and the muzhik put his lamp on the floor, unbuttoned the dead man's trousers, sliced off his sexual organs with a pocketknife, and stuffed them into the wife's mouth.

"*Tref*† wasn't good enough for you!" the muzhik said. "So now eat something kosher!"

The woman's soft throat swelled. She remained silent. The train was standing on the steppes. The furrowed snows swarmed with polar brilliance. Jews were being thrown out of the cars onto the rails. Shots rang out unevenly, like shouts. The muzhik in the fur cap with the dangling earflaps took me behind a pile of logs and began to search me. The darkened moon shone down on us. Smoke rose from the forest's lilac wall. Frozen wooden fingers crept stiffly over my body.

"A Yid or a Russian?" the telegrapher yelled from the car platform.

"Yeah, a Russian! So much so, he'd make a first-rate rabbi!" the muzhik muttered as he searched me.

He brought his wrinkled, anxious face close to mine, ripped out the four golden ten-ruble coins which my mother had sewn into my underwear for the journey, took my boots and my coat, and then, turning me around, hit me on the back of my neck with the edge of his palm and said in Yiddish, "*Antloyf, Chaim!*"**

I ran, my bare feet sinking in the snow. I felt him mark a target on my back, the nip of his aim cutting through my ribs. But the muzhik

---

* Anatoly Lunacharsky, 1875–1933, Marxist critic and playwright, was the USSR's first Commissar of Education.

† Food that is not kosher, and so is unfit to eat according to Jewish dietary laws.

** Yiddish: "Run away, Chaim."

did not shoot. A light was quavering within a garland of smoke among the columns of pine trees, within the covered cellar of the forest. I ran toward the hut. The smoke of burning dung patties rose from it. The forester groaned when I burst into his hut. Huddled in strips cut from furs and coats, he was sitting on a finely wrought bamboo armchair with velvet cushions, crumbling tobacco on his knees. Enveloped in smoke, the forester groaned again, got up, and bowed deeply.

"You mustn't come in here, my dearest friend! You mustn't come in here, dearest Comrade!"

He led me to a path and gave me some rags to wrap my feet in. By late next morning I had reached a shtetl. There was no doctor at the hospital to amputate my frostbitten feet. The medical orderly was running the ward. Every morning he came galloping over to the hospital on his short black stallion, tied it to the hitching post, and came over to us full of fire, sparks burning in his eyes.

"Friedrich Engels teaches us that there should be no nations," the medical orderly said, bending over the head of my bed, his pupils fiery coals. "And yet we say the opposite—nations have to exist."[*]

Ripping the bandages off my feet, he straightened his back, and, gnashing his teeth asked me in a low voice, "So where is it taking you, this nation of yours? Where? Why doesn't it stay in one place? Why is it stirring up trouble, making waves?"

The Soviets moved us out on a cart in the night: patients who had not seen eye to eye with the medical orderly and old Jewesses in wigs, the mothers of the shtetl commissars.

My feet healed. I continued along the destitute road to Zhlobin, Orsha, and Vitebsk. The muzzle of a howitzer acted as my shelter from Novosokolniki to Loknya.[†] We were riding on the uncovered cannon platform. Fedyukha, my chance traveling companion, a storyteller and witty jokester, was undertaking the great journey of the deserters. We slept beneath the powerful, short, upward-pointing muzzle, and warmed each other in the canvas pit, covered with hay like the den of

---

[*] The medical orderly is confusing Engels's concept of the nation state with nationality, in this case Russian versus Jewish nationality.

[†] Zhlobin, Orsha, and Vitebsk are towns, today in Belarus, that the narrator would have passed through on his way north from Kiev to Petersburg. Novosokolniki and Loknya are in Russia on the other side of the Belarus border.

an animal. After Loknya, Fedyukha stole my suitcase and disappeared. The shtetl soviet had issued me the suitcase along with two pairs of soldier's underwear, dried bread, and some money. Two days went by without food as we approached Petersburg. At the station in Tsarskoe Selo* I witnessed the last of the shooting. The defense detachment fired shots into the air as our train pulled in. The smugglers were led out onto the platform and their clothes were ripped off, and rubber suits filled with vodka came tumbling off of them onto the asphalt.

Shortly after eight in the evening, the Petersburg station hurled me from its howling bedlam onto the Zagorodny Boulevard. A thermometer on the wall of a boarded-up pharmacy across the street showed −24 degrees Celsius. The wind roared through the tunnel of Gorokhovaya Street; jets of gaslight faded over the canals. This frozen, basalt Venice stood transfixed. I entered Gorokhovaya Street, which lay there like a field of ice cluttered with rocks.

The Cheka[†] had installed itself at number 2, the former office of the governor. Two machine guns, iron dogs with raised muzzles, stood in the entrance hall. I showed the commandant the letter from Vanya Kalugin, my sergeant in the Shuysky Regiment. Kalugin had become an investigator in the Cheka, and had sent me a letter to come see him.

"Go to Anichkov Palace," the commandant told me. "He's there now."

"I'll never make it," I thought, and smiled at him.

The Nevsky Prospekt flowed into the distance like the Milky Way. Dead horses lay along it like milestones. Their legs, pointing upward, supported the descending sky. Their bare bellies were clean and shiny. An old man who resembled an Imperial guardsman trudged past me, dragging a wooden toy sledge behind him, driving his boots with difficulty into the ice. A Tyrolean hat was perched on his head, and he had tied his beard with a piece of string and stuck it into his shawl.

"I'll never make it," I said to the old man.

He stopped. His furrowed leonine face was filled with calm. He hesitated for a moment, but then continued dragging the sledge along the street.

---

* Today the city of Pushkin, fourteen miles south of St. Petersburg.
† The "Extraordinary Commission," formed in 1917 to investigate counterrevolutionary activities.

"Thus falls away the need to conquer Petersburg," I said to myself, and tried to remember the name of the man who had been crushed by the hooves of Arab stallions at the very end of his journey. It was Yehuda Halevi.*

Two Chinese men in bowler hats stood on the corner of Sadovaya Street with loaves of bread under their arms. They showed them to passing prostitutes, and with frozen fingernails drew lines across the crust. The women walked past them in a silent parade.

At Anichkov Bridge I sat on the base of the statue by Klodt's horses.†

I lay down on the polished flagstone, my elbow under my head, but the freezing granite blistered me, and drove, pushed, propelled me forward to the palace.

The portal of the raspberry-red side wing stood open. Blue gaslight shone above a lackey, who had fallen asleep in an armchair. His lower lip was hanging from an inky, moribund face filled with wrinkles, and his military tunic, flooded with light, hung beltless over livery trousers trimmed with gold lace. A splotchy arrow, drawn in ink, pointed the way to the commandant. I went up the stairs and passed through low, empty chambers. Women painted in somber black danced rounds on ceilings and walls. Iron grates covered the windows, their broken latches hung on the frames. At the end of the suite of chambers Kalugin was sitting at a table, lit as if on stage, his head framed by straw-colored muzhik hair. On the table in front of him was a heap of toys, colorful rags, and torn picture books.

"So here you are!" Kalugin said, raising his head. "Great! We need you here."

I brushed aside the toys piled on the table, lay down on the shining tabletop, and . . . woke up on a low sofa—perhaps a few minutes, perhaps a few hours later. The lights of a chandelier danced above me in a waterfall of glass. The wet rags that had been cut off me lay on the floor in a puddle.

"You need a bath," Kalugin told me, standing above the sofa. He lifted me up and carried me to a bathtub. It was an old-fashioned tub,

---

* Yehuda Halevi, 1075–1141, was a Jewish poet and religious philosopher from Toledo, who embarked on a pilgrimage to Palestine at the end of his life. He died in Egypt, slain, according to legend, by a horseman at the gates of Jerusalem.
† A sculpture of a group of horses by Peter Karlovich Klodt, 1805–1867.

with low sides. The water didn't flow from taps. Kalugin poured water over me with a bucket. Clothes were laid out on yellowish satin pouffes, on wicker stools—a robe with buckles, a shirt and socks of double-woven silk. The long underpants went all the way up to my head, the robe had been tailored for a giant, the sleeves were so long I tripped over them.

"So you're making fun of old Alexander Alexandrovich?" Kalugin said as he rolled up my sleeves. "The old boy weighed a good nine *pood*!"*

We somehow managed to tie Czar Alexander III's robe, and went back to the room we had been in before. It was the library of Maria Fyodorovna,† a perfumed box, its walls lined with gilded bookcases filled with crimson spines.

I told Kalugin which of our men in the Shuysky Regiment had been killed, who had become a commissar, who had gone to Kuban. We drank tea, and stars streamed over the crystal walls of our glasses. We chased our tea down with horsemeat sausages, which were black and somewhat raw. The thick, airy silk of a curtain separated us from the world. The sun, fixed to the ceiling, reflected and shone, and the steam pipes from the central heating gave off a stifling heat.

"You only live once," he said, after we had finished our horsemeat. He left the room and came back with two boxes—a gift from Sultan Abdul Hamid** to the Russian sovereign. One was made of zinc, the other was a cigar box sealed with tape and paper emblems. "*A sa majesté, l'Empereur de toutes les Russies,*" was engraved on the zinc lid, "from his well-wishing cousin."

Maria Fyodorovna's library was flooded with an aroma she had known a quarter of a century ago. Cigars twenty centimeters long and thick as a finger were wrapped in pink paper. I do not know if anyone besides the autocrat of all the Russias had ever smoked such cigars, but nevertheless I chose one. Kalugin looked at me and smiled.

"You only live once," he said. "Let's hope they've not been count-ed. The lackeys told me that Alexander III was an inveterate smoker. He loved tobacco, kvass, and champagne. But on his table—take a

---

* Czar Alexander III, 1845–94 lived in the Anichkov Palace. Nine *pood* is 325 pounds.
† Empress Maria Fyodorovna, 1847–1928, wife of Czar Alexander III.
** Abdul Hamid II, 1842–1918, the Sultan of the Ottoman Empire.

look!—there are five-kopeck clay ashtrays, and there are patches on his trousers!"

And sure enough, the robe I had been arrayed in was stained, shiny, and had been mended many times.

We passed the rest of the night going through Nicholas II's toys, his drums and locomotives, his christening shirt, and his notebooks with their childish scribbles. Pictures of grand dukes who had died in infancy, locks of their hair, the diaries of the Danish Princess Dagmar,* the letters of her sister, the Queen of England, breathing perfume and decay, crumbling in our fingers. On the title pages of the Bible and Lamartine,† her friends and governesses—the daughters of burgomasters and state councilors—bade farewell in laborious slanting lines to the princess leaving for Russia. Her mother, Louisa, queen of a small kingdom, had put much effort into seeing her children well settled. She gave one of her daughters to Edward VII, the Emperor of India and King of England, and the other to a Romanov. Her son George was made King of Greece. Princess Dagmar turned into Maria in Russia. The canals of Copenhagen and the chocolate sideburns of King Christian faded in the distance. Bearing the last of the sovereigns, Maria, a tiny woman with the fierceness of a fox, hurried through the palisades of the Preobrazhensky Grenadiers. But her maternal blood was to spill on Russia's implacable, unforgiving granite earth.

We could not tear ourselves from the dull, fatal chronicle till dawn. I had finished smoking Abdul-Hamid's cigar. In the morning, Kalugin took me to the Cheka, to Gorokhovaya Street, number two. He had a word with Uritsky.** I stood behind a heavy curtain that hung to the ground in cloth waves. Fragments of words made their way through to me.

"He's one of us," Kalugin said. "His father is a storekeeper, a merchant, but he's washed his hands of them. . . . He knows languages."

Uritsky came out of his office with a tottering gait. His swollen eyelids, burned by sleeplessness, bulged behind the glass of his pince-nez.

---

* Later Empress Maria Fyodorovna, wife of Czar Alexander III.

† Alphonse de Lamartine, 1790–1869, was a French Romantic poet and statesman.

** Mikhail (Mosey) Solomonovich Uritsky, 1873–1918, the son of a Jewish merchant, was the commissar of internal affairs for the northern district and the chairman of the Petrograd (Petersburg) Cheka.

They made me a translator in the Foreign Division. I was issued a military uniform and food coupons. In a corner of the Petersburg City Hall that was allocated to me I set about translating depositions of diplomats, agents provocateurs, and spies.

Within a single day I had everything: clothes, food, work, and comrades true in friendship and death, comrades the likes of which you will not find anywhere in the world, except in our country.

That is how, thirteen years ago, a wonderful life filled with thought and joy began for me.

THE *IVAN AND MARIA*

*I*n the summer of 1918 Sergei Vasilevich Malishev,[*] who was to become the chairman of the Nizhny-Novgorod Fair Committee, organized our nation's first produce expedition. With Lenin's approval, he loaded a series of trains with goods useful to peasants, and sent these trains to the Volga region to exchange the goods for wheat.

I ended up in the clerical department of this expedition. We chose the Novo-Nikolayev district in the province of Samara as our field of operation. According to the specialists, this province, if properly cultivated, was capable of feeding the whole Moscow region.

Near Saratov,[†] the goods were reloaded onto a barge at the river docks of Uvek. The hold of this barge became a makeshift department store. We pinned up portraits of Lenin and Marx between the curved ribs of our floating warehouse and framed the portraits with ears of corn, and we arranged bales of calico, scythes, nails, and leather goods on the shelves, even concertinas and balalaikas.

At Uvek we had been given a tugboat, the *Ivan Tupitsin,* named after a Volga merchant who had been its previous owner. The "staff," Malishev with his assistants and cashiers, made themselves at home on the tugboat, while the guards and sales clerks slept on the barge, under the counters.

It took a week to load the goods onto the barge. On a July morn-

---

[*] Sergei Vasilevich Malishev, 1877–1938, nicknamed "The Red Merchant," was one of the chief trade administrators during the early years of Soviet rule.

[†] Saratov, a city in western Russia, lies along the middle course of the Volga River.

ing the *Ivan Tupitsin,* gushing fat puffs of smoke, began to pull us up the Volga to Baronsk.* The local German settlers call it Katarinenstadt. It is now the capital of the Volga German Province, a wonderful region settled by hardy, taciturn folk.

The steppes outside Baronsk are covered with heavy, golden wheat, such as you can only find in Canada. They are filled with sunflowers and black oily clumps of earth. We had traveled from a Petersburg licked clean by granite flames to a California that was Russian through and through, and therefore even more outlandish. In our own California a pound of grain cost sixty kopecks, and not ten rubles as it did back in the north. We threw ourselves onto the loaves of bread with a savagery that nowadays is impossible to understand. We plunged our canine teeth, sharpened by hunger, into the bread's gossamer core. For two weeks we languished in a blissful drunkenness of indigestion. To me, the blood flowing through our veins had the taste and color of raspberry jam.

Malishev's calculations had been right: sales went well. Slow streams of carts flowed to the riverbank from all corners of the steppes. The sun crept over the backs of well-fed horses. The sun shone on the tops of the wheat-covered hills. Carts in a thousand dots descended to the Volga. Giants in woolen jerseys, descendants of the Dutch farmers who had settled in the Volga regions in the days of Catherine, strode beside the horses. Their faces looked just as they had back in Zaandam[†] and Haarlem. Drops of sparkling turquoise shone from within a mesh of leathery wrinkles beneath patriarchal mossy eyebrows. Smoke from tobacco pipes melted into the bluish lightning that flashed over the steppes. The settlers slowly climbed the gangplank onto the barge. Their wooden shoes clanged like bells heralding strength and peace. The goods were chosen by old women in starched bonnets and brown bodices. Their purchases were carried to the carts. Village painters had strewn armfuls of wildflowers and pink bull muzzles along the sides of the carts—the outer sides were usually painted a deep blue, within which waxen apples and plums gleamed, touched by the rays of the sun.

---

* Renamed Marks (Marx).
[†] Today Zaanstadt.

People from far away rode in on camels. These animals lay on the riverbank, their collapsed humps cutting into the horizon. Our trading always ended toward evening. We locked our store. The guards—war invalids—and the sales clerks undressed and jumped off the barges into the Volga burning in the sunset. On the distant steppes the wheat rolled in red waves. The walls of the sunset were collapsing in the sky. The swimming workers of the Samara Province Produce Expedition (that is what we were called in official documents) were an unusual spectacle. The cripples spouted silty pink streams from the river. Some of the guards were one-legged, others were missing an arm or an eye. They hooked themselves up in twos so they could swim. Two men would then have two legs, thrashing the water with their stumps, silty streams rushing in whirls between their bodies. Growling and snorting, the cripples rolled out onto the riverbank, frolicking, shaking their stumps at the flowing skies, covering themselves with sand, and wrestling, grabbing hold of each other's chopped extremities. After swimming, we went to the tavern of Karl Biedermayer. Our day was crowned by supper there. Two girls with brick-red hands, Augusta and Anna, served us meat patties—red flagstones quivering under whorls of seething butter and heaped with haystacks of fried potatoes. They spiced this mountain of village fare with onions and garlic. They placed jars of sour pickles in front of us. The smoke of the sunset wafted in from the marketplace through little round windows high up near the ceiling. The pickles smoldered in the crimson smoke and smelled of the seashore. We washed down the meat with cider. Every evening we, the residents of Peski and Okhta, men of the Petersburg suburbs that were frozen over with yellow urine, once again felt like conquerors. The little windows, cut into black walls centuries old, resembled portholes. Through them shone a courtyard, blissfully clean, a little German courtyard with rosebushes and wisteria, and the violet precipice of an open stable. Old women in bodices sat on stoops, knitting stockings for Gulliver. Herds were coming back from the pastures. Augusta and Anna sat down on stools beside the cows. Radiant bovine eyes glittered in the twilight. It was as if there had never been war on earth. And yet the front of the Ural Cossacks was only twenty versts from Baronsk.*

---

* The Red Army was fighting the White counterrevolutionary troops made up of Ural Cossacks and Czech divisions.

Karl Biedermayer had no idea that the Civil War was rolling toward his home.

At night I returned to our hold in the barge with Seletsky, who was a clerk, just as I was. He sang as we walked. Heads in nightcaps peered out of lancet windows. The moonlight flowed down the roof tiles' red canals. The muffled barking of dogs rose above this Russian Zaandam. Riveted Augustas and Annas listened to Seletsky's song. His deep bass carried us to the steppes, to the gothic enclosure of the wheat barns. Crossbeams of moonlight flickered on the river, and the breezy darkness swept over the sand of the riverbanks. Iridescent worms writhed in a torn sweep net.

Seletsky's voice was unnaturally powerful. He was an enormous fellow who belonged to that race of provincial Chaliapins,* of which so many, to our great fortune, have arisen throughout Russia. He even had the same kind of face as Chaliapin, part Scottish coachman, part grandee from the era of Catherine the Great. Seletsky was a simple man, unlike his divine prototype, but his voice resounded boundlessly, fatally, filled one's soul with the sweetness of self-destruction and gypsy oblivion. Seletsky preferred the songs of convicts to Italian arias. It was from him that I first heard Grechaninov's[†] song "Death." It resounded, menacing, relentless, passionate, over the dark water through the night.

> *She will not forget, she will come to you,*
> *Caress, embrace, and love you for all eternity.*
> *But a bridal wreath of thorns shall crown her head.*

This song flows within man's ephemeral shell like the waters of eternity. It washes away everything, it gives birth to everything.

The front was twenty versts away. The Ural Cossacks, joined by Major Vozenilek's Czech battalion, were trying to drive the dispersed Red detachments out of Nikolayevsk. Farther north, the troops of Komchuk—the Committee of the Members of the Constituent

---

* Fyodor Ivanovich Chaliapin, 1873–1938, a legendary bass, one of the most renowned opera singers of the early twentieth century.

[†] Alexander Tichonovich Grechaninov, 1864–1956, Russian composer and songwriter, noted for his religious works and children's music.

Assembly—were advancing from Samara.* Our scattered, untrained units regrouped on the left bank. Muravyov had just betrayed us. Vatsetis was appointed the Soviet commander in chief.†

Weapons for the front were brought from Saratov. Once or twice a week the pink and white paddle steamer *Ivan and Maria* docked at Baronsk. It carried rifles and shells. Its deck was full of boxes with skulls stenciled on them, under which the word "lethal" was written.

The ship's captain, Korostelyov, was a man ravished by drink, with lifeless flaxen hair. He was an adventurer, a restless soul, and a vagabond. He had traveled the White Sea on sailing vessels, walked the length and breadth of Russia, had done time in jail and penance in a monastery.

We always dropped by to see him on our way back from Biedermayer's if there were still lights on board the *Ivan and Maria*. One night, as we passed the wheat barns with their enchanted blue and brown castle silhouettes, we saw a torch blazing high in the sky. Seletsky and I were heading back to our barge in that warm, passionate state of mind that can only be spawned by this wondrous land, youth, night, and the melting rings of fire on the river.

The Volga was rolling on silently. There were no lights on the *Ivan and Maria,* and the hulk of the ship lay dark and dead, with only the torch burning above it. The flame was flaring and fuming above the mast. Seletsky was singing, his face pale, his head thrown back. He stopped when we came to the edge of the river. We walked up the unguarded gangplank. Boxes and gun wheels lay about the deck. I knocked on the door of the captain's cabin, and it fell open. A tin lamp without a glass cover was burning on the table, which was covered with spilled liquor. The metallic ring around the wick was melting. The windows had been boarded up with crooked planks. The sulfuric aroma of home-brewed vodka rose from cans under the table. Captain Korostelyov was sitting on the floor in a canvas shirt among green streams of vomit. His clotted, monastic hair stood around his head. He

---

* The Komchuk was a government formed in Samara by the anti-Soviet Social Revolutionary Party on June 18, 1918.

† Mikhail Artemevich Muravyov, 1880–1918, had been the commander in chief of the Southern Revolutionary Front, but began an anti-Soviet uprising in Simbirsk on July 10, 1918. He was killed the following day. Ioachim Ioachimovich Vatsetis, 1883–1938, took over from Muravyov immediately after his defection.

was staring fixedly up at Larson, his Latvian commissar, who was sitting, holding a *Pravda* in a yellowish cardboard folder open in front of him, reading it in the light of the melting kerosene flicker.

"You're showing your true colors!" Captain Korostelyov said from the floor. "Go on with what you were saying . . . go on torturing us if you have to."

"Why should I do the talking?" Larson answered, turning his back and fencing himself off with his *Pravda*. "I'd rather listen to you."

A redheaded muzhik, his legs dangling, was sitting on a velvet sofa.

"Lisyei! Vodka!" the captain said to him.

"None left," Lisyei said. "And nowhere to get none."

Larson put down his paper and burst out laughing, as if he were pounding a drum.

"A Russian man needs his drink, the Russian man's soul wants to carouse, but there's not a drop to be found anywhere around here!" the Latvian said in his thick accent. "And it still calls itself the Volga!"

Captain Korostelyov stretched out his thin, boyish neck, and his legs in their canvas trousers sprawled out across the floor. There was pitiful bewilderment in his eyes, and then they flashed. "Torture us," he said to the Latvian, barely audibly, stretching out his neck. "Torture us, Karl."

Lisyei clasped his plump hands together and peered at the Latvian. "Ha! He's trumping the Volga! No, Comrade, you will not trump our Volga, you will not bad-mouth her! Don't you know the song we sing: Mother Volga, Czarina of all rivers?"

Seletsky and I were still standing by the door. I kept thinking of retreating.

"Well, this is simply beyond my grasp!" Larson said, turning to us, but clearly continuing the argument. "Maybe these comrades here can explain to me why reinforced concrete is worse than birches and aspens, and airships worse than Kaluga dung?"

Lisyei's head twisted in his quilted collar. His legs didn't reach the floor. His plump fingers, pressed to his stomach, were knotting an invisible net.

"Ha! And what is it you know about Kaluga, my friend?" Lisyei asked in a pacifying tone. "I'll have you know there's famous folk that lives in Kaluga! Yes, fabulous folk!"

"Some vodka," Captain Korostelyov muttered from the floor.

Larson again threw back his piggish head and laughed out loud. "You win some, you lose some, " he muttered, pulling the *Pravda* closer. "Yes, you win some, you lose some."

Sweat was seething on his forehead, and oily streams of fire were dancing in his clotted, dirt-crusted hair.

"You win some, you lose some," Larson snorted again. "Yes, you win some, you lose some."

Captain Korostelyov patted the floor around him with his fingers. He began crawling forward, hauling himself along with his hands, dragging his skeletal body in its sackcloth shirt behind him.

"Don't you dare bait Russia, Karl," he whispered, crawling toward the Latvian, hitting him in the face with his clenched fist, and then, with a sudden shriek, beginning to flail at him. The Latvian puffed himself up and looked at us over his skewed glasses. Then he wound a silken rivulet of Korostelyov's hair around his finger and banged Korostelyov's head on the floor. He yanked his head up and banged it down again.

"There!" Larson said curtly, flinging the bony body to the side. "And there's more where that came from!"

The captain propped himself up on his hands and got on all fours like a dog. Blood was flowing from his nostrils, and his eyes were crossed, darting about. Suddenly he flung himself up and hurled himself with a howl under the table.

"Russia!" he mumbled from under the table, and started kicking and flailing. "Russia!"

The shovels of his bare feet thrashed about. Only one whistling, moaning word could be heard in his screeching.

"Russia!" he moaned, stretching out his hands, beating his head against the floor.

Redheaded Lisyei was still sitting on the velvet sofa.

"This has been going on since noon," he said, turning to Seletsky and me. "Fighting for Russia, feeling sorry for Russia."

"Vodka!" Korostelyov said harshly from under the table. He crawled out and stood up. His hair, dripping with blood, hung down on his cheeks.

"Where's the vodka, Lisyei?"

"The vodka, my friend, is forty versts away, in Voznesenskoe—forty versts by water or by land. There's a church there now, so there must be home brew to be had. Whatever you do, the Germans don't have none!"*

Captain Korostelyov turned around and walked out on rigid heron's legs.

"We're Kalugans!" Larson yelled out unexpectedly.

"He has no respect for Kaluga," Lisyei sighed, "whichever way you look at it. But me, I've been there in Kaluga! Proper folk live there, famous—"

Outside, someone yelled an order, and the clanking of the anchor was heard—the anchor was being weighed. Lisyei raised his eyebrows.

"We're not off to Voznesenskoe, are we?"

Larson burst out laughing, throwing his head back. I ran out of the cabin. Korostelyov stood barefoot on the bridge. The copper rays of the moon lay on his gashed face. The gangplanks fell onto the riverbank. Whirling sailors unwound the moorings.

"Dimitri Alekseyevich," Seletsky shouted up to Korostelyov. "At least let us get off! What do you need us along for?"

The engines erupted into erratic hammering. The paddlewheel dug into the river. A rotten plank on the pier creaked softly. The *Ivan and Maria* swung its bow around.

"So we're off," Lisyei said, coming out of the cabin. "So we're off to Voznesenskoe to get some home brew."

The *Ivan and Maria*'s uncoiling paddlewheel was gaining speed. The engine's oily clanking, rustling, and whistling grew. We flew through the darkness, forging straight ahead, plowing through buoys, beacons, and red signals. The water foamed beneath the paddles and went flashing back like the golden wings of a bird. The moon plunged into swirls of black water. "The Volga's waterway is full of bends" was a phrase I remembered from a schoolbook. "It abounds in sandbanks." Captain Korostelyov was shuffling about on the bridge. Blue shining skin stretched over his cheekbones.

---

* Lisyei is saying that the Volga German settlement of Wosnesenka, called Voznesenskoe by the Russians, now has a Russian community—hence the Orthodox church. And where there are Russians, there is home-brewed vodka, which one could not get from the Germans, who were mainly Mennonites.

"Full steam ahead!" he said into the tube.

"Full steam ahead it is!" a muffled invisible voice answered.

"I want even more steam!"

There was silence from the engine room.

"The engine will blow," the voice said, after a moment of silence. The signal torch toppled off the mast and streamed over the rolling waves. The steamer rocked. An explosion shuddered through the hull. We flew through the darkness, straight ahead. A rocket went soaring up from the riverbank, a three-inch gun started pounding us. A shell went whistling between the masts. The galley boy, dragging a samovar across the deck, raised his head. The samovar went skidding out of his hands and rolled down the stairs, split open, and a glittering stream poured down the dirty steps. The galley boy snarled, tottered over to the stairs, and fell asleep. The deadly aroma of home-brewed vodka came pouring from his mouth. Belowdecks, among the oily cylinders, the stokers, stripped to the waist, were roaring, waving their arms, and rolling on the floor. Their twisted faces shone in the pearly gleam of the pistons. The crew of the *Ivan and Maria* was drunk. Only the helmsman stood firmly at his wheel. He turned and looked at me.

"Hey, Yid!" he called out to me. "What's going to become of the children?"

"What children?"

"The children aren't going to school," the helmsman shouted, turning the wheel. "The children will turn into thieves!"

He brought his leaden, blue cheekbones close to my face and gnashed his teeth. His jaws grated like millstones. It was as if his teeth were being ground to sand.

"I'll rip you to pieces!"

I edged away from him. Lisyei came walking across the deck.

"What's going on here, Lisyei!"

"I guess he'll get us there," the redheaded muzhik said, and sat down on a bench.

When we got to Voznesenskoe, we sent him ashore. There was no "church" to be found, no lights, no carousel. The sloping riverbank was dark, covered by a low-hanging sky. Lisyei sank into darkness. He had been away for more than an hour when he resurfaced right by the water, hauling some large cans. A pockmarked woman, as well built as a horse, was following him. The child's blouse she was wearing was much too small and stretched tightly over her breasts. A dwarf in a pointed hat and tiny little boots was standing nearby, openmouthed, watching us haul the cans on deck.

"Plum liquor," Lisyei said, putting the cans on the table. "The plummiest home brew!"

And the race of our spectral ship began once more. We arrived in Baronsk toward daybreak. The river spread out boundlessly. Water trickled off the riverbanks, leaving a blue satin shadow. A pink ray struck the mist hanging on the ragged bushes. The bleak, painted walls of the barns and their thin steeples slowly turned and floated toward us. We steamed toward Baronsk among peals of song. Seletsky had cleared his throat with a bottle of the plummiest home brew, and was singing his heart out. Mussorgsky's *Flea* was in his song, Mephistopheles' booming laughter, and the aria of the crazed miller, "I am a raven, no miller am I."

The barefoot captain lay slumped over the railing of the bridge. His head was lolling, his eyelids shut tight, and his gashed face, a vague childish smile wandering over it, was flung up toward the sky. He regained consciousness when the boat began slowing down.

"Alyosha!" he shouted into the tube. "Full steam ahead!"

And we went charging toward the pier at full steam ahead. The gangplank we had mangled as we pulled out the night before went flying into the air. The engines stopped just in time.

"You see, he brought us back," Lisyei said, turning up beside me. "And there you were, all worried."

Chapayev's machine gun carts were already lining up on the riverbank.* Rainbow stripes darkened and cooled on the bank from which the tidewaters had just ebbed. In a heap next to the pier were boxes of cartridges left by boats that had come and gone. Makeyev, the commander of one of Chapayev's squadrons, was sitting beltless on a box in a peasant shirt and a tall fur hat. Captain Korostelyov went up to him with outspread arms.

"I was a real idiot again, Kostya," he said with his childlike smile. "I used up all the fuel!"

---

*Vasili Ivanovich Chapayev, 1887–1919, was commander of the Pugachov Brigade that was fighting the counterrevolutionary troops in the area.

Makeyev was sitting sideways on the box, scraps of his fur hat hanging over the yellow, browless arches of his eyes. A Mauser with an unpainted butt was lying on his knees. Without turning around, he fired at Korostelyov, but missed.

"What can I say?" Korostelyov whispered, with wide, shining eyes. "So you're angry with me?" He spread out his thin arms farther. "What can I say?"

Makeyev jumped up, turned around, and fired all the bullets in his Mauser. The shots rang out rapidly. There was something more Korostelyov had wanted to say, but he didn't manage to. He sighed and fell to his knees. He tumbled forward onto the rim of the spoked wheel of a machine gun cart, his face shattering, milky strips of brain bespattering the wheel. Makeyev, bending forward, was trying to yank out the last bullet which was jammed in the cartridge clip.

"They thought it was a good joke!" he said, eyeing the crowd of Red Army men and the rest of us who had gathered by the gangplank.

Lisyei crouched and went sidling over to Korostelyov with a horse blanket in his hands, and covered him as he lay there like a felled tree. Random shots rang from the steamer. Chapayev's soldiers were running over the deck, arresting the crew. The pockmarked woman, her hand pressed to her cheek, stood at the railing, peering at the shore with narrow, unseeing eyes.

"I'll show you too!" Makeyev yelled up at her. "I'll teach you to waste fuel!"

The sailors were led down one by one. German settlers, trickling from their houses, came out from behind their barns. Karl Biedermayer was standing among his people. The war had come to his doorstep.

We had much work to do that day. The large village of Friedental had come to trade. A chain of camels was lying by the water. In the far distance, windmills were turning on the colorless, metallic horizon.

We loaded the Friedental grain onto our barge until suppertime, and toward evening Malishev sent for me. He was washing on the deck of the *Ivan Tupitsin*. An invalid with a pinned-up sleeve was pouring water over him from a pitcher. Malishev snorted and chuckled, holding his cheeks under the stream of water. He toweled himself off and said to his assistant, obviously continuing a conversation, "And rightly so! You can be the nicest fellow in the world, have locked yourself up in monasteries, sailed the White Sea, been a desperado—but, please, whatever you do, don't waste fuel!"

Malishev and I went into the cabin. I laid out the financial records in front of me, and Malishev started dictating to me a telegram to be sent to Ilyich.

"Moscow. The Kremlin. To Comrade Lenin."

In the telegram we reported the dispatching of the first shipments of wheat to the proletariat of Petersburg and Moscow: two trainloads, each twenty thousand *poods* of grain.

GUY DE MAUPASSANT

*I*n the winter of 1916 I found myself in Petersburg with forged papers and without a kopeck to my name. Aleksei Kazantsev, a teacher of Russian philology, gave me shelter.

He lived on a frozen, reeking, yellow street in Peski.* To increase his meager income, he did Spanish translations—in those days the fame of Blasco Ibáñez[†] was on the rise.

Kazantsev had never been to Spain, not even once, but his whole being was flooded with love for the country—he knew every Spanish castle, park, and river. Besides myself, a large number of men and women who had fallen through the cracks of life flocked to him. We lived in dire poverty. From time to time our pieces on current events appeared in small print in the popular press.

In the mornings I lounged about in morgues and police stations.

But the happiest of us all was Kazantsev. He had a motherland— Spain.

In November I was offered the position of clerk at the Obukhovsky Factory,** not a bad job, bringing with it an exemption from conscription.

I refused to become a clerk.

* A poor suburb of Petersburg.
[†] Vicente Blasco Ibáñez, 1867–1928, was a Spanish novelist and anti-monarchist politician. His novels, with their themes of war and social injustice, were particularly popular in Soviet Russia.
** Steelworks founded in 1863. Its almost twelve thousand workers were to play an important role in the Revolution.

Even in those days, at the age of twenty, I said to myself: Better to suffer hunger, prison, and homelessness than to sit at a clerk's desk ten hours a day. There is no particular daring in making such a pledge, but I haven't broken it to this day, nor will I. The wisdom of my forefathers was ingrained in me: we have been born to delight in labor, fighting, and love. That is what we have been born for, and nothing else.

Kazantsev patted the short yellow down on his head as he listened to my sermon. The horror in his eyes was mixed with rapture.

At Christmas, fortune smiled upon us. Bendersky, a lawyer who owned the Halcyon Publishing House, had decided to bring out a new edition of Maupassant's works. His wife, Raisa, was going to do the translation. But nothing had yet come of the grand enterprise.

Kazantsev, as a Spanish translator, was asked if he knew anyone who might be able to help Raisa Mikhailovna. Kazantsev suggested me.

The following day, donning another man's jacket, I set out to the Benderskys'. They lived at the corner of the Nevsky Prospekt by the Moika River, in a house built of Finnish granite trimmed with pink columns, embrasures, and stone coats of arms. Before the war, bankers without family or breeding—Jewish converts to Christianity who grew rich on government procurements—had built a large number of such spuriously majestic, vulgar castles in Petersburg.

A red carpet ran up the stairs. Stuffed bears on their hind legs stood on the landings. Crystal lamps shone in their wide-open jaws.

The Benderskys lived on the third floor. The door was opened by a maid in a white cap and pointed breasts. She led me into a living room, decorated in old Slavic style. Blue paintings by Roerich,* prehistoric rocks and monsters, hung on the walls. Ancient icons stood on little stands in the corners. The maid with the pointed breasts moved ceremoniously about the room. She was well built, nearsighted, haughty. Debauchery had congealed in her gray, wide-open eyes. Her movements were indolent. I thought how she must thrash about with savage agility when she made love. The brocade curtain that hung over the door swayed. A black-haired, pink-eyed woman, bearing her large

---

*Nikolai Konstantinovich Roerich, 1874–1947, was a Russian painter and popular mystic who gained international fame for the sets he designed for Diaghilev's Ballets Russes.

breasts before her, came into the living room. It took me no more than a moment to see that Benderskaya was one of those ravishing breed of Jewesses from Kiev or Poltava, from the sated towns of the steppes that abounded with acacias and chestnut trees. These women transmute the money of their resourceful husbands into the lush pink fat on their bellies, napes, and round shoulders. Their sleepy smiles, delicate and sly, drive garrison officers out of their minds.

"Maupassant is the one passion of my life," Raisa told me.

Struggling to restrain the swaying of her large hips, she left the room and came back with her translation of "Miss Harriet." The translation had no trace of Maupassant's free-flowing prose with its powerful breath of passion. Benderskaya wrote with laborious and inert correctness and lack of style—the way Jews in the past used to write Russian.

I took the manuscript home with me to Kazantsev's attic, where all night, among his sleeping friends, I cut swaths through Benderskaya's translation. This work isn't as bad as it might seem. When a phrase is born, it is both good and bad at the same time. The secret of its success rests in a crux that is barely discernible. One's fingertips must grasp the key, gently warming it. And then the key must be turned once, not twice.

· · ·

The following morning I brought back the corrected manuscript. Raisa had not lied in speaking of her passion for Maupassant. She sat transfixed as I read to her, her hands clasped together. Her satin arms flowed down toward the ground, her forehead grew pale, and the lace between her struggling breasts swerved and trembled.

"How did you do this?"

I spoke to her of style, of an army of words, an army in which every type of weapon is deployed. No iron spike can pierce a human heart as icily as a period in the right place. She listened with her head inclined and her painted lips apart. A black gleam shone in her lacquered hair, parted and pulled smoothly back. Her stockinged legs, with their strong, delicate calves, were planted apart on the carpet.

The maid, turning away her eyes in which debauchery had congealed, brought in breakfast on a tray.

The glass sun of Petersburg reclined on the uneven, faded carpet. Twenty-nine books by Maupassant stood on a shelf above the table. The sun, with its melting fingers, touched the books' morocco leather bindings—the magnificent crypt of the human heart.

We were served coffee in little blue cups, and we began to translate "Idyll." Who can forget the tale of the hungry young carpenter sucking milk from the overflowing breasts of the fat wet-nurse. This took place on a train going from Nice to Marseilles, on a sultry midday in the land of roses, the motherland of roses where flower plantations stretch down to the shores of the sea.

I left the Benderskys' with a twenty-five-ruble advance. That evening our commune in Peski got as drunk as a flock of inebriated geese. We scooped up the finest caviar and chased it down with liver-wurst. Heated by liquor, I began ranting against Tolstoy.

"He got frightened, our count did! He lacked courage! It was fear that made him turn to religion! Frightened of the cold, of old age, the count knitted himself a jersey out of faith!"

"Go on," Kazantsev said, wagging his birdlike head.

We fell asleep on the floor next to our beds. I dreamt of Katya, the forty-year-old washerwoman who lived on the floor beneath us. In the mornings we would go and get boiling water from her. I'd never had a good look at her face, but in my dream Katya and I did God only knows what. We consumed each other with kisses. The following morning I could not resist going down to her for boiling water.

I came face-to-face with a wilted woman, a shawl tied across her chest, with disheveled ash-gray curls and sodden hands.

• • •

From then on I breakfasted every day at the Benderskys'. In our attic we now had a new stove, herring, and chocolate. Twice Raisa drove me out to the islands.* I couldn't resist telling her about my childhood. To my own surprise, my tale sounded doleful. Her frightened sparkling eyes peered at me from under her fur hat. The reddish hairs of her eyelashes quivered mournfully.

I met Raisa's husband, a yellow-faced Jew with a bald head and a

---

* Islands of the Neva and the Bay of Finland, on which St. Petersburg was built.

lean, powerful body that always seemed poised to surge up into the air. There were rumors that he was close to Rasputin. The profits he had made from military procurements had given him the look of a madman. His eyes wandered—the fabric of his reality had been rent. Raisa was embarrassed introducing her husband to new people. Because of my youth, it took me a week longer than it should have to realize this.

After the New Year, Raisa's two sisters came up from Kiev. One day I went to her house with the manuscript of "The Confession," and, not finding her there, dropped by again in the evening. They were in the dining room at the dinner table. I heard silvery neighing and the thunder of excessively jubilant men's voices. Dining is invariably boisterous in wealthy houses that lack pedigree. Their boisterousness was Jewish, with peals of thunder and melodious flourishes. Raisa came out to me in a ball gown, her back bare. Her feet tottered in wavering patent leather shoes.

"Oh, how drunk I am!" And she stretched out her arms draped in platinum chains and emerald stars.

Her body swayed like the body of a snake rising to music toward the ceiling. She shook her curly head, her rings tinkled, and suddenly she fell into an armchair with ancient Russian carving. Scars shimmered on her powdered back.

There was another explosion of women's laughter in the room next door. Out of the dining room came her sisters with their little mustaches, just as big-breasted and tall as Raisa. Their breasts were thrust forward, their black hair flowed free. Both were married to Benderskys of their own. The room filled with rambling female vivacity, the vivacity of mature women. The husbands wrapped the sisters in sealskin coats, in Orenburg shawls,* and shod them in black boots. Peering out from the snowy shields of their shawls were their burning, rouged cheeks, their marble noses, and eyes with a nearsighted Semitic sparkle. After some lively commotion, they left for the theater, where Chaliapin was appearing in *Judith*.†

•　•　•

* Delicate lac   wls, fashionable in Russia at the time, knitted from goat wool by Orenburg Tatars.
† Chaliapir   owned opera singer. *Judith* is an opera by Alexander Nikolayevich Serov, 1820–1871.

"I want to work," Raisa jabbered, stretching out her bare arms. "We've lost a whole week."

She brought a bottle and two glasses from the dining room. Her breasts lay loose in the silken sack of her dress. Her nipples stiffened, the silk impeding them.

"A cherished vintage," Raisa said, pouring the wine. "A Muscatel '83. My husband will kill me when he finds out!"

I had never had any dealings with a Muscatel '83 before, and did not hesitate to empty three glasses one after the other. I was immediately wafted off to a little side street where orange flames flickered and music played.

"Oh, how drunk I am. . . . What are we going to do today?"

"Today we're doing 'L'aveu.'"

In other words, "The Confession." The hero of this tale is the sun, *le soleil de France*. Incandescent drops of sun, falling on red-haired Céleste, turned into freckles. Wine, apple cider, and the sun with its steep rays had burnished the face of Polyte, the coachman. Twice a week, Céleste drove into town to sell cream, eggs, and chickens. She paid Polyte ten sous for the ride and four to carry her basket. And on every ride Polyte winked at her and asked, "When are we going to have a bit of fun, *ma belle*?"

"What do you mean by that, Monsieur Polyte?"

"Having fun means having fun, damn it!" Polyte explained, bouncing on the seat. "A man and a woman, no need for music!"

"I don't like such jokes, Monsieur Polyte," Céleste answered, and swept her skirts, which hung over her powerful, red-stockinged calves, away from the young man.

But Polyte, the devil, kept guffawing and coughing. "We'll have fun someday, *ma belle*!" And tears of mirth trickled down his face, which was the color of rust-red blood and wine.

I drank another glass of the cherished Muscatel. Raisa clinked glasses with me.

The maid with the congealed eyes walked through the room and disappeared.

*Ce diable de Polyte** . . . Over a period of two years Céleste paid him

* "That devil Polyte."

forty-eight francs. Two francs short of fifty! One day at the end of the second year, when they were alone together in the buggy, Polyte, who had drunk some cider before they set out, asked her as usual, "How about having some fun today, Ma'mselle Céleste?"

"I'm at your service, M'sieur Polyte."

Raisa laughed out loud, slumping over the table. *Ce diable de Polyte!*

The buggy was harnessed to a white nag. The white nag, its lips pink with age, walked a slow walk. The joyful sun of France embraced the buggy, shut off from the world by a faded brown cover. The young man and the girl—they needed no music.

•　•　•

Raisa handed me a glass. It was the fifth.

"To Maupassant, *mon vieux!*"

"Aren't we going to have some fun today, *ma belle?*"

I reached over to Raisa and kissed her on the lips. They trembled and bulged.

"You're so funny," Raisa muttered through her teeth, tottering backward.

She pressed herself against the wall, spreading her bare arms. Blotches flared up on her arms and shoulders. Of all the gods ever crucified, she was the most seductive.

"Be so kind as to seat yourself, M'sieur Polyte."

She pointed to the reclining blue Slavic armchair. Its back was made of interlaced carved wood on which tails were painted. I stumbled toward it.

Night obstructed my youth with a bottle of Muscatel '83 and twenty-nine books, twenty-nine petards crammed with pity, genius, and passion. I jumped up, knocking over the armchair and bumping into the shelf. Twenty-nine volumes came tumbling onto the carpet, falling onto their spines, their pages flying wild . . . and the white nag of my fate walked a slow walk.

"You're so funny," Raisa growled.

I left the granite house on the Moika Canal after eleven, just before her husband and sisters came back from the theater. I was sober and could have walked a thin plank, but stumbling was far better, and I swayed from side to side, singing in a language I had just invented.

Mists of fog rolled in waves through the tunnels of streets girded with a chain of street lamps. Monsters roared behind seething walls. The carriageways cut the legs that walked over them.

Back at home Kazantsev was asleep. He slept sitting up, his haggard legs stretched out in felt boots. The canary down was fluffed up on his head. He had fallen asleep by the stove, hunched over a 1624 edition of *Don Quixote*. There was a dedication on the title page to the Duke de Broglio. I lay down quietly so as not to wake Kazantsev, pulled the lamp toward me, and began to read Édouard de Maynial's book *The Life and Works of Guy de Maupassant*.*

Kazantsev's lips moved, his head lolled forward.

•   •   •

That night I learned from Édouard de Maynial that Maupassant was born in 1850 to a Norman nobleman and Laure Le Poittevin, Flaubert's cousin. At twenty-five, he had his first attack of congenital syphilis. He fought the disease with all the potency and vitality he had. In the beginning, he suffered from headaches and bouts of hypochondria. Then the phantom of blindness loomed before him. His eyesight grew weaker. Paranoia, unsociability, and belligerence developed. He struggled with passion, rushed about the Mediterranean on his yacht, fled to Tunis, Morocco, and central Africa, and wrote unceasingly. Having achieved fame, he cut his throat at the age of forty, bled profusely, but lived. They locked him in a madhouse. He crawled about on all fours and ate his own excrement. The last entry in his sorrowful medical report announces: "*Monsieur de Maupassant va s'animaliser* (Monsieur de Maupassant is degenerating to an animal state)." He died at the age of forty-two. His mother outlived him.

I read the book through to the end and got up from my bed. The fog had come to the window, hiding the universe. My heart constricted. I was touched by a premonition of truth.

---

* *La vie et l'oeuvre de Guy de Maupassant* was published by Société du Mercure de France in 1906.

PETROLEUM

I have a lot of news to tell you, as always. Sabsovich was given a prize at the oil refinery, walks about decked out in flashy "foreign" clothes, and has been given a promotion. When people heard about this promotion, they finally saw the light: the boy is moving up the ladder. This is the reason I stopped going out with him. "Now that he has moved up the ladder," the boy feels that he knows the truth hidden from us lesser mortals and has turned into "Comrade Perfect," so orthodox ("orthobox," as Kharchenko calls it) that you can't even talk to him anymore. When we ran into each other two days ago, he asked me why I hadn't congratulated him. I asked him whom I should congratulate, him or the Soviet government. He understood my point right away, hemmed and hawed, and said, "Well, call me sometime." But his wife was quick to pick up the scent. Yesterday I got a call. "Claudia, darling, if you need any underwear, we now have great connections at the Restricted Access Store." I told her that I was hoping to get by with my own underwear ration coupons till the outbreak of the World Revolution.

Now a few words about myself. You'll have heard by now that I am the section head at the Petroleum Syndicate. They dangled the position before me for the longest time, but I kept turning them down. My argument: no aptitude for office work, and then I also wanted to enroll at the Industrial Academy. Four times at Bureau Meetings they asked me to accept the position, so finally I had to accept. And I must say I don't regret it. From where I am I have a clear picture of the whole enterprise, and I've managed to get a thing or two done. I organized an expedition to our part of Sakhalin, stepped up the prospecting, and I deal a lot with the Petroleum Institute. Zinaida is with me. She's well. She'll be giving birth soon, and has been through quite a lot. She didn't tell her Max Alexandrovich (I call him Max-and-Moritz)* about the pregnancy until she was already in her third month. He put on a show of enthusiasm, planted an icy kiss on her forehead, and then gave her to understand that he was on the brink of a great scientific discovery, that his thoughts were far from everyday life, and that one could not imagine anyone less suited to family life than he, Max Alexandrovich Solomovich, but, needless to say, he wouldn't hesitate to sacrifice everything, etc., etc. Zinaida, being a woman of the twentieth century, burst into tears but kept her aplomb. She didn't sleep all night, gasping, her head thrashing about. The moment it was light, she put on a tattered old dress and rushed off to the Research Institute, looking dreadful, her hair in tangles. There she made a scene, begging him to forget what had happened the previous night, saying that she would destroy the child, but that she would never forgive the world—all this in the halls of the Research Institute, teeming with people! Max-and-Moritz goes bright red, then pale. "Let's discuss it on the phone, we'll get together for a chat," he mutters.

Zinaida didn't even let him finish, but rushed out and came running to me.

"I'm not coming to work tomorrow!" she told me.

I blew up, and, seeing no reason to control myself, bawled her out. Just think—she's over thirty, has no looks worth mentioning, no man worth his salt would even wipe his nose with her, and then this Max-and-Moritz fellow turns up (not that he's hot for her, he's hot for the fact that she's not Jewish and has aristocratic ancestors), she gets herself knocked up, so she might as well keep the baby and raise it. As we all know, Jewish half-castes come out quite well—just look at the specimen Ala produced. And when if not now does she intend to have a child, now when her gut muscles are still working and her breasts can still make milk? But she has only one answer to whatever I say: "I can-

---

* Two boys who terrorize the neighborhood with their funny practical jokes in the story in verse, *Max and Moritz*, by the German humorist Wilhelm Busch.

not bear the idea of my child growing up without a father." She tells me it's still like in the nineteenth century, "and my papa, the general, will come stalking out of his study carrying an icon and lay a curse on me (or maybe without an icon—I don't know how they used to curse back then), after which the women will take the baby to a foundling home or send it to a wet nurse in the countryside."

"Nonsense, Zinaida!" I tell her. "Times have changed, we'll make do without Max-and-Moritz!"

I was still in midsentence when I was called to a meeting. At that time the matter of Viktor Andreyevich had to be dealt with immediately. The Central Committee had decided to revoke the former Five-Year Plan and raise petroleum extraction in 1932 to forty million tons. The figures for analysis were handed to the planners, in other words to Viktor Andreyevich. He locks himself in his office, then calls me over and shows me his letter. Addressed to the Presidium of the Supreme National Economic Council. Contents: I hereby renounce all responsibility for the planning department. I consider the figure of forty million tons to be wholly unjustified. We're supposed to get more than a third of it from unprospected regions, which is like selling a bearskin not only before you've actually killed the bear, but even before you've tracked it down! Furthermore, from three oil refineries functioning today the new plan expects us to have a hundred and twenty up and running by the end of the Five-Year Plan. And all this with a shortage of metal and the fact that we have not yet mastered the extremely complex refinery system. And this is how he ended the letter: Like all mortals, I prefer to support accelerated production quotas, but my sense of duty, and so on and so forth. I read his letter to the end.

So then he asks me: "Should I send it, or not?"

And I tell him: "Viktor Andreyevich! I find your arguments and attitude completely unacceptable, but I do not see myself as having the right to advise you to hide your views."

So he sent the letter. The Supreme National Economic Council's hair stood on end. They called a meeting. Bagrinovsky himself came from the council. They hung a map of the Soviet Union on the wall, pinpointing new deposits and pipelines for crude and refined oil. "A country with fresh blood in its veins," Bagrinovsky called it.

At the meeting the young engineers of the "omnivore" type wanted to make a meal of Viktor Andreyevich. I stepped forward and gave a forty-five-minute speech: "Though I do not doubt the knowledge and good will of Professor Klossovsky, and even have the utmost respect for him, I spurn the fetishism of numbers that is holding him captive!" That was the gist of my argument.

"We must reject our multiplication tables as guidelines for governmental wisdom. Would it have been possible to foretell on the basis of mere figures that we were going to manage to fulfill our five-year crude-oil quarrying quota within just two and a half years? Would it have been possible to foretell on the basis of mere figures that by 1931 we would have increased the bulk of our oil export by nine times, putting us in second place after the United States?"

Muradyan got up and spoke after me, attacking the route of the oil pipeline from the Caspian Sea to Moscow. Viktor Andreyevich sat in silence, taking notes. His cheeks were covered with an old man's flush, a flush of venous blood. I felt sorry for him. I didn't stay to the end and went back to my office. Zinaida was still sitting there with clasped hands.

"Are you going to give birth or not?" I asked her.

She looked at me with unseeing eyes, her head shaking, and said something, but the words were soundless.

"I'm all alone with my sorrow, Claudia, as if they've just nailed my coffin shut," she tells me. "How quickly one forgets—I can't even remember how people live without sorrow."

That's what she said to me, her nose turning red and growing even longer, her peasant cheekbones (yes, some aristocrats do have them!) jutting out. I doubt Max-and-Moritz would get all fired up seeing you like that, I think to myself. I started yelling at her, and chased her off to the kitchen to peel potatoes. Don't laugh—when *you* come here, I'll have you peeling potatoes too! We were given such a stringent time frame for designing the Orsky factory that the construction crew and the draftsmen are working night and day, and Vasyona cooks them potatoes and herring and makes them omelets, and off they go to work again.

So off she went to the kitchen, and a minute later I heard a scream. I run—Zinaida is lying on the floor without a pulse, her eyes rolled up. I cannot even begin to tell you what she put us through—Viktor

Andreyevich, Vasyona, and me! We called in the doctor. She regained consciousness at night and touched my hand. You know Zinaida, how incredibly tender she can be. I could see that everything inside her had burned out and something new was about to well up. There was no time to lose.

"Zinusha," I tell her, "we'll call Rosa Mikhailovna (she's still our main specialist in these matters) and tell her that you've had second thoughts, that you won't go and see her. Can I call her?"

She made a sign—yes go ahead, you can. Viktor Andreyevich was sitting next to her on the sofa, taking her pulse incessantly. I walked away, but listened to what he said to her. "I'm sixty-five, Zinusha," he told her, "my shadow falls more and more weakly on the ground before me. I am an elderly, learned man, and God (God does have His hand in everything), God willed that the final five years of my life are to coincide with this—well, you know what I mean—this Five-Year Plan. So now I won't get a chance to have a breather or a quiet moment till the day I die. If my daughter didn't come to me in the evenings to pat me on the back, if my sons didn't write me letters, I would be unhappier than words could say. Have the baby, Zinusha, and Claudia Pavlovna and I will help raise it."

While the old man goes on mumbling, I call Rosa Mikhailovna—well, my dear Rosa Mikhailovna, I tell her, I know Zinaida promised to come see you tomorrow, but she's reconsidered. And I hear Rosa's sprightly voice on the phone: "Oh, I'm so happy she's reconsidered! That's absolutely marvelous!" Our specialist is always like this. Pink silk blouse, English skirt, hair neatly curled, showers, exercise, admirers.

We took Zinaida home. I tucked her in bed, made tea. We slept in each other's arms, we even cried, remembered things best forgotten, talked everything through, our tears mingling, until we fell asleep. All the while my "old devil" was sitting nice and quiet at his desk translating a German technical book. Dasha, you wouldn't recognize my "old devil"—he's all shriveled up, has run out of steam and become quiet. It really upsets me. He spends the whole day working himself to death on the Five-Year Plan, and then at night he does translations.

"Zinaida will have the baby," I tell him. "What shall we call the boy?" (It's definitely not going to be a girl.) We decided on Ivan. There are far too many Yuris and Leonids about the place. He'll most probably be a beast of a little boy, with sharp teeth, with teeth enough for sixty men. We've produced enough fuel for him, he'll be able to go on drives with young ladies to Yalta, to Batumi, while we've had to make do with the Vorobyovi Hills.* Good-bye, Dasha. My "old devil" will write you separately. How are things with you?

CLAUDIA.

P.S. I'm scribbling this at work, there's a great racket overhead, the plaster is falling from the ceiling. Our building still seems strong enough, and we're adding another four stories to the four that we have. Moscow is all dug up and full of trenches, pipes and bricks everywhere, a tangle of tram lines, machines imported from abroad are banging, rumbling, swinging their cranes, there's the stench of pitch, and there's smoke everywhere, like at a wildfire. Yesterday on Varvarskaya Square I saw a young man with sandals on his bare feet, his red, shaven head shining and his peasant shirt without a belt. He and I went hopping from one little mound to another, from one earth pile to another, climbing out of holes, falling back into them again.

"This is what it's like once a battle has begun," he tells me. "Moscow has now become the front, lady, Moscow is at the heart of the battle!"

He had a kind face, smiling like a child. I can still picture him before me.

* A Moscow neighborhood.

DANTE STREET

*T*he Hotel Danton, where I was staying, was rattled to its foundations by moans of love from five until seven in the evening. Experts were at work in the rooms. Having arrived in France with the conviction that its people had lost their spark, I was somewhat taken aback by their vigor. In our country, we do not bring women to such a boiling pitch. Nowhere near it.

"*Mon vieux,*" Monsieur Bienalle, my neighbor, once told me, "in our thousand years of history we have created woman, food, and literature. No one can deny this."

Jean Bienalle, a secondhand car dealer, did more for my knowledge of France than all the books I had read and all the French towns I had seen. The first time we met he asked me which restaurant I ate at, what café I went to, and which brothel I frequented. My answer appalled him.

"*On va refaire votre vie!*"*

And the changes were undertaken. We ate lunch at a tavern across the street from the Halles aux vins, frequented by cattle dealers and wine merchants.

Village girls in slippers served us lobster in red sauce, roast rabbit stuffed with garlic and truffles, and wine you could find nowhere else. Bienalle ordered, I paid, but I only paid as much as the French paid. It wasn't cheap, but it wasn't the foreigner's price. And I also paid the

* "We shall change your ways!"

Frenchman's price at the brothel funded by a group of senators next to the Gare St. Lazare. Bienalle had to put more effort into introducing me to the inmates of that house than if he had attempted to introduce me to a session of Parliament while a cabinet is being overthrown. We capped off the evening at the Porte Maillot at a café where boxing promoters and race car drivers gathered. My tutor belonged to the half of the nation that sells cars. The other half buys them. He was an agent for Renault and did most of his trade with the Balkans, those most ambiguous of countries, and with Rumanian speculators, the dirtiest of speculators. In his free time Bienalle taught me the art of buying a used car. According to him, one had to go down to the Riviera toward the end of the season, when the English were leaving for home, abandoning in local garages cars they had only used for two or three months. Bienalle himself drove a dilapidated Renault, which he drove the way a Siberian tribesman drives his sled dogs. On Sundays we drove 120 kilometers to Rouen in his bouncing vehicle to eat duck, which the locals there roast in its own blood. We were accompanied by Germaine, who sold gloves on Rue Royale. She spent every Wednesday and Sunday with Bienalle. She always came at five o'clock. Within seconds their room echoed with growls, the thud of tumbling bodies, frightened gasps, after which the woman's tender death throes began: "Oh, Jean . . ."

I added it all up: Germaine went into his room, closed the door behind her, they gave each other a kiss, she took off her hat and gloves, laid them on the table, and, according to my calculations, that was all there was time for. He wouldn't even have had time to undress. Not uttering a word, they bounced about like rabbits between the sheets. They moaned for a while, and then burst out laughing and chatted about everyday things. I knew as much as any neighbor living on the other side of a thin board partition. Germaine was having trouble with Monsieur Heinrich, the store manager. Her parents lived in Tours, where she visited them. On one Saturday she bought herself a fur wrap, on another she went to see *La Bohème* at the opera. Monsieur Heinrich had his saleswomen wear tailored dress suits. Monsieur Heinrich anglicized Germaine, turning her into one of those brisk, flat-chested, curly-haired businesswomen painted with flaming, brownish rouge. But her fine chunky ankles, her low, nimble laugh, the sharp gaze of her sparkling eyes, and that death-throe moan—"Oh, Jean!"—were all left untouched for Bienalle.

Germaine's powerful, lithe body moved before us in the smoke and gold of the Paris evening. She laughed, throwing back her head and pressing her delicate pink fingers to her breasts. My heart glowed during these hours. There is no solitude more desperate than solitude in Paris. This town is a form of exile for all who come to it from far away, and I realized that Germaine was more important to me than she was to Bienalle. I left for Marseilles with this thought in mind.

After a month in Marseilles, I returned to Paris. I waited for Wednesday to hear Germaine's voice.

Wednesday came and went, but nobody disturbed the silence of the room next door. Bienalle had changed his day. A woman's voice rang out on Thursday, at five o'clock as always. Bienalle gave his visitor time to take off her hat and gloves. Germaine had not only changed her day, she had also changed her voice. It was no longer the gasping, imploring "Oh, Jean!" followed by silence, the harsh silence of another person's happiness; it had turned into a hoarse domestic clamor with guttural exclamations. The new Germaine gnashed her teeth, flung herself heavily onto the sofa, and during the interludes pontificated in her thick, dragging voice. She said nothing about Monsieur Heinrich, growled until seven o'clock, and then got ready to go. I opened the door a crack to say hello to her, but saw a mulatto woman in the corridor with a cockscomb of horselike hair and large, dangling, hoisted-up breasts. She was coming down the corridor, her feet shuffling in worn-out shoes with no heels. I knocked on Bienalle's door. He was lolling about in bed in his shirt and washed-out socks, ashen and crumpled.

"So, *mon vieux*, you've pensioned off Germaine?"

"*Cette femme est folle*,"* he said with a shudder. "Mademoiselle Germaine does not care that on this earth there is winter and summer, a beginning and an end, and that after winter comes summer and then the opposite. She heaves a heavy burden on you and demands that you carry it—but where to, nobody but Mademoiselle Germaine knows!"

Bienalle sat up in bed. His trousers stretched over his thin legs. His pale scalp shimmered through his matted hair, and his triangular mustache twitched. A bottle of Macon, four francs a liter, lifted my friend's spirits again. As we waited for our dessert, he shrugged his shoulders

---

* "That woman is mad."

and said as if in answer to my thoughts, "There's more than everlasting love in this world—there are Rumanians, promissory notes, men who go bankrupt, cars with broken chassis. *Oh, j'en ai plein le dos!*"*

He grew more cheerful over a cognac at the Café de Paris. We sat on the terrace under a white awning with wide stripes running down it. The crowd streamed past over the sidewalk, blending with the electric stars. A car, long as a torpedo, stopped across the street from us. From it emerged an Englishman with a woman in a sable wrap. She sailed past in a cloud of perfume and fur, inhumanly long with a small, shining head of porcelain. Bienalle sat up when he saw her, stretched out his leg in his tattered trousers, and winked at her the way one winks at the girls on the rue de la Gaîté. The woman smiled with the corner of her carmine mouth, gave a barely visible nod with her tightly wrapped pink head, and, swinging and swaying her serpentine body, disappeared, with the stiff, crackling Englishman in tow.

"*Ah, canaille!*"† Bienalle said after them. "Two years ago anyone could have had her for an aperitif."

The two of us parted late. I had decided that I would go see Germaine that Saturday, take her to the theater, go to Chartres with her if she was in the mood. But as things turned out, I was to see Bienalle and his former girlfriend before then. The following evening, all the doors of the Hotel Danton were cordoned off by the police, their blue capes swirling through our vestibule. They let me go up after they verified that I was one of Madame Truffaut's lodgers. I found policemen standing outside my room. The door to Bienalle's room stood open. He was lying on the floor in a pool of blood, his lusterless eyes half closed. The stamp of street death was upon him. My friend Bienalle had been stabbed, stabbed to death. Germaine was sitting at the table in her tailored dress suit and her delicate, close-fitting hat. She greeted me and hung her head, and with it the feather on her hat hung too.

All this took place at six in the evening, the hour of love. There was a woman in every room. They hastily applied rouge and drew black lines along the edges of their lips before leaving half dressed, with stockings up to their thighs like pageboys. Doors opened and

* "Oh, I've had it up to here!"
† "Ah, the bitch!"

men with untied shoes lined up in the corridor. In the room of a wrinkled Italian racing cyclist a barefoot little girl was crying into the pillow. I went downstairs to tell Madame Truffaut. The girl's mother sold
newspapers on the Rue St. Michel. All the old women of our street,
the Rue Dante, misshapen piles of goiterous meat, whiskered, wheezing, with cataracts and purple blotches, had already gathered in the little office: market women, concierges, sellers of roasted chestnuts and
potatoes.

"*Voilà qui n'est pas gai*," I said as I went in. "*Quel malheur!*"*
"*C'est l'amour, monsieur. . . . Elle l'aimait.*"†

Madame Truffaut's lilac breasts tumbled in her lace blouse, her elephantine legs strode through the room, her eyes flashed.

"*L'amore!*" Signora Rocca, who ran a restaurant on Rue Dante,
called out from behind her like an echo. "*Dio castiga quelli, chi non
conoscono l'amore!*"**

The old women huddled together, all muttering at the same time.
A variolar flame lit their cheeks, their eyes bulging out of their sockets.

"*L'amour*," Madame Truffaut repeated, hobbling toward me. "*C'est
une grosse affaire, l'amour!*"‡

A siren sounded in the street. Skillful hands dragged the murdered
man downstairs and out to the ambulance. My friend Bienalle had
turned into a mere number, losing his name in the rolling waves of
Paris. Signora Rocca went over to the window and looked out at the
corpse. She was pregnant, her belly jutting out threateningly. Silk lay on
her protruding hips, and the sun washed over her yellow, puffy face and
soft yellow hair.

"*Dio*," Signora Rocca said. "*Tu non perdoni quelli, chi non amano!*"***

Dusk descended on the tattered net of the Latin quarter, the squat
crowd scuttling into its crevices, a hot breath of garlic pouring from its
yards. Darkness covered the house of Madame Truffaut, its gothic
facade with its two windows, and the remnants of turrets and volutes,
ivy turned to stone.

---

* "Well, this isn't very cheerful. How dreadful!"
† "It is love, monsieur. . . .She loved him."
** "Love! God punishes those who do not know love!"
‡ "Love is a nasty business!"
*** "God, you do not forgive those who do not love!"

Danton had lived here a century and a half ago. From his window he had seen the Conciergerie, the bridges strewn across the Seine, and the same cluster of little blind hovels huddling by the river. The same breath had wafted up to him. Rusty beams and signs of wayside inns had creaked, rattled by the wind.

DI GRASSO

I was fourteen years old. I belonged to the fearless battalion of theater ticket scalpers. My boss was a shark with an eye that always
squinted and a large, silky mustache. His name was Kolya Shvarts. I fell
in with him that dark year when the Italian Opera went bust. The
impresario, swayed by the theater critics, had not signed up Anselmi
and Tito Ruffo as guest stars, concentrating instead on a strong ensem-
ble. He was punished for this, went broke, and so did we. To set things
right, we were promised Chaliapin, but Chaliapin wanted three thousand a performance. So Di Grasso, the Sicilian tragic actor, came with
his troupe instead. They were taken to their hotel in carts loaded with
children, cats, and cages in which Italian birds fluttered.

"We can't push this merchandise!" Kolya Shvarts said when he saw
the motley procession rolling in.

The moment the actor arrived, he went down to the bazaar with his
bag. In the evening, carrying a different bag, he turned up at the theater. Barely fifty people came to the premiere. We hawked tickets at
half price, but could find no buyers.

That evening Di Grasso's troupe performed a Sicilian folk drama,
with a plot as humdrum as night and day. The daughter of a rich peasant became engaged to a shepherd. She was true to him, until one day
the squire's son came visiting from town in a velvet vest. The girl chatted with the visitor, tongue-tied and giggling at all the wrong moments.
Listening to them, the shepherd darted his head about like a startled
bird. Throughout the whole first act he crept along walls, went off

somewhere in his fluttering trousers, and then came back again, looking around shiftily.

"We have a turkey on our hands!" Kolya Shvarts said during the intermission. "This is merchandise for Kremenchug, not Odessa!"

The intermission gave the girl time to prime herself for the betrayal. In the second act she was unrecognizable. She became intolerant and dreamy, and eagerly gave back the engagement ring to the shepherd. The shepherd led her to a tawdry painted statue of the Holy Virgin.

"Signorina! It is the Holy Virgin's will that you hear me out!" he said in a bass voice in Sicilian dialect, turning away from her. "The Holy Virgin will give Giovanni, the visitor from town, as many women as he wills. But I, Signorina, need nobody but you! The Virgin Mary, our Immaculate Protectress, will tell you the same thing if you ask her."

The girl stood with her back to the painted wooden statue. As the shepherd talked, she tapped her foot impatiently. On this earth—oh, woe to us!—there isn't a woman who is not gripped by folly at the very moment when her fate is being decided. A woman is alone at such moments, with no Holy Virgin she can appeal to.

In the third act, Giovanni, the visitor from town, met his fate. The village barber was shaving Giovanni as he sat with his powerful masculine legs sprawled out over the proscenium. The pleats of his vest shone beneath the Sicilian sun. The stage set portrayed a village fair. The shepherd stood in the far corner. He stood there silently, among the carefree crowd. He hung his head, then raised it, and under the weight of his burning, fixed gaze, Giovanni began to fidget and squirm in his chair. He jumped up and pushed the barber away. In a cracking voice Giovanni demanded that the policeman remove all shady and suspicious-looking people from the village square. The shepherd—played by Di Grasso—hesitated for a moment, then smiled, soared into the air, flew over the stage of the Odessa City Theater, alighted on Giovanni's shoulders, and sunk his teeth into his neck. Muttering and squinting at the audience, he sucked the blood from the wound. Giovanni fell to the ground and the curtain came down in menacing silence, hiding the murderer and the murdered man. Not wasting a single moment, we rushed off to Theater Alley, Kolya Shvarts leading the pack. The box office was already selling tickets for the following day. Next morning the *Odessa News* informed the few people who had been at the performance that they had seen the most incredible actor of the century.

During his Odessa performances, Di Grasso was to play *King Lear*, *Othello*, *Civil Death*, and Turgenev's *Parasite*, convincing us with every word and movement that there was more justice and hope in the frenzy of noble passion than in the joyless rules of the world.

The tickets for these performances sold at five times their price. The public in its frantic quest for tickets ran to the taverns, where they found howling, red-faced scalpers spouting innocent blasphemies.

A stream of dusty pink heat poured into Theater Alley. Storekeepers in felt slippers brought green bottles of wine and casks of olives out onto the street. Macaroni was boiling in foaming water in cauldrons in front of stores, the steam melting into the distant skies. Old women in men's boots sold cockleshells and souvenirs, chasing wavering customers with their loud yells. Rich Jews, their beards combed and parted, rode in carriages to the Hotel Severnaya, and knocked discreetly at the doors of fat, black-haired women with mustaches—the actresses of Di Grasso's troupe. Everyone in Theater Alley was happy, except for one person, and that person was me. Disaster was hovering over me. It was only a matter of time before my father would realize that I had taken his watch and pawned it with Kolya Shvarts. Kolya had had enough time now to get used to the idea that the gold watch was his, and as he was a man who drank Bessarabian wine instead of tea at breakfast, he could not bring himself to return the watch, even though I had paid him back his money. That was the kind of person he was. His personality was exactly like my father's. Caught between these two men, I watched the hoops of other people's happiness roll past me. I had no choice but to escape to Constantinople. Everything had already been arranged with the second engineer of a steamer, *The Duke of Kent*, but before setting out to sea, I decided to bid Di Grasso farewell. He was to appear one last time in the role of the shepherd whisked into the air by an otherworldly force. Odessa's whole Italian colony had come to the theater, led by the trim, bald-headed consul, followed by fidgety Greeks and bearded externs staring fanatically at a point invisible to all. Long-armed Utochkin* was also there.

---

*Sergei Isayevich Utochkin, 1874–1916, an aviation pioneer, was a prominent and dashing Odessan figure.

Kolya Shvarts even brought his wife in her fringed, violet shawl, a woman as robust as a grenadier and as drawn-out as a steppe, with a crinkled, sleepy face peeking out at its borderland. Her face was drenched with tears as the curtain fell.

"You no-good wretch!" she shouted at Kolya as they left the theater. "Now you know what *real* love is!"

With mannish steps Madame Shvarts plodded heavily down Langeron Street, tears trickling from her fishlike eyes, her fringed shawl shuddering on her fat shoulders. Her head shaking, she yelled out for the whole street to hear a list of women who lived happily with their husbands. "Sugar puff—that's what those husbands call their wives! Sweetie pie! Baby cakes!"

Kolya walked meekly next to his wife, quietly blowing into his silky mustache. Out of habit, I walked behind them. I was sobbing. Catching her breath for a second, Madame Shvarts heard me crying and turned around.

"You no-good wretch!" she shouted at her husband, her fishlike eyes widening. "May I not live to see another happy hour if you don't give that boy back his watch!"

Kolya froze, his mouth falling open, but then he came to his senses, and, pinching me hard, shoved the watch into my hands.

"What does he give me?" Madame Shvarts's rough, tearful voice lamented, as it receded into the distance. "Low-down tricks today, low-down tricks tomorrow! I ask you, you no-good wretch, how long can a woman wait?"

They walked to the corner and turned onto Pushkin Street. I stayed back, clutching my watch, and suddenly, with a clarity I had never before experienced, I saw the soaring columns of the Town Council, the illuminated leaves on the boulevard, and Pushkin's bronze head with the moon's pale reflection on it. For the first time I saw everything around me as it really was—hushed and beautiful beyond description.

SULAK

*G*ulay's outfit had been crushed in the province of Vinnitsa in 1922.* His chief of staff was Adrian Sulak, a village schoolmaster. Sulak managed to cross the border into Galicia, and shortly thereafter the newspapers reported his death. Six years later, we found out that Sulak was alive, hiding in the Ukraine. Chernishov and I were commissioned to track him down. We set out for Khoshchevatoye, Sulak's village, with papers in our pockets saying that we were livestock specialists. The chairman of the village council turned out to be a demobilized Red Army man, a good, straightforward fellow.

"You'll be lucky if you can get your hands on a jug of milk in this place," he told us. "Here in Khoshchevatoye they chew people up, skin and bone!"

Chernishov asked him where we could spend the night, bringing the conversation around to Sulak's hut.

"Yes, that's an idea," the chairman said. "His widow's living there now."

He took us over to the edge of the village, to a house with a corrugated iron roof. Inside we found a dwarf in a loose white blouse sitting in front of a pile of sackcloth. Two boys in orphanage jackets sat with their heads bowed over books. A baby with a bloated white head lay asleep in a cradle. A cold monastic cleanliness lay over everything.

---

* General Diomid Gulay was the leader of the Ukrainian Liberation Movement. Vinnitsa is a province in west-central Ukraine.

"Kharitina Terentevna," the chairman said hesitantly. "I want to put these good people up with you."

The woman showed us the room and went back to her pile of sackcloth.

"This widow won't turn you away," the chairman told us when we were outside. "She's in a bind."

Looking around, he confided to us that Sulak had served with the Ukrainian nationalists, but had now gone over to the Pope of Rome.*

"What? The husband's with the Pope of Rome and the wife has a child a year?"

"That's life," the chairman said. He saw a horseshoe on the road and picked it up. "Don't be fooled just because the widow is a dwarf—she's got milk enough for five. Even other women come over for her milk."

At home the chairman fried some eggs with lard, and brought out some vodka. He got drunk, and climbed up onto the bench above the stove to go to sleep. We heard whispering and a child crying.

"Hannochka, I promise I will," our host whispered. "I promise I'll go see the schoolmistress tomorrow."

"Quiet up there!" shouted Chernishov, lying next to me. "We want to get some sleep!"

The bedraggled chairman peered over the edge of the stove bench. His shirt collar was unbuttoned and his bare feet hung down.

"The schoolmistress handed out some bunnies for breeding at school," he said apologetically. "She gave us a she-bunny, but no he-bunny. So there was the she-bunny, and then come spring, that's life, she hops off to the woods!"

"Hannochka!" the chairman suddenly shouted, turning to the girl. "I'll go to the schoolmistress tomorrow and I'll bring you a pair, and we'll make a cage for them!"

Father and daughter went on talking for a long time on the stove bench, and he kept shouting, "Hannochka!" Then he fell asleep. Next to me, Chernishov was tossing and turning in the hay.

"Let's go there now," he said.

---

* By the Pope of Rome he means the Polish partisans, who were Catholic, unlike the Ukrainian partisans, who were Russian Orthodox.

We got up. The moon shone in the clean, cloudless sky. The puddles were covered by spring ice. Bare cornstalks stood in Sulak's garden, which was overgrown with weeds and filled with scrap iron. A stable stood next to the garden. We heard a rustling noise coming from it, and a light shimmered through the cracks in the boards. Chernishov crept to the stable door, rammed it with his shoulder, and the lock gave way. We went inside and saw an open pit in the middle of the stable, with a man sitting at the bottom. At the edge of the pit stood the dwarf in her white blouse, a bowl of borscht in her hands.

"Hello, Adrian," Chernishov said. "Getting a bite to eat, are you?"

The dwarf dropped the bowl and hurled herself onto me, biting my hand. Her teeth were locked and she moaned and shook. A gunshot came from the pit.

"Adrian!" Chernishov shouted, jumping back. "We want to take you alive!"

Sulak struggled with the bolt of his gun at the bottom of the pit. The bolt clicked.

"I've been talking to you as a person," Chernishov said, and fired.

Sulak fell against the yellow, planed wall, scraping at it, blood flowing from his mouth and ears, and collapsed.

Chernishov stood guard. I ran to fetch the chairman. We took the dead man away that same night. Sulak's sons walked next to Chernishov along the wet, dimly shimmering road. The dead man's feet in Polish shoes with reinforced soles jutted out from the back of the cart. The dwarf sat stiffly by her husband's head. Her face, distorted by little bones, looked metallic in the dimming light of the moon. The baby slept on her tiny knees.

"Full of milk!" Chernishov suddenly said, as he marched down the road. "I'll show you milk!"

THE TRIAL

*M*adame Blanchard, a sixty-one-year-old woman, met Ivan Nedachin, a former lieutenant colonel, in a café on the Boulevard des Italiens. They fell in love. Their love was more a matter of sensuality than common sense. Within three months the lieutenant colonel had disappeared with Madame Blanchard's stocks and the jewelry she had given him to be appraised by a jeweler on the Rue de la Paix.

*"Accès de folie passagère,"** the doctor diagnosed Madame Blanchard's ensuing fit.

Regaining consciousness, the old woman confessed everything to her daughter-in-law. Her daughter-in-law went to the police. Nedachin was arrested in a wine cellar in Montparnasse where Moscow gypsies sang. In prison Nedachin turned yellow and flabby. He was tried in chamber number fourteen of the criminal court. First there was a case involving an automobile matter, followed by the case of sixteen-year-old Raymond Lepique, who had shot his girlfriend out of jealousy. The lieutenant colonel came after the boy. The gendarme pushed him out into the light, as a bear is pushed into a circus arena. Frenchmen in badly sewn jackets were shouting loudly at each other, and submissively rouged women fanned their teary faces. In front of them, on the podium beneath the republic's marble coat of arms, sat a red-cheeked man with a Gallic mustache, wearing a toga and a little hat.

* "A fit of temporary insanity."

"*Eh bien, Nedachin,*" he said, on seeing the accused man, "*eh bien, mon ami.*" And his fast burred speech washed over the shuddering lieutenant colonel.

"As a descendant of the noble line of the Nedachins," the presiding judge loudly proclaimed, "you, my friend, are listed in the heraldic books of the province of Tambov. An officer of the Czar's army, you immigrated with Wrangel* and became a policeman in Zagreb. Discrepancies in the question of what was government property and what was private property," the presiding judge continued sonorously, the tips of his patent leather shoes darting in and out under the hem of his gown. "These discrepancies, my friend, forced you to bid the hospitable kingdom of Yugoslavia farewell and set your sights on Paris."

"In Paris,"—here the judge ran his eyes over some papers lying before him—"in Paris, my friend, the taxi driver test proved a fortress you could not conquer, at which point you concentrated all the powers left to you on Madame Blanchard, who is absent from this hearing."

The foreign words poured over Nedachin like a summer shower. He towered over the crowd—helpless, large, with dangling arms—like an animal from another world.

"*Voyons,*"† the presiding judge said unexpectedly. "From where I am sitting, I can see the daughter-in-law of the esteemed Madame Blanchard.

A fat, neckless woman, looking like a fish jammed into a frock coat, hurried with lowered head over to the witness box. Panting, lifting her short little arms to heaven, she began listing the stocks stolen from Madame Blanchard.

"Thank you very much, madame," the presiding judge interrupted her, nodding to a gaunt man with a well-bred, sunken face, who was sitting next to him.

The public prosecutor, rising slightly, muttered a few words and sat down again, clasping his hands. He was followed by the defense attorney, a naturalized Kiev Jew, who ranted about the Golgotha of the Russian military officers in an offended tone, as if he were in the mid-

---

* Baron Peter Nikolayevich Wrangel, 1878–1928, commander of the White anti-Bolshevik army, was forced to evacuate 150,000 soldiers and civilians by sea from the Crimea to Constantinople in November 1920, which marked the end of the Russian Civil War.

 † "Let's see."

dle of an argument. Incomprehensibly pronounced French words came sputtering out of his mouth, sounding increasingly Yiddish toward the end of his speech. The presiding judge peered blankly at the attorney for a few moments without saying a word, and then suddenly lunged to the side—toward the gaunt old man in the toga and the little hat—then lunged to the other side, to another old man just like the first.

"Ten years, my friend," the presiding judge said meekly, nodding his head at Nedachin, and hurriedly grabbed the papers for the next case, which his secretary slid over to him.

Nedachin stood rigidly to attention. His colorless eyes blinked, his small forehead was covered with sweat.

"*T'a encaissé dix ans,*" the gendarme behind him said. "*C'est fini, mon vieux.*"* And, quietly pushing the crowd out of the way, the gendarme led the convicted man toward the exit.

---

* "He's locked you up for ten years. It's over, old boy."

MY FIRST FEE

*T*o be in Tiflis in spring, to be twenty years old, and not to be
loved—that is a misfortune. Such a misfortune befell me. I was
working as a proofreader for the printing press of the Caucasus Military
District. The Kura River bubbled beneath the windows of my attic. The
sun in the morning, rising from behind the mountains, lit up the river's
murky knots. I was renting a room in the attic from a newlywed
Georgian couple. My landlord was a butcher at the Eastern Bazaar. In
the room next door, the butcher and his wife, in the grip of love,
thrashed about like two large fish trapped in a jar. The tails of these
crazed fish thumped against the partition, rocking the whole attic,
which was blackened by the piercing sun, ripping it from its rafters and
whisking it off to eternity. They could not part their teeth, clenched in
the obstinate fury of passion. In the mornings, Milyet, the young bride,
went out to get bread. She was so weak that she had to hold on to the
banister. Her delicate little foot searched for each step, and there was a
vague blind smile on her lips, like that of a woman recovering from a
long illness. Laying her palm on her small breasts, she bowed to everyone she met in the street—the Assyrian grown green with age, the
kerosene seller, and the market shrews with faces gashed by fiery wrinkles, who were selling hanks of sheep's wool. At night the thumping
and babbling of my neighbors was followed by a silence as piercing as
the whistle of a cannonball.

To be twenty years old, to live in Tiflis, and to listen at night to the
tempests of other people's silence—that is a misfortune. To escape it, I

ran out of the house and down to the Kura River, where I was over-powered by the bathhouse steam of Tiflis springtime. It swept over me, sapping my strength. I roamed through the hunchbacked streets, my throat parched. A fog of springtime sultriness chased me back to my attic, to that forest of blackened stumps lit by the moon. I had no choice but to look for love. Needless to say, I found it. For better or worse, the woman I chose turned out to be a prostitute. Her name was Vera. Every evening I went creeping after her along Golovinsky Boulevard, unable to work up the courage to talk to her. I had neither money for her nor words—those dull and ceaselessly burrowing words of love. Since childhood, I had invested every drop of my strength in creating tales, plays, and thousands of stories. They lay on my heart like a toad on a stone. Possessed by demonic pride, I did not want to write them down too soon. I felt that it was pointless to write worse than Tolstoy. My stories were destined to survive oblivion. Dauntless thought and grueling passion are only worth the effort spent on them when they are draped in beautiful raiment. But how does one sew such raiment?

A man who is caught in the noose of an idea and lulled by its serpentine gaze finds it difficult to bubble over with meaningless, burrowing words of love. Such a man is ashamed of shedding tears of sadness. He is not quick-witted enough to be able to laugh with happiness. I was a dreamer, and did not have the knack for the thoughtless art of happiness. Therefore I was going to have to give Vera ten rubles of my meager earnings.

I made up my mind and went to stand watch outside the doors of the Simpatia tavern. Georgian princes in blue Circassian jackets and soft leather boots sauntered past in casual parade. They picked their teeth with silver toothpicks and eyed the carmine-painted Georgian women with large feet and slim hips. There was a shimmer of turquoise in the twilight. The blossoming acacias howled along the streets in their petal-shedding bass voices. Waves of officials in white coats rolled along the boulevard. Balsamic streams of air came flowing toward them from the Karzbek Mountains.

Vera came later, as darkness was falling. Tall, her face a radiant white, she hovered before the apish crowd, as the Mother of God hovers before the prow of a fishing boat. She came up to the doors of the Simpatia. I hesitated, then followed her.

"Off to Palestine?"

Vera's wide, pink back was moving in front of me. She turned around.

"What?"

She frowned, but her eyes were laughing.

"Where does your path take you?"

The words crackled in my mouth like dry firewood. Vera came over and walked in step with me.

"A tenner—would that be fine with you?"

I agreed so quickly that she became suspicious.

"You sure you have ten rubles?"

We went through the gates and I handed her my wallet. She opened it and counted twenty-one rubles, narrowing her gray eyes and moving her lips. She rearranged the coins, sorting gold with gold and silver with silver.

"Give me ten," Vera said, handing me back my wallet. "We'll spend five, and the rest you can keep to get by. When's your next payday?"

I told her that I would get paid again in four days. We went back into the street. Vera took me by the arm and leaned her shoulder against mine. We walked up the cooling street. The sidewalk was covered with wilted vegetables.

"I'd love to be in Borzhom right now in this heat," she said.

Vera's hair was tied with a ribbon. The lightning of the street lamps flashed and bounced off it.

"So hightail it to Borzhom!"

That's what I said—"hightail it." For some reason, that's the expression I used.

"No dough," Vera answered with a yawn, forgetting all about me. She forgot all about me because her day was over and she had made easy money off me. She knew that I wouldn't call the police, and that I wasn't going to steal her money along with her earrings during the night.

We went to the foot of St. David's Mountain. There, in a tavern, I ordered some kebabs. Without waiting for our food to be brought, Vera went and sat with a group of old Persian men who were discussing business. They were leaning on propped-up sticks, wagging their olive-colored heads, telling the tavern keeper that it was time for him to expand his trade. Vera barged into their conversation, taking the side of the old men. She was for the idea of moving the tavern to Mikhailovsky Boulevard. The tavern keeper was sighing, paralyzed by uncertainty and caution. I ate my kebabs alone. Vera's bare arms poured out of the silk of her sleeves. She banged her fist on the table, her earrings dancing among long, lackluster backs, orange beards, and painted nails. By the time she came back to our table, her kebabs had become cold. Her face was flushed with excitement.

"There's no budging that man—he's such a mule! I swear, he could make a fortune with Eastern cooking on Mikhailovsky Boulevard!"

Friends of Vera's passed by our table one after another: princes in Circassian jackets, officers of a certain age, storekeepers in heavy silk coats, and potbellied old men with sunburned faces and little green pimples on their cheeks. It was pushing midnight when we got to the hotel, but there too Vera had countless things to do. An old woman was getting ready to go to her son in Armavir. Vera rushed over to help her, kneeling on her suitcase to force it shut, tying pillows together with cords, and wrapping pies in oilpaper. Clutching her rust-brown handbag, the squat little old woman hurried in her gauze hat from room to room to say good-bye. She shuffled down the hallway in her rubber boots, sobbing and smiling through all her wrinkles. The whole to-do took well over an hour. I waited for Vera in a musty room with three-legged armchairs and a clay oven. The corners of the room were covered with damp splotches.

I had been tormented and dragged around town for such a long time that even my feeling of love seemed to me an enemy, a dogged enemy.

Other people's life bustled in the hallway with peals of sudden laughter. Flies were dying in a jar filled with milky liquid. Each fly was dying in its own way—one in drawn-out agony, its death throes violent, another with a barely visible shudder. A book by Golovin about the life of the Boyars lay on the threadbare tablecloth next to the jar. I opened the book. Letters lined themselves up in a row and then fell into a jumble. In front of me, framed by the window, rose a stony hillside with a crooked Turkish road winding up it. Vera came into the room.

"We've just sent off Fedosya Mavrikevna," she said. "I swear, she was just like a mother to all of us. The poor old thing has to travel all alone with no one to help her!"

Vera sat down on the bed with her knees apart. Her eyes had wandered off to immaculate realms of tenderness and friendship. Then she saw me sitting there in my double-breasted jacket. She clasped her hands and stretched.

"I guess you're tired of waiting. Don't worry, we'll do it now."

But I simply couldn't figure out what exactly it was that Vera was intending to do. Her preparations resembled those of a surgeon preparing for an operation. She lit the kerosene burner and put a pot of water on it. She placed a clean towel over the bed frame and hung an enema bag over the headboard, a bag with a white tube dangling against the wall. When the water was hot, Vera poured it into the enema bag, threw in a red crystal, and pulled her dress off over her head. A large woman with sloping shoulders and rumpled stomach stood in front of me. Her flaccid nipples hung blindly to the sides.

"Come over here, you little rabbit, while the water's getting ready," my beloved said.

I didn't move. Despair froze within me. Why had I exchanged my loneliness for this den filled with poverty-stricken anguish, for these dying flies and furniture with legs missing?

O Gods of my youth! How different this dreary jumble was from my neighbors' love with its rolling, drawn-out moans.

Vera put her hands under her breasts and jiggled them.

"Why do you sit half dead, hanging your head?" she sang. "Come over here!"

I didn't move. Vera pressed her shirt to her stomach and sat down again on the bed.

"Or are you sorry you gave me the money?"

"I don't care about the money."

I said this in a cracking voice.

"What do you mean, you don't care? You a thief or something?"

"I'm not a thief."

"You work for thieves?"

"I'm a boy."

"Well, I can see you're not a cow," Vera mumbled. Her eyes were falling shut. She lay down and, pulling me over to her, started rubbing my body.

"A boy!" I shouted. "You understand what I'm saying? An Armenian's boy!"

O Gods of my youth! Five out of the twenty years I'd lived had gone into thinking up stories, thousands of stories, sucking my brain dry. These stories lay on my heart like a toad on a stone. One of these stories, pried loose by the power of loneliness, fell onto the ground. It was to be my fate, it seems, that a Tiflis prostitute was to be my first reader. I went cold at the suddenness of my invention, and told her the story about the boy and the Armenian. Had I been lazier and given less thought to my craft, I would have made up a drab story about a son thrown out by his rich official of a father—the father a despot, the mother a martyr. I didn't make such a mistake. A well-thought-out story doesn't need to resemble real life. Life itself tries with all its might to resemble a well-crafted story. And for this reason, and also because it was necessary for my listener, I had it that I was born in the town of Alyoshki in the district of Kherson. My father worked as a draftsman in the office of a river steamship company. He toiled night and day over his drawing board so that he could give us children an education, but we took after our mother, who was fond of fun and food. When I was ten I began stealing money from my father, and a few years later ran away to Baku to live with some relatives on my mother's side. They introduced me to Stepan Ivanovich, an Armenian. I became friends with him, and we lived together for four years.

"How old were you then?"

"Fifteen."

Vera was waiting to hear about the evil deeds of the Armenian who had corrupted me.

"We lived together for four years," I continued, "and Stepan Ivanovich turned out to be the most generous and trusting man I had ever met—the most conscientious and honorable man. He trusted every single friend of his to the fullest. I should have learned a trade in those four years, but I didn't lift a finger. The only thing on my mind was billiards. Stepan Ivanovich's friends ruined him. He gave them bronze promissory notes, and his friends went and cashed them right away."

Bronze promissory notes! I myself had no idea how I came up with that. But it was a very good idea. Vera believed everything once she heard "bronze promissory notes." She wrapped herself in her shawl and her shawl shuddered on her shoulders.

"They ruined Stepan Ivanovich. He was thrown out of his apartment and his furniture was auctioned off. He became a traveling salesman. When he lost all his money I left him and went to live with a rich old man, a church warden."

Church warden! I stole the idea from some novel, but it was the invention of a mind too lazy to create a real character.

I said church warden, and Vera's eyes blinked and slipped out from under my spell. To regain my ground, I squeezed asthma into the old man's yellow chest.

"Asthma attacks whistled hoarsely inside his yellow chest. The old man would jump up from his bed in the middle of the night and, moaning, breath in the kerosene-colored night of Baku. He died soon after. The asthma suffocated him." I told her that my relatives would have nothing to do with me and that here I was, in Tiflis, with twenty rubles to my name, the very rubles she had counted in that entrance on Golovinsky Boulevard. The waiter at the hotel where I was staying promised to send me rich clients, but up to now had only sent me taproom keepers with tumbling bellies, men who love their country, their songs, and their wine and who don't think twice about trampling on a foreign soul or a foreign woman, like a village thief will trample on his neighbor's garden.

And I started jabbering about low-down taproom keepers, bits of information I had picked up somewhere. Self-pity tore my heart to pieces; I had been completely ruined. I quaked with sorrow and inspiration. Streams of icy sweat trickled down my face like snakes winding through grass warmed by the sun. I fell silent, began to cry, and turned away. My story had come to an end. The kerosene burner had died out a long time ago. The water had boiled and cooled down again. The enema tube was dangling against the wall. Vera walked silently over to the window. Her back, dazzling and sad, moved in front of me. Outside the window the sun was beginning to light the mountain crevices.

"The things men do," Vera whispered, without turning around. "My God, the things men do!"

She stretched out her bare arms and opened the shutters all the way. The cooling flagstones on the street hissed. The smell of water and dust came rolling up the carriageway. Vera's head drooped.

"In other words, you're a whore. One of us—a bitch," she said.

I hung my head.

"Yes, I'm one of you—a bitch."

Vera turned around to face me. Her shirt hung in twisted tatters from her body.

"The things men do," she repeated more loudly. "My God, the things men do. So . . . have you ever been with a woman?"

I pressed my icy lips to her hand.

"No. . . . How could I have? Who would have wanted me?"

My head shook beneath her breasts, which rose freely above me. Her stretched nipples bounced against my cheeks, opening their moist eyelids and cavorting like calves. Vera looked at me from above.

"My little sister," she whispered, settling down on the floor next to me. "My little whorelet sister."

Now tell me, dear reader, I would like to ask you something: have you ever watched a village carpenter helping a fellow carpenter build a hut for himself and seen how vigorous, strong, and cheerful the shavings fly as they plane the wooden planks? That night a thirty-year-old woman taught me her trade. That night I learned secrets that you will never learn, experienced love that you will never experience, heard women's words that only other women hear. I have forgotten them. We are not supposed to remember them.

It was morning when we fell asleep. We were awakened by the heat of our bodies, a heat that weighed the bed down like a stone. When we awoke we laughed together. That day I didn't go to the printing press. We drank tea in the bazaar of the old quarters. A placid Turk carrying a samovar wrapped in a towel poured tea, crimson as a brick, steaming like blood freshly spilled on the earth. The smoking fire of the sun blazed on the walls of our glasses. The drawn-out braying of donkeys mingled with the hammering of blacksmiths. Copper pots were lined up under canopies, on faded carpets. Dogs were burrowing their muzzles into ox entrails. A caravan of dust flew toward Tiflis, the town of roses and mutton fat. The dust carried off the crimson fire of the sun. The Turk poured tea and kept count of the rolls we ate. The world was beautiful just for our sake. Covered in beads of sweat, I turned my glass upside down. I paid the Turk and pushed two golden five-ruble coins over to Vera. Her chunky leg was lying over mine. She pushed the money away and pulled in her leg.

"Do you want us to quarrel, my little sister?"

No, I didn't want to quarrel. We agreed to meet again in the evening, and I slipped back into my wallet the two golden fivers—my first fee.

Since that day many years have passed, and I have often been given money by editors, men of letters, and Jews selling books. For victories that were defeats, for defeats that turned into victories, for life and death, they paid me a trivial fee, much lower than the fee I was paid in my youth by my first reader. But I am not bitter. I am not bitter because I know that I will not die until I snatch one more gold ruble (and definitely not the last one!) from love's hands.

XII

❧

Variations and Manuscripts

The variations in this section are early versions of pieces that Babel later revised for further publication. The first piece, "Roaming Stars: A Movie Tale," is a prose variation of Babel's screenplay of the same name, loosely based on Shalom Alechem's novel BLONDZNDE SHTERN (translated into English as WANDERING STAR). It is particularly interesting to compare the two variants, as Babel added many nuances, making the prose version an interesting key to the screen version and vice versa. The second piece in this section, "A story," published in ZHURNAL ZHURNALOV in 1917, appeared in a reworked version as "The Bathroom Window" in the magazine Silueti in 1923, and "Information" is an earlier variant of "My First Fee."

Babel was apparently intending to develop into novels the two unfinished manuscripts in this section, "Three in the Afternoon" and "The Jewess."

Variations

ROAMING STARS:
A MOVIE TALE

*B*riansky Station in Moscow. Night stretches above its glass roof. The train from Kiev pulls into the station. Platform jostling, platform love—the porters, transient witnesses of our love. The porters are pushing carts packed high with bundles, dead birds, live birds in cages. A girl who has arrived from the shtetl of Derazhny gets tangled in the grinding stream of carts and blocks their way. The girl's name is Rachel Monko. The carts swerve around her, sparks flashing from their wheels.

"Look who's come to town!" one of the porters yells into Rachel's ear, and he rumbles off with his cart. The porter is a short man, his hard face looks like every other face in the world and yet resembles none, but his voice is clear and loud, filled with triumph and rage.

"Look who's come to town from the sticks!" the porter yells, and rumbles off with his cart. The thunder machine roars over Rachel's head as she cowers, surrounded by platform love. All the squadrons of the night are galloping over the glass roof of Moscow's Briansky Station.

•　•　•

Rachel Monko has come to Moscow to enroll in the Women's Institute of Higher Education. If that does not work out, she intends to go to a school of dentistry. Rachel's face is like that of Ruth, wife of Boaz, like that of Bathsheba, concubine of David, King of Israel, or that of Esther, wife of Ataxerxes. Rachel has come to Moscow with a letter of recommendation from the Derazhny district agronomist to Ivan Potapich Butsenko, the owner of the Rossiya boardinghouse. One can say about Rachel that her love of science is as great as Lenin's, Darwin's, and Spinoza's love of truth.

. . .

Rachel takes a tram leaving from Briansky Station. She is stunned by the tram's glittering lights. It must be remembered that she had not once in her life left Derazhny. Rachel cannot control herself, and laughs with happiness. An old man is sitting next to her, an old man in a uniform cap. He is a police doctor. In his day he was loved by many women, and all the women who had loved him had been hysterical. The doctor has a tender, listless disposition. He looks at Rachel and thinks how she has yet to experience all that is already in his past, and yet how she knows more about life than he, an old man touched by a premonition of death. The girl knows more than he does, otherwise she wouldn't be laughing.

"Why are you laughing?" the doctor asks her, lifting his cap off his tender, balding head to her.

"It is such fun to be traveling on a Moscow tram," Rachel answers, her laughter growing stronger.

The doctor hurries away from her.

"Another hysterical woman," he says to himself. "Oh, God, they are all hysterical!"

. . .

The Rossiya boardinghouse is located in an old side street in the Varvarka quarter, near Staraya Square. It is run by an old couple, the Butsenkos: Ivan Potapich and Evdokiya Ignatevna. Life there has been clean and happy. They have had many healthy children, all of whom graduated from specialized institutes: the Institute of Land Surveying, the College of Mining, the Petrovsk-Razumovsky Academy. None of Butsenko's sons suffered from foolish Russian passions. None of them had joined the God-haters or hung themselves in railroad station washrooms or married Jewesses.

The boardinghouse of old Butsenko and his wife is outstanding for its cleanliness. Its cleanliness shines like the countenance of

Jesus Christ. In every room a little icon hangs on the prim bed curtains. Grain merchants from Liven, Yelets, and Ryazhsk stay at the Rossiya, men with unmenacing inclinations who expect their food to be brought up to their rooms and that the food be home cooking: it didn't matter how it was cooked, as long as it wasn't restaurant food.

The Butsenkos usually had kindhearted maids working for them. These were sickly women from faraway provinces—from Arkhangelsk, from the White Sea—and the Russian they spoke was so colorful and picturesque that if they weren't employed as maids they would have made good reciters of northern epics and sagas, and crowds would have flocked to the theaters to hear them.

That is what the Rossiya boardinghouse was like.

•   •   •

The Butsenkos' kitchen. Evdokiya Ignatevna, a crimson little old woman, is busy cooking at the stove. Ivan Potapich, enveloped by fluffy, aromatic gray hair, is writing out a menu for tomorrow. At the bottom of every page he writes, "Sincerely Yours." Both he and his wife are wearing aprons and have taut, neatly protruding bellies

The doorbell rings. Rachel Monko comes into the kitchen and timidly hands Butsenko a letter. He reads it standing, and with the seriousness of a judge listening to witnesses taking their oath, but the further he reads, the brighter and more tender his smile becomes.

"It's from Vladimir Semyonich," he tells the crimson little old woman, "our dear friend."

Here is Vladimir Semyonich's letter:

> Dearest Ivan Potapich. I recommend with all my heart the bearer of this letter, a girl from my town and a very dear person indeed, to be a lodger with full board at your boardinghouse. She left this godforsaken hole with the greatest difficulty, as she wants to pursue dentistry, or some other form of education that might be possible for her and to which this dear girl from my town might feel "an attraction, a consuming passion," and I hope that you will help her, you and your hardworking Evdokiya Ignatevna (who I remember as if it were yesterday, though if she remembers me I do not know, although I sincerely hope she does). . . .

Ivan Potapich finishes reading the letter, tenderly and with tears in his eyes, and then clasps Rachel's hands in his own soft, grandfatherly hands.

"How can I forget Vladimir Semyonich!" the old man says. "The year before last we celebrated Christmas together in Ostankino. . . ."

And Ivan Potapich can't say any more, because it would be hard to explain the tale of his acquaintance with Vladimir Semyonich, a tale of no interest whatsoever to anyone else, but which for him, Ivan Potapich, has many hidden treasures of the soul.

The year before last, in a wonderful, tranquil snowy winter, Ivan Potapich had gone to visit his eldest son in Ostankino for the Christmas feast, and there met an agronomist, Vladimir Semyonich, who was a friend of some friend or other. The guests had arrived, given presents to the children, thrown snow off the roof for fun, knocked icicles off the drainpipes, and drunk French wine. Vladimir Semyonich, increasingly intoxicated, began telling old Butsenko the kind of secrets one ought not to tell a stranger. But the agronomist spoke with such gravity and candor, so self-mockingly, that there was no shamefulness at all in his confidences, only warm esteem for a stranger, in other words for Ivan Potapich. The agronomist told the old man that his wife was a very silent sort of woman and had managed things in such a way that she would not have to bear his children, and other such secrets.

The following day the guests had gotten up at noon. Midday looked like morning. The snow glittered, the windows sparkled, and a plump nanny, battling to restrain her joy, kept shuffling and wheezing from one stove to another with more wood.

Ivan Potapich returned to Moscow with the agronomist in a small sledge pulled by well-trained gray horses with round cruppers, and the old man could not marvel enough at the fact that he had no heartburn or hangover from the wine he had drunk the night before, which made him like his chance companion all the more.

That was the extent of Butsenko's acquaintance with the agronomist. Vladimir Semyonich had sent two other letters from the provinces asking for little favors that Butsenko was glad to do. In the first letter, he asked for a seed catalogue, in the second he asked Butsenko to find out whether it was really true that the Siementhal milk cows from Derazhny had been given a favorable report at the Moscow

Agricultural Exhibition, and the third letter was about Rachel. Ivan Potapich is eager to fulfill the third request. He calls out loudly to his wife, "Mother, put the samovar on, and bring some pies!" And he leads Rachel to her room. Outside the window stands a little azure-colored church with yellow onion-shaped cupolas and dark blue stars on the domes. When she sees the church, Rachel realizes that everything in her life has changed for the better, and that her dream to see Moscow has finally come true. The old man, panting and bathed in glistening sweat, hurries in with a jug of water and stands there with a towel, waiting for Rachel to finish washing her face and hands. But she takes a long time. Girls raised in a strict family and who expect much from life take their time washing up. The old man, tired of waiting, leafs through Rachel's passport, which she has left lying on the table. The name in the passport is Rachel Hananevna Monko. The heading on the third page reads: "Zones in which Jews are permitted to reside."

Rachel has finished washing up and reaches out her strong red hands to take the towel the old man is holding. But the old man's face has become pitiful and angry.

"How shameful of you to try and trick us!" he says, hiding the towel behind his back. "How shameful!"

He hurries out of the room with weak steps, and outside the door comes face-to-face with his wife, who is holding a tray and is enveloped in the steam of a samovar, pies, and buns.

"Take those things back to the kitchen!" Ivan Potapich yells. "You can learn a lesson from people like her who've thrown their shame to the dogs!"

· · ·

Rachel has not found refuge at the Rossiya boardinghouse. She wanders through the streets till midnight looking for a place to stay. At midnight she arrives tired out at Voskresenskaya Square near Iverskaya Street, which is reverberating with the cheerful din of Moscow. Gypsy children dancing in the street rush over to Rachel and form a circle around her, singing and beating their tambourines. An old Persian man approaches Rachel and lays his hand on her shoulder. He slithers a regal finger with a painted nail down to her breast. A holy fool strides up to her on his bare, pink, monstrously thin legs, which are bent and creaking at the joints. Yellow spittle is bubbling in his tangled beard, and a blue ray glimmers on the chain bound around his neck. The blue ray glimmers on the chain the way a frozen tree-lined walk glimmers beneath the moon. In a chapel, candle wax glows and flares up, and the battle, the cheerful battle of Moscow's streets, rages around Rachel.

The Persian, fixing her with his eyes, pinches her with his painted fingers, and the gypsy children chase her and start pulling at the hem of her skirt. Rachel runs as fast as she can. She runs across Red Square, over the Moscow River, into the Zamoskvoreche quarter, and into a winding back alley. At the end of the alley hangs a smoking lantern over a ramshackle door. "Rooming house for travelers—every convenience," is written under the lantern. "The Hero of Plevna Rooming House."

The stars in this back alley are immense, the snow pure, the heavens deep.

•   •   •

In the office of the Hero of Plevna Rooming House, the attendant, a widower by the name of Orlov, is getting his son Matvei ready for bed. Matvei, a ten-year-old boy, is wrapped in purple and orange rags, his pants are multilayered, and his father pulls off each layer separately. Matvei has just learned a poem by heart as homework for school, and he cannot resist reciting it to his father.

"With his saber he pierced my soul," Matvei whispers as he dozes off. "He tore out my beating heart, and wrenching my wound apart, he plunged in some fiery coal."

"A beautiful little poem," Orlov says, and as a good-night blessing makes the sign of the cross three times over his son. "See, all of life can be squeezed into a little poem like that. It's about us too, you know, how we let every good-for-nothing step on our toes, and it's about God, and about mothers."

For a long time Orlov continues telling Matvei about life, about mothers and good-for-nothings, but Matvei is already asleep. Orlov shakes out his son's jacket and examines it to see if there are any tears in it, and Rachel enters the office.

"Could I have a room, please?" she asks timidly.

"We don't let in no girls without a fellow," Orlov answers. He bites off a thread and sits down to darn his son's jacket. "Who're you with? Where's your trick?"

Rachel has no idea what he means. She has no idea what Orlov is talking about. She goes down the stairs and out into the back alley. The stars in this back alley are immense, the snow pure, the heavens deep. A pregnant woman with a scalded face, her belly protruding crookedly, is sitting on the front step, softly singing a peasant wedding song. A student is standing next to her, a rakish, devil-may-care cap on his brown curls.

"Well, what have we here?" the student says to Rachel. "Who are you?"

"I'm a Jewess," Rachel answers.

If at this point the two of them had not been able to come to some kind of agreement, life wouldn't have been worth all the trouble.

"The man won't give you a room because you're without a fellow, and he won't give me a room because I'm without a girl," the student says to Rachel. "My name is Baulin, I'm a fellow you can trust."

If at this point Orlov had had enough fire in his soul to be taken aback by anything, then he would have been taken aback by how two people he had thrown out separately could reappear so quickly, and reappear together.

"We want a room, pops," Baulin calls out to him without coming into the reception area. Orlov puts down the jacket and spits on his finger, pricked by the needle.

"Ha! And she said she didn't have a john!" he mutters, and heads down the hallway with a candle to take them to their room.

The hallway of the Hero of Plevna smells of grain, bread, and apples, and a pile of broken chamber pots and tin washbasins lies against a wall. In another corner lies a pile of pictures in gold frames. Orlov shuffles down the hallway and opens the door to a room.

"There we go," he says. "Hand over the cash now."

"Change these holy chasubles here, will you?" Baulin tells Orlov, pointing at the stained sheets.

"We change the sheets after every client!" Orlov says, whisking off the dirty sheet, draping it over a table, and covering the bed with a damp rag that smells of garlic. Orlov slouches off and comes back clutching a chamber pot.

"Everything's in order," he says, stumbling back because Baulin has thumped him in the chest.

"Get out of here, you scum," Baulin whispers in despair, beating Orlov's arms. "Please, get out of here! Please!" Orlov hides the chamber pot behind his back and with bitter triumph says, "You were still dribbling snot all over your mother when I had a family of six to feed!"

Orlov's cheeks flush, he turns as red as a consumptive, and doesn't want to leave even after he has been paid for the room. Then he suddenly remembers that he has to wash Matvei's shirt and walks out of the room, leaving Baulin and Rachel alone. Outside the window lies the black water of the Moscow River and night pierced with golden holes. Rachel looks out the window, rubs the damp glass with the utmost tenderness in her trembling fingers, and begins to cry. She walks over to the mirror, but foul messages have been scratched all over it. One of them had been etched in cursive Church Slavonic script: "Tonight at midnight I had a session with a fabulous girl, but she won't tell me her name. I hope I didn't catch anything."

There are many messages etched onto the mirror, and Baulin pulls Rachel away from that shameful place.

"My dear friend," he says, his voice resounding, "you lie down on the bed, and I'll lie down by the door. We might even catch some sleep."

Out of his overcoat he takes a packet of illegal proclamations printed by the Moscow Committee of the Social Democratic Party and lays it under his head, laughs, and goes to sleep.

It's two in the morning. The cheerful Moscow bustle has come to an end, the candle has gone out. Baulin has begun to snore. Next door the tedious, melodious voice of a woman whines.

"You're such a Yid, Vanya!" the tedious voice whines. "You're up to your old tricks again! You say you'll pay me, but may I not live to see another day if I don't bite the coin you give me!"

A STORY

*This story is an earlier version of
"The Bathroom Window."*

I have an old acquaintance—Fanya Osipovna Kebchik. She had been a prostitute in her youth, but she assures me that "nothing in the world" would have induced her to take less than five rubles.

Now she has a "nice, respectable apartment." There are two girls there, Marusya and Tamara. Marusya is really nice, gentle, and with a delicate build. There are many requests for her. One of the windows in her room has a view of the street, the other—just a small one up by the ceiling—has a view of the bathroom. When I noticed this, I suggested the following deal to Fanya Osipovna Kebchik: for five rubles she would put a ladder by the little window in the bathroom, I would climb up the ladder, and for an hour or two, or for however long I wanted, I would peek into Marusya's room.

At first Fanya Osipovna was astonished at my suggestion, but then she said, "Oy, you rogue, you!" And . . . agreed.

She got her five rubles quite often. Needless to say, I only made use of the little window when Marusya had clients.

For me there is no greater bliss than passionlessly following the play of passion on people's faces.

What astonishing moments I spent! I remember an old, thickset man crying quietly on the edge of the bed, a drunken English soldier, coldly beating the girl with icy malice. There were disgusting types too. I particularly remember a drooling high school boy, his body covered with pimples, shivering with impatience and muttering bookishly, "Oh, how I want you! Give yourself to me!"

Recently something very unpleasant happened. I was standing on the ladder. Marusya had a client. Luckily they hadn't turned off the light. (They often do, which is bothersome.) Her guest was a fine fellow, cheerful, unassuming, with one of those large, harmless mustaches. He undressed in a funny way, very prim and proper: he took off his collar, looked in the mirror, noticed a pimple under his mustache, went closer to the mirror, studied the pimple, pressed it out, and then quite cheerfully made a few faces. He took off his boots and again rushed to the mirror—might there be a scratch? They lay down, kissed, tickled one another. All very ordinary. I was about to climb down, when I slipped. The ladder fell with a crash, and there I was, dangling in the air. The apartment was suddenly full of commotion. A hysterical screech came from Marusya's room. Everyone came running, Fanya Osipovna, Tamara, some official in a Ministry of Education uniform. They helped me down. My situation was pitiful. Marusya ran in half dressed, her lanky client in tow, his clothes thrown on hastily. Marusya guessed what had happened, and froze. She looked at me long and hard, and said quietly, and with surprise, "What a bastard, oh, what a bastard!"

She fell silent, stared at all of us, went over to the lanky man, and for some reason kissed his hand and started to cry softly.

"My dear, oh, God, my dear!" she said, between kisses and sobs, caressing him.

The lanky man stood there like a total idiot. My soul turned inside out. I went over to Madam Kebchik.

Within half an hour, Marusya knew the secret. All was forgiven and forgotten. But I was still wondering why Marusya had kissed the lanky fellow.

"Madam Kebchik," I said. "I'll give you ten rubles if you let me look again."

Madam Kebchik assured me that I was out of my mind, but ten rubles is ten rubles. So I stood again on top of the ladder, looked into the room, and saw Marusya, her thin white arms wrapped around her client, kissing him with long, slow kisses.

Tears were flowing from her eyes.

"My darling!" she whispered. "Oh, God, my sweet darling!" And she gave herself to him with all the passion of a woman in love.

She looked at him as if he, the lanky fellow, were the only man in the world.

And the lanky fellow wallowed in businesslike bliss.

INFORMATION

*This story is an earlier version of
"My First Fee."*

*I*n answer to your inquiry, I would like to inform you that I set out
on my literary career early in life, when I was about twenty. I was
drawn to writing by a natural affinity, and also by my love for a woman
named Vera. She was a prostitute from Tiflis, and among her friends
she had the reputation of being a woman with a good head for business.
People came to pawn things with her, she helped young women launch
their careers, and on occasion traded alongside Persians at the Eastern
Bazaar. She went out on the Golovinsky Boulevard every evening, hovering before the crowds—tall, her face a radiant white—as the Mother
of God hovers before the prow of a fishing boat. I saved up some
money, crept after her silently, and finally mustered the courage to
approach her. Vera asked me for ten rubles, leaned against me with her
soft, large shoulders, and forgot all about me.

In the tavern where we ate kebabs she became flushed with excitement, trying to talk the tavern keeper into expanding his trade by moving to Mikhailovsky Boulevard. From the tavern we went to a shoe-
maker to get some shoes, and then Vera went off to a girlfriend's for a
christening. Toward midnight we arrived at the hotel, but there too
Vera had things to do. An old woman was getting ready to go to her
son in Armavir. Vera knelt on her suitcase to force it shut, and wrapped
pies in oilpaper. Clutching her rust-brown handbag, the little old
woman hurried from room to room in her gauze hat to say good-bye.
She shuffled down the hallway in her rubber boots, sobbing and smiling through all her wrinkles.

I waited for Vera in a room with three-legged armchairs and a clay oven. The corners of the room were covered with damp splotches. Flies were dying in a jar filled with milky liquid, each fly dying in its own way. Other people's life bustled in the hallway, with peals of sudden laughter. It was an eternity before Vera came back into the room.

"We'll do it now," she said, closing the door behind her. Her preparations resembled those of a surgeon preparing for an operation. She lit the kerosene burner, put a pot of water on it, and poured the water into an enema bag that had a white tube hanging from it. She threw a red crystal into the enema bag, and began undressing.

"We've just sent Fedosya Mavrikevna off," Vera said. "I swear she was just like a mother to all of us. The poor old thing has to travel all alone, with no one to help her!"

A large woman with sloping shoulders lay in the bed, her flaccid nipples blindly pointing at me.

"Why are you sitting there so glum?" Vera asked, pulling me toward her. "Or are you sorry you gave me the money?"

"I don't care about the money."

"What do you mean, you don't care? You a thief or something?"

"I'm not a thief, I'm a boy."

"Well, I can see you're not a cow," Vera said with a yawn. Her eyes were falling shut.

"I'm a boy," I repeated, and went cold at the suddenness of my invention.

There was no going back, so I told my chance companion the following story:

"We lived in Alyoshki in the district of Kherson"—is what I came up with as a beginning. "My father worked as a draftsman, and tried to give us children an education. But we took after our mother, who was only interested in cards and good food. When I was ten I began stealing money from my father, and a few years later ran away to Baku to live with some relatives on my mother's side. They introduced me to an old man. His name was Stepan Ivanovich. I became friends with him, and we lived together for four years.

"How old were you then?"

"Fifteen."

Vera was expecting to hear about the evil deeds of the man who had corrupted me.

"We lived together for four years," I continued, "and Stepan Ivanovich turned out to be an extremely trusting man—he trusted everyone. I should have learned a trade during those years, but I only had one thing on my mind—billiards. Stepan Ivanovich's friends ruined him. He gave them bronze promissory notes, and they cashed them in right away."

I have no idea how I came up with bronze promissory notes, but it was a very good idea. The woman believed everything once I mentioned these promissory notes. She wrapped herself in her red shawl, and it trembled on her shoulders.

"They ruined Stepan Ivanovich. He was thrown out of his apartment and his furniture was auctioned off. He became a traveling salesman. When he lost all his money, I left him and went to live with a rich old man, a church warden."

Church warden! I stole the idea from some novel, but it was the invention of a lazy mind. To regain ground, I squeezed asthma into the old man's yellow chest—asthma attacks and hoarse whistling as he gasped for breath. The old man would jump up in the middle of the night and, moaning, breathe in the kerosene-colored night of Baku. He died soon after. My relatives would have nothing to do with me, so here I was, in Tiflis, with twenty rubles to my name. The waiter at the hotel where I was staying promised to send me rich clients, but up to now had only sent me tavern keepers.

And I started jabbering about low-down tavern keepers and their coarse, mercenary ways, bits of information I had picked up somewhere. Self-pity tore my heart to pieces; I had been completely ruined. I fell silent. My story had come to an end. The kerosene burner had died out. The water had boiled and cooled down again. The woman walked silently through the room, her back fleshy and sad.

"The things men do," Vera whispered, opening the shutters. "My God, the things men do!"

A stony hillside framed by the window rose with a crooked Turkish road winding up it. The cooling flagstones on the street hissed. The smell of water and dust came rolling up the carriageway.

"So, have you ever been with a woman?" Vera asked, turning to me.

"How could I have? Who would have wanted me?"

"The things men do," Vera said. "My God, the things men do!"

I shall interrupt my story at this point to ask you, my dear friends, if you have ever watched a village carpenter helping a fellow carpenter build a hut for himself and seen how vigorous, strong, and cheerful the shavings fly as they plane the wooden planks.

That night a thirty-year-old woman taught me her trade. That night I experienced a love full of patience and heard women's words that only other women hear.

It was morning when we fell asleep. We were awakened by the heat of our bodies. We drank tea in the bazaar of the old quarter. A placid Turk carrying a samovar wrapped in a towel poured tea, crimson as a brick, steaming like blood freshly spilled on the earth. A caravan of dust flew toward Tiflis, the town of roses and mutton fat. The dust carried off the crimson fire of the sun. The drawn-out braying of donkeys mingled with the hammering of blacksmiths. The Turk poured tea and kept count of the rolls we ate.

Covered in beads of sweat, I turned my glass upside down and pushed two golden five-ruble coins over to Vera. Her chunky leg was lying over mine. She pushed the money away and pulled in her leg.

"Do you want us to quarrel, my little sister?"

No, I didn't want to quarrel. We agreed to meet again in the evening, and I slipped back into my wallet the two golden fivers—my first fee.

Manuscripts

THREE IN

THE AFTERNOON

Three in the afternoon. Heat and silence. Outside the railroad car window silent, burned fields. Father Ivan is sitting by the window, drinking tea and wiping the sweat off his fat neck. A small group has gathered around him.

"Exploitation," Father Ivan says. "We moan, we groan. Bloodsucking spiders have trapped us in their webs! Think about it! The doctor is a Jew, the merchant dealing with trade and industry is a Jew, your young son's science teacher is a Jew—"

"A clever people," someone says from the corner.

"Yids!" a student with a hard face and a pale blond mustache says angrily.

"Take me, for instance," Father Ivan continues. "I have a little plot of land, a vegetable garden, a cow or two. And yet I can't turn a profit from my simple little farm. Why, I ask you, can't I turn a profit, while my tenant Yankel Rosenshrayr is managing quite nicely?"

"Because he's a Yankel," someone guffaws.

"The reasons are social and economic," another answers more slowly.

"So feast your eyes, gentlemen!" Father Ivan says, pointing at a skinny Jew in big galoshes. "My tenant lives like a pig in clover, feeds himself without the slightest effort, while I have to feed—"

Rosenshrayr, realizing that he has become the object of attention, carefully wraps the paper around his dried sausage, wipes his lips, brushes away the crumbs from his shiny suit, and knits his brow.

"*Oy*, even listening to your talk is disgusting to a man's ears!" he says.

He spreads out his red blanket and lies down, clasping his hands over his belly.

"We can't get by without Yids!" Father Ivan pronounces. "That is the tragic contradiction. A drunkard fell down the stairs into my cellar last month and passed away. Now my son has been arrested, because they say it was a punch in the face that sent the drunk man falling. That's why I've brought along the hooknose, for the defense."

"*Oy*, he's starting again!" Yankel mumbles. "What an amazement! How much this man can speak!"

The train nears the station. "Vinnitsa Station!" the conductor shouts. Yankel gets up, puts on his white cloak that reaches all the way down to his toes, and his chocolate-colored bowler hat that keeps slipping down to his nose. He picks up the priest's suitcases.

"*Oy gevalt*, these are not suitcases, they are lions!" he says, barely able to lift them.

They get off the train. From the train window Yankel is still visible for a long time, shuffling in his winter galoshes, barely managing to keep up with the majestic figure of the priest, who is heatedly pontificating about something.

"The devil and a babe in the woods, arm in arm!" someone in the railway car says, and guffaws.

In town the investigator informed Father Ivan that his son had been arrested for assault and battery and the murder of Vasili Kuzmichev, who had walked past the cellar door in a state of intoxication, and so on and so forth.

"Lord Almighty!" the priest said, his lips ashen, and sat down. "Jesus Christ in heaven, what are you saying!"

"Your Worship," Yankel said, moving toward the investigator. "Your Worship, this, if you will pardon me, is too terrible to even hear! He is a priest, if you will please look closely! He is at the end of his rope. That Vasili was, if you will pardon me, a drunkard—a feeble man!"

The investigator lifted his hands in resignation. Yankel, propping up the tottering priest, led him out into the waiting room.

"Yankel," Father Ivan said. "Yankel, I beg you—"

"Father," Yankel answered, "there is no need to grieve this way! I can't see you like this! Wait for me here a moment—a hog won't come running if you don't dangle no turnip."

Yankel went back to the investigator and sat down unhurriedly in an armchair opposite him.

"Him, the priest, he's a rich man. He needs all this nonsense here like you need to dance polkas on tabletops! So the drunkard came in and the priest's son says, 'You bastard, why are you drunk?' Someone had been eating a watermelon, the drunkard slipped on it and fell, and now we got to make a big song and dance of it? Your Worship—it's not like these people are some Yids or something! He's a priest, a rich man!"

Yankel took five ten-ruble notes out of his pocket and, peering at them, placed them under the inkwell.

"Get out of here, you lowlife!" the investigator said. "Go to hell!"

Yankel took back the notes and, treading softly, left the room.

"Father, these are not people!" he said to Father Ivan. "They are animals! Let's go home!"

By evening, all the worrying had given Father Ivan a bad stomachache, and his back hurt.

"*Oy,* that I should have to fear the hooligans as little as you have to fear all this here!" Yankel said, sitting on the priest and massaging his massive stomach. "There is no evidence, even if they stand on their heads twenty times. Tomorrow, with God's help, we will go to the lawyer and wipe the floor with their ugly mugs!"

"Yankel," Father Ivan said in a quiet voice, "so the drunkard came in, so Kostya yelled at him, he flew into a rage . . . where is justice in all of this?"

"Justice," Yankel said, sliding off the priest's stomach, "justice will win! If only everyone should have the kind of sweet life that you will have!"

He lay down on the sofa, curled up, and quietly fell asleep.

"Yankel!" Father Ivan called out to him. "I can't sleep, I am so unhappy. Quick, take me to the outhouse!"

Yankel awoke, swung his legs to the floor, and, disheveled, led the priest outside.

"It's his personality," he muttered, yawning. "The strangest personality. My brother has a wife, Cecilia, who's just the same. At the drop of a hat her stomach acts up. Yankel, she always tells me, when you die, Yankel, I won't be around no more to see you off!"

The following day Yankel started rushing around from the lawyer's office to the jail, from the jail to the government bureau, from the government bureau to the investigator's office. Father Ivan remained listless, depressed, and quiet.

Then came the day of the trial.

[. . .]*

* The manuscript breaks off at this point.

THE JEWESS

"The Jewess" is an unfinished manuscript of a novel that was found among the papers of Babel's friend Lev Ilich Slonim, in whose apartment in Leningrad Babel often stayed between 1927 and 1934. It is particularly interesting to follow Babel's creative process in this work-in-progress. Some passages read like notes that will be developed: "He took Boris aside, and peering at him with his blinking eyes (blinded from within), told him (he did this in an attempt to bond with his nephew who had strayed from the family) . . ." Much of the writing, however, already possesses a mature stylistic finish. "The Jewess" was never published in Russia, except for a Yiddish translation that appeared in the 1980s. Phrases in parentheses are Babel's.

1.

In observance of custom, the old woman sat on the floor for seven days. On the eighth day, she rose and went out onto the shtetl street. The weather was beautiful. A chestnut tree, drenched in sunlight, stood in front of the house, the candles on it already lit. When you think about the recently deceased on a beautiful day, the calamities of life seem even more cruel and inescapable. The old woman was wearing an old-fashioned black silk dress with a black floral print, and a silk kerchief. She had dressed up as she would have for her husband, who was now dead, so that the neighbors would not think that he and she were wretched in the face of death.

Old Esther Erlich headed to the cemetery. The withering petals of the flowers strewn across the burial mound had begun to curl. She touched them with her fingertips, and they crumbled and fell apart. Reb Alter, an old cemetery fixture, came hurrying up to her.

"Madame Erlich! For my prayers for the dead!"

She opened her bag, slowly counted out some silver coins, and handed them to Reb Alter in solemn silence.

Reb Alter, disconcerted by her silence, walked off on his crooked legs, holding a hushed conversation with himself. The sun followed his faded, crooked back. She stayed alone by the grave. The wind blew through the treetops, and they bent forward.

"I'm having a very bad time without you, Marius," Esther said. "I can't tell you how bad." She sat by the grave until noon, clutching some wilted flowers in her wrinkled hands. She clenched her fingers until they hurt, trying to dispel the memories. It is terrible for a wife to stand before a burial mound thinking back over thirty-five years of marriage, of the days and nights of marriage. Vanquished by her battle against these memories that were so painful to face, she trudged back home (in her silk dress) through the squalid shtetl.

Yellow rays filled the marketplace. Misshapen old men and women stood by their hawker's stands selling sunflower oil, withered onions, fish, and toffee for the children. In front of the house, Esther ran into her fifteen-year-old daughter.

"Mama!" the girl shouted in that particularly Jewish desperate woman's voice. "You're not going to torment us, are you? Boris has come!"

Esther's son stood fidgeting in the doorway in his military uniform, his chest covered with medals. The broken old woman, her damp face flushed and feverish, stopped in front of him.

"How dare you come too late to your father's deathbed! How dare you do that to him!"

Her children led her into the house.

She sat down on a little stool, the same stool she had sat on for seven days, and, staring into her son's eyes, tortured him with the tale of his father's death throes. It was an extremely detailed account. She left out nothing: the swelling in his legs, his nose turning blue the morning of the day he died, how she ran to the pharmacy to get oxygen balloons, the indifference of the people who stood around his deathbed. She left out nothing—not even how his father had called out for him as he died. She had knelt by his bed, warming his hands in hers. His father had weakly pressed her hand, ceaselessly uttering his son's name. He had stared with shining eyes, had repeated the name clearly, over and over. That one word, "Boris," had droned through the still room like the droning of a spindle. Then the old man had choked, there was a hoarse rattle in his breath, and he whispered, "Borechka." His eyes had bulged, and he wailed and moaned, "Borechka." The old woman had warmed his hands and said, "Here I am, your son is here!" The dying man's hand had filled with strength and began clutching and scratching the palms that were warming it. He began to shout that one word—"Borechka"—in a changed voice, high-pitched in a way it had never been during his life, and died with that word on his lips.

"How dare you come too late!" the old woman said to her son, who was sitting turned away from her at the table. They hadn't lit the lamps.

Boris sat in the dark, which had flooded the stillness. The old woman sat on the stool breathing heavily (with anger). Boris got up, his revolver rapping against the edge of the table, and left the room.

Half the night he roamed through the shtetl, his native shtetl. Clear serpentine reflections (of stars) quivered on the river. A stench rose from the hovels that stood along the bank. The three-hundred-year-old walls of the synagogue that had once withstood Khmelnitsky's hordes* had been battered with holes.

His native shtetl was dying. The clock of the centuries chimed the end of its defenseless life. "Is this the end, or is it a rebirth?" Boris asked himself. His heart was filled with so much pain that he didn't have the strength to answer this question. The school to which he had gone had been destroyed by Hetman Struk in 1919. The house in which Zhenya had once lived was now the labor exchange. He walked past the ruins, past the squat, crooked, sleeping houses, a hazy stench of poverty seeping out of their gates, and bade them farewell. His mother and sister were waiting for him at home. A dirty samovar was boiling on the table. A bluish piece of chicken lay next to it. Esther moved toward him with weak steps, pressed him to her, and wept. Her heart was pounding beneath her blouse, beneath her flabby, clammy skin—as was his heart, for their hearts were one. And the smell of his mother's shuddering flesh was so bitter, so pitiful, so typical of the Erlichs, that he felt a deep and boundless pity. The old woman cried, the all-embracing [one word illegible in the manuscript], shaking on his chest on which two Red Flag Medals hung. The medals were wet with her tears. That was the beginning of her recovery, and her resignation to loneliness and death.

---

* Bogdan Khmelnitsky, 1595–1657, a rebel Cossack leader who had led a successful Ukrainian rebellion against Polish rule in 1648. His army's ruthless massacre of Jews was still remembered centuries later in the shtetls of the region.

2.

The relatives, remnants of a large and ancient clan, arrived the following morning. There had been merchants in the family, adventurers, and
timid, poetic revolutionaries from the days of the People's Will Party.*
Boris's aunt, a medical orderly who had studied in Paris while living on
twenty rubles a month, had heard the speeches of Jaurès and Guesde.†
His uncle was a pitiful, luckless shtetl philosopher. Other uncles had
been grain merchants, traveling salesmen, and storekeepers, their liveli-
hoods knocked out from under them, a herd of confused, pathetic men,
a herd of men wearing long brown overcoats. Boris had to hear all over
again how his father's legs had become bloated, where he had developed bedsores, and who had run to the pharmacy to get oxygen. The
grain merchant, once a rich man, had been driven out of his house, and
now wrapped his old, thin legs in military leggings. He took Boris aside
and, peering at him with his blinking eyes (blinded from within), told
him (he did this in an attempt to bond with his nephew who had
strayed from the [one word illegible] family), that he had never expected that his father would manage to keep his body so smooth and clean.
They had looked at him while he was being washed, and he was as well
built and smooth as a young man. . . . And to think that some valve
somewhere in his heart, some tiny one-millimeter vein . . . His uncle
spoke these words probably thinking that as both he and the dead man
were born of the same mother, he probably had exactly the same heart
valve as his brother who had died a week ago.

The following day Boris's uncles asked him, first timidly, then with
the shudder of long suppressed-despair, if he could give them a recommendation so that they could join the trade union. Because of their former prosperity, none of the Erlichs were now accorded membership in
the trade union.

Their lives were indescribably sad. Their houses were collapsing
with leaks everywhere, they had sold everything, even their cupboards,

---

* Narodnaya Volya, the revolutionary terrorist organization that had assassinated Czar
Alexander II in 1881.
† Jules Guesde, 1845–1922, an early leader of the Marxist wing of the French Labor
Movement, and Jean Jaurès, 1859–1914, French socialist leader, were the foremost leftist orators
of the time.

and nobody would hire them. On top of that, they had to pay rent and water bills at much higher rates than members of the trade union. And they were old and suffering from terrible illnesses, harbingers of cancer and fatal disease, as were all members of ancient and dwindling Jewish families. Boris had long ago formed a theory about mankind—that people on their last legs should be put out of their misery as quickly as possible. But his mother was standing right next to him, her face resembling his face, her body like his was going to be in two or three decades, and through the closeness of his mother arose a feeling of fate, a feeling of their common fate, the fate of the bodies of all the Erlichs (in some respect all the same). He overcame his reservations and went to see the chairman of the Local Executive Committee. The chairman, a Petersburg worker, seemed to have been waiting all his life to tell someone how dismal it was to work on an Executive Committee in this damned former Jewish Pale of settlement, how difficult it was to resurrect these shtetls of the western provinces and lay the foundation for a new prosperity in these damned Jewish shtetls (of the damned southwest region) that were dying in misery (and like dogs).

For several days Boris kept seeing before him the cemetery of his native shtetl and the imploring eyes of his uncles, the former (devil-may-care?) traveling salesmen, who now dreamed of joining the trade union or the Labor Exchange. A few days passed. The Indian summer changed into autumn. A (slushy) shtetl rain was falling. Mud from the mountain, mud with rolling stones (like concrete) came flowing down from the mountain. The front room of the house was filled with water. Rusty bowls and Passover saucepans were put under the cracks in the roof. As they walked through the room they had to be careful where they stepped so they wouldn't trip over a bowl.

"Let's go," Boris said to his mother.

"Where to?"

"To Moscow, Mama."

"Aren't there enough Jews in Moscow?"

"Nonsense," Boris said. "Who cares what people say!"

She sat in the leaking room in her corner by the window from which she could see the pockmarked carriageway and her neighbor's collapsing house—and thirty years of her life. Sitting by the window and (sharing) her soul's tears and her old-woman's compassion for her sisters, brothers-in-law, and nephews, to whom fate had not granted a son like hers. Esther knew that sooner or later he would talk of going to Moscow and that she would give in. But before she did, she wanted to (torment herself and infuse her surrender with the sorrow of the shtetl . . .). She said that it pained her to death to leave without her husband, who had dreamed of Moscow as he had dreamed of leaving this godforsaken place to live (the rest of his life) more happily, from which you expect nothing more than peace and the happiness of others, to live with his son in this new (Promised) land. And now he lay in his grave, beneath the rain that had lashed down all night, while she was preparing to go to Moscow, where, word had it, people were happy, cheerful, spirited, full of plans (doing all kinds of special things). Esther said that it was hard for her to leave all her graves behind—of her fathers and her grandfathers, rabbis, *tsaddiks,* and Talmudists who lay under the gray (traditional) stones. She would never see them again. And how would he, her son, answer for her when her time came to die on foreign soil, among people who were so very foreign. . . . And then, how could she forgive herself if life in Moscow turned out to be pleasant? Her hands with their long (gout-ridden, twisted, soft, swollen) fingers trembled when Esther considered how unbearable it would be for her to be happy at such a time. Her damp, twisted fingers trembled, the veins on her yellow chest swelled and throbbed, the (shtetl) rain drummed on the iron roof. . . . For the second time since her son had come home, the little old Jewess in her galoshes wept. She agreed to go to Moscow because there was nowhere else for her to go, and because her son looked so (terribly) like her husband that she could not be parted from him, even though her husband, like everyone else, had had faults and pitiful little secrets, which a wife knows but never tells.

3.

Most of their arguments centered around what to take with them. Esther wanted to take everything, while Boris wanted to have done with it all and sell it off. But there was nobody in Kremenets to whom one could sell anything. The last thing the townsfolk needed was furniture. The dealers, angry men who had sprung up from God knows where, and who looked like undertakers, like visitors from the beyond, were only prepared to pay small change. They could only resell the merchandise to peasants. But Esther's relatives were quick to lend a helping hand. No sooner had they gotten over (the first doleful stirrings of soul) than they began to cart off whatever they could lay their hands on. And as, deep down, they were honest people, and not petty (pettily mercenary), the sight of this furtive (secretive) carting off was particularly sad (unbearable). Esther was taken aback. A sickly flush on her face, she tried to grab a snatching hand, but the quaking hand was covered in such pitiful sweat, and was so wrinkled, so old (edged with broken nails), that she (staggered back and in a flash) understood everything. She was horrified that anyone would have to stop someone in such a tormenting (offense), and that the people she had grown up with had gone out of their minds, trying to carry off cupboards and sheets.

Everything was sent to Moscow by train. Her relatives cried as they helped her tie her bundles. Sitting on the packed bales, they had come to their senses (their hearts were touched), and they said that they themselves would stay (in Kremenets)—they would never leave. The old woman [one word illegible] packed a kitchen trestle and a tub for boiling clothes. "You'll see, we'll need all this in Moscow!" she told her son. "After sixty years of life, am I supposed to remain with nothing but ashes in my soul and the kind of tears that flow even when you don't want to cry?" As their belongings were taken to the station, the old woman's hollow cheeks flushed, and a blind, urgent, passionate sparkle glittered in her eyes. She hurried through the besmirched, ransacked house, a force dragging her quaking shoulders along the wall from which torn strips of wallpaper hung.

The next morning, the day of their departure, Esther took her son and daughter to the cemetery, where, among oak trees that were centuries old, rabbis who had been killed by the Cossacks of Gonta and Khmelnitsky* lay buried under Talmudic gravestones. Esther went to her husband's grave, shuddered, and drew herself up. "Marius," she said (in a gasping voice), "your son is taking me to Moscow. Your son does not want me to be laid to rest at your side." Her eyes were fixed on the reddish mound, its earth spongy and crumbling. Her eyes grew wider and wider. Her son and daughter held her hands tightly. The old

---

*Ivan Gonta (d. 1768) and Bogdan Khmelnitsky, 1595–1657, were leaders of the Zaporozhian Cossacks who rebelled against Polish rule in Ukraine and were known for their ruthless massacres of Jews.

woman swayed, stumbled forward, and half closed her eyes. Her haggard hands, relinquished to her children, tensed, were covered in sweat, and grew limp. Her eyes grew wider and wider and blazed with light. She tore herself free, fell onto the grave in her silken dress, and began thrashing about. Her whole body was quaking, and her hand stroked the yellow earth and the withered flowers with greedy tenderness. "Your son, Marius, is taking me to Moscow!" she shouted, her shrill voice tearing through the Jewish cemetery. "Pray for him, that he will be happy!" She dragged her fingers, hooked and twisted as if she were knitting, over the earth that covered the dead man. Her son gave her his hand and she got up submissively. They walked along the path shaded by oak branches, and Boris's whole being blazed and surged as his tears pressed against his eyes and throat like rocks. He experienced the taste of tears that cannot break free and so must remain (inside a man). The old woman stopped by the gate. She freed her hand (pierced, drenched), on which sweat surged impetuously, like a subterranean spring, alternately boiling hot and deadly cold (frozen through), and waved to the cemetery and the grave as if she and her children were on a ship leaving port.

"Farewell, my sweet," she said (softly), without crying (or twitching). "Farewell."

And so the Erlich family left its native shtetl.

4.

Boris took his family to Moscow on the Sebastopol Express. He got tickets for a first-class compartment. They were taken to the station by Boychik, the shtetl comic, once known far and wide for his droll stories and massive black horses. He no longer had the horses, and his rickety cart was now drawn by a gigantic white jade with a drooping pink lip. Boychik himself had grown older, bent with rheumatism.

"Listen, Boychik, I'll be back next year," Esther said to his little bent back as the cart turned and pulled into the station. "You must keep well till then."

The hillock on Boychik's back became even more pointed. The white jade plodded through the mud on her stiff, gouty legs. Boychik turned around, his crimson eyelids raw and inflamed, his sash crooked, dusty tufts of hair growing out of the side of his face.—"(I don't think you will, Madame Erlich)," he said, and suddenly shouted to his horse: "The party's over! Off you go, now!"

The first-class railway car had been patched together out of several cars from Czarist times [one word illegible]. Through the wide, gleaming window Esther saw for the last time the huddled crowd of her relatives, rust-brown coats, soldiers' leggings, crooked smocks, her old sisters with their large, useless breasts, her brother-in-law Samuel, a former traveling salesman with his puffy, twisted face, her brother-in-law Efim, a former rich man whose withered, homeless feet were now wrapped in rags. They jostled each other on the platform (like . . .), and shouted words she could not hear as the train pulled out of the station. Her sister Genia went running after the train.

[One page of the original manuscript missing.]

[Boris showed] her Russia with so much pride and confidence, as if he, Boris Erlich, had himself created Russia, as if he owned it. And to some extent, he did. There was in everything a drop of his soul or of his blood, the blood of the corps commissar (of the Red Cossacks)— from the international train cars to the newly built sugar factories and refurbished train stations.

[Half a page in the manuscript crossed out.]

In the evening he ordered bed linen, and with childish pride showed his mother and sister how to turn on the blue night-light. With a big smile he revealed the secret of the little mahogany closet. Inside the closet there turned out to be a washstand—right there in the compartment! Esther lay beneath the cool sheets. Rocked by the oily bounce of the train's springs, she stared out into the blue darkness and (with her heart) listened to the breathing of her son. He tossed and called out in his sleep. Somebody, she thought, would definitely have to foot the bill for this palace hurtling through Russia with its lit chandeliers (and heated with sparkling copper tubes). This was a typically Jewish thought—such a thought would never have occurred to Boris. As they approached Moscow, he kept worrying whether Alexei Selivanov had received his telegram and would come to pick them up with the car. Alexei had received the telegram and did come with the car. The car was the Red Army headquarters' new thirty-thousand-ruble Packard, and in it the Erlichs drove to an apartment Boris had set up for them a while back in Moscow's Ostozhenka district. Alexei had even brought some furniture to the apartment. Esther was overwhelmed by the inexhaustible delight of the two-room apartment, as Boris showed her the kitchen with its gas stove, the bathroom with its own hot water boiler, and the pantry with its icebox. The rooms were beautiful. They were part of a house that had belonged to the deputy governor general of Moscow before the Revolution, and as Boris eagerly dragged his mother through kitchens, bathrooms, and mezzanines of the princely house, he was involuntarily fulfilling the call of his ancient Semitic blood. The cemetery and the grave of his luckless father, who had not lived to see happiness, had awakened in him the powerful passion for family which for so many centuries had sustained his people. At thirty-two, obeying this ancient command, he felt himself to be father, husband, and brother in one—the protector of the women, their breadwinner, their support—and he felt this with a passion, with the tormenting and stubborn tightening of the heart characteristic of his people. Boris was tortured by the thought that his father had not lived to see this, and wanted to make up for his having come too late to his father's deathbed by having his mother and sister pass from his father's hands into his own. And if his mother and sister were to fare better in his strong hands, that was simply due to the ruthlessness of life.

5.

Boris Erlich had been a student at the Institute of Psychology and Neurology (before the Revolution, all the other institutes had a restrictive enrollment quota for Jews). He had spent the summer of 1917 with his parents in the shtetl. He had trudged to all the restless villages nearby, explaining the basics of Bolshevism to the peasants. His propaganda rounds were hampered by his hooked nose, but not too much: back in 1917, people had more than noses on their minds. That same summer Alexei Selivanov, the son of a bookkeeper at the local council, came back from Siberian exile in Verkhoyansk. At home, while Alexei swallowed the cherry dumplings and liqueurs his mother made, he dug into the Selivanov family's history and found that they were descendants of

Selikha, a Zaporozhian Cossack commander.* Among the papers Alexei found there was even a lithograph of his ancestor wearing his Cossack jacket and sitting on a cardboard horse carrying his ceremonial mace. There was a faded inscription in Latin beneath the portrait, and Alexei claimed that he recognized the handwriting of Orlik, the Ukrainian chancellor in the days of Mazepa.† Alexei's romantic delving into the past coexisted with his membership in the Socialist Revolutionary Party.** His idols were Zhelyabov, Kibalchich, and Kalyayev.‡ At twenty-one, Alexei led a full life. His youthful passion fired up Erlich, the large-nosed student with the strange name. The two young men struck up a friendship, and Alexei became a Bolshevik when he realized that no other party in the world had as much battling, destroying, and rebuilding to do as the Bolshevik Party, filled as it was with mathematical and scientific passion. (Erlich supplied Alexei with books and the Communist Manifesto). After the Revolution, Alexei rounded up his shtetl friends: a nineteen-year-old Jew, who worked as a projectionist at the Chary Movie theater, a blacksmith, also a Jew, a few noncommissioned officers who were sitting around bored, and a few boys from a nearby village who had been discharged from the army. Alexei gave them horses, and their unit turned into the Insurgent Regiment of Red Ukrainian Cossacks. One of the former noncommissioned officers became the regiment's chief of staff, and Boris became its commissar. Alexei's regiment was fighting for a palpably good cause, its fighters lived together in camaraderie and died proudly in action, and each told taller tales than the next. Their ranks grew day by day, and the regiment experienced the fate of all the small rivulets that

---

* The Zaporozhian Cossacks, the Cossacks of the Dnieper River region, who during the sixteenth and seventeenth centuries had managed to stay politically autonomous both from Poland and Russia, briefly even forming a semi-independent state.

† Filipp Orlik, 1672–1742, served in the General Chancery of the Cossack government. Ivan Stepanovich Mazepa, 1644–1709, was a Cossack commander who became *hetman* (ruler) of Ukraine in 1687.

** The most important non-Bolshevik socialist party, suppressed by Lenin in 1921, after the Bolshevik victory in the Civil War.

‡ Andrei Ivanovich Zhelyabov, 1851–1881, Nikolai Ivanovich Kibalchich, 1853–1881, and Ivan Platonovich Kalyayev, 1877–1905, were leading members of the People's Will Party (Narodnaya Volya), a revolutionary terrorist organization. Kibalchich had been involved in the assassination of Czar Alexander II in 1881, and Kalyayev assassinated Grand Duke Sergei Alexandrovich, the governor general of Moscow in 1905.

flowed into the Red Army. The regiment turned into a brigade, the brigade into a division. Alexei's men battled renegade bands, Petlyura,* the White Army, and the Poles. By now all regiments already had their Political Divisions, Provision Units, Tribunals, and War Spoils Commissions.† In the campaign against General Wrangel's White Army, Alexei became a corps commander. He was twenty-four. Foreign newspapers wrote that Budyonny** and Alexei had invented new tactics and strategy of cavalry warfare. At the academy they began teaching the lightning raids of Alexei Selivanov. The students at the Military Academy went about solving exercises in strategy by studying the operations of the Ukrainian Cossack Corps. Alexei Selivanov and Boris Erlich, his irreplaceable commissar, were sent to study at the Military Academy, where they ended up studying their own operations along with the other students. In Moscow Alexei and Boris formed a commune with the former projectionist and one of the former noncommissioned officers. In the commune, as in the corps, honor and the spirit of camaraderie was high, and Boris clung to it with tormenting passion. Perhaps it was because his race had for so long been deprived of one of the most important human qualities—friendship, both behind the plow and on the field of battle. Boris experienced a need, a hunger for camaraderie and friendship—(to defend and be loyal to camaraderie)—with such vulnerability that his friendships were marked by fevered passion. But in his fervor, chivalry, and self-sacrifice, there was also something (attractive and) noble, which turned Boris's shabby room into a club for the "Red Marshals." This club truly blossomed when, instead of the standard-issue sausage and vodka, gefilte fish was served. The tin kettle was replaced by a samovar brought from Kremenets, and the tea was poured by the comforting hand of his old mother. It was many years

---

* Semyon Vasilevich Petlyura, 1879–1926, was one of the leading socialist leaders of Ukraine's unsuccessful fight for independence during the years of the Russian Civil War.

† In the new Soviet army, every regiment had representatives that reported back to Moscow and dealt with specialized day-to-day military issues. The Political Propaganda Division (Politotdel) dealt with the ideological education of the military, the Provision Units (Khoz-chast) with the acquiring and distribution of supplies, the Tribunals (Tribunaly) with military justice and the detection of counterrevolutionary activity in the ranks, and the War Spoils Commission (Trofeinaya Komissiya) was in charge of hindering looting and sending war spoils to the local military authorities.

** Semyon Mikhailovich Budyonny, 1883–1973, the commander of the First Cavalry and later a Marshal of the Soviet Union. One of the major figures in Babel's *Red Cavalry* stories.

since Alexei Selivanov and his brigade commanders had seen an old woman sitting behind a samovar. It was a pleasant change for them. The old woman was meek and timorous. And quiet as a mouse. But in her gefilte fish (and in her fingers that prepared the samovar) lay (the history of the Jewish people), a true history with a hefty dash of peppery passion.

6.

At first the gefilte fish caused trouble at their new apartment. One of the lodgers, a professor's wife, announced in the communal kitchen: God, did the apartment stink! And it was true. With the arrival of the Erlichs, even the hallway began to reek of garlic and fried onions.

I. BABEL.

XIII

✢

Plays

The events of 1926 proved to be a major turning point in Babel's career. In the previous three years his Odessa and RED CAVALRY stories had appeared in magazines and newspapers, making him one of the Soviet Union's most celebrated writers, and his collection of RED CAVALRY stories was published as a book. His first screenplay, SALT, based on the RED CAVALRY story of the same name, and the movie JEWISH LUCK, based on Shalom Aleichem's Menachem Mendel stories, for which Babel had written the subtitles, had premiered in 1925. Now Babel seized the opportunity to try his hand at playwriting. He based his first play, SUNSET, on his Odessa stories, whose protagonist was young Benya Krik, the "flamboyant" Jewish mobster who rules the Moldavanka (the Odessa neighborhood in which Babel was born) with an uncanny mix of ruthlessness, compassion, and his own peculiar brand of gangster chic. SUNSET premiered at the Baku Workers Theater on October 23, 1927, and played in Odessa, Kiev, and the celebrated Moscow Arts Theater. The reviews, however, were mixed. Some critics praised the play's powerful anti-bourgeois stance and its interesting "fathers and sons" theme. But in Moscow, particularly, critics felt that the play's attitude toward the bourgeoisie was contradictory and weak. SUNSET closed, and was dropped from the repertoire of the Moscow Arts Theater.

Babel wrote his second play, MARIA, in the early to mid-1930s. It was to be performed at the prestigious Vakhtangov Theater in Moscow, but was disallowed during rehearsals and subsequently never performed in the Soviet Union. Alexander Gladkov, an author present at a reading of the play that Babel gave, wrote in his diary that he felt the play's "simplicity and laconic quality" might be a problem. Babel also read the play to a small gathering in Sorrento, where he was visiting Gorky. After the reading, Gorky did not say anything critical to Babel, but in a scathing letter expressed his extreme doubts about the feasibility of staging it. "It is a well-crafted piece with many masterful traits and much subtle detail. But . . ." Gorky was shocked by Babel's "Baudelairean predilection for rotting meat. All the characters in your play, starting from the invalids, are putrid." He warned Babel of the play's dangerous subtexts. "Political inferences" would be made "that will be personally harmful to you."

SUNSET

A PLAY IN EIGHT SCENES

CHARACTERS

Mendel Krik — owner of a horse carting establishment. 62 years old.
Nekhama — his wife, 60.
Their children:
    Benya — a dandyish young man, 26.
    Lyovka — a hussar on leave, 22.
    Dvoira — an unmarried girl past her prime, 30.
Arye-Leib — *shamas* of the Carting Union Synagogue, 65.
Nikifor — the Kriks' chief driver, 50.
Ivan Pyatirubel — a blacksmith and friend of Mendel Krik, 50.
Ben Zkharia — a rabbi of the Moldavanka, Odessa's Jewish section, 70.
Fomin — a contractor, 40.
Evdokiya Potapovna Kholodenko — sells live and slaughtered chickens at
    the market. She is a corpulent old woman with a twisted hip, and an
    alcoholic. 50.
Marusia — her daughter, 20.
Ryabtsov — a tavern keeper.
Mitya — a waiter at the tavern.
Miron Popyatnik — a flute player at Ryabtsov's tavern.
Madame Popyatnik — his wife. A gossip with frantic eyes.
Urusov — clandestine solicitor. He rolls his *r*'s.
Semyon — a bald peasant.
Bobrinets — a loud Jew. He is loud because he is rich.
Weiner — a rich man with a speech impediment.
Madame Weiner — a rich woman.

Klasha Zubaryeva — a pregnant girl.
Monsieur Lazar Boyarsky — the owner of the Chef d'Oeuvre ready-to-wear
    clothes factory.
Senka Topun.
Cantor Zwieback.

The action takes place in Odessa in 1913

Scene One

The dining room in the KRIK *house. A low-ceilinged, homey, bourgeois room. Paper
flowers, chests of drawers, a gramophone, portraits of rabbis, and next to them photographs of the* KRIK *family: stony dark faces, bulging eyes, shoulders like cupboards.*

*The dining room has been prepared to receive guests. The table is covered with
a red tablecloth and bottles of wine, preserves, and pies.*

Old NEKHAMA KRIK *is making tea. To the side, on a small table, stands a boiling samovar.*

In the room, besides NEKHAMA, *are* ARYE-LEIB *and her son* LYOVKA, *in a hussar's
parade uniform. His peakless yellow cap is cocked to the side above his brick-red face, and
his military greatcoat is flung over his shoulders. Behind him he trails a curved sword.*
BENYA KRIK, *decked out like a Spaniard at a village fair, is knotting his tie.*

ARYE-LEIB: Ha, fine, Lyovka, very fine indeed! I, Arye-Leib the
    Moldavanka matchmaker and *shamas* at the carters' synagogue,
    am fully aware of what hacking things to pieces is all about!
    First they hack down reeds, then they start hacking down men!
    No one asks you whether you've got a mother or not! But
    explain this to me, Lyovka! Why can't a Hussar like you take an
    extra week off until your sister's happiness has been taken care
    of?

LYOVKA [*Laughs. His rough voice is thunderous.*]: An extra week? You're
    an idiot, Arye-Leib! An extra week off? The cavalry isn't the infantry,
    you know! The cavalry spits on the infantry! If I'm even an hour late,
    the sergeant major will drag me off to his office, squeeze the juice out
    of my soul and nose, and then have me court-martialed. Cavalrymen
    are judged by three generals, three generals covered with medals
    from the Turkish war.

ARYE-LEIB: Do they do this to everyone, or just to Jews?

LYOVKA: A Jew who climbs onto a horse stops being a Jew and becomes a Russian. You're such a blockhead, Arye-Leib! What's this got to do with Jews?

[DVOIRA's *face pokes through the half-opened door.*]

DVOIRA: Mama, a girl can beat her brains out in this house before she finds anything! Where did you put my green dress?

NEKHAMA [*Mumbles without looking up.*]: Look in those drawers.

DVOIRA: I've already looked, it's not there.

NEKHAMA: How about the wardrobe?

DVOIRA: It's not there either.

LYOVKA: Which dress is it?

DVOIRA: The green one with the frills.

LYOVKA: I guess Papa swiped it.

[DVOIRA *enters the room. She is half dressed,*
her face heavily rouged, her hair curled. She is tall and plump.]

DVOIRA [*In a dull voice.*]: Oy, I'm dying!

LYOVKA [*To his mother.*]: I bet you told him, you old cow, that Boyarsky is coming over today to take a look at Dvoira. Of course you did! Well, that's that, then! I saw Papa this morning. He harnessed Solomon the Wise and Muska, gulped some food, guzzled down his vodka like a hog, threw a green bundle into the cart, and drove off.

DVOIRA: *Oy,* I'm dying! [*She starts crying loudly, rips down the curtain from the window, jumps up and down on it, and throws it at her mother.*] There, take that!

NEKHAMA: May you die! May you die today!

[DVOIRA *runs out howling. The old woman shoves*
the curtain into a drawer.]

BENYA [*Knotting his tie.*]: Our darling papa, you see, won't cough up the dowry.

LYOVKA: The old bastard should have his throat cut, like a pig!

ARYE-LEIB: Is this the way you talk about your father, Lyovka?

LYOVKA: Well, he shouldn't be such a bastard!

ARYE-LEIB: Your father's at least a Sabbath older than you are!

LYOVKA: Then he shouldn't be such a boor!

BENYA [*Sticks a pearl pin into his tie.*]: Last year Syomka Munsh wanted Dvoira, but our dear papa simply wouldn't cough up the dowry, if you know what I mean. He made kasha with sauce out of him and threw him down the stairs!

LYOVKA: The old bastard should have his throat cut, like a pig!

ARYE-LEIB: As the sage Ibn Ezra once said of an unlucky matchmaker like myself, "Should you take it into your head to become a maker of candles, the sun will surely stick like a clod in the sky and never set again!"

LYOVKA [*To his mother.*]: A hundred times a day the old man kills us, and you stand there, dumb as a post! Dvoira's future bridegroom could turn up any minute now. . . .

ARYE-LEIB: It was about an unlucky man like myself that Ibn Ezra said, "Take it into your head to sew shrouds for the dead, and not one man will die from now to the end of time, amen!"

BENYA [*Has knotted his tie, taken off the crimson band that keeps his hair in place, donned a tight-fitting jacket, and poured himself a vodka.*]: Health to all present!

LYOVKA [*In a rough voice.*]: To our health!

ARYE-LEIB: May all go well!

LYOVKA: And may all go well!

[MONSIEUR BOYARSKY *rushes into the room.*
He is a cheerful, rotund man. He is an incessant talker.]

BOYARSKY: Greetings! Greetings! [*He introduces himself.*] Boyarsky, pleased to meet you, excessively pleased! Greetings!

ARYE-LEIB: Lazar, you said you would be here at four, and it's six o'clock already!

BOYARSKY [*Sits down and takes a glass of tea from old* NEKHAMA KRIK.]: God in heaven, we live in Odessa, and here in Odessa you have clients who squeeze the life out of you the way you squeeze pits out of a date—your best friends are ready to swallow you whole, suit and all, forget the salt! Cartloads of worries—a thousand scandals! When does a man have time to think about his health? You'll ask, what does a merchant need health for? I barely had time to get myself a hot seawater bath—and I came straight over!

ARYE-LEIB: You take seawater baths, Lazar?

BOYARSKY: Every day, like clockwork.

ARYE-LEIB [*To old* NEKHAMA.]: You can't get away for less than fifty kopecks a bath!

BOYARSKY: God in heaven, how fresh is the wine that flows in our Odessa! In the Greek Bazaar, Fankoni's—*

ARYE-LEIB: You eat at Fankoni's, Lazar?

BOYARSKY: I eat at Fankoni's.

ARYE-LEIB [*Triumphantly.*]: He eats at Fankoni's! [*To the old woman.*] You can't even get up from the table there for less than thirty kopecks—I won't tell you forty!

BOYARSKY: Forgive me, Arye-Leib, for daring—as a younger man—to interrupt you. Fankoni's costs me a ruble a day, even a ruble-and-a-half!

ARYE-LEIB [*Ecstatically.*]: What a spendthrift you are, Lazar! The world has never seen a rascal like you! A whole family can live on thirty rubles, send the children for violin lessons, and still save a kopeck—

[DVOIRA *rushes into the room. She is wearing an orange dress, and her powerful calves are squeezed into short, high-heeled boots.*]

ARYE-LEIB: This is our little Vera.

BOYARSKY [*Jumps up.*]: Greetings! Boyarsky!

DVOIRA [*Hoarsely.*]: Pleased to meet you.

[*Everyone sits down.*]

LYOVKA: Our Vera is a little dizzy today—too much ironing.

BOYARSKY: To get dizzy from ironing, that anyone can do, but not everyone can be a good person.

ARYE-LEIB: Thirty rubles a month up in smoke! . . . O Lazar, that you should ever have seen the light of day!

BOYARSKY: A thousand pardons, Arye-Leib, but this you must know about Boyarsky: he is not interested in capital. Capital is nothing.

---

* An elegant and expensive Odessan café that attracted a wealthy international clientele.

What Boyarsky is interested in is happiness! I ask you, dear friends, what good is it to me if my firm puts out a hundred—a hundred and fifty—suits, and then on top of that trousers to go with them, and then coats?

ARYE-LEIB [*To the old woman.*]: That's five rubles clean, a suit—I won't tell you ten!

BOYARSKY: So what good is my firm to me when my exclusive interest is happiness?

ARYE-LEIB: And my answer to you, Lazar, is that if we do business like human beings, and not like charlatans, then you will be guaranteed happiness till the day you die—may you live to be a hundred and twenty! And I tell you this as a *shamas*, and not as a matchmaker!

BENYA [*Pours wine.*]: May all our wishes come true!

LYOVKA [*In a rough voice.*]: To our health!

ARYE-LEIB: May all go well!

LYOVKA: And may all go well!

BOYARSKY: I was telling you about Fankoni's. Let me tell you a story, Monsieur Krik, about an impudent Jew. There I am, dropping in at Fankoni's, it's packed like a synagogue on Yom Kippur. Everyone is eating, spitting on the floor, worrying like crazy. One fellow worries because his business is bad, the next worries because business is good for his neighbor. And as for finding a place to sit down, forget it! . . . So then I bump into Monsieur Chapellon, a stately-looking Frenchman—and let me tell you, it's extremely rare for a Frenchman to be stately-looking—so he gets up to greet me, and invites me over to his table. Monsieur Boyarsky, he says to me in French, I hold your firm in the highest esteem, and I have some of the most marvelous coverings for coats—

LYOVKA: Coverings?

BOYARSKY: Coverings—heavy cloth for the outside of a coat—the most marvelous coverings for coats, he says to me, in French, and it would be an honor to invite you, as a firm, to drink two mugs of beer and eat ten crayfish with me—

LYOVKA: I love crayfish.

ARYE-LEIB: You'll be saying you love toads next.

BOYARSKY: —and eat ten crayfish with me—

LYOVKA [*In a rough voice.*]: I love crayfish!

ARYE-LEIB: Crayfish, toads—same difference.

BOYARSKY [*To* LYOVKA.]: Forgive me, Monsieur Krik, for saying this, but a Jew should not hold crayfish in high regard. This I am telling you from experience. A Jew who holds crayfish in high regard will go further with the female of the species than is right, he will utter obscenities at the table, and if he has children, then you can bet your last ruble that they'll turn into degenerates and billiard players. This I am telling you from experience. So let me tell you this story about an impudent Jew—

BENYA: Boyarsky.

BOYARSKY: Yes?

BENYA: Give me an estimate, off the cuff, how much a winter suit will cost me.

BOYARSKY: Double-breasted or single-breasted?

BENYA: Single-breasted.

BOYARSKY: What kind of coattails—round or pointed?

BENYA: Round coattails.

BOYARSKY: Whose cloth—yours or mine?

BENYA: Your cloth.

BOYARSKY: What cloth—English, Polish, or Muscovite?

BENYA: Which is best?

BOYARSKY: English cloth, Monsieur Krik, that's good cloth; Polish cloth is just sackcloth with a pattern on it; and Muscovite cloth is sackcloth without a pattern on it.

BENYA: I'll go for the English.

BOYARSKY: Your trimmings or mine?

BENYA: Your trimmings.

BOYARSKY: So how much will that cost you?

BENYA: How much will that cost me?

BOYARSKY [*Struck by a sudden idea.*]: Monsieur Krik, I'm sure we'll be able to give you a good deal!

ARYE-LEIB: I'm sure you'll be able to give him a good deal!

BOYARSKY: I'm sure we'll be able to give you a good deal—I was telling you about Fankoni's.

[*There is a clatter of metal-reinforced boot heels.* MENDEL KRIK *enters, carrying a whip, along with* NIKIFOR, *his head driver.*]

ARYE-LEIB [*Suddenly timid.*]: Let me introduce you. Mendel, this is Monsieur Boyarsky.

BOYARSKY [*Jumps up.*]: Greetings! Boyarsky!

[*Stomping with his boots, old* MENDEL *crosses the room, ignoring everyone. He throws down the whip, sits down on the couch, and stretches out his long, fat legs.* NEKHAMA *kneels down and begins pulling off her husband's boots.*]

ARYE-LEIB [*Stuttering.*]: Monsieur Boyarsky was telling us about his company. It puts out a hundred fifty suits a month—

MENDEL: So you were saying, Nikifor?

NIKIFOR [*Leaning against the doorpost, staring up at the ceiling.*]: I was saying, master, that people are laughing us out of town.

MENDEL: Why are they laughing us out of town?

NIKIFOR: People are saying that there are a thousand masters in your stable and seven Fridays in your week! Yesterday we carted wheat down to the harbor—so I went over to the office to get our money, and there they tell me—"Back off! The young master, Benchik, came over and gave us instructions to pay the money directly into the bank with a receipt."

MENDEL: Gave instructions?

NIKIFOR: Gave instructions!

NEKHAMA [*Has pulled off one of* MENDEL'*s boots and unwrapped his dirty leggings. He stretches out his other leg to her. She looks up at her husband with intense hatred and mutters through clenched teeth.*]: May you not live to see the light of day, you torturer!

MENDEL: So you were saying, Nikifor?

NIKIFOR: I was saying I was insulted by Lyovka today.

BENYA [*Drinks down his wine, his little finger extended.*]: May all our wishes come true!

LYOVKA: To our health.

NIKIFOR: We took the mare Freilin over to the blacksmith to be shod today. So Lyovka suddenly bursts in and starts shooting off his mouth, ordering Pyatirubel the blacksmith to line the horseshoes with rubber. So I say to him, excuse me, who does he think we are to be using rubber on our horseshoes? Police chiefs? Czars? Nicholas the Seconds?

The master, I tell him, said nothing to me about this. So Lyovka turns red as a beet and shouts: Who do you think *is* your master?

[NEKHAMA *has pulled off the second boot.* MENDEL *gets up. He yanks the tablecloth. Plates, pies, and preserves fall on the floor.*]

MENDEL: So who do you think *is* your master, Nikifor?

NIKIFOR [*Sullenly.*]: You are my master.

MENDEL: And if I am your master [*he goes over to* NIKIFOR *and grabs him by his shirt collar.*] . . . if I am your master, then tear to pieces anyone who dares set foot in my stables—tear out his heart, his tendons, his eyes!

[*He shakes* NIKIFOR *and then flings him to the side. Stooping forward, dragging his bare feet,* MENDEL *walks across the room to the door.* NIKIFOR *shuffles behind him. The old woman crawls on her knees to the door.*]

NEKHAMA: May you not live to see the light of day, you torturer!

[*Silence.*]

ARYE-LEIB: What if I told you, Lazar, that the old man didn't attend one of the better finishing schools?

BOYARSKY: I'd believe you, and you wouldn't even have to give me your word.

BENYA [*Gives* BOYARSKY *his hand.*]: I hope you'll come visit us some other time.

BOYARSKY: Well, families being what they are, there's always something going on—sometimes cold, sometimes hot. Good-bye! Good-bye! I'll come again some other time.

[BOYARSKY *hurries out.* BENYA *gets up, lights a cigarette, and throws his flashy coat over his arm.*]

ARYE-LEIB: Ibn Ezra once said about an unlucky matchmaker like myself, "Should you take it into your head to sew shrouds for the dead—

LYOVKA: The old bastard should have his throat cut, like a pig!

[DVOIRA *leans back in her chair and starts screaming.*]

LYOVKA: Ha, there you go! Dvoira is having a fit!

[*He pries open his sister's clenched teeth with a knife. She squeals louder and louder.* NIKIFOR *enters the room.* BENYA *flings his coat over his left arm, and with his right punches* NIKIFOR *in the face.*]

BENYA: Harness the bay horse to the buggy!

NIKIFOR [*A few drops of blood slowly trickle from his nose.*]: Give me my wages, I'm leaving.

BENYA [*Comes over to* NIKIFOR, *face-to-face, and speaks in a sweet and tender voice.*]: Nikifor, my dear friend, you will die today without eating supper!

Scene Two

Night. The KRIKS' *bedroom. Black wooden beams across the low ceiling. Blue moonlight weaves its way through the window.* MENDEL *and* NEKHAMA *are in a double bed. They are covered by a single blanket.* NEKHAMA, *her dirty gray hair disheveled, is sitting up in bed. She is grumbling in a low voice, grumbling endlessly.*

NEKHAMA: Other people live like people . . . other people buy ten pounds of meat for lunch, they make soup, they make meatballs, they make compote! The father comes home from work, everyone sits at the table, everyone eats, laughs. And us? God, oh, God, how dark my house is!

MENDEL: Let me be, Nekhama! Sleep!

NEKHAMA: And Benya, our little Benchik, as bright as the sun in the sky, and now look what he's come to! Today one policeman comes around, tomorrow another . . . one day people have a piece of bread in their hand, the next they find their legs in irons.

MENDEL: Let me breathe, Nekhama! Sleep!

NEKHAMA: And Lyovka! The child will come back from the army and also start marauding. What else is there for him to do? His father is a degenerate, he won't take his sons into his own business—

MENDEL: Let it be night, Nekhama! Sleep!

[*Silence.*]

NEKHAMA: The rabbi said, Rabbi Ben Zkharia . . . Come the new month, Ben Zkharia said, I won't let Mendel into the synagogue. The Jews won't allow me to—

MENDEL [*Throws off the blanket and sits up beside the old woman.*]: What won't the Jews allow?

NEKHAMA: Come the new moon, Ben Zkharia said—

MENDEL: What won't the Jews allow? And what have these Jews of yours ever given me?

NEKHAMA: They won't allow you in, into the synagogue.

MENDEL: A ruble with a chewed-off edge they gave me, these Jews of yours! And *you* they gave me, you old cow, and this bug-ridden grave!

NEKHAMA: And what did the Russian pork butchers give you? What did they give you?

MENDEL [*Lies back down.*]: Oh, this old cow is sitting on my head!

NEKHAMA: Vodka, that's what the pork butchers gave you, and a mouth full of foul language, a rabid dog's mouth. . . . He's sixty-two years old, God, sweet God, and he's as hot as an oven, strong as an oven!

MENDEL: Pull my teeth out, Nekhama! Pour Jewish soup into my veins! Break my back!

NEKHAMA: Hot as an oven. . . . God, how ashamed I am! [*She takes her pillow and lies down on the floor in the moonlight. Silence. Then her grumbling starts up again.*] Friday evening people go outside their gates, people play with their grandchildren—

MENDEL: Let it be night, Nekhama!

NEKHAMA [*Crying.*]: People play with their grandchildren . . .

[BENYA *enters the room. He is in his underwear.*]

BENYA: Haven't you had enough for today, my little lovebirds?

[MENDEL *sits up in bed. He looks at his son in shock.*]

BENYA: Or do I have to go to an inn to get some sleep?

MENDEL [*Gets out of bed. Like his son, he is in his underwear.*]: You ... you
dare come in here?

BENYA: Do I have to pay two rubles for a room in order to get some
sleep?

MENDEL: At night, at night you dare come in here?

BENYA: She's my mother. Do you hear me, you cheap bastard?

[*Father and son stand face-to-face in their underwear.
Slowly* MENDEL *moves closer and closer to his son. In the moonlight*
NEKHAMA's *disheveled head of dirty gray hair is trembling.*]

MENDEL: At night, at night you dare come in here. . . .

Scene Three

A tavern on Privoznaya Square. Night. RYABTSOV, *the tavern keeper—a stern, sickly
man—is at the counter reading the Bible. His drab, dusty hair is plastered down on both
sides of his head.* MIRON POPYATNIK, *a meek flutist, is sitting on a raised platform. They
call him the major. A weak, tremulous melody comes from his flute. Gray-haired, black-
mustached* GREEKS *sit at one of the tables playing dice with* SENKA TOPUN, BENYA
KRIK's *friend. In front of* SENKA *are a sliced watermelon, a Finnish knife, and a bottle of
Malaga wine. Two sailors are sleeping, their sculpted shoulders slumped on the table. In
a far corner* FOMIN, *the contractor, is meekly sipping soda water. A drunken woman—*
POTAPOVNA—*is heatedly trying to convince him of something.* MENDEL KRIK *is standing by a table in front. He is drunk, inflamed, colossal. With him is* URUSOV, *the solicitor.*

MENDEL [*Bangs his fist down onto the table.*]: It's dark! I feel like I'm in
a grave, Ryabtsov, in a black grave!

[MITYA *the waiter, a little old man with close-cropped silvery hair,
brings a lamp and puts it down in front of* MENDEL.]

MENDEL: I ordered all the lamps! I asked for singers! I ordered you to
bring me all the lamps in the tavern!

MITYA: They don't give us kerosene for free, you know. That's just how
it is—

MENDEL: It's dark in here!

MITYA [*To* RYABTSOV.]: He wants extra light.

RYABTSOV: That'll be a ruble.

MITYA: Here's a ruble.

RYABTSOV: Got it.

MENDEL: Urusov!

URUSOV: Present!

MENDEL: How much blood did you say runs through my heart?

URUSOV: According to science, two hundred *pood* of blood run through a man's heart every twenty-four hours. And in America they invented a—

MENDEL: Hold it! Hold it! . . . And if I want to go to America—is that free?

URUSOV: Totally free. You just up and go!

[POTAPOVNA *waddles over to the table, wiggling her crooked hip.*]

POTAPOVNA: Mendel, sweetie, it's not America we're going to, we're going to Bessarabia, to buy orchards.

MENDEL: You mean I just up and go?

URUSOV: According to science, you have to cross four seas—the Black Sea, the Ionian Sea, the Aegean Sea, the Mediterranean—and two world oceans, the Atlantic and the Pacific.

MENDEL: And you said a man can actually fly across the seas?

URUSOV: He can.

MENDEL: And can a man fly over mountains, high mountains?

URUSOV [*Sternly.*]: He can.

MENDEL [*Grabs his disheveled head.*]: There's no end, no limit. . . . [*To* RYABTSOV.] That's it, I'm going! I'm going to Bessarabia.

RYABTSOV: And what are you going to do in Bessarabia?

MENDEL: I'll do whatever I want!

RYABTSOV: What can you want?

MENDEL: Listen here, Ryabtsov, I'm still alive—

RYABTSOV: You're not alive if God killed you!

MENDEL: When is it he killed me?

RYABTSOV: How old did you say you were?

A VOICE FROM THE TAVERN: All in all, he's sixty-two!

RYABTSOV: It's sixty-two years that God's been killing you.

MENDEL: Listen Ryabtsov, I'm a lot cleverer than God.

RYABTSOV: Maybe you're cleverer than the Russian God, but not cleverer than the Jewish God.

[MITYA *brings in another lamp. Following him in single file are four fat, sleepy girls in grease-stained smocks. Each is carrying a lit lamp. A blinding light fills the tavern.*]

MITYA: Well, a bright and happy Easter to you! Girls! Surround this poor fool with lamps!

[*The girls put down the lamps in front of* MENDEL. *The radiance lights up his crimson face.*]

A VOICE FROM THE TAVERN: So we're turning night into day, Mendel?
MENDEL: There is no end!
POTAPOVNA [*Pulls* URUSOV *by the sleeve.*]: Sir, I beg you, please, have a drink with me. . . . You see, I sell chickens at the market, and those damn peasants always foist the oldest and scrawniest hens on me. Do I have to be chained to those damn hens? My daddy was a gardener, the best gardener that ever was! If an apple tree grows wild, you should see me prune it!
A VOICE FROM THE TAVERN: Are we turning Monday into Sunday, Mendel?
POTAPOVNA [*Her jacket has fallen open over her fat breasts. Vodka, heat, and rapture are stifling her.*]: Mendel will sell off his business and, with the Lord's help, we'll get some money and set off with my pretty daughter for those orchards. Lime blossoms, sir, will rain down on us, you know. . . . Mendel, darling, I'm a gardener, you know, I'm my daddy's daughter!
MENDEL [*Walks over to the counter.*]: Ryabtsov, I used to have eyes . . . listen to me, Ryabtsov, my eyes were stronger than telescopes, and what did I do with my eyes? My legs ran faster than locomotives, my legs could walk on water, and what did I do with my legs? I ran from eating slops to the outhouse, from the outhouse to eating slops. I've mopped floors with my face, but now I'm going to garden!
RYABTSOV: So go ahead and garden! Who's stopping you?

A VOICE FROM THE TAVERN: I'm sure there are one or two people at home who might very well stop him! They'll step on his tail, and that'll be that!

MENDEL: I ordered songs! Hey, you, musician! Let's have a military tune. . . . You're boring me to death! Come on, let's have some life here! Come on!

[*Quavering, faltering,* MIRON POPYATNIK's *flute lets out a piercing melody.* MENDEL *dances, stamping his iron-shod boots.*]

MITYA [*Whispering to* URUSOV.]: Are you ready for Fomin, or is it early yet?

URUSOV: It's early yet. [*To the musician.*] Go for it, Major!

A VOICE FROM THE TAVERN: There's no point him going for it, the singers are here. Pyatirubel has dragged in the singers.

[*The singers enter—blind men in red shirts. They bump into chairs, waving their canes in front of them.* PYATIRUBEL, *the blacksmith, is leading them. He is a boisterous man, a friend of* MENDEL's.]

PYATIRUBEL: I dragged these devils out of their beds. We're not going to play, they tell me. It's night, they tell me, night all over the world, we can't play anymore. . . . Do you know who I am, I tell them!

MENDEL [*Throws himself at the lead singer, a tall, pockmarked blind man.*]: Fedya, I'm going to Bessarabia!

THE BLIND MAN [*In a thick, deep bass.*]: Good luck, master!

MENDEL: A song, one last song for me!

THE BLIND MAN: Shall we sing "The Glorious Sea"?

MENDEL: One last song!

THE BLIND MEN [*Start tuning their guitars. They begin singing in deep bass voices.*]:

> "O holy Baikal—glorious sea,
> My barrel of salmon, my ship so free!
> Hey, oarsman, whip the waves to-and-fro,
> For this brave man has far to go."

MENDEL [*Hurls an empty bottle at the window. The window shatters.*]:
   Hit it!

PYATIRUBEL: Damn! He's a hero, the son-of-a-bitch!

MITYA [*To* RYABTSOV.]: How much shall we charge for the window?

RYABTSOV: That'll be a ruble.

MITYA: Here's a ruble.

RYABTSOV: Got it.

THE BLIND MEN [*Sing.*]:

> *"Long was I shackled in heavy chains,*
> *Over mountains I wandered in the rains.*
> *An old comrade helped me run,*
> *And I survived to see the sun."*

MENDEL [*With a blow of his fist he knocks out the window frame.*]: Hit
   it!

PYATIRUBEL: He's Satan incarnate, the old bastard!

VOICES FROM THE TAVERN:
   Go for it! Now he's really celebrating!
   What do you mean, really celebrating? For him this is normal!
   It can't be, someone must have died!
   No one's died! This is his normal celebrating!
   So, what's the reason? What's he celebrating?

RYABTSOV: Go find the reason! With one man it's money—he celebrates his wealth, with the next it's lack of money—he celebrates
   his poverty. People are always celebrating.

[*The song rings out louder and louder. The sound of the guitars reverberates*
   against the walls, and inflames hearts. A star flickers through the broken
   window. The sleepy girls stand by the door and sing, propping up
   their breasts with their rough hands. A sailor, his big legs
   spread apart, sways and sings in a clear tenor.]:

> *"Shilka and Nerchinsk no longer scare me,*
> *Guards in the mountains did not snare me,*
> *By beasts of the forest I wasn't torn apart.*
> *Henchmen's bullets didn't pierce my heart."*

POTAPOVNA [*Drunk and happy.*]: Mendel, darling, drink with me! Let's drink to my sweet pretty daughter!

PYATIRUBEL: He punched the post office clerk in the face! That's the way the old dog is! Then he ripped out the telegraph poles and carried them home on his back. . . .

> "I walked all night and all day long,
> With watchful eye through towns I flew.
> Village women gave bread to make me strong,
> And village men the tobacco they grew."

MENDEL: Break my back, Nekhama! Pour Jewish soup into my veins!

[*He throws himself onto the floor, rolls about, moans, laughs.*]

VOICES FROM THE TAVERN:
He's like an elephant . . .
I've seen elephants cry real tears . . .
You're lying! Elephants don't cry . . .
I tell you, I've seen them cry real tears . . .
At the zoo once I taunted an elephant . . .

MITYA [*To* URUSOV.]: Are you ready for Fomin, or is it early yet?

URUSOV: It's early yet.

[*The singers sing with all their might. The song thunders. The quivering, quaking guitars play full force.*]

> "O holy Baikal—O glorious sea,
> A glorious sail, my caftan fluttering free!
> Hey oarsman, whip the waves to and fro,
> I hear the thunder louder grow."

[*The blind men sing the last lines with vehement, joyful, weeping voices. Finishing the song, they rise and leave as one.*]

MITYA: Is that all?

THE LEAD SINGER: That's all.

MENDEL [*Jumps up.*]: I want a war song! Musicians, some life!

MITYA [*To* URUSOV.]: Is it time for Fomin, or is it early yet?

URUSOV: It's time.

[MITYA *winks at* FOMIN, *who is sitting in a far corner.*
FOMIN *quickly walks over to* MENDEL's *table.*]

FOMIN: I wish you a pleasant evening.

URUSOV [*To* MENDEL.]: Now, my dear friend, this is what we'll do—there's a time for work, and a time for play. [*He takes out a piece of paper covered with writing.*] Shall I read it out loud?

FOMIN: If you're not in the mood to dance, then I guess you should.

URUSOV: Should I just read the final amount?

FOMIN: I am in agreement with your suggestion.

MENDEL [*Stares at* FOMIN *and moves away.*]: I ordered some songs!

FOMIN: Don't worry, we'll sing, we'll celebrate, and when it's time to die, we'll die!

URUSOV [*Reads, rolling his r's.*]: "In accordance with the aforementioned points, I cede my carting establishment, with all its assets, as itemized below, to Vasili Eliseyevich Fomin—"

PYATIRUBEL: Fomin, you clown, do you realize what horses you're buying? These horses have carted millions of bushels of corn and half the world's coal! With these horses you're dragging away everything we've got here in Odessa!

URUSOV: "—in total, for the sum of twelve thousand rubles, of which a third is to be paid on signing, with the additional sum—"

MENDEL [*Points at the* TURK, *serenely smoking his hookah in the corner.*]: That man sitting there, he's judging me.

PYATIRUBEL: That's true, he's judging you. . . . Come on, let's drink to it! [*To* FOMIN.] Just watch, he's going to kill somebody!

FOMIN: I doubt it.

RYABTSOV: You're crazy, you fool! That man over there, that Turk, is a holy man!

POTAPOVNA: I'm daddy's little girl.

FOMIN: Right here, Mendel, that's where you have to sign.

POTAPOVNA [*Thumps* FOMIN *on the chest.*]: This is where he keeps his money, that's where it is!

MENDEL: I should sign, you said? [*Dragging his feet, he walks across the tavern to the* TURK *and sits down next to him.*] Ha, the girls I've had in my time, my dear fellow! The happiness I have seen! I built a house, I had sons—and the price they're offering me for all that, my dear fellow, is twelve thousand! And then that's that—you lie down and die!

[*The* TURK *bows, and with his hand touches first his heart and then his forehead.* MENDEL *kisses him tenderly on the lips.*]

FOMIN [*To* POTAPOVNA.]: Are you trying to make a Yenkel of me?
POTAPOVNA: He'll sell, Vasili Eliseyevich! On my life, he'll sell!
MENDEL [*Returns to his table, shaking his head.*]: How boring!
MITYA: What's boring is that you have to pay up!
MENDEL: Go away!
MITYA: No, you have to pay!
MENDEL: I'll kill you!
MITYA: Then you'll pay for that too!
MENDEL [*Lays his head on the table and spits. Saliva hangs from his mouth like a rubber band.*]: Go away, I want to sleep. . . .
MITYA: You won't pay? *Oy,* I'll kill him!
PYATIRUBEL: Hold on a minute before you start killing him! First, how much have you been swindling out of him per pint?
MITYA [*Flares up.*]: I'm no pushover! I'll rip you to pieces!

[*Without lifting his head,* MENDEL *pulls from his pocket some coins and throws them. They roll on the floor.* MITYA *runs after them, picking them up. A sleepy girl blows out the lamps. It is dark.* MENDEL *sleeps, his head resting on the table.*]

FOMIN [*To* POTAPOVNA.]: You couldn't hold back, could you? Your tongue scampers like a running dog! You ruined everything!
POTAPOVNA [*Wiping her tears from her deep, grimy wrinkles.*]: Vasili Eliseyevich. It's my daughter I'm sorry for!
FOMIN: You don't know what sorrow is yet!
POTAPOVNA: The Yids have surrounded us like lice!
FOMIN: A Yid is no obstacle for a clever man.

POTAPOVNA: He will sell, Vasili Eliseyevich! He'll swagger about a bit, but then he'll sell!

FOMIN [*Slowly, menacingly.*]: But if he doesn't sell, then I swear to you, old woman, by Jesus Christ our Lord, I will come for you and tear the skin off your back!

Scene Four

POTAPOVNA's *attic.* POTAPOVNA *is wearing a colorful new dress, and is leaning out the window chatting with a neighbor. There is a view of the harbor and the sparkling sea from the window. On the table is a big pile of purchases: rolls of cloth, shoes, a silk umbrella.*

NEIGHBOR'S VOICE: Come over and show off some of your new things!

POTAPOVNA: Don't worry, I'll be over to see you!

NEIGHBOR'S VOICE: Here we've been selling chickens in the same market row for nineteen years now, and suddenly—no more Potapovna!

POTAPOVNA: Maybe I won't have to stay chained to those damn chickens for the rest of my life after all. It looks now like I won't have to suffer all my life.

NEIGHBOR'S VOICE: It looks like you won't.

POTAPOVNA: I bet people can't believe my luck!

NEIGHBOR'S VOICE: No, they can't! Everyone would want to have your luck! You could bake it and sell it by the pound!

POTAPOVNA [*Laughs, her large body shaking.*]: Not everyone, you see, has a pretty daughter.

NEIGHBOR'S VOICE: They say, though, your daughter's a bit too skinny.

POTAPOVNA: Don't worry, dear! The nearer to the bone, the sweeter the meat!

NEIGHBOR'S VOICE: They say his sons are scheming against you.

POTAPOVNA: The girl will outweigh the sons.

NEIGHBOR'S VOICE: That's what I say, too!

POTAPOVNA: It's not like an old man will just drop a young girl like that.

NEIGHBOR'S VOICE: I hear he'll buy you some orchards.

POTAPOVNA: So, what else are people saying?

NEIGHBOR'S VOICE: Nothing, really, they're just prattling. I can't make heads or tails of it!

POTAPOVNA: I can! I definitely can! What are they saying about the linen?

NEIGHBOR'S VOICE: They say the old man set you up with fifteen yards.

POTAPOVNA: Thirty-five yards!

NEIGHBOR'S VOICE: A pair of shoes . . .

POTAPOVNA: Three pair!

NEIGHBOR'S VOICE: When old men fall in love—it's deadly!

POTAPOVNA: Yes, it looks like we won't have to stay chained to those damn chickens. . . .

NEIGHBOR'S VOICE: I guess you won't! Come on, dress up and hop over here to show off some of your new things.

POTAPOVNA: I'll be over in a bit! See you later, dear!

NEIGHBOR'S VOICE: See you later, dear!

[POTAPOVNA *leaves the window. She waddles about the room humming, and opens the closet. She climbs onto a chair and reaches up to the top shelf, where there is a big bottle of liquor. She drinks, and then eats a cream puff.* MENDEL, *festively dressed, enters the room with* MARUSIA.]

MARUSIA [*Boisterously.*]: Look where our little birdie has hopped up to! Mama, run over to Moseyka, will you?

POTAPOVNA [*Climbing down from the chair.*]: What do you want me to get?

MARUSIA: Some watermelons, and a bottle of wine, and half a dozen smoked mackerel. . . . [*To* MENDEL.] Give her a ruble!

POTAPOVNA: A ruble won't be enough.

MARUSIA: Don't try that on me! It'll be enough, there'll even be change!

POTAPOVNA: A ruble really won't be enough.

MARUSIA: It will! Come back in an hour. [*She shoves her mother out the door, slams it shut, and turns the key.*]

POTAPOVNA'S VOICE: I'll be sitting by the gate! If you need me, call!

MARUSIA: Fine! [*She throws her hat onto the table, shakes out her golden hair, and starts plaiting it into a braid. In a ringing voice full of strength and joy, she resumes her interrupted story.*] So we arrive at the cemetery, we look—it's one o'clock and the funeral is over. No one's there, only people kissing in the bushes. My godfather's grave was so pretty, you wouldn't believe it! So I took out the booze, the

Madeira you gave me, two bottles of it, and ran to get Father Yoann. You know Father Yoann—he's the little old man with little blue eyes.

[MENDEL *is watching* MARUSIA adoringly. He is trembling and mumbles something in answer—what, is unclear]

MARUSIA: Father Yoann sang the psalms for the dead, then I poured him a glass of Madeira, wiped the glass with a towel, and he drank. I poured him a second. [MARUSIA *has finished braiding her hair, and fluffs the end of her braid. She sits down on the bed, and unties the laces of her fashionable yellow boots.*] Xenia, in the meantime, is acting like she's forgotten she's at her father's grave. She's putting on airs, acting like a mouse in a bag of wheat, all made up and everything, ogling her fiancé, Sergei Ivanovich, who all the while is making me one sandwich after another! So to spite her I say: Excuse me, Sergei Ivanovich, shouldn't you be paying at least a little attention to your fiancée, Xenia Matveyevna? Though I said it straight out, it went in one ear and out the other! So we all drank the Madeira you gave me. [MARUSIA *takes off her boots and her stockings. She walks barefoot to the window and pulls the curtain shut.*] My godmother couldn't stop crying, but then got pink in the face like a little girl, so pretty, you wouldn't believe it! I was drinking too—so I say to Sergei Ivanovich [MARUSIA *uncovers the bed.*]: C'mon, let's all go to Langeron beach for a swim! And he says: Okay, let's go! [MARUSIA *laughs and struggles to take off her dress, which is too tight.*] And I bet you Xenia's back is covered with pimples, and she hasn't washed her feet in three years—you should have heard some of the things she called me! [MARUSIA *is hidden from her head to her waist by the dress she is trying to struggle out of.*] Ha, she tells me, you're just acting up, all snooty, hankering after the old man's money—ha, they won't let you get your hands on it! [MARUSIA *pulls off the dress and jumps into the bed.*] So I say to her—you know what, Xenia, darling—I say to her—let sleeping dogs lie! Sergei Ivanovich hears us and dies laughing! [*She stretches out her exquisite, bare, girlish arm to* MENDEL, *and pulls him toward her. She takes off his jacket, and throws it on the floor.*] So . . . come here and say, "Marusia darling!"

MENDEL: Marusia, darling!

MARUSIA: Say: "Marusia, my sweet little darling!"

[*The old man wheezes, shivers, half laughing, half crying.*]

MARUSIA [*Sweetly.*]: You ugly little pugface, you!

Scene Five

The Carting Union Synagogue in the Moldavanka, Odessa's Jewish quarter. Friday evening worship. Lit candles. CANTOR ZWIEBACK, *wearing a tallith and boots, is standing in the pulpit. The congregation—red-faced carters—is in deafening communion with God, rocking back and forth, spitting, wandering about the synagogue. Stung by the sudden bee of grace, they emit loud exclamations, sing along with the cantor in rough voices, falter and start muttering to themselves, and then loudly start lowing again, like oxen awakened from slumber. In the depths of the synagogue two ancient Jews—bony, hunchbacked giants, their long yellow beards swept to the side—are bent over a volume of the Talmud.* ARYE-LEIB, *the shamas, marches grandly back and forth between the rows of worshipers. A fat man with flushed, puffy cheeks is sitting on the front bench with his ten-year-old son between his knees. He is forcing the boy to look at the prayer book.* BENYA KRIK *is sitting on a side bench. Behind him sits* SENKA TOPUN. *They give no sign that they know each other.*

CANTOR [*Proclaims.*]: Lkhu nranno ladonai noriio itsur isheinu!

[*The carters start singing along. The drone of prayer.*]

CANTOR: *Arboim shono okut nbdoir vooimar* . . . [*In a throttled voice.*] Arye-Leib, rats!

ARYE-LEIB: *Shiru ladonai shir khodosh* . . . *Oy*, let's sing a new song to God! [*He goes over to a praying* JEW.] How are hay prices doing?

THE JEW [*Rocking back and forth.*]: They're up.

ARYE-LEIB: A lot?

THE JEW: Fifty-two kopecks.

ARYE-LEIB: We'll hold out—watch it hit sixty!

CANTOR: *Lifnei adonai ki vo, ki vo mishpoit goorets* . . . Arye-Leib, rats!

ARYE-LEIB: Enough already, you ruffian!

CANTOR [*In a throttled voice.*]: If I see one more rat, there'll be trouble!

ARYE-LEIB [*Serenely.*]: *Lifnei adonai ki vo, ki vo . . . Oy,* I am standing, *oy,* I am standing before God . . . where do oats stand?

SECOND JEW [*Without interrupting his prayer.*]: A ruble and four, a ruble and four!

ARYE-LEIB: I'm going crazy!

SECOND JEW [*Rocks back and forth bitterly.*]: It'll hit a ruble ten, it'll hit a ruble ten!

ARYE-LEIB: I'm going crazy! *Lifnei adonai ki vo, ki vo . . .*

[*Everyone is praying. In the silence, snippets of muffled conversation between* BENYA KRIK *and* SENKA TOPUN *are heard.*]

BENYA [*Bends over his prayer book.*]: Well?

SENKA [*From behind* BENYA.]: I have a job in the works.

BENYA: What job?

SENKA: Wholesale.

BENYA: What is it?

SENKA: Cloth.

BENYA: A lot?

SENKA: A lot.

BENYA: Police?

SENKA: Don't worry.

BENYA: Night watchman?

SENKA: He's in on it.

BENYA: Neighbors?

SENKA: They've agreed to be asleep.

BENYA: What cut d'you want?

SENKA: Half.

BENYA: Forget it.

SENKA: Why, as it is, you're about to lose your inheritance.

BENYA: I'm going to lose my inheritance, am I?

SENKA: So where do you stand?

BENYA: Forget it!

[*There is a gunshot—*CANTOR ZWIEBACK *has shot a rat that was running past the altar. The bored ten-year-old, trapped between his father's knees, flails about, trying to break loose.* ARYE-LEIB *stands*

frozen to the spot, his mouth hanging open. The TALMUDISTS
raise their large, indifferent faces.]

THE FAT MAN WITH THE FLUSHED CHEEKS: Zwieback! That's a pretty low-down trick!

CANTOR: My understanding was that I would pray in a synagogue, not a rat-infested pantry! [*He clicks open his revolver and throws the empty cartridge on the floor.*]

ARYE-LEIB: *Oy,* you bastard! *Oy,* you lout!

CANTOR [*Pointing at the dead rat with his revolver.*]: Look at this rat, O Jews, call in the people! Let the people judge if this is not a rat the size of a cow!

ARYE-LEIB: Bastard! Bastard! Bastard!

CANTOR [*Cold-bloodedly.*]: May there be an end to these rats!

[*He wraps himself up in the* tallith *and holds a tuning fork to his ear. The boy finally wriggles free from his father's knees, dashes over to the cartridge, snatches it up, and runs off.*]

FIRST JEW: All day long you break your neck working, you come to the synagogue to relax a little—and then this!

ARYE-LEIB [*Shrieks.*]: Jews, this is a sham! Jews, you know not what is taking place here! The Milkmen's Union is paying this bastard an extra ten rubles! So why don't you go to the milkmen, you bastard, and kiss their you-know-whats!

SENKA [*Bangs his fist down on his prayer book.*]: Can we have some quiet? This isn't a marketplace!

CANTOR [*Solemnly.*]: *Mizmoir ldovid!*

[*Everyone prays.*]

BENYA: So?

SENKA: There are people we can use.

BENYA: What people?

SENKA: Georgians.

BENYA: They have weapons?

SENKA: They have weapons.

BENYA: Where do you know them from?

SENKA: They live next to your buyer.

BENYA: What buyer?

SENKA: The one who's buying your business.

BENYA: What business?

SENKA: Your business—your lands, your house, your carting establishment.

BENYA [*Turns around.*]: Are you crazy?

SENKA: He said so himself.

BENYA: Who said?

SENKA: Mendel, your father, said so himself! He's going with Marusia to Bessarabia to buy orchards.

[*The hum of prayer. The* JEWS *are moaning intricately.*]

BENYA: Are you crazy?

SENKA: Everyone knows it.

BENYA: Swear it's true!

SENKA: May I not see happiness in this life!

BENYA: Swear on your mother!

SENKA: May I find my mother lying in a pool of blood!

BENYA: Swear again, you piece of shit!

SENKA [*Scornfully.*]: You're such a fool!

CANTOR: *Borukh ato adonai . . .*

Scene Six

The KRIKS' *courtyard. Sunset. It is seven o'clock in the evening.* BENYA *is sitting by the stable on a cart with its shafts raised, cleaning a revolver.* LYOVKA *is leaning against the stable door.* ARYE-LEIB *is explaining the profundities of* The Song of Songs *to* IVAN, *the boy who had run out of the synagogue on Friday evening.* NIKIFOR *is nervously pacing up and down the courtyard. He is obviously worried about something.*

BENYA: The time is coming! Make way for time!

LYOVKA: He should have his throat cut, like a pig!

BENYA: The time is coming. Step aside, Lyovka! Make way for time!

ARYE-LEIB: *The Song of Songs* teaches us: "By night on my bed I sought him whom my soul loveth"—What does the great commentator Rashi tell us about these words?

NIKIFOR [*Points at* BENYA *and* LYOVKA, *and says to* ARYE-LEIB]: Look at them! They've planted themselves by the stable like oak trees!

ARYE-LEIB: This is what the great Rashi tells us: "By night" means "by day and by night." "On my bed I sought"—who was seeking? Rashi asks. Israel was seeking! The People of Israel were seeking! "Him whom my soul loveth"—whom does Israel love? Rashi asks! Israel loves the Torah, and the Torah loves Israel!

NIKIFOR: What I want to know is, what are they loafing by the stable for?

BENYA: That's right, go on shouting!

NIKIFOR [*Pacing up and down the courtyard.*]: I know what I know. . . . My horse collars keep disappearing. I can suspect whoever I want!

ARYE-LEIB: Here an old man is trying to teach the law to a child, and you, Nikifor, keep interfering!

NIKIFOR: Why have they planted themselves by the stable like damn oak trees?

BENYA [*Takes his revolver apart and cleans it.*]: Nikifor, I see you're all nerves.

NIKIFOR [*Shouts, but his voice is weak.*]: I'm not your slave! If you want to know, I have a brother who lives out in the country, still in his prime! If you want to know, my brother would gladly take me in!

BENYA: Shout, shout as much as you want before you die!

NIKIFOR [*To* ARYE-LEIB.]: Old man, tell me why they're doing this to me!

ARYE-LEIB [*Raises his bleary eyes and looks at* NIKIFOR.]: I'm trying to teach the law, and you're bellowing like a cow! Is this how things should be in this world?

NIKIFOR: Your eyes are open, old man, but you do not see!

[NIKIFOR *leaves.*]

BENYA: Our Nikifor seems a little worried!

ARYE-LEIB: "By night on my bed I sought . . ." Whom was she seeking? What does Rashi teach us?

THE BOY: Rashi teaches us: "She was seeking the Torah."

[*Loud voices are heard.*]

BENYA: The time is coming. Step aside, Lyovka! Make way for time!

[MENDEL, BOBRINETS, NIKIFOR, *and* PYATIRUBEL
enter. PYATIRUBEL *is slightly tipsy.*]

BOBRINETS [*Deafeningly loud.*]: If you're not going to cart my wheat down to the harbor, Mendel, then who the hell will? If I'm not going to come to you Mendel, then who should I go to?

MENDEL: I'm not the only carter in the world. There's other carters besides me.

BOBRINETS: You're the only carter in Odessa—or are you trying to send me over to Butsis with his three-legged mules, or to Zhuravlenko with his broken-down tubs?

MENDEL [*Not looking at his sons.*]: Someone's hanging around my stables again!

NIKIFOR: They've struck root there, like damn oak trees.

BOBRINETS: You'll harness ten pairs of horses for me tomorrow, Mendel, you'll cart the wheat for me, you'll get the money, down a bottle of vodka, sing a few songs. . . . Ai, Mendel!

PYATIRUBEL: Ai, Mendel!

MENDEL: Why are people hanging around my stables?

NIKIFOR: Master, for God's sake!

MENDEL: Well?

NIKIFOR: Run for it, master . . . your sons . . .

MENDEL: My sons what?

NIKIFOR: Your sons are out to get you!

BENYA [*Jumps down from the cart. His head down, he speaks distinctly.*]: Papa, I happened to hear, from strangers, no less—both my brother, Lyovka, and I, we both heard—that you intend to sell the family business into which we have sunk a gold ruble or two and our own sweat!

[*Neighbors working in their yards come to see what is happening.*]

MENDEL [*Looking down.*]: People, neighbors . . .

BENYA: Did we hear right, me and my brother Lyovka?

MENDEL: People, neighbors, take a look at my own flesh and blood [*He

raises his head, and his voice gets stronger.], my very own flesh and
blood, lifting a hand to strike me. . . .

BENYA: Did we hear right, me and my brother Lyovka?

MENDEL: You won't get me! [*He throws himself at* LYOVKA, *punches him
in the face, and knocks him down.*]

LYOVKA: We will get you!

[*The sky is flooded by a blood-red sunset.* MENDEL *and* LYOVKA
*roll on the ground, punching each other in the face.
They roll behind a shed.*]

NIKIFOR [*Leaning against the wall.*]: Oh, what sin!

BOBRINETS: Lyovka! Hitting your own father!

BENYA [*In a desperate voice.*]: I swear to you on my life! He has thrown
everything—our horses, our house, our life—he has thrown everything at the feet of that whore!

NIKIFOR: Oh, what sin!

PYATIRUBEL: I'll kill anyone who tries to separate them! Don't anyone
dare touch them!

[*Wheezing and groaning is heard from behind the shed.*]

PYATIRUBEL: The man is yet to be born who can stand up to Mendel!

ARYE-LEIB [*To the boy.*]: Ivan, get out of the yard!

PYATIRUBEL: I'm ready to put a hundred rubles down—

ARYE-LEIB: Ivan, get out of the yard!

[MENDEL *and* LYOVKA *roll out from behind the shed. They jump
to their feet, but* MENDEL *knocks* LYOVKA *down again.*]

BOBRINETS: Lyovka! Hitting your own father!

MENDEL: You won't get me! [*He starts kicking his son.*]

PYATIRUBEL: I'm ready to put a hundred rubles down for anyone who's
interested!

[MENDEL *has won. Some of* LYOVKA's *teeth are broken,
tufts of his hair have been pulled out.*]

MENDEL: You won't get me!

BENYA: Just watch us!

[*With great force* BENYA *hits his father on the head with the
butt of his revolver.* MENDEL *falls down. Silence.
The sunset's blazing forests of cloud sink lower and lower.*]

NIKIFOR: They've killed him!

PYATIRUBEL [*Bends over* MENDEL, *who is lying motionless on the ground.*]:
Mendel?

LYOVKA [*Gets up, steadying himself with his fists. He is crying, stamping his
feet.*]: He kicked me below the belt, the bastard!

PYATIRUBEL: Mendel?

BENYA [*Turns to the crowd of bystanders.*]: What are you all doing here?

PYATIRUBEL: And I say it's not night yet! Night is still a thousand versts away!

ARYE-LEIB [*On his knees next to* MENDEL, *to* PYATIRUBEL.]: *Oy*, Russian
man, why say that it's not night yet when it is plain to see that this
man is as good as gone!

LYOVKA [*Crooked streams of tears and blood run down his face.*]: He kicked
me below the belt, the bastard!

PYATIRUBEL: Two against one! [*He staggers toward the exit.*]

ARYE-LEIB [*To the boy.*]: Get out of the yard, Ivan.

PYATIRUBEL: Two against one . . . it's a disgrace, a disgrace for all
Moldavanka! [*He stumbles off.*]

[ARYE-LEIB *wipes* MENDEL's *injured head with a wet handkerchief.
On the other side of the courtyard,* NEKHAMA—*wild, dirty-gray—
is hovering about in disbelief. She comes and kneels down
next to* ARYE-LEIB.]

NEKHAMA: Don't be silent, Mendel!

BOBRINETS [*To* MENDEL, *in a deep voice.*]: Stop fooling around, you old
clown!

NEKHAMA: Yell something, Mendel!

BOBRINETS: Get up, you old carter! Wet your whistle, down a bottle of
vodka!

[LYOVKA *is sitting on the ground with his legs apart. Slowly he spits out long ribbons of blood.*]

BENYA [*Chases the crowd of bystanders into a corner of the courtyard. He grabs a young man of about twenty by his shirt.*]: Get the hell out!

[*Silence. Evening. A blue darkness has fallen, but above the darkness the sky is still hot, crimson, and pitted with fiery holes.*]

Scene Seven

The KRIKS' *cart shed—a pile of horse collars, unharnessed buggies, harnesses. A part of the courtyard is visible.* BENYA *is sitting at a small table near the doors, writing something.* SEMYON, *an awkward, bald-headed peasant, is arguing with him, while* MADAME POPYATNIK *paces up and down.* MAJOR, *his legs dangling, sits out in the yard, on a cart with its shafts raised. A new sign is leaning against the wall. On it, in gold letters: "Horse-Carting Establishment, Mendel Krik & Sons." Garlands of horseshoes and crossed whips surround the letters.*

SEMYON: I don't care! What I want is my money!

BENYA [*Continues writing.*]: Why so rude, Semyon?

SEMYON: Give me my money, or I'll cut your throat!

BENYA: My dear man, I spit on you!

SEMYON: Where did you hide the old man?

BENYA: The old man is sick.

SEMYON: Right here on the wall, this is where he wrote how much he owed for the oats, how much for the hay—all nice and clear. And he always paid up! Twenty years I drove for him, and he was always fair and square!

BENYA [*Gets up.*]: You drove for him, but you're not going to drive for me—he wrote on the wall, but I'm not going to write on the wall—he paid you, but as for me, I very well might not pay you, because—

MADAME POPYATNIK [*Looks at the peasant with extreme disapproval.*]: When a man is such an idiot—it's disgusting!

BENYA: —because, with me, my dear fellow, you might well die before you eat your supper tonight!

SEMYON [*Frightened, but still defiant.*]: I want my money!

MADAME POPYATNIK: I am no philosopher, Monsieur Krik, but I can plainly see that there are people in this world who have no right to be alive!

BENYA: Nikifor!

[NIKIFOR *enters, looking about sheepishly. He speaks reluctantly.*]

NIKIFOR: Present.

BENYA: Settle up with Semyon and go over to Groshev's.

NIKIFOR: The day laborers are here and want to know who will be doing the hiring.

BENYA: I'll be doing the hiring.

NIKIFOR: And the cook is kicking up a fuss too because she pawned off her samovar to the master. Now she wants to know who she has to pay to get it back.

BENYA: She has to pay me. Settle up the business with Semyon, and bring back five hundred *poods* of hay from Groshev.

SEMYON [*Stunned.*]: Five hundred? Twenty years I've been carting—

MADAME POPYATNIK: When a man has money, he can buy hay, and oats, and even nicer things.

BENYA: And oats, two hundred *poods*.

SEMYON: I wouldn't say no to carting for you!

BENYA: Semyon, lose my address!

[SEMYON *kneads his hat, looks away, walks off, returns for a moment, and then walks off again.*]

MADAME POPYATNIK: A damn peasant giving you all this trouble! My God, if everyone suddenly remembered who owes them money! This very morning I was telling my husband, Major: "Husband, darling, I would never ask for those miserable two rubles that Mendel Krik owes us."

MAJOR [*In a hoarse, melodious voice.*]: One ruble, ninety-five kopecks.

BENYA: What two rubles?

MADAME POPYATNIK: Please, it's not even worth mentioning, really, good heavens, it's not even worth mentioning! Last Thursday, you see, Monsieur Krik was in a fabulous mood, and ordered marching tunes. . . . [*To her husband.*] How many were there?

MAJOR: Marching tunes? Nine.

MADAME POPYATNIK: And then he wanted dance tunes.

MAJOR: Twenty-one dance tunes.

MADAME POPYATNIK: That comes to one ruble, ninety-five. Paying musicians has always been a top priority with Monsieur Krik.

[NIKIFOR *enters, dragging his feet. He is looking to the side.*]

NIKIFOR: Potapovna is here.

BENYA: What do I care who's here and who isn't!

NIKIFOR: She's making threats.

BENYA: What do I care who's—

[POTAPOVNA *bursts in, hobbling, waving her enormous hip. She is drunk. She throws herself to the floor and stares up at* BENYA *with dull, fixed eyes.*]

POTAPOVNA: Czars in heaven!

BENYA: Yes, Madame Potapovna?

POTAPOVNA: Czars in heaven!

NIKIFOR: She's come to make trouble.

POTAPOVNA [*Winks.*]: Y-Y-Y-Yid bubbles are humming . . . the bubbles are bouncing about in my head—y-y-y.

BENYA: Get to the point, Madame Potapovna!

POTAPOVNA [*Bangs her fist on the floor.*]: You're right! You're right! Let the clever man measure, and the pig dance the measureka.

MADAME POPYATNIK: What a sophisticated lady!

POTAPOVNA [*Throws some coins on the floor.*]: Here are the forty kopecks I earned today. . . . I got up before dawn, it was still dark, and waited for the peasants on Baltskaya Street. . . . [*She lifts her head to the sky.*] I wonder what time it is now. Maybe three o'clock?

BENYA: Get to the point, Madame Potapovna!

POTAPOVNA: Y-Y-Y, blew bubbles . . .

BENYA: Nikifor!

NIKIFOR: Yes?

POTAPOVNA [*Wags her fat, weak, drunken finger at* NIKIFOR.]: And now, Nikisha, my own daughter is knocked up!

MADAME POPYATNIK [*Totters, burning with excitement.*]: Oh, what a scandal! What a scandal!

BENYA: What are you doing here, Madame Popyatnik? What do you want?

MADAME POPYATNIK [*Staggers, her eyes sparkling and fluttering with excitement.*]: I'm going, I'm going! God willing we will meet again . . . in happiness, in joy, in a blessed hour, in a happy minute!

[*She grabs her husband by the hand and starts backing out of the room. She turns around, her eyes crossed and flickering like black flames. MAJOR follows his wife, wiggling his fingers. They leave.*]

POTAPOVNA [*Smearing her tears over her flabby, wrinkled face.*]: At night I went to her, felt her breasts—I feel her breasts every night— they're already filled with milk, they don't even fit my hands anymore!

BENYA [*His sparkle has left him. He speaks quickly, glancing furtively behind him.*]: What month?

POTAPOVNA [*She stares fixedly up at BENYA from where she's lying on the floor.*]: Fourth.

BENYA: You're lying!

POTAPOVNA: Okay, third.

BENYA: What do you want from us?

POTAPOVNA: Y-Y-Y, blew bubbles . . .

BENYA: What do you want?

POTAPOVNA [*Tying her kerchief.*]: A cleanup costs one hundred rubles.

BENYA: Twenty-five!

POTAPOVNA: I'll bring in the dockworkers!

BENYA: You'll bring in the dockworkers? Nikifor!

NIKIFOR: Present.

BENYA: Go upstairs and ask my papa if I should hand over twenty-five—

POTAPOVNA: A hundred!

BENYA: —twenty-five rubles for a cleanup, or doesn't he want one?

NIKIFOR: I won't go.

BENYA: You won't?

[BENYA *rushes over to the calico curtains that divide the carting shed in two.*]

NIKIFOR [*Grabs* BENYA *by the arm.*]: Young man, I'm not afraid of God—I saw God and wasn't frightened—I will kill without being frightened!

[*The curtain stirs and parts.* MENDEL *enters. He is carrying his boots slung over his shoulder. His face is blue and swollen, like the face of a dead man.*]

MENDEL: Unlock the gates.

POTAPOVNA: Oh, my God!

NIKIFOR: Master!

[ARYE-LEIB *and* LYOVKA *approach the cart shed.*]

MENDEL: Unlock the gates.

POTAPOVNA [*Crawls on the floor.*]: Oh, my God!

BENYA: Go back upstairs to your wife, Papa.

MENDEL: Unlock the gates for me, Nikifor, old friend—

NIKIFOR [*Falls on his knees.*]: I beg you, master, don't grovel before me, a simple man!

MENDEL: Why won't you unlock the gates, Nikifor? Why won't you let me leave this courtyard where I have served my life sentence? [MENDEL'*s voice becomes more powerful, his eyes glitter.*] This court-yard, it has seen me be the father of my children, the husband of my wife, the master of my horses. It has seen my strength, and that of my twenty stallions and my twelve carts, reinforced with iron. It has seen my legs, huge as pillars, and my arms, my evil arms . . . but now unlock the gates for me, my dear sons, today let me for once do as I wish! Let me leave this courtyard that has seen too much. . . .

BENYA: Go back in the house, Papa, to your wife.

[*He approaches his father.*]

MENDEL: Don't hit me, Benchik.

LYOVKA: Don't hit him.

BENYA: What low-down people! [*Pause.*] How could you . . . [*Pause.*]
How could you say what you just said?

ARYE-LEIB [*To the onlookers.*]: Don't you all see that you shouldn't be
here?

BENYA: Animals! Animals!

[BENYA *rushes out.* LYOVKA *follows him.*]

ARYE-LEIB [*Leads* MENDEL *to the couch.*]: We'll rest a bit, Mendel, we'll
take a little nap. . . .

POTAPOVNA [*Gets up from the floor and begins to cry.*]: They've killed the
poor darling!

ARYE-LEIB [*Helps* MENDEL *onto the couch behind the curtain.*]: You'll take
a little nap, Mendel. . . .

POTAPOVNA [*Throws herself onto the floor by the couch, and starts kissing*
MENDEL's *hand, which is hanging down limply.*]: My little son, my
sweet little darling!

ARYE-LEIB [*Covers* MENDEL's *face with a kerchief, sits down, and begins
speaking in a quiet, distant voice.*]: Once upon a time, in the distant
past, there lived a man named David. He was a shepherd and then
he was a king, the King of Israel, of Israel's army and Israel's wise
men.

POTAPOVNA [*Sobbing.*]: My sweet darling!

ARYE-LEIB: David experienced wealth and experienced glory, but he
was not satiated. Strength brings thirst, only grief quenches the
heart. Having grown old, King David saw Bathsheba, General
Uriah's wife, on the roofs of Jerusalem, under the skies of
Jerusalem. Bathsheba's breasts were beautiful, her legs were beautiful, her gaiety was great. And General Uriah was sent into battle,
and the king coupled with Bathsheba, the wife of a man not yet
dead. Her breasts were beautiful, her gaiety was great . . .

Scene Eight

The KRIKS' *dining room. Evening. The room is brightly lit by a homemade hanging
lamp, candles in candelabras, and old-fashioned blue lamps fixed to the wall.*
MADAME POPYATNIK, *wearing a silk dress, is busy bustling about a table decorated
with flowers and filled with food and wine.* MAJOR *is sitting silently in the back of*

the room. His paper shirtfront is jutting out, his flute is lying on his knees. He is twiddling his fingers and bobbing his head from side to side. There are many guests. Some are strolling in groups about the open rooms, others sitting along the walls. The pregnant KLASHA ZUBARYEVA *enters the room. She is wearing a shawl with a gigantic flower pattern.* LYOVKA, *wearing a hussar's parade uniform, stumbles in after her, drunk.*

LYOVKA [*Barks out cavalry orders.*]:

> Horsemen, friends!
> Forward trot!
> If your horses are hungry,
> Then feed them a lot!

KLASHA [*Laughs out loud.*]: *Oy,* my belly! *Oy,* I'm going to miscarry!
LYOVKA:

> Mount your horses, left leg high,
> Hold on tight, or you will fly!

KLASHA: *Oy,* I'm dying!

[*They stroll on, passing* BOYARSKY, *who is wearing a frock coat, and* DVOIRA KRIK.]

BOYARSKY: Mademoiselle Krik, I don't call black white, nor am I the kind of man who would permit himself to call white black. With three thousand, we can set up a prêt-à-porter boutique on Deribasovskaya Street, and get happily married.
DVOIRA: It's got to be the whole three thousand, all at once?
BOYARSKY: Right now we're in the middle of July, and July isn't September. Light overcoats move in July, ladies' coats in September. And after September, you ask? Nothing! September, October, November, December. I don't call night day, nor am I the kind of man who would allow himself to call day night. . . .

[*They stroll on.* BENYA *and* BOBRINETS *enter.*]

BENYA: Is everything ready, Madame Popyatnik?

MADAME POPYATNIK: Even Czar Nicholas II wouldn't turn up his nose at such a table.

BOBRINETS: Explain your idea to me, Benya.

BENYA: This is my idea: A Jew no longer in the prime of life, a Jew who used to go about naked, barefoot, and filthy like a convict on Sakhalin island! And now that, thank God, he is getting up there in years, it is time to put an end to this life sentence of hard labor— it is time to turn the Sabbath into Sabbath.

[BOYARSKY *and* DVOIRA *stroll by.*]

BOYARSKY: September, October, November, December . . .

DVOIRA: But then, Boyarsky, I also want you to love me, at least a little.

BOYARSKY: What am I supposed to be doing with you if I won't be loving you? Turn you into meatballs? You make me laugh!

[*They stroll by. Near the wall, under a blue lamp, sit a poised cattle dealer
and a thick-legged young man in a three-piece suit.
The young man is carefully cracking sunflower seeds with his teeth
and putting the shells in his pocket.*]

THICK-LEGGED YOUNG MAN: Pow! A right hook in the face! Pow! A left hook—and wham, the old man went down!

CATTLE DEALER: Ha! Even the Tartars respect their elders! "Walking through life, oh the toil, oh the strife."

THICK-LEGGED YOUNG MAN: If he had lived by the book, but he . . . [*He spits out a shell.*] he did whatever he wanted. So what's there to respect?

CATTLE DEALER: You're an idiot!

THICK-LEGGED YOUNG MAN: Benya bought more than a thousand *poods* of hay.

CATTLE DEALER: For the old man a hundred was enough!

THICK-LEGGED YOUNG MAN: Either way, they're going to cut the old man's throat.

CATTLE DEALER: Yids? Their own father?

THICK-LEGGED YOUNG MAN: They'll slit the old man's throat, all right.

CATTLE DEALER: You're an idiot!

[BENYA *and* BOBRINETS *stroll by.*]

BOBRINETS: But what do you want, Benya?
BENYA: I want the Sabbath to be Sabbath. I want us to be people as
    good as anyone else. I want to walk with my legs on the ground and
    my head held high. . . . Do you understand what I'm saying,
    Bobrinets?
BOBRINETS: I understand what you're saying, Benya.

[*By the wall, next to* PYATIRUBEL, *sit* MR. AND MRS. WEINER,
smothered by the greatness of their wealth.]

PYATIRUBEL [*Seeking their sympathy in vain.*]: He used to rip the belts
    off policemen and beat the clerk at the main post office. He'd down
    a gallon of vodka on an empty stomach. He had all of Odessa by
    the throat. That's what the old man was like!

[WEINER *keeps rolling his heavy, slobbering tongue, but it's impossible to
    make out what he is saying.*]

PYATIRUBEL [*Timidly.*]: The gentleman has a speaking problem?
MADAME WEINER [*Viciously.*]: What do you think!
    [DVOIRA *and* BOYARSKY *stroll by.*]
BOYARSKY: September, October, November, December . . .
DVOIRA: And I *do* want a child, Boyarsky.
BOYARSKY: Absolutely! A child in a prêt-à-porter boutique is very pretty—
    it looks good. As for a child without a business, how will that look?

[MADAME POPYATNIK *bursts in with great excitement.*]

MADAME POPYATNIK: Ben Zkharia is here! Rabbi . . . Ben Zkharia!

[*The room fills with guests. Among them are* DVOIRA, LYOVKA, BENYA,
KLASHA ZUBARYEVA, SENKA TOPUN, *pomaded* CART DRIVERS, *waddling*
SHOPKEEPERS, *and giggling* PEASANT WOMEN.]

THICK-LEGGED YOUNG MAN: When money beckons, even the rabbi comes running. And here he is!

[ARYE-LEIB *and* BOBRINETS *wheel in a large armchair. Almost hidden in its plush depths is* BEN ZKHARIA'*s shriveled little body.*]

BEN ZKHARIA [*Shrilly.*]: Dawn has only sneezed, and in heaven the Lord is washing Himself with red water—

BOBRINETS [*Laughs out loud, expecting an intricate answer.*]: Why red, Rabbi?

BEN ZKHARIA: —and I am still lying on my back, like a cockroach—

BOBRINETS: Why on your back, Rabbi?

BEN ZKHARIA: Every morning God turns me on my back so I cannot pray. My prayers are getting on God's nerves. . . .

[BOBRINETS *roars with laughter.*]

BEN ZKHARIA: The chickens haven't gotten up yet, and Arye-Leib wakes me: Quick! Get over to the Kriks, Rabbi! They're having a feast! You'll get food, you'll get drink. . . .

BENYA: You'll get food, you'll get drink, whatever your heart desires, Rabbi!

BEN ZKHARIA: Whatever my heart desires? You mean you'll give away your horses too?

BENYA: I will give away my horses too!

BEN ZKHARIA: In that case, Jews, run to the Funeral Brotherhood and harness his horses to their hearse and take me to . . . where do you think?

BOBRINETS: Where to, Rabbi?

BEN ZKHARIA: To the Second Jewish Cemetery, you idiot!

BOBRINETS [*Roars with laughter, snatches the yarmulke off the* RABBI'*s head, and kisses his bald, pink pate.*]: Oy, he's a wild man! . . . Oy, he's a clever man!

ARYE-LEIB [*Introduces* BENYA.]: That's him, Rabbi, Mendel's son, Ben Zion.

BEN ZKHARIA [*Chews his lip.*]: Ben Zion . . . son of Zion . . . [*He is silent.*] Nightingales are not fed with fables, son of Zion, nor women with wisdom. . . .

LYOVKA [*In a deafening voice.*]: Get to your chairs, you riffraff, get your backsides to some stools!

KLASHA [*Shakes her head, smiles.*]: Oy, he's a lively one!

BENYA [*Throws his brother an indignant look.*]: My dear friends, please be seated! Monsieur Bobrinets will sit next to the rabbi.

BEN ZKHARIA [*Squirms in his armchair.*]: Why should I sit next to this Jew who's as long as our exile from the Holy Land has been? [*He points at* KLASHA.] Let the National Bank sit next to me. . . .

BOBRINETS [*Anticipating a new witticism.*]: Why National Bank?

BEN ZKHARIA: She's better than the National Bank. Make a nice deposit in her, and she'll yield such a percentage that wheat will wilt with envy. Make a bad deposit in her, and all her guts will creak in order to change your broken-down kopeck into a golden one! She's better than a bank, better than a bank!

BOBRINETS [*Raises his finger.*]: You must listen to his words!

BEN ZKHARIA: But where is our Star of Israel? Where is the master of this house? Where is Rabbi Mendel Krik?

LYOVKA: He is sick today.

BENYA: No, he is feeling well. . . . Nikifor!

[NIKIFOR *appears in the doorway in his shabby peasant coat.*]

BENYA: Have Papa and his wife come down.

[*Silence.*]

NIKIFOR [*In a desperate voice.*]: Ladies and gentlemen! . . .

BENYA [*Very slowly.*]: Have Papa come down.

ARYE-LEIB: Benya, we Jews don't cover our fathers with shame in front of everyone.

LYOVKA: Rabbi, no man has ever tortured a wild boar the way Benya is torturing Papa.

[WEINER *babbles indignantly, splattering spit.*]

BENYA [*Bends down to* MADAME WEINER.]: What is he saying?

MADAME WEINER: He is saying—"Shame and disgrace!"

ARYE-LEIB: Jews don't do such things, Benya!

KLASHA: You raise sons and—

BENYA: Arye-Leib, old man, old matchmaker, *shamas* of the Carters' Synagogue and funeral cantor, why don't you tell me how things should be done properly? [*He bangs his fist down on the table, and speaks with a pause after each word, accompanied by a thump of his fist.*] Have Papa come down!

[NIKIFOR *disappears.* BENYA *is standing in the middle of the room, his head hanging, his legs far apart. The blood is slowly rising to his head. Utter stillness. Only* BEN ZKHARIA'*s senseless muttering breaks the agonizing silence.*]

BEN ZKHARIA: God bathes in red water in heaven. [*He falls silent, squirms in his armchair.*] Why red, why not white? Because red is merrier than white. . . .

[*The two halves of the side door creak, groan, and then open. All faces turn in that direction.* MENDEL *appears, his face bruised and powdered. He is wearing a new suit. With him is* NEKHAMA, *wearing a bonnet and a heavy velvet dress.*]

BENYA: My friends, sitting here in my house! Permit me to raise this glass to my father, the hardworking Mendel Krik, and his wife, Nekhama Borisovna, who have walked thirty-five years along the road of life together. Dear friends! We know, we know full well, that no one has paved this road with cement, no one has placed benches along this long road! And then there's all the hordes of people who come running down that road, who haven't made it any easier, they've made it harder! My friends, sitting here in my house! What I ask is that you don't water the wine in your glasses, or the wine in your hearts!

[WEINER *babbles rapturously.*]

BENYA: What is he saying?

MADAME WEINER: He is saying—"Hurrah!"

BENYA [*Without looking at anyone.*]: Teach me, Arye-Leib. . . . [*He pours wine for his mother and father.*] Our guests are honoring you, Papa. Say a word or two!

MENDEL [*Looks around, and very quietly says.*]: To your health. . . .

BENYA: What Papa is trying to say is that he's donating a hundred rubles.

CATTLE DEALER: And then they talk about Jews. . . .

BENYA: Papa is donating five hundred! To whom should he donate, Rabbi?

BEN ZKHARIA: To whom? Jews! A girl's milk should not be left to curdle! He must donate the money to brides with no dowries!

BOBRINETS [*Bursts out laughing.*]: Oy, he's a wild man! . . . Oy, he's a clever man!

MADAME POPYATNIK: Do we want a flourish from the band now?

BENYA: Yes, we do!

[*A doleful flourish resounds through the room. A row of guests with glasses in their hands files toward* MENDEL *and* NEKHAMA.]

KLASHA ZUBARYEVA: To your health, Grandpa!

SENKA TOPUN: A wagonload of fun, Papa! A hundred thousand in pocket money!

BENYA [*Without looking at anyone.*]: Teach me, Arye-Leib!

BOBRINETS: Mendel, may God give me a son like your son!

LYOVKA [*Calls out across the table.*]: Papa! Don't be angry! Papa, you've had your fun and games. . . .

CATTLE DEALER: And then they talk about Jews! I know twice as much about Jews as you do!

PYATIRUBEL [*Makes his way across to* BENYA *and tries to kiss him.*]: You'll buy us and you'll sell us, you devil, you, and then tie us in a knot!

[*Loud sobbing is heard behind* BENYA. *Tears are flowing down* ARYE-LEIB'*s cheeks and into his beard. He shudders, and kisses* BENYA'*s shoulder.*]

ARYE-LEIB: Fifty years, Benchik! Fifty years together with your father! [*He shouts hysterically.*] He was a good father to you, Benya!

WEINER [*Suddenly attains the gift of speech.*]: Take him away!

MADAME WEINER: Well, I'll be damned!

BOYARSKY: Arye-Leib! You're mistaken, this is a time for laughter!

WEINER: Take him away!

ARYE-LEIB [*Sobs.*]: You had a good father, Benya. . . .

> [MENDEL *turns ashen under his powder. He holds out*
> *a new handkerchief to* ARYE-LEIB, *who*
> *uses it to wipe away his tears.*
> ARYE-LEIB *is laughing and crying.*]

BOBRINETS: You blockhead, you're not in your cemetery now!

PYATIRUBEL: You can search the whole world over, you'll never find a second Benchik! I'll wager anything. . . .

BENYA: Dear friends, be seated!

LYOVKA: Get your backsides to some stools, you riffraff!

> [*The thunder of chairs being moved. They seat* MENDEL *between the*
> RABBI *and* KLASHA ZUBARYEVA.]

BEN ZKHARIA: Jews!

PYATIRUBEL: Quiet, now!

BEN ZKHARIA: The old fool Ben Zkharia wants to say a word. . . .

> [LYOVKA *slumps forward onto the table, snorting with contempt,*
> *but* BENYA *shakes him, and he becomes quiet.*]

BEN ZKHARIA: Jews! Day is day, and night is night. Day drenches us with the sweat of our toil, but night offers its fans of divine coolness. Joshua, son of Nun, who stopped the sun, was nothing but a crazed fool! Jesus of Nazareth, who stole the sun, was an evil madman. And here is Mendel Krik, a member of our synagogue, who has turned out to be no cleverer than Joshua, son of Nun. He wanted to warm himself in the sun all his life, all his life he wanted to stand where he stood at midday. But God has policemen on every street, and Mendel Krik had sons in his house. The policemen come and see to it that things are as they should be. Day is day, and night is night. Jews! Everything is as it should be! Let's down a glass of vodka!

LYOVKA: Let's down a glass of vodka!

[*The shrill sound of flutes, the clinking of glasses, incoherent shouts, thunderous laughter.*]

MARIA

A PLAY IN EIGHT ACTS

Babel's second play, Maria, *is set during the Russian Civil War (1918-1920). Class distinctions had abruptly vanished, and aristocrats, smugglers, and Jewish mobsters were thrown together on the fringes of Soviet society.*

*Although it was felt that the play was too controversial to be performed in the Soviet Union, it was published in 1935 both as a book (*Goslitizdat*), and in the magazine* Teatr i dramaturgia.

CHARACTERS

Nikolai Vasilevich Mukovnin — a former aristocrat and quartermaster general in the Czar's army.
Ludmila Nikolayevna Mukovnina — his daughter.
Katerina Vyacheslavovna Felsen (Katya).
Isaac Markovich Dimshits.
Sergei Hilarionovich Golitsyn — a former prince.
Nefedovna — the Mukovnins' nanny.
Evstignevich — a disabled war veteran.
Bishonkov — a disabled war veteran.
Filip — a disabled war veteran.
Viskovsky — a former captain of the guards.
Yasha Kravchenko.
Madame Dora.
A police inspector.
Kalmikova — a maid in the hotel at Nevsky Prospekt, 86.
Agasha — a female janitor.
Andrei — a floor polisher.
Kuzma — a floor polisher.
Sushkin.
Safonov — a worker.

Elena — his wife.
Nyusha.
A policeman.
A drunk man — at the police station.
A Red Army fighter — just in from the front.

The action takes place in Petrograd during the first years of the Revolution.

Scene One

A hotel on the Nevsky Propekt. ISAAC MARKOVICH DIMSHITS's *hotel room: dirty and piled high with sacks, boxes, furniture. Two crippled war veterans,* BISHONKOV *and* EVSTIGNEVICH, *are unwrapping packets of food.* EVSTIGNEVICH, *a stout man with a large red face, has had both legs amputated above the knee.* BISHONKOV *has an empty, pinned-up sleeve. Both veterans are wearing medals and a St. George Cross on their chests.* DIMSHITS *is calculating profits on an abacus.*

EVSTIGNEVICH: They hassled us the whole way. Back when Zanberg was running the checkpoint at Viritsa* he used to let us do our thing, but they sent him packing.

BISHONKOV: We're being hassled too much, Isaac Markovich.

DIMSHITS: Is Korolev still there?

EVSTIGNEVICH: What d'you mean, still there? They finished him off. No wonder we're being hassled, what with all the checkpoint guards being new.

BISHONKOV: Getting our hands on produce is getting tougher, Isaac Markovich. The moment you get to know a checkpoint guard, he gets replaced by a new one. If they just snatched your stuff that would be one thing, but you never know when they're going to hold a gun to your head.

EVSTIGNEVICH: And you can't keep up with them. Every day they come up with new tricks. Last night we pulled in at Tsarskoye Selo Station† and they started shooting. We say, "Hey! What's going on?" We thought the government was being overthrown again, and that they were overthrowing it by shooting everyone in sight.

---

* A town to the south of Petersburg.
† Today the city of Pushkin, fourteen miles south of Petersburg.

BISHONKOV: Today they grabbed a lot of produce from us! For the street kids, they said. There's a whole colony of them at Tsarskoye Selo.

EVSTIGNEVICH: Yeah, right! Kids with beards on their faces!

BISHONKOV: If a man's hungry, he'll grab whatever food he can for himself! Yes, if he's hungry, for himself!

DIMSHITS: Where's Filip? I've been worried about him—why did you drop him and run?

BISHONKOV: We didn't drop him and run, Isaac Markovich. He got cold feet.

EVSTIGNEVICH: Someone's been talking to him.

BISHONKOV: It's tyranny, that's what it is!

EVSTIGNEVICH: Well, take Filip himself: he's a big, strong man, you notice him right away, but he's got no guts, his insides are weak. We drive up to the station—they're shooting, everyone's screaming, falling—I tell him, "Filip," I tell him, "we'll get over to Zagorodny Boulevard with no hassle—all the guards are friends!" But Filip's falling apart right before my eyes. "I'm afraid to go," he tells me. "Well, if you're afraid," I tell him, "then stay right where you are! Vodka smuggling is no big deal, you'll just get a kick in the pants, so what are you worried about? All you've got is one load of alcohol." But he was already lying there flat on his belly. A strong man, strong as a horse, but no guts.

BISHONKOV: We're all hoping he'll turn up. We haven't seen hide nor hair of him.

DIMSHITS: How much did you pay for the sausage?

BISHONKOV: We got sausage for eighteen thousand, Isaac Markovich, and it tastes awful. Nowadays you can be in Petrograd or out in Vitebsk, you get sausage from the same factory.

EVSTIGNEVICH [*Opens a secret cubbyhole in the wall and stashes the food there.*]: They're ruining Russia!

DIMSHITS: How much was the grain?

BISHONKOV: The grain was nine thousand. There's nothing you can do about it. They're not interested in selling. They're just waiting for you to open your mouth. I can't tell you how greedy these dealers have gotten.

EVSTIGNEVICH [*Hides loaves of bread in the wall.*]: My wife toiled over the oven to bake these. She sends her regards.

DIMSHITS: How're the kids? Doing well?

BISHONKOV: The kids are doing well. Very well indeed. They're all wearing fur coats, they're rich. . . . The wife asks if you'll come and visit.

DIMSHITS: Like I have nothing else to do. [*He flips the beads on the abacus.*] Bishonkov!

BISHONKOV: Yes?

DIMSHITS: I don't see no profits.

BISHONKOV: Getting our hands on food is getting tougher.

DIMSHITS: I don't see no profits.

BISHONKOV: You won't see no profits. Me and Evstignevich, we've been thinking that we should start handling some other product. There's a lot of bulk to this merchandise here: flour is bulky, grain is bulky, leg of veal is also bulky. We've got to move over to something else, saccharine, or gems. Diamonds are great. You pop them in your mouth and they're gone!

DIMSHITS: Filip's disappeared. . . . I'm worried about him.

EVSTIGNEVICH: I guess they must have broken all his bones by now.

BISHONKOV: Before the Revolution you could live quite well as a crippled veteran, but now . . .

EVSTIGNEVICH: Now you can forget it—it's all about education! In the past, soldiers got a hell of a lot of respect—now it's zilch. "How come you're an invalid?" this fellow asks me. "A shell blew both my legs off," I tell him. "What's so special about that?" he asks me. "Your legs got blown off right away without no suffering. You didn't have no suffering." So I ask him, "What d'you mean, no suffering?" "Well," he says, "it's common knowledge: you were chloroformed when they took your legs off, you didn't feel nothing. It's just that you can't come to grips with your toes—your toes kind of act up, itch, even though they've been chopped off, that's the only problem." "And how," I ask him, "do you happen to know all this?" "It's easy enough," he tells me, "everyone's educated now, thanks to those sons-of-bitches in charge." "Ha! I can tell how educated everyone is now, the way they kick crippled veterans off trains. . . . What do you want to kick me off the train for? I'm a cripple!" "We're throwing you off because goddamn Russia's sick and tired of all the cripples!" And he throws me off the train like a bundle of rags. I'm really upset at what our people have turned into.

[VISKOVSKY *enters in riding breeches and a jacket.*
His shirt is unbuttoned.]

DIMSHITS: Is that you?

VISKOVSKY: It's me.

DIMSHITS: So you forgot how to say hello?

VISKOVSKY: Did Ludmila Nikolayevna come to see you, Dimshits?

DIMSHITS: Did the dog grab your "hello" and run away with it? So what's it to you if she came to see me?

VISKOVSKY: I know you've got Mukovnin's ring, and her sister, Maria Nikolayevna, couldn't have given it to you—

DIMSHITS: Who says it had to be people who gave it me?

VISKOVSKY: How d'you get that ring, Dimshits?

DIMSHITS: I was given it to sell.

VISKOVSKY: So sell it to me.

DIMSHITS: Why should I sell it to you?

VISKOVSKY: Ever tried your hand at being a gentleman, Dimshits?

DIMSHITS: I'm always a gentleman.

VISKOVSKY: Gentlemen don't ask questions.

DIMSHITS: Those people want hard currency for the ring.

VISKOVSKY: You owe me fifty pounds sterling.

DIMSHITS: What for, if I may ask?

VISKOVSKY: For the thread deal.

DIMSHITS: You mean the deal you messed up?

VISKOVSKY: In the Cavalry Guard they didn't teach us the ins and outs of the thread trade.

DIMSHITS: You messed up the deal because you're hotheaded.

VISKOVSKY: So give me forty, Maestro, and I'll mend my ways.

DIMSHITS: How are you going to mend your ways if you never listen? You're told to do one thing, and you go do something completely different. In the war you were a captain or a count, whatever you were—maybe it's good to be hotheaded in war, but when pulling off a deal, a merchant has to watch where he puts his foot.

VISKOVSKY: Yessir!

DIMSHITS: And there's something else I'm pissed off about, Viskovsky! What was that trick you pulled with bringing me that princess?

VISKOVSKY: I thought the more refined, the better.

DIMSHITS: Didn't you know Ludmila Nikolayevna was a virgin?

VISKOVSKY: The best *tsimmes* you can get your hands on.

DIMSHITS: Thank you, I don't need that kind of *tsimmes*. I am a humble man, Captain Viskovsky, and I wouldn't want the princess to come to me like the Mother of God from an icon and look at me with eyes like silver spoons. Remember what we'd agreed on? Yes or no? I don't mind if it's a woman pushing thirty, that's what we agreed on, or thirty-five, a housewife who's having a hard time making ends meet and who'd take the grain and the bread I'd give her, along with the pound of cocoa for her kids, without yelling, "You goddamn bootlegger, you dirtied me, you used me!"

VISKOVSKY: There's still the younger Mukovnina.

DIMSHITS: That one's a liar. I don't like women who are liars. . . . Why don't you introduce me to the older one?

VISKOVSKY: Maria Nikolayevna has joined the army.

DIMSHITS: Now, Maria Nikolayevna, that's some woman! A feast for the eyes, a person you can talk to. . . . Why did you wait till she was gone?

VISKOVSKY: It's a tough call with her, Dimshits. Very tough.

EVSTIGNEVICH: "You got blown up without even getting shook up!" he said to me. "No suffering for you!" That's the kind of crap he was saying to me.

[*A shot is heard far away, then nearer. The shots become more frequent.*
DIMSHITS *turns out the light and locks the doors.*
Light shining through the windows, green glass, frost.]

EVSTIGNEVICH [*In a whisper.*]: You call this a life?

BISHONKOV: Goddamn it!

EVSTIGNEVICH: The damn sailors are on the loose again.

BISHONKOV: This is no life, Isaac Markovich.

[*There is a knock at the door. Silence.* VISKOVSKY *takes a revolver out of his pocket and releases the safety catch. A second knock.*]

BISHONKOV: Who's there?
FILIP [*From outside.*]: It's me.
EVSTIGNEVICH: Me who? Your name!
FILIP: Open up!
DIMSHITS: It's Filip.

[BISHONKOV *opens the door. An enormous, shapeless man enters the room and slumps wordlessly against the wall. A light flares up. Half of* FILIP's *face is scarred with burned flesh. His head has lolled onto his chest, his eyes are closed.*]

DIMSHITS: You been shot?
FILIP: No.
EVSTIGNEVICH: You look wasted, Filip.

[EVSTIGNEVICH *and* BISHONKOV *help* FILIP *out of his sheepskin coat and his outer clothes, and then take off his rubber suit filled with bootlegged vodka and throw it on the floor. The armless rubber dummy—a second* FILIP—*is lying on the floor.* FILIP's *fingers are lacerated, covered in blood.*]

EVSTIGNEVICH: They've really worked him over! And they call themselves human beings!
FILIP [*His head still lolling on his chest.*]: A man was following me . . . following me . . .
EVSTIGNEVICH: Following you?
FILIP: Yeah.
EVSTIGNEVICH: A man wearing leggings?
FILIP: Yeah.
EVSTIGNEVICH: We're done for. . . .
DIMSHITS: What, you brought him all the way here?
FILIP: No I didn't bring him all the way here. There was shooting, so he ran off to see what was up.

[BISHONKOV *and* EVSTIGNEVICH *lift up the wounded man and lay him on the bed.*]

EVSTIGNEVICH: I told you we'd have got through with no hassle.

[FILIP *is groaning. Faraway shots, machine gun fire, then silence.*]

EVSTIGNEVICH: You call this a life?

BISHONKOV: Goddamn it!

VISKOVSKY: Where's the ring, Maestro?

DIMSHITS: That ring's got you champing at the bit!

Scene Two

A room in the apartment of Mukovnin, a former aristocrat and quartermaster general in the Czar's army. The room serves as bedroom, dining room, and office—a typical room of the 1920s. Elegant antique furniture, but next to it a little makeshift tin stove, its pipes extending through the whole room. A pile of thinly chopped logs are stashed beneath the stove. Behind a screen, LUDMILA, *his daughter, is dressing for the theater. Curling tongs are heating over an oil lamp.* KATYA (KATERINA VYACHESLAVOVNA), *also a former aristocrat, is ironing a dress.*

LUDMILA: Darling, you are behind the times! Nowadays the audience at the Marinsky Theater is extremely elegant. The Krimov sisters and Varya Meindorf look as if they've just stepped out of a fashion magazine, and I can assure you that they live in the lap of luxury.

KATYA: No one is living well nowadays. No one.

LUDMILA: There you are wrong. You are behind the times, Katya, darling. The gentlemen of the proletariat are acquiring a taste for style. They want a woman to be elegant. Why, do you think Redko likes it when you run around dressed like a fishwife? You can bet your life he doesn't! No, Katya, darling, the gentlemen of the proletariat are definitely acquiring a taste for style!

KATYA: I wouldn't overdo the mascara if I were you, and I'm not at all sure about that sleeveless dress.

LUDMILA: You seem to be forgetting that I am being escorted by a gentleman.

KATYA: Well, your gentleman friend wouldn't know the difference.

LUDMILA: There you are wrong. He does have taste, and he is passionate too!

KATYA: Redheaded fellows are hot-blooded, everyone knows that.

LUDMILA: What do you mean, redheaded! My Dimshits's hair is chocolate brown.

KATYA: Does he really have that much money? I think Viskovsky is mistaken.

LUDMILA: Dimshits has six thousand pounds sterling to his name.

KATYA: What? He's conned all that from the cripples?

LUDMILA: He has conned nothing from the cripples! That is merely hearsay. They have formed a cooperative association, and all the profits are shared. Until recently, no crippled veteran was ever searched, so it was easier for them to carry things.

KATYA: Only a Jew could come up with a scheme like that!

LUDMILA: Oh, Katya, darling. Better a Jew than a cocaine addict, like most of the men of our set. This one is a cocaine addict, another has gotten himself shot, another has ended up as a coachman standing outside the Europa waiting for fares. *Par le temps qui court,** Jews have become the safest bet.

KATYA: I suppose you will not find a safer bet than Dimshits.

LUDMILA: Do not forget we are women, *ma chère*. We are just women, tired of "trolloping around," as the janitor's wife downstairs always says. We cannot just sit here twiddling our thumbs, can we? We can't—

KATYA: Are you thinking of having children?

LUDMILA: I shall have two little redheads.

KATYA: So we are talking marriage?

LUDMILA: You have to with these Jews, Katya, darling. They are obsessed with family—they lean on their wives, and their children are everything to them. Not to mention that a Jew is always grateful to the woman who has given herself to him. It's a really noble trait, this respect they have for women.

KATYA: How is it that you know the Jews so well?

LUDMILLA: Well, you know—from back then. When Papa commanded the troops back in Vilna, the whole place was full of Jews. Papa had a rabbi as a friend. They are all philosophers, these rabbis of theirs.

KATYA [*Hands her the ironed dress over the screen.*]: You'll be dining after the theater?

LUDMILA: I wouldn't be surprised.

---

* "The way things are now."

KATYA: I'm sure you'll have a drink or two, Ludmila Nikolayevna, passions will be excited, and the mists will engulf you.

LUDMILA: No mists will engulf me, *ma chère*. I shall let him call on me for a month, maybe two—that is how one handles Jews. I have not come to a decision yet as to whether I shall allow myself to be kissed.

[GENERAL MUKOVNIN *enters, wearing felt boots. His greatcoat with a red lining has been refashioned into a dressing gown. He is wearing two pairs of spectacles.*]

MUKOVNIN [*Reads.*]: "On the sixteenth day of October, in the year 1820, in the reign of our blessed Czar Alexander, a company of Life Guards from the Semyonovsky Regiment, forgetting their oath of allegiance and the military obedience they owed their commanders, had the effrontery to gather together without authorization at an advanced nocturnal hour. " [*He raises his head.*] And how did they forget their oath of allegiance? They forgot it by going out into the corridors after roll call with the intention of asking the company commander to call off the upcoming routine inspections of all the barracks. The regimental commander sometimes ordered these strict inspections. For this so-called mutiny, they were punished. And do you know how? [*He reads.*] "The men of lower rank, the ones considered ringleaders, were deprived of their lives, and the men of the first and second companies were sentenced to hang for setting a bad example, and the private soldiers that were specified in paragraph three had to run the gauntlet through the battalion six times, as an example to their peers."

LUDMILA: Oh, that's awful!

KATYA: We all know that there was much cruelty in the old days.

LUDMILA: If you ask me, the Bolsheviks would love Papa's book. They can use it most effectively to rant against the old army.

KATYA: All the Bolsheviks care about is the here and now.

MUKOVNIN: I am dividing the Semyonovsky tragedy into two chapters: the first is an analysis of the reasons for the mutiny, and the second a description of the insurrection, the torture, and banishment to the mines. My book will be a history of the barracks. It won't be a history of nations, but a history of all the Ivans and Sergeys that were handed over to Arakcheyev and sent off for twenty years of hard labor in military camps.*

LUDMILA: Papa, you must read Katya the chapter on Czar Paul. If Tolstoy were alive today, he'd be impressed. I am sure of it.

KATYA: All the newspapers care about is the here and now.

MUKOVNIN: Without knowledge of the past there is no road to the future. The Bolsheviks are continuing the work of Grand Prince Ivan Kalita,[†] unifying the Russian lands. They need skilled officers like myself, even if only to inform them of the mistakes we made.

[*The doorbell rings. There is bustling in the front hall.*
DIMSHITS *enters in a fur coat, carrying packages.*]

DIMSHITS: Greetings, General! Greetings, Katerina Vyacheslavovna! Is Ludmila Nikolayevna at home?

KATYA: She is expecting you.

LUDMILA [*From behind the screen.*]: I am dressing. . . .

DIMSHITS: Greetings, Ludmila Nikolayevna! The weather outside is so bad that no man would send his dog out in it. Hypolite drove me here, he talked my ears off, nothing but jabbering—what a strange bird! Isn't it getting late, Ludmila Nikolayevna?

MUKOVNIN: It's broad daylight, and they're off to the theater?

KATYA: Theaters start now at five in the afternoon.

MUKOVNIN: Saving on electricity, are they?

KATYA: Yes, they're saving on electricity. And then, if people go home late they're likely to get robbed.

DIMSHITS [*Unwrapping his packages.*]: Here is a nice leg of ham, General. It's not my specialty, but they told me it was corn-fed. Now, whether they fed it with corn or something else, it's not like I was there or anything.

[KATYA *goes to a corner and smokes a cigarette.*]

---

*Count Alexei Andreyevich Arakcheyev, 1769–1834, was a general and politician whose brutal tactics in reorganizing the Russian army led to his dismissal.

[†] Ivan Kalita [Ivan the Moneybag.] ruled Moscovy from 1325 to 1341, expanding Russian territory eastward into the trans-Volga regions.

MUKOVNIN: I must say, Isaac Markovich, you are being too good to us.

DIMSHITS: Some cracklings?

MUKOVNIN [*Not understanding.*]: Begging your pardon?

DIMSHITS: I'm sure they didn't serve no cracklings at your papa's table, but back in Minsk, in Vilsk, in Chernobyl, cracklings are held in the highest esteem. They are bits of goose. Have some and give me your opinion. . . . How is your book doing, General?

MUKOVNIN: The book is moving ahead. I have reached the reign of Czar Alexander I.

LUDMILA: It reads just like a novel, Isaac Markovich. In my opinion, it is reminiscent of *War and Peace*—the part where Tolstoy talks about the soldiers.

DIMSHITS: That's very nice to hear. Let them shoot in the streets, General, let them bang their heads against the walls—just keep on working. Finish the book and I'll throw you a feast, and I'll buy up the first hundred copies! How about a *délicieux petit* piece of sausage, General—it's homemade sausage, a German gave it to me—

MUKOVNIN: Isaac Markovich, you mustn't! I will become angry!

DIMSHITS: It would be a great honor if General Mukovnin were to get angry at me. It is an exquisite sausage! This German was quite a renowned professor, now he specializes in sausages. . . . Ludmila Nikolayevna, I have a strong feeling we'll be late.

LUDMILA [*From behind the screen.*]: I am ready.

MUKOVNIN: How much do I owe you, Isaac Markovich?

DIMSHITS: You don't owe me the horseshoe of the horse that dropped dead on Nevsky Prospekt earlier today.

MUKOVNIN: No, I am being serious, how much?

DIMSHITS: You are being serious? Fine—then let's make it two horse-shoes from two horses.

[LUDMILA *appears from behind the screen.*
She is dazzlingly beautiful, well built, with rosy cheeks.
She is wearing diamond earrings and a sleeveless black velvet dress.]

MUKOVNIN: Isn't my daughter beautiful, Isaac Markovich?

DIMSHITS: I wouldn't say she isn't.

KATYA: She is a real Russian beauty, that's what she is, Isaac Markovich.

DIMSHITS: It's not my specialty, but I can see the quality.

MUKOVNIN: I also want to introduce you to my older daughter, Maria.

LUDMILA: I must warn you, Maria is the favorite here, and yet, believe it or not, our favorite went off to join the army.

MUKOVNIN: What are you talking about, Ludmila, darling? She joined the army's Political Propaganda Division.*

DIMSHITS: Your Excellency—anything you want to know about the Political Propaganda Division, you ask me! They are soldiers too.

KATYA [*Taking* LUDMILA *to the side.*]: I would not wear those earrings if I were you.

LUDMILA: You think so?

KATYA: Of course not. Don't forget there's that dinner afterward. . . .

LUDMILA: Have no fear, *ma chère*. No need to teach a Viennese how to waltz. [*She kisses* KATYA.] Katyusha, you sweet, silly girl. [*To* DIMSHITS.] My boots. [*She turns away and takes off her earrings.*]

DIMSHITS [*Rushing to help her.*]: At your service!

[*She puts on her boots, fur coat, and knitted wool kerchief.*
DIMSHITS *eagerly bustles about, helping her.*]

LUDMILA: I still can't believe that we haven't sold all these things yet. Papa, don't forget to take your medicine. And Katya, don't let him do any work.

MUKOVNIN: Katya and I are going to spend a cozy evening at home.

LUDMILA [*Kisses her father on the forehead.*]: How do you like my papa, Isaac Markovich? Isn't he precious?

DIMSHITS: The general is not a mere man, he is a jewel!

LUDMILA: We are the only ones who truly appreciate him. Where did you leave Prince Hypolite?

DIMSHITS: I left him outside the door. I ordered him to wait there, it's a question of discipline. We'll be there in a minute. So long, Nikolai Vasilevich!

KATYA: Don't drink too much.

DIMSHITS: We won't—there's not much chance of that nowadays.

---

* Polit-otdel, a political organ of the new Soviet government charged with the ideological education of the military during the Russian Civil War and the Russian-Polish War of 1920.

LUDMILA: Good-bye, Papa, darling.

[GENERAL MUKOVNIN *escorts* DIMSHITS *and his daughter to the front hall; voices and laughter are heard.* MUKOVNIN *returns.*]

MUKOVNIN: What a charming and virtuous Jew.

KATYA [*Curled up at the edge of the sofa, smoking.*]: They all seem to be somewhat lacking in tact.

MUKOVNIN: Katya, darling! Where do you expect them to have picked up tact? They were only allowed to live on one side of the street, and if they ever crossed over to the other side, the police would immediately chase them back. That is how it used to be in Kiev on Bibikovsky Boulevard. So where do you expect them to have picked up tact? What is really surprising is their energy, their vitality, their resilience!

KATYA: That energy has poured into Russian life. But we, after all, are different. It's all so foreign to us.

MUKOVNIN: One thing that isn't foreign to us is fatalism. Another, that Rasputin and the German Czarina destroyed the Romanov dynasty. And yet nothing but good has come from that wonderful Jewish race, which has given us Heine, Spinoza, and Christ.

KATYA: You used to praise the Japanese too, Nikolai Vasilevich.

MUKOVNIN: The Japanese? They are a great nation, there is much we can learn from them!

KATYA: It is clear enough who Maria takes after. You are a Bolshevik, Nikolai Vasilevich.

MUKOVNIN: I am a Russian officer, Katya, and I ask the simple question: gentlemen, please tell me when it was that the rules of war became foreign to you? We tortured and murdered these people, is what I tell them, they defended themselves, they attacked, fighting with resourcefulness, circumspection, desperation—they are fighting in the name of an ideal, Katya!

KATYA: An ideal? I'm not so sure about that. We're unhappy, and it doesn't look like that will change. We've been sacrificed, Nikolai Vasilevich.

MUKOVNIN: So let them shake up Russia's Vanyas and Petrushkas. That would be wonderful. Time is running out, Katya. Peter the Great, the only true Russian Czar, once said, "Delay is death!" What a maxim. And if this is so, my dear fellow officers, shouldn't you have the courage to look at your field maps and figure out which of your flanks faltered, and where and why you were defeated? I have a right to look the truth in the eye, and I shall not renounce that right.

KATYA: You have to take your medicine.

MUKOVNIN: What I tell my comrades in arms, the men I fought shoulder to shoulder with is, "*Tirez vos conclusions**—delay is death!"

[*He exits. Next door a Bach fugue is being played coldly and with precision on a cello.* KATYA *listens, then gets up and walks over to the telephone.*]

KATYA: Could you connect me with the District Headquarters? . . . Redko, please. . . . Is that you, Redko? . . . I just wanted to tell you . . . Don't forget you're not the only man fighting for the Revolution, and yet you're the only one who never has time to see a person . . . a person at whose house you spend the night whenever you need to. . . . [*Pause.*] Take me out, Redko. Come and pick me up in your car. . . . Well, if you're busy . . . No, I'm not angry. Why should I be angry?

[*She hangs up. The music stops.* GOLITSYN, *a lanky man in a soldier's jacket and leg wrappings, enters, carrying a cello.*]

KATYA: What did they tell you in the tavern—"Don't play weepy tunes"?

GOLITSYN: "Don't play weepy tunes, don't pull at our heartstrings."

KATYA: They need something cheerful, Sergei Hilarionovich. People want to forget their worries, they want to rest. . . .

GOLITSYN: Not all of them. Some ask for plaintive tunes.

KATYA [*Seats herself at the piano.*]: What kind of audience do you have?

GOLITSYN: Dockworkers from the Obvodny Canal.

KATYA: I suppose you go to their trade union. . . . They give you some supper there, don't they?

---

*"Draw your own conclusions."

GOLITSYN: Yes, they do.

KATYA [*Plays a popular tune.*]:

> *"Through wind and wave our ship sails free,*
> *As we throw the damn Whites to the fish in the sea."*

Try playing this. It should go down well at that tavern of yours.

[GOLITSYN *tries to play the tune, misses a few notes, then gets it right.*]

KATYA: Would it be worth me learning stenography, *mon prince*?

GOLITSYN: Stenography? I have no idea.

KATYA:

> *"I sit on a barrel crying tears of dismay,*
> *The boys don't want marriage,*
> *Just a roll in the hay."*

They need stenographers right now.

GOLITSYN: I wouldn't know. [*He tries to follow her tune.*]

KATYA: Maria is the only true woman of all of us. She is strong, gutsy, a real woman. We sit around here sighing, while she's happy in her Political Propaganda Division. . . . What have people come up with to replace happiness? There isn't anything.

GOLITSYN: Maria Nikolayevna has always sat in the driver's seat. That's always been her strong point.

KATYA: And right she is.

> *"Oh sweet little apple, whither did you roll?"*

And then, she is involved with Akim Ivanich.

GOLITSYN [*K tops playing.*]: Who is this Akim Ivanich?

KATYA: Their division commander, a former blacksmith. She mentions him in every letter.

GOLITSYN: How do you know she's involved with him?

KATYA: I have read it between the lines, I'm certain of it. . . . Or should I maybe move to my family in Borisoglebsk? At least it's home.

You, for instance, you go to that monastery to see that monk—what was his name?

GOLITSYN: Sioni.

KATYA: Yes, to Father Sioni. What does he teach you?

GOLITSYN: You just mentioned happiness. Well, he teaches me that there is no happiness in having power over people, or in this never-ending greed—this unquenchable greed.

KATYA: Let's play, Sergei Hilarionovich!

> *"I sit on my barrel,*
> *While the market hags bicker,*
> *Not a kopeck in my pocket*
> *But I'm thirsty for liquor."*

Sioni is a beautiful name.

Scene Three

LUDMILA *and* DIMSHITS *in his hotel room. Bottles and the remains of their meal stand on the table. Part of an adjacent room is visible in which* BISHONKOV, FILIP, *and* EVSTIGNEVICH *are playing cards.* EVSTIGNEVICH'S *little invalid cart has been placed on a chair; his legs, amputated above the knee, are jutting out.*

LUDMILA: Felix Yusupov* was as beautiful as a god—a tennis player, a Russian champion. Though his beauty was not really masculine enough . . . there was something doll-like about it. Well, I met Vladimir Bagalei at Felix's. Right to the very end the Czar simply could not understand what a gallant nature that man had. We used to call him the "Teutonic Knight." Fredriks† was a friend of Prince Sergei, you know Prince Sergei—he's the one who plays the cello. That evening there was another surprise *hors programme*: Archbishop Ambrosii. The old man started flirting with me, can you imagine? He kept topping up my glass and peering at me with such a crafty, pious twinkle in his eye! At first Vladimir was not particularly impressed with me. "In my eyes you were only a snub-

---

* Prince Felix Yusupov, 1887–1967, gained international notoriety for his involvement in the assassination of Rasputin.

† Count Vladimir Borisovich Fredriks, 1832–1927, descendant of a distinguished line of Baltic barons, was Czar Nicholas II's Minister of the Imperial Court and Domains.

nosed little girl," he admitted, "*si démesurement russe,** with flushed cheeks." At dawn we drove out to the Czar's palace at Tsarskoye Selo, left the car in the park, and rode on in a buggy. Vladimir drove it himself. "I could not take my eyes off of you all evening, Ludmila Nikolayevna." "Of which Nina Buturlina is well aware, *mon prince.*" I knew they were having a liaison—more probably a flirtation. "Buturlina, *c'est le passé!*"† "*On revient toujours à ses premiers amours, mon prince.*"** Vladimir had never been accorded the title of Grand Duke, as he was the offspring of a morganatic marriage, and the Czarina refused to meet his family. Vladimir always called her "an evil genius." Furthermore, he was a poet, naive, and had no head for politics. We arrived at Tsarskoye Selo. It was dawn. Somewhere, right over the pond, a nightingale was singing. Vladimir told me again: "*Mademoiselle Boutourline c'est le passé.*"‡ "The past, *mon prince,* has a tendency to return at times, and when it does, it does so with a vengeance."

[DIMSHITS *turns out the light, pushes* LUDMILA *back onto the sofa, and throws himself on her. There is a struggle. She frees herself, straightens her hair, her dress.*]

BISHONKOV [*Throws down a card.*]: Try beating this!

FILIP: Nope, no one can beat that!

EVSTIGNEVICH: Well, they lead him up to the fence, his hands tied. "So, my friend," they tell him. "Turn around!" And he tells them, "There's no need for me to turn around. I'm a fighting man, finish me off as I am." Their fence is just a tiny wattle fence, really, about hip high. It's night, they're at the edge of the village, beyond the village are the steppes, at the edge of the steppes is a forest—

BISHONKOV [*Throws down another card.*]: That's it! You're out!

FILIP: Not so fast!

EVSTIGNEVICH: So they lead him out there and take aim. He is standing by the fence, and suddenly it's as if he'd been snatched up from

---

* "so overly Russian."

† "is a thing of the past."

** "One always returns to one's first loves, my prince."

‡ "Mademoiselle Buturlina is a thing of the past."

the earth, his hands still tied! It was as if God Almighty whisked him away. He jumped over the wattle fence and off he scampered! They fired, but it was night, darkness everywhere, and he was running and dodging, so he got away.

FILIP [*Puts down his cards.*]: What a hero!

EVSTIGNEVICH: A real hero! A great horseman. I knew him as well as I know you. He was on the run for half a year before they finally caught him.

FILIP: So they finished him off?

EVSTIGNEVICH: They did. It's unfair, if you ask me. When a man manages to crawl out of the grave after coming face-to-face with his maker, it goes against the grain to kill him.

FILIP: No one gives a damn nowadays.

EVSTIGNEVICH: It's unfair, if you ask me. It's the law in every country in the world: if a firing squad misses you, then fortune has smiled on you and they set you free.

FILIP: Not here they don't! Give them half a chance and they'll finish you off!

BISHONKOV: Yeah, give them half a chance—

LUDMILA: Turn on the light!

[DIMSHITS *switches it on.*]

LUDMILA: I am leaving. [*She turns around, looks at* DIMSHITS, *and bursts out laughing.*] Don't pout. Come here. You have to understand—I must get used to you first.

DIMSHITS: I'm not a boot one has to get used to.

LUDMILA: I will admit that you have awakened within me feelings of warmth toward you. But these feelings need time to develop. Maria is about to come back on leave, and you will meet her. Nothing in our family is ever done without her. . . . Papa is well disposed toward you, but, as you yourself saw, he is helpless. . . . And then, there is much that still remains unresolved. Your wife, for instance.

DIMSHITS: What's my wife got to do with all this?

LUDMILA: I am aware that Jews are attached to their children.

DIMSHITS: What are you bringing that up for?

LUDMILA: And that is why for the time being you must sit next to me quietly, and be patient.

DIMSHITS: Since the day the Jews began waiting for the Messiah, they have been patient. Have another glass.

LUDMILA: I've already had too much.

DIMSHITS: They brought me this wine from a battleship. The grand duke had a case on board. . . .

LUDMILA: How do you manage to get all these things?

DIMSHITS: I can get stuff where no one else can. Drink up.

LUDMILA: Gladly—that is, if you sit there nice and quiet.

DIMSHITS: Is this some synagogue, for me to sit nice and quiet or something?

LUDMILA: I must say, this frock coat you are wearing is the kind I imagine one would wear to a synagogue. Frock coats, Isaac, darling, are worn by headmasters at graduation ceremonies, and by merchants at memorial dinners.

DIMSHITS: I'll stop wearing frock coats.

LUDMILA: And then those tickets. Never buy front-row tickets. It's the mark of a social climber, a parvenu.

DIMSHITS: I *am* a social climber.

LUDMILA: But you have an inner nobility, and that makes all the difference. However, your name is unfitting. When we put our announcement in the papers, the *Izvestia*, for instance . . . you could, you know, change Isaac to Alexei. Do you like Alexei?

DIMSHITS: I like it. [*He turns out the light again, and throws himself on* LUDMILA.]

EVSTIGNEVICH: The two of them are at it.

FILIP [*Listens.*]: It looks like she's finally . . .

BISHONKOV: I like Ludmila Nikolayevna best of all. She treats you like a person, which is more than I can say for some of those other hags around here . . . She even remembers my name.

[VISKOVSKY *enters the room, stands behind* EVSTIGNEVICH'*s back, and watches the cards being played.*]

LUDMILA [*Tearing free.*]: Call me a cab!

DIMSHITS: Yeah, right away! Like I got nothing better to do!

LUDMILA: Call me a cab this minute!

DIMSHITS: It's thirty below zero outside—you wouldn't send a rabid dog out in such weather.

LUDMILA: All my clothes are torn! How can I show myself at home like this?

DIMSHITS: You made your bed, now lie in it!

LUDMILA: How vulgar! You're knocking on the wrong door.

DIMSHITS: Just my luck.

LUDMILA: I told you I have a toothache, an unbearable toothache!

DIMSHITS: That's apples and oranges. What's teeth got to do with things?

LUDMILA: Will you find me some drops for my toothache? I am suffering!

[DIMSHITS *exits. He bumps into* VISKOVSKY *in the adjacent room.*]

VISKOVSKY: Congratulations.

DIMSHITS: Her teeth's hurting her.

VISKOVSKY: That can happen.

DIMSHITS: What can happen is that they don't hurt.

VISKOVSKY: It's all an act, Isaac Markovich. It's definitely all an act.

FILIP: The toothache is an invention of hers, Isaac Markovich, and not a real toothache at all.

LUDMILA [*Fixes her hair in front of the mirror. Singing a song, she walks about the room, regal, cheerful, flushed.*]

> "*My sweetheart is a man who is tall and brash,*
> *My sweetheart is a man both gentle and cruel,*
> *He thrashes and whips me with a silken lash . . .*"

DIMSHITS: I'm not a boy—a lot of time has passed since I last was a boy!

VISKOVSKY: Yessir!

LUDMILA [*Picks up the telephone.*]: 3-75-02. Papa, darling, is that you? . . . I'm very well. . . . Nadia Johanson was at the theater with her husband. Isaac Markovich and I are having dinner. . . . You must see Spessivtseva, she's far better than Pavlova! . . . Did you take your medicine? You must go to bed. . . . No, your daughter knows exactly what she is doing. . . . Katya, darling, is that you? . . . I am following your instructions, *ma chère. Le manège continue, j'ai mal aux dents ce soir.**[She walks about the room, singing, and patting her hair into place.]*

DIMSHITS: She shouldn't be surprised if I'm not home next time she comes around!

VISKOVSKY: Well, it's up to you, after all.

DIMSHITS: Because, though I don't mind other people asking about my wife and children, I won't take that sort of thing from her!

VISKOVSKY: Yessir!

DIMSHITS: For your information, these people don't deserve to tie my wife's shoelace! Not even her shoelace!

Scene Four

In VISKOVSKY's *room. He is wearing riding breeches and boots, but no jacket. His shirt collar is undone. There are bottles on the table—there has been much drinking.* KRAVCHENKO, *a tiny, flushed man in a military uniform, is lounging on the sofa with* MADAME DORA, *a gaunt woman dressed in black wearing large dangling earrings and with a Spanish comb in her hair.*

VISKOVSKY: Just for one deal, that's all, Yasha!

> *"I was possessed by one power alone,*
> *A single passion, a passion that consumes."*†

KRAVCHENKO: How much d'you need?

VISKOVSKY: Ten thousand pounds sterling. For one deal. You ever seen sterling pounds, Yasha?

KRAVCHENKO: All that cash just for thread?

VISKOVSKY: Forget the thread! We're talking diamonds. Three carat, blue water diamonds, clean, no sand. That's all they take in Paris.

KRAVCHENKO: There's none like that left here.

VISKOVSKY: There's diamonds in every house. You just have to know how to get at them. The Rimsky-Korsakovs have them, the

---

* "The circus is continuing, I have a toothache tonight."
† A quotation from Lermontov's poem *Mtsyri.*

Shakhovskys have them. No, there's still enough diamonds in imperial St. Petersburg!

KRAVCHENKO: You'll never make a Red merchant.

VISKOVSKY: Just you wait and see. My father used to trade—he traded estates against horses. . . . The horse guards may surrender, but they do not die.

KRAVCHENKO: Go and bring in Ludmila Nikolayevna. She's at the end of her rope in the corridor.

VISKOVSKY: I will arrive in Paris like a count.

KRAVCHENKO: Where the hell did Dimshits disappear to?

VISKOVSKY: He's hanging out in the outhouse, or playing cards with Shapiro and the Finn. [*He opens the door.*] Hey, miss, come warm yourself at our fire. [*He goes out into the corridor.*]

DORA [*Kisses* KRAVCHENKO's *hands.*]: My sunshine! My everything!

[VISKOVSKY *enters with* LUDMILA, *who is wearing her fur coat.*]

LUDMILA: This is beyond comprehension. We had an agreement.

VISKOVSKY: And an agreement is more precious than money.

LUDMILA: We agreed that I would be here at eight. It's quarter to ten now . . . and he didn't even leave me a key . . . where could he be?

VISKOVSKY: A bit of speculating and he'll be back.

LUDMILA: Be that as it may, these people are no gentlemen.

VISKOVSKY: Have a vodka, sweetheart.

LUDMILA: Yes, I will have one, I'm frozen through . . . still, all this is simply beyond comprehension!

VISKOVSKY: Allow me, Ludmila Nikolayevna, to introduce you to Madame Dora, a citizen of the republic of France—*Liberté, Égalité, Fraternité.* Among her other good qualities, she is also the owner of a foreign passport.

LUDMILA [*Extends her hand.*]: Mukovnina.

VISKOVSKY: You know Yasha Kravchenko. He was an ensign in the Czar's army, now he's a Red Artillerist. He's with the ten-inch gun detachment at Kronstadt, and you can turn those guns every which way.

KRAVCHENKO: Viskovsky has been on a roll all evening.

VISKOVSKY: Every which way! Who knows what can happen, Yasha.

They might ask you to blow up the street you were born on, and you would blow it up, or to blast an orphanage to bits, and you'd say, "A two-zero-eight fuse!" and blast that orphanage to bits. That's what you'd do, Yasha, as long as they let you live your life, strum your guitar, and sleep with thin women. You're fat but you like them thin. You'll do anything, and if they tell you to renounce your mother three times, you would renounce her three times. But that's not the point, Yasha! The point is they will want more: they won't let you drink vodka with the people you like, they'll make you read boring books, and the songs they'll teach you will be boring too! Then you'll be mad, my dear Red Artillerist! You'll be furious, your eyes will start rolling! Then two citizens will come visiting: "Let's go, Comrade Kravchenko." "Should I take any personal effects with me, or not?" you'll ask them. "No, you needn't take any personal effects with you. It'll be a quick interrogation, over in a minute." And that will be the end of you, my dear Red Artillerist. It'll cost them four kopecks. It's been calculated that a Colt bullet costs four kopecks and not a centime more."

DORA [*In broken Russian.*]: Jacques, take me to home.

VISKOVSKY: To your health, Yasha! To victorious France, Madame Dora!

LUDMILA [*Her glass has already been topped up a few times.*]: I'll quickly go see if he's back yet.

VISKOVSKY: A bit of speculating and he'll be back. Hey, Countess, did you think up that trick with the teeth yourself?

LUDMILA: Yes, I did . . . good, wasn't it? [*She laughs.*] I had no choice. Those Jews don't know how to respect a woman they want to be close to.

VISKOVSKY: When I look at you, Ludmila, I think of a little tomtit. Let's have a drink, my little tomtit!

LUDMILA: Are you trying to corner me? You've put something in this vodka, Viskovsky, haven't you?

VISKOVSKY: My little tomtit. All the strength of the Mukovnins went to Maria. All you were left with was a row of delicate teeth.

LUDMILA: That's cheap, Viskovsky.

VISKOVSKY: And I don't like your small breasts. A woman's breasts should be beautiful, large, helpless, like those of a ewe.

KRAVCHENKO: We'll be going, Viskovsky.

VISKOVSKY: No, you're not. . . . Why don't you marry me, my little tomtit?

LUDMILA: No, I'd be better off marrying Dimshits. I know exactly how things would turn out if I married you: you'd be drunk the first day, have a hangover the second, then you'd go off to God knows where, and then you'd end up shooting yourself. No, I think I'll stick to Dimshits.

KRAVCHENKO: We want to go, Viskovsky. Please!

VISKOVSKY: You're not going anywhere! A toast! A toast to all women! [*To* DORA.] This here is Ludmila . . . her sister's name is Maria.

KRAVCHENKO: I think Maria Nikolayevna has joined the army.

LUDMILA: She's at the Polish border right now.

VISKOVSKY: At the front! At the front, Kravchenko! They've got a waiter for a division commander.

LUDMILA: That is not true, Viskovsky! He's a metalworker.

VISKOVSKY: The waiter's name is Akim. Let's have a drink in honor of women, Madame Dora! Women love ensigns, waiters, petty officials, Chinamen. . . . A woman's business is love—the police will sort out what's what. [*He raises his glass.*] To all sweet women, wonderful women, who love us, even if only for an hour! Not even an hour, if you think about it. A veil of gossamer. Then the gossamer is torn. . . . Her sister is called Maria. . . . Imagine, Yasha, that you fall in love with the Czarina. "You're scum!" the Czarina says. "Go away!"

LUDMILA [*Laughs.*]: That sounds just like Maria.

VISKOVSKY: "You're scum! Go away!" She spurned the horse guardsman and decided to go to Furshtadskaya Street, 16, apartment 4.

LUDMILA: Don't you dare, Viskovsky!

VISKOVSKY: Let's drink to the Kronstadt Artillery, Yasha! . . . That's when she decided to go to Furshtadskaya Street. Maria Nikolayevna went out in a gray tailored dress suit. She had bought some violets by Troitsky Bridge, and pinned them to the lapel of her jacket . . . The prince—the one who plays the cello—the prince got his bachelor pad all nice and tidy, crammed his dirty clothes under the sideboard, put all the dirty dishes on a top shelf. . . . Then coffee and petit fours were served at Furshtadskaya Street. They drank their coffee. She had brought violets and spring with her, and curled her legs up on the sofa. He took a shawl, covered those strong, tender legs, and was met by a dazzling smile—a heartening, humble, sad, but still encouraging smile . . . she embraced his graying head. . . . "Prince! What is the matter, my Prince?" And his voice issued like that of a Papal choirboy. "*Passe, rien ne va plus.*"*

LUDMILA: You're such a bastard!

VISKOVSKY: Imagine, Yasha, right before your eyes the Czarina is removing her corset, her stockings, and her bloomers. . . . Even you, Yasha, might well blush and not know where to look.

[LUDMILA *laughs out loud, throwing her head back.*]

VISKOVSKY: She left 16 Furshtadskaya Street. . . . Where were her footprints for me to kiss? Where were they? But let us hope that Akim's voice rings deeper than that of a papal choirboy. . . . What do you think, Ludmila Nikolayevna?

LUDMILA: You put something in this vodka, Viskovsky! My head is spinning. . . .

VISKOVSKY: Come here, girly. [*He grabs her shoulders and pulls her toward him.*] How much did Dimshits pay you for that ring?

LUDMILA: What are you talking about?

VISKOVSKY: It's not your ring, it's your sister's. You sold a ring that wasn't yours.

LUDMILA: Let me go!

VISKOVSKY [*Pushes her through a side door.*]: Come with me, girly!

[DORA *and* KRAVCHENKO *remain alone in the room.*
In the window, the slow beam of a searchlight.
DORA, *puffy and disheveled, leans over to* KRAVCHENKO
and kisses his hands, babbling and moaning. FILIP,
with his scarred face, comes tiptoeing in unhurriedly on his bare feet,
and quietly takes the wine, sausage, and bread from the table.]

FILIP [*In a low voice, his head bent to the side.*]: You don't mind, do you, Yasha?

---

* The croupier's call when bets are closed at the roulette table.

[KRAVCHENKO *shakes his head, and* FILIP *carefully tiptoes out.*]

DORA: You are my sunshine! My life! My everything!

[KRAVCHENKO *remains silent. He hears steps outside.* VISKOVSKY *enters, smoking a cigarette, his hands shaking. The door to the adjacent room is open.* LUDMILA *is lying on the sofa, crying.*]

VISKOVSKY: Calm down, Ludmila Nikolayevna. You'll get over it.

DORA [*In broken Russian.*]: Jacques, I want our room. . . . Take me to home, Jacques!

KRAVCHENKO: In a minute, Dora.

VISKOVSKY: One for the road, Comrades?

KRAVCHENKO: In a minute, Dora.

VISKOVSKY: One for the road—to all the l-ladies . . .

KRAVCHENKO: This is very bad, Captain.

VISKOVSKY: To all the ladies, Yasha!

KRAVCHENKO: This is very bad, Captain.

VISKOVSKY: What is very bad, if I may ask?

KRAVCHENKO: Men with the clap should not sleep with women, Mr. Viskovsky.

VISKOVSKY [*In a military tone.*]: Would you care to repeat that?

[*Pause.* LUDMILA *stops sobbing.*]

KRAVCHENKO: What I said was: men infected with gonorrhea—

VISKOVSKY: Remove your glasses this instant, Kravchenko! I am going to punch your ugly mug.

[KRAVCHENKO *pulls out his revolver.*]

VISKOVSKY: Fine, if that's the way you want it!

[KRAVCHENKO *fires. Curtain. Behind the curtain: shots, falling bodies, a woman's scream.*]

Scene Five

At the MUKOVNINS' *apartment. The* OLD NANNY *is lying curled up on a trunk in the corner. She is asleep. A lamp casts a pool of light onto the table.* KATYA *is reading a letter from* MARIA *to* MUKOVNIN.

KATYA: "At dawn the bugle from squadron headquarters wakes me. By eight I have to be in the Political Propaganda Division, I'm in charge there—I edit the articles of the divisional newspaper, I run the literacy classes. Our reinforcements are all Ukrainians. They remind me of Italians, the way they talk and act. Russia has been suppressing and destroying their culture for centuries. In our house in Petersburg, opposite the Hermitage and the Winter Palace, we might as well have been living in Polynesia for all we knew anything at all about our people! Yesterday I read aloud in class the chapter in Papa's book about the murder of Czar Paul. It was so clear that the Czar deserved his fate that nobody in class questioned it. What they asked me instead—in their typically forthright way—was about the disposition of the regiment, the rooms in the palace, which regimental guard it had been that had stood watch that night, who were the conspirators, and in what way the Czar had wronged them. I keep hoping that Papa will come out here in the summer, as long as the Poles don't start acting up again. You will see a new army, Papa, new barracks, quite the opposite of what you are describing. In summer our garden here will be green and blossoming, the horses will regain their strength in the pastures, and their saddles will have been mended. I have already spoken to Akim Ivanovich, and he has agreed that you should come. Let's hope that you'll be well enough. It's night now. I came off duty late and climbed the worn, four-hundred-year-old stairs to my room. I live up in the tower, in a vaulted hall that was once Count Krasnicki's armory. The castle was built on a ledge below which a river flows. Meadows stretch into infinity, with a misty forest wall in the distance. There are lookout niches on every floor of the castle from which the approaching Tatars and Russians were observed, and from which boiling oil was poured onto the heads of the besiegers. Old Hedwig, the housekeeper of the last Krasnicki, cooked me some dinner and lit the fireplace, deep and black as a dungeon. The horses are stomping and dozing in the park below. Kuban Cossacks are sitting around a fire, eating and singing. The trees are covered with snow, the oak and chestnut branches hang heavy, and an uneven, silver blanket is lying over the snowy walks and statues. The statues are still unscathed—youths throwing javelins, and nude, frozen goddesses, their arms curved, their hair flying in waves, their eyes blind. Hedwig is dozing, her head shaking, the logs in the fireplace flare up and crumble. The centuries have made the bricks of this building resonant as glass, and they sparkle with gold as I sit here writing to you. I have Alyosha's photograph beside me on the table. My comrades here are the very people who didn't think twice about killing him. I was with them just a few minutes ago, working to set them free. Am I doing the right thing, Alyosha? Am I fulfilling your command to live a life of courage? The immortal essence of Alyosha keeps egging me on. It is late, but I cannot sleep. An inexplicable fear for you and a dread of my dreams keep me awake. I see pursuit, torture, and death. I live a strange dichotomy: closeness to nature and anxiety for you. Why does Ludmila write so rarely? A few days ago I sent her a paper signed by Akim Ivanovich, stating that as I am on active duty the authorities have no right to requisition my room at home. Furthermore, we must see to the official document allowing Papa to keep his library. If the document has expired, it has to be renewed at the People's Commissariat for Education at Chernishev Bridge, room 40. I would be so happy if Ludmila were to settle down and start a family, but the man should be a frequent guest at our house so that Papa can get to know him; Papa's heart won't deceive him. And Nanny should meet him too. Katya keeps complaining about Nanny, saying that she isn't doing any work. Katya, Nanny is old. She has raised two generations of Mukovnins. She has her own opinions and feelings about things, and she's no simpleton. I always felt that she did not have much of a peasant's soul in her, though if you think about it, what did we, tucked away in our Polynesia as we were, know about the peasantry? I hear that finding provisions in Petersburg has become even harder, and that the rooms and linen of everybody who is not working are being requisitioned. I am ashamed that we here at the front are living so well. Akim Ivanovich has taken me hunting twice, and I have a horse, a Don Cossack horse. . . ." [KATYA *raises her head.*] So you see how well things stand, Nikolai Vasilevich? [MUKOVNIN *covers his eyes with his palms.*] Don't cry. . . .

MUKOVNIN: I am asking God—we all have a God of our souls—why he gave me, egotistical, foolish man that I am, such wonderful children as Maria and Ludmila.

KATYA: But that is good, Nikolai Vasilevich. There is no need to cry.

Scene Six

A police station at night. A DRUNK *lies huddled under a bench. He is waving his fingers in front of his face and holding a conversation with himself. A thickset* OLD MAN *is dozing on the bench. He is wearing an expensive raccoon coat and a tall fur hat. The coat is open wide, revealing the old man's bare, gray chest. A* POLICE INSPECTOR *is cross-examining* LUDMILA. *Her fur hat is askew, her hair disheveled, and her coat has been tugged off one of her shoulders.*

INSPECTOR: Name?

LUDMILA: I want to go home.

INSPECTOR: Name?

LUDMILA: Barbara.

INSPECTOR: Father's name?

LUDMILA: Ivan.

INSPECTOR: Where do you work?

LUDMILA: At Laferme, the tobacco factory.

INSPECTOR: Your union card.

LUDMILA: I don't have it on me.

INSPECTOR: Why are you dealing in smuggled goods?

LUDMILA: I'm a married woman. . . . I want to go home!

INSPECTOR: What makes you want to deal in smuggled goods? Have you known Brilyov for a long time?

LUDMILA: I do not know any Brilyov. I have never heard of him.

INSPECTOR: Brilyov signed for the shipment of thread that passed through you to Gutman. Where did you stash the thread?

LUDMILA: What are you talking about? What do you mean, stash?

INSPECTOR: I'll tell you right away what I mean by stash! [*To a policeman.*] Call in Kalmikova!

[*The policeman brings in* SHURA KALMIKOVA, *the maid in the hotel at Nevsky Prospekt, 86, where* DIMSHITS *and his men are staying.*]

INSPECTOR: Are you a hotel maid?

KALMIKOVA: I am just standing in for someone else.

INSPECTOR: Do you recognize this woman?

KALMIKOVA: I most certainly do.

INSPECTOR: What can you tell me?

KALMIKOVA: I can answer your questions—her father's a general.

INSPECTOR: Does she work?

KALMIKOVA: She steams up men, that's her job.

INSPECTOR: Does she have a husband?

KALMIKOVA: Yeah, she got married in the bushes—she's got quite a few husbands. One of them spent a whole night in the outhouse because of her teeth.

INSPECTOR: What teeth? What are you going on about?

KALMIKOVA: She knows perfectly well what teeth.

INSPECTOR [*To* LUDMILA.]: You been arrested before? How many times?

LUDMILA: I have been infected. . . . I am ill.

INSPECTOR [*To* KALMIKOVA.]: We need to ascertain how many times she's been arrested before.

KALMIKOVA: That I don't know. I can't tell you that. I can't tell you what I don't know.

LUDMILA: I am exhausted. . . . Let me go home!

INSPECTOR: Calm down! Look at me!

LUDMILA: My head is spinning. . . . I'm going to faint.

INSPECTOR: Look at me!

LUDMILA: My God, why do I have to look at you?

INSPECTOR [*Furious.*]: Because I haven't had any sleep for five nights, that's why! Do you understand?

LUDMILA: Yes, I understand.

INSPECTOR [*Moves closer to her, grabs her by the shoulders, and looks into her eyes.*]: How many times have you been arrested?

Scene Seven

At the MUKOVNINS' *apartment. There are shadows on the walls.* GOLITSYN *is praying in front of an illuminated icon. The* NANNY *is sleeping on the trunk.*

GOLITSYN: Verily, verily, I say unto you, except a corn of wheat fall into the ground and die, it abideth alone: but if it die, it bringeth forth much fruit. He that loveth his life shall lose it; and he that hateth his life in this world shall keep it unto life eternal. If any man serve me, let him follow me; and where I am, there shall also my servant be: if any man serve me, him will my Father honor. Now is my soul troubled; and what shall I say? Father, save me from this hour: but for this cause came I unto this hour.

KATYA [*Comes up to him silently, stands next to him, and rests her head on his shoulder.*]: I always meet Redko at the headquarters in what used to be an antechamber. There's an oilskin sofa there. I go in, Redko locks the door, and afterward he unlocks it.

GOLITSYN: I see.

KATYA: I am going home to Borisoglebsk, *mon prince.*

GOLITSYN: That would be for the best.

KATYA: Redko keeps lecturing me on whom to love, whom to hate. He says that the law of big numbers is now in effect. But I, you see, am a small number. What do I matter?

GOLITSYN: But you do matter.

KATYA: Yes, I do matter! I should count! I am free now, Nanny. . . . Wake up. Please wake up. You'd sleep right through the Second Coming!

NEFEDOVNA [*Raises her head.*]: Where's Ludmila?

KATYA: Ludmila will be back soon, and I'm leaving town, so there'll be nobody to give you a hard time.

NEFEDOVNA: Why give me a hard time? What is there for me to do? I was born to be a nanny, hired to raise children, but there are no children here. The house is full of women, but there's not a single child in sight. One's gone off to fight a war, as if there's no one else who can do the fighting, the other one is roaming around lost. What kind of a house is this to be without children?

KATYA: We'll have some children by Immaculate Conception.

NEFEDOVNA: All you girls do is talk! You think I don't see what's going on? With you girls, nothing ever amounts to anything.

GOLITSYN: Go to Borisoglebsk, they need you. It's a wasteland there, with beasts devouring each other.

NEFEDOVNA: Look at the Molostovs—two-bit merchants, but they saw to it that their nanny was given a pension. Fifty rubles a month! Prince, why don't you see to it that I get a pension too?

GOLITSYN [*Lights the makeshift tin stove.*]: No one would listen to me now, Nanny. I have no connections these days.

NEFEDOVNA: But they were just two-bit merchants!

[MUKOVNIN *enters. The front door opens, and* MUKOVNIN *staggers back at the sight of* FILIP, *large and shapeless, hooded and wrapped in rags. Half of* FILIP's *face is covered in raw scar tissue. He is wearing felt boots.*]

MUKOVNIN: Who are you?

FILIP [*Moves closer.*]: One of Ludmila Nikolayevna's acquaintances.

MUKOVNIN: How may I help you?

FILIP: There has been a small disaster, Your Excellency.

KATYA: Did Mr. Dimshits send you?

FILIP: Yes, he sent me. The whole thing started from nothing.

KATYA: What about Ludmila Nikolayevna?

FILIP: They were all there together. . . . They were having a little fun, Your Excellency, but things got out of hand. Captain Viskovsky and, well, Kravchenko . . . they went at each other, both were a little tipsy—

GOLITSYN: General Mukovnin, let me have a word with our Comrade here.

FILIP: It's not like anything special happened. It was a misunderstanding. Both were a little tipsy, both had weapons—

MUKOVNIN: Where is my daughter?

FILIP: We are not sure, Your Excellency.

MUKOVNIN: Tell me where my daughter is! You need not hold anything back from me!

FILIP [*Barely audibly.*]: She's been arrested.

MUKOVNIN: I have looked death in the eye. I am a soldier!

FILIP [*Louder.*]: They've arrested her, Your Excellency.

MUKOVNIN: You mean they've arrested her? What for?

FILIP: Some illness or something got them going. Kravchenko says, "You gave her that illness, Captain Viskovsky, so I'll shoot you!" And they had weapons on them, so she—

MUKOVNIN: The Cheka* came for her?

---

*The "Extraordinary Commission" set up in 1917 to investigate counterrevolutionary activities. The Cheka later became the KGB.

FILIP: Some men came and took her away, who knows who they were. . . . nowadays no one wears no uniform, Your Excellency. You can't tell who's who.

MUKOVNIN: Katya, I must go to Smolny!*

KATYA: You're not going anywhere, Nikolai Vasilevich! You mustn't!

MUKOVNIN: I must go to Smolny immediately!

KATYA: Please, Nikolai Vasilevich—

MUKOVNIN: The thing is, Katya, that my daughter must be returned to me immediately. [*He goes to the telephone.*] Would you please connect me to Military Headquarters!

KATYA: You mustn't!

MUKOVNIN: I would like to speak to Comrade Redko. . . . This is Mukovnin. . . . All I can tell you, Comrade, is that in former days I was quartermaster general of the Sixth Army. . . . Hello, is that you, Comrade Redko? Hello, Comrade Redko! This is Mukovnin speaking. I hope you are well. . . . I am very sorry to disturb you. . . . The thing is that yesterday evening some armed men came and arrested my daughter Ludmila at a hotel on Nevsky Prospekt, number 86. I am not asking you to pull strings, Comrade Redko, I know that that sort of thing is frowned upon in your organization, I simply wish to announce that it is vital I see my oldest daughter, Maria Nikolayevna. You see, I have been somewhat unwell recently, and I feel it essential that I consult with her. We have sent telegrams and express letters to her—I know Katya has asked for your help in that—but we've received no answer. I would like to request to speak to her directly. . . . I should add that General Brusilov[†] has invited me to come to Moscow to discuss my return to active duty. . . . Oh, you say our letters were delivered? On the eighth? Well, I am very grateful to you! The best of luck, Comrade Redko! [*He hangs up.*] Everything is fine. They have found Maria and our telegram was delivered to her on the eighth! She'll be in Petersburg tomorrow, or the day after tomorrow at the latest. Nanny, we must tidy up Maria's room—tomorrow you will have to get up at the crack of

---

* The Petrograd Council, the seat of Lenin's government, situated in the former Smolny Institute for Girls of the Nobility.

† Alexei Alekseyevich Brusilov, 1853–1926, was a Soviet general who was also of aristocratic birth.

dawn and tidy it up! Katya is right—this apartment is a mess. We really have let it go, there's dust everywhere! We have to put covers on all the furniture. . . . Do we have covers, Katya?

KATYA: We have some, but not for all the furniture.

MUKOVNIN [*Rushing around the room.*]: We must cover the furniture at all cost! It will be nice for Maria to find everything just as she left it. Why not make things comfortable, if one is able to? Not to mention, at our place there's no chance to at least *s'amuser* a little. You have no penchant whatsoever for *amusement*, Katya, darling, you'll lag behind the times if you don't go to the theater.

KATYA: When Maria comes back, I shall go to the theater.

MUKOVNIN [*To* FILIP.]: I'm sorry, what is your name?

FILIP: Filip Andreyevich.

MUKOVNIN: Why don't you take a seat, Filip Andreyevich? We didn't even thank you for all your trouble. We must offer Filip Andreyevich something to eat. Nanny, do we have anything we can offer him? We always like having guests, Filip Andreyevich, though you must forgive our simple hospitality. Please, make yourself comfortable. We must introduce you to Maria Nikolayevna—

KATYA: You must get some rest, Nikolai Vasilevich. You must go and lie down.

MUKOVNIN: And for your information, I'm not in the least bit worried about Ludmila. It will be a lesson for her, a lesson because of her childishness, her lack of experience. . . . For your information, I'm even glad. . . . [*He shudders, stops, collapses into a chair.* KATYA *rushes over to him.*] Don't worry, Katya, don't worry. . . .

KATYA: Are you all right?

MUKOVNIN: It's nothing, it's just my heart. . . .

[KATYA *and* GOLITSYN *help him up and lead him out.*]

FILIP: He looks a bit rattled.

NEFEDOVNA [*Laying out plates on the table.*]: Were you there when they arrested our young lady?

FILIP: Yes, I was.

NEFEDOVNA: Did she fight back?

FILIP: At first she did, but then she just went with them.

NEFEDOVNA: I'll give you some potatoes and some fruit pudding too.

FILIP: Believe it or not, Grandma, we had a whole tubful of meat noodles back at our place, and then with all these troubles, we looked away for a second and they'd disappeared into thin air.

NEFEDOVNA [*She puts the potatoes in front of him.*]: They boiled off your face during the Civil War?

FILIP: No, it got boiled off a while back, during the civil peace.

NEFEDOVNA: So, you think there'll be another war? What do your people say?

FILIP [*Eating.*]: There'll be war in August.

NEFEDOVNA: What, with the Poles?

FILIP: With the Poles.

NEFEDOVNA: Haven't we already given them all the land they want?

FILIP: What they want is for their country to stretch from sea to sea. They want it to be like it was in old times again.

NEFEDOVNA: What idiots!

[KATYA *enters.*]

KATYA: The general is in very bad shape. We must call the doctor.

FILIP: Doctors, miss, don't come at such an hour.

KATYA: He is dying, Nanny! His nose has turned blue. . . . He already has the look of death on him!

FILIP: The doctors have all bolted their doors. You couldn't get them to come out at night even at gunpoint.

KATYA: We must go and get some oxygen from a pharmacy!

FILIP: Is His Excellency a union member?

KATYA: I don't know. We don't know anything about such things here.

FILIP: If he's not a union member, then they won't give him any.

[*The doorbell rings sharply.* FILIP *goes to open the door, and then returns.*]

FILIP: It's . . . it's . . . Maria Nikolayevna. . . .

KATYA: Maria?

[KATYA *goes toward the door with outstretched arms, bursts into tears, stops, covers her face with her hands, and then drops them. In front of her stands a* RED ARMY FIGHTER, *about nineteen years old, with long legs. He is dragging a sack behind him.* GOLITSYN *enters and stops by the door.*]

RED ARMY FIGHTER: Greetings!

KATYA: My God! What happened to Maria!

RED ARMY FIGHTER: Maria Nikolayevna has sent you some supplies.

KATYA: Where is she? Is she with you?

RED ARMY FIGHTER: Maria Nikolayevna is with the division—everyone's at their positions now. I've got something here for you—some boots—

KATYA: She didn't come with you?

RED ARMY FIGHTER: No, of course not. We're in the middle of a battle, Comrade.

KATYA: We've sent her letters, telegrams. . . .

RED ARMY FIGHTER: You can send what you want, it makes no difference. The units are on the move night and day.

KATYA: Are you going to see her?

RED ARMY FIGHTER: Sure I am. Do you want me to tell her something?

KATYA: Yes, please tell her . . . tell her that her father is dying—that there is no hope of saving him. Tell her that he called out to her on his deathbed . . . and that her sister, Ludmila, is no longer living with us, as she's been arrested. Tell Maria Nikolayevna that we wish her all the best, and that she mustn't feel remorse about not being here with us in our hour of need. . . .

[*The* RED ARMY FIGHTER *looks around, and steps back—*MUKOVNIN *comes staggering out of his room. His eyes are wandering, his hair disheveled, there is a smile on his face.*]

MUKOVNIN: You see, Maria, all the time you were away I wasn't in the least bit sick! On best behavior! [*He sees the* RED ARMY FIGHTER.] Who is this? [*He repeats his question louder.*] Who is this? Who is this? [*He collapses.*]

NEFEDOVNA [*Sinks to her knees beside* MUKOVNIN.]: Are you leaving me, my little Kolya? Aren't you going to wait for your poor old Nanny?

[MUKOVNIN *wheezes. Death throes.*]

Scene Eight

Noon. Blinding light. Outside the window, the sun-drenched columns of the Hermitage and a corner of the Winter Palace. The empty apartment of the MUKOVNINS. ANDREI *and his apprentice* KUZMA, *a fat-faced young man, are polishing the floor upstage.* AGASHA *is shouting out of the window.*

AGASHA: Damn you, Nyusha, don't let the child get all dirty down there! Where are your eyes, you sitting on them or something? A grown wench and still a fool! Tikhon! Hey, Tikhon! Why did you leave the shed door open? Lock the shed! Hello, Yegorovna! Is there any way I can get some salt from you till the first? I'll have my coupons by then and you'll get it back. I'll send my girl over to you with a little jar, and you can put the salt in it. . . . Tikhon! Hey, Tikhon! Have you been by the Novoseltsevs? When are they moving out?

TIKHON'S VOICE: They say they have nowhere to go!

AGASHA: They knew how to live nice and grand, now let them move out nice and grand! Tell them they've got till Sunday. Tell them that if they're still there after Sunday, things will get ugly! Nyusha! Damn you! Open your eyes! The child is stuffing dirt up its nose! Bring the child up here this instant, and come and wash windows instead! [*To the floor polisher.*] So, how are things moving along?

ANDREI: We're putting some muscle into it.

AGASHA: Then how about putting some muscle into those corners too? You haven't done them!

ANDREI: What corners?

AGASHA: All four corners. And you've turned the whole floor rusty brown. Is it supposed to be like that? The color's off!

ANDREI: We don't have the right materials to work with nowadays.

AGASHA: You think I was born yesterday? If there was money in it, you'd come up with the right materials in a second.

ANDREI: If it was up to me, I wouldn't ask my worst enemy to clean floors after the Revolution! During the Revolution the dirt grew to three inches thick on these floors—you couldn't shave it off with a plane! I should get a medal for cleaning floors after the Revolution, and all you do is bark.

[KATYA, *wearing mourning, enters upstage with* SUSHKIN.]

SUSHKIN: The only reason I'm buying all this stuff is because I'm a furniture fanatic. I'm nuts about furniture! I simply can't walk past an antique piece and resist it. Antiques make me crazy. But as we all know, buying anything large nowadays is like hanging a millstone around your neck and jumping into a lake, you get dragged right to the bottom. So you buy something, you're full of enthusiasm, and then the next morning, in the cold light of day, you don't know what to do with all the stuff.

KATYA: You forget that everything here is of exquisite quality. The Stroganoffs had this furniture brought from Paris a hundred years ago.

SUSHKIN: And that is why I'm giving you a billion two hundred rubles for it.

KATYA: How many loaves of bread does that buy?

SUSHKIN: Well, but you can't count these things in loaves of bread—you have to take into consideration the fact that I'm buying these pieces as a madman, as an enthusiast. I'm sure you know well enough what a risk I'm taking, owning grand pieces of furniture—I'll be the first in line to get carted off. [*Changes his tone.*] I've brought some young men with me. [*Shouts downstairs.*] Okay, everyone, you can come up now! And bring some ropes!

AGASHA [*Steps forward.*]: And where d'you think you're going to drag this off to?

SUSHKIN: I don't believe I have had the pleasure . . .

KATYA: This is our caretaker.

AGASHA: I'm the janitor here.

SUSHKIN: Pleased to meet you. How about this: you help us carry down the furniture, and we'll take care of you.

AGASHA: That will not be possible, Comrade.

SUSHKIN: What do you mean, not possible?

AGASHA: There's people moving in here from the basement.

SUSHKIN [*Dismissively.*]: Really? Fascinating!

AGASHA: And where are they going to get furniture from, if I may ask?

SUSHKIN: That is of no concern to us, Comrade.

KATYA: Agasha, Maria Nikolayevna has authorized me to sell all the furniture.

SUSHKIN [*To* AGASHA.]: Excuse me, Comrade, but does this furniture belong to you?

AGASHA: The furniture isn't mine, just as it isn't yours.

SUSHKIN: Listen, lady, first of all, you and I haven't shat in the same hole, okay? Secondly, your attitude is going to get you into trouble.

AGASHA: You bring a warrant, and I'll let you cart off the furniture.

KATYA: Agasha, this furniture belongs to Maria Nikolayevna, and as you know—

AGASHA: Everything I knew, madame, I have forgotten—I've had to relearn everything.

SUSHKIN: Careful, you're getting into deep waters!

AGASHA: You raise your voice to me and you're out of here!

KATYA: Let us go, Mr. Sushkin.

SUSHKIN [*To* AGASHA.]: You're a bit above yourself.

AGASHA: Bring me a warrant, and then you can cart everything out.

SUSHKIN: We'll be discussing this elsewhere.

AGASHA: Yes, down at the police station.

KATYA: Let us go, Mr. Sushkin.

SUSHKIN: I will go, but of one thing you can be sure: when I come back, I won't be alone.

AGASHA: Madame, what you're doing isn't right.

[*They leave.* ANDREI *and* KUZMA *finish polishing the floor. They gather their equipment.*]

KUZMA: She sure gave it to him.

ANDREI: That little lady knows how to throw punches.

KUZMA: Was she here when the general was around?

ANDREI: Back then she kept her head low and her mouth shut.

KUZMA: I'm sure the general was a nasty customer!

ANDREI: No, he wasn't! He never was! Whenever you went up to him, he'd say hello, shake hands with you. We all loved him.

KUZMA: What are you saying? How could you all love a general?

ANDREI: Because we're a bunch of fools! He didn't do any more harm than was to be expected. He chopped his own firewood.

KUZMA: Was he old?

ANDREI: Not really.

KUZMA: Then why did he die?

ANDREI:

> *"Man doesn't die because he's infirm*
> *He dies because he's served his term."*

And the general had served his term.

[*Enter* AGASHA, SAFONOV—*a bony, young, taciturn worker—and his*
pregnant wife ELENA, *a tall woman, not more than twenty, with*
a small, bright face. She is in the final stages of her pregnancy. They are
loaded with household goods: stools, mattresses, a little paraffin stove.]

ANDREI: Wait a second, wait a second—let me spread something on the
floor!

AGASHA: Come in, Safonov, don't be afraid! This is where you are going
to live!

ELENA: This is so fancy, couldn't we get a place that's less . . .

AGASHA: It's time you got used to better things.

ANDREI: You'll be surprised how fast you'll get used to better things.

AGASHA: The kitchen's to the left, and the bath where you can wash is
over there. Come on, young man, let's go get the rest of the stuff.
You stay here, Elena, and don't walk around—you'll lose your baby.

[AGASHA *and* SAFONOV *exit.* ANDREI *is gathering up his things—*
brushes, buckets. ELENA *sits down on a stool.*]

ANDREI: Well, good luck in your new home.

ELENA: It doesn't really look all that comfortable—it's so big.

ANDREI: When are you due?

ELENA: I'm going in tomorrow.

ANDREI: It'll be easy enough for you. You'll be going to the palace on
the Moika Canal, right?

ELENA: That's right, the Moika Canal.

ANDREI: That palace is now called "Mother and Child"—a Czarina had
it built for a shepherd, now women go there to give birth.
Everything's nicely fixed up, it'll be no hassle.

ELENA: I have to go in tomorrow. One minute I'm frightened, the next
I'm not.

ANDREI: What's there to be frightened of—you're going in to give birth, one hiccup and it'll be out. You squeeze all your insides, you give birth, then you'll be as good as new.

ELENA: It's just that I have such narrow hips.

ANDREI: When push comes to shove, they'll widen. You should see some of those pretty little women, tiny, with lots of nice hair, the prettiest little hands and feet, and they give birth to large roughnecks who can drink vodka by the bucket and fell a bull with a single punch. Giving birth is what women are here for. [*He swings his sack onto his shoulder.*] You want a girl or a boy?

ELENA: I don't mind either way.

ANDREI: You're right, both are fine. What I say is that all kids born today have a good life to look forward to. That's a sure thing nowadays! [*He picks up the rest of his tools.*] Let's go, Kuzma! [*To* ELENA.] One hiccup and it'll be out.

> [*The floor polishers exit.* ELENA *opens the windows,
> and the sun and the noise of the street come pouring in.
> Sticking out her belly, she carefully walks along the walls,
> touching them, peeks into adjacent rooms, turns on the chandelier,
> and turns it off again.* NYUSHA, *an enormous crimson-faced girl,
> comes in carrying a bucket and a rag to wash the windows.
> She climbs up onto the windowsill and tucks in her skirt above
> her knees. She is bathed in sunlight. She stands against the
> background of the springtime sky like a statue holding up an arch.*]

ELENA: Will you come to our housewarming party, Nyusha?

NYUSHA [*In a bass voice.*]: You ask me—I'll come. What're you going to serve?

ELENA: Not much, whatever I can get my hands on.

NYUSHA: What I want is some red wine, nice and sweet. [*She suddenly bursts into song with a loud, piercing voice.*]

> "*A Cossack galloped through valleys unseen
> Into cold and distant Manchurian lands,
> He galloped through gardens and orchards green,
> A precious ring clasped in his powerful hands.*

The precious ring was from his sweetheart true:
'Think of me as you ride through those distant lands,
And in a year forever I shall belong to you.'

Alas, a year had come and gone. . ."

[*Curtain*]

XIV

❧

Screenplays

B*abel began working for the Soviet cinema in the mid-1920s. He had achieved literary fame with his Odessa and* RED CAVALRY *stories, and was approached by Pyotr Chardynin, the renowned director of such silent film classics as* QUEEN OF SPADES *and* HOUSE OF KOLOMNA, *to write a screenplay version of his* RED CAVALRY *story "Salt." The Ukrainian State Film Company (VUKFU) produced the movie in 1925. The same year, Babel provided the subtitles for the movie* JEWISH LUCK, *based on Shalom Aleichem's Menachem Mendel stories. Alexander Granovsky of the Moscow State Yiddish Theater, along with Grigori Gricher-Cherikover, directed the movie. The cinematography was by Eduard Tissé, who was Sergei Eisenstein's cinematographer on classics such as* BATTLESHIP POTEMKIN, OCTOBER 1917, *and* ALEXANDER NEVSKY.*

Not all Babel's screenplays have come down to us. In 1925, he began working on the first screenplay in this section, ROAMING STARS, *loosely based on Shalom Aleichem's novel of the same name (translated into English as* WANDERING STAR). *Grigori Gricher-Cherikover also directed this movie.*

In ROAMING STARS, *Babel kept to the basic technique of silent movie scenario writing, numbering the scene sequences and writing out the subtitles in capital letters. But unlike other screenwriters of the period, who confined themselves to dry description and technical stage directions, Babel's scenario writing had literary subtlety and stylistic depth: "She is a gaunt German woman with yellow puffed-up hair and an unblinking glass eye. The telephone rings. She lifts the receiver. Her face uncoils like a long spring, at the end of which is a gush of prefabricated delight." The movie was a box office success, but the critics were not pleased with the director's work, accusing him of smoothing out and prettifying Babel. As the movie magazine* SOVIETSKOE KINO *wrote, "The movie will do well, and it will bring in the public, but there is nothing, or almost nothing left of Shalom Aleichem or Isaac Babel."*

The second screenplay in this section, BENYA KRIK, *which Babel based on his Odessa stories, was to be filmed by the Soviet Union's most renowned director, Sergei Eisenstein. Babel, however, transferred the movie from* GOSKINO *(the State Committee for Cinematography) in Moscow, to the Ukrainian State Film Company (VUKFU), which had just filmed* ROAMING STARS, *and Vilner directed* BENYA KRIK.

Babel's movie THE CHINESE MILL, *directed by Levshin, was released in 1928.* NUMBER 4 STARAYA SQUARE *is Babel's only screenplay for a talkie that has come down to us.*

Among Babel's screenplays that have not yet been located are: JIMMY HIGGINS, *adapted from Upton Sinclair's novel (1928), a movie that Babel coscripted with Tasin, and* PILOTS *(1935). In 1939, Babel worked on the scenario for Mark Donskoi's famous Gorky trilogy with Ilya Gruzdev, Gorky's biographer. A few months later Babel was arrested, and when the film came out in 1940 his name was removed from the credits.*

ROAMING STARS

Thoughout the early 1920s, Isaac Babel had been involved in promoting the translation and publication of Shalom Aleichem's work in Russian. He had written the subtitles for the 1925 silent movie Jewish Luck, *based on Shalom Aleichem's Menachem Mendel stories, had translated some of his stories from Yiddish, and had put together and edited an extensive selection of translations of Aleichem's stories by Solomon Gekht.*

The silent movie Roaming Stars *premiered in 1926. The screenplay was only loosely based on Shalom Aleichem's novel of the same name (translated into English as* Wandering Star*). In the novel, Leibel and Reizl (the movie's Lev and Rachel) run away from the "Bessarabian shtetl of Holeneshti" with a traveling Yiddish theater. Leibel proves to be an actor of unprecedented talent who, in Aleichem's words, "can turn snow into lumps of cheese." His performances make the traveling theater world famous, the theater leaves for New York, and Leibel and Reizl live happily ever after. In Babel's screenplay there is no happy ending. Young Lev becomes a world famous violinist who ultimately pays a high price for his fame and fortune in the capitalist West, while Rachel, by a twist of fate, joins the struggle for the Revolution.*

Part One

1. The edge of a double bed. Night. The broad back of old Ratkovich, the rich man of the shtetl. He is asleep. Somebody's bare arm slithers over his pillow. Old Ratkovich rolls over, and in his sleep traps the thief's hand, moves again, the hand frees itself, snatches a bundle of keys from under the pillow, and disappears.
2. A well-furnished room (but one smacking of the shtetl) in Ratkovich's house. It is a summer night. A moonbeam falls on the spotless floor. The door opens slowly. Lev Ratkovich, the rich man's eighteen-year-old son, enters the room on tiptoe. The

flame of the candle flickers. The young man puts the candle on the table, and goes over to the safe.

3. A large pier glass cabinet, a family heirloom, stands against the wall. In it flicker the moonbeams and the candle's flame.

4. Lev opens the safe. He takes out his father's silken money pouch. A wad of banknotes falls out of the pouch and onto the floor. A thud is heard. The young man drops the pouch and throws himself in terror on the floor, covering the money with his body.

5. Old Ratkovich's black-fringed silk pouch is lying on the floor in the moonlight.

6. The young man is still lying on the floor. The mirror reflects his distorted, terrified face. Behind him a white apparition begins swaying. It sways more and more, moves toward him, is about to grab him. Lev cowers as close to the floor as possible.

7. A cat, sleeping in a deep armchair, wakes up, stretches, jumps onto a hanging lamp draped in a white sheet. The lamp sways. This is the white apparition that has frightened Lev.

8. The reflection of the swaying lamp in the mirror.

9. The cat jumps from the lamp onto the back of the young man lying on the floor. He squirms, lifts his head, comes to his senses. He grabs the money and rushes out of the room.

10. The candle has burned itself down. It goes out. The cat curls itself into a ball, and dozes off.

11. Old Ratkovich's bedroom. He is asleep next to his wife in a very large featherbed. Both of them are wearing nightcaps. Lev tiptoes through the room. He is barefoot, as before, his shoes hanging over his shoulder. He is holding a violin and a bow wrapped in cloth. He carefully opens the door to the next room, where his brothers and sisters are asleep.

12. AND YOUR DESCENDANTS, O ISRAEL, WILL BE MORE ABUNDANT THAN THE GRAINS OF SAND BY THE OCEAN.

13. The room where the Ratkovich children sleep looks more like a boarding-school dormitory than a bedroom. A multitude of beds of every shape and size. A multitude of children of different ages and proportions. The fugitive makes his way among the beds, kisses his youngest sister on the forehead, and climbs out the window.

14. A maze of rooftops of small shacks stretches out in front of the window that Lev has climbed out of. The shacks are huddled close together. Their roofs are slanting, covered with slippery moss, and are reminiscent of Indian pagodas. Young Ratkovich jumps from the window onto the first roof.

15. The earth illuminated by moonlight. The roofs cast shadows. The shadow of Ratkovich's jump.

16. Ratkovich jumps from roof to roof. He jumps like a gymnast on a flying trapeze. Finally—he reaches the ground.

17. The deserted street of a little Ukrainian border shtetl. The bewitching lights of the night flood the crooked little alleys and the tightly packed hovels; the streets look as if they are from a stage set of a fairy-tale play. Staggering through the mud, holding his violin tightly, young Ratkovich runs in zigzags down the street, as if he were running for his life.

18. He comes across two drunken peasants. Holding on to each other, the peasants are standing with their legs apart and their foreheads together, like two crossed rifles. They separate with extreme difficulty, grope for the gates of their houses, which are God knows where. Their drunken faces are forlorn.

19. "THERE WAS A DOOR LATCH HERE THIS MORNING, BUT NOW IT'S GONE . . . JESUS-MARY-AND-JOSEPH!"

20. The drunken peasants, giving up the idea of finding their houses, slowly kiss each other and sink to their knees. They kiss each other's beards with utmost tenderness, scrupulousness, and care. Unable to stop kissing, they tumble, holding on to each other, into the torpid shtetl mud, and fall asleep.

21. In the distance, young Ratkovich's slender figure flashes through dark back streets. He creeps toward a rickety two-story house of strange Ukrainian-Polish architecture, with cellars, sheds, and a pen for animals on the ground floor.

22. The drunkards lie there kissing each other from time to time as they sink deeper and deeper into the mud. Their hair is disheveled. Their mud-caked boots stick out like sunken stakes in a flooded field. Their beards are tousled. There is a deeply pensive expression on their faces.

23. Ratkovich enters a dark, reeking corridor, which lies below the

living quarters of the two-story house. Deep in the back—in the shed—a cow's muzzle.

24. A woman wrapped in a cloak is crouching in the dark corner of the cowshed, which is filled with barrels, buckets, and paints.

25. Ratkovich approaches the shed, bangs the roof with a pole.

26. The figure in the corner shudders, jumps up, tips over a pail. A thick, white stream of milk flows onto the floor from the pail.

27. Ratkovich bangs against the roof with the pole. A woman's hand grabs the pole, and out of the shed comes Rachel Monko, the seventeen-year-old daughter of the *belfer*, the assistant to the *melamed* at the Hebrew school. The cloak covers her face and body.

28. Rachel uncovers her face and rushes to Ratkovich. Her lips reach for his lips, but at that very moment the girl stops in her tracks. There are tears in her eyes. She looks at the young man with unusual tenderness.

29. "IS IT DECIDED, LEV?"

30. Ratkovich takes Rachel's slender hand in his. Their hands tremble—it is a lingering, nervous, unstoppable trembling.

31. The stream of milk slowly twists its way along the dirt floor of the shed.

32. Ratkovich bends toward Rachel. He says:

33. "IT IS DECIDED. . . . I WILL GO ABROAD WITH OTS-MAKH. HE WILL STAGE HIS TRAGEDIES, AND I SHALL BE THE SOLO VIOLINIST IN THE ORCHES-TRA. . . . AND IN TWO YEARS, RACHEL, YOU AND I WILL GET MARRIED!"

34. Ratkovich and Rachel's faces come closer. Their eyes are closed, their eyelids quiver. They approach one another, but again they stop: the agonizing game of young men and women before their first kiss. Ratkovich awkwardly presses his lips against Rachel's cheek. Her eyes, wide open and fixed, look to the side, and tears flow down her happy face. Ratkovich moves his lips closer and closer to her mouth. The violin falls out of his hands. Rachel stands rigid, she doesn't move. He kisses her lips. Rachel smiles, shudders, and suddenly embraces him with all her might.

35. The violin is lying on the ground. The stream of milk slowly flows around it.

36. The first kiss. The cow thrusts her short muzzle out of the shed and licks the lovers with her long tongue. CUT

37. The steppe, the moon. A high-framed cart, draped with torn rags, stands by a bluff. This cart is in fact a covered wagon from a gypsy camp. A driver is slumbering on the wagon box. In his sleep he furiously scratches himself, twists his legs, and scrapes his back against the leather hood of his wagon.

38. The sky. Full moon. The clear light of the moon. Swanlike clouds float slowly by.

39. Far in the background, near the horizon, the running figures of Ratkovich and Rachel.

40. The driver scratches himself furiously, but doesn't wake up. One of his violent movements almost capsizes the wagon. The lively face of an old woman appears between the rags.

41. "WHAT'S GOING ON, MEYER?"

42. The driver wakes up, and turns his imperturbable face to the old woman.

43. "NOTHING, FLEAS!"

44. The glistening face of the moon.

45. The river. Strips of moon on the water.

46. Ratkovich and Rachel stand on a bluff overlooking the river. Their arms are stiff and shivering. Ratkovich is pressing his violin to his chest. The lovers walk off in different directions. First they tread warily, slowly, then more quickly, then they run as fast as they can.

47. The wagon. The sleeping driver.

48. Panting, Ratkovich approaches the wagon. He throws his violin onto a bundle of rags and, exhausted, climbs into the wagon. The old woman nudges the dozing driver in the back.

49. "LET'S GO, MEYER!"

50. The driver raises his whip over the impassive horses. They don't move. Then he wallops each of them over the tail, and they begin galloping. The wagon rattles over rocks and stones down the slope toward the glistening river.

51. Deep inside the wagon Ratkovich and the old woman huddle close together. He gives her the bundle of banknotes. The old woman's kerchief slips off, revealing the bald head and expressive

face of Otsmakh, a Jewish vaudeville actor. Otsmakh hoists up a whole series of frocks and petticoats he is wearing, unfastens his bloomers rather indecently, and tucks the money into little pouches sewn into his drawers. He rearranges his frocks, and blissfully cuddles up to Ratkovich's shoulder.

52. The horses cross the river, going deeper and deeper into the water. The moonlight lies on the waves. Meyer stands upright on the wagon box, the horses wade up to their stomachs in the shining, seething water. Otsmakh, frightened, crawls to the very top of the wagon. With one hand he is holding on to Meyer, with the other he is clutching the money pouches in his bloomers. His face shows an excessive amount of fear. The river becomes deeper and deeper.

53. The steppe. Rachel stands on the precipice. Far in the distance, the wagon is rolling out onto the opposite bank of the river.

Part Two

54. OTSMAKH TRANSFORMS HIMSELF INTO A TRAGIC ACTOR.

55. A mirror. Over the mirror, an electric lamp. The powerfully lit face of Otsmakh. He is making up his face. The makeup: a long gray beard parted in two like a majordomo's beard, low-hanging bushy eyebrows, cheeks covered in rouge, on his ears gigantic fake earrings, on his head a powdered wig of the kind worn at the French court in the eighteenth century.

56. KING LEAR, FROM SHAKESPEARE TO . . . OTSMAKH!

57. Otsmakh in all his glory. He is pleased with himself. He is wearing lacquered officers' boots with spurs, white buckskin breeches, and a page's velvet jacket.

58. A squalid dressing room. Ratkovich is tuning his violin next to Otsmakh. Otsmakh turns to him:

59. "MAY I CEASE BEING OTSMAKH, IF TODAY I DO NOT WIPE THE FLOOR WITH THAT FAMOUS POSSARD PERFORMANCE!"

60. Otsmakh rings the bell, and dashes backstage. He runs past three women wearing the most bizarre stage makeup.

61. THE THREE DAUGHTERS OF KING LEAR.

62. Two of the daughters are stout, middle-aged Jewish women, the third is a girl of about six. Like Otsmakh, the actresses are also wearing lacquered officer's boots with spurs. Their stomachs are squeezed into satin vests. One of the women is wearing a kind of helmet from which two braids hang down; the second woman, a cap full of feathers. The third of King Lear's daughters—the six-year-old—has her hair loose, and is wearing a garland of paper flowers. The girl has on a simple peasant tunic. The Jewish women are having a quick snack before the curtain rises. Otsmakh runs past them with the bell.

63. Otsmakh runs onto the stage, the curtain is down.

64. AT THE COURT OF KING LEAR.

65. King Lear's throne stands to the side of the stage. Above the throne hang Japanese fans and family photographs of God knows who, mostly military figures. Right in front of the audience is a case with Hebrew inscriptions, like the cases in synagogues where the Torah scrolls are kept. Otsmakh rings the bell, and looks through a hole in the curtain at the audience.

66. The eighth row of the orchestra. The audience is from a little ramshackle Galician town. Hasidic men, old women in brown wigs and headdresses, young men with swank sideburns, opulent Jewish women in tightly corseted dresses. A multitude of children. Babies make up a third of the audience. They are squealing, crying, or sleeping. One baby is causing a particularly loud ruckus. Suddenly it calms down. Its face takes on a deeply pensive, thoughtful expression. The man sitting in the next seat jumps up in a fury. He points at his wet suit and at the puddle on the seat. The woman wrings her hands and carries the child off.

67. The woman rushes through the theater and the foyer holding the peeing, hollering child out in front of her. She runs out onto a balcony that overlooks the town, which is submerged in mist. She seats the child on the railing.

68. Otsmakh continues looking over the audience. The theater manager rushes up to him.

69. "PROFESSOR RETI IS IN THE AUDIENCE!"

70. Otsmakh looks blankly at the manager. The manager elucidates:

71. "THE FAMOUS PROFESSOR RETI FROM THE BERLIN CONSERVATORY!"

72. Otsmakh wraps himself in his black cloak embroidered with butterflies and skulls. He rushes backstage, and from there to the professor's box, where, with deep bows he greets the professor and his daughter as they enter the box. The professor is an old man in a tailcoat, with long wavy gray hair. Otsmakh kowtows before him.

73. "TODAY, MY DEAR PROFESSOR, YOU WILL HAVE THE OPPORTUNITY TO SEE OTSMAKH WIPING THE FLOOR WITH POSSARD'S FAMOUS PERFORMANCE!"

74. Otsmakh disappears as suddenly as he appeared. The stupefied professor watches him leave.

75. The lights go out in the auditorium. The audience seats itself, the children play in the aisles. Otsmakh comes out onto the ramp in front of the curtain. He takes a deep bow and proclaims:

76. "NOW, DEARLY BELOVED CLIENTS, WE WILL PRESENT THE LATEST CREATION OF THE RENOWNED NEW YORK AUTHOR AND VAUDEVILLIST, JACOB SHAKESPEARE, 'KING LEAR,' OR 'THEY WERE THICK AS THIEVES'!"

77. Otsmakh finishes his speech, takes a deep bow, and disappears behind the curtain. At that moment the conductor's baton appears above the rim of the orchestra pit. The baton turns out to be an everyday walking stick with a silver monogram and a small strap on the end.

78. The conductor is wearing an Austrian officer's uniform and has a yarmulke on his head. He stands rigidly, his hands barely moving; he doesn't conduct, he simply winks at the musicians whose turn it is to play.

79. The orchestra in action. The musicians: Hasidim wearing coats. Young Ratkovich stands in a prominent place. In the corner, the German drummer is waving his drumsticks about in the air. The drummer is drunk.

80. The conductor winks gravely at the drummer.

81. The drunk German hurries back to his drum and gives it a pow-

erful blow. Ignoring the conductor's anxious winks, the German continues beating the drum. The German's wife is standing behind him and pulls him away from the drum. She holds her drunken husband tightly by his coattails, and only lets him go when it is his turn to beat the drum.

82. Professor Reti and his daughter are watching the drummer and are shaking with laughter. They are sitting in the front loge. The old man is leaning back in his seat laughing out loud.

83. The orchestra falls silent. The conductor winks at Ratkovich. He begins to play.

84. His solo.

85. Ratkovich's intense face, the violin, thin fingers flying over the strings.

86. Professor Reti, still leaning back in his seat, stops laughing. The old man sits upright and peers at Ratkovich.

87. The solo.

88. Ratkovich's thin fingers rushing over the strings.

89. The drummer's wife leans against her dozing husband's back and listens with rapture to Ratkovich's playing.

90. The professor leans forward over the railing of his theater box. His eyes are fixed on Ratkovich. He grabs hold of his daughter's hand.

91. "PAPA, WHAT'S WRONG?"

92. The professor, elated, stands up, sings, conducts, sways.

93. "HOW HE CAN PLAY! OH, HOW THIS BOY CAN PLAY!"

94. Ratkovich has jumped up from his stool. He plays standing. Inspiration rocks him. His thin, intense face is distorted, pale, and beautiful. His fingers fly over the neck of the violin with diabolic speed. He finishes.

95. The conductor, his mouth open, lowers his baton and stands frozen in the orchestra pit.

96. The musicians, crouching, trudge toward the exit. Ratkovich shuffles out behind them. The drummer wakes up, shudders, and gives the drum a powerful blow. At that moment, the curtain rises.

97. The professor rushes out of the box. He gets caught on the door handle and his jacket tears. He hurries on.

98. The curtain is up. Otsmakh is lounging in a relaxed but mournful pose on his throne. His three daughters are at his feet, look-

ing up at him adoringly. In the opposite corner is a group of doleful courtiers wearing a wild medley of costumes. The court jester stands next to the throne. He is an incredibly lanky, red-haired Jew. He is wearing American checkered pants, a Tyrolean hat, and is holding a rattle. Otsmakh, emerging from profound thoughts, claps his hands.

99. A coquettish maid in an apron and a frilly cap moves a small table with little snacks and a bottle of wine next to the throne. There is a label on the bottle. Otsmakh pours himself some wine, his little finger delicately lifted, and drinks half a glass. With a majestic sweep he pours the rest on the floor. The maid grabs a broom, rushes toward the throne, and begins sweeping at the wine.

100. The musicians, crouching, hobble toward the exit along a narrow corridor beneath the stage. Professor Reti comes rushing up to Ratkovich, and grabs him by the lapel:

101. "WHO ARE YOU? WHERE ARE YOU FROM?"

102. Ratkovich looks at the old man in astonishment. The professor is tugging harder and harder at his lapel.

103. "WHO IS YOUR TEACHER?"

104. Ratkovich bows awkwardly, stiffly, very self-consciously.

105. "I . . . I STUDIED WITH RABBI ZALMAN IN DERAZHNY, IN THE DISTRICT OF VOLHYNIA."

106. The old professor's coat is torn. The old man is intense—he clasps his head, shakes Ratkovich's hand, pats his shoulder.

107. "PLAY SOMETHING, PLAY SOMETHING FOR ME, MY DEAR BOY!"

108. Ratkovich looks about helplessly. The obsequious conductor motions him to play. Ratkovich places his violin under his chin.

109. The tragedy of King Lear is unfolding. His eldest daughter, the stays of her corset jutting out, is dancing before the king. She strikes voluptuous poses. The courtiers clap and sing as at a Jewish wedding. But suddenly one of the courtiers—he is wearing a top hat and a coat of armor—commits an act of unprecedented effrontery. He pinches the king's daughter's breast. Otsmakh notices this. He pulls his sword out of its sheath and throws himself on the miscreant. A bloody duel ensues. The king and the courtier engage in a sword fight.

110. Professor Reti is sitting backstage on a pile of ropes in a corner. Covering his face with his hands, he is listening to Ratkovich play. The young man has finished playing. The old man lowers his hands from his face, which is twisted with emotion. He jumps up, grabs Ratkovich's hand, drags him to a large office calendar hanging on the wall. The date on the calendar is Thursday, August 19, 1909. Pointing at the calendar, the old man says:

111. "COME STUDY WITH ME! I SWEAR TO YOU THAT WITHIN THREE YEARS YOU WILL BE A GREAT ARTIST!"

112. A close-up of the calendar. A hand slowly lifts up the top page and bends it back.

Part Three

113. Briansky Station in Moscow. A crowd of porters and people who have come to meet the train. In the background, a grid with a board showing the arrival times of the trains.

114. The board. The date: December 11, 1912. Time of arrival: 1.57 P.M.

115. THE DATE ON THE BOARD.

116. The train pulls into the station. The porters and the waiting crowd rush toward the arriving train.

117. Jostling and shoving on the platform. The unloading of passengers. Family scenes.

118. A tall, flushed Russian girl descends from a third-class car. Her whole family rushes to embrace her: an old colonel, a flamboyant student, two little cadets wearing large caps, an old maid wearing a hat with dangling ribbons. They kiss the girl, push flowers at her, call over porters. All their faces are filled with emotion. Right behind her, Rachel gets off the train with all her bundles.

119. A wave of people carries Rachel to the exit. She is weighed down by her bundles and bags.

120. Porters are wheeling carts packed high with bags along the plat-

form. On one of the carts is a live bird in a cage. A grinding stream of carts flows past Rachel. She is blocking their way. The bewildered girl is trapped between mountains of speeding baggage. The porters yell and curse at her for all they are worth. One porter shouts:

121. "LOOK WHO'S COME TO TOWN FROM THE STICKS!"
122. Stunned, Rachel staggers back. The carts fly past, sparks flashing from their wheels.
123. At the baggage checkroom. Rachel is checking all her things. Over her head fly bales, bundles, a bag.
124. Rachel is standing on the square in front of the Briansky Station. The crowd at the station disperses. A provincial girl in Moscow. She goes up to a policeman and asks him the way. The policeman, wearing cotton gloves, explains very politely which tram she has to take. She hurries to catch a tram.
125. Rachel in the tram. She is surrounded by tram passengers, the most hard-hearted people in the world. Ecstatically, Rachel drinks in the never-before-seen splendor of the tram.
126. The man standing next to Rachel is a doleful, red-nosed bureaucrat wearing a uniform cap. He asks her in a sour voice:
127. "WHAT'S THERE TO BE SO CHEERFUL ABOUT?"
128. Rachel answers, beaming:
129. "IT IS SUCH FUN TO BE TRAVELING ON A MOSCOW TRAM!"
130. The bureaucrat raises his eyebrows and moves away from her. He is under the impression that she is a lunatic.
131. Rachel gets off the tram, goes to an old, two-story building with a sign: "Rossiya. Rooms to Let. I. P. Butsenko."
132. The kitchen in the Rossiya boardinghouse. Bright cleanliness. The boardinghouse is owned by Butsenko and his wife, an old couple with neatly protruding bellies. Both are wearing clean aprons. They are busy preparing potato dumplings.
133. Rachel is standing at the entrance of the Rossiya boardinghouse. She takes a letter out of her bag and rings the bell.
134. The kitchen. The doorbell rings. Butsenko takes off his apron and patters to the front door.
135. Butsenko opens the door: "May I help you?" Rachel timidly hands

him the letter. The old man leads her over to his desk, takes his copper-rimmed spectacles out of a drawer, and begins to read. As he reads, a tender smile brightens his face.

136. A close-up of the letter: "DEAREST IVAN POTAPICH. WITH ALL MY HEART I RECOMMEND THE BEARER OF THIS LETTER, A GIRL FROM MY TOWN, TO BE A LODGER AT YOUR BOARDINGHOUSE. SHE LEFT OUR TOWN WITH GREAT DIFFICULTY AND HAS HEADED FOR MOSCOW IN ORDER TO CONTINUE HER EDUCATION, FOR WHICH SHE HAS AN UNQUENCHABLE PASSION. . . ."

137. The little old man throws down the letter, takes Rachel's hands in his, squeezes them gently, bursts into an endless fit of laughter, and takes her into the kitchen to meet his wife.

138. In the kitchen. Butsenko takes Rachel over to the old woman:

139. "VLADIMIR SEMYONICH HAS SENT US A LODGER."

140. The old woman clasps her plump hands together, dries her fingers on her apron, and kisses Rachel on both cheeks. Butsenko pulls Rachel away from his wife.

141. "MOTHER, YOU'LL SMOTHER THE POOR GIRL WITH YOUR KISSES! WHY NOT GO PUT ON THE SAMOVAR?

142. Butsenko takes the girl to her room. It is a cozy, old-fashioned room. There are icons and an icon lamp in the corner. Another icon, a tiny one, is hanging on the headboard of the bed. Butsenko rushes around, puts things away, and hurries off with a jug to get water.

143. The tiny icon hanging on the headboard.

144. Rachel is alone. She takes off her hat and walks over to the window.

145. Outside the window stands an ancient Moscow church with its onion-shaped domes.

146. Butsenko, panting and beaming, comes in with the jug of water and a clean towel. Rachel washes up. She brushes her teeth, thoroughly washes her face and hands. She gasps with pleasure. The old man looks tenderly at her unbound hair and the wonderful, virginal nape of her neck. Rachel continues washing for a long

time, and the old man, tired of standing with the towel in his hands, walks over to the table and looks at Rachel's passport. A change comes over his face.

147. Rachel is washing, gasping with pleasure.

148. Old Mrs. Butsenko comes bustling through the corridor, carrying a tray with steaming pies, tea glasses, and a samovar that envelops her head with a cloud of steam.

149. Butsenko is holding Rachel's passport in his hands. He peers at Rachel, and then, with a nasty expression on his face, continues leafing through her passport.

150. A close-up of the passport: RACHEL KHANANEVNA MONKO, 19 YEARS OF AGE, UNMARRIED.

151. There is a look of surprise on the old man's face. He adjusts his spectacles on his nose, and reads page three of her passport.

152. The heading on page three: ZONES IN WHICH JEWS ARE PERMITTED TO RESIDE.

153. The old woman puts the pies, glasses, and samovar on the table. Rachel has just finished washing up. She laughs, and with her bare, strong hands reaches out for the towel which the old man is holding. But Butsenko won't give her the towel, he pulls it away. There is anger, fear, and reproach in his meek face. Shaking his head, he says:

154. "A JEWESS! THE SHAME OF IT!"

155. Rachel's face. Having been refused the towel, she dries her wet face with the hem of her skirt.

156. Butsenko stamps his foot and shouts to his wife, "Take all of that away!" The indignant old woman removes the tray she had prepared for Rachel. The old woman's head is enveloped by the samovar's steam. Cut.

157. Evening. Boisterous, prerevolutionary Moscow crowds. To one side stands a little chapel. Lit candles, sparkling icons, worshipers bowing and praying. Rachel appears from around the corner.

158. Three tiny gypsy girls are dancing in the street, beating tambourines. They are draped in coin necklaces and are wearing long dresses that reach to the ground. The gypsy girls see Rachel, rush over to her, and dance all around her.

159. Rachel tries to break out of their noisy circle.

160. She gives the gypsy girls a coin and escapes. An old Persian man in an embroidered caftan blocks her way. He directs an equivocal, old-man's smile at her, and touches her breast with the painted nail of his finger.

161. The half-dressed figure of a holy fool emerges next to Rachel and the Persian. The holy fool's body is shivering vigorously. His bald, egg-shaped head is wagging.

162. The Persian's fingers with their painted nails slither slowly over Rachel's breasts.

163. Three faces: Rachel's, the Persian's, the holy fool's.

164. The holy fool is grimacing, spittle is bubbling in his tangled beard, he asks threateningly for alms. Rachel runs away.

165. Rachel runs in a panic through the streets, the holy fool stumbling after her.

166. Night. Rachel runs over the Zamoskvoretsky Bridge.

167. The Moscow River, the embankment. The glitter of the snow. Black iron gratings over the snow. Far away the illuminated windows of factories and homes.

168. A quiet back alley in the Zamoskvoretsky quarter. A line of gas lamps. A well-dressed man in a fur coat is leaning against a wall, drinking vodka out of a bottle.

169. The door of the Hero of Plevna rooming house in the depths of the alley.

170. The sign: "FAMILY ROOMING HOUSE FOR TRAVEL-ERS—EVERY CONVENIENCE."

171. Rachel hurries over to the entrance and reaches for the door handle. The door opens unexpectedly. A man of about twenty-four comes out. He has a round, cheerful face, and the devil-may-care cap of a vagabond student on his curls. Stopping at the entrance, he peers at Rachel, scrutinizing her carefully. Rachel goes into the rooming house.

172. The office of the Hero of Plevna rooming house. Orlov, the attendant, a drowsy fellow in a vest, is playing draughts with a solemn old man who has the appearance of an Old Believer.* Orlov is wearing galoshes on his bare feet and cavalry breeches tied at the

---

*The Old Believers were an archconservative Christian sect that had split from the Russian Orthodox Church in the seventeenth century.

bottom with string. Over the usual squeamish expression of his face there is now a powerful, feverish streak. The old man is deeply pensive, but sure of himself. It is clear that he is winning.

173. The game board. The situation is hopeless for the attendant. His hand making a desperate move.

174. Rachel enters. She asks:

175. "COULD I HAVE A ROOM, PLEASE?"

176. The attendant, without raising his head:

177. "WE DON'T LET IN NO GIRLS WITHOUT A FELLOW."

178. Rachel does not understand. The attendant yells furiously:

179. "WHO'RE YOU WITH? WHERE'S YOUR TRICK?"

180. Rachel's dumbfounded face.

181. The attendant and the old man are playing feverishly. The old man makes the winning move.

182. Baulin, the young man with the student's cap, is pacing up and down in front of the rooming house. Rachel comes out. She stops, leans against the wall, and closes her eyes. The young man takes off his cap and asks her:

183. "WHO ARE YOU? WHAT ARE YOU DOING HERE IN THIS . . . THIS DEN?"

184. Rachel opens her eyes.

185. "I'M . . . I'M A JEWESS."

186. Baulin scratches his forehead pensively.

187. "WELL, COMRADE . . . THEY WON'T LET ME GO INTO THIS PLACE WITHOUT A GIRL, AND THEY WON'T LET YOU IN WITHOUT A MAN. MY NAME IS BAULIN, I'M AN HONEST FELLOW, YOU CAN TRUST ME."

188. Rachel looks at him mistrustfully. She hesitates, but then smiles at him and gives him her hand.

189. The attendant is staring shattered at the game board. He has lost the game. The old man is snidely sipping his tea. The galoshes fall off the attendant's feet. He scratches one foot with a toenail of the other. Rachel and Baulin come into the office. Baulin:

190. "WE WANT A ROOM, POPS."

191. The attendant gets up and stretches himself.

192. "HA! AND SHE SAID SHE DIDN'T HAVE NO JOHN!"

193. A dirty hallway in the hotel. The attendant walks down the hallway, carrying a candle. Rachel and Baulin are following him.

194. One of the doors in the hallway opens, a woman's trembling hand and bare shoulder jut out, but are immediately yanked back into the room, the door slamming shut.

195. The attendant takes Rachel and Baulin to the door of their room. In the corner of the hallway stands a pile of chamber pots, broken tin washbasins, and pictures in gold frames. The attendant unlocks the door.

196. The attendant, Baulin, and Rachel enter the room of this "nighttime" hotel. The attendant switches on the light. Baulin comments on the questionable cleanliness of the bed linen.

197. "CHANGE THESE HOLY CHASUBLES HERE, WILL YOU?"

198. The attendant, offended, inspects the stained sheets.

199. "WE CHANGE THE SHEETS AFTER EVERY CLIENT!"

200. The attendant changes the sheets, and slyly manages to use an old one as a tablecloth.

201. While the attendant is busy changing the sheets, Rachel reads a note nailed to the mirror.

202. The note: TONIGHT AT MIDNIGHT I HAD A SESSION WITH A FABULOUS GIRL, BUT SHE WON'T TELL ME HER NAME. I HOPE I DIDN'T CATCH ANYTHING.

203. Rachel steps back from the mirror. Baulin tries to block her view of the graffiti covering the walls. The attendant leaves. Baulin locks the door and turns to Rachel:

204. "GO TO SLEEP, MY FRIEND. I'LL SEE TO IT THAT YOU'LL BE SAFE."

205. Trembling, Rachel climbs onto the bed without taking off her shoes, and curls up. Baulin spreads out his coat by the door, and furtively takes out a bundle of printed leaflets and a batch of proclamations.

206. A close-up of the illegal proclamations printed by the Moscow Committee of the Social Democratic Party.

207. Baulin lies down by the door, puts the bundle of leaflets and proclamations under his head, and furtively slips a revolver under his makeshift pillow.

208. "WE MIGHT EVEN GET SOME SLEEP. . . ."

209. Rachel lies curled up on the bed listening with horror to the rooming house's habitual night noises.

210. The room next door. On a disheveled bed, a half-dressed officer in riding breeches and boots is grappling with a woman wearing a prim, high-buttoned, black silk dress. He has pinned her arms behind her back.

211. Baulin smokes a cigarette, chuckles, reaches out to the switch, and turns out the light. Fadeout.

Part Four

212. Night. A squad of policemen enters the back alley.

213. The policemen silently jimmy the Hero of Plevna's front door.

214. They climb the stairs, trying to make as little noise as possible.

215. Orlov, the attendant, is sleeping sonorously beneath an icon. He is again wearing his galoshes. One of the policemen lays his hand on his shoulder. Policeman:

216. "ANY ILLEGALS* OVERNIGHT?"

217. The attendant jumps up. Scratching his head, he answers:

218. "NO, I DON'T THINK THERE'S NO ILLEGALS STAY-ING HERE."

219. The policemen and the attendant leave the office.

220. In the hallway. A sudden slamming of a door, then silence.

221. Baulin, lying on his overcoat, is sleeping in the room by the door-way. Hearing the commotion, he jumps up and grabs his revolver.

222. The policemen's stamping feet in the corridor. Their swords are sticking out.

223. Baulin's bundle is lying on the floor along with the package of proclamations.

224. Rachel lies curled up on the bed, immersed in a sleep of youth and blissful ignorance.

225. Baulin is listening by the door.

226. THE RAID.

*Individuals without a residence permit that allows them to reside in Moscow.

227. Window, sky, stars. Baulin jumps onto the windowsill.

228. The deserted street. A shoeshine man, an old Assyrian, dressed in colorful rags, is shining a policeman's shoes. The dozing policeman has settled down on the bench. Suddenly he leaps up.

229. Baulin jumps out of a second-floor window. He falls to the ground and breaks his leg.

230. The policeman grabs his whistle and blows it.

231. Another policeman, a very short man wearing a lot of medals and a very large cap, comes running out of the back alley to assist him.

232. The crimson, puffed-up face of the first policeman. He does not dare to approach Baulin, who is lying sprawled on the ground, and blows his whistle with ecstasy and voluptuousness, like a cockerel among his hens.

233. The old teary-eyed Assyrian timidly pulls his shoeshine box toward the policeman's boot, which he hasn't finished shining yet.

234. Baulin's broken leg. Baulin is clawing the dirty street snow covered in dog's urine.

235. Two policemen, keeping a few steps back, are priming themselves to jump on the defenseless man. They fire themselves up with shouts, wave their revolvers around, and finally throw themselves on Baulin. One begins to strangle him while blowing his whistle with increasing passion, the other begins tying up Baulin's broken leg.

236. Baulin's leg, broken at the knee, twisted to the side.

237. A room in the Hero of Plevna. The figure of a man covered in a sheet lying facedown on a wide bed. The only thing glistening in the dark is his bald pate, and on his bald pate is a bump. On either side of the "guest" lie two frightened prostitutes, about sixteen years old.

238. The raid on the rooming house continues. The policemen knock furiously on the door of a room. The door opens.

239. The man wrapped in the sheet does not change his position. He shoves his hand out from under the sheet, his face is not visible, only his glistening bald pate, and on it the bump.

240. The stretched-out hand holding a passport. The policeman's hand takes the passport.

241. The policeman reads the passport. On his face, suspicion changes to gravity and respect.

242. A close-up of the passport issued to Apollon Silych Gustovaty, Honorary Guardian and State Councilor.

243. The "figure" wrapped in the sheet and the prostitutes lie motionless. The policeman respectfully places the passport on top of the figure and, bowing, leaves the room.

244. In another room. A prostitute of about forty-five sits sleepily smoking a cigarette as she waits for the police to raid her room. She is wearing a long nightgown with torn lace. A schoolboy of about sixteen is cowering in terror by the wall. He has managed to throw on his school jacket—under his jacket he is wearing his long underwear. The policemen come barging into the room. The inspector asks the boy:

245. "AND WHAT, IF I MAY BE SO BOLD, ARE YOU DOING HERE, DEAR SIR?"

246. The schoolboy hiccups:

247. "IT WAS . . . RAINING . . . SO I THOUGHT . . . I'D COME IN HERE FOR A BIT. . . ."

248. The inspector gives the old prostitute a push: "Get outside!"

249. The schoolboy gets a fatherly scolding from the inspector, who then hands him his trousers.

250. Strastnaya Square. Night. The policemen are leading off the prostitutes they have arrested during the raid.

251. Street prostitutes run the moment they see the policemen coming. They grab hold of the first pedestrian they find and pretend to be out walking with their husbands, their bonafide companions.

252. Two prostitutes rush over to an elderly Jew in a large fur coat, each pulling him in a different direction. The Jew, deep in mirthless thought, looks first at one woman, then at the other with his tired old eyes, takes them both by the arm, and walks off with them as if he were out walking with his daughters.

253. A cab stand on Tverskaya Street. The prostitutes are badgering the cabbies.

254. A swaggering hunchback cabby in flashy greatcoat. A girl in a fluffy white hat and a beauty spot on her chin comes running up to him. She tells the hunchback she wants him to drive her away as fast as possible. The hunchback:

255. "THAT'LL BE A TENNER DOWN!"

256. The woman steps onto the cab's footboard. She says:

257. "I DON'T HAVE ANY MONEY ... BUT THERE'S OTHER WAYS I CAN PAY YOU. . . ."

258. The hunchback sizes her up with his blue eyes. "Fair enough," his blue eyes say, and he whips his horses into a gallop.

259. One cab after another goes flying up Tverskaya Street with fleeing prostitutes.

260. The hunchback pulls into a cul-de-sac next to a vacant plot. He halts the horses, gets up from his box, and climbs into the back of the cab where the woman is sitting. Cut.

261. The policemen are herding the prostitutes they arrested during the raid into the police station.

262. A large, shadowy room, divided in half by iron bars, behind which the women are gathered.

263. The prostitutes' faces pressing against the bars. Among the women: the old prostitute who was spending the night with the schoolboy, Rachel, and the woman wearing the prim, high-buttoned dress who had been fighting in the room with the officer. Her presence at the rooming house and at the police station is inexplicable. She paces up and down nervously, and asks a guard for a cigarette. The guard rolls a cigarette for her, lights a match, and tenderly looks at the "lady," and then turns away so as not to offend her with his sympathy. The woman shudders, puffs at the cigarette, and immediately throws it away with a sob.

264. The room in which the prostitutes undergo a medical checkup. A bright electric lamp hangs over the examining chair. Next to it stands a doctor in a white coat (the doctor happens to be the sour bureaucrat with whom Rachel had spoken in the tram), and a medical assistant. A little farther away a clerk is sitting behind a desk. A policeman brings in the prostitute who was spending the night with the schoolboy. She goes over to the examining chair and lies down on it without even being asked. The doctor bends over her. He is holding a medical instrument. Fadeout.

265. The clerk, a pen behind his ear, is waiting for the diagnosis.

266. The examination is over. The woman gets up from the chair. The doctor to the clerk:

267. "SYPHILIS . . . SECOND STAGE . . . NEXT!"
268. The woman walks humbly over to the clerk, who writes something in her papers. The policemen drag in Rachel, her clothes tattered and torn.
269. The doctor, who has seen it all before, prepares his instruments.
270. The policemen place her on the examining chair. An old policeman with a kind face says to her:
271. "THIS IS FOR YOUR OWN GOOD, YOU SILLY GIRL, OTHERWISE GOD KNOWS HOW MANY YOU'LL INFECT!"
272. Rachel's terrorized face beneath the electric lamp.
273. The doctor's face emerges from the darkness. He has recognized her and asks:
274. "WHO ARE YOU? WHAT ARE YOU DOING HERE?"
275. Her lips tremble.
276. "I'M . . . I'M A JEWESS."
277. The clerk with the pen behind his ear is waiting for the diagnosis.
278. Rachel on the examining chair. The perplexed doctor tells the clerk:
279. "SHE'S . . . SHE'S HEALTHY. . . . NEXT!"
280. Rachel walks over to the clerk's desk. He hands her a stamped piece of paper. Rachel staggers back, asks him, "What's this?" The clerk:
281. "A YELLOW SLIP FOR YOUR EXCELLENCY."
282. Rachel looks around in dismay, clutching the stamped piece of paper. Suddenly an inspector's face, overgrown with rampant black hair, moves down toward her. The hair surrounds the fat, hard, greedy face like a shaggy halo. The inspector points at the packet found in her room.
283. "ARE THESE YOUR PROCLAMATIONS, SWEETHEART?"
284. The inspector is holding the packet of proclamations.
285. He is waiting for an answer, his lips apart. On his face, the entreaty of a man not good at his profession: please, confess, I beg you, you sweet little girl you, help me by confessing. Rachel turns her dumbfounded face toward him.
286. A dark, vaulted room in the police station. A flickering kerosene

lamp with a ripped standard-issue lampshade is hanging above a table. Baulin is writhing on a torn, oilskin armchair by the wall. He is lying with his back to the audience, his broken leg has been carelessly bandaged. The old policeman with the kind face is leaning over him. He is pouring water into Baulin's mouth from the spout of a large sooty teapot.

287. The inspector brings Rachel into the room and makes a sign to the policeman that the two prisoners should be placed in front of each other. The inspector leans his tousled, shaggy head under the lamp, shoves the proclamations close to Baulin's face, and with the same greedy, ingratiating face demands an answer.

288. "TELL ME HERE AND NOW, MY DEAR FRIEND . . . ARE THESE YOUR PROCLAMATIONS, YOU SON-OF-A-BITCH?"

289. Baulin squirms in the armchair. He slips, falls on the floor, moans. The old policeman leans over him once more. Baulin's fingers squeeze, caress, scratch the policeman's plump hand.

290. Baulin's contorted face turns toward the audience. He moans:

291. "MAMA!"

292. The policeman whispers into Baulin's ear:

293. "PLEASE, I BEG YOU, CONFESS! WE HAVE TO GET YOU TO A HOSPITAL!"

294. The inspector sidles up closer to Baulin. The inspector needs a confession, and so, his face pitiful, his eyes fixed on Rachel, he begins squeezing Baulin's broken leg.

295. "ARE THESE YOUR PROCLAMATIONS?"

296. Baulin's face. His whispering lips:

297. "MAMA!"

298. Rachel moves toward the inspector. She tells him:

299. "THEY ARE MY PROCLAMATIONS."

300. The inspector stops squeezing Baulin's leg and eagerly nods his head.

301. "GOOD GIRL!"

302. the inspector says, his face brightening and filling with joy. He wants to hear more.

303. Rachel makes a false deposition. Her words are crisp and clear, her face lit by the fitful oily light of the lamp.

304. "I GOT HOLD OF THOSE PROCLAMATIONS!"

305. she says, and stops to think what she should say next.

306. The inspector, fearing that Rachel has had second thoughts about giving a deposition, walks over to Baulin and starts squeezing his broken leg again. Baulin bounds up, cries out in pain, loses consciousness. Rachel immediately begins talking. She prattles and babbles without stopping to catch her breath. The inspector's fat legs are twisting under the table with impatience. With one hand he is caressing Baulin's broken leg, and with the other he is patting, twirling, and tugging at his tousled locks of hair. His face is lit with joy, his lips are moving, his eyebrows are quivering, his eyes are sparkling.

Part Five

307. A THOUSAND MILES AWAY FROM THE ROSSIYA BOARDINGHOUSE.

308. A street in Berlin. A crowd of people walking past a billboard. A gigantic poster is announcing a concert to be given by Leo Rogdai.

309. A street in Berlin. The majestic building of the Hotel Imperial. On the fifth floor a wall cleaner is moving along the hotel's facade, cleaning the sign. The cleaner, a pleasant, cheerful fellow, is caged on a wooden scaffold secured with pulleys to the edge of the roof. The cleaner is singing at the top of his voice. Then he stops and listens.

310. The street, shot from a fifth-floor perspective, as the cleaner would see it.

311. The poster. Its date: September 4, 1912.

312. The cleaner lowers himself to the third floor. He stops his scaffold at an open window, from which come the sounds that have captivated him.

313. Ratkovich's room on the third floor of the Hotel Imperial. Ratkovich no longer exists—he has turned into Leo Rogdai, the renowned virtuoso. Noon. The virtuoso's room: a low, wide, unmade bed, flowers and gifts strewn about, a laurel crown in a

case. By the fireplace, a photograph of Rachel. On the table, the remains of a meal and an uncorked bottle of wine. The walls are covered with posters and schedules of concerts in Berlin, Hamburg, and Munich. Rogdai has changed—he has aged, grown thinner. He is pacing up and down the room half dressed, strums at his violin, and places it under his chin. Fadeout.

314. A repeat of scene 105: Professor Reti listening to Ratkovich play backstage at the provincial theater.

315. Rogdai is playing. The cleaner's face, filled with reverence, appears outside the window. He takes off his cap and kneads it in his hands.

316. "MR. VIOLINIST, CAN YOU PLAY A *PAS D'ESPAGNE*?"

317. Rogdai smiles, walks over to the window, and plays a *pas d'Espagne*.

318. The cleaner kneads his dirty cap, his fingers snapping faster and more cheerfully.

319. Two billiard balls rolling over a billiard table.

320. A cupped hand is resting on the cushioned rail of the billiard table. A large, well-groomed hand with a diamond ring on its little finger. The cue rolling back and forth in the cup of the palm.

321. The billiard room of the Imperial. Rogdai's impresario, Vittorio Maffi, takes aim at one of the two remaining billiard balls. A large crowd has gathered around the table. Maffi is extremely tall, lean, supple, black-haired, wrinkled. His partner, Herr Kalnischker, exudes gentleness, patience, and dignity. Herr Kalnischker is a short man. The lines of his tiny body are round, his stomach bulges, but not too much, his legs patter unhurriedly. Neither player is wearing a jacket. Maffi hits the ball. A miss. He grimaces, steps back, or rather jumps to the side. An old gaffer standing there gaping is hit in the mouth by the end of Maffi's cue. Maffi turns around and jams the cue deeper into the mouth of the old man, who is now beside himself with fear, pushing him against the wall.

322. Herr Kalnischker's small, fat hand on the cushioned rail of the billiard table. A cue is rolling back and forth in the cup of his palm.

323. The crucified old man with the cue jammed in his mouth. He is

pressed against the wall. Maffi, unruffled, driving his cue deeper into the man's mouth, turns his back on him.

324. Kalnischker hits the ball. The ball drops into one of the side pockets. One ball—number fifteen—is left on the billiard table. Kalnischker takes a sip of milk from a glass, puts the glass down unhurriedly, and says:

325. "THE FIFTEEN: TWO CUSHIONS, CORNER POCKET."

326. With murderous deliberation Kalnischker chalks his cue tip.

327. Maffi's back, his cue jutting out of the old man's mouth. The desperate face of the man, his teeth gnawing at the cue.

328. Kalnischker, wearing down his partner, spends a lot of time taking aim, pulling back his cue, again taking aim. The ball lies near the opposite cushion of the table. A small man, Kalnischker has to put an inordinate amount of effort into reaching the ball. He leans over the table with his stomach, balancing on tiptoe, one of his tiny legs trembling in the air. Kalnischker hits the ball. The ball drops. Kalnischker bows deeply to his partner.

329. A grimace flashes over Maffi's face. Without turning around, he pulls the cue out of the old man's mouth. The man lunges at Maffi waving his fists, but the others drag him back just in time. Someone tells him:

330. "ARE YOU MAD? THAT IS VITTORIO MAFFI, IMPRESARIO TO CHALIAPIN AND ROGDAI, HIGH STAKES GAMBLER, AND SWASHBUCKLING DUELIST EXTRAORDINAIRE!"

331. The old man falls silent and looks around the room. A large tear rolls down his wrinkled cheek, trickles through his beard, and sparkles on the tip of a hair. An attendant comes rushing over and wipes away the tear with a napkin.

332. Attendants help the players into their jackets. Little Herr Kalnischker takes the gigantic Signor Maffi aside. Herr Kalnischker ingratiatingly tilts his neatly combed head:

333. "WILL YOU SEE TO IT THAT OUR ACCOUNTS ARE SETTLED, MY DEAR SIGNOR MAFFI?"

334. Maffi looks down at his partner from the height of his gigantic stature. He is not sure how to proceed—whether to hit Kalnischker or pay him. Kalnischker mumbles even more ingratiatingly:

335. "WILL YOU SEE TO IT, MY VERY DEAR SIGNOR MAFFI?"

336. Maffi walks off without uttering a word. He picks up a suitcase he has left by the door, and stalks toward the exit. Kalnischker shuffles after him tenaciously. Maffi turns around and mumbles through clenched teeth:

337. "COME TO VILLA GRENNIER ON SUNDAY, AND YOU'LL GET YOUR DAMN FIVE HUNDRED MARKS!"

338. Maffi rushes off. Kalnischker bows to the Italian's vanishing back, walks over to the table, and with small sips finishes his glass of milk.

339. Rogdai is playing for the cleaner, who is snapping his fingers to the rhythm of the tune.

340. The luxurious lobby of the Hotel Imperial. Maffi, suitcase in hand, hurries up the stairs, three steps at a time. The bellhops and attendants bow to him.

341. The concierge behind his counter. He looks like Napoleon Bonaparte. He has cultivated this resemblance down to the minutest detail—even a wave of hair lies across his forehead like Napoleon's. On the desk, in all its splendor, stands a portrait of Napoleon. A pince-nez is hanging on a wide ribbon on the porter's chest.

342. The cleaner's wooden scaffold and his dangling legs, shot from below.

343. Rogdai is playing for his simple listener with enthusiasm. The cleaner, filled with bliss, hurls his cap down into the street. Suddenly the window blinds roll down, cutting off Rogdai from the cleaner.

344. Rogdai turns around. Maffi is standing in the doorway, the cord of the blinds in his hand. Maffi throws his suitcase into the middle of the room, swats his thighs with his riding whip, and mutters through clenched teeth:

345. IT'S SIX MONTHS NOW THAT THE LITTLE YID RATKOVICH TURNED INTO THE FAMOUS LEO ROGDAI, AND YET THE FAMOUS LEO ROGDAI HAS NO SILK UNDERWEAR, NO THOROUGHBRED HORSES, NO HIGH-SOCIETY MISTRESS! WHEN ARE YOU GOING TO TURN INTO A MAN, ROGDAI?"

346. Maffi walks over to the fireplace, kicking the things strewn on the floor out of his way. He picks up Rachel's picture, grimaces, and looks around the room.

347. Rachel Monko's picture.

348. Rogdai has flushed a deep crimson. He snatches Rachel's picture out of Maffi's hand and hides it in one of his jacket pockets. There is a barely noticeable smile on Maffi's face. With his riding whip he scoops up one of Rogdai's bedroom slippers. On the tip of his whip, the Italian twirls the old slipper with its large hole where the big toe is and throws it out the window.

349. Rogdai's bedroom slipper falls onto the roof of the house next door.

350. Maffi points at the suitcase he has brought with him.

351. "THIS IS FOR YOU—TO HELP TURN YOU INTO A MAN!"

352. Rogdai opens the suitcase, takes out of it a saddle and a revolver. He stares at Maffi with a dumbfounded look on his face. The Italian taps his own legs with his whip.

353. "YES! YES! BE A MAN!"

354. Rogdai continues unpacking the suitcase. He takes out a bottle of cologne, razors, a mustache night-band, ladies' garters, frilled bloomers, and another item that the young man immediately throws back into the suitcase. Maffi stamps his foot:

355. "BE A MAN!"

356. Rogdai pulls a bottle of absinthe out of the suitcase. Maffi pours two glasses, hands one to Rogdai, and shouts fiercely:

357. "CHILDREN DRINK MILK, HORSES WATER, AND MEN DRINK ABSINTHE! BE A MAN!"

358. Rogdai, perplexed, clinks glasses with the impresario, who shouts:

359. "A TOAST TO MANHOOD!"

360. They drink. Maffi's powerful, long leg is resting on the leather armchair, the cushions sinking deeper and deeper under its weight. The leather cracks, the springs come bouncing out.

361. Rogdai drinks down his glass of absinthe, sways. The Italian pours him another and makes him drink it. Maffi's face, distorted by a sudden tic, imperiously watches Rogdai drink. The young man drinks down the whole glass, sways, laughs. Maffi leans over Rogdai.

362. "AND NOW, MY YOUNG WHIPPERSNAPPER, WE SHALL GO TO A WOMAN WHO WILL MAKE YOU A MAN!"

363. Maffi's face slowly turns toward the viewer, who can now see that one of his ears has been chopped off.

364. The cheek where the ear has been chopped off. Cut.

365. The lobby of the Hotel Imperial. The concierge who resembles Napoleon is studying himself in the mirror. He fixes his Napoleonic lock of hair and lifts the telephone receiver.

366. A placement agency for maids and wet nurses. Three sleepy German wet nurses are sitting by the wall. All three have their hands clasped over their bellies: they are propping up their heavy breasts with their fat workers' hands. The proprietress of the agency is sitting at her desk. She is a gaunt German woman with yellow puffed-up hair and an unblinking glass eye. The telephone rings. She lifts the receiver. Her face uncoils like a long spring, at the end of which is a gush of prefabricated delight.

367. The concierge on the telephone:

368. "GOOD MORNING, FRAU PUTZKE. I NEED A CHEAP WASHERWOMAN AND AN EVEN CHEAPER BOILER-ROOM STOKER."

369. Frau Putzke's eyes. One eye is boisterously twirling in its orb, the other, her glass eye, rests in blue immobility.

369a.Frau Putzke bows and shakes the receiver:

370. "I AM EXPECTING A GROUP OF RUSSIAN IMMI-GRANTS FROM KOENIGSBERG ANY DAY NOW. THEY ARE DREADFUL PEOPLE, BUT VERY, VERY CHEAP."

371. One of the wet nurses falls asleep. Her hands unclasp and her immense breasts tumble down, covering her stomach.

372. The concierge agrees to take on two of the "dreadful" but cheap people. He places the receiver back on the hook and busies himself with filling out bills, but his counter is wobbling, one its legs is a little shorter than the others.

373. Maffi walks down the stairs with Rogdai, who is tipsy.

374. Maffi's car comes speeding around the corner. In its quavering headlights, an old postman, somewhat hard of hearing, staggers from side to side. The car rolls up to the entrance of the hotel.

375. Maffi and Rogdai make their way toward the car. Rogdai, drunk, stops the postman, lays his hand on the postman's shoulder, and asks him with a blissful smile:

376. "WERE YOU EVER A HAPPY MAN, MISTER POST-MAN?"

377. The startled postman hasn't quite caught what Rogdai said. He is a little hard of hearing. He is holding a packet of letters and newspapers. The old man quickly pulls some cotton wool out of his ears.

378. A close-up of the newspapers that the postman is holding. The first lines of a classified advertisement: "Immigrant Rachel Monko seeks . . ."

379. Rogdai laughs and repeats his question. The postman shrugs his shoulders. Was he ever happy? Not really. The postman bows to the tipsy gentlemen, stuffs the cotton wool back in his ears, and enters the hotel.

380. Maffi and Rogdai get into the car and are driven off.

381. In the lobby of the hotel. The postman places the pile of letters and newspapers on the concierge's counter, and leaves. The concierge is engrossed in his work, infuriated by the counter's constant wobbling. He tears a piece from one of the newspapers that the postman has just delivered, and jams it under the counter's leg. Now his counter is stable. A shred of newspaper has fallen and is lying nearby.

382. A close-up of the torn shred of newspaper. It is the beginning of the advertisement:

383. IMMIGRANT RACHEL MONKO, HAVING FINISHED HER TERM IN A LABOR CAMP IN NERCHINSK, IS SEEKING LEV RATKOVICH FROM DERAZHNY IN VOLHYNIA. PLEASE SEND ANY INFORMATION TO THE FOLLOWING ADDRESS: KOENIGSB . . .

384. The concierge is writing, leaning on the counter that is no longer wobbling.

385. The sparkling lights of Berlin by night. High up, a rotating electric circle: LEO ROGDAI.

386. Maffi's car weaves through a stream of carriages, trams, and trucks.

387. The inside of the car. Drunken Rogdai and Maffi are playing a high-stakes card game. Money is lying on the floor of the car. The car jolts, but the players don't even notice. Their heads bang against the roof as they continue playing.

388. A heavy jolt. Rogdai flies up, his top hat rams into a hook jutting down from the roof of the car and stays hanging there. Rogdai pulls out one banknote after another and throws them onto the seat. His top hat is hanging a foot over his head. Maffi is keeping the bank.

389. The driver turns his head and looks back. Smiling, he watches the unusual game.

390. The game continues. Maffi is winning.

391. Far away on the black backdrop of the sky, the rotating electric letters—LEO ROGDAI—receding in the distance.

392. Rogdai throws down a bundle of banknotes, among them the picture of Rachel Monko. Rogdai, drunk, does not notice her picture. Maffi's large hand covers the money. He deals the cards, wins, and rakes the banknotes together, brushing the photograph aside.

393. The entrance of Villa Grennier. An electric lamp hangs above the sign: VILLA GRENNIER.

394. A walk lined with plane trees. A shaft of light. The illuminated leaves of the trees. Maffi's car speeds up a hill.

395. The inside of the car. Rachel's picture is lying on the floor. Rogdai pulls his top hat off the hook, and flops it crookedly onto his head.

396. Maffi's car pulls up to the entrance of Villa Grennier. Maffi and Rogdai go inside.

397. The lobby of Baroness Grennier's home. The doorman, a well-built fellow with a handsome, dubious face, opens the door. Rogdai and Maffi enter and hand their coats to the doorman.

398. The coat stand in Baroness Grennier's front hall. A row of top hats.

399. The top hats shot from above—the dull sheen on the black silk. There is a hole in Rogdai's top hat.

400. Maffi hurries up the stairs, three steps at a time.

401. The doorman asks Rogdai—"Whom may I announce?"

402. "TELL THE BARONESS THAT ROGDAI IS HERE."

403. A painting of Christ lit with mysterious, dull light. The painting is by an Italian master of the quattrocento. Just below Christ's pierced feet are the heads of two adolescent girls with luxuriant ribbons in their hair, leaning over their embroidery.

404. Evening. Baroness Grennier's salon. The decor is simple, rich, dignified, and elegant. A mellow pastor is reading from Alphonse Daudet's *Tartarin of Tarascon.**

405. The book's title page.

406. Listening to the pastor are: the old baroness, a majestic woman with a solemn face, and her two adolescent daughters (luxuriant ribbons in their hair, low-heeled slippers on their feet, and so on). The old woman is listening carefully. On her lips is a gentle smile, barely visible. Her daughters are giggling. Two elderly aristocratic gentlemen with rosettes are standing near the opposite wall. One is thin and lanky, with a rich mane of hair, the other corpulent and squat, with a bald patch—and yet, in an elusive way, they resemble one another. The doorman enters and announces:

407. "THE COUNT DE ROGDAI."

408. The baroness puts down her embroidery and walks up to her guest. The elderly gentlemen with the rosettes assume a dignified air. The pastor stops reading. The baroness introduces Rogdai to her daughters.

409. "IT IS A GREAT HONOR INDEED TO MEET SUCH A FAMOUS VIRTUOSO!"

410. The girls curtsy. The baroness introduces Rogdai to the pastor, and then to the thin elderly gentleman.

411. "COUNT SAN SALVADOR."

412. Rogdai and the thin elderly gentleman bow to each other with the utmost punctiliousness. The baroness introduces Rogdai to the squat elderly gentleman.

413. "BARON SANT' IAGO."

414. Rogdai and the squat elderly gentleman bow to each other with the utmost punctiliousness. Rogdai is offered a chair, and asked to listen to the reading of *Tartarin of Tarascon.*

*Alphonse Daudet, 1840–1897, French author and short story writer.

415. A hallway in the Villa Grennier. Maffi walks up to a door, knocks, and shouts, "Open up!"

416. A corner in the room of Helene, one of Baroness Grennier's daughters. A mirror. Helene's exquisite bare shoulders are visible in the mirror.

417. Helene, half dressed. She is young and very beautiful. She has heard the knock on her door. She rushes in distress to her closet, riffles frantically through her dresses, and throws them on the floor. The pile of dresses on the floor. Helene stops at a simple black dress.

418. Maffi outside the closed door. He is swatting his whip against his leg. Helene comes out of her room. With superb maidenly grace, she stretches both hands out to Maffi. Her feeling of strength, youth, and beauty fills her with joy. Maffi mutters something to her, takes her by the hand, and slowly turns her around.

419. "WHAT A HORRIBLE DRESS!"

420. he says, swatting his whip harder and harder against his leg. Helene staggers back.

421. A close-up of the painting of Christ. A girl, one of the baroness's daughters, is peering carefully through a lorgnette at . . .

422. . . . Rogdai squirming in his armchair.

423. The pastor is reading with rapture. When he comes to a particularly wonderful passage, he raises his finger.

424. The velvet curtain separating the salon from the adjacent room is drawn apart. Helene's face, dazzling and pale, appears.

425. Maffi enters the salon followed by Helene, who is wearing a low-cut dress. A long sash embroidered with gold thread is trailing behind her on the floor. Rogdai jumps up. He is staring at Helene. Maffi, swatting his whip, says to Helene:

426. "HERE, STANDING BEFORE YOU, BARONESS, IS LEO ROGDAI IN PERSON, WHOSE PHENOMENAL MASTERY OF THE VIOLIN . . ."

427. The young man cannot tear his dazzled eyes from Helene. He slowly kisses her hand. At that very instant, the doorman hands him Rachel's picture.

428. "THE GENTLEMAN DROPPED THIS," the doorman says with a bow. Embarrassed, Rogdai takes the picture and puts it in

his pocket. Helene turns and looks at Maffi, her eyes filled with fear and adoration.

Part Six

429. A Christmas tree is standing on the table. Little ornaments are hanging on the branches.
430. In Baroness Grennier's salon. Rogdai, Helene, and her younger sister Augusta are decorating the tree. They are pulling Christmas favors in a happy, playful mood.
431. Helene climbs onto the table, places a Santa Claus on top of the Christmas tree, and strews artificial snow over it. Rogdai is arranging the candles. He stops and gazes at laughing, rosy-cheeked Helene. His gaze is very tender.
432. The front hall of the baroness's home. The doorman is polishing his nails.
433. Little Herr Kalnischker rings the doorbell.
434. The doorman lets him in. Kalnischker asks him:
435. "IS SIGNOR MAFFI IN?"
436. The doorman is not favorably impressed with Kalnischker. Not deigning to answer, he continues polishing his nails, and mumbles offhand:
437. "SIGNOR MAFFI IS NOT RECEIVING VISITORS."
438. Little Herr Kalnischker is not in the least discouraged by the doorman's chilly reception. He bows and says meekly:
439. "I SHALL WAIT."
440. Kalnischker unhurriedly takes off his coat, tries to hang it on the coat rack, but does not manage, as he is too short to reach the hook. He pushes a velvet footstool to the coat rack, climbs onto it, hangs his coat and his bowler hat, and sits on a high armchair that is standing to the side. His short little legs do not reach the floor. There is an expression of unflappable patience on his face.
441. The doorman turns his back on him in contempt.
442. Kalnischker's short little legs are dangling above the floor.
443. Helene and Rogdai are dressing a doll, putting stockings and

fashionable garters on its legs. They step back and marvel at their work.

444. Kalnischker's short little legs are dangling above the floor.

445. The doorman's demeanor is as unruffled as Kalnischker's. The doorman gets up, pulls the pocket watch out of Kalnischker's vest pocket, takes a look—"What time is it?" Kalnischker fixes him with his expressionless eyes.

446. "I SHALL WAIT," Kalnischker says, his little legs dangling.

447. At that moment the door flies open and Maffi comes bursting into the hall. His face darkens the instant he sees Kalnischker. The little man approaches the Italian with tiny steps and bows deeply.

448. Rogdai and Helene are still dressing the doll for the Christmas tree. It is a large baby doll with puffed-up cheeks and a round belly. Laughing, they put a brassiere and bloomers on the doll, and puff up its hair.

449. Maffi peers at Kalnischker. A tic flashes across his face. He pulls Kalnischker's pocket watch out of Kalnischker's vest pocket, just as the doorman had done before, and takes a look—"What time is it?" He wonders whether he should hit him or pay his debt. Kalnischker is still standing there with his neatly combed head in a deep bow. Maffi hurries toward the staircase, and Kalnischker follows him with quick little steps.

450. Helene and Rogdai have finally dressed the doll. It is now wearing a dress and a coat and holding a parasol. Rogdai laughs and presses the doll to his chest. At that moment Maffi enters the salon. Helene takes another doll out of a box and rushes toward Maffi, her face radiant and happy. She stretches her arms out to him, but Maffi steps aside to make way for Kalnischker. Maffi:

451. "BARONESS HELENE, MAY I INTRODUCE HERR KALNISCHKER? HE IS EXTREMELY INTERESTED IN YOUR PORCELAIN COLLECTION."

452. Helene turns ashen, and the doll drops from of her hands. Kalnischker picks up the doll. Helene shudders, offers Kalnischker her arm, and they leave the room. Rogdai rushes after them. Maffi stops him:

453. "AS PER OUR CONTRACT . . ."

454. Maffi says, looking Rogdai in the eye.

455. Kalnischker and Helene are walking down the corridors lined with statues and palm trees. Kalnischker, still holding the doll, keeps up a playful flow of witticisms. Helene is silent. Her face is rigid and pale.

456. Maffi is speaking with Rogdai, who is pressing the dressed doll against his chest:

457. "AS PER OUR CONTRACT, MY DEAR FELLOW, YOU ARE TO LEAVE TODAY FOR A TOUR OF FRANCE AND BRITAIN, AND THEREFORE . . ."

458. Kalnischker and Helene enter her private boudoir. She asks him to take a seat.

459. Rogdai is still clutching the doll. Maffi turns toward him and stands in profile. The stub of his cut-off ear is partially visible to the viewer.

460. ". . . AND THEREFORE, YOU DO NOT HAVE ENOUGH TIME TO LOOK AT BARONESS HELENE'S PORCE-LAIN COLLECTION."

461. Maffi fully turns his grotesquely deformed cheek toward the viewer.

462. The cut-off ear. Out of it . . .

463. . . . trotting on shaky little legs, comes a tiny, shaggy, horribly grotesque, aristocratic little pooch.

464. Six dogs covered in ribbons and frills, followed by two tiny old Englishwomen, sail through the lobby of the Hotel Imperial toward the exit. The concierge rushes out from behind his counter to the revolving doors and ushers out the two Englishwomen, who are followed by one exhausted dog after another. The door revolves slowly, and the last dog disappears behind its turning panels, at which point Baulin, holding a bundle, comes staggering into the lobby with a bewildered look on his face. And right behind Baulin is Rachel. The concierge rushes up to Baulin— "What are you doing here?" Baulin hands him a letter.

465. "FROM FRAU PUTZKE . . ."

466. The concierge clips his pince-nez, dangling on a silk ribbon, onto his nose. He reads the letter and eyes Baulin critically. Baulin has aged, grown weaker, and has a beard. The concierge:

467. "WE'LL HIRE YOU AS A THIRD-GRADE BOILER ROOM STOKER."

468. Then the concierge turns to Rachel. He is pleasantly surprised by her simple, slender face. He wants to convince her that he is a man of uncommon subtlety. He rearranges his silk ribbon and, bowing and scraping, says:

469. "AH, MADEMOISELLE, IT WAS BUT A CENTURY AGO THAT MEN OF MY APPEARANCE WERE EMPERORS, BUT NOW . . ."

470. The concierge shrugs his shoulders. He is displeased with the twentieth century.

471. Rogdai and Maffi enter the lobby of the hotel. Rachel is standing with her back to them. They climb the stairs. After a few steps, Rogdai stops Maffi:

472. "I DIDN'T KNOW THAT BARONESS HELENE HAD A PORCELAIN COLLECTION!"

473. Maffi waves his hands scornfully and leaves, going up the stairs three steps at a time. Rogdai stays back. He cannot stop thinking about Baroness Helene's porcelain collection.

474. Rachel continues her conversation with the concierge. Suddenly she asks him:

475. "MAY I CALL DIRECTORY INQUIRIES?"

476. The concierge is surprised, but says—"Please, go ahead." Rachel enters the telephone booth and lifts the receiver.

477. Rogdai slowly walks down the stairs. He enters the telephone booth next to the one Rachel is in.

478. Rachel on the telephone:

479. "DIRECTORY INQUIRIES? COULD YOU PLEASE GIVE ME THE ADDRESS OF LEV RATKOVICH, A RUSSIAN CITIZEN?"

480. The little glass panel separating the two booths. Rachel's nape and Rogdai's back can be seen through the glass.

481. Rogdai on the telephone.

482. Baroness Grennier's salon. The baroness walks to the telephone.

483. Rogdai on the telephone:

484. "COULD I PLEASE SPEAK TO BARONESS HELENE?"

485. The old woman nods and walks away from the telephone.

486. The directory-inquiries office. A young woman is looking for the name "Ratkovich." Her finger stops at "Rogdai" but moves on. She cannot find "Ratkovich," and says into the telephone:

487. "WE HAVE NO LISTING FOR A LEV RATKOVICH, IMMIGRANT FROM RUSSIA. . . ."

488. Rachel puts the receiver back on its hook and comes out of the booth.

489. The concierge says to Rachel:

490. "WE WILL HIRE YOU AS A FIRST-GRADE WASHER-WOMAN. . . ."

491. The concierge has an attendant take Rachel to the maids' quarters. Rachel, Baulin, and the attendant leave.

492. Rogdai is waiting on the telephone.

493. The matte glass door to Helene's room. The old baroness walks up to the door, wants to knock, but at that moment the light in Helene's room goes out.

494. Rogdai is waiting on the telephone.

495. The old baroness walks back to the telephone:

496. "I AM SORRY, HELENE IS HAVING HER ENGLISH LESSON RIGHT NOW."

497. Rogdai slowly lowers the telephone, forgetting to hang up.

498. The receiver dangling against the wall.

499. The attendant and Rachel are going down into the cellar. The marble flight of stairs, covered by a carpet, changes into cement stairs, which then change into slimy, dark, crumbling steps littered with junk of every kind. Rachel and the attendant cross the cellar and go to a dilapidated door nailed together with planks. The attendant opens the door. A cloud of steam comes pouring out of the room. Rachel staggers back.

500. "WHAT IS THIS?" she asks the attendant.

501. "IT'S THE LAUNDRY," he answers. He takes her by the hand . . .

502. . . . and leads her into a thick, reeking curtain of smoke and steam. Wavering outlines of hunched-up forms can be seen through the immense cellar's powerful, all-engulfing pillars of steam. In the distance, the moving silhouettes of Rachel and the attendant, barely visible in the impenetrable fog.

503. The attendant takes Rachel to a large ironing table. Next to it is the gaping aperture of the tube through which the dirty linen is conveyed to the laundry. Nightshirts and soiled sheets come tumbling out. Rachel steps back.

504. "I WILL NOT WORK IN THIS HELL!" she cries.

505. The attendant laughs.

506. "WELL, MADAME, PERHAPS YOU SHOULD TAKE A LUXURY SUITE INSTEAD."

507. Delighted with his witticism, he laughs louder and louder. One after another Chinese men, their torsos bare, their arms steaming and covered in suds, emerge from the billowing fog. They approach Rachel and stand very close to her, the dim lines of their yellow bodies wavering in the puffs of steam. They stare at the laughing attendant, slowly stretch their mouths wide, and begin to grin. At that instant, a large pile of linen comes tumbling out of the tube, burying Rachel under it.

508. The movie screen is shrouded with steam. Two fiery beams penetrate this shroud, move, and grow.

509. A car is rushing along the dazzling Friedrichstrasse. There is a pile of luggage next to the driver's seat. Maffi and Rogdai are in the car. They are heading for the railroad station.

Part Seven

510. AFTER A TRIUMPHANT TOUR OF THE CAPITALS OF EUROPE, ROGDAI RETURNS TO BERLIN AND GIVES HIS FIRST CONCERT THERE.

511. Berlin. Night. The square in front of the theater. The theater's massive facade is illuminated. The crowd is storming the main entrance.

512. The ushers are keeping the jostling crowds back from the locked doors. There are posters announcing Leo Rogdai's concert on pillars on both sides of the entrance. Street urchins have gathered by these pillars. They are waiting for a chance to plunge into the crowd and steal their way into the theater.

513. The urchins clambering up the billboards. The date on the poster announcing Leo Rogdai's concert: March 9, 1914.

514. The entrance to the theater. A chain of green gas lamps. High society is arriving.

515. A row of cars and carriages outside the entrance.

516. The ticket office. The line outside the ticket office. The clerk sells the last ticket, hangs up a sign saying "Sold Out," and pulls the ticket window shut.

517. The surging crowds in front of the entrance. Mounted policemen cut into the crowd.

518. Rogdai is sitting in the corner of his dressing room. Low lights. A table lamp with a lampshade. Rogdai is sitting with his back to the viewer. His long legs are stretched out, his head is hanging. Rogdai slowly turns his face toward the viewer: spectral, passionate, thin— it has become almost unrecognizable in the space of a year.

519. THE RESULT OF A YEAR OF FAME, AND A YEAR OF FRIENDSHIP WITH SIGNOR MAFFI.

520. Rogdai reaches for a bottle of wine. Next to the bottle lie his violin and bow. He is wearing a coat and tails and elegant shoes. He studies the label on the bottle, and his face twitches. He makes a sign to the attendant, who comes hurrying over to him:

521. "TAKE AWAY THIS WATERY STUFF AND BRING ME SOME ABSINTHE!"

522. The attendant takes away the wine.

523. The violin, the bow. Rogdai's fingers flit over the strings.

524. The attendant brings in another bottle. Rogdai pours himself some absinthe and drinks.

525. Rogdai's long, extended neck, bulging out as he gulps down the alcohol.

526. The main entrance of the theater. The ushers open the doors. The crowd pours into the lobby, people jostling and elbowing one another.

527. The street urchins hop off the pillars, and go scampering over and under the crowd into the lobby.

528. One of the theater's flights of stairs. Disheveled, excited people are rushing up the steps. A man in front is waving the remnants of a walking stick in the air.

529. Another flight of stairs. A mass of people, among them Baulin and Rachel, are running toward the upper balconies.

530. The dazzlingly lit auditorium. The audience is pouring in from all sides.

531. In the foyer. Professor Reti, who has not lost an iota of his enthusiasm, is addressing a group of young people crowding around him:

532. "HE WAS MY PUPIL, LADIES AND GENTLEMEN!"

533. The crowd gathers around the old man. He talks to them enthusiastically about his pupil and the incredible story of his career.

534. A group of Russians are sitting in the cheapest seats in the top balcony. They laugh, jostle one another, and act the way happy young people sitting in balcony seats do all over the world. Baulin gives Rachel an orange, which she bites into.

535. The plush railing of a theater box. On it lie a carved fan, opera glasses studded with pearls, a long box of sweets. Helene's hands unwrap a sweet and then push it aside.

536. In Baroness Grennier's theater box. Helene, in a low-cut gown, is sitting motionless and breathtakingly pale next to her mother, who is wearing an elegant black hat. In the depths of the box, Count San Salvador and Baron Sant' Iago are serenely sleeping, decked out in their inevitable medals and ribbons.

537. The first rows of seats, expensive theater boxes. Women in low-cut gowns eyeing each other through their lorgnettes. Immaculately washed and shaven men.

538. The Russians have finally sat down. Rachel has finished eating her orange. She turns to Baulin:

539. "THEY SAY THAT HE'S ORIGINALLY RUSSIAN."

540. Baulin answers, "I don't know." He hands her another orange. Laughing, she gives him half of it.

541. Rogdai is tuning his violin in his dressing room.

542. The audience sitting in its seats. The ushers close the doors. The chandeliers slowly extinguish.

543. The extinguishing chandeliers. Their yellow, dying light.

544. The curtain rises. On the stage, the symphony orchestra is waiting for the conductor.

545. Rogdai has tuned his violin. He plucks a few chords, one quieter than the next, puts his violin down, and disappears behind a curtain. An attendant comes rushing in:

546. "YOU'RE ON!"

547. Behind the curtain Rogdai is injecting himself with morphine.

548. On stage. The conductor walks up to his podium. His eyes dart about, looking for Rogdai.

549. The attendant running frantically back and forth in Rogdai's dressing room.

550. "YOU'RE ON!"

551. Rogdai comes out from behind the curtain. He picks up his violin and runs out toward the stage.

552. The auditorium. Darkness. Silence. Hundreds of hands begin to clap.

553. The lit-up stage, shot from a distance. Rogdai, a tiny shape diminished by the distance, walks toward the footlights and bows.

554. Rachel's hands unclasp, dropping a program and a piece of orange.

555. The program, swaying in the air, floats down from the top balcony and lands on somebody's head.

556. Rachel's face. She lunges forward in the grip of a terrible emotion. She shouts:

557. "LEV!"

558. Baulin covers her mouth.

559. The stage, shot from a distance. Rogdai plays.

560. The cashier is running down the corridor. He is holding an iron strongbox filled with money.

561. A corner of Rodgai's dressing room. Maffi is checking the stubs of the sold tickets. The cashier comes running in and triumphantly puts the money box in front of Maffi.

562. "FULL HOUSE, SIGNOR MAFFI! THE THEATER'S FILLED TO THE RAFTERS!"

563. Maffi takes a pile of banknotes out of the box, a tic flashing across his face. The whole table is littered with banknotes.

564. The pile of money on the table. Maffi's large white hands cover the scattered banknotes, a magnificent ring of unusual shape sparkling on his index finger.

565. The sparkling diamond in Maffi's ring. Within the diamond. . .

566. . . . Rogdai's fingers flying with diabolic speed over the strings.

567. Professor Reti, filled with enthusiasm, is annoying his neighbors. He is gesticulating, humming along, flapping his arms.

568. Rogdai's pale, distorted, inspired face. His chin is pressed against the violin.

569. Maffi's fingers, counting the money.

570. Rogdai's violin, his singing bow, his hair tousled.

571. Maffi's fingers, counting the money. Helene's hand touches them.

572. Maffi raises his head. Helene is standing in front of him.

573. "VITTORIO,"

574. she says tenderly.

575. "YOU DON'T LOVE ME, VITTORIO."

576. A suppressed yawn bulges Maffi's jaw and cheekbones. He battles the yawn spreading over his face without lowering his intent eyes from Helene.

577. "I . . . DO LOVE YOU . . ."

578. he mutters, reluctantly bending over and kissing her hand, on which there are four bloody marks scratched by her hysterical nails.

579. Rogdai's fingers flying over the strings.

580. The chandeliers, their lights extinguished, hanging below the ornate ceiling of the theater. Their lamps begin to fill with yellow light and burn brightly.

581. Hundreds of applauding hands. The first part of the program has ended.

582. The flight of stairs. Bare, gray walls. Rachel is running down the stairs.

583. Rogdai in his dressing room. He is surrounded by a crowd of admirers. The women are clapping their hands right in front of his face. Gesticulating, enthusiastic Professor Reti comes lunging toward him. Helene passes between them. Rogdai pushes away the people crowding around him and takes Helene to the other side of the dressing room. He asks her with a gasp:

584. "FOR THE LAST TIME, HELENE—YES OR NO?"

585. Helene pulls away her hand, and vacantly answers:

586. "YES, YES, YES . . ."

587. And she leaves.

588. Rachel is running down the stairs along the dull, gray walls.

589. Rogdai turns to one of the fops clapping in his face:

590. "TONIGHT I WANT TO GET DRUNK!"

591. The fop stands to attention and salutes:
592. "AYE-AYE, CAPTAIN!"
593. Outside Rogdai's dressing-room door. An attendant stops Rachel, who is trying to enter.
594. "I WANT TO SEE ROGDAI!"
595. she shouts, pushing back the attendant. He raises his arm threateningly. Maffi juts his head out of the dressing room.
596. "WHAT'S ALL THIS RACKET?"
597. Rachel rushes to Maffi, begging him to let her in. Maffi bows to her. His bow is very refined, elegant, and barely perceptible.
598. "MAY I BE SO BOLD AS TO ASK YOUR NAME, MADE-MOISELLE?"
599. Rachel:
600. "I AM RACHEL MONKO, A . . . A COMPATRIOT OF ROGDAI'S."
601. The Italian bows to her a second time, takes her rough, red hand with its badly cut fingernails, and, before lifting it to his lips, glances at her slyly, holding her shivering fingers in his large, calm hand. She tugs her hand away, he kisses her wrist, bows a third time, and says:
602. "WE MUST NOT PERTURB ROGDAI DURING HIS CONCERT. IF YOU WOULD NOT MIND COMING TO MY PLACE, HE SHOULD BE THERE IN ABOUT AN HOUR. . . ."
603. Rachel presses Maffi's hands. He takes a powder box and some lipstick out of his vest pocket and hands them to Rachel, who looks at him in dismay.
604. "WOULD YOU NOT LIKE TO FIX YOUR FACE A LIT-TLE?"
605. Rachel shrinks back. A pocket in her dress opens and the muzzle of a small Browning peers out.
606. Maffi's fingers snap the powder box shut.
607. The muzzle of the Browning, peering out of Rachel's pocket.
608. Maffi slips the powder and the lipstick back into his vest pocket, and accompanies Rachel out.
609. The main entrance of the theater. Maffi's car. The driver is dozing inside—neither his face nor his hands are visible. The driver

is wrapped in a fur coat that rises above the steering wheel like a formless, furry lump. It is hard to guess if there is a man hidden beneath that rough, protruding mound. Maffi and Rachel walk up to the car. Maffi helps her into the car and slams the door shut, waking up the driver. The driver's small, wrinkled, and surprisingly indifferent face slowly emerges out of the incredible heap of fur. Maffi tells him where to drive to and jumps into the car. The car's lights flare up. Two swift rays light up the street. The car drives off.

610. Night. A Berlin street. High up, dazzling electric lights are gyrating in the form of a violin and the letters "LEO ROGDAI."

611. The car. It is leaving the city center, weaving its way through carts carrying butchered pigs to market.

612. The walk lined with plane trees outside Villa Grennier. Night. The swaying treetops. Below, Maffi's car is flying through the streets, its headlights' two fiery shafts flying before it.

613. The baroness's salon. Night. A Venetian window. The moon, floating past the window, casts its deathly rays on a statue standing in a niche by the window, on the eyeless marble face of Apollo.

614. Maffi and Rachel get out of the car. The Italian takes a rose from a little vase fixed to the inside of the car and offers it to Rachel.

615. The lobby of the Villa Grennier. The bell rings. The doorman opens the door. Maffi takes him aside and, with a severe air, orders him to do something. The doorman, a well-built fellow with a handsome, dubious face, gives Rachel a sidelong glance.

616. The Grennier salon. The doorman turns on the light. Maffi points Rachel to a chair next to the statue of Apollo, and makes himself comfortable in a chair opposite her. He lights a cigar. Rachel:

617. "I THINK WE HAVE TO GET ROGDAI TO END HIS CONTRACT WITH HIS IMPRESARIO. HE IS ILL, HE HAS TO RECUPERATE! DON'T YOU AGREE?"

618. Maffi nods his head. The door of the salon opens a crack. Rachel jumps up and stands rigidly by the statue.

619. A police officer enters the room. Rachel, ready to bolt, sees the policeman and the parting of his hair, combed down to a meticu-

lous shine. Maffi bows to the policeman, pulls the revolver out of Rachel's pocket, lays it on the table, and, pointing at Rachel, says:

620. "ALLOW ME TO INTRODUCE YOU TO RACHEL MONKO, A CRIMINAL FUGITIVE FROM RUSSIA WHO IS TO BE IMMEDIATELY DELIVERED INTO THE HANDS OF THE RUSSIAN AUTHORITIES."

621. Rachel's face, turned toward Maffi. She throws away the flower that Maffi had given her. The crushed rose falls onto the Browning.

622. The rose and the revolver.

Part Eight

623. A platter with a roasted fowl exquisitely laid out with its plumage. The fowl has been used as an ashtray by a group of drinkers, cigarette butts sticking out all over it.

624. The platter is lying in the middle of the table, which is covered with plates and spilled wine. Rogdai's hand stubbing out a smoking cigarette in the fowl.

625. A private room in the restaurant. Dawn. The remains of the shameful banquet. Rogdai, swaying, takes a few steps.

626. He steps over the unconscious body of a man lying on the floor. The man's legs are bent in a sitting position: he had been about to bite into a chunk of beefsteak speared on the end of his fork when he fell asleep and off his chair.

627. The sky lights up. The sun is rising.

628. A street in Berlin. A lone janitor is sweeping the sidewalk outside the Hotel Imperial. He leans on his broom, pulls up his shirt and scratches his belly, and, raising his tousled head to the sky, opens his mouth in a long, obstinate, shuddering yawn.

629. The barrel of a cement mixer can be seen through branches lit by the sun. A group of homeless children are sleeping in the barrel, their filthy little bodies in a tangle. One of them wakes up, sneezes, stretches his thin blackened hands to the sky, and winks at a drunkard who is leaning against the barrel. The drunkard is Rogdai. He is wearing a coat and tails, elegant shoes, and a battered top hat that is slipping off his head.

630. Rogdai lifts his top hat, his dull eyes fixed vacantly on the winking boy. He walks off, swaying.

631. Baulin's cramped little room next to the boiler. Bloated veins—the boiler pipes—cut through Baulin's room; the room is clenched between the pipes' dusty paws. A shabby, bearded man, obviously Russian, is pacing up and down the room. His endless pacing smacks of lengthy imprisonment. He has worn a path from one corner to the other. This polished path shines against the rough-hewn floor. Next to the room is the boiler for central heating. Baulin is shoveling coal into the boiler.

632. Baulin lights the fire and crushes some coal with a hammer. He is working absentmindedly, and by mistake keeps hitting an old shoe lying next to the coal. Sadness has made him incapable of work. He has battered the shoe to a pulp without even noticing. He throws down the hammer and heads back to his room. The bearded man stops pacing the room and, looking Baulin in the eye, says:

633. "WELL, COMRADE BAULIN, WE HAVE NO OBJECTION TO YOUR RETURNING TO RUSSIA TO UNDERTAKE CLANDESTINE WORK FOR OUR CAUSE."

634. Baulin nods his head. He walks over toward the window located high up, right under the ceiling. Outside the window, stumbling feet in elegant shoes—Rogdai's feet.

635. The laundry in the Hotel Imperial. A Chinese man has fallen asleep on a heap of starched men's shirts he has ironed. A thin stream of spittle is trickling from the sleeping man's mouth and onto a shining shirtfront. Rachel's workbench is empty. Baulin enters the laundry. He leans over Rachel's workbench, looks at the clock. It is three in the morning.

636. The sun is rising above the walk lined with plane trees leading to the Villa Grennier.

637. Rogdai, bumping into trees, is stumbling toward the villa.

638. The lobby in the baroness's home. The furniture is in complete disorder. The house is being cleaned. Chairs are standing on tables, the coat stand has been moved to the side. Rogdai is creeping along a wall.

639. In the hallway. Rogdai stumbles into the velvet curtain separating

one of the rooms from the hallway. Loud voices are coming from the room. Rogdai listens, becomes rigid.

640. Baroness Grennier's room. Maffi, in a rage, strikes the table with his whip. The baroness, Count San Salvador, and Baron Sant' Iago stand cowering and servile before him. Maffi shouts:

641. "YOUR STINKING DUMP HERE IS SWALLOWING EVERY LAST PENNY I EARN FROM ROGDAI'S CONCERTS! STARTING SUNDAY I WANT YOU TO RAISE THE PRICES ON THE GIRLS, ESPECIALLY HELENE!"

642. Maffi swishes his whip a few inches from the baroness's nose.

643. Rogdai has entangled himself in the curtain.

644. Maffi is shaking Count San Salvador.

645. "I'M GOING TO SEND YOU PACKING AND HIRE THE EX-KING OF PORTUGAL INSTEAD!"

646. The winding and flapping curtain. Rogdai's body struggling among its heavy folds.

647. The disheveled Count San Salvador staggers back from his infuriated master. The old man, frightened to death, keeps crossing himself delicately.

648. Rogdai creeps along the wall. Only his hunched-over back is visible.

649. An ancient cuckoo clock in the hallway strikes four. The cuckoo waggles its head boisterously.

650. Rogdai opens the door to Helene's room and staggers back.

651. A patch of sky in the window. The sun is rising.

652. Helene's room. Helene is lying asleep in bed with Kalnischker.

653. Rogdai creeps to the nightstand, where Kalnischker's false teeth are lying in a glass of water. He picks up the false teeth, his fingers clenching them tightly.

654. Rogdai's fingers clenching Kalnischker's false teeth. Fadeout into:

655. The eyeless marble face of Apollo.

656. An escritoire arranged with unusual thoroughness and love: an inkwell, a pen-and-pencil holder, a piece of cloth for wiping pen nibs, neatly cut paper, a paperweight, and a machine for sharpening pencils.

657. The baroness's salon. Rachel is being questioned by the policeman. Rachel is huddling against the statue. The policeman has

spent hours writing out a statement. He is writing slowly, calli-graphically, forgetting everything else in the world. His hand-writing is of diabolical beauty.

658. "SO YOU'RE A POLITICAL FUGITIVE, NOT A CRIMI-NAL ONE?"

659. the policeman asks, and, receiving a positive answer, begins once more decorating the filled sheets of paper, which look more like Japanese etchings than sheets of paper filled with writing.

660. Rachel embraces Apollo's marble legs. The statue moves very slightly on its wooden podium.

661. Rogdai enters Helene's boudoir. He opens her closet and riffles through the gowns hanging on clothes hangers.

662. Helene's open closet. The personal toilette of a young woman of the world: shoes, dresses, perfume bottles, and gloves.

663. Rogdai finds the dress that Helene was wearing when they first met, the dress with the long sash embroidered with gold thread.

664. Baroness Grennier and the old gentlemen come shuffling out of the room one after the other. The infuriated Italian hurls the whip after them, and it lands on San Salvador's bent back.

665. In Helene's boudoir. Rogdai takes down the portrait of him that was painted in the days when he was young and strong.

666. The hook on the wall on which the portrait had hung.

667. In the salon. The policeman has finished the fourth page and is about to embark on the fifth. He unhurriedly blots the ink on the sheet filled with writing, eyes it with admiration, shakes it. Maffi enters the room.

668. "WHAT? YOU'RE STILL HERE?"

669. The policeman, hurled down from the heights of heaven:

670. "THE FRÄULEIN MAINTAINS THAT SHE HAS THE HONOR OF BEING A POLITICAL CRIMINAL. THIS BEING SO, I AM WRITING A SMALL SUMMING-UP OF HER STATEMENT."

671. Maffi yawns and waves his hands dismissively.

672. "FINISH WHAT YOU'RE DOING AND TAKE HER AWAY. IT'S TIME TO GO TO BED."

673. Maffi takes off his evening jacket and shakes it out. It gets caught on Apollo's hand and hangs there. A bed has been made up for

Maffi on the sofa. Arranged on a nightstand are all the things that a forty-year-old man might need during the night: wafers, a bottle of soda water, a French novel, a dressing gown, and so on. Maffi unbuttons his collar. He grimaces—the collar is too tight.

674. Rachel, still huddling next to the statue, asks Maffi:

675. "WHERE IS ROGDAI?"

676. Maffi hurls the collar away, pours himself some soda water, and says:

677. "YOU THINK I'M MY BROTHER ABEL'S KEEPER?"

678. The statue of Apollo moves. Rachel, leaning against it with her shoulder, topples the enormous statue from its pedestal. The statue tumbles over, falling onto the sofa, fracturing Maffi's skull, shattering into a thousand pieces.

679. Rachel pushes Maffi onto his back. She claws at his face, yelling:

680. "WHERE IS ROGDAI?"

681. Maffi's skull is fractured, his eyes bloody. Rachel begins strangling him, but the police officer lunges at her and puts handcuffs on her.

682. Maffi, covered in blood, his eyes unseeing, is waving his arms in the air. He slumps off the sofa and crawls on all fours toward Rachel.

683. The policeman drags Rachel, who is struggling hysterically, across the floor. He pushes open a door and at the curtain separating the rooms bumps into someone's legs.

684. Rogdai's body, hanging from the gold-embroidered sash, has been set swaying by the policeman's bumping into it. Rogdai's asphyxiated face turns toward the viewer.

685. Rachel looks into the dead man's face, throws her handcuffed hands into the air, and collapses on the floor.

686. Maffi comes crawling in after Rachel. He gropes for the revolver in his pocket, takes it out, and shoots without aiming.

687. Rogdai's hand clutching Kalnischker's false teeth. The bullet pierces the dead man's hand and the fingers unclench, dropping the false teeth. The hanging man's body turns its back to the viewer. Cut.

688. Baulin's dingy little room. His bearded companion, crouching between the pipes, is mending his pants with stitches that are

clumsy, masculine, and soldierly. From time to time he looks over to the boiler where Baulin is stoking the furnace.

689. Baulin in front of the blazing furnace. Rachel quietly comes into the cellar. She takes off her kerchief. Her hair has turned gray. She steadies herself on the wall. After a few moments of silence she asks without raising her head:

690. "WHERE SHALL WE GO TO NOW?"

691. The flame of the burning coals. Baulin answers:

692. "BACK TO RUSSIA!"

693. Among the tangle of pipes, the bearded man's face bent over his pants. His eyes dart in Baulin's direction and then back.

694. The polished strip of floor, trodden by Baulin and his bearded comrade.

BENYA KRIK

A TREATMENT FOR A FILM

The silent movie Benya Krik, *directed by Vilner, premiered in January 1927. The screenplay is based on the Odessa stories, and is divided into sections that bear the names of individual stories. As in Babel's other screenplays, the writing style in* Benya Krik *reads more like a literary work than a scenario. "Dvoira throws herself onto the cringing groom, drags him toward her as a dockworker might drag a sack of flour down a gangplank, and devours him with a long, wet, predatory kiss." It is particularly interesting to read this screenplay in connection with the Odessa stories and the play* Sunset, *as it develops and varies their themes. The Odessa story "How Things Were Done in Odessa" opens with, "Let's talk about Benya Krik. Let's talk about his lightning-quick beginning and his terrible end." But the screenplay* Benya Krik *is the only surviving work in which we find out what his terrible end is after the Bolsheviks take over Odessa in 1919.*

Part One

THE KING

Chief of Police Sokovich, off Duty

Chief of Police Sokovich's room. A canary is swinging in a cage, which is hanging from the ceiling near a window lined with potted geraniums.

An old woman in a cap is sitting by the grand piano, knitting. The needles move quickly. The piano is partially visible, its lacquered cover glistening.

The chief of police plays with unusual pathos—he moves his lips, lifts his shoulders, and opens his mouth.

The keyboard. Sokovich's fingers, covered in rings in the shape of skulls, hooves, and Assyrian seals, are racing over the keys.

The canary in its cage is bursting with song. Sokovich is swaying as he plays, and with him sway the room, the canary, the knitting needles, and the old woman.

Marantz, a Jew in a tattered suit, emerges from the depths of the room. He coughs, shuffles, and scrapes his feet, but the enraptured chief of police doesn't hear him.

Sokovich's fingers pound the keys tempestuously. Marantz's doleful, indecisive face bends down toward the keyboard.

The chief of police begins playing in a tender *piano*. Marantz cannot contain himself. Overcome with emotion, he grabs Sokovich's head and presses it against his chest.

Sokovich jumps up. Marantz whispers something into his ear, or, to be more precise, he whispers something somewhere below Sokovich's ear.

"MAY I NOT LIVE TO SEE THE DAY I LEAD MY OWN DAUGHTER UNDER THE FLOWER CANOPY . . . IF . . . IF I AM NOT . . . TODAY . . . "

Marantz steps back, cowers, swivels on his shaky feet. Sokovich looks at him gravely. Marantz:

"THE KING IS GIVING AWAY HIS SISTER TODAY. EVERYONE WILL GET BLIND DRUNK, AND YOU CAN PULL OFF AN EXCELLENT RAID!"

Sokovich slams down the piano cover. He peers at the Jew's grimacing, twitching face.

A young gypsy woman with layers of tattered skirts is sitting on the edge of the sidewalk in front of the chief of police's house. She is covered in ribbons and coin necklaces. She is eating bread rolls and taking swigs from a wine bottle. Next to her a monkey on a chain is jumping up and down. Excited children are running in circles around her.

Sokovich's front door opens and Marantz sneaks out into the street. He looks around furtively, and walks away along the wall.

The gypsy grabs the monkey and runs after Marantz. She catches up with him and starts begging and coaxing him for money.

"GIVE US SOMETHING, YOUR EXCELLENCY! GIVE US SOME-
THING, YOU HANDSOME MAN!"

Marantz spits and walks on. The gypsy stands looking after him for
a long time. The monkey jumps onto her shoulder, and also watches
Marantz walk away.

A street in the Moldavanka, the Jewish quarter of Odessa. Mendel
Krik's cart comes charging around the corner. The old man is drunk.
He whips the horses, and they gallop with thundering hooves.
Pedestrians scramble out of the way.

Mendel Krik, known as a ruffian even in carting circles

Mendel Krik brandishes his whip. Legs astride, the old man stands
upright in the cart. Crimson sweat steams on his face. He is tall, stout,
drunk, and jolly.

The cart flies at full speed. "Look out!" the drunk old man yells to
the pedestrians. The gypsy girl, singing, swaying her hips, comes
toward him. On her shoulder the monkey is busy cracking one nut after
another. The gypsy gives the old man a slight, barely visible sign.

The reins in Mendel's hands. Clenched in his iron grip, they stop
the horses in full gallop.

Mendel's face, suddenly sober, turns toward the gypsy.

The gypsy walks past Mendel. She throws him a sidelong glance,
and sings:

"MARANTZ! A HUNDRED DEVILS UPON HIS MOTHER!"

The gypsy sways her hips, pets the monkey, and sings:

"MARANTZ HAS SEEN THE CHIEF OF POLICE. . . ."

Mendel jerks the reins and drives on. Now the horses are trotting
slowly.

A close-up of a flaking sign: "Horse-Carting Establishment, Mendel
Krik & Sons." Painted on the sign are a chain of horseshoes, and an
English lady in riding habit holding a whip. The lady is cavorting on a
cart horse—the cart horse is flinging its front legs high in the air.

Under the sign, two young men sit cracking sunflower seeds on a
bench in front of a shabby one-story house. They sit in deep silence,

staring blankly in front of them. One is a young Persian with an olive-brown face and bushy eyebrows. The other is Savka Butsis. Butsis is missing an arm, and a flapping sleeve has been sewn over the stump. With his other arm, his good arm, he scoops the sunflower seeds with unusual dexterity and bravura out of his pocket and, without even aiming, slings them into his mouth. He never misses.

Mendel Krik drives up to the house. The young men, Savka and the Persian, salute Mendel Krik silently and without turning their heads. The gates open for Mendel. The man opening them is hidden from view.

The courtyard of Mendel Krik's house is wide, and edged with old, squat buildings cluttered with dovecotes, carts, and unharnessed horses. Young women are milking cows in a corner.

Three pink, spotted udders, and women's hands, pulling at the teats. Spurts of milk splutter into the pails.

One of the girls has finished milking. She straightens her back and stretches. A ray of sun illuminates the freckled skin of her lively face. She narrows her eyes. Mendel flies into the yard with his heated stallions. He jumps down from the cart, throws the reins to the girl, and, his fat legs stumbling, rushes to the house.

The girl unharnesses the stallions with nimble fingers and slaps the muzzles of the playful ones.

His Majesty, the King

A double or, to be more precise, quadruple bed fills the room of the bride-to-be, Dvoira Krik. This giant contraption is covered with a countless number of embroidered pillows. Benya Krik is leaning with his back against the bed. The back of his shaved neck is visible.

Benya Krik is playing the mandolin. He is wearing slick, lacquered shoes, and his feet are resting on a stool. His suit bears the mark of refined gangster chic.

The voluminous bed—the cradle of the clan, of battle and love. Old Krik bursts into the room. He pulls off his boots. He unwinds his unbelievably dirty foot bindings, and stares at them in disbelief. He thinks to himself, "I can't believe how dirty some people are!" Mendel stretches his hot, sticky toes and, slightly intimidated in his son's "kingly" presence, mutters:

"MARANTZ SAW THE CHIEF OF POLICE TODAY!"

Benya's fingers, plucking the mandolin strings, become rigid. A string breaks and spirals around the neck of the mandolin. The mandolin flies onto the bed and is buried in the cushions.

FADEOUT

An empty sleeve, fastened with a ruby pin in the shape of a snake, is hanging from Savka Butsis's shoulder.

A street in the Moldavanka. Savka and the Persian are sitting on a bench outside Marantz's front door. They are immersed in their favorite pastime—cracking sunflower seeds. A buggy pulls up to Marantz's house. A portly coachman with a patriarchal backside and a flowing beard is sitting on the box. Something about the coachman reminds one in a strange way of the gyspy woman in the earlier scenes.

Benya steps out of the buggy and rings the doorbell. A little hatch in the door opens and Marantz's head comes jutting out, a head still safeguarding a few tufts of hair and covered with ink stains and pillow feathers. A terrible fear suddenly streaks across his face. Benya raises his hat to the broker with unsettling politeness.

The coachman's indifferent face. Bored, he jingles the coin necklace the gypsy woman had been wearing.

Marantz comes stumbling out into the street. Benya greets him, takes hold of his shoulders, and says in a friendly tone:

"THERE'S MONEY TO BE MADE, MARANTZ!"

Benya rubs his thumb and index finger together, signifying that a profitable deal is at hand.

Marantz hesitates. Struggling to guess the reason for this unexpected visit, he peers into Benya's impenetrable face.

Benya's thumb and index finger rub slower and more mysteriously.

"THERE'S MONEY TO BE MADE, MARANTZ!"

The broker has been won over. His wife comes out of the house with his coat, his chocolate-brown bowler hat, and a canvas umbrella. A gaggle of children is peeking out the front door. Clean and nimble Semitic eyes sparkle from their grimy faces. Marantz and Benya get into the buggy. Marantz's wife bows to the "King." Her long breasts swing, like washing hung to dry in a yard on a windy day. The coachman whips the horses.

The buggy driving off. We see the coachman's burly, reassuring back, Marantz's bowler, and Benya's panama. The buggy drives past a policeman. The policeman salutes Benya.

One-armed Savka motions one of Marantz's sons to come over. The little fellow, wavering between terror and delight at the unknown, comes hobbling up to him in a crooked, halting line.

The seashore. A crashing wave. Above, white dachas with colonnaded facades. The buggy is riding along the edge of the seashore. Benya and Marantz are chatting affably. The bowler and the panama hat bob amicably. The horses are trotting in a brisk canter. The area becomes more and more deserted.

Marantz's misgivings have gradually turned into joy at the beauty of the sea and the rocks. He has sprawled out on the leather cushions and unbuttoned his shirt to catch a little sun. Benya takes out his cigarette case, offers Marantz a cigarette, and casually says:

"WORD HAS IT THAT YOU'VE BEEN BLABBING TO THE INSPECTOR ABOUT ME."

Marantz's quaking fingers tap the cigarette on the silver top of Benya's case.

The buggy rolls to a hidden, deserted spot on the shore. Rocks, bushes. The coachman stops the horses, turns his bearded face to the passenger, and swings his legs back into the buggy.

Benya offers Marantz a match. The terrified Jew begins smoking his cigarette. He looks first at Benya, then at the coachman, who is now sitting on the box with his legs dangling into the buggy. The coachman slowly places his feet on Marantz's shoulders and lifts the bowler hat off his head.

The Persian is playing a game favored by all children with Marantz's little son: the little boy lays his palms on those of the Persian and then quickly pulls them back. The Persian pretends he is too slow to hit the little boy's palms, and little Marantz squeals with delight. The boy is perfectly happy.

The seashore. A wave breaks beneath the cliffs. Marantz's bowler hat falls into the water.

The buggy drives along the seashore. Benya is wearing his panama hat as before, but Marantz is no longer wearing a hat. His head is lolling disheveled. The coachman raises the buggy's top.

The bowler hat is floating on the broad, blue, melting waves.

The horses' straining, foaming muzzles.

The Persian and the boy are still playing. Savka is tirelessly cracking sunflower seeds.

The buggy, its top up, drives past the policeman. He again salutes.

Savka sees the buggy from a distance. He pats the little boy on the cheek, gives him a fiver, and sends him off with a playful little nudge of his knee.

The buggy stops outside Marantz's house. Benya gets out and walks to the front door.

Savka and the Persian get up from the bench and walk off, their arms over each other's shoulders.

"Madame" Marantz opens the door.

"WORD HAS IT, MADAME MARANTZ, THAT YOUR LATE HUS-BAND HAS BEEN BLABBING ABOUT ME."

The woman's distorted face in the doorway.

Marantz's body slowly rolls out of the buggy.

The backs of Savka and the Persian as they lazily trudge along the street.

Marantz's body sprawled out on the ground.

A little heap of the husks of the sunflower seeds that Savka cracked.

Part Two

The King's friends come to Dvoira Krik's wedding

The police station building. A brick wall, three stories high. Jail-cell windows, covered with bars, are on the third floor. Prisoners' faces are peering out of them. The prisoners, overwhelmed by sudden excitement, begin waving to someone with handkerchiefs.

A street in the Moldavanka. A side view of the police station. An old Jewess is sitting on the corner, delousing her granddaughter's hair. There is a sudden noise. The old woman raises her head and looks at the approaching procession.

Gangsters are heading to old Krik's house in archaic wedding carriages. Savka and the Persian are sitting in the first carriage, each holding a gigantic bouquet of flowers in his extended, steely hand. They are dressed in the style of Benya Krik, but instead of panama hats they are wearing tiny bowler hats, cocked to the side. The coachman is wearing a bow tie, and looks more like the best man at a wedding than a coachman.

The second carriage is a gigantic, swaying, black box. Lyovka Bik, one of the King's closest associates, is sprawled out in the back. He is holding a bouquet of flowers in his hands, and his coachman is wearing a bow tie.

A crowd of well-wishing policemen are standing at the gates of the police station. They watch the opulent procession with envy and respect.

The third carriage. One-eyed Froim Grach is sitting in it (his left eye is missing, gouged out and dried up), presenting a striking antithesis to the other gangsters. He is wearing a canvas cloak and well-polished boots. Next to sullen and drowsy Grach is the coquettish, wrinkled face of sixty-year-old Manka, the matriarch of the Slobodka* bandits. She is wearing a lace kerchief. Urchins and loafers are running behind their carriage.

Froim Grach and Manka, the matriarch of the Slobodka bandits

The episcopal carriage of Froim and Grandma Manka slowly rolls past the police station.

The prisoners wave their handkerchiefs in a frenzy.

The old woman bows with the poise of an empress surveying her troops.

Sokovich's sullen face at a second-floor window.

Sokovich's office. A portrait of Czar Nicholas II is hanging on the wall. Sokovich's squirming back at the window. Glechik, his deputy, a fat man with a soft, rolling stomach, is sitting at the desk in a wide arm-

---

* Slobodka was a rough shantytown neighborhood on the outskirts of Odessa.

chair. His shortsighted eyes blinking, he sucks at fruit drops, of which he has a whole box. The chief of police's back manifests extreme excitement, twisting and shuddering as if a flea had bitten it.

Glechik shoves a heap of fruit drops into his mouth. They don't all immediately fit in the opening, which is covered with a lush drooping mustache The chief of police turns around abruptly, walks over to Glechik, and prods him:

"IT'S CURTAINS FOR BENCHIK! WE'LL GRAB THEM TODAY AT THE WEDDING!"

Glechik's forlorn face. Blinking, he asks:

"WHY BOTHER GRABBING THEM?"

The chief of police waves his hands disparagingly and rushes out of the office. Fat Glechik lifts his rolling stomach and trudges dejectedly after Sokovich. A piece of chicken wrapped in oilpaper is sticking out of his bulging pocket, and a dirty bit of string is hanging down and dragging along the floor.

The chief of police runs down the stairs, Glechik waddling after him.

The peaceful existence of a police station backyard. A fat-faced policeman is washing a pair of long underpants in a tub by the wall; in another corner of the yard, a group of Odessans, among them sage old Jews and stout market women, are eagerly saying good-bye and shaking the hand of a clerk. The handshaking takes a long time, the hands of the Odessans come darting out to him in the strangest ways, and after every convulsive handshake the clerk slips a fifty-kopeck coin into his pocket. Sokovich trots past the sage old men and the stout market women.

The policemen have lined up along the courtyard wall. The chief of police walks up to them. They stare at him intently. He gives them a speech:

"FELLOW OFFICERS! WHEN YOU HAVE HIS MAJESTY THE CZAR, YOU CAN'T HAVE A KING TOO!"

The row of well-fed, mustached faces. The chief of police continues his speech, and the more his enthusiasm grows, the more the faces of the policemen droop.

A flock of doves by a dovecote. Someone shoos them away with a stick.

Glechik pokes a long stick into the dovecote and then throws the stick away. Nothing can cheer him up. Passion and doubt are battling in his fat face.

Deputy Chief Glechik's tormented soul

Glechik takes a card out of his pocket and reads it with sadness and a sort of secret voluptuousness.

A close-up of the wedding invitation with a noble crown on it. Written in ink on the side: "To his Excellency, Monsieur Glechik." The printed text:

"Monsieur and Madame Mendel Usherovich Krik, and Monsieur and Madame Tevya Hananevich Shpilgagen request the honor of your presence at the wedding of their children Vera Mikhailovna Krik and Lazar Timofeyevich Shpilgagen, on Tuesday, June 5, 1913. Sincerely, the Parents."*

Glechik reads the invitation with sadness. A heavy sigh shakes the doleful thicket of his mustache. He is tormented by doubts. He turns his head, closes his eyes, and begins to twiddle his thumbs.

"TO GO OR NOT TO GO . . ."

Glechik's twiddling thumbs. One thumb bumps against the other: so he *will* go.

Gripped by a powerful emotion, he throws his chicken to a dog and hurries away.

Glechik hurrying through the yard. He is practically knocked off his feet by a group of policemen who are dragging in a young man by the scruff of the neck. It is Kolka Pakovsky, the same fellow we have already seen in the guise of the gypsy woman and Benya's coachman. Kolka's clothes are in tatters, he is drunk, his legs are dragging as he stumbles after the policemen. He takes the hand of the man propping him up and carefully licks it with drunken tenderness.

---

*A comic twist in the invitation is that the couple marrying is announced with Russian patronymics, although the parents have clearly Jewish names. Though Vera's father is called Mendel, she is referred to as Vera Mikhailovna, and though Lazar's father is called Tevya, Lazar is referred to as Lazar Timofeyevich.

Sokovich jerks his leg briskly and continues his speech:

"WE'VE GOT TO CATCH BENYA KRIK'S WHOLE GANG IN TODAY'S RAID!"

The policemen's dejected faces.
Kolka, propped up by the policemen, is dragged before the chief. They tell the chief of police:

"A KNIFE FIGHT IN BROAD DAYLIGHT, YOUR EXCELLENCY!"

Sokovich looks at Kolka absentmindedly.

"LOCK HIM UP OVERNIGHT. WE'LL DEAL WITH HIM TOMORROW."

The exchange between the handshakers and the clerk is still continuing.

The policemen are dragging Kolka through the corridors of the police station. Kolka keeps trying to kiss the boots of the men dragging him away.

The policemen open the door of a cell and thrust Kolka in. He goes tumbling head over heels into the cell.

The cell. Kolka tumbling into it. The other prisoners jump up as if on a silent order, and hug their new cell mate.

Kolka calms down in the arms of his cell mates. He takes a few swaggering steps, and collapses on the floor. His cell mates look at him eagerly, as at the bearer of blessed news. Their circle closes over Kolka as he falls.

Shot from above: tousled heads leaning over Kolka. The circle of prisoners slowly opens, Kolka gets up, yet a body is still lying sprawled on the floor.

On the cell floor lies a bloated rubber suit, somewhat reminiscent of a diving suit, and filled with some kind of liquid.

FADEOUT

Puffs of steam and smoke cloud the screen. Two pregnant bellies covered in striped smocks emerge from the fog. The bellies rest side by side against the bar of a stove.

Turkeys, geese, and every dish imaginable are roasting and steaming on the stove. The pregnant cooks are placing food on plates. Tiny eighty-year-old Reizl is reigning over them. Her withered little face, enveloped in puffs of steam, is filled with grandeur and holy impassivity. Reizl is holding a big knife, with which she slices open the stomachs of large sea fish writhing about on the table.

The pregnant cooks with their striped bellies pass the dishes to shabby Jewish waiters wearing white gloves and paper shirtfronts that keep curling up. Warts glow on their cheeks, and tufts of hair stand up in inappropriate places. They grab the dishes and run out of the kitchen.

The dying fish flop over the table, thrashing with their sparkling tails.

The wedding feast in the Kriks' courtyard. Chinese lanterns are hanging everywhere. The waiters run past tables of beggars and cripples, who are drunk, pulling wild grimaces, banging their crutches, and grabbing hold of the waiters, who tear themselves loose and head for the main table, where the King's retinue is wreaking havoc. The newlyweds sit at the place of honor: forty-year-old Dvoira, a large-breasted woman with goiter and bulging eyes, and Lazar Shpilgagen, a feeble little creature with a haggard face and thinning hair. Next to them sit Benya, Papa Krik, Lyovka Bik, Savka, the Persian, and their ladies—guffawing Moldavanka women in flaming red shawls. Papa Krik bellows:

"OY, A SWEET KISS FOR THE BRIDE!"

The drunken bride plunks her fat breasts onto the table, takes a few swigs of wine directly from the bottle, scratches her legs under the table, and slips her hand into meek Shpilgagen's shirt. The guests echo Papa Krik's call:

"OY, A SWEET KISS FOR THE BRIDE!"

The gangsters jump onto the chairs and pour vodka straight from the bottles into their mouths. Dvoira throws herself onto the cringing groom, drags him toward her as a dockworker might drag a sack of flour down a gangplank, and devours him with a long, wet, predatory kiss. The gangsters break plates.

Dvoira kissing Shpilgagen. A lame beggar comes crawling over to the newlyweds and stares at their kiss with blunt attention.

A policeman is dragging a bucket of boiling water through a corridor in the police station.

The cell. The policeman takes the boiling water inside. Kolka grabs the bucket out of the policeman's hands and pours the boiling water over his head. The scalded policeman collapses.

Kolka runs out into the corridor. He throws the rubber suit on a pile of slop pails lying in a corner, slits it open, and sets fire to the kerosene that is pouring out of it.

Glechik, the deputy chief of police, is wavering in uncertainty outside the gates of the Kriks' house. His stomach is squeezed into a new uniform, he is dragging a saber behind him, and on his head is a large, old-fashioned cap with a patent-leather peak. Glechik's chest is covered in medals: one for saving someone from drowning, another issued by Empress Maria in commemoration of the three-hundred-year reign of the Romanovs, and so on. Glechik timidly opens the gate a little.

A very bizarre musician, a large Turkish drum in front of him, stands a few paces away from the main table. He has a piece of string tied to his foot with which he makes copper plates on the drum clash, while he pounds the drum with a stick attached to his knee. The top part of his body is devoted to a gigantic tuba, more reminiscent of the coils of a boa constrictor. The sun's blue baton is blazing on the tuba. The musician is resting.

Glechik appears at the far end of the courtyard. Benya rushes over to him, and they kiss each other three times on the cheeks.* Benya makes a sign to the musician.

The musician starts up and jumps into action: he blows into the tuba, tugs at the string and thumps the stick attached to his knee against the drum.

Benya brings Glechik over to the other wedding guests. The delight of the guests that the deputy chief of police is present. The bride, covered in spilled wine, throws herself on Glechik's chest, Papa Krik thumps him on the back with all his might, and sixty-year-old Manka places a maternal kiss on his forehead. Savka comes hurrying over to Glechik with two bottles of vodka. Savka's woman tries to snatch one of them away, but he breaks the bottle over her head, and

* A traditional Russian sign of friendship, the three kisses symbolizing the Holy Trinity, an idiosyncratic act at a Jewish wedding.

then rushes over to Glechik and places the other bottle to his lips, as if he were giving a baby a bottle of milk. Papa Krik comes hurrying over with a cucumber.

The musician goes into a frenzy, his limbs bouncing every which way.

The rollicking Moldavanka women dance in a circle around Glechik, plying him with vodka, cucumbers, gefilte fish, and oranges. The women's hips are blossoming out, and old Krik and Grandma Manka dance face-to-face in the circle. Lyovka Bik, crazed with merriment, shoots bullets into the air, plunges into the circle, grabs hold of the old woman, and presses the revolver into her hand. Manka tenderly narrows her eyes and pulls the trigger.

The old woman's wrinkled hand, her finger pulling the trigger.

The shot. The dance reaches a crazed pitch. Papa Krik suddenly stops, sniffs at the air, and takes Benya aside:

"BENYA! YOU KNOW WHAT? I THINK I SMELL FIRE!"

Conducting the dance, Benya calms his father:

"PAPA! PLEASE EAT AND DRINK AND DON'T LET THESE FOOLISH THINGS BE WORRYING YOU!"

The musician in full swing, his leg is jerking, his tuba sends shivers through the sun.

The Moldavanka dance with its bravura, gunshots, breaking plates, and money flying between the dancers' feet.

The edge of the sky, reddened by the fire.

The fire brigade dashes through the streets of the Moldavanka. The crowd in front of the burning police station. The policemen are throwing boxes out the windows, a shower of paper is flying through the air. Sokovich, crazed, is galloping on his horse.

Inside the smoke-filled building, three fat bottoms are sliding with desperate speed down a slanting plank.

The wall of the police station. Prisoners are jumping out of smashed windows. Their wives run up to them and hug them.

The musician in full swing.

The Moldavanka amazons abducting their husbands. The women drag the prisoners to their houses.

The dancing in the Kriks' courtyard.

The firemen uncoil a long rubber hose and attach it to a fire hydrant on the street. They point the hose menacingly in the direction of the blaze, turn on the faucet, and . . . a few drops of water dribble with great effort onto the ground. The fire hydrant is not working.

Against the backdrop of the sky, filled with the glow of the fire, two black crossbeams twist and come crashing down.

Sokovich's mustache is singed. He is watching the blaze. Benya Krik walks past him with Kolka Pakovsky, whose clothes are ripped and covered in kerosene and water. Benya raises his hat.

"AI-AI-AI! WHAT BAD LUCK! A NIGHTMARE!"

Benya shakes his head mournfully. Sokovich fixes him with his dull, puzzled eyes.

FADEOUT

In the Kriks' courtyard. Sunrise. The lanterns are going out. Drunken guests are lying on the ground like collapsed stacks of fire-wood.

Dvoira Krik's quadruple bed. She is pulling Shpilgagen toward it. He turns pale, struggles to get away, but his resistance weakens and he falls onto the bed.

The musician, entangled in his bits of string, sticks, and copper plates, is sleeping, slumped over his drum.

Part Three

HOW THINGS WERE DONE IN ODESSA

Much water and blood have flowed since the day of Dvoira Krik's wedding.

A sea of banners. On these banners: "Long Live the Provisional Government!"*

---

* The Provisional Government came to power after the Russian Revolution of February 17, and introduced freedom of speech, assembly, press, and religion, and instituted universal suffrage and equal rights for women.

A big-breasted lady in a military uniform is carrying a banner proclaiming: "We shall fight for victory to the bitter end!"

A battalion of women of the Kerensky era.* The battalion is made up of ladies and streetwalkers. The ladies' faces are filled with resolve and inspiration—the streetwalkers' faces are puffy and tired.

A gigantic safe, taking up the whole screen. Its compartments are filled with stocks, foreign currency, and diamonds. Someone's hands place piles of gold coins into the safe.

Rubin Tartakovsky, proprietor of nineteen bakeries, clarifies his attitude toward the Revolution

Tartakovsky's office. The safe covering the whole wall. Tartakovsky, an old man with a silver beard and powerful shoulders, is handing money to Muginshtein, his assistant, who is placing the money in various compartments in the safe.

The raised revolutionary breasts of the women's battalion are streaming down the street, which is filled with loafers and hollering children.

The safe's heavy metallic door slowly falls shut.

"AND NOW, MUGINSHTEIN, WE SHALL GO AND CONGRATU-LATE THE WORKERS!"

the old man tells his assistant, and they leave the office.

Tartakovsky's bookkeeping department. A prereform setup reminiscent of Dickens's London. None of the clerks are wearing jackets. They have pen holders behind their ears and cotton wool in their ears. They are all either very fat or very thin. The fat workers are wearing sweaters and dirty vests, the thin workers shirtfronts and bow ties. Some have uncommonly rich heads of hair, others are bald. Some are sitting on tattered armchairs covered with pillows, others are perching on high, three-legged stools, but they all look as if they had just swallowed something very bitter. Only one bookkeeper, an Englishman, keeps an inviolable calm. He is gnawing at a pipe that envelops him with billows of the most vicious smoke. A boy is turning a press wheel

---

*Alexander Fyodorovich Kerensky, 1881–1970, was a leading figure in the Provisional Government, and served as Prime Minister of Russia from June 1917 until the Bolsheviks seized power four months later in the October Revolution.

in the corner, copying letters. A fleshy lady, Greek-looking because of her aquiline nose, is sitting at a window with the sign "Cashier" over it. Tartakovsky and Muginshtein walk up and down the room. The workers sit up. The boy, seeing his boss, begins turning the press with great vigor. He is holding his breath and turns red.

A large number of snot-nosed, rachitic children squirming in a heap. Half naked, their legs rickety, they are teeming on the ground like worms.

A large, four-story building on Moldavanka's Prokhorovskaya Street, where unimaginable Jewish poverty has gathered. Green, shivering old men dressed in rags are warming themselves in the sun, a watchmaker in tattered shoes has set up his table in the yard, bald-headed Jewesses in torn smocks cook food in battered pails. Tartakovsky and Muginshtein walk through the yard. The ragged old men rise from their seats, train their pus-filled eyes covered with thick bloody fluid on Tartakovsky, and bow to him. A disheveled Jewess in men's boots comes running up to him:

"WHAT ABOUT THE TOILET, MONSIEUR TARTAKOVSKY?"

she asks the old man. Tartakovsky shrugs his shoulders.

"WHAT ABOUT THE TOILET?"

he answers. The Jewess grabs him by the hand and takes him to her apartment.

She leads Tartakovsky up stairs that are covered in the dirt and trash of abject poverty. Wild, scraggly cats are flitting up and down the stairs.

The woman drags Tartakovsky to her toilet. There is no toilet bowl, only a hole in the cement floor. Reeking liquid is dribbling from the ceiling. Next to the toilet, almost within the toilet area itself, stands a bed heaped with tattered blankets. A hunchbacked girl with carefully plaited hair is lying on the bed. Tartakovsky pats the woman approvingly on the back:

"NOW THAT YOUR NIKOLAI HAS BEEN SNATCHED AWAY BY THE CHOLERA, WE'LL ALL BE BETTER OFF, YOU TOO!"

The hunchbacked girl looks at Tartakovsky. Water is streaming down the side of the wall next to her bed.

Children are crawling on the floor—the naked, rachitic, snot-nosed children of the ghetto.

Tartakovsky and Muginshtein walk through the teeming heap of children, Tartakovsky struggling to find a place to tread. In the depths of the courtyard is the entrance to the cellar where the bakery is.

The sign above the cellar: "Bakery and Pastry Shop No. 16, Joint Stock Company, Rubin Tartakovsky." Next to it hangs another sign: "Fancy Cakes Made to Order."

A slimy staircase, many of its treads broken, leads to the cellar. A little boy working at the bakery is dragging a 150-pound sack down the stairs. The sack begins sliding down the stairs, and he lies down in front of it and blocks it with his head.

The bare backs of two dough kneaders: the sweat-lacquered back of young Sobkov, and an old man's crooked back with cracked shoulder blades. The old man's shoulder blades are not moving in the directions they ought to be moving in. The smooth, endless play of the dough kneaders' back muscles.

Muginshtein and Tartakovsky walk down the stairs and enter the bakery. They slip and stumble, but Muginshtein zealously props up his boss.

The backs of the dough kneaders. Young Sobkov, as he kneads, is reading the *Newspaper of the Odessa Council of Workers' Deputies*, which he has nailed to the wall above the dough trough. The newspaper is lit by the restless flame of a kerosene lamp.

The bakery is a foul-smelling cellar. Scant rays of light pierce the dusty hatches in the ceiling. Uncovered kerosene lamps are smoking in the corner. The bakers are stripped to the waist. Kochetkov, a cheerful, bowlegged fellow, is stoking a flaming oven, and the head baker is pulling baking paddles lined with ready loaves of bread out of another oven.

The head baker pulling the baking paddles with the baked bread out of the oven. Tartakovsky and Muginshtein entering the bakery. Workers, looking more like spirits of the netherworld than men, crowd around them. Tartakovsky proclaims:

"GENTLEMEN! I CONGRATULATE YOU ON OBTAINING YOUR BELOVED FREEDOM! NOW WE TOO CAN BREATHE FREELY!"

Tartakovsky fervently begins shaking his workers' hands, and they line up as a crowd will line up outside a store.

The bakers, not used to being treated so well, eagerly wipe their hands on their aprons to shake their master's hand with pitiful clumsiness, quickly brushing off any flour that might have settled on him.

Sobkov's back. The young man is still kneading the dough and reading his newspaper. Tartakovsky gives the bronzed back with its rippling muscles a friendly slap, and then holds out his hand to him. The young man pulls his hands very slowly out of the sticky dough, turns his sly face, framed by a shock of curls, to his master, and slowly, with solemn formality, holds out a dough-caked hand to him. Kochetkov, the cheerful fellow stoking the oven, rushes over to Sobkov and quickly begins to clean the dough off Sobkov's fingers. Sobkov laughs and looks his master in the eye. Tartakovsky abruptly turns around and leaves. Kochetkov winks at Sobkov.

Little snakes of dough writhe on Sobkov's shapeless and monstrously enlarged palm.

FADEOUT

Café Fankoni.* Businesswomen with large handbags, stockbrokers, an Odessa crowd. A dapper young man waving shackles in the air is standing on a platform where the orchestra usually plays. A gloomy man with an asymmetrical face sits behind him, holding a chain cutter in his hands. The chain cutter is for cutting through the shackles.

"CITIZENS OF FREE RUSSIA! FOR GOOD LUCK BUY A PIECE OF THE LEGACY LEFT US BY THE ACCURSED REGIME AND HELP OUR WOUNDED WAR HEROES! FIFTY RUBLES! WHO WILL BID MORE?"

Three disabled veterans—three close-cropped, armless mannequins—are sitting next to each other on a plush sofa by the wall across from the platform.

A girl wearing a low-cut blouse and a large hat with a sagging brim is walking among the tables carrying a jar in which she collects money "for the Revolution." Her blouse is disarranged and her shoes are worn

*An elegant and expensive Odessan café that attracted a wealthy international clientele before the Revolution.

through. Enthusiasm, spring, and fervor have covered her long nose with delicate pearls of sweat. Tartakovsky is sitting at a table, surrounded by a flock of fawning brokers. The table is heaped with samples: wheat, strips of leather, karakul fur. He drops a twenty-kopeck coin in the girl's jar.

The auctioneer on the platform waves the shackles in the air.

The girl with the low-cut blouse weaves her way among the tables. Benya Krik is lounging at a table by the window, carefully writing something on a napkin. Drunken Savka is sitting next to him, eating one cream puff after another. The young lady comes up to Benya. With an elegant flick of the wrist, the King throws a golden coin into her jar. The auctioneer quickly comes down from his platform and brings Benya a link from the shackles. The veterans come hobbling after the auctioneer and thank Benya with lifeless voices. Drunken Savka stares at the spectacle. He gets up, his legs faltering, and peers down the young lady's blouse.

The low-cut blouse and Savka's sullen, resolute face above it.

Sobkov, dressed in his Sunday best, walks past Benya's table. Benya asks him to sit down.

"YOU'VE WAITED LONG ENOUGH FOR YOUR REVOLUTION, SOBKOV, AND HERE IT IS!"

Sobkov grins and motions with his head toward the patrons of the café.

"THE REVOLUTION WILL BE HERE ONCE WE'VE TAKEN THEIR COINS FROM THEM."

Benya wipes the nib of his pen on Savka's jacket and grimaces very expressively.

"WHAT YOU SAY ABOUT THE COINS IS TRUE, SOBKOV!"

he says, and begins writing again. Savka has fallen asleep. Sobkov eyes the patrons of the café.

Tartakovsky's table. One of the brokers pours a pile of gold crosses and amulets onto it.

"AND HERE, MONSIEUR TARTAKOVSKY, I HAVE A CONSIGNMENT OF RELIGIOUS RELICS AT HALF PRICE!"

Tartakovsky looks unwillingly at the merchandise and weighs the crosses on his palm.

Benya folds the note, calls the waiter, and asks him to hand the note to Tartakovsky.

Tartakovsky is not interested in the merchandise. He pushes away the "consignment of religious relics." The waiter hands him Benya's note.

Benya's note, scribbled on a flowered napkin:

Monsieur Tartakovsky, I ordered one person to find tomorrow morning by the gate of number 17, Sofiyevskaya Street, fifty thousand rubles. If he does not find it, then something awaits you, the like of which has never before been heard, and you will be the talk of all Odessa. Sincerely yours, Benya the King.

Outraged, Tartakovsky crumples the letter, and makes indignant signs at Benya, furiously tugging at his shirt collar as if to say, "Go ahead, rip the last shirt I own off my back!" And he furiously sets about writing a reply.

The waiter gives the invalids three glasses of grenadine with straws in them. The armless mannequins slurp the grenadine through the straws.

The waiter hands Tartakovsky's reply to Benya.

Tartakovsky's epistle, also written on a napkin:

Benya, If you were an idiot, I would write you as to an idiot. But from what I know of you, you aren't one, and may the Lord prevent me from changing my mind. I have no money, all I have is ulcers, sores, worries, and no sleep! Drop your foolish thoughts, Benya. Your friend, Rubin Tartakovsky.

Benya puts Tartakovsky's letter in his pocket, pays the check, and wakes Savka. Savka jumps up, his eyes bulge, and he grabs Benya by the throat. Savka had dreamed that the police descended upon him in the night. He comes to his senses and immediately calms down. Benya, Savka, and Sobkov head for the exit. Tartakovsky is still tugging at his shirt collar—"Go ahead, rip the last shirt I own off my back!" The King spreads out his arms, as if to say: "Well, I did my best!"

The corner of Ekaterininskaya and Deribasovskaya Streets. A beautiful spring day. The strolling Odessa crowd. Benya calls out to a cabbie—*shteiger* in Odessa slang—and points at drunken Savka. He tells the *shteiger*:

"DRIVE HIM ABOUT TILL HE COMES TO, VANYA!"

Savka is lolling back on the cab seat with all the hauteur and chic he can muster. The horse starts off at a fast trot.

A group of flower girls on the corner of Ekaterininskaya and Deribasovskaya Streets. The playful women and their flowers against the backdrop of the shop windows of Wagner's, the most elegant store in Odessa. Foreign goods are displayed in the windows: elegant luggage, porcelain, bibelots, little bottles of perfume in boxes lined with blue satin. Among the women selling flowers is a girl of about fifteen, dressed in rags. The King goes up to her, buys some violets, and, while Sobkov is not looking, slips some pieces of paper with messages scribbled on them among her bouquets. The girl watches Benya tensely.

Benya and Sobkov turn into Nikolayevsky Boulevard. The Odessa crowd is surging around them. The flower girl is trudging along in the distance, her dirty thin legs are bare. She is watching Benya with spellbound eyes.

Nikolayevsky Boulevard. Benya and Sobkov walk up to the railings of the Vorontsov Palace.* Beyond the railings are lilac bushes not yet in bloom.

"TELL ME, SOBKOV, WHAT ELSE BESIDES COINS DO THE BOLSHEVIKS NEED?"

Benya asks him. The young baker takes one of Lenin's books out of his pocket, but Benya pushes it away.

Benya's lips slowly part:

"I DON'T NEED NO BOOKS, JUST TELL ME WHAT'S WHAT, PLAIN AND SIMPLE, AND TAKE ME TO YOUR COMRADES. WHERE ARE THEY?"

---

*Prince Mikhail Semyonovich Vorontsov, the governor-general of Novorossia and Odessa from 1823 to 1844, had commissioned the building of this palace in the 1820s. By the time of the screenplay the palace had become an engineering institute.

Sobkov opens his arms wide and points to the docks, to Peresip, and to the factories,* and says:

"THAT'S WHERE THEY ARE!"

A panoramic shot of Peresip, the shipbuilding yards, and the smoking steamships. Workers are loading cargo. They are enveloped in the smoke that is pouring out of the steamships' funnels.

FADEOUT

The port. A group of carts is waiting by the pier. Sacks of oats are tied to the horses' muzzles. Midday sun. Froim Grach is sleeping on the warm flagstones under one of the carts. The little flower girl appears at the street corner.

The girl walks toward Grach's cart. She tickles him with a bouquet of flowers. Grach wakes up and immediately assumes an expression as if he had not been sleeping at all. The girl quickly hands him a note and runs away.

The note:

"GRACH, THERE'S SOMETHING TO TALK TO YOU ABOUT. BENYA."

Grach jumps onto his cart and whips his horses into a gallop.

FADEOUT

A Persian teahouse on Provozhnaya Square. Carters and merchants are drinking tea. The Persian, who appeared in Part One, is standing behind the counter. The flower girl enters the teahouse with stumbling steps. The Persian pours her a glass of strong tea, and the girl hands him a note:

"ABUDULLAH, THERE'S SOMETHING TO TALK TO YOU ABOUT. BENYA."

The Persian hides the note. His face is distorted. He begins clear-

---

*Benya and Sobkov are standing at the intersection of Nikolayevsky Boulevard and Ekaterininskaya Street, in Odessa's most elegant quarter, and are looking down toward the docks and the poorer Odessa neighborhood of Peresip, beyond which lay the impoverished factory neighborhoods of Near Mills (*Blizhiye Melnitsy*) and Far Mills (*Dalniye Melnitsy*).

ing away the tea glasses of his customers, many of whom haven't finished drinking yet. He pours out the tea, shouts, runs about the teahouse, and begins shoving his customers, who are staring at him in astonishment, toward the door. An old man with side-whiskers wants to pick a fight with him, but the moment he sees the Persian's terrible face, the old man suddenly stops in his tracks. Only the flower girl calmly continues drinking her tea.

The Persian extinguishes the samovar's flame and pours water into its pot.

FADEOUT

Lyovka Bik, the animal slaughterer, is standing in his overalls on a platform with a bloody knife in his hand. A crowd of Jewesses have gathered below. They hand the slaughterer (the *shoykhet*) their chickens and ducks to be slaughtered.

Lyovka slits a chicken's throat.

Old Reizl hands the *shoykhet* a cockerel. The cockerel is beating its wings. Lyovka raises his knife to its throat. At that moment the flower girl comes tiptoeing into the slaughterhouse. She is holding a bouquet of flowers. She treads timidly on the cement floor, which is covered in blood.

The knife trembles in the *shoykhet*'s hand and his eyes widen. He stiffens. In his hands the cockerel is still beating its wings.

FADEOUT

Part Four

Tartakovsky's bookkeeping office. Muginshtein, his assistant, is sitting at the main desk. The Englishman sits working in his cubicle in a cloud of smoke. A clerk brings Muginshtein some papers to be signed. Muginshtein signs them with a flourish. One of the letters, however, does not meet with his approval. He hurls it on the floor and spits in the direction of the clerk who brought it. The clerk, not in the least put out, spits back. Suddenly, four masked men with revolvers in their hands climb in through the open windows from the street.

Four masked gangsters, drawn up to their full heights, stand on four windowsills.

"HANDS UP!"

A medley of raised hands.

Froim Grach, the Persian, Lyovka Bik, and Kolka Pakovsky are guarding the exits. They are wearing droll masks made of bright calico. They are easy to recognize, particularly Grach, whose mask keeps slipping down.

Benya enters. He walks over to Muginshtein.

"WHO'S IN CHARGE HERE WHEN THE BOSS IS OUT?"

Muginshtein, shivering:

"I'M IN CHARGE HERE WHEN THE BOSS IS OUT."

Benya takes hold of Muginshtein's raised arms and lowers them. He shakes hands with him pleasantly and leads him to the safe.

"IN THAT CASE, WITH GOD'S HELP, PLEASE OPEN THE SAFE."

Muginshtein, at the end of his tether, shakes his head. Benya takes his revolver out of his pocket and orders Muginshtein:

"OPEN YOUR MOUTH!"

Muginshtein slowly opens his mouth. His crooked teeth are visible.

Benya jams the revolver into Muginshtein's mouth and slowly, without lowering his eyes, cocks the safety catch. Spittle trickles out of Muginshtein's mouth, and his hands slither down toward his trousers. He pulls out a bunch of keys from a secret hiding place, a little pouch sewn into his long johns.

The medley of raised hands.

The massive doors of the safe open. Tartakovsky's riches come into view. The Persian's distorted face floats toward the safe, his eyes wide beneath the black arches of his brows.

Benya wipes the barrel of his revolver, which is dripping with spit, on Muginshtein's jacket flap. He puts the revolver away, sits down in an armchair, crosses his legs, and opens a leather bag. Muginshtein hands him a diamond brooch. Benya gets up and walks over to the cashier, whose fat arms are raised, and pins the brooch to her chest.

The cashier's powerful chest is panting.

She is bewildered. She looks at Benya and then at the brooch. Her arms are raised. There are large sweat stains around her armpits. Grach walks over to the woman, sniffs at her, and wrinkles his nose. His mask has slipped down to his chin. Benya goes back to his armchair.

The handing over of the valuables has begun. Muginshtein gives Benya money, stocks, and diamonds. Benya drops the loot into his bag. They work unhurriedly.

A panoramic view of the office. Lyovka Bik is squabbling with an old clerk who is shouting that he can no longer keep his arms in the air. The old man howls:

"YOU DAMN ROBBERS! I HAVE A HERNIA!"

Lyovka carefully probes the old man's stomach and allows him to lower his arms.

The old man hurries over to the cashier and peers at her brooch. Smacking his lips, he says:

"A SUPERLATIVE TWO-CARAT!"

The handing over of the valuables continues without interruption. The hands of Muginshtein and Benya move smoothly.

Lyovka Bik is strolling through the office. The Englishman, tormented by his inability to smoke, makes imploring signs, nodding his head toward his pipe. Lyovka slides the pipe between the Englishman's yellow teeth and lights a match.

The movement of Muginshtein's and Benya's hands.

The Englishman's pipe simply will not light—this is because his hands are raised, which keeps him from pressing down the tobacco in his pipe. Lyovka lights one match after another. The lit match in his fingers freezes.

Drunken Savka has just jumped through the window. He roars and waves his revolver.

Lyovka's match is burning to the end. It singes his fingers.

Drunken Savka fires his revolver and Muginshtein collapses. Benya, gripped by horror and rage, shouts:

"EVERYONE OUT!

The King grabs Savka by the lapel, pulls him toward him, and shakes him harder and harder.

"I SWEAR TO YOU ON MY MOTHER'S HAPPINESS, SAVELI, YOU'LL BE LYING NEXT TO HIM!"

The gangsters run. Muginshtein lies writhing on the floor. The old man with the hernia comes crawling toward him from under a desk.

Muginshtein's death throes, fading into . . .

. . . the cover of a book: *Hygiene and Marriage.*

A curly-headed young maiden is bending over the book. She has an insignificant, freckled face, and she is staring so intently that she looks gloomy.

*The police headquarters of Kerensky, the lawyer**

Inside the police headquarters. Young women and puny students with Jewish features are sitting at desks, among them Lazar Shpilgagen, now looking even more haggard than on the day of his marriage. The curly-headed young woman is sitting by the telephone, deeply engrossed in questions of hygiene and marriage. For a long time she ignores the rattling telephone bell (the telephone is an old model with a bell on the outside). Finally she lifts idly the receiver.

"SHPILGAGEN, TELL THE CHIEF THAT TARTAKOVSKY IS BEING RAIDED."

she tells Shpilgagen, who is sitting next to her, puts back the receiver, and immerses herself once more in her book.

Shpilgagen totters weakly toward the chief. His shoelaces are undone, and he stops to tie them.

Chief of Police Tsitsin, also a lawyer

The office of the chief of police. Tsitsin, a brown-haired man with a haggard, aristocratic face, is holding forth before three crippled war veterans, the same three men for whose benefit the shackles had been auctioned off at Café Fankoni. A stream of flowery words washes over

---

*A humorous, irreverent reference to Kerensky, Prime Minister of the provisional government in the four months leading up to the Bolshevik Revolution in October 1917. He had been a lawyer by profession.

the war veterans. Shpilgagen enters. At first the chief does not pay attention to what Shpilgagen is saying, but then he becomes extremely agitated.

The chief runs down the corridor, waving his arms.

The old man with the hernia is pouring water out of a brass teapot over the fainted cashier, who has fainted. She covers the brooch with her hand.

A tank slowly rolls out of the courtyard of the police headquarters. Tsitsin's inspired face is peeking out of one of the tank's embrasures.

The bakers, with Sobkov at their head, come running toward Tartakovsky's office.

A crowd of thousands in Tartakovsky's yard: women, crawling children, idlers, orators. The tank rolls with arduous slowness. Tsitsin jumps out of the tank. Sobkov calls out to him:

"GIVE ME A FEW FIGHTING MEN AND WE'LL GRAB THE KING!"

Tsitsin waves him away and runs off, the crowd trailing behind him. Only a watchmaker in tattered shoes stays behind. With a bored expression he raises his eyes, fortified with a watchmaker's glass, to the sky. The sun with its flaming rays pierces the glass.

A room in the Kriks' house. Framed portraits of Tolstoy and General Skoblev are hanging on the wall. Old Reizl is serving soup to Benya and Froim Grach. Grach dips a large piece of bread into the soup and devours it with gusto. Benya pushes his plate away. Reizl places roasted gizzards and sliced eggs in front of him, but Benya refuses everything—his mind is not on gizzards. Sobkov comes bursting into the room.

"WE DON'T NEED NO CRIMINALS!"

the baker shouts, and fires at Benya. He misses. Grach throws himself on Sobkov, pushes him down under him, and begins strangling him. Benya pulls Grach off Sobkov.

"LET HIM GO, FROIM! TRY FIGURING OUT THESE BOLSHE-VIKS AND WHAT THEY WANT!"

Grach gets up. Sobkov, half strangled, remains lying on the floor. Reizl brings in the main course, stepping over Sobkov's sprawled-out body without bothering to glance down, and pours some stew onto their plates. Benya drums his fingers on the table.

FADEOUT

Two days later Muginshtein's funeral took place. Such a funeral Odessa had never seen, nor will the world ever see the like of it

A cantor in somber raiment. Behind him march the little synagogue choirboys in black overcoats and tall velvet hats.

An opulent carriage, three pairs of horses with plumes on their heads, and men from the Funeral Brotherhood in top hats.

The crowd walking behind the coffin. In the first row, Tartakovsky and another reputable merchant are propping up old Auntie Pesya, the mother of the murdered man.

The crowd: lawyers, members of the Society of Jewish Shop Assistants, and women wearing earrings.

Benya Krik's red automobile is tearing through the streets of Odessa.

Tartakovsky and the coworkers of the deceased, among them the old man with the hernia and the Englishman, are carrying the coffin along the cemetery path. Benya Krik's automobile pulls up at the gates of the cemetery. Benya, Kolka Pakovsky, Lyovka Bik, and the Persian jump out. Benya is carrying a wreath.

Tartakovsky and the other men carrying the coffin. Benya and his associates catch up with them. The gangsters push away Tartakovsky, the old man with the hernia, and the Englishman, and slide their steel shoulders under the coffin. The procession collapses in disorder. Tartakovsky disappears. The gangsters carrying the coffin tread slowly, sorrowfully, with fiery eyes.

The whole screen is filled with the coffin swaying on the gangsters' shoulders.

By the cemetery gates. Tartakovsky's coachman has left his post to answer the call of nature. His broad back is looming by the corner of the cemetery wall. Tartakovsky comes running out through the gateway. He jumps into his carriage and whips the horses.

The cantor is praying above the grave. Benya is propping up Auntie Pesya. The cantor takes a handful of earth to throw onto the coffin, but his hand suddenly stops cold. Two fellows come trudging toward him, carrying the deceased Savka Butsis. Benya turns to the cantor:

"PLEASE PERFORM THE LAST RITES FOR SAVELI BUTSIS, A MAN UNKNOWN TO YOU, BUT ALREADY DECEASED.

The cantor, his whole body shaking, his eyes darting left and right in search of an escape, totters toward Savka's coffin. The gangsters have surrounded the corpse and warily follow the prayers, ready to stave off any attempts the cantor might make to cut corners in the funeral service. The crowd is receding. The people fall back to about ten paces or so from the coffins, and then turn and run.

Tartakovsky is whipping the horses. His coachman is running after the carriage.

The cemetery path. Tombstones, praying angels, pyramids, marble Stars of David. The running, panicking crowd.

The cantor is stammering over Savka's coffin, Auntie Pesya is crying bitter tears, and the gangsters are praying in the tradition of their fathers.

By the cemetery gates the crowd is trampling down every obstacle in its path: carriages, a tram, even transport wagons are taken by storm.

The worn-out coachman has given up all hope of catching up with his carriage. He parts the flaps of his padded coat and sits down on the ground to catch his breath.

The stream of buggies and carts. People are standing on the carts, swaying as if they were standing on the deck of a ship during a storm.

Two elegantly dressed ladies standing on a coal cart.

The red automobile plunges into the running crowd and disappears.

FADEOUT

The bare backs of Sobkov and his lanky neighbor. The movement of their back muscles.

In the bakery. Kochetkov is throwing firewood into the blazing oven and the head baker is pulling out finished loaves. Benya enters. He takes Sobkov aside.

The storeroom. Loaves of bread are cooling in long rows on shelves. Benya and Sobkov enter.

"TAKE ME TO YOUR COMRADES, SOBKOV, AND I SWEAR ON MY MOTHER'S HAPPINESS THAT I'LL GIVE UP GANGSTER-ING!"

Sobkov runs his fingers over the crust of a steaming loaf.

"WORDS, NOTHING BUT WORDS!"

He looks at Benya and immediately looks away again. The King comes up very close to him and lays his delicate, ring-covered hand on the baker's bare, dirty shoulder.

"I SWEAR TO YOU ON MY MOTHER'S HAPPINESS!"

he repeats forcefully.

The long rows of bread cooling on the shelves. The bread's perfume rolls like a green wave through the storeroom. A ray of sunlight cuts through the mist.

Benya's and Sobkov's heads close together behind a hedge of lac-quered loaves.

Part Five

THE END OF THE KING

A telegram ribbon is unfurling against a black background.
The ribbon is sliding out of the telegraph apparatus:

"IN THE YEAR OF OUR LORD, 1919."

The telegraph operator is receiving a direct dispatch. Sobkov, now a military commissar, is leaning over the unfurling ribbon. A loaf of black bread, threaded through with veins of straw, lies on a table next to the apparatus, and ration-issue herring is soaking in a basin of water. The telegraph operator is wearing the kind of woolen hat that skiers and skaters wear, and his torn coat is tied over his belly with a wide, monkish cord. He is wearing a backpack filled with provisions, indicat-ing that he was just about to leave.

The loaf of bread, the soaking herring. The telegraph operator's fingers dig into the loaf.

Sobkov reads the ribbon that is uncoiling over the machine gun next to the telegraph apparatus. Sobkov is also digging his fingers deep into the loaf, trying to fish out the doughy inside.

The telegram ribbon:

"TO MILITARY COMMISSAR SOBKOV STOP. ANITICIPATING ENEMY PRESSURE STOP. FIND A PRETEXT TO LURE . . ."

The machine gun tangled in the telegram ribbon. Kochetkov is sitting in a corner, mending a tattered boot. Without taking it off, he is trying to reattach the flapping sole with a piece of wire.

The continuation of the telegram:

". . . TO LURE BENYA KRIK'S UNITS OUT OF ODESSA AND DIS-ARM THEM STOP."

Kochetkov's boot: Neatly twisted and clipped wire knots run the whole length of the sole along the welt.

Sobkov stuffs the telegraph ribbon into his pocket. He tears a chunk off the loaf and chews it as he walks away. He leaves the telegraph room with Kochetkov.

The dazzling telegraph ribbon is continuing to unfurl against a black background. The ribbon's end slides . . .

. . . into an uncovered car engine.

In the yard of the telegraph office. A graveyard of trucks and countless mobile field kitchens. One field kitchen is operating. A Red Army fighter is boiling cabbage soup. He is stoking the oven, using wooden wheels torn off other field kitchens. Sobkov's driver, also in the yard, is struggling to start the battered, dilapidated car. The hood is missing. The driver is trying to fix the engine, but all his efforts seem to be in vain.

The car's engine: a smoking 1919 contraption, held together with wires and straps.

Sobkov and Kochetkov enter the yard. They get into the car. Sobkov tells his driver:

"TO THE BARRACKS, ON THE DOUBLE!"

The driver turns the crank, but the engine will not start. He wipes streams of sweat from his crimson face. He glares with hatred at the engine, fiddles with some valves, and suddenly spits with all his might into the heart of the motor. Sobkov and the cook come to help him. They turn the crank, but to no avail. Finally Kochetkov manages to crank up the engine. The driver jumps into his seat, steps on the gas pedal, a gigantic cloud of smoke pours from the exhaust, and the car moves off with a groan.

The car rolls out through the gates. The driver yanks the steering wheel convulsively. The cloud of smoke grows thicker and fills the screen. Well-thumbed playing cards fanned out in a sinewy hand emerge with unusual clarity from the yellowish fog. One of the fingers on the hand is broken and crooked. A ray of sunlight pierces the cards.

The N. "Revolutionary" Regiment is preparing for the final battle

The barracks of Benya Krik's "revolutionary" regiment. The soldiers' underwear is hanging to dry on ropes strung across the whole length of the barracks. The underwear has government stamps on it. A crooked card game is under way beneath the ropes where the government-issue underwear is hanging most densely. The two players are the goggle-eyed Persian and Papa Krik, who has donned a minute military cap with a Red Army star on it. The crowd of gangsters we have already met at Dvoira Krik's wedding is standing around the table. The Persian, convinced that his trumps are unbeatable, is dealing the cards with triumph and passion. Meek gloom is on Papa Krik's face. He deliberates for a long time, wrinkles his forehead, closes one eye, and finally "kills" one of the Persian's cards.

The sun-drenched cards in old Krik's hand.

The old man despondently "kills" the Persian's second card. Kolka Pakovsky's bare back leans toward him.

Kolka Pakovsky is sitting, stripped to the waist, on a high stool next to Mendel Krik. An old Chinese man is giving him a tattoo. He has already etched a mouse onto Kolka's right shoulder blade, and is now coiling a long and limber mouse tail over the shoulder.

Mendel Krik is "killing" his opponent's cards one after another. The Persian's face has darkened. He pays Mendel with new gunmetal watches. On the table next to him lies a heap of new watches, fresh from a store shelf and still in their boxes.

The barracks filled with drying underwear. In the far corner stands Lyovka Bik in a blood-smeared leather apron, cutting up a recently butchered bull. He plies his trade even in the barracks. He is surrounded by "Red Army fighters" waiting for their portion. The heads of market women standing in line outside the window. They are also waiting for their portions. Lyovka hands out meat dripping with blood to the Red Army men. From time to time he skewers a monstrous piece of meat with his knife and, without turning around, hurls it out the window, as a lion tamer might hurl a chunk of horsemeat into a lion's cage.

The card game is continuing. It is now the Persian's turn to triumph. Twitching, guffawing, trembling with excitement, he trumps the old man's cards and demands his winnings. Papa Krik pays with new banknotes, which he pulls out of a packet tied together as they are in banks. Two notes turn out to be blank on one side, only their tops are printed. The old man calls over one of the gangsters and gives him the worthless notes.

"TELL YUSSIM HE'LL BE WASHING HIS FACE IN BLOOD IF HE KEEPS CHURNING OUT BILLS LIKE THESE! TELL HIM TO FIX THESE!"

The gangster slips the notes into his pocket and leaves. At the door he bumps into Tartakovsky, and makes way for him to pass into the barracks. Tartakovsky is wearing a battered soldier's cap. His face bears the traces of an astonishing disguise—he has shaven off his mustache, but has left his beard intact in the fashion of a Dutch skipper.

Tartakovsky tiptoes along the wall. He is holding a velvet pouch with something in it. The old man has dyed his hair and is dressed in the spirit of the times: he is wearing a torn coat, his shoes are tattered, and only his belly is as majestic as before. Two reputable Jews are tiptoeing behind him. One is wearing a cyclist's cap, an overcoat, and leggings, the other a slightly smaller cap and a cape fastened with a military ornamental clasp.

The captain of the N. "Revolutionary" Regiment

The inner courtyard of the Red Army barracks. On one of the doors to the barracks hangs the sign: "Infantry Regiment Honoring the Glorious French Revolution." (And written in chalk next to it: "The

German one too.") Benya, wearing an outlandish uniform, is riding a horse. Froim Grach is standing in the middle of the yard cracking a coachman's whip. Benya is riding at full gallop in neat circles around the yard, as if he were in a riding ring.

A low door. Three fat bellies squeeze through the narrow opening.

The galloping continues. Tartakovsky and his quivering companions enter the yard. They bow to Benya, the Captain of the N. "Revolutionary" Regiment, who is riding tirelessly in circles. He spurs his horse, brandishes his whip, and gallops toward the cringing fat men. Tartakovsky holds out the velvet pouch to Benya.

There is a flowery, embroidered inscription on the velvet pouch:

"FROM THE REVOLUTIONARY ARTISANS OF ODESSA."

Benya pulls a Torah scroll out of the velvet pouch, its parchment wound around carved, lacquered sticks. He hands the Torah to Froim Grach. Tartakovsky steps closer, caresses the horse's muzzle with a trembling hand, and launches into his speech:

"WE, THE REVOLUTIONARY ARTISANS, BEG YOU . . ."

Benya's impassive face. His arms, folded majestically, are leaning on the pommel of his saddle. Froim is unwinding the scroll in the background.

Tartakovsky continues:

". . . BEG YOU TO DEFEND REVOLUTIONARY ODESSA WITHIN REVOLUTIONARY ODESSA ITSELF AND . . ."

Froim is unwinding the Torah, pulling out one Czarist hundred-ruble bill after another.

Benya watches Froim from the corner of his eye. Tartakovsky continues:

". . . WITHIN REVOLUTIONARY ODESSA ITSELF, AND NOT TO SET OFF FOR ANOTHER . . . ANOTHER FRONT."*

---

*In 1919 the Civil War was raging all around Odessa as the armies of the Bolsheviks, the Ukrainian Nationalists, the Czarist Whites, and the foreign intervention forces battled each other near Odessa. Throughout much of 1919, the Czarist armies of General Denikin seemed to be gaining the upper hand. In this scene, Tartakovsky is trying to bribe Benya with Czarist banknotes to stay in Odessa and help the Whites reestablish the former status quo.

The thunder of gates flung open. A column of smoke comes pouring into the yard and interrupts the artisan's speech. Three fire brigade horses enveloped in smoke trot into the yard. They are towing Sobkov's car, which caught fire on the way to the barracks. A Red Army fighter wearing felt slippers on his bare feet is sitting on one of the horses. Sobkov and Kochetkov jump off the other two horses and hurry toward the barracks. The driver walks over to the smoking engine, glares at it, lifts his bleary eyes to the sky, and spits intently time and again into the magneto.

Sobkov and Kochetkov hurry through the same door through which the three bellies of the revolutionary artisans had squeezed with such difficulty.

Tartakovsky's voice has dropped to a whisper. He pats the horse's muzzle with increasing cheerfulness and affection, while the other delegates caress its flanks. Benya bends down closer to them. Froim is rolling up the parchment in his corner.

The card game inside the barracks is continuing with unremitting passion. A young man with bandaged legs, his face rough and his mustache close-cropped, is lathering one of his cheeks by the opposite wall not far from Lyovka, who is still flinging slices of meat through the air. Next to the young man, a short plump woman in fashionable knee-length boots is lying asleep on a couch with her back to the audience. Sobkov and Kochetkov come bursting into the barracks. Sobkov jumps onto a platform beneath a pair of crossed flags:

"COMRADES!"

The newly hatched "comrades" gather lazily around Military Commissar Sobkov. Lyovka wipes his knife on his apron and walks over to the platform. The other men in the barracks also come forward, among them the young man with the lathered cheek, the Chinese man, and Kolka Pakovsky, still stripped to the waist. Only the Persian and Papa Krik stay where they are, continuing their card game, still exchanging their new watches and new banknotes.

"COMRADES!"

the military commissar repeats. The "comrades" stare at him with dull eyes. A view from behind: all the men, as if by silent command, scratch one bare foot against the other. Sobkov says:

"THE WORKERS' GOVERNMENT IS PREPARED TO FORGIVE YOUR PAST CRIMES, AND DEMANDS THAT YOU COMMIT YOURSELVES TO HONESTLY SERVE THE PROLETARIAT!"

The young man with the lathered cheek is standing in front of Sobkov in profile, his face sullen, his thumbs twiddling. Lyovka Bik is polishing his knife to a shine. The military commissar continues:

"THE EXECUTIVE COMMITTEE HAS PUT ITS TRUST IN YOU AND HAS DECIDED TO TURN YOUR REGIMENT INTO A PROVISIONS ACQUISITION DETACHMENT."

Sobkov stops in order to gauge the effect of his sudden announcement on the gangsters. The gangsters applaud. The applause is lively, they like the announcement and clap with mounting fervor. The military commissar, fired up, slides his hand into his pocket for his handkerchief, but his hand slides deeper and deeper without impediment. Someone has sliced off his pocket.

The expertly sliced-off pocket.

Military Commissar Sobkov stands riveted to the spot, his mouth hanging open. The gangsters return to their places. The young man with the bandaged legs, the rough face, and the close-cropped mustache lathers his other cheek. His lady friend stirs, wakes up, and turns her creased face and tousled curls toward the military commissar. Sobkov, shaken, looks first at the gangsters and then at the yawning woman, who swings her fat legs in their fashionable boots off the couch.

The young man whom Papa Krik had sent off with the banknotes comes running through the barracks bringing back the amended bills. He gives them to Papa Krik.

Sobkov comes back to his senses and pulls out his revolver. Kolka Pakovsky, sprawled out in his armchair, looks at him, turning his head in profile, and then looks away again. The Chinese man is still working on his shoulder, adding color to the mouse's tail, which is coiling around Kolka's nipple like a snake. Kochetkov grabs hold of Sobkov's hand.

Sobkov's fingers, in Kochetkov's grip, weaken and drop the revolver.

Part Six

Tempted by the prospect of doing some "provision acquisition," Benya Krik's regiment decides to set out from Odessa

A deserted Odessa street. The stores lining it are boarded up with planks, bolts, and locks. A picture of the King of Greece is nailed to the door of a ramshackle little store, and under the picture hangs the sign: "Here trades Meir Grinberg, foreign subject." A solitary dog lies in the middle of the street next to some cut telegraph wires. They lie before the dog like banners before a victorious commander in chief. A fat, lame man is limping quickly along the street. He is stepping heavily on one leg, which is curved like a wheel. His back can be seen receding down the length of the deserted street in the red dust of the sun.

Benya Krik comes riding around the corner on a thoroughbred horse. A multitude of ribbons is plaited into its mane. Next to him ride Sobkov on a sleepy Siberian pony, and one-eyed Grach in riding breeches. The rest of Grach's outfit—his canvas cloak, his well-polished boots, and his whip—have remained unchanged. Kochetkov is marching behind them. His flopping soles tear their doleful jaws wide open. Behind the horsemen ride musicians perched on mules. These mules are from the time when Odessa was occupied by the Nationalists. The mules are twirling their long ears. They have no saddles or stirrups— they are covered with simple carpets. The musician from Dvoira Krik's wedding is marching in front of the band, raising to the skies his shining tuba, which, as previously mentioned, resembles a boa constrictor more than a musical instrument.

The receding back of the lame man shot from a distant perspective in the fiery dust of the sunset. He arrives at a plumbing store, the only store that has not been boarded up, and turns his red, sweating, good-natured face toward the viewer.

Benya Krik's horde of men is marching behind the band. The former gangsters are wearing helmets and machine gun belts, and their pants are rolled up. Some are barefoot, others are wearing shoes that are torn and tattered, but made of patent leather. An unruly, shrieking throng of mothers, brides, wives, and prams is tangling up the lines.

Kolka Pakovsky's mother, a little old woman carrying his rifle and backpack for him, is hobbling behind him, struggling to keep up. Lyovka Bik is pushing a baby carriage carrying his one-year-old son. Next to him is his wife, a lively Moldavanka woman wrapped in a red shawl. Lyovka Bik and his family leave the marching horde. He gazes sadly at the long line of boarded-up stores.

The "artillery" arrives—*tachankas* with machine guns mounted on them. Behind the "artillery" rolls a cart on which some kind of booth has been mounted. Written in large letters is: "Political Education Unit of the N. Infantry Regiment Honoring the Glorious French Revolution." Inside the booth a sailor, his puffed-up chest covered in ribbons, is playing a ramshackle little piano. Two midgets, a man and a woman dressed in elegant evening wear, are holding out to the bystanders little buckets with "For Decorating our Barracks" written on them.

Inside the only store that has not been boarded up. The merchandise for sale: porcelain toilet bowls, drain pipes, toilet seats. A lanky young fellow with greenish freckles and a thin neck is sprinkling the floor with a brass kettle, making elaborate water designs of numbers and human forms. The German store owner, the lame man, wipes his broad, helpless face with a towel. The quick walk has exhausted him. Profuse sweat seethes on his fiery, hanging cheeks—the sweat of a good-natured fat man. Having wiped his face, he slides the towel into his open shirt. At that moment the door opens and Lyovka Bik, accompanied by his family, comes bursting into the store.

The kettle shakes in the young fellow's hand. The elegant loops are interrupted, and water pours at random onto the floor.

A row of sparkling toilet bowls. Lyovka's inquisitive face bending over them. He sees that there is nothing to take, hesitates, walks away, returns, and, so as not to leave empty-handed, takes one of the toilet bowls that is lavishly decorated with pink flowers. He tosses it into his son's baby carriage and leaves. The German stands rooted to the spot, the towel inside the opening of his shirt.

At the corner of Deribasovskaya and Ekaterininskaya Streets, Café Fankoni is boarded up and there are no flower girls to be seen. A barefoot girl draped in a sack, the same girl who delivered Benya's notes, is huddling against Wagner's display window. The first regimental row—Benya, Froim, and Sobkov—is riding past her. Trembling, she quickly pulls a rose wrapped in newspaper out from under her blouse. Darting between the horses, she runs up to Benya and hands him the rose.

The port. The wharves of the so-called Watermelon Harbor are lined with boats. The sunset is gilding the dirty sails, the water filled with rinds, and the heaps of watermelons, the myriad of watermelons. Little boats are piled to the brim with them.

The unloading of watermelons. The owner of the boat, a Greek, throws a watermelon to a stevedore on the dock, who throws it to another stevedore, who then throws it to another, all the way to the railroad car. The distance between one stevedore and another is two to three paces.

The watermelons, thrown from one hand to another.

Some of Benya's men are watching the unloading of the watermelons with stony faces. A barely visible ripple runs through their ranks. Suddenly, with astonishing speed, they push the stevedores into the water and form their own line from the vessel to the railroad car. A momentary pause and the unloading of the watermelons continues with its former smoothness.

The watermelons, thrown from one hand to another.

The stevedores, veteran dockworkers, are thrashing about in the water. The Greek owners of the vessels hoist their sails and prepare to escape. Evening. The lights in the port are lit.

Benya Krik's regiment is boarding railroad boxcars. The future "provision acquisition detachment" has filled a boxcar with piles of empty sacks.

Kochetkov is standing guard at the door of a passenger car, the first car after the locomotive. Benya and Froim climb in. Kochetkov locks the door behind them. Froim hears the rasping of the key in the lock, turns, and peers through the window at Kochetkov's simple, high-cheekboned face. Froim knocks on the window:

"HEY, KOCHETKOV! WHAT IF I NEED TO GO FOR A YOU-KNOW-WHAT?"

Kochetkov stands at attention with his rifle.

"THERE'S NO TIME FOR YOU-KNOW-WHATS IN THE WAR!"

Froim eyes Kochetkov and disappears into the depths of the railroad car.

The boats, hurriedly hoisting their sails, pull out to sea. The drenched stevedores crawl onto the shore. Evening.

Gas lamps have been lit on the platform. Lyovka Bik is dragging a pile of empty sacks to the train. Sobkov comes up to him and asks:

"WHY SO MANY SACKS, LYOVKA?"

Lyovka, bent beneath the weight of his load, looks at the slow-witted military commissar.

"YOU NEED SACKS IF YOU'RE GOING TO FIGHT THE SMUG-GLERS AND THEIR SACKS!"

he answers, and hurries on. Old Manka, the matriarch of the Slobodka bandits, bustles after him carrying a basket.

Benya is standing by a compartment window. Manka, gasping for breath, comes rushing up to him. She takes a quart of liquor and a mandolin out of her basket and gives them to him.

The locomotive whistles.

Benya Krik's men are pushing the railroad car loaded with watermelons along the track. They couple it to the train.

The regiment has boarded. Red Army fighters from regular units are closing the doors of the boxcars. Slowly, unstoppably, the doors roll shut on their iron rollers. The jaws of the boxcars all close at the same instant. The Red Army fighters jump onto the brake platforms.

The locomotive whistles one last time and begins to move.

More Red Army fighters, hidden behind the warehouses, jump onto the brake platforms and climb onto the roofs of the railroad cars.

Faraway sails on the nocturnal sea. The slashed moon in an avalanche of clouds.

The train gathers speed.

Odessa receding in the distance—the winding line of lights in the port, the winking eye of the lighthouse, the reflection of the moon on the black water, the swaying hulls of the fishing boats, and the gaps between their sails through which the stars shine.

A private first-class railroad car. The roomy, frayed interior retaining signs of recent grandeur. A gilded bath adorned with imperial eagles stands in a corner, fixed to the floor. A quart of liquor and a suckling pig roasted whole are on the table. Sobkov pours vodka into cracked mugs. The midgets, dressed in their evening wear, are also present at the feast. There are no forks or knives to be seen. Froim is pulling the suckling pig apart with his hands.

Kochetkov is making himself comfortable in a little anteroom outside the private compartment. He has put his rifle between his legs, spread a dirty tablecloth over a little table, laid out tobacco and cigarette papers, and carved a little rod for packing the tobacco into the cigarettes.

Sobkov, Benya, Froim, and the midgets toast, clinking together their many-shaped mugs. The rims of the mugs have been smashed off and their bottoms secured with wire. Everyone has drunk down their liquor except for Sobkov, who has poured it down his shirt. Benya and Froim notice his ruse, glance at each other, and slip their revolvers under the area map lying on the table.

Kochetkov is rolling cigarettes, his fingers moving unhurriedly. He stacks them in neat little piles.

Froim pours vodka. The group toasts, their eyes fixed on one another. The revolvers are bulging beneath the area map.

Only the midgets are drinking cheerfully and with gusto.

The hurtling train. Night. The slithering silhouettes of the Red Army fighters glitter on the roofs of the railroad cars, on the brake platforms, and on the couplings. The last car uncouples from the train and rolls back, a spark flitting over the rails in its wake.

In the private first-class car. The company is drinking. This time Benya and Froim have poured away their vodka, but they do it with more skill than Sobkov, and nobody sees them.

Kochetkov, rolling cigarettes in the hall outside. Everyone in the compartment pretends to be drunk. Sobkov gives Benya and Froim flabby, slobbering kisses. The midgets, truly drunk, attempt to dance. Froim lifts them with outstretched arms and, jerking his legs in his big boots, dances a mysterious, somber, ponderous dance.

A second railway car uncouples and rolls back into the night. A spark chases after it, sputtering over the rails.

Benya is playing his mandolin, his head hanging low, his expression fixed. Sobkov, lolling in an armchair as if he were completely drunk, is clapping to the music. Froim is dancing with the midgets. The tiny woman flings her little arms around Froim's brick-red neck and kisses him on the lips.

A stream of poured-out vodka trickles out from under the table. Kochetkov, rolling cigarettes.

The drunken midgets collapse. They embrace one another and fall asleep.

Benya flings his mandolin to the side, and pours vodka. Froim, Sobkov, and Benya intertwine their arms and drink to brotherhood.

"TO BROTHERHOOD!"

The three men lift their mugs to their lips. At that instant the train stops. The sharp jolt makes the vodka spill, and the men slowly disentangle their intertwined arms. Sobkov rushes to the window and pulls back the curtains. The night is flooded with the flames of a large campfire. Crimson rays streak across the faces of Benya and Froim.

The train has stopped in a field. All that is left of the train is the locomotive and the first-class car. All the other cars have been uncoupled. Red Army fighters are teeming over the roof of the first-class car—they are on the roof, the steps, the brake platforms, and the windows. The campfire is flaming fifty paces from the tracks.

Two shepherds are boiling a peaceful stew in a sooty pot. Red Army fighters—shaggy, squat, barefoot muzhiks—crawl out of the ripened wheat and, their rifles at the ready, run toward the train.

Sobkov steps away from the window and throws his mug of vodka into the gilded tub.

"DON'T BE ANGRY, BENYA."

he says, and leaves the compartment. Benya looks first at Froim, then at the bath, and then at the midgets, who are sleeping in the corner in each other's arms. Froim makes a fist and sticks his thumb through his rough, scarred index and middle fingers, and raises it in front of the King's face.

Kochetkov is standing on the steps of the first-class car holding out his hat filled with cigarettes to the shaggy muzhiks. They eagerly snatch at them.

Benya appears at the window.

The muzhiks' hands grappling for the cigarettes in Kochetkov's hat.

Benya eyes the Red Army fighters swarming around the car, their rifle barrels pointing at him. He looks at a barefoot muzhik sitting on the coupling where the car is hooked to the train, and then at Sobkov, standing rigidly in front of the window, the receiver of a field telephone in his hands.

Inside the compartment. Froim is smashing open the floor of the car with demonic speed. The one-eyed carter wants to make a getaway through a hole in the floor. Kochetkov creeps up to him and shoots him in the head. Froim turns his resigned, reproachful, blood-drenched face to him.

Sobkov keeps his eyes fixed on the open window. He is still holding the field telephone in his hands. Benya slowly pulls the curtains shut. The midgets have jumped up, awakened by the shot. Kochetkov raises his finger to his lips. "Shh," he says, and goes over to Benya, taking him by the hand.

"WE'VE BEEN THROUGH THICK AND THIN TOGETHER!"

Kochetkov says, and turns Benya around to face him. The Red Army fighters enter the compartment, their rifles aimed.

The back of Benya's shaved neck. A spot appears on it, a gaping wound with blood spurting in all directions.

FADEOUT

In the study of the chairman of the Odessa Executive Committee. A kerosene lamp is burning beneath a sumptuous dead chandelier. The chairman, a drowsy man wearing a loose-hanging white shirt, a scarf around his neck, and a tall sheepskin hat, is leaning over a diagram.

"THE PRODUCTION CURVE OF ODESSAN LEATHER FACTORIES IN THE FIRST HALF OF 1919."

An engineer from the National Economics Council is explaining the diagram to him. The telephone rings and the chairman lifts the receiver.

In the field by the campfire. Sobkov, lying on the ground, is speaking into the telephone. The bodies of Benya and Froim lie next to him, covered with a bast mat. Their bare feet are jutting out from under the mat.

The chairman listens to the report and puts the receiver back on the hook. He raises his sleepy eyes to the engineer.

"PLEASE CONTINUE, COMRADE."

Two heads, one close-cropped, the other in a shaggy sheepskin hat, lean over the diagram.

THE CHINESE MILL

(AN ATTEMPTED MOBILIZATION)

The silent movie The Chinese Mill, *directed by Levshin, premiered in July 1928. It is a comedy based on the misguided enthusiasm of a young provincial, Egor Zhivtsov, the secretary of the Young Communist League of his village, an outpost deep in the Russian hinterland. Zhivtsov hears that a revolution is brewing in capitalist China, and mobilizes the village yokels into a large, disorganized troop that is eager to set out to help bring Communism to China.*

Part One

The top of a haystack; an eagle of the steppes illuminated by the sun. Clouds. Their fringes are lit by the setting sun. Sasha Panyutin, a provincial enthusiast and inventor, is installing a wireless antenna on the rickety roof of a former manor house. On the roof there is a sign:

"HOMETOWN OF EGOR ZHIVTSOV—THE VILLAGE OF POVARENSHINO."

The village, surrounded by forests through which a glistening river winds. Unharvested fields, haystacks.

Panyutin has finished working—the antenna is installed, he has hammered the final nail.

The antenna cuts into the fleecy clouds.

The former manor's main hall—now the village reading room.

On the carved table legs are columns with cupids. The face of one of the cupids is half hidden by a copy of *Pravda*.

On the table stands a wireless radio built into a metallic candy box, along with a loudspeaker.

Peasants are sitting on benches, preparing to hear good tidings.

The large callused hands of the peasants.

Stacks of plows in the shed.

Plow handles.

On another bench sit the Komsomols,* tousled hair, laughing eyes.

In opposite corners are two rows of arms—young and old.

Cherevkov, one of the Komsomols and the village librarian—a tall, good-natured fellow—is standing by the radio. He lifts his hand.

"LISTEN TO MOSCOW, COMRADES!"

The Moscow radio station—a web of steel crossbeams.

The candy box, the spark indicator, and knobs. Panyutin's hand is fiddling with them.

A row of wrinkled old village women are sitting in the village reading room.

The peasants are sitting restlessly on the benches.

Village girls in their finery.

Young men with accordions.

An old, gray-haired man wearing bast sandals and a fur stands in the back by the wall where the newspaper is posted. He drags the fur along the floor behind him, like a Roman patrician.

Cherevkov, inspired:

"LISTEN TO MOSCOW, COMRADES!"

The roofs of one of Moscow's main streets. A forest of antennas.

An old woman wearing a patched shawl is holding the headset to her ears. Her head is enclosed by the metallic hoop.

"IT'S SPEAKING!"

Large beads of sweat roll down the old woman's face.

The Bolshoi Theater in Moscow.

The stage of the Bolshoi Theater.

A Chinese orator has taken the stand. In front of him is the radio microphone.

* Members of the Komsomol, the Young Communist League.

"THIS MEETING OF CHINESE NATIONALS LIVING IN MOSCOW IS A PROTEST AGAINST BRITISH VIOLENCE!"

The theater is jam-packed with Chinese.

Spotlights on high-cheekboned faces.

A line of horn-rimmed spectacles.

A row of Chinese students wearing horn-rimmed spectacles.

The chandeliers of the Bolshoi Theater are mirrored in the spectacles.

The Chinese orator. Above him a statue of Lenin with a raised arm. The light glows on Lenin's bronze head.

The eighty-year-old fingers of the old woman grip the radio headset.

The old woman's perturbed face.

"THEY'RE SAYING SOMETHING HOLY, BUT I CAN'T TELL WHAT ABOUT!"

The old woman crosses herself.

The Chinese orator.

A row of heavy village beards.

A rake has gotten tangled in a beard.

The hands of the Chinese students on the velvet balustrade of the balcony.

Among the students, Zhivtsov, the secretary of the Komsomol cell of the village of Povarenshino, is applauding wildly. He is in Moscow as a delegate to the Congress of Aviakhim.* He has dropped by the Chinese gathering between meetings. His jacket, worn over a peasant blouse, flies open. The chain of his grandfather's pocket watch hangs across his chest.

He is short, pimply, long-haired, wearing large, shabby shoes. His chest is covered with badges: from K.I.M.,† from AVIAKHIM, from M.O.P.R.,** a medal for rescuing someone from drowning, and many more.

The Chinese orator is speaking passionately.

Zhivtsov echoes all the orator's gestures.

"DOWN WITH WOR-R-R-LD IMPERIALISM!"

---

* The Association for the Furthering of Chemistry and Aviation.
† The International Communist Youth Movement.
** The International Revolutionary Aid Society.

Zhivtsov shouts in a trance.

Zhivtsov's gaping, distorted mouth, his thirty-two flawless teeth.

Zhivtsov's neighbor, a Chinese student, takes off his glasses, wipes them, and with joyful, shortsighted eyes looks at Zhivtsov and grabs his hand.

Zhivtsov and the Chinese student shake hands passionately.

A street in Moscow. Thick steam pours from the window of a laundry. "All work performed on premises by Su Chi Fo."

A mountain of dazzling white linen rises out of the steam.

The sunlight cuts through the moving clouds of steam and rests on the linen.

The inside of the Chinese laundry. A Chinese man, stripped to the waist, with a scraggly Asiatic beard, is washing stacks of pretentious bloomers.

Hanging in a golden frame above the Chinese man is an oleograph titled "A Night in Venice."

Tears run down the cheeks of the gondolier. They are condensation from the steam.

An airfield on the banks of the Moscow River.

A sign: "Orientation flights for the delegates of the Aviakhim Congress."

A group of Kirghiz tribesmen wearing long robes enter the cabin of the airplane.

The flap of a multicolored Kirghiz robe flutters over an airplane wheel.

An old Chinese woman, Su Chi Fo's wife, is ironing. Tears fall onto the linen.

She irons them away.

The wings of a flying airplane.

Su Chi Fo's son enters the laundry. He is the student who sat next to Zhivtsov at the Bolshoi Theater.

Another teardrop falls onto the linen. The old woman irons it away.

Su Chi Fo places a brand-new tin teapot in a suitcase.

Moscow seen from an airplane.

Su Chi Fo takes a train ticket from the labyrinthine pockets of his wife's jacket and gives it to his son.

The train ticket says "Moscow-Chita-Manchuria."

The quivering hand of the old Chinese woman is ironing lace.

Zhivtsov ecstatic with joy in the cabin of the flying airplane.

The Moscow River shot from above. Its banks are covered with newspapers.

Swimmers sun themselves, reading newspapers.

Zhivtsov knocks on the pilot's cabin door.

"THIS IS SO INTERESTING, COMRADE, ABSOLUTELY FASCINATING! BUT I HAVE TO CATCH THE TRAIN TO POVARENSHINO!"

The airplane descends.

Lace hanging from the ironing board. The iron in the Chinese woman's hand.

A tear falls on the iron and sizzles.

Su Chi Fo's departing son bids his father farewell—he clasps his father's hand, which is covered in a cloud of soap suds.

He goes over to his crying mother.

The airplane touches down.

The door opens, Zhivtsov jumps out.

A soapy mark left on the Chinese woman's shoulder.

Airplane wheels.

The turning wheels of a streetcar.

Crutches on the steps of the streetcar.

The turning wheels of a bus.

Powerful locomotive wheels.

A signal: a railroad worker swings a lantern three times.

The wheels of the locomotive shake, begin moving.

Zhivtsov's bags fly into the train's corridor and he jumps in behind them.

Zhivtsov bumps into the Chinese student on the platform of the railway car.

The switches are thrown. A multitude of tracks in the large Moscow station.

Zhivtsov speaks:

"ARE YOU GOING FAR?"

The Chinese student is holding a foreign-made suitcase in one hand and the tin teapot in the other. He answers:

"TO HANGCHOW."

Suburban buildings flow by the train.

The switches are thrown. (The general plan.)

Zhivtsov presses the accordion he bought in Moscow to his chest. He says:

"AND I'M GOING TO POVARENSHINO—IT HAPPENS TO BE IN THE SAME DIRECTION."

The Chinese student smiles, showing his dazzling teeth.

The train picks up speed.

The moon has plunged into a lake, the reeds flicker.

A bird swims in the middle of the lake.

Zhivtsov and the Chinese student are sitting on the vestibule steps of the rushing train.

A lively discussion.

The Chinese student is talking to Zhivtsov.

Dazzlingly lit, steeply rising mountains drenched by recent torrential downpours. With all his strength an old trembling coolie hauls a rickshaw up the mountain.

An Englishman and a bulldog sit in the rickshaw.

The thin lacquered wheels jiggle and stop.

The coolie is at the end of his tether.

Then the wheels start rolling up the mountain again—rolling slowly, with difficulty. The Chinese student goes on talking.

The Russian landscape flies past the train: a river bathed in moonlight, a hedge running up a hill.

On the train's vestibule step the Chinese student continues telling the amazed Zhivtsov about his country.

A cattle shed. A barrel full of water. The fires of the racing train in the water. A cow drinks from the water, scattering the flames. Drops fall from her hairy lips, and in the drops the train's fires still sparkle.

The agonizing climb of the coolie up the mountainside.

Part Two

Cows in a river.

Above the surface of the water, a multitude of cows' muzzles, tormented by the heat, turn up into the air.

A field. Intense heat. A flock of sheep covered in dust.
The sheep nestle their muzzles under each other's bellies.

Midday. The burning sun. The sleepy kingdom of Povarenshino.

The deserted market square littered with vegetable skins, scraps of hay, manure.

The cooperative store is boarded up.

There's a lock on the door.

A note hangs on the lock:

"I'M YONDER EATING."

In the locked store a hog is digging his snout into a barrel of oatmeal. A passerby wearing a dolman tears off a corner of the sign, rolls himself a cigarette, and starts smoking.

A stream of smoke stretches up to the sun's blinding disk.

An oncoming locomotive at full speed.

A train station in the hinterlands. Glimpses of railroad buildings.

The platform, filled with a mass of milk cans.

Local "society" girls walk up and down the platform.

Each of them has a conspicuous flaw: a large nose, bowed legs, pimples.

The train flies into the station. It towers and quivers above the small, dilapidated huts like a wonderful, intricate, glittering moutain.

The Chinese student bids Zhivtsov farewell.

Zhivtsov says:

"BROTHER! WRITE TO ME IF ANYTHING HAPPENS IN CHINA,
AND WE'LL THINK OF SOMETHING!"

The Chinese student takes off his Kuomintang* badge and pins it on Zhivtsov.

Zhivtsov instantly envisions himself as a helpless fighter under the Kuomintang flag.

He pulls the cherished accordion he bought in Moscow off his shoulder and hands it to the Chinese student. The student tries to refuse it, but it is too late—the train pulls out.

---

* A Chinese radical nationalist party, succeeded by the Chinese Communist Party in 1949.

An Englishman in the window of the international train's car flows past the faces of the local girls.

The perplexed Chinese student holding the large accordion flows past.

The hitching post outside the tavern.

"SELF-SERVICE CANTEEN, FULL WAITER SERVICE. SECOND CATEGORY."

In the background of the interior shot of the tavern, an uneven, dilapidated, homemade billiard table with wooden billiard balls.

A muzhik's hand crushes a peeled egg.

Leaning over the billiard table is Yeryoma, a dreamy muzhik with a bald head fringed with apostolic hair . . .

. . . he throws the crushed egg at a brood of chicks gathered on the billiard table.

On the corner of the billiard table, the remains of Yeryoma's meal.

A teapot is standing on three billiard balls with worn-off numbers.

Zhivtsov cheerfully rides to the tavern, pats the sleepy mare. He knocks on the window.

"YERYOMA!"

Yeryoma looks up, startled.

He runs out of the tavern.

The billiard table. The clatter of his steps sets one of the billiard balls under the teapot rolling and it falls into a pocket.

A worn-out drunkard lies sleeping in the dust in the middle of the market square.

A dog rubs itself against him as if he were a doorpost, yawns, lies down.

The serene Russian plain, crisscrossed by winding roads.

Yeryoma and Zhivtsov, talking energetically, rattle along the country road in a cart. A huge camellike horse is pulling it. It is harnessed to the tiny cart. It must be said of the horse that it is an old and thoughtful creature that looks askance at its flighty master, Yeryoma.

Zhivtsov asks Yeryoma:

"THE MILL—DID THE WORK GROUP FIX IT UP?"

Yeryoma answers, waving a billiard stick that has a strap tied to it, turning it into a whip:

"AN OWL, THEY SAY, HATCHED A BROOD OF OWLETS AT THE MILL—SO HOW CAN WE FIX IT?"

A tarred log is lying on the square.
It is oozing beads of sweat.
The market square.
A little muzhik—bitterly poor—is milking a small mangy cow harnessed to a cart. The little muzhik is drunk and lies down to sleep under the cart.
Zhivtsov bursts in on the man's sleeping paradise.
With his whip he hits the man and the dog that are sleeping in the middle of the square.

"EVERYONE'S SNORING AWAY WHEN I'M NOT AROUND!"

Zhivtsov yells, waving the billiard stick.
The sleeping man and the dog roll over and scamper away.
Zhivtsov drums on the locked door of a store.
The watchman looks out the window of the village reading room and, seeing Zhivtsov, quickly starts running around.
The store assistant's pudgy face, covered with feathers, emerges from inside the store, and immediately darts away again.
Anxious, scampering chickens.
The store assistant feverishly starts lowering the prices in the locked store. He tears off the price tags . . .
. . . and rewrites the prices, cutting them by ten percent.
Zhivtsov drums on the door of the village reading room.
The adept watchman cranks up the gramophone.
Anxious chickens flutter through the wicker fence.
A peasant woman lifts the hem of her skirt and runs across the square.
The gramophone record revolves.
Zhivtsov waves the billiard stick.

"EVERYONE'S SNORING AWAY WHEN I'M NOT AROUND! DAMN THEM!"

The milked cow starts galloping.

Under the cart, the startled muzhik.

An endless chain of wagons carrying grain is rolling toward the cow and the muzhik.

The harvest, quite clearly, has been good.

On one wagon, on which the grain has been loaded without sacks, two round-bellied naked infants frolic in the rye that is glittering in the sun.

The chain of wagons crosses the market square.

"LORD IN HEAVEN! HOW MUCH MOONSHINE VODKA THIS COULD MAKE, OH, HOW MUCH MOONSHINE VODKA!"

Yeryoma says with emotion . . .

. . . following the flow of wagons.

The frolicking infants.

The grain in the sun.

"BUT WHO'LL GRIND ALL THIS NOW, THE LANDOWNING OGRES?"

Zhivtsov yells desperately.

"OFF TO THE MILL, YERYOMA!"

The revolving gramophone record.

Zhivtsov's cart flies along the road to the mill at full speed.

The slow and majestic flow of wagons.

A strap tears in Yeryoma's harness.

He doesn't notice and keeps whipping his horse.

At the edge of the horizon, on the banks of a river, the dilapidated mill with its battered mill wheel.

On top of the mill's attic sits a motionless owl.

"FASTER, YERYOMA!"

Zhivtsov shouts.

In front of the mill is a little plank bridge, which has been unreliable these past four years. The cart rushes toward the bridge.

Yeryoma crosses himself . . .

. . . the cart rushes onto the bridge . . .

. . . the planks break . . .

. . . Yeryoma's sign of the cross flashes in the air.

Zhivtsov, the horse, the cart, all fall into the ditch.

The owl.

The loose wheel of the cart rolls across a swath dividing two unharvested fields.

The swath separates a field in which there is a tall thick wall of undulating wheat from a scraggly, poorly tended field.

The rolling wheel.

EXPERIMENTAL FIELD OF THE POVARENSHINO ALL-UNION LENINIST COMMUNIST YOUTH LEAGUE.

The harvest. In the experimental field, the ears are thick, heavy, tall.

Two American harvesters are at work.

On one of them sits young Cherevkov, the village librarian.

On the other, Panyutin.

Komsomol girls are tying the sheaves.

THE "EXPERIMENTAL" FIELD OF OLD GERASIM CHEREVKOV.

The poorly tended field has yielded a scraggly, sparse crop.

Gerasim is a heated, anxious little muzhik and . . .

. . . Gerasim's father is a decrepit old man wearing a hemp shirt and wide pants. They are cutting with sickles.

The old man wields his sickle weakly.

Gerasim's wife—a boisterous, large peasant woman—is tying sheaves.

She says to her husband venomously:

"YOUR SON'S WHEAT OVER THERE WILL BE A LOT WHEATER!"

The high wall of wheat, and Gerasim's pitiful crop.

The sweeping and efficient work of the harvesters.

Gerasim's father's antiquated sickle moves feebly. The strain makes the old man keel over onto his back, he cannot get up, he only wiggles his feet. Gerasim looks at his father and spits spitefully.

His wife says viciously:

"YOUR SON'S WHEAT OVER THERE WILL BE A LOT WHEATER!"

Gerasim furiously throws down his sickle and jumps across the swath.

He runs to the harvester on which his son is working and blocks its path.

"WHY DON'T YOU WORK FOR YOUR FATHER, INSTEAD OF FOR OTHER PEOPLE, YOU SON-OF-A-BITCH? I'LL GIVE YOU A GOOD WHIPPING!"

he shouts, pounding his pants.

Young Cherevkov, a hearty giant, grabs his small father, wedges him under his arm, and continues working.

Cherevkov's grandfather is sitting on his bony behind, his lips chewing. His faded eyes fill with tears. Gerasim's wife is shouting at him.

One of Gerasim's bast sandals flies off his dangling legs, as his son is still holding him under his arm.

Yeryoma, carrying the remains of his cart on his shoulders, approaches the working harvesters.

Zhivtsov, filthy and covered with scratches, and Yeryoma's melancholic horse, dragging the wreckage of the shaft in which the billiard stick and the strap are tangled.

When they see Zhivtsov, the Komsomols come running over to him.

Young Cherevkov, forgetting his father, drops him.

"WHY DON'T YOU WORK FOR YOUR FATHER, YOU SON-OF-A-BITCH, INSTEAD OF FOR OTHER PEOPLE!"

Gerasim, disheveled, attacks his son again.

The swath separates two fields.

"WORK WITH YOUR SON, YOU NUMBSKULL! YOU'D GET MORE OUT OF IT!"

Zhivtsov says to Gerasim, as one by one he shakes the hands of all the Komsomols.

The grandfather sitting on the ground.

A row of cut stalks of wheat.

The undulating wall of wheat. . . .

In front of a herd walks Teryosha, a very blond shepherd.

The ripe ears of wheat beat against his chest, against his International Communist Youth League badge.

The shepherd is immersed in studying an arithmetic textbook.

A page of the arithmetic textbook moving through the tall wheat.

Part Three

The Komsomol cell is threshing the grain harvested from the experimental field.

The harmonious work of young frenzied hands.

The flying sheaves paint a rainbow in the sunset sky.

Arms swinging up.

Shirts sticking to sweating backs.

Young men, covered in thick dust, heaving the sheaves.

Girls on top of the threshing machine catching the sheaves.

Laughing among themselves, the girls jostle each other, spicing up their sheaf-catching with risqué provincial jokes.

A girl throwing sheaves bungles a throw.

The sheaf flies over the threshing machine.

She laughs and curses.

There is a mug nailed to the threshing machine with a sign on it: "To Reach the Goals of our Cultural Battle for Swearing—One Kopeck in Gold."

The spirited girls throw kopecks into the mug.

The sacks gradually fill with grain pouring out of the threshing machine.

The young men carry away the sacks on their sweaty muscular shoulders.

On a gigantic haystack:

Cherevkov.

Seen from the haystack, the serene Russian plain—harvested fields, a wood, a stream.

Steel cables carry the hay to Cherevkov.

The sun shines and moves over the wires.

Teryosha the shepherd is still studying. He has buried himself in the golden hay. He copies a problem from his arithmetic textbook: 4 + 4 + 4 + 7, which, according to Teryosha, equals 24.

Barefoot urchins on foaling mares are taking the hay to the haystack. Their feet dangle playfully on the bulging sides of the mares.

The urchins have brought the hay. Cherevkov pulls it up with the cables and . . .

. . . also drags up diligent Teryosha with his arithmetic book, notebook, and pencil.

Next to the threshing machine, sacks filling with grain.

The village church, turned into a granary.

The young men carry the sacks there.

The church is filled with grain up to the eyebrows of St. Nicholas.

A grimy little banner with the letters "R.S.F.S.R."*

The banner has been fastened to a locomotive. By Panyutin the engineer.

He is tinkering around with the locomotive's blazing firebox.

The wild rolling of the locomotive's wheels.

The sacks filling with grain.

A boy of about ten wearing a belt. On his belt hangs a saber.

Sitting on a sheaf of hay, he is riding up to Cherevkov.

He hands him a note.

The note: The agenda of the plenary session of the Povarenshino Komsomol Village Cell:

1. The international situation in China—speaker, Comrade Zhivtsov.
2. The electrification of the water mill and, if possible, global electrification—speaker, Comrade Zhivtsov.
3. Sexual excesses and deviation in the unit—speaker, Comrade Varya.

The boy jumps off the haystack and hands Zhivtsov the note.

He reads it in the light of some burning hay.

Sheaves flying up into the sky.

---

*U.S.S.R.

The boy with the saber has gone over to the girls on the threshing machine.

The girls, black with dust, their eyes and lips sparkling like those of Negroes.

They read the note with religious solemnity.

Replay from Part One—a Chinese rickshaw coolie's agonizing, endless climb up a mountain.

In front of the dilapidated, shattered mill wheel, next to the mill-race destroyed by pigs and filled with every kind of village refuse—animal skeletons, buckets without bottoms, the rotting rims of military caps—stands Zhivtsov.

He is bending over a Chinese issue of *Prozhektor*.

Yeryoma is standing dreamily by the door of the mill. With his whip he counts . . .

. . . jackdaws flying in the sky.

Yeryoma's horse is tearing apples off somebody's apple tree and eating them.

Zhivtsov's contorted face above some photographs.

Close-up: the face of the rickshaw coolie, covered in sweat.

Flying sheaves.

WORK'S OVER!

The young men throw the last sheaf.

The area around the threshing machines where the Komsomols had been working is deserted. Not a single person is in sight. (Zoom in.)

The Komsomols have finished their threshing and are washing themselves by a barrel.

The water becomes blacker than soot, but the sun and laughing faces are reflected in it.

The haystack. A round ditch.

The cook sets down an enormous bowl of cabbage soup.

Floating in the middle of the bowl, among the greasy cabbage, the shimmering disk of the sun.

Close-up: the climbing rickshaw coolie.

Zhivtsov's face leaning over the photograph. Seen through the mesh of his tousled hair, the newspaper page showing Chinese workers killed in a skirmish with foreign troops.

The cheerful meal of the Komsomols, chewing mouths, laughing eyes, glittering drops fall from spoons. The young men crack jokes and . . .

. . . the mug that collects fines in the "Cultural Battle" against swearing dances as if possessed.

The bowl of cabbage soup is half empty, but the sun floats in it as before.

Zhivtsov appears on top of the haystack.

His face is contorted with sorrow and inspiration. He proclaims from the haystack:

"AT THE VERY MOMENT WHEN . . ."

The face of the rickshaw coolie.

". . . WHEN THE CHINESE REVOLUTION IS AWAITING YOUR HELP . . ."

Teryosha's full mouth, his motionless cheeks, his goggling eyes.

A girl's fat, barefooted leg prods one of the young men's legs under the table. More playful prodding.

Zhivtsov begins sinking into the haystack. His speech becomes increasingly angry:

". . . WHEN PRIVATE CAPITAL GRABS US BY THE THROAT AND BRAZENLY GRINDS OUR PROLETARIAN WHEAT . . ."

The Komsomols put down their spoons.

Two gypsies look out of the forge: one of them is a blacksmith, the other has brought his horse to be shod.

Zhivtsov has sunk up to his knees in the hay, he is waving his arms:

". . . WHEN INTERNATIONAL CAPITAL WILL NOT LET US REBUILD OUR MILL . . ."

A semicircle of laid-down spoons.

Under the table, a girl is kicking her neighbor. The young man's leg does not move.

The horse's hoof twitches in the blacksmith's hand.

Zhivtsov stands waist-deep in hay. Dust and sun . . .

". . . WHEN THE BLOOD OF OUR CHINESE BROTHERS IS
BEING SHED . . ."

The face of the rickshaw coolie—dreadful, bare, black, round, like
a polished cast-iron ball, sun and sweat glistening on it.
The Komsomols stand up and approach the haystack.
Young backs, young heads, curly forelocks.

"WHILE YOU HERE—YOU . . ."

A slice of raisin cake.
The rickshaw coolie falls and crawls on all fours, he crawls right
up to Zhivtsov. Zhivtsov's face. His eyes move, his inspiration seeks
an escape, his inspiration has to break free, and it manages to break
free.

". . . AND THIS IS WHY I DECLARE THE MOBILIZATION OF
ALL VOLUNTARY MEMBERS OF THE LENINIST KOMSOMOL
FOR THE DEFENSE OF THE CHINESE REVOLUTION. ALL
VOLUNTEERS RAISE THEIR HANDS!"

The hands of the Komsomols fly into the air.
Sasha Panyutin lifts his crippled hand.
In the sky, against a fiery cloud, Panyutin's hand with a chopped-
off finger.
Komsomol member Varya, who had been tying sheaves, heartily
kisses the woman next to her.
The horse has torn its hoof away from the blacksmith.
The gypsy jumps onto the shod horse and rides off.
A festive, swaying forest of raised hands is closing in on Zhivtsov.
The Komsomols look as solemn as if they are about to take an oath.
While Zhivtsov . . . Zhivtsov realizes that he has managed to pull
off an unusual, completely unexpected feat.
Somewhat perplexed, up to his waist in hay, he shrinks back from
the exultant comrades who are closing in on him.
The gypsy rides wildly through the village streets. Two old women
carrying buckets on yokes come toward him. One old woman is large,
the other small.

"WAR!"

the gypsy shouts to them, and rides on.

The small old woman is drenched from head to toe by water from her large companion's bucket.

Clouds of dust behind the galloping gypsy.

Part Four

Night in Povarenshino. A strange and significant night. Flames flicker in the windows.

Smoke rises from all the chimneys and spreads into the starry sky.

The meadow. Flowers sway beneath the moon. The gypsy rides through the flowers on his horse.

The flowers beneath the horse's hooves.

A campfire rises toward the sky.

Around the campfire in a clearing in the forest, a gypsy camp.

An old man, illuminated by the flames of the fire, is telling the young people a tale of great horse thieves and great singers.

The village cemetery. Crosses bathed in moonlight.

Yeryoma is hurriedly digging.

The horse's mouth is foaming.

The gypsy rushes toward the campfire.

Circling around and around on his foaming horse, he shouts:

"WAR!"

The face of an old gypsy woman looks out from inside a covered wagon facing the campfire.

The reflection of a new moon ripples in a puddle of rainwater in the forest near the camp.

On the floor, mountains of worn-out village shoes that need mending.

A dim oil lamp lights the cobbler's hovel.

He and his daughter, a girl of about ten, are working feverishly.

An old man's hand and a child's hand are alternately hammering shoe soles with all their might.

Somebody's hand darts in the window and throws three more gigantic pairs of shoes onto the pile.

The girl, waxed threads in her mouth, turns her serious, absorbed face toward us:

Flames flicker in the houses.

A map of China lit by wavering candlelight.

A large finger moves over the map.

Cherevkov, Teryosha, and one other "volunteer" are leaning over the map.

Cherevkov is running his finger over the map. He explains the following strategic plan:

"WE WILL HEAD RIGHT ON TO PEKING THROUGH SZECHUAN. . . ."

Teryosha is leaning toward a more careful strategy:

"NO! WE NEED TO GO AROUND THE DAMN PLACE!"

Old Mrs. Cherevkov, in tears, is packing pies into a bag.

Cherevkov, trying to console his mother, takes her in his arms and starts dancing with her:

"AH, MAMA! WE'LL GET SOMETHING GOING HERE!"

The old woman dances, laughs, cries.

The face of the village sorceress.

Inside a rich man's cottage.

The sorceress pours a brew made of flies into glasses, and hands them to the horrified young men.

"DRINK THIS WITH A PRAYER. . . . LORD WILLING, YOU WILL VOMIT IT OUT TOMORROW . . . AND YOU WON'T GO TO NO WAR!"

The sorceress, a mistress of her trade, spits in all four directions and whispers a spell.

A young man, crazed with fear, paces about frantically, crosses himself, and drinks.

Cherevkov is still dancing with his crying and laughing mother.

"AH, MAMA! WE'LL GET SOMETHING GOING HERE!"

The boy is writhing on the floor . . .

. . . his face is contorted with spasms, there is foam on his lips.

A snow-white model of the Volkhovstroi Power Station, carved by the inspired chisel of Sasha Panyutin. Through the mica window of the model electric power station, the flame of a one-kopeck candle.

The heads of Zhivtsov and Panyutin, seen through the window of the electric power station.

In Zhivtsov's room. A dilapidated bunk, a bookcase filled with books, a briefcase, dried ears of wheat. The only good thing in the room is the splendid Volkhovstroi model and the shelves of books.

The bookcase is filled with the collected works of Lenin.

The spines of numerous Lenin books.

With Zhivtsov is Sasha Panyutin, who is very much aware that something momentous but dubious has taken place.

"THIS TIME YOU'VE REALLY STARTED SOMETHING, EGOR!"

Panyutin says, looking around glumly.

His eyes fall on a three-legged chair.

Sighing, he takes the chair, examines it, and starts working.

Zhivtsov himself is aware that he has started something. He paces about the room, deep in thought.

Panyutin is fixing the chair. He sighs.

"YOU'VE REALLY MESSED THINGS UP, EGOR!"

The village fool is sounding the alarm in the belfry.

The band of gypsies, lamps flickering in their covered wagons, cross the river.

The abandoned gypsy camp. Pegs stuck in the ground, manure, the smoldering embers of the campfire.

In the cemetery Yeryoma is digging with all his might.

Zhivtsov's abundant, inexhaustible hair. He runs his pensive, irresolute fingers through it.

"EGOR, YOU'VE REALLY MESSED THINGS UP!"

Panyutin says, engrossed in repairing the chair.

The spines of the Lenin books.

Zhivtsov walks hesitantly to the bookcase, takes a book, opens it.

The title page. A picture of Lenin, squinting, sly.

Zhivtsov's head leaning over Lenin's picture. He tosses his abundant hair out of the way.

In a shed, furrowed with moonlight—tiny, tipsy Gerasim Cherevkov. He is looking through the harnesses for a strap.

Cherevkov's tiny, tattered father bursts into his son's hut. He rushes at his giant of a son, brandishing his strap.

"I'M GOING TO WHIP YOU THIS VERY MINUTE FOR THIS MESS YOU MADE!"

The young giant carefully sits his old father on a bench and hands him a pie.

Without letting go of the strap, the little old muzhik resentfully starts eating, but is somewhat delighted, as this is such an unusual situation.

A slow leafing-through of the Lenin book.

Light falls on Panyutin's humorous* face.

"WHEN THE SECRETARY OF A VILLAGE KOMSOMOL UNIT DECREES A GENERAL MOBILIZATION—WHAT CHOICE DOES ONE HAVE?"

Panyutin says.

Cherevkov's bewildered fingers running through his hair.

Lenin's sly, squinting face.

A slow leafing-through of the book.

Zhivtsov's face above the turning pages.

Panyutin, humming a tune, attaches the fourth leg to the chair.

A page turns, stays. Here a quote from Lenin should appear that bears relation to the unusual situation in Povarenshino.

Quote.

Cherevkov's decrepit grandfather lies huddled in sheepskins on the sleeping bench in Cherevkov's hut. He also demands some pies. His grandson gives him some.

A quote from Lenin.

Zhivtsov's brightening face.

The grandfather lying on the bench is chewing the pies. Peas fall onto the sheepskin.

---

* Babel is using the word "yumoristicheskii" in a slightly subversive way, as it is unclear if Panyutin's face is "humorous," or if he has a wry, amused expression on his face in reaction to what he is reading in Lenin's works.

Yeryoma's horse is wandering about the village, knocking on windows, looking for its master.

A window opens, and a voice shouts:

"YERYOMA ISN'T HERE! BEAT IT!"

And the horse trots on.

Yeryoma has dug up something long from the grave, wrapped in a bast mat.

He is very pleased. He wipes his sweat away with his arm.

The horse, his bony friend, approaches him, dragging its shaft behind it. The horse has finally found him.

The horse looks at its master with reproachful eyes, as if to say: "Really, Yeryoma, you're out of your mind! Totally unreliable!"

The horse grabs him by the collar with its teeth and tugs at him.

"I'M COMING, I'M COMING!"

Yeryoma mumbles, ashamed.

Zhivtsov closes the book and slowly looks up again, his face lit with a sudden, happy thought that will settle everything. The model of the Volkhovstroi Power Station. Zhivtsov's face through the mica window.

Panyutin sets down the chair, which stands soundly on its four legs.

The four legs of the chair.

The new moon ripples in a puddle of rainwater among the flowers. In front of the paling sky, the chimneys of Povarenshino are smoking.

Part Five

The sky. Sunrise.

A cock flies up onto a fence, crows.

The cock's claw with its spur.

A bast shoe with a spur.

Teryosha, wearing the bast shoe with the spur, is walking along the road.

In front of Teryosha's herd walks a new shepherd—he is old, sooty, and dirty.

An endless chain of carts is crossing the river.

The river seethes, glitters, flows between the wheels.

On one of the carts in the water, young peasant men and women. The girls' ribbons flutter in the wind.

Flowers float in the river.

Three singing youths, their arms over each other's shoulders, are on their way to "report for duty" at the gathering point. They are covered with weapons and accordions. On the edge of the horizon, crowds of peasants are flowing along the winding roads.

The young men are growing in number. There are now five.

They knock on the rich man's window.

"COME ALONG, MAX! WE HAVE TO REPORT FOR DUTY!"

In a locked chamber, stretched out on the floor, the son of a kulak. His deathly, contorted face.

The young men walk on, there are now seven of them.

There is a sign on a closed wine store:

"Because of civil war in China, the sale of Russian vodka is banned for three days."

In front of the sign the blissfully drunk, disheveled heads of Cherevkov's father and grandfather.

"HEY, YOU, RUSSIA! YOU GREAT POWER, YOU! O RUSSIA, YOU GREAT POWER, YOU!"

The Cherevkovs dance wildly.

Crowds of people are streaming from the hills. A mass migration of the peoples of Povarenshino.

In the crowd, two giant peasants resembling each other, surely brothers.

"WOULD YOU GIVE ALL THIS BACK TO THE LANDOWNERS?"

one of them says, pointing at . . .

. . . the vast and beautiful expanse of Russia stretching before them.

"WE WILL NOT GIVE IT BACK!"

the other one answers.

Four strong feet strutting in bast shoes.

Cherevkov's old mother gives him a cross. The boy is ashamed—it is hard to turn it down, but there is no point in taking it.

"SEE YOU DON'T HARM THE CHINESE. . . . JUST BRING BACK
A PACKET OF TEA WITH YOU—THAT'LL BE ENOUGH!"

the old woman says to her son.

The young man surreptitiously slips the cross into his boot.

The road is filled with singing young men, their arms around each
other's shoulders.

There are no longer seven, but fifteen.

Flowers float on the river. Fadeout.

Egor, covered in every conceivable badge, holding his briefcase, a
fur hat on his head, is solemnly marching to the mill—the gathering
point.

He is followed by an incalculably large army of men marching in
orderly rows.

Among them are Komsomols carrying a banner, hunting rifles, and
accordions.

Among them are also the bearded village infantry, marching in bast
shoes, entangled with howling women,

squawking infants,

barking dogs.

Among them is also the cavalry: five mounted forest wardens with
German helmets, remnants of the Great War.

Zhivtsov climbs onto a mound and lifts his arm majestically.

The troops fall silent.

All eyes are trained on Egor, the commander in chief.

Yeryoma, panting, pushes his way through the troops. He is holding in his arms the item wrapped in a bast mat that he dug up from the
cemetery. With a sweeping gesture, he places it in front of Zhivtsov and
unwraps it—it turns out to be a machine gun.

"I'VE KEPT IT FOR EIGHT YEARS—I SACRIFICE IT TO THE
SOVIET STATE!"

Yeryoma says, his ecstatic words gushing out of him.

The troops present their arms.

The gypsy is galloping through the streets of a backwater town.

THE CHIEF OF POLICE OF THE DISTRICT OF "N," BUSY FER-
VENTLY BUILDING THE PEACEFUL SOCIALIST FUTURE.

The courtyard of the town's police station.

The chief of police, in striped military pants and with galoshes on his bare feet, is shearing a sheep.

The gypsy gallops into the courtyard.

"WAR!"

he yells, and, turning around and around with his horse, informs the stunned chief of the developing military deployment in the neighboring district against the warmongers occupying Shanghai.

Zhivtsov by the mill on top of a mound.

Yeryoma is caressing the machine gun.

Zhivtsov raises his arm:

"CITIZEN VOLUNTEERS! LAST NIGHT I CONFERRED WITH THE CENTRAL EXECUTIVE COMMITTEE. . . . OUR CHINESE BROTHERS ARE MANAGING WELL ENOUGH ON THEIR OWN. . . . THE CENTRAL EXECUTIVE COMMITTEE OF THE U.S.S.R. ADVISES US PLAIN AND SIMPLE TO TAKE CARE OF OUR OWN CURRENT AFFAIRS—SUCH AS THE HUNDRED-PERCENT FIX-UP OF THE MILL."

Teryosha's dog yawns, wags its tail, leaves.

Yeryoma, deeply disappointed, moves his eyes from . . .

. . . the machine gun to Zhivtsov . . .

. . . from Zhivtsov to the machine gun.

A group of brightening old women's faces.

A row of Komsomol faces, their expressions: at first dumbfounded, then grinning.

"HE TRICKED US . . . THE POCKMARKED DEVIL!"

In his shed, Panyutin is working with his tools: shovels, axes, saws, sacks of sand.

Teryosha, delighted, takes the spurs off his bast shoes and puts them in his pocket.

"HE TRICKED US . . . IVANICH!"

Varya shouts at Teryosha:

"WHAT'RE YOU KEEPING THOSE FOR? THROW THEM OUT!"

Teryosha answers:

"THEY MAY COME IN HANDY. . . ."

A spur makes Teryosha's pocket protrude.
Cherevkov rushes to his mother.

"TAKE IT BACK, MAMA!"

He gives the old woman the cross—he has finally managed to get rid of it.

Yeryoma, indignant, in the company of drunken Gerasim Cherevkov, is dragging off the machine gun.

"I ABSOLUTELY MUST DEFEAT SOMEONE TODAY!"

Yeryoma yells.

CURRENT AFFAIRS OF THE CENTRAL EXECUTIVE COMMITTEE OF THE U.S.S.R.

An open shed next to the mill. The Komsomols are sorting out the tools: shovels, axes, saws, wheelbarrows.
Mounted policemen are riding along the road behind their chief.
A half-shorn sheep.
Yeryoma and Gerasim Cherevkov are sitting at the bottom of the ditch.
They are trying out the machine gun.
The bullets hit the sheer walls of the ditch.

CURRENT AFFAIRS OF THE CENTRAL EXECUTIVE COMMITTEE OF THE U.S.S.R.

Shovels swinging up.
Arms swinging up.
Shovels swinging up.
Arms swinging up.
Tumbling soil.
The efficient work of the Komsomols by the millrace.
The spur has pierced Teryosha's pocket and is sticking out.
A pile of discarded accordions.
A pile of discarded weapons.

Shovels swinging up.

Arms swinging up.

Work at the mill—columns of dust—hammering.

Among the columns of dust, a frenzied Zhivtsov.

A thin stream of water is trickling into the dirty pond.

With adroit maneuvers, the police surround the ditch in which Yeryoma was shooting.

The police officers are crawling on their stomachs, pointing their rifles.

In the ditch, Yeryoma and his companion are in deep sleep in each other's arms, the machine gun between them.

The police officers, pointing their rifles, reach the edge of the ditch.

They throw themselves on Yeryoma, who is fast asleep.

Yeryoma, buried under a pile of fluttering police officers.

"HURRAH!"

shouts Yeryoma, waking up, not realizing what is happening.

CURRENT AFFAIRS OF THE CENTRAL EXECUTIVE COMMIT-
TEE OF THE U.S.S.R.

Cherevkov is nailing new planks to the dilapidated mill wheel.

The millrace is constantly growing, sacks of sand fall into the water.

The work inside the mill.

An agitated owl . . .

. . . flies away from its dark shelter.

The muzzle of a rifle—a shot.

A stream, formerly flowing to the side, now flows into the pond.

An increasingly powerful stream flows into the pond.

Rotten planks, heaps of rags, and all kinds of garbage from the village float up to the surface—clean water appears.

Yeryoma's horse stands above the stream, waits, and, when the dirty water has receded, starts drinking.

The water has risen—the pond is full.

Zhivtsov lifts the barrier.

Sparkling water flows onto the mill wheel, which is covered with a mix of old and new planks. The wheel comes alive, moves, turns.

The dead owl. Fadeout.

CURRENT AFFAIRS OF THE CENTRAL EXECUTIVE COMMIT-
TEE OF THE U.S.S.R.

The turning millstones, repaired.
The rotating mill wheel, the sparkling water glittering in the sun.
Flour pours from the millstones.
The peasants are carrying the grain from the church that has been
turned into a granary.
St. Nicholas is slowly uncovered.

"HEY, RUSSIA! YOU GREAT POWER, YOU!"

Father and grandfather Cherevkov are dancing.
Flour is flowing from the millstones.
A village street. Among the rows of thatched roofs, one new roof is
glittering beneath the sun.
Flowers are floating down the river.
Through the spinning wheel, through the streams of water—the
tired, sweating, happy faces of the Komsomols.

NUMBER 4
STARAYA SQUARE

Babel wrote Number 4 Staraya Square *a few months before his arrest. It was a talkie for Soyuzdetfilm, the movie studio that was also bringing out the famous Gorky trilogy, which Babel had just finished working on. After Babel's arrest, the movie did not go into production. "Number 4 Staraya Square" was the address in Moscow of the Central Committee of the Soviet Communist Party. With his choice of title, Babel indicated how deeply involved the Central Committee was in controlling all the elements of the Soviet Union's race for technical supremacy in the world. Although Communism triumphs in the end, the screenplay takes dangerous digs at bureaucratic inefficiency and corruption in Stalinist Russia.*

1.

A lean man in a leather coat came out of the Central Committee of the Soviet Communist Party at number 4 Staraya Square.

Above his head in huge letters on the building: "CCSCP."

The unblinking eyes of the man in the leather coat stared straight ahead.

A woman carrying a package bumped into him as she hurried past; without noticing, he slowly walked on toward a long line of cars parked across the street from the Central Committee building.

He found his car, opened the door, and got in next to his driver.

The driver, a gangly man with a likable, snub-nosed, devil-may-care face, started the engine.

The car drove through Moscow.

Driving past the Kremlin, the driver threw a sidelong glance at the man in the leather coat.

"The outskirts?"

The lean man shook his head.

"No, Moscow."

The car plunged into one side street after another.

"Well, Comrade Murashko, who are we now?" the driver asked without turning his head.

The man in the leather coat shook himself out of deep thought.

"Who are we now? We are the Airship Construction Team."

"Great!" the driver said, nodding his head.

The lights of Moscow sparkled.

"How does an airship work, I mean scientifically?" the driver asked, looking straight ahead.

"Scientifically? Well, Vasya, it's lighter than air."

"Great!" Vasya said, nodding his head again.

"Let's just hope this airship project won't have *us* ending up lighter than air!" Murashko said, shifting in his seat.

"You're right, we might well end up lighter than air," Vasya said, turning the steering wheel.

The car drove through the streets of Moscow.

"Which way should I head, Comrade Murashko?"

"Head to the highway we took to get to the dacha last summer, and we'll go as far as the twelfth kilometer."

The car left Moscow behind. On both sides of the highway the fields of early spring poured forth their emeralds.

Vasya stopped the car at the twelfth kilometer. Murashko got out and walked along the strip of wet grass lining the highway. Vasya followed him, his long legs stepping clumsily.

Murashko walked to the middle of a vast, empty field. The wet grass was sticking to his shoes. Vasya stood next to him.

Both men were silent. Murashko looked around, running his eyes over the field. The field was completely desolate. Only a single, bent willow tree and the ruins of an old barracks blackened the horizon.

"Our launch pad," Murashko said.

Vasya stared at the "launch pad," and said with a tone both commiserating and gloating, "Once a field, now a launch pad!"

"I see it all," Murashko said. "The dock, the hangar, the gas purification unit, the gas reservoirs, the project design center—an entire airship construction complex!"

"So why are they stalling?" Vasya interrupted him, flaring up. "They sent you to take over Workshop 26, and you managed things quite well over there. Then you got to be deputy director of Workshop 24, and there too no one could hold a candle to you! So, what's the problem? Even if the thing has to be lighter than air—"

"That's exactly what the Central Committee keeps saying," Murashko cut in, half agreeing, half pondering.

2.

The wooden barracks on the airship construction site. Inside it, sheets of plywood formed a partition for a room with a sign that said: "Director of Airship Construction."

The long black pipe of a makeshift stove cut through the plywood partition and ran the whole length of the room.

In the director's "office," Murashko was sitting in an opera chair inlaid with mother-of-pearl. In front of him stood a rickety table heaped with papers, drafts, and samples. In the office: noise, commotion, and a throng of construction workers.

"They don't want to, and that's that!" a foreman with rubber boots, spattered with mortar and lime, announced in a morose bass.

Murashko suddenly looked up at him.

"What do you mean, they don't want to?"

"And why should they want to?" the foreman continued. "At the Anilin construction site, workers are raking in fourth-level wages, while we here are forced to work for second-level pay! And then our mess hall . . . well . . . it just isn't good enough!"

"How's that?"

"Well, Comrade Murashko, it just isn't good enough. Take your average ditch digger, for instance: one wants meatballs, and the next wants beef Stroganoff. It's every man for himself!"

Murashko jotted down something in his notebook and turned to another foreman, a pockmarked little man with a metal rule in his hands.

"What do you want?"

The incessant onslaught of construction problems have instilled a somber steeliness in the foreman's words: "What do I want? In two days things here will grind to a halt."

"Is it the cement?"

"That's right. I can scrape together forty barrels, but then it's curtains!"

Murashko's secretary, a rosy, hefty, well-built woman, was sitting on a crate serving as a chair on the other side of the partition. On a second, larger crate were papers and a telephone that looked like an army field telephone and smacked of war and frontline action.

"Comrade Murashko," the secretary said in a placid voice through the partition. "The director of the Fourth Regional Construction Supply Department."

Murashko picked up the receiver.

"Murashko speaking."

• • •

The large office of the director of the Fourth Regional Construction Supply Department . The director was a man with a surprisingly milky, porcine face. His deputy, a man with shiny black hair and the inordinately expressive face of a provincial actor, was standing behind his chair. He whispered something into the director's ear.

The director whined into the telephone in an offended, high-pitched voice.

"All I can say, Comrade Murashko, is that you're acting as if you come from another planet!"

"Well, I *am* an airship man, after all."

The deputy bent forward to his boss's ear and hissed, "You've got to be tougher!"

The director puffed himself up.

"I'm telling you this one last time: there is no cement, nor are we anticipating there being any!"

The deputy, in his boss's ear: "Tougher!"

"For your information . . ." Murashko's calm, dispirited voice came streaming out of the receiver, "for your information, according to invoice number 94611, two hundred tons of cement were shipped to you from Novorossisk on the fourteenth. They arrived at your Moscow depot on the twenty-first." And Murashko hung up.

The director's porcine face was gripped by an expression of extreme astonishment and offense.

"He said that . . . that it was shipped on the fourteenth," he stammered in dismay, "and that it arrived at our depot on the twenty-first!"

The deputy with the inordinately expressive face turned beet red and then went pale.

"Um, well, Ivan Semyonovich," he whispered, quickly looking around, "a little note was sent to us, and so . . ."

• • •

Murashko's "office." A squat little bookkeeper, with the air of a goose about to bounce into flight, stood in front of Murashko's desk.

"We figure the general estimate at twenty-eight million," he said in a sugary voice, preening himself.

A resonant voice outside the window: "Aksinya, give me forty kopecks so I can get myself some tea."

Murashko looked at the preening bookkeeper.

"That's too low," he said. "We have to go with my figure of thirty-five million."

The bookkeeper recoiled as if he had been lashed with a whip.

"Comrade Murashko, permit me to add—"

The appeasing voice of Murashko's secretary rang out from the other side of the partition: "Please pick up the telephone. It is the Central Committee of the Komsomol. . . ."*

• • •

The office of the Secretary of the Central Committee of the Komsomol. The secretary, a young blond woman with braids coiled into a crown over her head, was sitting in a chair. She looked through the papers lying on the table, and said with an energy filled with youth, cheerfulness, enthusiasm, and competence, "Let me see, Comrade Murashko. Are you the one who needs . . . just a minute . . ." The young woman quickly ran her eyes over the papers again. "Are you the one who needs an airship construction crew, hangars, mooring masts, airship navigators, gas purification unit mechanics . . . just a minute . . ." She turned the page and continued reading out the roster with even more energy. "As well as both engineers and draftsmen with airship expertise."

* The Communist Youth Organization of the Soviet Union. Its members were sent to work on construction projects throughout the country.

"Yes, I'm the one!" Murashko answered, won over by the woman's unbridled cheerfulness and youth.

She put away the papers.

"What we'll provide you with, Comrade, is nice strong boys and girls from the ranks of the Komsomol, but with no expertise."

"But what am I supposed to do with them?" Murashko asked her defiantly.

"Exactly what everyone else does," the secretary said, looking out the window to where Moscow lay. "You'll simply have to reshuffle them to fit your bill."

"And what about all that highfalutin help you were going to give me?" Murashko asked.

"We're going to give you a Komsomol team leader," the young woman answered. "A tried-and-tested construction foreman from an electrical power plant."

Murashko put the receiver back on the hook. There was still a residue of animation in his face.

"All I can say is that, notwithstanding instruction 380, they're finishing us off with their budget restrictions, plain and simple," the bookkeeper said suddenly, hopping from foot to foot in front of Murashko's desk.

A feisty little woman of about eighteen, with an unruly mop of flaxen curls and an unyieldingly obstate face, came bursting into Murashko's office.

"I'd like to make it clear here and now that I've never seen one before!" she announced, standing by the door.

"Seen what?" Murashko asked, unperturbed.

"An airship!"

"And what would you have needed to see one for?"

"Well, I like that!" the young woman snapped. "Here I am, the Komsomol team leader sent by the Central Committee to run the airship construction team, and I'm asked what I need to have seen an airship for!"

"*You* are the Komosomol team leader the Central Committee sent?"

"Yep," the girl answered. "Pleased to meet you!"

She shook Murashko's hand, and then headed for the door.

"I'll go take a look at the workers' dormitory—the place looks like a real dump to me!" she said, scuttling out of the office.

"That one's a troublemaker!" the chief bookkeeper said, watching her disappear.

"A ticking time bomb!" the foreman added, making space for the bookkeeper, who was hopping about more and more agitatedly.

"I'll have you know, Comrade Murashko, the government's position is crystal-clear to me. As for the budget restrictions, you'll simply have to—"

"Put in for thirty-five million," Murashko interrupted him in a tone that allowed for no discussion.

The secretary opened the door and admitted a blue-eyed, rosy-cheeked old man.

"This is Professor Polibin," she said, with a streak of fear and respect in her face.

Murashko chased all the other people out of his office. He and the professor remained alone. Murashko pushed the opera chair with the inlaid mother-of-pearl, the only chair in his office, toward the professor, and sat down on some parquet planks tied into a bundle.

Professor Polibin looked first out the window, then around the office, and said in a mellifluous voice, "I think one could go so far as to say that you have already launched your project."

•   •   •

The bookkeeper, about to bounce into flight, was pouring his heart out to the secretary on the other side of the partition.

"I'll have you know that I'm fully aware of the government's point of view. . . ."

In the "office," Professor Polibin, running his blue eyes over Murashko, was holding forth in his sugary voice: "In my view, my dear Alexei Kuzmich, the problem of who is to occupy the post of chief airship builder is a tricky question indeed. Who would be the top specialist in this field in the Soviet Union?"

Murashko slid closer on the bundle of parquet planks.

"Well, there is always Ivan Platonovich Tolmazov," Professor Polibin continued, peering at Murashko even more intently. "He's a renowned scientist and theoretician of the highest quality."

"I wouldn't even dare consider asking a man of his standing!"

"Well, as for Tolmazov's students," Polibin's tenor flowed on, "I would single out Vasilyev. Though I must say . . . he is young, so intolerably young!"

"A shortcoming that a few years will put right," Murashko pointed out. "Who else besides Tolmazov's students might we consider?"

Polibin's eyes gazed into the distance as if he were plumbing the depths of his consciousness.

"Pyotr Nikolayevich Zhukov. He is a *perpetuum mobile,* a visionary, a maniac, I should say. And then there's Yastrezhemsky, but I don't really think he'd be the right man . . . he's not a Party man."

"No, he's not one of us," Murashko agreed.

A pause.

"What would you say, my dear professor, if we tried twisting *your* arm into accepting the position?"

An expression of intense beatitude washed over Professor Polibin's rosy face. He opened his mouth, but at that very moment a battle broke out on the other side of the partition. Murashko's docile secretary was being accosted by a middle-aged woman with a beret on her head and a tattered fur boa around her neck.

"Professor Polibin might well be a great man!" the woman with the boa yelled, waving her handbag at the secretary. "But I, Comrade, I am a mother! Yes, before you stands a mother!"

In Murashko's office the courtship was winding down.

"In conclusion, I would like to stress"—a ripple of intense emotion ruffled the balm in Polibin's voice—"to stress my twenty-eight years of experience as a scientist, my extensive volunteer work, and my status as a Party sympathizer since the year 1927."

Murashko tapped his finger on his knee and got up.

"Yes, my dear professor, we'll take all of that into account. I promise. We'll discuss it further at a later date."

Polibin bowed, stretched out his thin palm to shake Murashko's broad hand, and, still bowing, backed out of the office. By the door he collided with the middle-aged woman wearing the boa. She made way for him, and then, her body blocking the door, launched her attack.

"Comrade Director!"

Murashko slapped his cap onto his head.

"Come back in two days. I'm leaving now."

But under the circumstances, leaving was not a simple matter. The woman blocking the door was triumphantly roused and ready for battle.

"When a mother comes to you in deep sorrow, then your little trip can wait!" And she pulled a letter out of her bag. "This isn't a letter from just anyone! It is a letter from Eliseyev!"

Murashko glanced at the letter and looked at the woman with interest.

"So, you are Friedman's mother?"

"I'm the mother of one of those damn daredevils, that's who I am!" the woman answered mournfully.

Murashko grabbed some papers and stuffed them into his briefcase.

"Comrade Friedman . . . Raisa Lvovna, is it?"

"Yes, Raisa Lvovna."

"It's all been taken care of. We will hire your son as a pilot, it's all been settled. But the whole thing will start a year from now, not before. And then, your son is up in the substratosphere, while we're down here building an airship."

But Raisa Friedman did not move.

"I have one question, and do you know what it is? My question is: doesn't a mother have the right to want her one and only son to open his parachute three hundred meters up instead of fifty?" Raisa Friedman sobbed. "If I were Comrade Voroshilov,* I would rip the men who order our boys to do such things into little pieces, but as a mother I have no choice but to endure it all!"

Murashko picked up his briefcase brusquely.

"Raisa Lvovna, I am late as it is, I really am!"

The woman blew her nose and wiped her eyes. "I suppose you must have a mama too, no? I'm sure your mama would understand me. . . . *Oy*, what I went through to raise him!" she suddenly shrieked unexpectedly. "Why don't you ask me what I had to go through to raise him? I fed him nothing but the creamiest butter, the nicest chicken patties,

---

*Kliment Efremovich Voroshilov, 1881–1969, close associate of Stalin and Marshal of the Soviet Union. He frequently appears in the Red Cavalry stories, as he had been General Budyonny's military commissar.

everything bursting with vitamins! I poured my soul into those patties, I poured everything I had into them, so they would not, God forbid, end up overcooked, or, God forbid, undercooked! And what do I end up with? Today my boy is free-falling out of the sky, tomorrow he'll be free-falling from the moon!"

"You know what, Raisa Lvovna?" Murashko suddenly interrupted her.

"What?" Friedman's mother sobbed.

"You know what?" Murashko repeated, his eyes twinkling, and he came up very close to her. "What you should do is run our kitchen. And when your Lev gets stationed here, you can make chicken patties bursting with good vitamins for him and all the other boys."

Friedman's mother staggered back in astonishment.

"I see you're just as devil-may-care as everyone else, Comrade Director. I came to you with my sorrow—"

But Murashko launched a counterattack.

"Nothing but the creamiest butter bursting with vitamins! How about that, Comrade Friedman?"

3.

Night. A moving train. A first-class compartment.

Murashko was immersed in an English technical book. Next to him sat a quiet woman of about twenty-six with chestnut-colored hair that was neatly parted in the middle. She was crocheting a collar for a dress.

The woman looked at her watch: "It's after midnight."

"I will go outside, Comrade, so that you can lie down," Murashko said. He went out into the corridor and lit a cigarette.

A tall, dark, long-legged fellow in an Aeroflot uniform came out of the washroom. A towel hung from his shoulder, and he was holding a soap container.

"Murashko! Hello there! Where are you heading?"

"To Voronezh."

"Anyone sharing your compartment—a man, a woman?"

"A woman."

"What kind?"

Murashko gave the question some thought.

"The domestic animal kind."

"Forget it," the man with the towel said, and went to his compartment.

Murashko stood by the window, smoking his cigarette. Wet, black, quivering fields flew by.

In the meantime, Murashko's traveling companion had managed to change into pajamas and brush her soft hair. She took out a black leather cylinder containing blueprints, put it on the edge of the bed by the wall, and covered it with the sheet. Then she opened her handbag, took out a small revolver, and made sure that it was loaded. She placed the revolver under her pillow, lay down, and covered herself with the blanket.

4.

An indescribable rumpus. Two little boys of about five or six were wielding wooden swords, a nine-year-old was banging on a makeshift drum. The leader of the pack, twelve-year-old Igor, was flying through the room, hanging from a wooden model airship fastened to the ceiling with ropes. Only an old, shaggy dog, dozing stoically by the door, kept his calm.

The small windows were fitted with geraniums and cacti. Above the flowers hung cages with birds: starlings, thrushes, canaries, and birds of an unidentifiable kind. They all sang, chirped, and whistled.

A tub stood on two stools in the corner. A plump woman with puffed-up hair was washing clothes in it, slowly and evenly kneading soap into them, as she read a book propped up on the windowsill.

Murashko, astonished at the strange sight, stopped in his tracks as he opened the door. No one noticed his arrival, only the dog opened one eye and then closed it again.

"Hello, Comrade, I was ringing the doorbell but nobody came."

Hearing a stranger's voice, the children stopped playing and stared at Murashko in genuine astonishment. The flying boy let himself drop down to the floor, startling the dog.

"Our door's never locked," the woman with the puffed-up hair answered simply, shaking the suds off her red hands. "What's there to steal? You want Zhukov? Pyotr!" she shouted. "Pyotr!"

The starling whistled angrily at her.

"Isn't he here?" Murashko asked, disappointed.

The woman dried her hands on her apron.

"He is here. He's just not answering. He never answers when I call him. Why don't you come in?"

And, forgetting Murashko, she continued reading.

• • •

Zhukov's room. His windows too were decorated with geraniums and birdcages. Wooden shelves were lined with test tubes, retorts, and vials. In the corner stood a lathe. The floor was littered with stacks of books, and the bed, the table, and the chairs were heaped with blueprints. A man of about fifty, with steel-rimmed spectacles, a black mane of hair, and a futile little beard, sat at a table that was covered in a piece of torn oilskin, sketching with quick movements.

Murashko cleared his throat, waited, shuffled noisily, but the man sitting at the table didn't notice him, or, more probably, was immersed in a mysterious music only he could hear. Murashko cleared his throat more loudly, and Zhukov looked up from his blueprint.

"Yes?"

"I've come from Moscow, and . . ." Murashko began.

"Well?" Zhukov interrupted him.

"I would like to offer you a job."

Zhukov threw back his head, laughed out loud, and suddenly fell silent.

"I already have a job," he said abruptly. "I am busy building captive balloons. I don't do odd jobs on the side."

"You've got me wrong," Murashko interrupted him. "Did you not submit a project proposal for a new airship design to the Council of the People's Commissars?"

"The council? Damn you! So you're from the council!" he shouted, jumping up. He grabbed a pile of papers from an open box and hurled them at Murashko.

"There! That's what you wanted!"

"What are these?" Murashko asked.

"Notes from doctors, damn you! Notes saying that I'm of sound mind! I will have you know that Professor Tolmazov and his gang have not managed to drive me insane!" he shrieked in a sudden falsetto. "Nor will they!"

Murashko's calm brought Zhukov back to his senses, but he quickly became flustered again. His eyes flashed angrily beneath his spectacles, and he turned away. "What did you come here for?"

"To invite you to work on our Airship Construction Project."

Zhukov took his sketch pencil and drew a sharp line, leaned back, thought for a few moments, and then said in a calm voice that was more a statement than a question, "You are inviting me to work for you? Are *you* mad?"

Murashko took out an identity card.

Zhukov recoiled in horror.

"What's that?" he gasped.

"No, no, it's only my identity card proving that I am director of the Airship Construction Project."

Zhukov glared at Murashko. Tempestuous, stubborn thoughts were blazing behind Zhukov's steel-rimmed spectacles. He ran his fingers through his hair, quickly rolled up a few blueprints, took two document cases, tied everything together with a piece of string, and put on his hat and coat.

"Let's go," he said.

The two men went into the next room.

"Katya, I'm off to Moscow," he muttered vaguely, and clumsily patted one of his children on the head.

Zhukov's wife dried her hands, came over to her husband, and kissed him on his beard.

"Bring me back some lemons," she told him.

"Don't forget Cicero's linseed . . . Cicero is our starling," he said absently to Murashko over the children's heads, and suddenly roared at them: "And don't give your mother a hard time!"

"Good-bye, Comrade Zhukova," Murashko said, bowing to Zhukov's wife, who was once more immersed in her book.

"Good-bye!" she said, stopped reading, and asked with childish curiosity: "But what are you taking him away for?"

"I really need him," Murashko told her.

The dog opened both eyes at the same time. The starling whistled wildly.

• • •

Murashko and Zhukov stopped at the corner of a deserted provincial street to let a car pass.

"Your position will be—"

"When it comes to airship construction, I'm even prepared to sweep the floors," Zhukov quickly cut in.

Murashko smiled. "You will be our chief engineer, Pyotr Nikolayevich."

Zhukov's beard quivered.

"All that is not important! The main thing is that we'll send them up!"

"Send who up?"

"The Soviet airships."

5.

The reception area of the Economic Council of the People's Commissars. Groups of representatives, directors, and specialists who had come to propose projects—people from all corners of the Soviet Union—sat surrounded by stacks of paper.

A man with a Mongolian face walked past, his embroidered caftan flashing by.

The hallowed doors opened and a man came hurrying out of the conference room, his service jacket awry, his briefcase hanging open with a bundle of papers on the brink of falling out. His deputy, who had been waiting by the door, rushed up to him.

"We have to stick to instruction 380!" the man leaving the conference room whispered angrily.

His deputy stood to attention.

"But allow me to—"

"They won't allow a thing," the first man said in a hollow voice.

Murashko was sitting at a table in the reception area studying some papers. His chief bookkeeper glanced at him with fiery eyes and moaned, "Did you hear that, Comrade Murashko?"

The director of Construction Project Four came hurrying out through the hallowed doors, wiping the sweat from his forehead. His black-haired deputy materialized in front of him in a well-tailored suit.

"They've killed it!" the director stammered.

"On what grounds did they kill it?" his deputy asked, stiffening.

"On the grounds that we need to work within the set budget limits."

Murashko's chief bookkeeper groaned again: "Did you hear that, Comrade Murashko?"

The hallowed doors swung open.

"Airship Construction Project!" the secretary's voice screeched.

The project specialist, a tall man with a pince-nez hanging on a cord, jumped up. He dragged Murashko after him. The doors closed behind them.

Murashko's bookkeeper went over to the deputy of Construction Project Number Four, and in an instant saw him to be a man of his own way of thinking.

"One thing they simply refuse to take into account is that if a man sees things from the government's standpoint, then that man *has* to be taken into account!"

•   •   •

The conference room. Some ten people were sitting at a round table. The project specialist, ingratiating, tugging at the pince-nez hanging on the black cord, poured forth a stream of officialese: "For the most part, our Airship Construction Project has stayed within the parameters of instruction 380. However, given the specificity of the project, some alterations had to be effected on the numbers. As your commission has declared itself ready to increase the maximum on the construction budget, and now proposes a projected funding of 32,446,000 rubles, we would like . . ."

•   •   •

In the reception area, the bookkeeper was jumping up and down outside the hallowed doors of the conference room.

•   •   •

In the conference room, the concluding words of the chairman's response to the project specialist: "In my opinion, Comrades, as your project proposal is insufficiently fleshed out, and as the miserly cost estimate does not offer realistic possibilities for such an important enterprise as the Airship Construction Project, it is my opinion, Comrades, that you must go back and rework the proposal. The time limit for the construction of the airship should be set at eighteen months. For the time being, the amount of capital investment should be fixed at ninety million rubles. We suggest that the Airship Construction Project submit a reworked proposal and cost estimate based on these criteria. Any objections?"

"No," Murashko stammered in a suddenly hoarse voice. "No, none."

The chairman made a sign to the secretary, who was taking the minutes: "No objections."

6.

A car raced along the highway at incredible speed.

A policeman stopped the car at a crossing.

"Your license."

Vasya, sitting in the driver's seat, immediately began to haggle: "I was doing sixty-five, Comrade, and not a kilometer more!"

"You were doing a hundred and twenty," the policeman said. "Whose car is this?"

"Mine!" said Raisa Friedman's voice, and a shoulder draped in a fur boa jutted out of the window.

"And who are you?"

"I'm with the Airship Construction Project," Raisa Friedman answered.

As the car moved on, the shoulder with the fur boa jutted out of the window again: "You should realize who you can stop and who you can't!"

•   •   •

The car pulled into the airship construction area, steering with difficulty among piles of bricks, planks, logs, and vats of cement. It drove past brick walls under construction, excavators gnawing at the earth, and tractors dragging loaded platforms. The car stopped for an instant to let a miniature train pass that was running on a narrow-gauge track. Window frames and standard-issue doors were stacked in a small, open wagon. The rumbling of the excavators, the grinding of the winches, the music of construction. Raisa Friedman was having a production meeting with Vasya as the car stood waiting by the barrier at the rail crossing.

"What would you say if we were to serve some chopped herring as an hors d'oeuvre tomorrow for the engineering and technical staff?"

"Beautiful!" Vasya said.

"And then chicken broth with meatballs."

"Excellent!" Vasya confirmed.

"And then, as a second course, sweet-and-sour stew."

Here Vasya hesitated.

"Well . . . I'm not so sure about that."

"It's a fabulous dish!" Raisa Friedman assured him. "And then for dessert, a strudel."

"Beautiful!" Vasya said, tossing back his head. "Now that you've come here, life will be sweet!"

At the bend in the road, Raisa Friedman jumped out of the car.

"Yes, but think of the price I must pay!" she said as she walked away. "I don't even get to see my husband during the day anymore!"

Raisa Friedman walked past the remains of the barracks and a lone willow tree that was still whole as if by a miracle. The barracks were being dismantled with the speed of lightning.

Raisa Friedman walked majestically up to the foreman.

"Comrade, where can I find the second mess hall?"

"This is it," the foreman said, pointing at the workers demolishing the barracks.

"What? They're tearing it down?"

"That's exactly what they're doing, tearing it down," the foreman agreed.

"And what about my new mess hall?" Raisa Friedman asked in a faltering voice.

"We haven't built it yet. Where are you going, Comrade?"

Hopping through the ruins of the barracks, Raisa Friedman made her way to the main office building. Murashko had a new office there—an unfinished room in which the workers were installing the fourth prefabricated wall with the door in it. But Murashko was already at his desk. Two cleaning women were laying out a carpet on the floor.

Raisa Friedman rushed past Murashko's secretary.

"Comrade Murashko! We don't have one!"

"One what?"

"We don't have a mess hall! This is an outrage!"

"We'll build one!"

"But you told me you were hiring me to run it!"

"There'll be time enough for that. In the meantime, you can round up all the builders and outfitters, and see to it that they—"

They were interrupted by Murashko's secretary, who came staggering in with a flushed face.

"Professor Tolmazov is here," she said in a terrified whisper.

Murashko jumped up, and buttoned his work jacket.

"Well, Raisa Lvovna, the heat is on. Have you ever heard of Tolmazov?"

"Of course I have! Who do you think I am?" she said with dignity.

"Well then, let's start work! I take it I don't have to show you too how things need to be done," Murashko said, quickly riffling through the papers on his desk, hiding a plate of cookies in the drawer, and hurriedly throwing the crumpled-up bits of paper lying on the floor into the wastepaper basket.

"No, I do not have to be shown how things need to be done," Raisa Friedman said with a touch of doubt in her voice. "But you hired me to run that mess hall."

And she left the office.

Murashko pulled the soft armchair closer to the desk.

• • •

In the reception room two men stood talking near the flushed secretary. One, a middle-aged man exuding an air of calm, had short-cropped hair and was wearing an expensive, loose-fitting suit. This was the celebrated Tolmazov. Next to him sat a heavy, wide-shouldered, rough-hewn young fellow with prominent cheekbones and a dour face. This was Tolmazov's student, Vasilyev.

"Ivan Platonovich, I place all my hopes in you," Vasilyev said to Tolmazov. "All it will take is a single word from you!"

"And I will say that single word," Tolmazov answered in a voice as loose-fitting as the suit he was wearing. "I will say that word, Seryozha. We won't let these people here snatch you away from our institute!"

Murashko appeared at the door.

"Please come in, Ivan Platonovich!"

•   •   •

Murashko sat at his desk, Tolmazov in the armchair.

"One sees you so seldom nowadays, Ivan Platonovich," Murashko said.

"But this time around, *I* am the one who is coming for a favor," Tolmazov replied, with almost more coquetry than an academic can permit himself.

"All the luckier for us," Murashko let slip.

Tolmazov looked at him in surprise.

"Having the opportunity, I mean, of doing you a favor," Murashko quickly added. "It would be a great pleasure. There aren't that many pleasures left to us."

The professor smiled.

"That is very kind of you," he said. "I have come to you on account of Vasilyev, one of my students at the institute. He defended his dissertation just recently—a wonderful defense! It was on the subject of my vortex theory."

Murashko nodded sympathetically.

"Vasilyev combines his deep knowledge of aerodynamics with a great meticulousness and exactitude in his work."

Murashko nodded again.

"And then we suddenly find out that Vasilyev is taken away from the institute as a member of the Komsomol and assigned to your Airship Construction Project! I hope, Comrade . . . um . . ."

"Murashko," Murashko prompted him.

". . . Comrade Murashko, that you will not object to him remaining on our faculty at the institute."

"But I do object!" Murashko said. "To be perfectly honest with you,

I did have some misgivings at first about his coming to us, but after the splendid reference you have just given him . . . Well, you'll simply have to let our Airship Construction Project have him."

A shadow flashed over Professor Tolmazov's face. He got up.

"I have no option but to address myself to a higher authority."

Suddenly Zhukov, disheveled, came tearing into the office.

"Comrade Murashko, how could you do that? What a blockhead! On the launch pad, we again have—"

Tolmazov, taken aback, stepped to the side, but Zhukov had already seen him. Both men froze.

"Hello, Ivan Platonovich," Zhukov said after a few moments of silence in an unexpectedly high-pitched voice.

Tolmazov bowed. Then Zhukov bowed too, but bolts of lightning were already flashing in his eyes.

"As you can see, I am alive and have not gone insane."

"Judging by your last article, one might well—"

Zhukov came bounding forward. "You disagree with my position?"

Tolmazov nodded. "I completely and utterly disagree."

"I can't believe you didn't even try to understand what I was saying!" Zhukov shouted, marching toward Tolmazov.

Tolmazov turned to Murashko and explained in a condescending tone, "Pyotr Nikolayevich and I have been arguing for some twenty years now."

"I am aware of that," Murashko said.

"I am trash, that's what I am! Worthless!" Zhukov began yelling, almost in delirium. "While you, you have been blossoming! Handsome! A handsome youth! A handsome man! A handsome old man! A god! Yes, Ivan Platonovich is a god!"

Zhukov squirmed, waved his arms, and ran in circles around the office.

Professor Tolmazov grimaced.

"Are you also here visiting Comrade Murashko?" Tolmazov asked, in an attempt to change the subject.

"Visiting! I'm here because of the airship!" Zhukov sputtered furiously.

"Pyotr Nikolayevich is the chief engineer of our Airship Construction Project," Murashko said, leaning forward slightly.

"Ah," Tolmazov said, visibly shaken.

"Ah, indeed!"

Zhukov's eyes flashed with boyish fire and he ran out of the office, muttering under his breath.

"A dangerous decision," Tolmazov said, completely dropping his official tone. "He is a dreamer, an autodidact! A dangerous man indeed!"

"And yet we have found a counterbalance for him," Murashko said, glancing at Tolmazov. "I received a phone call today. A council of scientists has been appointed to oversee our Airship Construction Project, and it is to be headed by the highly esteemed Professor Tolmazov."

"Me? You're joking!" Tolmazov said.

"No, I'm not joking," Murashko answered. "The main thing for us is to send them up."

"Send who up?" Tolmazov asked.

"The Soviet airships."

7.

A panoramic view of the airship dockyard: hangars scattered over its vast area, gas reservoirs, a mooring mast. Some of the buildings were ready, some were being finished, others were still surrounded by scaffolding. A gigantic excavator was tearing at the earth with its prehistoric jaws and then moving on, tirelessly hacking a path for itself.

The office buildings, the aerodynamics laboratory, and the new mess hall.

The design department. Hot shafts of light were falling onto the drafting tables and the heads of the young women working there.

In the corner stood a desk with a sign above it: "Chief Engineer of Fledgling Bird."

Fate had thrown Natasha Maltseva into a train compartment together with Comrade Murashko, and now this twenty-six-year-old woman with chestnut hair neatly parted in the middle was occupying the position she deserved—that of chief engineer of operations.

• • •

A brightly lit corridor. The shine of the walls, and a hospitallike silence.

Disheveled Zhukov hurried down the corridor with the chief bookkeeper at his heels.

"Comrade Zhukov! Your cleaning woman has sent a request for an advance on her pay!

"Aksinya . . . oh, yes, she's a good woman. A very good woman! Give her five thousand!" Zhukov stammered as he hurried on.

The chief bookkeeper was on the brink of extending his stubby little wings and bouncing into the air.

"Comrade Zhukov, she's only asking for eighty rubles!"

But Zhukov had already disappeared behind the doors of the design department.

Natasha Maltseva raised her calm, intent eyes to Zhukov, and without saying a word handed him a large blueprint with the heading: "High-speed airship *USSR 1*, designed by Zhukov." She made a sign to one of the cleaning women. "Get me Comrade Vasilyev!"

Zhukov quickly riffled through a pile of supplementary blueprints lying on a nearby desk. Then he caught sight of an outline sketch of the cross-section of the airship.

"A fabulous piece of work!"

"Brilliant," Natasha said, with the same calm, intent stare fixed on Zhukov.

Zhukov's spectacles sparkled angrily. "Girlish enthusiasm!"

Natasha shrugged her shoulders. "It's obvious enough that it's brilliant."

Vasilyev entered the office. Zhukov turned to him energetically: "What we need now is your okay to launch this baby!"

"As you can see, Comrade Vasilyev, we have reached the stage of aerodynamics computations," Natasha said quietly. "And that's your field."

Vasilyev walked over to the blueprints and bent over them.

"I don't quite understand this. You are intending to put the gondola—"

"To hell with the gondola!" Zhukov shouted. "Everyone will be inside! Forget the gondolas! Get inside!"

"The fuel tanks—" Vasilyev continued.

"There are no tanks! There is no fuel! There'll be hydrogen engines . . . running on their own gas."

"You see, Comrade Zhukov's basic idea is—" Natasha began.

"I know Comrade Zhukov's basic ideas," Vasilyev interrupted her.

"Nevertheless, I would still like to know where the ship's steering system is!"

Zhukov's eyes flashed beneath his spectacles.

"Well, I'm sorry, but you won't find one!"

"In that case, I would be grateful if you would enlighten me as to how you intend to steer the ship," Vasilyev asked with undisguised derision.

Zhukov came tearing forward, but the drafting table cut off his path.

"You're still living in the eighteenth century! I'm going to install a ring at the tail of the ship which will replace the steering system—the ring will be eight meters in diameter. It will control the ship's direction, speed, and mobility!" And looking at his watch he suddenly shouted, "Good God, it's past four already! And God Almighty, I'm sure, is waiting impatiently. . . . So, Comrade Vasilyev, get working!"

And he rushed off. "A-e-ro-dy-na-mic!" he shouted in a voice that ran from declamation to cock's crow.

Vasilyev stared after him until the door fell shut.

"I don't know who one should contact first, the psychiatric ward or the NKVD,"* he said to Natasha. "Is he insane or a saboteur?"

"He is a genius," Natasha said.

"One that denies that two times two equals four."

"Does two times two equaling four have anything to do with Professor Tolmazov's vortex theory?" Natasha asked archly.

Vasilyev furiously grabbed the table with both hands.

"No, my highly esteemed Comrades," he shouted, as if he were addressing the committee of scientists. "No, Comrades, science plays no role whatsoever here! This is now a matter for the Party to decide!"

"Everything is decided by our Party," Murashko said, appearing suddenly in the doorway. "Calm down, young man."

"Young man? Why, are you old or something?" Aksinya mumbled from a corner.

"Comrade Murashko!" Vasilyev said, drawing himself up. "I am speaking for my whole group when I tell you that we will not attempt

---

* The People's Commissariat for Internal Affairs, which was to become the KGB in 1955.

to work our way through these ravings. I demand that an expert be brought in."

"As in Professor Tolmazov?" Natasha asked, narrowing her eyes.

"Do you know of anyone who is more of an authority in this field?" Vasilyev answered, barely able to contain his anger.

8.

The aerodynamics laboratory of the Airship Construction Project. Airship models hung from the ceiling. A sleek, silver, cigar-shaped model, suspended from a wire, was swaying gently, the gondola and engine within it. Next to it, near the aerodynamics air pumps, stood the airship design commission: Tolmazov, Zhukov, Murashko, Vasilyev, Maltseva, Polibin, and the engineers from the design department. The engines of the air pumps were droning. All heads were turned to the indicator panel.

Maltseva switched off the machine.

Tolmazov walked over to where the models were hanging, and the rest followed him. He stood by the wall, and checked the notes in his notebook.

"Now to the air pump results. I accept the hydrogen engine, it is a risk worth taking. I admit that it does offer a chance for a slight increase in speed."

"A slight increase?" Zhukov interrupted him. "You call going from fifty kilometers an hour to three hundred a slight increase in speed?"

"As for the rest," Tolmazov continued, turning to Zhukov, "I will remind you of some basic facts that every schoolboy knows. The way you have designed the ring that is to replace the steering system, it will inevitably stall in the contiguous stratum of air. In other words, the airship will be unnavigable. I would like to refer you to the handbook issued by the Armstadt Firm in Mannheim."

"I see what you are saying!" Zhukov snapped. "Even the moon was invented by the Germans!"

"You're the one who is aiming for the moon, Comrade Zhukov!" Tolmazov retorted.

"One day we'll even get that far," Zhukov muttered.

Seeing that the discussion was veering from its scientific course, Polibin stepped in.

"I think one could go so far as to say," he began in his mellifluous voice, "that there might be a touch of dilettantism in the model of our highly esteemed Comrade Zhukov. . . ."

"You'll have to get rid of that ring, Comrade Zhukov!" Tolmazov said roughly.

"I must say that my inclination is to agree with Comrade Tolmazov on this point," Polibin's voice purred.

Zhukov sat down in an armchair, clasped his head in his hands, and shut his eyes.

"Years," he whispered, jumping up. "A whole decade . . . pitfalls . . . desperation . . . Am I to be tormented, tormented all my life?"

His thin body began to shake and his eyes filled with pain.

"High priests of science! Archimandrites!" he shouted. "Two fingers, three fingers . . . Old Believers! Followers of Nikon!"*

"Are these the arguments you are proffering?" Tolmazov asked him coldly.

Zhukov closed his eyes and fell silent.

"My argument," he said with unexpected clarity, "is that the airship we are building, I am building, she is building"—he pointed at Natasha Maltseva—"she over there is building"—he pointed at the cleaning woman—"will fly above your damn clerics' heads! It will fly higher, faster, and farther than any other airship has ever flown before!"

Tolmazov shrugged his shoulders.

"That's poetry, not science. In my opinion, the possibility of launching this airship in its present design is completely out of the question."

"I suggest we call a meeting of our committee of scientists," Murashko said in his usual, calm voice.

"A complete waste of time, if you ask me," Tolmazov said, getting up and pushing away his chair.

"This is the first time I find myself in agreement with the highly esteemed Professor," Zhukov said.

---

*Nikita Minin, 1605–1681, Patriarch Nikon of Moscow, initiated reforms in the Russian Orthodox Church that led to a schism. The Old Believers (Starover) refused to accept his liturgical reforms. One of Nikon's most controversial reforms was to change the practice of crossing oneself using the index and middle finger into crossing oneself using thumb, index, and middle finger.

Murashko slowly looked at the others.

"As the results of the aerodynamics experiment were inconclusive," he said in a completely offhand manner, "we will conduct further experiments once the airship is airborne."

"In that case, I have a question," Vasilyev said, dashing toward Murashko. "I have only one very simple question: who will you send up in this flying coffin?"

9.

"The test-flight crew of the airship *USSR 1* reporting for duty! Present are: Eliseyev, captain; Friedman, altitude pilot; Petrenko, navigational pilot; Bityugov, airship engineer; Alexeyev, navigator; Asparyan, radio operator; Gulyayev, first flight engineer; and Borisov, second flight engineer!" Eliseyev, the test pilot, announced, saluting Murashko. Lined up next to Eliseyev outside the closed gates of the hangar stood eight men in Aeroflot uniforms.

A bright July morning. The airfield. A formation of airplanes in the sky.

"Greetings, Comrades!" Murashko said.

"Greetings!" the flight crew replied.

"Which one of you is Friedman?"

Eliseyev took Murashko to a blue-eyed giant.

"This is our altitude pilot Lev Friedman."

"I see our little boy here has grown into quite a man!" Murashko said.

Friedman blushed.

"I hope my mom hasn't been kicking up a fuss again," he said.

The immense gates of the hangar parted. The silver airship *USSR 1* hung suspended from girders.

The assembly crew, its foreman the feisty girl with the unruly mop of curls in front, stood by the airship. Next to her stood Natasha, struggling to contain her excitement. Zhukov was sitting in a chair near the stern of the ship.

The pilots walked around the airship, their eyes filled with hungry curiosity. Friedman furtively shook Mop-head's hand as he walked past. Murashko and the pilots walked over to the front of the ship.

"Go on, Natasha, show them the ropes," Zhukov called out to Maltseva, waving to her to come over. "I'm bound to make a mess of things!"

"Comrades! You see before you the airship *USSR 1,* designed by Engineer Zhukov!" Natasha's unexpectedly powerful voice rang out. "This design is based on a new concept that will guarantee a considerable increase in speed, range, altitude, and, most importantly, safety and ease of navigation."

Zhukov's face, as he listened with closed eyes.

• • •

The new mess hall bathed in light. Starched tablecloths, scrubbed floors, an abundance of flowers.

Raisa Friedman, never missing an opportunity to hold a production meeting: "What would you suggest as a first course?" she asked the chief bookkeeper. "Chopped herring or chopped liver?"

"Cabbage soup, my dear Mrs. Raisa!" the bookkeeper said to her with fervor. "When will you make us some plain and simple cabbage soup?"

• • •

The sun stood high in the sky. The test pilots and construction crew crossed the airfield and walked toward the mess hall. Murashko and Eliseyev, who were both from the same town, were walking next to each other.

"Have you been back home recently?"

"I was just there," Eliseyev said.

"How's everyone doing?"

"They're blossoming," Eliseyev said. "Fedya Kostromi is now secretary of the District Committee."

"Amazing!"

"Vitka is a machine tool operator. Word has it that he has managed to produce several times the required quota."

"What about Varyukha?" Murashko asked.

"She got married. A good fellow, except for Saturday evenings."

"He hits the bottle?"

"And how."

"What about Ponomaryev?"

Behind them, Mop-head and Friedman, walking next to each other: "If you really want to go out with me," she said in a didactic tone, "you don't have to come up with anything fancy. Just figure out how you can get your hands on two *Anna Karenina* tickets, and on Sunday I want to go to Khimki."*

Petrenko, a young pilot, and Agniya Konstantinovna walking together: "Personally, I disagree with Volodya Kokkinaki on the speed issue. But when it comes to range, the airship is a winner. That's what I said to Volodya. . . ."

Borisov, the second flight engineer, a somewhat sad, dour-looking man, was walking next to Vasilyev.

"An interesting machine," he said thoughtfully. "Very interesting indeed. After all, Tolmazov's vortex theory doesn't quite—"

"I disagree with you!" Vasilyev hissed through clenched teeth, quickly looking around. "It's a coffin! A flying coffin! Though I'm not even sure if it can actually fly!"

Borisov's lackluster eyes fixed on Vasilyev with dumb astonishment. Vasilyev again quickly looked around.

"Amateurishness! Recklessness!"

"Wait a minute . . ." Borisov mumbled, dragging out his words. "You—"

"Later," Vasilyev said, noticing Natasha and Mop-head approaching.

"Comrade Vasilyev!" Natasha called out to him. "That's treason! Why, that's worse than treason! It's idiocy!"

"I shall call a Komsomol committee meeting this evening," Mop-head announced, shaking her curls.

Vasilyev flared up: "I will gladly discuss the situation with the Komsomol committee, and I won't stop there either!"

Natasha looked at him as if this were the first time she had ever set eyes on him.

"Are you really such a blockhead?" she asked him slowly and distinctly, with a probing tone as if she were asking herself the question.

---

* A recreational area on the Moscow River.

Vasilyev wanted to answer, but managed to restrain himself. He marched off, but then turned and came back.

"Could you please give me a clean handkerchief?"

Natasha gave him a clean handkerchief, took his dirty one, and dropped it into her handbag.

Mop-head stared at them in amazement.

"What a bastard!"

"What do you mean?" Natasha asked her, surprised.

"He just gave you his dirty handkerchief!"

"He left home in such a hurry this morning that he didn't have a chance to take a clean one," Natasha explained. "Once you get married, you too will be thinking of handkerchiefs and such things."

"He's your husband?" Mop-head gasped.

"You guessed it!" Natasha said, and laughed out loud. "We've been married for over three years now!"

. . .

The entire catering staff stood waiting by the entrance of the mess hall, with Raisa Friedman standing in front.

"Comrade Pilots!" she said to the approaching group, launching into the speech she had prepared. "Allow me to welcome you in the name of the Stakhanovite* Mess Hall Collective . . ." And then she saw her son. "My son! My daredevil son is here!" Mother Friedman shouted.

"Mama," Friedman said, annoyed. "I see you're coasting down the runway again!"

10.

The pilots' dormitory. The night before the test flight.

Petrenko was holding forth: "I told Mishka straight to his face!"

"Which Mishka?"

"Mishka Gromov. Which Mishka did you think? No, Mishka, I

---

*A system named after a coal miner, Alexei Grigoryevich Stakhanov, 1906–1977, in which workers endeavored to increase their efficiency and productivity, for which they were rewarded with bonuses.

told him, I don't agree with you when it comes to altitude procedures. We can reach quite an altitude without those oxygen masks. As long as we keep a cool head."

"You're chattering away when you are about to climb into a coffin," Borisov, the second flight engineer, commented dryly, sitting on his bed.

"What kind of coffin? A brocaded one?" Friedman asked. "Custom-made! Engineer Zhukov's flying coffin with a ring on its tail! I too studied the vortex theory, and I can tell you for a fact that with the ring adhering to the contiguous stratum of air, the ship will be unnavigable."

"Well, it would be nice if Vasya heard what you were saying!" Petrenko yelled.

"Which Vasya?" Borisov asked angrily.

"Molokov, who else!"

"Why don't you just leave me alone!" Borisov said gloomily. "A whole scientific theory is falling apart here."

Eliseyev appeared at the door.

"A committee meeting right before a flight? Off to bed!"

"Aye-aye, Captain!" Friedman replied, and stretched himself out on his bed.

"Comrade Captain, I request permission to make a statement!" Borisov said, his eyes blinking nervously. "On the basis of the flight codex of the Soviet Union, I refuse to take part in the flight, on account of the unreliability of the ring steering system."

Pause.

Silence. Eliseyev's cheekbones rippled, and then froze.

"Fine," he said. "You have every right to refuse. Any more refusals?"

Silence.

"There are no more refusals," Friedman said.

"So there are no more refusals," Eliseyev repeated. "Off to bed, then!" He turned to Borisov: "You will relocate to the Fourth Dormitory."

Eliseyev left the room.

Borisov quickly gathered his things.

Silence. The silence became unbearable.

"Fair enough," Borisov muttered, as he continued gathering his things together. "After all, the flight codex wasn't drawn up for laughs!"

●　●　●

The hydrogen engines were being tested in the hangar. Eliseyev suddenly appeared in front of Murashko.

"The second flight engineer refuses to participate in the test flight on the grounds of the unreliability of the steering system."

"Comrade Captain," Mop-head said, her voice trembling. "As I assembled the whole propeller mechanism with my own hands, I would like—"

"I cannot take anyone without pilot's training on a flight!" Eliseyev said.

" 'I cannot take anyone without pilot's training,' " Zhukov parroted derisively. "Well, who do you intend to take, if not her? That girl isn't reaching for the clouds, she's reaching for the stars."

"Reaching for the stars is not one of the specifications in the service regulations," Eliseyev said with a smile.

"You will go up as a member of the test-flight commission," Murashko told her firmly.

"You expect a thank-you?" Mop-head muttered.

"I can do without one."

"She's reaching for the stars," Zhukov grumbled. "What more do you want?"

11.

Early morning. The slanted rays of the sun. The launch crew maneuvered the airship out of the hangar. The committee of scientists stood nearby.

"I think one could go so far as to say that the contraption has the most original shape imaginable."

This phrase could have been uttered by none other than Professor Polibin.

Tolmazov, standing to the side, noticed Vasilyev nearby and lifted his eyebrows in surprise.

"Aren't you flying?"

"I officially voiced my opinion about this airship," Vasilyev said morosely.

The powerful droning of the engines.

"I would say—" Professor Polibin began.

"So go ahead and say it!" Professor Tolmazov interrupted him so brusquely that Polibin remained speechless.

• • •

Eliseyev, Friedman, and Petrenko were in the airship's control room.

The flight engineer and Mop-head were standing next to the engine crew.

Murashko and Natasha walked through the airship's inner gangway.

"So we'll finally get off the ground, Comrade Murashko!"

"Though it was tough enough to get the go-ahead," Murashko said. "Tolmazov and Vasilyev pulled all kinds of strings to have things stopped."

Eliseyev's command: "Release the lines!"

"Aye-aye, Captain! Releasing the lines!" the starter replied.

"Takeoff!" the starter yelled.

"Aye-aye! Taking off!" Eliseyev answered.

The airship soared into the air.

Zhukov stood by the porthole, his beard quivering, then, his unseeing eyes fixed straight ahead, he stumbled toward the control panel.

• • •

"Increase altitude!"

"Aye-aye, Captain! Increasing altitude!"

"Maintain altitude at eight hundred!"

The smooth, powerful drone of the engines.

Mop-head's rapid, nimble, confident movements as she worked the controls.

Eliseyev's voice: "Full speed ahead!"

"Aye-aye, Captain! Full speed ahead!" the pilot's voice came echoing back.

• • •

On the ground.

The committee of scientists were following the airship's progress.

"I think one could go so far as to say," Professor Polibin's voice came filtering through, "that the atmospheric effect is more or less incapable of paralyzing Zhukov's ring."

• • •

In the airship.

Eliseyev's distant voice: "Keep the course at a hundred and twenty!"

An answer came echoing back immediately: "Aye-aye, Captain! Keeping the course at a hundred and twenty!"

Zhukov glanced at the instruments.

"We've reached a speed of three hundred!" he shouted to the airship crew. He slung open his arms, and Mop-head ran and embraced him, kissed him, and hurried back to the engines.

"Oh, I'm so happy!" Natasha said, looking intently at Zhukov as she always did.

• • •

On the ground.

Polibin could not resist the pleasure of announcing to Professor Tolmazov: "I think one could go so far as to say that the airship is navigating perfectly well along a horizontal plane, which to some extent could be seen as contravening your vortex theory."

• • •

In the air.

Eliseyev's voice over the megaphone: "I'm preparing for a touch-down!"

"Go ahead," Murashko answered joyfully.

Eliseyev's voice, sounding clearer: "Prepare for touchdown! Adjust steering!"

Obedient voices responded immediately: "Aye-aye, Captain! Adjusting steering!"

But there was no loss of altitude.

The airship made another circle. Friedman turned the steering wheel again. Zhukov looked at the altimeter. There was no loss of altitude.

"Comrade Captain!" Friedman announced in a soft voice. "The altitude steering system is not functioning!"

Eliseyev's face flushed.

"Navigate for abrupt altitude loss!"

"Aye-aye, Captain! Navigating for abrupt altitude loss!"

The airship made another circle. Friedman turned the steering wheel. The ring on the tail end of the ship was now shaking. There was still no loss of altitude.

"Good-bye, my little ringlet," Eliseyev sang to himself, "Good-bye, true love of mine!"

The airship made another circle.

· · ·

On the ground.

"What is going on, Comrade Tolmazov?" Vasilyev asked with fear in his voice.

"They cannot land," Professor Tolmazov said, "which was to be expected."

"I beg your pardon?" Professor Polibin barked. "What you said was that they would not be able to take off!"

· · ·

In the air.

"The wind seems to be pushing us upward," Eliseyev said with his customary calm. Then, in an abruptly altered voice: "Navigate for all-out altitude loss!"

Friedman turned the steering wheel with all his might. The ring on the tail end of the ship was now rattling loudly. The steering cables tore.

"I'm turning off the power and going for a static landing," Eliseyev said to Murashko with his usual aplomb. There's no other way I can land with this ring."

The airship went hurtling over the airfield. Eliseyev looked down at the swaying earth.

"Pilots Friedman and Petrenko! Climb up into the body of the airship, check the tail unit, and fix the steering cables!"

"Aye-aye, Captain!"

Eliseyev and the navigator took over the controls. Friedman and Petrenko climbed into an internal shaft in the airship's body and crawled along it, steadying themselves on shroud lines that were fluttering in the wind. Holding on to each other, they crawled toward the tail, groped for the torn pieces of cable, and tied them together in a knot.

The wind began to push the airship down toward the ground.

"How are we doing?" Murashko asked.

"Couldn't be better," Eliseyev answered. "The steering system is functioning again." Then he turned and said into the megaphone, "The whole crew, except for the pilots, prepare to jump!"

"Aye-aye, Captain! Ready to jump!"

"Jump? What for?" Murashko shouted.

"There's no time for explanations!" Eliseyev shouted back, his face crimson. "You will do as you are ordered! You will jump according to emergency guidelines!"

•　•　•

The first to jump was Murashko. After him came the flight engineer, the navigator, the radio operator, and the airship engineer.

Mop-head managed to shake Friedman's hand as she hurried to the escape hatch.

Natasha hesitated for an instant at the hatch.

"What about you, Comrade Eliseyev?"

"Don't ask questions!" he shouted.

And Natasha jumped.

The parachutists hung in the air like little white clouds.

The airship was empty, except for Eliseyev, Zhukov, and the pilots sitting rigidly at the controls.

"Jump, Comrade Zhukov!"

Zhukov refused with a wave of his hand: "Don't talk nonsense! I'm staying to the end!"

A sharp tug at the gas lever. The gas valve opened with a loud clank. The airship began to descend. Eliseyev's face with its high cheekbones flashed for a second—Friedman's wide-open eyes.

•　•　•

On the ground.

Raisa Friedman came out of the mess hall building in her uniform jacket. Behind her came two mess hall workers carrying a large platter with a chocolate cake in the shape of an airship.

"Hurry!" Raisa Friedman said. "They are coming home!"

· · ·

The airship was descending.

"Cast the anchor ropes!" Eliseyev commanded.

The anchor ropes were cast. The airship swayed and shook a few meters from the ground.

The launch crew came running across the field, grabbing for the ropes swinging in the air. The airship's nose bumped against the ground. Eliseyev went tumbling to the side, the control panel split and fell on him. Zhukov fell onto the gangway. The pilots grabbed hold of their control posts.

"Good-bye, my little ringlet," Eliseyev said. "Everything is fine." He wiped the sweat from his forehead.

Friedman was trying to turn the steering wheel with all his might.

"You can get off now, we've landed!" Eliseyev said to him.

· · ·

The parachutists touched down one after another. Vasilyev, distraught, came running up to Natasha.

"Tell me, Seryozha, do you remember which formula we used to calculate the Reynolds Factor?" she asked him, gasping for air.

People were running to the airship. Eliseyev and Friedman lowered Zhukov's motionless body out of the hatch.

Friedman's mother was sobbing. Light tears fell onto the cake.

A fiery, scarlet stream of blood was trickling from under Zhukov's black mane of hair and down his high forehead. His snapped spectacles were hanging limply.

"Zhukov, can you hear me?" Professor Tolmazov, running in front of the others, called out.

The stream of blood on Zhukov's face was now flowing down his cheeks.

12.

Night. Three blinding rays of light from hanging lamps illuminated the inclined heads of Natasha, Varya from the draft department, and Leibovich, an old, kindly, bald, gaunt engineer.

Mop-head's inextinguishable eyes shone from a corner plunged in darkness.

"Are you almost done, Natasha?" she said, barely audibly and without moving.

"Yes."

Natasha's team was looking for a flaw in the airship's design. At the other end of the corridor, in Murashko's office—his new office with heavy furniture, carpets, and portraits hanging on the walls—another team was also searching for flaws in the design.

It was a stormy meeting, as it is in countless commissions where passions reach the pitch that heralds ominous changes in an institution.

Murashko was sitting rigidly at the conference table. He was unusually pale. Hands clenched into fists were being shaken at him, criticism came flying from all sides.

"We signaled you a thousand times!" Borisov yelled.

"We had every right to take chances," Friedman shouted, slamming the water jug down on the table.

Friedman's words were drowned in the roar of voices. An unruffled tenor cut through the roar.

"A tempest in a teacup!" Polibin said, entering the room. Taking out a handkerchief, he dusted off an armchair and sat down.

The scorn, self-importance, and primness bordering on squeamishness with which Polibin settled into the armchair were so incompatible with his usual demeanor that the members of the meeting fell silent.

"Carry on, my dear colleague," Polibin said, putting away his handkerchief and nodding to Murashko. "Please carry on, you have my full attention."

• • •

The design department, filled with the specters of distress and silence.

"Natasha, are you almost done?"

Natasha got up and, hesitating, walked on legs that seemed not her own to Leibovich's drafting table, placed a blueprint on it, and with her eyes motioned to Mop-head.

"Leibovich, I think this is where the problem is!"

The lamps illuminated their heads leaning over the blueprint.

•   •   •

In Murashko's office. Murashko was talking, his head thrown back, his hands leaning on the edge of the table: "I object, and I shall continue to object until the very end!"

"Do get to the point, dear colleague," Polibin interrupted him.

•   •   •

In the design department.

Varya, Natasha, and Leibovich jumped back, as if they had seen a snake slithering over the blueprint.

Natasha closed her eyes and then opened them, her face wet with tears.

"My sweet little Mop-head!" she said, stretching her arms out to her.

"So that's all it was," Varya said, shaking her boyish head bitterly. "So that's why it crashed."

Mop-head looked at Leibovich, then at Varya and Natasha.

"Leibovich! We have found the flaw!" Natasha said. She braced herself, grabbed the blueprint, and went running out of the room.

•   •   •

The committee members came pouring out of Murashko's office and into the corridor in a noisy crowd.

"I will burn that damn airship to a crisp!" Friedman said with uncharacteristic gravity to Petrenko, who was walking next to him. "There won't even be anything left for the gravediggers. You don't know what I'm capable of!"

"Yes, I do," Petrenko said.

Murashko walked past them. Polibin, running with dainty steps, caught up with him and took him by the arm. "Polibin asked to join your Airship Construction Project," Polibin said, "and how was he treated? He was sent packing! But here I am again! I think you will find you haven't gained anything by picking a fight with me!"

And he hurried on with mincing, pattering steps. Natasha came rushing past him, borne on the wings of happiness. These wings brought her to Murashko.

"Well, that's that!" Murashko said to her. "They listened to what I had to say, and their verdict: Murashko will have to suspend all work until everything has been looked into. I'm to get rid of Zhukov, and drag the airship to the nearest scrap heap, or find some pawnshop to pawn it off to."

"Alexei Kuzmich!" Natasha interrupted him, her whole body trembling.

"And that isn't even all! We are to hand over everything to the Justice Department."

"Alexei Kuzmich," Natasha went on in a hushed voice, taking him by the arm. "I found the flaw."

13.

Zhukov was drafting. His face was bent low over the table. The magic light of the lamp fell on his mane of hair and the bandage, through which blood was seeping.

The doorbell.

"Come in," he called, lowering his face even closer to the blueprint.

But it was the front doorbell that was ringing. Natasha, Friedman, and Mop-head were standing outside.

Night. The face of Vasya the driver shimmered through the windshield of his car.

The incessant ringing of the bell.

"He doesn't hear the bell," Friedman said, tugging at the door handle.

The door opened. It wasn't locked. Tiptoeing in, they crossed the hallway and the children's room in which the four little Zhukovs were asleep.

Zhukov raised his head from the blueprint and saw his guests.

"Comrade Zhukov," Mop-head said in a trembling voice filled with clumsy severity and emotion. "In the name of the Komsomol

Committee, and in the name of all our Komsomol members, we would like to express our sympathy, and to affirm—"

"I found the flaw," Natasha said in her caressing voice.

"The airship will fly, Maestro!" Friedman shouted, suddenly stopping short. Zhukov's absent face. The bloodstain, like a star, on his bandage, his eyes fixed over the heads of his guests.

"Comrade Zhukov," Mop-head said, stepping closer. "We must continue working on the project right away."

"This is what we have to continue working on!" Zhukov answered, unrolling a blueprint containing the drawing of a strangely shaped monstrosity. "We have to work on the space capsule of the future."

He tugged at his bandage.

"Here is the realization of interplanetary flight. The flight to the moon! A speed of a thousand kilometers an hour in the outer atmosphere!"

"The moon can wait, Comrade Zhukov," Friedman said. "Come back with us to the airship dockyard."

Friedman and the other Komsomols looked troubled, almost frantic.

"While you are hiding here, Murashko is being put under incredible pressure!" Mop-head said, distressed. "Tomorrow another team is coming to take over, and it will be too late."

"What you are doing is wrong, Comrade Zhukov," Natasha said.

The sound of Natasha's steady, hushed voice made Zhukov shrink, then jump up and stiffen.

"It is of vital importance that the *USSR 1* pass the test," she continued.

"Show me what you have there," Zhukov said, reaching for the notebook with her calculations that she was holding.

Natasha handed it to him.

Mop-head tiptoed into the next room. She picked up the telephone receiver and quickly dialed a number.

"The Central Committee of the Party? Number 518. I want to speak to Comrade Murashko of the Airship Project. . . . Comrade Murashko? We're trying to bring Zhukov back."

"What state is he in?" Murashko's voice came from the receiver.

"His state? He's talking interplanetary space travel. But we're going to drag him over to the airship dockyard now."

Zhukov was sitting silently in front of Natasha's calculations. He got up, and looked about dispiritedly. There was an expression of sadness and helplessness on his face.

"Comrade Zhukov," Mop-head said timidly. "We are all waiting for you. The whole assembly crew is waiting."

Zhukov closed his eyes.

"New aerodynamics calculations," he said, as if speaking to himself. "Changes to the ring. Impossible . . .we'll never manage."

He walked up and down the room with uncharacteristic slowness and fatigue. He smiled unexpectedly at Natasha. He tossed his head back, marched off into the adjoining room, picked up the telephone, and dialed a number. Awkwardly, he spoke provincial words into the receiver: "Have I managed to put a call through to the apartment of the academic, Tolmazov? Should Ivan Platonovich wish to come to the telephone, could he please do so?"

The phone in Tolmazov's apartment had been answered by an elderly woman, a typical Moscow professor's wife, wearing a bright, youthful smock.

"Ivan Platonovich has been asleep for some two hours now. May I ask who is calling?"

"This is Zhukov, who has some business to discuss with Ivan Platonovich, business which in the Soviet Union nobody but he can attend to."

"I would prefer that you did not disturb Ivan Platonovich at this hour," Tolmazov's wife said, and hung up.

"She would prefer . . ." he stammered. "She would prefer that I didn't disturb him. . . ."

14.

Anna Nikolayevna, the professor's wife, was wrong. Tolmazov was not asleep. Zhukov's blueprints were spread out on his long table.

Tolmazov was studying one blueprint after another. He was disheveled, and his fingers were trembling. His trembling fingers picked up an ashtray. The ashtray fell.

Anna Nikolayevna's heavily painted and powdered face appeared in the doorway.

"You're not in bed, Ivan Platonovich?"

"As you can see . . ."

"That Zhukov fellow called. I didn't call you—"

"Call him back immediately!"

"I simply cannot understand you!" she said in a hurt voice. "One minute you're yelling that he's stark-raving mad, and the next . . ."

Tolmazov was poring over the blueprints.

"As you're not sleeping, I'd like to have a little talk about Tamara. She wants to go to a resort."

Tolmazov raised his head from the blueprints.

"Zhukov is mad," he said. "But Tamara is normal, you're normal, Polibin is normal, and along with all of you I too have become normal—I have stopped being Tolmazov!"

"Lord in heaven, Ivan Platonovich! What are you saying?" Anna Nikolayevna gasped, almost in tears. "Everyone is saying that the airship couldn't land, and here you are—"

"You fool!" Tolmazov said in a stifled voice. "So how come it took off, then?"

"You're the one who should answer that question," a voice came from the door.

Tolmazov turned around. Murashko was standing in the doorway.

"How did you get in here?" Anna Nikolayevna whispered.

"The maid let me in."

The maid, half dressed and flustered, appeared behind him.

"Go away," Tolmazov said to his wife.

Anna Nikolayevna left the room, bursting into tears the moment the door closed.

Tolmazov stood in front of the blueprints as if he were guarding them.

"We need your help," Murashko said.

"Why should I get involved?"

"So that we can see the *USSR 1* through its test flight, so that the Tolmazov Vortex Theory can be modified and developed, and so that the Soviet Union will recognize that Pyotr Zhukov is one of its most outstanding engineers. These are the reasons why Professor Tolmazov must work on the aerodynamics computations of Zhukov's ring."

"I don't quite understand what you mean."

Tolmazov's hands were shaking.

"I think you do understand. And what you must also understand is that it is of the utmost importance . . ."

Tolmazov's baffled face.

". . . of the utmost importance that the airships fly. The Communist Party, the Soviet Union, charged me with this enterprise. And I shall . . . how should I put it . . . I shall carry it out, come what may!" Murashko sat down. "I am waiting for an answer."

15.

Polibin leaned back in the seat of a very elegant car. Next to him sat Vasilyev, with an even more dour expression than usual.

Fields of ripened rye flew past.

"My young friend," Polibin proclaimed. "I think one could go so far as to say that you are not quite satisfactory in your position. People come, people go. I personally would prefer to see a little more self-confidence, indeed, aplomb, in a deputy chief engineer. . . . You should model yourself on Professor Tolmazov."

"Not much point in that. That test flight really shook him up."

"It's all plain and simple, my young friend. The test flight totally compromised Zhukov and victoriously brought to the fore our celebrated Professor Tolmazov's vortex theory. It is what billiard players call a lethal combo, when the cue tears the cloth, smashes the lamp hanging over the billiard table, and goes plunging into the opponent's eye. But I have to say that you should have shown more spirit in the high position you were accorded. Had you done so, Zhukov and company would not have strutted about the way they did!"

The car sped past dimly flowing fields toward the airship construction site.

• • •

On the airship dockyard Mop-head's assembly brigade was disassembling components of the ring.

"Keep up the good work, Comrades!" Mop-head's echoing voice rang out. "We, the Komsomol brigade, must not flag!"

"When did we ever flag?" a gangly fellow covered in engine grease said in a deep voice.

Aksinya, ever-present, appeared at the door: "The design department wants you."

Mop-head hurried off. She had to run fast, as the new director of construction did not like to be kept waiting.

The new director of construction was Ivan Platonovich Tolmazov.

"Comrade Maltseva, we shall now test the side sections! Comrade Leibovich, you have four hours to complete the calculations! Where is the assembly brigade leader?"

"Here I am," Mop-head said timidly.

"What is your name?"

"Anya Ivanova."

"Hey, did you hear that, everyone?" someone called out. "Mop-head has a name!"

"The ring has to be dismantled by six o'clock, Comrade Ivanova! Zhukov! Are you asleep?"

"No, I'm not asleep," Zhukov answered.

He looked at Tolmazov, who had taken off his jacket, and peered at him shyly and filled with admiration. Then he went hurrying aimlessly from one drafting table to the next.

"Seryozha," Tolmazov called out to Vasilyev, who was standing transfixed by the door. "Where did you disappear to? Go check the progress on the ring. We're flying tomorrow!"

"Flying on what?" Polibin's tenor resounded from behind Vasilyev.

Polibin scuttled over to Tolmazov on his little legs, leaned toward him, and, unable to contain his rage, shrieked, "Involvement is very praiseworthy in an academic, but in this case possibly too late!"

Murashko appeared at the door. Polibin shuffled his little legs. "Greetings, Comrade Murashko!" he said. "I have come from the Central Office. The investigative commission charged with looking into the crash has been appointed, and I am the chairman of this commission. First things first: I want you to seal the hangar and issue an order for all work to cease immediately!"

"Not until I have that in writing," Murashko said.

"The written order has already been dispatched," Polibin, who seemed to have grown in height, announced.

16.

In the building next to the hangar, Vasilyev and Natasha were working quickly and silently linking two cables.

Mop-head and Friedman were crouching behind some bushes next to the gas container and hastily uncoiling an electric cable from a metal container.

In a booth not far from the airship project's main building, Vasya the driver and Varya from the design department were joining wires and attaching a lever to a marble slab.

Vasya looked at his watch and pulled the lever down.

A thick cloud of smoke rose from the metal container in the bushes.

Petrenko sat reading a book in the control room of the airship project building.

A siren wailed, followed by loud bells. Little red lights began to flash, the emergency telegraph system rattled into action, and the many phones on the control-room table began to ring.

Petrenko grabbed two receivers at the same time: "A fire at the gas purification unit? And also in the first and second hangars? And in the depot?"

Petrenko dropped both receivers and picked up the only one that wasn't ringing.

"Connect me to Murashko's apartment! The director of the Airship Construction Project! The director!"

Petrenko's howl reverberated through the control room.

Clouds of black smoke covered the sky.

Fire engines sped toward the gas purification units.

• • •

"The smoke is nearing the hangar, Comrade Murashko," Eliseyev's calm voice came over the phone.

"What action do you propose?" Murashko asked.

"I propose that the airship be launched."

"Follow all the emergency procedures," Murashko said, placing the receiver back on the hook, and for the first time in many days smiled.

The airmen pulled their uniforms on as they ran.

The launch crew brought the airship out of the hangar as quickly as possible.

A group of Komsomols from Mop-head's brigade came running with fire extinguishers.

Oily black smoke rose, forming a spreading row of clouds in the sky.

The airship went soaring up into the air.

It flew over the highway along which Polibin's car was speeding.

Hearing the drone of the engines, Polibin looked out the window and saw the rising airship.

Murashko came out of his office and turned to his secretary: "Have them turn off the fire alarm."

Mop-head radioed Murashko from the airship: "Perfect steering! Speed 240! Everything in order!"

The airship unexpectedly turned toward the wind.

"Set the course at 120!" Eliseyev ordered.

"Aye-aye, Captain! Setting the course at 120!" Petrenko replied.

The airship responded smoothly to all the commands, gradually picking up speed.

Then came time to test the toughest maneuver.

"Descend in a spiral!" Eliseyev ordered.

"Aye-aye, Captain! Descending in a spiral!" Friedman answered, anxiously gritting his teeth.

The two-hundred-meter-long silver cigar went into a spiraling nosedive, stopped short in the nick of time, and swung up again in a steep ascent.

Natasha radioed Murashko: "The spiraling descent was successful, Comrade! Everything in order!"

Murashko was leaving the main building when he ran into Polibin, who was carrying a package.

"I wonder what we're paying these firemen for! They are not doing much good!" Murashko said to him, and walked off into the field.

Two old men were sitting on an empty, upturned crate outside the hangar, shading their eyes from the sun as they watched the airship floating high in the sky. A group of workers and airship builders was standing nearby. An old metallurgist from the assembly crew came over and sat down next to the old men, and, shading his eyes, also watched the airship. The two old men were Zhukov and Tolmazov.

The airfield filled with airmen, journalists, and air force workers, all of whom had come in from Moscow.

It was now the third hour of *USSR 1*'s test flight. The records in height and speed had already been broken.

A plain-looking man of about fifty came up to Murashko. He had been the chairman of the commission at the Economic Council of the People's Commissariat, which had authorized the higher funding estimates for the Airship Construction Project.

"Well, Comrade, I've been transferred from the Economic Council," he said to Murashko.

"Where to?"

"I'm now back at the Central Committee of the Communist Party. I'm telling you this because I want you to come and see me over there. After all, the Airship Construction Project is no longer a 'construction project.'"

The last view of the silvery airship *USSR 1* in the fiery sky.

17.

A lean man came out of the Central Committee of the Soviet Communist Party at number 4 Staraya Square. He stopped for a moment, and then headed for the line of cars parked outside the entrance.

The car drove off.

"Moscow?" Vasya asked.

"No, the outskirts."

Pause.

"Well, Comrade Murashko? Who are we now?"

"We're the high-altitude bomber project, that's who we are. Factory number . . ."

Moscow flew past the windows.

TWO SCENES FROM
THE FORGING OF STEEL

The following two pieces, "The Germans in the Ukraine" and "In Petlyura's Prison," are scenes from a screenplay Babel was working on between November 1937 and February 1938 with the actress Yulia Solntseva. It was based on Ostrovsky's best-selling novel The Forging of Steel *(translated into English as* The Making of a Hero*). Ostrovsky's novel is a Socialist Realist bildungsroman about a young man achieving maturity as a model Communist during the years of the Russian Civil War (1918–20).*

The complete screenplay has not survived. The movie The Forging of Steel, *directed by Mark Donskoi, with whom Babel had worked on the Gorky trilogy, premiered in 1942. It is not clear, however, whether Babel's screenplay was in any way used.*

The Germans in the Ukraine

Kaiser Wilhelm II's soldiers are marching along the main street of Shepetovka, stamping their boots. They are wearing dark gray uniforms. On their heads, steel helmets. On their rifles, bayonets broad as knives. The officers march in front of the rows of soldiers, their long legs flying high. Small, white, stony faces shudder on thin necks; colorless stares are fixed straight ahead, past people cowering against walls. These are typical shtetl people of the time: hunched-over Jews in yarmulkes and coats tied with string; boys from cheder, their sap already drained by the *Principles of the Torah,* with chestnut-brown *peyes* hanging in a curls down the sides of large-eyed, doleful faces; workers' wives wrapped in heavy shawls; peasants in white smocks and wide-brimmed hats made of coarse straw. Next to them lies, bitterly twisted, a world of monstrously crisscrossing, rotting beams, Hasidic hovels, and wooden synagogues stretching up narrowly to the sky.

Drums roll. The rectilinear roar of marching bands ricochets down the jagged streets. The artillery comes rumbling loudly onto the main street.

"What power!" an old man in a torn shirt sighs.

"We'll have to figure out something," a youth answers vaguely, and disappears into the crowd.

. . .

At Shepetovka Station. Germans in helmets with eagles atop are dragging struggling animals to boxcars: gray Ukrainian oxen, offended squealing pigs, and meek calves. Weapons, machine guns, and soldiers are being loaded onto another train.

From a trackman's hut two Ukrainians are watching the soldiers embark.

"Even if the partisans tried their hand," one of them says slowly, "how could they hope to tackle such a force?"

A broad-chested, red-faced commandant in a new belt and a high gray Prussian-style military cap with a patent leather brim is furiously striding down the platform alongside the trains.

The doors of the boxcars slowly open. The commandant jumps onto the step of a first-class car. A dark blue, oily locomotive, enveloped in steam, is quivering in front of the train. The commandant raises a whistle to his lips.

"*Abfahrt!*"*

The train does not move.

"*Donnerwetter!*"† the German mumbles, flushing a deep red.

He rushes up and down the platform, his bottom wobbling, his meaty purple face stuck on his stiff neck. Gasping for breath, he hurries to the locomotive. There is an unbearably shrill whistle as steam escapes. The dials on the instruments swing wildly. The locomotive stands empty, the engineer has disappeared.

"*Das ist Russland!*"** the commandant says to an orderly. He steadies himself on the handrails, thrusts out his fat legs, and climbs down from the locomotive.

* German: "Depart!"
† German: "Damn it!"
** German: "That's Russia for you."

· · ·

At the railroad depot, two metalworkers are working on adjacent work-benches: Artyom Korchagin, a giant with a perpetually guilty look on his face, and Zhukhrai, a stocky, well-proportioned man in a Ukrainian peasant shirt, with a powerful, even glow in his eyes.

"So, what's your take on the Communist Party?" Zhukhrai asks Artyom, looking him straight in the eye.

Artyom's face looks even more guilty than usual.

"I don't really have much of a take on any of those parties, Fyodor Ivanovich," he says in an unsure voice. "They need help, so I help . . ."

"Are you going to join the strike?" Zhukhrai asks him, still staring him in the eye.

"I'll do whatever the other men will do."

"How about leading the other men for a change?" Zhukhrai says, peering at him slyly.

Suddenly the doors of the depot open with a loud rumble. The commandant comes marching through the work hall with stomping, echoing steps, his aiguillettes and buttons sparkling, his boots immaculately polished. Two Prussian sergeant majors, inhumanly large living pillars, come marching behind him, followed by a pathetic figure who comes scurrying on feeble legs clad in tattered trousers, his mustache drooping and the tip of his nose quivering.

The commandant, his neck rigid, barks out a tirade of chopped German words.

"*Übersetsen! Übersetzen Sie, bitte!*"* he says over his shoulder to the man with the quivering nose.

· · ·

INTERPRETER: Well, what the German general is saying is that you
   laborers can dream all you want—nothing's gonna happen."
COMMANDANT [*Unleashes another tirade of German—wheezing, barking,
   with a cascade of chopped words. Single phrases can be made out:* Seine
   Majestät, Kaiser und König.]: His majesty, our King and Kaiser . . .
   His Excellency, the Grand Field Marshal and Commander of . . .

---

* German: "Translate! Translate, please!"

in opposing Germany, you oppose God. In opposing God, you
oppose Germany!

INTERPRETER: Well, what he's saying is, get all the engineers and the
trains set up, 'cause Germany's got to be fed.

[*The* COMMANDANT *points at* ARTYOM KORCHAGIN.]

INTERPRETER [*To* ARTYOM.]: You!

[*The two* SERGEANT MAJORS *march toward* ARTYOM *like moving pillars.
The* COMMANDANT *points his finger at* POLENTOVSKY, *a lean,
stooped old man with a silver-gray, short-cropped head of hair.*]

INTERPRETER [*To* POLENTOVSKY.]: You too, old man!
ARTYOM [*His eyes still fixed on the ground.*]: What do you want us for?
INTERPRETER: Let's go!
ARTYOM [*His eyes fixed on the ground.*]: Where to?
INTERPRETER: You're going to run the military train for the Germans.
ARTYOM [*Turning away.*]: I'm a sick man.
INTERPRETER [*Pointing at the two* SERGEANT MAJORS.]: We've got doc-
tors here who know how to take care of a sick man.
COMMANDANT [*His face flushing a deep crimson.*]: *Donnerwetter!** We
know how to show our appreciation for service!
INTERPRETER: He says he'll give you a nice tip.
ARTYOM: I told you I'm a sick man.
INTERPRETER [*To one of the* SERGEANT MAJORS.]: You take over, Doc-
tor!

•   •   •

Artyom, his large arms dangling by his side, walks with gray-headed
Polentovsky through the depot steeped in heavy metallic twilight. The
sergeant majors and the commandant with the rigid neck are marching
behind them.

"Artyom," Zhukhrai says in a low voice, his eyes fixed straight
ahead.

---

*"Damn it!"

"How dreadful," Artyom whispers sadly.

"They're taking the train into battle," Zhukhrai says in an even lower voice.

A painfully harsh roll of drums. A forest of short bayonet knives moves past the railroad workshop.

The depot gates roll toward each other hopping on narrow rails, and suddenly, with a thundering hullabaloo, the whole workshop jumps to life.

"Well, boys, time to go home!" Zhukhrai says in his usual rough voice, throwing his overalls on the ground. "Okay, boys! The party's over!"

"Sergey, we're striking!" a cheerful, ringing boyish voice flies through the workshop.

"We'll be done for, Fedya," says a pensive older worker wearing an apron and a black leather strap over his clean, high forehead.

"We won't run the train for the Germans!" Zhukhrai answers. "We're not running anything that's against the Workers' Cause!"

"What are you teaching the people with your black soul?" A crimson face with a heavy mustache rises before Zhukhrai.

"We won't run the train!" Zhukhrai says in a low voice, raising his face, which turns pale. A dull, growing hissing, the clanking of steel, the spasm of an underground rumble, keeps coming nearer.

A swanlike cloud of smoke flies past the window, flares up in a flash, and dissipates. The blue locomotive with its oily, darkening sides floats past the window.

"How did we get into this bind, Artyom?" Zhukhrai mutters.

• • •

A train with gun cars rolls past the window, their squat gun barrels threatening the sky, armored train cars with blindly sparkling headlights, airtight boxcars with people's souls sealed in them.

The train has passed. The night outside the window is clear. Above it the ghastly, narrow lamp of the moon has lit up. The slackening crackle of transmission in the workshop, the slackening movement around the workbenches.

The train carrying the soldiers of Kaiser Wilhelm II hurtles through the darkness of the Ukrainian steppes. Flashing by are forests, ravines, a hamlet—little hovels shining blue in the moonlight—blue trees in blossom.

"They're taking this train into battle," Artyom says, throwing coal into the firebox. "What a mess we're in!"

Illuminated by the flames' rosy gold, he bangs shut the iron hatch, wipes his face covered in sweat and coal dust with his sleeve, sits down on a stool, and lets his black hands fall. A German soldier, wearing a helmet with an eagle on it, is sitting on the coal tender, his fat legs dangling down. Night. The sparkling moon has sunk into a lake, on land sunflowers are hanging their dark heads.

• • •

ARTYOM: We've gone about twenty versts.
POLENTOVSKY [*Looking out the window.*]: We're at the crooked gully.
ARTYOM: Yes, we are. [*Suddenly with all the desperation of his dark, kind soul.*]. This German's a human being, just like you and me!

[*The* GERMAN *puffs up his cheeks; he is smoking a long, black, two-kopeck cigar.*]

ARTYOM: What has he ever done to anyone?
POLENTOVSKY: What have *we* ever done to anyone?
ARTYOM [*Dejectedly.*]: It's a sin, that's what it is.
POLENTOVSKY: Sin's got nothing to do with it.

[*The* GERMAN, *puffing out his fat cheeks, sucks on the cigar, snorts, and, nestling his rifle, dozes off.* ARTYOM *towers over him, blocking out the sky, a crowbar in his hands. The* GERMAN'*s body topples onto the platform of the tender.*]

POLENTOVSKY [*Straightens up, his eyes shining.*]: No, sin's got nothing to do with it.

• • •

The train hurtles through meadows, among indistinctly lit flowers. The moon floats effortlessly in the thundering expanse. Two shadows hurl themselves from the locomotive and go rolling down the embankment.

The train, liberated, with no one running it, quakes, goes tearing toward a ravine, screeches over a bridge, and, its indicator arrows spinning, flies out of control, is illuminated, surges into the air.

Explosion.

Crates of ammunition explode one after the other in the pile of flaming debris.

In Petlyura's Prison

People lying motionless on bunk beds and in shadowy corners. Weak light trickles through a little window high up by the ceiling. An old man is sleeping huddled by the wall, his open mouth twisted. One of his cheeks is covered with raw scar tissue. Across the cellar from the window, a woman with a shawl wrapped around her plump round shoulders is delousing a girl whose head is resting on her lap. Pavel, his face slashed, is lying in the far corner on the rough dirt floor. A peasant girl in a kerchief and bast shoes comes tiptoeing quietly and timidly up to him.

"So, what's your name?" the old man by the wall, waking up, asks her in a hoarse voice.

"Krista," the girl answers, barely audibly.

The old man's snoring echoes once more through the cellar.

The girl squats down to give Pavel a cup of water. Pavel's thin hand shudders, his teeth are chattering.

"People are saying there is no God," Krista whispers, her eyes fixed on Pavel, who is lying stretched out on the floor. "Can there be a God when young people suffer like this?"

She spreads out her skirts the way peasant girls do and sadly rests her head on her hand. Outside the cellar door there is a burst of loud voices, soldiers' laughter. The bolt of the door clanks, and Krista shudders. She gets up. A Cossack captain wearing a blue sleeveless jacket, his head shaved except for a long forelock,* enters the cellar, his clumsily fastened spurs clattering on the floor. He is a fat young man with a pink, flabby face. He winks at Krista, and, wiggling his finger, beckons her to come over. She comes toward him, tottering in zigzags like an injured bird.

"So, you want to stay cooped up in here forever?" the captain says, nudging her with his fat shoulder.

---

* Ukrainian Cossacks shaved their heads, leaving only a forelock, known as a *chub*.

"Please, sir, don't," Krista says, raising eyes filled with unbearable, sparkling anguish to the captain.

The red-cheeked Petlyura fighter bends closer to her and winks at her again slowly, while his other eye stares lifelessly straight ahead.

"I could maybe arrange things, if you'd like me to."

"Please, sir, no!"

"Well, if it's 'Please, sir, no!' then I'll have to hand you over to the Cossacks."

His spurs jingling like bells, the captain marches out, broad, fat-legged, his back round. Krista watches him leave, her face filling with pitiful, childlike perplexity. Then, silently, without warning, she collapses on the floor.

"They're going to torment her," the woman with the shawl over her shoulders sighs.

"What's there to cry about?" the old man, who had been sleeping, says complacently. "Give the bosses whatever they want, and they'll go easy on you!"

"You're an old man, Grandpa, an old man, but still a fool," the woman delousing the little girl's thick hair says.

Pavel's burning eyes are fixed on the woman. Thoughts are battling within those eyes. Pavel raises himself up from the floor, his parched lips part.

"Don't give in, Krista!"

Curled up with her head on her knees, Krista rocks back and forth endlessly, monotonously, inconsolably.

"How can I stand up to all of them?" Her voice, barely audible, sounds as if it were coming from far away. "Oh, what a hard life this is! Oh, how they will torture me, those cursed . . ."

"If you had played your cards right, you could've been home by now," the old man says with indifference, and nestles up closer to the wall.

"But I'm a virgin," Krista says, raising her head.

The bolt of the opening cellar door clanks again. A very tall, haggard, stooping clerk with a pince-nez enters the cellar, warily sniffing the air.

In his hand he is holding a sheet of paper covered with writing.

"Christina Filipovna Gnatyuk?"

He runs his blazing eyes over the sheet of paper:

"District?"

Krista shrinks back toward the wall.

"Kiev, Shepetovsky District."

"Russian Orthodox?"

"Yes."

"How much land do you own?"

"We're landless."

"You know how to sign your name?"

Krista nods.

"Then sign these discharge papers."

"Oh, thank you, sir!"

The girl rushes over to the stooped clerk with the pince-nez and kisses his large, vein-covered hand, straightens up, and turns to the other prisoners.

"Farewell, good people."

She turns to Pavel: "Farewell, sweet boy."

The door closes behind her and the bolt clanks. The old man lights a shriveled cigarette and blows out a vigorous stream of smoke.

"She'll go to her village, to her father's house, and make herself four, five dozen *piroshkis*."

Outside the door, Krista's piercing shriek, rushing steps, thudding bodies. The old man lifts his head, cups his ear, and listens. "They're ruining the poor girl."

The dull thuds of Pavel throwing himself against the door. He thrusts himself against it with all his might, crazed, his head reeling, banging his fists against it. A guard slides open the grill in the door, his face appears.

"You want me to hit you with my rifle butt?"

AFTERWORD

A PERSONAL MEMOIR

by Nathalie Babel

*The Arrest of My Mother**

My mother, Evgenia Borisovna Babel, née Gronfein, was arrested a few months before my twelfth birthday. It was in the spring of 1941, just after the collapse of the German-Soviet Pact. Stalin and Hitler were no longer allies, and all persons of Russian origin resid-

---

* I have adapted some of the material in the first section of this memoir from my introduction to the second edition of *The Lonely Years,* published in 1995 by Verba Mundi Books, David Godine, Boston.

ing in occupied France were now thought to be politically dangerous. Many were arrested. The provincial town of Niort in the west of France, where the 1939 *exode* had deposited us, had little experience with political prisoners in those days. The local French police just rounded up the dozen or so Russian women of the town and took them to the local jail. There were only women, no men. The children were left at home alone or with neighbors. I was left alone. Sometimes concerned neighbors invited me for meals or to spend the night. But most of the time, I managed by myself.

As I remember them, these Russian women were middle-aged or aged women of the old Russian Orthodox intelligentsia, the bygone bourgeoisie, and even one tall, impressive-looking lady with a mane of white hair, who had been in attendance at the court of the late Empress Alexandra. Together, this genteel and distinguished group was put into the jail with a variety of criminals. The prison warden understood quite quickly that these ladies had little in common with the usual population there, and so he decided to separate them from the ordinary inmates. They did not partake in the routine activities of prison life, were allowed in the courtyard at odd periods, and had different visiting hours than the rest of the prisoners.

Clearly, these women were not dangerous, but nevertheless, rules had to be followed when it came to visits. A permit was required before I could visit my mother, to be issued by both the French and German authorities. I remember going from office to office, taking the necessary steps to obtain the right to visit my mother—visits that lasted only a few minutes. I was allowed to come and see her twice a week, if my memory serves me correctly. My mother, flanked by two policemen, would be brought to a gate. I was behind another gate, accompanied by another policeman. The two gates were separated by a kind of ditch across which we spoke. Sometimes we were permitted to embrace and kiss each other, a favor for which I had obtained authorization in a special section of the police.

This went on for a few weeks, settling into a routine. Then one day, at the very beginning of the visit, my mother said to me very quickly in Russian, "The others have been freed. If you don't get me out right away, I will perish." The guard cut her off after these few words. But I had understood perfectly.

I looked for help, but there was none. I spoke with people. They were all afraid. I went to the French authorities. I saw the mayor. I attempted without success to see the *Préfet*, the highest administrator of the whole area *(département)*. However, I did meet the official door-keeper *(huissier)* of this august personage, and was so dazzled by the gold braids of his uniform that I mistook him for the *Préfet* himself. Each of these officials said that he was powerless, that the problem stemmed from the larger problems between Germany and the Soviet Union.

Then I met a man who had helped me at the jail. Sometimes we had waited together to see our respective relatives—his wife had been arrested for black-market chicken trading. We used to talk, and one day he noticed that I was distraught and crying. "Only the Germans can solve your problem," he told me. Then he wrote out on a piece of paper the name of the head of the local *Kommandantur*, saying that this person was an older career officer. "You must go to the *Kommandant* of our town. He is a decent man, and you have a chance."

The German *Kommandant* happened to be of old French ancestry and was married to an Englishwoman. His name, I recall, was Du Barry. Everyone advised me against going to see him, saying it was much too dangerous. So I went alone.

It was a brilliant summer day. Birds were singing, and drops of water from a garden hose were playing on the windowpanes of the officers' receiving rooms. How I managed to get inside the *Kommandant*'s office, I cannot remember. But I imagine that each soldier of whom I asked directions was too startled to do anything but give them to me. And then, there he stood inside his chamber. Huge maps with small flags covered the walls. I can still see his uniform, his medals, and his aide, whom he dismissed after taking a look at me, the petitioner.

He came forward from behind his desk and astonished me with some words of welcome in French. I told him that my mother was innocent, that I had no one else, and that he had to let her go. Two days later, on July 16, the day before my twelfth birthday, my mother walked into the courtyard of our small house. The weather was beautiful. I was standing outside chatting with a few of the neighbors. She opened the gate and walked in with a smile, as if everything were normal. We all stood transfixed, before moving toward her. I remember the sensation of being in a slow-motion picture, before I started experiencing enormous relief and joy. I did not feel surprised, because in my heart I knew that she had to return for us to have the chance to survive.

How did it happen that she was released? *Kommandant* Du Barry had summoned her, interviewed her, and could not have failed to be surprised by her refined and completely fluent German. She had acquired it many years before, thanks to the ministrations of a Prussian *Kinderfräulein*, a most energetic mentor in my grandfather's household. *Kommandant* Du Barry made my mother promise not to escape, asked her to come every day to the *Kommandantur* to sign her name in a register, and then let her go. She gave him her word of honor, and every day until the German army fled in tatters and panic, she came in to sign.

But why was my mother not released with the other Russian ladies? Why was she and none of the others kept in jail, clearly destined to go somewhere else where they would process her and her case? It was because the other prisoners were émigré Russian Whites, whereas she was Red. She was the wife of Isaac E. Babel, the well-known Soviet writer and a Jew. Although I was born in Paris, I was his daughter, and therefore I was Red, too. By the time the historical and political events I am describing took place, my mother had already lived in Paris for over fifteen years. But she had always kept her Soviet passport, which had to be periodically renewed. Each visit to the Soviet Embassy was such an ordeal that she had let her papers expire, a fact which created more obstacles for her, and even more complications for her husband.

And why did she keep her Soviet nationality? She had very little choice. She could have applied for a Nansen passport.* But as the wife of the writer Isaac Babel, she was dependent on the money he sent from Russia to support us, while she lived in Paris, ostensibly temporarily to study art. She could not very easily sever all her ties with the Soviet Union without bringing severe harm to her husband. And like so many others, she could not renounce forever the possibility of returning one day to Russia.

---

* The Nansen passport was devised in 1922 by a High Commission for Refugees under the League of Nations headed by the Norwegian explorer Fridtjof Nansen. This passport, which was provided to all Russians claiming émigré status, certified the holder's identity and category of statelessness. It was officially adopted in France in 1924, the same year France formally recognized the Soviet Union.

My first official encounter with the Soviet authorities had taken place with my father years before. When he came to Paris in 1932 and met me for the first time (I was three years old), he took me to the Soviet Embassy and had my name entered into his passport, making me de facto a Soviet citizen. It was undoubtedly a cautious political move on his part. But on the other hand, we also knew, from the hundreds of letters he sent to his relatives abroad, that he harbored the utopian dream of having his whole family around him back in Russia. Yet he had been instrumental in obtaining exit visas for his mother, his sister, and his wife. I believe that this dream was anchored in some reality until Gorky's death in 1936. After that time, my father's repeated calls for us to join him in Moscow were no doubt for the benefit of a very vigilant censorship. There were clearly various hypotheses as to why he registered me as a Soviet citizen. Still, for many years, my mother resented this step he had taken on my behalf.

While I was growing up during the 1930s, we belonged neither to the White émigré group, most of whom were Russian Orthodox, nor to the Reds—the Communist colony in Paris. There was a social ambiguity in this position, and also a moral challenge for my mother. The Whites knew who she was, and that her husband had been celebrated by the hated regime. So they were not always comfortable with her. The Reds knew of Evgenia Borisovna's feelings of detestation for them, and certainly did not expect her to join them even socially. Nonetheless, a large part of our daily experience was Russian: language, stories, recollections of the Gronfeins' family life in Kiev before the Revolution, Russian customs and foods.

My mother also had to explain my father's absence to me. The main reason she gave was that, as a writer, Babel could not separate himself from his land and native language, which were indispensable tools for his creative art. She convinced me of the nobility of his beliefs, and made sure that I felt love and respect for him and his commitment to his writing. It was only much later in my life that I was able to look at this idealized image of my father with a more critical eye.

In addition to our Russian world, there was the indisputable fact that we lived in France. I have always felt comfortable in both worlds, although there were many differences between my classmates and myself. First of all, besides French, I could speak another language incomprehensible to them. This alone marked me as being different. Moreover, when I was asked at the beginning of each school year about what were my parents' professions, I answered, "Both of my parents are artists. My father a writer, and my mother a painter." This also drew attention, as well as the fact that I had a cosmopolitan education. As early as I can remember, I heard about literature, painting, exhibits, geography, and travels to faraway countries from my mother's conversations with her friends. Among them were Alexandra Exter, who painted set designs for the *Ballets Russes,* the sculptor Constantin Brancusi, the writer Joseph Kessel, and many others. My mother often took me to visit artists in their ateliers, where I could see them painting, sculpting, and creating various objets d'art. I began my formal schooling at the age of seven, which was the custom in Russia, but considered very late in France. I never read stories for little girls, but started out with real literature. My first two books were *Uncle Tom's Cabin* in a French version for children and the classic *Lettres de mon moulin* by Alphonse Daudet. I received no religious education, following my father's orders. I studied neither Judaism nor Catholicism, and did not go to church on Sundays. I envied my classmates, with their pretty dresses and flowers going to Mass.

My ignorance of religion could be a danger at times, when our Jewish identity had to be kept a secret. Once, during the war, a Russian lady came to visit my mother in Niort on Easter Sunday. On seeing me, she gave the customary Russian Orthodox Easter greeting, "Christ is risen." Puzzled but polite, I answered, "Thank you very much, the same to you," rather than "He has risen indeed," the customary reply which all Russian Orthodox children would know by heart. My mother blanched, and the lady looked embarrassed, but did not say a word. From such near-catastrophic incidents, I learned early the importance of the meaning of words.

I also understood that Russia was a warm, creative, unique country, whose people had deep feelings and lofty sentiments—peasants as well as nobles. But from the political conversations I overheard at home, I knew before many others that the Russian Revolution of 1917 had degenerated into something monstrous, that the Bolshevik regime was not a temporary stage leading to a magnificent future, and that millions of people were being deceived. Many others, including my father, I believe, remained optimistic, especially in the early years of Soviet rule.

Although I received a partial Russian education and have lived for many years in the United States, I remain also French. The culture of France and its language are integral to my sense of self. I believe that the country of one's childhood education puts its stamp upon a person forever. The first alphabet, the first children's songs and rhymes, the first counting and adding two plus two, one's first prejudices and loyalties, all make one a member of that culture, like it or not.

All of these contradictions illustrate what I have known throughout my entire life—that there was never anything simple about being the daughter of Isaac Babel. My father was similarly filled with many contradictions, which are apparent in his stories and books. Perhaps his future biographer will explore further the many inconsistencies that marked his brief life. I do believe, however, that these countervailing themes endowed his fiction with a resonance and richness, thereby creating literature of the highest order.

The Yellow Star

There is a story about which I have always felt uncomfortable, because I never tried to find out enough to bring it to a proper closure. Like the first section of this memoir, "The Arrest of My Mother," it deals with my childhood.

It happened during the time when the German authorities decreed that all French citizens of Jewish ancestry had to declare themselves officially and to wear a Yellow Star. French Jewry has traditionally been one of the most assimilated Jewish groups in Western Europe. Prominent Jewish families have been French for many generations, and they certainly could never imagine that there could ever be any persecution organized against them. They considered, at least at the beginning, that having to register with the authorities was just one of the many troublesome inconveniences of the war.

My mother, however, had gone through the Civil War, the Revolution, and the implementation of the Soviet regime, and felt otherwise. She was quite distrustful of such a political decree. She considered that having a Soviet passport was already quite enough of a handicap, so she never "declared" us. Neither she nor I ever wore a Yellow

Star. It is amazing now to think that we were never denounced, a common enough occurrence in those days.

At that time, we were living in Niort. One of the town's "local glories" was the celebrated writer Ernest Pérochon,* who had once received the Prix Goncourt, France's most prestigious literary prize. I mention him because his family owned a large beautiful house, and rented a few of the rooms to an elderly lady who had come from Paris because of the war. Her name was Madame Lazareff. She was the widow of a banker, and therefore had the money to rent space in one of the town's most important residences. We knew that she had a son who had disappeared. But nobody knew, including Madame Lazareff herself, what had become of him. Was he a prisoner? Was he hiding somewhere? No one knew.

When the decree of the Yellow Star came, Madame Lazareff, of course, began to wear hers. I should mention that she was very friendly with my mother, all the more so since she was also of Russian origin.

One spring afternoon—probably in 1942—Madame Lazareff was having tea with us. We were living in a little house at the end of a courtyard, behind a larger house. Someone rang the bell and I went to open the gate. I found myself in front of two French policemen. I was told, "We understand that there is a Madame Babel here." In those days, whenever you saw the police, especially when they entered your home, your knees started to buckle. And then they said, "We have come for Madame Lazareff. We were told that she is here." And indeed she was right there. They told her, "You have been reported for not wearing your Yellow Star. And we can see that it's true. You aren't wearing it."

Madame Lazareff, who was smaller than I was as a child, and dressed in her usual mourning black, answered, "Yes, yes. I am wearing it, but it's on my coat."

"Well," they said, "that's not enough. You're supposed to have it on every garment."

They didn't let her return to her place. They just took her away, and no one ever saw her again. How long did she survive? Did she die on the train? In a concentration camp? Surely, given her frailty, she must have perished very quickly.

---

* Ernest Pérochon, 1885–1942, French writer, winner of the Prix Goncourt in 1920 for his novel *Nêne*. He lived in Niort from 1921 until his death.

Just before the policemen left, I opened my big mouth and told them, "You are really *des oiseaux de malheur*" (messengers of grief). Then one of them asked my mother, "Is this your daughter? How old is she?"

"She is twelve," my mother answered.

"You are lucky," he replied. "If she were a year older, we would take her also."

And how could they have known that Madame Lazareff was having tea with my mother? That son of hers had a wife and daughter, who occasionally came to visit from Paris. I remember his wife's elegance and beauty, but do not recall whether she was Jewish. The daughter was a few years older than I was, very pretty with copper curls. A spoiled city girl, clearly from a rich family. I remember that she talked about nothing but boys—she was really boy crazy, which seemed completely stupid to me. But then, she really was stupid, or at least very naïve. We learned later that she had been the one who had sent the policemen over to our house. It was during one of her visits to Niort to see her grandmother. The policemen arrived at the house of Ernest Pérochon and she was the one who answered the door. They demanded, "Where is Madame Lazareff?" In those days, any fifteen-year-old facing that situation would have said, "I really don't know. Let me find someone else to help you."

"And who is Madame Babel?" they continued, after she had informed them. "And where is Madame Babel?" And so they came to us.

This incident, so fraught with danger and so common then, still makes me shudder. And I have never felt that the story was quite over. Charles de Gaulle, of course, came back from London in 1944, when Paris was barely liberated. Many political dissidents *(résistants)* who had fled occupied France soon followed as well. One of them was a journalist named Pierre Lazareff. Born in France of parents of Russian origin, he had spent the war years as the head of the War Information Office in the United States. He returned to Paris in September 1944 and became the publisher of one of the leading postwar newspapers born out of the *Résistance* movement, called *France-Soir*.

I have always wondered if he was the mysterious son of the old lady that we had known in Niort. For many years afterward, I was tempted to contact him to find out. But, if my intuition was correct, how could I possibly tell him that his own daughter had been the instrument of his mother's death? Perhaps if Madame Lazareff had been warned, she would have had time to hide somewhere. Such a conversation would only have been terribly upsetting to both of us. And so I never went to see him.

The End of the War

As the liberation of Paris approached in the summer of 1944, clouds of planes passed over our heads with a deafening noise, occasionally dropping a bomb, perhaps on some local railroad. We did not know whether those planes were going toward their destinations or coming back from them. But even after the retreat of the German army from France, the war was still not over for us. Food rationing continued for at least two more years. War was still being fought over large parts of Europe. The chronic shortages, the hunger and disease continued. But the immediate and constant danger and fear were gone, and that changed everything. What began as a trickle turned into an enormous movement of displaced persons—people going home, people looking for people, survivors released from concentration camps or prisoner of war camps wandered in search of their families. Sometimes a person who had disappeared reappeared, amazingly.

My mother and I had little choice except to stay in the provincial town where we had spent over four years and where we had survived the Nazi occupation. We were homeless, penniless, and displaced. We had not yet been able to get into contact with anyone. The few valuables which my mother had taken with us in the fall of 1939 when we fled Paris had been sold—some jewelry, the last gifts from her father which had been saved during the Revolution, a good stamp collection, a fur coat. Some old friends from Paris and Brussels managed to send us some money, when they could figure a way to do so. There were times when we ate very frugally indeed.

We remained in the town of Niort for at least another year, although my memories of this time are vague. I must have gone to school for another year. I do, however, remember the atmosphere of our life at that time. We were living in a kind of limbo. It was a purgatory, as we waited for the door to open for us to return to a normal life. We stayed in the same little house, without a toilet or bathroom—without hot water or heating.

I have often been asked whether I ever went back to Niort. Never. It has remained for me a place out of time, out of space, out of tangible reality. I do not actually remember where that town is on the map— somewhere not too far from the Atlantic Ocean. Of course, I do remember the streets, some specific places, the market, where I stood in line at five in the morning in winter. Like most French towns, Niort had its covered produce market, with separate stalls for the different merchants. In those days, the market was allowed to open for one or two days a week. Peasants and farmers brought whatever victuals they had to sell. But there were too many people and very little to buy. In order to have the chance to buy anything, you had to be right at the head of the line, which began to form in the middle of the night. When the gates opened at seven, you had to race at top speed to your target-ed booth. We kids made arrangements among ourselves, since even those at the head of the line could not reach two stalls at the same time. "Look, I'll buy the potatoes, if you can get me the eggs. . . ." There was a playful element to this, but if you lost the game, you might not eat at all that day. For years, I was obsessed by these recollections. It took a very long time for those of my generation—who were between the ages of ten and fifteen during the war, the occupation, and the terror—to adapt to a more normal life.

Early in 1946, my mother took a trip to Paris, a journey which was quite an odyssey at the time. The trains were still so overcrowd-ed. I remember pushing her through the window to get a seat in the train. She wanted to find out whether we had anything left there and, above all, to see if she could find out something about the fate of her husband. She did learn that we had lost all claim to our small house in Plessis Robinson, a suburb south of Paris. Another family had occupied it for some time, and there was nothing she could do about it. In addition to the house, we had lost all our furnishings. This included a very good library, which today would be invaluable, as it contained all of my father's first editions. There was also my mother's art collection, along with her own works of art—paintings, which might now be still on walls somewhere in Europe—a retrospective compliment, perhaps.

While in Paris, my mother was told through the Montparnasse*
grapevine that Ilya Ehrenburg† wanted to see her. She had known him
since the mid-1920s, when he was living in Paris, and by which time he
had already established a significant place for himself in Soviet literature. She disliked him intensely, considering him the ultimate spokes-
men for the Soviet regime. Since the beginning of the war, when he
returned to Moscow, he was the most famous and widely read journalist in the USSR, read avidly even by Stalin himself. He was one of the
few writers to escape the Stalinist purges.

Despite her feelings, she went to see him, hoping for news of her
husband. He told her—quite amazingly—that Babel was alive, that he
had spent the war in exile, and was now living under surveillance not
far from Moscow.

And so she returned to Niort with renewed hope about her husband. It was the first news she had received of him since his last letters
in 1939. There were many reasons to believe Ehrenburg, because he
was such a prestigious and well-informed person. She harbored these
hopes and illusions until 1949 or 1950, since there was never any official announcement of my father's death. Meanwhile, American organi-
zations were also searching for displaced persons. And in 1948, they let
us know that no traces of Babel could be found in Russia after 1939.

We left Niort at last in the late spring of 1946. An old family friend
let us have what used to be the summer residence of his rich relatives,
who had never returned after the war. It was in the small village of
Bois-le-Roi, just at the edge of the vast forest of Fontainebleau, south
of Paris. The house was big, with a large garden full of fruit trees.
Everything was abandoned and neglected, yet lovely. We harvested
many different varieties of apples, and prepared them in all sorts of
ways. I remember that when my mother planted corn, a neighbor asked
her if she was planning to raise pigs. The French did not consider corn

---

* Montparnasse: favorite Left Bank "*quartier*" of Paris for the bohemian and artistic crowd.
Artists, painters, writers, poets, and émigrés from all over the world passed their days and nights
in its famous cafés—La Rotonde, La Coupole, Le Dôme. The Russian crowd ("*Les Russes*"),
including many famous artists and writers, was especially well known there.

† Ilya Grigorievich Ehrenburg: 1891–1967, famous Soviet novelist, essayist, journalist. Paris
correspondent for *Izvestia* in the 1930s. Author of *The Fall of Paris* (1941), for which he won the
Stalin Prize for Literature. Recipient of the Order of Lenin in 1944 for his efforts as a wartime
journalist. Member of the French Legion of Honor. Winner of the Stalin Peace Prize (1953).
Author of *The Thaw* (1954).

on the cob fit for human consumption in those days. My mother began to take in paying guests, including her friends and acquaintances. She was an excellent cook, and often fed a dozen people a day. I helped with the cleaning. By that time, I was ready to enter the tenth grade. The fact that I had continued my schooling throughout the war years is astonishing, and sheds another light on my mother's character. She never considered that I could not go to school, even in times when it was dangerous to step outside our home, when anti-Semitism was raging everywhere, even in the elementary school classes. I had to continue my education, no matter what hardship or risk it entailed.

Whenever the school year began, I had to be sent away somewhere, and was put into boarding school. The Lycée de Versailles was the choice, although I do not remember why. I was allowed to return home on the weekends. It was an excellent school, very upscale, and it was very hard to gain admittance. The discipline was extremely strict. The staff consisted mostly of elderly spinsters, not very attuned to the needs of traumatized adolescents. For me, boarding school life was far from easy, like being in a Charles Dickens novel. Everything had to be done according to detailed rules and regulations. You had to get up at a certain time, and had so many minutes to get dressed, then breakfast at an appointed time, and so on, until lights out at nine o'clock. This discipline created the sense of ropes tied around my body. We had to walk to class two by two, as if we were little girls. I do not remember a single thing that I learned or studied there, but I do recall being deeply unhappy. I had been living such a close and protected life with my mother for so long—living in fear during the Nazi occupation, but also in great independence. I longed for the weekends, when I would go home to that big, beautiful, frigid house, where Mother was waiting for me after a week alone. I was becoming emotionally and mentally unbalanced. I think that it was not so much what we now call post-traumatic stress as it was the living trauma of being in that school, and away from my mother and from my first great love. My nerves, already frayed, became live electric wires. Mercifully, this painful episode lasted less than three months. I was expelled before the Christmas break. Expelled for rebellious behavior, bad character, and loose morals.

It seems that my correspondence was being monitored, and a passionate letter from my boyfriend had been discovered and opened. My mother and I were summoned by Madame La Directrice and given a full treatment of humiliation. Watching my mother in that situation was more painful to me than all my problems. She was told, among other things, that I could only be destined to a life of menial labor, given my "condition of moral turpitude." That she had obviously not been able to raise a decent girl—and that if I were not destined for a life of whoredom, I might at best become a seamstress, which seemed to be for the headmistress barely above the bottom. I was fifteen years old! I was given a certificate with the statement "Conduct to be watched" *(conduite à surveiller)*. This was a horrible stigma in those days, almost certainly preventing acceptance at any other school. And so my mother and I went back to the big, empty house in Bois-le-Roi.

The end of the year passed—long, dark, and dreary. Finally, on New Year's Day 1947, we were reunited with my auntie and uncle from Belgium. It was the first time they had been able to leave Brussels since the end of the war to visit us. They, of course, knew of my situation and decided, together with my mother, that the only solution was for me to return to Belgium with them. Belgium seemed to be one of the European countries which "normalized" very quickly after the war and, in 1947, no longer had the same great shortages of food, clothing, and heating, which still existed in France. We were still using rationing coupons to buy things, whereas Belgium had already done away with them.

And so, as an adolescent, I was to go to Belgium. But this turned out not to be so simple. There was the question of what kind of official papers I possessed, since a special visa was needed. My father had registered me as a Soviet citizen, by putting me in his passport, during his stay in Paris in 1932. This meant that in 1947, although I had been born in France, I was not a French citizen—and this was certainly an obstacle to freedom. However, I had to wait until my eighteenth birthday to petition for French citizenship—to which I was entitled. By this time, my mother had given up her Soviet passport and was "a citizen without a country"—an *apatride,* even after living over twenty years in France.

As I had no permission to enter Belgium legally, my uncle arranged for me to enter the country illegally. He must have paid someone to get me across the border into Belgium from the northeast part of France. I remember having to cross a field of snow, crawling flat on my belly to get underneath the rows of barbed wire, which still separated the two countries. I do not know whether this was really necessary, or whether the man in charge of this mission wanted to impress on my uncle that he was really earning his money. But for me, after the Nazi danger, it was one of the darkest moments of my life. This whole long passage of events—the boarding school, the winter in the forest, the continued absence of my father, the illegal crossing—was a bitter experience, and made me feel that the war was far from over for me. It took years for me to feel free from the memory of so many fears, losses, and sorrows.

I was admitted to the Lycée Français in Brussels, based only on papers from my school in Niort. The fact that I had been expelled from a French national school was to remain a deep and shameful secret for years. I was much too afraid to talk about it, for fear that my trickery would be discovered. I learned later that the Directrice of the Lycée de Versailles was known for being anti-Semitic and xenophobic. And it was rumored that, during the occupation, she had reported on Jewish students. Perhaps, she had only used my love letter as a pretext to expel me.

In contrast, the Lycée Français was a wonderful school. The teachers, who were still young and had themselves just gone through the war, understood that our generation was a bit different—that strict discipline was not the best approach. My classmates were all between the ages of fifteen and seventeen, and we were a fairly motley group. Many of us had already seen a great deal in our short lifetimes. One of my classmates had lost all of his hair—we never knew exactly how—some ordeal, I suppose. Once, as I was climbing the stairs behind him, he suddenly turned around, all white, upset, and belligerent. He explained that the sound of my heavy boots (I did not have new shoes yet) was intolerable to him, awakening memories of other boots. Another classmate stuttered badly. We could all be pretty rude and difficult. We were prone to fits of anger, probably unjustified. I outdid myself the day that I put my fist into a classmate's face hard enough to make his nose bleed. And he was quite a peaceful fellow, as I recall. I admire the teachers at that school, who never punished us, always tried to establish a good rapport with us, and who understood our excesses and their causes.

I spent two-and-a-half years there, and did well in my studies, passing both of the baccalaureate examinations required for entrance to a French university.

Revelations

At the beginning of 1956, I went to London for several months to study English. When I returned to Paris in the summer, I found my mother looking very poorly. In fact, she was already extremely ill, having been diagnosed with cancer. It was discovered much too late, and she died less than a year later. On my arrival, my mother was very distressed and agitated about an event which, unfortunately, had taken place during my absence.

I soon learned what had happened during my stay in England. My mother had received an invitation—or a summons, I don't know—for a second meeting with Ilya Ehrenburg, whom she had last seen in 1946, ten years earlier. She had no reason to change her feelings of mistrust, shared by many others. But by then he was an even more powerful and important person in the Soviet literary world and had the authority of the official regime behind him. He was able to travel quite freely between Moscow and Paris. He was an important cultural link between the two countries, and was greatly favored in French leftist literary circles. He was the one person in that intellectual milieu who could have known the truth about Babel's disappearance in 1939. Actually, during the 1950s, my mother had been stopped in the street several times by total strangers, who seemed to know very well who she was, and who would say, "I can give you news of Babel." The stories varied—he was in camp, in prison, in Siberia, and so on. I don't think my mother ever believed these strangers, and indeed suspected that they were Soviet plants. But it always unnerved us, because they said what we wanted to believe—that Babel was still alive. It was also after Stalin's death in 1953 when we started hearing about the process of "rehabilitations."[*]

Since she still harbored suspicions about Ehrenburg, and also because she was already quite ill, she asked a friend, a Madame Shakoff, to accompany her on this visit. Thus, there was a witness to her encounter with him. The story of this meeting has never ceased to disturb me.

Ehrenburg informed my mother that Babel had been rehabilitated two years earlier in 1954, and that the official date of his death was March 17, 1941.[†] He then asked my mother to sign a paper certifying

---

[*] "Rehabilitation" was a new Soviet term, indicating that all criminal charges against a person condemned and "repressed" under the Stalinist regime were dropped in the absence of evidence.

[†] This was the officially accepted death date for Babel until KGB archives opened after perestroika revealed the actual date of January 27, 1940. See *La Parole ressuscitée. Dans les archives littéraires du K.G.B.*, by Vitali Chentalinski, Editions Robert Laffont, Paris, 1993.

that she and my father had been divorced since before the war. He knew perfectly well, of course, that no such divorce had taken place between the time of Babel's last visit to Paris in the winter of 1935–1936 and his arrest in May 1939. Even living in Moscow, how could he have divorced his wife without informing anyone in his family, with whom he was in constant correspondence? Ehrenburg then told her, apparently with great brutality, that my father had a second wife living in the Soviet Union, by whom he had another child—a daughter. When my mother asked the name of the child, he answered, "Natasha," which is, of course, my name. I honestly don't know whether this was just a mistake on his part or whether he said this on purpose to upset her even more. What I do know is that my mother then spat in his face and fainted. All of these dramatic and dreadful details were confirmed to me by Madame Shakoff—also a rather emotional old Russian lady. My mother never recovered from this episode, which contributed greatly to the pain she was already enduring in the final months of her illness before her death in May 1957.

During my whole childhood, I suffered from having neither a brother nor a sister. I used to invent them with such intensity that I managed to convince even my most skeptical classmates of the existence of a big brother and a small sister. Some judiciously chosen photographs of attractive children totally unknown to me helped to make my illusions real. There is a painful irony in this faraway past. As an adult, I learned within a relatively short period of time that fate indeed had given me an older brother and a younger sister.

I thought I had always known all the reasons why my mother left Russia in 1925. She despised and feared the Soviet regime, and as an artist, she wanted to paint and study abroad. Paris was the obvious choice for that purpose. My mother kept her secrets well. She had to be dying in a public ward of the St. Antoine Hospital in Paris to share with me emotional regions of her life that had always been relegated to the shadows. She did this not because she felt that she owed me these private truths, but because she feared that in an uncertain future, my ignorance could do me harm.

"You should know," my mother said, "that you have a half-brother. I left Russia mostly because of an affair your father was having with an actress, a very beautiful woman. She pursued him relentlessly, and didn't care that he was married. She wanted him and his fame, and had a son by him. Perhaps one day you might meet this man, and you should know he is your half-brother and not someone you could fall in love with."

At the time of their acquaintence, Tamara Vladimirovna Kashirina, a beautiful and well-known actress, was twenty-five years old, with a pleasant husband, a small daughter, and a full social calendar. She had only one problem: she was "bored." With Babel courting her insistently, with his gift as an "incomparable raconteur," her boredom vanished. While Babel apparently convinced her that he was really in love for the first time, the circumstances of his family life were complicated and required a good deal of his attention. Babel told her that he was planning to send his wife to France, where she could study painting. His mother would be going to live with her married daughter, who by this time had settled in Brussels. While taking care of all of these family arrangements in 1925 and 1926, Babel traveled frequently. He was always moving to the country or to another city, searching for that elusive place where he could work in peace. In 1925 alone, Babel wrote to Tamara from seven different cities. Their own encounters were infrequent, short, and often postponed.

On July 13, 1926, their son Mikhail was born in Leningrad. Babel, who was then in Moscow, expressed his enthusiasm from a distance. "The long-awaited telegram arrived last night. Well done, Tamara! It's great that it's a boy. Girls are common enough, but a boy can turn out to be a real provider. . . . I'm dying to know how it all went, how you are feeling, where you had the baby. Please tell me everything quickly. It's such a bitter feeling not to know, but I'm tied down here completely and just can't break away for the time being. . . . God bless you, dear Tamara, and get well soon—and when I come, I shall be so happy for you. Letters, letters, letters! I kiss you warmly, my dear soul."*

By the time their son was born, Tamara thought that he had finished all the necessary arrangements for his family's departure. She believed, not unreasonably, that the moment had arrived when Babel could start a real family life with her and Mikhail. But this was never to happen.

Later in 1926 and 1927, Babel wrote to Tamara mostly from Kiev, where he had temporarily settled. They celebrated together Mikhail's

---

* Memoirs of Tamara Ivanova, published in the literary journal *Oktyabr* (*October*), May, June, July 1992, Moscow.

first birthday on July 13, 1927, and again Tamara made plans for their future together. But it was the last time that Babel was ever to see his son. Two weeks later, he was already in Paris with his wife.

The Soviet Way

Four years after my mother's death, in 1961, I traveled to the USSR for the first time. There, I found out that in Moscow my mother's deepest secret was common knowledge. Everybody in the literary and cultural milieu knew that Mikhail V. Ivanov was Babel's natural son. He was still a small child when his mother, Tamara Vladimirovna Kashirina, married the Soviet writer Vsevolod Ivanov, who adopted, raised, and loved Mikhail as his own. For this reason, Tamara Ivanova never permitted Babel to see his son again. When Mikhail was about eighteen, some well-intended soul told him the truth about his origins. Such a revelation must have caused him much pain and confusion. He later became a painter, and was known for his cityscapes of Moscow. We never met and never will, although I always felt a lot of fraternal sympathy with him. I learned recently of his death in Moscow in the spring of 2000.

That first trip to the Soviet Union in 1961 was a sort of pilgrimage for me. My primary motivations were to learn something more about the fate of my father, and I still wanted to find out what really lay behind that last meeting between my mother and Ehrenburg. I went in an official capacity, a modest one, but one which provided the protection of the French government. I was a guide-interpreter for the first postwar national exhibition organized by the French Chamber of Commerce. The exhibition was intended to show off all the advances of French industry, from fountain pens to radios to tractors to cars. It was a momentous occasion. Two hundred guide-interpreters were eventually chosen by the Soviet embassy, out of four hundred candidates, all of whom had been preselected and trained by the French. The selection, as we learned later, had been carried out according to very specific criteria: a certain percentage of actual Russian émigrés (by 1961, these persons had already reached middle age); a certain percentage of their children, born in France, who were bearing Russian surnames; a certain number of women of Russian origin, who had married Frenchmen, thereby acquiring French surnames; and Frenchwomen who had acquired Russian surnames through marriage! How I stayed on that list, I do not know and I never asked.

Before our departure, a large group of French laborers were sent to Moscow to work on the construction site for the exhibition, which was to be located in the huge Sokolniki Park. The French authorities gave preference to members of the French Communist Party, who were so very eager to visit the USSR. Soon after their arrival, they became appalled by the work habits of the Soviets, whom they considered slow, lazy, unskilled, incompetent, etc. It took three or four Soviets to produce the output of a single French worker. I served as an interpreter for a number of French workers, when they answered questions about their way of life in France. Their fellow Communists could not believe what they said. One lodging for one family, their own kitchen, perhaps a *quatre-chevaux* car to drive to the farm on weekends to visit their parents. . . . All lies, of course. And the French were foaming at the mouth.

A big celebration was held in Sokolniki Park when the construction site was finally completed. Everyone was invited, including the Soviet workers. The French government had flown in wonderful food and wine for this festive occasion. All of us went, of course. There was a beautiful bonfire and the party ended when our French workers ceremoniously threw their Communist Party membership cards into the flames. The experiment in political enlightenment had been a huge success.

As guide-interpreters, we had to work very hard, since there were over eighty thousand visitors a day. All plans for organized shifts had to be forgotten, and sometimes we worked twelve hours a day, instead of the expected six. During the exhibition, I was assigned to the very large book section. We had a huge quantity of paperbacks and many beautiful hardbound art books. There were three copies of each. After the first display had disappeared, we installed the second. For the third display, we had enough paperbacks, but we decided to nail down the art books by their covers, so visitors should still enjoy them. In the end, we were left with the nailed bookcovers. Needless to say, the book section did not have much to pack for the return to Paris. Nevertheless, it was an unforgettable experience. None of my later visits to Moscow as an individual scholar, with a grant to work in the Lenin Library, at least ostensibly, can match the encounters, and surprises, of those few summer months of 1961—the time of my first meetings with my half-sister Lydia and her mother.

In the late 1950s, my aunt, Meri Chapochnikoff, née Babel, my father's only sister, began a correspondence with her niece Lydia, and her mother Antonina Nikolayevna Pirozhkova. She too had somehow learned about their existence. Not wanting to hurt or offend my mother, she did not write to them until after her death. In 1961, knowing that I was going to Moscow, she tried to tell me about them, but I would not hear of it. Yet despite my deep resentment, Aunt Meri told me just before my departure that she had informed them that I was coming. She gave me their telephone number and tried her best to convince me to meet them. I was furious at her for what I considered her betrayal of my mother's life and memory. I felt full of conflicts, and expressed my confusion to Boris Souvarine,* an old friend of my father's and a wise man. He said to me, "Trust your father's judgment and trust your heart."

There is one particularly striking difference between Babel's family in Paris and his family in Moscow, specifically, our ignorance of their existence. Antonina Nikolayevna learned of Babel's wife and daughter on the first day she met him at a luncheon at a friend's house in 1932. As she recalled their first meeting in her memoirs, "Over lunch, Babel told us how difficult it had been for him to get permission to go abroad, and how long the process had dragged on. Going was an absolute necessity for him, since his family lived abroad with no means of support, and it was very difficult to help them from Moscow."[†]

As it turned out, she learned about my existence right from the beginning. " 'I'm going there to meet a little three-year-old miss,' he said. 'I'd like to bring her back to Russia, as I fear they might turn her into a monkey there.' He was speaking of his daughter Natasha, whom he had not seen."[**]

In her memoirs, Antonina notes that Babel never spoke to her about his son Misha, about whose existence she learned from friends. On the other hand, she learned a great deal more about us over the years. "By contrast, I knew everything about Natasha. Babel would always show me her photographs and repeat everything that Evgenia Borisovna wrote in her letters about her, and would ask me to buy toys and little books for her."[‡] Her daughter Lydia naturally knew of us all her life.

* See the second footnote of my preface to this volume.
[†] *At His Side, The Last Years of Isaac Babel,* p. 2, by A. N. Pirozhkova, Steerforth Press, South Royalton, Vermont, 1996, paperback edition
[**] Op. cit., p. 2.
[‡] Op. cit., p. 92.

Their awareness of us contrasted with our lack of it. In his personal correspondence, Babel wrote practically every day to relatives and friends. I figure that he must have written at least twelve personal letters a day—often using postcards. But there was never a word about his other life in Moscow, not even when his second daughter was born in January 1937—an event which must have made him very happy.

On my first day in Moscow, I realized that if I did not call this family immediately, I would never do it. So I called. Lydia and I agreed to meet in front of the Bolshoi Theater the next day. She would wear red and I would wear blue—and thus we would know each other. She arrived with a friend—and so did I. My friend was Tanya Parrain,* who was also an exhibition guide, and was also in the Soviet Union for the first time. It seemed that each of us needed reinforcement. We were both young, pretty, I think, and nicely dressed. We resembled each other in some unexpected way. Once during that summer, when we were trying to squeeze together into a crowded phone booth, an irate citizen called us "useless doubles."

On the day of our first encounter, we walked around the city, making conversation, testing the ground for emotional land mines. She was a young architect. I was teaching French language and literature. Then Lydia said, "My mother is expecting us for tea." It was one of those moments of decision that one remembers forever—an existential moment that can change your whole life. I accepted.

So we went to what had been my father's last home, a large two-story stone house in the heart of Moscow. At the time I met them, they each had a room on the second floor with access to a communal bath and kitchen. I remember their rooms as being quite cozy, in a cluttered, friendly Russian manner. Their eating and sleeping in the same room did not surprise me, as I had done the same with my mother for many years, as had many other Russian émigrés. This old part of the city has since been torn down to make way for modern apartment buildings.

As we walked into a dark entry and climbed a flight of stairs, I saw a woman standing at the top of the landing and crying. I looked at her, and what suddenly came out of my mouth has never failed to astound

---

*Tanya Parrain is the daughter of Brice Parrain, French writer and philosopher, and also a specialist in Russian and Soviet literature. Her maternal grandfather, George Chelpanov, was well-known founder of the Institute of Psychology in Moscow.

me. "You look so much like my mother!" I blurted out. I have compared photos of both of them in their youth, and indeed there was a physical resemblance. We both started to cry. I was amazed and felt deeply touched to meet another woman who, like my own mother, had never stopped loving my father—who appeared never to have wavered in her devotion to him. For many years and across the Iron Curtain, we remained a part of each other's lives as best we could, despite the obstacles. Lydia and her mother eventually emigrated to the United States in 1996.

Returning to the subject of Ehrenburg and his encounters with my mother, I quote from a recent biography of this enigmatic figure by Joshua Rubenstein:

> Ehrenburg saw Babel's first wife Yevgeniya Borisovna in France on two occasions after the Second World War. When he visited Paris in 1946, according to Nathalie Babel, he conveyed the message that he [Babel] was alive and had spent the War in exile, under house arrest, not far from Moscow.*

There is no doubt in my mind that on this occasion, Ehrenburg knew he was lying to my mother. He of all people had sufficiently high stature and connections to know the truth about Babel's fate. In 1944, he had just won the Lenin Prize for his work as a war correspondent, and had won the Stalin Prize for Literature a few years earlier. He was at the height of his fame and power. Rubenstein himself noted in his book that by the end of the war, "No other private citizen [in the USSR] reached such unique stature."[†] He considered Babel to be among his closest friends. Surely he would have been able to find out if Babel was really alive and living so close by.

Why did he mislead my mother? Certainly not to spare her feelings, as he knew she absolutely despised him. I believe strongly that he was following orders to pass on false information. After all, he had done just that during his whole professional life. Babel was well known in the literary community in France, the USSR's wartime ally, and was admired by many eminent men of letters, such as André Gide, Romain Rolland, and André Malraux. These same writers had been very force-

---

* *Tangled Loyalties: The Life and Times of Ilya Ehrenburg,* p. 288, by Joshua Rubenstein, Basic Books, a Division of HarperCollins, New York, 1996.
† Op. cit., p. 218.

ful in insisting that Babel be sent to Paris as a delegate in 1935 to the International Congress of Writers for the Defense of Culture and Peace. They surely would have asked Ehrenburg about Babel's fate. De Gaulle had made Ehrenburg a member of the French Legion of Honor after the liberation of Paris. The Soviet government could hardly have found a more credible messenger of the news that the Soviet Union had spared Babel's life. And what better way to publicize this message than to inform his wife?

Ehrenburg met with my mother in 1956, ten years after their first encounter. He was working hard on the rehabilitation of Babel's works and was the de facto chairman of a Commission of the Writers' Union to look after Babel's legacy. He was indeed instrumental in getting Babel republished at last in the USSR. Antonina Nikolayevna was also a member of this commission. I believe that in 1956, Ehrenburg, a survivor, decorated with every possible honor the Soviet system could bestow, miraculously still alive at the age of sixty-five, felt that he had nothing to fear anymore, and that he was trying to ease his conscience. He did act on behalf of many people who were victimized by the Soviet regime, and he did help in the rehabilitation of some of the maligned dead. Babel was his great friend and a great writer, whom he professed to love. He did everything he could to break the silence surrounding Babel's name, his memory, and his work and to introduce Babel to new generations of readers who had never heard of him. He wrote the introduction to the 1957 edition, the first edition in the USSR after the war. His introduction was bold for the time, and he knew that it would not be met favorably by everyone. His introduction and Babel's stories were in fact very much criticized by the Communist literary establishment. It took ten years for another volume of Babel's work to be published again in 1966.

In 1956, Ehrenburg informed my mother of Babel's date of death and his rehabilitation. But why did he want to tell her about a second family and to ask her to sign a falsified admission of divorce? It was a cruel act on his part. There was certainly no love lost between them. Ehrenburg undoubtedly considered Antonina a more suitable widow than my mother, who by then had lived in Paris for more than thirty years as an émigré artist. After all, Antonina was the epitome of the new Soviet woman, having been the first woman construction engineer employed to work on the Moscow subway system. Now that Babel was rehabilitated, perhaps he thought she could receive a pension as his legitimate wife. Perhaps Ehrenburg had other reasons for trying to establish her social position and status, all honorable from his point of view.

Over the years following our first meeting in 1961, I developed a great admiration for Antonina Nikolayevna and respect for her efforts and perseverance. She was one of the main editors of the publication of two volumes of Babel's collected works in 1990–1991, when she was eighty years old. These two volumes are still the most complete compilation of Babel's work in Russian. Unfortunately, certain omissions, which were made understandably in the 1957 publication, are found again in the later edition.

I am thankful to her that she shared with me a few of my father's unpublished stories. These stories had resurfaced little by little and had been given to her. Babel had left these stories with friends (perhaps as gifts). They had kept them, and after the rehabilitation of Babel, they entrusted the stories to her. Indeed, over the years she became the repository of Babel's work in the Soviet Union. As a result, and with Ehrenburg's help, she established her social position as an important personage.

America

Being Russian, French, American, and Jewish has meant that wherever I am, part of me could be somewhere else. Living in so many worlds can lead to varied confusions, mistakes, emotional misperceptions, and in my case it has also led to impulsiveness and a tendency toward pessimism. However, when the United States offered the opportunity, I decided to try to benefit from my "multicultural identity." I soon learned that New York City was an ideal place to put my confusions to good use, particularly on upper Broadway.

After mother died, I was poor and restless, and decided to leave the past behind. My decision was crystallized by an invitation to teach in the Department of French at Barnard College. I flew to New York in early September 1961, arriving with a suitcase in hand, my winter coat on my arm, and twenty dollars in my purse. I had just returned from that first momentous visit to Moscow, which had made me miss the first week of the fall semester.

I had written to the chairman, the late and admired Leroy Breunig, about a one-week delay in my arrival, explaining that I was coming to the States via the USSR. This led him to remark at the first departmental meeting, "This woman has a very original sense of geography."

As a faculty member, I was able and encouraged to take classes at Columbia University. I had access to so many fascinating topics and professors, and loved the idea of being an *auditeur libre*, an intellectual *flâneur* in the manner of the French. I registered for six courses, without knowing what this entailed.

I remember in particular a seminar on English romantic poetry, about which I knew almost nothing, which was taught with a heavy dose of Freudian theory. I understood very little, but enjoyed it very much. I found the discussions in class on hidden images, double entendres, and erotic metaphors immensely challenging. My bliss began to evaporate when my professors started to ask about my midterm essays. "Midterm" was a new concept for me, yet I learned its meaning quickly after I discovered the nonexistence of the status of *auditeur libre* at Columbia. My transcript still bears witness to my prompt retreat from most of these courses. I appeared, as I was later told, "to be very nice and very lost."

While I enjoyed campus life, I was shocked on several occasions when a total stranger would approach me and ask abruptly, "Can you tell me where and how your father died?"

I became a regular student, first for an American MA in the Department of Slavic Studies, then for a doctoral program in English and comparative literature. I was readily admitted, because I already had earned degrees from the Sorbonne and the École des Langues Orientales. I chose the English Department so as not to become a pure Slavicist, and certainly not to become an expert on Babel, a role for which many people thought I was predestined. My specialty areas were nineteenth century French and Russian prose—an ambitious choice, considering the number and normal output of important writers of that time. The English Department had never had a Ph.D. student without English literature as a major area of study, and few professors in the department spoke French or Russian, let alone both. This situation led to many farcical episodes, or at least they seem so in retrospect. For example, the department was not ready to consider that English could serve as one of the two foreign language requirements. The consternation was general when I refused adamantly to study Chaucer and Spencer, which were always required courses for all students in the English Department. I made another error when I answered glibly to the Professor of Italian Renaissance that I already had a passable *culture générale* of his sacred field. He countered with an eight-page, single-spaced mandatory reading list. I countered with hysterics in the office of the chairman, while he stood slightly agog, being himself a self-controlled New England gentleman. The requirement for the Italian Renaissance was waived.

My dissertation examined some of the psychological and literary affinities between Hugo and Dostoyevsky. In the end, everybody had fun with it, I think, and discovered something new. I went on to become a professor of comparative literature at the University of Texas and later at the University of California, also teaching American southern writers as well as Latin American literature. But the Russian novel kept tugging at my coat. Little by little, I found myself becoming a Slavicist and also a Babel scholar. In spite of my reluctance, and even a pathological resistance, my father finally caught up with me! Some of his correspondence was being translated, and I ended up being the only one who could identify all the people mentioned in those letters.

This knowledge led me to becoming in 1964 the editor of *The Lonely Years: 1925–1939*, a collection of almost four hundred letters that Babel wrote to my aunt and grandmother (his sister and mother), whom I knew very well. This volume revealed many facets of Babel's character, as well as his whereabouts during the 1920s and 1930s. In 1966, I edited *You Must Know Everything*, which brought a number of new and forgotten stories to the public.

That is how I started doing Babel scholarship, which I have continued sporadically for over three decades. After a long silence, here I am at it again.

NATHALIE BABEL
Washington, D.C.
March 2001

ISAAC EMMANUELOVICH BABEL

A CHRONOLOGY

by Gregory Freidin

1894   Isaac Babel is born (June 30) in Moldavanka, a poor district near the harbor of Odessa, to Feiga and Man Yitzkhovich Bobel, a dealer in agricultural machinery. Soon after, the family, now under the name Babel, relocates to Nikolayev (150 kilometers from Odessa). Babel studies English, French, and German; private Hebrew lessons.

1899   Babel's sister, Meriam, born on July 16.

1905   The October Manifesto of Czar Nicholas II establishes a constitutional monarchy. Pogroms in southern Russia, including Nikolayev, witnessed by Babel. But the family is untouched.

1906   Babel's family, now considerably more prosperous, moves back to Odessa and settles in the residential center of the city. Babel enrolls in the Nicholas I Commercial School in Odessa; begins writing stories in French.

1911   After an unsuccessful attempt to enroll at the University of Odessa (due to the restrictions on Jews), Babel enters the Institute of Finance and Business Studies in Kiev. Meets Evgenia Borisovna Gronfein, his future wife.

1913   First publication: the story "Old Shloyme."

1914   World War I begins.

1915   Babel follows his institute's evacuation from Kiev to Saratov.

1916   After graduating from the institute, moves to St. Petersburg, meets Maxim Gorky, and begins to contribute stories and sketches to Gorky's journal *Letopis* and other periodicals (stories: "Mama, Rimma, and Alla," "Elya Isaakovich and Margarita Prokofievna"). Babel's stories receive a favorable response from reviewers.

1917   Charged with writing pornography (story "The Bathroom Window"), but the charge is made moot by the political turmoil.

       The February Revolution.* Czar Nicholas II abdicates. Russia is ruled by the provisional government. Babel briefly volunteers for the Rumanian front. Bolshevik coup d'état in October.†

       Babel abandons the disintegrating front in November, returns to Odessa, and takes a dangerous journey to Petrograd** (his story "The Road," 1932). Reaches Petrograd in December 1917 and joins the newly organized Cheka for a brief stint as a translator for the counterintelligence department.

1918   In March, Babel becomes a regular contributor of sketches about life in the city to Maxim Gorky's anti-Leninist newspaper *Novaya zhizn* until the publication is shut down by the Bolsheviks on July 6 (Babel's last contribution is in the July 2 issue).

       Contributes stories to newspaper *Zhizn iskusstva* (Petrograd) in November.

1918–19 Serves in the food requisitioning detachments during the Civil War; returns to Odessa. Marries Evgenia Gronfein (August 9, 1919).

1920   Odessa Party Committee issues Babel the credentials of a war correspondent under the name of Kiril Vasilievich Lyutov, assigned to Budyonny's Cavalry Army on the Polish front. Babel spends June through September with the Budyonny Cavalry.‡

       Returns to Odessa severely ill (lifelong asthma). Travels with his wife in Georgia and the Caucasus, contributes to local periodicals.

1921   End of the Civil War. The tolerant New Economic Policy replaces War Communism.

       Babel does editorial work for a publishing house, contributing stories and essays to Odessa periodicals.

* March, according to the Gregorian calandar, adopted subsequently.
† November 7, according to the Gregorian calandar.
** Formerly St. Petersburg.
‡In August 1920, the Red Army reaches the outskirts of Warsaw but is soon after repelled and by September defeated by Pilsudski's troops, aided by the Western powers; an armistice is signed in October 1921; the Treaty of Riga, finalizing the Russian-Polish border and ceding parts of the Ukraine and Belarus to Poland, is signed on March 18, 1921.

1923   Most of the Benya Krik stories (the Odessa stories) written and published in Odessa.
        Father dies (July 13).

1923–24 After finishing the Odessa stories, Babel begins work on the *Red Cavalry* stories (June 1923), the publication of his stories in the avant-garde *Lef* and the fellow traveler *Krasnaya Nov*; the beginning of Babel's fame.

1924   Lenin dies on January 21; Stalin, the Communist Party's General Secretary since 1922, begins his ascent to power.
        Budyonny's first attack on *Red Cavalry* stories (March).
        Babel publication in the first issue of Evgeny Zamiatin's independent journal *Russkii sovremennik*.
        Meriam Chapochnikoff (Babel's sister) emigrates to Brussels.

1925   First two childhood stories (the cycle *The Story of My Dovecote*) are published with a dedication to Maxim Gorky.
        Evgenia Babel (Gronfein), Babel's wife, emigrates to Paris.

1926   *Red Cavalry* is published as a book. Babel's mother emigrates to Brussels. Babel is Russia's "most famous writer."

1925–27 Babel's liaison with Tamara Kashirina (later, Mrs. Vsevolod Ivanov).

1926   Mikhail (Ivanov) is born to Babel and Tamara Kashirina in July.
        Babel finishes his play *Sunset* in August.
        Works on the film script of *Benya Krik*; the beginning of Babel's career as a screenwriter (script based on Shalom Aleichem's *Roaming Stars* and others).

1927   The film *Benya Krik* is released and soon taken out of circulation. In subsequent publications of the script, Babel disowns the film.
        Babel is in Kiev on family business; possibly works on *The Jewess* (a novel) of which only the beginning is extant. Plans a work on the French Revolution, hints that he is working on a novel about the Cheka; continues work on the "childhood" story cycle (referred to by Babel as "my true legacy").
        Babel leaves Russia for Paris in July; a brief affair with E. Khaiutina (future Mrs. Nikolai Yezhov) in Berlin; rejoins his wife in Paris.
        Sunset staged successfully in Baku (October 23), in two theaters in Odessa (October 25 and December 1).

1928   Moscow production of *Sunset* at the Moscow Art Theater II (February 28) fails.
        The Shakhty Trial. End of the liberal New Economic Policy era and beginning of the Stalin Revolution.
        Babel returns to Russia in October. General Budyonny resumes attacks on the *Red Cavalry* stories. Gorky comes to Babel's defense.
        The Chinese Mill, a film comedy based on a script by Babel, premieres in July.
        Continues work on the childhood story cycle (according to Babel, "part of a larger whole").
        Critic Alexander Voronsky, an early patron and admirer of Babel, chides him in print for his low productivity, or "silence."
        Completes the story "My First Fee" (1922–28); plans *Kolya Topuz*, a long narrative about an Odessa bandit who is reformed during the period of socialist construction (late 1920s–early 1930s).

1929   Trotsky is exiled from Soviet Russia in January.

Babel's daughter, Nathalie, born in Paris to Evgenia Borisovna Babel on July 17.

Red Cavalry is published in English translation in the United States (following German and French editions), preceded by the appearance of some stories in literary magazines.

1929–30 "In search of new material," Babel, like many other Soviet writers, travels in the industrial heartland to observe "socialist construction"; witnesses the brutal collectivization and famine in the Ukraine (February–summer 1930).

1930   Babel is publicly accused of granting an anti-Soviet interview to a Polish newspaper while on the French Riviera. He insists, apparently successfully, that the interview was a fabrication. Attempts to receive permission to return to Paris fail in part due to the author's continued "silence."

1931   Resumes contacts with Khaiutina.

Spends early spring in the Ukraine.

Publishes two more childhood stories (the *Dovecote* cycle) and a "collectivization" story, "Gapa Guzhva."

Impending publication of a series of stories is announced at the end of the year, only one of them subsequently published.

1932   Publication of the story "Guy de Maupassant." Babel lives in Molodenovo, a village outside Moscow, close to Gorky's summer estate.

Babel meets Antonina Nikolayevna Pirozhkova, a young engineer.

After many pleas, Babel finally is allowed to return to his family in France.

1932–33 In Paris, Babel sees his daughter for the first time. Collaborates on a script about a famous socialist-revolutionary double agent, Yevno Azef, for a French movie studio (continues this work later in Russia). Close friendship with Ilya Ehrenburg, who introduces Babel to André Malraux. Babel visits Gorky in Sorrento. Travels through France, Italy, Germany.

Returns to Moscow in August in response to Gorky's request for assistance in organizing the First Congress of Soviet Writers.

In the fall, Babel travels, with Antonina Pirozhkova, through the Caucasus on the way to Kabardino-Balkaria (a small Caucasus republic).

1934   Babel travels to the Donbass region (January).

During the 17th Communist Party Congress, "The Congress of Victors," opposition to Stalin becomes manifest, but is ultimately defeated.

Publication of Babel's story "Dante Street."

Osip Mandelstam recites his anti-Stalin verses to his friends and is arrested in May.

At the First Congress of Soviet Writers (August), Babel obliquely criticizes the cult of Stalin. Speaking about his modest output, Babel calls himself "a great master of the genre [of literary silence]." He is grateful to the Soviet establishment for being able to enjoy the high status of a writer despite his "silence," which, in the West, would have forced him to abandon writing and "sell haberdashery." Babel spends time with André Malraux, who attended the congress.

Assassination of Sergei Kirov on December 1. Beginning of the great purges.

1935   Babel attends the Congress of Soviets in Moscow (February).

Babel completes *Maria*, his second play, which is published in March.

Babel and Pasternak are dispatched, on the insistence of André Malraux and André Gide, to the anti-Fascist International Congress of Writers for the Defense of Culture and Peace in Paris (June).

On July 14, Babel witnesses huge demonstrations in Paris (Popular Front and the pro-Fascist Croix de Feu*), seeing in them the signs of an impending revolution.

Along with his wife and daughter, Babel visits his mother and sister in Brussels (July). Babel makes plans to bring his entire family back to the Soviet Union. These plans do not materialize.

Babel returns to the Soviet Union (August) and travels, with Antonina Pirozhkova, to the Kiev region and on to Odessa. After returning to Moscow, Babel and Pirozhkova establish a household.

Ilya Ehrenburg, on a visit to Moscow from Paris, queries Babel about the mounting repression and the purges of the old Bolshevik intellectuals from the leadership. Babel attributes the changes to the preparations for war, which calls for a more decisive, military-style government and a kind of art that could best serve the goals of total mobilization of society.

Babel collaborates with Sergei Eisenstein on the film *Bezhin Meadow*, about a young peasant Communist who is murdered for denouncing his father as a kulak (winter 1935–36).

1936   Attack on Dmitri Shostakovich's opera *Lady Macbeth of the Mtsensk District* (January) inaugurates the "Campaign against Formalism," a purge in the cultural sphere.

Together with André and Roland Malraux, Babel visits Gorky in the Crimea and, along with Mikhail Koltsov, serves as Malraux's interpreter (March). Afterward Gorky complains to Stalin that the "Campaign against Formalism" represents a harmful cultural policy.

Babel spends time with André Gide in Moscow and occasionally interprets for him.

Maxim Gorky dies on June 18.

As one of the leading figures in the Writers' Union, Babel receives a country house (dacha) in Peredelkino.

Spanish Civil War begins in July.

The trial of Lev Kamenev, Grigory Zinoviev, and other famous party and military leaders, including several Civil War heroes (some friends of Babel's) takes place in August. The accused are sentenced to death.

Nikolay Yezhov (now the husband of E. Khaiutina) replaces Genrikh Yagoda in September as the head of the NKVD (Stalin's secret police).

According to an NKVD informer, Babel is critical of the trials, saying that the prosecution failed to make a convincing case against the accused.

*Ilya Ehrenburg, *Memoirs: 1914–1941*, translated by Tatyana Shebunina (NY: Grosset & Dunlap, 1966), p. 317.

1937   Daughter Lydia is born to Babel and Antonina Pirozhkova (January).

Babel publishes stories "Sulak," "Di Grasso" (thematically, part of the childhood story cycle), and "The Kiss" (a new concluding story of *Red Cavalry*).

Show trials of political and military leaders continue.

1938   In a meeting with Ilya Ehrenburg, Babel recounts how banned books are pulped in a Moscow factory. Ehrenburg, who has just been recalled to Moscow from Spain, suggests to Babel that if Fascism wins in Spain, the repressive USSR would be the only place left for people like Babel and himself, and "so much the worse for us."[*]

Last meeting with Ehrenburg (May).

Yezhov is replaced by Lavrenty Beria as the head of the NKVD and is soon afterward arrested. He gives evidence against Babel.

Babel publishes a story "The Trial" (August).

Collaborates on scripts for the film version of Gorky's autobiographical trilogy (he is chiefly responsible for the script of the volume *My Universities*, released in 1939–40).

Signs a contract for an edition of his collected works.

1939   Babel completes a film script for a military-industrial spy thriller, *Number 4 Staraya Square* (the title referring to the address of the Communist Party Central Committee Headquarters in Moscow).

Babel is arrested on May 15 and is soon charged with spying for France and Austria. The accusation is based, in part, on the evidence provided by Yezhov and Babel's fellow writers Boris Pilnyak and Mikhail Koltsov, who had been arrested earlier.

Molotov-Ribbentrop Pact is signed in Moscow in August. In September, the armies of Germany and the Soviet Union invade and partition Poland.

1940   Babel is executed in the Lubyanka prison on January 27.

1941   Germany invades the Soviet Union on June 22.

1948   Rumors circulate about Babel's imminent release from prison.

1953   Stalin dies (March 5).

1954   Babel is officially exonerated on December 23. The death certificate misleadingly states that he died under unknown circumstances on March 17, 1941.

1955   *Collected Stories by Isaac Babel*, with an introduction by Lionel Trilling, is published in New York.

1956   Nikita Khrushchev denounces Stalin at the 20th Party Congress (February).

1957   A volume of selected stories is published in Moscow with the introduction by Ilya Ehrenburg, at last opening the way for subsequent editions, albeit censored and incomplete.

1964   *Isaac Babel, The Lonely Years: 1925–1939: Unpublished Stories and Correspondence*, edited and introduced by Nathalie Babel. Revised edition published in 1995.

---

[*] S. Povartsov, *Prichina smerti—rasstrel* (*Cause of Death: Execution by the Firing Squad*), M. 1966, p. 130.

1966   *You Must Know Everything,* edited by Nathalie Babel, published in New York.

1989   *Vospominania o Babele* (*Babel Remembered*), edited by Antonina Pirozhkova, is published in Moscow, including Pirozhkova's essay "Years Spent Together (1932–1939)."

1990   The two-volume *Sochineniia* (*Works*) edition is published in Moscow, the most comprehensive uncensored edition of Babel to date, albeit incomplete.

   Details of Babel's interrogation and death begin to reach Soviet press (publications by Arkady Vaksberg and Vitaly Shentalinsky based on their research in the KGB archives).

1994   The centenary of Babel's birth is marked by international conferences in Russia and the United States.

1996   Pirozhkova publishes *At His Side: The Last Years of Isaac Babel,* translated by Anne Frydman and Robert L. Busch (Royalton, Vermont).

GREGORY FREIDIN

NOTES

I. Early Stories

OLD SHLOYME
Original title: "*Starii Shloyme*". First published in *Ogni* 6, 1913.

AT GRANDMOTHER'S
Original title: "*Detstvo. U babushki.*" First published in *Literaturnoye Nasledstvo*, Nauka, 1965, dated: Saratov, November 12, 1915.

ELYA ISAAKOVICH AND MARGARITA PROKOFIEVNA
Original title: "*Elya Isaakovich i Margarita Prokofievna.*" First published in *Letopis* 11, 1916.

MAMA, RIMMA, AND ALLA
Original title: "*Mama, Rimma, i Alla.*" First published in *Letopis* 11, 1916.

THE PUBLIC LIBRARY
Original title: "*Publichnaya biblioteka.*" First published in *Zhurnal zhurnalov* 48, 1916, under the heading "My Notes." Signed Bab-El.

NINE
Original title: "*Devyat.*" First published in *Zhurnal zhurnalov* 48, 1916, under the heading "My Notes." Signed Bab-El.

ODESSA
Original title: "*Odessa.*" First published in *Zhurnal zhurnalov* 51, 1916, under the heading "My Notes." Signed Bab-El.

THE AROMA OF ODESSA
Original title: "*Listki ob Odesse.*" First published in *Vechernyaya zvezda*, March 8, 1918.

INSPIRATION
Original title: "*Vdokhnovenie.*" First published in *Zhurnal zhurnalov* 7, 1917, under the heading "My Notes." Signed Bab-El.

DOUDOU
Original title: "*Doudou.*" First published in *Svobodniye mysli* 2, March 13, 1917, under the heading "My Notes."

SHABOS-NAKHAMU
Original title: "*Shabos-Nakhamu.*" First published in *Vechernyaya zvezda,* March 16, 1918, under the subheading "From the Hershele Cycle." Babel was working on a series of stories on Hershele, a trickster figure in Jewish lore, who was also reputed to be the court jester Reb Borukhl Tulchiner, the grandson of the Baal Shem Tov, the founder of Hasidism. The manuscripts of these stories, however, have not survived.

In the *Red Cavalry* story "Rabbi," the narrator tells the rabbi, " 'I am putting the adventures of Hershele of Ostropol into verse.' 'A great task,' the rabbi whispered, and closed his eyelids."

See also *1920 Diary* entry for July 23.

ON THE FIELD OF HONOR
Original title: "*Na pole chesti.*" First published in *Lava* 1, 1920.

THE DESERTER
Original title: "*Dezertir.*" First published in *Lava* 1, 1920.

PAPA MARESCOT'S FAMILY
Original title: "*Semeistvo papashi Maresko.*" First published in *Lava* 1, 1920.

THE QUAKER
Original title: "*Kvaker.*" First published in *Lava* 1, 1920.

THE SIN OF JESUS
Original title: "*Iisusov grekhi.*" First published in *Na khleb,* August 29, 1921.

AN EVENING WITH THE EMPRESS
Original title: "*Vecher u imperatritsy.*" First published in *Siluety* 1, 1922, under the heading "From the Petersburg Diary."

CHINK
Original title: "*Khodya.*" First published in *Siluety* 6–7, 1923, under the heading "From the Petersburg Diary."

A TALE ABOUT A WOMAN
Original title: "*Skazka pro babu.*" First published in *Siluety* 8–9, 1923. The story is an earlier version of "The Sin of Jesus."

THE BATHROOM WINDOW
Original title: "*V shchelochku.*" First published in *Siluety* 12, 1923, with the subtitle "From the Book *Oforty.*" See also its earlier version, "A Story," in the section Variations and Manuscripts.

BAGRAT-OGLY AND THE EYES OF HIS BULL
Original title: "*Bagrat-Ogly i glaza ego byka.*" First published in *Siluety* 12, 1923, with the subtitle "From the Book *Oforty.*"

LINE AND COLOR
Original title: "*Liniya i tsvet.*" First published in *Krasnaya nov* 7, 1923, with the subtitle "A True Occurrence."

YOU MISSED THE BOAT, CAPTAIN!
Original title: "*Ty promorgal, kapitan!*" First published in *Izvestiya Odesskogo Gubispolkoma,* February 9, 1924. Signed Bab-El.

THE END OF ST. HYPATIUS
Original title: "*Konets sv. Ipatiya.*" First published in *Pravda,* August 3, 1924, under the heading "From My Diary."

II. THE ODESSA STORIES

THE KING
Original title: "*Korol.*" First published in *Moryak,* June 23, 1921, with the subtitle "From the Odessa Stories."

JUSTICE IN PARENTHESES
Original title: "*Spravedlivost v skobkakh.*" First published in *Na pomoshch!,* August 15, 1921, with the subtitle "From the Odessa Stories."

HOW THINGS WERE DONE IN ODESSA
Original title: "*Kak eto delalos v Odesse.*" First published in *Izvestiya Odesskogo Gubispolkoma,* May 5, 1923.

LYUBKA THE COSSACK
Original title: "*Lyubka Kazak.*" First published in *Krasnaya nov* 5, 1924, with the subtitle "From the Odessa Stories."

THE FATHER
Original title: "*Otets.*" First published in *Krasnaya nov* 5, 1924, with the subtitle "From the Odessa Stories."

FROIM GRACH
Original title: "*Froim Grach.*" First published in *Vozdushnye puti,* Volume 3, New York, 1963.

THE END OF THE ALMSHOUSE
Original title: "*Konets bogadelni.*" First published in *30 Dnei* 1, 1932, with the subtitle "From the Odessa Stories," dated 1920–1930.

SUNSET
Original title: "*Zakat.*" First published in *Literaturnaya Rossiya,* November 20, 1964. The last page of the manuscript was missing.

III. THE RED CAVALRY STORIES

The stories are presented in the order in which they appeared in the first edition of the book *Konarmiya (Red Cavalry),* May 1926, by which time all the stories had been published in magazines and newspapers as indicated below.

CROSSING THE RIVER ZBRUCZ
Original title: *Perekhod cherez Zbruch.* First published in *Pravda,* August 3, 1924. Dated Novograd-Volynsk, July 1920.

   Savitsky: The altered name Babel used in his later editions of the *Red Cavalry* stories for Semyon Konstantinovich Timoshenko, 1895–1970, the commander of the Sixth Division of the Red Cavalry. He was later to become a Marshal of the Soviet Union and Commissar of Defense. He appears as Savitsky in the *Red Cavalry* stories "My First Goose," "The Commander of the Second Brigade," "The Story of a

Horse," and "The Continuation of the Story of a Horse," and as Timoshenko throughout the *1920 Diary*. In the original publication of the stories, Babel used Timoshenko's name.

THE CHURCH IN NOVOGRAD
Original title: "*Kostel v Novograde.*" First published in *Izvestiya Odesskovo Gubispolkoma*, February 18, 1923.

See also *1920 Diary* entry for July 15.

A LETTER
Original title: "*Pismo.*" First published in *Izvestiya Odesskovo Gubispolkoma*, February 11, 1923. Dated Novograd-Volynsk, June 1920.

See also *1920 Diary* entry of August 9, 1920.

Pavlichenko: The altered name of Iosif Rodionovich Apanasenko, 1890–1943, who took over the command of Division Six after Timoshenko. Mentioned throughout the *1920 Diary* and in the *Red Cavalry* stories "The Life of Matvey Rodionovich Pavlichenko" and "Czesniki." In the original publication of the stories, Babel used Apanasenko's name.

THE RESERVE CAVALRY COMMANDER
First published in *Lef* 4, 1923. Babel changed the original title "*Dyakov*" to "*Nachalnik konzapasa*" ("The Reserve-Cavalry Commander") in later story editions. Dated Belyov, July 1920.

See also *1920 Diary* entries for July 13, 14, and 16.

PAN APOLEK
Original title: "*Pan Apolek.*" First published in *Krasnaya nov* 7, 1923.

ITALIAN SUN
First published in *Krasnaya nov* 3, 1923. Babel changed the original title "*Sidorov*" to "*Solntse Itali*" ("Italian Sun") in later story editions. Dated Novograd-Volynsk, July 1920.

GEDALI
Original title: "*Gedali.*" First published in *Krasnaya nov* 4, 1924. Dated Zhitomir, June 1920.

See also *1920 Diary* entries for June 6 and July 7.

MY FIRST GOOSE
Original title: "*Moi pervii gus.*" First published in *Izvestiya Odesskovo Gubispolkoma*, May 4, 1924. Dated July 1920.

See also *1920 Diary* entry for August 9.

THE RABBI
Original title: "*Rabbi.*" First published in *Krasnaya nov* 1, 1924.

See also *1920 Diary* entry for June 3.

THE ROAD TO BRODY
Original title: "*Put v Brody.*" First published in *Izvestiya Odesskovo Gubispolkoma*, June 17, 1923. Dated Brody, August 1920.

See also *1920 Diary* entries for August 18 and 31.

THE *TACHANKA* THEORY
Original title: "*Ucheniye o tachanke.*" First published in *Izvestiya Odesskovo Gubispolkoma*, February 23, 1923.

DOLGUSHOV'S DEATH

Original title: "*Smert Dolgusheva*." First published in *Izvestiya Odesskovo Gubispolkoma*, May 1, 1923. Dated Brody, August 1920.

Korotchayev: Was demoted by General Budyonny from provisional commander of the Fourth Cavalry Division to one of the brigade commanders of the Sixth Cavalry Division. See also *1920 Diary* entries for August 2, 8, and 13.

THE COMMANDER OF THE SECOND BRIGADE

First published in *Lef* 4, 1923. Babel changed the original title "*Kolesnikov*" to "*Kombrig 2*" ("The Commander of the Second Brigade"). Dated Brody, August 1920.

See also *1920 Diary* entry for August 3, in which Budyonny threatens to shoot Kolesnikov and Grishin. In the original edition of this story in *Lef*, Babel had used Grishin's name, which in later editions Babel changed to Almazov.

SASHKA CHRIST

Original title: "*Sashka Khristos*." First published in *Krasnaya nov* 1, 1924.

See also *1920 Diary* entry for July 28.

THE LIFE OF MATVEY RODIONOVICH PAVLICHENKO

Original title: "*Zhiznyeopisaniye Pavlichenki, Matveya Rodionicha*." First published in *Shkval* 8, 1924.

Matvey Rodionovich Pavlichenko: the altered name of Iosif Rodionovich Apanasenko, 1890–1943, who took over the command of the Sixth Cavalry Division in August 1920. Mentioned throughout the *1920 Diary*, particularly the entries for August 5, 8–13. See also Sketches for the *Red Cavalry* Stories, "Apanasenko's Life Story" (p. 482).

THE CEMETERY IN KOZIN

Original title: "*Kladbishche v Kozine*." First published in *Izvestiya Odesskovo Gubispolkoma*, February 23, 1923.

See also *1920 Diary* entries for July 18 and 21.

PRISHCHEPA

Original title: "*Prishchepa*." First published in *Izvestiya Odesskovo Gubispolkoma*, June 17, 1923. Dated Demidovka, July 1920.

See also *1920 Diary* entries for July 23, 24. See also the two sections on Demidovka in Sketches for the *Red Cavalry* Stories (pp. 482–84).

THE STORY OF A HORSE

First published in *Izvestiya Odesskovo Gubispolkoma*, April 13, 1923. Babel changed the original title "*Timoshenko i Melnikov*" ("Timoshenko and Melnikov") to "*Istoriya odnoi loshadi*" ("The Story of a Horse") in later editions. Dated Radzivillov, July 1920. The story was republished in *Krasnaya nov* 3, 1924.

In a letter to the editor, Parfenti Melnikov denied that he had ever written a letter renouncing his membership in the Communist Party. Babel wrote an apology, published in the literary magazine *Oktyabr*. See "A Letter to the Editor," (p. 362).

KONKIN

Original title: "*Konkin*." First published in *Krasnaya nov* 3, 1924. Dated Dubno, August 1920.

See also *1920 Diary* entry for July 13.

BERESTECHKO
Original title: "*Berestechko.*" First published in *Krasnaya nov* 3, 1924. Dated Berestechko, August 1920.
　　See also *1920 Diary* entries for August 7 and 8.

SALT
Original title: "*Sol.*" First published in *Izvestiya Odesskovo Gubispolkoma*, November 25, 1923.

EVENING
First published in *Krasnaya nov* 3. Babel changed the original title "*Galin*" to "*Vecher*" ("Evening") in later editions. Dated Kovel, 1920.
　　See also *1920 Diary* entries for September 10 and 11.

AFONKA BIDA
Original title: "*Afonka Bida.*" First published in *Krasnaya nov* 1, 1924.
　　See also *1920 Diary* entry for August 1.

AT SAINT VALENTINE'S
Original title: "*U Svyatogo Valentina.*" First published in *Krasnaya nov* 3, 1924. Dated Berestechko, August 1920.
　　See also *1920 Diary* entry for August 7.

SQUADRON COMMANDER TRUNOV
　　Original title: "*Eskadronnii Trunov.*" First published in *Krasnaya nov* 2, 1925.
　　See also "And Then There Were Nine," "And Then There Were Ten," and the *1920 Diary* entry for August 30. See also "Sokal 1" and "Sokal 2" in Sketches for the *Red Cavalry* Stories (pp. 478–79).

IVAN AND IVAN
Original title: "*Ivany.*" First published in *Russkii Sovremenik* 1, 1924.
　　See also *1920 Diary* entry for August 3.

A CONTINUATION OF THE STORY OF A HORSE
First published in *Krasnaya nov* 3, 1924 as part of the story "*Timoshenko i Melnikov*" ("Timoshenko and Melnikov"), which Babel changed to "*Prodolzhenie istorii odnoi loshadi*" ("A Continuation of the Story of a Horse") in later editions.

THE WIDOW
First published in *Izvestiya Odesskovo Gubispolkoma* 15, 1923. Babel changed the original title "*Shevelyov*" to "*Vdova*" ("The Widow") in later editions.
　　See also *1920 Diary* entry for August 9.

ZAMOSC
Original title: "*Zamostye.*" First published in *Krasnaya nov* 3, 1924. Dated Sokal, September 1920.
　　See also *1920 Diary* entries for August 29 and 30.

TREASON
Original title: "*Izmena.*" First published in *Izvestiya Odesskovo Gubispolkoma*, March 20, 1923.

CZESNIKI
Original title: "*Chesniki.*" First published in *Krasnaya nov* 3, 1924.
　　See also *1920 Diary* entries for August 28–31.

AFTER THE BATTLE
Original title: "*Posle boya*." First published in *Prozhektor* 20, 1924. Dated Galicia, September 1920.
See also *1920 Diary* entry for August 31.

THE SONG
First published in *Krasnaya nov* 3, 1925. Babel changed the original title "*Vecher*" ("Evening") to "*Pesnya*" ("The Song"). Dated Sokal, August 1920.

THE RABBI'S SON
Original title: *Syn Rabbi*. First published in *Krasnaya nov* 1, 1924.
See also *1920 Diary* entry for September 12.

IV. THE RED CAVALRY CYCLE:
ADDITIONAL STORIES

MAKHNO'S BOYS
Original title: "*U batko nashego Makhno*." First published in *Krasnaya nov* 4, 1924, dated 1923.

A HARDWORKING WOMAN
Original title: "*Staratelnaya zhenshchina*." First published in *Pereval* 6, 1926.
See also *1920 Diary* entry for July 16.

GRISHCHUK
Original title: "*Grishchuk*." First published in *Izvestiya Odesskovo Gubispolkoma*, February 23, 1923, subtitled "From the *Red Cavalry*," dated July 16, 1920.
See also *1920 Diary* entries for July 14, 19, and 21–29.

ARGAMAK
Original title: "*Agarmak*." First published in *Novii mir* 3, 1932, subtitled "An Unpublished Chapter of the *Red Cavalry*," dated 1924–1930.

THE KISS
Original title: "*Potselui*." First published in *Krasnaya nov* 7, 1937

AND THEN THERE WERE NINE
Original title: "*Ikh bylo devyat*." First published in *Novii Zhurnal* 95, New York, June 1969.
See also "And Then There Were Ten," "Squadron Commander Trunov," and the *1920 Diary* entry for August 30.

AND THEN THERE WERE TEN
Original title: "*Ikh bylo desyat*." First published in *Petersburg 1918,* 1989, Michigan, Ardis Publishers.

A LETTER TO THE EDITOR
First published in *Oktyabr* 4, 1924.

V. *THE RED CAVALRYMAN:* ARTICLES

WHAT WE NEED IS MORE MEN LIKE TRUNOV!
Original title: "*Pobolshe takikh Trunovikh!*" First published in *Krasnii kavalerist*, August 13, 1920, signed "War correspondent for the Sixth Cavalry Division, K. Lyutov."

THE KNIGHTS OF CIVILIZATION
Original title: "*Ritsari tsivilizatsii.*" First published in *Krasnii kavalerist,* August 14, 1920, signed K.L.
   See also *1920 Diary* entry for August 8.

DISPATCH OFFICE, SHAPE UP!
Original title: "*Ekspeditsiya podtyanis.*" First published in *Krasnii kavalerist,* September 11, 1920.

MURDERERS WHO HAVE YET TO BE CLUBBED TO DEATH
Original title: "*Nedobitiye ubiitsy.*" First published in *Krasnii kavalerist,* September 17, 1920, signed "War correspondent for the Sixth Cavalry Division, K. Lyutov."

HER DAY
Original title: "*Yeyo den.*" First published in *Krasnii kavalerist,* September 18, 1920, signed K. Lyutov.
   See also *1920 Diary* entry for August 3.

VI. *1920 Diary*

First full publication in *Isaak Babel: Sochineniya v dvukh tomakh,* Moscow 1990.

JUNE 3
"Love in the kitchen": see the *Red Cavalry* story "Evening."
   "The Bazaar in Zhitomir": see the *Red Cavalry* stories "Gedali" and "The Rabbi's Son."

JULY 13
Dyakov: see the *Red Cavalry* story "The Reserve Cavalry Commander."

JULY 14
Grishchuk: see the *Red Cavalry* stories "The Tachanka Theory" and "Dolgushov's Death."
   Semyon Konstantinovich Timoshenko: Appears as Savitsky in the *Red Cavalry* stories "My First Goose," "The Commander of the Second Brigade," "The Story of a Horse," and "The Continuation of the Story of a Horse."

JULY 16
"A terrible incident, soldiers' love": see "A Hardworking Woman" from the Red Cavalry Cycle.
   "If it gets up, then it's a horse": see the *Red Cavalry* story "The Reserve Cavalry Commander," and "Grishchuk" from The *Red Cavalry* Cycle.

JULY 18
"The Jewish cemetery outside Malin": see the *Red Cavalry* story "The Cemetery in Kozin."

JULY 19
Nikolai Petrovich Kolesov (also referred to as Kolesnikov in the diary entries for August 3, 13, and 18, and in the Sketches for the Red Cavalry Stories) appears as Kolesnikov in the *Red Cavalry* story "The Commander of the Second Brigade."

JULY 21
"A cemetery, the destroyed house of Rabbi Azrail": see the *Red Cavalry* story "The Cemetery in Kozin."

JULY 23

Prishchepa: See the *Red Cavalry* story "Prishchepa" and the two sections on Demidovka in Sketches for the *Red Cavalry* Stories (pp. 482–84).

JULY 24

"My tale about the Chinese": Babel's friend Viktor Shklovsky wrote in an essay volume (*Gamburgsky shchet*, 1928) that throughout 1919 Babel "talked of nothing but two Chinese men in a brothel." See also the story "Chink" (p. 112).

AUGUST 1

"Our infantry is in the trenches": See the *Red Cavalry* story "Afonka Bida."

AUGUST 2

Korotchayev: See the *Red Cavalry* story "Dolgushov's Death."

AUGUST 3

"Budyonny to Kolesnikov and Grishin: 'I'll shoot you!' "—see the *Red Cavalry* story "The Commander of the Second Brigade."

AUGUST 4

"We have a new division commander, Apanasenko"—appears in the *Red Cavalry* stories as Pavlichenko. See "A Letter," "The Life of Matvey Rodionovich Pavlichenko," and "Czesniki."

AUGUST 7

"The looting of the church": See also the *Red Cavalry* story "At Saint Valentine's."

   "*Notre petit héros achève 7 semaines*": See also the *Red Cavalry* story "Berestechko."

AUGUST 8

"Scorched the pharmacist's body with white-hot iron pokers": See the *1920 Diary* entry for August 8.

AUGUST 9

"The tale of how he whipped his neighbor Stepan": See the *Red Cavalry* story "The Letter."

   "Shurka's lover is heavily wounded": See the *Red Cavalry* story "The Widow."

   Alexander Nikolayevich Vinokurov: Appears as Vinogradov in the *Red Cavalry* stories "Berestechko" and "After the Battle."

AUGUST 11

"Must write . . . the life story of Apanasenko": See the *Red Cavalry* story: "The Life of Matvey Rodionovich Pavlichenko."

AUGUST 18

"Interrogation of prisoners": See stories "Squadron Commander Trunov," "And Then There Were Nine," and "And Then There Were Ten."

   "Smashed, smoked-out beehives": See "The Road to Brody."

AUGUST 30

"And then there were nine": See stories "Squadron Commander Trunov," "And Then There Were Nine," and "And Then There Were Ten."

AUGUST 31

Captain Yakovlev: See "The Widow," "After the Battle," "Murderers Who Have Yet to Be Clubbed to Death."

SEPTEMBER 12
"Panic at the train station": See "The Rabbi's Son."
  "The nurse's story": See "After the Battle."

VII. SKETCHES FOR THE RED CAVALRY STORIES

First published in *Literaturnoe Nasledstvo* 74, 1965.

VIII. REPORTS FROM PETERSBURG, 1918

FIRST AID
Original title: "*Pervaya pomoshch.*" First published in *Novaya zhizn*, March 9, 1918, under the heading "Diary."

HORSES
Original title: "*O loshadyakh.*" First published in *Novaya zhizn*, March 16, 1918, under the heading "Diary," and signed I.B.

PREMATURE BABIES
Original title: "*Nedonoski.*" First published in *Novaya zhizn*, March 26, 1918, under the heading "Diary."

THE DEAD
Original title: "*Bitye.*" First published in *Novaya zhizn*, March 29, 1918, under the heading "Diary."

THE PALACE OF MOTHERHOOD
Original title: "*Dvorets materinstva.*" First published in *Novaya zhizn*, March 31, 1918, under the heading "Diary."

EVACUEES
Original title: "*Evakuirovanniye.*" First published in *Novaya zhizn*, April 13, 1918, under the heading "Diary."

MOSAIC
Original title: "*Mozaika.*" First published in *Novaya zhizn*, April 21, 1918, under the heading "Diary."

QUITE AN INSTITUTION
Original title: *Zavedenitse.* First published in *Novaya zhizn*, April 25, 1918, under the heading "Diary."

THE GEORGIAN, THE KERENSKY RUBLES, AND THE GENERAL'S DAUGHTER (A MODERN TALE)
Original title: "*O gruzinye, kerenkye, i generalskoi doche.*" First published in *Novaya zhizn*, May 4, 1918.

THE BLIND
Original title: "*Slepiye.*" First published in *Novaya zhizn*, May 19, 1918, under the heading "Diary."

THE EVENING
Original title: "*Vecher.*" First published in *Novaya zhizn*, May 21, 1918, under the heading "Diary."

I WAS STANDING AT THE BACK
Original title: "*Ya zadnim stoyal.*" First published in *Novaya zhizn,* June 7, 1918, under the heading "Petersburg Diary."

A BEAST CAN'T TALK
Original title: "*Zver molchit.*" First published in *Novaya zhizn,* June 9, 1918, under the heading "Diary."

FINNS
Original title: "*Finny.*" First published in *Novaya zhizn,* June 11, 1918, under the heading "Diary."

A NEW LIFE
Original title: "*Novii byt.*" First published in *Novaya zhizn,* June 20, 1918, under the heading "Diary."

AN INCIDENT ON THE NEVSKY PROSPEKT
Original title: "*Sluchai na Nevskom.*" First published in *Novaya zhizn,* June 27, 1918, under the heading "Diary."

THE MOST HOLY PATRIARCH
Original title: "*Svyateishii patriarch.*" First published in *Novaya zhizn,* July 2, 1918, under the heading "Diary."

AT THE STATION: A SKETCH FROM LIFE
Original title: "*Na stantsii: Nabrosok s naturi.*" First published in *Era* 6, July 13, 1918.

ON PALACE SQUARE
Original title: "*Na Dvortsovoi Ploshchadi.*" First published in *Zhizn Iskusstva,* November 11, 1918, under the heading "Diary."

THE CONCERT IN KATERINENSTADT
Original title: "*Kontsert v Katerinenshtadte.*" First published in *Zhizn Iskusstva,* November 13, 1918, under the heading "Diary."

IX. REPORTS FROM GEORGIA, 1922–1924

AT THE WORKERS' RETREAT
Original title: "*V dome otdykha.*" First published in *Zarya Vostoka,* June 24, 1922, signed K. Lyutov.

KAMO AND *SHAUMIAN*
Original title: "*Kamo i Shaumian.*" First published in *Zarya Vostoka,* August 31, 1933, under the heading "A Letter from Batum." Signed K. Lyutov.

WITHOUT A HOMELAND
Original title: "*Bez rodiny.*" First published in *Zarya Vostoka,* September 14, 1922, under the heading "A Letter from Batum." Signed K. Lyutov.

MOSLEM SEMINARIES AND SOVIET SCHOOLS
Original title: "*Medresse i shkola.*" First published in *Zarya Vostoka,* September 14, 1922, under the heading "Letters from Ajaria." Signed K. Lyutov.

TOBACCO
Original title: "*Tabak.*" First published in *Zarya Vostoka,* October 29, 1922, under the heading "A Letter from Abkhazia." Signed K. Lyutov.

GAGRY
Original title: "*Gagry.*" First published in *Zarya Vostoka,* November 22, 1922, under the heading "Abkhazian letters." Signed K. Lyutov.

IN CHAKVA
Original title: "*V Chakve.*" First published in *Zarya Vostoka,* December 3, 1922, under the heading "From a Caucasian Diary."

RENOVATIONS AND REFURBISHMENT
Original title: "*Remont i chistka.*" First published in *Zarya Vostoka,* December 14, 1922, under the heading "Abkhazian letters."

PARIS AND *JULIET*
Original title: " '*Parizot' i 'Yuliya'* ". First published in *Izvestiya Odesskogo Gubispolkoma,* March 17, 1924. Signed Bab-El.

X. REPORTS FROM FRANCE, 1935

The following pieces were originally published in *Pioner* 3, 1937, under the heading "A Trip to France."

THE CITY OF LIGHT
Original title: "*Gorod-Svetoch.*"

FRENCH SCHOOLS
Original title: "*Shkola vo Frantsii.*"

TOWN AND COUNTRY
Original title: "*Goroda i derevni.*"

COURT OF JUSTICE AND PARLIAMENT
Original title: "*Pravosudiye i parlament.*"

THE POPULAR FRONT
Original title: "*Narodnii front.*"

THE POWER OF MONEY
Original title: "*Vlast deneg.*"

THE RED BELT
Original title: "*Krasnii poyas.*"

XI. STORIES, 1925–1938

THE STORY OF MY DOVECOTE
Original title: "*Istoriya moyei golubyatni.*" First published in *Krasnaya gazeta,* May 18, 19, 20, 1925, evening edition. Dated 1925.

FIRST LOVE
Original title: "*Pervaya lyubov.*" First published in *Krasnaya gazeta,* May 24, 25, 1925, evening edition. Dated 1925.

KARL-YANKEL
Original title: "*Karl-Yankel.*" First published in *Zvezda* 7, 1931.

THE AWAKENING
Original title: "*Probuzhdeniye*." First published in *Molodaya gvardiya* 17–18, 1931, under the heading "From the Book *The Story of My Dovecote*." Dated 1931.

IN THE BASEMENT
Original title: "*V podvale*." First published in *Novii mir* 10, 1931, under the heading "From the Book *The Story of My Dovecote*." Dated 1929.

GAPA GUZHVA
Original title: "*Gapa Guzhva*." First published in *Novii mir* 10, 1931, under the heading "The First Chapter from the Book *Velikaya Krinitsa*." Dated spring 1930.

KOLYVUSHKA
Original title: "*Kolyvushka*." First published in *Vozdushniye puti*, Volume 3, New York, 1963.

THE ROAD
Original title: "*Doroga*." First published in *30 dnei* 3, 1932. Dated 1920–1930.

THE *IVAN AND MARIA*
Original title: "*Ivan-da-Mariya*." First published in *30 dnei* 4, 1932. Dated 1920-28.

GUY DE MAUPASSANT
Original title: "*Gyui de Mopassan*." First published in *30 dnei* 6, 1932. Dated 1920–22.

PETROLEUM
Original title: "*Nefts*." First published in *Vechernaya Moskva*, February 14, 1934.

DANTE STREET
Original title: "*Ulitsa Dante*." First published in *30 dnei* 3, 1934.

DI GRASSO
Original title: "*Di Grasso*." First published in *Ogonyok* 23, 1937.

SULAK
Original title: "*Sulak*." First published in *Molodoi kolkhoznik* 6, 1937.

THE TRIAL
Original title: "*Sud*." First published in *Ogonyok* 23, 1938, under the heading "From My Notebook."

MY FIRST FEE
Original title: "*Moi pervii gonorar*." First published in *Vozdushniye puti*, Volume 3, New York, 1963.

XII. Variations and Manuscripts

ROAMING STARS: A MOVIE TALE
Original title: "*Bluzhdayushchiye zvezdi*." First published in *Shkval* 3, 1925. See also the screenplay *Roaming Stars*.

A STORY
Original title: "*Moi listki. Raskaz I. Babelya*." First published in *Zhurnal zhurnalov* 16, 1917. See also "The Bathroom Window," of which this is an earlier variant.

INFORMATION
Original title: "*Spravka.*" First published in the book *Izbrannoye,* Issac Babel, Moscow, 1966.

THREE IN THE AFTERNOON
Original title: "*Tri chasa dnya.*" First published in *Filologicheskii zbornik,* Alma Ata, 1971.

THE JEWESS
Original title: "*Evreika.*" First published in *Novii zhurnal* 95, New York, 1969.

XIII. PLAYS

SUNSET
Original title: *Zakat.* First published in *Novii mir* 2, 1928.

MARIA
Original title: *Mariya.* First published in *Teatr i dramaturgiya* 3, 1935.

XIV. SCREENPLAYS

ROAMING STARS
Original title: *Bluzhdayushchiye zvezdi.* First published as the book *Bluzhdayushchiye zvezdi,* Kino-pechat, Moscow 1926.

BENYA KRIK
Original title: *Benya Krik.* First published in *Krasnaya nov* 6, 1926.

THE CHINESE MILL (AN ATTEMPTED MOBILIZATION)
Original title: *Kitayskaya melnitsa.* First published in *Ulbandus Review* 1–2, New York, 1978.

NUMBER 4 STARAYA SQUARE
Original title: *Staraya Ploshchatd, 4.* First published in *Iskusstvo kino* 5, 1963.
From The Forging of Steel

THE GERMANS IN THE UKRAINE
Original title: *Nemtsi na Ukraine.* First published in *Krasnoarmeyets* 9–10, 1938.

IN PETLYURA'S PRISON
Original title: *V tyurmye u Petlyury.* First published in *Krasnoarmeyets* 12, 1938.